RETAIL MANAGEMENT

A STRATEGIC APPROACH

EIGHTH EDITION

Barry Berman

Hofstra University

Joel R. Evans

Hofstra University

Prentice Hall

Upper Saddle River, NJ 07458

Acquisitions Editor: Leah Johnson
Assistant Editor: Anthony Palmiotto
Editorial Assistant: Rebecca Calvert
Marketing Manager: Shannon Moore
Marketing Assistant: Kathleen Mulligan
Senior Production Editor: M.E. McCourt
Managing Editor (Editorial): Bruce Kaplan
Managing Editor (Production): John Roberts
Production Manager: Arnold Vila
Assoc. Dir., Manufacturing: Vincent Scelta
Design Manager: Pat Smythe
Interior Design: Michael Jung
Cover Design: Michael Jung/Michael Fruhbeis
Composition: York Graphic Services, Inc.

Library of Congress Cataloging-in-Publication Data

Berman, Barry.
   Retail management: a strategic approach / Barry Berman, Joel R. Evans. — 8th ed.
     p. cm.
   Includes index.
   ISBN 0–13–026334–6
   1. Retail trade—Management.   I. Evans, Joel R. II. Title.
HF5429..B45 2001
658.8′7—dc21   00-055065

Credits and acknowledgments for materials borrowed from other sources and reproduced, with permission, in this textbook appear on pages C1–C2. Credits and acknowledgments for line art and textual materials borrowed from other sources and reproduced, with permission, in this textbook appear on the appropriate page within text.

Printed in the United States of America
10 9 8 7 6 5 4 3 2
ISBN 0-13-026334-6

To LINDA, GLENNA AND PAUL, AND LISA AND BEN

To LINDA, STACEY, AND JENNIFER

Thank you for your enduring
patience and understanding.

Barry Berman

Joel R. Evans

Barry Berman (Ph.D. in Business with majors in Marketing and Behavioral Science) is the Walter H. "Bud" Miller Distinguished Professor of Business and Professor of Marketing and International Business at Hofstra University. **Joel R. Evans** (Ph.D. in Business with majors in Marketing and Public Policy) is the RMI Distinguished Professor of Business and Professor of Marketing and International Business at Hofstra University.

While at Hofstra, each has been honored as a faculty inductee in Beta Gamma Sigma honor society, received multiple Dean's Awards for service, and been selected as the Teacher of the Year by the Hofstra M.B.A. Association. For several years, Drs. Berman and Evans were co-directors of Hofstra's Retail Management Institute and Business Research Institute. Both regularly teach undergraduate and graduate courses to a wide range of students.

Barry Berman and Joel R. Evans have worked together for more than 20 years in co-authoring several best-selling texts, including *Retail Management: A Strategic Approach,* Eighth Edition. They have also consulted for a wide variety of clients, ranging from small "mom-and-pop" retailers to *Fortune 500* companies. They are co-founders of the American Marketing Association's Special Interest Group in Retailing and Retail Management, and currently serve on its board. They recently co-chaired the Academy of Marketing Science/American Collegiate Retailing Association's triennial conference, "Retailing 2000: Launching the New Millennium." In 1999, they were featured speakers at the annual meeting of the National Retail Federation, the world's largest retailing trade association. Each has a chapter on retailing in the most recent edition of Dartnell's *Marketing Manager's Handbook.*

Barry and Joel are both active Web practitioners (and surfers), and they have written and developed all of the content for the comprehensive, interactive Web site that accompanies *Retail Management* (www.prenhall.com/bermanevans). They may be reached through the Web site or by writing to mktbxb@Hofstra.edu (Barry Berman) and mktjre@Hofstra.edu (Joel R. Evans).

PREFACE

As we enter the new millennium, we are delighted by the continuing positive response to this text, as evidenced by adoptions at hundreds of colleges and universities around the world. In the eighth edition, we have set out to capture the new spirit of retailing in an E-commerce world. *This edition represents the most sweeping revision of the text since its first edition.*

We have worked hard—eagerly, in fact—to produce a cutting-edge text, while retaining the coverage and features most desired by professors and students, *and* maintaining the length of prior editions. The concepts of a strategic approach and a retail strategy remain our cornerstones. With a strategic approach, the fundamental principle is that the retailer has to plan for and adapt to a complex, changing environment. Both opportunities and constraints must be considered. A retail strategy is the overall plan or framework of action that guides a retailer. Ideally, it will be at least one year in duration and outline the mission, goals, consumer market, overall and specific activities, and control mechanisms of the retailer. Without a pre-defined and well-integrated strategy, the firm may flounder and be unable to cope with the environment that surrounds it. The major goals of our text are to enable the reader to become a good retail planner and decision maker and to help focus on change and adaptation to change.

Retail Management is designed as a one-semester text for students of retailing or retail management. In many cases, such students will have already been exposed to marketing principles. We feel retailing should be viewed as one form of marketing and not distinct from it.

THE DAWN OF A NEW ERA FOR RETAIL MANAGEMENT: A STRATEGIC APPROACH

As Bob Dylan once said, "The times, they are a changing." When we look back on how we wrote the first edition of *Retail Management,* we lived in a different time. We wrote out our drafts long-hand and had them typed. We didn't have our own PCs because they were too expensive and they didn't really do much. We photocopied research articles one by one in the library, often relying on dated material. We shopped at stores that were typically open from 10:00 A.M. to 7:00 P.M., Monday through Saturday. That meant always waiting in lines, settling for what merchandise local stores carried, and little opportunity to comparison shop. And believe it or not, there was no Internet or World Wide Web.

Now, in preparing the eighth edition of *Retail Management,* this is how we spent a typical day: At 7:00 A.M. one morning, we decided we needed new high-speed printers to replace our older model. Unlike earlier days, we didn't visit five stores searching for the right model at the right price, we went right to the Web. First stop: CNET, a leading online computer and electronics "shopping bot." There, we typed in "laser printers" and read detailed reviews and specification sheets for the leading models. While still at CNET, we decided to comparison shop for a particular printer model. Instantly, up popped a listing of 43 online retailers that carried the model, along with their prices, shipping policies, and in-stock positions. We clicked on Buy.com and, zoom, we went right to the link for the printer. At Buy.com, we ordered two printers and expanded memory cards. The next day, the printers arrived. The time we started at CNET to the time we finished with Buy.com was no more than 30 minutes. No lines, no parking problems, no wait for the store to open, no hassle!

After buying the printers, it was back to work. We consulted our free automatic daily E-mails of the business section of the *New York Times* (which you, too, can get for free by subscribing at www.nytimes.com), visited various retail magazine sites for their regular news updates (take a look at www.discountstorenews.com, for example), and did our usual search of retailer sites (look at the revamped site of Wal-Mart, the world's largest retailer, at www.wal-mart.com). As we did research on particular retailing topics, we went to search engines such as Yahoo! (www.yahoo.com) and online library resources such as Uncover Web (uncweb.carl.org).

What does this all mean? The "E" word—electronic—permeates our lives. From a consumer perspective, gone are the old Smith-Corona typewriters, replaced by word processing software on PCs. Snail mail is giving way to E-mail. Looking for a new music CD? Well, we can go to the store—or we can order it from CDnow (www.cdnow.com) or Amazon.com (www.amazon.com) or maybe even download some tracks as we create our own CDs. Are you doing research? Then hop on the Internet express and have access to millions of facts at our fingertips. The Web is a 24/7/365 medium that is transforming and will continue to transform our behavior.

From a retailer perspective, we see four formats—all covered in *Retail Management*—competing in the new millennium (cited in descending order of importance):

- Combined "bricks-and-mortar" and "clicks-and-mortar" retailers. These are store-based retailers that also offer Web shopping, thus providing customers the ultimate in choice and convenience. Over 90 percent of the world's largest retailers, as well as many medium and small firms, fall into this category or will shortly. This is clearly the fastest-growing format in retailing, exemplified by such different firms as Barnes & Noble (www.barnesandnoble.com), Costco (www.costco.com), and Wal-Mart (www.wal-mart.com).
- Clicks-and-mortar retailers. These are the new breed of Web-only retailers that have emerged in recent years, led by Amazon.com (www.amazon.com). Rather than utilize physical store facilities, these companies promote a "virtual" shopping experience: wide selections, low prices, and convenience. Among the firms in this category are grocery retailer Peapod (www.peapod.com), Priceline (www.priceline.com)—the discount airfare, hotel, and more retailer, and toy retailer eToys (www.etoys.com). By 2003, total annual Web retailing revenues from all formats are expected to reach $140 billion.
- Direct marketers with clicks-and-mortar retailing operations. These are firms that have relied on traditional nonstore media such as print catalogs, direct selling in homes, and TV infomercials to generate business. Almost of them have added Web sites, or will be shortly, to enhance their businesses. Leaders include Lands' End (www.landsend.com) and Spiegel (www.spiegel.com). In the near future, direct marketers will see a dramatic increase in the proportion of sales coming from the Web.
- Bricks-and-mortar retailers. These are companies that rely on their physical facilities to draw customers. They do not sell online, but use the Web for customer service and image building. Ikea uses its Web site to provide company information and store locations. Home Depot sells gifts, gives extensive advice on do-it-yourself projects, and has store directions. Firms in this category represent the smallest grouping of retailers. Many will need to rethink their approach as online competition intensifies.

On a personal level, we have spent the last few years striving to disprove the adage that you can't teach old dogs new tricks. And we've had loads of fun doing so. We both have developed our own Web sites (in addition to the Prentice Hall site—www.prenhall.com/bermanevans—accompanying *Retail Management*). We are active "surfers." We are always looking for new links. There's even time for an occasional "intellectual" game such as Out of Order at Sonystation.com.

Has this helped us as authors? You bet. We have access to more information sources than ever before, from international trade associations to government agencies. The information in *Retail Management,* Eighth Edition, is more current than ever because we are using the original sources themselves and not waiting for data to be published months or a year after being compiled. We are also able to include a greater range of real-world examples because of the information at company Web sites.

Will this help you, the reader? Again, you bet. Our philosophy has always been to make *Retail Management* as reader-friendly, up-to-date, and useful as possible. In addition, we want you to benefit from our experiences, in this case, our E-xperiences.

E-xciting E-features

To reflect these E-xciting times, *Retail Management: A Strategic Approach,* Eighth Edition, incorporates a host of E-features throughout the book.

With regard to content, each chapter includes important practical applications of the Web within the context of that chapter. Here are some examples of how the discussion of the Web is integrated into *Retail Management:*

- *Chapter 1:*   Careers in retailing (www.careersinretailing.com) and the Web addresses of the largest ten U.S. retailers.
- *Chapter 2:*   How retailers can conduct customer satisfaction surveys (customersat.com).
- *Chapter 3:*   The Guitar Center (www.guitarcenter.com), the largest U.S. retailer of musical instruments.
- *Chapter 4:*   The retailer assistance that is available through the Small Business Development Center (sba.gov/sbdc).
- *Chapter 5:*   Why Ikea (www.ikea.com) does not sell products at its Web site.
- *Chapter 6:*   Web retailing for small and large retailers, such as blindsdepot.com (www.blindsdepot.com). There is also a detailed discussion of E-commerce.
- *Chapter 7:*   Family Dollar's (www.familydollar.com) focused target market strategy.
- *Chapter 8:*   MicroStrategy (www.microstrategy.com), one of many firms that market information systems software.
- *Chapter 9:*   How retailers can learn about trading areas from government (tiger.census.gov) and nongovernment (www.esri.com) online sources.
- *Chapter 10:*   The International Council of Shopping Centers (www.icsc.org), the world's largest shopping center association, with a variety of resources for retailers.
- *Chapter 11:*   Retailers such as Target (www.target.com/jobs) that have entire sections of their Web sites devoted to retailing jobs.
- *Chapter 12:*   Barnes & Noble's (www.barnesandnoble.com) return policy for online purchases.
- *Chapter 13:*   Retail Technologies (www.retailpro.com), one of the firms that markets inventory management software.
- *Chapter 14:*   The Doneger Group (www.doneger.com), the largest independent resident buying office.
- *Chapter 15:*   How retailers often visit merchandise marts such as AmericasMart (www.americas.com) and CaliforniaMart (www.californiamart.com) when making buying decisions.
- *Chapter 16:*   Why the *New York Times on the Web* (www.nytimes.com) reports that online retailers are modifying their return policies.
- *Chapter 17:*   How shopping bots such as mySimon (www.mysimon.com) are revolutionizing the way in which people comparison shop.
- *Chapter 18:*   How small retailers can benefit from free or low-cost Web store development by Bigstep.com (www.bigstep.com) and others.

- *Chapter 19:*   Blockbuster's (www.blockbuster.com) use of its Web site in a very promotional manner.
- *Chapter 20:*   How retailers can learn about the benefits of benchmarking (www.eprs.com/benchmarking.htm).
- *Appendix A:*   How retail job opportunities may be found online from sources such *Retail Jobnet* (www.retailjobnet.com).

But, that's not all! *Retail Management,* Eighth Edition, is packed with other E-features:

- A comprehensive Web site (www.prenhall.com/bermanevans), with an interactive study guide, more than 1,000 "hot links," a glossary, and much more.
- End papers with Web addresses of search engines, career banks, and more.
- Margin notes throughout each chapter keyed to important text concepts highlight the addresses of a variety of Web sites. Companies such as CDnow, Cheap Tickets, eBay, Macy's, Old Navy, Papa John's, Rainforest Café, REI, Tuesday Morning, and Williams-Sonoma are featured. You can also look at Web sites that show what it takes to be a franchisee (carvel.com/franchise_faq.asp), draw an online map of your community (tiger.census.gov/cgi-bin/mapbrowse-tbl), take an online demo from an outside buying office (www.buying-office.com/files/demo), and shop at an online auction (http//www.haggle.com). There are about 250 Web-based margin notes in all.
- A "Technology in Retailing" box in each chapter. Many of these relate to companies engaging in Web retailing, such as All the Right Gifts (http://www.alltherightgifts.com), Follett (www.efollett.com), Food.com (www.food.com), and Varsitybooks.com (www.varsitybooks.com).
- A Web-based exercise at the end of each chapter, involving the Web sites of such diverse organizations as Lettuce Entertain You (www.leye.com/restaurants/index.html), Starbucks (www.starbucks.com), and Supercuts (www.supercuts.com).
- Two comprehensive cases on Web-based retailing (Part Two and Part Three).
- A listing of 45 FREE online sources of retailing information (Table 8.2).

BUILDING ON A STRONG TRADITION

Besides the E-features just mentioned, *Retail Management,* Eighth Edition, carefully builds on its heritage as the market leader.

The Foundation of *Retail Management: A Strategic Approach*

These features have been retained from earlier editions of *Retail Management: A Strategic Approach:*

- Full coverage of all major retailing topics including consumer behavior, information systems, store location, operations, service retailing, the retail audit, retail institutions, franchising, human resource management, computerization, and retailing in a changing environment.
- A strategic decision-making orientation, with many flowcharts, figures, tables, and photos. The chapter coverage is geared to the six steps used in developing and applying a retail strategy, which are first described in Chapter 1.
- A real-world approach focusing on both small and large retailers. Among the well-known firms discussed are Amazon.com, Bloomingdale's, Costco, Gap, Home Depot, Lands' End, The Limited, McDonald's, Neiman Marcus, Spiegel, Starbucks, Tiffany, and Wal-Mart.
- Real-world boxes on current retailing issues in each chapter. These boxes further illustrate the concepts presented in the text by focusing on real firms and situations.
- A numbered summary keyed to chapter objectives, a key terms listing, and discussion questions at the end of each chapter.

- Thirty-eight end-of-chapter cases involving a wide range of retailers and retail practices.
- Eight end-of-part comprehensive cases.
- Up-to-date information from such sources as *Advertising Age, Business Week, Chain Store Age, Direct Marketing, Discount Store News, Entrepreneur, Inc., Journal of Retailing, Progressive Grocer, Stores,* and *Wall Street Journal.*
- A convenient, one-semester format.
- "How to Solve a Case Study," following Chapter 1 in the text.
- An appendix on franchising, following Chapter 4.
- An end-of-text appendix on careers in retailing and another with a detailed glossary.

New to the Eighth Edition

Since the first edition of *Retail Management: A Strategic Approach,* we have sought to be as contemporary and forward-looking as possible. We are proactive rather than reactive in our preparation of each edition. That is why we still take this adage of Wal-Mart's founder, the late Sam Walton, so seriously: "Commit to your business. Believe in it more than anybody else."

For the eighth edition, there many changes in *Retail Management:*

1. The organization of the text has been revamped.
   a. There are new chapters on building and sustaining relationships (Chapter 2) and on merchandise management (Chapter 14). Relationships are covered early in the text to signify their importance in retail planning.
   b. There are substantially revised chapters on Web, nonstore, and other nontraditional retailing (Chapter 6); identifying and understanding consumers (Chapter 7); information gathering and processing in retailing (Chapter 8); implementing merchandising plans (Chapter 15); and establishing and maintaining a retail image (Chapter 18).
   c. There are new end-of-chapter appendixes on service retailing (Chapter 2) and global retailing (Chapter 3), both with a strategic flavor. These appendixes amplify the discussions in their respective chapters and give extended attention to these topics.
   d. All of the chapters have been streamlined so they flow better and truly capture the spirit of retailing in the 21st century.
   e. Appendix A on careers is updated. Appendix B describes the contemporary Web site that accompanies the text. Appendix C (Glossary) includes several hundred key terms.
   f. The end papers are totally updated.

2. The in-chapter boxed material—which is all new—is more topical and includes thought-provoking questions. Every chapter contains a "Technology in Retailing" box, a "Retailing Around the World" box, and an "Ethics in Retailing" box. And there is a ***New!*** boxed feature in each chapter ("Careers in Retailing"), a real-life look at people from all walks of retailing life.

3. All chapter-opening vignetters are new.

4. All of the chapter-ending cases are new or revised and all are now based on real retail situations and firms. Nineteen cases have a video component; they are denoted by a video symbol in the text.

5. All of the part-ending comprehensive cases are new and based on real retail situations and firms.

6. There is a ***New!*** case and exercise book that is bundled free with the text.

7. These substantive chapter changes have been made:
   a. Each chapter begins with an opening vignette relating customer service and customer relationships to the topics in that chapter. These are the modern-day linchpins of successful retailing.
   b. Chapter 1 (An Introduction to Retailing) is more tightly written and sets the stage for the new Chapter 2.
   c. *New!* Chapter 2 (Building and Sustaining Relationships in Retailing) examines concepts that are critical for today's retailers, including value, the chain, the value delivery system, customer satisfaction, customer and channel relationships, and ethics. The chapter concludes with a *New!* appendix on planning for the unique aspects of service retailing.
   d. Chapter 3 (Strategic Planning in Retailing) has been repositioned, so that it now follows the new material on relationship retailing. It concludes with a *New!* appendix on the special dimensions of strategic planning in a global retailing environment.
   e. Chapter 4 (Retail Institutions by Ownership) is more tightly written, examines recent institutional trends, and deals with food and general merchandise retail strategies.
   f. Chapter 5 (Retail Institutions by Store-Based Strategy Mix) is more tightly written, examines several recent institutional trends, and deals exclusively with food and general merchandise retail strategies.
   g. *Substantially revised!* Chapter 6 (Web, Nonstore-Based, and Other Forms of Nontraditional Retailing) places the E-commerce revolution in perspective, with considerably more discussion of Web retailing—including the role of the Web, the scope of online retailing, characteristics of Web users, factors to consider in planning whether to have a Web site, and several examples of Web retailing in action. There is also a more in-depth discussion of video kiosks and a new section on the emergence of airport retailing.
   h. *Substantially revised!* Chapter 7 (Identifying and Understanding Consumers) has a much tighter and more focused retailing orientation. There are new sections on consumer needs and desires, shopping attitudes and behavior, retailer actions, and environmental factors affecting consumers.
   i. *Substantially revised!* Chapter 8 (Information Gathering and Processing in Retailing) has more material on building and using a retail information system, data-base management, data warehousing, data mining, and micromarketing and the roles of different channel members in acquiring data.
   j. Chapters 9 and 10 (Trading-Area Analysis and Site Selection) have more discussion of the technology available for site selection (especially geographic information systems) and the uses of computerized census data. New visual examples are provided throughout these chapters.
   k. Chapter 11 (Retail Organization and Human Resource Management) has new material on women and minorities in retailing. More real-world examples are provided.
   l. Chapter 12 (Operations Management: Financial Dimensions) is updated, and talks more about retail bankruptcies, consolidations, and restructurings.
   m. Chapter 13 (Operations Management: Operational Dimensions) is more tightly focused, with merchandising topics such as category management and inventory management moving to Chapters 14 and 15.
   n. *New!* Chapter 14 (Developing Merchandise Plans) discusses the premise of a merchandising philosophy, presents a framework for merchandise planning, describes category management, and looks at merchandising software.
   o. *Substantially revised!* Chapter 15 (Implementing Merchandise Plans) emphasizes the application of a merchandising strategy, logistics, and inventory management.

p. Chapter 16 (Financial Merchandise Management) is more tightly written and updated.

q. Chapter 17 (Pricing in Retailing) focuses more on the concept of value and the different ways in which price strategies may reflect a good value to consumers.

r. ***Substantially revised!*** Chapter 18 (Establishing and Maintaining a Retail Image) has more on the relationship between atmospherics and retail positioning, as well as how to keep the customer in the store—or at the Web site. There is a new section on atmospherics and Web retailing.

s. Chapter 19 (Promotional Strategy) has enhanced illustrations of promotion efforts in a retail setting and covers the latest trends in retail promotion—including the use of electronic media.

t. Chapter 20 (Integrating and Controlling the Retail Strategy) adds to the previous coverage of benchmarking and gap analysis, and introduces a retailing effectiveness checklist.

A WEB SITE FOR THE 21ST CENTURY:

www.prenhall.com/bermanevans

We are E-xtremely E-nergized (like the E-nergizer Bunny) about the Web site that accompanies *Retail Management: A Strategic Approach*, Eighth Edition. The site is a lively learning, studying, interactive tool. It is easy to use (see Appendix B for more details), provides hands-on applications, and has easy downloads and hot links. We believe the supplement will be of great value to you.

The Web site has several elements, including:

- **Career and Company Information:** Advice on resumé writing, how to take an interview, jobs in retailing, retail career ladders, and a comprehensive listing of retailers (about 500 companies, complete with their addresses, phone numbers, and Web addresses). There are "hot links" that go directly to the career sections of the Web sites of 120 retailers.
- **Study Materials:** Chapter objectives and summaries, and chapter-by-chapter listings of key terms.
- **Interactive Study Guide:** 20 multiple choice, 20 true-false, and 15 fill-in questions per chapter. You can get page references for wrong answers, check your score, and send the results to yourself or your professor.
- **Glossary:** All of the key terms from *Retail Management* with their definitions. Terms may be accessed alphabetically through an easy-to-use search feature.
- **Web Site Directory:** Hundreds of retailing-related Web sites, divided by topic. The sites range from search engines to government agencies to retail firms to trade associations.
- **Computerized Exercises:** 16 user-friendly exercises. These are keyed to the text and noted by a computer icon throughout *Retail Management*.
- **Free Downloads and Demos:** Encourage you to visit specific Web sites to gather useful information and try out innovative software.

HOW THE TEXT IS ORGANIZED

Retail Management: A Strategic Approach has eight parts. Part One introduces the field of retailing, the basics of strategic planning, the importance of building and maintaining relations, and the decisions to be made in owning or managing a retail business. In Part Two, retail institutions are examined in terms of ownership types, as well as store-based, nonstore-based, electronic, and nontraditional strategy mixes. The wheel of retailing, scrambled merchandising, the retail life cycle, and the World Wide Web are covered. Part Three focuses on selecting a target market and information gathering methods, including discussions of why and how consumers shop and the retailing information system. Part Four presents a four-step approach to location planning: trading-area analysis, choosing the most desirable type of location, selecting a general locale, and deciding on a specific site.

Part Five discusses the elements involved in managing a retail business: the retail organization structure, human resource management, and operations management (both financial and operational). Part Six deals with merchandise management—developing merchandise plans, implementing merchandise plans, the financial aspects of merchandising, and pricing. In Part Seven, the ways of communicating with customers are analyzed, with special attention on retail image, atmosphere, and promotion. Part Eight deals with integrating and controlling a retail strategy.

At the end of the text, Appendix A highlights career opportunities in retailing, Appendix B explains the components of the Web site and how to use it, and Appendix C is a comprehensive glossary.

FOR THE PROFESSOR

A complete teaching package is available. It includes a comprehensive Web site for instructors, a detailed instructor's manual, color PowerPoint files, transparency masters, a large test bank, and notes for video lectures. All of the instructional materials have been developed or written by the authors (except for the videos, which we personally selected).

Please feel free to send us comments regarding any aspect of *Retail Management* or its package: Barry Berman (E-mail at mktbxb@hofstra.edu) or Joel R. Evans (E-mail at mktjre@hofstra.edu), Department of Marketing and International Business, Hofstra University, Hempstead, N.Y., 11549. We promise to reply to any correspondence.

B. B.
J. R. E.

ABOUT THE BOXED MATERIAL

IN *RETAIL MANAGEMENT: A STRATEGIC APPROACH*

As noted earlier, there are four applications boxes per chapter: "Technology in Retailing," "Retailing Around the World," "Ethics in Retailing," and "Careers in Retailing." Through these boxes, a wide variety of thought-provoking situations are presented.

"TECHNOLOGY IN RETAILING" BOXES

"RETAILING AROUND THE WORLD" BOXES

"ETHICS IN RETAILING" BOXES

"CAREERS IN RETAILING" BOXES

ABOUT THE VIDEOS

THAT ACCOMPANY
RETAIL MANAGEMENT: A STRATEGIC APPROACH

Every chapter (except Chapter 1) has two end-of-chapter cases, 19 of which have optional video components. In addition, a video for Chapter 1, on Lands' End, augments the discussion of that firm.

These are the cases that have a video component:

ACKNOWLEDGMENTS

Many people have assisted us in the preparation of this book, and to them we extend our warmest appreciation.

We thank these individuals for contributing cases and exercises to the supplement that accompanies *Retail Management: A Strategic Approach.*

Patricia M. Anderson, Quinnipiac College
Joe K. Ballenger, Stephen F. Austin State University
Mary A. Bartling, Mount Mary College
Anne Heineman Batory, Wilkes University
Stephen S. Batory, Bloomsburg University
Marianne C. Bickle, Colorado State University
Doreen Burdalski, Philadelphia University
John Callahan, Eastern Financial Federal Credit Union
James W. Camerius, Northern Michigan University
Kenny K. Chan, California State University, Chico
James W. Clinton, University of Northern Colorado
Dean Cohen, Johannesburg, South Africa
Howard W. Combs, San Jose State University
Andrew Cullen, The Penmore Group
William P. Darrow, Towson University
John D' Auria, Metro-Dade County
Roger Dickinson, University of Texas at Arlington
Molly Eckman, Colorado State University
Jack D. Eure, Jr., Southwest Texas State University
Larry Goldstein, Iona College
Jonathan N. Goodrich, Florida International University
Michele M. Granger, Southwest Missouri State University
Edward Heler, Heler2 Consultancy, LLC
Lisa A. Henderson, Drexel University
Terence L. Holmes, Murray State University
David C. Houghton, Northwest Nazarene University
Brian R. Hoyt, Ohio University

Gail Hudson, Arkansas State University
Michelle Smoot Hyde, Brigham Young University
Karen Hyllegard, Colorado State University
Gale A. Jaeger, Marywood University
Carol Felker Kaufman, Rutgers University, Camden
William W. Keep, Quinnipiac College
Patrick Kemp, Medic Aid Communications
Doris H. Kincade, Virginia Tech University
Algin B. King, Towson University
Gail H. Kirby, Santa Clara University
Antigone Kotsiopulos, Colorado State University
Mark R. Leipnik, Sam Houston State University
Richard C. Leventhal, Metropolitan State College
Michael R. Luthy, Bellarmine College
Kathryn L. Malec, Manchester College
Raymond A. Marquardt, Arizona State University East
Suzanne G. Marshall, California State University, Long Beach
Sanjay S. Mehta, Sam Houston State University
Allan R. Miller, Towson State University
Deborah M. Moscardelli, Central Michigan University
Jennifer Paff Ogle, Colorado State University
Sharon S. Pate, Western Illinois University
Melodie Philhours, Arkansas State University
Carolyn Predmore, Manhattan College
Stan Rapp, Cross Rapp Consulting Group
Lynn Samsel, University of Nebraska–Lincoln
Sangeeta Sarma, University of Kentucky
Bridgette Shields, Crucial Technology
Leslie Stoel, University of Kentucky
Susan C. Strickler, South Dakota State University
Rodney L. Stump, Morgan State University
William R. Swinyard, Brigham Young University
Kellye D. Threlfall, Old Dominion University
Connie Ulasewicz, San Francisco State University
Ginger Woodard, East Carolina University

We thank the following reviewers, who have reacted to this or earlier editions of the text. Each has provided us with perceptive comments that have helped us crystallize our thoughts:

M. Wayne Alexander, Morehead State University
Larry Audler, University of New Orleans
Ramon Avila, Ball State University
Betty V . Balevic, Skidmore College
Stephen S. Batory, Bloomsburg University
Joseph Belonax, Western Michigan University
Ronald Bernard, Diablo Valley College
Charlane Bomrad, Onondaga Community College
John J. Buckley, Orange County Community College
David Burns, Youngstown State University
Joseph A. Davidson, Cuyahoga Community College
Peter T. Doukas, Westchester Community College
Jack D. Eure, Jr., Southwest Texas State University
Letty Fisher, Westchester Community College
Myron Gable, Shippensburg University
Linda L. Golden, University of Texas at Austin
J. Duncan Herrington, Radford University
Mary Higby, Eastern Michigan University
Charles A. Ingene, University of Washington
Marvin A. Jolson, University of Maryland
Ruth Keyes, SUNY College of Technology
J. Ford Laumer, Jr., Auburn University
Richard C. Leventhal, Metropolitan State College
John Lloyd, Monroe Community College
James O. McCann, Henry Ford Community College
Frank McDaniels, Delaware County Community College
Ronald Michman, Shippensburg University

Howard C. Paul, Mercyhurst College
Roy B. Payne, Purdue University
Dawn Pysarchik, Michigan State University
Curtis Reierson, Baylor University
Barry Rudin, Loras College
Julie Toner Schrader, North Dakota State University
Steven J. Shaw, University of South Carolina
Gladys S. Sherdell, Montgomery College
Jill F. Slomski, Gannon University
John E. Swan, University of Alabama in Birmingham
Anthony Urbanisk, Northern State University
Lillian Werner, University of Minnesota
Kaylene Williams, University of Delaware
Terrell G. Williams, Utah State University

Special thanks and acknowledgment are due to the Prentice Hall people who have worked on this edition, especially editor Leah Johnson, production editor Mary Ellen McCourt, Web site coordinator Cindy Harford, assistant editor Anthony Palmiotto, and administrative assistant Rebecca Calvert. We also appreciate the efforts of Diane Schoenberg, Michael Polis, and Allan Randmae for their editorial assistance; and Linda Berman for compiling the indexes.

Barry Berman
Joel R. Evans
HOFSTRA UNIVERSITY

BRIEF CONTENTS

CONTENTS

PART TWO
SITUATION ANALYSIS 113

PART EIGHT

PUTTING IT ALL TOGETHER   671

AN OVERVIEW OF STRATEGIC RETAIL MANAGEMENT

◼ In Part One, the field of retailing, establishing and maintaining relationships, and the basic principles of strategic planning and the decisions made in owning/managing a retail business are explored.

◼ Chapter 1 describes retailing's framework, shows why it should be studied, and examines its special characteristics. The value of strategic planning is noted, including a detailed review of Lands' End. The elements of the retailing concept are presented, as well as the nature of the total retail experience, customer service, and relationship retailing. The focus and format of the text are detailed. At the end of the chapter, hints for solving case studies are offered.

◼ Chapter 2 looks at the complexities involved in retailers' relationships— with both customers and other channel members. These topics are examined: value and the value chain, customer relationships and channel relationships (including the customer base, customer service, customer satisfaction, and loyalty programs), the differences in relationship-building between goods and service retailers, the impact of technology on retailing relationships, and the interplay between ethical performance and relationships in retailing. The chapter ends with an appendix on planning for the unique aspects of service retailing.

◼ Chapter 3 shows the usefulness of strategic planning for all kinds of retailers. Each aspect of the planning process is studied: situation analysis, objectives, identifying consumers, overall strategy, specific activities, control, and feedback. The controllable and uncontrollable parts of a retail strategy are detailed. Strategic planning is shown as a series of interrelated steps that are continuously reviewed. At the end of the chapter, there is an appendix on the strategic implications of international retailing.

CHAPTER 1

An Introduction to Retailing

CHAPTER OBJECTIVES

1. To define retailing, consider it from various perspectives, demonstrate its impact, and note its special characteristics
2. To introduce the concept of strategic planning and apply it
3. To relate the marketing concept to retailing, with an emphasis on the total retail experience, customer service, and relationship retailing.
4. To indicate the focus and format of the text

As Carl Steidtmann, director and chief economist of PricewaterhouseCoopers, says, retailers must be "customer-focused, not product-focused" if they are to create a retailing experience that is enjoyable for shoppers and encourages them to return to those retailers in the future. Close attention to customer service will help keep the retailer's eye on the consumer. Here is a six-step approach for doing so:

1. *Create a Great Environment*—The Ritz-Carlton hotel chain authorizes its employees to handle complaints according to their best judgment. Each staff member "owns" a complaint and is empowered to make sure it's properly resolved.

2. *Listen to Your Customers*—One way of listening is to place executives on the sales floor. An owner of 15 supermarkets in Ireland listens by spending several hours per week packing grocery bags and asking if everything is okay.

3. *Consider the "Lifetime Value" of Your Customers*—Supermarkets, for example, must view customer service from the perspective of a customer's lifetime purchases (roughly $250,000), *not* the $20 or so average purchase per visit.

4. *Use Direct Mail*—Saks and Nordstrom effectively use direct mail to thank their customers. When is the last time *you* received a thank-you letter from a retailer?

5. *Employ Relationship Marketing Principles*—Retailers need to establish relationships with existing customers to motivate them to come back regularly.

6. *Provide Rewards to Your Best Customers*—Reward programs encourage long-term customer patronage. According to Stanley Marcus, "once you establish excellent service, you provide a safe harbor to which customers can always return."[1]

Please Note: Web site addresses are constantly changing.
The links in this chapter are current as of the publication of this book.

OVERVIEW

Retailing consists of the business activities involved in selling goods and services to consumers for their personal, family, or household use. It includes every sale of goods and services to the *final* consumer—ranging from automobiles to apparel to meals at restaurants to movie theater tickets. Retailing is the last stage in the distribution process. In contrast, **wholesaling** is an *intermediate* stage in the distribution process during which goods and services are not sold to final consumers but to business customers—such as manufacturers and retailers—for their use in running the business or for resale to others.

Retailing today is at an interesting crossroads. On the one hand, retail sales are at their highest point in history. Wal-Mart is the first $150 billion retailer (with annual worldwide revenues reaching that amount in 1999). New technologies are improving retail productivity. There are many opportunities to start a new retail business—or work for an existing one—and to join a franchise. Global retailing possibilities abound. On the other hand, retailers face numerous challenges. Many consumers are bored with shopping or do not have much time for it. Some localities have too many stores (making it harder for them to succeed); retailers often seem to spur one another into frequent price cutting (and lower profit margins). Consumer expectations about customer service are high—while retailers are offering more self-service and automated systems (such as voice mail) to handle customer interactions. At the same time, many retailers are not yet sure what to do with the Internet; even those with Web sites often do not know whether to use them for image purposes, customer information and feedback, and/or sales transactions.

Here's the way the *U.S. Industry & Trade Outlook* puts it:

> The retail industry is one of the most competitive in the United States, which means retailers will continue competing in any way possible. For instance, some will pursue the strategy of providing better customer service, while others will try to make shopping more pleasant by investing in entertainment; some will invest heavily in new technologies to try to reduce costs and pass savings on to consumers, while others may expand the merchandise mix or develop a store-specific brand; some may consolidate or merge to have better service. Retailers may focus on such strategies, but it is expected that they will continue investing in their business to ensure that customers return. In short, retailers will compete to raise the value people receive from shopping with a particular firm.[2]

Can retailers flourish in this setting? You bet! Just look at your favorite restaurant, dry cleaner, and supermarket. Look at the rapid growth of Bed Bath & Beyond, Gymboree, and Old Navy. What do they have in common? A desire to please the customer and a strong market niche. See what the new Great Lakes Crossing mall is doing (Figure 1.1). To prosper in the long term, they all need a solid strategic plan and a willingness to adapt to change, both central thrusts of this book.

In Chapter 1, we will look at the framework of retailing, the importance of developing and applying a sound retail strategy, and the focus and format of the text.

Visit Wal-Mart (www.wal-mart.com) and see what drives the world's largest retailer.

Old Navy (www. oldnavy.com) has a distinctive style—in the store and on the Web.

THE FRAMEWORK OF RETAILING

To better understand retailing's role and the range of retailing options that are possible, let us look at it from these perspectives:

- Suppose we manage a manufacturing firm that makes vacuum cleaners. How should we sell these items to our customers? We could distribute via big chains such as Circuit City or small neighborhood appliance stores, have our own sales force visit people in their

Figure 1.1
The Allure of Retailing

To flourish, retailers need to be appealing and have a strong market niche. Great Lakes Crossing is Michigan's first enclosed value-regional shopping/entertainment mall. It is quickly establishing itself as the state's most popular tourist destination. Since the center's grand opening in November 1998, Great Lakes Crossing's fashion, food, and fun have been attracting customers from an extended 100-mile trading area. In this photo montage, clockwise from upper left: Stores are arranged in a series of named and numbered merchandise "zones." Gameworks, a creation of Sega and Steven Spielberg, is one of the center's entertainment venues. Bass Pro Outdoor World is expected to draw over 4 million visitors annually to the mall. Rainforest Café is one of over 30 dining options.
Reprinted by permisssion of The Taubman Company.

homes (as Electrolux does), or set up our own stores (if we have the ability and resources to do so). We could even sponsor TV infomercials or magazine ads, complete with a toll-free phone number.

- Suppose we have an idea for a service, such as a new way to teach first graders to use computer software for spelling and vocabulary. How should we set it up? We could lease a store in a strip shopping center and run ads in a local paper, rent space in a Y and rely on teacher referrals, or do mailings to parents and visit children in their homes. In each case, the service is offered "live." But now, there is another option: We could use an animated Web site to teach children "online."

- Suppose that we, as consumers, want to buy apparel. What choices do we have? We could go to a department store or to one specializing in apparel. We could shop with a full-service retailer or a discounter (even a flea market). We could go to a shopping center because of the store variety or order from a catalog to maximize convenience. We could look to retailers with a broad assortment of clothing (if we like to buy complete outfits) or look to retailers with a deep assortment of clothing in one category (if we like to buy items such as shoes and outerwear at different stores). We could even zip around the Web and visit the growing list of retailers with sites—including ones around the globe.

Service businesses such as Avis (www. avis.com) often engage in retailing.

There is a tendency to think of retailing as primarily including the sale of tangible (physical) goods. However, it is essential to recognize that retailing also encompasses the sale of services. A service may be the shopper's primary purchase (such as a haircut or airline travel) or it may be part of the shopper's purchase of a good (such as delivery or training). Retailing does not have to involve a store. Mail and phone orders, direct selling to consumers in their homes and offices, Web transactions, and vending machine sales all fall within the scope of retailing. Lastly, retailing does not have to include a "retailer." Manufacturers, importers, nonprofit firms, and wholesalers act as retailers if they sell goods or services to final consumers. On the other hand, purchases made by manufacturers, wholesalers, and other organizations for their use in the organization or further resale are not part of retailing.

Let us now examine various reasons for studying retailing and its special characteristics.

Reasons for Studying Retailing

Learn more about the exciting array of retailing career opportunities (www. careersinretailing. com).

Among the reasons for studying retailing are its impact on the economy, its functions in distribution, and its relationship with firms selling goods and services to retailers for their resale or use. These factors are discussed next. A fourth element for students of retailing is the broad range of career opportunities, as highlighted with a "Careers in Retailing" box in each chapter and in Appendix A at the end of this book. See Figure 1.2.

The Impact of Retailing on the Economy Retailing is a major part of U.S. and world commerce. Retail sales and employment are key economic contributors, and retail trends often mirror trends in a nation's overall economy.

Figure 1.2
Career Pathways to Success

Reprinted by permission.

A Career in Retailing Is a Best Buy

When he started with the company nearly 30 years ago, Brad Anderson—the president and chief operating officer of Best Buy—never thought he would be sitting in his current office: "I take great pride in only having done one job interview in my life. I am not a person who started off with a specific ambition to be very successful in business or knew what I wanted in terms of a career." His current position is due to his vision in helping Best Buy grow from a small specialty audio store to a 312-store consumer electronics and appliance powerhouse.

Anderson believes new products and innovations will be the driving force of the future in retailing; and this will have major implications for retailers: "The biggest thing for us as retailers is to try and figure out how to change as fast as the products we sell and as our consumers' education requires us to change. And it isn't just the retail environment. There's virtually nothing we do that won't be impacted over the course of the next 10 years by the products that are coming out of this industry."

Anderson also thinks the retail industry must overcome its traditional resistance to change in order to keep up with the new environment. In the past, retailers set a course and maintained it. "Now you're constantly adjusting your course."

Source: Laura Heller, "A Top-Drawer Exec with Ground-Floor Perspective," *Discount Store News* (May 24, 1999), pp. 38, 72.

According to the Department of Commerce, annual U.S. retail store sales are about $3 trillion. Telephone and mail-order sales by nonstore retailers, vending machines, direct selling, and the Web generate another $250 billion in yearly revenues. Furthermore, personal consumption expenditures on financial, medical, legal, educational, and other services account for another several hundred billion dollars in annual retail revenues. Outside the United States, retail sales are trillions of dollars per year.

Durable goods stores—including the automotive group, furniture and appliance group, and lumber, building materials, and hardware group—account for 42 percent of total U.S. retail store sales, with the automotive group alone responsible for one-fourth of all U.S. retail store sales. Nondurable goods and services stores—including the general merchandise group, apparel group, gasoline service stations, eating and drinking places, food group, drug and proprietary stores, and liquor stores—together account for the other 58 percent of U.S. retail store sales, with the food group, general merchandise group, eating and drinking places, and apparel group contributing nearly 45 percent of all U.S. retail store sales.

French-based Carrefour (www. carrefour.com) is the largest non-U.S. retailer on the planet.

The world's 100 largest retailers generate $1.75 trillion annually in revenues. These firms represent 15 nations and such categories as diversified retailing, supermarkets, specialty stores, department stores, drugstores, convenience stores, mail order, and membership clubs. Forty-two of the 100 are based in the United States (including three of the top six), 11 in Great Britain, 10 in France, 9 in Germany, and 9 in Japan.[3] Table 1.1 shows the 1998 performance of the 10 largest U.S. retailers. They accounted for $401 billion in sales—one-seventh of U.S. retail store sales—and operated more than 20,200 stores.

Retailing is a major source of jobs. U.S. Bureau of Labor Statistics' data show that more than 22 million people are employed by traditional retailers. Yet this figure understates the true number of people working in retailing because it does not include the several million persons employed by service firms, seasonal employees, proprietors, and unreported workers in family businesses or partnerships. Among the leading retail employers in the United

Table 1.1 The 10 Largest Retailers in the United States, 1998

Rank	Company	Web Address	Major Retail Emphasis	Sales (thousands)	After-Tax Earnings (thousands)	Number of Stores
1	Wal-Mart	www.wal-mart.com	Full-line discount stores, membership clubs	$137,634,000	$4,430,000	3,599
2	Sears Roebuck	www.sears.com	Department stores, specialty stores	41,322,000	1,048,000	3,043
3	Kmart	www.bluelight.com	Full-line discount stores	33,674,000	518,000	2,161
4	Target Corporation (formerly Dayton Hudson)	www.targetcorp.com	Department stores, full-line discount stores	30,951,000	935,000	1,182
5	J.C. Penney	www.jcpenney.com	Department stores, drugstores, catalog	30,678,000	594,000	3,904
6	Home Depot	www.homedepot.com	Home centers	30,219,000	1,614,000	761
7	Kroger	www.kroger.com	Supermarkets, convenience stores	28,203,000	411,000	2,207
8	Safeway	www.safeway.com	Supermarkets	24,484,000	807,000	1,497
9	Costco	www.costco.com	Membership clubs	24,270,000	460,000	278
10	American Stores	www.americanstores.com	Supermarkets, drugstores	19,867,000	234,000	1,580

Source: Company annual reports.

States—and other nations, as well—are eating and drinking places, food stores, general merchandise stores, auto dealers and service stations, apparel and accessory stores, and furniture and home furnishings stores.

From another perspective—costs—retailing is a key field of study. In the United States, on average, 32 cents of every dollar spent in department stores, 45 cents of every dollar spent in furniture and home furnishings stores, and nearly 25 cents of every dollar spent in grocery stores go to the retailers to pay for the operating costs incurred, activities performed, and profits earned. Costs include rent, store displays, wages, ads, and store maintenance. Only a small part of each sales dollar is retailer profit. In 1998, the 10 largest U.S. retailers' after-tax profits averaged 2.8 percent of sales.[4] Thus, a change in retail productivity can have a big impact on consumers and the economy. Figure 1.3 shows 1998 costs and profits for J.C. Penney, a firm with department stores, drugstores (most notably Eckerd), and a large catalog business.

Retail Functions in Distribution Retailing is the last stage in a **channel of distribution,** which comprises all of the businesses and people involved in the physical movement and transfer of ownership of goods and services from producer to consumer. A typical distribution channel is shown in Figure 1.4.

In a distribution channel, retailers play a key role as the contact between manufacturers, wholesalers, and other suppliers and the final consumer. Here's how: Many manufacturers would like to make one basic type of item and sell their entire inventory to as few buyers as

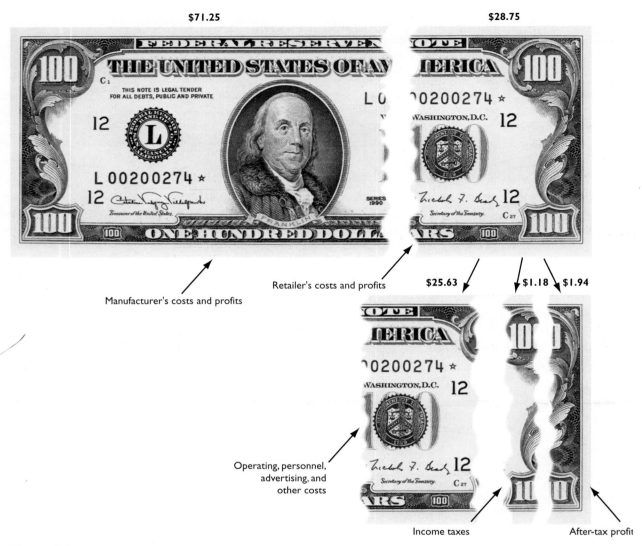

Figure 1.3

The High Costs and Low Profits of Retailing—Where the Typical $100 Spent with J.C. Penney in 1998 Went

The data are based on the averages for all J.C. Penney businesses: department stores, drugstores, and catalog.

Source: Computed by the authors from *J.C. Penney Company 1998 Annual Report.*

possible. Yet, final consumers usually want to choose from a variety of goods and services and purchase a limited quantity. So, retailers collect an assortment of goods and services from various sources, buy them in large quantity, and offer to sell them in small quantities to consumers. This is the **sorting process.** See Figure 1.5.

As a result, each manufacturer (wholesaler) becomes more efficient, and final consumers are pleased with the available selection. Wide retail assortments let customers do one-stop shopping; and they can choose and buy the product version and amount desired. The word *retailing* is actually based on this breaking-bulk function. It is derived from the old French word *retailler*, which means "to cut up."

Figure 1.4
A Typical Channel of
Distribution

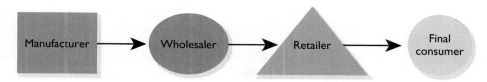

Handwritten margin note: Communication

Another function for retailers is communicating both with customers and with manufacturers and wholesalers. From ads, salespeople, and displays, shoppers learn about the availability and characteristics of goods and services, store hours, sales, and so on. Manufacturers, wholesalers, and others are informed about sales forecasts, delivery delays, customer complaints, defective items, inventory turnover (by style, color, and size), and more. Many goods and services have been modified due to feedback received by suppliers.

Handwritten margin note: service (store, transport, advert, pre-pay marking)

For small manufacturers and wholesalers, retailers can provide assistance by transporting, storing, marking, advertising, and pre-paying for merchandise. However, small retailers may need the same type of help from their suppliers. The number of functions performed by retailers has a direct bearing on the percentage of each sales dollar they need to cover their costs and profits.

Handwritten margin note: custom. service (delivery, install.)

Retailers also complete transactions with customers. This means striving to fill orders promptly and accurately and often involves processing customer credit via the retailers' or another charge plan. In addition, retailers may provide customer services such as gift wrapping, delivery, and installation.

Handwritten margin note: adv./benefit of manuf/ws.

For these reasons, in most cases, goods and services are sold via retail firms not owned by manufacturers (wholesalers). This lets the manufacturer (wholesaler) reach more customers, reduce costs, improve cash flow, increase sales more rapidly, and focus on its area of expertise.

Figure 1.5
The Retailer's Role in
the Sorting Process

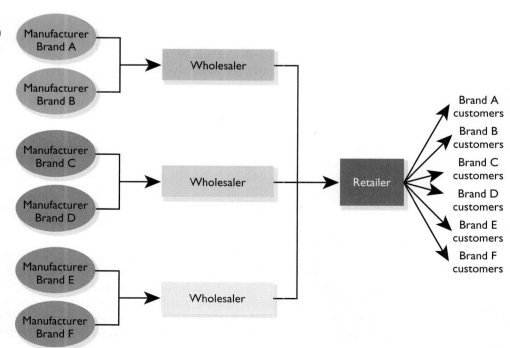

Sherwin-Williams (www.sherwin-williams.com) is not only a manufacturer but also a retailer.

Manufacturers such as Sherwin-Williams and Polo Ralph Lauren do operate their own retail facilities (besides selling at traditional retailers), and are excellent at it. In running their stores, these firms complete the full range of retailing functions and compete with conventional retailers: They consider how many final consumers will buy their products, how geographically dispersed those people are, what expenditures are needed to fulfill retailing functions, what level of service is required by consumers, and other factors. Yet, due to the scope of retailing tasks, even strong manufacturers can fail as retailers. Liz Claiborne had to close its First Issue women's clothing store chain. It had too limited an assortment, an inadequate number of stores (77 nationally), unexciting decors, and other weaknesses. In short, Liz Claiborne learned that designing clothing and selling it in department stores and specialty stores were not the same as actually operating retail stores. Liz Claiborne really did not know how to be a good retailer.

The Relationships Among Retailers and Their Suppliers The complex relationships among retailers and their suppliers must be understood. On one hand, retailers are part of a distribution channel; thus, manufacturers and wholesalers must be concerned about retail coverage of the consumer market, the caliber of displays, the level of customer services, store hours, and retailers' reliability as business partners. On the other hand, retailers are also major customers of goods and services for resale, store fixtures, computer equipment, management consulting, and insurance.

Retailers and their suppliers may have divergent viewpoints that need to be reconciled. Control over the distribution channel, profit allocation, the number of competing retailers handling suppliers' products, display space and locations, promotion support, payment terms, and operating flexibility are just a few issues over which retailers and suppliers may have different priorities. Due to the large number of regional, national, and global chains, retailers now have more power in the distribution channel than ever.

Channel relations are generally smoothest if **exclusive distribution** is involved, whereby suppliers enter into agreements with one or a few retailers designating the latter as the only companies in specified geographic areas to carry certain brands or product lines. This arrangement stimulates both parties to work together in maintaining an image, assigning shelf space, allotting profits and costs, advertising, and so on. Yet, it also usually requires that retailers limit their assortment of goods and services in the product categories covered by an agreement; thus, retailers might have to decline to handle other suppliers' items. From the manufacturers' perspective, exclusive distribution may limit their long-run total sales potential.

Channel relations tend to be most volatile if **intensive distribution** is used, whereby suppliers sell through as many retailers as possible. This often maximizes suppliers' sales and lets retailers offer many brands and product versions. As a result, competition among retailers selling the same items is high; and retailers may use tactics not beneficial to individual suppliers, as they are more concerned about their own revenues than sales of any brand. They may assign shelf space, set prices, and advertise in a way that is adverse to specific brands (giving them little space, using them as sale items, or not advertising them).

With **selective distribution,** suppliers sell through a moderate number of retailers. This combines aspects of exclusive and intensive distribution. It allows suppliers to have higher sales than in exclusive distribution and lets retailers carry some competing brands. It encourages suppliers to provide marketing support and retailers to give adequate shelf space. Yet, this approach generally does not have the channel cooperation of exclusive distribution or the sales potential of intensive distribution. See Figure 1.6.

Unless suppliers know retailers' attributes and needs, they cannot have good rapport with them; and as long as retailers have a choice of suppliers, they will select those that best understand and react to their needs. The following illustrate several issues in retailer–supplier relations:

Figure 1.6
Comparing Exclusive,
Intensive, and
Selective Distribution

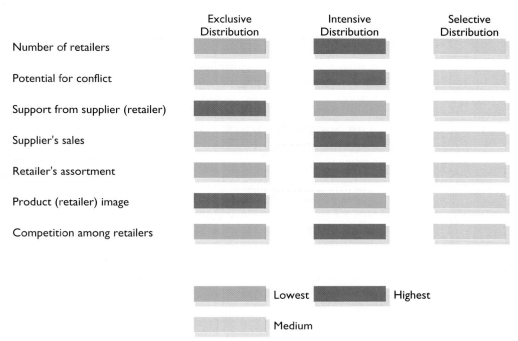

	Exclusive Distribution	Intensive Distribution	Selective Distribution
Number of retailers	Medium	Highest	Lowest
Potential for conflict	Medium	Highest	Lowest
Support from supplier (retailer)	Highest	Medium	Lowest
Supplier's sales	Medium	Highest	Medium
Retailer's assortment	Medium	Highest	Medium
Product (retailer) image	Highest	Medium	Lowest
Competition among retailers	Medium	Highest	Lowest

Lowest   Highest

Medium

- Competition in the marketplace—Many manufacturers thought the Web would deliver a lot of good news. Here was a way to generate new customers, interact directly with shoppers, increase market share, and reduce selling costs: "There's just one hitch. Those same thoughts terrify retailers. They fear that their role between company and customer will be rendered obsolete by the virtual marketplace."[5]
- Product image—Baccarat, the maker of fine crystal, has engaged in a long-running dispute with Ross-Simons, an off-price retailer with store and catalog operations. Ross-Simons carries jewelry and fine housewares with such prestige names as Lenox, Wedgwood, Reed and Barton, Waterford, and Baccarat. However, to protect its high-quality image, Baccarat no longer wants to sell through off-price retailers such as Ross-Simons. As a result, the two firms have been in litigation for a number of years.[6]
- Slotting allowances—Some large book retailers, including Barnes & Noble and Amazon.com, are requiring publishers to pay slotting allowances for prime space in their stores or at their Web sites. This makes the space expensive and difficult to secure for small publishers: With Amazon.com, publishers pay up to $10,000 for a prominent listing on its Web site.[7]
- Distribution rights—Until the early 1990s, Goodyear sold its tires predominantly through a distribution network of 3,000 independent dealers. Since then, Goodyear has added such major retail chains as Wal-Mart, Sears, and Kmart. Accordingly, a number of dealers felt Goodyear's adding these firms hurt their own customer base and reduced their profits. Some sued Goodyear. But today, the situation has turned around because Goodyear offers them exclusive tire lines and enhanced marketing programs.[8]

Manufacturers of goods that are used in retail businesses should also have a working knowledge of retailing. Thus, a fixture manufacturer has to understand the operations of its retailers with regard to store layout, linear feet of shelf space, the use of self-service merchandising, routing of customer traffic, and storage specifications. Both a knowledge of basic retailing principles and the special factors relative to a given type of retailer are necessary for the fixture manufacturer to succeed.

Similarly, firms that sell services, such as insurance, to retailers can benefit from a good understanding of retailing. Inventory valuation, employee job functions, construction costs, crime rates, and depreciation are some relevant factors that must be examined. For example, how should merchandise that has been marked down in price be valued if there is water damage? Or how much will fire insurance premiums be reduced if new sprinklers are installed in a store?

The Special Characteristics of Retailing

Several special characteristics distinguish retailing from other types of business. Three of them are noted in Figure 1.7 and discussed here: The average amount of a sales transaction for retailers is much less than for manufacturers. Final consumers make many unplanned purchases; those who buy for resale or for use in manufacturing products or running a business are more systematic and plan ahead. Most retail customers must be drawn to a retail location; salespeople often visit manufacturers, wholesalers, and other firms to initiate and complete transactions. Each factor imposes unique requirements on retail firms.

Average sales transactions per shopping trip are well under $100 for department stores, specialty stores, and supermarkets. These low amounts create a need to tightly control the costs associated with each transaction (such as credit verification, sales personnel, and bagging); to maximize the number of customers drawn to the retailer, which may place more emphasis on ads and special promotions; and to increase impulse sales by more aggressive selling. However, low average sales and high costs cannot always be controlled by the retailer. For example, over the past decade, the average amount of a sales transaction in a department store has gone up only slightly more than the rate of inflation. And, despite their high costs, one-half of specialty store sales are on credit.

Inventory management is often difficult for retailers because of the many small sales transactions to a large number of different customers. As an illustration, a typical supermarket has 6,000 to 7,000 customer transactions *per week*. This makes it harder for retailers to determine the levels of existing stock and the popularity of various brands, sizes, and prices of merchandise. For that reason, retailers are expanding their use of computerized inventory systems.

Retail sales often involve unplanned or impulse purchases. Surveys show that a large percentage of consumers do not look at ads before shopping, do not prepare shopping lists (or deviate from the lists once in stores), and make purchases that are fully unplanned. This

Figure 1.7
Special
Characteristics
Affecting Retailers

behavior indicates the value of point-of-purchase displays, attractive store layouts, and well-organized stores, catalogs, and Web sites. Candy, cosmetics, snack foods, magazines, and other items can be sold as impulse goods if they are placed in visible, high-traffic places in a store, catalog, or Web site. Since consumers buy so many goods and services in an unplanned manner, the retailer's ability to forecast, budget, order merchandise, and have the proper number of personnel on the selling floor is made tougher.

Macy's (www.macys. com) recently added a Web site to accompany its traditional stores and catalogs.

Retail customers usually visit a store, even though mail, phone, and Web sales have increased in recent years. The large number of final consumers, the interest of many consumers in shopping in person and in comparison shopping among brands and models, the small average transaction, the unplanned nature of purchases, and consumers' desire for privacy at home are just some reasons for the popularity of stores. And since people must be attracted to a store, the retailer needs to consider such factors as location, transportation, hours, proximity of competitors, product assortment, parking, and advertising.

THE IMPORTANCE OF DEVELOPING AND APPLYING A RETAIL STRATEGY

A **retail strategy** is the overall plan guiding a retail firm. It influences the firm's business activities and its response to market forces, such as competition and the economy. Any retailer, regardless of size or type, can and should utilize these six steps in strategic planning:

1. Define the type of business in terms of the goods or service category and the company's specific orientation (such as full-service or "no frills").

2. Set long-run and short-run objectives for sales and profit, market share, image, and so on.

3. Determine the customer market to which to appeal on the basis of its characteristics (such as gender and income level) and needs (such as product and brand preferences).

Doing Well by Doing Good

Macy's 16th annual Passport Show, staged in both Los Angeles and San Francisco, raised a record $2 million for AIDS research. The sold-out events, both called "Different Together," included a fashion show, as well as a parade of fashion, entertainment, sports celebrities, and political figures. The fashion show featured designs from Laundry by Shelli Segal, Tahari, Makins Hats, Hugo Boss, Levi Strauss, and Calvin Klein. Models were dressed in fashions representing each decade of the 20th century. In both cities, speakers included the chairman and chief executive officer of Macy's West, Elizabeth Taylor, Magic Johnson, and k.d. lang. Close to 3,000 people attended the event at each location.

Despite the show's success, the chairman of Macy's West says, "It was more difficult this year to get people involved because there's a feeling that with the advances we've made on AIDS research, that we've gotten there, but we haven't."

Additional funds were raised through Macy's West's annual Passport In-Store promotion. With that program, customers who contributed $10 received a 15 percent discount on all Macy's West purchases that day. Macy's West acknowledges that the Passport In-Store is one of its busiest sales days of the year.

Evaluate the ethics of Macy's Passport In-Store promotion.

Source: Teena Hammond, "Macy's Raises $2 Million for Aids Research," *Women's Wear Daily* (October 16, 1998), p. 17.

4. Devise an overall, long-run plan that gives general direction to a firm and its employees.

5. Implement an integrated strategy that combines such factors as store location, product assortment, pricing, and advertising and displays to achieve objectives.

6. Regularly evaluate performance and correct weaknesses or problems as they are observed.

To illustrate these points, the background and strategy of Lands' End—one of the world's foremost retailers—are presented. Then, the marketing concept is defined and applied to retailing.

At Lands' End (www.landsend.com), satisfaction is guaranteed. Period.

Lands' End: Where Customer Satisfaction Is Guaranteed. Period.[9]

Company Background Gary Comer worked at an ad agency for 10 years, but his true vocation was sailing. So, he left the agency in 1963 and with his sailing partner opened a catalog outlet store in Chicago specializing in sailing equipment. The name Lands' End (rather than the intended Land's End) was due to a typographical error in an early catalog! After five years and only moderate success, Gary Comer bought out his partner and began tinkering with the catalog. He added clothing, accessories, and luggage aimed at full-time and weekend sailors. The inaugural full-color catalog (30 pages) appeared in 1975.

1976 saw Lands' End shift direction. Comer decided to no longer carry sailing items and instead turned to recreational and informal clothing, accessories, shoes, and soft-sided luggage—and broadened the customer base. Unlike many apparel-based retailers, most Lands' End clothing was (and is) traditionally styled, with only slight seasonal variations. In 1978, headquarters were moved to Wisconsin and a toll-free 800 number established (with 24-hour service commencing in 1980). National ads were introduced in 1981, and the firm went public during 1986. Three specialty catalogs were launched in 1990, with the first foreign catalog mailed in 1991. During 1995, the firm opened a state-of-the-art World Wide Web site (www.landsend.com)—which in 1999 was named one of the most outstanding sites in the apparel field in a consumer study conducted by Vanderbilt University's Owen School of Management.

Today, Lands' End is a giant. Annual sales (by mail order, phone, outlet stores, and the Web) are $1.4 billion; it has facilities in Germany, Great Britain, and Japan; and it ships products to 175 nations around the globe. It sends 250 million catalogs a year and its Web site is visited 16 million times yearly; online sales more than tripled from 1998 to 1999. Lands' End has 1,100 phone lines and handles up to 50,000 calls daily (100,000 in December). Its Wisconsin distribution center is the size of 16 football fields.

The Lands' End Strategy: Keys to Success Throughout its nearly 40 years of existence, during the ups and downs facing any retailer, Lands' End has followed a consistent, far-sighted, customer-oriented strategy—one that has paved the way for its long-term achievements. Here are some of Lands' End's keys to a successful strategy:

- Growth-oriented objectives—The firm seeks annual long-run growth of 10 to 15 percent. To reach that goal, it is seeking greater volume from existing customers and trying to get more customers from its data base who have not bought in the past three years to do so. The firm hopes to expand its international operations even further and move much more rapidly into online sales.
- Appeal to a prime market—The firm is strong with 35- to 64-year-old customers, who have a median household income of $55,000. About 70 percent of customers are professionals or managers.
- Outstanding customer service—The firm prides itself on offering the best possible customer service, as exemplified by the "principles of doing business" shown in Figure 1.8.

Figure 1.8
The Guiding
Philosophy of Lands'
End

Reprinted by permission.

The Lands' End Principles of Doing Business.

Principle 1.
WE DO EVERYTHING WE CAN TO MAKE OUR PRODUCTS BETTER. WE IMPROVE MATERIAL, AND ADD BACK FEATURES AND CONSTRUCTION DETAILS THAT OTHERS HAVE TAKEN OUT OVER THE YEARS. WE NEVER REDUCE THE QUALITY OF A PRODUCT TO MAKE IT CHEAPER.

Principle 2.
WE PRICE OUR PRODUCTS FAIRLY AND HONESTLY. WE DO NOT, HAVE NOT, AND WILL NOT PARTICIPATE IN THE COMMON RETAILING PRACTICE OF INFLATING MARK-UPS TO SET UP A FUTURE PHONY "SALE."

Principle 3.
WE ACCEPT ANY RETURN FOR ANY REASON, AT ANY TIME. OUR PRODUCTS ARE GUARANTEED. NO FINE PRINT. NO ARGUMENTS. WE MEAN EXACTLY WHAT WE SAY: GUARANTEED. PERIOD.

Principle 4.
WE SHIP FASTER THAN ANYONE WE KNOW OF. WE SHIP ITEMS IN STOCK THE DAY AFTER WE RECEIVE THE ORDER. AT THE HEIGHT OF THE LAST CHRISTMAS SEASON THE LONGEST TIME AN ORDER WAS IN THE HOUSE WAS 36 HOURS, EXCEPTING MONOGRAMS WHICH TOOK ANOTHER 12 HOURS.

Principle 5.
WE BELIEVE THAT WHAT IS BEST FOR OUR CUSTOMER IS BEST FOR ALL OF US. EVERYONE HERE UNDERSTANDS THAT CONCEPT. OUR SALES AND SERVICE PEOPLE ARE TRAINED TO KNOW OUR PRODUCTS, AND TO BE FRIENDLY AND HELPFUL. THEY ARE URGED TO TAKE ALL THE TIME NECESSARY TO TAKE CARE OF YOU. WE EVEN PAY FOR YOUR CALL, FOR WHATEVER REASON YOU CALL.

Principle 6.
WE ARE ABLE TO SELL AT LOWER PRICES BECAUSE WE HAVE ELIMINATED MIDDLEMEN; BECAUSE WE DON'T BUY BRANDED MERCHANDISE WITH HIGH PROTECTED MARK-UPS; AND BECAUSE WE HAVE PLACED OUR CONTRACTS WITH MANUFACTURERS WHO HAVE PROVEN THAT THEY ARE COST CONSCIOUS AND EFFICIENT.

Principle 7.
WE ARE ABLE TO SELL AT LOWER PRICES BECAUSE WE OPERATE EFFICIENTLY. OUR PEOPLE ARE HARD-WORKING, INTELLIGENT, AND SHARE IN THE SUCCESS OF THE COMPANY.

Principle 8.
WE ARE ABLE TO SELL AT LOWER PRICES BECAUSE WE SUPPORT NO FANCY EMPORIUMS WITH THEIR HIGH OVERHEAD. OUR MAIN LOCATION IS IN THE MIDDLE OF A 40-ACRE CORNFIELD IN RURAL WISCONSIN.

Calls are answered promptly, almost all merchandise is available in stock, and most orders are delivered in two days. Salespeople undergo 80 hours of training when hired, and regular training thereafter. Trousers are hemmed free and lost buttons are replaced, also for free. Lands' End has the simplest, most comprehensive guarantee in the industry: "GUARANTEED. PERIOD." Customers can return products at any time for any reason.

- Personalized company image—Unlike other mail-order retailers, which just show pictures of products, present brief descriptions, and cite prices, Lands' End adds a personal touch. An entry for slacks may contain a story on "why the chino slacks may be the best 'hanging out' pants you'll ever put on." Its catalogs include short stories by notable writers such as Elmore Leonard. The Lands' End guarantee is stated in each catalog and on its Web site, as is its toll-free number. Shoppers who call usually reach full-time, year-round operators, who provide information, answer questions, and process orders.

- Employee relations—Lands' End is rated as one of *Fortune*'s "Top 100 Best Companies to Work For."

- Extensive promotion—The firm mails new catalogs every few weeks. Besides general catalogs, it has specialty catalogs for narrower target markets and to reduce seasonality, as well as catalog and mailing costs. It runs ads in magazines and newspapers; and its Web site has been featured in TV ads. See Figure 1.9.

- Honest value—The firm says, "Value is more than price. *Value* is the combination of product quality, world-class customer service, and a fair price."

- Commitment to technology—The firm is devoted to new technologies that cater to the changing marketplace. Lands' End was one of the first retailers to engage in electronic shopping systems, with touch-screen kiosks in train stations, office buildings, and hotel lobbies. In addition, ordering, warehousing, and other operations are highly automated and computerized.

- Responsiveness to unsatisfactory performance—In 1999, after a tough 1998 (sales were up from 1997, but profits were down), Lands' End aggressively restructured the com-

Figure 1.9
Lands' End's
Dominant Business:
Mail-Order Retailing

Lands' End is one of the leading mail-order retailers in the world, with a large and growing global presence. It regularly promotes its catalogs in a number of media.
Photo by Barry Berman.

pany by function and by channel of distribution to accelerate online sales, reduce organizational layers and duplication, and cut costs.

The Marketing Concept Applied to Retailing

As just described, Lands' End has a sincere long-term desire to please customers. In doing so, it uses a customer-centered, companywide approach to strategy development and implementation; it is value-driven; and it has clear goals. Together, these principles form the **marketing concept.**

The marketing concept can be transformed into the retailing concept, which should be understood and applied by all retailers. See Figure 1.10. The **retailing concept** comprises these four elements:

1. *Customer orientation*—The retailer determines the attributes and needs of its customers and endeavors to satisfy these needs to the fullest.

2. *Coordinated effort*—The retailer integrates all plans and activities to maximize efficiency.

3. *Value-driven*—The retailer offers good value to customers, whether it be a discounter or upscale. This means having prices appropriate for the level of products and customer service.

4. *Goal orientation*—The retailer sets goals and then uses its strategy to attain them.

Technology in Retailing

Consumers Find It's a "Bot" Comparison Shopping

Shopping robots, called "bots," are computerized comparison programs that enable online shoppers to search hundreds of Web sites in seconds and learn which Web-based retailer offers the best price. As a result, bots are putting increased pressure on Web retailers to offer the best price. They have also resulted in a "fundamental shift in power to the consumer," according to one consultant.

Let's look at how a typical bot such as mySimon (www.mysimon.com) works. Suppose you are interested in purchasing a novel. You just go to the bot's Web site and type the title. The program then searches through its listing of Web retailers, ranging from large bookstores to small specialty bookstores. The bot then provides a list of retail prices for that title, along with shipping times and shipping costs. You can, thus, choose the retailer based on a combi-

nation of overall costs and shipping time. Comparison shopping is also available on RoboShopper (www.roboshopper.com) and through Excite and Infoseek, among others.

Although bots are very useful, they are not without their limitations. For example, some merchants have prevented bots from entering their sites. Others have tried to thwart bot comparison shopping by offering products in special configurations that are not available with other firms (such as adding a case or a battery pack to a camera).

As a small Web book retailer, you are considering offering rock bottom prices on best-sellers to increase traffic on your site. What are the pros and cons of this tactic?

Sources: Chris Taylor, "Bot Till You Drop," *Time* (October 11, 1999), pp. 52–53; and Rebecca Quick, "Buying the Goods: The Attack of the Robots," *Wall Street Journal* (December 7, 1998), p. R14.

Figure 1.10
Applying the Retailing
Concept

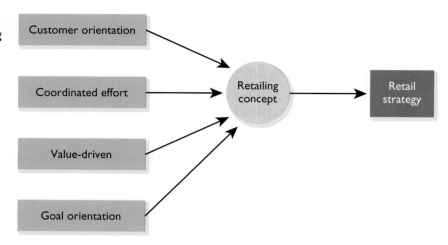

Unfortunately, this concept is not grasped by every retailer. Some are indifferent to customer needs, plan haphazardly, have prices that do not reflect the value offered, and have unclear goals. Too often, retailers are not receptive to change, or they blindly follow strategies enacted by competitors. Some retailers do not get feedback from customers; they rely on supplier reports or their own past sales trends.

The retailing concept is fairly easy to adopt. It means communicating with shoppers and viewing their desires as critical to the firm's success, having a consistent strategy (such as offering designer brands, plentiful sales personnel, attractive displays, and above-average prices in an upscale store), offering prices perceived as "fair" (a good value for the money) by customers, and working to achieve meaningful, specific, and reachable goals. However, the retailing concept is only a strategic guide. It does not deal with a firm's internal capabilities or competitive advantages but offers a broad planning framework.

Let's look at three issues that relate to a retailer's performance in terms of the retailing concept: the total retail experience, customer service, and relationship retailing.

The Total Retail Experience   While one person may shop at a discount retailer, another at a neighborhood store, a third at a full-service firm, and so on, these diverse shoppers have something crucial in common: They each encounter a total retail experience (including everything from parking to checkout counter) in making a purchase.

The **total retail experience** includes all the elements in a retail offering that encourage or inhibit consumers during their contact with a retailer. Many elements, such as the number of salespeople, displays, prices, the brands carried, and inventory on hand, are controllable by a retailer; others, like the adequacy of on-street parking, the speed of online shopping, and sales taxes, are not. If some part of the total retail experience is unsatisfactory, consumers may not buy a given good or service—they may even decide not to patronize a retailer again. As one disgruntled shopper remarked, "While visiting a department store, I was amazed at how the only salesperson in the area was chatting on the telephone. I roamed around the area near the counter trying to catch her attention. This didn't work. Finally, I approached the counter and stood directly in front of her. She refused to make eye contact and actually turned away from me. At this point, I stormed out of the store, vowing never to return."[10]

In planning a customer-oriented, integrated strategy, a retailer must be sure all strategic elements are in place. For the shopper segment to which a particular firm appeals, the total retail experience must be aimed at fulfilling customer expectations—and it must meet them. That means a discount store should have ample stock on hand when it runs sales, but not plush carpeting on the floor; a neighborhood store should be open late hours, but not have overly trendy products; and a full-service store should have knowledgeable personnel, but not have them seen as haughty by customers. Some retailers have not learned the lesson. This is why many theme restaurants are having trouble now that the novelty has worn off. People are noticing that food may be only so-so, while prices may be high.[11]

One of the biggest challenges for today's retailers is generating customer "excitement," since many people are bored with shopping or have little time for it. Here is what one shopping center, highlighted in Figure 1.11, is doing:

> Parque Corredor is one of the modern shopping centers popping up on the outskirts of Madrid, Spain. As the population seeks wide open spaces, more families are flooding into the suburbs. Parque Corredor is one of the few Spanish shopping centers that has embraced entertainment as the new anchor. Parque Corredor is supported by a health club, with a full Olympic-sized pool, a 12-cinema theater, a youth center with 2 basketball courts, and a running field. The shopping center incorporates the entertainment and leisure elements into the shopping atmosphere and uses these features to pull some 250,000 shoppers from the nearby suburbs.[12]

Customer Service **Customer service** refers to the identifiable, but sometimes intangible, activities undertaken by a retailer in conjunction with the basic goods and services it sells. It has a strong impact on the total retail experience. Among the factors comprising a firm's customer service strategy are store hours, parking access, shopper-friendliness of the store layout, credit acceptance, level and caliber of salespeople, amenities such as gift wrapping, rest room availability, employee politeness, handling special orders, delivery policies, the amount of time shoppers spend on checkout lines, and customer follow-up. The list is not all inclusive; and it differs in terms of the value-driven approach taken—discount versus full service. Customer service is discussed further in Chapter 2, "Building and Sustaining Relationships in Retailing."

Satisfaction with customer service is affected by expectations (based on the type of retailer) and past experience; and people's assessment of customer service depends on perceptions—not necessarily reality. Different people may evaluate the same service quite differently. The same person may even rate a firm's service differently at different times due to the intangibility, although the service remains constant.

According to many studies, the leading retailer in customer service is Nordstrom: "In answer to our annual survey, more than 30,000 *Consumer Reports'* readers told us about 55,000 shopping experiences they had in department stores, specialty stores, mass merchandisers, off-price stores, and warehouse clubs. Nordstrom was the highest-rated firm. In fact,

1-800-Flowers.com (www.1-800-flowers.com) is a big believer in bringing "excitement" to retailing. Take a store tour online.

Figure 1.11
Enhancing the Total Retail Experience: A Youth Center at Parque Corredor Shopping Center

Reprinted by permission of PricewaterhouseCoopers LLP.

the only department store in our survey to stand out for service was Nordstrom. Salespeople there work on commission—unlike staff at most department stores—and have the freedom to accompany a shopper from one department to another if need be. The policy is for returns to be as easy as purchases. Items are generally taken back, no questions asked."[13]

Interestingly, despite a desire to provide excellent customer service, a number of outstanding retailers are now wondering if "the customer is always right." Are there limits? Ponder these situations:

Wal-Mart has abandoned open-ended returns and set a 90-day limit for most items. The revised policy is designed to combat customers who take their time returning items, such as the shopper who got a refund for a battered thermos. The store later learned that the thermos had been bought in the 1950s, before the first Wal-Mart opened. L.L. Bean, which for years didn't question customers about returns, has decided to crack down. Some shoppers were returning goods they had purchased at garage sales. One even tried to return worn clothes dug out of the closet of a relative who died.[14]

Relationship Retailing Today's best retailers realize it is in their interest to engage in **relationship retailing,** whereby they seek to establish and maintain long-term bonds with customers, rather than act as if each sales transaction is a completely new encounter with them. This means the retailers must concentrate on the total retail experience, monitor satisfaction with customer service, and stay in touch with customers. Table 1.2 shows a customer respect checklist that retailers could use to assess their relationship efforts.

To be effective in relationship retailing, a firm has to keep these two points in mind: First, because it is harder to lure new customers than to make existing ones happy, a "win–win" approach should be enacted. For the retailer to "win" in the long run (attract shoppers, make

As with the retailers profiled in this book, we want to engage in relationship retailing. So, visit our Web site (www.prenhall.com/ rm_student).

Now THIS Is Customer Service—In America or Japan

The story of an American couple who bought a faulty CD player at a Tokyo department store shows the lengths to which a retailer truly committed to customer service will go to satisfy a customer.

Shortly after buying the product, the couple realized it was defective and missing parts. Annoyed, the husband planned to call the department store at 10:00 A.M. the next day, when the store opened. Instead, at 9:59 A.M., the couple received a phone call from the store's vice-president who said he was on the way over to their hotel with a replacement. In less than an hour, the vice-president and a junior employee were at the couple's doorstep.

The junior employee explained the steps he had taken to correct the problem. On the day the couple purchased the CD player, he had learned it was defective. When he tried to reach them before they left the store, he found that they were already gone. The clerk called 32 Tokyo hotels hoping to locate the couple. Fortunately, he learned their Tokyo address after contacting American Express (the CD player was charged on an American Express card) and then calling their home in the United States. In addition to replacing the defective CD player, the executive and sales clerk gave the couple a number of gifts. They then apologized for having the customers wait while the clerk rewrote the sales slip.

What could be learned from the way this incident was handled? Did the store overreact? Why or why not?

Source: Jill Griffin, "Customer Loyalty: Earning It and Keeping It," *Discount Merchandiser* (March 1998), p. 98.

Table 1.2 A Customer Respect Checklist

✔ Do we trust our customers? Do we operate our business to effectively serve the vast majority of customers who are honest or to protect ourselves from the small minority who are not?

✔ Do we stand behind what we sell? Are we easy to deal with if a customer has a problem? Is there a sense of urgency to make a customer whole? Are frontline workers empowered to respond properly to a problem? Do we guarantee what we sell? Do we guarantee our service?

✔ Do we stress promise-keeping in our firm? Is keeping commitments to customers—from being in-stock on advertised goods to being on time for appointments—important in our company?

✔ Do we value customer time? Do we anticipate periods of maximum demand for our offerings and staff accordingly to minimize customer waiting? Are our facilities and service systems convenient and efficient for customers to use? Do we prepare new employees to provide efficient, effective service before putting them in front of customers? Do we teach employees that serving customers supersedes all other priorities, such as paperwork or stocking shelves?

✔ Do we communicate with customers respectfully? Are signs informative and helpful? Are our statements clear and understandable? Is advertising above reproach in truthfulness and taste? Are contact personnel professional in appearance and manner? Does our language show respect, such as "I will be happy to do this" and "It will be my pleasure"? Do we answer and return calls promptly—with a smile in our voice? Is our voice mail caller-friendly?

✔ Do we respect all customers? Do we treat all customers with respect, regardless of their appearance, age, race, gender, status, or size of purchase or account? Have we taken any special precautions to minimize discriminatory treatment of certain customers?

✔ Do we thank customers for their business? Do we say "thank you" at times other than after a purchase? Do our customers feel appreciated?

✔ Do we respect employees? Do our human resources policies and practices pass the employee-respect test? Do employees, who are expected to respect customers, get respectful treatment themselves? Would employees want their children to work for us when they grow up?

Source: Adapted by the authors from Leonard L. Berry, "Retailers with a Future," *Marketing Management* (Spring 1996), p. 43. Reprinted by permission of the American Marketing Association.

sales, earn profits), the customer must also "win" in the long run (receive good value, be treated with respect, feel welcome by the firm). Otherwise, the retailer loses (shoppers patronize competitors) and customers lose (by having to spend time and money to learn about other retailers). Second, due to the advances in computer technology, it is now much easier to develop a customer data base—complete with information on people's attributes and past shopping behavior. Thus, ongoing customer contact can be better, more frequent, and more focused. This topic is covered further in Chapter 2, "Building and Sustaining Relationships in Retailing."

THE FOCUS AND FORMAT OF THE TEXT

There are various approaches to the study of retailing: an institutional approach, which describes the types of retailing and their development; a functional approach, which concentrates on the activities that retailers perform (such as buying, pricing, and personnel practices); and a strategic approach, which centers on defining the retail business, setting objectives, appealing to an appropriate customer market, developing an overall plan, implementing an integrated strategy, and regularly reviewing operations.

We will study retailing from each perspective, but center on a *strategic approach*. Our basic premise is that the retailer has to plan for and adapt to a complex, changing environment. Both opportunities and threats must be considered. By engaging in strategic retail management, the retailer is encouraged to study competitors, suppliers, economic factors, consumer changes, marketplace trends, legal restrictions, and other elements. A firm prospers if its competitive strengths match with the opportunities in the environment, weaknesses are eliminated or minimized, and plans look to the future as well as the past.

Retail Management: A Strategic Approach is divided into eight parts. The balance of Part One looks at both building relationships and strategic planning in retailing. Part Two characterizes retailing institutions on the basis of their ownership, store-based strategy mix, and Web, nonstore-based, and other nontraditional retailing formats. Part Three deals with consumer behavior and information gathering in retailing. Parts Four to Seven discuss these specific elements of a retailing strategy: planning the store location; managing a retail business; planning, handling, and pricing merchandise; and communicating with the customer. Part Eight shows how a retailing strategy may be integrated, analyzed, and improved. Four topics receive special coverage with end-of-chapter appendixes: how to solve a case study (Chapter 1), service retailing (Chapter 2), international retailing (Chapter 3), and franchising (Chapter 4). There are three end-of-text appendixes: retailing careers, about the Web site accompanying *Retail Management,* and a glossary.

To further underscore the exciting nature of retailing, these real-world boxes appear in every chapter: "Careers in Retailing," "Ethics in Retailing," Retailing Around the World," and "Technology in Retailing."

SUMMARY

In this and every text chapter, the summary is linked to the objectives stated at the beginning of the chapter.

1. *To define retailing, consider it from various perspectives, demonstrate its impact, and note its special characteristics.* Retailing comprises the business activities involved in selling goods and services to consumers for personal, family, or household use. It is the last stage in the distribution process, whereas wholesaling is an intermediary stage. Today, retailing is at an interesting crossroads, with many challenges ahead.

Retailing may be viewed from multiple perspectives. It includes tangible and intangible items, does not have to use a store, and can be done by manufacturers and others—as well as by retailers.

Annual U.S. store sales are $3 trillion, with other forms of retailing accounting for hundreds of billions of dollars in added revenues. The world's 100 largest retailers generate $1.75 trillion in yearly revenues. About 21 million people in the United States work for retailers, which understates the number of those actually employed in a retailing capacity. Retail firms receive up to 45 cents of every sales dollar as compensation for operating costs, the functions performed, and the profits earned.

Retailing encompasses all the businesses and people involved in physically moving and transferring ownership of goods and services from producer to consumer. In a distribution channel, retailers do valuable functions as the contact for manufacturers, wholesalers, and final consumers. They collect assortments from various suppliers and offer them to customers. They communicate with both customers and other channel members. They may ship, store, mark, advertise, and pre-pay for items. They complete transactions with customers and often provide customer services.

Retailers and their suppliers have complex relationships because retailers serve in two capacities. They are part of a distribution channel aimed at the final consumer; and they are major customers for suppliers. Channel relations are smoothest with exclusive distribution; they are most volatile with intensive distribution. Selective distribution is a way to balance sales goals and channel cooperation.

Retailing has several special characteristics. The average sales transaction is small. Final consumers make many unplanned purchases. Most customers visit a store location.

2. *To introduce the concept of strategic planning and apply it.* A retail strategy is the overall plan guiding the firm. It has six basic steps: defining the business, setting objectives, defining the customer market, developing an overall plan, enacting an integrated strategy, and evaluating performance and making modifications. Lands' End's strategy has been particularly well designed and carried out.

3. *To relate the marketing concept to retailing, with an emphasis on the total retail experience, customer service,* *and relationship retailing.* The marketing concept (known as the retailing concept when applied to retail situations) should be understood and used by all retailers. This requires a firm to have a customer orientation, use a coordinated effort, and be value-driven and goal-oriented. Yet, despite its ease of use, many firms do not adhere to one or more elements of the retailing concept.

The total retail experience consists of all the elements in a retail offering that encourage or inhibit consumers during their contact with a retailer. Some elements are controllable by the retailer; others are not. Customer service includes identifiable, but sometimes intangible, activities undertaken by a retailer in association with the basic goods and services sold. It has an effect on the total retail experience. In relationship retailing, a firm seeks long-term bonds with customers, rather than acting as if each sales transaction is a totally new encounter with them.

4. *To indicate the focus and format of the text.* Retailing may be studied by using an institutional approach, a functional approach, and a strategic approach. Although all three approaches are utilized in this text, the focus is on the strategic approach. The underlying principle is that a retail firm needs to plan for and adapt to a complex, changing environment.

Key Terms

retailing (p. 3)
wholesaling (p. 3)
channel of distribution (p. 7)
sorting process (p. 8)
exclusive distribution (p. 10)

intensive distribution (p. 10)
selective distribution (p. 10)
retail strategy (p. 13)
marketing concept (p. 17)
retailing concept (p. 17)

total retail experience (p. 18)
customer service (p. 19)
relationship retailing (p. 20)

Questions for Discussion

1. Which of these involve retailing? Explain your answers.
   a. A music store targeting college students.
   b. An appliance store selling to hospitals.
   c. An insurance company specializing in automobile insurance for small businesses.
   d. A fast-food restaurant.

2. Comment on the sorting process from the manufacturer's perspective. From the retailer's.

3. What kinds of information do retailers communicate to customers? To suppliers?

4. What are the pros and cons of a firm such as Coach (leather-goods) having its own retail facilities, as well as selling through traditional retailers?

5. Why would one retailer seek to be part of an exclusive distribution channel while another seeks to be part of an intensive distribution channel?

6. Describe how the special characteristics of retailing offer unique opportunities and problems for supermarkets.

7. What is a retail strategy? How could it be utilized by a small florist?

8. On the basis of the chapter description of Lands' End, present five suggestions that a new retailer should consider.

9. Explain the retailing concept. Apply it to a convenience store such as 7-Eleven or Circle K.

10. Define the term "total retail experience." Then, describe a recent retail situation where you were dissatisfied and state why.

11. Do you believe that customer service in retailing is improving or declining? Why?

12. How could a small Web-based retailer engage in relationship retailing?

13. What checklist item(s) in Table 1.2 do you think would be most difficult for Wal-Mart, as the world's largest retailer, to address? Why?

14. Distinguish among these approaches to the study of retailing:
    a. Institutional.
    b. Functional.
    c. Strategic.

WEB-BASED EXERCISE

Amazon.com (www.amazon.com)

Questions

1. Evaluate Amazon.com's site from the perspective of the total retail experience.

2. What are the best features of the site? Why?

3. What features can be improved? How?

4. Discuss Amazon.com's safe shopping guarantee. (This section is within the "Our Guarantee" section of the site.)

CHAPTER ENDNOTES

1. Murray Raphel, "Make Your Store the Brand!" *Direct Marketing* (February 1999), pp. 34–37.

2. *U.S. Industry & Trade Outlook '99* (New York: McGraw-Hill, 1999), pp. 42-1–42-2.

3. Estimated by the authors from data in "Global Powers of Retailing," *Stores* (October 1999), Section 2.

4. *Annual Retail Trade Survey 1998* (Washington, D.C.: U.S. Census Bureau, 1999); and retailer annual reports.

5. Rochelle Garner, "Mad as Hell," *Sales & Marketing Management* (June 1999), p. 55.

6. Russell Garland, "Rhode Island-Based Retailer's Dispute with French Firm Headed for Trial," *Knight-Ridder/Tribune Business News* (October 6, 1998), p. OKRB98279124.

7. David Bank and George Anders, "Amazon.com Is Charging up to $10,000 to Plug Publishers' Books on Web Site," *Wall Street Journal* (February 9, 1999), p. B10.

8. John Russell, "Akron, Ohio-Based Goodyear Works on Rocky Relationship with Dealers," *Knight-Ridder/Tribune Business News* (January 18, 1999), p. OKRB9901805.

9. The material in this section is drawn from Lands' End company literature; *Lands' End 1999 Annual Report*; Erika Rasmusson, "The Lands' End Difference," *Sales & Marketing Management* (October 1998), p. 138; De'Ann Weimer, "Lands' End Tacks Again," *Business Week* (December 14, 1998), pp. 90–98; Eleena de Lisser, "Masterminding the Mazes of Package Delivery," *Wall Street Journal* (December 23, 1998), pp. B1, B4; Patricia Winters Lauro, "Lands' End's Cybercatalog Is Focus of New Campaign," *New York Times on the Web* (May 20, 1999); and "Lands' End and Victoria's Secret Tie for First in Catalog Sellers Online Customer Support," *PR Newswire* (July 6, 1999).

10. Constance L. Hays, "Service Takes a Holiday," *New York Times* (December 23, 1998), p. C4.

11. Charles V. Bagli, "Novelty Gone, Theme Restaurants Are Tumbling," *New York Times* (December 7, 1998), pp. 1, 38.

12. Kathryn Grambling, "What's Hot, What's Not: Innovative and Interesting in Latin America, Europe, and Asia," *Winning Strategies for the New Global World of Retailing* (Columbus, Ohio: PricewaterhouseCoopers, 1999), p. 11.

13. "Sorting Out the Stores," *Consumer Reports* (November 1998), pp. 12–17.

14. Louise Lee, "Without a Receipt You May Get Stuck with That Ugly Scarf," *Wall Street Journal* (November 18, 1996), p. A1.

APPENDIX ON HOW TO SOLVE A CASE STUDY

A case study is a collection of facts and data based on a real or hypothetical business situation. The goal of a case study is to enhance your ability to solve business problems, using a logical framework. The issues in a case are generally not unique to a specific person, firm, or industry, and they often deal with more than one retail strategy element. Sometimes, the material presented in a case may be in conflict. For example, two managers may disagree about a strategy or there may be several interpretations of the same facts.

In all case studies, you must analyze what is presented and state which specific actions best resolve major issues. These actions must reflect the information in the case and the environment facing the firm.

Steps in Solving a Case Study

Analysis should include these sequential steps:

1. Presentation of the facts surrounding the case.

2. Identification of the key issues.

3. Listing of alternative courses of action that could be taken.

4. Evaluation of alternative courses of action.

5. Recommendation of the best course of action.

PRESENTATION OF THE FACTS SURROUNDING THE CASE

It is helpful to read a case until you are comfortable with the information in it. Rereadings often are an aid to comprehending facts, possible strategies, or questions that need clarification and were not apparent earlier. In studying a case, assume you are a retail consultant hired by the firm. While facts should be accepted as true, statements, judgments, and decisions made by the individuals in a case should be questioned, especially if not supported by facts—or when one individual disagrees with another.

During your reading of the case, you should underline crucial facts, interpret figures and charts, critically review the comments made by individuals, judge the rationality of past and current decisions, and prepare questions whose answers would be useful in addressing the key issue(s).

IDENTIFICATION OF THE KEY ISSUE(S)

The facts stated in a case often point to the key issue(s) facing a retailer, such as new opportunities, a changing environment, a decline in competitive position, or excess inventories. Identify the characteristics and ramifications of the issue(s) and examine them, using the material in the case and the text. Sometimes, you must delve deeply because the key issue(s) and their characteristics may not be immediately obvious.

LISTING ALTERNATIVE COURSES OF ACTION THAT COULD BE TAKEN

Next, alternative actions pertaining to the key issue(s) in the case are listed. Consider courses of action based on their suitability to the firm and situation. Thus, the promotion strategy for a small neighborhood stationery store would not be proper for a large gift store located in a regional shopping center.

Proposed courses of action should take into account such factors as the business category, goals, the customer market, the overall strategy, the product assortment, competition, legal restrictions, economic trends, marketplace trends, financial capabilities, personnel capabilities, and sources of supply.

Evaluation of Alternative Courses of Action

Evaluate each potential option, according to case data, the key issue(s), the strategic concepts in the text, and the firm's environment. Specific criteria should be used and each option analyzed on the basis of them. The ramifications and risks associated with each alternative should be considered. Important data not included in the case should be mentioned.

Recommendation of the Best Course of Action

Be sure your analysis is not just a case summary. You will be critiqued by your professor on the basis of how well you identify key issues or problems, outline and assess alternative courses of action, and reach realistic conclusions (that take the retailer's size, competition, image, and so on into consideration). You need to show a good understanding of both the principles of strategic retail management and the case. Be precise about which alternative is more desirable for the retailer in its current context. Remember, your goal is to apply a logical reasoning process to retailing. A written report must demonstrate this process.

Note: The cases in *Retail Management* have questions to guide you. However, your analysis should not be limited by them.

CHAPTER 2

Building and Sustaining Relationships in Retailing

CHAPTER OBJECTIVES

1. To explain what "value" really means and highlight its pivotal role in retailers' building and sustaining relationships
2. To describe how both customer relationships and channel relationships may be nurtured in today's highly competitive marketplace, with a special emphasis on the customer base, customer service, customer satisfaction, and loyalty programs
3. To examine the differences in relationship building between goods and service retailers
4. To discuss the impact of technology on relationships in retailing
5. To consider the interplay between retailers' ethical performance and relationships in retailing

Department stores such as Neiman Marcus and Saks Fifth Avenue reward their key customers with distinctive gifts and other benefits to entice them to continue being loyal. One retail consultant says that upscale stores are "shooting for a class of people who spend $6,000 for a dress. You have to coddle these people constantly because you cannot afford to lose even a few of them as customers."

This is a sampling of the rewards offered by department stores:

- Neiman Marcus' In Circle program gives its 150,000 members one point for every dollar spent. Members who spend $100,000 can choose tickets to the Super Bowl or the Kentucky Derby. Both of these rewards include first-class air travel and hotel rooms. Those that spend $1 million get to choose among a Jaguar S-type car, a one week annual stay for life (and for the lives of their children) at a luxury resort, or one million frequent flier points.
- Saks Fifth Avenue recently invited its 40 platinum members (who spend at least $10,000 per year) to dinner at a top New York restaurant with their spouses and friends. Among the invited guests were designer Donna Karan, who personally offered to help the guests select their spring wardrobe at Saks.
- Bloomingdale's, Target Corporation, and Nordstrom have recently begun loyalty programs that provide special discounts or gift certificates. For example, Nordstrom offers a $20 merchandise certificate for every $1,000 in Nordstrom purchases.[1]

OVERVIEW

As the linchpins of its business, a retailer must understand and properly apply the concepts of "value" and "relationship" from the perspective of the customer and other channel members, as well as itself. The goal is (a) to have customers strongly believe the retailer offers

Please Note: Web site addresses are constantly changing.
The links in this chapter are current as of the publication of this book.

good value for the money and (b) to have both customers and channel members like doing business with that retailer. Some firms grasp this well. Others still have some work to do. Consider the following:

Value means more than knocking off five cents from a product. It means identifying life-style experiences. Look at Saturn. Its value isn't in selling the best-made car or the cheapest. Its value is in selling relationships. The world seems to be changing faster and we have to change with it. We need to better address our most important partnership—our customers—and we need to be reminded how central we are to their lives. In an era when interaction between humans is more impersonal—phone, fax, voice mail, E-mail—the [store] is still a place where we can come together.[2]

90 percent of shoppers with incomes above $70,000 shop in discount stores, according to a survey by WSL Strategic Retail. Five years ago, that percentage was half as large. The best of the lower-priced stores let shoppers get in and out quickly, yet enjoy the service and some ambience of department stores. "Ten years ago, you had places like [the now defunct] Woolworth's where people thought they had to trade courtesy, clean stores, and wide aisles for price," said Candace Corlett, a partner at WSL. "They don't have to do that anymore—thank you very much, Target Stores and Wal-Mart."[3]

Gap (www.gap.com) is a value-driven retailer even though it is not a discounter.

Gap doesn't sell anything not available elsewhere. It does market those things better than anyone. At the Banana Republic store in San Francisco, the letters B-O-X-E-R-S were splashed, big and bold, across six store windows. Behind the glass, suspended, were 47 pairs of boxer shorts—dark blue with white golf balls, red gingham, light blue with dolphins, dark green with goldfish. They're only men's underpants. But, in this window, they're turned into pop art. Gap plays at elevating the ordinary.[4]

The two biggest U.S. furniture store operators, Helig-Meyers and Levitz, stress low prices and easy credit in advertising. "We've Gone Nuts!" said an ad from a Helig chain. "Don't Pay Anything Until April!" shouted a Levitz ad for a leather living-room set on sale for $1,799. The message many consumers read: The stuff must be overpriced most of the time. "We don't talk about how easy it can be to make your home attractive," says Jerry Epperson, an investment banker who specializes in the furniture industry. "All we talk about is sale, sale, sale and credit terms, credit terms."[5]

The bottom line: "Consumers unabashedly define themselves in terms of their ability to get the best value out of every shopping experience [and store]: 'Does it have the selection I want every time?' 'Can I depend on it consistently to fulfill my needs?' 'Is my time well spent?' 'Is it indispensable to me?' 'Did I get what I paid for?' If the value is not there, they will move on."[6] See Figure 2.1.

This chapter looks at value and the value chain, relationship retailing—in terms of customer relationships (including customer service and loyalty programs) and channel relationships, the differences in relationship building between goods and service retailers, technology and relationships, and ethics and relationships. There is also an end-of-chapter appendix on service retailing.

VALUE AND THE VALUE CHAIN

In many distribution channels, there are several parties: manufacturer, wholesaler, retailer, and customer. Transactions are most apt to be pleasing to all parties when they have similar beliefs about the value provided and received, and the payments for that level of value.

Figure 2.1
Tim Hortons:
Providing Extra Value
for Customers

Tim Hortons offers the
convenience of modern
facilities and 24-hour
drive-through service at
most locations. The
restaurant styles include
full-sized units, double
drive-throughs, kiosks,
and carts.
Reprinted by permission.

From the manufacturer, wholesaler, and retailer perspectives, **value** is represented by a series of activities and processes—a value chain—that *provides* a given level of value for the consumer. It is the totality of the tangible and intangible product and service attributes offered to customers. For these firms, the value provided is closely related to their desire to earn a fair profit and the type of strategy pursued (such as discount vs. upscale). Where the firms may differ is in assigning the value each provides—as well as in allocating the activities undertaken in the value chain.

From the customer's perspective, **value** is the *perception* the shopper has of a value chain. It is the customer's view of all the benefits gotten from a purchase (formed, largely, by the total retail experience). Value is based on perceived benefits received versus prices paid. It varies by type of shopper. There are price shoppers who want low prices, as well as service-oriented shoppers who will pay higher prices to receive superior service and status-oriented shoppers who will pay more to buy at certain prestigious stores.

Why is "value" such a meaningful concept for every retailer in any kind of setting?

- Offering good value is a must for any retailer. Customers must always believe they got their money's worth. This is true whether a retailer sells $20,000 Rolex watches or $40 Casio watches.
- Retailers must work to ensure that customers perceive the level of value provided in the same manner the retailers intend.
- Value is desired by all customers—however, value means different things to different customers.
- It is easy for customers to comparison shop for prices through ads and the World Wide Web. Thus, prices have moved closer together for different types of retailers.
- Meaningful retail differentiation is essential. It is not enough to be a "me too" retailer. Competitive advantages in the form of greater value must be presented to customers.
- A specific value/price point is required. Is the retailer looking to offer $100 worth of benefits for a $100 item or $125 worth of benefits for the same item accompanied by better ambience and services and a $125 price tag? Either approach can succeed if properly enacted and marketed.

A retail **value chain** represents the total bundle of benefits offered to consumers through a channel of distribution. It comprises many elements, including store location and parking,

Figure 2.2
MotoPhoto®: Preserving Memories and
Serving the Customer

Moto Photo, Inc. is engaged in the franchising and ownership of
stores offering one-hour photo processing services, portraiture,
and related imaging services and merchandise. To ensure the
best possible processing quality, the stores have certified techni-
cians examine each negative and uses state-of-the-art equipment. MotoPhoto® can correct for many color and exposure
situations that occur when photos are shot. There is a big choice
of print sizes and finishes: "Which do you prefer? The choice is
yours—$3\frac{1}{2} \times 5$ or 4×6 or ask about new Advanced Photo
System™ sizes. Glossy finishes are standard and make the most
vibrant prints, but matte finishes are available upon request."
Reprinted by permission of Moto Photo, Inc.

retailer ambience, the level of customer service, the products/brands carried, product quality, the retailer's in-stock position, shipping, prices, the retailer's image, and so forth. As a
rule, consumers are concerned with the results of a value of chain not the process. Food
shoppers who buy online via Peapod care only that they receive the brands ordered when
desired, not about the steps needed for home delivery at the neighborhood level. See Figure 2.2.

Some elements of a retail value chain are visible to shoppers. These include the store windows, store hours, in-store personnel, and computerized point-of-sale equipment. Some
value chain elements are not visible to shoppers. These include credit processing, store
maintenance, company warehouses, and many merchandising decisions. Various cues are

Kennys Covers the World of Irish Books

With over 150,000 titles, Kennys Book Shop in Galway, Ireland, houses the largest Irish literary collection in the world. The retailer added a direct marketing operation after realizing the need to expand its customer base beyond Europe; and Kennys recently started a Web site (www.kennys.ie). The firm has annual sales exceeding $3 million.

Kennys was founded in 1940, and business grew slowly during its first 40 years. A major opportunity occurred in 1980 when the U.S. Library of Congress asked Kennys to supply it with a copy of every book published in Ireland. Now, 140 U.S. libraries and many U.S. universities are steady customers.

Kennys began its direct marketing operation when a U.S. librarian asked for a catalog. To comply with the librarian's request, Kennys prepared a list of its most popular titles and distributed the list to 100 American libraries. The store's direct marketing program was expanded when another U.S. customer asked Kennys to send him packages of books in his special interest area on a monthly basis. Today, Kennys has almost 1,500 members in its book club. All members receive books on approval; and they can return or exchange unwanted titles.

What relationship retailing and customer service tips could be garnered from studying Kennys?

Source: Murray Raphel, "How an Irish Book Store Found a Niche
—and Filled It," *Direct Marketing* (March 1999), pp. 18–22.

surrogates for value: upscale store ambience and plentiful sales personnel for high-end stores; linoleum floors, shopping carts, and self-service for discounters.

There are three complementary components to a value-oriented retail strategy: expected, augmented, and potential. An *expected retail strategy* represents the minimum value chain elements a given customer segment expects from a given type of retailer. As an example, what bundle of benefits must every mid-price retailer provide for customers? For most retailers, these are expected value chain elements: cleanliness of the store, convenient store hours, knowledgeable employees, timely service, popular merchandise in stock, parking, and return privileges. If not performed properly, expected elements cause customer dissatisfaction and relate to why shoppers avoid certain retailers.

An *augmented retail strategy* encompasses the extra elements in a value chain that differentiate one retailer from another. As an example, what does Target Stores do to differentiate itself from Wal-Mart? For many retailers, these are augmented value chain elements: valet parking, free delivery, personal shoppers and other special services, exclusive brands, superior salespeople, and loyalty programs. Augmented items are a complement to—not a substitute for—expected value chain elements. By being different from competitors, augmented features are the key to continued customer patronage.

A *potential retail strategy* comprises value chain elements not yet perfected by a competing firm in the retailer's industry category. As an example, what customer services could a new upscale apparel chain offer that no other chain has? In many retail situations, these are potential value chain elements: 7-day/24-hour store hours (an augmented strategy for supermarkets), unlimited customer return privileges, full-scale customization (mass customization), instant fulfillment of rain checks by placing in-store orders and offering free delivery, customer self-checkouts, and in-mall trams to make it easier for shoppers to navigate in enormous regional shopping centers. Potential value chain elements represent opportunities not yet being exploited by competitors—and the first firms to capitalize on them gain a solid head start over their adversaries. Barnes & Noble and Borders took advantage of an opportunity by opening the first book superstores, and Amazon.com has become a darling of Wall Street by being the first online bookstore. Yet, even as pioneers, for these firms to grow in the long run, they must do an outstanding job of both satisfying customers' basic expectations and offering differentiated features from competitors.

When applying value-oriented retailing principles, there are five potential pitfalls to avoid:

- *Planning value with just a price perspective*: Value is tied to two factors: benefits and prices. Most discounters accept credit cards today because shoppers want to purchase with them. A discounter not accepting credit cards would have a competitive disadvantage in the eyes of many customers.
- *Providing value-enhancing services that customers do not want or will not pay extra for*: Ikea knows most of its customers do not want to pay for having furniture pre-assembled. They want to spend less and assemble the furniture themselves.
- *Competing in the wrong value/price segment*: Neighborhood retailers generally have a tough time competing in the low-price part of the market. They are better served by offering a number of augmented benefits and charging somewhat more than large chains.
- *Believing augmented elements alone create value*: Many retailers think that if they offer a benefit not available at competitors that they will automatically prosper. Yet, they must never lose sight of the importance of expected benefits. Many theme restaurants are having trouble now that the novelty has worn off. Customers are noticing that food is often only so-so, while prices tend to be high.
- *Paying lip service to customer service*: Most firms say, and even believe, customers are always right. Yet, they act contrary to this philosophy, by having a high turnover of salespeople, charging for returned goods that have been opened, and not giving rain checks if items are out of stock.

Target Stores (www.target.com) is a value-driven retailer that is a discounter.

Will Rainforest Café (www.rainforestcafe.com), a novelty restaurant chain, thrive in the long run?

Table 2.1 A Value-Oriented Retailing Checklist

Answer Yes or No to Each Question

✔ Is value defined from a consumer perspective?

✔ Does the retailer have a clear value/price point?

✔ Is the retailer's value position competitively defensible?

✔ Are channel partners capable of delivering value-enhancing services?

✔ Does the retailer distinguish between expected and augmented value chain elements?

✔ Has the retailer identified meaningful potential value chain elements?

✔ Is the retailer's value-oriented approach aimed at a distinct market segment?

✔ Is the retailer's value-oriented approach consistent?

✔ Is the retailer's value-oriented approach effectively communicated to the target market?

✔ Can the target market clearly identify the retailer's positioning strategy?

✔ Does the retailer's positioning strategy consider tradeoffs in sales versus profits?

✔ Does the retailer set customer satisfaction goals?

✔ Does the retailer periodically measure customer satisfaction levels?

✔ Is the retailer careful to avoid the pitfalls in value-oriented retailing?

✔ Is the retailer always on the lookout for new opportunities that will create value for consumers?

Any question that is answered "no" requires corrective action on the part of the retailer or other channel members.

To sidestep these pitfalls, a retailer could use the checklist shown in Table 2.1. This checklist poses a number of questions that a retailer must honestly address. It can be answered by an owner/corporate president, a team of executives, or an independent consultant. The checklist should be reviewed at least once a year—more often if a major development, such as the emergence of a strong competitor, occurs.

RETAILER RELATIONSHIPS

In Chapter 1, we introduced the concept of relationship retailing, whereby retailers seek to form and maintain long-term bonds with customers, rather than act as if each sales transaction is a new encounter with them. But for relationship retailing to work properly, enduring value-driven relationships are needed with other channel members, as well as with customers. Both jobs are challenging. See Figure 2.3.

Customer Relationships

Many retailers realize loyal customers are the backbone of business: "In general, the longer a customer stays with a firm, the more he or she is worth. Long-term customers buy more, take less of a firm's time, are less price sensitive, and bring in new shoppers. Best of all, there is no acquisition cost. Good long-term customers are worth so much that reducing customer defections by as little as five points—from, say 15 percent to 10 percent yearly—may double profits."[7] As a result, "Retailers have to stop thinking in terms of customers being loyal to the store and concentrate on the retailer being loyal to the customer."[8]

Figure 2.3
4,000 Places to Bring the Care Back to Health Care

In conjunction with its channel partners, CVS uses the latest technology to service its customers and foster relationships with them. Since its introduction in 1994, CVS has invested over $200 million in its proprietary Rx2000 pharmacy system. One of the most successful innovations has been CVS' launch of the Rapid Refill system, which enables customers to order prescription refills using a touch-tone phone. Rapid Refill now accounts for 50 percent of refills. In addition to providing an added convenience for customers, one of the most important benefits of Rapid Refill is that it significantly reduces the time pharmacists spend on the phone, so they can spend more time doing what they do best—counseling patients on medications and addressing their total health care needs.
Reprinted by permission.

In applying relationship retailing, there are four factors to keep in mind: the customer base, customer service, customer satisfaction, and loyalty programs and defection rates. Let's explore these next.

The Customer Base   Retailers must regularly analyze their customer base in terms of population and life-style trends, attitudes toward and reasons for shopping, the level of loyalty, and the mix of new versus loyal customers.

The U.S. population is aging. A fourth of households have only one person, a sixth of people move annually, most people live in urban and suburban areas, the number of working women is rising, middle-class income has been rising slowly, and the African-American, Hispanic-American, and Asian-American segments are expanding. Thus, gender roles are changing, shoppers demand more, market segments are more diverse, there is less interest in shopping, and time-saving goods and services are desirable.[9]

There are various factors that influence people's shopping behavior. According to recent research,

- Seventy percent of women and 40 percent of men enjoy shopping; and men shop more quickly than women. Only 37 percent of consumers believe service today is better than it used to be.
- Consumers' most important reasons for shopping at a given *apparel retailer* are product availability, ease in finding products, confidence in products, ease of shopping, and convenience of the location.

- Consumers' most important reasons for shopping at a given *discount department store* are convenience, price, and assortment and quality of merchandise.
- Consumers' most important reasons for shopping at a given *supermarket* are cleanliness, prices, accuracy in price scanning at the register, and how clearly prices are labeled.
- Sixty-four percent of consumers like retailers to be organized by product category, half like retailers to organize by occasion or end use, and only 15 percent like retailers organized by brand.[10]

All consumers are not equal. It is more worth nurturing relationships with some than with others; they are the retailer's **core customers**—its best customers. And they should be singled out by the firm: "The most practical way to get started is by answering three questions. First, which of your customers are the most profitable and the most loyal? Look for those who spend more money, pay their bills promptly, are reasonable in their service requests, and seem to prefer stable, long-term relationships. Second, which customers place the greatest value on what you have to offer? Some customers will have found that your products, services, and special strengths are simply the best fit for their needs. Third, which customers are worth more to you than to your competitors? Some warrant extra effort and investment. Conversely, no firm can be all things to all people: Customers who are worth more to a competitor will eventually defect."[11] About 70 percent of shoppers say they are loyal to mass merchants, 56 percent to specialty stores, 49 percent to home improvement stores, and 35 percent to PC/electronics stores.[12]

A retailer's desired mix of new versus loyal customers depends on that firm's stage in its life cycle, goals, resources, and its competitors' actions. A mature firm is more apt to rely on core customers, supplementing revenues with new shoppers. An entrepreneur faces the dual tasks of attracting shoppers and building a loyal following; it cannot do the latter without the former. If goals are growth-oriented, the customer base must be expanded by adding stores, greater advertising, and so on; the challenge is to do this in a way that does not deflect attention away from core customers. It is more costly to attract new customers than to serve existing ones; this does not mean core customers are cost-free. If competitors try to take away a firm's existing customers with price cuts and special promotions, it may feel it must pursue competitors' customers in the same way. Again, it must be careful not to alienate its core customers.

Nordstrom (www. nordstrom.com) is widely viewed as the king of customer service.

Customer Service   As described in Chapter 1, *customer service* refers to the identifiable, but sometimes intangible, activities undertaken by a retailer in conjunction with the goods and services it sells. It strongly affects the total retail experience provided to customers. Consistent with the value chain philosophy of retailing, it is imperative that firms view customer service as comprising two components—expected service and augmented service. **Expected customer service** is the level of service that customers want to receive from any retailer, such as basic employee courtesy. Yet, how many employees are trained to always say, "Hello, how may I help you?" and "Thank you for shopping at our store." *Thank you* sometimes seems to be disappearing from the retail vocabulary. Often, **augmented customer service**—which encompasses the actions that enhance the shopping experience and give retailers a competitive advantage—is stressed without enough attention placed on expected customer service.

The attributes of personnel who interact with customers (such as politeness and knowledge), as well as the number and variety of customer services offered, have a strong impact on the relationship created. Here are two opposite consumer perceptions, related to the caliber of their customer service experiences:

> My wife likes to shop at the local Safeway. Is it because of the prices? Yes, that's part of it. Is it because of the location? Yes, that's part of it too. She also likes their produce department. But the biggest reason she likes to shop at the local Safeway is "Marshall."

Now Marshall is a very good checkout person. He's fast, efficient, and seldom makes a mistake. But his competency is not why my wife keeps going back. She goes back because Marshall always has a warm and friendly smile. And because when Marshall asks, "How are you today?" you know he's sincere about it. For those few minutes while she is a customer in his checkout line, Marshall makes my wife feel genuinely valued and appreciated. And week after week she buys our groceries at "Marshall's" Safeway.[13]

I know what it feels like to be an item with a barcode, being run across the scanner. I learn this every time I shop in my neighborhood's gargantuan supermarket. Whenever I go through the checkout line, the young clerks don't look at me. They don't say hello. They don't even acknowledge my humanity. At the end of the transaction, they don't tell me what the total is. I'm to read it myself from the video display in front of me. They don't say thank you or goodbye. Sometimes, they miss my hand with the change and receipt. Most customers seem resigned to the treatment. After all, it only makes sense that workers who are extensions of machines should retaliate by treating customers the same way.[14]

Planning the most appropriate customer service strategy can be complicated because retailers often face situations such as these: "In this era of consolidation, retailers—department stores in particular—have been obsessed about cutting costs, systematically slicing the areas on which service relies. Though experts say quality service depends, first and foremost, on sales help being available at the drop of a hat, retailers in the early 1990s sharply reduced staffing on the sales floor. Numbers are hard to come by, but analysts estimate the cuts at 10 to 30 percent. Now some firms are siphoning money from other activities to expand sales staffs. Also, after a long period during which department stores were esteemed for training buyers and executives in merchandising, today the retail industry spends less training its employees than any other major business sector. Finally, even as many other industries embrace pay-for-performance systems, retailers have been slow to experiment with new ways to motivate workers and focus attention on the customer. Several have scaled back sales commissions as a way of cutting costs."[15]

Some retailers have found that customer service can be improved if they empower personnel. In **employee empowerment,** workers have discretion to do what they believe is necessary—within reason—to satisfy the customer, even if this means bending some rules. At Nordstrom, "our aim is to constantly attract and retain people with a passion for retailing and serving every customer. We want knowledgeable salespeople who personalize customer interaction and make shopping fun and rewarding."[16] At Direct Tire, a salesperson may pay for a cab to get a stranded customer to his or her destination. Home Depot has built employee empowerment into its way of business. Every worker on the selling floor gets several weeks training prior to meeting their first customer. Employees have wide latitude in making on-the-spot decisions. They can freely talk with individual customers and act as consultants and problem solvers.

To apply customer service properly, a firm must first outline an overall service strategy and then plan individual services. Figure 2.4 shows one way a retailer may view the customer services it offers.

Developing a Customer Service Strategy In devising a strategy, a retailer has to make decisions involving the range, level, choice, price, measurement, and retention of its services.

What services are expected and what services are augmented for a particular retailer? Because expected customer services are a basic part of a retail strategy, they must be provided. Examples are credit for a furniture retailer, new-car preparation for an auto dealer, and a liberal return policy for a gift shop. Those retailers could not stay in business without

Figure 2.4
Classifying Customer Services

Source: Adapted by the authors from Albert D. Bates, "Rethinking the Service Offer," *Retailing Issues Letter* (December 1986), p. 3. Reprinted by permission.

Cost of Offering Service

	High	Low
Value of Service to Customer High	**Patronage builders—** High-cost activities that are the primary factors behind customer loyalties. Examples: transaction speed, credit, gift registry	**Patronage solidifiers—** The "low-cost little things" that increase loyalty. Examples: courtesy (referring to the customer by name and saying thank you), suggestion selling
Value of Service to Customer Low	**Disappointers—** Expensive activities that do no real good. Examples: weekday deliveries for two-earner families, home economists	**Basics—** Low-cost activities that are "naturally expected." They don't build patronage, but their absence could reduce patronage. Examples: free parking, in-store directories

them. Because augmented services are extra elements that enhance a retail strategy, a retailer could cater to its target market adequately without such services; but using them improves its competitive standing. Examples are home delivery for a supermarket, an extra warranty for an auto dealer, gift wrapping for a toy store, and credit for a flea market booth. It is vital for each retailer to determine which customer services are expected and which are augmented for its situation. Expected services for one firm, such as delivery, may be augmented for another. See Figure 2.5.

What level of customer service is proper to complement a firm's image? An upscale retailer would offer more services than a discounter since people expect the firm to have a wide range

Figure 2.5
Augmented Services: Going Above and Beyond the Norm

To upgrade their customer service, some supermarkets have installed self-service NCR Price Verifiers, which enable shoppers to check the prices of items they have selected —before they go to the checkout center.
Reprinted by permission of NCR Corporation. NCR is a copyright of NCR Corporation.

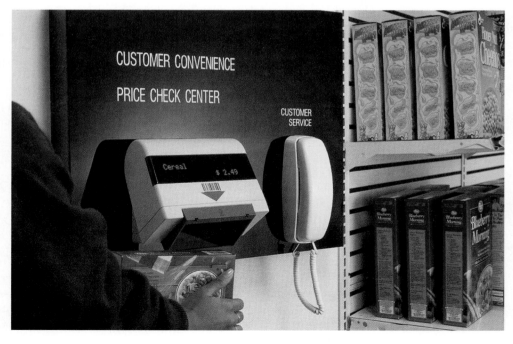

of services as part of its basic strategy. This is not true of a discounter. In addition, service performance would be different. Customers of an upscale retailer may expect elaborate gift wrapping, valet parking, a restaurant, and a ladies' room attendant, while discount shoppers may expect cardboard gift boxes, self-service parking, a lunch counter, and an unattended ladies' room. Service categories are the same; the service level is not.

Should there be a choice of customer services? Some firms let customers select from various levels of service; others provide only one level. A retailer may honor several credit cards or only its own. Trade-ins may be allowed on some items or all. Warranties may have optional extensions or fixed lengths. A firm may offer one-, three-, and six-month payment plans or insist on a one-month payment period.

Staples (www.staples. com) offers free delivery on orders of $50 or more.

Should customer services be free? Two factors cause retailers to charge for some services: costs and consumer behavior. Delivery, gift wrapping, and other services are labor intensive, and their costs are steadily rising. And it has been found that people are more apt to be home for a delivery or service call if a fee is imposed. Without a fee, retailers may have to attempt a delivery two or three times. In settling on a free or fee-based strategy, a firm must determine which services are expected (these are often free) and which are augmented (these may be offered for a fee), competitors and profit margins should be watched closely, and the target market studied. In setting fees, a retailer must also decide if its goal is to break even or to make a profit on the services. As one retail observer noted, "Expecting free customer service today is a lot like challenging a school of piranhas to a game of water polo."[17]

How can a retailer measure the benefits of providing customer services against their costs? The purpose of customer services is to attract and retain shoppers, thus maximizing sales and profits. This means augmented services should not be offered unless they raise a firm's total sales and profits. Unfortunately, little research on the benefit–cost ratios of various services has been done. Thus, a retailer should plan augmented services based on experience, competitors' actions, and customer comments; and when the costs of providing these services increase, higher prices should be passed on to the consumer.

How can customer services be terminated? Once a retailer establishes a customer service strategy, shoppers are likely to react negatively to any reduction of services. Nonetheless, inefficient and costly augmented services may have to be discontinued. In dropping customer services, a firm's best strategy is to be forthright—explaining why services are being terminated and how the customer will benefit via lower prices. Sometimes, a firm may choose a middle ground, charging for previously free services and allowing those who want the services to continue to receive them.

Planning Individual Services Once a broad customer service plan is outlined, individual services are planned. For example, a department store may offer all these services: credit, layaway, gift wrapping, a bridal registry, parking, pay phones, a restaurant, a beauty salon, carpet installation, dressing rooms, clothing alterations, rest rooms and sitting areas, the use of baby strollers, home delivery, and fur storage. The range of typical customer services is shown in Table 2.2 and described next.

Today, most retailers let their customers make credit purchases. Even some supermarkets and fast-food chains—two of the last major holdouts—allow credit-card transactions. And many firms accept personal checks with proper identification. About 40 to 60 percent of department and specialty store purchases are on credit, with consumers' use of credit rising greatly as the amount of a purchase goes up.

Retailer-sponsored credit cards have three key advantages. One, the retailer saves the sales fee it would pay for outside card sales. Two, people are encouraged to shop with a given firm because its card is usually not accepted elsewhere. Three, contact can be maintained with customers and information learned about them. There are also disadvantages to retailer credit cards: startup costs are high, the firm must worry about unpaid bills and slow cash

Table 2.2 Typical Customer Services

Credit	Miscellaneous	
Delivery	• Bridal registry	• Rest rooms
Alterations and installations	• Interior designers	• Restaurant
Packaging (gift wrapping)	• Personal shoppers	• Baby-sitting
Complaints and returns handling	• Ticket outlets	• Fitting rooms
Gift certificates	• Parking	• Beauty salon
Trade-ins	• Water fountains	• Fur storage
Trial purchases	• Pay phones	• Shopping bags
Special sales for regular customers	• Baby strollers	• Information
Extended store hours		
Mail and phone orders		

Visa (www.visa.com) is the widest-circulating commercial credit card today.

flow, credit checks and follow-up tasks must be performed, and customers without the firm's card may be discouraged from buying.

Bank and other commercial credit cards let small and medium retailers offer credit, generate added business for all types of retailers, appeal to tourists and mobile shoppers, provide advertising support from the sponsor, reduce bad debts, eliminate startup costs for the retailer, and provide data. Yet, these cards charge a fee per transaction (based on the retailer's sales volume) and do not yield retailer loyalty.

All bank cards and most retailer cards involve revolving accounts. With a **revolving credit account,** a customer charges items and is billed monthly on the basis of the outstanding cumulative balance. An **option credit account** is a form of revolving account; no interest is assessed if a person pays a bill in full when it is due. However, should a person make a partial payment, he or she is assessed interest monthly on the unpaid amount. Some credit-card firms (such as American Express) and some retailers emphasize open credit accounts. With an **open credit account,** a consumer must pay the bill in full when it is due. Partial, revolving payments are not permitted. A person with an open account also has a credit limit.

For a retailer whose products, its customers, or both require that items be delivered, there are three decisions in setting up delivery service: the transportation method, equipment ownership versus rental, and timing. The shipping method can be car, van, truck, train, boat, mail, and/or plane. The costs and appropriateness of methods depend on the merchandise involved. Large retailers often find it economical to own delivery vehicles. This also lets them advertise the company name, have control over schedules, and have their employees handle deliveries. Small retailers serving limited trading areas may use their personal vehicles. However, many small, medium, and even large retailers use firms such as United Parcel Service if consumers live away from a delivery area, transportation is used sporadically, and shipments are not otherwise efficient (because small amounts are sent). Last, the retailer must decide how quickly to process orders and how often to deliver to different locales.

For certain firms, alterations and installations are expected services, and treated accordingly—though more retailers now charge fees. However, many discounters have stopped offering alterations of clothing and installations of heavy appliances on both a free and a fee basis. They feel the services are too ancillary to their business and not worth the effort. Other retailers offer only basic alterations: shortening pants, taking in the waist, and lengthening jacket sleeves. They do not adjust jacket shoulders or width. Some appliance retailers may hook up washing machines but not do plumbing work.

Within a store, packaging (gift wrapping)—as well as complaints and returns handling—can be centrally located or decentralized. Centralized packaging counters and complaints and returns areas have several advantages: they may be situated in otherwise dead spaces; the main selling areas are not cluttered; specialized personnel can be used; and a common store policy is enacted. The advantages of decentralized facilities are that shoppers are not inconvenienced; people are kept in the selling area, where a salesperson may resolve problems or offer different merchandise; and extra personnel are not required. In either case, a clear policy as to the handling of complaints and returns must be stated.

Gift certificates encourage new and existing customers to shop with a given retailer. Many firms require gift certificates to be spent and not redeemed for cash. Trade-ins also induce new and regular shoppers to patronize a retailer. People get the feeling of a bargain. Trial purchases let shoppers test products before purchases are final, thus reducing risks. If customers like the products, they are kept and paid for; if customers dislike them, they can be returned. Some mail-order firms allow trial purchases.

Retailers are increasingly offering special services to regular customers. Special sales, not open to the general public, are run to increase customer loyalty. Extended hours, such as evenings and weekends, are provided. This lengthens in-store shopping time and decreases rushing. Mail and phone orders from regular customers are handled for convenience.

Other useful customer services include a bridal registry, interior designers, personal shoppers, ticket outlets, free (or low-cost) and plentiful parking, water fountains, pay phones, baby strollers, rest rooms, a restaurant, baby-sitting, fitting rooms, a beauty salon, fur storage, shopping bags, and in-store information counters. The latter should not be

Careers in Retailing

Building Customer Relationships Means Diversity in the Workforce

The Director of College Relations for Sears has this view toward diversity in the workplace: "At Sears, we understand that the diversity of our associates is critically important, enabling us to maintain a workforce that meets the needs of our customers and the communities in which we work and live. For that reason, we are committed to recruiting the best students from all cultures to be our future executives."

According to the president of the National Retail Federation, "African-Americans, Hispanics, and other minorities will find prime opportunities for career development and advancement in this dynamic industry as retailers recognize the need for that diversity to be reflected on the retail selling floor and in upper management."

Two leading retail career paths are buying and store management. A buyer often manages millions of dollars of merchandise and is perpetually trying to anticipate what styles and colors consumers will want. Every week (or more frequently), the buyer evaluates performance based on sales for the prior week. If sales are up compared to the corresponding period last year, "you celebrate." If sales are down, the buyer innovates and finds new ways to sell merchandise. Store managers, on the other hand, typically manage from 10 to 120 part-time and full-time employees. There are personnel, legal, advertising, community relations, security, and credit issues for them to address. If the store manager is successful, there are larger stores and higher-level positions that await.

Source: Richard Feinberg, "The Retail Industry: A Giant, Hidden Career Opportunity," *The Black Collegian Online* (February 1997).

undervalued; confused customers are less apt to be satisfied or complete their shopping trips. A retailer's willingness to offer some or all of these services indicates to customers its concern for them. Therefore, firms need to consider the impact of excessive self-service.

Customer Satisfaction **Customer satisfaction** occurs when the value and customer service provided through a retailing experience meet or exceed consumer expectations. If the expectations of value and customer service are not met, the consumer will be dissatisfied. Furthermore, retailers should always keep in mind that customer expectations move continuously upward[18]—and that only "very satisfied" customers are likely to remain loyal in the long run. How well are retailers doing in customer satisfaction? Many have a lot of work to do. It is imperative for retailers to avoid the kinds of complaints cited in Table 2.3, which invariably lead to customer dissatisfaction. Consider the results of two large-scale consumer surveys:

- The American Customer Satisfaction Index annually questions thousands of people to link customer expectations, perceptions of quality, and perceived value to satisfaction. Overall, retailers consistently have scored about 75 on a scale of 100. Fast-food firms usually rate lowest (with scores in the 60s).
- Shopping incidents may be categorized as critical—where a negative experience may keep a shopper from returning; marginal—where an experience is unsatisfying, but the customer is apt to return; and satisfactory—where the experience is acceptable and the customer would definitely shop again. More than one-third of respondents said they recently had faced a marginal or critical incident.[19]

Unfortunately for retailers, most consumers do not complain when dissatisfied. They just shop elsewhere. Why don't shoppers complain more? (1) Most people feel complaining produces little or no positive results. So they do not bother to complain. (2) Complaining is not

Table 2.3 Common Customer Complaints About Retailers: Tactics to Avoid

True Lies	Blatant dishonesty or unfairness, such as selling unneeded services or purposely quoting fake, "lowball" cost estimates.
Red Alert	Retailers who assume customers are stupid or dishonest and treat them harshly or disrespectfully.
Broken Promises	Service retailers who do not show up as promised. Careless, mistake-prone service.
I Just Work Here	Powerless employees who lack the authority—or the desire—to solve basic customer problems.
The Big Wait	Waiting in a line made long because some of the checkout lanes or service counters are closed.
Automatic Pilot	Impersonal, emotionless, no-eye-contact, going-through-the-motions nonservice.
Suffering in Silence	Employees who don't bother to communicate with customers who are anxious to hear how a service problem will be resolved.
Don't Ask	Employees unwilling to make any extra effort to help customers, or who seem put out by requests for assistance.
Lights On, No One Home	Clueless employees who do not know (will not take the time to learn) the answers to customers' common questions.
Misplaced Priorities	Employees who visit with each other or conduct personal business while the customer waits. Those who refuse to assist a customer because they're off duty or on a break.

Source: Adapted by the authors from Leonard L. Berry, "Retailers with a Future," *Marketing Management* (Spring 1996), p. 43. Reprinted by permission of the American Marketing Association.

easy. Consumers have to find the party to whom they should complain, access to that party may be restricted, and forms may have to be completed—each of these factors adds to customer frustration and takes time on the person's part.[20]

To remedy the lack of consumer feedback, retailers must make it easier for shoppers to complain, make sure shoppers believe their concerns are being addressed, and deploy ongoing customer satisfaction surveys. As suggested by consulting firm CustomerSat.com (www.customersat.com), retailers should ask such questions as these and then take corrective actions reflecting their shoppers' feelings:

1. "How satisfied are you with our customer service?" [very satisfied, satisfied, neither satisfied nor dissatisfied, dissatisfied, very dissatisfied]

2. "Please rate our customer service." [excellent, very good, good, fair, poor]

3. "We provide good customer service." [strongly agree, agree, neither agree nor disagree, disagree, strongly disagree]

4. "How often does customer service exceed expectations?" [very frequently, frequently, neither frequently nor infrequently, infrequently, very infrequently]

5. "What do you like most about our customer service?" "What do you like least?"

Loyalty Programs **Consumer loyalty (frequent shopper) programs** reward a retailer's best customers, those with whom it wants long-lasting relationships. Programs must be well-conceived and part of a value-driven strategy:

Lettuce Entertain You (www.leye.com) places a great emphasis on consumer loyalty programs.

Because they seem simple, consumer loyalty programs have popped up everywhere. Today, it seems, no self-respecting retailer is without one. Spend $100 at Waterstone's Books & Music, get a $10 gift certificate. Purchase a tall espresso at Starbucks in the morning, come back in the afternoon and get the next size larger for the price of a tall. Rack up enough points in the Frequent Diners Club at Lettuce Entertain You restaurants in several cities and receive tickets to Honolulu, plus five nights in a hotel. Do loyalty programs also work for smaller firms? Yes, no, and maybe. Relationship retailing is a strategy, not a short-term program. Firms that enact a system of rewards but neglect to have a companywide devotion to customer service, fail. Firms believing a "Dear Preferred Customer" letter is all it takes to communicate with high-value clientele, fail. Only those retailers delivering genuine benefits based on intimate knowledge of their best customers and creating a "customer-first" mentality at all levels of their organization reap the ultimate benefit: greater customer loyalty.[21]

What do good customer loyalty programs have in common? Their rewards are useful and appealing to customers; and they are attainable in a reasonable time frame. The programs honor shopping behavior (the greater the purchase amounts, the greater the benefits). A data base tracks behavior (it "keeps score"). The programs have features that are unique to particular retailers and not redeemable elsewhere. There is a range of rewards to stimulate short- and long-run purchases. Communications with customers are personalized. Frequent shoppers are made to feel "special." Participation rules are publicized and rarely changed. The programs are promoted and membership is encouraged. See Figure 2.6.

The better loyalty programs include three complementary elements: *Rewards*—Many loyalty programs reward purchases with merchandise, travel, partner gift certificates, or more of the company's product. *Value-added benefits*—These are perquisites that build interactive relationships with shoppers. These include special offers, newsletters, and member events. *Customer recognition*—Personalization is at the center of recognition. This means acknowledging customers by name and understanding their needs, wants, and concerns. Members are made to feel unique. Rewards, value-added benefits, and recognition all build

Figure 2.6
The Discovery Club:
A Loyalty Program
from wine.com

Reprinted by permission.

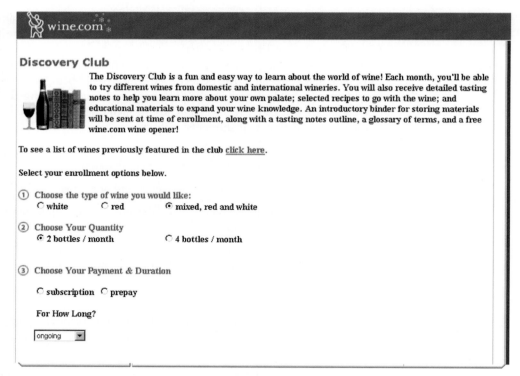

customer loyalty. Each type of benefit, however, serves a different role. Typically, rewards serve as the most compelling reason for customers to participate in a program. The promise of a reward is what motivates customers to find out more about a retailer's offer and take advantage of it.[22]

Studying customer defections, by tracking data bases or doing consumer surveys, contributes valuable information. Such analysis shows a firm how many customers it is losing and (with surveys) why they are no longer patronizing a given retailer. Customer defections may be expressed in absolute terms (people who no longer buy from the firm at all) or in relative terms (people who shop less often with the firm). Each retailer must determine what its acceptable defection rate is. Remember, not all customers are "good" customers. It may better serve a retailer if shoppers who always look for sales, return items without sales receipts, expect fee-based services to be free, and so on, become defectors.

The more knowledge a firm gathers about defecting customers, the more it can learn and, thus, the better it can serve current and future customers. Unfortunately, too few retailers review defection data or survey defecting customers, due to the complexity of doing so and an unwillingness to hear "bad news."

Channel Relationships

Within the framework of a value chain, members of a distribution channel (manufacturers, wholesalers, and retailers) jointly represent a **value delivery system,** which comprises all the parties that develop, produce, deliver, and sell and service particular goods and services. This has ramifications for retailers:

● Each channel member is dependent on the other. When consumers shop with a certain retailer, they often do so because of both the characteristics of that retailer and the products it carries.

- Every value delivery system activity must be enumerated and responsibility assigned for them.
- Small retailers may have to use suppliers outside the normal distribution channel to get the products they want and gain adequate supplier support. While large retailers may be able to buy directly from manufacturers, smaller retailers may have to buy through wholesalers that handle small accounts.
- A value delivery system is as good as its weakest link. No matter how well a retailer performs its activities, it will still have unhappy shoppers if suppliers deliver late or do not honor warranties.
- The nature of a given value delivery system must be related to target market expectations.
- Channel member costs and functions are influenced by each party's role in a value delivery system. Long-term cooperation and two-way information flows foster efficiency.
- Value delivery systems are more complex than ever due to the vast product assortment of superstores, the many forms of retailing, and the use of multiple distribution channels by some manufacturers.
- Nonstore retailing (such as mail order, phone transactions, and the Web) requires a different delivery system than store retailing. Though there is no "store," shoppers have high hopes as to the caliber of catalogs, Web pages, delivery time, product assortments, convenience, and customer service.
- Due to conflicting goals about profit margins, shelf space, and so on, some channel members are adversarial—to the detriment of the value delivery system and channel relationships. In recent years, there has been a move toward greater channel power by large retail chains.

When they forge strong positive channel relationships, members of a value delivery system can better serve each other and the final consumer. Here's how:

> Traditionally, the relationship between retailers and suppliers was, at best, arm's length, if not at times adversarial. The manufacturers' goal was to move the greatest volume of goods at the highest price. The retailers' goal was to negotiate the lowest price for the goods. Competitive pressures led to the development of a new paradigm. It focused on a simple idea: make sure the right product at the right price is on the shelf when the customer enters the store, while maintaining the lowest possible inventory at all points in the pipeline from suppliers to retailer. Since this has to do with managing the pipeline of merchandise flow, it requires cooperation between retailers and upstream suppliers.[23]

Blockbuster (www.blockbuster.com) guarantees that popular movies will be in stock, due to its novel approach with vendors.

> The new strategy for Blockbuster is deceptively simple: stock more of the new releases that customers want. Before, the average customer had to visit a store five consecutive weekends to get the movie wanted. To change that, Blockbuster overhauled its business model. In the past, it bought tapes from studios for about $65 apiece. Since each store has 10,000 tapes, inventory got expensive, thus limiting its willingness to invest in too many copies of one film. Now Blockbuster has revenue sharing with all but a couple of major studios. The deals dramatically lower Blockbuster's up-front costs to $6 to $7 a tape. In exchange, Blockbuster hands over roughly 40 percent of revenue.[24]

> Where retailers were solely responsible for negotiating prices, choosing products, paying for them, placing them on the sales floor, and advertising in the 1980s, retailers now must rapidly respond to people's needs. Shoppers are driven by immediacy, value, and easy access. Major retailers have closer ties, joint relationships, and partnerships with suppliers. They're providing selling space and working jointly with wholesalers to design, advertise, maintain inventory, and share in profits. If a retailer doesn't perform as expected, manufacturers will feel that the sale is one-sided.[25]

Figure 2.7
Elements
Contributing to
Effective Channel
Relationships

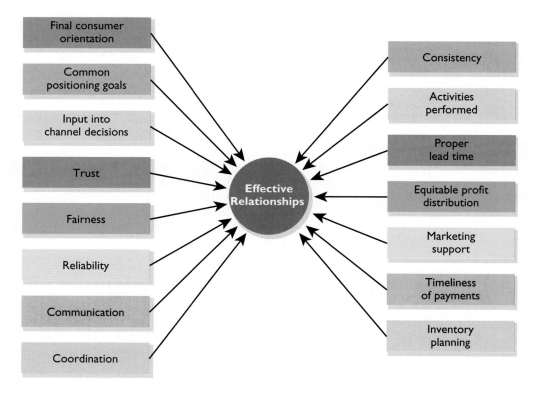

One relationship-oriented practice that some manufacturers and retailers are trying to use, especially supermarket chains, is *category management*. With this approach, channel members collaborate to maximize product category performance by offering product assortments and prices that better address consumer needs. Products are managed by category rather than by individual item. For retailers, category management is based on these principles: First, rather than just buy goods and services, retailers listen more to customers and stock what they want. Second, profitability is improved because inventory follows demand closer. Third, by being better focused, each department can become more desirable for shoppers. Fourth, retail buyers are assigned more responsibilities and accountability for category performance. Fifth, retailers and their suppliers must share data and be more computerized. Sixth, retailers and their suppliers must plan together for the best assortments. Category management is discussed further in Chapter 14.

Figure 2.7 shows various factors that contribute to effective channel relationships.

THE DIFFERENCES IN RELATIONSHIP BUILDING BETWEEN GOODS AND SERVICE RETAILERS

Given consumers' heightened interest in services, it is now more crucial than ever to understand the differences in relationship building between retailers marketing services and those marketing goods. This applies to store-based and nonstore-based retailers, as well as to firms offering only goods *or* services and those offering goods *and* services.

Goods retailing focuses on the sale of tangible (physical) products. **Service retailing** involves transactions in which consumers do not purchase or acquire ownership of tangible products. Some retailers engage in either goods retailing (such as hardware stores) or service retailing (such as travel agencies); others offer a combination of the two (such as video stores that rent, as well as sell movies). The latter format is the fastest-growing. Consider how many pharmacies offer film developing, how many department stores have beauty salons, how many computer stores run fee-paid training classes, how many stationery stores sell lottery tickets, how many hotels have gift shops, how many golf driving ranges sell equipment, and so on.

Service retailing encompasses such diverse businesses as personal services, hotels and motels, auto repair and rental, and recreational services. In addition, although several services have not been commonly considered a part of retailing (such as medical, dental, legal, and educational services), they should be when they entail a transaction with a final consumer.

There are three kinds of service retailing: **rented-goods services,** in which consumers lease and use goods for specified periods of time; **owned-goods services,** in which goods owned by consumers are repaired, improved, or maintained; and **nongoods services,** in which intangible personal services (not goods) are offered to consumers—who experience the services rather than possess them. The terms *customer service* and *service retailing* are not interchangeable. Customer service refers to the activities undertaken *in conjunction with* the retailer's main business; they are part of the total retail experience. Service retailing refers to situations in which services *are sold to* the consumer.

Examples of rented-goods service retailing are Hertz car rentals, carpet cleaner rentals at a supermarket, and video rentals at a 7-Eleven. In each case, a tangible good is leased for a fixed time. The consumer may enjoy the use of the item, but ownership is not obtained and the good must be returned when the rental period is up. Owned-goods service retailing illustrations include repair of a watch mainspring, lawn care to eliminate weeds, and an annual air-conditioner tune-up to maintain performance. In this grouping, the retailer providing the service never owns the good involved. In nongoods service retailing, personal services, involving the use of the owner's or employee's time in return for a fee, are offered; tangible goods are not involved. Some examples are stock brokers, tutors, travel agents, real-estate brokers, and personal trainers. In each case, the seller offers personal expertise for a specified time.

Cheap Tickets (www.cheaptickets.com) makes itself more tangible through its descriptive name.

The unique aspects of services, which influence relationship building and retention, are that (1) the intangible nature of many services makes a consumer's choice of competitive offerings tougher than with goods; (2) the service provider and his or her services are sometimes inseparable (thus localizing marketing efforts); (3) the perishability of many services prevents storage and increases risks; and (4) the human nature of many services makes them more variable.

The intangible (and possibly abstract) nature of services makes it harder for a firm to develop a clear consumer-oriented strategy, particularly since many retailers (such as opticians, repairpeople, and landscapers) start service businesses on the basis of their product expertise. The inseparability of the service provider and his or her services means the owner-operator is often indispensable and good customer relations are pivotal. Perishability presents a risk that in many cases cannot be overcome. Thus, revenues from an unrented hotel room are forever lost. Variability means service quality may differ for each shopping experience, store, or service provider. See Figure 2.8.

More than goods retailers, service firms usually recognize that long-term customer relationships are essential to their well-being. After all, service retailing is much more dependent on personal interactions and word-of-mouth communication:

Relationship marketing benefits the customer, as well as the firm. For continuously or periodically delivered services that are personally important, variable in quality, and/or complex, many customers will desire to be "relationship customers." High-involvement services also hold relationship appeal to customers. Medical, banking, insurance, and hairstyling services illustrate some or all of the significant factors—importance, variability, complexity, and involvement—that would cause many customers to desire continuity with the same provider, a proactive service attitude, and customized service delivery. All are potential benefits of relationship marketing. The

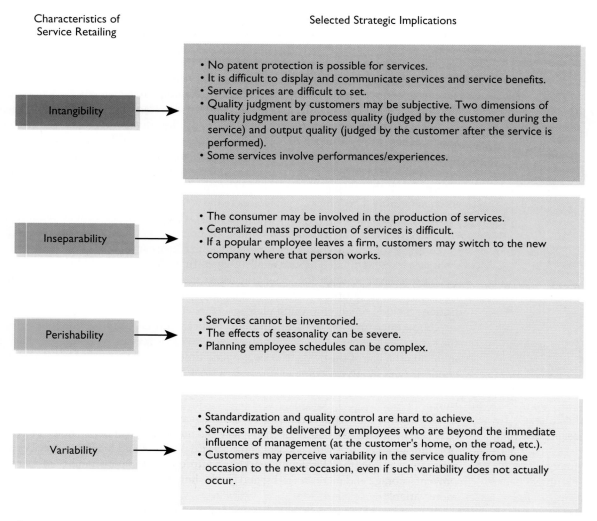

Characteristics of
Service Retailing

Selected Strategic Implications

Intangibility
- No patent protection is possible for services.
- It is difficult to display and communicate services and service benefits.
- Service prices are difficult to set.
- Quality judgment by customers may be subjective. Two dimensions of quality judgment are process quality (judged by the customer during the service) and output quality (judged by the customer after the service is performed).
- Some services involve performances/experiences.

Inseparability
- The consumer may be involved in the production of services.
- Centralized mass production of services is difficult.
- If a popular employee leaves a firm, customers may switch to the new company where that person works.

Perishability
- Services cannot be inventoried.
- The effects of seasonality can be severe.
- Planning employee schedules can be complex.

Variability
- Standardization and quality control are hard to achieve.
- Services may be delivered by employees who are beyond the immediate influence of management (at the customer's home, on the road, etc.).
- Customers may perceive variability in the service quality from one occasion to the next occasion, even if such variability does not actually occur.

Figure 2.8

Characteristics of Service Retailing That Differentiate It from Goods Retailing and Their Strategic Implications

Source: Adapted by the authors from Valarie A. Zeithaml, A. Parasuraman, and Leonard L Berry, "Problems and Strategies in Service Marketing," *Journal of Marketing,* Vol. 49 (Spring 1985), p. 35. Reprinted by permission of the American Marketing Association.

intangible nature of services makes them difficult for customers to evaluate prior to purchase. The heterogeneity of labor-intensive services encourages customer loyalty when excellent service is experienced. Not only does the auto repair firm want to find customers who will be loyal, but customers want to find an auto repair firm that evokes their loyalty. Relationship marketing allows service firms to be more knowledgeable about customers. Knowledge of the customer combined with social rapport built over a series of service encounters facilitate the tailoring or customizing of service to the customer's specifications. Relationship marketing does not apply to every service situation. However, for those services distinguished by the characteristics discussed here, it is a potent marketing strategy.[26]

Figure 2.9 highlights 10 factors that consumers may consider in forming their perceptions of the caliber of the relationship experiences offered by particular retailers. The appendix at the end of this chapter presents an additional discussion on the unique aspects of operating a service retailing business.

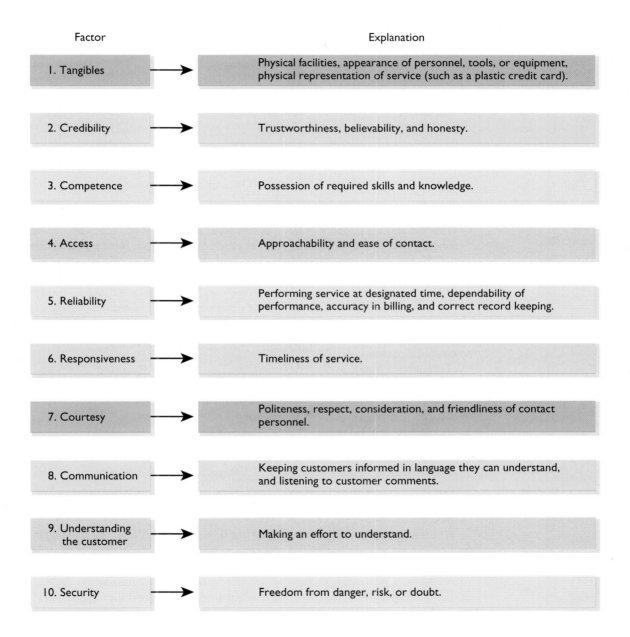

Factor	Explanation
1. Tangibles	Physical facilities, appearance of personnel, tools, or equipment, physical representation of service (such as a plastic credit card).
2. Credibility	Trustworthiness, believability, and honesty.
3. Competence	Possession of required skills and knowledge.
4. Access	Approachability and ease of contact.
5. Reliability	Performing service at designated time, dependability of performance, accuracy in billing, and correct record keeping.
6. Responsiveness	Timeliness of service.
7. Courtesy	Politeness, respect, consideration, and friendliness of contact personnel.
8. Communication	Keeping customers informed in language they can understand, and listening to customer comments.
9. Understanding the customer	Making an effort to understand.
10. Security	Freedom from danger, risk, or doubt.

Figure 2.9
Ten Factors Consumers Use to Determine Service Quality

Source: Adapted by the authors from Valarie A. Zeithaml, A. Parasuraman, and Leonard L. Berry, *Delivering Quality Service: Balancing Customer Perceptions and Expectations* (New York: Free Press, 1990), pp. 21–22. Free Press is a division of Simon & Schuster. Reprinted by permission.

TECHNOLOGY AND RELATIONSHIPS IN RETAILING

Technology is beneficial to relationships in retailing if the result is a better information flow between retailers and customers, as well as between retailers and suppliers; and there are faster, more dependable transactions. Nonetheless, this comment sums up the complexities of and concerns about technology:

> Why isn't anyone correct about technological predictions? Because a key new technology changes the standard. It's not a matter of the old world, plus something new. It's a matter of a whole new world. The car, phone, and TV all redid the world (and retailing!). Today's technologies are redoing the world in ways we can't predict, save to say that they're going to be important. And technology creates instant dependency, a panic-stricken feeling of loss if it doesn't work. As a retailer or consumer, have you ever put a card in an ATM and the machine refused to give you the card back? Even though you're sophisticated and educated, you still get a surge of technology-induced panic.[27]

In general, these two points should be taken into account in studying technology and its impact on relationships in retailing. One, in each firm, the roles of technology and "humans" must be clear and consistent with the objectives and style of business. Although technology can be a great aid in providing a high level of customer service, it can also become overloaded and break down—and it is viewed as impersonal or "cold" by some consumers. Setting up new technology needs to be as efficient as possible, with minimal disruptions to suppliers, employees, and customers. Two, customers expect certain advances to be in place, so they can rapidly complete credit transactions, get feedback on product availability, and so on. Firms have to deploy some advances (such as the ones just mentioned) simply to be competitive. By enacting other advances, they can carve out differential advantages—consider the paint store with computerized paint-matching equipment for customers who want to touch up old jobs and the stationery store with an interactive video kiosk that allows people to customize greeting cards.

Throughout *Retail Management*, in the "Technology in Retailing" boxes and in chapter discussions, we devote a lot of attention of technological advances. Here, we look at technology's effects in terms of electronic banking and customer–supplier interactions.

Electronic Banking

Electronic banking involves both the use of automatic teller machines (ATMs) and the instant processing of retail purchases. It allows centralized recordkeeping and lets customers complete transactions 24 hours a day, 7 days a week at a variety of bank and nonbank locations (including home or office). As Figure 2.10 indicates, payment systems technology has certainly evolved over the years.

At present, in the United States alone, there are 230,000 ATMs (up from 60,000 in 1985) and people make 11 billion ATM transactions per year (up from 3.6 billion in 1985), numbers that are sure to keep growing.[28] ATMs are located in banks, shopping centers, department stores, supermarkets, convenience stores, hotels, and airports; on college campuses; and at other sites. With sharing systems, consumers can make transactions at ATMs outside their local banking areas. For instance, the Cirrus and Plus networks each make it possible for consumers to have access to tens of thousands of ATMs worldwide.

Besides its use in typical financial transactions (such as check cashing, deposits, withdrawals, and transfers), electronic banking is increasingly being used in retailing situations. More retailers (especially those that previously accepted only cash or check payments, such as supermarkets) are accepting some form of electronic debit payment plan, whereby the purchase price is immediately deducted from a consumer's bank account by computer and

Figure 2.10
The Evolution of
Electronic Banking

Reprinted by permission of
Carolina First Corporation.

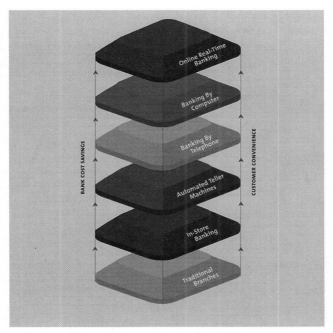

transferred to a retailer's account. There are now 1 billion such electronic transfers at U.S. stores each year, versus about 8 billion transactions with traditional credit cards.[29]

One highly touted, but thus far limited in use, new version of electronic payment is called the **smart card** by industry observers. The smart card contains an electronic strip that stores and modifies information as transactions take place. The version being tested in the United States by Visa, MasterCard, American Express, and others is similar to pre-paid phone cards, whereby consumers buy computer-coded cards in denominations of $10, $20, $50, $100, and more. Then, as they shop, retail card readers deduct the purchase amounts from the cards. After being used up, the cards are thrown away or they can be recoded. One big limitation for consumers is that few firms now handle smart card transactions; unlike cash payments, retailers pay a fee for smart card transactions. In the future, "smarter" smart cards are expected to be more permanent and store more information (such as frequent shopper points).[30]

The role of individual retailer credit cards is declining due to the popularity of such financial services providers as Visa and MasterCard, which together have 170 million cardholders (many of whom have both cards). Yet, numerous retailers still stress their own credit programs since they believe they may lose their identities if these programs are used less frequently by customers.

Customer and Supplier Interactions

Technology is changing the nature of retailer–customer and retailer–supplier interactions. If applied well, benefits accrue to all parties. If not, there are negative ramifications. Here are several illustrations.

Point-of-sale scanning equipment is widely utilized by supermarkets, department stores, specialty stores, membership clubs, and others—hundreds of thousands of firms in all. Why? By electronically scanning merchandise (rather than having cashiers "ring up" each product), retailers can quickly complete customer transactions, amass sales data, give feedback to suppliers, place and receive orders more quickly, reduce costs, and adjust inventory figures. But there is a downside to scanning: the error rate. And this can be upsetting to consumers. According to a Federal Trade Commission (FTC) study, scanner errors in reading prices occurred 9.2 percent of the time in department stores, 6.3 percent of the time in drugstores, 5.4 percent of the time in home centers, 4.6 percent of the time in discount stores, 3.5 percent of the time in food stores, and 1.8 percent of the time in toy stores. Yet, although consumer perceptions are that errors cause overcharges, the FTC found undercharges were more likely than overcharges. These results were confirmed by another study of 2,000 retail stores.[31] One way to assure consumers about scanner accuracy is to display more information at the point of purchase.

A novel experiment now underway involves self-scanning, a concept whose future success is by no means certain. Here's how it works:

> With self-checkout, customers feel they're getting in and out of a store faster because they don't have to wait for assistance. Retailers benefit, too. NCR Self-Checkout is designed to boost profitability by speeding throughput. More lanes are open all the time, even in short, high-traffic periods. Lines are shorter and shoppers spend less time at checkout. Costs are reduced because more lanes are open—with less staff. NCR Self-Checkout is an expanded ATM with an integrated point-of-sale solution. The scanner/scale is easy to use—even the first time—and helps customers scan with confidence. The touchscreen display guides shoppers intuitively through a transaction. Built-in security features are designed to protect cash and monitor inventory. In addition to a security camera showing an on-screen image of customers performing transactions, comprehensive security software, including an optional weight data base, further identifies inconsistencies in scanning and bagging.[32]

Figure 2.11 shows another self-scanning station, this one from Stores Automated Systems.

Figure 2.11
A Self-Checkout Station

This self-checkout, from Stores Automated Systems, Inc., is stationary. Shoppers scan goods across a scanner and place them into a bag on a scale. The weight of the bagged items is compared to the weight of the scanned items, ensuring the shopper has scanned all items. A signature-capture device lets shoppers pay for purchases by credit or debit card without needing a cashier. Reprinted by permission.

Other technological innovations are also influencing retail interactions. Here are two examples:

Neiman Marcus pioneered the electronic gift card (www.neimanmarcus.com/assistance/gift_card.jhtml).

- A growing number of retailers think they have the answer to the problem of finding the perfect gift—the electronic gift card: "They're supposed to be easier to use, cutting-edge enough to appeal to kids, and with a big advantage to retailers. If the recipient buys less than the full value of the gift, the balance stays on the card, rather than being returned in cash to the consumer. Neiman Marcus is credited as being the first retailer to use the electronic gift card. 'When we launched our card in 1994, we were looking for something to replace the traditional paper certificate, which had outlived its marketing value,' said Billy Payton, vice-president of marketing and customer programs. 'The cards proved so popular with customers, that within 90 days we completely dropped paper certificates.' Gift cards generally are imprinted with magnetic strips or barcodes, machine-readable at the cash register. Some retailers offer a toll-free number for customers to call to get balance information. Many cards are rechargeable, so they can be given added value when the original limit is reached."[33]
- Interactive electronic kiosks (discussed further in Chapter 6) are gaining in popularity: "You arrive at an airport and use electronic check-ins to board the plane. You reach your destination, electronically access your rental car, and are on the road. Now, some hotels are betting they can speed up one of traveling's great ordeals with check-in kiosks. When Tim Probus arrived at MainStay Suites in Plano, Texas, late on a Sunday, the hotel had locked up for the night. He made a beeline for a computerized kiosk outside the lobby. 'I put my credit card in, and the key came out,' he says. It took 40 seconds to be checked in. About 80 percent of the guests use the kiosk at the MainStay Suites in Plano."[34]

Another fascinating technological advance, still in its infancy, is appealing to manufacturers, retailers, and consumers—when it works easily and inexpensively. It involves **mass**

Technology in Retailing   The Lure of Electronic Gift Cards

Federated Department Stores now offers electronic gift cards at every cash register in all of its more than 400 department stores—Bloomingdale's, Bon Marche, Burdines, Macy's, Rich's/Lazarus/Goldsmith's, and Stern's. In the past, these cards were offered on a limited basis and only at gift wrap or customer service stations. As Federated's senior vice-president of marketing services says, "While we know this type of payment appeals to the younger segment of our customers, gift cards are a contemporary idea and we have many customers, regardless of age, who are contemporary in their life-style." Because each division of Federated operates in different regions and serves different markets, the promotional plan for electronic gift cards is decentralized.

There are several major benefits of the electronic cards over traditional paper gift certificates. First, electronic cards are easier to purchase and redeem. Second, gift givers can recharge the cards with a new balance once purchases have been made. Third, parents can give these cards to their college-bound children to enforce spending limits and to make sure these monies are spent in particular stores. Despite the advantages of the electronic gift cards, Federated still offers paper certificates for those customers who are more comfortable with this method of gift giving.

Do you agree with Federated's decision to continue with paper gift certificates? Why or why not?

Source: "Contemporary Gifts," *Chain Store Age* (February 1999), p. 152.

customization, the ability to efficiently and economically offer goods and serves more tailored to individual consumers:

> In theory, mass customization benefits consumers, manufacturers, and retailers. Consumers receive a product fulfilling their needs better than a mass-produced one. Manufacturers have fewer markdowns and returns from retailers. Retailers have fewer markdowns and less inventory investment. Most importantly, retailers and manufacturers have more consumer loyalty. In addition, customization can remove some guesswork from doing business. Firms that mass customize know exactly what people buy and do not buy every day and can plan and react accordingly. And finally, mass customization provides a sustainable competitive advantage. The Industrial Age model of making things cheaper by making them the same does not always hold for manufacturers and retailers today because competitors can copy product and store innovations faster than ever.[35]

Among the leading practitioners of mass customization are the Dell and Gateway PC firms, Levi Strauss at its company-owned retail stores, Web-based music retailers, and General Nutrition Centers.

ETHICAL PERFORMANCE AND RELATIONSHIPS IN RETAILING

Ethical challenges fall into three interconnected categories: ethics, social responsibility, and consumerism. Ethics relates to the retailer's moral principles and values. Social responsibility involves acts benefiting society. Consumerism entails protecting consumer rights. "Good" behavior depends not only on the retailer but also on the expectations of the community in which it does business.

Throughout *Retail Management*, in "Ethics in Retailing" boxes and chapter discussions, we look at many ethical issues. Here, we study the broader effects of ethics, social responsibility, and consumerism.

Ethics

In dealing with their constituencies (customers, the general public, employees, suppliers, competitors, and others), retailers have a moral obligation to act ethically. Furthermore, due to the heightened societal and media attention now paid to firms' behavior—and the high expectations people have today, a failure to be ethical may lead to adverse publicity, lawsuits, the loss of customers, and a lack of self-respect among employees. Each of these events happened to Sears after it was discovered that the firm was illegally collecting credit card debt from 200,000 of its customers who had declared for personal bankruptcy.

When a retailer has a sense of **ethics,** it acts in a trustworthy, fair, honest, and respectful manner with each of its constituencies.[36] For this to occur, executives must articulate to employees and channel partners which kinds of behavior are acceptable and which are not. The best way to avoid unethical acts is for firms to have written ethics codes, to distribute them to employees and channel partners, to monitor behavior, and to punish poor behavior—and for top managers to be highly ethical in their own conduct. See Figure 2.12.

Often, society may deem certain behavior to be unethical but laws may not forbid it. Most observers would agree that practices like these are unethical (and sometimes illegal, too):

- Raising prices on scarce products after a natural disaster such as a hurricane or earthquake.
- Not having adequate stock when a sale is advertised.
- Charging high prices in low-income areas because consumers there do not have the transportation mobility to shop out of their neighborhoods.
- Selling alcohol and tobacco products to children.

Figure 2.12
Eddie Bauer: Strong
Ethical Sensibilities

Reprinted by permission of
Eddie Bauer, Inc.

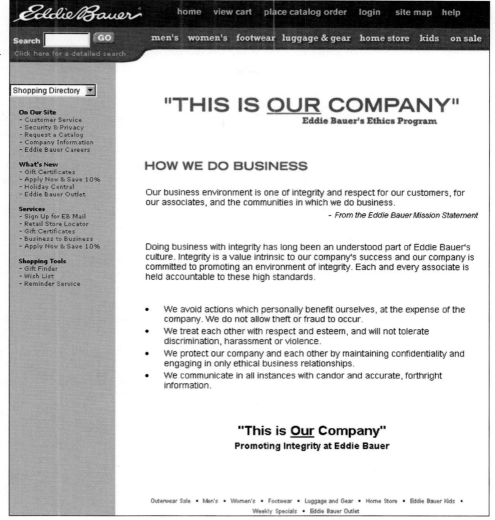

- Having a salesperson pose as a market researcher when engaged in telemarketing.
- Defaming competitors.
- Selling refurbished merchandise as new.
- Pressuring employees to push high-profit items to shoppers, even if they are not best for them.
- Selling information from a customer data base.

The Direct Marketing Association makes its complete ethics code available at its Web site (www.the-dma. org/library/ guidelines).

Many trade associations promote ethics codes to member firms. For example, the Direct Marketing Association has a code that members are encouraged to use. Here are some of its provisions: *Article 1:* All offers should be clear, honest, and complete. *Article 5:* Disparagement of anyone on grounds of race, color, religion, national origin, gender, marital status, or age is unacceptable. *Article 8:* All contacts should disclose the sponsor and the purpose of the contact; no one should make offers or solicitations in the guise of one purpose when the intent is another purpose. *Article 12:* Offers suitable for adults only should not be made to children. *Article 23:* Sweepstakes prizes should be advertised in a clear, honest, and complete way so the consumer may know the exact offer. *Article 27:* Merchandise should not be shipped without receiving customer permission. *Article 36:* A telemarketer should not knowingly call a consumer with an unlisted or unpublished phone number. *Article 42:* Firms should operate in accordance with the laws and regulations of the United States Postal Service, the Federal Trade Commission, the Federal Communications Commission, the Federal Reserve Board, and other applicable jurisdictions.[37]

Social Responsibility

A retailer exhibiting **social responsibility** acts in the best interests of society—as well as itself. The challenge is to balance corporate citizenship with a fair level of profits for stock-holders, management, and employees. Some forms of social responsibility are virtually cost-free to the firm, such as having employees participate in community events or disposing of waste products in a more careful way. Some are more costly, such as making donations to charitable groups or giving away goods and services to a school. Still others mean going above and beyond the letter of the law, such as having free loaner wheelchairs for disabled persons besides legally mandated wheelchair accessibility to retail premises.

Most retailers know socially responsible acts do not go unnoticed by consumers. Though the acts may not stimulate greater patronage for firms with weak strategies, they can be a customer inducement for retailers otherwise viewed as "me too" entities. It may also be possible to profit from good deeds. If a retailer donates excess inventory to a charity that cares for the ill, poor, or infants, it can take a tax deduction equal to the cost of the goods plus one-half the difference between the cost and the retail price. To do this, a retailer must be a corporation and the charity must use the goods and not sell or trade them.

This is what a cross-section of retailers are doing to be socially responsible. McDonald's founded the Ronald McDonald House program, which serves people around the world. Families can stay at a low-cost Ronald McDonald House instead of a more costly hotel when their seriously ill children receive medical treatment outside their own community. Target Stores no longer carries cigarettes; and A&P has removed cigarette machines from its super-markets to reduce sales to minors. At Wal-Mart, "we believe it is our responsibility to be a part of the collective effort to protect and preserve our natural resources. That's why we have a four-part commitment to: Provide environmentally improved products to our customers. Look for better ways to build and operate Wal-Mart stores and offices. Support and encourage local community and environmental activities. Support educational programs for children."[38] J. C. Penney requires domestic and foreign suppliers to sign a code of conduct stipulating that underage labor is not used.

Hannaford Bros.' pledge nicely sums up the role of a socially involved retailer:

> To succeed, we must satisfy our customers, associates, communities, and shareholders. To achieve this, we must practice the highest level of ethical, social, legal, and professional behavior. We must constantly anticipate the changing needs and desires of customers and respond quickly and effectively to them. We are committed to distributing the goods and services consumers want with prices and quality that represent superior value. We are committed to the growth of all associates. To accomplish this, we need a growing business, a sharing of common goals, and an atmosphere of mutual trust, openness, and encouragement. We will support and participate in the efforts of local, state, and national groups which best contribute to the quality of life. In the long run, we will best serve the interests of our shareholders by serving well our customers, associates, and communities.[39]

Consumerism

Consumerism relates to the activities of government, business, and other organizations that are designed to protect individuals from practices infringing upon their rights as con-

The Ronald McDonald House program (www.rmhc.com) is one of the most respected community outreach efforts in retailing.

sumers. This definition is based on the premise that consumers have basic rights that should be safeguarded. As President Kennedy said 40 years ago, consumers have the *right to safety* (protection against hazardous goods and services), the *right to be informed* (protection against fraudulent, deceptive, and incomplete information, advertising, and labeling), the *right to choose* (access to a variety of goods, services, and retailers), and the *right to be heard* (consumer feedback, both positive and negative, to the firm and to government agencies).

Retailers—and their channel partners—need to avoid business practices violating these rights and to do all they can to understand and protect them. These are some reasons why:

- Retailing is so competitive that people are more apt to patronize firms perceived as customer-oriented and not to shop with ones seen as greedy.
- Because consumers are more knowledgeable and selective than in the past, retailers must offer fair value, provide detailed information, and be prepared to handle questions and complaints.
- Consumers are becoming more price-conscious. The popularity of discount retailing is also heightening consumer awareness of prices.
- Large retailers may be viewed as indifferent to consumers. They may not provide enough personal attention for shoppers or may have inadequate control over employees.
- The use of self-service is increasing, and it can cause frustration for some shoppers.
- The rise in new technology is unsettling to many consumers, who must learn new shopping behavior (such as how to use electronic video kiosks).
- Retailers are in direct customer contact, so they are often blamed for and asked to resolve problems caused by manufacturers (such as defective products). They must reconcile the interests of suppliers and customers. In addition, they can pass on safety, information, and recommendations to suppliers.

Consider the negative feelings that consumers have about how some retailers are handling the issue of customer privacy:

Ethics in Retailing

The Changing Role of Pharmacists

In the past, licensed pharmacists restricted their advice to how and when a client should take a particular medication. Today, pharmacists are seeking—and in some cases obtaining—the right to counsel patients and to change and even initiate prescriptions.

The Health Care Financing Administration (HCFA), the government organization that oversees both federal and state insurance for the poor, recently gave pharmacists in Mississippi the right to be reimbursed under Medicaid for advising patients with a number of ailments (such as diabetes, asthma, and high cholesterol). The HCFA is also considering whether to give pharmacists in other states similar authority. In addition, 21 states have already granted pharmacists the right to initiate and modify a patient's drug treatment as long as they have a collaborative agreement with a physician. In such an agreement, the physician provides the pharmacist with a detailed program of patient care and allows the pharmacist to modify it.

Pharmacists say that patients benefit from their advice and availability; and they can also can reduce health care costs by performing routine procedures, such as checking a patient's blood pressure. Many physicians, on the other hand, question the ability of the pharmacist to diagnose an illness and then prescribe drugs.

What are the ethical issues of a pharmacist diagnosing an illness and then prescribing a medication?

Source: Robert Berner, "Pharmacists Start to Vie for a Broader Range of Powers," *Wall Street Journal* (January 28, 1999), pp. B1, B18.

The controversy began for CVS when the pharmacy chain hired a company called Elensys to handle the administrative functions involved with tracking compliance and mailing marketing information. CVS provided names and addresses of pharmacy customers to Elensys, which then sent mailings on appropriate chain letterhead. The type of information that patients received included refill reminders and information about new drugs related to their own condition. A person with diabetes, for example, could learn about a new type of syringe. Drug companies partially funded the mailings. To some people, however, the direct mail program smacked of Big Brother. Privacy groups complained that the transfer of data to the marketing firm violated patient confidentiality, raising the possibility that information on the medications people are taking could become available to employers and others. The program sparked a public outcry after the *Washington Post* ran a series of articles and editorials about it, with more than 200 CVS customers calling the chain to voice their concern. Within a week, CVS canceled the use of Elensys to manage compliance programs.[40]

To avoid the preceding situation, many retailers have devised programs to protect consumer rights without waiting for government or consumer pressure to do so. Following are examples of these actions.

J.C. Penney adopted the "Penney Idea" in 1913 and still adheres to its seven basic concepts:

To serve the public, as nearly as we can, to its complete satisfaction; to expect for the service we render a fair remuneration and not all the profit the traffic will bear; to do all in our power to pack the customer dollar with value, quality, and satisfaction; to continue training ourselves and our associates so the service we give will be more intelligently performed; to improve constantly the human factor in our business; to reward men and women in our firm by participation in what the business produces; and to test our every policy, method, and act—"Does it square with what is right and just?"[41]

In the 1970s, Giant Food—a leading supermarket chain—hired Esther Peterson (once President Johnson's consumer affairs advisor) at a rank equal to vice-president. It then devised a consumer bill of rights, patterned on President Kennedy's, to which it has adhered ever since:

1. Right to safety—Giant's product safety standards, such as age-labeling toys, go far beyond those required by government agencies.

2. Right to be informed—Giant has a detailed labeling system.

3. Right to choose—Consumers who want to purchase possibly harmful or hazardous products (such as foods with additives) can do so.

4. Right to be heard—A continuing dialog with reputable consumer groups is in place.

5. Right to redress—There is a money-back guarantee policy on all products.

6. Right to service—Customers should receive good in-store service.[42]

A number of retailers have voluntarily enacted their own product-testing programs, whereby merchandise is tested for such attributes as value, quality, misrepresentation of contents, safety, and durability before being placed for sale. Sears, Wal-Mart, J.C. Penney, A&P, Macy's, Target Stores, and Giant Food are just a few of those doing testing. See Figure 2.13. Among the other consumerism activities undertaken by various retailers are setting clear procedures for handling customer complaints, reviewing advertising message clarity, sponsoring consumer education programs, and training personnel on how to interact properly with customers.

Figure 2.13
Voluntary Product
Testing at Target
Stores

Reprinted by permission of
Target Stores.

Target's Responsibility

At Target, toys are an important part of our business. We want the toys you buy to meet Target's and the U.S. Government's high standards of quality, value, and safety. Therefore, we abide by all U.S. Consumer Product Safety Regulations. Target also utilizes an independent testing agency. They test samples of all toys we sell to help ensure your child's safe play.

All toys sold at Target are tested to be certain they are free from these dangers:

Sharp edges

Toys of brittle plastic or glass can be broken to expose cutting edges. Poorly made metal or wood toys may have sharp edges.

Small parts

Tiny toys and toys with removable parts can be swallowed or lodged in child's windpipe, ears, or nose.

Loud noises

Noise-making guns and other toys can produce sounds at noise levels that can damage hearing.

Sharp points

Broken toys can expose dangerous points. Stuffed toys can have barbed eyes or wired limbs that can cut.

Propelled objects

Projectiles and similar flying toys can injure eyes in particular. Arrows or darts should have protective soft tips.

Electrical shock

Electrically operated toys that are improperly constructed can shock or cause burns. Electric toys must meet mandatory safety requirements.

Wrong toys for the wrong age

Toys that may be safe for older children can be dangerous when played with by little ones.

Consumer-oriented activities are not limited to large chains; small firms can also be involved. A local toy store can separate toys by age category. An independent supermarket can have special displays featuring environmentally safe detergents. A neighborhood restaurant can cook foods in low-fat vegetable oil and emphasize menu items with reduced sodium. A sporting goods store can give a money-back guarantee on exercise equipment, so people can try it out in their homes.

SUMMARY

1. *To explain what "value" really means and highlight its pivotal role in retailers' building and sustaining relationships.* To the manufacturer, wholesaler, and retailer, value is represented by a series of activities and processes providing a given level of value for the consumer. It consists of the tangible and intangible product and service attributes offered to customers. To the customer, value is the perception the shopper has of a given value chain. It

SUMMARY (CONTINUED)

is the customer's view of all the benefits received via a particular purchase (formed, to a large extent, by the total retail experience). Value is based on perceived benefits received versus prices paid. It varies by type of shopper.

A retail value chain represents the total bundle of benefits offered by a channel of distribution. It comprises many elements, including: store location, ambience, customer service, the products/brands carried, product quality, the in-stock position, shipping, prices, the retailer's image, and so forth. Some elements of a retail value chain are visible to shoppers. Others are not.

An expected retail strategy represents the minimum value chain elements a given customer segment expects from a given type of retailer. An augmented retail strategy encompasses the extra elements in a value chain that differentiate one retailer from another. A potential retail strategy includes value chain elements not yet perfected by a competitor in the retailer's industry category.

2. *To describe how both customer relationships and channel relationships may be nurtured in today's highly competitive marketplace, with a special emphasis on the customer base, customer service, customer satisfaction, and loyalty programs.* For relationship retailing to work properly, enduring relationships are needed with other channel members, as well as with customers. More retailers than ever now realize loyal customers are the backbone of their business.

In applying relationship retailing with consumers, there are four central factors to keep in mind: the customer base, customer service, customer satisfaction, and loyalty programs and defection rates. All consumers are not equal. Some are more worth nurturing long relationships with than others; they are a retailer's core customers. And they should be singled out in a firm's data base.

Firms should view customer service as having two components—expected services and augmented services. The attributes of personnel who interact with customers, as well as the number and variety of services offered, have a strong impact on the relationship created. Some firms have improved customer service by empowering personnel, giving them the authority to bend some rules. In devising a strategy, a retailer must make broad decisions and then enact specific tactics with regard to credit, delivery, and so forth.

Customer satisfaction occurs when the value and customer service provided in a retail experience meet or exceed expectations. If expectations of value and cus-

tomer service are not met, the consumer will be dissatisfied. According to recent surveys, retailers have work to do in this area.

Consumer loyalty programs reward the best customers, those with whom a retailer wants to form long-lasting relationships. To succeed, they must complement a sound value-driven retail strategy. By studying customer defections, a retailer can gain valuable information. Such analysis shows a firm how many customers it is losing and why they are no longer patronizing a given retailer.

Members of a distribution channel jointly represent a value delivery system, comprising all the parties that develop, produce, deliver, and sell and service particular goods and services. Each one is dependent on the others; and every activity must be enumerated and responsibility assigned. Small retailers may have to use suppliers outside the normal channel to get the items they want and gain supplier support. A delivery system is as good as its weakest link. Member costs and functions are influenced by each party's role in a delivery system. A relationship-oriented technique that some manufacturers and retailers are trying, especially supermarket chains, is category management.

3. *To examine the differences in relationship building between goods and service retailers.* It is essential to see the differences in relationship building between retailers marketing goods and those marketing services. Goods retailing focuses on selling tangible products. Service retailing involves transactions where consumers do not purchase or acquire ownership of tangible products.

There are three kinds of service retailing: rented-goods services, in which consumers lease goods for a given time; owned-goods services, whereby goods owned by consumers are repaired, improved, or maintained; and nongoods services, in which intangible personal services are offered—consumers experience services rather than possess them. Customer service refers to activities that are part of the total retail experience. With service retailing, services are sold to the consumer.

The unique features of services that influence relationship-building and retention are the intangible nature of many services, the inseparability of some service providers and their services, the perishability of many services, and the variability of many services.

4. *To discuss the impact of technology on relationships in retailing.* Technology is advantageous when it leads to an improved information flow between retailers and suppliers, and between retailers and customers, and to faster, smoother transactions.

Electronic banking involves both the use of automatic teller machines (ATMs) and the instant processing of retail purchases. It allows centralized record keeping and lets customers complete transactions 24 hours a day, 7 days a week at a variety of bank and nonbank locations. The smart card may be the wave of the electronic future. Technology is also changing the nature of supplier/retailer/customer interactions through point-of-sale scanning equipment, self-scanning, electronic gift cards, interactive kiosks, mass customization, and other innovations.

5. *To consider the interplay between retailers' ethical performance and relationships in retailing.* Retailer challenges fall into three related categories: ethics, social responsibility, and consumerism. Ethics relates to a firm's moral principles and values. Social responsibility has to do with benefiting society. Consumerism entails the protection of consumer rights. "Good" behavior is based not only the firm's practices, but also on the expectations of the community in which it does business.

Ethical retailers act in a trustworthy, fair, honest, and respectful way. Firms are more apt to avoid unethical behavior if they have written ethics codes, communicate them to employees, monitor and punish poor behavior, and have ethical executives. Retailers perform in a socially responsible manner when they act in the best interests of society through recycling and conservation programs, and other efforts. Consumerism activities involve government, business, and independent organizations. Four consumer rights are basic: to safety, to be informed, to choose, and to be heard.

Key Terms

value (p. 29)
value chain (p. 29)
core customers (p. 34)
expected customer service (p. 34)
augmented customer service (p. 34)
employee empowerment (p. 35)
revolving credit account (p. 38)
option credit account (p. 38)

open credit account (p. 38)
customer satisfaction (p. 40)
consumer loyalty (frequent shopper) programs (p. 41)
value delivery system (p. 42)
goods retailing (p. 44)
service retailing (p. 44)
rented-goods services (p. 45)

owned-goods services (p. 45)
nongoods services (p. 45)
electronic banking (p. 48)
smart card (p. 49)
mass customization (p. 51)
ethics (p. 52)
social responsibility (p. 54)
consumerism (p. 54)

Questions for Discussion

1. When a consumer shops at a discount store, what factors determine whether the consumer feels that he or she got a fair value? How does the perception of value differ when that same consumer shops at an upscale store?

2. What are the expected and augmented value chain elements for each of these retailers?
   a. Supermarket.
   b. Movie theater.
   c. Blockbuster video store.

3. Why should a retailer devote special attention to its core customers? How should it do so?

4. What is the connection between customer service and employee empowerment? Is employee empowerment always a good idea? Why or why not?

5. How would you measure the level of customer satisfaction with your college's bookstore?

6. Devise a consumer loyalty program for a local dry cleaner.

7. What is a value delivery system? How may it be improved?

8. Describe the three different kinds of services that retailers may offer.

9. What are the unique aspects of service retailing? Give an example of each.

10. Should dental, accounting, and other services be considered a part of retailing? Why or why not?

11. What are the pros and cons of ATMs? As a retailer, would you want an ATM in your store? Why or why not?

12. Will the time come when most consumer purchases are made with self-scanners? Explain your answer.

13. Describe three unethical, but legal, acts on the part of retailers that you have encountered. How have you reacted in each case?

14. Differentiate between social responsibility and consumerism from the perspective of a retailer.

15. How would you deal with consumer concerns about privacy in their relationships with retailers?

WEB-BASED EXERCISE

Blockbuster (www.blockbuster.com)

Questions

1. What features of Blockbuster's Web site enhance relationship retailing?

2. What features should Blockbuster consider adding to its Web site to further foster relationship retailing?

3. Evaluate Blockbuster's Web site from the perspective of getting shoppers to revisit it on a regular basis.

4. Evaluate Blockbuster's Web site from the perspective of getting customers to buy videos.

CHAPTER ENDNOTES

1. Jane Wolfe, "If You Spend a Million, They'll Throw in a Jaguar," *New York Times* (March 21, 1999), Section 3, p. 10.

2. Michael Sansolo, Food Marketing Institute, as quoted in "Feel-Good Solutions," *Progressive Grocer* (August 1998), p. 22.

3. Jennifer Steinhauer, "The Stores That Cross Class Lines," *New York Times* (March 15, 1998), Section 3, p. 1.

4. Nina Munk, "Gap Gets It," *Fortune* (August 3, 1998), p. 81.

5. James R. Hagerty and Robert Berner, "Ever Wondered Why Furniture Shopping Can Be Such a Pain?" *Wall Street Journal* (November 2, 1998), p. A18.

6. Wendy Liebmann, "How America Shops," *Vital Speeches of the Day* (July 15, 1998), pp. 595–98.

7. Frederick R. Reichheld, "Learning from Customer Defections," *Harvard Business Review*, Vol. 74 (March–April 1996), p. 57.

8. Murray Raphel, "Pressed into Service," *Direct Marketing* (June 1999), pp. 42–44.

9. PricewaterhouseCoopers, *Deconstructing Demographics: Key Trends for the Next Decade* (August 1998); and Murray Raphel, "Who Is Tomorrow's Customer?" *Direct Marketing* (November 1998), pp. 52–54.

10. Kurt Salmon Associates, *Consumer Outlook '98* and *Consumer Outlook '99*; Robert Verdisco, "Gender-Specific Shopping," *Chain Store Age* (February 1999), p. 26; and Barry Janoff, "Targeting All Ages," *Progressive Grocer* (April 1999), pp. 37–39.

11. Reichheld, "Learning from Customer Defections," p. 61. See also Rasmussen Ericka, "Wanted: Profitable Customers," *Sales & Marketing Management* (May 1999), pp. 28–34.

12. Valerie Soranno, "Customer Profiles Are Key to Loyalty," *Discount Store News* (February 8, 1999), p. 14.

13. Ernest W. Nicastro, "The 'Marshall' Plan—Or Customer After-Care: How to Spend Less and Sell More," *Direct Marketing* (April 1999), p. 62.

14. Alison Kirk, "The Invisible Customer," *Across the Board* (October 1998), p. 9.

15. Jennifer Steinhauer, "Whatever Happened to Service?" *New York Times* (March 4, 1997), pp. D1–D2. See also Mary M. K. Fleming, "When Customer Service Goes Bad," *Business Horizons* (July–August 1999), pp. 43–52.

16. *Nordstrom 1998 Annual Report*, p. 8.

17. Gene Hoffman, "Commercializing the Helping Hand," *Progressive Grocer* (July 1999), p. 112.

18. Donald W. Jackson, Jr., "One More Time: How Do You Satisfy Customers," *Business Horizons*, Vol. 42 (May–June 1999), pp. 71–76.

19. "American Customer Satisfaction Index Scores by Industry Sector 1994–99," *acsi.asq. org/results.html* (March 7, 2000); and Faye Brookman, "Satisfaction Equals Retention," *Discount Store News* (November 11, 1998), p. 17.

20. Shirley Bednarz, "Fine Whine," *Entrepreneur* (February 1999), p. 103.

21. Mary Connors, "Dear Preferred Customer," *Dividends* (May 1996), pp. 13–14.

22. Kurt Johnson, "Making Loyalty Programs More Rewarding," *Direct Marketing* (March 1999), pp. 24–26; and Nancy Stephenson, "Holding All the Cards," *American Demographics* (February 2000), pp. 35–37.

23. Robert D. Buzzell, "Channel Partnerships Streamline Distribution," *Sloan Management Review*, Vol. 36 (Spring 1995), p. 86. See also Judy A. Siguaw, Penny M. Simpson, and Thomas L. Baker, "Effects of Supplier Market Orientation on Distributor Market Orientation and the Channel Relationship: The Distributor Perspective," *Journal of Marketing*, Vol. 62 (July 1998), pp. 99–111; and Matt Nannery, "The Peacemakers," *Chain Store Age* (August 1999), pp. 67–72.

24. Daniel Kadlec, "How Blockbuster Changed the Rules," *Time* (August 3, 1998), p. 48; and Geraldine Fabrikant, "Viacom's Weak Link Grows a Bit Stronger," *New York Times* (October 5, 1998), pp. C1, C12.

25. "Executives Praise Quick Response Technology," *SHOWCASE International* (April–May 1998), pp. 30–31.

26. Leonard L. Berry, "Relationship Marketing of Services—Growing Interest, Emerging Prospects," *Journal of the Academy of Marketing Science*, Vol. 23 (Fall 1995), pp. 237–38. See also Glenn B. Voss, A. Parasuraman, and Druv Grewal, "The Roles of Price, Performance, and Expectations in Determining Satisfaction in Service Exchanges," *Journal of Marketing*, Vol. 62 (October 1998), pp. 46–61; Stephen S. Tax and Stephen W. Brown, "Recovering and Learning from Service Failures," *Sloan Management Review*, Vol. 40 (Fall 1998), pp. 75–88; and Rajiv P. Dant, James R. Lumpkin, and Mohammed Y. A. Rawwas, "Sources of Generalized Versus Issue-Specific Dis/Satisfaction in Service Channels of Distribution: A Review and Comparative Investigation," *Journal of Business Research*, Vol. 42 (May 1998), pp. 7–23.

27. James R. Rosenfield, "Technology: Terrific When It Works, Really Awful When It Doesn't," *Direct Marketing* (November 1995), pp. 38–39.

28. "Despite Rise in Units, ATM Transactions Drop," *ATMmagazine.com* (July 23, 1999).

29. See "Debit, Pre-Paid Card Usage Growing," *Chain Store Age* (July 1999), p. 172.

30. David P. Schulz, "Credit Industry Seeks New Approaches to Promise of Smart Cards," *Stores* (December 1998), pp. 58–59; Marcia Stepanek, "What Smart Cards Couldn't Figure Out," *Business Week* (November 30, 1998), p. 142; and Becky Bull, "Getting Smarter?" *Progressive Grocer* (May 1999), pp. 131–32.

31. "Department Stores Trail Supermarkets in Scanner Accuracy," *Chain Store Age* (December 1996), p. 125; and Guy Richard Clodfelter, "Pricing Accuracy at Grocery Stores and Other Retail Stores Using Scanners," *International Journal of Retail & Distribution Management*, Vol. 26 (October–November 1998), pp. 412–20.

32. *NCR Self-Checkout*, company brochure (1999).

33. Lisa Cornell, Associated Press, "Retailers Have High Hopes for Electronic Gift Cards," *Marketing News* (January 4, 1999), p. 33.

34. Neal Templin, "Electronic Kiosk Checks in Guests at More Hotels," *Wall Street Journal* (February 16, 1999), p. B1.

35. "Just for You: The Status of Mass Customization," *PricewaterhouseCoopers Intelligence Update* (March 1999), p. 4.

36. N. Craig Smith, "Ethics and the Marketing Manager" in N. Craig Smith and John A. Quelch, *Ethics in Marketing* (Homewood, Illinois: Irwin, 1993), pp. 3–34.

37. *Direct Marketing Association Guidelines for Ethical Business Practices* (New York: Direct Marketing Association, revised August 1999).

38. "Wal-Mart Good Works: Our Environment," *www/walmartfoundation.org/environment.html* (March 8, 2000).

39. "Hannaford Company Facts," *www.hannaford.com/compfact* (March 9, 2000).

40. Faye Brookman, "Drug Chains Contend with Thorny Privacy Issue," *Stores* (June 1998), p. 70.

41. J.C. Penney public relations.

42. Giant Food public relations.

CASE 1

CUSTOMER SERVICE THE RITZ-CARLTON WAY

Since its 1983 incorporation, the Ritz-Carlton Hotel Company has received a number of prestigious awards from both the hospitality industry and leading consumer organizations. In 1998, for example, 11 of the American Automobile Association's 57 prestigious five-diamond awards went to Ritz-Carlton hotels (in that year, there were only 35 hotels in the Ritz-Carlton chain). On several occasions, Zagat's annual *U.S. Hotels, Resorts & Spas Survey* has recognized Ritz-Carlton as the "Best Hotel Group."

Ritz-Carlton's preoccupation with customer service and employee training is somewhat unusual in an industry characterized by low wages and a high level of employee turnover. Across the industry, annual hotel employee turnover is estimated to range from 51 percent to 300 percent. According to Leonardo Inghilleri, a Ritz-Carlton senior vice-president, "Customers who come to our hotel pay a premium for perfection. We have a tremendous challenge to meet and exceed customer expectations. That's why we discuss customer service every single day of our lives."

Ritz-Carlton's philosophy is embodied in the core values it calls the "Gold Standards," a vital part of which is the firm's credo. It states: "The Ritz-Carlton Hotel is a place where the genuine care and comfort of our guests is our highest mission. We pledge to provide the finest personal service and facilities for our guests who will always enjoy a warm, relaxed yet refined ambiance. The Ritz-Carlton experience enlivens, instills well-being, and fulfills even the unexpressed wishes and needs of our guests."

Ritz-Carlton's quest for superb service begins with employee selection. It has identified specific behavioral traits that would lead to successful employees in each position. The firm recognizes that the desired traits differ by position. Thus, housekeepers are expected to be exact, attentive to detail, and take pride in their work. In contrast, a doorman has to be more of a "people person" and be able to convey friendliness to patrons, even from a distance. Exactness is not a crucial aspect of a doorman's position.

The firm uses a well-designed selection and interview process to determine if an applicant meets the requirements for a given position. This process is so demanding that Ritz-Carlton hires only 1 in 10 applicants.

Although Ritz-Carlton's customer service standards are first communicated to all new employees at an orientation session, the standards also provide the basis for continuous employee training. All 16,000 employees undergo 120 hours of training per year, divided into two general areas: technical training (such as how to properly make a bed or serve a meal at a first-class restaurant) and customer service training that addresses how guest challenges can be best resolved (such as dealing with a broken TV). The training is reinforced with 10- to 15-minute daily meetings that explain why the firm is in business and its continued commitment to "Gold Standards" customer service.

Every Ritz-Carlton employee is empowered to resolve guest problems, whether or not the matter of concern immediately falls into that employee's immediate area of responsibility. For instance, a waiter hearing that a guest's TV is performing poorly is expected to call the hotel's engineering department to resolve the problem. Ritz-Carlton's research has found that the most loyal customers are those who have had a minor problem quickly resolved.

Ritz-Carlton also recognizes the need to retain employees by providing a good compensation package and through its concern with satisfying employees' personal needs. The company recently initiated new programs that improve their employees' personal growth.

Questions

1. Why do you think that more hotels have not copied Ritz-Carlton's approach to customer service?

2. What other aspects of relationship retailing can Ritz-Carlton utilize?

3. Present an outline for a customer service philosophy for a local dry cleaner based on the information in this case.

4. How can Ritz-Carlton use its customer data base to further improve its customer service?

Video Questions on Ritz-Carlton

1. Describe how Ritz-Carlton uses employee empowerment as a component of its customer service strategy.

2. Discuss the pros and cons of Ritz-Carlton's quest for a 100-percent customer satisfaction rating.

NOTE The material in this case is drawn from Scott Hays, "Exceptional Customer Service Takes the 'Ritz' Touch," *Workforce* (January 1999), pp. 99–103; and www.ritzcarlton.com.

CASE 2

LUCY'S LAUNDRYMART: CARING FOR CUSTOMERS *AND* THEIR CLOTHES

Lucy's LaundryMart believes it can build profits by thinking outside the traditional laundromat box. Located in Los Angeles' inner-city communities, it serves residents of high-density apartment complexes. Most of its customers are women between the ages of 29 and 45, often with children in tow. When they come in for their weekly visits, they tend to stay for about 90 minutes.

"No one really wants to do the laundry. We want to make it as enjoyable as possible. We want to give our customers plenty of things to do and hopefully keep the entire family entertained," says Simon Smith, senior vice-president. How? By adding convenience to the six-store chain's mix. In most laundromats, there is little to do besides watch the spin cycle. Lucy's, on the other hand, features children's play areas and convenience stores in every unit.

In keeping with the family environment Lucy's has created, the convenience stores do not sell alcohol. In addition, video games in the "Kid Zones" are geared toward younger

CASE 2
(CONTINUED)

children. No violent arcade games are installed. These nuances are appreciated in Lucy's urban neighborhoods. They help deter the "wrong element" from loitering, Smith says.

Another convenience is the ability for customers to not have to carry pocketfuls of change. Customers use Lucy's own smart cards at any of the company-owned stores. The cards are rechargeable with values from $1 to $99 at vending machines in the laundromats. There is no more need to collect quarters all week or hope that the bill changer accepts crumpled singles. Smith says the smart cards provide peace of mind for customers in addition to convenience. "If a customer loses a card and is a member of the Lucy's club," he explains, "we can look up the value and deactivate the lost card, as well as issue a new card with the remaining balance."

In line with wanting to give customers plenty to do, the chain has made a practice of co-branding its stores with noncompetitive, service-oriented firms. Partners helping to enhance Lucy's destination appeal include Wells Fargo bank branches and Starbucks, Burger King, and Subway outlets. "By combining services that consumers use frequently in one location," says Lucy's chairman Bill Cunningham, "we feel we can reduce daily hassles and increase the perception of time that people feel they have available."

All the added conveniences come at a cost. Where most laundromats may have one or two people operating the store, Lucy's staffs each unit with an average of 10 people at any given time. But some of those costs are minimized by the co-branding arrangements. Lucy's and its partners benefit from reduced occupancy costs in the shared spaces. Lucy's LaundryMarts currently operate in spaces no bigger than 9,000 square feet, including its brand partners.

The newfangled laundromat box seems to be working. Smith says the convenience stores are operating with gross margins of 35 percent; the National Association of Convenience Stores pegs the industry average at 32 percent. While the convenience store segment at Lucy's has sales per square foot of slightly below the industry average, the laundry segment of the business operates at three times the industry average. The numbers have earned Lucy's the notice and financial backing of heavyweight firms such as InterWest Partners, San Francisco; Centre Partners, New York City; and JP Morgan Capital, New York City. Since its founding, Lucy's had opened only one or two stores a year. However, in 1999, the chain wanted to add 25 stores, and to have another 40 to 50 stores operational by the end of 2000.

Questions

1. Evaluate the pros and cons of emphasizing smart cards instead of cash at Lucy's.

2. What aspects of Lucy's strategy can be transferred to more affluent suburban areas?

3. What other types of retail operations (aside from Starbucks, Burger King, and Subway stores) are ideal for co-branding? Explain your answer.

4. Comment on Lucy's expansion plans. How can it keep its level of customer service as it grows?

NOTE

APPENDIX ON PLANNING FOR THE UNIQUE ASPECTS OF SERVICE RETAILING

This appendix is presented because service retailing in the United States and elsewhere in the world is growing steadily and represents a large portion of overall retail trade. In the United States, consumers spend three-fifths of their after-tax income on such services as travel, recreation, personal care, education, medical care, and housing. Three-quarters of the labor force works in the service sector. Consumers spend billions of dollars each year to rent such products as power tools and party goods (coffee urns, silverware, wine glasses, etc.).

Sites such as Internet Travel Network (www. itn.com) and Travel-=ocity (www. travelocity.com) are revolutionizing the travel services industry.

People annually spend $125 billion to maintain their cars. There are 90,000 beauty and barber shops, 56,000 laundry and cleaning outlets, 50,000 hotels and motels, 20,000 video-rental stores, and 15,000 sports and recreation clubs. During the past 25 years, the prices of services have risen more than the prices of many goods. Due to technological advances, automation has substantially reduced manufacturing labor costs; but many services remain rather labor-intensive due to their personal nature.[1]

In particular, a service retailer must understand how to plan for the differences between goods and service retailing. See Table 1.

Here, we will look at the abilities required to be a successful service retailer and how to improve the performance of service retailers.

Abilities Required to Be a Successful Service Retailer

The personal abilities required of a service-oriented retailer are usually quite distinct from those of a goods-oriented retailer:

- With service retailing, the major value provided to the customer is some type of service, not the ownership of a physical product.
- Specific skills may be required, and the skills may not be transferable from one type of service to another. For example, TV repairpeople, beauticians, and accountants cannot easily change businesses or transfer skills. The owners of appliance stores, cosmetics stores, and toy stores (all goods-oriented firms) would have an easier time changing and transferring their skills to another area.
- More service operators must possess licenses or certification to run their businesses. Barbers, real-estate brokers, dentists, attorneys, plumbers, and others must pass exams in their fields.
- Owners of service businesses must enjoy their jobs and have the aptitude for them. Because of the close personal contact with customers, these elements are essential and difficult to feign.

Many service retailers can operate on lower overall investments and succeed on less yearly revenues than goods retailers. A service station can function with one gas attendant and one skilled mechanic. A tax-preparation firm can succeed with one accountant. A watch repair business needs one repairperson. In each case, the owner may be the only skilled worker. Costs can be held down accordingly. On the other hand, a goods retailer needs an adequate assortment and supply of inventory, which may impose financial obligations, require storage, and be costly.

The time commitment of a service retailer differs by type of business opportunity. Some businesses, like a self-service laundromat or a movie theater, require a low time commitment. Other businesses, like house painting or a travel agency, require a large time commitment because personal service is the key to profitability. More service retailers fall into the high rather than the low time-investment category.

TABLE 1 Special Managerial Considerations for Service Retailers in Seven Key Strategic Areas

Service Retailing as Compared with Goods Retailing	Managerial Adjustments Needed by Service Retailers
Store organization	
More specialized supervision is needed.	Separate management for service areas will be required.
More specific search for service employees is needed.	Nontraditional sources for identification of employees must be used.
Lower employee turnover is needed.	Frequent salary and performance reviews must be carried out.
Higher pay for skilled craftspeople than for merchandising personnel is needed.	Pay levels will need to be adjusted upward over periods of longevity for service employees.
Service production	
More involvement in producing the service is needed.	Production skills will need to be obtained by supervisors.
More emphasis on quality control is needed.	Supervisors must be able to assess the quality of a service performed for a customer.
There is more need to monitor consumer satisfaction.	Prior customers should be researched to measure their satisfaction with the service.
There is more need to refine scheduling of employees.	Maximizing employee time requires matching consumer purchasing with the ability to produce the service.
Quality must be consistent among all outlets.	Standards for consistency of the service must be set and continually evaluated; central training may be required for workers in branch operations.
Pricing	
Services vary in cost; therefore, pricing is harder.	Prices may be quoted within a range before the purchase.
There is more difficulty in price competition or promotion based on price.	Services should be promoted in terms of criteria other than price.
Promotion	
Value is more difficult for consumers to determine.	Consumers need to be convinced of value through personal selling.
It is difficult to display services within a store.	In-store signs or a service center is required to show services' availability.
Visual presentation is more important.	Before-and-after photographs may be possible with some services. Testimonials may be possible with other services.
Cross-selling with goods is important.	A quota or bonus for goods-oriented salespersons who suggest services will lead to increased service selling.
It is more difficult to advertise in catalogs.	Service features and conditions must be specified.
Complaints	
It is harder to return a service.	Policies must be set for adjusting the service purchased by a dissatisfied customer.
A customer is more sensitive about services involving a person (rather than a good)	Specific guarantees and policies about adjustments must be set; new types of insurance must be added to cover liabilities.
Controls	
There is a greater opportunity to steal customers.	Employees' assurances of loyalty must be established. Protection of store loyalty must be sought.
Measuring performance	
Capital expenditures vary widely for different services.	Return on net worth may not be the most important measurement of the value of a service to the retailer.
Small or no inventories are required to offer services.	Turnover, markdown controls, and other goods-related controls are not as appropriate.
Higher labor costs exist for services.	Profit after labor costs replaces the gross margin of goods retailing.
Some services support the sale of goods.	Sales-supporting services should be assessed differently from revenue-producing ones.
Cost accounting is more important.	Job-specific records are required to assess the profits of each sale.

Source: Adapted by the authors from J. Patrick Kelly and William R. George, "Strategic Management Issues for the Retailing of Services," *Journal of Retailing*, Vol. 58 (Summer 1982), pp. 40–42. Reprinted by permission.

Improving the Performance of Service Retailers

Service tangibility can be increased by stressing service provider reliability, promoting a continuous slogan (for instance, Hertz #1 Club), describing specific service accomplishments (such as a car tune-up's improving gas consumption by one mile per gallon), and offering warranties (such as some hotels giving automatic refunds to unhappy guests). American Airlines (www.aa.com) offers a program at its Web site whereby customers can select flights and make their reservations interactively. This program is a tangible representation of American Airlines and its logos.

Demand and supply can be better matched by offering similar services to market segments with different demand patterns (such as Manhattan tourists and residents), new services with demand patterns that are countercyclical from existing services (such as cross-country skiing during the winter at Denver golf resorts), new services that complement existing ones (such as beauty salons adding tanning booths), special deals during nonpeak times (such as midweek movie theater prices), and new services not subject to existing capacity constraints (such as a 10-table restaurant starting a home catering service).

Midas (www.midas.com) has created a consistent image and presence for its far-flung auto services business.

Standardizing services reduces their variability, makes it easier to set prices, and improves efficiency. Services can be standardized by clearly defining each of the tasks involved, determining the minimum and maximum times needed to complete each task, selecting the best order for tasks to be done, and noting the optimum time and quality of the entire service. Standardization has been successfully applied to such firms as quick-auto-service providers (oil change and tune-up firms), legal services (for house closings and similar proceedings), and emergency medical care centers. If services are standardized, there is often a trade-off: more consistent quality and convenience in exchange for less of a personal touch.

Besides standardizing services, retailers may be able to make services more efficient by automating them, thereby substituting machinery for labor. For instance, attorneys are increasingly using computerized word processing for common paragraphs in wills and house closings. This means more consistency in the way documents look, time savings, and neater—more error-free—documents. Among the service firms that have automated at least part of their operations are banks, car washes, bowling alleys, airlines, phone services, real-estate brokers, and hotels.

The store location of a service retailer must be carefully considered. Sometimes, as with TV repairs, house painting, and lawn care, the service is "delivered" to the customer. The firm's location becomes the client's home, and the actual office of the retailer is rather insignificant. Many clients might never even see a firm's office; they make contact by phone or personal visits, and customer convenience is optimized. In these instances, the firm incurs travel expenses, but it also has low (or no) rent and does not have to maintain store facilities, set up displays, and so on. Other firms are visited on "specific-intent" shopping trips. Although a customer may be concerned about the convenience of a location, he or she usually does not select a skilled practitioner such as a doctor or a lawyer based on the location. It is common for doctors and attorneys to have offices in their homes or near hospitals or court buildings. A small store can often be used because little or no room is needed for displaying merchandise. A travel agency may have 12 salespeople and book millions of dollars in trips, yet fit into a 500-foot store.

Too often, "Pricing mismanagement plagues service industries because many service firms ignore the special challenge of pricing intangible products. Three distinct but related concepts for service pricing can help firms capture and communicate value through their pricing":

- *Satisfaction-based pricing* recognizes and reduces customer perceptions of uncertainty that service intangibility magnifies. It involves service guarantees, benefit-driven pricing, and flat-rate pricing.

- *Relationship pricing* encourages long-term relationships with valuable customers. It entails long-term contracts and price bundling.
- *Efficiency pricing* shares cost savings with customers that arise from the firm's efficiently executing service tasks. It is related to the concept of cost leadership.[2]

Negotiated pricing occurs when a retailer works out pricing arrangements with individual customers because a unique or complex service is involved and a one-time price must be agreed on. Unlike traditional pricing (whereby each consumer pays the same price for a standard service), each consumer may pay a different price under negotiated pricing (depending on the nature of the unique service). A moving company charges different fees, depending on the distance of the move, who packs the breakable furniture, the use of stairs versus an elevator, access to highways, and the weight of furniture.

Contingency pricing is an arrangement whereby the retailer does not get paid until after the service is performed and payment is contingent on the service's being satisfactory. A real-estate broker earns a fee only when a house purchaser (who is ready, willing, and able to buy) is presented to the house seller. Several brokers may show a house to prospective buyers, but only the broker who actually sells the house earns a commission. This technique presents risks to a retailer since considerable time and effort may be spent without payment. A broker may show a house 25 times, not sell it, and therefore not be paid.

Until the late 1970s, many professional associations did not let members advertise. Since then, the courts and the Federal Trade Commission have ruled that lawyers, physicians, pharmacists, accountants, and others may advertise. Today, when advertising, professionals are expected to exhibit high standards of ethics, explain when services should be sought, and state what they can realistically provide to clients.

One customer type is often beyond the reach of some service firms: the do-it-yourselfer. And the number of do-it-yourselfers in the United States is growing, as service costs increase. The do-it-yourselfer does a car tune-up, paints the house, mows the lawn, makes all vacation plans, and/or sets up a darkroom for developing film. Goods-oriented discount retailers do well by selling supplies to these people, but service retailers suffer since the major service (labor) is done by the customer. Segmentation is desirable, and perhaps necessary, to avoid this segment or to serve it by offering low prices for basic services.

Although some dentists don't believe in promoting their services, the American Association of Orthodontists (www.aaortho.org) helps those who do.

Retail strategies used by service professionals vary greatly. On the one hand, there are many doctors, lawyers, dentists, and others who do not believe in retailing tactics and do not use them. They do not view themselves as involved with service retailing, think activities such as advertising are demeaning, deplore competitive tactics, and do not understand all the elements in retail planning. They believe their skills market themselves. On the other hand, there are a growing number of service professionals who are quite involved in retail strategies in response to the competition in their fields. For example, the number of U.S. dentists has grown dramatically over the past 30 years. Yet, due to better prevention measures (such as fluoride toothpaste and fluoridated water), the number of cavities has dropped significantly. Many dentists have adapted by advertising in local papers, offering free initial examinations, locating in shopping districts or shopping centers, and adding new products for adults (such as "invisible" braces).

APPENDIX ENDNOTES

1. *Statistical Abstract of the United States 1999* (Washington, D.C.: U.S. Department of Commerce, 1999), various pages.

2. Leonard L. Berry and Manjit S. Yadav, "Capture and Communicate Value in the Pricing of Services," *Sloan Management Review*, Vol. 37 (Summer 1996), pp. 41–51.

Strategic Planning
in Retailing

CHAPTER OBJECTIVES

1. To show the value of strategic planning for all types of retailers
2. To explain the steps in strategic planning for retailers: situation analysis, objectives, identification of consumers, overall strategy, specific activities, control, and feedback
3. To examine the individual controllable and uncontrollable elements of a retail strategy
4. To present strategic planning as a series of integrated steps

In the past, banks and other service companies attempted to attract and keep as many customers as possible. Some of these same firms are now becoming much more selective in targeting their efforts at the most profitable customers. According to one bank consulting firm, the top 20 percent of a typical bank's customers produce as much as 150 percent of its total profits. In contrast, the bottom 20 percent drain 50 percent of the bank's profits.

Today, when a customer calls First Union Corporation, for example, to inquire about a lower interest rate for his or her credit card or to ask for a waiver on a bounced-check fee, the response depends on the color of a tiny square appearing next to the customer's name on a computer screen. A red square indicates the bank is losing money on the account. A green square means the customer is profitable and should be granted concessions. And a yellow square is for customers who are in between the red and green designations. Customer service personnel are free to negotiate with these customers.

First Union's computer system takes about 15 seconds to classify each customer based on his or her account balance, level of activity, number of visits, and other variables. On average, the most profitable customers keep several thousand dollars in their accounts, use a teller less than once a month, and hardly ever use the call center.[1]

OVERVIEW

As noted in Chapter 1, a **retail strategy** is the overall plan or framework of action that guides a retailer. Ideally, it will be at least one year in duration and outline the mission, goals, consumer market, overall and specific activities, and control mechanisms of the retailer. Without a defined and well-integrated strategy, the firm can flounder and be unable to cope with marketplace factors.

The process of strategic retail planning has several attractive features:

The U.S. Small Business Administration (www.sba.gov) has a lot of useful planning tools for retailers on its Web site.

- It provides a thorough analysis of the requirements for different types of retailing.
- It outlines the goals of the retailer.

> *Please Note:* Web site addresses are constantly changing.
> The links in this chapter are current as of the publication of this book.

69

- The firm learns how to differentiate itself from competitors and develop an offering that appeals to a group of customers.
- The retailer studies the legal, economic, and competitive environment.
- The firm's total efforts are coordinated.
- Crises are anticipated and often avoided.

Strategic planning can be conducted by the owner of the firm, professional management, or a combination of the two. As a person moves up the retail career ladder, a key indicator of performance and advancement potential is whether increased planning responsibility is undertaken and how well it is completed. Even among family businesses, the majority of high-growth companies have strategic plans.

The steps in planning and enacting a retail strategy are interdependent; a firm often starts with a general plan that becomes more specific as options and payoffs become clearer. In this chapter, we cover each step in the development of a comprehensive, integrated retail strategy, as shown in Figure 3.1. Because of the growing importance of global retailing, the appendix at the end of this chapter explores the special dimensions of strategic planning in a global retailing environment.

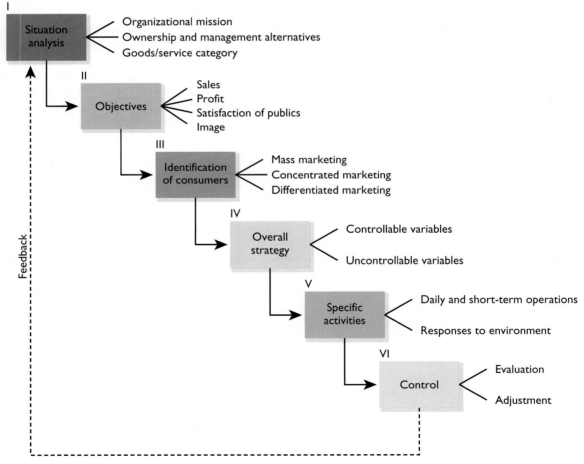

Figure 3.1
Elements of a Retail Strategy

SITUATION ANALYSIS

Situation analysis is a candid evaluation of the opportunities and threats facing a prospective or existing retailer. It seeks to answer two general questions: What is the firm's current status? In which direction should it be heading? For a retailer, situation analysis means being guided by an organizational mission, evaluating ownership and management options, and outlining the goods/service category to be sold.

To succeed, a retail strategy must anticipate and adapt to the changing business environment. As such, a good firm fully analyzes emerging opportunities and threats. **Opportunities** are the marketplace openings that exist because other retailers have not yet capitalized on them. Ikea does well because it is the pioneer firm in offering a huge selection of furniture at discount prices. **Threats** are environmental and marketplace factors that can adversely affect retailers if they do not react to them (and sometimes, even if they do). Single-screen movie theaters have virtually disappeared in some areas since they have been unable to fend off inroads made by multiscreen theaters.

A firm needs to spot trends early enough to satisfy customers and stay ahead of competitors, yet not so early that customers are not ready for changes or that false trends are perceived. A late response could mean a firm might miss out on profitable opportunities but minimize its risks. Strategic planning should consider the nature of marketplace factors in terms of the certainty of occurrence and the magnitude of change, their effect on a retailer's business, and the time required to react properly. The time a firm takes to react to marketplace challenges depends on the part of a strategy needing modification. Merchandising shifts—such as stocking a very popular fad item—are more quickly enacted than adjustments in a firm's overall location, pricing, or promotion strategy. A new retailer can adapt to trends more easily than existing firms with established images, ongoing leases, and space limitations. Although the marketplace is often quite challenging for small retailers, ones that prepare well can stand up to competition from larger firms.

During situation analysis, especially for a new retailer or one thinking about making a major strategic change, an honest, in-depth self-assessment is needed. It is all right for a person or company to be ambitious and aggressive, but overestimating one's abilities and prospects may be harmful—if the results are entry into the wrong retail business, inadequate resources, and misjudging competitors.

Organizational Mission

An **organizational mission** is a retailer's commitment to a type of business and to a distinctive role in the marketplace. It is reflected in the firm's attitude toward consumers, employees, suppliers, competitors, government, and others. A clear organizational mission lets a firm gain a customer following and distinguish itself from competitors. See Figure 3.2.

One major decision a retailer must make is whether to base its business around the goods and services sold or around consumer needs. For example, a retailer entering the hardware business must decide if, in addition to hardware products, a line of bathroom vanities should be stocked. A traditionalist would probably opt not to carry vanities because they seem unconnected to the proposed business. But a firm viewing a hardware store as a do-it-yourself home improvement center sees the vanities as a logical part of its product mix. The latter would carry any relevant items that the consumer, not the retailer, wants.

A second major decision for a retailer is whether it wants a place in the market as a leader or a follower. The firm could seek to offer a unique strategy, such as Taco Bell becoming the first national quick-serve Mexican food chain. Or it could emulate standard practices of competitors in its category but do a better job in executing them, such as a neighborhood fast-food Mexican restaurant offering five-minute guaranteed service and a cleanliness pledge.

By focusing on quick-serve Mexican food, available at convenient locations around the United States, Taco Bell (www.tacobell.com) has become the leading retailer in its category.

Figure 3.2

The Focused Organizational Mission of Frisch's Restaurants

The company operates and licenses family restaurants under the trade name Frisch's Big Boy. These facilities are located in Ohio, Indiana, and Kentucky. Additionally, the firm operates two hotels with restaurants in metropolitan Cincinnati, where it is headquartered. Trademarks which the company has the right to use include "Frisch's," "Big Boy," "Quality Hotel," and "Golden Corral."

Reprinted by permission.

Our mission is to be a respected leader in the food service and hospitality industries. We guarantee our customers quality products that provide real value, with the service they expect, in clean, pleasant surroundings. We dedicate ourselves to sound management practices and effective human relations, while returning maximum earnings to our stockholders.

A third basic decision involves a firm's market scope. Large chains often seek a broad customer base (due to their resources and recognition). It is usually best for small retailers—and most startups—to focus on a narrower customer base. By doing so, they may compete well with bigger firms that tend not to adapt strategies as well to local markets.

Although the development of an organizational mission is the first step in a retailer's planning process, the mission should be continually reviewed and adjusted to reflect changing company goals and a dynamic retail environment.

Careers in Retailing

Amazon.com Pours It On

When George Aposporos joined Amazon.com as vice-president of business development in 1997, the firm was a privately held Web-based book retailer that was about to go public. Now, Amazon.com has become a diversified seller of books, music, videos, electronic greeting cards, and auctioned goods—and the number of customers who regularly visit Amazon.com has grown from 330,000 to 8.5 million.

George Aposporos believes the best part of his job is the creative aspect: "What's exciting about working with the Internet is that the rules are constantly changing, giving creative people like me a receptive medium to make their ideas a reality." His professional background includes being a producer for television and independent videos, as well as a co-founder of a firm that advised advertisers and advertising agencies on the use of interactive media. In 1995, he set up a consulting firm for electronic commerce.

Aposporos says "Amazon.com is very well positioned in the E-commerce area. One of the hardest things to do for a company is to develop itself into a brand people trust, and I think we've accomplished that. But there is still a lot more to be done, and we are working hard to keep operating effectively."

Source: Cecile B. Corral, "The Empire's Architect," *Discount Store News* (May 24, 1999), pp. 35, 54.

Here is the well-conceived mission of Guitar Center, the largest U.S. retailer of musical instruments, with stores in 20 states, as paraphrased from its Web site (www. guitarcenter.com):

> You'll find far more than guitars at each of our locations. You'll find a vast selection of keyboards, midi peripherals, music software, pro audio, recording equipment, dance music gear, drums, percussion, amplifiers, basses, acoustic guitars, accessories, and vintage instruments. Guitar Center is a pioneer in the development of the musical instrument superstore. The stores feature high ceilings and lots of open floor space to support massive displays of products. They also have private acoustic rooms and innovative demonstration areas that foster a "hands on" environment. Each department has people whose job it is to specialize—drummers deal with drummers, guitarists with guitarists, and so on. At Guitar Center, total satisfaction is the number one concern. To prove it, Guitar Center has a guarantee of total satisfaction. If you're not satisfied—for any reason—simply bring back the product for a full refund. No questions, no hassles. We guarantee the lowest prices in the Nation. Period. And we won't be undersold. Not by another retailer, not by mail order, not by anyone.

Ownership and Management Alternatives

An essential aspect of situation analysis is assessing ownership and management alternatives. Ownership options include whether to operate as a sole proprietorship, a partnership, or a corporation—as well as whether to start a new business, buy an existing business, or become a franchise.[2] Management options include owner-manager versus professional manager and centralized versus decentralized structures. As two legal experts remarked, "People dealing with a firm may not notice whether it's a sole proprietorship, a partnership, or a corporation. The form chosen, though, can make a big difference when it's time to pay taxes, respond to a law suit, or split up the business."[3]

A **sole proprietorship** is an unincorporated retail firm owned by one person. All benefits, profits, risks, and costs accrue to that individual. It is simple to form, fully controlled by the owner, operationally flexible, easy to dissolve, and subject to single taxation by the government. It makes the owner personally liable for legal claims from suppliers, creditors, and others; and it can result in limited capital and expertise.

A **partnership** is an unincorporated retail firm owned by two or more persons, each of whom has a financial interest. Partners share benefits, profits, risks, and costs. A partnership allows responsibility and expertise to be divided among multiple principals, provides a greater capability for raising funds than a proprietorship, is simpler to form than a corporation, and is subject to single taxation by the government. Depending on the type of partnership, it, too, can make owners personally liable for legal claims, can be dissolved due to a partner's death or a disagreement, binds all partners to actions made by any individual partner acting on behalf of the firm, and usually has less ability to raise capital than a corporation.

A **corporation** is a retail firm that is formally incorporated under state law. It is a legal entity apart from individual officers (or stockholders). Corporate status means funds can be raised through the sale of stock, legal claims against individuals are not usually allowed, ownership transfer is relatively easy, the firm is assured of long-term existence (if a founder leaves, retires, or dies), the use of professional managers is encouraged, and unambiguous operating authority is outlined. Depending on the type of corporation, it is subject to double taxation (company earnings and stockholder dividends), faces more government rules than other ownership forms, can require a complex and costly process when established, may be viewed as impersonal, and may separate ownership from management. A closed corporation is typically operated by a limited number of persons who control ownership; stock is not available for public purchase. In an open corporation, stock is widely traded and available for public purchase.

Sole proprietorships account for 74 percent of all retail firms in the United States that file tax returns, partnerships for 4 percent, and corporations for 22 percent. However, in terms of sales volume, sole proprietorships account for 9 percent of total U.S. retail store sales, partnerships for 4 percent, and corporations for 87 percent.[4]

Starting a new business—being entrepreneurial—offers a retailer flexibility in location, operating style, product lines, customer markets, and other factors; and it lets a strategy be fully tailored to the owner's desires and strengths. It can also mean having construction or renovation costs, having a time lag until the business is ready to open and then until profits are earned, beginning with an unknown name and image, and having to form supplier relationships and amass an inventory of goods. Figure 3.3 presents several factors to consider when starting a business.

Buying an existing business allows a retailer to acquire an established company name, a customer following, a good location, trained personnel, and standing facilities; to operate

Figure 3.3
Selected Factors to Consider When Starting a New Retail Business

Source: Adapted by the authors from *Small Business Management Training Instructor's Guide,* No. 109 (Washington, D.C.: U.S. Small Business Administration).

NAME OF BUSINESS_____

A. SELF-ASSESSMENT AND BUSINESS CHOICE
  1. Evaluate your strengths and weaknesses.
  2. Commitment paragraph: Why should you be in business for yourself? Why open a new business rather than acquire an existing one or become a member of a franchise chain?
  3. Describe the type of retail business that fits your strengths and desires. What will make it unique? What will the business offer for customers? How will you capitalize on the weaknesses of competitors?

B. OVERALL RETAIL PLAN
  1. State your philosophy of business.
  2. Choose an ownership form (sole proprietorship, partnership, or corporation).
  3. State your long- and short-run goals.
  4. Analyze your customers from their point of view.
  5. Research your market size and store location.
  6. Quantify the total retail sales of your goods/service category in your trading area.
  7. Analyze your competition.
  8. Quantify your potential market share.
  9. Develop your retail strategy: store location and operations, merchandising, pricing, and store image and promotion.

C. FINANCIAL PLAN
  1. What level of funds will you need to get started and to get through the first year? Where will they come from?
  2. Determine the first-year profit, return on investment, and salary that you need/want.
  3. Project monthly cash flow and profit-and-loss statements for the first two years.
  4. What sales will be needed to break even during the first year? What will you do if these sales are not reached?

D. ORGANIZATIONAL DETAILS PLAN (ADMINISTRATIVE MANAGEMENT)
  1. Describe your personnel plan (hats to wear), organizational plan, and policies.
  2. List the jobs you like and want to do and those you dislike, cannot do, or do not want to do.
  3. Outline your accounting and inventory systems.
  4. Note your insurance plans.
  5. Specify how day-to-day operations would be conducted for each aspect of your strategy.
  6. Review the risks you face and how you plan to cope with them.

immediately; to generate ongoing sales and profits; and to possibly get good lease terms or financing (at favorable interest rates) from the seller. It also means fixtures may be older, there is less flexibility in developing and enacting a strategy tailored to the new owner's desires and strengths, and the growth potential of the business may be limited. Figure 3.4 shows a checklist of questions to consider when purchasing an existing retail business.

By being a franchisee, a retailer can combine independent ownership with franchisor management assistance, thorough strategic planning, a known company name and a loyal customer following, cooperative advertising and buying, and a regional, national, or global (rather than local) image. It also means a contract may specify rigid operating standards, limit the product lines sold, and restrict the choice of suppliers; the franchisor is usually paid continuously (royalties); advertising fees may be required; and there is a possibility of termination by the franchisor if the agreement is not followed satisfactorily.

From a strategic perspective, the management format chosen also has a dramatic impact. In an owner-manager system, planning tends to be less formal and more intuitive, and many tasks are reserved for the owner-manager (such as employee supervision and cash management). With a professional manager system, planning tends to be more formal and systematic. However, a professional manager is usually more constrained in his or her authority than an owner-manager. In a centralized structure, planning clout is limited to top management or ownership; for a decentralized structure, managers in individual departments have

Figure 3.4
A Checklist for
Purchasing an Existing
Retail Business

NAME OF BUSINESS _____

These questions should be considered when purchasing an existing retail business:

1. Why is the seller placing the business up for sale?
2. How much are you paying for goodwill (the cost of the business above its tangible asset value)?
3. Have sales, inventory levels, and profit figures been confirmed by your accountant?
4. Will the seller introduce you to his/her customers and stay on during the transition period?
5. Will the seller sign a statement that he/she will not open a directly-competing business in the same trading area for a reasonable time period?
6. If sales are seasonal, are you purchasing the business at the right time of the year?
7. In the purchase of the business, are you assuming existing debts of the seller?
8. Who receives proceeds from transactions made prior to the sale of the business but not yet paid by customers?
9. What is the length of the lease if property is rented?
10. If property is to be purchased along with the business, has it been inspected by a professional engineer?
11. How modern are the storefront and store fixtures?
12. Is inventory fresh? Does it contain a full merchandise assortment?
13. Are the advertising policy, customer service policy, and pricing policy of the past owner similar to yours? Can you continue old policies?
14. If the business is to be part of a chain, is the new unit compatible with existing units? How much trading-area overlap is there with existing stores?
15. Has a lawyer examined the proposed contract?
16. What effect will owning this business have on your life-style and on your family relationships?

major input into decisions. Regardless of management format, a retailer is best able to prepare and enact a proper strategy only if there is ample information and communication.

A comprehensive discussion of independent retailers, chains, franchises, leased departments, vertical marketing systems, and consumer cooperatives appears in Chapter 4.

Goods/Service Category

Entrepreneur Magazine (www.entrepreneur mag.com) addresses many of the issues facing new and growing firms as they plan their strategies.

Before a prospective retail firm can fully design a strategic plan, it selects a **goods/service category**—the line of business—in which to operate. Figure 3.5 shows the diversity of goods/service categories from which a retailer may choose. Chapter 5 examines the attributes of food-based and general merchandise store retailers. Chapter 6 focuses on Web, nonstore, and other forms of nontraditional retailing.

At this stage of planning, it is advisable (for most retailers) to specify both a general goods/service category and a niche within that category. For example, Jaguar dealers are luxury auto retailers catering to upscale customers. Wendy's is an eating and drinking chain famous for its quality fast food, with a menu emphasizing hamburgers. Motel 6 is a hotel chain whose forte is inexpensive rooms with few frills.

When selecting the goods/service category, the potential retail business owner should select a type of business that will allow him or her to match personal abilities, financial resources, and time availability with those required by that kind of business.

Personal Abilities Personal abilities depend on an individual's aptitude—the preference for a type of business and the potential to do well; education—formal learning about retail practices and policies; and experience—practical learning about retail practices and policies.

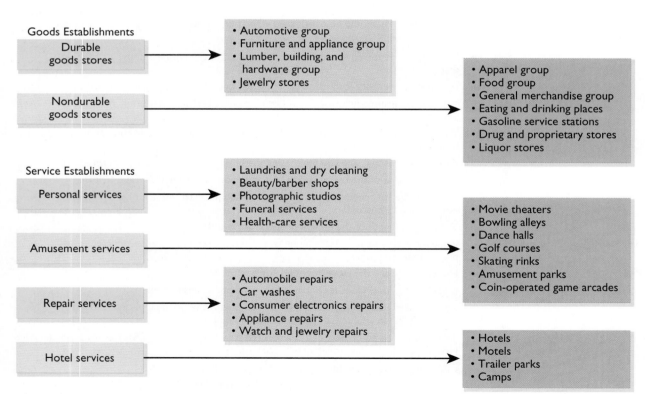

Figure 3.5
Selected Kinds of Retail Goods and Service Establishments

A person should have an aptitude for the business to be entered. Thus, an individual who wants to run a store, likes to use initiative, and has the ability to react quickly to competitive developments will be suited to a different type of situation than a person who depends on others for advice and does not like to make decisions. The first individual could be an independent operator, in a dynamic business like apparel; the second might seek partners or a franchise and a business that is stable, such as a stationery store. In addition, some people enjoy personal interaction with customers; they would dislike the impersonality of a self-service operation. Still others enjoy the relative impersonality of mail-order or Web-based retailing.

In certain fields, education and experience requirements are specified by law. Insurance brokers, stockbrokers, real-estate brokers, barbers, beauticians, certified public accountants, pharmacists, and opticians represent a cross-section of the kinds of retailers who must satisfy educational or experience standards to demonstrate professional competency. For example, real-estate brokers have to be licensed. This involves examining their ethical character, as well as their knowledge of real-estate practice. Yet, the designation "broker" does not depend on the ability to sell or have a customer-oriented demeanor.

Some skills can be learned by education or experience; others are inborn. Accordingly, potential retail owners have to review their personal skills and match them with the demands of a given business. This is a tough process that involves careful reflection and insight into oneself. Strengths and weaknesses must be weighed in this matching process. Partnerships may arise when two or more parties possess complementary skills. A person with extensive selling experience may join with someone who has the operating skills necessary to open a store. Each partner would have valued skills but may be unable to operate a retail entity without the expertise of the other.

Financial Resources Another primary factor in selecting the goods/service category for a retail business is the level of financial resources required. Many enterprises, especially new, independent ones, fail because the owners do not adequately project the financial resources needed to open and operate the firm. Table 3.1 outlines some of the typical investments for a new retail venture.

Novice retailers frequently underestimate the need for a personal drawing account. This is used for the daily, weekly, and monthly living expenses of the owner and his or her family in the early, unprofitable stage of a business. Because few new ventures are immediately profitable, the budget must include such expenditures. The costs of renovating an existing facility often are miscalculated by new retailers. Underfunded firms tend to invest initially in only essential renovations. Other improvements wait until the firms are prospering, and renovations are paid from profits. This practice reduces the initial investment, but it can give the retailer a poor image.

Merchandise assortment, as well as the types of goods and services sold, has an impact on the financial outlay required of a new retailer. The use of a partnership, corporation, or franchise agreement also will affect the initial investment.

Table 3.2 illustrates the financial requirements for a hypothetical used-car dealer. The initial personal savings investment of $300,000 to enter the business would force many potential owners to rethink the choice of product category, as well as the format of the firm. First, the plans for a 32-car inventory reflect this owner's desire for a balanced product line. If the firm concentrates on subcompact, compact, and intermediate cars—and does not stock full-size cars and sports utility vehicles—it can be more specialized and reduce inventory size. This would mean a lower investment. Second, an entering used-car dealer can reduce the initial investment by seeking a site whose facilities do not have to be modified, such as the site of a previous used-car dealer. Third, fewer of a person's financial resources are needed if he or she enters into a partnership or corporation with others, which lets costs—and profits—be shared.

Table 3.1 Some of the Typical Financial Investments for a New Retail Venture

Use of Funds	Source of Funds
Land and building (lease or purchase)	Personal savings, bank loan, commercial finance company
Inventory	Personal savings, manufacturer credit, commercial finance company, sales revenues
Fixtures (display cases, storage facilities, signs, lighting, carpeting, etc.)	Personal savings, manufacturer credit, bank loan, commercial finance company
Equipment (cash register, marking machine, office equipment, computers, etc.)	Personal savings, manufacturer credit, bank loan, commercial finance company
Personnel (salespeople, cashiers, stockpeople, etc.)	Personal savings, bank loan, sales revenues
Promotion	Personal savings, sales revenues
Personal drawing account	Personal savings, life insurance loan

Miscellaneous
  Equipment repair
  Credit sales (bad debts)
  Professional services
  Repayment of loans
	Personal savings, manufacturer and wholesaler credit, bank credit plan, bank loan, commercial finance company

Note: Collateral for a bank loan may be a building, fixtures, land, inventory, or a personal residence.

American Express (www.americanexpress.com/homepage/smallbusiness.shtml) offers financial support and advice for small firms.

The U.S. Small Business Administration (www.sba.gov) assists businesses by guaranteeing over 50,000 loans per year. In addition, such private companies as Wells Fargo and American Express now have financing programs specifically aimed at small businesses.[5]

Time Demands Time demands on retail owners (or managers) differ significantly by goods or service category. They are influenced both by consumer shopping patterns and by the ability of the owner or manager to automate operations or delegate activities to others.

Many retailers must have weekend and evening hours—and may be open on holidays—to serve today's busy consumers. Gift shops, toy stores, housepainters, and others have extreme seasonal shifts and keep long hours during prime seasons. Mail-order firms and those selling through the Web, that can process orders during any part of the day, have more flexible hours.

The ability or inability to automate operations or delegate duties also affects the number of hours worked. Some businesses require less owner involvement, including gas stations with no repair or maintenance services, coin-operated laundries, movie theaters, and motels. The emphasis on automation, self-service, standardized goods and services, and financial controls lets the owner reduce the time investment. Other businesses require active owner involvement. Hair salons, TV repair stores, butcher shops, restaurants, and jewelry stores are time-consuming businesses.

Intensive owner participation can be due to several factors:

- The owner may be the key worker, with patrons attracted by his or her skills (the major competitive advantage). In that case, delegating work to others will lessen consumer loyalty. Associated with this situation are the attention and expertise only an owner can give to certain customers.

Table 3.2 Financial Requirements for a Used-Car Dealer

Total Investments (first year)

Lease (10 years, $60,000 per year)	$ 60,000
Beginning inventory (32 cars, average cost of $12,500)	400,000
Replacement inventory (32 cars, average cost of $12,500)[a]	400,000
Fixtures and equipment (painting, paneling, carpeting, lighting, signs, heating and air-conditioning system, electronic cash register, service bay)	60,000
Replacement parts	75,000
Personnel (one mechanic)	45,000
Promotion (brochures and newspaper advertising)	35,000
Drawing account (to cover owner's personal expenses for one year; all selling and operating functions except mechanical ones performed by the owner)	40,000
Accountant	15,000
Miscellaneous (loan payments, etc.)	100,000
Profit (projected)	40,000
	$1,270,000

Source of Funds

Personal savings	$ 300,000
Bank loan	426,000
Sales revenues (based on expected sales of 32 cars, average price of $17,000)	544,000
	$1,270,000

[a]Assumes that 32 cars are sold during the year. As each type of car is sold, a replacement is bought by the dealer and placed in inventory. At the end of the year, inventory on hand remains at 32 units.

- Some types of retailing, such as personal services, are not easy to automate. In these instances, owner involvement is necessary to provide the services.
- Because many small retailers are underfunded, the owner and his or her family must often undertake all the functions of the firm. Spouses and children work in 40 percent of family-owned businesses.
- In a business that operates on a cash basis and has weak financial controls, the owner must be around to avoid being cheated. For a firm with weak inventory procedures, it may be difficult to match sales with inventory levels, making it easy for employees to pocket cash sales if not watched by the owner.

It is sometimes assumed that a person running a retail firm works only when it is open for business. However, off-hours activities are often essential. A butcher must go to a meat wholesaler at least once a week to make purchases. That is why these wholesalers are busiest very early in the morning. At a restaurant, some foods must be prepared in advance of the posted dining hours. An antique dealer spends nonstore hours hunting for goods. An owner of a small store cleans, stocks shelves, and does the books during the hours the firm is not serving customers. A prospective retail owner also has to examine his or her time preferences regarding stability versus seasonality (some would rather work 40-hour weeks, 48 weeks a year; others would rather work 80-hour weeks for 6 months and relax the other 6 months), ideal working hours (days and times), and personal involvement (absentee ownership or on-site management).

OBJECTIVES	After situation analysis, a retailer sets **objectives,** the long-run and short-run performance targets it hopes to attain. Stating objectives helps mold a strategy and translates the organizational mission into action. A firm can pursue one or more of these goals: sales (growth, stability, and market share), profit (level, return on investment, and efficiency), satisfaction of publics (stockholders and consumers), and image (customer and industry perceptions). Each goal is sought by many retailers. Some strive to achieve all the goals fully; others attend to a few and want to achieve them really well. Think about this array of goals set by Target Stores:

According to Gerald L. Storch, president of new business development and credit operations at Target Corporation (Target Stores' parent), Target Corporation could hit annual sales of $46 billion—twice its current volume—in the next 5 to 10 years: "From the store base we have now, we could double our sales—and we could also double our store base. If you layer in Super Target Stores, there is virtually unlimited growth potential. It is very clear for Target Corporation that Target Stores is our key growth vehicle. For years, we have been reinvesting cash into Target Stores. Now, Target Stores is generating positive cash flow, and that's one reason that we're buying back $1 billion of Target Corporation stock." Specific Target Stores' goals include:

- Filling out the United States with Target Stores in new and existing markets. The biggest gaps are in the Northeast and the Plains and Rocky Mountain states.
- Acquiring clusters of stores "on an opportunistic basis"—when the economics are better than building from scratch or sites are hard to find.
- Offering more sophisticated design throughout the assortments, based on a new finding by Target Stores that design is fast becoming a key catalyst of purchasing at discount stores.
- Developing merchandise aimed at winning younger customers.
- Making the Target Stores' Guest Card a "focal point" for profit growth. Twelve million cards have been launched since 1995; 20 million are expected to be issued by 2001.[6]

Sales

Sales objectives are related to the volume of goods and services a retailer sells. Growth, stability, and market share are the sales goals most often sought.

Some retailers set sales growth as a top priority. They look to expand operations and increase revenues. There may be less emphasis on short-run profits. The assumption is that investments in the present will yield profits in the future. A small or large retailer that does well often becomes interested in opening new units and enlarging revenues. However, too active a pursuit of expansion can result in problems. Many retailers successful in their current business fail as they open new units. Management skills and the personal touch are sometimes lost with improper expansion. Sales growth is a legitimate goal, but it should not be too fast or preclude considering other objectives.

Stability in annual sales and profits is the goal of a wide range of retailers that place emphasis on maintaining their sales volume, market share, price lines, and so on. Small retailers often seek stable sales that enable the owners to make a satisfactory living every year, without the pressure of sharp downswings or upsurges. And certain retailers develop a loyal customer following and are intent not on expanding but on continuing the approach that attracted the original consumers.

For some firms, market share—the percentage of total retail-category sales contributed by a given company—is another goal. In retailing, it is often an objective only for large retailers or retail chains. The small retailer is more concerned with competition across the street or down the block than with total sales in a metropolitan area.

Sales objectives may be expressed in dollars and units. To achieve dollar goals, a retailer can engage in a discount strategy (low prices and high unit sales), a moderate strategy (medium prices and medium unit sales), or a prestige strategy (high prices and low unit sales). In the long run, having sales units as a performance target is vital. Dollar sales over a several-year period may be difficult to compare due to changing retail prices and the rate of inflation; but unit sales are easier to compare from year to year. A firm with sales of $350,000 three years ago and $500,000 today might assume it is doing well, until unit sales figures are computed: 10,000 three years ago and 8,000 this year.

Profit

With profitability objectives, retailers seek at least a minimum profit level during a designated time period, usually a year. Profit may be expressed in dollars or as a percentage of sales. For a firm having yearly sales of $5 million and total yearly costs of $4.2 million, pre-tax dollar profit is $800,000 and profits as a percentage of sales are 16 percent. If the profit goal is equal to or less than $800,000, or 16 percent, the retailer is satisfied. If the goal is greater than $800,000, or 16 percent, the company has not attained the minimum desired level of profits and is dissatisfied.

Firms with substantial capital expenditures in land, buildings, and equipment often set return on investment (ROI) as a goal. ROI is the relationship between company profits and investment in capital items. It is used similarly to any profit statistic: A satisfactory rate of return is pre-defined and then compared with the actual rate of return at the end of the year or other designated period. For a retailer with annual sales of $5 million and expenditures (including monthly long-term payments for capital items) of $4 million, the yearly profit is $1 million. If the total investment to the retailer for land, buildings, and equipment is $10 million, then ROI equals $1 million/$10 million, or 10 percent per year. The goal must be 10 percent or less for the retailer to be satisfied.

Increased operating efficiency is many firms' goal. It may be expressed as $1 -$ (operating expenses/company sales); the higher the result, the more efficient the firm. A retailer with sales of $2 million and operating costs of $1 million has a 50 percent efficiency rating ($[1 - (\$1 \text{ million}/\$2 \text{ million})]$). Of every sales dollar, 50 cents goes for such nonoperating costs as merchandise purchases and to profits, and 50 cents for operating expenses. The retailer might set a goal to increase operating efficiency to 60 percent. On sales of $2 million, operating costs would have to drop to $800,000 ($[1 - (\$800,000/\$2 \text{ million})]$). Sixty cents of every sales dollar would then go for nonoperating costs and profits, and 40 cents for operations. Better efficiency would lead to better profits. However, a firm must be careful. If expenses are cut too much, customer service may decline; and this may lead to a sales decline and a resulting profit drop.

Satisfaction of Publics

A retailer may strive for satisfaction of publics' objectives. Publics include stockholders, consumers, suppliers, employees, and government.

Stockholder satisfaction is a vital goal for any publicly owned retail firm. It is up to top management to set and attain goals consistent with stockholder wishes. Many firms set policies leading to small annual increases in sales and profits (because these goals can be sustained over the long run and indicate good management), rather than ones introducing innovative ideas that can lead to peaks and valleys in sales and profits (indicating poor management). Stable earnings lead to stable dividends for stockholders.

Today customer satisfaction with the total retail experience is a goal most firms set, although some have awakened to this only recently. It is crucial to satisfy consumers and not have a policy of *caveat emptor* ("Let the buyer beware"). Retailers must listen to criticism and adapt properly. They can do this by gearing their overall mission and goals to customer satisfaction. If shoppers are pleased, other goals are more easily reached. However, this goal ranks too low for many retailers, large and small alike. For them, the other objectives cited rate higher in the list of priorities.

Good supplier relations is also a key goal. Retailers must understand and work together with their suppliers if favorable purchase terms, new products, good return policies, prompt shipments, and cooperation are to be received. Good relations are particularly important for small retailers due to the many services that suppliers provide for them.

Cordial labor relations is another vital goal—often basic to retailers' performance, whether they are small or big. Good employee morale means less absenteeism, better treatment of customers, and lower turnover. Relations can be improved by effective selection, training, and motivation.

Because all levels of government impose rules affecting retailing practices, a significant goal should be to understand and adapt to these policies. In some cases, firms can influence rules by acting as members of large groups, such as trade associations or chambers of commerce.

Image (Positioning)

A main goal for virtually any retailer is to create and maintain the image it feels is proper for the specific type of business involved. An **image** represents how a given retailer is perceived by consumers and others. A firm may be seen as innovative or conservative, specialized or broad-based, discount-oriented or upscale. The key to a successful image is that consumers view the retailer in the manner the retailer intends.

Through **positioning,** a retailer devises its strategy in a way that projects an image relative to its retail category and its competitors, and elicits consumer responses to that image. Thus, a firm selling women's apparel could generally position itself as an upscale or mid-priced specialty store, a department store, a discount department store, or a discount specialty store, and it could specifically position itself with regard to any nearby retailers carrying women's apparel.

For some retailers, such as McDonald's, Hertz, or the market-leading drugstore chain in your area, industry leadership (which may be local) is a positioning goal. It often results in two benefits for a firm. First, it may enhance company image because consumers are apt to place the leader on a higher pedestal than competitors. Second, other retailers may follow the pricing and other strategies of the leader rather than their own distinctive approaches. A subsidiary benefit is the internal morale boost that accompanies being "number one," and this motivates all to work harder.

Two opposite positioning philosophies have gained popularity in recent years: mass merchandising and niche retailing. **Mass merchandising** is a positioning approach whereby retailers offer a discount or value-oriented image, a wide and/or deep merchandise assortment, and large store facilities. (For example, Wal-Mart has a wide, deep merchandise mix while Sports Authority has a narrower, deeper assortment.) These firms want to appeal to a broad customer market, attract a lot of customer traffic, and generate high stock turnover. Because mass merchants have relatively low operating costs, achieve economies in operations, and appeal to value-conscious shoppers, their continuing popularity is forecast.

In **niche retailing,** retailers identify specific customer segments and deploy unique strategies to address the desires of those segments. A given retailer concentrates its efforts on a market segment and not the mass market. Niching creates a high level of loyalty and shields retailers from more conventional competitors. This approach will also have a large future presence since it lets many retailers stress factors other than price in their strategies and encourages more focus by firms such as department stores. The growth of boutique-type stores and compartmentalized department stores should continue. See Figure 3.6.

Figure 3.6
Bloomingdale's
Positioning: Trendy
and Upscale

Bloomingdale's has 24
department stores in 10
states. It features
upscale fashion apparel,
as well as home-related
goods, with an emphasis
on distinctive merchan-
dise. Bloomingdale's has
been described as
"more a life-style than a
store."
Reprinted by permission of
Simon Property Group.

Because both mass merchandising and niche retailing are well-liked, some observers call this the era of **bifurcated retailing.** They believe this may mean the decline of middle-of-the-market retailing. Firms that are neither competitively priced nor particularly individualistic may have difficulty competing.

Let us further examine the concept of positioning through these examples:

J.C. Penney (www.
jcpenney.net/
company/position/
index.htm) has
devoted a lot of
attention to commu-
nicating its position-
ing message.

- "J.C. Penney dedicates itself to satisfying the needs and expectations of our targeted customer segments. We will offer fashion and basic apparel, accessories, and home furnishings in a customer-friendly environment in our stores, in our catalog, and on the Internet. We seek to provide our target customers with a timely and competitive selection of fashionable, quality merchandise with unquestionable day-in, day-out value. Within this positioning framework, we will begin with our target customers' point of view in developing merchandise offerings, quality standards, branding and pricing strategies, visual merchandising, and service levels. We will position J.C. Penney uniquely in a niche of our own by exceeding the fashion, quality, selection, and service components of the discounter; equaling the merchandise intensity of the specialty store; and providing the selection and under-one-roof shopping convenience of the department store."[7]

- "Everybody knows the shoe shop image. A gray-haired guy with grubby nails and a grubbier apron is bent over a grimy, clattering old machine. Worn-out shoes are jumbled on dusty shelves. Everything smells like glue and shoe polish. Then there is Marcy's Shoes and Quik Fix Repair in Merchant's Walk shopping center in Cape Girardeau, Missouri. Cobbler Gene Benthal mends shoes on the latest European- and American-made machinery in a tidy workplace that's tucked in the back of the store. Out front, customers wait in comfortable wooden chairs, wiggling their toes in soft gray carpet. Marcy's is no hole-in-the-wall fix-it shop. The store is a roomy 2,000 square feet. Owner Marcy Dockins also sells men's and women's footwear in modern, shoe salon-like surroundings."[8]

- Figure 3.7 shows a positioning map with a number of retailers depicted. The figure is based on the results of a study of the women's fashion market in Chicago involving more than 2,000 female apparel shoppers. It was conducted by Babson College and sponsored by 15 firms. The map highlights consumer perceptions regarding the comparative position of each chain on a "value scale" and on a "fashion scale." Value is based on both the caliber of clothing and the shopping experience relative to product prices. Fashionability is based on the freshness, styling, and assortment of clothing. Respondents commented only on the stores at which they actually shopped.[9]

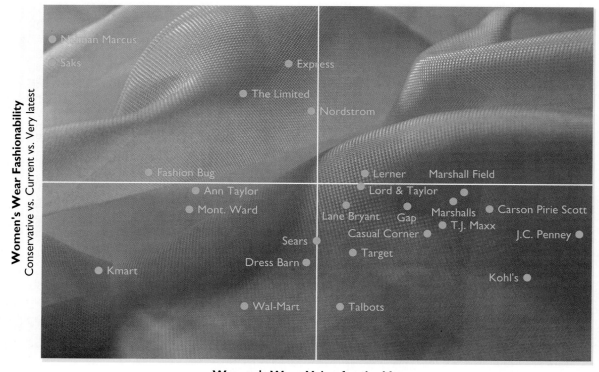

Women's Wear Fashionability
Conservative vs. Current vs. Very latest

Women's Wear Value for the Money
Worst value (left)   Best value (right)

Figure 3.7
How Chicago Retailers Are Positioned in the Women's Fashion Market

Reprinted by permission from *Chain Store Age.* Copyright Lebhar-Friedman, Inc., 425 Park Avenue, New York, NY 10022.

Selection of Objectives

The objective(s) a retailer selects will greatly influence the development of its overall strategy. A firm that clearly defines objectives and devises a strategy to achieve them improves its chances of success.

An example of a retailer with clear goals and a proper strategy to attain them is Papa John's, the pizza chain. As reported at its Web site (www.papajohns.com):

Papa John's (www.papajohns.com) is the fastest-growing U.S. quick-service pizza chain. Look at its Web site to see why.

> In 1983, 22-year-old John Schnatter had a vision: he wanted to create the perfect pizza, made from the best ingredients, delivered hot and fresh to the customer's door. With less than $1,600 in capital, but equipped with 100 percent determination, Schnatter installed an oven in a converted broom closet in the back of an Indiana tavern and began delivering pizza. In the company's first year, he sold 300 to 400 pizzas a week. One year later, he opened the first Papa John's restaurant. Presently, Papa John's has expanded to an $860 million pizza chain with over 1,900 locations in 46 states, the District of Columbia, Mexico, and Puerto Rico. Today, Papa John's is the fastest-growing pizza delivery and carryout company in the nation, adding an average of 30 new stores each month. And Papa John's has an unwavering focus on a limited menu of high-quality products; and its streamlined operations and distribution system and its training and development programs have resulted in increasing respect from customers, franchisees, investors, and employees alike. (See Figure 3.8.)

Technology in Retailing

The Sports Authority Is in New Balance

Sports Authority and New Balance have begun a chain-wide partnership to improve inventory planning, forecasting, and replenishment. The program, called CPFR, is an acronym for collaborative planning, forecasting, and replenishment.

Under CPFR, Sports Authority shares vital data relating to sales, inventory levels, and forecasts with New Balance. Sports Authority and New Balance will use the program to jointly generate sales forecasts for particular products based on their sales history and the effects of price changes and promotional activities on sales. According to a Sports Authority senior vice-president, sharing this information on a regular basis "will give us better knowledge of our inventory. We'll see what is selling and what isn't, and gain a better knowledge of [product] assortment." The two parties hope the program will improve Sports Authority's in-stock positions, reduce markdowns, and yield better product assortments. Sports Authority hopes CPFR will help raise its in-stock levels from 89 percent to 92 percent.

Sports Authority also plans to extend its CPFR program to three other large vendors. And it is preparing performance benchmarks for each of these vendors: "When you can apply the right space to the right product, and when you're also talking to the vendor, it's pretty powerful."

Present five performance standards for Sport Authority's CPFR program.

Source: Adam Blair, "TSA, New Balance Join Interactive Partnership," *Women's Wear Daily* (June 2, 1999), p. 13.

Team Members: People are our most important asset. Papa John's will provide clear, consistent, strategic leadership, and career opportunities for our Team Members who (a) exhibit passion toward their work, (b) uphold our core values, (c) take pride of ownership in building the long-term value of the Papa John's brand, and (d) have ethical business practices. *Customers:* Papa John's will create superior brand loyalty by

Figure 3.8

Papa John's: Fulfilling Its Vision

Reprinted by permission.

(a) authentic, superior-quality products, (b) legendary customer service, and (c) exceptional community service. *Franchisees:* We will partner with franchisees to create continued opportunity for growth to those who (a) adhere to Papa John's proven core values and systems, (b) exhibit passion in running the business, and (c) take ownership pride in building the long-term value of Papa John's brand. *Shareholders:* We will produce superior long-term value for shareholders.

IDENTIFICATION OF CONSUMER CHARACTERISTICS AND NEEDS

The retailer or prospective retailer next must identify consumer characteristics and needs. The customer group that a retailer seeks to attract and satisfy is called the **target market.** In selecting its target market, a firm may use one of three techniques: **mass marketing,** selling goods and services to a broad spectrum of consumers; **concentrated marketing,** zeroing in on one specific group; or **differentiated marketing,** aiming at two or more distinct consumer groups, with different retailing approaches for each group.

Conventional supermarkets and drugstores are examples of retailers defining their target markets broadly. They sell a wide assortment of medium-quality items at popular prices. In contrast, a small upscale men's shoe store exemplifies the retailer selecting a well-defined and specific consumer group and offering a narrow, deep product assortment at above-average prices (or in other cases, below-average prices). A retailer aiming at one segment does not try to appeal to everyone.

Department stores are among the retailers seeking multiple market segments. They cater to several customer groups and provide unique goods and services for each. Accordingly, men's apparel may be sold in a number of distinctive boutiques in the store. Also, large retail chains frequently have divisions that appeal to different market segments. Target Corporation has traditional department stores for customers interested in full service and discount department stores for those interested in low prices.

The choice of target market and the approach for attracting it give direction to strategic decisions. See Table 3.3. After choosing the target market, a firm can determine the best competitive advantages and allot resources. The significance of **competitive advantages**— the distinct competencies of a retailer relative to competitors—must not be overlooked. Why? The selection of a target market and its satisfaction by a unique retail offering are needed for goals to be achieved. Some examples will demonstrate this.

Kmart (www.kmart. com/corp) uses discount department stores and its Web site to target middle-class, price-conscious shoppers.

Tiffany defines its target market as upper-class, status-conscious consumers. It situates stores in prestigious shopping areas, offers high-quality products, uses elegant print ads, has extensive customer services, and sets relatively high prices. Kmart targets middle-class, value-conscious consumers. Thus, it locates in midrange shopping centers and districts, offers national brands and Kmart brands of medium quality, features good values in its ads, maintains some customer services, and charges below-average to average prices. Off-price stores aim at extremely price-conscious consumers. Many locate in low-rent strip shopping centers or districts, offer national brands (sometimes manufacturer overruns or items not sold by other retailers) of average to below-average quality merchandise, emphasize low prices in ads, offer few or no customer services, and set very low prices. The key to the success of each of these retailers is its ability to define customers and cater to their needs in a distinctive manner.

A retailer is better able to select a target market and satisfy customer needs if it has a good understanding of consumer behavior. This topic is discussed in Chapter 7.

Table 3.3 Target Marketing Techniques and Their Strategic Implications

Strategic Implications	TARGET MARKET TECHNIQUES		
	Mass Marketing	**Concentrated Marketing**	**Differentiated Marketing**
Retailer's location	Near a large pupulation base	Near a small or medium population base	Near a large population base
Goods and service mix	Wide assortment of medium-quality items	Deep assortment of high-quality or low-quality items	Distinct goods/services aimed at each market segment
Promotion efforts	Mass advertising	Direct mail, subscription	Different media and messages for each segment
Price orientation	Popular prices	High or low	High, medium, and low—depending on market segment
Strategy	One general strategy directed at a large homogeneous (similar) group of consumers	One specific strategy directed at a specific limited group of customers	Several specific strategies, each directed at different (heterogeneous) groups of consumers

OVERALL STRATEGY

After completing a situation analysis, setting objectives, and selecting the target market, the retailer is ready to develop an in-depth overall strategy. This involves two components: those aspects of business the firm can directly affect (such as hours of operation and sales personnel) and those to which the retailer must adapt (such as competition, the economy, and laws). The former are called **controllable variables,** and the latter are called **uncontrollable variables.** See Figure 3.9.

A strategy must be prepared with both kinds of variables in mind. The ability of retailers to grasp and predict the effects of controllable and uncontrollable variables is greatly aided by the use of suitable data. In Chapter 8, information gathering and processing in retailing are described.

Controllable Variables

The controllable parts of a retail strategy consist of the basic categories shown in Figure 3.9: store location, managing a business, merchandise management and pricing, and communicating with the customer. A good strategy integrates these areas so a unified plan is devised and followed. These elements are comprehensively covered in Chapters 9 to 19.

Store Location A retailer has several store location decisions to make. The initial one is whether to use a store or nonstore (e.g., mail-order or the Web) format. Next, for store-based

Figure 3.9
Developing an Overall
Retail Strategy

retailers, a general location and a specific site are determined. Competitors, transportation access, population density, the type of neighborhood, nearness to suppliers, pedestrian traffic, and store composition are among the factors to be considered in picking a location. See Figure 3.10.

The terms of tenancy (such as rent, operating flexibility, and length of contract) are reviewed and a build, buy, or rent decision made. The locations of multiple outlets, an increasing phenomenon today, may be considered if expansion is a goal. Each of these aspects of location can cause problems if inadequately outlined in the strategy phase.

Managing a Business The second area of strategic planning, managing a business, entails two major elements: the retail organization and human resource management, and operations management. Tasks, policies, resources, authority, responsibility, and rewards are outlined via a retail organization structure. Practices regarding employee hiring, training, compensation, supervision, and so on are instituted through human resource management. Job descriptions and functions are detailed and communicated, along with the authority and responsibility of all personnel and the chain of command.

Operations management strives to efficiently and effectively perform the tasks and policies necessary to satisfy customer, employee, and management goals. The financial dynamics of operations involve asset management, budgeting, and resource allocation. Other specific aspects of operations management include store format and size, personnel use, store maintenance, energy management, store security, insurance, credit management, computerization, and crisis management.

Merchandise Management and Pricing The third aspect of strategic planning deals with merchandise management and pricing. In merchandise management, the general quality of the goods and services offered is determined. Decisions are made as to the width of assortment (the number of different product categories carried) and the depth of assortment (the variety of products carried in a given category).

Policies are set with respect to how innovative the retailer is going to be in introducing new items. Criteria for buying decisions (how often, what terms, which suppliers, and so on) are established. Forecasting, budgeting, and retail accounting procedures are outlined, as is

Figure 3.10
The Sheraton Safari Hotel: Capitalizing on Its Location

This very successful hotel is situated just outside the entrance to Walt Disney World in Florida. It has 489 rooms, a lush décor inside and out, and meeting facilities for conventions. The location is appealing because of its proximity to Walt Disney World, despite the large number of competing hotels and motels.
Reprinted by permission of MeriStar Hospitality Corporation.

the level of inventory for each type of merchandise carried. Finally, the retailer devises procedures to assess the success or failure of each item sold.

With regard to pricing, a retailer chooses from among several pricing techniques (such as leading/following, cost-plus/demand-oriented, and so on); and it decides what range of prices to set, consistent with the firm's image and the quality of goods and services offered. The number of prices within each product category is determined, such as how many prices of luggage to carry. Psychological pricing may be used. And the use of markdowns is planned in advance.

Communicating with the Customer The fourth area of planning involves building and maintaining a distinctive image, as well as the promotion techniques deployed. As mentioned earlier, image is critical for retailers. Therefore, a distinctive and desirable (by the target market) image must be sought. This image can be created and sustained by applying several techniques.

The physical attributes, or atmosphere, of a store and its surrounding area greatly influence consumer perceptions of a retailer. The impact of the storefront (the building's exterior) should not be undervalued, as it is the first part of a store seen by the customer. Inside the store, layouts and displays (the arrangement and positioning of merchandise), wall and floor colors, lighting, scents, music, and the kind of sales personnel also contribute to store image. Customer services and community relations generate a favorable image for the retailer.

The right use of promotional techniques enhances a firm's sales performance. Techniques can range from inexpensive flyers for a take-out restaurant to an expensive national ad campaign for a franchise chain. Three forms of paid promotion are available: advertising, personal selling, and sales promotion. In addition, a retailer can obtain free publicity when stories about it are written, televised, or broadcast.

Retailing Around the World

A Starbucks Decision About Entering Kuwait

Nasser Al-Mutair is a young graduate from a university in the state of Washington with a degree in marketing. As a student in the United States, Nasser often visited Starbucks and thought that a specialty coffee shop would be very successful in Nasser's native Kuwait. In addition to the Arab fondness for coffee, Nasser understood that there are a large number of foreigners living in Kuwait. Traditional Kuwaiti restaurants are viewed as inadequate for this population. After graduation, Nasser had serious conversations with his uncle about a number of potential businesses. One of these opportunities was Starbucks Coffee.

Nasser and his uncle looked forward to a meeting with Howard Behar, the president of Starbucks International Coffee Company, who flew to Kuwait to meet them. While Behar had not previously visited the Middle East, he was interested in expanding Starbucks' international operations. Two of Behar's concerns about opening in Kuwait were Starbucks' image in the Middle East and the potential profitability of this market.

Nasser knew Behar would be in Kuwait for less than one day and that his uncle would ask some detailed questions about the proposed Kuwaiti operation. He also understood that Howard Behar had mixed feelings about Kuwait.

What factors should Nasser Al-Mutair and Howard Behar each consider before making a decision about opening a Starbucks in Kuwait?

Source: Dianne H. B. Welsh, Peter Raven, and Nasser Al-Mutair, "Starbucks International Enters Kuwait," *Journal of Consumer Marketing*, Vol. 15 (No. 2, 1998), pp. 191–97.

While the preceding discussion outlined the controllable portions of a retail strategy, uncontrollable variables must also be kept in mind. A description of uncontrollable variables is next.

Uncontrollable Variables

The uncontrollable parts of a strategy are composed of the factors shown in Figure 3.9: consumers, competition, technology, economic conditions, seasonality, and legal restrictions. Farsighted retailers monitor the external environment and adapt the controllable parts of their strategies to take into account elements beyond their immediate control. The uncontrollable nature of these variables is explained next.

Consumers Once a target market is picked, a firm sets its strategy accordingly. A skillful retailer knows it cannot alter demographic trends or life-style patterns, impose tastes, or "force" goods and services on people. Rather, that firm learns about its target market and forms a strategy consistent with consumer trends and desires. Selecting a target market is within a retailer's control; but the firm cannot sell goods or services that are beyond the price range of its customers, not wanted, or not displayed or advertised in the proper manner.

Competition After the type of business and location are chosen, there is little most retailers can do to limit the entry of competitors. In fact, a retailer's success may encourage the entry of new firms or cause established competitors to modify their strategies to capitalize on the popularity of that retailer. A heavy increase in competition should lead a company to re-examine its strategy, including the definition of its target market and its merchandising focus, to ensure that it sustains a competitive advantage. An error too many retailers make is assuming that being first is a sufficient advantage in fighting off new entrants. A continued willingness to satisfy the target market better than any competitor is fundamental.

Technology In today's world of retailing, technology is advancing rapidly. Computer systems are available for inventory control and checkout operations. Electronic surveillance may be used to reduce shoplifting. Barcoding has revolutionized merchandise handling and inventory control. There are more efficient ways for warehousing and transporting merchandise. Toll-free 800 numbers are more popular than ever for consumer ordering. And, of course, there is the Web. Nonetheless, some advancements are expensive and may be beyond the reach of small retailers. For example, although small firms may be able to use computerized checkouts, they will probably be unable to use fully automated inventory systems or toll-free numbers. As a result, their efficiency may be less than that of larger competitors. They must adapt by providing more personalized service (because prices may be above-average to reflect operating costs).

Economic Conditions Economic conditions are beyond any retailer's control, no matter how large it is. Unemployment, interest rates, inflation, tax levels, and the annual Gross Domestic Product (GDP) are just some economic factors with which a retailer copes and which it cannot change. In outlining the controllable parts of its strategy, a retailer needs to consider and adapt to forecasts about international, national, state, and local economies.

Seasonality A constraint on certain retailers is the seasonality of their goods and services and the possibility that unpredictable weather will play havoc with sales forecasts. Retailers selling sports equipment, clothing, fresh food, travel services, and car rentals cannot control the seasonality of consumer demand or bad weather. A solution to this uncontrollable part of planning may be for these retailers to diversify offerings, such as carrying a goods/service mix with items that are popular in different seasons. A sporting goods retailer can emphasize ski equipment and snowmobiles in the winter, baseball and golf equipment in the spring, scuba equipment and fishing gear in the summer, and basketball and football supplies in the fall. The impact of seasonality and weather are reduced by adapting the controllable part of the retail strategy.

Legal Restrictions   All retailers should be familiar with the legal restrictions they face. Table 3.4 shows how each of the four controllable aspects of a retail strategy are affected by the legal environment.

The Telecommunications Act of 1996 (www.fcc.gov/ telecom.html) places significant restrictions on telemarketers. Learn more about it.

Retailers that operate in more than one state are subject to federal laws and agencies. The Sherman Act and the Clayton Act are intended to reduce monopolies and restraints of trade. The Federal Trade Commission deals with unfair trade practices and consumer complaints. The Robinson-Patman Act prohibits suppliers from giving unjustified merchandise discounts to large retailers that could adversely affect small retailers. The Telephone Consumer Protection Act, Food and Drug Administration rules for food labeling, and the Telecommunications Act of 1996 all are designed to protect consumers. In addition, there are various other consumer protection acts in such areas as door-to-door sales, product safety, packaging, consumer credit, and warranties and guarantees. Although these acts are mostly geared to manufacturers, they affect retailers using deceptive selling practices or selling private-label items.

At the state and local levels, retailers have to deal with many restrictions. Zoning laws prohibit firms from operating at certain sites and demand that building specifications be met. Blue laws limit the days or hours during which retailers can conduct business. Construction, fire, elevator, smoking, and other codes are imposed on retailers by the state and city. The licenses to operate some businesses are under state or city jurisdiction. Minimum-price laws sometimes require that specified items not be sold for less than a floor price. Other laws restrict direct selling practices. Many states and municipalities engage in consumer protection; they police

---

Ethics in Retailing

The Continuing Saga of Sears' Questionable Sales Practices

In 1997, Sears paid a $580,000 fine, but did not admit liability, to resolve a Florida criminal investigation of phantom tire-balancing at its auto centers. Then, in 1999, an Illinois civil suit was filed against Sears, accusing the firm of charging customers for tire-balancing services that were not performed. The Illinois lawsuit also charged that Sears had destroyed tire-balancing machines containing evidence of the number of tires that actually were balanced.

Both the Florida and Illinois suits charged that Sears did not perform the full two-part tire balancing process on as many as 30 million vehicles. The first step, the one Sears allegedly skipped, involved correcting a flaw in "out of round" tires by shaving off a thin layer of rubber. Although Sears charged customers $12.50 per tire, according to one attorney, the company omitted the procedure because the machines were finicky and slow. It was very difficult for a customer to determine whether the full process was performed.

With regard to other matters involving auto-center work, in 1992, Sears paid a $15 million fine (without admitting liability) related to pushing unnecessary auto repairs on unsuspecting customers. In April 1999, Sears paid a $980,000 fine (without admitting liability) to resolve the Florida Attorney General's investigation that Sears misrepresented the sale of used auto batteries as new.

How can Sears avoid similar business practices in the future?

Source: Joseph B. Cahill, "Sears Is Sued Again on Auto-Center Work," *Wall Street Journal* (June 17, 1999), pp. A3, A10.

Table 3.4 The Impact of the Legal Environment on Retailing[a]

Controllable Factor Affected	Selected Legal Constraints on Retailers	Ramifications
Store Location	Zoning laws	Restrict the potential choices for a location and the type of facilities that may be constructed.
	Blue laws	Restrict the days and hours during which retailers may operate.
	Environmental laws	Limit the retail uses of certain sites.
	Door-to-door (direct) selling laws	Limit the hours and manner of business to protect consumer privacy.
	Local ordinances	Involve fire, smoking, outside lighting, capacity, and other rules.
	Leases and mortgages	Require parties to abide by stipulations in tenancy documents.
Managing the Business	Licensing provisions	Mandate minimum education and/or experience requirements for personnel in certain retail businesses.
	Personnel laws	Involve nondiscriminatory hiring, promoting, and firing of employees.
	Antitrust laws	Limit mergers and expansion.
	Franchise agreements	Require parties to abide by legal precedents with regard to purchase terms, customer service levels, etc.
	Business taxes	Include real-estate and income taxes.
	Recycling laws	Mandate that retailers participate in the recycling process for various containers and packaging materials.
	Delivery laws	Penalties for late deliveries are imposed in some states.
Merchandise Management and Pricing	Trademarks	Provide retailers with exclusive rights to the brand names they develop.
	Licensing agreements	Allow retailers to sell goods and services created by others in return for royalty payments.
	Merchandise restrictions	Forbid some retailers from carrying or selling specified goods or services.
	Product safety laws	Prohibit retailers from selling items that have been inadequately tested or that have been declared unsafe.
	Product liability laws	Allow retailers to be sued if they sell defective products.
	Warranties and guarantees	Must adhere to federal standards.
	Lemon laws	Specify consumer rights if products, such as autos, require continuing repairs.
	Sales taxes	In most states, consumers required to pay state and/or local taxes on items, in addition to the prices set by retailers.
	Tax-free days	Some locales have been doing this to encourage consumer shopping.
	Unit-pricing laws	Require price per unit to be displayed (most often applied to supermarkets).
	Price-marking laws	Specify that discounted and sale items must be marked properly.
	Dual pricing	Occurs when the same item has different prices on different containers (to reflect the higher prices of new goods). In some areas, this is not permitted.
	Collusion	Retailers not allowed to discuss selling prices with competitors under any circumstances.
	Sale prices	Defined as a reduction from the retailer's normal selling prices. Calling anything else a sale is illegal.
	Minimum-price and loss-leader laws	Require that certain items not be sold for less than their cost plus a markup to cover retail overhead costs.
	Price discrimination	Suppliers generally not allowed to offer unjustified discounts to large retailers that are unavailable to smaller ones.
	Item-price-removal laws	Mandate that prices be marked on each item, as well as on store shelves.

(CONTINUED)

Table 3.4		
Controllable Factor Affected	**Selected Legal Constraints on Retailers**	**Ramifications**
Communicating with the Customer	Truth-in-advertising and -selling laws	Require retailers to be honest and not omit key facts in ads or sales presentations.
	Truth-in-credit laws	Require that consumers be fully informed of all terms when buying on credit.
	Telemarketing laws	Intended to protect the privacy and rights of consumers with regard to telephone sales transactions.
	Comparative advertising	Retailers expected to provide complete documentation when making claims about their offerings versus competitors (e.g., lower prices).
	Bait-and-switch laws	Make it illegal to lure shoppers into a store to buy low-priced items and then to aggressively try to switch them to higher-priced ones.
	Inventory laws	Mandate that retailers must have sufficient stock when running sales.
	Labeling laws	Require merchandise to be correctly labeled and displayed.
	Cooling-off laws	Allow customers to cancel completed orders, often made by in-home sales, within three days of a contract date.
	Other restrictions	Prohibit some goods and services from being advertised in certain media (e.g., no tobacco ads on radio or TV).

[a] This table is broad in nature and omits a law-by-law description. Many laws are state- or locally-oriented and apply only to certain locations; the laws in each place differ widely. The intent here is to give the reader some understanding of the current legal environment as it affects retail management. For more specifics, contact the sources named in the chapter.

retailers from this vantage point. In addition, a number of states and cities have stepped up their efforts to restrict unfair or socially undesirable retailing practices.

A retail strategy must be pursued in a way that satisfies all levels of government. A firm adhering to the spirit and letter of the law will maintain a customer following and be less apt to get bad publicity. For more information, contact the Federal Trade Commission (www.ftc.gov), state and local bodies, the Better Business Bureau (www.bbb.org), the National Retail Federation (www.nrf.com), or a specialized group such as the Direct Marketing Association (www.the-dma.org).

Integrating Overall Strategy

What do you think about H&R Block's (www.handrblock.com) overall strategy?

At this point, the retailer has finished devising an overall strategy. It has chosen an organizational mission, an ownership and management style, and a goods/service category. Sensible long-run and short-run goals have been set. A consumer market has been designated, and its attributes and needs studied. General decisions have been made about the store location, managing the business, merchandise management and pricing, and communications. These elements must be coordinated to have a consistent, integrated strategy and to systematically account for uncontrollable variables (consumers, competition, technology, economic conditions, seasonality, and legal restrictions).

The company is then ready to perform the specific tasks to carry out its strategy productively.

SPECIFIC ACTIVITIES

Short-run decisions are now made and enacted for each controllable part of the strategy in Figure 3.9. These actions are known as **tactics** and encompass a retailer's daily and short-term operations. They must be responsive to the uncontrollable environment. Here are some tactical moves a retailer may make:

Chain Store Age (www. chainstoreage.com) tracks all kinds of tactical moves made by retailers.

- Store location: Trading-area analysis gauges the geographic area from which a firm draws its customers. The level of saturation in a trading area is studied regularly. Relationships with nearby retailers are optimized. Lease terms and provisions are negotiated and fulfilled. A chain carefully decides on the sites of new outlets. Facilities are actually built or modified.
- Managing the business: There is a clear chain of command from senior managers to entry-level workers. An appropriate organizational structure is set into place. Personnel are hired, trained, and supervised. Asset management tracks assets and liabilities. The budget is spent properly (and throughout the year). Systematic operating procedures are used and adjusted as required.
- Merchandise management and pricing: The assortments within departments and the space allotted to each department require constant decision making. Innovative firms look for new merchandise and are willing to clear out slow-moving items. Purchase terms may have to be negotiated often, and new suppliers sought. Selling prices reflect the firm's image and target market. Price alternatives can offer consumers some choice. Adaptive actions are needed to sell slow-moving items, respond to higher supplier prices, and react to competitors' prices.
- Communicating with the customer: The storefront and display windows, store layout, and merchandise displays need constant attention. These elements help gain consumer enthusiasm, present a fresh look, introduce new product categories, and reflect changing seasons. Ads are designed and then placed during the proper time and in the appropriate media. The deployment of sales personnel varies by merchandise category and season.

The essence of excellence in retailing is building a sound strategy and fine-tuning it as the environment changes. A retailer that stands still is often moving backward. Tactical decision making is discussed in more detail in Chapters 9 through 19.

CONTROL

A firm's strategy and tactics should be evaluated and revised continually. In the **control** phase, a semiannual or annual review of the retailer takes place (Step VI in Figure 3.1), with the strategy and tactics (Steps IV and V) that have been developed and implemented being evaluated against the business mission, objectives, and target market (Steps I, II, and III). This procedure is called a retail audit, which is a systematic process for analyzing the performance of a retailer. The retail audit is covered in Chapter 20.

A retailer's strengths and weaknesses are revealed as performance is assessed. The aspects of a strategy that have gone well stay in place; those that have gone poorly are revised, consistent with the mission, goals, and target market. If possible, minor adjustments are made, because major ones may confuse customers. The adjustments are reviewed in the firm's next retail audit.

FEEDBACK

During each stage in a strategy, an observant management receives signals or cues, known as **feedback,** as to the success or failure of that part of the strategy. Refer to Figure 3.1. Positive feedback includes high sales, no problems with the government, and low employee turnover. Negative feedback includes falling sales, government sanctions (like fines), and high turnover.

Retail executives look for positive and negative feedback so they can determine the causes and then capitalize on opportunities or rectify problems.

SUMMARY

1. *To show the value of strategic planning for all types of retailers.* A retail strategy is the overall plan that guides a firm. It consists of situation analysis, objectives, identification of a customer market, broad strategy, specific activities, control, and feedback. Without a well-conceived strategy, a retailer may stumble or be unable to cope with environmental factors.

2. *To explain the steps in strategic planning for retailers.* Situation analysis is the candid evaluation of the retailer's opportunities and threats. It looks at the firm's current position and where it should be heading. This analysis consists of defining and adhering to an organizational mission, evaluating ownership and management options, and outlining the goods/service category. An organizational mission is a commitment to a type of business and a place in the market. Ownership/management options include sole proprietorship, partnership, or corporation; starting a business, buying an existing one, or being a franchisee; owner management or professional management; and being centralized or decentralized. The goods/service category depends on personal abilities, finances, and time resources.

Objectives are the retailer's long- and short-run goals. A firm may pursue one or more of these objectives: sales (growth, stability, and market share), profit (level, return on investment, and efficiency), satisfaction of publics (stockholders, consumers, and others), and image/positioning (customer and industry perceptions).

Next, consumer characteristics and needs are determined, and a retailer selects a target market. A firm can sell to a broad spectrum of consumers (mass marketing); zero in on one customer group (concentrated market-

ing); or aim at two or more distinct groups of consumers (differentiated marketing), with separate retailing approaches for each.

A broad strategy is then formed. It involves controllable variables (aspects of business a firm can directly affect) and uncontrollable variables (factors a firm cannot control and to which it must adapt).

After a general strategy is set, a firm makes and implements short-run decisions (tactics) for each controllable part of that strategy. Tactics must be forward-looking and respond to the environment.

Through a control process, strategy and tactics are evaluated and revised continuously. A retail audit systematically reviews a strategy and its execution on a regular basis. Strengths are emphasized and weaknesses minimized or eliminated.

An alert firm seeks out signals or cues, known as feedback, that indicate the level of performance at each step in the strategy.

3. *To examine the individual controllable and uncontrollable elements of a retail strategy.* There are four major controllable factors in retail planning: store location, managing the business, merchandise management and pricing, and communicating with the customer. The principal uncontrollable factors affecting retail planning are consumers, competition, technology, economic conditions, seasonality, and legal restrictions.

4. *To present strategic planning as a series of integrated steps.* Each stage in the strategic planning process needs to be performed, undertaken sequentially, and coordinated in order to have a consistent, integrated, unified strategy.

Key Terms

retail strategy (p. 69)
situation analysis (p. 71)
opportunities (p. 71)
threats (p. 71)
organizational mission (p. 71)
sole proprietorship (p. 73)
partnership (p. 73)
corporation (p. 73)
goods/service category (p. 76)

objectives (p. 80)
image (p. 82)
positioning (p. 82)
mass merchandising (p. 82)
niche retailing (p. 82)
bifurcated retailing (p. 83)
target market (p. 86)
mass marketing (p. 86)
concentrated marketing (p. 86)

differentiated marketing (p. 86)
competitive advantages (p. 86)
controllable variables (p. 87)
uncontrollable variables (p. 87)
tactics (p. 93)
control (p. 94)
feedback (p. 94)

Questions for Discussion

1. Why is it necessary to develop a thorough, well-integrated retail strategy? What could happen if a firm does not develop such a strategy?

2. How would situation analysis differ for a small home center and Home Depot?

3. What are the pros and cons of starting a new business versus buying an existing one?

4. Develop a checklist to help a prospective service retailer choose the proper service category in which to operate. Include personal abilities, financial resources, and time demands.

5. Why do retailers frequently underestimate the financial and time requirements of a business?

6. Draw and explain a positioning map showing the kinds of retailers selling home PCs.

7. Differentiate between mass merchandising and niche retailing. Why is it possible for both approaches to succeed?

8. Discuss local examples of retailers applying mass marketing, concentrated marketing, and differentiated marketing.

9. Marsha Hill is the store manager at a popular flower shop. She has saved $100,000 and wants to open her own store. Devise an overall strategy for Marsha, including each of the controllable factors listed in Figure 3.9 in your answer.

10. A competing small appliance retailer has a better location than yours. It is in a modern shopping center with a lot of customer traffic. Your store is in an older neighborhood and requires customers to travel further to reach you. How could you use a merchandising, pricing, and communications strategy to overcome your disadvantageous location?

11. How could each of these minimize the effects of seasonality?
    a. Swimming pool retailer.
    b. Mail-order greeting card business.
    c. College bookstore.

12. Describe how a retailer can use fine-tuning in strategic planning.

13. How are the control and feedback phases of retail strategy planning interrelated? Give an example.

14. Should a store-based firm (such as a bank) use the strategic planning process differently from a Web-based retailer? Why or why not?

WEB-BASED EXERCISE

Smart Business Supersite (www.smartbiz.com)

Questions

1. How helpful is this site in developing a home-based retail business? Explain your answer. (Refer to the material in the "Browse SBS" section of the site.)

2. Develop a retail strategy for a new computer service business that targets a local college dormitory student population. The service business installs components, offers training, and conducts troubleshooting services. (Refer to the "Computing in Business" material in the "Browse SBS" section of the site.)

3. Under the "Management" section, choose "Company Policies," "Company Mission," and "Forecasting." Evaluate these modules. (This material is in the "Browse SBS" section of the site.)

4. Using the information you gathered in answering Question 3, present a retail strategy for a college store.

CHAPTER ENDNOTES

1. Rick Brooks, "Alienating Customers Isn't Always a Bad Idea, Many Firms Discover," *Wall Street Journal* (January 7, 1999), pp. A1, A12.

2. For additional information, beyond that provided in this chapter, see Peter A. Karl III, "Twenty Questions on Selection of a Legal Entity," *CPA Journal*, Vol. 69 (August 1999), pp. 40–45; and Jill Andresky Fraser, "Perfect Form," *Inc.* (December 1997), pp. 155–58.

3. Steven C. Bahls and Jane Easter Bahls, "In Good Form," *Entrepreneur* (September 1996), pp. 75–79.

4. *Statistical Abstract of the United States 1999* (Washington, D.C.: U.S. Department of Commerce, 1999).

5. David R. Evanson, "Bucking the System," *Entrepreneur* (June 1998), pp. 77–79; and Cynthia E. Griffin, "Breaking the Bank," *Entrepreneur* (March 1998), pp. 110–15.

6. Valerie Seckler, "Target's Trend Line: $46 Billion in Sales by 2009," *Women's Wear Daily* (July 7, 1999), p. 17.

7. "Positioning Statement," *www.jcpenney.net/company/position/index.htm* (March 9, 2000).

8. Berry Craig, "Marcy's Shines Up Shoe Image," *Shopping Centers Today* (May 1999), p. 180.

9. "Shopping Chicago: Who Fills Women's Apparel Needs?" *Chain Store Age* (October 1996), Section Three; and James Mammarella, "Value Rules Apparel Decisions as Battle for Market Share Sharpens," *Discount Store News* (October 7, 1996), pp. 21–29.

CASE 1

LONG LIVE THE (BURGER) KING!

In an attempt to improve its image, food quality, and sales, Burger King is in the midst of equipping its U.S. restaurants with kitchens that permit customers to view their food being cooked. Burger King is also redesigning its drive-through windows, store exteriors, and logo. In totality, these changes are regarded by some retailing analysts as among the most sweeping in the chain's 45-year history and some of the most thoroughgoing in the fast-food industry. Burger King has begun the transformation by converting 40 company-owned units in Orlando, Florida. It is estimated that the full implementation of the plan would take between two and three years.

Burger King's new prototype has been designed to specifically address consumer concerns. For example, the kitchen redesign is in response to consumers wanting faster service and to emphasize the chain's grilling its beef and chicken (versus McDonald's frying). Burger King is also adding a "customer courtesy zone" to provide a space for customers to temporarily park their vehicles while they wait for additional ketchup or salt. This space quickens service by letting customers in other cars order and receive items while these requests are being addressed. Currently about 60 percent of Burger King's sales are made at the drive-through window.

Although they have always liked the food, many Burger King customers have complained about difficult-to-read menu boards, crowded eating areas, tables bolted to the floor, and a "boring" environment. In response, Burger King is changing its tan-and-brick exteriors to cobalt blue and redecorating interiors with mustard yellow walls, gray countertops, and red waste containers. Burger King is even updating its Burger King in-a-bun logo.

To appeal to children, Burger King's new prototype contains a "virtual" fun center with an electronic kiosk loaded with interactive games. This equipment eventually will enable children at one Burger King location to communicate with children at other units. The new prototype also features three computer-controlled broilers instead of the current one-speed system. The multiple-speed broiler will allow Burger King to more slowly heat products. Slower heating is required for its planned half-pound burger, the Great American. Burger King hopes this new food item will increase dinner sales.

CASE 1

(CONTINUED)

Burger King says it is a coincidence that its kitchen renovation is going on at the same time as McDonald's, but many retailing analysts believe these changes are a defensive strategy. The average Burger King outlet now has sales of $1.1 million per year versus $1.5 million at the average McDonald's. Burger King hopes its changes will increase the average unit's sales to $1.6 million.

Burger King estimates that the cost of building the new prototype is at least $15,000 more per unit than the prior prototype. Thus, some franchisees question the economics of the new format. Says one franchisee, "We need to see what the return is. If we get the kind we think we're going to get, we're going to be warming up the bulldozers." To help franchisees pay for the upgrades, Burger King is considering offering a combination of "investments and incentives." It also plans to increase the number of company-owned restaurants from 500 to 2,000 by purchasing some from existing franchisees and building others.

In contrast to McDonald's, with its almost 13,000 U.S. restaurants and 44 percent share of the U.S. quick-serve burger market, Burger King has 7,800 U.S. restaurants and a 21.9 percent market share—up from 17.2 percent in 1993.

Questions

1. Evaluate Burger King's overall plan.

2. How will the new prototype affect Burger King's target market strategy? Explain your answer.

3. What are the pros and cons of Burger King's increasing the number of company-owned units?

4. What types of control mechanisms does Burger King need to monitor the success of its plan?

NOTE

The material in this case is drawn from Constance L. Hays, "Burger King Plans Overhaul of Restaurants and Image," *New York Times* (April 15, 1999), p. C10; and Richard Gibson, "Burger King Seeks New Sizzle," *New York Times* (April 14, 1999), pp. B1, B6.

CASE 2

LANDS' END: ENTICING MILLIONS OF CUSTOMERS TO SHOP OUR WAY

Lands' End is a mail-order and Web retailer of informal clothing for men, women, and children. In addition, it sells shoes, soft luggage, and bed-and-bath items. Unlike other mail-order firms, most of Lands' End's offerings stress traditional "classic apparel" that "does not mimic the changing fads of the fashion world."

Unlike many other retailers that purchase from wholesalers, Lands' End works directly with mills and manufacturers. All of its customers also shop directly with Lands' End by phone, mail, fax, or the Web.

Lands' End prides itself on its consumer orientation. This is evidenced by three dimensions. One, everything sold by Lands' End is guaranteed. Consumers can return any item purchased, at any time, and for any reason. Lands' End's guarantee is so simple that it has no fine print. Two, the retailer covers the credit card risk to consumers in the event of credit card fraud involving a Lands' End purchase. Three, Lands' End has a stated goal of shipping at least 90 percent of items at the time a customer places an order. Even though this requires a high inventory investment, it instills a high degree of customer confidence in the firm. Each of these strategy elements are especially important to a direct marketer.

The majority of Lands' End's customers are between 35 and 64 years of age. Lands' End's target market is also upscale. The median household income of its customers averages $55,000. About 88 percent of its customers have a college education and they are three times as likely as the general population to have some level of post-graduate education. Lands' End's customers are also two times as likely as the general population to live in a household with online access.

Lands' End operations consist of three segments: core, specialty, and international. The core segment is comprised of adult apparel offered through regular monthly and prospecting catalogs and the retailer's two catalogs of fine tailored clothing: *First Person Singular* for working women and *Beyond Buttondowns* for men. Sales in the core business were $862 million in fiscal 1999, $826 million in fiscal 1998, and $754 million in fiscal 1997.

The specialty segment contains three catalogs—*Kids*, comprised of casual clothing for children; *Corporate Sales*, made up of embroidered items for company incentive programs or group apparel for firms, clubs, and athletic teams; and *Coming Home*, bed-and-bath items. Sales in the specialty sector were $365 million in fiscal 1999, $307 million in fiscal 1998, and $270 million in fiscal 1997.

Lands' End's international segment is highlighted by sales in Japan, Great Britain, and Germany. Catalogs are mailed in these countries and denominated in local currencies. Sales in the international segment were $146 million in fiscal 1999, $132 million in fiscal 1998, and $96 million in fiscal 1997.

The fastest growth at Lands' End is through its Web-based business. Lands' End currently offers over 1,000 products from its core and specialty segments on the Web. Internet sales were $61 million in fiscal 1999, more than three times the $18 million sales in fiscal 1998. These revenues are credited to the firm's appropriate business segment.

Lands' End's overall performance in fiscal year 1999 was satisfactory. Sales growth was 8.5 percent (compared with 13 percent in the prior year), while net income as a percent of sales slipped to 2.3 percent (from 5.1 percent). The firm attributed much of the decline in profits to the need for above-average markdowns due to excess inventories.

Questions

1. Describe and evaluate Lands' End's organization mission.

2. What are the pros and cons of Lands' End's not using channel intermediaries such as wholesalers?

3. Comment on Lands' End's performance in terms of sales, profits, and positioning.

4. What are the pros and cons of Lands' End's chosen target market?

Video Questions on Lands' End

1. Describe the evolution of Lands' End from its inception to now.

2. Discuss the role of Lands' End's Dodgeville, Wisconsin, location in its overall retail strategy.

NOTE   The material in this case is drawn from *Lands' End, Inc., 1999 Annual Report;* and *www. landsend.com.*

APPENDIX ON THE SPECIAL DIMENSIONS OF STRATEGIC PLANNING IN A GLOBAL RETAILING ENVIRONMENT

Michigan State University's CIBER (ciber.bus.msu.edu) is an excellent source of information on global business practices.

There are about 270 countries—encompassing 6 billion people and a $30 trillion economy—in the world. The United States accounts for less than 5 percent of the worldwide population and nearly 30 percent of the worldwide economy. This means that although the United States is a very attractive marketplace, there are also many other appealing markets around the globe. That is why global retailing is growing dramatically. It is expected that annual worldwide retailing sales will reach $9.2 trillion by 2009.[1] When we talk about the global environment of retailing, we are referring to both U.S. firms operating in foreign markets and foreign retailers operating in U.S. markets.

The challenge of strategic planning in a global retailing environment is clear: "The world economy is a crazy-quilt of retail markets in which promising new territories are closely mingled with potential quagmires for retailers looking to expand beyond their home countries." There are many differences among countries despite "the growing similarity of consumer tastes and the development of sophisticated information systems."[2] Thus, in embarking on an international retailing strategy, firms should thoroughly consider each of the factors shown in Figure 1.

The Strategic Planning Process and Global Retailing

Retailers looking to operate in global markets should follow these four steps *in conjunction with* the strategic planning process described in Chapter 3.

1. *Assess Your International Potential:* "Because international growth requires an extension of your firm's resources, you must first focus on assessing your international potential. This should give you a picture of the trends in your industry, your domestic position in that industry, the effects that international activity may have on your current operations, the status of your resources, and an estimate of your domestic and international sales potential. In general, you should not get into international retailing unless you have a secure base of operations in the United States. Find out about candidate countries by using research. It's easy to ruin an otherwise well-conceived plan by making fundamental cultural, partnering, or resource allocation mistakes. It's far better to put the time into research at the beginning rather than learn when it's too late that you did not do enough homework."

2. *Get Expert Advice and Counseling:* "Once you have assessed your international potential and made a decision to commit time and resources, the next step is to get expert advice and counseling. Many groups in the private sector and government provide guidance to companies planning to go international. Industry trade associations are also useful, as are private consulting firms and the business departments of major universities. If you are entirely new to international retailing, call the U.S. government's Trade Information Center, toll-free, at (800) USA-TRADE (800-872-8723). If you are further along, contact the nearest district office of the Commerce Department's International Trade Administration. State governments are another source of assistance."

The CIA World Fact Book (www.cia.gov/cia/publications/factbook/index.html) has a wealth of useful data on the characteristics of individual countries around the world.

3. *Select Your Countries:* "After reviewing your research and digesting the advice, the next decision is about which country or countries to enter. You need to prioritize information about each country's environment, including economic strength, political stability, regulatory environment, tax policy, infrastructure development, population size, and cultural factors to reflect influences on the candidate countries. For example, the economy of a country is generally considered critical to most businesses and is normally ranked high in importance. Equally critical are political factors, particularly government regulations. Others are

Figure 1
Factors to Consider
When Engaging in
Global Retailing

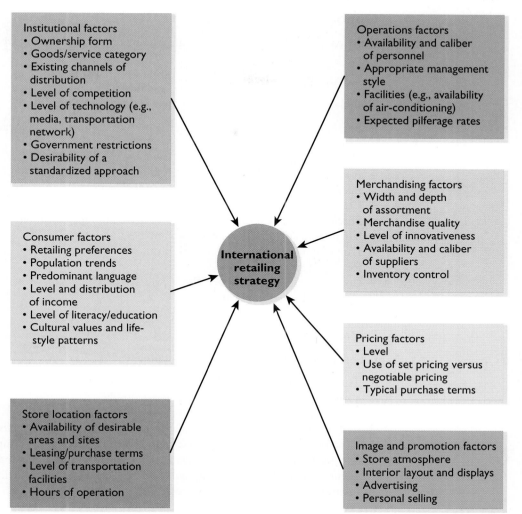

more dependent on which product you market. For example, the technological stage of a country plays a more influential role for computers than for cosmetics.

4. *Develop, Implement, and Review an International Retailing Strategy:* "In developing an international retailing strategy, write a business plan that lists short- and long-term goals, the competitive niche you're seeking, and how you're going to position your offering. In general, a successful strategy identifies and manages your objectives, both immediate and long range; specifies tactics you will use; schedules activities and deadlines that reflect your objectives and tactics; and allocates resources among those activities. The plan should cover a two-to-five-year period, depending on what you are selling, the strength of competitors, conditions in the target countries, and other factors. Keep your strategy flexible because often it is only after entering a country that you realize that your way of doing business needs modification. Successful strategies are those in which plans can be changed to exploit unique local conditions and circumstances. Set realistic sales goals. Don't underestimate the local competition, but don't overestimate it either."[3]

Opportunities and Threats in Global Retailing

For participating firms, there are wide-ranging opportunities and threats in global retailing.

OPPORTUNITIES

Global retailing opportunities exist for several reasons:

- Foreign markets may represent better growth opportunities (because of population and other trends).
- Domestic markets may be saturated or stagnant.
- A retailer may be able to offer goods, services, or technology not yet available in foreign markets.
- Competition may be less in foreign markets.
- Foreign markets may be used to supplement, not replace, domestic sales.
- There may be tax or investment advantages in foreign markets.
- Due to government and economic shifts, many countries are more open to the entry of foreign firms.
- Communications are easier. The World Wide Web enables retailers to reach customers well outside their domestic markets.

THREATS

Global retailing threats exist for several reasons:

- There may be cultural differences between domestic and foreign markets.
- Management styles may not be easily adaptable.
- Foreign governments may place restrictions on some operations.
- Personal income may be poorly distributed among consumers in foreign markets.
- Distribution systems and technology may be inadequate (for example, poor roads, lack of refrigeration, and a weak mail system). In some instances, this may minimize the effectiveness of the Web as a selling tool—because part of the value delivery chain is lacking.
- Institutional formats may vary greatly among countries.

STANDARDIZATION: AN OPPORTUNITY AND A THREAT

When devising a global strategy, a retailer must pay particular attention to the concept of *standardization*. Can the strategy followed in the firm's home market be standardized and directly applied to foreign markets, or do personnel, the physical structure of facilities, operations, advertising messages, product lines, and other factors have to be adapted to local conditions and needs? Table 1 shows how the economies differ in 20 countries. And consider this,

> Compared to the 50 states [in the United States], with their principal language of English and overall federal law and tax systems, Europe is a jigsaw puzzle of cultures, languages, and nationalistic differences that are not instantly diluted by the removal of internal trade barriers. This patchwork includes those who have a general suspicion of financial institutions and thus a low use of credit (the French); a nation of families who wouldn't dream of driving out to breakfast on a Sunday morning (the British); a nation with longer trading hours than the 10:00 A.M. to 10:00 P.M. of the United States, but where a majority of shops close for three hours in midday (Spain); and Europe's most economically powerful country, whose citizens are notoriously price-conscious and do much of their food shopping in no-frills discount stores (Germany).[4]

Table 1 The Global Economy, Selected Countries

Country	1999 Population (millions)	1999 Pop. Density (per sq. kilometer)	1998 Per Capita GDP (U.S. $)	Annual GDP Growth 1998–2002 (%)	1997 Per Capita Retail Sales (U.S. $)	1999 World Competitiveness Ranking Among the Twenty Countries Listed
Brazil	172	20	6,100	3.0	1,364	12
Canada	31	3	22,400	2.8	4,157	3
China	1,250	134	3,600	7.3	272	8
France	59	108	22,600	2.3	5,601	6
Germany	82	234	22,100	2.1	5,683	2
Great Britain	59	244	21,200	1.9	5,236	4
India	1,001	337	1,720	5.6	191	15
Indonesia	216	118	2,830	−3.1	313	19
Italy	57	195	20,800	2.2	5,504	9
Japan	126	336	23,100	0.2	10,390	5
Malaysia	21	65	10,300	0.2	868	7
Mexico	100	52	8,300	4.0	906	13
Philippines	79	265	3,500	3.3	584	10
Poland	39	127	6,800	5.3	2,038	17
Russia	146	9	4,000	−1.3	1,023	20
South Africa	43	36	6,800	2.4	740	16
South Korea	47	475	12,600	0.6	1,440	14
Thailand	61	120	6,100	1.4	658	11
United States	273	30	31,500	2.3	6,320	1
Venezuela	23	26	8,500	2.7	1,056	18

GDP is a country's Gross Domestic Product. Per Capita GDP is expressed in terms of purchasing power parity.
World Competitiveness Ranking is based on a country's domestic economy, internationalization, government, finance, infrastructure, management effectiveness, science and technology, and population and labor force characteristics.

Sources: Compiled by the authors from *CIA World Factbook 1999;* IMD, *1998 World Competitiveness Yearbook;* Economist Intelligence Unit, *1998 and 1999 World Outlook;* and *Euromonitor.*

Factors Affecting the Success of a Global Retailing Strategy

Generally speaking, several factors can affect the level of success of an international retailing strategy:

- *Timing:* "Being first in a market doesn't ensure success, of course, but being there before the serious competition does increase one's chances."
- *A balanced international program:* "While timing is important, market selection is even more critical. One factor firms must consider is the stability of a nation's currency and government."

- *A growing middle class:* "A rapidly growing middle class means expendable income, which translates into sales."
- *Matching concept to market:* "In *developed* retail markets, where quality and fashion are more appreciated, specialty operations are entering with success. On the other hand, when entering *developing* markets, discount/combination (food and general merchandise) retailers have been successful. Consumers in these markets are more interested in price, assortment, value, and convenience." See Table 2.
- *Solo or partnering:* "When establishing a presence in many countries, retailers have often chosen the route of joint ventures with local partners. The joint venture appeases countries and populations whose cultural sensitivity is particularly acute. The joint venture makes it easier to establish government contacts and learn the ways of getting things done."
- *Store location and facilities:* "Foreign retailers often have to adapt their concepts to different real-estate configurations in other markets." Shopping malls may be rare in some places.
- *Product selection:* "Consumers in most parts of the world would be overwhelmed by the product assortment in North American stores."
- *Service levels:* "Consumers in some areas do not expect anything close to the level of service American shoppers have come to demand." This can be a real point of distinction.[5]

Table 2 Preparing for Different Global Markets

DEVELOPED, MATURE MARKETS

Issues

- Increasing competition, deteriorating margins, and saturation
- Consolidation and rationalization (cost cutting), forcing poor performers out of the market
- New enabling technologies
- Demanding customers
- Limited growth

Implications

- Retailers must focus on maximizing operational efficiencies, vendor relationships, infrastructure, and technology
- For growth, large retailers are expanding regionally then globally into developed or developing markets

DEVELOPING, IMMATURE MARKETS

Issues

- Minimal purchasing power per capita, yet strong economic growth and pent-up demand
- Huge customer base, representing up to 70 percent of the world's population
- Infrastructure issues (transportation, communication, etc.) may pose problems
- Disorganized, fragmented retail structures that are vulnerable to new entrants
- The number of indigenous large retailers is small to none
- Strong protectionist measures may exist

Implications

- Tremendous opportunity for large retailers; limited competition, huge growth potential
- Initial entry may need to be through intermediary: joint venture, etc.

Source: Deloitte & Touche, "Global Powers of Retailing," *Stores* (January 1998), Section 3, p. S15. Reprinted by permission.

U.S. Retailers and Foreign Markets

Here are examples of U.S. retailers with high involvement in foreign markets.

Until 1991 when it opened its first store in Mexico, Wal-Mart operated stores only in the United States. By 1999, it had greatly increased its global presence outside the United States—including outlets in Argentina, Brazil, Canada, Germany, Mexico, China, and Korea. These stores generated $12.5 billion in annual sales. According to the firm's Web site (www.wal-mart.com): "Wal-Mart's global expansion has been achieved through a combination of building retail outlets from the ground up and through a series of acquisitions at the right time and right place. Both approaches have yielded excellent market penetration and financial growth for Wal-Mart Stores, Inc. Wal-Mart International has found that the retailer's culture is transportable to other cultures worldwide. As a global brand, customers recognize that Wal-Mart stands for low cost, best value, and the greatest selection of quality merchandise. Wal-Mart's highest standards of customer service have also been exported and adopted by international associates around the globe." In the future, Wal-Mart plans to be even more aggressive outside the United States.

Toys "R" Us has been active internationally for years, and now has more than 450 stores abroad (up from about 75 in 1990). Among the more than 25 nations in which it has well-established stores are Australia, Canada, France, Germany, Great Britain, Japan, Singapore, Spain, and Sweden. In 1994, it signed its first foreign franchising agreements, thus entering the United Arab Emirates and other Middle Eastern nations. During 1996, it entered Indonesia, Italy, South Africa, and Turkey. Why the emphasis on franchising? As its Web site (www.tru.com) said, "Their local knowledge of the retail market combined with the Toys "R" Us expertise in the management of children's megastores should provide a powerful combination to fully cover the potential of the market and increase the availability of toys."

Many of the world's leading mail-order retailers are U.S.-based—including American Express, Avon, Citicorp, Franklin Mint, and Reader's Digest. These firms are efficient and have a clear handle on customers and distribution methods. However, as of now, total worldwide mail-order sales (for both U.S. and foreign firms) outside the United States are less than those in the United States. Thus, there is great growth potential in foreign markets.

Blockbuster (www.blockbuster.com) operates more than 2,000 video stores in 26 foreign countries in Europe, Asia, the Pacific Rim, and North and South America. According to its Web site, it employs over 14,000 people at those stores—and at least 12 different languages are spoken at Blockbuster stores: "The first international Blockbuster store opened in London in 1989. The foreign country with the most Blockbuster stores is Great Britain, with more than 700. The foreign country with the fewest Blockbuster stores is Uruguay, with one. Blockbuster's newest foreign market was Poland."

For the past 15 years, the majority of McDonald's new restaurants have opened outside the United States. Today, sales at 12,500 outlets in 115 foreign nations account for one-half of total systemwide revenues. Besides Western Europe, McDonald's also has outlets in such places as Argentina, Australia, Brazil, Brunei, Canada, China, Costa Rica, Czech Republic, Hungary, India, Japan, Malaysia, Mexico, New Zealand, Philippines, Poland, Russia, Turkey, Venezuela, and Yugoslavia. The 15 restaurants in India are unique because "cows are sacred and most people don't eat beef. McDonald's ditched the Big Mac for an Indian stand-in, the Maharaja Mac. That's two all-mutton patties, special sauce, lettuce, cheese, pickle, and onions, all on a sesame seed bun."[6]

Foreign Retailers and the U.S. Market

A large number of foreign retailers have entered the United States, in order to appeal to the world's most affluent mass market. Here are three examples.

Ikea (www.ikea.com) is a Swedish-based home-furnishings retailer with stores in nearly 30 countries. In 1985, Ikea opened its first U.S. store in Pennsylvania. Since then, it has added stores in such cities as Baltimore, Chicago, Elizabeth (New Jersey), Hicksville (Long Island, New York), Houston, Los Angeles, San Francisco, Seattle, and Washington, D.C. The firm offers durable, stylish ready-to-assemble furniture at low prices. Because Ikea positions itself as a dominant furniture retailer, its stores are large and have enormous selections. For example, the outlet in Elizabeth, New Jersey, is 270,000 square feet and has a playroom for children and other customer amenities. The firm generates nearly 90 percent of its sales from international operations, including about $700 million dollars at its U.S. stores.

The Netherlands' Royal Ahold (www.ahold.com) is a supermarket operator ranking among the world's top retailers with $35 billion in annual retail sales. It has stores in 17 countries and serves 25 million shoppers weekly. In the United States, rather than introducing its own stores, Royal Ahold has acquired several chains, making it the leading supermarket firm along the eastern seaboard. Its more than 1,000 U.S. stores include these chains: Stop & Shop, Giant Food, Tops Markets, and Bi-Lo.

Body Shop International (www.the-body-shop.com) is a British-based chain that specializes in natural cosmetics and lotions such as Vitamin E Cream, Tea Free Oil, Banana Shampoo, and Aloe Vera Lotion—"products that cleanse, beautify, and soothe the human form." There are 1,600 Body Shop stores in 48 countries, including the United States. The firm has more than 400 U.S. stores (55 percent of which are company-owned and 45 percent of which are franchised), which generate roughly one-quarter of Body Shop's total company revenues.

Besides extending their traditional businesses into the United States, a number of foreign firms (such as Royal Ahold) have acquired ownership interests in U.S. retailers. Although the revenues of U.S.-based retailers owned by foreign firms are hard to measure, they certainly exceed $100 billion annually. Foreign ownership in U.S. retailers is highest for general merchandise stores, food stores, and apparel and accessory stores. Examples of U.S.-based retailers owned by foreign firms are shown in Table 3.

Both U.S. retailers operating in foreign markets and foreign firms operating in the U.S. market need to be careful in their approach:

> Retailers considering operations abroad must carefully study demographic, economic, and cultural trends; must be flexible in choosing retail formats; and must be willing to enter into partnerships with local operators. Retailers also must be prepared to commit capital resources to sustain what may be losing operations for several years before consumers accept them. To be sure, overseas expansion is risky and requires a long-term outlook, particularly in countries with a great potential for growth in the next century. The prospective profits in those markets is so large, however, that many retailers cannot afford to miss these opportunities.[7]

Table 3 Selected Ownership of U.S. Retailers by Foreign Firms

U.S. Retailer	Principal Business	Foreign Owner	Country of Owner
Eddie Bauer	Mail order and specialty stores	Otto Versand Gmbh	Germany
Brooks Brothers	Apparel	Marks & Spencer	Great Britain
Burger King	Restaurants	Diageo	Great Britain
Carvel	Ice cream	Investcorp	Bahrain
Citgo	Gas stations	Petroleos de Venezuela	Venezuela
Crate & Barrel	Housewares stores	Otto Versand Gmbh	Germany
Food Lion	Supermarkets	Delhaize Le Lion	Belgium
Giant Food	Supermarkets	Royal Ahold	Netherlands
Great Atlantic & Pacific (A&P)	Supermarkets	Tengelmann	Germany
Hannaford Brothers	Supermarkets	Delhaize Le Lion	Belgium
LensCrafters	Optical stores	Luxottica	Italy
Motel 6	Economy motels	Accor	France
7-Eleven	Convenience stores	Ito-Yokado	Japan
Shaw's Supermarkets	Supermarkets	J. Sainsbury	Great Britain
Spiegel	Mail order	Otto Versand Gmbh	Germany
Stop & Shop	Supermarkets	Royal Ahold	Netherlands
Talbots	Apparel	Jusco Ltd.	Japan

APPENDIX ENDNOTES

1. Valerie Seckler, "Study: Giants Will Grow Fast," *Women's Wear Daily* (June 9, 1999), p. 13.

2. "Target: Global Opportunities," *Stores* (September 1998), p. 20.

3. William J. McDonald, "Five Steps to International Success," *Direct Marketing* (November 1998), pp. 32–36.

4. Ian Waddell, "Global Challenges Set the Scene for 1992," *Chain Store Age* (May 1990), p. 190. See also Len Lewis, "Going Global," *Progressive Grocer* (March 1997), pp. 28–34.

5. "Global Powers of Retailing," *Chain Store Age* (December 1996), Section 3, pp. 10B–13B. See also "Global Powers of Retailing," *Chain Store Age* (October 1999), Section 2.

6. *McDonald's 1998 Annual Report*; and Dan Biers and Miriam Jordan, "McDonald's in India Decides the Big Mac Is Not a Sacred Cow," *Wall Street Journal* (October 14, 1996), p. A14.

7. *U.S. Industry & Trade Outlook '99* (New York: McGraw-Hill, 1999), p. 42–6.

PART ONE
COMPREHENSIVE CASE
Sears' Strategy for Continuing Renewal

INTRODUCTION

At Sears, we're guided by a simple and brief, yet all-encompassing vision: to be a compelling place to shop, a compelling place to work, and a compelling place to invest. We believe that if we can engage the customer and the sales associate, the financials will follow. I'm sure that many of you will agree with me completely here. In much less time than anyone expected, we achieved a turnaround for the company that is a very real recovery in the short-term financial sense. Over the long term, however, moving into the new century, our primary focus is a total transformation of our company.

In January 1993, we undertook this transformation based on five strategic principles. Each would transcend the organization and each of our key constituencies: customers, associates, and shareholders. Briefly, they are to 1) concentrate where Sears enjoys equity with the public; 2) make Sears a more exciting place to shop; 3) develop a local market focus; 4) concentrate on cost/asset productivity; and 5) cultivate a winning culture. I told our management at the time that they might as well memorize the list because it wasn't going to change.

THE SECOND REVOLUTION

Based on these strategies, we made tremendous strides in our image, customer relations, and morale. Despite this progress, however, after five years of continually increasing revenues and profit, we clearly hit some stall points in our business in 1998. Things got a bit more "interesting" than we expected. I found myself facing the toughest question in my Sears career: "Are we the

growth company we anticipated, or are we just another mature company enjoying a growth spurt?" Frankly speaking, we don't have a definitive answer yet and it might take a while. The solution to the puzzle lies in understanding the difference between the two and examining what steps we'll be taking to be fully in the growth mode.

Conventional wisdom defines a mature company as having growth but stalling out. Companies, particularly large ones, often experience stall points. They are, more accurately, a downward inflection in the growth rate they've experienced. Much is undesirable in a mature organization. Incrementalism is the guiding philosophy: the notion of doing slightly better every year. We've certainly been guilty of this. "Must top last year by 3 percent, 4 percent, 5 percent" is a difficult internal issue we've struggled with longer than we'd like to admit. So, how can we insure that we are growing and not just plodding along?

A company's growth vision must extend far beyond merely improving performance. It's a matter of reinvention: not just better—but different, as well. Different, not just better. Courage and innovation, not just improvement. If customer satisfaction continues to improve bit by bit, we're doing better. Just "better" is insufficient. We'd be victims of incrementalism, positioning ourselves for further stall points. Our strategy is, and will remain, to be different and better. Our performance must generate the degree of value growth correspondent with our customers' evolving expectations and the upheaval in the market.

It's not always a matter of coming up with new answers to old questions. It involves turning your perspective around. It's asking the right people the right questions. We need to ask our target customer, for example, is the same venue you've always shopped still best for you? Are there alternative means of delivering value that will generate greater satisfaction for you and, ultimately, better results for us? Is that store concept that served your needs five years ago still viable for maintaining a relationship with Sears?

Until now, it was incumbent on customers to come to our stores, where we built them, and at the times we selected for their shopping. We made a lot of decisions on their behalf. That's a privilege we're forced to relinquish in this new age. The customers rule. We need to bring the mountain to them, whenever they want. That's what's happening in our world today. I call this strategy "convergence."

Today it is totally insufficient to be merely a store or a catalog retailer. You must operate in all channels with equal intensity and equal velocity. Your multiple channels must converge at a single source of service and value to the customer. For us, it's what we call "serving anyone, anywhere, anytime." At Sears, we have big stores to go with small stores to go with catalogs to go with E-commerce.

Consider Amazon.com. Through a stunning burst of innovation and marketing savvy, it was the first to seize category authority in electronic book retailing. It was out there—unprotected and available. Today, traditional booksellers are scrambling to catch up. Again, it's not just being better, but different. Amazon.com is living proof that a retailer's competition is constantly changing. It took action while others learned a hard lesson.

At Sears, we learned a valuable lesson from the Amazon episode. Consider that Sears holds a 35 percent share of the appliance business. Incredibly, one of every three appliances sold in the United States is bought from Sears—at least at this moment. Kenmore is America's favorite appliance brand—at least at this moment. In fact, 60 percent of America's kitchens feature a Kenmore nameplate—at least at this moment. We know success can be fleeting. We're not sitting still. We know, so far anyway, there are no limits to what can be sold on the Internet. So guess who just added its appliance business to the Web? Right—Sears. We won't be beaten to the punch. It's a matter of serving anyone, anywhere, anytime.

An organization planning on growth must be ready to reply when opportunity presents itself. Your eyes must be wide open, your peripheral vision keen. You have to be a dedicated early adopter. Occasional failure is a very reasonable trade-off. Recall that innovation is but one part of being different: Courage is the other—courage to take risks. When the topic is stall points, an "ounce of prevention" most certainly applies. Competition, the marketplace, the economy are of minor consequence when a company hits such barriers. The material factors are generally internal.

From my experience, there are strategies for avoiding these internally generated stall points going in. Embrace innovation in product offering, ambience, and service levels. Develop a distaste for the status quo. Outside our industry, Intel is an excellent example of a major corporation that survives, thrives, and grows its value through change. It quickly identifies and responds to a perplexing dilemma we all face: to admit that what got us to where we are today—things that worked well as recently as two years ago—won't necessarily perform as well in the future. Nothing is untouchable anymore, especially in retailing. We must be willing to reconsider and, if necessary, abandon not-so-very-old ideas, even while they're still working. I've been preaching constant rein-

vention for years now, and we're beginning to appreciate the power of questioning everything. Really sticking our necks out!

The most severe impediment to continuous reinvention is ego. Pride can play havoc with the best of ideas. Some people can't let go of a process where they were instrumental in its development. Our decision making must reflect a sense of our fallibility and humility, or else we're living in the past, and the past, quite frankly, is the home of the dinosaur.

There always will be stall points in any industry. We have to be realistic. Despite the best of intentions, every firm will encounter them. The great ones deal with them and rebound. There are two marvelous retailing examples: Wal-Mart and Gap were hit with major stall points in the mid-'90s, but drove through with great success. On the other hand, there are numerous examples of companies that hit stall points and couldn't rebound. I don't have to list the stores no longer in business.

It all boils down to challenging yourself. Apple Computer is a wonderful example of a company that had been written off as down and out, but look at its restoration to health. Reinvention, innovation, challenging yourself—all working closely in sync.

PRIORITIES REVISITED

Hand in hand in the battle against stall points stands the need to re-examine the core principles of your firm. You'll recall I mentioned our transformation was undertaken on the strategic principles I listed. Earlier this year, my executive team and I held several strategy summits to determine if these pillars were still relevant as this organization goes forward.

Feedback from our management team uncovered that we, as an enterprise, weren't truly acting in concert. We asked ourselves: Were those original five priorities still valid? After careful analysis, we reconfirmed their relevance to our business today and our business tomorrow. However, they were not fully meaningful to each of our associates. Many of our people were simply unfamiliar with them. Over the years, we've experienced turnover in our management. Concurrently, we had not relentlessly communicated the principles on a renewed basis. Plus, the competitive situation had changed dramatically from the scenario of 1993.

We decided it was time to revisit these priorities, and update and clarify their interpretation as the foundation for Sears' "Second Revolution." Let's review these initiatives from today's perspective:

Our First Priority: Focus Our Business Where We Can Win

- In 1993, winning was about merchandise. Today, it is about winning with customers.
- As each of you has learned, leverage today is in the hands of shoppers—not the merchants or manufacturers. (The Internet is a great facilitator here.)
- We must redefine our value proposition (the totality of the value package we deliver, as understood by the customer).
- We must develop specific customer acquisition and retention goals, especially for younger shoppers.
- We must be relevant to customers and engage their power to form a relationship with us.
- In the end, it will be innovation that creates the winning focus for us.

Second: Position Sears as a Compelling Place to Shop

- Original consideration was the physical environment of the stores. But today's customer has far more options regarding the time, place, and means of connecting with a purveyor of goods and services.
- Contemporary interpretation of a compelling place to shop goes back to the notion of serving anyone, anywhere, anytime.
- If customers want to get on the Web in the middle of the night for information or to make a transaction in a category where we have strength, more power to them!
- We must be ready to live in the world of technology and be ready for whatever comes along.
- Technology—whatever you didn't grow up with.
- Today's 15-year-olds will be critical Sears shoppers within 10 years. We must be digitally capable of reaching them on their terms.
- Faster, quicker, better—we must be all three.

Third: Achieve Local Market Focus

- Original: Tailor our proposition, presentation, and assortment to meet the unique and special needs of the marketplace.
- Over time, the focus shifted from mass market to targeted basis.

- 1999 task: Construct individualized, relevant, specific customer offers.
- Our "unfair" competitive advantage: the depth of knowledge we have about our customers—the power of information. Richest data base of any retailer in the world.
- Very precise information across all facets of our merchandise and services.
- The task before us: Release the power of that information in pursuit of deeper, more profound, and lasting relationships with our customers.

Fourth: Cost and Asset Productivity

- Original efforts were successful. Seems to have flattened out over time.
- Asset productivity is a facilitator for shareholder value creation in the marketplace today.
- Make our assets (real and human) work for us efficiently in this changing market.
- Asset productivity—long term, not a slash and burn event.
- Must ask ourselves: What processes drive nonvalue-added activities and associated costs? What can we eliminate or simplify? Be innovative!

Fifth: Build a Winning Culture

- Results often define. The last two years, we've witnessed a plateauing of morale in our organization.
- In our competitive retail environment, the winners enjoy the energy, spontaneity, and associate engagement that Sears absolutely must have.
- Management must demonstrate its commitment to associates.
- In a winning culture, associates know how to win customers and transfer that knowledge to others.
- The collective thinking of 320,000 associates is enormous. We must listen to their ideas, and encourage their thoughts, questions, and challenges.
- Turnover: Must stabilize the work force—keep that institutional learning in-house. Turnover cost is astronomical, not just in hiring and training. Operational ripples affect all of our cost initiatives.
- A winning culture is a diverse culture. It must mirror the populace we seek to serve; there cannot be any confusion in this regard. We've made progress, but insufficient to get to where we need to be.

PROGRESS TO DATE

With our strategies set in place, where do we stand operationally as we begin the next phase of our transformation, our Second Revolution?

Since 1993, we've added more than $12 billion in annual retail sales. For most of this time, Sears was among the retail leaders in comparable-store sales—although we've been challenged significantly over the past year. Comp-store sales are reflected in our customer service levels. Here, we've achieved parity with target competitors and progress in our goal of meeting and eventually overtaking "the best in class."

Concurrently, worker morale remains very high, compared to where we began. The vast majority of our associates tell us of their pride in working for Sears, the sense of accomplishment they feel, and that they understand their individual efforts are linked to our corporate strategic objectives.

Our long-term prospects look strong. We expect good earnings per share. This reinforces the crux of our vision. It bears repeating: putting the customer and the associate front and center will create the financial results. After a period of stabilization and revitalization, we've begun to focus on growth again. We want to take the best of Sears and its brands, such as Craftsman, and bring that directly to the customer's neighborhood. There are two important considerations with this approach. First, we are not merely transferring business—rather, we are creating opportunities to expand our market share. Second, the formats must be built around our traditional strengths and reflect the five strategic pillars.

These new concepts include: *Sears Hardware Stores*—now numbering 265, they combine the convenience of a traditional hardware store with the value and assortment of a Sears hardware department. *Sears Dealer Stores*—our fastest-growing segment—have become the appliance and electronics superstore of rural America. We have close to 700 stores, and revenues are over $1 billion here, well in advance of anyone's expectations. Our most innovative concept is *The Great Indoors*. In our huge suburban Denver prototype, we've incorporated every element of decorating and remodeling for all the rooms in our target customer's home. Behind our success here, second and third stores are under way. We believe the Great Indoors concept is, ultimately, a $10 billion revenue opportunity.

GETTING BACK ON TRACK

Today, Sears enjoys a unique position:

1. We're the only true national chain of department stores, soft goods and hard goods, as well as automotive. No national company enjoys this breadth of merchandise and breadth of relationship.
2. We have the brands people want—a balanced mix of renowned national brands and respected private brands in both hard lines and soft lines.
3. We offer the widest variety of credit options, including the Sears Card—certainly the most popular private card in America. Here, our reach extends to 65 million households.
4. No one provides service like Sears: delivery, installation, and repair. No matter where the customer bought an item, we can fix it, and we do so 48,000 times a day.
5. We provide all this at a price people want to pay.
6. We're at those locations we're expected to be—with 900 full-line department stores in the majority of the country's leading malls, off the mall in locations convenient to customers' neighborhoods, and directly and aggressively to customers through specialty catalogs and the Internet.

It's a matter of blending convergence with innovation: anyone, anywhere, anytime.

THE EIGHT LESSONS OF TRANSFORMATION

Since the very first steps in our transformation journey, we've learned, and continue to learn, a number of insights that have practically universal application throughout the business world. I call these our "Eight Lessons of Transformation."

First and foremost in any successful transformation, you must develop a passion for the customer. Everything must be squarely focused on the customer. As I learned as a teenager stocking groceries, a decision in the customer's favor is ultimately to your advantage. Surveys and statistics will tell you lots, but are no panaceas. They don't translate into a passion for the customer.

Our second principle of transformation is that your vision must be simple, straightforward, and inclusive. Ours reflects the direct relationship that links Sears' constituencies. As such, we fully accept that each of us must develop a passion for the customer, understand that people add value, and provide performance leadership for our shareholders.

Third, engaged people will take the bold steps that make us a compelling place to shop, work, and invest. Our greatest potential for differentiating ourselves is our people. Each Sears manager needs to master the art of listening. This is our best source for ideas that will improve how we go to market. We believe strongly in ownership, taking a personal stake. We're doing this today with special stock purchase programs for all associates and stock options for managers. Education and training are critical. Before someone can accept a vision, they must understand it. People must be educated regarding the tasks and goals ahead of them, along with some understanding of the underlying philosophy.

Fourth, get decision making as close as possible to the consumer. We have a very aggressive effort in progress in our full-line stores to find ways to get our store people more firmly into the decision-making process. We empower people through training as well as flexible regulations arid procedures.

Fifth, foster a spirit of innovation for your firm to thrive. This follows the previous two lessons: Engage people and get decision making close to the customer. I've charged our top 200 managers to tackle specific challenges we face enterprisewide. These range all the way from work/life balance issues to E-commerce to designing a store from scratch that would attract the younger customers we must cultivate. Many of our best ideas come from sales associates who deal directly with the customer.

Concentrate on the positive is our sixth lesson. While it's important to learn from mistakes, it's even more important to learn from your successes. We must know what created the particular success and how to recreate the environment where success can be replicated.

Seventh, unleash the power of your people into the community. Plant the seeds of a strong community volunteerism program in your organization.

A final lesson: Two years ago, much to our shock, we were caught in an ethical dilemma that we never dreamed of. My advice: Assume nothing, and have your house in order ethically. Don't be caught short. Insure that your culture both allows for the admission of failure and facilitates the communication of bad news upstream. Sears was unprepared. We learned the hard way. Admit failures early. At Sears, we want everyone to know that we expect them to do the right thing—for the right reason. I encourage you: Avoid the ethics paradox. Don't create too many rules and regulations. It becomes more and more difficult for your people to understand what you want.

Questions

1. Before reading the case, what was your perception of Sears? Did the case change this perception? Explain your answer.
2. How does Sears apply the retailing concept?
3. Relate these concepts to Sears' stated strategy: value, value chain, customer base, and customer service.
4. What are the pros and cons if Sears decides to introduce ATMs in its department stores?
5. In a situation analysis of today's Sears, identify several opportunities and threats facing the firm.
6. In your view, how is Sears positioned (what is its image) compared to Wal-Mart—whose revenues are several times greater than Sears?
7. Comment on this remark by Arthur C. Martinez: "Encourage everyone to abandon old ways of doing things before they turn into a distraction and drag a performance."

PART TWO

SITUATION ANALYSIS

■ In Part Two, the organizational missions, ownership and management alternatives, goods/service categories, and objectives of a broad range of retail institutions are presented. By understanding the unique attributes of these institutions, prospective and ongoing retailers are better able to develop and adapt their own strategies.

■ Chapter 4 examines the characteristics of retail institutions on the basis of ownership type: independent, chain, franchise, leased, vertical marketing, and consumer cooperative. The methods used by manufacturers, wholesalers, and retailers to obtain control in a distribution channel are also discussed. An end-of-chapter appendix has added information on franchising.

■ Chapter 5 describes retail institutions in terms of their strategy mix. Three key concepts are introduced: the wheel of retailing, scrambled merchandising, and the retail life cycle. Strategic responses to the evolving marketplace are noted. Several strategy mixes are then studied, with food and general merchandise retailers reviewed separately.

■ Chapter 6 focuses on Web, nonstore retailing, and other forms of nontraditional retailing approaches. Direct marketing, direct selling, vending machines, the World Wide Web, video kiosks, and airport retailing are among the topics included. The explosion of Web-based retailing is featured.

CHAPTER 4

Retail Institutions by Ownership

CHAPTER OBJECTIVES

1. To show the ways in which retail institutions can be classified
2. To study retailers on the basis of ownership type and examine the characteristics of each
3. To explore the methods used by manufacturers, wholesalers, and retailers to exert influence in the distribution channel

Stephen Adams and his wife Taisa are co-owners of a Pet Valu franchise. Prior to his current position, he was the night shift manager at a steel-fabrication factory looking for a new career. According to Stephen, the acquisition of the Pet Valu franchise "was really an easy decision because the business was so compatible (with our personalities). We love pets and enjoy talking to pet owners. In the beginning, I was putting in 80 hours a week. Now I'm down to 60 hours and have five part-timers, mostly teenagers, helping me out. But the hard work doesn't bother me because I love the business and pet owners are easy and fun to deal with. We relate to them because we're pet owners, too. Our customers like dealing with people who share the same passion."

There are 82 Pet Valu stores in the United States and 400 worldwide. Pet Valu's vice-president of franchise development describes the firm's typical 3,000-square-foot stores as "neighborhood stores with superstore prices." The real draw "is that Pet Valu offers customized services, which you don't get in the large stores. The large stores can't offer personalized service. Every time you visit one of them, you have a different salesperson taking care of you." In contrast, the Adamses know every regular customer on a first-name basis.[1]

OVERVIEW

The term **retail institution** refers to the basic format or structure of a business. In the United States, about 2.3 million different firms are defined as retailers by the Bureau of the Census, and they operate more than 2.8 million establishments.

An institutional discussion shows the relative sizes and diversity of different kinds of retailing, enables firms to better understand and enact their own strategies, and indicates how various types of retailers are affected by the external environment. In particular, institutional analysis is important in these phases of strategic planning: selecting an organizational mission, choosing an ownership alternative, defining the goods/service category, and setting objectives.

In the next three chapters, retail institutions are viewed from these perspectives: ownership (Chapter 4); store-based retail strategy mix (Chapter 5); and nonstore-based, electronic, and nontraditional retailing (Chapter 6). Figure 4.1 shows a breakdown of each category. Classifications are not mutually exclusive; that is, an institution may be correctly placed in

---

Please Note: Web site addresses are constantly changing.
The links in this chapter are current as of the publication of this book.

Figure 4.1
A Classification
Method for Retail
Institutions

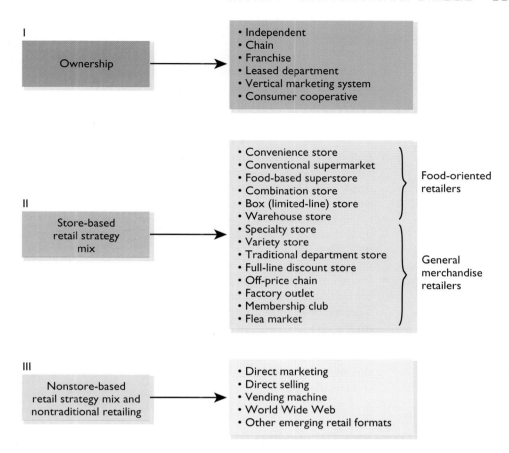

more than one category. For example, a department store unit may be part of a chain, have a store-based strategy, accept mail-order sales, and have a Web site.

Please interpret the data in Chapters 4 to 6 carefully. Because some institutional categories are not mutually exclusive, care should be taken in combining statistics to aggregate data so double counting does not occur. While data are as current as possible, not all information corresponds to a common date and the last U.S. government retailing census (as of this writing) is the *1997 Census of Retail Trade.*

RETAIL INSTITUTIONS CHARACTERIZED BY OWNERSHIP

Retail firms may be independently owned, chain-owned, franchisee-operated, leased departments, owned by manufacturers or wholesalers, or consumer-owned.

Although retailers are primarily small (80 percent of all stores are operated by firms with one outlet and over one-half of all firms have two or fewer paid employees), there are also very large retailers. In 1998, the five leading U.S. retailers totaled $275 billion in sales and employed 1.9 million people.

Opportunities in retail ownership abound. For example, according to the National Foundation for Women Business Owners (www.nfwbo.org), U.S. retail firms owned by women generate revenues of $525 billion annually and employ 5.4 million people. Sales of women-owned U.S. retail businesses have grown by 90 percent over the past decade, far faster than the overall growth rate of U.S. retailers.

From positioning and operating perspectives, each ownership format serves a marketplace niche and presents certain advantages and disadvantages. Retail executives must not lose sight of this in playing up their strengths and working around their weaknesses:

- Independent retailers should capitalize on their targeted customer base and do all they can to please shoppers in a friendly, folksy way. Word-of-mouth communication is important. These retailers should not try to serve too many customers or enter into price wars.
- Chain retailers should capitalize on their widely known image, make sure each store lives up to that image, and take advantage of economies of scale and mass promotion possibilities. They should not become too inflexible in adapting to the changes in the marketplace.
- Franchisors should capitalize on the vastness of their geographic coverage—made possible by franchisee investments—and the motivation of franchisees as owner-operators. They should not get bogged down in policy disputes with franchisees or charge excessive royalty fees.
- Leased departments should enable store operators and outside parties to join forces and offer an enhanced shopping experience, while sharing expertise and expenses. They should not hurt the image of the store or place too much pressure on the lessee to bring in store traffic.

Small Retailers Beware

Although the number of frauds committed against small retailers cannot be accurately estimated, there has been a rise in the amount of complaints to the Better Business Bureau. For example, complaints concerning promises of capital upon payment of a loan fee more than doubled over a recent six-year period. According to the head of the consumer law section of the California Attorney General's office, "There is less protection for small business owners than consumers."

Here's a brief summary of some popular scams directed at small retailers:

- "Be Your Own Boss"—These scams promise assistance in setting up a business. Typically, the schemes overstate possible earnings or list fictitious names of successful franchisees.

- "Paper Pirates"—These are firms that sell copier paper and other office supplies at inflated prices. Worse, some firms never deliver the paid-for supplies.
- "Banking on Deposit"—A small business owner receives a phony letter offering a share of money in a foreign bank as payment for a short-term loan.
- "Slam Dancing"—A business owner's long-distance carrier is switched without permission.
- "Capital for a Fee"—A business owner is asked to pay a fee in advance of receiving a large loan.

How can a small retailer avoid being ripped off?

Source: John R. Emshwiller, "Ripped Off!" *Wall Street Journal* (May 21, 1998), p. R29.

- A vertically integrated channel should give a firm greater control over sources of supply, but it should not provide the consumer with too little choice of products or too few outlets. The opposite is true for a nonintegrated channel.
- Cooperatives should provide members with significant price savings. They should not expect too much involvement on the part of members or add facilities that raise costs too much.

Independent

An **independent** retailer owns only one retail unit. In the United States, there are almost 2.2 million independents—accounting for nearly 40 percent of total retail store sales. One-half of independents are run entirely by the owners and/or their families; these firms generate just 3 percent of total U.S. store sales (averaging $65,000–$75,000 in annual revenues) and have no paid workers (there is no payroll).

The high number of independent retailers is associated with the **ease of entry** into the marketplace. Due to low capital requirements and no, or relatively simple, licensing provisions, entry for many kinds of small retail firms is easy. The investment per worker in retailing is usually much lower than for manufacturers. Retailer licensing, although somewhat more stringent in recent years, is still pretty routine. Each year, tens of thousands of new retail businesses, most independents, open in the United States. The ease of entry into retailing is reflected in the low market shares of the leading firms in many goods/service categories as a percentage of total category sales. For example, in the grocery store category—where large chains are quite strong, the five largest grocery retailers account for only about 22 percent of sales.[2]

Since a great deal of competition is due to the relative ease of entry into retailing, it is undoubtedly a big factor in the high rate of retail business failures among newer firms. The Small Business Administration estimates that one-third of new U. S. retailers do not survive their first year and two-thirds do not continue beyond their third year. Most of these failures involve independents. On an annual basis, about 15,000 retailers (of all sizes)—roughly 75 per 10,000 firms—file for bankruptcy protection, in addition to the thousands of small retailers that just close their doors.[3]

The U.S Small Business Administration has a Small Business Development Center (SBDC) Program to provide assistance for current and prospective small business owners (www.sba.gov/sbdc): "SBDCs supply a wide variety of information and guidance in central and easily accessible branch locations. The program is a cooperative effort of the private sector, the educational community, and federal, state, and local governments. It enhances economic development by giving small firms management and technical assistance. There are 57 SBDCs—one in every state (Texas has four), the District of Columbia, Guam, Puerto Rico, and the U.S. Virgin Islands—with a network of nearly 1,000 service locations. In each state, there is a lead organization which coordinates services through a network of subcenters and satellite sites in each state. Subcenters are at colleges, universities, community colleges, vocational schools, chambers of commerce, and economic development corporations." The SBA also has many free downloadable publications at its Web site. See Figure 4.2.

Competitive Advantages and Disadvantages of Independents Independent retailers have a variety of advantages and disadvantages. These are among their advantages:

- There is a great deal of flexibility in choosing retail formats and locations, and in devising strategy. Because only one store location is involved, detailed specifications can be set for the best location and a thorough search undertaken. Uniform location standards are not needed, as they are for chain stores, and independents do not have to worry about being too close to other company stores. In setting strategy, independents have great latitude in

The CCH Business Owner's Toolkit (toolkit.cch.com) is an excellent resource for the independent retailer.

Read the Stew Leonard's story—from a small dairy business to a retail powerhouse (www.stew leonards.com/stew_ leonards/funfact. html).

Figure 4.2
Useful Online
Publications for Small
Retailers

Go to *www.sba.
gov/library/pubs.html* and
download any of the
U.S. Small Business
Administration's publica-
tions at this Web site.
They're free!

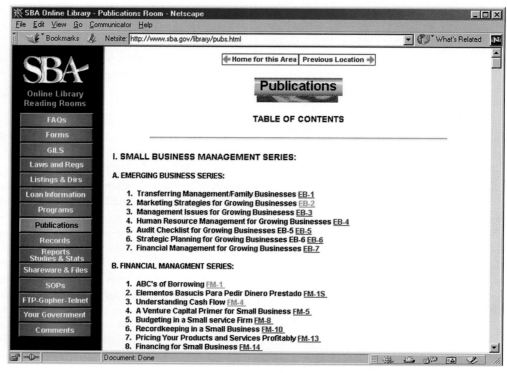

selecting target markets. Because many independents have modest goals, small customer segments may be selected rather than the mass market. Product assortments, prices, store hours, and other factors are then set consistent with the market.

- Inasmuch as independents run only one store, investment costs for leases, fixtures, workers, and merchandise can be held down. In addition, there is no duplication of stock or personnel functions. Responsibilities are clearly delineated within a store.

- Independents often act as specialists and acquire skills in a niche of a particular goods/service category. They are then more efficient and can lure shoppers interested in specialized retailers.

- Independents exert strong control over their strategies; and the owner-operator is typically on the premises. Decision making is usually centralized and layers of management personnel are minimized.

- There is a certain image attached to independents, particularly small ones, that chains find difficult to capture. This is the image of a personable retailer with a comfortable atmosphere in which to shop.

- Independents are able to sustain consistency in their efforts since only one geographic market is served and just one strategy is carried out. For example, there cannot be problems due to two branch stores selling identical items at different prices.

- Independents have "independence." Owner-operators tend to be in full charge and do not have to fret about stockholders, board-of-director meetings, and labor unrest. They are often free from union work and seniority rules. This can enhance labor productivity.

- Owner-operators usually have a strong entrepreneurial drive. They have personal investments in their businesses, success or failure has huge implications, and there is a lot of ego involvement.

These are some of the disadvantages of independent retailing:

- In bargaining with suppliers, independents may not have much power because they often buy in small quantities. They may even be bypassed by suppliers or limited in the products made available to them. Reordering may also be tough if minimum order requirements are too high for them to qualify. To overcome this problem, a number of independents, such as hardware stores, have formed buying groups to increase their power in dealing with suppliers.
- Independents typically cannot gain economies of scale (low per-unit costs due to handling many units at one time) in buying and maintaining inventory. Due to financial constraints, small assortments are bought several times per year rather than large orders once or twice per year. Thus, transportation, ordering, and handling costs per unit are high.
- Operations are often very labor intensive, sometimes with little computerization. Ordering, taking inventory, marking items, ringing up sales, and bookkeeping may be done manually. This is less efficient than computerization (expensive for some small firms in terms of the initial investment in hardware and software—although costs have fallen significantly). In many cases, owner-operators are unwilling or unable to spend time learning how to set up and apply computerized procedures.
- By virtue of the relatively high costs of TV ads and the large geographic coverage of magazines and some newspapers (too large for firms with one outlet), independents are limited in their access to advertising media and may pay higher fees per ad compared to regular users. Yet, there are various promotion tools available for creative independents (see Chapter 19).
- A crucial problem for family-run independents is an overdependence on the owner. Often, all decisions are made by this person, and there is no continuity of management when the owner-boss is ill, on vacation, or retires. The leading worries at family-run firms involve identifying successors, the role of nonfamily workers, and management training for family members. Long-run success and employee morale can be affected by overdependence on the owner.
- There is a limited amount of time and resources allotted to long-run planning. Since the owner is intimately involved in daily operations of the firm, responsiveness to new legislation, new products, and new competitors frequently suffers.

Chain

There are 7,000 Radio Shack (www. radioshack.com) stores in the United States. See if there is one near you.

A **chain** retailer operates multiple outlets (store units) under common ownership; it usually engages in some level of centralized (or coordinated) purchasing and decision making. In the United States, there are roughly 90,000 retail chains that operate about 650,000 establishments.

The relative strength of chains is great, and their popularity is rising, even though the number of retail chains is small (4 percent of all U.S. retail firms). Chains today operate almost one-quarter of retail establishments; and because stores in chains tend to be considerably larger than those run by independents, chains account for more than 60 percent of total store sales and employment.

While the majority of chains have 5 or fewer outlets, the several hundred firms with 100 or more outlets account for well over one-third of U.S. retail sales. Forty or so U.S. retailers have at least 1,000 outlets each (not including franchises like McDonald's). There are also many large foreign chains. See Figure 4.3.

The dominance of chains varies greatly by type of retailer. Retailers operating multiple outlets generate 75 percent or more of total category sales for department stores, discount department stores, and grocery stores. On the other hand, stationery, beauty salon, furniture, and liquor store retailers with multiple outlets produce far less than 50 percent of total retail sales in their categories.

Figure 4.3

Carrefour: The Largest Non-U.S.-Based Retailer in the World

After its recent merger with Promodès, France's Carrefour now operates 9,000 stores in 26 countries (including Europe, the Americas, and Asia), employing 240,000 people. The stores include 680 huge hypermarkets and 3,200 other discount stores.
Reprinted by pemission of PricewaterhouseCoopers LLP.

Competitive Advantages and Disadvantages of Chains There are abundant competitive advantages for chain retailers:

Sears' Craftsman brand is so powerful, that it sells 3,500 different Craftsman tools online (www.sears.com.craftsman).

- Many chains have bargaining power with suppliers due to their volume of purchases. These chains receive new items as soon as they are introduced, have reorders promptly filled, get proper service and selling support from suppliers, and obtain the best prices. Large chains may also gain exclusive rights to selling certain items and may have suppliers make goods under their own brands. Sears has manufacturers produce appliances with its Kenmore name and tools with its Craftsman name.

Fostering an Entrepreneurial Spirit at Starbucks

Howard Schultz, the chief executive officer and the chairman of Starbucks Coffee, is a strong believer in the old cliché, "You never get a second chance to make a good first impression." So, as part of his responsibilities, he tells all new employees that he is delighted to welcome them to Starbucks. Since Starbucks hires about 500 employees per month, Schultz welcomes them with a video message. Even part-time employees (called "partners") are repeatedly informed of how much they are valued during the 24 hours of training they must successfully complete during their first 80 hours of employment.

Schultz's concern about training and treating employees well dates from his own first experiences in 1982 as a Starbucks employee, when Starbucks was a small firm. According to Schultz, "What struck me most is how much people cared. It was the passion everyone had about coffee that tied us together." He left Starbucks in 1985 to create his own coffee firm. In 1987, Howard Schultz bought the Starbucks chain.

Difficult though it may be, Schultz tries to keep a uniform culture among Starbucks' 26,000-person staff. Looking for evidence of his success in nurturing worker morale? Starbucks' employee turnover rate is about one-third that of other specialty coffee retailers.

Source: Stephanie Gruner, "Lasting Impressions," *Inc.* (July 1998), p. 126.

- Chains can achieve cost efficiencies by doing wholesaling functions themselves. Buying directly from manufacturers and in large volume, shipping and storing goods, and attending trade shows sponsored by suppliers to learn about new offerings are just some wholesaling activities that can be fulfilled by chains. Thus, they can sometimes bypass wholesalers, with the result being lower supplier prices.

- Efficiency in multiple-store operations can be gained via shared warehousing facilities; large purchases of standardized store fixtures, employee uniforms, and so on; centralized purchasing and decision making; and other factors. Chains typically give headquarters executives broad authority for overall personnel policies—as well as for buying, pricing, and advertising decisions.

- Chains, because of their resources, can use computers in ordering merchandise, taking inventory, forecasting, ringing up sales, and bookkeeping. This increases efficiency and reduces overall costs.

- Chains, particularly national or regional ones, can take advantage of a variety of media, from TV to magazines to traditional newspapers. Large revenues and geographic coverage of the market allow chains to utilize all forms of media.

- Most chains have defined management philosophies. There tend to be detailed strategies, and employee responsibilities are clear. Continuity is usually ensured when managerial personnel are absent or retire because there are qualified people to fill in and succession plans in place. See Figure 4.4.

Figure 4.4
MasterCuts: A Well-Defined Management Philosophy

MasterCuts Family Haircutters is a provider of value-priced haircuts within the shopping mall environment. Professionally trained stylists are available on a walk-in basis to serve price-sensitive families looking for fast and convenient quality haircutting services. There is a strong emphasis on staff training, field management, and the presentation of retail products. Artistic training is very important to the success of MasterCuts. Stylists are encouraged to keep abreast of new trends, techniques, and professional hair care products through regularly scheduled workshops. "We are working to deliver great value and consistently good customer service."
Reprinted by permission of Regis Corporation.

- Many chains expend considerable time and resources in long-run planning. Frequently, specific staff are assigned to planning on a permanent basis. Opportunities and threats are carefully monitored.

Chain retailers do have a number of disadvantages:

- Once chains are established, their flexibility may be limited. Additional nonoverlapping store locations may be hard to find. Consistent strategies must be maintained throughout all branches—prices, promotions, and product assortments must be similar for each store. For chains that use centralized decision making, there may be difficulty in adapting to local needs, such as taking into account differences in life-styles among city, suburban, and rural customers.
- Investments may be high. There are multiple leases, fixtures, product assortments, and employees. The purchase of merchandise may be costly because a number of store branches must be stocked.
- Managerial control can be hard, especially for chains with geographically dispersed branches. Top management cannot maintain the control over each branch that independents have over their single outlets. Lack of communication and time delays in making and enacting decisions are particular problems.
- Personnel in large chains may have limited independence in their jobs. In many cases, there are several management layers, unionized employees, stockholders, and boards of directors. Some chains empower their personnel to give them more independence and better address special customer needs when they arise. As the director of the SBDC at the University of Memphis said: "The key similarity between children and chains is this. The more you have—children or stores—the less attention you have for each one, so you have to empower them more and trust them more. They won't turn out to have the same personality, but if you raise them right, they'll each do you proud in their own way."[4]

Franchising

Franchising involves a contractual arrangement between a *franchisor* (which may be a manufacturer, a wholesaler, or a service sponsor) and a retail *franchisee,* which allows the franchisee to conduct a given form of business under an established name and according to a given pattern of business. In a typical arrangement, the franchisee pays an initial fee and a monthly percentage of gross sales in exchange for the exclusive rights to sell goods and services in a specified area. Franchising is a retail organizational form in which small businesses can benefit by being part of a large, multiunit chain-type retail institution. See Figure 4.5.

There are two types of franchising: product/trademark and business format. In **product/trademark franchising,** franchisees acquire the identities of franchisors by agreeing to sell the latter's products and/or operate under the latter's names. Franchisees operate rather autonomously from their franchisors. Although they must adhere to certain operating rules, they set store hours, choose locations, determine store facilities and displays, and otherwise run the business. Product/trademark franchising represents two-thirds of retail franchising sales. Examples are auto dealers and many gasoline service stations.

With **business format franchising,** there is a more interactive relationship between franchisors and franchisees. The franchisees receive assistance on site location, quality control, accounting systems, startup practices, management training, and responding to problems—besides the right to sell goods and services. The use of prototype stores, standardized product lines, and cooperative advertising let these franchises achieve a level of coordination previously found only in chains. In recent decades, most growth in franchising has involved business format arrangements—which are common for restaurants and other food outlets, real estate, and service retailing. Due to the small size of many franchisees, business format fran-

Figure 4.5
Franchising the
AmeriHost Way

There are about 100
AmeriHost Inn Hotels
in 16 states, which gen-
erate more than $65
million in annual room
revenues.
Reprinted by permission of
AmeriHost Properties, Inc.

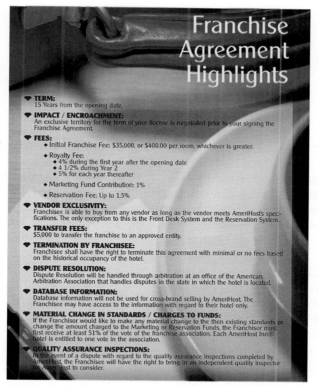

Franchise Agreement Highlights

TERM:
15 Years from the opening date.

IMPACT / ENCROACHMENT:
An exclusive territory for the term of your license is negotiated prior to your signing the Franchise Agreement.

FEES:
- Initial Franchise Fee: $35,000, or $400.00 per room, whichever is greater.
- Royalty Fee:
  - 4% during the first year after the opening date
  - 4 1/2% during Year 2
  - 5% for each year thereafter
- Marketing Fund Contribution: 1%
- Reservation Fee: Up to 1.5%

VENDOR EXCLUSIVITY:
Franchisee is able to buy from any vendor as long as the vendor meets AmeriHost's speci-fications. The only exception to this is the Front Desk System and the Reservation System.

TRANSFER FEES:
$5,000 to transfer the franchise to an approved entity.

TERMINATION BY FRANCHISEE:
Franchisee shall have the right to terminate this agreement with minimal or no fees based on the historical occupancy of the hotel.

DISPUTE RESOLUTION:
Dispute Resolution will be handled through arbitration at an office of the American Arbitration Association that handles disputes in the state in which the hotel is located.

DATABASE INFORMATION:
Database information will not be used for cross-brand selling by AmeriHost. The Franchisee may have access to the information with regard to their hotel only.

MATERIAL CHANGE IN STANDARDS / CHARGES TO FUNDS:
If the Franchisor would like to make any material change to the then existing standards or change the amount charged to the Marketing or Reservation Funds, the Franchisor must first receive at least 51% of the vote of the franchise association. Each AmeriHost Inn® hotel is entitled to one vote in the association.

QUALITY ASSURANCE INSPECTIONS:
In the event of a dispute with regard to the quality assurance inspections completed by AmeriHost, the Franchisee will have the right to bring in an independent quality inspector for AmeriHost to consider.

chising accounts for more than 75 percent of outlets (though just one-third of total sales).

Though variations in franchising exist, McDonald's (www.mcdonalds.com/corporate/franchise) is a good example of a business format franchise arrangement. The firm provides

Technology in Retailing — Churchs Reaches Out and Touches Its Franchisees

Churchs is a 1,350-unit fast-food res-taurant chain—mostly operated by franchisees—featuring chicken. Recently, the firm realized that it had to overhaul communications between its headquarters staff and franchisees. Many new franchisees had questions on construction, equipment needs, and staffing. In addi-tion, existing franchisees had questions on financing, marketing programs, and vendor agreements.

Churchs' Chicken Business Support Center was created as the single point of contact with fran-chisees. The center handles phone, E-mail, and Intranet communication. The system involves three forms of specialists: the opening consultant, the busi-ness consultant, and the field consultant. The opening consultant deals with correspondence on new restaurant locations. The business consultant handles financial issues. The field consultant provides advice relating to onsite openings and operations support.

Besides these specialists, the center houses oper-ating manuals, architectural drawings, and marketing promotions that are available to franchisees 24 hours a day. Another key feature of the center is a software package that provides advice on developing a business plan. At the end of the first year of opera-tion, each franchisee is expected to have completed a business plan using this software and the advice of Churchs' business consultants.

What are the pros and cons for franchisees in using this center rather than a traditional phone-based franchisee support staff? For Churchs?

Source: Michael Hartnett, "Churchs Reaches Out to Franchisees with Advanced Support Center," *Stores* (October 1998), pp. 94, 98.

each new franchisee with intensive training at "Hamburger U," a detailed operating manual (complete down to the most minute facets of running machinery), regular visits by service managers, and repeat trips to Hamburger U for brush-up training. In return for a 20-year franchising agreement with McDonald's, a conventional franchisee has an initial cash investment of $150,000 and pays ongoing royalty fees totaling at least 12.5 percent of gross sales directly to McDonald's.

Size and Structural Arrangements Retail franchising began in the United States in 1851, when Singer Sewing Machine first franchised dealers. It did not become popular until the early 1900s, as underfinanced auto makers started using franchising to expand their distribution. Although auto and truck dealers still provide more than one-half of all U.S. retail franchise sales, few retail sectors have not been affected by franchising's growth. In the United States, there are now 2,500 retail franchisors doing business with 250,000 franchisees. They operate 600,000 franchisee- and franchisor-owned U.S. outlets, employ several million people, and generate over one-third of total store sales. In addition, hundreds of U.S.-based franchisors currently have foreign operations, with tens of thousands of outlets.

About 85 percent of U.S. franchising sales and franchised outlets involve franchisee-owned units; the rest are from franchisor-owned outlets. If franchisees operate only one outlet, they are classified as independents by the U.S. Department of Commerce; franchisees that operate two or more outlets and franchisor-owned stores are classed as chains. Today, a large number of franchisees operate as chains.

Three structural arrangements dominate retail franchising. Figure 4.6 presents examples of each:

- Manufacturer-retailer—A manufacturer gives independent franchisees the right to sell goods and related services (subject to conditions) through a licensing agreement.
- Wholesaler-retailer
  a. Voluntary—A wholesaler sets up a franchise system and grants franchises to individual retailers.
  b. Cooperative—A group of retailers sets up a franchise system and shares the ownership and operations of a wholesaling organization.
- Service sponsor-retailer—A service firm licenses individual retailers to let them offer specific service packages to consumers.

Want to learn more about what it takes to be a franchisee? Check out the Carvel Web site (carvel.com/franchise_faq.asp).

Competitive Advantages and Disadvantages of Franchising Franchisees receive several benefits by investing in successful franchise operations:

- Individual franchisees can own retail enterprises with relatively small capital investments.
- Franchisees acquire well-known names and goods/service lines.
- Standard operating procedures and management skills may be taught to the franchisees.
- Cooperative marketing (e.g., national advertising) is often used that could not otherwise be afforded.
- Franchisees obtain exclusive selling rights for specified geographical territories.
- Franchisee purchases may be less costly per unit due to the volume bought by the overall franchise.

Some potential problems do exist for franchisees:

- Oversaturation could occur if too many franchisees are in one geographic area; the sales and profits of each unit would then be adversely affected.
- Due to overzealous selling by some franchisors, the income potential and required managerial ability, initiative, and investment of franchised units may be incorrectly stated.
- Franchisees may be locked into contract provisions whereby purchases must be made through franchisors or certain approved vendors.

Figure 4.6
Structural
Arrangements in
Retail Franchising

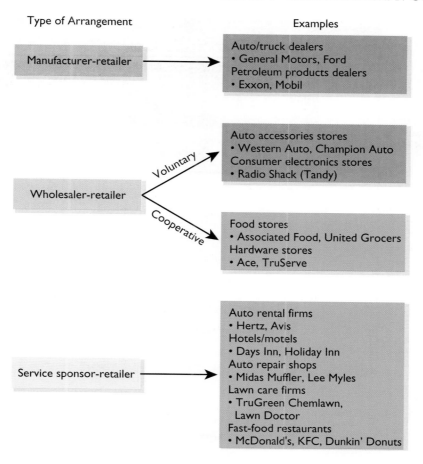

Type of Arrangement

Manufacturer-retailer

Wholesaler-retailer
— Voluntary
— Cooperative

Service sponsor-retailer

Examples

Auto/truck dealers
• General Motors, Ford
Petroleum products dealers
• Exxon, Mobil

Auto accessories stores
• Western Auto, Champion Auto
Consumer electronics stores
• Radio Shack (Tandy)

Food stores
• Associated Food, United Grocers
Hardware stores
• Ace, TruServe

Auto rental firms
• Hertz, Avis
Hotels/motels
• Days Inn, Holiday Inn
Auto repair shops
• Midas Muffler, Lee Myles
Lawn care firms
• TruGreen Chemlawn,
  Lawn Doctor
Fast-food restaurants
• McDonald's, KFC, Dunkin' Donuts

- Cancellation clauses may give franchisors the right to void individual franchises if provisions of franchise agreements are not met.
- In some industries, franchise agreements are of short duration.
- Under most contracts, royalties are a percentage of gross sales, regardless of franchisee profits.

The preceding factors contribute to **constrained decision making,** whereby franchisors can exclude franchisees from or limit their involvement in the strategic planning process.

To curb unfair franchisor sales practices, the Federal Trade Commission (FTC) has a disclosure requirements and business opportunities rule. It applies to all U.S. franchisors and is intended to provide adequate information to potential franchisees prior to making investments. Though the FTC does not regularly review disclosure statements, several states do check them and may require corrections. Also, a number of states have fair practice laws that do not allow franchisors to terminate, cancel, or fail to renew franchisees without just cause. Arizona, California, Indiana, New Jersey, Virginia, Washington, and Wisconsin are among the states with fair practice laws. The FTC has an excellent Web site on franchising (www.ftc.gov/bcp/franchise/netfran.htm) as highlighted in Figure 4.7.

Franchisors accrue lots of benefits by having franchise arrangements:

- A national or global presence can be developed quickly and with less franchisor investment.
- Franchisee qualifications for ownership can be set and enforced.

Figure 4.7
Franchises and Business Opportunities

At the FTC's franchising site, *www.ftc.gov/bcp/ franchise*, there are many free downloads about opportunities—and warnings, as well.

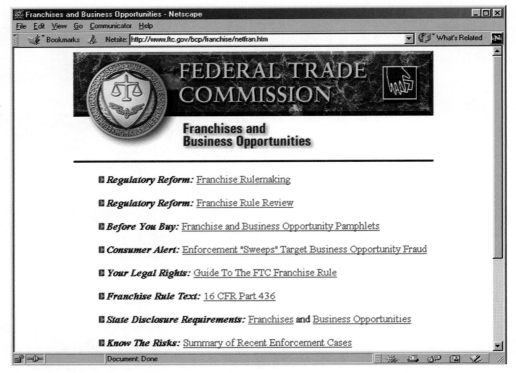

- Money is obtained when goods are delivered rather than when they are sold.
- Agreements can be drawn up requiring franchisees to abide by stringent rules set by franchisors.
- Because franchisees are owners and not employees, they have a greater incentive to work hard.
- After franchisees have paid for their franchised outlets, franchisors still receive royalties and may sell products to the individual proprietors.

Franchisors also face potential problems:

- Franchisees could harm a firm's overall reputation if they do not adhere to company standards.
- A lack of uniformity among outlets could adversely affect customer loyalty.
- Intrafranchise competition is not desirable.
- The resale value of individual units is injured if franchisees perform poorly.
- Ineffective franchised units directly injure their franchisors' profitability from selling services, materials, or products to the franchisees and from royalty fees.
- Franchisees, in greater numbers, are seeking independence from franchisor rules and regulations.

Additional information on franchising is contained in the appendix at the end of this chapter.

Leased Department

A **leased department** is a department in a retail store—usually a department, discount, or specialty store—that is rented to an outside party. The proprietor of a leased department is usually responsible for all aspects of its business (including fixtures) and normally pays the store a percentage of sales as rent. The store has operating restrictions for the leased department to ensure overall consistency and coordination.

In most situations, leased departments are used by existing store-based retailers to broaden their merchandise or service offerings into product categories requiring highly specialized skills or knowledge not possessed by the retailers themselves. Thus, leased departments often operate in categories that are on the fringe of the store's major product lines. They are most common for in-store beauty salons, banks, photographic studios, and shoe, jewelry, cosmetics, watch repair, and shoe repair departments. Leased departments are also gaining popularity in shopping center food courts They account for $15 billion in annual department store sales. Unfortunately, data on overall leased department sales are not available.

Meldisco Corporation (www.footstar.com) is a leading operator of leased departments. It runs leased shoe departments in more than 2,500 stores and has annual sales of $1.8 billion. Many of its leased departments are at Kmart stores nationally and in Rite Aid Drug Stores on the West coast. In these departments, Meldisco owns the inventory and display fixtures, staffs and merchandises the departments, and pays fees for the space occupied. The stores where Meldisco has its leased departments cover the costs of utilities, maintenance, advertising, and checkout services.

Competitive Advantages and Disadvantages of Leased Departments
From the stores' perspective, having leased departments has a number of benefits:

- Store personnel might lack the merchandising ability to handle and sell certain goods and services.
- The market can be enlarged by providing one-stop customer shopping.
- Leased department operators pay for inventory and personnel expenses, thus reducing store costs.
- Personnel management, merchandise displays, the reordering of items, and so on are undertaken by the lessees.
- A percentage of revenues is received regularly.

There are also some potential pitfalls, from the stores' perspective:

- Leased departments may use operating procedures that conflict with those of the stores.
- Lessees may adversely affect stores' images.
- Customers may blame problems on the stores rather than on the lessees.

For leased department operators, there are these advantages:

- Existing stores are usually well known, have a large number of steady customers, and generate immediate sales for leased departments.
- Some costs are reduced through shared facilities, such as security equipment and display windows.
- There are economics of scale (volume savings) through pooled ads. Lessees' images are aided by their relationships with popular stores.

Lessees face these possible problems:

- There may be inflexibility as to the hours they must be open and the operating style they must utilize.
- The goods/service lines they are allowed to offer will usually be restricted.
- If lessees are successful, the stores may raise the rent or may not renew leases when they expire.
- The in-store locations may not generate the sales expected.

A leased department may be viewed from two perspectives: as an element in a shopping center and as a part of a franchise system. In the shopping center context, a leased department operator is renting an area with a given traffic flow to conduct its business. The lessee must examine the character of the traffic flow and its relationship to the chosen target market; the lessor must examine the extent to which the leased department will either create added traffic or be a parasite and live off the traffic generated by other parts of the store. The franchise analogy relates to a leased department's ability to blend with the merchandise philosophy of another retailer and the need to set a broad policy for all departments, so an entire store's image is not injured by one operator.

An example of a thriving long-term lease arrangement is one shared by CPI Corporation and Sears. For over 40 years, CPI (www.cpicorp.com) has had photo studios in Sears stores. In exchange for the use of space in more than 900 U.S. and Canadian Sears stores, CPI pays Sears 15 percent of its gross sales. CPI's annual sales per square foot are much higher than Sears' overall average. CPI has a five-year licensing agreement with Sears, that has been renewed several times. Its yearly revenues via leased departments in Sears outlets exceed $300 million—amounting to 84 percent of CPI's total revenues.

Vertical Marketing System

A **vertical marketing system** consists of all the levels of independently owned businesses along a channel of distribution. Goods and services are normally distributed through one of these types of vertical marketing systems: independent, partially integrated, and fully integrated. See Figure 4.8.

Figure 4.8
Vertical Marketing Systems: Functions and Ownership

Type of Channel	Channel Functions	Ownership
I • Independent systems	Manufacturing ↓ Wholesaling ↓ Retailing	Independent manufacturer / Independent wholesaler / Independent retailer
II • Partially integrated systems	Manufacturing ↓ Wholesaling ↓ Retailing	Two channel members own all facilities and perform all functions.
III • Fully integrated systems	Manufacturing ↓ Wholesaling ↓ Retailing	All production and distribution functions are performed by one channel member.

In an independent vertical marketing system, there are three levels of independently owned firms: manufacturers, wholesalers, and retailers. Such a system is most often used if manufacturers or retailers are small, intensive distribution is sought, customers are widely dispersed, unit sales are high, company resources are low, channel members want to share costs and risks, and task specialization is desirable. Independent vertical marketing systems are used by many stationery stores, gift shops, hardware stores, food stores, drugstores, and many other firms. They are the leading form of vertical marketing system.

With a partially integrated vertical marketing system, two independently owned businesses along a channel perform all production and distribution functions without the aid of the third. The most common form of this system is when a manufacturer and a retailer complete transactions and shipping, storing, and other distribution functions in the absence of an independently owned wholesaler. A partially integrated system is most apt if manufacturers and retailers are large, selective or exclusive distribution is sought, unit sales are moderate, company resources are high, greater channel control is desired, and existing wholesalers are too expensive or unavailable. Partially integrated systems are often used by furniture stores, appliance stores, restaurants, computer retailers, and mail-order firms.

Kroger, the food retailer, manufactures 5,000 food and non-food products in over 25 plants (www. kroger.com/ manufacturing/ manufacturing.htm).

Through a fully integrated vertical marketing system, a single company performs all production and distribution functions without the aid of any other firms. In the past, this system was usually employed only by manufacturers, such as Avon, Goodyear, Sherwin-Williams, and major gasoline refiners. At Sherwin-Williams, the paint manufacturer, its 2,250 company-owned stores account for 57 percent of the firm's sales.[5] Today, more retailers have fully integrated systems for at least some products. For example, Kroger (the food retailer) produces dairy items, baked goods, ice cream, and other items; and Sears has ownership shares in an appliance maker, a paint and detergent maker, an apparel maker, and others.

A fully integrated vertical marketing system lets a firm have total control over its strategy, have direct contact with final consumers, have higher retail markups without raising prices (by eliminating channel members), be self-sufficient and not rely on others, have exclusivity over goods and services offered, and keep all profits within the company. By making many of

Bodying in for the Long Haul

When Patrick Gournay, Body Shop International's chief executive officer, joined the firm in 1998, he instituted a number of strategies to improve the firm's bottom line. As part of the firm's reorganization, the company formed a joint management venture in the United States with Adrian Bellamy. Under Bellamy's direction, Body Shop's central U.S. office was reorganized, a product and marketing team was formed, the company repurchased 28 stores from franchisees, and it closed 11 underperforming units. In addition, three warehouses were closed, inventory levels were reduced by more than 30 percent, and the firm's U.S. bottle-filling factory was transferred to a third party.

Central to Body Shop's strategy was the desire to increase the number of company-owned stores and decrease the number of franchisees. Gournay said, "If we do a better job than any of our current franchisees, we should be planning to buy them back." In addition, Body Shop realized that it lacked focus. "We tried too many jobs at once—manufacturing, distributing, and retailing. So a decision was made: We decided to become a brand retailer, not a manufacturer. We'll still develop products, but we're outsourcing a lot of manufacturing."

Evaluate Body Shop's decision to change its vertical marketing system.

Source: Julie Naughton, "Body Shop Digs In," *Women's Wear Daily* (June 18, 1999), p. 10.

the products sold in its stores, Ben & Jerry's (the ice cream firm) maximizes product visibility, trains and supervises store personnel, has exclusivity over brands, and controls retail ads and prices. However, there may be some difficulties with a fully integrated system, including high investment costs and a lack of expertise in both manufacturing and retailing.

Some firms (including many cited in this section) use a **dual vertical marketing system,** whereby they are involved in more than one type of distribution arrangement. Thus, Sherwin-Williams has a fully integrated system for its Sherwin-Williams' paints and sells them only at company-owned stores. Sherwin-Williams also sells its Dutch Boy paints in home improvement stores, full-line discount stores, hardware stores, and others via an independent vertical marketing system (which includes wholesalers). This means Sherwin-Williams can appeal to different consumers, increase revenues, share some of its costs, and maintain a good degree of control over its strategy. See Figure 4.9.

Besides partially or fully integrating a vertical marketing system, a firm can exert power in a distribution channel because of its economic, legal, or political strength; superior knowledge and abilities; customer loyalty; or other factors. **Channel control** occurs when one member of a distribution channel can dominate the decisions made in that channel by the power it possesses. Manufacturers, wholesalers, and retailers each have a combination of tools to improve their positions relative to one another.

Manufacturers can exert control by franchising, whereby marketing programs are closely scrutinized; developing strong brand loyalty, wherein retailers must stock items due to demand; pre-ticketing items, thereby designating suggested list or selling prices; and exclusive distribution, with retailers voluntarily agreeing to adhere to given standards in exchange for sole distribution rights in given geographic areas.

Wholesalers have the ability to exert influence over manufacturers and retailers in these situations. If wholesalers are large, their businesses are important and they can put pressure on suppliers and buyers. They can introduce their own private brands and circumvent manufacturers. A franchise system and/or brand loyalty can be developed to control the distribution system. Wholesalers can become the most efficient members in the channel for the functions they perform, such as shipping and processing reorders.

Retailers can exert clout with other channel members in these instances:

Figure 4.9
Sherwin-Williams'
Dual Vertical
Marketing System

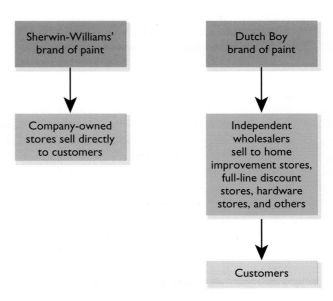

- When one retailer represents a large percentage of a supplier's sales volume, channel control may be applied. For example, there are a number of independent firms from which Sears purchases a large proportion of their output. One such firm is Whirlpool, the maker of major appliances, which produces Sears' Kenmore brand of appliances. As a result, Sears has a strong bargaining position.
- Private brands can enable retailers to have channel control, improve competitive positioning, and raise profit margins. For instance, over one-half of apparel bought by national chains and one-fifth of apparel bought by specialty retailers involve private brands. In a typical supermarket, private brands (including "no-name" generics) account for up to 20 percent of purchases. At Sainsbury, a British supermarket chain, two-thirds of the products it buys are private brands. With private brands, retailers can obtain brand loyalty for their own products, convert brand loyalty to store loyalty, and require that items be made to specifications. Private brands let retailers switch vendors with no impact on customer loyalty, as long as the same product features are included. Just the threat of switching vendors is often enough to get a supplier in line on a retailer's price, delivery, or terms request.

Clearly established channel roles often have benefits for all parties. Long-term relationships allow for scheduling efficiencies and let retailers receive supplier financing and vendors obtain bank loans (due to pre-sold inventories). Some economies result because activities are eliminated, simplified, or shared. Advertising, financing, and billing are dramatically simplified, and many tasks, such as merchandise marking, can be performed by the manufacturer.

Consumer Cooperative

As an REI member (www.rei.com/YOUR_COOP/joinrei.html), look at what $15 will get you!

A **consumer cooperative** is a retail firm owned by its customer members. In a cooperative arrangement, a group of consumers invests in the company, elects officers, manages operations, and shares the profits or savings that accrue. In the United States, there are several thousand consumer cooperatives, ranging from small buying clubs to Recreational Equipment Inc. (REI), with $600 million in annual sales. Consumer cooperatives have been most popular in food retailing. However, the 500 or so U.S. food cooperatives account for only a fraction of 1 percent of total retail store sales (and less than 1 percent of total grocery sales).

Consumer cooperatives exist for these basic reasons: Some consumers feel they can operate stores as well as or better than traditional retailers. They believe existing retailers are inadequately fulfilling customer needs for healthful, environmentally safe products. They also assume existing retailers often make excessive profits and that they can sell merchandise for lower prices.

This is how REI operates: It sells outdoor recreational equipment, such as backpacks and bicycles, to 1.6 million active members. It has 6,000 employees in 55 stores, runs a mail-order business, and has a Web site (www.rei.com). Unlike other cooperatives, REI is operated by a professional staff that adheres to the policies set by the member-elected board. There is a $15 one-time membership fee, which entitles customers to shop at REI, elect people to the board of directors, and share in profits (based on the amount spent by each member). REI's goal is to distribute a 10 percent dividend to members.

Cooperatives have not grown beyond their current level because they involve a lot of consumer initiative and drive; consumers are usually not expert in buying, handling, and selling goods and services; cost savings and low selling prices have not been as expected in many cases; and consumer boredom in running or working for the cooperatives frequently sets in. Traditional retailers are also now doing a better a job of appealing to consumer niches in categories such as grocery products.

SUMMARY

1. *To show the ways in which retail institutions can be classified.* There are 2.3 million retail firms in the United States operating 2.8 million establishments. They can be classified on the basis of ownership, store-based strategy mix, and nonstore-based, electronic, and nontraditional retailing. These categories are not mutually exclusive; many retailers can be placed in more than one category. This chapter deals with retail ownership. Chapters 5 and 6 report on the other classifications.

2. *To study retailers on the basis of ownership type and examine the characteristics of each.* Eighty percent of U.S. retail establishments are independents, each operating only one store. This number is mostly due to the ease of entry. Among independents' competitive advantages are their flexibility, low investments, specialized offerings, direct strategy control, image, consistency, independence, and entrepreneurial spirit. Disadvantages include limited bargaining power, few economies of scale, labor intensity, reduced media access, overdependence on the owner, and limited planning.

Chains are multiple stores under common ownership, usually with some centralized purchasing and decision making. They account for nearly a quarter of retail outlets, but over 60 percent of U.S. retail sales. Chains have these advantages: bargaining power, wholesale function efficiencies, multiple-store efficiencies, computerization, media access, well-defined management, and long-range planning. They face these potential problems: inflexibility, high investments, reduced control, and limited independence of personnel.

Franchising embodies contractual arrangements between franchisors (manufacturers, wholesalers, or service sponsors) and franchisees that let the latter conduct given businesses under established names and according to specified rules. It accounts for over one-third of U.S. store sales. Franchisees have these benefits: small investments, well-known company names, standardized operations and training, cooperative marketing efforts, exclusive selling rights, and volume purchases. They may face constrained decision making due to oversaturation, lower than promised profits, strict contract provisions, cancellation clauses, short-term contracts, and continuing royalty fees. Franchisors benefit by more quickly and cheaply expanding their businesses, setting franchisee qualifications, improving cash flow, outlining operating procedures, gaining high

franchisee motivation, and receiving ongoing royalties. They may suffer if franchisees hurt the company image, do not operate uniformly, compete with one another, lower resale values and franchisor profits, and seek greater independence.

Leased departments are in-store locations rented to outside parties. They usually exist in categories on the fringe of their stores' major product lines. Stores gain these advantages: expertise of lessees, greater traffic, reduced costs, merchandising support, and revenues. Potential disadvantages are conflicts with lessees and adverse effects on store image. Benefits for lessees are well-known store names, steady customers, immediate revenues, reduced expenses, economies of scale, and an image associated with the store. Potential problems are inflexibility, restrictions on items sold, lease nonrenewal, and poorer results than expected.

Vertical marketing systems consist of all the levels of independently owned firms along a channel of distribution. Independent systems have separately owned manufacturers, wholesalers, and retailers. In partially integrated systems, two separately owned firms, usually manufacturers and retailers, perform all production and distribution functions without the aid of a third. With fully integrated systems, single firms do all production and distribution functions. Some firms use dual vertical marketing systems, whereby they are involved in more than one type of system.

Consumer cooperatives are retail firms owned by their customers, who invest, elect officers, manage operations, and share savings or profits. They account for a tiny piece of retail sales. Cooperatives are formed if consumers think they can do retailing functions, offerings of traditional retailers are inadequate, and prices are high. They have not grown because consumer initiative is required, expertise may be lacking, expectations have frequently not been met, and boredom occurs.

3. *To explore the methods used by manufacturers, wholesalers, and retailers to exert influence in the distribution channel.* Even without an integrated vertical marketing system, channel control can be exerted by the most powerful firm(s) in a channel. Manufacturers, wholesalers, and retailers each have ways to increase their impact in a channel. Retailers' influence is greatest when they are a large part of their vendors' sales, private brands are used, and economic power due to order volume exists.

Key Terms

retail institution (p. 114)
independent (p. 117)
ease of entry (p. 117)
chain (p. 119)
franchising (p. 122)

product/trademark franchising
   (p. 122)
business format franchising (p. 122)
constrained decision making (p. 125)
leased department (p. 126)

vertical marketing system (p. 128)
dual vertical marketing system
   (p. 130)
channel control (p. 130)
consumer cooperative (p. 131)

Questions for Discussion

1. What are the characteristics of each of the owner-ship forms discussed in this chapter?

2. How may a retailer be categorized by more than one ownership form? Give two examples.

3. Why does the concept of ease of entry usually have a greater impact on independent retailers than on chain retailers?

4. How can an independent retailer overcome the problem of overdependence on the owner?

5. What difficulties might an independent encounter if it tries to expand into a chain?

6. What competitive advantages and disadvantages do regional chains have in comparison with national chains?

7. Do you expect retail chains with 100 or more outlets to continue to increase their percentage of U.S. retail sales? Explain your answer.

8. What are the similarities and differences between chains and franchising?

9. From the franchisee's perspective, under what circumstances would product/trademark franchising be advantageous? When would business format franchising be better?

10. Why would a department store want to lease space to an outside operator rather than run a business, such as shoes, itself? What would be its risks in this approach?

11. What are the pros and cons of Sherwin-Williams' using a dual vertical marketing system?

12. At many retail apparel chains, store brands account for more than 50 percent of sales. What are the pros and cons of this strategy from a channel control perspective?

13. How could a small independent restaurant increase its channel control?

14. Why have consumer cooperatives not expanded much? What would you recommend to change this?

WEB-BASED EXERCISE

Franchise Handbook (www.franchise1.com)

Questions

1. Evaluate two of the featured dry cleaning and laundry franchises listed on this site from the perspective of a franchisee. (Select "Featured Franchises and Consultants," then "By Category," and then "Dry Cleaning/Laundries.")

2. Read and summarize two articles on franchising that are contained in the "Articles" section.

3. Discuss the entries in the "Directory of Franchise Opportunities" from the vantage point of a new college graduate with limited capital.

4. Discuss the entries in the "Directory of Franchise Opportunities" from the vantage point of an investor who wants low involvement in the day-to-day operations of a retail business.

CHAPTER ENDNOTES

1. Bob Weinstein, "Survival of the Biggest," *Entrepreneur* (August 1999), pp. 138–41.

2. "State of the Industry," *Chain Store Age* (August 1999), Section Two, p. 12A; and *Annual Benchmark Report for Retail Trade: January 1989 to December 1998* (Washington, D.C.: U.S. Department of Commerce, 1999).

3. *Statistical Abstract of the United States 1999* (Washington, D.C.: U.S. Department of Commerce, 1999).

4. Dennis Rodkin, "Chain Reaction," *Entrepreneur* (August 1999), p. 124.

5. *Sherwin-Williams 1999 Annual Report.*

CASE 1

SAVE-A-LOT: A NEW OPPORTUNITY FOR FOOD RETAILERS

Supervalu's long-run objective is to grow its Save-A-Lot 1,200-item limited assortment stores into a national chain. However, unlike other wholesalers, Supervalu plans to use Save-A-Lot as an expansion vehicle for its independent operators as opposed to building a company-owned retail chain. Of the 740 Save-A-Lots now being operated, only 140 are owned by Supervalu.

Asked if the expansion plans will call for more company-owned stores, Save-A-Lot's executive vice-president, Dave Boehnen, says "Because of our wholesale heritage, we're very comfortable in supporting independents. We believe Save-A-Lot is going to become increasingly important to them as they position themselves against new competitive forces in the market. It's a unique format, and while we will grow corporate stores, it is primarily intended to be a licensed program."

In addition to opening new Save-A-Lot stores, Supervalu hopes that independents will convert some of their existing operations to the Save-A-Lot model as a way of enhancing their competitive advantage. According to Boehnen, "If an independent is in a competitive situation where the future of a conventional store is in jeopardy, we believe Save-A-Lot may have some unique competitive advantages, and we'd encourage them to convert, even though it would cannibalize some of our existing wholesale business." One big advantage of the Save-A-Lot prototype is its low capital requirements. Depending on the amount of leasehold improvements, the capital investment for a typical store ranges from $500,000 to $600,000.

Supervalu plans to have more than 800 Save-A-Lot stores in the near future, many of them in such new marketing areas as Colorado, Arizona, and New York. Besides opening in new areas, Save-A-Lot has shifted its location strategy from rural locations in Kentucky and Tennessee to inner city sites in such places as Philadelphia. Plans are to target households with under $35,000 annual income in all locations.

Save-A-Lot's operation includes several fundamental elements:

- Each store carries approximately 1,200 high-volume items. Only one SKU (stock-keeping unit) is stocked for each product. This limits selection and helps improve the store's inventory turnover.
- The prototype's 15,000-square-foot space limitation means that when one item is added to store inventory, another is removed. For example, the chain's TNT ("Temporary and Terrific") promotions often feature such national brands as Folger's Coffee and Kellogg's cereals for short time periods.
- Aside from TNT promotions, most of the products featured are private brands that are unique to Save-A-Lot. A private brand strategy limits direct price competition and promotes store loyalty.

- The chain has 11 of its own distribution centers, separate from those for other Supervalu units. According to Boehnen, "It's completely different dealing with 1,200 SKUs than full-line grocery."
- Save-A-Lot uses everyday low pricing. Products are generally sold for the same price each week. Steady prices simplify sales forecasting and improve efficiency due to more predictable sales.
- The stores offer a focused total shopping experience. Accordingly, Save-A-Lot sells both meat and produce. Aldi, a key competitor, does not sell either of these items. The total shopping experience means that a shopper can complete all of his or her food shopping at one Save-A-Lot store.

Questions

1. Evaluate Supervalu's decision to make its Save-A-Lot strategy available to its independent retailers rather than grow a corporate-owned chain.

2. Discuss the pros and cons of Save-A-Lot's overall retail strategy.

3. How can Supervalu enforce constrained decision making with the independent Save-A-Lot units?

4. What are the pros and cons of Supervalu's dual vertical marketing system strategy for Save-A-Lot?

NOTE   The material in this case is drawn from Len Lewis, "Expansion Vehicle," *Progressive Grocer* (January 1999), pp. 69–70.

CASE 2

MAACO: EVALUATING FRANCHISING OPPORTUNITIES

Maaco Auto Painting and Bodyworks was founded in 1972 by Anthony A. Martino, who created Aamco Transmissions in the 1950s. After Martino sold his interest in Aamco in the 1960s, he observed that another segment of the auto after-market was ripe for franchising: auto paint and collision repair. At the time, auto body and painting service businesses were fragmented—with thousands of small independent body shops, one national company that performed cheap jobs, and custom shops specializing in restoring expensive vehicles.

As Martino saw it, the low-priced and high-priced ends of the market were saturated, while the huge middle market was underrepresented. So, he devised the methods, manuals, and systems for an auto painting and collision repair franchise business in a pilot shop he opened in Wilmington, Delaware. Today, there are about 565 independently owned and operated Maaco franchises in the United States, Canada, and Mexico. These centers paint over 650,000 vehicles per year.

Maaco is the only national firm in the $24 billion a year paint and collision business. It repaints cars that are typically between three and seven years old, restores rust-damaged cars, and repairs cars that have been involved in accidents. Although it offers paint jobs for as low as $199, Maaco is most involved with the middle-market price range of $500 paint jobs on cars. According to Anthony Martino, "Maaco's strategy of painting 40 cars a week at $500 per car is more profitable than painting three or four cars a week at $1,200." The success of Maaco is due to its positive image, the consistency and uniformity of operations, and the support programs provided to franchisees.

CASE 2

(CONTINUED)

Maaco is the best-known U.S. auto paint and collision repair chain. Its strong reputation is based on the quality of work conducted by its local franchisees and a national limited warranty. The firm's image is reinforced by a national advertising program and public relations conducted by Maaco, as well as local ads and public relations activities by franchisees.

Maaco instills consistency and uniformity throughout its franchised locations. Each location has the same manner of operation (that includes hand and machine sanding, chemical washing, proper masking, painting in a modern spray booth, and baking in a temperature-controlled oven), and the same caliber of supplies. Each new franchisee receives four weeks of formal training at corporate headquarters and three weeks of on-site training.

The Maaco customer support team works with franchisees on financing assistance, site selection, installation of equipment, lease negotiations, placing ads for workers, crew training, and problem solving. During training, franchisees receive operations, sales, advertising, and promotional manuals; and they meet and discuss their store opening with department heads from every major support area. After store openings, Maaco provides ongoing support for sales and marketing, public relations, purchasing, operations, weekly reports, and quality control. The firm's training process is an ongoing one.

The total costs for a Maaco franchise are $289,000—$60,000 is the minimum cash required, with the balance financed. This includes all equipment, an initial inventory of supplies, a $30,000 franchise fee, and take-home pay for the franchisee for his or her first year of business. In addition, franchisees pay a royalty fee of 8 percent of sales to Maaco and are obligated to spend $850 per week in local advertising. Some franchisees pool their budgets to advertise on TV.

Maaco's goal is for each franchised unit to have an annual net profit of $100,000. Although the costs (based on rents and local labor rates) and income (based on the number of paint jobs, the percent of insurance claim work, and the percent of fleet business) differ by location, Maaco's profit expectations are based on an average franchise location repairing/painting 25 to 40 cars per week. Maaco also assumes that each franchised outlet can convert 60 percent of the estimates it prepares into completed business, with an average price of $450 per car, including bodywork.

The average franchise has weekly sales of between $10,000 and $15,000 for all but the first three months of each year, when business is slower on a nationwide basis. Franchisees generally run special sales during the winter season to keep their full-time work crews busy.

Questions

1. What are the pros and cons of an individual becoming a Maaco franchisee rather than opening an independent auto paint and body shop?

2. Develop a checklist of factors a person should consider in evaluating a Maaco franchising opportunity.

3. What additional information, besides that in the case, should a prospective franchisee acquire before purchasing a Maaco franchise? Cite sources to acquire this information.

4. Evaluate the financial data provided in this case from the perspective of a potential franchisee.

Video Questions on Maaco

1. Describe the challenges and opportunities that Maaco faces in the future.

2. Assess the video as a means of attracting potential franchisees.

NOTE   The material in this case is drawn from *www.maaco.com;* Roberta Maynard, "Building a Winner from Scratch," *Nation's Business* (October 1997), pp. 65 – 71; and 1999 phone interviews with Maaco staff.

APPENDIX ON THE DYNAMICS OF FRANCHISING

This appendix is presented because of franchising's strong growth and exciting opportunities. To illustrate: In 1986, the Serruya brothers (Aaron, Michael, and Simon—who then ranged in age from 14 to 20) opened their first Yogen Früz frozen yogurt stand in a Toronto mall. Today, due to the Serruyas' assertively franchising their concept, Yogen Früz World-Wide has 5,000 outlets—less than 100 company-owned—under various trade names, including I Can't Believe It's Yogurt (ICBIY), Bresler's, Swensen's, and Yogen Früz. Its outlets have revenues in the hundreds of millions of dollars (U.S.). The company has stores throughout the United States and Canada, as well as outlets in 80 other countries. None of this would have been possible without the use of franchising (and a great concept, of course).[1]

And how about Blockbuster? It has a base of company-owned outlets, but also 1,000 franchised stores. Most of its growth is from franchises. Consider these "fun facts" (www.blockbuster.com):

Visit Blockbuster's "franchise opportunities" section of its Web site (www.blockbuster.com/co/franchise_jhtml). While you're there, access the preliminary online franchise application.

Blockbuster has a store within a 10-minute drive of virtually every major U.S. neighborhood. More than 38 million American households are active Blockbuster members. Nearly 1,500 videos are rented from U.S. Blockbuster stores each minute, 24 hours a day, 365 days a year. Houston is the city with the most stores. The busiest domestic store is in Charlotte, North Carolina. The store located in the city with the smallest population is in Rapid City, South Dakota. The store located farthest south is in Christchurch, New Zealand. The store located farthest north is in Fairbanks, Alaska.

Here, we go beyond the discussion of franchising in Chapter 4, and provide information on managerial issues in franchising and on the relationships between franchisors and franchisees.

Since 1980, annual U.S. retail franchising sales have more than tripled. As noted in the chapter, 600,000 retail establishments in the United States are affiliated with 2,500 franchisors and employ several million full-and part-time workers (including the proprietors). A number of business format franchisors have at least 1,000 outlets. The U.S. Department of Commerce predicts that retail franchising will continue to grow sharply for at least the next decade.

U.S. franchisors are now situated in over 150 countries worldwide, a number that keeps rising. This trend is due to these factors: U.S. franchisors recognize the growth potential in foreign markets. Franchising is becoming accepted as a retailing format in more nations. Trade barriers among nations have been reduced due to such pacts as NAFTA—the North American Free Trade Agreement that is making it easier for U.S.-, Canada-, and Mexico-based firms to operate in each other's marketplaces.

Here are some outstanding Web sites for you to get additional background information on a variety of topics related to franchising:

- International Franchise Association—www.franchise.org
- Franchising.org—www.franchising.org

- *Entrepreneur Magazine's* Franchise Channel—www.entrepreneurmag.com/ franchise
- U.S. Small Business Administration Franchise Workshop—www.sbaonline.sba.gov/ work-shops/franchises

Managerial Issues in Franchising

Franchising appeals to many owners and potential owners (franchisees) of small businesses for several reasons. Most franchisors have easy-to-learn, standardized operating methods they have perfected over the years. This means new franchisees do not have to learn from their own trial-and-error methods, which may be costly and time-consuming. Franchisors often have training facilities where franchisees are taught how to operate equipment, manage employees, maintain records, and improve customer relations; they usually follow up with field visits by a service staff.

A new outlet of a nationally advertised franchise (such as Subway fast food, Fantastic Sam's hair salons, or Midas auto service stores) can develop a large customer following rather quickly and easily because of the reputation of the firm. And not only does franchising result in good initial sales and profits, it also reduces franchisees' risk of failure *if the franchisees affiliate with strong, supportive franchisors.*

What kind of individual is best suited to being a franchisee? This is what one expert believes:

> Owning a franchise is not for everyone. The right person in the wrong program can lead to profound unhappiness. Because the time investment can involve one's life savings and a long-term legal commitment, this is not a step that should be taken lightly. Fiercely independent entrepreneurs are rarely happy in the franchise world. If one is interested in running and designing every aspect of an operation, he or she should think twice before buying a franchise. That person may be better off with an independent business. Most franchising programs impose a strict regimen on franchisees, dictating everything from how to greet customers to how to prepare and present the product or service. If one chafes at any restrictions, he or she may find franchise life too confining. But for a person used to the security of a full-time job, being a franchisee can offer the support needed to make a transition to entrepreneurship. These days, many downsized middle managers are bringing a wealth of business savvy to the franchise world. Thousands are at that stage in their careers where they have some capital to invest and are not interested in inventing a new (and risky) business concept, yet are attracted to the dream of self-employment.[2]

Want to be a McDonald's franchisee (McDonald's was rated as the best franchise operator for the past 20 years by *Entrepreneur*)? Then, read on:

> McDonald's is successful because it involves a mixture of system standards and individual opportunities. As a franchisee, you agree to work within the McDonald's system. McDonald's franchisees must personally devote their full time and best efforts to the day-to-day operation of the business. You cannot qualify for a franchise if you intend to be an absentee or part-time owner. Only individuals can qualify for a franchise. McDonald's does not grant franchises to corporations or partnerships. The franchise agreement allows you to operate a specific McDonald's restaurant, according to McDonald's standards, for a period of years (usually 20). McDonald's locates, develops, and constructs the restaurant under its own direction based on a nationwide development plan which seeks to be responsive to changing demographic factors, customer convenience, and competition. McDonald's retains control of the restaurant facilities it has developed. You equip the restaurant at your own expense with kitchen equipment, lighting, signage, seating, and decor. While none of this equipment is pur-

chased from the Company, it must meet McDonald's specifications. To maintain uniformity, franchisees must use McDonald's:

- Formulas and specifications for menu items,
- Methods of operation, inventory control, bookkeeping, accounting, and marketing,
- Trademarks and service marks, and
- Concepts for restaurant design, signage, and equipment layout.[3]

The investment and startup costs for a franchised outlet can be as low as a few thousand dollars for a personal service business to as high as several million dollars for a hotel. In return for its expenditures, any franchisee usually gets exclusive selling rights for a geographic area; a business format franchisee also gets training, store equipment and fixtures, and assistance in picking out a store site, negotiating with suppliers, advertising, and so on.

An example of how inexpensive franchising can be is Novus Windshield Repair, a Minneapolis-based firm with 2,500 franchised outlets. A typical franchisee makes an initial payment of $25,000 to $40,000 (including equipment and supplies) and ongoing royalty payments of about 8 percent of sales. The franchisees engage in the repair of vehicle windshields.

Table 1 shows the franchise fees, startup costs, and royalty rates for new franchisees at 13 leading franchisors in a wide variety of business categories. At present, financing support—either in-house financing or arranging third-party financing—is offered by most franchisors. All of the firms cited in Table 1 provide or arrange financing. In addition, through its guaranteed loan program, the U.S. Small Business Administration is a good financing

Although Novus' franchise fees are rather low, it has a lot to offer its franchisees (www.novuswsr.com).

Table 1 The Costs of Becoming a New Franchisee with Selected Franchisors (as of 1999)

Franchising Company	Franchise Fee	Other Startup Costs	Royalty Fee as a % of Sales	Franchisee-Owned Outlets as a % of All Outlets	Offers Financing Support
Aamco Transmissions	$30,000	$136,800–$145,900	7	99+	Third party
Dunkin' Donuts	$40,000	$91,990–$840,800	4.9	100	Third party
Fantastic Sam's	$10,000–$30,000	$45,000–$154,000	$209/week fee	99+	Third party
Jazzercise	$325–$650	$850–$19,775	Up to 20	99+	In-house
Lawn Doctor	$35,500	$5,600–$10,600	10	100	In-house
Mail Boxes Etc.	$30,000	$88,000–$169,250	5	100	In-house and third party
Medicine Shoppe	$10,000–$18,000	$48,600–$107,000	2 to 5.5	99	In-house and third party
Molly Maid	$16,900 and up	$46,600	3-6	99+	In-house and third party
Moto Photo	$15,000	$85,000–$260,000	6	91	In-house and third party
Petland	$25,000	$131,500–$460,000	4.5	99+	Third party
Super 8 Motels	$20,000 and up	$231,400–$2,280,000	5	100	Third party
Wicks 'N' Sticks	$25,000	$155,500–$272,500	6	95	Third party
Yogen Früz	$25,000	$0–$225,000	6	99	Third party

Source: Computed by the authors from "21st Annual Franchise 500," *Entrepreneur* (January 2000), various pages.

option for prospective franchisees; and some banks offer special interest rates for franchisees affiliated with established franchisors.

Besides receiving fees and royalties for allowing franchisees to run one or more outlets, franchisors may sell goods and services to their franchisees. Sometimes, this is required; more often, for legal reasons, such purchases are at the franchisees' discretion (subject to franchisor specifications). Each year, franchisors sell billions of dollars worth of items to franchisees.

Franchisors can set detailed standards covering every aspect of business, such as signs, product freshness, merchandise selection, the time involvement expected of franchisees, and employee uniforms. Half of U.S. business format franchisors require franchisees to be owner-operators and work full-time at the business. The franchisors' standards must be adhered to by franchisees. Thus, franchisor concerns about systemwide consistency and franchisee desires to conduct their own business may lead to conflicts.

Franchised outlets can be purchased (leased) directly from franchisors, master franchisees, or existing franchisees. Franchisors sell either new locations or company-owned outlets (some of which may have been taken back from unsuccessful franchisees). At times, they sell the rights to develop outlets in entire geographic regions or counties to master franchisees, which then deal with individual franchisees. Existing franchisees usually have the right to sell their units if they first offer them to their franchisor; if potential purchasers meet all financial and other criteria, and/or if purchasers undergo training. Of particular interest to prospective franchisees is the emphasis a company places on franchisee-owned outlets versus franchisor-owned ones. This helps indicate the commitment of the firm to franchising. As indicated in Table 1, leading franchisors typically own a small percentage of outlets.

One last point regarding managerial issues in franchising concerns the failure rate of new franchisees. For many years, it was believed that becoming a success as a franchisee was virtually a "sure thing"—and much safer than starting a business from scratch—due to the franchisor's well-known name, its years of experience, its training programs, and so on. However, some recent research has shown franchising to be as risky as opening a new business. Why? Some franchisors have oversaturated the market with stores and not provided promised support, and unscrupulous franchisors have preyed on unsuspecting investors.

With the preceding in mind, Figure 1 has a checklist by which potential franchisees can assess opportunities. In using the checklist, franchisees should also obtain full prospectuses and financial reports from all franchisors under consideration, and talk to existing franchise operators and customers.

Franchisor-Franchisee Relationships

Many franchisors and franchisees have good relationships because they share goals regarding company image, business operations, the goods and services offered, cooperative advertising, and sales and profit growth. This two-way relationship is illustrated by the actions of Taco John's International (www.tacojohns.com), a franchisor with 450 franchised pizza restaurants in about 20 states:

> Our customers are our franchisees, their employees, and their customers. Everything we do is aimed at helping franchisees better serve customers:
>
> - *Franchise Development*—The design of our restaurants is the result of careful, independent research and hands-on development with company prototypes. We provide site sketches and standard building plans. We also provide construction consultation during the project.
> - *Marketing and Advertising*—The Marketing Department plans and distributes materials to help you grow your business and build the Taco John's brand image. Our national campaign is funded by Taco John's, suppliers, and franchisees. Every

Figure 1
A Checklist for Prospective Franchisees to Evaluate Franchise Opportunities

1. What are the required franchise fees: initial fee, advertising appropriations, and royalties?

2. What degree of technical knowledge is required of the franchisee?

3. What is the required investment in time by the franchisee? Does the franchisee have to be actively involved in the day-to-day operations of the franchise?

4. What is the extent of control of a franchise by a franchisor in terms of materials purchased, sales quotas, space requirements, pricing, the range of goods to be sold, required inventory levels, and so on?

5. Can the franchisee accept the regimentation and rules of the franchisor?

6. Are the costs of required supplies and materials purchased from the franchisor at market value, above market value, or below market value?

7. What degree of name recognition do consumers have of the franchise? Does the franchisor have a meaningful advertising program?

8. What image does the franchise have among consumers and among current franchisees?

9. What are the level and quality of services provided by the franchisor to franchisees: site selection, training, bookkeeping, human relations, equipment maintenance, and trouble-shooting?

10. What is the franchisor policy in terminating franchisees? What are the conditions of franchise termination? What is the rate of franchise termination and nonrenewal?

11. What is the franchisor's legal history?

12. What is the length of the franchise agreement?

13. What is the failure rate of existing franchises?

14. What is the franchisor's policy with regard to company-owned and franchisee-owned outlets?

15. What policy does the franchisor have in allowing franchisees to sell their business?

16. What is the franchisor's policy with regard to territorial protection for existing franchisees? With regard to new franchisees and new company-owned establishments?

17. What is the earning potential of the franchise during the first year? The first five years?

restaurant also belongs to a regional marketing co-op to help them participate in advertising that would otherwise not be cost-effective for a single restaurant. Field managers work with the co-ops and franchisees in setting marketing plans. Promotions for individual units are part of the Local Store Marketing program. The overall goal of marketing is "One Message. One Voice." throughout the Taco John's system.

• *Franchise Business Consultants*—Each restaurant is assigned a Franchise Business Consultant whose main job is to provide support to help franchisees acquire, develop, and nurture their business and operational skills to build sales, retain customers, and maintain profits.

- *Human Resources*—Our Human Resources Department will provide you with materials to help attract, motivate, and retain people. Programs have been developed to ensure your crew will be the best possible. The Training Department teaches franchisees and their team members the Taco John's operating system and how to effectively deliver the Taco John's promise to each customer. Initial training involves classroom and restaurant training during which you get a set of manuals.
- *Your New Restaurant Opening*—A Grand Opening Team will work with you in your restaurant, just before and during your opening.
- *Research and Development*—The Research and Development Department's primary focus is consumer research, operations testing, and customer feedback during initial in-store testing.
- *Purchasing and Distribution*—Company purchasing and distribution personnel negotiate with manufacturers and distribution centers to make sure our system receives the best possible quality, service, and purchase prices. A nationwide system of approved distributors warehouse all the products needed to operate a restaurant. Weekly orders are delivered to each restaurant's door.

Nonetheless, for several reasons, tensions do exist between various franchisors and their franchisees. These are just some of the reasons why:

- The franchisor-franchisee relationship is not one of employer to employee. Franchisor controls are often viewed as rigid.
- Many agreements are considered too short in duration by franchisees. Nearly half of U.S. agreements are 10 years in duration or less (one-sixth are 5 years or less), usually at the franchisor's request.
- For the franchisees that lease their outlets' property from their franchisors, the loss of a franchise license generally means eviction; and the franchisee receives nothing for "goodwill."
- Some franchisees feel franchisors want to buy back their units due to higher profit potential.
- Some franchisors believe their franchisees do not reinvest enough in their outlets and that this results in a poor image for the firm.
- Franchisees may not be concerned enough about overall company image and the consistency of operations from one outlet to another.
- Franchisors may not give adequate territorial protection and may open new outlets near existing ones.
- Franchisees may refuse to participate in cooperative advertising programs.
- Franchisees may offer substandard service.
- Some franchisors use minor contract infractions to oust franchisees.
- Franchised outlets up for sale must usually be offered first to franchisors, which also have approval of sales to third parties.
- Some franchisees believe franchisor marketing support is low.
- Franchisees may be prohibited from operating competing businesses.
- Restrictions on purchases and suppliers may cause franchisees to pay higher prices and have limited product assortments.
- Franchisees may band together to force changes in policies and exert pressure on franchisors.
- Sales and profit expectations may not be realized.

Tensions can lead to conflicts—even litigation. Potential negative franchisor actions include terminating agreements; reducing promotional and sales support; and adding unneeded red tape for orders, information requests, and warranty work. Potential negative franchisee actions include terminating agreements, adding competitors' product lines, refusing to promote goods and services, and not complying with franchisor information requests.

Each year, business format franchisors terminate the contracts of 10 percent of the franchisee-owned stores that opened within the prior five years; and the American Arbitration Association is asked to mediate hundreds of franchising disputes—at the request of both franchisors and franchisees. Since 1990, the number of franchisee complaints to the Federal Trade Commission about poor business franchisors on the part of their franchisors has grown dramatically.

Although franchising has historically been characterized by franchisors' having more power than franchisees, this inequality has been reduced. Why? First, franchisees affiliated with specific franchisors have joined together. For example, the Association of Kentucky Fried Chicken Franchisees, National Coalition of Associations of 7-Eleven Franchisees, Vision Care Franchisee Association, and Supercuts Franchisee Association represent thousands of franchisees. Second, large umbrella organizations, such as the American Franchisee Association (www.franchisee-org) and the American Association of Franchisees and Dealers (www.aafd.org), have been formed. Third, many franchisees now operate more than one outlet, so they have greater clout. Fourth, there has been a substantial rise in litigation between franchisors and franchisees. Fifth, when dissatisfied, some franchisee groups have sought to purchase their franchisors. For instance, a franchisee group at Straw Hat Pizza acquired their franchisor.

Improved communication and better cooperation are necessary to resolve these issues. One innovative approach to doing so is used by AlphaGraphics Printshops of the Future, a franchisor with 350 outlets. At AlphaGraphics, "the franchisor no longer decides by itself how every penny of royalties will be used. Instead, 25 percent of royalty fees are set aside for services of each franchisee's choosing, such as help from computer consultants or promotional mailings." In return, "franchisees must keep current with royalty payments, submit monthly financial statements, and prepare annual budgets."[4]

Another progressive approach is the code of ethics by the International Franchise Association. If the IFA's 32,000 franchisor, franchisee, and supplier members adhere to this voluntary code, the conflicts between franchisors and franchisees will decline substantially. These are some of the standards of conduct recommended in the IFA code (www.franchise.org/welcome_about/code.asp):

- Franchisors' offering circulars shall be complete, accurate, and not misleading.
- Franchisors and franchisees shall deal with each other honestly, ethically, and respectfully.
- Franchisors shall not prohibit franchisees from forming or participating in any franchisee association.
- Franchisee agreements may only be terminated for good cause. Franchisees shall be given a reasonable opportunity to remedy their shortcomings before they are actually terminated.
- Prior to opening new outlets, franchisors shall consider the potential impact of those outlets on existing franchisees if the new outlets would be in close proximity to them.

APPENDIX ENDNOTES

1. "Yogen Früz World-Wide, Inc.," *Hoover's Online* (October 14, 1999); and "Press Releases," *www.yogenfruz.com* (March 9, 2000).

2. Andrew A. Caffey, "Opportunity Knocks," *Entrepreneur Magazine's Buyers Guide to Franchise & Business Opportunities 1997*, p. 3.

3. *McDonald's Franchising Brochure*, p. 3.

4. Jeffrey A. Tannenbaum, "To Pacify Irate Franchisees, Franchisers Extend Services," *Wall Street Journal* (February 24, 1995), pp. B1–B2; and *www.alphagraphics.com* (March 9, 2000).

CHAPTER 5

Retail Institutions by Store-Based Strategy Mix

CHAPTER OBJECTIVES

1. To describe the wheel of retailing, scrambled merchandising, and the retail life cycle and show how they can help explain the performance of retail strategy mixes
2. To discuss some ways in which retail strategy mixes are evolving
3. To examine a wide variety of food-oriented retailers involved with store-based strategy mixes
4. To study a wide range of general merchandise retailers involved with store-based strategy mixes

Who says supermarket retailing is stagnant? Not Piggly Wiggly. Sixty percent of its shoppers carry the supermarket chain's loyalty card. These customers account for 80 percent of the firm's overall sales. The loyalty program, which was instituted at the beginning of 1998, has helped Piggly Wiggly retain its most profitable customers despite increased competition from Wal-Mart Supercenters and Publix.

As Piggly Wiggly's director of loyalty marketing said, "Our primary goal has been to reward our best customers by giving them a greater piece of the promotional pie. Why should someone who walks in off the street get the same discount we give someone who spends $150 a week with us?" In addition to sending birthday cards to the top 10 percent of its customers, Piggly Wiggly tailors promotions to individual customer preferences. For example, a person who regularly buys flowers will receive a coupon redeemable in the store's flower department.

An important feature of Piggly Wiggly's strategy is its "Greenbax" program, which provides a running total of a customer's total points and the amount added by the current transaction at the bottom of each cash register receipt. The customer can scan a loyalty card at any Piggly Wiggly store to determine the redemption choices and print out Greenbax certificates. These certificates can be used at a variety of stores, restaurants, and movie theaters or applied for further discounts at Piggly Wiggly.[1]

OVERVIEW

In Chapter 4, retail institutions were described by type of ownership arrangement. In this chapter, we discuss three key concepts in planning retail strategy mixes: the wheel of retailing, scrambled merchandising, and the retail life cycle. We then look at some ways in which retail strategies are evolving and study the basic strategies of a number of store-based retail institutions. Chapter 6 deals with nonstore-based, electronic, and nontraditional retailing strategies.

> *Please Note:* Web site addresses are constantly changing.
> The links in this chapter are current as of the publication of this book.

CONSIDERATIONS IN PLANNING A RETAIL STRATEGY MIX

A retailer may be classified by its **strategy mix.** This mix is a firm's particular combination of these factors: store location, operating procedures, goods/services offered, pricing tactics, store atmosphere and customer services, and promotional methods.

Store location refers to the use of a store or nonstore format, placement in a geographic area, and the kind of site (such as a shopping center versus an isolated store). Operating procedures include the kinds of personnel employed, management style, store hours, and other factors. The goods/services offered may encompass several product categories or just one, and quality may be low, medium, or high. Pricing refers to a retailer's comparative strategy: prestige pricing (creating a quality image by high prices), competitive pricing (setting prices at the level of rivals), or penetration pricing (underpricing other retailers to attract value-conscious consumers). Store atmosphere and customer services are reflected by a firm's physical facilities and the level of personal attention provided, credit, return policies, delivery, and other factors. Promotion involves the retailer's activities in such areas as advertising, displays, personal selling, and sales promotion. By combining these elements, a retailer can develop a unique strategy.

To flourish in today's environment, a retailer should strive to be dominant in some aspect of its strategy. The firm may then be able to reach **destination retailer** status—whereby consumers view the company as distinctive enough to become loyal to it and go out of their way to shop there. We tend to link "dominant" with "large." Yet, both small and large retailers can dominate in their own way. There are several ways to be a destination retailer:

1. Be price-oriented and cost-efficient to attract price-sensitive shoppers.

2. Be upscale to attract full-service, status-conscious consumers.

3. Be convenient to attract those interested in shopping ease, nearby locations, or long store hours.

4. Offer a dominant assortment with an extensive selection in the product lines carried to appeal to consumers interested in variety and in-store shopping comparisons.

5. Offer superior customer service to attract those frustrated by the decline in retail service—as they perceive it.

6. Be innovative or exclusive and provide a unique way of operating (such as video kiosks at airports) or carry products/brands not stocked by others to reach people who are innovators, bored, or looking for items not in the "me too" mold.

Combining two or more of these approaches can yield even greater appeal for a given retailer.[2]

Before we look at specific retail strategy mixes, three significant concepts that help explain the use of these mixes are presented: the wheel of retailing, scrambled merchandising, and the retail life cycle. We also look at ways in which retail strategies are evolving today.

The Wheel of Retailing

According to the **wheel of retailing** theory, retail innovators often first appear as low-price operators with a low-cost structure and low profit margin requirements. Over time, these innovators upgrade the products they carry and improve their facilities and customer service (by adding better-quality items, locating in higher-rent sites, accepting exchanges and allowing refunds, providing credit and delivery, and so on), and prices rise. As innovators mature, they become vulnerable to new discounters with lower cost structures, hence, the wheel of retailing.[3] See Figure 5.1.

Figure 5.1
The Wheel of
Retailing

As a low-end retailer
upgrades its strategy, to
increase sales and profit
margins, a new form of
discounter takes its
place.

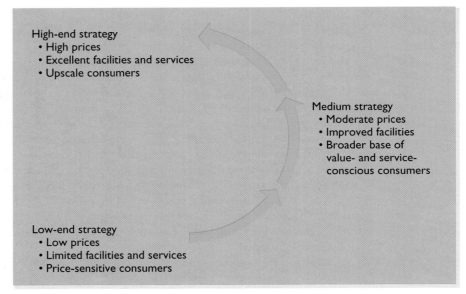

High-end strategy
• High prices
• Excellent facilities and services
• Upscale consumers

Medium strategy
• Moderate prices
• Improved facilities
• Broader base of
  value- and service-
  conscious consumers

Low-end strategy
• Low prices
• Limited facilities and services
• Price-sensitive consumers

The wheel of retailing is grounded on four basic premises:

1. There are many price-sensitive shoppers willing to trade customer services, wide selections, and convenient locations for lower prices.

2. Price-sensitive shoppers are often not loyal and are willing to switch to retailers with lower prices. Other, prestige-sensitive, customers like shopping at retailers with high-end strategies.

3. New institutions are frequently able to have lower operating costs than existing institutions.

4. As retailers move up the wheel, they typically do so to increase sales, broaden the target market, and improve store image.

In the 1950s and again in the 1970s, traditional department store prices rose to levels that spurred the growth of two new institutions: the full-line discount store and the retail catalog showroom. These firms could stress low prices because of such cost-cutting techniques as having a small sales force, situating in lower-rent store locations, using inexpensive fixtures, emphasizing high stock turnover, and accepting only cash or check payments for goods.

Where would you place Kohl's (www.kohls.com) along the wheel of retailing?

As full-line discount stores and retail catalog showrooms succeeded, they typically sought to move up along the wheel. This meant enlarging the sales force, improving locations, upgrading fixtures, carrying lower-turnover merchandise, and granting credit. These improvements led to higher costs, which, in turn, led to higher prices. In the 1980s, the wheel of retailing again came into play as newer types of discounters, such as off-price chains, factory outlets, and permanent flea markets, expanded to satisfy the needs of the price-conscious consumer. The 1990s have seen an explosion of a retail institution known as the "category killer" store (a huge discount-oriented outlet specializing in one or a few product lines), which appeals to people who are interested in low prices and a large selection in the line(s) carried. The category killer's size lets it operate very efficiently. We are now also witnessing the birth of discount Web retailers—some of whom have very low costs because they do not have "bricks-and-mortar" facilities.

Figure 5.2
Retail Strategy
Alternatives

Low-End Strategy		High-End Strategy
Low rental location—side street	⟷	High rental shopping center or central business district location
No services or services charged at additional fee (or services may be limited to credit and returns)	⟷	Elaborate services available included in price, such as: credit decorating delivery gift wrapping alterations layaway
Spartan fixtures and displays	⟷	Elaborate fixtures and displays
Simple retail personnel organization	⟷	Elaborate retail personnel organization
Price emphasis in promotion	⟷	No price emphasis in promotion
Self-service or high sales per store personnel ratio	⟷	Product demonstrations, low sales per store personnel ratio
Crowded store interior	⟷	Spacious store interior
Most merchandise visible	⟷	Most merchandise in back room

As indicated in Figure 5.1, the wheel of retailing reveals three basic strategic positions: low end, medium, and high-end. The medium strategy may have some difficulties if retailers in this position are not perceived by consumers as distinctive. Figure 5.2 shows the opposing alternatives a retailer faces in considering a strategy mix. Through this dichotomy, one can differentiate between the two extreme cases of strategic emphasis: low end and high end. The wheel of retailing suggests that established firms should be wary in adding services or converting their strategy from low end to high end. Because price-conscious shoppers are not usually store loyal, they are apt to switch to lower-priced firms. Furthermore, retailers may be eliminating the competitive advantages that have led to profitability. As discussed below, this occurred with the retail catalog showroom, which is now a defunct format in the United States.

Scrambled Merchandising

Whereas the wheel of retailing focuses on strategic orientation in terms of product quality, prices, and customer service, scrambled merchandising involves a retailer's increasing its width of assortment (the number of different product lines carried). **Scrambled merchandising** occurs when a retailer adds goods and services that may be unrelated to each other and to the firm's original business. See Figure 5.3.

The popularity of scrambled merchandising today is due to many factors: retailers are

How much of a practitioner of scrambled merchandising is Williams-Sonoma (www.williams-sonoma.com)?

interested in increasing overall sales volume, goods and services that are fast-selling and have high profit margins are usually the ones added, consumers may make more impulse purchases, people are attracted to one-stop shopping, different target markets may be reached, and the impact of seasonality and competition may be reduced. In addition, the popularity of a retailer's original product line(s) may be insufficient to sustain long-term growth, causing that firm to scramble to maintain and grow its customer base. That is why Blockbuster, because of the advent of pay-per-view and premium movie channels on cable TV, now carries CDs, magazines, movie merchandise, candy, video games and game players, and more.

Scrambled merchandising is contagious. For example, drugstores, bookstores, florists, video stores, and photo-developing firms are all affected by supermarkets' scrambled mer-

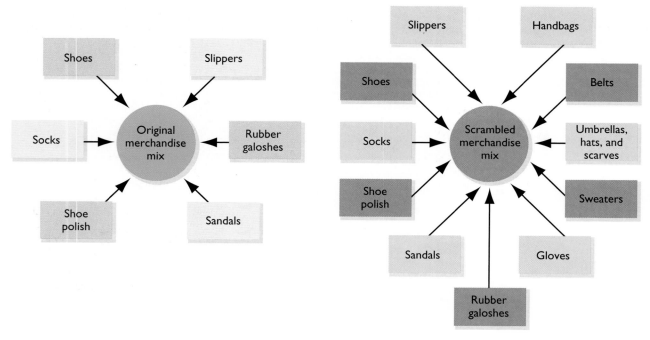

Figure 5.3
Scrambled Merchandising by a Shoe Store

chandising. About 11 percent of U.S. supermarket sales are from general merchandise, health and beauty aids, and other nongrocery items, such as pharmacy products, books and magazines, flowers, video rental, and seasonal goods.[4] In response, the aforementioned retailers are compelled to use scrambled merchandising to fill the sales void caused by supermarkets. They have added unrelated items, like toys and gift items, greeting cards, batteries, and cameras. This then creates a void for other retailers, which are also forced to scramble.

The prevalence of scrambled merchandising means that competition among different types of retailers is increasing and that distribution costs for manufacturers are affected as sales are dispersed over more retailers. There are other limitations to scrambled merchandising, such as the potential lack of retailer expertise in buying, selling, and servicing items with which they are unfamiliar, the costs associated with a broader product assortment (including lower inventory turnover); and the possible damage to a retailer's image if scrambled merchandising is ineffective.

The Retail Life Cycle

A third concept in understanding diverse retail strategy mixes is the **retail life cycle.** It states that retail institutions—like the goods and services they sell—pass through identifiable life cycle stages: innovation, accelerated development, maturity, and decline.[5] The direction and speed of institutional changes can be interpreted from this theory. Table 5.1 summarizes the stages of the retail life cycle.

From an industrywide perspective, in the United States:

The *initial retail era* focused on merchandise. Money was made when goods were bought. Stores located in the inner city. Market reach was limited and local. Advertising was mostly by word of mouth or in local media. This era came to an end

Table 5.1 The Retail Life Cycle

		STAGE IN THE LIFE CYCLE			
	Area or Subject of Concern	Innovation	Accelerated Development	Maturity	Decline
Market characteristics	Number of competitors	Very few	Moderate	Many direct competitors; moderate indirect competitors	Moderate direct competitors; many indirect competitors
	Rate of sales growth	Very rapid	Rapid	Moderate to slow	Slow or negative
	Level of profitability	Low to moderate	High	Moderate	Very low
	Duration of stage	3–5 years	8 years	Indefinite	Indefinite
Appropriate retailer actions	Investment/growth/ risk decisions	Investment minimization; high risks accepted	High level of investment to sustain growth	Tightly controlled growth in untapped markets	Marginal capital expenditures, and only if essential
	Central management concerns	Concept refinement through adjustment and experimenting	Establishing a pre-emptive market position	Excess capacity and overstoring; prolonging maturity and revising the business concept	Engaging in a run-out strategy
	Use of management control techniques	Minimal	Moderate	Extensive	Moderate
	Most successful management style	Entrepreneurial	Centralized	Professional	Caretaker

with the Great Depression. The *next retail era* hit its growth phase in the post-World War II era. It was expansion-oriented. Opening new stores was the focus. Money was made when goods were sold. Stores followed their customers to suburbs and the regional mall was born. Market reach was national, as was advertising. The beginning of the end for this era was the 1987 stock market crash and the collapse of Campeau (then owner of Federated Department Stores). The *new era* in retail development reflects the industry's informationalization. It represents a shift in focus from market expansion to information intensification, from geography to communication-focused technologies, from return on investment to return on customers, from sales growth to profit growth, from increasing individual transactions to establishing long-term customer relationships. Third-wave retailers share these attributes: global focus, obsession with technology, and organizational restructuring around the customer.[6]

Let us now study the stages of the retail life cycle as they apply to individual institutional formats and show specific examples. During the first stage of the cycle (innovation), there is a strong departure from the strategy mixes of existing retail institutions. A firm in this stage significantly alters at least one element of the strategy mix from that of traditional competitors. Sales and then profits often rise sharply for the first firms in a category. There are risks that new institutions will not be accepted by shoppers, and there may be large initial losses due to heavy investments. At this stage, long-run success is not assured.

Are you ready yet for online grocery shopping with a company such as Peapod (www.peapod.com)? Check it out.

An example of an institution in the innovation stage is the online grocery store, such as Peapod. How will the format do? There are conflicting views: "Consumers these days think nothing of buying books or Barbies online. But will they also E-shop for eggs? Online grocers think so and are racing to build the warehouses and Web sites to capitalize on what they see as the next big trend in dot.com commerce. But there are a chorus of doubters in the next aisle. Within a few years, the firms say, consumers in virtually any metropolitan area will be able to buy food staples and household products by PC with the same quality and prices offered at Safeway or Kroger. Though analysts are skeptical, most predict they will be profitable. But online grocers face an uphill battle. The challenge will be to attract and retain enough repeat customers in a volume-driven business with razor-thin profit margins. It will take more than the ease of pointing and clicking to get people in the habit of ordering bread and milk online. Firms must overcome die-hard shopping habits, limited selections, and a preference among some people simply to squeeze their own melons. In addition, price is apt to be a factor for many budget-conscious shoppers."[7]

 In the second stage (accelerated development), both the sales and profits of a retail institution exhibit rapid growth. Existing firms expand their geographic bases of operations, and newer companies of the same type enter the marketplace. Toward the end of accelerated development, cost pressures (to cover a larger staff, a more complex inventory system, and extensive controls) may begin to affect profits.

The interactive electronic video kiosk is an institution in the growth stage. Kiosks are selling everything from clothing to magazines to insurance to PCs. According to Robert Chomentowski, a market analyst with Frost & Sullivan, an international marketing and consultant firm, "The interactive video kiosk market is expanding at a formidable pace. In 1996, the U.S. interactive kiosk market grew to $370 million. And the market is expected to grow to $3 billion in 2003, with a compound annual growth rate of 35 percent over the forecast period."[8] This institution is examined further in Chapter 6.

 The third stage (maturity) is characterized by a slowdown in sales growth for the institutional type. Though overall sales may continue to go up, the rise is at a much lower rate than during the introduction and growth stages. Profit margins may have to be reduced to stimulate purchases. Maturity is brought on by market saturation caused by the high number of firms in an institutional format, competition from newer institutions, changing societal interests, and inadequate management skills to lead mature or larger firms. Once maturity is reached, the goal is to sustain it as long as possible and not to fall into decline.

The liquor store, a form of specialty store, is an institution in the maturity stage; sales are rising, but very slowly as compared to earlier years. From 1990 to 1999, U.S. liquor store sales went up an average of 2 percent annually—far less than the rate for all U.S. retailers. The slowdown is due to competition from membership clubs, mail-order wine retailers, and supermarkets (in states allowing wine or liquor sales); changing life-styles and attitudes regarding liquor; the lifting of the drinking age from 18 to 21 in all 50 states; and limitations on the nonalcoholic items that liquor stores are permitted to sell in some locales.

The final stage in the retail life cycle is decline, whereby industrywide sales and profits for a format fall off, many firms abandon the format, and newer formats attract consumers previously committed to that retailer type. In some cases, a decline may be hard or almost impossible to reverse. In others, it may be avoided or postponed by repositioning the institution.

The retail catalog showroom's U.S. popularity peaked in the mid-1980s. In a catalog showroom, consumers chose items from a catalog, shopped in a warehouse setting, and wrote up orders. By 1998, the U.S. catalog showroom had virtually vanished. Of the big three firms, Best Products and Consumers Distributing went out of business and Service Merchandise switched to a traditional store format. Why? Many other retailers aggressively cut costs and prices, so showrooms were no longer low-price leaders. Showrooms had a tough time reacting to price cuts by competitors because catalogs had to be printed far in advance. To reach more consumers, advertising costs rose. Too many items were slow-sellers or had low profit margins. Some consumers found showrooms crowded and disliked writing orders, the lack of displays reduced browsing time, and the paucity of apparel goods also held down revenues.[9] On the other hand, conventional supermarkets have slowed their decline by placing new units in suburban shopping centers, redesigning interiors, lengthening store hours, having low prices, expanding the use of scrambled merchandising, closing unprofitable smaller units, and converting to larger outlets.

The retail life cycle concept is valuable in indicating the proper retailer response as institutions evolve. Expansion should be the focus in the initial stages, administrative skills and operations become critical in maturity, and adaptation is essential at the end of the cycle: "No matter how successful an organization has been in the past, that is no guarantee of future success. If anything, past greatness creates a barrier to future change. For retailers that understand the changes which are taking place in their business environment, the future represents an unprecedented landscape of opportunity."[10]

HOW RETAIL INSTITUTIONS ARE EVOLVING

Forward-looking firms know their individual strategies must be modified as retail institutions evolve over time. Complacency is not desirable. Many retailers have witnessed shrinking profit margins due to intense competition and consumer interest in lower prices. This has put pressure on them to tighten internal cost controls and to promote higher-margin goods and services while eliminating unprofitable items.

Here are two views of the strategic challenges facing retail institutions:

Gone are the days in which a retailer could stuff merchandise onto shelves warehouse-style and reap instant success. Faced with a mature, saturated market where sales gains often come at one another's expense, retailers must vie to win consumer dollars. Due to overstoring, we expect a major shakeout to continue in various segments as

Technology in Retailing

Using Common Systems to Segment Uncommon Customers

Delia's owns three apparel chains: TSI Soccer, Jean Country, and Screem. All three chains were acquired between 1996 and the end of 1998, and will remain as separate entities. Although each chain focuses on teenagers, they cater to different target markets.

Delia's recently introduced a unified point-of-sale, back office, and information system for the three chains. As Delia's director of retail systems states, "We'll have one system for reporting and analysis across all stores, but the chains get to act and feel like their own businesses." Previously, each chain used the system in place before their acquisition by Delia or used a modified version of Delia's catalog system.

The new arrangement stores and analyzes infor-

mation captured at the point-of-sale. With a unified approach, Delia's can gather and review customer demographic data from shoppers at all three chains. These data include purchases at a store, catalog, or Web site.

The unified data base gives Delia's opportunities for cross-selling among the chains. In addition, the integrated system will save considerable time since information technology personnel can work with just one system. The new system also has data to help personnel prepare a yearly buying plan for each store.

What are the pros and cons of a unified information system for three different specialty store chains?

Source: Jean Thilmany, "Delia's Single System Powers Three Chains," *Women's Wear Daily* (April 7, 1999), p. 13.

less-competitive firms drop out or merge with other retailers. The gap will widen between the top and bottom performers of various retail formats.[11]

Until fairly recently, retailing was characterized by formats that were easily distinguished because of their pricing and service strategies and their products. Consumers went to drugstores for prescription drugs and supermarkets for food. People's expectations about the shopping experience in each type of store were fairly standard. Today, distinctions among retail sectors have blurred as firms expand their offerings to meet customer needs for convenience, generate more traffic, and try to get a larger share of customers' pocketbooks. We see increased competition for product categories that once were the exclusive or primary domain of a particular store type. The need for a strong competitive advantage is greater than ever. Firms must broaden their perception of who competitors are and act accordingly.[12]

Let us see how firms are reacting to this formidable environment via mergers, diversification, and downsizing, as well as cost containment and value-driven retailing.

Mergers, Diversification, and Downsizing

Some firms have used mergers and diversification to sustain sales growth in a highly competitive environment (or when the institutional category in which they operate matures). For stronger firms, this trend is expected to carry over into the future.

Mergers involve the combination of separately owned retail firms. Diversification mergers take place between retailers of different types, such as the ones between J.C. Penney (the department store chain) and Thrift Drug, Eckerd, and Genovese (drugstore chains). Specialization mergers occur between similar types of retailers, such as two local banks or two department store chains (as took place when Federated Department Stores acquired R.H. Macy). By merging, retailers hope to jointly maximize resources, enlarge their customer base, improve productivity and bargaining power, limit weaknesses, and gain competitive advantages. This is a way for resourceful retailers to grow more rapidly and for weaker ones to enhance their long-term prospects for survival (or gain some return on investment by selling assets). See Figure 5.4.

Figure 5.4
J.C. Penney's Eckerd: A Growing Drugstore Power Through Mergers

J.C. Penney has been in the drugstore business since 1969 when it acquired Thrift Drug. In 1996, the company acquired Eckerd, Fay, Kerr, and a number of Rite Aid drugstores. In 1997, it purchased Revco drugstores; and in 1999, it acquired Genovese drugstores. As of now, J.C. Penney operates nearly 3,000 drugstores—all converted to the powerful Eckerd name—and it is the largest drugstore operator in the world.
Reprinted by permission of Eckerd Corporation.

Through its various divisions, The Limited, Inc. (www.limited.com) is an apparel retailing dynamo.

With **diversification,** retailers become active in businesses outside their normal operations—and add stores in different goods/service categories. For example, to expand beyond its core business, The Limited, Inc., developed Express (for young women), Structure (for men), and Bath & Body Works (toiletries). In addition, it acquired Victoria's Secret (a mail-order and store-based lingerie business), Henri Bendel (upscale women's clothing), and Lane Bryant (full-figured women's clothing).

Because of mergers and diversification, the size of many retail chains has grown dramatically. And they have not all done well with that approach. As in the manufacturing sector, even though stronger firms are expanding, we are also now witnessing **downsizing**—whereby unprofitable stores are closed or divisions are sold off—by retailers unhappy with performance. Because Kmart's diversification did not meet expectations, it closed or sold off virtually all ventures outside the discount department store field (including Borders' bookstores, Builders Square, Office Max, Pay Less drugstores, and Sports Authority).

For several reasons, the interest in downsizing is expected to continue. First, various retailers have overextended themselves and do not have the resources or management talent to succeed without retrenching. Second, in their quest to open new stores, certain firms have chosen poor sites (because they have already saturated the best locations). Third, retailers such as Barnes & Noble are becoming more interested in operating fewer, but much larger, stores and operating on the Web. Fourth, retailers such as supermarkets are finding they can do better if they focus attention regionally rather than nationally. Fifth, once-diversified firms such as Kmart have decided to return more to their roots.

This means many "retailers have grown accustomed to shifts in what the consumer wants and are well acquainted with economic cycles. Even as they shutter unprofitable stores, they are opening newer, profitable formats and converting existing units to these formats."[13]

Cost Containment and Value-Driven Retailing

With a cost-containment approach, retailers strive to hold down both initial investment costs and ongoing operating costs. In recent years, more firms have enacted this strategy because of intense competition from discounters, the need to control complicated chain or franchise operations, high land and construction costs, the volatility of the economic environment, and the desire to maximize productivity.

Cost containment can be accomplished through one or more of these strategy mix decisions:

- Standardizing operating procedures.
- Standardizing store layouts, size, and product offerings.
- Using secondary locations, freestanding units, and locations in older strip centers and by occupying sites abandoned by others (second-use locations).
- Placing stores in smaller communities where building regulations are less strict, labor costs are lower, and construction and operating costs are reduced.
- Using inexpensive construction materials, such as bare cinder-block walls and concrete floors.
- Using plainer fixtures and lower-cost displays.
- Buying refurbished equipment.
- Joining cooperative buying and advertising groups.
- Encouraging manufacturers to finance inventories.

Consolidated Stores' cost-containment approach even extends to its austere Web site (www.cnstore.com).

A major driving force behind cost containment is the quest to provide good value to customers: "However value is defined, price clearly plays a big role in what consumers buy and where they buy it. Indeed, retailers' pricing policies—particularly those of discounters—have encouraged consumers to shop for bargains and to distrust traditional sales and sale prices. In the 1980s, quality was largely a matter of status. A designer name, a good image, and even a high price were acceptable or desirable. But today's savvy, more pragmatic consumers have discovered they can get reasonable quality at everyday low prices. According to a study by Kurt Salmon Associates, a retail consulting firm, three-quarters of respondents said they shop at apparel discounters either regularly or occasionally."[14]

RETAIL INSTITUTIONS CATEGORIZED BY STORE-BASED STRATEGY MIX

Selected aspects of the strategy mixes of 14 store-based retail institutions are highlighted in this section and Table 5.2. These strategy mixes are divided into food-oriented and general merchandise groups. While not all-inclusive, the strategy mixes do provide a good overview of store-based retailing strategies.

Food-Oriented Retailers

Six major strategic formats are used by food-oriented retailers: convenience store, conventional supermarket, food-based superstore, combination store, box (limited-line) store, and warehouse store. Each is discussed in the following subsections.

Convenience Store A **convenience store** is usually a food-oriented retailer that is well located, is open long hours, and carries a moderate number of items. This type of retailer is small (only a fraction of the size of a conventional supermarket), has average to above-average prices, and average atmosphere and customer services. The ease of shopping at convenience stores and the impersonal nature of many large supermarkets make convenience stores particularly appealing to their customers, many of whom are male.

In 1998, there were 97,000 convenience stores (excluding the thousands of stores where food was a very small fraction of revenues); and total annual sales at those stores were $75 billion (excluding gasoline). Today, U. S. convenience stores account for 7 percent of retail grocery sales, 5 percent of fast-food sales, and 20 percent of gasoline sales.[15]

7-Eleven (www.7-eleven.com) dominates the convenience store category.

Items such as milk, eggs, and bread once represented the major portion of sales; now, sandwiches, tobacco products, snack foods, soft drinks, newspapers and magazines, beer and wine, video rentals, lottery tickets, and a car wash are also often key items. In addition, gasoline generates 20 to 40 percent or more of total sales at many stores, At one time, virtually no convenience stores carried gasoline; now 77 percent do. A number of convenience stores have installed ATMs and expanded nonfood offerings to remain attractive to shoppers. See Figure 5.5.

7-Eleven, Circle K, Ultramar Diamond Shamrock, and Casey's General Store are among the largest food-based convenience store chains in the United States, with 7-Eleven alone having 5,500 outlets. Texaco's Food Mart and Amoco's Food Shops are among the convenience store chains operated by oil companies at their gas station locations.

The convenience store's natural market advantages are its usefulness for fill-in merchandise when a consumer does not want to travel to or spend time shopping at a supermarket, the ability of customers to buy gas and fill-in merchandise at the same time, the use of drive-through windows, and the long store hours. Most of the items sold by a convenience store are used within 30 minutes of purchase. Many customers shop there at least two or three times a week and the average sales transaction is small. Due to limited shelf space, stores receive multiple weekly deliveries and prices reflect the small sale amounts and the high handling costs. Because customers are less price-sensitive than those shopping at other food-oriented retailers, gross margins are much higher than those of conventional supermarkets.

Lately, the industry has faced various problems: some areas are saturated with stores; supermarkets are providing more competition due to longer hours and better stocking of nonfood items; a number of stores have become too big, making shopping less expeditious;

Table 5.2 Selected Aspects of Store-Based Retail Strategy Mixes

Type of Retailer	Location	Merchandise	Prices	Atmosphere and Services	Promotion
Food-Oriented					
Convenience store	Neighborhood	Medium width and low depth of assortment; average quality	Average to above-average	Average	Moderate
Conventional supermarket	Neighborhood	Extensive width and depth of assortment; average quality; manufacturer, private, and generic brands	Competitive	Average	Heavy use of newspapers, flyers, and coupons, self-service
Food-based superstore	Community shopping center or isolated site	Full assortment of super-market items, plus health and beauty aids and general merchandise	Competitive	Average	Heavy use of newspapers and flyers, self-service
Combination store	Community shopping center or isolated site	Full selection of supermarket and drugstore items or super-market and general merchandise; average quality	Competitive	Average	Heavy use of newspaper and flyers; self-service
Box (limited-line) store	Neighborhood	Low width and depth of assortment; few perishables; few national brands	Very low	Low	Little or none
Warehouse store	Secondary site, often in industrial area	Moderate width and low depth; emphasis on manufacturer brands bought at discounts	Very low	Low	Little or none
General Merchandise					
Speciality store	Business district or shopping center	Very narrow width of assortment; extensive depth of assortment; average to good quality	Competitive to above-average	Average to excellent	Heavy use of displays; extensive sales force
Traditional department store	Business district, shopping center, or isolated store	Extensive width and depth of assortment; average to good quality	Average to above-average	Good to excellent	Heavy ad and catalog use, direct mail; personal selling
Full-line discount store	Business district, shopping center, or isolated store	Extensive width and depth of assortment; average to good quality	Competitive	Slightly below-average to average	Heavy use of newspapers; price-oriented; moderate sales force
Variety store	Business district, shopping center, or isolated store	Good width and depth of assortment; below-average to average quality	Average	Below-average	Heavy use of newspapers; self-service
Off-price chain	Business district, suburban shopping strip, or isolated store	Moderate width, but poor depth of assortment; average to good quality, low continuity	Low	Below-average	Use of news-papers; brands not advertised; limited sales force
Factory outlet	Out-of-the-way site or discount mall	Moderate width, but poor depth of assortment; some irregular merchandise; low continuity	Very low	Very low	Little; self-service
Membership club	Isolated store or secondary site (industrial park)	Moderate width, but poor depth of assortment; low continuity	Very low	Very low	Little; some direct mail; limited sales force
Flea market	Isolated site, racetrack, or arena	Extensive width, but poor depth of assortment; variable quality; low continuity	Very low	Very low	Limited; self-service

Figure 5.5
Wendy's and Pilot: A New Combination for Convenience Stores

Wendy's and Pilot have combined their facilities in some locales to offer expanded products for convenience store customers.
Reprinted by permission of Wendy's International.

the traditional target market (35-year-old blue-collar workers) has been shrinking; and several chains have had financial difficulties.

The Food Marketing Institute (www.fmi.org) is the leading industry association for food retailers.

Conventional Supermarket The Food Marketing Institute defines a **supermarket** as a self-service food store with grocery, meat, and produce departments and minimum annual sales of $2 million. Included are conventional supermarkets, food-based superstores, combination stores, box (limited-line) stores, and warehouse stores. See Figure 5.6.

A **conventional supermarket** is a departmentalized food store with a wide range of food and related products; sales of general merchandise are rather limited. This institution started in the 1930s when it was recognized that only a large-scale operation would let a retailer combine volume sales, self-service, and low prices. Self-service allowed supermarkets to cut costs, as well as increase volume. Personnel costs were reduced, and impulse buying

Figure 5.6
The Food Retailing World of A&P

The Great Atlantic & Pacific Tea Company, Inc. (A&P), based in Montvale, New Jersey, operates conventional supermarkets, superstores, combination food and drug stores, and limited assortment food stores in U.S. states, the District of Columbia, and Ontario, Canada, under the A&P, Waldbaum's, Super Foodmart, Food Emporium, Super Fresh, Farmer Jack, Kohl's, Sav-A-Center, Dominion, Ultra Mart, and Food Basics trade names.
Reprinted by permisson.

increased. The car and the refrigerator contributed to the supermarket's success by lowering travel costs and adding to the life span of perishables. Easy parking and lower prices (for consumers buying in bulk) were tactics used by the supermarket to exploit these inventions.

Since the early 1960s, overall supermarket sales have stabilized at about three-quarters of U.S. grocery sales, with conventional supermarkets now yielding 43 percent of supermarket sales. In 1998, there were 18,200 conventional units, with sales of $143 billion.[16] Chains account for the majority of sales. Among the leaders are Kroger, Safeway, Albertson's, and Winn-Dixie. Many independent supermarkets are affiliated with cooperative or voluntary organizations, such as IGA and Supervalu.

Conventional supermarkets have generally relied on high inventory turnover (volume sales). Their profit margins are low. In general, average gross margins (selling prices less merchandise costs) are 20 to 22 percent of sales and net profits are 1 to 3 percent of sales.

Conventional supermarkets must deal with intense competition from other types of food stores: convenience stores offer greater customer convenience; food-based superstores and combination stores have more product lines and greater variety within them, as well as better gross margins; and box and warehouse stores have lower operating costs and prices. Membership clubs (discussed later), with their discount prices, also provide competition— especially now that they have much expanded food lines. Over the past 25 years, thousands of conventional supermarkets have closed; many others have changed their strategy mix to another format. Variations of the supermarket are covered next.

Food-Based Superstore A **food-based superstore** is larger and more diversified than a conventional supermarket but usually smaller and less diversified than a combination store. This format originated in the 1970s as supermarkets sought to stem sales declines by expanding store size and the number of nonfood items carried. Some supermarkets merged with drugstores or general merchandise stores, but more grew into food-based superstores. There were 7,300 food-based U.S. superstores in 1998, with sales of nearly $120 billion.[17]

The typical food-based superstore occupies 25,000 to 50,000 square feet of total space and obtains 20 to 25 percent of revenues from general merchandise items, such as garden supplies, flowers, small household appliances, wine, and film developing. It caters to consumers' complete grocery needs and offers them the ability to buy fill-in general merchandise.

Like combination stores, food-based superstores are efficient, offer people a degree of one-stop shopping, stimulate impulse purchases, and feature high-profit general merchandise. But they also offer other advantages: It is easier and less costly to redesign and convert supermarkets into food-based superstores than into combination stores. Many consumers feel more comfortable shopping in true food stores than in huge combination stores. Management expertise is better focused in food-based superstores.

In the past 15 years, all the leading U.S. supermarket chains have turned more to food-based superstores. They have expanded and remodeled existing supermarkets and built numerous new stores. Many independent supermarkets have also converted facilities to food-based superstores.

Combination Store A **combination store** unites supermarket and general merchandise sales in one facility, with general merchandise typically accounting for 25 to 40 percent of total sales. The introduction of these stores can be traced to the late 1960s and early 1970s, when common checkout areas were developed for independently owned supermarkets and drugstores or supermarkets and general merchandise stores. A natural offshoot of this was to fully integrate the two operations under one management. In 1998, there were 2,000 U.S. combination stores (including supercenters), and annual sales were $40 billion.[18]

Combination stores are popular for the following reasons. They are very large, from 30,000 up to 100,000 or more square feet. This leads to operating efficiencies and cost savings. Consumers like one-stop shopping and will travel further to get to the store. Impulse sales are high. Many general merchandise items have better gross margins than traditional supermarket items. Supermarkets and drugstores have many commonalities in customers served and the kinds of low-price, high-turnover items sold. Drugstore and general merchandise customers are drawn to the store more frequently than they would be otherwise.

A **supercenter** is a combination store blending an economy supermarket with a discount department store. It is the U.S. version of the even larger **hypermarket** (the European institution pioneered by firms such as Carrefour that did not succeed in the United States). At least 40 percent of supercenter sales are from nonfood items. These stores usually range from 75,000 to 150,000 square feet in size and they stock up to 50,000 and more items, much more than the 30,000 or so items carried by other combination stores.

Among the firms with combination stores are Meijer, Fred Meyer, Wal-Mart, Kmart, and Albertson's.

Meijer's (www.meijer.com) combination stores are quite popular with shoppers. They carry 120,000 items.

Box (Limited-Line) Store The **box (limited-line) store** is a food-based discounter that focuses on a small selection of items, moderate hours of operation (compared to other supermarkets), few services, and limited manufacturer brands. There are usually less than 1,500 items, few or no refrigerated perishables, and few sizes and brands per item. Price marking is on the shelf or on overhead signs. Items are displayed in cut cases. Customers do their own bagging. Checks are usually not accepted. Box stores depend on low-priced private-label brands. They aim to price merchandise 20 to 30 percent below supermarkets.

The box-store concept originated in Europe around 1970 and was exported to the United States in the mid-1970s. The growth of these stores has not been as anticipated, as sales rose modestly in the 1990s. Other food stores, in some cases, have matched box-store prices. Many people are loyal to manufacturer brands and box stores cannot fulfill one-stop shopping needs.

There were 850 box stores in the United States in 1998, with sales of $3 billion.[19] The leading box store operator is Aldi.

Warehouse Store A **warehouse store** is a food-based discounter offering a moderate number of food items in a no-frills setting. Unlike box stores, warehouse stores appeal to one-stop food shoppers. These stores concentrate on special purchases of manufacturer brands. They use cut-case displays, provide little service, post prices on shelves, and locate in secondary sites (like industrial districts).

Warehouse stores began in the late 1970s. As of 1998, there were 1,750 U.S. stores with $30 billion in sales.[20] There are three warehouse store formats in terms of size: 15,000 to 25,000 square feet, 25,000 to 35,000 square feet, and 50,000 to 65,000 square feet.

The largest store is known as a super warehouse. There are 475 of them in the United States. They have annual sales exceeding $20 million each and contain a variety of departments, including produce. High ceilings are used to accommodate pallet loads of groceries. Shipments are made directly to the store. Customers pack their own groceries. Super warehouses can be profitable at gross margins that are far lower than those for conventional supermarkets. The leading super warehouse chain is Cub Foods.

A potential problem, which has limited the growth of warehouse stores, is the lack of brand continuity. Since products are usually bought when special deals are available, brands may be temporarily or permanently out of stock. In addition, many consumers do not like shopping in warehouse settings.

Table 5.3 shows selected operating data for convenience stores, conventional supermarkets, food-based superstores, combination stores, box stores, and warehouse stores.

General Merchandise Retailers

There are eight store-based general merchandise strategic formats shown in Table 5.2; each is covered in the following subsections: specialty store, traditional department store, full-line discount store, variety store, off-price chain, factory outlet, membership club, and flea market.

Table 5.3 Selected Typical Operating Data for Food-Oriented Retailers, 1998

Factor	Convenience Store	Conventional Supermarket	Food-Based Superstore	Combination Store[a]	Box (Limited-Line) Store	Warehouse Store
No. of stores	97,000	18,200	7,300	2,000	850	1,750
Total annual sales	$75 billion[b]	$143 billion	$120 billion	$40 billion	$3 billion	$30 billion
Average store selling area (sq. ft.)	5,000 or less	15,000–20,000	25,000–50,000	30,000–100,000+	5,000–9,000	15,000+
No. of checkouts per store	1–3	6–10	10+	10+	35	5+
Gross margin	25–30%	20–22%	20–25%	25%	10–12%	12–15%
No of items stocked per store	3,000–4,000	12,000–17,000	20,000+	30,000+	Under 1,500	2,500+
Major emphasis	Daily fill-in needs; dairy, sandwiches, tobacco, gas, beverages, magazines	Food; only 5% of sales from general merchandise	Positioned between supermarket and combo store; 20–25%of sales from general merchandise	One-stop shopping; general merchandise is 25–40% of sales	Low prices; few or no perishables	Low prices; variable assortments; may or may not stock perishables

[a] Including supercenters.
[b] Excluding gasoline.

Source: "66th Annual Report of the Grocery Industry," *Progressive Grocer* (April 1999); and authors' estimates.

Specialty Store A **specialty store** concentrates on selling one goods or service line, such as apparel and accessories, toys, furniture, or muffler repair. In contrast to a mass marketing approach, specialty stores usually carry a narrow, but deep, assortment in their chosen category and tailor the strategy to selective market segments. This enables specialty stores to maintain better selections and sales expertise than competitors, which are often department stores. It also lets them control investments and have a certain amount of flexibility. Among the popular categories of specialty stores are apparel, personal care, auto supply, home furnishings, electronics, books, toys, home improvement, pet supplies, jewelry, and sporting goods.

This is how the U.S. specialty store has progressed as an institution:

In the 1950s and 1960s, retailing was dominated by giant department stores that carried just about every type of merchandise—from apparel to appliances and electronic equipment. The more limited amount of products available permitted them to do this rather easily. For example, TV sets were offered in about 20 different models, compared with more than 200 today. During the late 1960s and early 1970s, specialty stores focusing on narrow product lines began to emerge. The first to do so were apparel shops targeting teens and children. As a result of the bulge of baby boomers, the teenage and junior apparel industry rocketed to new heights. Initially, the growing pie was comfortably shared by department stores and new specialty stores. However, young, price-conscious shoppers began to favor smaller, more focused chains that offered better customer service and more new models and

Sweden's Ikea Stays Offline

Ikea, the Swedish furniture giant, has no plans to sell its colorful and decorative furniture and accessories online. Despite its zealous concern for efficiency, Ikea views online retailing with much trepidation.

Although Ikea has had a Web site (www.ikea.com) since 1997, the site is basically an online catalog. Its online visitors must still go to an Ikea store to purchase furniture and accessories. Even phone orders are not accepted. According to the person responsible for Ikea's international Web development, Ikea has no plans to update its site into E-commerce: "The range of items and low prices, the stores, and the printed Ikea catalogs are the big issues in our marketing mix and a lot remains to be done within these areas first to improve our business."

Two reasons why Ikea has not ventured more into E-commerce are its large "experience" stores and its focus on customer service. Ikea has made significant investments in stores by including such amenities as day care centers, cafeterias, and sample rooms. It does not want to lose these customer services. Ikea is also unconvinced that it can offer Web customers the same level of service as in-store customers.

Comment on Ikea's approach to the Web.

Sources: Sami Kuusela, "Offline. On Target?" *Business 2.0* (December 1998), pp. 43 – 44; and *www.ikea.com* (March 7, 2000).

brands. As suburban shopping malls grew in the late 1970s and early 1980s, specialty chains quickly populated the new complexes, duplicating their store concepts nationwide. During the economic growth of the 1980s, mall occupancy escalated, and just about everybody raked in big profits. By the early 1990s, the retail climate was becoming overstored and profits were declining. The recession of 1990-91 exacerbated the overstoring problem and led to the demise of many department stores and specialty store chains. After a wave of store closings and industry consolidation, today's retail environment is more benign. For department stores and specialty retailers, competition remains. Several specialty retailers, such as Abercrombie & Fitch, American Eagle Outfitters, and Gap, have once again taken the lead as the preferred shopping destination among young people by offering styles that these consumers are seeking, at the prices they want.[21]

Consumers often shop at specialty stores because of the knowledgeable sales personnel, the variety of choices within the goods/service category, customer service policies, intimate store size and atmosphere (although this is not true of the category killer store), the lack of crowds (also not true of category killer stores), and the absence of aisles of merchandise unrelated to their purchase intentions—they do not have to go by several departments looking for the desired product. Some specialty stores have elaborate fixtures and upscale merchandise for affluent shoppers, while others are discount-oriented and aim at price-conscious consumers.

Total specialty store sales are difficult to estimate because these stores sell almost all kinds of goods and services, and aggregate specialty store data are not compiled by the U.S. Department of Commerce. However, annual nonfood specialty store sales in the United States exceed $1 trillion (including auto dealers). During 1998, the top 100 specialty store chains (excluding auto dealers) had sales of $175 billion and operated about 90,000 outlets. Among the 100 chains, about one-quarter were involved with apparel. Specialty store leaders include Toys "R" Us (toys), The Limited, Inc., and Gap (apparel),

Best Buy and Circuit City (consumer electronics), and Barnes & Noble and Borders (books).[22]

As noted earlier in the chapter, one type of specialty store—the category killer—has been gaining in strength. A **category killer** (also known as a **power retailer**) is an especially large specialty store. It features an enormous selection in its product category and relatively low prices; and consumers are drawn from wide geographic areas. Toys "R" Us, The Limited, Gap, Sam Goody, and Barnes & Noble are just a few of the many specialty store chains opening new category killer stores to complement existing stores. Blockbuster, Sephora (depicted in Figure 5.7), Sports Authority, and Staples are among the chains almost fully based on the category killer store concept. Sports Authority's 225 stores all have more than 40,000 square feet of selling space. With annual sales of over $1.6 billion, it is the world's leading specialty store chain for sporting goods. In an environment with thousands of sporting goods stores, the category killer format enables Sports Authority "to provide under one roof an extensive selection of merchandise for sports and leisure activities that ordinarily are associated with specialty shops and pro shops, such as golf, tennis, snow skiing, cycling, hunting, fishing, bowling, archery, boating, and water sports, as well as for activities ordinarily associated with traditional sporting goods retailers, such as team sports, physical fitness, and men's, women's, and children's athletic and active apparel and footwear. Each megastore offers about 45,000 active items (excluding discontinued ones) across 18 major departments."[23]

Nonetheless, smaller specialty stores (even ones with under 1,000 square feet of space) can prosper if they are focused, offer strong customer service, and avoid being imitations of

Figure 5.7
Sephora: A Power in Beauty Care

French-based Sephora operates category killer stores in France, Luxembourg, Spain, Italy, Portugal, Poland, and Asia-Pacific. It entered the United States in 1998 with stores in New York and Miami. Since then, it has expanded rapidly in the United States.

Reprinted by permission of PricewaterhouseCoopers LLP.

larger firms. Many consumers do not like shopping in huge stores: "Some companies mistakenly believe that increasing the size of a store will automatically translate into increased sales. Tandy discovered the error in this thinking with its Incredible Universe chain. The 17-store chain was a new interactive concept in the retailing of name brand consumer electronics and appliances. The behemoth stores averaged 184,000 square feet in size and carried over 85,000 different items. After slumping sales hurt profits at the parent company, Tandy exited the business and closed all the stores in mid-1997. Because category killers may not be practical for a consumer who is looking for only one or a few specific items, Home Depot is hoping to attract this market by opening a chain of smaller Villager Hardware stores."[24]

Any size specialty store can be adversely affected by seasonality or a decline in the popularity of its product category because its offering is so concentrated. This type of store may also fail to attract consumers who are interested in one-stop shopping for multiple product categories.

Traditional Department Store A **department store** is a large retail unit with an extensive assortment (width and depth) of goods and services that is organized into separate departments for purposes of buying, promotion, customer service, and control. It has the greatest selection of any general merchandise retailer, often serves as the anchor store in a shopping center or district, has strong credit card penetration, and is usually part of a chain. To be defined as a department store by the U.S. Bureau of the Census, a store has to meet four criteria. First, it must employ at least 50 people. Second, apparel and soft goods (nondurables) must account for at least 20 percent of total sales. Third, the merchandise assortment must include some items in each of these lines: furniture, home furnishings, appliances, and radio and TV sets; a general line of apparel for the family; and household linens and dry goods. Fourth, if annual sales are under $10 million, no more than 80 percent can be from any one line. If sales are at least $10 million, there is no limitation on the percentage from a line, as long as combined sales of the smallest two lines are at least $1 million.

Two types of retailers satisfy the Bureau of Census definition: the traditional department store (introduced by Macy's, Wanamaker, and others in the 1860s) and the full-line discount store (introduced by firms such as Kmart, Target Stores, and Wal-Mart in 1962). Together, they accounted for more than $280 billion in 1998 sales—including supercenters and leased departments. This was 10 percent of U.S. retail sales.[25] The traditional department store is discussed here; the full-line discount store is examined next.

At a **traditional department store,** merchandise quality ranges from average to quite good. Pricing is moderate to above-average. Customer service ranges from medium levels of sales help, credit, delivery, and so forth to high levels of each. For example, Macy's targets middle-class shoppers interested in assortment and moderate prices, while Bloomingdale's aims at upscale consumers through more trendy merchandise and higher prices. A dwindling number of traditional department stores (such as Sears) sell all of the product lines that the category used to carry. Most place greater emphasis on apparel and do not carry such lines as furniture, consumer electronics, and major appliances.

Over its history, the traditional department store has been responsible for many innovations, including advertising prices, enacting a one-price policy (whereby all shoppers pay the same price for the same good or service), developing computerized checkout facilities, offering money-back guarantees, adding branch stores, decentralizing management, and moving into suburban shopping centers.

However, during the past several years, industrywide sales growth of traditional department stores has lagged behind that of full-line discount stores. Today, traditional department store sales, which were $96 billion in 1998, represent a little over one-third of total department store sales. These are some reasons for the institution's difficulties:

Saks Incorporated (www.saks incorporated.com) operates several department store chains around the country, including Carson Pirie Scott, Parisian, Proffitt's, and Saks Fifth Avenue.

- They no longer have brand exclusivity for a lot of the items they sell; manufacturer brands are available at specialty and discount outlets.
- Many firms have been too passive with private-label goods. Instead of creating their own brands, they have signed exclusive licensing agreements with fashion designers to use the latter's names. This perpetuates customer loyalty to the designer and not the store.
- There are more price-conscious consumers than before, and they are attracted to discount retailers.
- The popularity of shopping malls has aided specialty stores since consumers can accomplish one-stop shopping through several specialty stores in the same mall or shopping center.
- Large specialty chains have strong supplier relations and extensive advertising campaigns; department stores do not dominate the smaller stores around them as they once did.
- Many discounters, which did not previously, now accept credit cards.
- Customer service has deteriorated. Store personnel are not as loyal, helpful, or knowledgeable.
- Some stores are too big and have too much unproductive selling space and low-turnover merchandise.
- The scrambled merchandising of food retailers has drawn away sales.
- Unlike specialty stores, many department stores have had a weak focus on customer market segments and a fuzzy image. Too often, departments have been organized by supplier brand name rather than according to customer needs.
- Such chains as Sears have repeatedly changed strategic orientation, confusing consumers as to their image. (Is Sears a traditional department store chain or a full-line discount store chain?)
- Chain management has sometimes been too decentralized—leading to different merchandising strategies in branch stores (which blur the chain's image).
- Some companies are not as innovative in their merchandise decisions as they once were; they react to suppliers rather than make suggestions to them.
- Specialty stores often have better assortments in the lines they carry. No traditional department store has the toy selection of Toys "R" Us or the sporting goods assortment of Sports Authority.
- Leveraged buyouts saddled several chains with significant debt, causing a poor cash flow; limited funds for store renovations, advertising, and (in some cases) adequate merchandise assortments; and adverse publicity.

To overcome these problems, traditional department stores need to clarify their niche in the marketplace (retail positioning); place greater emphasis on customer service and sales personnel; present more exciting, better-organized store interiors and displays—and change them frequently; use space better by downsizing stores and eliminating slow-selling, space-consuming items (such as J.C. Penney dropping consumer electronics products); and open outlets in smaller, underdeveloped towns and cities (as Sears has done). They can also centralize more buying and promotion functions, do better research, and reach customers more efficiently (via such tools as targeted mailing pieces).

Full-Line Discount Store A **full-line discount store** is a type of department store with these features:

- It conveys the image of a high-volume, low-cost, fast-turnover outlet selling a broad merchandise assortment for less than conventional prices.
- It is more apt to carry the range of product lines expected at department stores, including consumer electronics, furniture, and appliances. There is also greater emphasis on such items as auto accessories, gardening equipment, and housewares.

On the Fast Track at Federated Department Stores

In the current quick-paced retailing climate, young managers are emerging as stars. Take the case of Love Goel, who at age 27 became the chief operating officer of Federated Department Store's E-commerce division—overseeing 500 employees nationwide. By 2002, Goel anticipates his division's generating $3 billion to $4 billion in annual revenues.

Goel says, "We are building the future. We are at the beginning of the journey. I'm the kind of person you bring in to blow the place up. I'm not encumbered by a lot of the traditional baggage." He is 10 years younger than most of his senior managers and had just 10 months' experience in retailing before assuming his position. Goal has bachelor degrees in computer science and finance, but not an MBA. "I sometimes ask myself, 'How did an old-line company let a guy this young get to the top?'"

Despite his lofty position at Federated, Love Goel does have his weaknesses. One of his bosses, William Lansing, chief executive officer of Federated Direct, says "Love is a somewhat immature manager. He breaks a lot of glass. There are people who think he's arrogant. But I think he'll lose the rough edges. We tolerate the bad part of it because the good part is very good."

Source: Jonathan Kaufman, "What Happens When a 20-Something Whiz Is Suddenly the Boss," *Wall Street Journal* (October 8, 1999), pp. A1, A10.

- Centralized checkout service is provided.
- Customer service is not usually provided within store departments, but at a centralized area. Products are normally sold via self-service with minimal assistance in any single department.
- The nondurable (soft) goods carried tend to feature private brands, whereas the durable (hard) goods are well-known manufacturer brands.
- Less fashion-sensitive merchandise is carried.
- Buildings, equipment, and fixtures are less expensive; and operating costs are lower than for traditional department stores and specialty stores.
- There is somewhat less emphasis on credit sales than in full-service stores.

Full-line discount store revenues were $186 billion in 1998 (including supercenters and leased departments), nearly two-thirds of all U.S. department store sales. Together, Wal-Mart, Kmart, and Target Stores operated 5,300 full-line discount stores (including supercenters) with $140 billion in full-line discount store sales. Overall, about a dozen full-line discount chains had sales of at least $1 billion in 1998.[26]

The success of full-line discount stores is due to a number of factors. They have a clear customer focus: middle-class and lower-middle-class shoppers looking for good value. The stores feature popular brands of average- to good-quality merchandise at competitive prices. They have added new goods and service categories and often have their own, well-advertised brands. Firms have worked hard to improve their image and make more customer services available. The average outlet (not the supercenter) tends to be smaller than a traditional department store, which improves productivity. Sales per square foot are often higher than in traditional department stores. Many full-line discount stores are located in small towns, where competition is reduced. Chains have been well managed, with standardized branch outlets and good employee relations. Facilities are often newer than those of many traditional department stores.

The greatest challenges facing full-line discount stores are the strong competition from other retailers (particularly lower-priced discounters and new store formats, such as category killers), too rapid expansion of some firms, saturation of prime locations, and the dominance of Wal-Mart, Kmart, and Target Stores. As a result, the industry has had a number of consolidations, bankruptcies, and liquidations.

Variety Store   A **variety store** handles a wide assortment of inexpensive and popularly priced goods and services, such as stationery, gift items, women's accessories, health and beauty aids, light hardware, toys, housewares, confectionery items, and shoe repair. Transactions are often on a cash basis. There are open displays and few salespeople. Variety stores do not carry full product lines, may not be departmentalized, and do not deliver products.

In 1998, variety store sales were $12 billion, well under 1 percent of total U.S. retail store sales. Among conventional variety store chains, McCrory, with 160 stores, is the leader. Woolworth exited the variety store business in 1997 after more than a century of operations.

Over the past 25 years, conventional variety stores have shown the poorest performance of any store category. This is due to heavy competition from specialty stores and discounters, the older facilities of many stores, the low profit margins of some items, and the decision of firms such as Woolworth to leave the category. At one time, Woolworth had 1,200 variety stores with annual sales of $2 billion.

One interesting spin-off from the conventional variety store has been gaining popularity. Dollar discount stores and closeout chains are becoming more prevalent. These stores often sell similar items to those sold in conventional variety stores, but in plainer surroundings and at much lower prices. Dollar General and Family Dollar are leading dollar discount store chains and Consolidated Stores (with its Odd Lots/Big Lots/Pick 'n Save stores) is a major closeout chain. Among the three firms, 1998 sales were $8 billion.[27]

Off-Price Chain   An **off-price chain** features brand-name (sometimes designer label) apparel and accessories, footwear (primarily women's and family), linens, fabrics, cosmetics, and/or housewares and sells them at everyday low prices in an efficient, limited-service environment. It frequently has community dressing rooms, centralized checkout counters, no gift wrapping, and extra charges for alterations. Merchandise is bought opportunistically, as special deals occur. Other retailers' canceled orders, manufacturers' irregulars and overruns, and end-of-season items are often purchased for a fraction of their original wholesale prices.

Off-price chains usually aim at the same type of shoppers as traditional department stores, but offer prices up to 40 to 50 percent lower. And as a T.J. Maxx executive once noted, shoppers are lured by the promise of new merchandise on a regular basis, "Every T.J. Maxx store gets thousands of items of new, quality merchandise in every week."[28] In addition, various off-price shopping centers now appeal to people's interest in one-stop shopping.

The most crucial aspect of their strategy for off-price chains involves buying merchandise and establishing long-term relationships with suppliers. To succeed, the chains must secure large quantities of merchandise at reduced wholesale prices and have a regular flow of goods into the stores. Their inventory turnover is far higher than that of department stores.

Sometimes, manufacturers use off-price chains to sell samples and products that have not done well (this generally occurs three to four weeks after the beginning of a season) and merchandise remaining on hand near the end of a season. In this way, manufacturers have access to quick cash, gain a market for closeouts and discontinued items, and have relationships with retailers promising not to mention brands or prices in ads (so as to not alienate department store or specialty store clients). Off-price chains tend to be less demanding than department stores in terms of the advertising support requested from suppliers, do not return products, and pay promptly.

Other times, off-price chains employ a more active buying strategy. Instead of waiting for closeouts and canceled orders, they convince manufacturers to make merchandise such as garments during off-seasons and pay cash for items before they are produced (or delivered).

TJX (www.tjx.com) operates two of the biggest off-price apparel chains: T.J. Maxx and Marshall's.

In 1998, the total sales of U.S. off-price apparel stores were $20 billion. The four biggest chains had sales of $12 billion and operated 1,660 stores.[29] The leaders are T.J. Maxx and Marshalls (both owned by TJX), Ross Stores, and Burlington Coat Factory.

Off-price chains have faced some marketplace pressures because of growing competition from other institutional formats (such as department stores running special sales throughout the year), the discontinuity of their merchandise, poor management at some firms, insufficient customer service for some shoppers, and the shakeout of underfinanced companies.

Factory Outlet A **factory outlet** is a manufacturer-owned store selling manufacturer closeouts, discontinued merchandise, irregulars, canceled orders, and, sometimes, in-season, first-quality merchandise. Manufacturers' interest in outlet stores has risen for four basic reasons. First, a manufacturer can control where its discounted merchandise is sold. By placing outlets in out-of-the-way locations, depressed areas, or areas with low sales penetration of the firm's brands, factory outlet revenues are unlikely to affect the sales at a manufacturer's key specialty and department store accounts. Second, outlets can be profitable despite prices up to 60 percent less than customary retail prices. This is due to low operating costs—as a result of few services, low rent, limited displays, and plain store fixtures. In addition, the manufacturer does not have to pay wholesalers or retailers. Third, at factory outlets, manufacturers can decide on store visibility, set promotion policies, remove labels, and be sure that discontinued items and irregulars are disposed of properly. Fourth, since many specialty and department stores are increasing their use of private labels, manufacturers may need revenue from outlet stores to sustain their own growth.

In recent years, more factory outlet stores have been locating in clusters or in outlet malls to expand customer traffic and use cooperative ads. Large outlet malls are in Connecticut, Florida, Georgia, New York, Pennsylvania, Tennessee, and a number of other states. In 1998, there were 13,000 U.S. factory outlet stores representing 500 manufacturers—many in the 300 outlet malls nationwide; and these stores had $13 billion in sales, three-quarters from apparel and accessories.[30] See Figure 5.8. Manufacturers with factory outlets include Bass

Figure 5.8
Outlet Malls

Tanger Factory Outlet Centers owns and operates 30 outlet centers in 22 states totaling more than 5.0 million square feet of outlet retail space. Tanger Outlet Centers are characterized by a tenant mix of leading designer and brand name manufacturers. Each facility provides a one-stop shopping experience for consumers to purchase a variety of brand name products for the entire family directly from the manufacturer at substantial savings.
Reprinted by permission.

(footwear), Gap (apparel), Harry & David (fruits and gift items), Levi's (apparel), Liz Claiborne (apparel), Pepperidge Farm (food), Samsonite (luggage), and Totes (rain gear).

When determining whether to enter into or expand factory outlets, manufacturers need to be cautious. They must evaluate their expertise in retailing, the investment costs, the impact on existing retailers that buy from them, and the response of final customers. Certainly, manufacturers will not want to jeopardize their products' sales at full retail prices.

Membership Club A **membership (warehouse) club** appeals to price-conscious consumers, who must be members to shop there. It straddles the line between wholesaling and retailing. Some members of a typical club are small business owners and employees who pay a nominal annual fee (such as $35 each) and buy merchandise at wholesale prices; these customers make purchases for use in operating their firms or for personal use. They yield 60 percent of total club sales. The bulk of members are final consumers who buy exclusively for their own use; they represent 40 percent of overall club sales. These consumers also usually pay a nominal membership fee and must belong to a union, be municipal employees, work for educational institutions, or belong to other specified groups to become members (in reality, eligibility is so broad as to exclude few consumers). Sometimes, their prices are slightly more than those paid by business customers.

The membership club is a derivative of the membership-based discount retailer popular in the 1950s and 1960s in the United States and the giant European warehouse outlet catering to small food and drugstore retailers. The operating strategy of the current membership club began in the mid-1970s and centers on large store facilities (up to 100,000 or more square feet), inexpensive isolated or industrial park locations, opportunistic buying (with some merchandise discontinuity), a fraction of the items stocked by full-line discount stores, little or no advertising, plain fixtures, wide aisles (to give forklift trucks access to shelves), concrete floors, limited or no delivery, fewer credit options than in many other stores, goods sent directly from manufacturers to stores, and very low prices.

A membership club sells three kinds of goods: general merchandise, such as consumer electronics, appliances, computers, housewares, tires, and apparel (35 to 60 percent of sales); food (20 to 35 percent of sales); and sundries, such as health and beauty aids, tobacco, liquor, and candy (15 to 30 percent of sales). Today, it may also have a pharmacy, photo developing, a car-buying service, and other items formerly viewed as frills for this format. Its inventory turnover rate is several times that of a department store.

Sam's (www. samsclub.com) is Wal-Mart's membership club division. It has lower prices and plainer settings than Wal-Mart's full-line department stores.

In 1998, there were 1,000 membership club stores. The retail aspect of these clubs accounted for sales of $22 billion to $25 billion. Together, the two leaders, Sam's and Costco (formerly PriceCostco), yield 90 percent of industry sales.[31]

The major retailing challenges faced by membership clubs relate to the limited size of their final consumer market segment, the allocation of efforts between business and final consumer accounts (without antagonizing one group or the other, and without presenting a blurred store image), the lack of interest by many consumers in shopping at warehouse-type stores, the power of the two industry leaders, and the potential for saturation caused by overexpansion.

Flea Market A **flea market** has many retail vendors offering a range of products at discount prices in plain surroundings. It is rooted in the centuries-old tradition of street selling—shoppers touch, sample, and haggle over the prices of items. Once, flea market vendors sold only antiques, bric-a-brac, and assorted used merchandise. Today, they also frequently sell new goods, such as clothing, cosmetics, watches, consumer electronics, housewares, and gift items. Many flea markets are located in nontraditional sites not normally associated with retailing: racetracks, stadiums, and arenas. Others are at sites abandoned by supermarkets and department stores. They may be indoor or outdoor.

Are Flea Markets Fair Competitors?

After a two-month investigation, the Queens, New York, district attorney raided a flea market and confiscated more than 100,000 counterfeit items which carried such labels as Polo, Ralph Lauren, Calvin Klein, Nike, Nautica, and Timberland. Among the counterfeit items that were seized were T-shirts, jackets, sweatpants, sunglasses, and backpacks.

As stated by the president of a private investigation firm involved with the raid, manufacturers and designers need to "roll up their sleeves and come up with a solid investigative plan" to crack down on counterfeiters. "They need to do their homework, bring information to proper law enforcement agen-

cies, and follow-up with civil and criminal action."

This comment was disputed by a firm that works as an outside counsel for several manufacturers of clothing that have been the subject of counterfeiting: "They all have productive, cost-effective programs. It's like fighting the war against drugs. You start with the little guy with the hope of meeting the bigger guys, and these days we're hitting more big guys." The International Anti-Counterfeiting Coalition says counterfeiters cost the apparel industry alone an estimated $8 billion in retail sales.

What is the obligation of a flea market owner in verifying that goods sold there are legitimate?

Source: Rosemary Feitelberg, "Flea Market Raid Bags $2 Million in Bogus Goods," *Women's Wear Daily* (October 29, 1998), p. 4.

At a flea market, individual retailers rent space on a daily, weekly, or seasonal basis. For example, a flea market might rent 20-foot-by-40-foot spaces for $30 to $50 or more per day, depending on the location. Some flea markets impose a parking fee or admission charge on consumers shopping there.

There are a few hundred major flea markets in the United States, such as the Rose Bowl Flea Market in California, but overall sales data are not available. The improved credibility of permanent flea markets, consumer interest in bargaining, Sunday hours, the broader product mix, the availability of some brand-name goods, and consumer price sensitivity all contribute to this institution's appeal. The Rose Bowl Flea Market (www.rgcshows.com/ rose-bowl.asp) has 1,500 vendors and attracts 20,000 shoppers a day:

> The flea market is held the second Sunday of every month, rain or shine, at the World Famous Rose Bowl in Pasadena. All selling spaces are 10 feet deep × 20 feet frontage with additional room for one car. Vendors may line up after 1:00 A.M. and move in from 5:30 A.M. to 7:00 A.M. The only restricted items are food, animals, guns, ammunition, and pornography. The price of available selling space is as follows: Our best available high traffic spaces are $70.00 reserved pink spaces located around the main perimeter. Also, for new merchandise sellers, we have $50.00 yellow spaces located in front of the main entrance. They are 10 feet × 20 feet; however, no cars may remain there. We also have $50.00 white spaces located across a bridge from our other flea market areas. Rose Bowl Flea Market regular admission starts at 9 A.M. for the general public at $6.00 per person. Children under 12 are admitted free with an adult. We also have an early admission from 7:30 A.M. to 9:00 A.M. for $10.00 per person and a special preview VIP admission from 6:00 A.M. to 7:30 A.M. for $15.00 per person. Group rates are available. The public may shop for those last minute bargains until 4:30 P.M.

At any flea market, price haggling is encouraged, cash is the predominant currency, and many vendors gain their first real experience as retail entrepreneurs. *Goodridge's Guides to*

Flea Markets lists more than 5,500 flea markets, big and small, around the United States. The newest trend in flea markets involves Web-based flea markets such as eBay (www.ebay.com) and Amazon.com with its zShops.

Some traditional retailers are not happy about flea markets. They believe flea markets represent an unfair method of competition since the quality of merchandise may be misrepresented or overstated, consumers may buy items at flea markets and return them to other retailers for refunds that are higher than the prices paid, suppliers are often unaware their products are sold there, state and federal taxes can be easily avoided, and operating costs are quite low. Flea markets may also cause traffic congestion.

The high total sales volume from off-price chains, factory outlets, membership clubs, and flea markets can be explained by the wheel of retailing. All of these institutions are low-cost operators appealing to price-conscious consumers who are not totally satisfied with other retail formats that have upgraded merchandise and customer service, raised prices, and moved along the wheel.

SUMMARY

1. *To describe the wheel of retailing, scrambled merchandising, and the retail life cycle and show how they can help explain the performance of retail strategy mixes.* In Chapter 4, retail institutions were examined by type of ownership. This chapter views retailing from the perspective of store-based strategies. A retail strategy mix involves a combination of factors: location, operations, goods/services offered, pricing, atmosphere and customer services, and promotion. To flourish, a firm should strive to be dominant in some aspect of its strategy and thus reach destination retailer status

Three important concepts help explain the performance of diverse retail strategy mixes. According to the wheel of retailing, retail innovators often first appear as low-price operators with a low-cost structure and low profit margins. Over time, they upgrade their offerings and customer services and raise prices. They then become vulnerable to new discounters with lower cost structures that take their place along the wheel. Scrambled merchandising occurs as a retailer adds goods and services that are unrelated to each other and the firm's original business to increase overall sales and profit margins. Scrambled merchandising is contagious, and retailers often use it in self-defense. The retail life cycle states that retail institutions pass through identifiable stages of innovation, development, maturity, and decline. Attributes and strategies change as institutions mature.

2. *To discuss some ways in which retail strategy mixes are evolving.* Many institutions are adapting to the dynamics of the marketplace. Each of these approaches has been popular for different firms, depending on their strengths, weaknesses, and goals: mergers—by which separately owned retailers join together; diversifi-

cation—by which a retailer becomes active in businesses outside its normal operations; and downsizing—whereby unprofitable stores are closed or divisions are sold. Sometimes, single companies use all three approaches. More firms are also utilizing cost containment and value-driven retailing. They strive to hold down investment costs, as well as operating costs. There are many ways to do this.

3. *To examine a wide variety of food-oriented retailers involved with store-based strategy mixes.* Retail institutions may be classified by store-based strategy mix and divided into food-oriented and general merchandise groupings. In all, 14 store-based strategy mixes are covered in this chapter.

These are the food-oriented store-based retailers: A convenience store is well located, is open long hours, and offers a moderate number of fill-in items at average to above-average prices. A conventional supermarket is departmentalized and carries a wide range of food and related items; there is little general merchandise; and prices are competitive. A food-based superstore is larger and more diversified than a conventional supermarket but smaller and less diversified than a combination store. A combination store unites supermarket and general merchandise in a large facility and sets competitive prices; the supercenter (known as a hypermarket in Europe) is a type of combination store. The box (limited-line) store is a discounter focusing on a small product selection, moderate hours, few services, and few manufacturer brands. A warehouse store is a discounter offering a moderate number of food items in a no-frills setting that can be quite large (for a super warehouse).

S U M M A R Y (CONTINUED)

4. *To study a wide range of general merchandise retailers involved with store-based strategy mixes.* These are the general merchandise store-based retailers: A specialty store concentrates on one goods or service line and has a tailored strategy; the category killer is a special kind of specialty store. A department store is a large retailer that carries an extensive assortment of goods and services. The traditional one has a range of customer services and average to above-average prices. A full-line discount store is a department store with a low-cost, low-price

strategy. A variety store has an assortment of inexpensive and popularly priced items in a plain setting. An off-price chain features brand-name items and sells them at low prices in an austere environment. A factory outlet is manufacturer-owned and sells that firm's close-outs, discontinued merchandise, and irregulars at very low prices. A membership club appeals to price-conscious shoppers, who must be members to shop there. A flea market has many vendors offering items at discount prices in nontraditional settings.

Key Terms

strategy mix (p. 145)
destination retailer (p. 145)
wheel of retailing (p. 145)
scrambled merchandising (p. 147)
retail life cycle (p. 148)
mergers (p. 152)
diversification (p. 153)
downsizing (p. 153)
convenience store (p. 154)

supermarket (p. 156)
conventional supermarket (p. 156)
food-based superstore (p. 157)
combination store (p. 157)
supercenter (p. 158)
hypermarket (p. 158)
box (limited-line) store (p. 158)
warehouse store (p. 158)
specialty store (p. 159)

category killer (power retailer) (p. 161)
department store (p. 162)
traditional department store (p. 162)
full-line discount store (p. 163)
variety store (p. 165)
off-price chain (p. 165)
factory outlet (p. 166)
membership (warehouse) club (p. 167)
flea market (p. 167)

Questions for Discussion

1. Describe how a small drugstore could be a destination retailer.

2. Explain the wheel of retailing. Is this theory applicable today? Why or why not?

3. Develop a low-end retail strategy mix for a shoe store. Include location, operating procedures, goods/services offered, pricing tactics, and promotion methods.

4. The shoe store in Question 3 wants to upgrade to a high-end strategy. Outline the changes that must be made in the firm's strategy mix. What are the risks facing the retailer?

5. How could these retailers best apply scrambled merchandising? Explain your answers.
   a. Bakery.
   b. TV repair firm.
   c. Carpet store.
   d. Bowling alley.

6. Contrast the strategy emphasis that should be used by institutions in the innovation and accelerated developement stages of the retail life cycle with the emphasis by institutions in the maturity stage.

7. What alternative approaches are there for institutions that are in the decline phase of the retail life cycle?

8. Contrast the strategy mixes of convenience stores, conventional supermarkets, food-based superstores, and warehouse stores. Is there room for each? Explain your answer.

9. Do you think U.S. supercenters will succeed in the long-run? Why or why not?

10. What are the pros and cons of Sports Authority's operating 40,000+-square-foot stores?

11. Contrast the strategy mixes of specialty stores, traditional department stores, and full-line discount stores.

12. Comment on the decision of many traditional department stores to stop carrying such items as furniture, consumer electronics, and appliances.

13. What must the off-price chain do to succeed in the future?

14. Do you expect factory outlet stores to keep growing? Explain your answer.

WEB-BASED EXERCISE

Supercuts (www.supercuts.com)

Questions

1. Based on its Web site, what target market is the Supercuts specialty store chain seeking? Explain your answer.

2. Evaluate the Supercuts Web site from the perspective of attracting consumer clients.

3. Assess the Supercuts Web site from the perspective of attracting franchisees.

4. If there is one near you, visit a Supercuts store. Compare your perception of the physical store to your perception based on its Web site.

CHAPTER ENDNOTES

1. Matt Nannery, "Pigging Out," *Chain Store Age* (July 1999), pp. 77, 79.

2. Joel R. Evans and Barry Berman, "Power Retailing: Not Just for Large Firms," *Tips for Better Retailing*, Vol. 1 (Number 1, 1995).

3. The pioneering works on the wheel of retailing are Malcolm P. McNair, "Significant Trends and Developments in the Postwar Period," in A. B. Smith (Editor), *Competitive Distribution in a Free High Level Economy and Its Implications for the University* (Pittsburgh: University of Pittsburgh Press, 1958), pp. 17–18; and Stanley Hollander, "The Wheel of Retailing," *Journal of Marketing*, Vol. 25 (July 1960), pp. 37–42. For a more recent analysis of the concept, see Stephen Brown, "The Wheel of Retailing: Past and Future," *Journal of Retailing*, Vol. 66 (Summer 1990), pp. 143–49; and Stephen Brown, "Postmodernism, the Wheel of Retailing, and Will to Power," *International Review of Retail, Distribution, and Consumer Research*, Vol. 5 (July 1995), pp. 387–414.

4. "1999 Nonfoods Sales Manual," *Progressive Grocer* (August 1999), p. 21.

5. William R. Davidson, Albert D. Bates, and Stephen J. Bass, "The Retail Life Cycle," *Harvard Business Review*, Vol. 54 (November–December 1976), pp. 89–96. See also, James R. Lowry, "The Life Cycle of Shopping Centers," *Long Range Planning*, Vol. 30 (January–February 1997), pp. 77–86; Nirmalya Kumar, "The Revolution in Retailing: From Market Driven to Marketing Driving," *Long Range Planning*, Vol. 30 (December 1997), pp. 830–35; and "The Metamorphosis of American Retailing," *Women's Wear Daily* (September 28, 1998), p. 154S.

6. Carl Steidmann, "Third-Wave Retailers Find New Way to Do Business," *Chain Store Age Executive* (August 1993), p. 9A.

7. Dana Canedy, "Need Asparagus? Just Click On It," *New York Times on the Web* (September 10, 1999).

8. "Any Questions?" *www.kiosks.org/faqs.html* (March 9, 2000).

9. Tony Lisanti, "What If Service Merchandise Had Done Things Differently?" *Discount Store News* (April 5, 1999), p. 11.

10. Steidmann, "Third-Wave Retailers Find New Way to Do Business," p. 11A.

11. "Retailing: Specialty," *Standard & Poor's Industry Surveys* (May 27, 1999), pp. 14–15.

12. Linda Hyde, "Cross-Competition Escalates Battle for Market Share," *Chain Store Age Executive* (August 1993), pp. 11A–13A.

13. "Retailing: Current Analysis," *Standard & Poor's Industry Surveys* (January 27, 1994), p. 70.

14. "Retailing: General," *Standard & Poor's Industry Surveys* (May 20, 1999), p. 14.

15. *1999 State of the Industry* (Alexandria, Virginia: National Association of Convenience Stores, 1999).

16. "66th Annual Report of the Grocery Industry," *Progressive Grocer* (April 1999), p. 10.

17. Estimated by the authors from the "66th Annual Report of the Grocery Industry," p. 10.

18. Ibid.

19. Ibid.

CHAPTER ENDNOTES

20. Ibid.

21. "Retailing: Specialty," p. 16.

22. Computed by the authors from David P. Schulz, "Top 100 Specialty Stores," *Stores* (August 1999), pp. S1–S19.

23. Marianne Wilson, "Sephora's Strategic Revolution," *Chain Store Age* (January 2000), pp. 53–54; and *Sports Authority 1999 Annual Report*.

24. "Retailing: Specialty," p. 13.

25. *Annual Benchmark Report for Retail Trade: January 1989 to December 1998* (Washington, D.C.: Department of Commerce, 1999).

26. Ibid; and "The DSN Annual Industry Report," *Discount Store News* (July 12, 1999), p. 58.

27. See Kelly Barron, "Wal-Mart's Ankle Biters," *Forbes* (October 18, 1999), pp. 86–92.

28. Alice Z. Cuneo, "T.J. Maxx Fashions Ads to Battle Off-Price Pack," *Advertising Age* (September 16, 1996), p. 20.

29. "The DSN Annual Industry Report," p. 51.

30. "Outlet Industry Data," *www.valueretailnews.com/data.html* (March 9, 2000).

31. "The DSN Annual Industry Report," pp. 51, 58.

CASE 1

STARBUCKS IS STILL HOT

Some retailing analysts have compared Starbucks to other restaurant chains that grew too fast and collapsed (such as Planet Hollywood, Rainforest Café, and Boston Chicken) or say that its market in big cities is saturated. Other analysts feel Starbucks is still hot. One sees strong parallels between Starbucks and McDonald's, including "the singular focus on one product, the overseas opportunities, and the rapid emergence as the dominant player in a new niche." Some proponents of Starbucks point to its high stock price and its large expansion program both in the United States and in foreign locations.

For 1999 and 2000, Starbucks planned to open at least one store per day, every day in the United States alone. And while many observers concede that Starbucks' markets may be saturated in major U. S. cities, they feel Starbucks has significant growth opportunities in "mid America" and abroad. As of 1999, Kansas City had only two Starbucks outlets, Indiana had only one, and there were no Starbucks outlets in Tennessee, Mississippi, and Alabama. In addition, Starbucks' retail concept is applicable around the world. In 1999, it had 102 stores in Asia and forecasts having 500 units there by 2004.

The new store openings are just one part of Starbucks' overall retail strategy. Starbucks has also opened kiosks in 30 U.S. airports and operates 375 coffee shops in Barnes & Noble's bookshops. In an effort to increase sales in supermarkets, Starbucks recently launched a partnership wherein Kraft distributes Starbucks' beans and ground coffees to more than 20,000 supermarkets.

Ultimately, the success or failure of Starbucks will depend on how well it executes its strategy. One looming challenge is its need to increase sales in existing stores at the same time it expands its store base. This may be hard due to the cannibalization of sales at existing units by new units. Another challenge will be Starbucks' ability to differentiate itself in a competitive landscape including not only other high-quality, high-priced coffee houses but also low-cost coffee available at diners and luncheonettes.

To aid in the execution of its strategy, Starbucks has hired John Richards, a former industry consultant with significant hotel experience, to run its North American retail division. Richards is a hands-on executive who carefully reviews specific performance criteria, such as the percent of sales that are made before 11 A.M. (40 percent), same-store annual sales growth (6 percent), and the average bill ($3.50). Richards thinks that Starbucks has plentiful opportunities in both the southern and western United States due to warmer weather bringing higher evening sales and the growing popularity of iced drinks, which also offer higher profit margins than regular drip coffee.

One significant competitive advantage of Starbucks is its cadre of loyal customers. As one industry expert says, "Ten percent of Starbucks customers come in twice a day. That's a pretty remarkable figure for a retailer." Unlike Planet Hollywood and Rainforest Café, companies that saw their customer base fall when the novelty wore off, it is clear that good coffee is not a fad. Some cynics even suggest that coffee drinking may even be the last socially acceptable addiction.

Questions

1. Evaluate Starbucks' overall retail strategy, based on information in the case and at its Web site (www.starbucks.com).

2. What should be the role of food such as sandwiches and pastries in Starbucks' overall retail strategy?

3. Can Starbucks be considered a category killer? Explain your answer.

4. How easy is it for a competitor to copy Starbucks' retail strategy? Explain your answer.

Video Questions on Starbucks

1. Discuss Starbucks' "everything matters" philosophy.

2. Describe Starbucks' retail positioning as a coffee house.

NOTE   The material in this case is drawn from Nelson D. Schwartz, "Still Perking After All These Years," *Fortune* (May 24, 1999), pp. 203–10.

CASE 2

WILL THE MEGAPLEX KILL OFF THE MULTIPLEX?

Many people are flocking to the spacious new movie megaplex complexes and avoiding the multiplexes that have been a mainstay of shopping centers. In contrast to the multiplexes, the megaplexes usually offer more than a dozen screens, digital sound systems, stadium seating (armchairs arranged in tiers that offer viewers an unobstructed view), arm rests that can hold drinks and be tilted up to convert individual seats into a love-seat format, and screens with ceiling-to-floor and wall-to-wall dimensions.

In response to consumer demand, many theater chains are converting multiplexes to megaplexes—where feasible. If conversions are not possible, operators have chosen to either keep marginally profitable theaters open while waiting for their leases to expire, to sell the theaters, or to take write-offs and build new megaplexes at other sites. Many times, the long-term leases at shopping centers require the movie theater operator to take a substantial write-off when a multiplex takes the equivalent of "early retirement."

According to Summer Redstone, chairman of Viacom, a major entertainment conglomerate: "Stadium seating is a breakthrough in the industry. Where we have built them, we are

CASE 2
(CONTINUED)

doubling and tripling our business. For example, in Cincinnati, where we have a 20-screen stadium seating complex, we are doing three to four times as much business as we did a year ago, before we converted the multiplex." Research by National Amusements indicates that audiences will bypass a multiplex closer to home to see a film at a megaplex that is further away.

The costs of constructing a new megaplex—which can include as many as 24 or more screens with 3,000 or more seats—is now estimated at $1 million a screen. This compares with $600,000 a screen for a multiplex with 8 to 12 screens and 2,500 seats. In both instances, the figures do not include land costs.

Movie theater chains realize they need to protect their market areas with new megaplexes or risk losing business to competitors. For example, Loews states that although about a quarter of its U.S. movie screens are now in megaplexes, the firm expects the majority of its screens to be in the new format within the next few years.

Some industry analysts strongly believe that the United States is already "overscreened." Part of the reason for this is that, "Everybody is building new screens, and the old screens are not coming off line as quickly as possible." There are currently about 34,000 U.S. movie screens, roughly one for every 8,000 people. And while the number of movie tickets sold has increased by 40 percent since 1988, the number of screens has increased by 47 percent. Due to overscreening, many movie chains are investing in foreign markets.

Overscreening benefits movie distributors, who apportion films among movie houses. Distributors typically share movie revenues with the movie houses. Although theater owners typically get as little as 10 percent of revenues when a major film opens, they keep an increasingly larger percent of revenues as a film runs. Generally, distributors and movie houses aim to each keep 50 percent of revenues over a movie's entire run.

Questions

1. Develop a retail strategy for a multiplex to compete with a new megaplex theater located nearby.

2. What factors do you think contribute to the high profitability of megaplexes relative to multiplexes?

3. What are the cash flow implications of the switch from multiplexes to megaplexes for the movie theater chains?

4. Can megaplexes be considered category killers? Do you think we will ever see the return of single-screen theaters? Explain your answers.

NOTE

The material in this case is drawn from Geraldine Fabrikant, "Plenty of Seats Available," *New York Times* (July 12, 1999), pp. C1–C2.

CHAPTER 6

Web, Nonstore-Based, and Other Forms of Nontraditional Retailing

CHAPTER OBJECTIVES

1. To look at the characteristics of the three major retail institutions involved with nonstore-based strategy mixes: direct marketing, direct selling, and vending machines—with an emphasis on direct marketing
2. To explore the emergence of electronic retailing through the World Wide Web
3. To discuss two other nontraditional forms of retailing: video kiosks and airport retailing

According to estimates by industry executives and analysts, those who shop on the World Wide Web abandon between one-half and two-thirds of the purchases they begin to make. For example, at 911gifts.com, 45 percent of potential transactions are halted by customers prior to checkout; and 30 percent of those shoppers bail out at the first page of the billing process: "We're still in the early phase of E-commerce adoption, so a lot of people just get into the process and panic."

Two factors contributing to the high level of transaction terminations are shipping and handling fees and customer resistance to registration procedures. Many sites do not disclose shipping and handling fees until late in the buying process. Says one E-commerce consultant, "It's sticker shock. A lot of people just aren't willing to pay what is essentially a 30 percent to 40 percent markup." Although Web retailers like complex registration forms because they provide them with useful data, customers often find the process time-consuming and an invasion of privacy. Some online merchants are experimenting with ways to simplify registration. Excite lets users shop at a number of merchants after typing in their credit card information only once.

The large proportion of customers bailing out is particularly critical since the Web has been a medium for impulse purchases. Thus, Web retailers must "make a consumer's purchase decision as slippery as possible," referring to the speed with which sites should finalize transactions.[1]

OVERVIEW

In this chapter, we examine nonstore-based retailing, electronic retailing, and two other emerging types of nontraditional retailing: video kiosks and airport retailing. These formats all influence the strategies of current store-based retailers, as well as newly formed retailers. Thus, the discussion in Chapter 6 builds on the material covered in Chapter 5.

> *Please Note:* Web site addresses are constantly changing.
> The links in this chapter are current as of the publication of this book.

Retailers engage in **nonstore retailing** when they use strategy mixes that are not store-based to reach consumers and complete transactions. It occurs via direct marketing, direct selling, and vending machines. Some firms, such as J.C. Penney, Borders, and Home Depot , combine both store and nonstore activities to expand their customer markets and sales. See Figure 6.1. Others, such as Mary Kay and QVC, stick to nonstore retailing to better target segments and hold down operating costs. During 1998, nonstore retailing sales were $233 billion, with 77 percent of that from direct marketing (hence, the direct marketing emphasis in this chapter).

The fastest-growing form of direct marketing involves electronic Web-based retailing. From sales of $500 million in 1996 and $20 billion in 1999, Web-based retailing is expected to reach revenues of $140 billion in 2003. Nonetheless, it will take some time to determine the full long-term impact of the Web on retailing. As Sir Richard Greenbury, chief executive of Great Britain's Marks & Spencer, said recently:

> Right now, opinions about the impact of the Internet on conventional bricks-and-mortar retailers, catalogs, and even door-to-door selling—are extremely different. One school of thought maintains that E-commerce will affect all retailers and all types of products, that the Internet will change the face of retailing thoroughly and permanently. Another

While Marks & Spencer (www.marks-and-spencer.co.uk) operates department stores in Europe and Brooks Brothers in the United States, it is also a leading direct marketer.

Figure 6.1
Home Depot: Combining Bricks-and-Mortar with Clicks-and-Mortar

Home Depot, the leader in home center retailing, has developed a full-feature Web site, *www.homede-pot.com*, to complement its category killer chain of stores. Interestingly, the major item sold online by Home Depot is gift cards. The major purpose of the site is to provide detailed hints on how to undertake various do-it-yourself home improvement projects, complete with suggestions about the necessary tools and supplies to complete these projects, and to provide store locations and directions.
Reprinted by permission.

school believes the Internet is not as much an issue for bricks-and-mortar retailers as for direct marketers, that it will prove easier for consumers to switch from catalog shopping to online shopping, but that most people who currently enjoy shopping face-to-face will not find the new medium particularly attractive. I believe the Internet has brought about a revolution in retailing. And I don't believe that anyone can predict with even a modicum of certainty how it will end. But, I would venture to say, any school of thought, like the two above, that paints the picture in black and white is off the mark. The truth is that the Internet's effect on retailing is many, many shades of gray. And that means senior managers' responses should range accordingly. Some have already felt the impact of the Net. For others, the eye of the storm is a long way off.[2]

Nontraditional retailing also comprises two newer formats that do not fit neatly into the conventional types of retailing considered as "store-based" or "nonstore-based." These are the video kiosk and airport retailing. Sometimes they involve store-based retailing; other times they do not. What they have in common is their departure from traditional retailing, which makes a separate discussion of them valuable.

DIRECT MARKETING

Direct marketing is a form of retailing in which a customer is first exposed to a good or service through a nonpersonal medium (such as direct mail, broadcast or cable TV, radio, magazine, newspaper, or PC) and then orders by mail, phone (usually with a toll-free number), or fax—and increasingly by computer. In 1998, U.S. sales to final consumers were $180 billion (including the Web). More than half of U.S. adults make one or more direct marketing purchases during a typical year. Japan, Germany, Great Britain, France, and Canada are among the leaders in direct marketing revenues outside the United States. Among the products bought most frequently are gift items, apparel, magazines, books and music, sports equipment, home accessories, food, and insurance.[3] See Figure 6.2.

Figure 6.2
Golf Day: Direct Marketing and Sports Equipment

Sports equipment is one of the best-selling product categories for direct marketers; and Golf Day is a leading direct marketer of golf equipment and apparel. It mails out catalogs on a regular basis and takes orders through its toll-free 800 phone number. It also sells products through its E-store at *www.golfday.com*.
Reprinted by permission.

Direct (www.directmag.com) and *Catalog Age* (www.catalogagemag.com) are two vital sources of direct marketing information.

In the United States, direct marketing customers are more apt to be married, upper middle class, and 36 to 50 years of age. Mail shoppers are more likely to live in areas far from malls. Phone shoppers are more likely to live in upscale metropolitan areas and to call in orders to avoid traffic and save time. Although the share of direct marketing purchases made by men is small, it is growing. For instance, 30 percent of catalog shoppers are now men, up from less than 20 percent a few years ago. About 43 percent of those shopping direct spend at least $300 per year in this manner; and they most desire convenience, unique merchandise, and good prices.[4]

Although direct marketing is one of the largest and fastest-growing retail institutions in the United States, it is also one of the most misunderstood: "What an exciting time to be working in the area of direct marketing—as the old gives way to the new and the old ways are considered in a new light. Just a few years ago, you had to explain what you meant if you said you were working in the area of 'direct marketing.' It used to be thought of quite narrowly, as synonymous with the term 'mail order.' For those from a retail background, it is fairly common to define the parameters of direct marketing in terms of nonstore formats. From a retail perspective, direct marketing is just that—direct without the necessity of a store to conduct exchanges."[5]

Direct marketers can be divided into two broad categories: general and specialty. General direct marketing firms offer a full line of products and sell everything from clothing to housewares. J.C. Penney (with its mail-order and Web businesses) and QVC (with its cable TV and Web businesses) are examples of general direct marketers. Specialty firms focus on more narrow product lines, like their specialty store counterparts. Spiegel, L.L. Bean, Publishers Clearinghouse, and Franklin Mint are among the thousands of U.S. specialty direct marketers. See Figure 6.3.

Direct marketing has a number of strategic business advantages:

- Many costs are reduced—startup costs can be rather low; reduced inventories can be held; no fixtures or displays are needed; a prime store location is unnecessary; regularly staffed store hours do not have to be kept; a sales force may not be needed; and a firm may be run out of a garage or basement.

Figure 6.3
Micro Warehouse: Specializing in Personal Computers and Accessories

Micro Warehouse is a specialty direct marketer. But specialty does not mean small. The company offers more than 30,000 different microcomputer hardware, software, and peripheral products and supplies. As one satisfied customer says, "It doesn't matter what I need or when I need it, Micro Warehouse has the products, and it's always able to deliver them immediately." Reprinted by permission.

- It is possible for a firm to offer lower prices (due to reduced costs) than store-based retailers carrying the same items. A very large geographic area can be covered inexpensively and efficiently.
- Customers are given a convenient method of shopping—without crowds, parking congestion, or lines at cash registers.
- Customers do not have to be concerned about safely shopping early in the morning or late at night.
- Specific consumer segments can be pinpointed through mailings.
- Sometimes, consumers can legally avoid paying sales tax by buying from direct marketers not having retail facilities in their state (however, a number of states are interested in eliminating this loophole[6]).
- A store-based retailer can supplement its regular business and expand its geographic trading area (even becoming a national or global firm) without adding outlets.

There are limitations to direct marketing, but they are not as critical as those for direct selling firms:

- Products cannot be examined prior to purchase. Thus, the range of items sold is usually more limited than that sold in stores, and direct marketers need liberal return policies to attract and keep customers.
- Prospective direct marketers may underestimate entry costs. Catalogs can be expensive; printing and mailing may be several dollars per catalog. A computer system may be required to track shipments, monitor purchases and returns, and keep mailing lists current. A 24-hour phone staff may be needed.
- Even the most successful catalogs draw purchases from less than 10 percent of recipients. The high costs and relatively low response rates have caused some merchants to charge for their catalogs (with the fee usually reimbursed after the first order is placed).
- Direct marketing clutter exists. In 1998, 17 billion catalogs were mailed in the United States alone—about 65 apiece for every man, woman, and child in the United States!
- Because printed catalogs are prepared well in advance, prices and styles may be difficult to plan.
- Some firms have given the industry a bad name due to delivery delays and shipping damaged goods.

The full 30-day rule is available online (www.ftc.gov/bcp/conline/pubs/buspubs/mailordr/index.htm).

The "30-day rule" is a U.S. federal regulation that greatly affects direct marketers. The Federal Trade Commission (FTC) requires firms to ship orders within 30 days of their receipt or notify customers of delays. If an order cannot be shipped in 60 days, the customer must be given a specific delivery date and offered the option of canceling the order and getting a refund or continuing to wait for the order to be filled. The rule includes orders placed by mail, phone, fax, and computer.

Despite these limitations, long-run growth for direct marketing is projected for several reasons. Consumer interest in convenience and the difficulty in setting aside time for shopping are expected to continue. More direct marketers will be offering 24-hour operations for orders. Product standardization and the prominence of well-known brands are reducing consumer perceptions of risk when buying on the basis of a catalog, Web, or other nonpersonal description. Direct marketers have rapidly improved their skills and efficiency; they are more effective than before. Technological breakthroughs and new approaches, such as in-home computerized purchases, are expected to attract more consumer shopping.

Due to its vast presence and immense potential, our detailed discussion of direct marketing is intended to give the reader an in-depth look into this retail institution. We next cover the domain of direct marketing, emerging trends, steps in a direct marketing strategy, and key issues facing direct marketers.

The Domain of Direct Marketing

As defined earlier in this chapter, direct marketing is a form of retailing in which a consumer is exposed to a good or service through a nonpersonal medium and then orders by mail, phone, fax, or computer. It may also be viewed in this manner: "Direct marketing is an interactive system of retailing which uses one or more advertising media to effect a measurable response and/or transaction at any location, with this activity stored on a data base."[7]

Accordingly, we include these as forms of direct marketing: any catalog; any mail, TV, radio, magazine, newspaper, phone directory, fax, or other ad; any computer-based transaction; or any other nonpersonal contact that stimulates customers to place orders by mail, phone, fax, or computer.

We do not include these as forms of direct marketing:

- Direct selling—Consumers are solicited by in-person selling efforts or seller-originated phone calls. In both cases, the firm uses personal, rather than nonpersonal, communication to initiate contact.
- Conventional vending machines—Consumers are exposed to nonpersonal media but do not complete transactions via mail, phone, fax, or computer. Thus, people do not really interact with the firm, and a data base cannot be generated and kept.

Direct marketing is involved in many video kiosk transactions; when items are mailed to consumers, there is interaction between the firm and the customer, and a data base can be formed. Direct marketing is also in play when consumers originate phone calls based on catalogs or ads they have seen.

Online Comes to College Bookstores

A new company, Varsitybooks.com (www.varsity books.com) has contracts with a number of small universities, colleges, preparatory schools, and distance learning programs to handle their textbook sales. In some instances, the schools are closing their own book-selling operations and sending students to Varsitybooks.com's Web site. As Varsitybooks.com's president says, "They can quite literally shut the door on their bookstores." In addition, at more than 200 schools where it does not have contracts, Varsitybooks.com's Web site lists the required texts for each course. Each of these institutions will be paid a commission based on Varsitybooks.com's sales.

According to the National Association of College Stores, textbook sales are the least profitable aspect of operating a college store. Furthermore, traditional bricks-and-mortar bookstores are now facing competition from other Web booksellers such as Big Words, Inc. (www.bigwords.com) and ecampus.com (www.ecampus.com).

Another major competitor is Follett (www.efollet.com), a bookstore chain that provides online ordering for 600 of its own stores and 150 independent stores that want Follett to maintain their Web operations. This alternative lets the independents establish Web operations while running their traditional stores—and most schools are not ready to give their book-selling operations to an online company.

As a college store manager, would you turn over your textbook sales to Varsitybooks.com? Explain your answer.

Source: Lisa Guernsey, "Bookseller Is Ready to Offer Textbooks Online," *New York Times on the Web* (July 5, 1999).

The Customer Data Base: Key to Successful Direct Marketing

Because direct marketers initiate contact with customers (in contrast to many store shopping trips that are initiated by the consumer), it is imperative that they develop and maintain a comprehensive customer data base. By doing so, they can pinpoint their best customers, make offers aimed at specific customer needs, avoid costly mailings to nonresponsive shoppers, and track sales by customer. A good data base is the major asset of most direct marketers; and *every* thriving direct marketer has a strong data base.

Data-base retailing is a way of collecting, storing, and using relevant information about customers. Such information typically includes the person's name, address, background data, shopping interests, and purchase behavior (including the amounts bought, how often, and how recently). Though customer data bases are often associated with large computerized information systems, they may also be used by small firms that are not overly computerized.

Here's how data-base retailing can be beneficial:

In many situations, a version of the 80–20 principle probably applies, whereby 80 percent of sales are made to 20 percent of customers. With data-base retailing, a firm could identify those 20 percent and better satisfy them by superior product selection, announcements of special sales, more personalized correspondence, etc. In addition, the firm could identify and place heightened emphasis on the next 40 percent of its customers, a group that has often been ignored. Through data-base marketing, a retailer could also learn which people no longer patronize it and which shop less often. In these instances, people may be called or sent letters—in a cordial manner—to see why they are no longer shopping (or shopping less). Based on the reasons given, a retailer could undertake special promotions geared directly to those customers. What's the key to successful data-base retailing? It must be viewed in a positive way as a beneficial tool—not as an unwelcome and burdensome chore. Knowledge is power and power leads to profits.[8]

Data-base retailing is discussed further in Chapter 8.

Emerging Trends

Several trends are relevant for direct marketing: the evolving attitudes and activities of direct marketers, changing consumer life-styles, increased competition, the greater use of dual distribution channels, newer roles for catalogs and TV, technological advances, and mounting interest in global direct marketing.

Evolving Attitudes and Activities of Direct Marketers A few years ago, the Direct Marketing Association (DMA) (www.the-dma.org) conducted a landmark study of direct marketing professionals and published the results in *Direct Marketing Practices and Trends*. The DMA looked at current practices, future plans, and opinions regarding industry trends. In all, 3,000 direct marketing professionals participated in the project.

Table 6.1 reports some of the DMA's findings.

Changing Consumer Life-Styles From a direct marketing perspective, the life-styles of American consumers have shifted dramatically over the past 30 years, mostly due to the large number of women who are now in the labor force and the longer commuting time to and from work for suburban residents. Today, many consumers do not have the time or the inclination to shop at retail stores. They are attracted by the convenience and ease of purchases through direct marketing.

Because consumers are now more satisfied with their direct marketing experiences than in the past (owing to improved company performance), sales should continue to be strong. A

Table 6.1 Direct Marketing Practices: The View from the Field (Based on a Study of 3,000 Direct Marketing Professionals)

When selling goods and services, direct marketers have specific goals in mind and engage in certain strategies to meet them. They often focus on improving customer retention, reactivating customers, and increasing purchase frequency. Three-quarters say they are doing more along these lines than they did before, and that they plan to do more in the future.

About 80 percent think lifetime customer value is a more significant operating principle today than it was before, and that it will be even more so in the future.

Three-quarters think frequency programs are an effective means to obtain buyer loyalty and that there will be more of them in the future. Yet, many say they currently are not using such programs.

Over one-half say their firms usually take a product-driven approach, while 44 percent take a market-driven approach. Moreover, 80 percent expect their firms will have a more market-driven approach in the future.

Sixty-one percent of firms used direct mail, 39 percent catalogs, 25 percent package/statement stuffers, and 25 percent magazines.

Sixty-eight percent say their firm's marketing data base was centralized in their organization.

Thirty-one percent indicate their firm spent under $100,000 to build a marketing data base (including hardware, software, internal resources, external consulting, development time, and external data), 28 percent spent between $100,000 and $499,999, and 18 percent spent $500,000 or more. Twenty-three percent did not provide an estimate.

In maintaining the data base, 35 percent spent under $50,000 annually, 16 percent spent between $50,000 and $99,999, 14 percent spent between $100,000 and $249,999, and 14 percent spent $250,000 or more. Twenty-one percent did not provide estimates.

Customer service remains an important issue—61 percent think customers expect more service from direct marketing than from stores. Ninety-two percent feel service will become even more critical in the future.

Source: Direct Marketing Best Practices (New York: Direct Marketing Association, 1996). Reprinted by permission of the DMA Marketing Council.

1999 survey of catalog shoppers found that 29.7 percent of them thought catalog shopping was more satisfying than shopping in a store, 61.7 percent thought the two experiences were equally satisfying, and only 8.5 percent thought shopping in a store was more satisfying.[9]

These are just some of the factors consumers consider in selecting a direct marketer:

- Company reputation (image).
- Ability to shop whenever the consumer wants.
- Types of goods and services offered.
- Assortment.
- Brand names carried.
- Availability of a toll-free phone number for ordering.
- Credit card acceptance.
- Speed of promised delivery time.
- Comparable store prices.
- Satisfaction with past purchases.

Spiegel (www.spiegel. com) has largely been a direct marketer since the early 1900s. It faces more competition now than ever before.

Increased Competition Among Firms As direct marketing sales have risen, so have the number of competitors. And although there are a number of big firms, such as J.C. Penney and Spiegel, there are also thousands of small ones. According to the Direct Marketing Association, there are over 10,000 U.S. mail-order companies.

The high level of competition exists because entry into direct marketing is both easier and less costly than entry into store retailing. A direct marketer does not need a store location;

can function with a limited staff; and can place inexpensive one-inch ads in the back of leading magazines, send out brochures to targeted customers, and have a low-cost Web site. It can keep low inventory and place orders with suppliers after people have paid for items (as long as the firm abides by the FTC's 30-day rule).

It is estimated that one out of every two new direct marketers fails. This is because direct marketing lures many small firms that may inadequately define their market niche, offer nondistinctive goods and services, have limited experience, underestimate the effort required, have trouble with supplier continuity, and receive a large share of consumer complaints.

Greater Use of Dual Distribution Channels Another contributor to the intense competition in direct marketing is the expanded use of dual distribution channels. In the past, most stores used ads to draw customers to their locations. Now, many stores supplement revenues by using ads, brochures, catalogs, and Web sites to obtain mail-order, phone, and computer-generated sales. They see that direct marketing is efficient, targets specific segments, appeals to people who might not otherwise shop with those firms, and needs a lower investment to reach other geographic areas than opening branch outlets.

Bloomingdale's and Nordstrom are examples of store-based retailers that have successfully entered into direct marketing. Bloomingdale's by Mail was established in 1982 and has seen sales grow rapidly since then, as the customer data base has grown to 3 million people. It is now accompanied by a Web site (www.bloomingdales.com). Nordstrom's The Catalog was begun in 1994 to capitalize on the firm's legendary reputation for customer service: toll-free 24-hour shopping, same-day shipments for orders placed before 11:00 A.M., second-day air delivery via Federal Express, and complementary gift boxes. In 1998, Nordstrom introduced a Web site (www.nordstrom.com) with the same goals as the catalog.

These comments sum up direct marketing's lure for store retailers: "While having a selling Web site is not yet a life-or-death issue for most retailers, store-based firms must explore direct distribution if they want to thrive in the years ahead. 'To maintain or enhance market share, the store retailer must consider direct channels to capitalize on the opportunity presented by peoples' desire to shop anywhere, anytime, and exactly the way they want,' says Jannita Watson of Kurt Salmon Associates. 'Over the next 10 to 15 years, there will be a huge shift to nonstore retailing of all types, from traditional phone order, this time on a wireless personal communicator with interactive video screen anytime, anywhere, to interactive in-home shopping, or anywhere shopping.' Watson knows some retailers with growing chains and rising comparable-store sales may ask why they should be concerned about nonstore channels. But, she says, 'The gradual increase in nonstore shopping is over; we're heading into rapid growth. This means a smaller portion of the consumer's wallet is available to store retailers.'"[10]

Newer Roles for Catalogs and TV Direct marketers have been recasting the ways in which they use their catalogs, as well as their approach to TV retailing. Here's how.

Retailers are revamping the ways in which they use their catalogs in three basic areas. First, many firms now print "specialogs"—in addition to or instead of the annual catalogs that feature all of their offerings. Each year, such firms as Spiegel, L.L. Bean, and Travelsmith send out multiple catalogs, including separate specialogs by market segment or occasion. By using a **specialog,** a retailer can cater to the specific needs of different customer segments, emphasize a limited number of items, and reduce catalog production and postage costs (as a specialog may be 8 to 50 pages in length, as compared to 100 pages or more for a general catalog).

Second, to help defray their catalog costs, some companies accept ads from noncompeting firms that are compatible with their own images. For instance, Bloomingdale's by Mail has had ads for fine liquors, luxury cars, and vacation travel. Overall, catalog ads provide several million dollars in revenues for direct marketers.

Third, both to stimulate sales and to defray costs, some catalogs are sold in bookstores, supermarkets, and airports, as well as at company Web sites. Thousands of stores carry an assortment of the catalogs made available to them. The percentage of consumers buying a catalog who actually make a product purchase is many times higher than that for those who get catalogs in the mail.

TV retailing has two components: shopping networks and infomercials. On a shopping network, the only regular programming involves merchandise presentations and their sales (usually by phone). The two biggest players are the cable giants QVC and Home Shopping Network (HSN), with combined annual revenues of $3.5 billion. Each company has access to a TV audience of 70 million households. Only 5 percent of U.S. consumers bought goods through TV shopping programs in 1988; more than twice as many are doing so today. The popularity of TV-based home shopping is expected to rise as the number of channels increases and as interactive shopping technology (which lets people browse through channels and ask for data and advice) becomes available. Once regarded as a medium primarily for shut-ins and the lower middle class, the typical TV-based shopper is now younger, more fashion-conscious, and as apt to be from a high-income household as the overall U.S. population.[11]

QVC's and HSN's strategies are similar. Both feature jewelry, women's clothing, and personal-care products, and do not emphasize nationally recognized brands. Most items must be bought from QVC and HSN during the limited time the products are advertised. This practice encourages consumers to act immediately, but it also forces some consumers to watch programs for long hours in the hope that specials are repeated. The two firms also have active Web sites (www.iqvc.com and www.hsn.com).

An **infomercial** is a program-length TV commercial (most often, 30 minutes in length) for a specific good or service that airs on cable television or on broadcast television, often at a fringe time. As they watch an infomercial, shoppers call in their orders, which are then delivered directly to them. Infomercials are particularly worthwhile for products that benefit from visual demonstrations. Good infomercials work because they present detailed information on the product, include customer testimonials, are entertaining, and are divided into neatly timed segments (since the average viewer watches only a few minutes of the "show" at a time)—with ordering information flashed on the screen in every segment.

It is estimated that infomercials (which first appeared in the mid-1980s) now account for over $1 billion in annual U.S. revenues. Extremely successful infomercials include those for the Ronco Pasta Maker, the George Foreman Grill, Tony Robbins motivational tapes and books, K-Tel "oldies" music, Time-Life books, Ginsu knives, and a variety of exercise equipment. In general, infomercial shoppers are "less risk averse, more price-conscious, and more convenience-seeking than nonshoppers. They are also more brand-conscious, innovative, impulsive, and variety-seeking than nonshoppers."[12] The Electronic Retailing Association (www.retailing.org) is the trade association for infomercial firms.

Technological Advances Direct marketing is in the midst of a technological revolution that is improving operating efficiency and offering enhanced sales opportunities. These are just some advances taking place:

- Market segments can be better targeted. Through selective binding, longer catalogs can be sent to the best customers and shorter catalogs to new prospects.
- Firms can inexpensively use computers to enter customer mail and phone orders, arrange for shipments, and monitor inventory on hand.
- It is now simple for direct marketers to set up and maintain computerized data bases.
- Huge, automated distribution centers can more efficiently accumulate and ship out orders.

Ron Popeil has become a very rich man through his Ronco (www.ronco.com) infomercials.

- Customers can dial toll-free phone numbers to place orders and get information. The cost per call for the direct marketer is quite low.
- Consumers can conclude transactions from many more locations, including phones on airlines that have automatic links to particular direct marketers.
- Cable TV programming lets consumers view 24-hour shopping channels and place orders.
- In-home/at-office PC-based shopping transactions can be conducted at retailer Web sites.

Mounting Interest in Global Direct Marketing Many more retailers have become involved with global direct marketing over the past several years because of the opportunities in foreign markets and the growing consumer acceptance of nonstore retailing in those countries. Among the booming number of U.S.-based direct marketers with a significant international presence are Eddie Bauer, Lands' End, Sharper Image, and Williams-Sonoma.

Outside the United States, annual mail-order sales (by both domestic and foreign firms) from final consumer transactions are in excess of $100 billion. Although German and Japanese consumers account for half of total non-U.S. spending, there are a number of potential areas for direct marketers, including China, Brazil, South Africa, France, and Spain.[13]

Consider this:

> The United States is the most advanced direct marketer in the world today, with Europe close behind and Japan learning quickly. When one considers the enormous impact direct marketing has had on U.S. commerce, the prospects in developing nations are exciting. Small firms can afford to operate across international lines, competing with large rivals. Mail-order companies whose catalogs now draw 1 or 2 percent response in the United States may get 10 to 20 percent in other countries where competing products aren't available or catalog glut isn't a problem. Before these efforts can become reality, several major obstacles need to be overcome. These include major gaps in addressing information, a lack of standards, different currencies, wide variations in postal rates and procedures, and the need for uniformity that can ensure the smooth flow of mass mailings the world over.[14]

Lands' End has many different Web sites to service customers around the world, such as its German site (www.landsend.de). Because of Lands' End's customer commitment, this site is in German.

The Steps in a Direct Marketing Strategy

A direct marketing strategy has eight steps: business definition, generating customers, media selection, presenting the message, customer contact, customer response, order fulfillment, and measuring results and maintaining the data base. See Figure 6.4.

Figure 6.4
Executing a Direct
Marketing Strategy

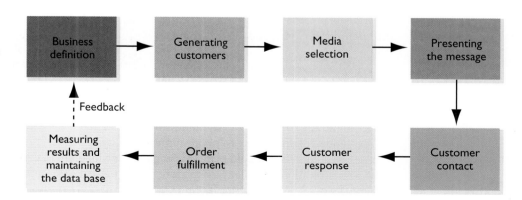

Business Definition First, a company makes these two decisions regarding its business definition:

- Is the firm going to be a pure direct marketer or is it going to engage in a dual distribution channel (involving both store-based and direct marketing)? If the firm chooses the latter, it must clarify the role of direct marketing in its overall retail strategy.
- Is the firm going to be a general direct marketer and carry a broad product assortment, or is it going to specialize in one goods/service category? Either way, a merchandising approach must be conceived.

Generating Customers A mechanism for generating customers is devised next. Several options are available. A firm can

- Buy a mailing list from a broker. For one mailing, a list usually costs $50 to $100 or more per 1,000 names and addresses; it is supplied in mailing-label format. Brokers annually rent or sell billions of names and addresses to direct marketers—which can buy broad lists or ones broken down by gender, location, and so on. In purchasing a mailing list, the direct marketer should check its currency.
- Buy a list on a CD-ROM disk from a firm such as infoUSA (www.infoUSA.com), which sells a CD for $59.95 with data on 100 million U.S. households. With such a disk, the direct marketer can use the list multiple times, but it is responsible for selecting names and printing labels.
- Send out a blind mailing to all the residents in a particular area. This method can be expensive and may receive a very low response rate.
- Advertise in a newspaper, magazine, Web site, or other medium and ask customers to order by mail, phone, fax, or computer.
- Contact consumers who have previously bought from the firm or requested information. For years, J.C. Penney has managed a multimillion customer data base. This is very efficient, but it takes a while to develop a data base. And if a company wants to grow, it cannot rely solely on these consumers.

Media Selection Several media are available to the direct marketer. They include

- Printed catalogs.
- Direct-mail ads and brochures.
- Inserts with monthly credit card and other bills ("statement stuffers").
- Freestanding displays with coupons, brochures, or catalogs (such as magazine subscription cards at the supermarket checkout counter).
- Ads or programs in the mass media: newspapers, magazines, radio, TV.
- Banner ads or "hot links" on the World Wide Web.
- Video kiosks.

In choosing among alternatives, the direct marketer should consider costs, distribution, the required lead time, and other factors.

Presenting the Message At this point, the firm develops and presents its message in a way that engenders consumer interest, creates (or maintains) the proper image, points out compelling reasons for a purchase, and provides data about the goods or services offered (such as prices, sizes, and colors). The message must also contain complete ordering instructions, including a method of payment, how to designate the items purchased, shipping charges, and the firm's address/phone number/Web site.

The direct marketer should plan a message and the medium in which it is presented in the same way a traditional retailer plans a store. The latter uses a storefront, lighting, carpeting, the store layout, and displays to foster a particular atmosphere and image. In direct marketing, the headlines, message content, use of color, paper quality, personalization of mail, space devoted to each item, and order in which items are presented are among the elements affecting a firm's shopping atmosphere and image.

Customer Contact Next, for each campaign it runs, a direct marketer decides whether to contact all customers in its data base or to seek specific market segments (with different messages and/or media aimed at each). It can classify prospective customers as *regulars* (those who have purchased on a continuous basis); *nonregulars* (those who have purchased on an infrequent basis); *new contacts* (those who have never been sought before by the firm); and *nonrespondents* (those who have been contacted before but never made a purchase).

Regulars and nonregulars are the most apt to respond to any future offerings from a firm. Furthermore, a direct marketer can better target its efforts to these people since it has purchase histories on them. Thus, customers who have bought clothing in the past are prime prospects for specialogs. New contacts probably know little about the firm. Messages to them must create interest, accurately portray the firm, and present meaningful reasons for consumers to buy. This group is important if growth is sought.

Nonrespondents who have been contacted repeatedly by a firm without making purchases are highly unlikely to buy in the future. Unless a firm can present a message in a very different way, it is inefficient to continue seeking this group. Firms such as Publishers Clearinghouse annually do millions of mailings to people who have never bought; in their case, this is proper because they are selling inexpensive impulse items and need only a small response rate to succeed.

Customer Response Customers can respond to direct marketers in one of three ways: (1) They can buy through the mail, phone, fax, or computer. (2) They can request further information, such as a catalog. (3) They can ignore the message. Purchases are generally made by no more than 2 to 3 percent of those contacted. The rate is higher for specialogs, mail-order clubs (e.g., for music), and firms focusing on repeat customers.

Order Fulfillment A firm needs a system to process orders. When orders are received by mail or fax, the firm must sort them, determine if payment is enclosed, check whether the item is in stock, mail announcements if items cannot be sent on time, coordinate shipments, and replenish inventory. If phone orders are placed, the firm must have a trained sales staff available at times during which people may call. Salespeople answer questions, make suggestions, enter orders, note the payment method, see whether items are in stock, coordinate shipments, and replenish inventory. If orders are placed by computer, there must be a process for handling credit transactions, issuing receipts, and forwarding orders to a warehouse in a prompt, efficient way. In all cases, names, addresses, and purchase data are added to the data base for future reference.

During peak seasons, additional warehouse, shipping, order processing, and sales personnel are needed to supplement regular employees. Direct marketers that are highly regarded by consumers fill orders promptly (usually within two weeks), have knowledgeable and courteous personnel, do not misrepresent product quality, and provide liberal return policies.

Measuring Results and Maintaining the Data Base The last step in a direct marketing strategy is analyzing results and maintaining the data base. Most forms of direct marketing yield such clearly measurable results as these:

- Overall response rate—It can be determined what number and percentage of the people reached by a particular brochure, catalog, Web site, and so forth actually purchase.

Payment Security and the Web— The Retailers' Perspective

Up to 5 to 6 percent of the average Web retailer's transactions are affected by consumer fraud, according to Cyber-Source, a developer of software systems that detect online fraud. And for those Web businesses that sell software and other digital goods, attempted fraud is even greater. One estimate is that as much as 30 percent of sales transactions for these items result in an attempt at credit card fraud.

Limiting fraud is much more difficult for Web retailers than for store-based merchants. For example, store-based merchants can compare signatures, look at pictures on credit cards (where available), and have the opportunity to ask for additional forms of identification. On the other hand, E-commerce merchants face two potential problems when they accept a credit card as payment. First, the processing charge for these firms is greater than for bricks-and-mortar retailers due to the higher rate of fraud. Second, Web retailers are entirely responsible for making sure the credit card user is not unauthorized. Although a defrauded customer has no liability, Visa USA says a merchant is liable for fraudulent transactions. Most banks also will not protect a Web business from consumer fraud.

How can an E-commerce retailer protect itself against credit card fraud?

Source: Cecile B. Corral, "Online Security, Payment Services Aid E-tailers Stung by Fraud," *Discount Store News* (April 19, 1999), pp. 20, 25.

- Average purchase amount—This can be analyzed by customer location, gender, and so forth.
- Sales volume by product category—Sales can be related to the space allotted to each product in brochures, catalogs, and so forth.
- Value of list brokers—The revenues generated by various mailing lists can be compared.

After measuring results, the direct marketer reviews its customer data base and makes sure new shoppers are entered into it, address changes have been noted for existing customers, purchase and customer background information is current and available in various segmentation categories, and nonrespondents are purged from the data base (when desirable).

This stage provides feedback for the direct marketer as it plans for each new campaign.

Key Issues Facing Direct Marketers

In planning and enacting their strategies, direct marketers must keep the following points in mind.

A large number of people still dislike one or more aspects of direct marketing. The greatest levels of consumer dissatisfaction deal with late delivery or nondelivery, deceptive claims, items broken or damaged in transit, the wrong items being delivered, and the lack of information provided. Yet, as already noted, in most cases, the leading direct marketers are highly rated by consumers.

Most U.S. households report that they open all direct mail, but many would like to receive less of it. Since the average American household is sent nearly 200 catalogs a year, besides hundreds of other direct mail pieces, firms have to be concerned about marketplace clutter. It is hard to be distinctive and to increase customer response rates in this kind of environment.

Many consumers are concerned about their names and background information being sold by list brokers, as well as by some direct marketers to other direct marketers. They feel the practice is an invasion of privacy and that the decision to make a direct marketing purchase does not constitute permission to pass on personal information. To counteract this, the direct marketing industry has agreed to remove people's names from mailing list circulation if they make a request to the Direct Marketing Association. Clearly, direct marketers will have to address this issue more squarely in the near future.

Dual distribution retailers must sustain a consistent image for both store-based and direct marketing efforts. They must also recognize the similarities and the differences in the strategies for each approach.

The steady increase in postal rates has made the mailing of catalogs, brochures, and other promotional materials expensive for some firms. Thus, many direct marketers are turning more to newspapers, magazines, and cable TV—and the Web.

Finally, direct marketers must carefully monitor the legal environment. They must be aware that, in the future, more states will probably require residents to pay sales tax on out-of-state direct marketing purchases; the firms would have to remit the tax payments to the affected states.

DIRECT SELLING

The Direct Selling Association (www.dsa.org) is working hard to promote the image and professionalism of this retail format.

Direct selling includes both personal contact with consumers in their homes (and other nonstore locations such as offices) and phone solicitations initiated by a retailer. Cosmetics, jewelry, vitamins, household goods and services (such as carpet cleaning), vacuum cleaners, dairy products, and magazines and newspapers are among the items sometimes sold in this way. In 1998, the industry had $23 billion in U.S. sales and employed 10 million people (90 percent part-time).[15] Table 6.2 shows an industry overview.

The strategy mix for direct selling emphasizes convenience in shopping and a personal touch. Many times, detailed demonstrations can be made. Consumers are often more relaxed in their homes than in stores. They are also likely to be attentive and are not exposed to competing brands (as they are in stores). For some shoppers, such as older consumers and parents with young children, in-store shopping is difficult to undertake because of limited mobility. For the retailer, direct selling has lower overhead costs because store locations and fixtures are not necessary.

Nonetheless, direct selling revenues in the United States have risen relatively slowly over the past several years. Here are some reasons why:

- More women now work; and they may not be interested in or available for in-home purchases.
- Improved job opportunities in other fields and the interest in full-time career-oriented positions have reduced the pool of people interested in direct-selling jobs.
- A firm's market coverage is limited by the size of its sales force. Many firms are able to reach fewer than one-half of potential customers.
- Sales productivity is low since the average transaction is small and most consumers are unreceptive to this type of selling—many will not open their doors to salespeople or talk to telemarketers.
- Sales force turnover is high because the bulk of employees are poorly supervised part-timers.
- To stimulate sales personnel, compensation is usually 25 to 50 percent of the revenues they generate. This means average to above-average prices.
- Various legal restrictions are in effect due to deceptive or high-pressure sales tactics. There are stringent requirements with respect to telemarketing under the FTC's Telemarketing Sales Rule (described at www.ftc.gov/bcp/telemark/rule.htm); in particular, firms must promptly disclose their identity, that the purpose of the call is selling, the

Table 6.2 A Snapshot of the U.S. Direct Selling Industry

Major Product Groups (as a percent of sales dollars)

Home/family care products (cleaning products, cookware, cutlery, etc.)	32.2
Personal care products (cosmetics, jewelry, skin care, etc.)	25.9
Services/miscellaneous/other	18.2
Wellness products (weight loss products, vitamins, etc.)	17.9
Leisure/educational products (books, encyclopedias, toys/games, etc.)	5.8

Place of Sales (as a percent of sales dollars)

In the home	69.5
Over the phone	10.9
In a workplace	10.7
At a temporary location (such as a fair, exhibition, shopping mall, etc.)	6.1
Other locations	2.8

Sales Approach (method used to generate sales, as a percent of sales dollars)

Individual/one-to-one selling	71.9
Party plan/group sales	26.3
Customer placing order directly with firm	1.6
Other	0.2

Demographics of Salespeople (as a percent of all salespeople)

Independent contractors/Employees	99.8/0.2
Female/Male	73.0/27.0
Part-time/Full-time (30 hours and up per week)	90.0/10.0

Source: Fact Sheet: 1999 Direct Selling Industrywide Growth & Outlook Survey (Washington, D.C.: Direct Selling Association, 1999). Reprinted by permission.

nature of the goods or services being sold, and that no purchase or payment is necessary to win a "free" prize.

- A poor image is associated with the term *door-to-door,* hence, the industry preference for the term *direct selling.*

Firms are responding to these issues in various ways. For example, Avon is placing greater emphasis on workplace sales, offering free training to sales personnel (it used to charge a fee), rewarding the best workers with better territories, rapidly expanding internationally (which now accounts for 60 percent of its revenues), and placing cosmetics kiosks in shopping centers. Mary Kay and Tupperware hire community residents as salespeople and have a party atmosphere rather than a strict door-to-door approach; this requires networks of family, friends, and neighbors. Fuller Brush salespeople reach two-thirds of U.S. households; the company uses mail-order catalogs to reach the other one-third. It also advertises for sales positions in its catalogs. And virtually every major direct selling firm also has a Web site. In fact, after decades of door-to-door selling in the United States, *Encyclopaedia Britannica* decided to abandon those efforts and concentrate instead on direct mail, catalogs, telemarketing, and the Web. Its online encyclopedia (www.britannica.com) is now available at no charge.

Among the leading direct sellers are Avon and Mary Kay (cosmetics), Amway (household supplies), Tupperware (plastic containers), Shaklee (health products), Fuller Brush (small household products), Kirby (vacuum cleaners), and Welcome Wagon (greetings for new residents sponsored by groups of local retailers). Some stores, such as J.C. Penney, also use direct selling. Penney's decorator consultants sell a complete line of furnishings, not available in its stores, to consumers in their homes. See Figure 6.5.

Figure 6.5
Direct Selling and
Mary Kay

Throughout the world
(in approximately 30
countries), Mary Kay
Cosmetics employs
more than 500,000
direct sales "consul-
tants," who mostly visit
customers in their
homes and account for
$1 billion in revenues.
Through its Web site,
www.marykay.com, the
company even provides
links to the home pages
of its U.S. consultants.
Reprinted by permission of
Mary Kay Cosmetics.

VENDING MACHINES

A **vending machine** is a retailing format involving the coin- or card-operated dispensing of goods (such as beverages) and services (such as life insurance sales at airports). It eliminates the use of sales personnel and allows for around-the-clock sales. Machines can be placed wherever they are most convenient for consumers—inside or outside a store, in a motel corridor, at a train station, or on a street corner.

According to the National Automatic Merchandising Association (www.vending.org), the major industry organization, "In 1888, Thomas Adams of the Adams Gum Company installed penny gum dispensing machines on New York's elevated train platforms, and gave vending its start in the United States. Today, vending machines are operated by thousands of firms nationwide and worldwide. They range from relatively simple to highly sophisticated, and offer an enormously diverse array of products."

Although many attempts have been made to "vend" clothing, magazines, and other general merchandise, 85 percent of the $30 billion in 1998 U.S. vending machine sales involved hot and cold beverages and food items. Because of health-related issues, between 1980 and 1998, cigarettes' share of vending machine sales fell from 25 percent to just 2 percent. The greatest sales volume is achieved in factory, office, and school lunchrooms and refreshment areas; public places such as service stations are also popular sites for machines. Newspapers on street corners and sidewalks, various machines in hotels and motels, and candy machines in restaurants and at train stations are highly visible aspects of vending, but they account for a small percentage of U.S. vending machine sales.[16] Two of the leading vending machine operators are Canteen Corporation and Aramark Services.

Items priced above $1.50 have not sold well in vending machines because too many coins are required for each transaction, and only one-quarter of U.S. vending machines are equipped with dollar bill changers. Many consumers have been reluctant to purchase more expensive items that they cannot see displayed or have explained. However, consumers' expanded access to and use of debit cards (whereby customer bank balances are immediately reduced to reflect purchases) are expected to have a major impact on resolving the payment issue, and the new video-kiosk-type of vending machine lets people see product displays and

*Aramark (www.
refreshment.aramark.
com) vending
machines sell 400
million servings of
soda and 200 million
snacks per year.*

Vending Machines Face the Euro Challenge

Luca Adriani, the chief executive of Coges S.R.L., a manufacturer of vending machines, sees the advent of Europe's euro currency as both an opportunity and a threat. In preparation for January 2002, when euro coins and bills will be introduced (the euro will then be the common currency for 11 nations), orders for his new vending machines are very strong. However, because Coges also operates vending machines, his firm will have to bear the high costs of replacing the coin boxes in its existing machines. In addition, Coges will lose revenues during the period when its machines are converted to accept the euro. Says Adriani, "I'm laughing on one side of my face, and crying on the other."

The main question, according to a spokesperson for the German vending machine industry, is "When do you convert your machines? If you do it too early, your customers don't have the coins and go elsewhere. It's a problem unique to vending." European industry officials also worry about whether there will be an adequate number of euro coins as of 2002—in the denominations used by most vending machines. Some firms are promoting cashless machines using smart cards (debit cards) instead of coins.

Acting as a consultant to Coges S.R.L, discuss the pros and cons of a vending machine strategy based on smart cards instead of coins.

Source: John Tagliabue, "Vending Machines Face an Upheaval of Change," *New York Times* (February 16, 1999), p. C4.

get detailed information (and then place a credit card or debit card order). Popular brands and standardized nonfood items are best suited to increasing sales via vending machines.

To improve productivity and customer relations, vending machine operators are deploying a variety of innovations. For instance, machine malfunctions have been reduced by the application of electronic mechanisms to coin-handling and dispensing controls. Microprocessors track consumer preferences, trace malfunctions, and record receipts. Some machines even have voice synthesizers that are programmed to say such phrases as "Thank you, come again" or "Your change is 25 cents."

Operators must still deal with theft, vandalism, stockouts, above-average prices, and the perceptions of a great many consumers that vending machines should be patronized only when they need fill-in convenience items.

ELECTRONIC RETAILING: THE EMERGENCE OF THE WORLD WIDE WEB

The world of retailing and how people shop are undergoing enormous changes from the days when retailing meant simply visiting a store, shopping from a printed catalog, greeting the Avon lady in one's home, or buying candy from a vending machine. Who would have thought that a person could "surf the Web" to get data for a school or work project, learn how to set a VCR timer, search for bargains, and save a trip to the store? Well, these activities are real and they're here to stay. Let's take a look at the World Wide Web from a retailing perspective, remembering that selling there is a form of direct marketing.

We begin by defining two terms that seem to cause a lot of confusion: Internet and World Wide Web. The **Internet** is a global electronic superhighway of computer networks that use a common protocol and that are linked by telecommunications lines and satellite. It functions as a single, cooperative virtual network and is maintained by universities, governments, and businesses. The **World Wide Web (Web)** is one way of accessing information on the Internet, whereby people work with easy-to-use Web addresses (sites) and pages. Web users see words, colorful charts, pictures, and video, and hear audio—turning their computers into interactive multimedia centers. People can easily move from one site to the next by pointing at the proper spot on the computer screen and clicking a mouse button. Web browsing software, such as Netscape and Microsoft Internet Explorer, facilitate surfing the Web.

Both *Internet* and *World Wide Web* convey the same central theme: online interactive retailing. Since almost all online retailing is done by the World Wide Web, the word *Web* is used in our discussion, which is comprised of these topics: the role of the Web, the scope of online retailing, characteristics of Web users, factors to consider in planning whether to have a Web site, and examples of Web retailers.

The Role of the Web

From the vantage point of the retailer, the World Wide Web can serve one or more of these roles:

- Project a retail presence.
- Generate sales—as the major source of revenue for an online retailer or as a complementary source of revenue for a store-based retailer.
- Enhance the retailer's image.
- Reach geographically dispersed consumers, including foreign ones.
- Provide information to consumers—about products carried, store locations, usage information, answers to common questions, customer loyalty programs, and so on.
- Promote new products and fully explain and demonstrate their features.
- Furnish customer service in the form of E-mail, "hot links," and other communications.
- Be more "personal" with consumers by letting them point and click on topics they choose.
- Conduct a retail business in a cost-efficient manner.
- Obtain customer feedback.
- Give special offers and send coupons to Web customers.
- Describe employment opportunities.
- Present information to potential investors, potential franchisees, and the media.

The role assigned to the Web by a given retailer depends on whether its major goal is to interactively communicate with consumers or to sell goods and services, it is predominantly a traditional retailer that wants to have a Web presence or a newer firm that wants to derive most or all of its revenues from Web transactions, and the level of resources the retailer is willing to commit to Web site development and maintenance. There are more than 4 million Web sites worldwide, hundreds of thousands of which are retail-related. More retail sites are added every day. Virtually all large store-based retailers—in addition to thousands of nonstore Web specialists—already have Web sites or are actively working on them.

The Scope of Online Retailing

What we are witnessing now is the enormous expansion of "clicks-and-mortar" Web-based retailing compared with the slower growth of "bricks-and-mortar" store-based retailing. Consider the online efforts of Gap (www.gap.com), a very successful store-based retailer:

Gap has been widely praised for its online efforts. Visit its Web store (www.gap.com/onlinestore/gap).

> Diane Young wanted to buy a three-quarter-sleeve black shirt from Gap. But the $19 item was not in her local store. So Young went back to her office, logged on to the Web site, and bought it there. With just a few clicks, she was assured it was on its way. Ever since, shopping at gap.com has become a habit for the 28-year-old Manhattan Web-advertising producer. Twice a month, Gap sends her tailored E-mails promoting its latest specials. And thanks to the site's graphics and easy-to-use format, Young figures she is spending 10 to 15 percent more at Gap these days. What's Gap's secret? The same sort of compelling marketing and customer focus that has brought it success in the offline world. The Web site is promoted at every cash register and, recently, in window displays with the slogan "surf.shop.ship." Clerks are trained to refer shoppers to

Gap's site. In some high-traffic Gap and GapKids stores, the retailer has installed "Web lounges" that lure buyers with comfortable couches and sleek gray computer terminals hooked up to gap.com. Online customers can return items purchased on the Net the old-fashioned way by walking into any neighborhood Gap. These moves persuade consumers to think, "Hey, it's the online version of what I see on the street."[17]

Let us look at some statistics showing the Web's scope (keeping in mind that the data are rough estimates): As of the end of 2000, there are projected to be 150 million Web users in North America, 87 million in Western Europe, 58 million in Asia-Pacific, 11 million in South/Central America, 10 million in Eastern Europe, and 8 million in the Middle East/Africa. In 1999, 17 million U.S. households purchased online. In 1999, store-based retailers accounted for 62 percent of U.S. online retail sales, a figure expected to rise to 80 percent or more in 2004. During 1998, U.S. shoppers represented 75 percent of worldwide online retail sales, an amount that should fall to 50 percent in 2003. As noted at the beginning of the chapter, U.S. retail Web sales should rise from $20 billion in 1999 to $140 billion in 2003. European online retail sales should go from $8 billion in 1999 to an amount up to ten times higher in 2003. By 2002, it is estimated that 5 percent or more of the retail sales of the following goods and services will be made online: apparel, banking, books, computer hardware and software, consumer electronics, gifts, greeting cards, insurance, music, newspapers/magazines, sporting goods, toys, travel, and videos.[18] Figure 6.6 indicates online sales projections for several product categories.

Yet, despite these glowing projections, the Web now accounts for only a fraction of one percent of total U.S. retail sales, a figure that—under the best-case scenario—will reach less

Figure 6.6
Web-Based Retail
Sales Projections for
Selected Product
Categories

Source: Chart developed by
the authors from data by
Forester Research, 1999.

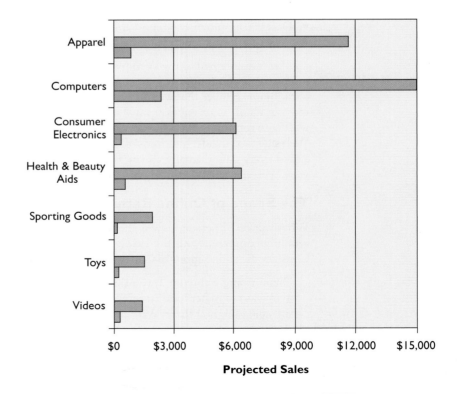

than 5 percent in 2003! The Web will not be the death knell of store-based retailing but another choice for shoppers, like other forms of direct marketing:

> Yes, there is a lot of growth, excitement, and substance to the Internet economy. There is also a lot of hype and many failed startups. That is part of the process of entrepreneurial endeavor. Hype encourages investment, which accelerates the innovation cycle of trial and error, leading to growth-creating breakthroughs. For all the attention given to Internet firms, they are mainly an innovative ferment on the surface of the U.S. economy. As Kevin Kelly (editor at large of *Wired* magazine and author of *New Rules for the New Economy*) notes, the new economy doesn't replace the old economy; it builds on top of the old, and its technologies eventually permeate underlying layers.[19]

No matter what they are selling, Web merchants want to complete as many transactions as possible. However, on the Web, a smaller percentage of shoppers actually make a purchase than in a traditional retail store—most simply click to the next site.[20]

Characteristics of Web Users

Web users have these characteristics, some of which are highlighted in Figure 6.7:

- Gender and age—There are about as many males and females surfing the Web; however, males are more apt to purchase. Among adult Web users, 41 percent are 18 to 34 years old, 49 percent are 35 to 54 years old, and 10 percent are 55 and older.
- Income and education—In 1998, U.S. households with an annual income above $50,000 accounted for 47 percent of total retail sales but 74 percent of Web sales. As of 2003, they will represent 65 percent of Web sales. Only one-quarter of U.S. Web users have not attended college. About 95 percent of college students say they use the Web, 60 percent daily.
- Purchase behavior—Among those making Web purchases, 35 percent spend at least $250 on the Web each year and 51 percent shop at least 5 times.
- Reasons for *using* the Web—People seek information, entertainment, and interactive communications.
- Reasons for *shopping* on the Web—Shoppers are attracted by prices, convenience, choice, and the "fun" of Web retailing.
- Reasons for *not shopping* on the Web—Nonshoppers are concerned about transmitting credit information, like to see products first, want to talk to salespeople, and feel they cannot get enough information on the Web.[21]

What will drive repeat business for Web retailers? Shoppers feel the most important aspects for their continued patronage are value and customer service. As the senior editor of *Stores*, the publication of the National Retail Federation, says: "If an online retailer is true to its value proposition, shopper loyalty will follow. But as retailers across all channels can attest, today's shoppers are fickle, eclectic, value-driven, and in search of new experiences. That puts increasing pressure on retailers to be consistent in their value propositions and vigilant of the fulfillment activities that weigh heavily on the likelihood to buy again. Surveys underscore that loyalty on the Web remains suspect. If online retailers want to turn the tide, they must find ways to offer loyalty programs based on rewards, personalization, quality customer support for the online shopping experience, and privacy policies that protect customers and establish trust."[22]

According to a large-scale consumer study by NFO Interactive, Web users can be enticed to shop more often if they are assured of privacy, there are larger price discounts, they are able to return a product to a bricks-and-mortar store, they can speak with sales representatives, and download time is faster.[23]

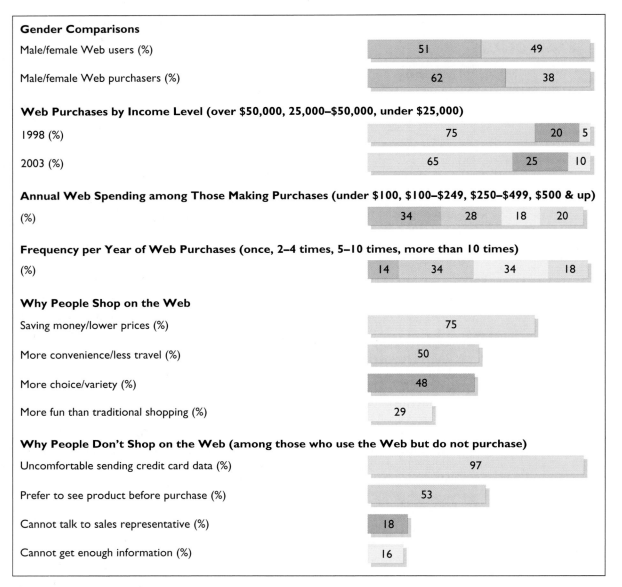

Figure 6.7
A Snapshot of U.S. Web Customers

Sources: Chart developed by the authors from data in *Second Annual Ernst & Young Internet Shopping Study* (New York: Ernst & Young, 1999); Bob Tedeschi, "E-Commerce Report," *New York Times* (July 12, 1999), p. C4; Heather Green, " 'Twas the Season for E-Splurging," *Business Week* (January 18, 1999), p. 40; and "Internet at a Glance," *Business 2.0* (April 1999), p. 108.

Factors to Consider in Planning Whether to Have a Web Site

In general, the Web offers many positive features for retailers. It is usually less costly to have a Web site than a store. The potential marketplace is huge and dispersed, yet relatively easy to reach. Web sites can be quite exciting, with all types of bells and whistles, due to their multimedia capabilities. People can visit Web sites at any time, and their visits can be as short or long as they desire. Information can be targeted, so that, for example, a person visiting a toy store's Web site could click on the icon labeled "Educational Toys—ages three to six." A customer data base can be established and customer feedback obtained.

The Web also has negative features for retailers: If consumers do not know a firm's Web address, it may be cumbersome to find. Many people are not yet willing to buy online, for privacy, security, and other reasons. There is tremendous clutter with regard to the number of Web sites, and it is sure to get worse. Because Web surfers are easily bored, a firm must regularly update its Web site to ensure repeat visits. The more multimedia features a Web site has, the slower it may be for people to access. Some firms have been overwhelmed with customer service requests and questions from E-mail. It may be hard to coordinate store-based and Web-based transactions. There are few standards or rules as to what may be portrayed at Web sites. Consumers expect online services to be free and are reluctant to pay for them.

There is a large gulf between full-scale, integrated Web selling and a basic telling (rather than selling) Web site. During a recent National Retail Federation Information Technology Power Summit, a preliminary model was formulated so retailers could envision the development of a Web site as a five-step process. The five stages are described in Figure 6.8. The president of the National Retail Federation believes that: "Today, many retailers are in Stage 1 or Stage 2. Many large, successful retailers are happy to be at Stage 2, and find that it brings them new customers and increased visibility. The Stage 3 Web presence, where the Web becomes simply another channel, was, for a time, the ideal that retailers sought. Stages 4 and 5 will represent the next steps on the road to retail nirvana— the total integration of the virtual with the physical. And as history tells us, Stages 6, 7, 8 and beyond are out there, waiting for the technology to mature and new applications to be developed."[24]

Potential (and existing) Web retailers should carefully consider these recommendations from a leading industry observer:

Just what does it take to be a cyberretailer? Here are 15 tips:

1. Brand identity—This can be accomplished by the strength of the retail brand, as Nordstrom.com exemplifies, or it can be done under a multibrand umbrella strategy like Brandsforless.com that serves as a portal for other online stores.

2. Convenience—The ultimate model of convenience is Streamline.com, which offers groceries, dry cleaning, video rentals, and other merchandise delivered almost anytime.

3. Cross-merchandising—Some retailers do this better than others. Avon.com suggests items that either complement a purchase or offer a better value.

4. Culture—Kudos to Office Depot for realizing the importance of the technology side of the business and setting up a separate base for Officedepot.com.

5. Customer service—Ultimatefootballshop.com gets my nod for customer service. I ordered an NFL team logo golf umbrella that was produced in the old team color. They credited my account and told me to keep the umbrella with their compliments.

6. Design—The look of an online storefront is important because of the medium's wow factor, but it also must be right for the audience. Delias.com marries both elements as the hot cataloger has created a cool site for its teen audience.

7. Free shipping—Office Depot, like some catalogers and direct marketers, applies this strategy to Officedepot.com.

8. Fashion—Gap has transformed its core business from the traditional storefront to the Web, at Gap.com, without sacrificing any element of its fashion palettes and displays.

Stage 1: Brochure Web Site

A site is built rapidly, on a small budget. It may sell a few items but really exists to see if Web sales will work for the retailer. Customers are directed to the nearest store. At some point, these sites often move to Stage 2.

Stage 2: Commerce Web Site

This site involves full-scale selling, possibly with more items on the Web than in the store. The site also has customer service support, and describes the retailer's history and community efforts. It is not integrated with information systems. As a result, customers may order and later find an item is not in stock.

Stage 3: Web Site Integrated with Existing Processes

The site is integrated with the retailer's existing purchasing, inventory, and accounting systems. That lessens the need to have separate reports, and ensures that out-of-stock items are automatically deleted from the site.

Stage 4: The "Webified" Store

Network systems bring Web connectivity to browser-based point-of-sale, kiosk, or in-store terminals. This lets the retailer sell items it carries but that are not to be stocked in a given store, directs customers to the items at other stores where they are available, enables Web-assisted sales, and provides information from manufacturer Web sites.

Stage 5: Site Integrated with Manufacturer Systems

The site now combines all the information sources necessary for collaborative sales. Thus, manufacturers automatically replenish fast-selling merchandise and ship directly to consumers, if so desired by the retailer.

Figure 6.8

The Five Stages of Developing a Retail Web Presence

Source: Chart developed by the authors from the discussion in Tracy Mullin, "Determining Web Presence," *Chain Store Age* (October 1999), p. 42.

9. Fulfillment—Being in stock and providing on-time delivery are critical. eToys.com immediately informs the customer if a product is in stock, not hours later after the order is processed.

10. Fun and entertainment—Auction sites are making shopping a real game of chance and a treasure hunt that has resulted in eBay.com becoming one of the 10 most heavily trafficked Web sites.

11. Information integration—Whatever you want to know about car stereos and other electronics, Crutchfield.com provides it and integrates cleverly with the shopping experience.

12. Personalization—Everyone wants to be treated specially, and the Web is the perfect vehicle for one-to-one service. With its E-mail capability, customization is offered effectively by several cyberretailers, including Landsend.com.

Small Businesses Take Off on the Internet

As of mid-1999, there existed approximately 30,000 small retail businesses—defined as firms with annual sales of less than $10 million—taking orders over the Web. This number is expected to rise to 400,000 small businesses online by 2003, up from only 200 in 1996.

The Web is attractive to small retailers due to the ease of getting a business started. The simplest way to start a Web business is to become an affiliate of a larger business such as Amazon.com. Its 260,000 affiliates display an Amazon.com banner or button on their home pages. When a visitor clicks on the link and then purchases a product from Amazon.com, the affiliate gets a commission ranging from 5 to 15 percent. The key to becoming a successful affiliate is to develop a site that is so intriguing that it not only has heavy traffic, but also is used as a connection to purchase related goods.

Another strategy is to sell goods on an auction site such as eBay. According to eBay, more than 10,000 people make all or a large proportion of their total income at its site alone. HyperMart has plans to make it simpler for small retailers to sell through the Web by using the firm's security systems and electronic shopping cart technologies.

Source: David Leonhardt, "Lemonade Stands on Electric Avenue," *Business Week E.Biz* (July 26, 1999), pp. EB 64, EB 66.

13. Public relations/marketing—Although many cyberretailers have gotten publicity, no firm has created quite as much buzz as Victoriassecret.com. In four days, following its Super Bowl TV commercial and live Web fashion show, its site attracted an estimated 200 million visitors.

14. One-click ordering—Amazon.com has set the standard. Once you enter the appropriate data, all it takes to make a purchase is a simple click on the appropriate icon.

15. Selection—Like store retailers, product selection for cyberretailers is critical, but shouldn't be overwhelming. There isn't any rationale that a store's entire assortment be available online or vice versa. For example, Costco.com offers products not available in its clubs.[25]

> Shopping for a $25,000 diamond ring or $25 jeans? Costco Online (www.costco.com) has them both!

See Figures 6.9 and 6.10.

Consistent with the preceding discussion, a retailer has many decisions to make if it wants to utilize the Web. These are enumerated in Table 6.3. A firm cannot just put up a site and wait for consumers to visit it in droves and expect that they will happily return. In many cases: (1) It is still difficult for people to find what they are looking for. "Even if you know what you want to buy and you simply need to find a site that has the item in stock at a decent price, using the Web is not simple." (2) Once the person finds what he or she wants, it may be hard to see what is being bought. "Subtleties of color and texture often don't come across well on the Web. Until someone figures out how to send a cashmere scarf digitally, you won't be able to touch it." (3) Customer service is lacking. "In the bricks-and-mortar world, customer service is paramount. On the Web, it's often an afterthought." (4) Web sites and their store siblings are often not in sync. "Send someone a gift from CompUsanet.com and the recipient may be surprised to find it can't be returned or exchanged at a CompUSA store." (5) Privacy policies are frequently not consumer-oriented. "Lots of sites don't respect customer privacy. Order from a site, fill out a survey, or merely browse, and you can find your E-mail box swamped with unsolicited advertising and other junk."[26]

Figure 6.9
mySimon: Shopping
Bot Extraordinaire

mySimon, *www.mysimon. com,* is a shopping service (a shopping bot) that enables consumers to have access to the products of thousands of online merchants. mySimon is very easy to use, gives shopping tips, provides product reviews, and shows multiple vendors for each product requested. It is paid a referral fee by the retailers participating in its service.

Reprinted by permission.

Examples of Web Retailing in Action

These examples show the breadth of retailing on the World Wide Web.

Wal-Mart (www.wal-mart.com) has had a Web presence for years. However, until recently, the site was not much of a player—attracting only 1.3 percent of U.S. Web users, who stayed at the site for an average of six minutes per visit. In 1999, Web sales represented a fraction of one percent of total company revenues. But as of 2000, Wal-Mart is placing great emphasis on the Web through its dramatically revamped and enhanced Web site, saying that the site "will be the shot heard around the retail world." It plans to integrate its store and Web operations. Wal-Mart's goal is simple: "To reign over the Web."[27]

At the opposite end of the spectrum from Wal-Mart is the tiny business of Rosa Simon. Nonetheless, in 1998, she opened a Web site (www.blindsdepot.com) for her window-treatments business, which she had operated by herself through direct selling: "A technology neophyte, she looked first at Yahoo Stores. As with other companies, Yahoo enables users to build a Web site in minutes by filling out a series of forms online. For $100 a month, entrepreneurs can post their store on Yahoo's site and offer as many as 50 products for sale. What Ms. Simon could not get from Yahoo—or any other provider—was placement high on the results pages of search engines. Seeking more shoppers, she opted for an all-in-one package from iMall, which guarantees placement on its shopping site. When that failed to generate sales, she built a store using software from Concentric Network, an Internet service provider that hosted the site for $50 a month. Concentric software was limited for her purposes, so she spent $500 to build a more sophisticated site with ShopSite software, from Open Market. With the help of a consultant, she also learned how to increase site visibility on search engines. The payoff came when sales started to roll. 'I'm making much more than before,' she said. 'And I'm working much less.'"[28]

Figure 6.10
Online Adventures in
Wine Shopping

The wine.com Web site,
www.wine.com, makes
the purchase of wine
and related products a
very pleasant experi-
ence. The site is packed
with interesting infor-
mation. Wine.com has
created a shopping envi-
ronment that rivals that
of the best store-based
wine retailers.
Reprinted by permission.

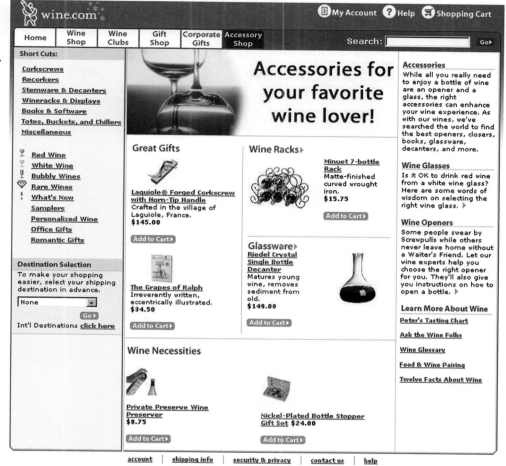

Another illustration of how small firms can exploit the Web is the Fine Grind: "Having your own Web site does not have to be hard or expensive. I know, since I helped my friend Dave Wolff—who runs a coffee shop but doesn't know from Java software—put his business online (www.finegrind.net), with lots of links and pictures and other bells and whistles, for next to nothing. Since then, the price has gone down. Dave still doesn't even own a working computer. Now that he's online, Dave uses the Web to research sources of bagels and egg-cream syrup, lure customers with promotions, and sell coffee-related items. More impor-tant, the site is helping the coffee shop, the Fine Grind, act as a focal point for an otherwise scattered community of people interested in poetry, music, and art in the rural area around Bel Air, Maryland, 45 miles north of Baltimore. And creating that kind of community was the fantasy Dave had in mind when he gave up his career managing an office high-rise to open a coffee shop."[29]

Finally, glimpse these lively Web happenings:

- Priceline.com (www.priceline.com), eBay (www.ebay.com), and Amazon.com (www.amazon.com) are just a few of the retailers with large-scale online auctions, featuring everything from hotel rates and air fares to consumer electronics and textbooks. Even nonprofit Goodwill has an auction Web site (www.shopgoodwill.com) that sells donated items to the highest bidders.

Table 6.3 Retailer Decisions in Utilizing the Web

What are the company's Web goals? At what point is it expected that the site will be profitable?

What budget will be allocated to developing and maintaining a Web site?

Who will develop and maintain the Web site, the retailer itself or an outside specialist?

Should the firm set up an independent Web site for itself or should it be part of a "cybermall"?

What features will the Web site have? What level of customer service will be offered?

What information will the Web site provide?

How will the goods and services assortment differ at the Web site from the firm's store?

Will the Web site offer benefits not available elsewhere?

Will prices reflect a good value for the consumer?

How fast will the user be able to download the text and images from the Web site, and point and click from screen to screen?

How often will Web site content be changed?

What staff will handle Web inquiries and transactions?

How fast will turnaround time be for Web inquiries and transactions?

How will all of the firm's information systems be integrated?

How will the firm coordinate store and Web transactions and customer interactions?

What will be done to avoid crashes and slow site features during peak shopping hours and seasons?

Will shoppers have to call a toll-free number to conclude a transaction after seeing an item on the Web?

How will online orders be processed?

How easy will it be for shoppers to enter and complete orders?

What online payment methods will be accepted?

What search engines (such as Yahoo, Infoseek, and Excite) will list the retailer's Web site?

How will the site be promoted: (a) on the Web and (b) by the company?

How will Web data be stored and arranged?

How will Web success be measured?

How will the firm determine which Web shoppers are new customers and which would otherwise visit a company store?

How will the firm ensure secure (encrypted) transactions?

How will consumer privacy concerns be handled?

How will returns and customer complaints be handled?

- NetGrocer (www.netgrocer.com), Peapod (www.peapod.com), and Webvan (www. Webvan.com) are among the leaders in online food stores. Analysts predict that annual online grocery sales could reach $11 billion by 2003, once the kinks in delivery are worked out.
- To better compete with movies on cable TV, Blockbuster (www.blockbuster.com) is beginning to allow customers to use the Web to reserve the videos they want to rent. It also hopes to be able to rent videos for Web viewing in the future, once the technology is available to do so.[30]

OTHER NON-TRADITIONAL FORMS OF RETAILING

Two other emerging, fast-growing nontraditional retail institutions merit special discussion: video kiosks and airport retailing. Although both of these formats have existed for several years, they have recently become much more important aspects of retailing. They appeal to retailers' desires to utilize new technology (video kiosks) and to locate in sites with high pedestrian traffic (airports).

Video Kiosks

Kiosks.org (www.kiosks.org) is tracking the phenomenal growth of video kiosks.

The **video kiosk** is a freestanding, interactive, electronic computer terminal that displays products and related information on a video screen; it often uses a touchscreen for consumers to make selections. Although some video kiosks are located in stores to enhance customer service, others enable consumers to place orders, complete transactions (typically with a credit card), and arrange for products to be shipped. Kiosks can be linked to retailers' computer networks or tied in to the Web.

Video kiosks can be situated practically anywhere (from a store aisle to the lobby of a college dormitory to a hotel lobby), require little or no personnel besides maintenance workers, and are an entertaining and easy way for people to shop. As two industry observers remarked, "The interactive kiosk is like an ATM but used for any end other than dispensing cash." "Kiosks can really enrich the shopping experience. They add a lot of flash and dazzle, a unique dimension to shopping."[31] See Figure 6.11.

According to North Communications, a kiosk manufacturer, "'Kiosk' is derived from a Turkish word, referring to an open summerhouse or pavilion; it was first popularized in France in the 1870s, when tall columns, often housing newsstands and bearing posters advertising galleries and theaters, began to emerge on the streets of Paris. Today, an electronic kiosk is distinguished by several minimum characteristics: a powerful CPU, often networked to a proprietary telecommunications system or the Internet, with full-motion video and audio, usually with MPEG hardware, a receipt printer, and magstripe card reader. Kiosks are appearing in bewildering variety now, with high-resolution laser printers, video teleconferencing, fingerprint and barcode readers, smart cards, and more. The line is beginning to blur between kiosks and ATMs, as the demand for public access to cyberspace begins to grow."[32]

At the beginning of 1999, there were about 250,000 video kiosks in use throughout the United States. It is estimated that there will be 1.7 million U.S. kiosks by the end of 2003. It is also forecast that U.S. video kiosk sales will rise from $830 million in 1999 to $3 billion in 2003. Worldwide, nearly 80 percent of kiosks are involved with retail-related transactions. North America accounts for 59 percent of kiosk sales, the Pacific Rim for 20 percent, Europe for 16 percent, and the rest of the world for 5 percent.[33]

The average hardware cost to a retailer for a video kiosk is $8,000. This does not include content development and kiosk maintenance. Hardware prices range from under $1,000 per kiosk to $15,000 to $20,000 per kiosk, depending on its functions—the more "flash and dazzle," the higher the price.[34]

Many shopping centers and individual store-based retailers are putting their hallways and back office space to better, more profitable use by setting up video kiosks in what previously were open hallways. These kiosks carry everything from gift certificates to concert tickets to airline tickets:

Today's kiosks are smaller, sleeker, and more high-tech and interactive than in the past. The next breed of kiosks will give retailers the power to offer products not in the store, provide superior service, and move merchandise direct to consumer. Toys "R" Us' initiative includes Internet kiosks in its stores. Shoppers can use them to browse low-volume items, collectibles, and other items. Borders Group is rolling out to its stores a new kiosk called Title Sleuth. The kiosks marry store inventory with that of borders.com—the two systems share data bases and fulfillment. Kmart is breaking in its Kmart Solutions in-store shopping network. The kiosks feature touchscreen menus that let shoppers electronically purchase everything from toys and books to cash wire transfers and flowers. OfficeMax kiosks let customers order more than 25,000 office supplies, furniture, and other items. Wal-Mart and Pottery Barn offer gift-registry kiosks. New digital download and fulfillment kiosks at Virgin Megastores

Figure 6.11
Virgin on Demand

There are Virgin Megastores in Europe, the United States, and Japan. Many of them have in-store "Virgin on Demand" video kiosks. With these kiosks, customers can make their own CDs compiling music from their favorite artists.
Reprinted by permission of PricewaterhouseCoopers LLP.

allow customers to create custom CDs in-store from Internet music sites, a first for any music retailer. Interactive kiosks can be found in the Microsoft store in San Francisco, in Hastings Entertainment units, in Gap stores (shoppers register on the kiosks in return for discounts, birthday reminders, and fashion updates), and at Circuit City, where shoppers use kiosks to search for PCs. Polo Ralph Lauren's new stores serve up special promotions on Polo Jeans kiosks.[35]

Airport Retailing

While there are no definitive financial statistics on the extent of airport retailing, this is one of the fastest-growing sectors of retailing. Not long ago, the leading retailers at airports were fast-food outlets, tiny gift stores, and newspaper/magazine stands. Today, airports are a major mecca of retailing. At virtually every large airport, as well as at many medium ones, there are full-blown shopping areas. And most small airports still have at least a fast-food retailer and vending machines for newspapers, candy, and so forth.

The potential retail market is huge. U.S. airports alone fly 3.2 million passengers a day and employ 1.6 million people (who often buy something for their personal use at the airport). There are 410 primary commercial U.S. airports, 30 of which are large hubs, 40 of which are medium hubs, 70 of which are small hubs, and 270 of which are nonhubs:

Today, many airports commonly encompass several thousand acres of land, have all of the functions and physical infrastructure of a modern city, share many governmental responsibilities with their host communities, and provide essential, if not indispensable, public services. The airport may have hundreds of tenants and concessionaires engaged in a wide array of aeronautical and general business enterprises located on, and generating revenue for, the airport. Annual operating budgets may run into the tens or hundreds of millions of dollars, with capital projects accounting for many millions more. The terminal complex, aviation facilities, support facilities, and areas such as runways, taxiways, and aprons are easily valued in the hundreds of millions of dollars for even a modest-sized airport. Modern airports are big business, impacting the social, economic, and political life of communities.[36]

New York's Kennedy Airport (www.panynj. gov/aviation/ jfkshopsframe.htm) typifies the retailing environment at the world's major airports.

These are some of the distinctive features of airport retailing:

- There is a very sizable group of prospective shoppers. In a typical year, a big airport may have 20 million people passing through its concourses. A regional mall is likely to attract 5 million to 6 million annual visits.
- Air travelers are a temporarily captive audience at the airport, looking for a way to fill their waiting time—which could be up to several hours. Air travelers tend to be above-average in income.
- Sales per square foot of retail space at airports is usually three to four times higher than at regional malls. Rent is about 20 to 30 percent higher per square foot for airport retailers.
- Airport stores are smaller, carry fewer items, and have higher prices than stores located elsewhere.
- Replenishing merchandise and stocking store shelves are sometimes difficult at airport stores because they are physically removed from delivery areas and there is limited storage space.
- Airport stores have excellent sales of gift items and forgotten travel items, from travelers not having the time to shop elsewhere. Brookstone, which sells garment bags and travel clocks at its airport shops, calls these products "I forgot" merchandise.
- Some passengers are at the airport at any time of day. Longer store hours are possible.
- There are special security issues, as well as opportunities for and restrictions on duty-free shopping for international travelers.[37]

SUMMARY

1. *To look at the characteristics of the three major retail institutions involved with nonstore-based strategy mixes: direct marketing, direct selling, and vending machines—with an emphasis on direct marketing.* Firms employ nonstore retailing when they use strategy mixes that are not store-based to reach customers and complete transactions. Such retailing encompasses direct marketing, direct selling, and vending machines.

In direct marketing, a consumer is first exposed to a good or service through a nonpersonal medium and then orders by mail, phone, fax, or computer. The 1998 U.S. retail sales from direct marketing were $180 billion. Direct marketers fall into two broad categories: general and specialty. Among the strengths of direct marketing are its reduced operating costs, large geographic coverage, customer convenience, targeted segments, and more. Among the limitations of direct marketing are the consumer's inability to examine items before purchase, the costs of printing and mailing, the low response rate, marketplace clutter, and more. Under the "30-day rule,"

there are stipulations to the policies a firm must follow as to shipping speed. The long-run prospects for direct marketing are strong because of consumer interest in reduced shopping time, 24-hour ordering, the stocking of well-known brands, improvements in operating efficiency, and technological breakthroughs.

The key to successful direct marketing is the customer data base, with data-base retailing being a way of collecting, storing, and using relevant shopper information. Several trends are vital to direct marketers: their attitudes and activities, changing consumer life-styles, increased competition, the use of dual distribution, the roles for catalogs and TV, technological advances, and the growth in global direct marketing. Specialogs and infomercials are two tools being used more by direct marketers.

A direct marketing plan has eight stages: business definition, generating customers, media selection, presenting the message, customer contact, customer response, order fulfillment, and measuring results and maintaining the data base. Firms also must consider that

SUMMARY (CONTINUED)

many people dislike shopping this way, feel overwhelmed by the amount of direct mail they receive, and are concerned about their privacy.

Direct selling includes personal contact with consumers in their homes (and other nonstore sites) and phone calls by the seller. It yielded $23 billion in 1998 U.S. retail sales, covering many goods and services. The strategy mix stresses convenience, a personal touch, demonstrations, and more relaxed consumers. U.S. sales have not gone up much due to the rise in working women, the labor intensity of the business, sales force turnover, government rules, and the poor image of some firms.

A vending machine uses coin- and card-operated dispensing of goods and services. It eliminates salespeople, allows 24-hour sales, and may be put anywhere convenient. Beverages and food items represented 85 percent of the $30 billion in 1998 U.S. vending revenues. Efforts in other product categories have met with some customer resistance; and items priced above $1.50 have not done well.

2. *To explore the emergence of electronic retailing through the World Wide Web.* The Internet is a global electronic superhighway that acts as a single, cooperative virtual network. The World Wide Web (Web) is one way of accessing information on the Internet, whereby people turn their computers into interactive multimedia centers. From a retailer perspective, the Web can serve one or more purposes, from projecting an image to presenting information to potential investors. The purpose chosen depends on the goals and focus. There is a great contrast between "clicks-and-mortar" retailing and "bricks-and-mortar" retailing.

The growth of Web-based retailing has been—and will continue to be—enormous. In 2003, revenues from retailing on the Web will be $140 billion in the United States and as much as $80 billion in Europe. Nonetheless, the Web will still garner less than 5 percent of U.S. retail sales in the year 2003.

More males than females shop on the Web, and purchasers are above-average in income and education. Shoppers are attracted by prices and convenience.

Nonshoppers worry about transmitting credit information and not seeing products first.

The Web offers these positive features for retailers: It can be inexpensive to have a Web site. The potential marketplace is huge and dispersed, yet easy to reach. Sites can be quite exciting. People can visit Web sites at any time. Information can be targeted. A customer data base can be established and customer feedback obtained. Yet, if consumers do not know a firm's Web address, it may be hard to find. Many people are not yet willing to buy online. There is clutter with regard to the number of retail sites. Because Web surfers are easily bored, a firm must regularly update its site to ensure repeat visits. The more multimedia features a Web site has, the slower it may be to access. Some firms have been overwhelmed with customer service requests. Improvements are needed to coordinate store- and Web-based transactions. There are few standards or rules as to what may be portrayed at Web sites. Consumers expect online services to be free and are very reluctant to pay for them.

A Web strategy can move through five stages: brochure site, commerce site, sited integrated with existing processes, the "Webified" store, and site integrated with manufacturer systems.

3. *To discuss two other nontraditional forms of retailing: video kiosks and airport retailing.* The video kiosk is a freestanding, interactive computer terminal that displays products and other information on a video screen; it often uses a touchscreen for people to make selections. Although some kiosks are in stores to upgrade customer service, others let consumers place orders, complete transactions, and arrange shipping. Kiosks can be put almost anywhere, require few personnel, and are an entertaining and easy way for people to shop. They will yield $3 billion in annual U.S. revenues by 2003.

Due to the huge size of the air travel marketplace, airports are gaining in popularity as retail shopping areas. Travelers (and workers) are temporarily captive at the airport, often with a lot of waiting time to fill. Sales per square foot, as well as rent, are high. Gift items and "I forgot" merchandise sell especially well.

Key Terms

nonstore retailing (p. 176)
direct marketing (p. 177)
data-base retailing (p. 181)
specialog (p. 183)

infomercial (p. 184)
direct selling (p. 189)
vending machine (p. 191)
Internet (p. 192)

World Wide Web (Web) (p. 192)
video kiosk (p. 203)

Questions for Discussion

1. How could a local stationery store use both nonstore retailing and store-based retailing?

2. Do you think nonstore retailing will continue to grow faster than store-based retailing? Explain your answer.

3. How would you increase a direct marketer's response rate from 2 percent of those receiving a mail catalog to 5 percent?

4. Explain the "30-day rule" for direct marketers.

5. What is data-base retailing?

6. What are the two main decisions to be made in the business definition stage of a planning a direct marketing strategy?

7. How should a bank that uses direct marketing handle consumer concerns about their privacy?

8. Differentiate between direct selling and direct marketing. What are the strengths and weaknesses of each?

9. As an industry consultant, what would you propose to increase sales volume via direct selling?

10. Select a product not heavily sold through vending machines and present a brief plan for doing so.

11. From a consumer's perspective, what are the advantages and disadvantages of the World Wide Web?

12. From a retailer's perspective, what are the advantages and disadvantages of having a Web site?

13. What must retailers do to improve customer service on the Web?

14. What future role do you see for video kiosks? Why?

WEB-BASED EXERCISE

Electronic Commerce Guide (www.ecommerce.internet.com)

Questions

1. Read two articles from the "E-Commerce News" section. Discuss the implication of these articles for Web-based retailers, as well as store-based retailers.

2. Develop a presentation for a local chamber of commerce on the opportunities and pitfalls in Web-based retailing using the materials at this Web site.

3. Discuss three important technical trends in retail E-commerce using the materials in the "EC Tech Advisor" section of the Web site.

4. Using the information at this Web site, describe five E-commerce retail trends related to consumers.

CHAPTER ENDNOTES

1. Bob Tedeschi, "E-Commerce Report: Internet Retailers Are Attracting Lots of Window Shoppers," *New York Times* (March 8, 1999), p. 14.

2. Sir Richard Greenbury, "Retailing: Confronting the Challenges That Face Bricks-and-Mortar Stores," *Harvard Business Review*, Vol. 77 (July–August 1999), p. 160.

3. Arnold Fishman, *Annual Guide to Mail Order 1998* (Homewood, Ill : Marketing Logistics, 1999); Direct Marketing Association, *www.the-dma.org* (March 9, 2000); "1999 Consumer Catalog Shopping Survey," *Catalog Age* (May 1999); and "State of the Industry," *Chain Store Age* (August 1999), Section Two, p. 32A.

4. "1999 Consumer Catalog Shopping Survey;" and Mary Ann Eastlick and Richard A. Feinberg, "Shopping Motives for Mail Catalog Shopping," *Journal of Business Research*, Vol. 45 (July 1999), pp. 281–90.

5. Harry Timmermans and Michelle A. Morganosky, "Special Issue on Direct Marketing: Where the Old Meets the New," *Journal of Business Research*, Vol. 45 (July 1999), p. 247.

6. See Robert Cohen, "Beware of Taxable Presence in Online and Catalog Arenas," *Discount Store News* (April 5, 1999), p. 12.

7. *Direct Marketing.* This definition appears in every issue of the monthly magazine.

**CHAPTER
ENDNOTES**

8. Joel R. Evans and Barry Berman, "Using Data-Base Marketing to Target Repeat (Loyal) Customers," *Tips for Better Retailing,* Vol. 1 (Number 3, 1995).

9. "1999 Consumer Catalog Shopping Survey."

10. David P. Schulz, "Growth of Direct-to-Consumer Channels Reshapes Retail Distribution," *Stores* (March 1999), p. 48.

11. Debra Aho Williamson, "Home Shopping Master QVC Struts Its Stuff Online, Too," *Advertising Age* (September 20, 1999); and Robert Scally, "Retail TV's Pioneer Pitchman," *Discount Store News* (May 24, 1999), p. 50.

12. Naveen Donthu and David Gilliland, "Observations: The Infomercial Shopper," *Journal of Advertising Research,* Vol. 36 (March–April 1996), p. 76.

13. Melissa Campanelli, "Leavy: Direct Mail Opportunities Thrive Overseas," *www.dmnews.com* (October 14, 1999); and Michelle A. Morganosky and John Fernie, "Mail Order Direct Marketing in the United States and the United Kingdom: Responses to Changing Market Conditions," *Journal of Business Research,* Vol. 45 (July 1999), pp. 275–79.

14. "Mail-Order Marketing: A Worldwide View," *Direct Marketing* (May 1996), pp. 31–32.

15. *Fact Sheet: 1999 Direct Selling Industrywide Growth & Outlook Survey* (Washington, D.C.: Direct Selling Association, 1999).

16. *Vending 101* (Chicago: National Automatic Merchandising Association, 1999); and Rodney Ho, "Vending Machines Make Change," *Wall Street Journal* (July 7, 1999), pp. B1, B4.

17. Louise Lee, "Clicks and Mortar at Gap.com," *Business Week* (October 18, 1999), pp. 150, 152.

18. *The Internet Data Services Report* (New York: Morgan Stanley Dean Witter, August 11, 1999); *The European Internet Report* (New York: Morgan Stanley Dean Witter, June 1999); John Tagliabue, "Foie Gras and Chips, Anyone?" *New York Times* (March 27, 1999), pp. C1, C5; Amy McMillan Tambini, "Online Shopping Soars into '99," *Discount Store News* (January 25, 1999), p. 3; Steve Lohr, "In E-Commerce Frenzy, Brave New World Meets Old," *New York Times* (October, 10, 1999), Section 4, p. 5; Michael J. Mandel, "The Internet Economy: The World's Next Growth Engine," *Business Week* (October 4, 1999), pp. 72–77; and *Business Week e.biz* (February 7, 2000).

19. Steve Lohr, "The Web Hasn't Replaced the Storefront Quite Yet," *New York Times on the Web* (October 3, 1999).

20. "O Commerce Pioneers!" *Fortune Technology Buyer's Guide* (Summer 1999), pp. 199, 202.

21. *Second Annual Ernst & Young Internet Shopping Study* (New York: Ernst & Young, 1999); Bob Tedeschi, "E-Commerce Report," *New York Times* (July 12, 1999), p. C4; "Retailing: Specialty," *Standard & Poor's Industry Surveys* (May 27, 1999), p. 7; "Young Minds, Big Money," *Business 2.0* (September 1999), p. 190; Heather Green, " 'Twas the Season for E-Splurging," *Business Week* (January 18, 1999), p. 40; "Internet at a Glance," *Business 2.0* (August 1999), p. 164; and "Internet at a Glance," *Business 2.0* (April 1999), p. 108.

22. Susan Reda, "Research Probes Links Between Online Satisfaction and Customer Loyalty," *Stores* (August 1999), p. 65.

23. Dana James, "From Clicks to Coin," *Marketing News* (October 11, 1999), p. 3.

24. Tracy Mullin, "Determining Web Presence," *Chain Store Age* (October 1999), p. 42.

25. Tony Lisanti, "The 15 Laws of Cyberretailing," *Discount Store News* (February 22, 1999), p. 11.

26. Jodi Mardesich, "The Web Is No Shopper's Paradise," *Fortune* (November 8, 1999), pp. 188–98.

27. Emily Nelson, "Overhauling Its Web Site, Wal-Mart Will Push Toys and Electronics," *Wall Street Journal* (October 1, 1999), pp. B1, B4; Alice Z. Cuneo, "Wal-Mart's Goal: To Reign Over Web," *Advertising Age* (July 5, 1999), pp. 1, 27; and Dan Scheraga, "Wal-Mart, Kmart Go Electronic," *Chain Store Age* (February 2000), pp. 184–85.

28 Bob Tedeschi, "Turning Small Businesses' Web Dreams into Reality," *New York Times on the Web* (October 11, 1999).

29. Marty Katz, "For a Perky Do-It-Yourself Web Site, The Price Was Right," *New York Times* (September 22, 1999), Special Section on E-Commerce, p. 29.

30. Robert D. Hof, Heather Green, and Paul Judge, "Going, Going, Gone," *Business Week* (April 12,

1999), pp. 30–32; Associated Press, "Goodwill Branch Looks to Web Auctions," *New York Times on the Web* (August 17, 1999); Barry Janoff, "Point, Click, Shop," *Progressive Grocer* (June 1999), pp. 31–34; and Associated Press, "Blockbuster Moves onto Internet," *New York Times on the Web* (October 22, 1999).

31. Dow Jones News, "Developers Broaden Uses of Interactive Kiosks," *Newsday* (May 10, 1999), p. C7; and Richard Sale, "Adding Flash and Dazzle," *Promo* (July 1999), p. 37.

32. North Communications, *www.kioskstore.com* (1998).

33. *Interactive Kiosk Markets* (San Francisco: Frost & Sullivan, 1999).

34. Gail Walker, "Kiosks Can Add Flash and Dazzle," *www.kiosks.org/newsbits* (April 8, 1999).

35. Dan Hanover, "Clicks and Mortar," *Chain Store Age* (September 1999), pp. 172–73.

36. *Economic Impact of U.S. Airports* (Washington, D.C.: Airports Council International, 1998).

37. Jennifer Steinhauer, "It's a Mall . . . It's an Airport," *New York Times* (June 10, 1998), pp. D1, D4; "Airport Retail Poses Design Challenge," *Chain Store Age* (May 1997), pp. 138–39; and Philana Patterson, "Brookstone Expects to Beat Estimates, Buoyed by Steady Airport Store Stores," *Wall Street Journal* (August 13, 1999), p. B5A.

CASE 1

DELIA'S: FROM CATALOG STARTUP TO A LEADING PLAYER OF APPAREL AND ACCESSORIES

Stephen Kahn has been able to build Delia's, a catalog retailer that sells funky clothes and accessories (such as cybernail polish and a millennium mouse pad) to 10- to 24-year-old females, into the nation's leading direct marketer to teenage girls. In just four years, the firm's annual sales skyrocketed from $150,000 to $150 million. And there is still a lot of potential. There are 28 million U.S. teenage females who spend an estimated $60 billion per year.

Delia's began when Kahn decided to quit his job at Paine Webber and set up a catalog operation that sold clothing to young women on college campuses. He then enlisted Christopher Edgar as a partner to specialize in developing the catalog and the overall retail strategy. After preparing a retail business plan, Kahn and Edgar decided to test the market by placing direct response advertisements in such magazines as *Cosmopolitan*, *Seventeen*, and *YM*. Much to their surprise, the phones rang off the hook. The number of callers was so great that the partners had to hire college students to handle the communications, as well as to gather information on the callers' birthdays, buying habits, credit history, and so on. At the same time, they hired young graphic artists and magazine editors to design the catalogs. As Edgar remarked, "Right away we knew that we stumbled onto a consumer group that was itching to be tapped."

Delia's direct marketing approach has enabled the partners to bypass distributors and quickly reach out to consumers. Its private-label strategy has let Delia's generate brand and retailer loyalty. At an early stage, the partners even decided to establish their own warehouse facility so the firm could better manage the order fulfillment process.

Despite the positives, success has not been easy. In Delia's early days, Stephen Kahn had a difficult time getting funding. Venture capitalists, for instance, believed that teenagers were a fickle group whose tastes were both difficult to define and constantly changing. The lack of access to credit cards by teenagers was another frequently cited obstacle by potential financiers. Unable to get traditional financing, Kahn went to friends and family members to raise the needed $1 million in startup capital so that he could produce, print, and distribute catalogs.

Competitors are well aware of Delia's prowess. Several key competitors have even copied Delia's marketing strategy. Delia's has responded by adding teenage boys to its target market by acquiring a direct retailer of boys' soccer clothing and equipment, a chain of mall stores

CASE 1

(CONTINUED)

that target young male shoppers, and a grouping of catalogs for young boys and girls. These acquisitions added 6 million names to Delia's customer data base and increased annual sales by almost $50 million. Recently, Delia's set up a number of Web sites, including Delia's online boutique (www.delias.com), a boys' apparel store (www.droog.com), and a children's home furnishings store (www.contentsonline).

Although some retailing analysts question whether new competitors will strike at Delia's target market and siphon off sales, others feel a shakeout among some of the newcomers is inevitable. For example, Claire's Stores, a $500 million chain of teenage apparel and accessories with its own Nikki catalog, recently closed down. Compared to its competitors, Delia's has the advantage of a strong position in multiple channels: mall stores, on the Web, and through traditional catalogs.

Questions

1. Discuss the synergy between Delia's female and male clothing operations.

2. How do Delia's store, catalog, and Web operations complement one another? What potential conflicts must be avoided? Explain your answers.

3. What unique problems does Delia's face in maintaining its data base?

4. Evaluate Delia's strategy of using private labels.

NOTE   The material in this case is drawn from David S. Murphy, "Delia's Next Big Step," *Fortune* (February 15, 1999), pp. 192[C]–192[H].

CASE 2

ADVERTISING
AND MARKETING
ON THE INTERNET

When Tracy O'Such received a large bonus, she decided it was time to purchase a new Mercedes C280. After using the Web to research prices, she visited several dealerships seeking a comparable $38,000 deal. One salesperson told her that the over $40,000 price she negotiated there was a "giveaway." Undeterred, O'Such contacted a Web buying service and, within 12 hours, she was quoted the $38,000 price. Coincidentally, the $38,000 quote was from the same dealer she visited, but from a different salesperson. She called the first salesperson back and said, "Guess what? I've found the car for my price." The salesperson argued that the price quote was impossible. At that point, Tracy told the salesperson, "It's in your showroom." There was silence at the other end of the phone.

According to marketing research, the number of households using Web referral services (such as www.autoweb.com and www.autobytel.com) to shop for cars increased from 800,000 in 1998 to 1.2 million in 1999. This figure was projected to increase to 1.7 million in the year 2000 and 5.2 million by 2003. About 94 percent of all car purchase requests submitted over the Web come from one of the referral services.

Many consumers believe auto referral services provide valuable information. In addition to price quotes, these services typically inform consumers about the invoice cost of each vehicle. This information was once a closely guarded secret. The Web sites also give information on vehicle specifications and "test drive" testimonials that are useful in helping shoppers pare down the number of car choices they face to a reasonable level and in deciding which model and brand are most appropriate to their needs.

Dealers benefit from the large volume of sales leads supplied by the referral services. On average, dealers collect 37 leads a month from referral services and make sales with about 15 percent of the leads. Dealers generally pay $25 per inquiry or a flat monthly fee. Many dealers view Web-generated sales in a positive way since they are connected with customers who are really ready to buy. The dealers' sales costs are lower due to the savings on sales commissions and in negotiating time.

The success of auto referral services has been observed by car dealers and car manufacturers. Dave Thomas (not Wendy's Dave Thomas!), who owns 16 dealerships in Oregon, is one of the thousands of dealers who have established their own Web sites. Thomas' site lets customers list the model and exact accessories they want and request a quote from one of his dealerships. More than 25 percent of the new vehicles sold or leased by Thomas' dealerships originate through his Web site. These transactions are conducted by a separate staff of eight salespeople who conduct only Web-driven sales transactions.

Ford has established a BuyerConnection section at its Web site (www2.ford.com), where prospective customers can tailor their vehicles and contact dealers. Similarly, General Motors has a GMBuyPower site (www.gmbuypower.com) and DaimlerChryslerAG has a GetAQuote site (www.getaquote.com). The General Motors' site allows shoppers to determine which specific dealer has the exact car configuration they desire. Although this site does not yet enable consumers to purchase a car online, they can communicate with dealers by E-mail and apply for financing online.

There are predictions that by the year 2004 consumers will be able to buy new cars directly from manufacturers through the Web and bypass dealers. In the meantime, there is always CarsDirect.com (www.carsdirect.com). It offers 2,500 different models (via agreements with a network of dealers), lets shoppers pick colors and options online, has haggle-free competitive prices, can arrange financing and insurance, and will deliver a car to the customer or let the customer pick up the vehicle from a dealer.

Questions

1. As a dealer, what are the pros and cons of affiliating with Web referral services?

2. Should a dealer charge the same price for a vehicle sold in its showroom as through a Web referral service? Explain your answer.

3. Select two auto referral services and evaluate their Web sites.

4. React to this statement: "There are predictions that by the year 2004 consumers will be able to buy new cars directly from manufacturers through the Web and bypass dealers."

Video Questions on Advertising and Marketing on the Internet

1. According to the video, what are the major pros and cons of advertising and marketing on the Web?

2. Discuss the major Web-based promotional strategies that are available to a regional department store chain.

NOTE   The material in this case is drawn from John Dodge, "The Driver's Seat," *Wall Street Journal* (July 12, 1999), p. R40; Fara Warner, "New Tactics Shake Up Online Auto Retailing," *Wall Street Journal* (October 18, 1999), p. B1; and Sana Siwolop, "Online, Few Kick Tires, But Many Look," *New York Times* (March 28, 1999), p. BU11.

PART TWO
COMPREHENSIVE CASE
Humanizing Cyberspace

INTRODUCTION

One Tuesday afternoon, Jessica Perlman bought a foam-green silk blouse from a national retailer. For Mrs. Perlman, the blouse was just the thing to wear to her anniversary dinner on Friday night. For the retailer, the transaction was the start of a data trail leading to the very heart of the corporation.

Mrs. Perlman's choice registered at several places in the store's daily sales reports. The blouse was tallied as a unit sale in the women's department. It made the reports as a part of the day's receipts. It even became a hand-written note to the department manager, which would later appear as part of the inventory report. None of this mattered to Mrs. Perlman, who was unaware of her blouse's notoriety.

By Wednesday, the records regarding Mrs. Perlman's blouse had been added to, subtracted from, and averaged into a variety of data fields in computers housed in district and regional offices. In addition to Mrs. Perlman's blouse, the records tracked birthday presents, wardrobe upgrades for job interviews, shower gifts, and replacements for favorite shirts from which jelly stains could not be removed. By Thursday, all of this information had been merged with even more information, tallied in more ways than any one person knew, split out, and sent to a variety of desktop computers in offices scattered throughout the retailer's national headquarters two time zones away.

On Friday, as Mrs. Perlman prepared for her romantic evening, a fashion coordinator mulled the viability of foam-green as a bridge color into the next season's assortment. In another office, a corporate buyer noted the continuing strong performance of silk. A divisional president compared sales activity in women's sizes to the rest of the division. Other people used data (including Mrs. Perlman's blouse) to analyze inventory, distribution strategies, advertising effectiveness, and consumer segmentation.

Commerce was not always like this. Back in 1902, James Cash Penney kept his first store open as long as someone was around who might want to shop. Within his first few months in Kemmerer, Wyoming, he knew the names and faces of nearly everyone in town. He soon knew who liked cotton, who liked wool, and who would not be caught dead in calico. In time, retail dynamics changed. Larger communities meant larger stores. Customers were more apt to find just what they wanted. But to do so, they would have to settle for less personalized service. In the 1950s, when Penney stores began expanding into suburban strip centers, in the 1960s when full-sized department stores became the norm, and in the 1970s when the typical Penney store became more common in a regional shopping mall, the customer-to-associate ratio continued to increase. Truly personalized service became increasingly difficult.

Meanwhile, on that anniversary Friday night, Mrs. Perlman was not aware of the experts in their far away offices. Nor was she aware of their perceptions of her. As she looked in the mirror, she did not see an age bracket, an income level, a preference in fabrication, or a trend in coloration. She saw a pleasant person preparing to celebrate a special occasion wearing a blouse that showcased her eyes perfectly.

None of the people at headquarters knew Mrs. Perlman as a person. They knew about her purchases. They knew her name. But with all the data they had, nobody knew if she would want another special garment at the same time next year, that she was especially fond of smooth fabrics and pastels, or that her husband almost always wore navy blue. They did not know whether she would ever return. Regardless of all the things they knew, none of them had figured out a way to know the individual customer.

"COMMON SENSE" TRAP

Somewhere along the line, many retailers have fallen victim to common sense. But common sense is based on experience. When those experiences or the reasons behind them change, common sense often becomes nonsense.

Dress shirts serve as an example. When suit coats first came into vogue, dress shirts were worn as undergarments. They were immensely practical. Coats were often coarse and heavy. The shirt protected the coat from

The material in this case is adapted by the authors from Michael Ponder, Internet Commerce Division, J.C. Penney, "Humanizing Cyberspace: The Cautionary Tale of Mrs. Perlman's Blouse," *Arthur Andersen Retailing Issues Letter* (March 1999), pp. 1–6. Reprinted by permission.

perspiration. More importantly, it protected the gentleman's skin from the itchy coat. To do this effectively, the shirt had to extend beyond the jacket's collar and sleeves. Dress shirts were white because they were undergarments. Shirt collars and cuffs were stiff and neatly pressed to show that the gentleman was clean and that his station in life did not require manual labor.

As technology progressed (particularly heating and air conditioning), shirts became more socially acceptable as outer garments. They came in colors. They even came with short sleeves. But when a suit coat is involved, social conventions remain. Shirt collars and cuffs are stiff. A colored dress shirt is considered a bit flamboyant by many, and short sleeves under a suit coat seem vaguely scandalous.

The moral? Beware of changing experiences that render common sense obsolete. Sometimes the anachronism lingers, as with the dress shirt. Sometimes it does not. A good example of this is "IBM's World Avenue," an online shopping mall.

ONLINE MALL

The IBM venture opened with a fair amount of fanfare a few years ago. Online retailing was going to become a major economic boom. Retailing meant stores. World-level retailing meant many stores. Many stores meant a mall. It was only common sense.

The online mall mimicked bricks-and-mortar retail space. No one stopped to think that, because cyberspace is new, the common sense rules applying to three-dimensional selling space don't always work. In the physical world, from which most retailers draw their experiences, malls work to the customers' benefit. With major anchors and a large assortment of specialty stores, shoppers can be fairly certain of finding anything they want while only having to park once. True, a shopping trip can last for hours (hence the need for restaurants and amusements). But it can also save hours of driving, parking, shopping, driving, parking, shopping, and then driving some more.

In the cyber-world, listing a variety of online stores on one menu is also a convenience. It can save shoppers seconds. The very nature of being online means the shopping experience will differ from the physical one. Still, we see retailers trying to force traffic flow and establish merchandise adjacencies in cyberspace just as they do in the physical world. We see them laboring to figure just "where" on their "site" (two physical terms in a nonphysical environment) certain merchandise belongs. In short, we see many of them trying to operate just as they do bricks-and-mortar stores and glossy paper catalogs.

Some say online shopping is like physical shopping. Retailers offer merchandise. Customers buy. However, there are differences. The forces leading to retailers' selections are changing (time-to-market pressures, for example). The very nature of customer service is changing. And sitting in front of a computer screen in pajamas in a living room differs from walking through a store. Others say online shopping is more like a catalog experience. But that comparison also falls short of the mark. By simply placing a catalog online, retailers allow people to do the same thing as before except that image resolution is poorer. To be truly valuable, an electronic retailing site must be more than a copy of existing selling channels. It must have benefits and its own intuitive sense.

Sense will work in this new environment but not common sense. While the concept is familiar, the details are new. That is why IBM's World Avenue did not work. It closed about a year after it began. This is not a reflection of the viability of online retailing, but rather it does speak to the future. New phenomena require a new application of sense. Common sense works only when looking backward.

ACTIVE CONSUMER

The first key to serving the online customer is to realize he or she is an individual human being and not a statistical target. The second is to realize that he or she is busy. These points make many of our common sense assumptions obsolete. People online seldom sit waiting to be entertained. More than three-quarters of the people online at any moment are there to do something. They may be looking for news, checking investments, or booking a trip. In this environment, ads do not work like television commercials. When an individual human being is actively trying to accomplish something, that same entertaining ad will be a distraction and annoyance. Or more likely, it will be ignored. Instead of placing a message in front of the greatest number of eyeballs, a successful online advertiser will place the message where it pertains to what a customer might be doing when exposed to the ad.

Beyond placement, the very nature of an effective online ad also changes. Typically, a TV ad tries to accomplish two or three objectives. The first is to engage the viewer, to catch his or her attention. The advertiser then tries to establish the brand or product name. Then, if there is still time, the ad can communicate factual content. This approach does not work with an active viewer. If the ad is relevant, the viewer will pay attention. Dancing logos are unnecessary and often annoying to someone trying to accomplish a task. Establishing the brand or product name in a banner ad is important, but only if it contains relevant content beyond the name.

The difference is even greater one step past a banner ad. When people click on a banner and go to a retail site, they want information. Brand establishment is secondary. They have already come to you. Entertainment value is a distant third and counterproductive unless it enhances the content. This suggests much more than a change in advertising. It is a fundamental step in redefining who the customer really is and how a business can relate to him or her. It also suggests that the Internet is not a mass medium. At its best, the Web is a personal communication channel with massive numbers of individuals using it.

THE REAL BOSS

Another key to figuring out how to serve the online customer is extremely daunting for most businesses. It is the recognition that companies do not control their businesses: customers do, one at a time. This has always been true. Mrs. Perlman's mother remembers merchants speaking to her by name and stocking her favorite sweets. But until the advent of E-commerce, technology and mathematics conspired to hide the fact that customers dominate the business.

Businesspeople have always said it is crucial to know the customer. But the traditional language of retailing suggests an arms-length relationship at best. While there is talk of "relationship retailing," "one-to-one selling," and "personalized online experiences," most seasoned professionals speak of tracking customer groups, targeting them, and at the most opportune moment launching a campaign, often in the form of a blitz intended to leverage a dominant position. The terminology and the mindset behind it are more like a military attack than an effort to build individual customer relationships.

Throughout the process, individual customers (such as Mrs. Perlman) remain anonymous. Businesses try to manipulate customer behavior on a mass scale. Limited-time sale pricing and special events are two examples. They then evaluate sales data to see if they guessed right.

Some basic fallacies flaw this reasoning. Outselling a competitor does not always mean that you offered what customers actually wanted. It only means your assortment was closer to what they wanted than your competitors' offering. To find out what people really want, you have to ask them, one at a time. You have to give individuals an active part in decision making beyond multiple choice. This change goes far beyond the retail world. Perhaps the most profound effect of the Internet explosion is that personal empowerment has grown into a very real force.

In the retail world, this empowering aspect of life online is not only enabling one-to-one interactions between retailers and customers, it is necessitating them.

SOCIAL EVOLUTION

Today's customers want what they want the way they want it right now and preferably at a competitive price. This is not new. People have always wanted immediate gratification. But in the past, they had to compromise this desire with the practical limitations of product fulfillment. That is not the case anymore.

It is ironic that the computer, which supported the volume that depersonalized retailing, has begun to mature so that it can now deal with smaller numbers. It is now possible for technology to track, reach out to, and interact with people as individuals again. Retailers will soon be able to choose whether they want to be mass merchants or establish one-to-one relationships with massive numbers of individuals. It is a major choice, one spelling the difference between success and bankruptcy.

Because retailers have better tools now, it is becoming more feasible (and necessary) to deal with people as they have always shopped—as individuals. The best companies during the next decade will be the ones that understand this. The ones that don't—the ones that insist on using new tools to do business the old way—will be written about as they announce staffing cutbacks and asset sales to stay profitable.

Business is not only about cost control anymore. Newspapers are littered with tales of companies discovering that if they save enough money in their operations over a long enough period of time, they go out of business. The new paradigm, which customers are demanding, revolves around service. They want businesses to serve their needs on their terms. They want to be heard (and understood) at a level beyond mathematical analysis and demographic groupings. They want to be treated like people.

Some feel the Internet has caused this shift in customer perspective. I don't. If the Internet had never moved from a military research project to a public, individualizable tool, something else would have been invented. It is not a matter of people loving technology. They don't. What they love are the possibilities technology offers them—the ability to do the things they want in their own way. As technology improves, the desire to be empowered is becoming a more fundamental part of the social landscape.

EMILY DIETZ AND THE MODERN LUDDITES

During her first class on Introduction to Computers, a student named Emily Dietz decided to compose an E-mail note to her fellow seventh-grader, Mary Ellington. After a few moments of concentration, when she was satisfied that her text carried the perfect degree of understated nuance, Emily clicked on the "send" button. The note disappeared from her screen. The computer, which had seen the note as a long string of zeroes and ones, converted that string into a coded stream of electrons. This stream was then released onto the Internet. Traveling at the speed of light, the digitally encoded stream flew through the school's server and several routers, each of which read a small segment of the code and sent the message to its first destination: another server that processed the note and logged it into Mary's electronic mailbox. Still working at the speed of light, the second server composed a note of its own. This note, informing Mary that she had mail, went back onto the Internet, following a different route back to the school's server. It sat there until fourth period, when Mary Ellington had some computer time.

Seeing that she had mail waiting, Mary touched a button that sent yet another stream of electrons on a light-speed journey of indeterminate length, asking the second server to send the note back to her computer. After a delay so short that it seemed not to be a delay at all, a representation of Emily's text appeared on Mary's screen. It read, "Josh is cute, and he likes you." After a suppressed giggle, Mary composed a reply. It read, "Shut up." Then, at the touch of a button, the entire process—digital encoding, electron streams, servers, and routers—repeated itself.

In another time, this communication would have been handled with scraps of paper, surreptitiously passed from hand to hand like a scene from a black-and-white prison movie. The two girls would have had the giddy sense of risk stemming from the very real possibility of detection, embarrassment, and possibly detention. But in today's world, E-mail works better. Neither girl realized she was taking part in something much more far-reaching than Josh's real or imagined interest. Their use of technology is the embodiment of today's positive version of Ned Lud's eighteenth-century vision of the machine as enemy.

Lud was a weaver in a little village near Leicestershire, England. He was unemployed. He was angry, believing that machines had taken away his livelihood. Then, one night in 1779, Lud broke into a house and destroyed two machines used to knit hosiery. To the people who distrusted automation, Lud's act was every bit as heroic as Rosa Parks' refusal to step to the back of the bus would be to civil rights advocates 176 years later. Luddites proclaimed that machines were soulless, intrusive things and that people should not be made to serve them. They advocated a retreat from technology and a return to the "good old days."

The industrial age is fading. We are now in the information age. To many, the transition to this new age is every bit as disorienting, discomforting, and intimidating as the last transition was to Ned Lud and his compatriots. And after all these years, his name is coming back into popular conversation. Organized groups of classical Luddites raise the same concerns and arguments about computers as earlier groups did about industrial machinery. Ironically enough, you can find many of these groups on the Web.

At the same time, another group (unorganized) is taking the Luddite manifesto one step farther. They agree that people should not serve machines. They agree that computers can be soulless and intrusive. But they also concede that computers are extremely convenient. Rather than advocating a retreat from technology, as the classical Luddites do, they seek technologies so advanced that they become invisible.

Rather than stressing technology, they stress function. They may not know how a microwave works, but they know how to use one. They may not be able to explain E-mail, but they know it is safer than passing notes in class. They want to do what they want to do when they want to do it and still be treated as individuals. Without articulating it, these neo-Luddites are escaping the tyranny of machines by transcending it—by letting the machines serve them.

Emily Dietz and her peers are not only demanding this personalized vision enabled by transparent technologies: they are helping to create it. Her grandmother, Mrs. Perlman, who at Emily's age saw personalized customer service—practiced without technology—fading away, approves of the world Emily is helping to create.

Questions

1. What can an independent retailer learn from the information in this case?
2. What can a chain retailer learn from the information in this case?
3. Is it easier or harder to become a destination retailer today than it was 20, 50, or 100 years ago? Explain your answer.
4. How can a firm use a computerized data trail to improve its scrambled merchandising decisions?
5. Comment on this statement: "Somewhere along the line, many retailers have fallen victim to common sense. But common sense is based on experience."
6. Amazon.com is moving from an online specialty category killer in books to an online mall selling a wide variety of products, including electronics, toys, and games on its Web site. What must it do to succeed where others have failed?
7. Why is the online shopper considered an active customer? What are the ramifications of this for both Web retailers and store-based retailers?

TARGETING CUSTOMERS AND GATHERING INFORMATION

■ In Part Three, various details related to identifying and understanding consumers, and developing an appropriate target market plan, are first presented. Information-gathering methods—which can be used in identifying and understanding consumers, as well as in developing and implementing a retail strategy—are then described.

■ Chapter 7 discusses the many influences on retail shoppers: demographics, life-styles, needs and desires, shopping attitudes, and behavior, retailer actions that influence shopping, and environmental factors. These elements are placed within a retail target marketing framework. It is critical for retailers to recognize what makes their customers and potential customers tick—and for them to act accordingly.

■ Chapter 8 deals with information gathering and processing in retailing. The difficulties that may arise from basing a retail strategy on nonsystematic research are considered. The retail information system, its components, and recent advances in information systems are then reviewed in depth. Particular emphasis is placed on data warehousing and data mining. The chapter concludes by outlining and describing the marketing research process, as well as the critical information role of retailers in the distribution channel.

CHAPTER 7

Identifying and Understanding Consumers

CHAPTER OBJECTIVES

1. To discuss why it is important for a retailer to properly identify, understand, and appeal to its customers
2. To enumerate and describe a number of consumer demographics, life-style factors, and needs and desires—and to explain how these concepts can be applied to retailing
3. To examine consumer attitudes toward shopping and consumer shopping behavior, including the consumer decision process and its stages
4. To look at retailer actions based on target market planning
5. To note some of the environmental factors that affect consumer shopping

Sports Authority's new 50,000-square-foot store in Clifton, New Jersey, is the chain's prototype that will serve as a model for future stores. To increase its sales among women, a number of the store's features have been designed to better appeal to female shoppers. According to Sports Authority's president, "Physically, sporting goods stores have been intimidating and not terribly interesting to women."

The new prototype has adapted many merchandising techniques from department stores. These include hanging signs to identify specific departments, displays depicting active figures, full-length mirrors on the sales floor, and banners imprinted with "Just Ask" signs to encourage shoppers to seek out sales personnel. This store places a greater emphasis on footwear and apparel than other Sports Authority units; and it has also increased its offerings of such special services as skateboard tune-ups, paint-ball refills, and winding lines on fishing reels.

To facilitate self-service shopping, maps are positioned at the store's entrance. Footwear is displayed in the center ring, apparel in the middle ring, and sporting goods and accessories in the outer ring. In addition, footwear, apparel, and equipment are displayed according to activity: fitness, racquet sports, extreme, ski/water sports, outdoor, fishing, team sports, sports stadium, fan shop, and golf.[1]

OVERVIEW

A retailer's ability to devise and apply a sound strategy depends on how well that firm identifies and understands its customers, and forms its retail strategy mix to appeal to them. This entails identifying the characteristics, needs, and attitudes of consumers, as well as recognizing how people make purchase decisions—and then devising an appropriate target market plan. It also means studying the environmental factors that affect purchase decisions. Consider the following:

> *Please Note:* Web site addresses are constantly changing.
> The links in this chapter are current as of the publication of this book.

Retailers have long depended on their ability to size up people when they walk in the door. Customers give themselves away by their clothing, speech, and mannerisms. While gut instinct still works for some retailers, the era of successful scrutiny has passed. You can no longer pigeonhole at a glance because increasing consumer diversity has made stereotyping futile. You need a more systematic way to understand customers. In 1800, a typical American had access to fewer than 300 products on sale in his or her hometown, one retail establishment (a country store), and about 500 feet of retail space. In contrast, a typical American in a city of a million people now has access to over a million products, thousands of retailers, and over 20 million square feet of selling space.[2]

Today's consumers know what they want. They are tough critics, savvy purchasers, value-driven spenders, and practical thinkers. The demands on their time at work and home have made them extremely selective about how they spend their leisure hours. They also have greater, more pressing demands on their dollars as they face retirement, college costs, and growing families. Shopping is also vying with leisure activities, from vacations and dining out to videos and hobbies. This means retailers must be that much better. Better at knowing their consumers, predicting their needs and wants, and delivering products and shopping experiences that consistently exceed their expectations. This is the biggest challenge for the next decade. And it all begins and ends with the consumer.[3]

Consumer shopping is influenced by a number of factors. In this chapter, we explore—in a retailing context—the impact on shoppers of each of the elements shown in Figure 7.1: demographics, life-styles, needs and desires, shopping attitudes and behavior, retailer actions that influence shopping, and environmental factors. By studying these elements, a retailer can devise the best possible target market plan and do so in the context of its overall strategy.

Please note: In this chapter, we use "consumer," "customer," and "shopper" interchangeably.

Figure 7.1
What Makes Retail
Shoppers Tick

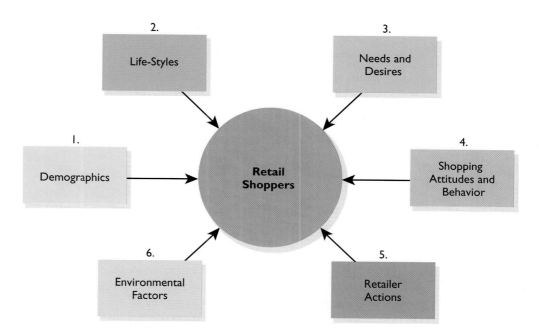

CONSUMER DEMOGRAPHICS AND LIFE-STYLES

Demographics are objective, quantifiable, easily identifiable, and measurable population data. **Life-styles** are the ways in which individual consumers and families (households) live and spend time and money.

Consumer Demographics

To learn what information retailers could easily obtain about your community, visit *The Rite Site* (www.easidemographics.com/reports/easi_free_reports.phtml), select "Zip Codes" under "Geographies," and press "Go!" On the next page, enter your zip code.

Groups of consumers and individual consumers can be identified in terms of such demographic variables as gender, age, growth rate, life expectancy, literacy, language spoken, household size, marital and family status, income, retail sales, mobility, place of residence, employment status, occupation, education level, and ethnic/racial background. These variables strongly affect people's retail shopping and retailer actions.

A retailer should have some basic knowledge of overall demographic trends, as well as the demographic attributes of its own target market. Table 7.1 indicates countrywide demographics for 20 nations around the world and Table 7.2 contains U.S. demographics by region. Regional data are a useful starting point for retailers, since most firms are local and regional in nature.

In understanding U.S. demographics, it is also vital to know about these other facts:

- The typical U.S. household has annual after-tax income of $35,000. The top one-sixth of households have incomes of $75,000 or more; the lowest one-fifth earn under $15,000. If income is high, people are more apt to have **discretionary income**—money left after paying taxes and buying necessities.
- One-sixth of people change residences each year, yet 60 percent of all moves are in the same country.
- There are 6 million more females than males, and three-fifths of females aged 16 and older are in the labor force (many full-time).
- Most U.S. employment is in services. In addition, there are now more professionals and white-collar workers than before and fewer blue-collar and agricultural workers.
- More adults have attended some level of college, with one-quarter of all U.S. adults aged 25 and older at least graduating from a four-year college.
- The population comprises a number of different ethnic and racial groups. African-Americans, Hispanic-Americans, and Asian-Americans account for more than one-quarter of U.S. inhabitants—a figure that is steadily rising. Each of these groups represents a large potential target market.[4]

Although the preceding gives a basic picture of the United States, consumer demographics vary by area. Within the same state or city, some locales have larger populations and more affluent, older, and better-educated residents than others. Because most retailers are local or operate in only parts of particular regions, they must compile data about the people living in their particular trading areas and those most likely to patronize them. A retailer could identify its target market based on some combination of these demographic factors—and plan its retail strategy accordingly:

- Market size—How many consumers are in the target market?
- Gender—Is the target market predominantly male or female, or are they equal in proportion?
- Age—What are the prime age groups to which the firm appeals?
- Household size—What is the average size of households?
- Marital and family status—Are consumers single or married? Do families have children?
- Income—Is the target market lower income, middle income, or upper income? Is discretionary income available for luxury purchases?
- Retail sales—What is the retail sales potential for the retailer's goods/services category?

Table 7.1 Population Demographics: A Global Perspective—Selected Countries

Country	1999 Male/ Female (%)	1999 Age Distribution(%) 0–14 Years	15–64 Years	65 Years & Over	Annual Population Growth (%)	1999 Life Expectancy in Years	1999 Literacy Rate (%)	Principal Languages Spoken
Brazil	49.2/50.8	30	65	5	1.16	64.1	83	Portuguese, Spanish, English, French
Canada	49.5/50.5	20	68	12	1.06	79.4	97	English, French
China	51.7/48.3	26	68	6	0.77	69.9	82	More than a dozen versions of Chinese
France	48.7/51.3	19	65	16	0.27	78.6	99	French
Germany	49.0/51.0	15	69	16	0.01	77.2	99	German
Great Britain	49.2/50.8	19	65	16	0.24	77.4	99	English
India	51.7/48.3	34	61	5	1.68	63.4	52	Hindi, English, 22 other languages spoken by at least one million people
Indonesia	50.0/50.0	30	65	5	1.46	62.9	84	Bahasa Indonesia, English, Dutch
Italy	48.5/51.5	14	68	18	−0.08	78.5	97	Italian
Japan	49.0/51.0	15	68	17	0.20	80.1	99	Japanese
Malaysia	50.2/49.8	35	61	4	2.08	70.7	84	Bahasa Melayu, English, Chinese
Mexico	49.2/50.8	35	61	4	1.73	72.0	90	Spanish
Philippines	49.7/50.3	37	59	4	2.04	66.6	95	Filipino, English
Poland	48.7/51.3	20	68	12	0.05	73.1	99	Polish
Russia	46.8/53.2	19	68	13	−0.33	65.1	98	Russian
South Africa	49.5/50.5	34	61	5	1.32	54.8	82	Afrikaans, English, 9 other languages
South Korea	50.5/49.5	22	71	7	1.00	74.3	98	Korean, English
Thailand	49.2/50.8	24	70	6	0.93	69.2	94	Thai, English
United States	49.0/51.0	22	66	12	0.85	76.2	97	English, Spanish
Venezuela	50.5/49.5	33	62	5	1.71	73.0	91	Spanish

The literacy rate is the percentage of people who are 15 and older who can read and write.

Sources: Compiled by the authors from *CIA World Factbook 1999.*

Table 7.2 Selected U.S. Demographics by Region (as of 1999)

Region	Percent of U.S. Population	Percent of U.S. Household Income	Percent of U.S. Retail Sales	Percent of Population 18 to 34 years old	Percent of Population 50 & Older	Percent of Population Living in Metropolitan Areas	Population Per Square Mile of Land Area	Percent Change in Population 1990–1999
New England	4.9	5.8	5.2	24.4	28.3	89.4	214.5	+ 2.0
Middle Atlantic	14.0	15.5	13.1	23.1	29.7	91.2	386.0	+ 2.1
East North Central	16.2	16.5	16.9	23.0	27.6	79.4	181.8	+ 5.4
West North Central	6.9	6.7	7.3	22.5	28.4	59.0	36.8	+ 5.7
South Atlantic	18.1	17.9	19.5	23.5	28.5	79.1	183.4	+12.1
East South Central	6.1	5.4	5.7	22.8	28.0	57.5	92.1	+ 8.3
West South Central	11.1	10.2	10.5	23.8	24.9	76.6	70.0	+11.8
Mountain	6.3	5.8	6.7	23.0	25.0	72.2	19.3	+20.5
Pacific	16.4	16.2	15.1	24.9	24.5	91.5	51.6	+11.8

New England = Connecticut, Maine, Massachusetts, New Hampshire, Rhode Island, Vermont; Middle Atlantic = New Jersey, New York, Pennsylvania; East North Central = Illinois, Indiana, Michigan, Ohio, Wisconsin; West North Central = Iowa, Kansas, Minnesota, Missouri, Nebraska, North Dakota, South Dakota; South Atlantic = Delaware, District of Columbia, Florida, Georgia, Maryland, North Carolina, South Carolina, Virginia, West Virginia; East South Central = Alabama, Kentucky, Mississippi, Tennessee; West South Central = Arkansas, Louisiana, Oklahoma, Texas; Mountain = Arizona, Colorado, Idaho, Montana, Nevada, New Mexico, Utah, Wyoming; Pacific = Alaska, California, Hawaii, Oregon, Washington.

Sources: Computed by the authors from U.S. Bureau of the Census data; except for household income and retail sales data, which are from "1999 Survey of Buying Power," *Sales & Marketing Management* (1999), p. 58.

- Birth rates—How important are birth rates for the retailer's goods/services category?
- Mobility—What percentage of the target market moves each year (into and out of the trading area)?
- Where people live—How large is the trading area from which customers can realistically be drawn?
- Employment status—Does the target market contain working women, retirees, and so on?
- Occupation—In what industries and occupations are people working? Are they professionals, office workers, or of some other designation?
- Education—Are customers college-educated?
- Ethnic/racial background—Does the target market consist of a distinctive racial or ethnic subgroup?

Consumer Life-Styles

The General Social Survey of U.S. households (www.icpsr.umich.edu/gss) annually interviews people to learn about their life-styles and attitudes. See the results.

Consumer life-styles are based on both social and psychological factors. They are affected by people's demographic backgrounds. As with demographics, a retailer should first have some basic knowledge of various consumer life-style concepts and then determine the life-style attributes of its own target market.

These social factors are useful in identifying and understanding consumer life-styles.

- A **culture** is a distinctive heritage shared by a group of people. It passes on a series of beliefs, norms, and customs. In the United States, there is an overall culture, which stresses individuality, success, education, and material comfort. There are also different subcultures for various demographic groups (such as Hispanic and Asian) due to the many countries from which residents have come.

Asian Men Tour the Grocery Aisles

According to a Hong Kong marketing research firm, which surveyed more than 1,000 consumers in each of 12 Asian markets, 31 percent of the grocery store decision makers in all regions are male. The highest proportion of male decision makers are in Malaysia (47 percent), Singapore is second, with males comprising 41 percent of decision makers, and Shanghai is third with 40 percent. In contrast, far fewer grocery store decision makers in Western markets are male. The Asian findings are contrary to the traditional retailing strategy that targets only female shoppers in Asian markets. The research suggests that Asian males view shopping as a family activity and accompany their wives and children.

The large number of male grocery shoppers means that stores should re-examine their overall approach in Asia. One consultant suggests that grocery stores should stock more male-oriented products, such as car accessories. The stores can also benefit from a value-pricing appeal to males who want more impact on family spending.

Some experts do not fully believe the study's findings. A Unilever marketing executive says that "men may claim they're the decision makers, but what they say and what is reality may be miles apart."

As vice-president of marketing for an Asian grocery chain, prepare a marketing plan to capitalize on the male market.

Source: Louise Lee, "Men in Asia Grocery Shop, Survey Finds," *Wall Street Journal* (February 19, 1999), p. B5B.

- **Social class** involves an informal ranking of people based on income, occupation, education, and other factors. There are people with similar values and life-styles in each social class category.
- **Reference groups** influence people's thoughts and behavior. An aspirational group is one to which a person does not belong but wishes to join. A membership group is one to which the person does belong. A dissociative group is one to which the person does not want to belong. Reference groups that are face-to-face, such as families, have the most impact on people. In addition, within reference groups, there are opinion leaders whose views are especially respected and sought.
- The **family life cycle** describes how a traditional family moves from bachelorhood to children to solitary retirement. At each stage, attitudes, needs, purchases, and income change. Besides planning for this cycle, retailers must be responsive to the many adults who never marry, divorced adults, single-parent families, childless couples, and so on. That is why more attention is being paid to the **household life cycle,** which incorporates the life stages of both family and nonfamily households.
- *Time utilization* refers to the types of activities in which a person is involved and the amount of time allocated to them. Some of the broad categories of time utilization are work, transportation, eating, recreation, entertainment, parenting, sleeping, and (retailers hope) shopping. Today, many consumers allocate much less time to shopping activities than in the past.

These psychological factors are helpful in identifying and understanding consumer life-styles:

Retailers can study consumer psychology with tools such as the Keirsey Temperament Sorter. Take the online test (www. keirsey.com/cgi-bin/ keirsey/newkts.cgi) to gain insights about yourself.

- A **personality** is the sum total of an individual's traits, which make that individual unique. These traits include a person's level of self-confidence, innovativeness, autonomy, sociability, emotional stability, and assertiveness. Together, these attributes have a big impact on a person's life-style.
- **Class consciousness** is the extent to which a person desires and pursues social status. It helps determine the use of reference groups and the importance of prestige purchases. A class-conscious person values the status of particular goods, services, and retailers more than one who is not.
- **Attitudes (opinions)** are the positive, neutral, or negative feelings a person has about the economy, politics, goods, services, institutions, and so on. They are also feelings consumers have about a given retailer and its activities. Does the consumer feel a retailer is desirable, unique, and fairly priced?
- **Perceived risk** is the level of risk a consumer believes exists regarding the purchase of a specific good or service from a given retailer, whether or not the belief is actually correct. There are six types: *functional* (Will a good or service perform as expected?), *physical* (Can a good or service hurt me?), *financial* (Can I really afford the purchase?), *social* (What will peers think of my shopping with this retailer?), *psychological* (Am I doing the right thing?), and *time* (How much effort must I exert to make a purchase?). Perceived risk is highest if the retailer or the brands it carries are new, a person is on a budget, a person has little experience, there are many choices, a purchase is socially visible or complex, and so on. See Figure 7.2. Retailers can reduce perceived risk by giving ample information.
- The importance of a purchase to the consumer affects the amount of time he or she will spend to make a decision and the range of alternatives considered. If a purchase is seen as important, perceived risk tends to be higher than if it is viewed as unimportant; and the retailer must act appropriately.

A retailer can develop a life-style profile of its target market by answering these questions and then use the answers in developing its strategy:

Figure 7.2
The Impact of
Perceived Risk on
Consumers

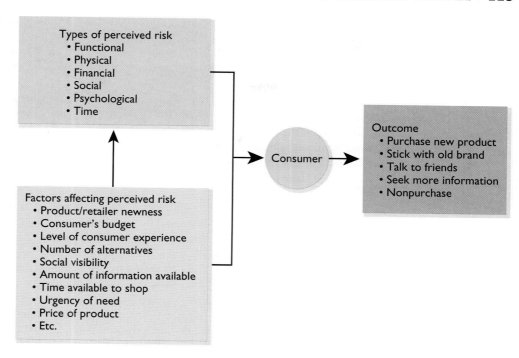

- Culture—What cultural values, norms, and customs are most important to the target market?
- Social class—Are consumers lower, middle, or upper class? Are they socially mobile?
- Reference groups—To whom do people look for purchasing advice? Does this differ by good or service category? How can a firm target opinion leaders?
- Family (or household) life cycle—In what stage(s) of the cycle are the bulk of customers?
- Time utilization—How do people spend time? How do they view the time spent shopping?
- Personality—Do customers have identifiable personality traits?
- Class consciousness—Are consumers status-conscious? What does this signify for purchases?
- Attitudes—How does the target market feel about the retailer and its offerings in terms of specific strategy components?
- Perceived risk—Do customers feel risk in connection with the retailer? Which goods and services have the greatest perceived risk?
- Importance of the purchase—How important are the goods/services offered to the target market?

Retailing Implications of Consumer Demographics and Life-Styles

Retailers need to consider demographic and life-style factors from several perspectives. Here are some illustrations. By no means do the examples cover the full domain of retailing.

Gender Roles: The greater number of working women, who put in 60 to 70 hours or more each week between their job and home responsibilities, is altering life-styles significantly. Compared to women who have not worked outside the home, they tend to be more self-confident and individualistic, more concerned with the convenience and ease of household duties, more interested in sharing household and familial tasks with spouses or significant others, more knowledgeable and demanding as consumers, more interested in leisure activities and travel, more involved with improving themselves and their educational background, more appearance-conscious (concerned with the way they dress), and more indifferent to small price differences among stores or merchandise. They are much less interested in leisurely shopping trips.

Due to the trend toward working women, the life-styles of males are also changing. Large numbers of men now take care of children, shop for food, do laundry, wash dishes, cook for the family, vacuum the house, and clean the bathroom. Today, 28 percent of U.S. males are either the primary grocery shopper in the family (16 percent) or share that responsibility (12 percent).[5] See Figure 7.3. The future will see still more changes in men's and women's roles (and in their conflicts over them). Furthermore, the clout and duties of husbands and wives will be shared with greater frequency than before. Retailers need to understand and adapt to this trend.

Consumer Sophistication and Confidence: Many shoppers are now more knowledgeable and cosmopolitan; more aware of national and worldwide trends in tastes, styles, and goods and services; and more sophisticated. Nonconforming behavior is more widely accepted since increased education has led to the self-assurance that shoppers require to reduce their need for conformity, while providing an appreciation of available choices. Confident shoppers depend less on brands and labels and are more apt to experiment: "Today's customer is someone, not anyone. They want personnel with knowledge of the product they sell. Customers have long passed the point where they ask, 'What's the difference between this VCR for $199 and the one for $249?' and are satisfied with the answer, 'Fifty dollars.'" "While consumers have money to spend, they are very selective about where and on what they spend it."[6]

Poverty of Time: For some households, the increased of number of working women, the desire for personal fulfillment, the commute between work and home, and the greater number of people working at second jobs contribute to their feeling time-pressured. Many customers are thus apt to place a high value on goods and services that minimize time expenditures: "Time, or rather the lack of it, is the single greatest problem consumers face today. It affects the choices they make every day as they confront demands at work and at home. Consequently, leisure time has become a precious commodity. As a result, both women and men are cutting hours for various discretionary activities as they try to squeeze out a little

Figure 7.3
Blurring Gender Roles

Due to changing life-styles, more husbands and wives shop together now, as at this A&P store.
Reprinted by permission.

more time for family and for themselves. Time is so precious that many people agree that, given the choice, they would rather have more free time than more money!"[7]

There are various ways for retailers to respond to the poverty-of-time concept. For instance, they can increase the number of branch stores to limit customer travel time; have longer hours of operation, including evening and weekend openings; add on-floor sales personnel; reduce checkout time; and utilize mail order, Web site, and other direct marketing practices. See Figure 7.4.

Component Life-Styles: This is a concept of growing significance for retailers. In the past, shoppers tended to be typecast based on their overall demographics and life-styles. However, it is now recognized that shopping behavior is less predictable and more individualistic. It is more situation-based, hence, the phrase *component life-style:* "Have you wondered of late what's going on with consumers? Why they are so full of contradictions when it comes to spending money? Why they will buy a $500 leather jacket at full price but wait for a $50 sweater to go on sale? Will buy a top-of-the-line sports utility vehicle then go to Costco to buy new tires? Will eagerly pay $3.50 for a cup of coffee but think $1.29 is too expensive for a hamburger? Will spend $2.00 for a strawberry-smelling bath soap but wait for a coupon to buy a $0.99 twin pack of toilet soap?" "It doesn't matter how much money they have or where they went to school. People with money don't just buy expensive things anymore. A man might buy a $2,000 suit at Armani at full-price, but he'll wait until underwear and shirts go on sale. A mother from a low-income family may routinely shop at a mass merchandiser for her kids' clothes, housewares, or diapers and wait for sales and coupons when she shops for food. But if she see a gold bracelet she 'must' have, she will buy it—as long as she feels she's getting her money's worth."[8]

Consumer Profiles

Considerable research has been aimed at describing consumer profiles in a way that is useful for retailers. Here are three examples.

Even though only a few years separate them from baby boomers, 18- to 34-year-olds—Generation X and Generation Y—couldn't be more different. This demographic subset has been described as much more spontaneous, responsive, spirited, passionate,

VALS (future.sri.com/vals/valsindex.shtml) classifies life-styles into several profiles. Visit the site to learn about the profiles and take the survey to see where you fit.

Figure 7.4
Responding to Consumers' Poverty of Time

Today, A&P supermarkets offer the "Outgoing Chef" program for time-pressured customers. Through this program, people can purchase complete made-to-order meals that they can just heat up and have on the table in minutes. As the store sign says, "Take Home Convenience...Plus Restaurant Quality."
Reprinted by permission.

and action-oriented than boomers. As these and other distinctions become clearer, retailers have started to look closely at the buying power they represent. This group will never know a world without computers and view PCs as basic equipment. Which brings up the question: Now that they have purchasing power, what will they be buying, and how will they be buying it? Today's 18- to 34-year-olds are eating out or bringing takeout food home in record numbers. They are part of a generation whose domestic skills have generally not been developed. When faced with the decision to sew a hem or take pants to a tailor, most will opt for the latter because they lack the skill or interest to do it. The same holds true for cooking.[9]

Hispanic-Americans shop for groceries 1.5 times per week, spend an average of $102 per primary shopping trip vs. $85 for other groups, lean toward traditional foods, are concerned about health, and place a high value on courtesy and respect. They reward those values with loyalty. Almost 60 percent will pay more for a well-known brand. They tend to shop in evenings and on weekends, and have strong family values and a close-knit family. Shopping is more of a social event for the family.[10]

One-third of the shoppers with each retail institution drive the majority of sales, and it is this group of "heavy shoppers" that retailers should take into consideration. Who are they? Their demographics vary. Convenience stores and drugstores tend to attract smaller households (one or two members), while heavy grocery store shopper households tend to be larger (three or four members). Drugstores are more likely to have heavy shoppers who are older—26 percent of heavy drugstore shoppers are aged 65 and older—while other channels see their heavy shoppers primarily coming from households headed by those under 55 years old. Upscale shoppers are more likely to shop heavily at membership clubs, while the poor are more apt to be heavy convenience store shoppers than any other segment.[11]

Ethics in Retailing

Diversity Means "Share the Mall"

When Sheila Hunter, the marketing director for Fiesta Mall, a 1.1-million-square-foot mall in Mesa, Arizona, invited two customer groups to focus group interviews, she did not expect to hear that they both shared the same concern. The first group, comprised of teenagers in baggy pants with pierced body parts and rainbow-colored hair, claimed to be pre-judged by their appearance. The second group, made up of baby boomer parents and senior citizens, also felt misunderstood. Both groups wanted to be accepted for who there were, not by their appearance.

In response to the interviews, Fiesta Mall created a community awareness campaign called "Share the Mall," the intent of which is to increase people's tol-erance for diversity. One component of the campaign is an interactive, visual stack of cubes that lets shoppers mix and match the faces and clothing of four very different-looking shoppers. The display's theme is "We all look different, and that's OK."

Fiesta Mall employees have been involved in cultural diversity and sensitivity seminars. As Sheila Hunter says, "One reason the modern shopping center was created in the first place was to have a retail diversity that satisfies a broad range of customers. That's basically what a shopping center does, and that's really what we're trying to emphasize now."

Design a cultural diversity and sensitivity seminar for a nearby regional shopping center.

Source: Kevin Kenyon, "Center Helps Diverse Customers 'Share the Mall,'" *Shopping Centers Today* (May 1999), pp. 132, 134.

CONSUMER NEEDS AND DESIRES

Nike works hard to satisfy both consumer needs and desires, especially the latter. Its Web site (www.nike.com) reflects this.

In developing a profile of its target market, the retailer should also identify the most essential consumer needs and desires. From a retailing perspective, *needs* are a person's basic shopping requirements consistent with his or her present demographics and life-style. *Desires* are discretionary shopping goals that have an impact on a person's attitudes and behavior. For example, a person may need a new car to get to and from work and seek out a dealer with Saturday service hours to address his or her need for weekend hours. The person may desire a Porsche and a free loaner car when the vehicle is serviced—and be happy with a Saturn that can be serviced on the weekend and fits within the budget.

Consider this: "Because of their life stage needs and inherent attitudes, first-wave baby boomers will be in their peak spending years throughout much of the next decade. Compared with other age groups, those aged 45 to 54 spend at a level far exceeding their share of the total population. They spend more on all key categories and are particularly strong spenders on "desires" (wants) as opposed to "needs"—categories such as gifts, entertainment, and personal care products. Retailers that want to benefit from this group's fat wallets will work to make the shopping experience easier through new location strategies, new approaches to merchandising, and upgraded service. Rather than enticing people through advertising or price promotion to go out their way to visit a store, retailer focus will increasingly shift toward intercepting customers at more convenient times and places."[12]

When the retailer gears its strategy toward satisfying consumer needs and desires, it is appealing to their **motives,** the reasons for their behavior. These are just a few of the questions to resolve:

- How far will customers travel to get to the retailer?
- How important is convenience?
- What store hours are desired? Are evening and weekend hours required?
- What level of customer services is preferred?
- How extensive a goods/service assortment is desired?
- What level of goods/service quality is preferred?
- How important is price?
- What retailer actions are necessary to reduce perceived risk?
- Do different market segments have special needs? If so, what are they?

Let us address the last question by looking at three particular market segments that are drawing greater retailer attention: in-home shoppers, online shoppers, and outshoppers.

In-Home Shopping: The in-home shopper is not always a captive audience. Shopping is often discretionary, not necessary. Convenience in ordering an item, without traveling for it, is important. These shoppers are often also active store shoppers, and they are affluent and well-educated. Many in-home shoppers are self-confident, younger, and venturesome. They like in-store shopping but have low opinions of local shopping. For some catalog shoppers, time is not an important shopping variable. In households with young children, in-home shopping is more likely if the female is employed part-time or not at all than if she works full-time. In-home shoppers often have a limited ability to comparison shop; may not be able to touch, feel, handle, or examine products firsthand; are concerned about customer service (such as returns); and may not have a salesperson from whom to acquire information.

Check out the results of the latest GVU survey (www.gvu.gatech.edu/user_surveys) to find out more about Web users.

Online shopping: People who shop online are well-educated, have above-average incomes, and so on (as noted in Chapter 6). However, retailers must also recognize that unlike many other retail formats, the Web has multiple uses for people that go beyond purchasing online: "Companies selling or contemplating selling online must regard the Internet in a broader context—as a medium through which people not only buy but also sort through their buying decisions. While many online households have actually bought goods or services online, a much higher number have researched goods or services on the Internet, only to buy the items at a store or fax or phone the order in. In fact, of 12 online activities we asked online consumers about, only 10 percent of consumers said they used the Web often or all the time to purchase, while 37 percent said they used the Web often or all the time to research items they might purchase later. More often, consumers went online to send E-mail (73 percent) or to retrieve current news or specialized information (44 percent). Retailers that view the Web as an 'either-or' proposition are missing the point. It's really important to avoid judging the success of an online presence simply in terms of sales."[13]

Outshopping: Out-of-hometown shopping, **outshopping,** is important for both local and surrounding retailers to study. The former want to minimize this behavior, whereas the latter want to maximize it. Outshoppers are often male, young, members of a large family, and new to the community. Income and education vary by situation. Outshoppers differ in their life-styles from those who patronize neighborhood or hometown stores. They enjoy fine foods, like to travel out-of-town, are active, like to change stores, and read out-of-town newspapers more than hometown shoppers. They also downplay hometown stores and compliment out-of-town stores. This is critical information for suburban shopping centers. Outshoppers have the same basic reasons for patronizing out-of-town shopping areas whether they reside in small or large communities—easy access, liberal credit, store diversity, product assortments, prices, the presence of large chain outlets, entertainment facilities, customer services, and product quality.

SHOPPING ATTITUDES AND BEHAVIOR

Retail shopping is affected by consumer attitudes toward retailing. In this section, we look at people's attitudes toward shopping, where they shop, and the way in which they make purchase decisions.

Attitudes Toward Shopping

Over the years, considerable research has been done on people's attitudes toward shopping. Such attitudes have a considerable impact on the ways in which people act in a retail setting. In particular, retailers must strive to turn around some negative consumer perceptions that now exist. Let us highlight some of the recent research findings.

Shopping Enjoyment: Many people (55 percent) do not enjoy shopping, certainly not as much as in the past. As one retailing consultant says, "For too many consumers, visiting stores becomes a crowded, unpleasant endeavor. It all boils down to ease of shopping. I want to go in there and I don't want to come out with sweaty palms and stress. The store should provide pleasure rather than the opposite." When the International Mass Retailing Association asked shoppers what would make them choose one retailer from a grouping of four similar retailers situated near each other, the shoppers said: the retailer whose layout they knew best, the retailer with no stuff in the aisles, the retailer with the best employee attitudes, the cleanest retailer, and the retailer that appeared neatest and nicest inside.[14]

Attitudes Toward Shopping Time: Retail shopping is viewed as a chore by many people. Half of them "feel hassled to shop." When asked to rank several activities in terms of how they like to spend their leisure time away from home, women place shopping third—after dining out and vacations—and men place it last—after vacations, dining out, sports and recreation, movies/theater, children's activities, and social events.[15]

Shifting Feelings about Retailing: There has been a major change in people's attitudes toward spending, value, and shopping at established retail outlets over the past decade. People no longer believe high prices accurately reflect value. Thus, "Retailers' pricing policies—particularly those of discounters—have encouraged consumers to shop for bargains and to distrust traditional sales and sale prices. In the 1980s, quality was largely a matter of status. A designer name, a good image, and even a high price were acceptable or desirable. But today's savvy, more pragmatic shoppers have discovered they can get reasonable quality at everyday low prices. And more people are waiting for sales to make their purchases. As price has become the critical driver in purchasing decisions, consumers who were once loyal to a particular store are willing to turn on a dime if a well-stocked, lower-priced competitor comes along."[16]

Why People Buy or Do Not Buy on a Shopping Trip: When making a purchase with a particular retailer, both apparel and consumer electronics customers say they were most influenced by an item's being on sale—or having a good price even if not on sale—and the retailer's carrying the style/look/brand sought. In deciding not to make a purchase with the first retailer visited, apparel and consumer electronics customers both say they were looking for lower prices or could not find anything they liked. More than two-thirds of apparel customers say they have visited retailers with a clear notion of what they wanted. Yet, only half of those shoppers actually found what they were seeking. Furniture shoppers are most interested in return policies, advertised items being in stock, prices, and knowledgeable salespeople.[17]

Attitudes by Market Segment: Grocery shoppers can be divided into several categories, such as: shopping avoiders—those who dislike grocery shopping; time-starved shoppers—those who will pay more for convenience; responsible shoppers—those who feel grocery shopping is one of their key household tasks; and traditional shoppers—those who plan store trips carefully. Web consumers feel more comfortable with technology, like comparison shopping, and are more trusting of online security than nonshoppers. Overall enthusiasm for shopping is much higher in Europe than in the United States. Two-thirds of Europeans say they like or love to shop, compared with just over one-half of Americans.[18]

Attitudes Toward Private Brands: About two-thirds of consumers believe retailer brands are as good as or better than manufacturer brands: "'Brand' has recently taken on a new meaning. It used to mean a distinctive and familiar national name. Consumers bought branded items because they saw them as having a particular image, quality, and consistency not found in other items. Today, store brands and private labels are finding favor with many consumers. To them, these nontraditional brands offer quality, style, and consistency at affordable prices. Bottom line: These 'nontraditional labels' are winning favor with consumers as brands and providing stiff competition for true 'traditional' national brands."[19]

Where People Shop

Consumer patronage differs sharply by the product category purchased. It is vital for retailers to know where consumers are buying various goods and services, and plan accordingly. Table 7.3 shows where America shops for a range of product categories.

Many consumers do **cross-shopping** where they (a) shop for a product category through more than one retail format or (b) visit multiple retailers on one shopping trip. (a) occurs because these consumers feel comfortable shopping at different formats, their objectives vary by occasion (for example, they may want bargains on everyday clothes and fashion-forward items for weekend wear), they shop wherever sales are offered, and they have a favorite format for themselves and another one for other household members. (b) occurs because consumers want to save travel time and shopping time, both of which can be reduced when visiting more than one retailer per shopping trip. Here are cross-shopping examples:

- Some supermarket customers also regularly buy items carried by the supermarket at convenience stores, full-line department stores, drugstores, and specialty food stores.
- Some department store customers also regularly buy items carried by the department store at factory outlets and full-line discount stores.

Table 7.3 Where America Shops—Selected Product Categories

Retailers Where Primary Household Shoppers Purchased Home Goods Within the Past Year (% of primary shoppers)

Hardware store	64.4	Toy superstore	44.6
Card/gift store	63.0	Traditional department store	39.2
Mail-order catalog	62.5	Furniture store	24.7
Full-line discount store	53.4	Sporting goods superstore	20.5
Membership club	46.3	Upscale department store	18.0

Retailers Where Primary Household Shoppers Purchase Consumables at Least Monthly (% of primary shoppers)

Supermarket	52.0	Conventional drugstore	16.0
Convenience store	30.0	Warehouse supermarket	6.0
Full-line discount store	29.0	Membership club	5.0
Supercenter	17.0	Deep discount drugstore	5.0

Where Apparel Is Purchased (% of all revenues) / **Where Books Are Purchased (% of all books)**

Traditional department store	34.7	Large chain bookstore	36.2
Specialty store	22.2	Independent/small chain bookstore	26.2
Full-line discount store	19.4	Book club	25.3
Off-price retailer	6.6	Discount stores	12.3
Factory outlet	3.9	Total	100.0
Other	13.2		
Total	100.0		

Sources: Compiled by the authors from Pricewaterhouse Coopers, *Retail Preview: Home Goods* (August 1998), p. 7; Pricewaterhouse Coopers, *Retail Preview: Consumables* (September 1998), p. 4; NPD, "Measuring the Market," *Discount Stores News* (December 14, 1998), p. A45; and Shannon Dortch, "Ready Readers, Reluctant Readers," *American Demographics* (May 1998), p. 8.

- In shopping centers, one-sixth of the people who visit music/electronics stores also shop at shoe stores, one-sixth at family apparel stores, and 11 percent at bookstores. Of those who visit hobby stores, 18 percent also shop at sporting goods stores. As a result, "In the older days, stores were purposely spread apart to force shoppers to walk the distance. Today, stores should be close together to keep shopping as efficient as possible."[20]

The Consumer Decision Process

In addition to identifying the characteristics of its target market, the retailer should know how people make decisions. This requires some familiarity with **consumer behavior,** which involves the process by which people determine whether, what, when, where, how, from whom, and how often to purchase goods and services. Such behavior is influenced by a person's background and traits.

The retailer must grasp the consumer's decision process from two different perspectives: (a) what good or service the consumer is thinking about buying and (b) where the consumer is going to make the purchase of that item (if the person opts to buy). A consumer can make the decisions separately or jointly. If made jointly, he or she relies on the retailer for support (information, assortments, knowledgeable sales personnel, and so on) over the entire decision process. If the decisions are made independently—what to buy versus where to buy—the person then gathers information and advice before visiting a retailer and views the retailer merely as a place to buy (and probably more interchangeable with other firms).

In choosing whether or not to buy a given item ("what"), the consumer considers features, durability, distinctiveness, value, ease of use, fashion, and so on. In choosing which

The U.S. Consumer Information Center facilitates consumer decision making for such products as cars by providing free online information (www.pueblo.gsa. gov/cars.htm).

retailer to patronize for that item ("where"), the consumer considers location, assortment, credit availability, sales help, hours, customer service, and so on. Thus, the manufacturer and retailer have distinct challenges: The manufacturer wants people to buy its brand ("what") at any location carrying it ("where"). The retailer wants people to buy the product, not necessarily the manufacturer's brand ("what"), at its store or nonstore location ("where").

The **consumer decision process** consists of two parts: the process itself and the factors affecting the process. The decision process has six basic steps: stimulus, problem awareness, information search, evaluation of alternatives, purchase, and post-purchase behavior. Factors that affect the process are a consumer's demographics and life-style. The complete consumer decision process is shown in Figure 7.5.

The best retailers are those that assist the consumer at each stage in the process: stimulus (newspaper ads), problem awareness (stocking new models that are better than existing ones), information search (point-of-sale displays and good salespeople), evaluation of alternatives (clearly noticeable differences among products), purchase (acceptance of credit cards), and post-purchase behavior (extended warranties and money-back returns). The greater the role a retailer assumes for itself in the decision process, the more loyal the consumer will become to that retailer, which is then viewed as indispensable.

Each time a person buys a good or service, he or she goes through a decision process. In some cases, all six steps in the process are utilized; in others, only a few of the steps are employed. For example, a consumer who has previously and satisfactorily bought luggage at a local store may not use the same extensive process as a person who has never bought luggage.

The decision process outlined Figure 7.5 assumes that the end result is the purchase of a good or service. However, at any point in the process, a potential customer may decide not to buy; the process then stops. A good or service may be unneeded, unsatisfactory, or too expensive. Before we consider the different ways in which the consumer uses the decision process, the entire process is explained.

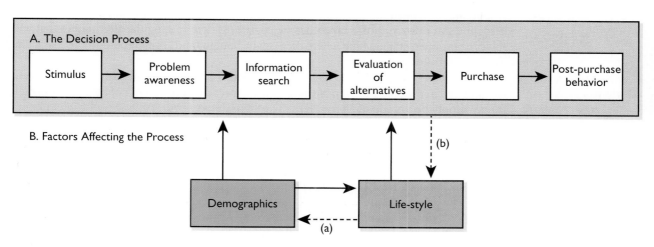

Note: Solid arrows connect all the elements in the decision process and show the impact of demographics and life-style on the process. Dashed arrows show feedback. (a) shows the impact of life-style on certain demographics, such as family size, location, and marital status. (b) shows the impact of a purchase on elements of life-style, such as social class, reference groups, and social performance.

Figure 7.5
The Consumer Decision Process

Stimulus: A **stimulus** is a cue (social or commercial) or a drive (physical) meant to moti-vate or arouse a person to act. When one talks with friends, fellow employees, and so on, a social cue is received. The special attribute of a social cue is that it comes from an interper-sonal, noncommercial source. A commercial cue is a message sponsored by a retailer or some other seller. Ads, sales pitches, and store displays are commercial stimuli. Such cues may not be regarded as highly as social ones by consumers because they are seller-controlled. A third type of stimulus is a physical drive. It occurs when one or more of a person's physical senses are affected. Hunger, thirst, cold, heat, pain, or fear could cause a physical drive. A potential consumer may be exposed to any or all three stimuli for any good or service. If aroused (motivated), he or she will go to the next step in the decision process. If a person is not suffi-ciently aroused, he or she will ignore the stimulus—terminating the process for the given good or service.

Problem Awareness: At **problem awareness,** the consumer not only has been aroused by social, commercial, and/or physical stimuli, but also recognizes that the good or service under consideration may solve a problem of shortage or unfulfilled desire. It is sometimes hard to learn why a person is motivated enough to move from a stimulus to problem aware-ness. Many people shop with the same retailer or buy the same good or service for different reasons, they may not know their own motivation, and they may not tell a retailer their real reasons for shopping there or buying a certain item.

Recognition of shortage occurs when a person discovers a good or service should be repurchased. A good could wear down beyond repair or the person might run out of an item such as milk. Service may be necessary if a good such as a car requires a repair or a CPA ser-vice is used each year during tax season. Recognition of unfulfilled desire takes place when a person becomes aware of a good or service that has not been bought before—or a retailer that has not been patronized before. An item such as contact lenses may improve a person's life-style, self-image, and so on in an untried manner, or it may offer new performance features, such as a voice-activated computer. People are more hesitant to act on unfulfilled desires than on shortages. Risks and benefits may be tougher to see. Whether a person becomes aware of a shortage or an unfulfilled desire, he or she will act only if it is a problem worth solving. Otherwise, the process will end.

Information Search: If a shortage or unfulfilled desire merits further thought, information is sought. An **information search** has two parts: (1) determining the alternatives that will solve the problem at hand (and where they can be bought) and (2) ascertaining the character-istics of each alternative.

Nonprofit Consumer World has an online, noncommercial guide catalog with over 2,000 sources to aid the consumer's infor-mation search (www. consumerworld.org).

First, the person compiles a list of various goods or services that address the problem encountered in the previous step of the decision process. This list does not have to be formal. It may simply be a group of alternatives the person thinks about. A person with a lot of pur-chasing experience will normally utilize an internal search of his or her memory to determine the goods or services—and retailers—that would be satisfactory for solving the current problem. A person with little purchasing experience will often use an external search to develop a list of goods or services and retailers that would solve the current problem. An external search can involve commercial sources such as the mass media and retail salespeo-ple, noncommercial sources such as *Consumer Reports* and government publications, and social sources such as family and friends. Second, the person gathers information relating to the attributes of each alternative. An experienced shopper will search his or her memory for the attributes (pros and cons) of each good or service alternative. A consumer with little experience or a lot of uncertainty will search externally for information about each alterna-tive under consideration.

The extent to which a person searches for information depends, in part, on his or her per-ceived risk relative to the purchase of a specific good or service. Risk varies among individu-als and by situation. For some it is inconsequential; for others it is quite important. The retailer's role in a consumer's search process is to provide enough information for him or her to feel comfortable in making decisions, thereby reducing perceived risk. Point-of-purchase advertising, product displays, and knowledgeable sales personnel help provide consumers with the information they need to make decisions.

Once the consumer's search for information is completed, he or she must decide whether the current shortage or unfulfilled desire can be met by any of the alternatives. If one or more are satisfactory, the consumer moves to the next step in the decision process. However, the consumer will discontinue the process if no satisfactory goods or services are found.

Evaluation of Alternatives: Once a person has enough information, he or she can select one option from among the choices. This is easy if one alternative is clearly superior to the others on all features. An item with excellent quality and a low price is a certain pick over expensive, average-quality ones. However, a choice is not often that simple, and the person would engage in an **evaluation of alternatives** before making a decision. If two or more options seem attractive, the person determines the criteria to evaluate and their relative importance. Then the alternatives are ranked and a choice made.

The criteria for a decision are those good or service attributes that the person considers to be relevant. They may include price, quality, fit, color, durability, warranty, and so on. The person sets standards for these characteristics and rates each alternative according to its ability to meet the standards. The importance of each criterion is also determined by the consumer, and the attributes of a good or service are usually of different importance to each person. For example, one shopper may consider price to be the most important factor while another places greater importance on quality and durability.

At this point, the person ranks the alternatives under consideration from most favorite to least favorite and selects one from among the list. For some goods or services, it is hard to evaluate the characteristics of the available alternatives because the items are technical, intangible, new, or poorly labeled. When this occurs, shoppers often use price, brand name, or store name as an indicator of quality, and choose an alternative based on this criterion. Once a person examines the attributes of alternatives and ranks them, he or she chooses the good or service that is most satisfactory. In situations where no alternative proves adequate, a decision not to purchase is made.

Purchase Act: After the choice of the best alternative, the person is ready for the **purchase act**—an exchange of money or a promise to pay for the ownership or use of a good or service. Important decisions are still made during this step. From a retailing perspective, the purchase act may be the most crucial aspect of the decision process because the consumer is mainly concerned with three factors, as highlighted in Figure 7.6:

- Place of purchase—This may be a store or a nonstore location. Many more items are bought at stores than at nonstore locations, although the latter are growing more quickly. The place of purchase is evaluated in the same way as the good or the service itself: alternatives are listed, their characteristics are defined, and they are ranked. The most desirable place of purchase is then chosen. Criteria for selecting a store-based retailer include such factors as store location, store layout, customer service, sales help, store image, and prices. Criteria for selecting a nonstore retailer include such factors as image, customer service, prices, hours, interactivity, and convenience. A consumer will shop with the firm that has the best combination of criteria, as defined by that consumer.
- Purchase terms—These include the price and method of payment. Price is the dollar amount a person must pay to achieve the ownership or use of a good or service. Method of payment is the way the price may be paid (cash, short-term credit, long-term credit).
- Availability—This relates to stock on hand and delivery. Stock on hand is the amount of an item that a place of purchase has in inventory. Delivery is the time span between the order and the receipt of an item and the ease with which an item is transported to its place of use.

Figure 7.6
Key Factors in the
Purchase Act

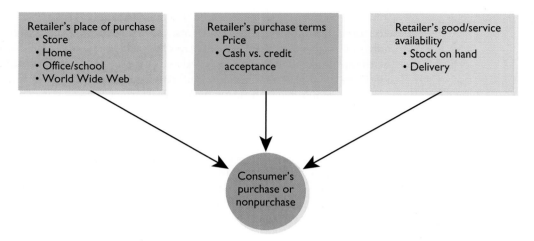

If a person is pleased with these three components of the purchase act, the good or service will be bought. If there is dissatisfaction with the place of purchase, the terms of purchase, or availability, the consumer may not buy, although there is contentment with the item itself:

> Karen wanted to buy a stereo system. She knew which system to get and had saved $100 for a down payment. But, after a month of trying, Karen gave up in disgust: "The system I wanted was sold in only three stores in my area and through an online firm. Two of the stores overpriced the stereo by $75. The third store had a really good price, but the owner insisted I pay in cash. In addition, I would have had to drive to the warehouse, 20 miles away, to pick up the system. The Web retailer had a very good deal— low price, credit, and delivery. But it ran out of the model I wanted and told me the wait would be two months. When I heard that, I just gave up. My portable CD player will have to suffice."

Post-Purchase Behavior: After buying a good or service, a consumer may engage in **post-purchase behavior,** which falls into either of two categories: further purchases or re-evaluation. In some situations, buying one item leads to further purchases and consumer decision making continues until the last purchase is made. For instance, a car purchase leads to buying insurance; and a retailer that uses scrambled merchandising by stocking nonrelated items may also stimulate a shopper to make further purchases, once the primary good or service is bought.

A person may also re-evaluate the purchase of a good or service. Does it perform as promised? Do its actual attributes match the expectations the consumer had of these attributes? Has the retailer done as expected? Satisfaction may lead to contentment, a repurchase when the good or service wears out, and favorable conversations with friends interested in the same item. Dissatisfaction may lead to unhappiness, brand or store switching when the good or service wears out, and unfavorable conversations with friends interested in the same item. The latter situation (dissatisfaction) may result from **cognitive dissonance**—doubt that the correct decision has been made. A consumer may regret that the purchase was made at all or may wish that another alternative from the list had been chosen. To overcome cognitive dissonance and dissatisfaction, the retailer must realize that the consumer decision process does not end with a purchase. Customer aftercare (by a phone call, a service visit, or E-mail) may be as important as anything a retailer can do to complete the sale. When items are expensive or important to a consumer, after-care takes on added significance because the person really wants to be right. In addition, the more alternatives from which to choose, the greater the doubt after a decision is made and the more important the after-care.

Many retailers realize consumers often have doubts and second thoughts about recent purchases. Decades ago, department stores pioneered the concept of a money-back guarantee, so customers could return merchandise if cognitive dissonance became too great. Realistic sales presentations and ad campaigns can also minimize dissatisfaction because consumer expectations do not then exceed reality. If overly high expectations are created, a consumer is more apt to become unhappy because a good or service does not perform at the level promised. The coupling of an honest sales presentation with good after-care of the consumer should reduce or eliminate cognitive dissonance and dissatisfaction.

Types of Consumer Decision Making

Every time a person purchases a good or service or visits a retailer, he or she uses a form of the decision process just described. Often, the process is used subconsciously, and a person is not even aware of its use. Also, as indicated in Figure 7.5, the process is affected by the characteristics of the consumer. For example, older people may not spend as much time as younger ones in making decisions due to their experience. Well-educated consumers may search out many information sources before making a decision. Upper-income consumers may spend little time making a decision because they can afford to buy again if a purchase is unsatisfactory. In a family with children, each member may have input into a decision, thereby lengthening the process. Class-conscious consumers may be more interested in social sources. Consumers with low self-esteem or high perceived risk may use all the steps in the process in detail. People who are under time pressure may skip steps in the process to save time.

Finding Out What Customers Really Want

E-Lab (the "E" stands for experience) is a consulting firm that specializes in consumer research and works with a host of retailers. According to Rick Robinson, one of E-Lab's co-founders, "Every consumer behavior has a particular framework and a theory that it is based upon. Our job is a matter of finding the meaningful patterns that exist. Often, we don't ask customers what they want. We watch what they do." On a typical project, E-Lab researchers may review thousands of hours of tapes showing people shopping in a convenience store aisle or buying an item in a sporting goods store. E-Lab has created special software to search for key words and phrases that the research team has identified as important.

In comparison with other research firms, the backgrounds of many E-Lab employees are rather nontraditional. They may be actors, musicians, and professionals with a background in theology. All of them are chosen on the basis of their ability to tell stories and their interaction skills as interviewers: "They're not afraid to draw a story out of people who may be reluctant to talk."

E-Lab researchers have interesting and varied jobs. They often visit consumers in their homes or otherwise go out in the field. For example, one E-Lab employee has intensively studied how people use cooking utensils: "The Cuisinart food processor just doesn't have the same cultural meaning for people as an older wooden spoon. It does not evoke memories of mother or grandmother or the home."

Source: Gene Koprowski, "The Science of Shopping," *Business 2.0* (June 1999), pp. 139–42.

The decision process is used differently depending on the situation. One situation—such as the purchase of a new home—may necessitate a thorough use of each step in the process; perceived risk will probably be high regardless of the consumer's background. Another situation—such as buying a magazine—may let the consumer skip certain steps in the process; perceived risk will probably be low regardless of the person's background. There are three types of decision processes: extended decision making, limited decision making, and routine decision making. They are explained next.

Extended decision making occurs when a consumer makes full use of the decision process in Figure 7.5. Considerable time is spent gathering information and evaluating alternatives—both what to buy and where to buy it—before a purchase is made. The potential for cognitive dissonance is great. In this category are expensive, complex items with which the person has had little or no experience. Perceived risk of all kinds is high. Examples of items requiring extended decision making are a house, a first car, and a life insurance policy. At any point in the purchase process, a consumer can stop, and for expensive, complex items, this occurs often. Consumer characteristics (such as age, education, income, and class consciousness) have their greatest impact with extended decision making.

Because their customers tend to use extended decision making, such retailers as real-estate brokers and auto dealers emphasize personal selling, printed materials, and other methods of communication to provide as much information as possible. A low-key approach should be enacted, so shoppers feel comfortable and not threatened. In this way, the consumer's perceived risk can be minimized.

Limited decision making occurs when a consumer uses each step in the purchase process but does not spend a great deal of time on each of them. It requires less time than extended decision making since the person typically has some experience with both the what and the where of the purchase. In this category are items that have been purchased before, but not regularly. Risk is moderate, and the consumer will spend some time shopping. Priority is sometimes placed on evaluating known alternatives according to the person's desires and standards, although information search is also important for some. Examples of items requiring limited decision making are a second car, clothing, a vacation, and gifts. Consumer attributes have an impact on decision making, but the effect lessens as perceived risk falls and experience rises. Income, the importance of the purchase, and motives play strong roles in limited decision making.

This form of decision making is quite relevant to such retailers as department stores, specialty stores, and nonstore retailers that want to sway shopping behavior and that carry goods and services that people have bought before. The shopping environment and assortment of the retailer are very important. Sales personnel should be available for questions and to differentiate among brands or models.

Routine decision making takes place when the consumer buys out of habit and skips steps in the purchase process. He or she wants to spend little or no time shopping, and the same brands are usually repurchased (often from the same retailers). In this category are items bought regularly. They have little risk because of consumer experience. The key step for this type of decision making is problem awareness. When the consumer realizes a good or service is needed, a repurchase is often automatic. Information search, evaluation of alternatives, and post-purchase behavior are less likely than in limited or extended decision making. These steps are not undertaken as long as a person is satisfied. Examples of items often requiring routine decision making are groceries, newspapers, and haircuts. Consumer attributes have little impact on buying. Problem awareness almost inevitably leads to a purchase.

This type of decision making is most relevant to such retailers as supermarkets, dry cleaners, and fast-food outlets. For them, these strategic elements are crucial: a good location, long hours, clear product displays, and, most important, product availability. Ads should be reminder-oriented. The major task for personnel would be completing the transaction quickly and precisely.

Impulse Purchases and Customer Loyalty

Two other aspects of consumer behavior merit special attention: impulse purchases and customer loyalty.

Impulse purchases occur when consumers buy products and/or brands they had not planned on buying before entering a store, reading a mail-order catalog, seeing a TV shopping show, turning to the Web, and so forth. With impulse purchases, at least part of consumer decision making is influenced by the retailer. There are three kinds of impulse shopping:

Discover more about impulse shopping. Go to www.american demographics.com, select "Demographics Back Issues," click on April 1999, and choose "Meet You in Aisle Three."

- *Completely unplanned*—A consumer has no intention of making a purchase in a goods or service category before he or she comes into contact with a retailer.
- *Partially unplanned*—A consumer intends to make a purchase in a goods or service category but has not chosen a brand before he or she comes into contact with a retailer.
- *Unplanned substitution*—A consumer intends to buy a specific brand of a good or service but changes his or her mind about the brand after coming into contact with a retailer.

With the partially unplanned and substitution kinds of impulse purchases, some decision making takes place before a person interacts with a retailer. In these cases, the consumer may be involved with any type of process (extended, limited, or routine). Completely unplanned shopping is usually related to routine decision making or limited decision making; there is little or no time spent shopping, and the key step is problem awareness.

Impulse purchases are more susceptible to retailer displays than pre-planned purchases: "For most shoppers, the checkout lane is the final hurdle—choosing the right lane and getting out of the store quickly is a major objective. Retailers, however, view the checkout lane as a 'last chance' area—the place to sell impulse items such as candy and magazines, as well as small, but profitable, necessities such as batteries and razor blades." Nearly one-half of supermarket shoppers say they buy items located at the checkout lane, even though two-thirds agree with the statement that "The checkout counter contains a lot of products I don't need."[21]

In studying impulse buying, these are some of the consumer attitudes and behavior patterns that retailers should take into consideration:

- In-store browsing is positively affected by the amount of time a person has to shop.
- Some individuals are more predisposed toward making impulse purchases than others.
- Those who enjoy shopping are more apt to make in-store purchase decisions.
- Impulse purchases are greater when a person has discretionary income to spend.[22]

When **customer loyalty** exists, a person regularly patronizes a particular retailer (store or nonstore) that he or she knows, likes, and trusts. Such loyalty lets a person reduce decision making because he or she does not have to invest time in learning about and choosing the retailer from which to make purchases. Over the years, research has addressed various aspects of shopper loyalty: Loyal customers tend to be time-conscious, like shopping locally, do not often engage in outshopping, and spend more per shopping trip. In a service setting, such as an auto repair shop, customer satisfaction with service quality often leads to shopper loyalty; price has little bearing on decisions.

In today's competitive marketplace, it is a challenge for a retailer to gain customer loyalty—the greatest asset a firm can have. Applying all facets of the retailing concept certainly enhance a firm's chances of gaining and keeping loyal customers: customer orientation, coordinated effort, value-driven, and goal orientation. Practicing relationship retailing helps also!

According to Harte-Hanks Market Research,

- Customer satisfaction is a crucial aspect of customer loyalty. It is hard for any retailer to obtain customer loyalty without shoppers first having a high degree of satisfaction with that retailer.
- Even if retailers get high satisfaction scores, this does not mean they also will earn customer loyalty. Among the factors that will create a sense of loyalty beyond satisfaction is the retailer's "value proposition" and an ability to communicate a caring attitude to customers.
- Retailers can receive a higher-than-average degree of loyalty by targeting shoppers who are especially predisposed to being loyal.
- Although two retailers may have the same number of very loyal customers, one of them may deal with more shoppers who are indifferent and who do not exhibit any loyalty.[23]

RETAILER ACTIONS

A *target market*, as defined in Chapter 3, is a customer group a retailer seeks to satisfy. With *mass marketing*, a firm such as a supermarket or a drugstore sells goods and services to a broad spectrum of consumers; it does not really focus efforts on any one kind of customer. In *concentrated marketing*, a retailer tailors its strategy to the needs of one distinct consumer group, such as young working women; it does not attempt to satisfy people outside that segment. With *differentiated marketing*, a retailer aims at two or more distinct consumer groups, such as men and boys, with a different strategy mix for each; it can do this by operating more than one kind of outlet (such as separate men's and boys' clothing stores) or by having distinct departments grouped by market segment in a single store (as a department store might do). In deciding on the target market approach to use, a retailer considers its goods/service category and goals, competitors' actions, the size of various segments, the relative efficiency of each target market alternative for the particular firm, the resources required, and other factors. See Figure 7.7.

After choosing a target market method, the retailer selects the target market(s) to which it wants to appeal; identifies the characteristics, needs, and attitudes of the target market(s); seeks to understand how its targeted customers make purchase decisions; and acts appropriately. The process for devising a target market strategy is shown in Figure 7.8.

Below we present several examples of retailers' target market activities.

Retailers with Mass Marketing Strategies

Murray's Discount Auto Parts and Target Stores are retailers that engage in mass marketing by appealing to a broad range of customers.

Murray's is a Michigan-based regional chain with more than 75 auto parts stores. Unlike most of its competitors, the firm actively strives to attract a broad array of customers—not just seasoned, male do-it-yourselfers. Murray's offers personal shoppers, computer-assisted ordering, and big 10,000-square-foot stores with everyday low prices and merchandise piled high in the aisles. It is the exception to the stereotype of the intimidating auto parts store and is visited by many people who are not typical auto parts shoppers: "Murray's wants to make the auto parts shopping experience enjoyable for even the novice do-it-yourselfer. Its clean, brightly lighted stores feature multiple checkout lanes with a customer service desk in the back of the store, giving the space the appearance of a grocery store rather than an auto parts shop." The chain's president says, "We are not intimidating. One of the greatest compliments I get is from men who tell me, 'I can send my wife to Murray's and I trust you guys will treat her well.'"[24]

See how Target Stores' department store heritage (target.com/company/history.asp) has guided the chain for nearly 40 years.

Target Stores is one of the big three in the full-line discount store chain sector, along with Wal-Mart and Kmart. However, unlike its competitors, Target draws a broader customer base. As its chairman says, "People's tastes are not determined by income, obviously. A lot

Figure 7.7
Afterthoughts: A Retailing Strategy Geared to a Young Female Target Market

The Afterthoughts chain has achieved a strong growth rate by listening to the voice of its customer, understanding who she is, and then responding with merchandise that gives her what she wants when she wants it. The store formats reflect a sense of exploration and discovery that most teenagers undergo as they try on different looks. The merchandise they find captures an essential feeling of freshness in the latest colors and patterns. Afterthoughts offers fashion jewelry, accessories, cosmetics, and gift items for pre-teen and teenage girls.
Reprinted by permission.

of people want to be 'with it.' " Although it sticks to low prices, Target is more contemporary than Wal-Mart or Kmart. Experts note that "Target's merchandising brilliance owes to its department store heritage. It is always looking to have the latest things, whether a camera or a skirt. This sort of life-style merchandising helps Target do more than nibble the market share of the Kmarts or even the J.C. Penneys of the world. It also allows Target to challenge specialty stores like Crate & Barrel and Banana Republic, as well."[25]

Retailers with Concentrated Marketing Strategies

Family Dollar and Reading Glass Express are retailers that engage in concentrated marketing by appealing to a narrow range of customers.

| Determine Target Market Approach | → | Select Specific Target Market(s) | → | Study Characteristics, Needs, and Attitudes of Target Market(s) | → | Examine How Consumers Make Decisions—by Product Category | → | Develop and Enact Appropriate Retail Strategy Mix(es) for the Target Market(s) Chosen |

Figure 7.8
Devising a Target Market Strategy

Casual Male Big & Tall (www.casualmale.com) is another retailer with a concentrated marketing strategy. It appeals to "big guys."

Family Dollar operates a chain of 3,400 dollar discount stores (a type of variety store) in 38 states. The firm has a very focused target market strategy, stated at its Web site (www.familydollar.com): "The typical Family Dollar customer is a female who shops for a family with a median annual income of less than $25,000, and in many cases under $15,000. With their limited income, price is the single most important factor in our customers' shopping decisions. These families depend on Family Dollar to provide them with the good values they must have to make every dollar they spend count." Stores are rather small and are often situated in rural areas and small towns, as well as in urban areas. Most items are priced under $17.99 and sold in a no-frills environment.

Reading Glass Express is a small, but growing, California-based optical chain. It concentrates on middle-aged baby boomers by specializing in high-end, high-fashion nonprescription reading glasses and sunglasses. The stores carry 350 different frames, with prices ranging from $29 to $499; and customers can pick from among such designer brands as Gucci, Versace, Armani, Donna Karan, and Alain Mikli. The shops' interiors are well lit and plushly furnished. Says the firm's chief executive, "Our customers treat eyewear as a fashion accessory and they are always stopping in to see what's new."[26]

Retailers with Differentiated Marketing Strategies

Through its KFC, Pizza Hut, and Taco Bell chains, Tricon (www.triconglobal.com) is another retailer that practices differentiated marketing—segmenting customers by food preference.

Zale Corporation and J.C. Penney are retailers that engage in differentiated marketing by appealing to multiple customer segments.

Zale operates three jewelry chains, each with a distinct consumer group. Zales Jewelers has stores in shopping malls nationwide. Stores appeal to moderate-income customers and feature classic, traditional styles. Merchandise is standardized across the chain. Gordon's Jewelers is located in 27 markets and is an upper-moderate regional chain. It has a more contemporary product mix than Zales, and key items vary by market. Bailey Banks & Biddle is a high-end chain with an upscale clientele and product assortment.[27]

J.C. Penney is now emphasizing two main market segments, as noted at one of its Web sites (www.jcpenney.net): "modern spenders" and "starting outs." Modern spenders are dual-earner households with up to two children. They are 35 to 54 years of age, are consumption-oriented, have strong purchase patterns, and are time-starved. Starting outs are usually single or young families with up to one child. They are under 35 years of age, have emerging shopping patterns, and do not yet have strong retail loyalties. Both segments are middle class in terms of income.

ENVIRONMENTAL FACTORS AFFECTING CONSUMERS

There are several environmental factors that influence shopping attitudes and behavior, including the:
- State of the economy.
- Rate of inflation (how quickly prices are rising).
- Quality of the infrastructure where people shop, such as the level of traffic congestion, the crime rate, and the ease of parking.
- Price wars among retailers.
- Emergence of new retail formats.
- Trend toward more people working at home.
- Government and community regulations regarding shopping hours, new construction, consumer protection, and so forth.
- Evolving societal values and norms.

Technology in Retailing

From Comfort Creatures to Looky-loos: The Many Faces of Internet Shoppers

According to Personify, a marketing research firm, Web customers can be categorized into specific segments. Some people can be placed into more than one category, depending on the situation:

- Comfort creatures—sensory-oriented people concerned with colors and features.
- Connected suits—savvy executives who use a site's most advanced features.
- Country clubbers—status-oriented people who seek discounts on name-brand merchandise.
- Credit checkers—young people who are concerned about their credit card balances.
- Detail drivers—people who want to know how things work.
- Electrons—people with a wide range of interests who "zap" all over the site with no real logic.
- Explorers—people who visit all the areas of a site ("Lewis or Clark in another life").
- Gear heads—people who want the latest cool gizmo, but are uninterested in its technology.
- Geeks—well-informed people who use the Web to keep ahead of their friends.
- Gift boxers—people who shop for someone else.
- Knowledge workers—people who gather information as part of their job.
- Novices—enthusiastic people who are low on information and high on enthusiasm.
- Surgical shoppers—people who know exactly what they want and seek an easy buying process.
- Looky-loos—Impulsive people who often respond to a banner ad.

As the marketing manager for a small electronics Web retailer that targets stereo enthusiasts, how should your firm design its Web site to appeal to detail drivers, gear heads, and surgical shoppers?

Source: James Ryan, "Your Online Shadow Knows," *Business 2.0* (June 1999), pp. 49–55.

While all these elements may not necessarily have an impact on any particular shopper, they do influence the retailer's overall target market.

When considering the value chain they offer to their customers, retailers should also keep the following in mind about the standard of living in the United States[28]:

Product	Amount of Time a Typical U.S. Worker Had to Labor in 1998 to Earn the Product	Amount of Time a Typical U.S. Worker Had to Labor in 1960 to Earn the Product
New home	6.5 years	3.6 years
New car	46.8 weeks	35.7 weeks
Year's tuition at a private college	38.0 weeks	9.1 weeks
New men's suit	23.5 hours	40.7 hours
Color TV	22.1 hours	187.6 hours
Week's worth of groceries	12.3 hours	15.5 hours
10 gallons of gasoline	0.8 hour	1.5 hours

SUMMARY

1. *To discuss why it is important for a retailer to properly identify, understand, and appeal to its customers.* In order to properly develop and apply a retail strategy mix, a firm must identify the characteristics, needs, and attitudes of consumers; understand how consumers make decisions; and devise the proper target market plan. It must study environmental influences, too.

2. *To enumerate and describe a number of consumer demographics, life-style factors, and needs and desires—and to explain how these concepts can be applied to retailing.* Demographics are easily identifiable and measurable population statistics. Life-styles are the ways in which consumers live and spend time and money.

Consumers can be described in terms of such demographic factors as gender, age, life expectancy, literacy, languages spoken, income, retail sales, education, ethnic/racial background, and so forth. To be useful for retailers, demographic data usually has to be localized. Consumer life-styles are comprised of social and psychological elements and are greatly affected by demographics. Social factors include culture, social class, reference groups, the family life cycle, and time utilization. Psychological factors include personality, class consciousness, attitudes, perceived risk, and the importance of a purchase. As with demographics, a retailer can generate a life-style profile of its target market by analyzing these concepts.

There are several interesting demographic and life-style trends going on that apply to retailing. These involve gender roles, consumer sophistication and confidence, the poverty of time, and component life-style. Considerable research has been done to enumerate consumer profiles in a useful way for retailers.

In developing a target market profile, the retailer should identify essential consumer needs and desires. Needs are basic shopping requirements and desires are discretionary shopping goals. When a firm gears a strategy toward satisfying consumer needs, it is appealing to their motives—the reasons for behavior. The better needs and desires are addressed, the more apt people are to make purchases.

3. *To examine consumer attitudes toward shopping and consumer shopping behavior, including the consumer decision process and its stages.* Many people do not enjoy shopping, view shopping as a chore, no longer believe high prices accurately reflect value, and are quite interested in sales and items being in stock. Different consumer segments have different attitudes toward shopping. More people now feel that private brands are of good quality.

Consumer patronage differs by product category bought. People often engage in cross-shopping, whereby they shop at more than one retail format for the same product category or visit multiple retailers on the same shopping trip.

Retailers require a knowledge of consumer behavior—the process whereby individuals decide whether, what, when, where, how, from whom, and how often to purchase goods and services. In particular, the consumer's decision process must be grasped from two different perspectives: (a) what good or service the consumer is thinking about buying and (b) where the consumer is going to make the purchase of that item. The consumer can make these two decisions separately or jointly.

The consumer decision process has six basic steps: stimulus, problem awareness, information search, evaluation of alternatives, purchase, and post-purchase behavior. The process is influenced by a person's background and traits.

A stimulus may be a social or commercial cue or a physical drive meant to motivate a person to act. At problem awareness, the consumer not only has been aroused by a stimulus, but further recognizes that the good or service under consideration may solve a problem of shortage or unfulfilled desire. Next, an information search determines the available alternatives and the characteristics of each. The alternatives are then evaluated and ranked. In the purchase act, a consumer considers the place of purchase, terms, and availability. After a purchase is made, there may be post-purchase behavior in the form of additional purchases or re-evaluation. The consumer may have cognitive dissonance if there is doubt that a correct choice has been made.

Extended decision making occurs if a person makes full use of the six steps in the decision process. In limited decision making, each step is used, but not in great depth. Routine decision making takes place when a person buys out of habit and skips steps in the purchase process. Impulse purchases occur when shoppers buy items they had not planned on purchasing before coming into contact with the retailer. With customer loyalty, a person regularly patronizes a given retailer.

4. *To look at retailer actions based on target market planning.* Retailers can deploy a mass marketing, concentrated marketing, or differentiated marketing plan. Murray's and Target Stores typify mass marketing retailers. Family Dollar and Reading Glass Express exemplify concentrated marketing retailers. Zale and J.C. Penney illustrate differentiated marketing in action.

5. *To note some of the environmental factors that affect consumer shopping.* Shopping attitudes and behavior are swayed by the economy, the inflation rate, the infrastructure where people shop, and other factors. Retailers also need to take into account how the standard of living has changed, as reflected in the amount of time people must work to earn various goods and services.

Key Terms

demographics (p. 220)
life-styles (p. 220)
discretionary income (p. 220)
culture (p. 223)
social class (p. 224)
reference groups (p. 224)
family life cycle (p. 224)
household life cycle (p. 224)
personality (p. 224)
class consciousness (p. 224)

attitudes (opinions) (p. 224)
perceived risk (p. 224)
motives (p. 229)
outshopping (p. 230)
cross-shopping (p. 231)
consumer behavior (p. 232)
consumer decision process (p. 233)
stimulus (p. 234)
problem awareness (p. 234)
information search (p. 234)

evaluation of alternatives (p. 235)
purchase act (p. 235)
post-purchase behavior (p. 236)
cognitive dissonance (p. 236)
extended decision making (p. 238)
limited decision making (p. 238)
routine decision making (p. 238)
impulse purchases (p. 239)
customer loyalty (p. 239)

Questions for Discussion

1. Comment on this statement: "Retailers have long depended on their ability to size up people as they walk in the door. Today, you need a more systematic way to understand customers."

2. Analyze the global population data in Table 7.1 from a retailing perspective.

3. How could a national department store chain use the U.S. population data presented in Table 7.2?

4. Explain how a retailer selling do-it-yourself furniture (with pre-cut wood) could reduce the six types of perceived risk.

5. Why is it important for retailers to know the difference between "needs" and "desires?"

6. Distinguish between in-home shopping and outshopping. In each case, what should be the strategic emphasis of retailers?

7. Is cross-shopping good or bad for a retailer? Explain your answer.

8. What two different perspectives should a retailer have in studying the consumer decision process? Why is this useful?

9. Describe how the consumer decision process would operate for these goods and services. Include "what" and "where" in your answers: a laser printer, a lawn service, and a used car. Which elements of the decision process are most important to retailers in each instance? Explain your answers.

10. Why should a real-estate broker care whether clients have cognitive dissonance? The seller moves after a transaction and the buyer will not be in the market for another house again until a great many years have elapsed.

11. Differentiate among the three types of impulse purchases. Give an example of each.

12. Contrast the mass market approach used by a supermarket with the concentrated marketing approach used by a bakery featuring expensive pastries and breads. Could a retailer combine these two approaches? If so, how?

13. Visit the Web site of Home Depot (www.homedepot.com) and then evaluate its target market strategy.

14. Why is it valuable for retailers to know how much time people must work to afford various goods and services?

WEB-BASED EXERCISE

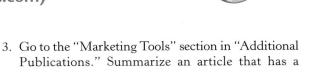

American Demographics (www.demographics.com)

Questions

1. Enter the *"American Demographics* Back Issue" section of the Web site. Prepare a bibliography with all of the articles that have a retail focus within the past year.

2. Select one *American Demographics* article from the past year that has significance for a department store. What could the key executives of a department store chain learn from this article?

3. Go to the "Marketing Tools" section in "Additional Publications." Summarize an article that has a major implication for a national fast-food franchisor. Explain your choice of article.

4. Refer to the "Forecast" section in "Additional Publications." Summarize an article that has a major implication for a shopping center developer. Explain your choice of article.

CHAPTER ENDNOTES

1. Rosemary Feitelberg, "Sports Authority Looks Out for Ladies," *Women's Wear Daily* (April 22, 1999), p. 10.

2. Marvin Nesbit and Arthur Weinstein, "How to Size Up Your Customers," *American Demographics* (July 1986), p. 34; and James H. Snider, "Consumers in the Information Age," *Futurist* (January–February 1993), p. 15.

3. Kurt Salmon Associates, *Consumer Outlook '98*, p. 2.

4. *Statistical Abstract of the United States 1999* (Washington, D.C.: U.S. Department of Commerce, 1999), various pages.

5. Barry Janoff, "Targeting All Ages," *Progressive Grocer Annual Report* (April 1999), p. 37.

6. Murray Raphel, "Meet the Millennium Customer," *Direct Marketing* (December 1998), p. 48; and Wendy Liebmann, "How America Shops," *Vital Speeches of the Day* (July 15, 1998), p. 595.

7. Kurt Salmon Associates, *Consumer Outlook '98*, p. 3.

8. Liebmann, "How America Shops," pp. 595–96.

9. Carol Radice, "Targeting Tomorrow's Consumers," *Progressive Grocer* (July 1998), p. 55.

10. Terry Hennessy, "Traditional Wisdom," *Progressive Grocer* (February 1999), p. 90.

11. Marcia Mogelonsky, "Hard-Core Shoppers," *American Demographics* (September 1998), p. 49.

12. Ira P. Schneiderman, "Splitsville: As the Population Becomes Highly Segmented, Retailers Will Have to Choose the Groups They Focus On," *Women's Wear Daily* (March 24, 1999), p. 30.

13. *Second Annual Ernst & Young Internet Shopping Study* (New York: Ernst & Young, 1999), pp. 9–11.

14. Dick Silverman, "Consumers Are Becoming More Shopworn," *Daily News Record* (July 6, 1998), p. 12; and Calmetta Y. Coleman, "Making Malls (Gasp!) Convenient," *Wall Street Journal* (February 8, 2000), pp. B1, B4.

15. Kurt Salmon Associates, *Consumer Outlook '98*, pp. 4–5.

16. "Retailing: General," *Standard & Poor's Industry Surveys* (May 20, 1999), p. 14.

17. PricewaterhouseCoopers, *Retail Preview: Soft Goods* (October 1998), p. 22; and PricewaterhouseCoopers, *Retail Preview: Home Goods* (August 1998), pp. 14, 16–17.

18. Victor J. Orler and David H. Friedman, "The Consumers Behind Consumer-Direct," *Progressive Grocer* (February 1998), p. 40; and "Comparison Shoppers," *Women's Wear Daily* (July 8, 1998), p. 6.

19. Kurt Salmon Associates, *Consumer Outlook '98*, p. 14.

20. PricewaterhouseCoopers, *Retail Preview: Consumables* (September 1998), p. 6; Jennifer Steinhauer, "The Stores That Cross Class Lines," *New York Times* (March 15, 1998), Section 3, pp. 1, 11; and "Mall Shopping Patterns Shift," *Chain Store Age* (February 1998), p. 147.

21. Marcia Mogelonsky, "Keep Candy in the Aisles," *American Demographics* (July 1998), p. 32; and Mark Dolliver, "I'll Just Grab This," *Adweek* (May 25, 1998), p. 19.

22. Sharon E. Beatty and M. Elizabeth Ferrell, "Impulse Buying: Modeling Its Precursors," *Journal of Retailing*, Vol. 74 (Summer 1998), pp. 169–91.

23. Harry Seymour and Laura Rifkin, "Study Shows Satisfaction Not the Same as Loyalty," *Marketing News* (October 26, 1998), p. 40.

24. Isabelle Sender, "Auto Parts For Novices, Supermarket Style," *Chain Store Age* (May 1998), p. 48.

25. Shelly Branch, "How Target Got Hot," *Fortune* (May 24, 1999), pp. 170, 172.

26. Marianne Wilson, "Quick-Start Successes," *Chain Store Age* (June 1999), p. 43.

27. Marianne Wilson, "Putting the Sparkle Back in Zale," *Chain Store Age* (January 1999), pp. 48–49.

28. Robert Fresco, "Whose Standard of Living?" *Newsday* (September 19, 1999), p. A19.

CASE 1

SUPERMARKETS SEEK A LARGER SHARE OF PERSONAL CARE SALES

In recent years, the sales of personal care products have been growing. In 1999, the total unit sales of health care products carried at mass merchants, drug chains, and supermarkets rose by 5.6 percent from 1998—while unit hair coloring sales rose 12.4 percent and unit sales of facial cosmetics rose 10.4 percent.

Although the sales of personal care products at supermarkets have historically lagged behind those at mass merchants and drug chains, supermarket prospects for these items are now strong. Research indicates that 63.7 percent of households buy soap in a supermarket, 50.0 percent buy shampoo, 33.1 percent buy hair conditioners, 25.8 percent buy hair spray, and 25.1 percent buy hand and body lotions. Furthermore, the 1998 to 1999 sales increase at supermarkets was at least 10 percent for each of these categories: hair coloring (14.3 percent), women's fragrances (11.3 percent), and skin care (10 percent).

In 1999, the sales of specialty bath and body personal care items were $384 million for mass merchants (up 44 percent from 1998), $175 million for drug chains (up 35 percent), and $88 million for supermarkets (up 22 percent). Tom Zimmerman, a sales director for Dial's specialty personal care division, says that even though revenues at specialty stores (such as Body Shop) continue to grow, the food-drug-mass channel is growing faster. Zimmerman predicts that this segment will catch up to specialty store sales within the next three to five years.

Nancy Lund, the category manager for a natural fruit-and-floral bath and body products marketer, expects that category to feature more value-based products "that are pretty and smell nice." Such products, she notes, will be especially important in supermarkets and in mass channels "where the customer is looking for good value. If she wants a high-end product, she'll go elsewhere—a specialty chain or department store."

Dial's Tom Zimmerman thinks supermarkets will have a greater role in the future for bath and body categories: "They appeal to women of all ages and offer above-average margins and a high dollar ring. They can also enhance the store image and make shopping more fun." He further believes that supermarkets should create a dedicated section for specialty bath products that is 8 to 16 linear feet in length. This will enable them to stock a variety of different brands and to target different age groups: "Supermarkets are a very important channel, with a tremendous growth opportunity, but the category is highly underdeveloped in food stores." Zimmerman suggests that the lagging response is due to supermarkets' reliance on private labels and the inability of many private-label producers to develop high-quality fragrances, a continuous stream of new products, and appropriate gift pack presentations.

In their quest for personal care sales, supermarkets have the advantage of the high volume of shopping visits versus drug and discount chains. They also have a price edge on beauty

CASE 1
(CONTINUED)

care products as compared with drug chains. An unknown factor in the competitive balance among various retail formats is Web sales. Two sites in particular, drugstore.com and Beauty Buys.com, are attempting to attract beauty care shoppers through price appeals.

Questions

1. To what target market(s) should supermarkets appeal when selling personal care products?

2. Why do you think that many consumers do not buy personal care products at supermarkets, despite their frequent shopping trips?

3. What type of decision-making process applies to these personal care products? Why?

   a. Lipstick for self.
   b. Shampoo for child.
   c. A gift of perfume or cologne.

4. How can supermarkets stimulate both impulse purchases and store loyalty for personal care products?

NOTE   The material in this case is drawn from Nancy Brumback, "Getting Personal," *Progressive Grocer* (June 1999), pp. 37–42.

CASE 2

RETAILING IN EUROPE

When comparing retailing in Europe with retailing in the United States, a number of similarities and differences are readily apparent. According to many experts, European retailing is edging closer to U.S.-style retailing as evidenced by Europe's increase in self-service merchandising and the steady decline of small retailers at the expense of larger chains. On the other hand, those who believe that retailing in Europe still differs substantially from the United States look at the contrasts in store size, the use of scrambled merchandising as a retail strategy, the degree of customer service, retail location strategy, and store hours. Let's examine these similarities and differences.

Similarities:

- Heightened European emphasis on self-service merchandising—To reduce retail personnel costs and increase impulse purchases, more European retailers are turning to self-service operations, a practice that was socially unacceptable in the past, when the shopping trip was more of a leisurely ritual.
- Rising market share for large European chains at the expense of small independent retailers—Retail analysts generally attribute the growing strength of European chains to more auto ownership in Europe (which lets shoppers travel greater distances to shopping centers filled with chain store tenants) and to the higher proportion of working women (who are pressed for time and desire one-stop shopping in larger chain stores).

Differences:

- Store size—On average, European stores are still much smaller than U.S. stores, and there is more consumer respect for independent stores.
- Scrambled merchandising—Although scrambled merchandising is very popular in the United States, particularly in supermarkets and general merchandise retailers, European retailers tend to specialize in a narrower product mix. As a result, European shoppers usually make separate trips to a bakery, meat market, and pharmacy. While many U.S. shoppers would view the lack of scrambled merchandising as an inconvenience, many Europeans see the separate shopping trips as an opportunity to get the freshest food possible, to examine a larger selection, or to receive better customer service. The small store size and the high number of independent retailers in Europe contribute to the low degree of scrambled merchandising there.
- Customer service—Some observers say that European shoppers still like to browse and resent being rushed to make a decision. Thus, what appears to be slow service to a U.S. consumer is seen by a European consumer as an opportunity to browse.
- Malls versus central business districts—In the United States, the success of suburban malls has come at the expense of central business districts. At many European cities, the central business districts have benefited from the creation of city-based shopping malls by closing traffic on side streets, and the popularity of central business districts due to the presence of restaurants with outside dining.
- Store hours—Seven-day store openings and extended hours of operation are common in most parts of the United States. However, in Europe, many stores are closed from noon to 2 P.M. during the week, from noon on during Saturday, and all day on Sunday.

Questions

1. Do you think U.S. and European retailing will move closer together in the future? What is the impact for the consumer? Explain your answer.

2. As a consumer, what European retailing practices would you want to see come to the United States? Why?

3. Discuss how U.S. and European shoppers might use the consumer decision process differently.

4. How could a European retailer utilize self-service merchandising to increase impulse purchases?

Video Questions on Retailing in Europe

1. What factors account for the success of U.S.-based franchises in Europe?

2. What are the basic differences in retailing between Northern versus Southern European counties? How do these differences affect consumer behavior?

CHAPTER 8

Information Gathering and Processing in Retailing

CHAPTER OBJECTIVES

1. To show why retailers should systematically collect and analyze information when developing and modifying their strategies
2. To examine the role of the retail information system, its components, and the recent advances in such systems
3. To describe the marketing research process: problem definition, secondary data search, generating primary data (if needed), data analysis, recommendations, and implementing findings
4. To discuss the retailer's data collection role

David Richey is a hotel mystery shopper whose job is to check on the customer service of leading hotels on behalf of his firm, Richey International. The company has contracts with 2,000 luxury hotels throughout the world. Many of these hotels share common reservations systems, such as Preferred Hotels & Resorts Worldwide (which serves 120 independently owned luxury hotels). Preferred requires that all participating hotels meet at least 80 percent of its customer service standards in an annual test that is conducted by Richey International.

Among the physical and social aspects of a hotel stay that Richey International evaluates are whether front-desk personnel use a guest's name during the check-in process, whether the correct minibar charges are posted at the checkout area, whether the bathroom tub and shower are spotlessly clean, how long it takes for baggage to be delivered to a room after a guest checks in, and the waiting time for coffee to be served at breakfast after a guest is seated.

To avoid detection and special treatment, David Richey registers under an alias. He also uses an extensive "bag of tricks" to evaluate each hotel. For example, he whacks a light bulb against the bedspread to make sure that the filament is broken and then screws it back to determine if the hotel's staff will notice and replace the "burned-out" bulb. And he carries a hidden tape recorder to record his reflections on the quality of the dining experience at the hotel restaurant.[1]

OVERVIEW

When a retailer forms a new strategy or adjusts an existing one, gathering and reviewing information is quite valuable. The firm can study such aspects of its strategy as the attributes and buying behavior of current and potential customers, alternative store and nonstore sites, store management and operations, product offerings, pricing, and store image and promotion—so as to prepare the best possible approach.

> *Please Note:* Web site addresses are constantly changing.
> The links in this chapter are current as of the publication of this book.

Acting on the basis of good information reduces a retailer's chances of making wrong decisions. Without proper information, a firm's risk of poor performance is higher because it may act on the basis of too little knowledge or on knowledge gained nonsystematically. Research activity should, to a large degree, be determined by the risk involved in a decision. For instance, while it may be risky for a department store to open a new branch store, there is much less risk if a retailer is deciding whether it should carry a new line of sweaters. In the branch store situation, thousands of dollars for research and many months of study may be proper. In the case of the new sweaters, limited research may be sufficient.

Information gathering and processing should be conducted in an ongoing manner, yielding enough data for planning and control. Unless information is obtained regularly, it may focus on short-run problems (crises), rather than the firm's long-range strategic planning needs:

> Retailers can gain a competitive edge through information support tools. J.C. Penney wants to decipher over 1.2 million rows of sales data. CVS, the drugstore chain, has the challenge of managing 25,000 items sold in 1,400 stores in 15 states. Levi Strauss tracks the sales of its 10,000 products and monitors the performance by channel across its 30,000 U.S. retailers that collect point-of-sale data. Nordstrom's handles over 1 million SKUs per store. How can executives in these firms manage such huge product volumes? They use retail information systems. Merchandisers, financial planners, inventory planners, buyers, and forecasters all clamor for the data they need to increase margins and inventory turnover and to ensure availability for hot items.[2]

In this chapter, the shortcomings of nonsystematic research are noted. The retail information system, data-base management and data warehousing, and the marketing research process are then described.

RETAIL STRATEGIES BASED ON NONSYSTEMATIC RESEARCH

Retailers are often tempted to rely on nonsystematic or incomplete ways of obtaining information due to time constraints, cost constraints, and the lack of research skills. Here are examples:

- Using intuition (e.g., "My gut reaction is to order 100 dozen quartz watches and sell them for $75 each as Christmas gifts.")
- Continuing what was done before (e.g., "We never sold luggage on the Web. Why should we now?")
- Copying a successful competitor's strategy (e.g., "Bloomingdale's has had great success with the sale of gourmet foods. We should stock and promote those products.")
- Devising a strategy after speaking to a few individuals about their perceptions (e.g., "My friends feel our prices are too high. We ought to lower them to improve sales and profits.")
- Assuming past trends will continue in the future (e.g., "The wholesale prices of CD burners keep on falling. If we wait a month to make a purchase, we can underprice competitors who are buying now.")

Let us take a look at the negative ramifications of the decisions made by several retailers that have not obtained information in a systematic way and analyze their strategic errors.

A movie theater charges $7 for tickets throughout the entire week. The manager cannot understand why attendance is poor on weekday afternoons. She feels that because all patrons are seeing the same movie, prices should be the same for a Monday matinee as a Saturday evening. Yet, by looking at data stored in the theater's retail information system, she would learn attendance is much lower on Mondays than on Saturdays, indicating that because people prefer Saturday evening performances, they are willing to pay $7 to see a movie then. Weekday customers have to be lured, and a lower price is a way to do so.

A toy store orders conservatively for the holiday season because the previous year's sales were weak. The store sells out two weeks before the peak of the season, and additional items cannot be delivered to the store in time for the holiday. This retailer uses a technique employed by many firms: incremental budgeting. Under that policy, a percentage is added to or subtracted from the prior year's budget to arrive at the present year's budget. The store owner assumed the previous year's poor sales would occur again. However, a survey of consumers would have revealed a sense of optimism and an increased desire to give gifts. A research-oriented retailer would have planned its inventory accordingly.

A chain bookstore opens a new branch unit 70 miles from its closest current store. The decision is based on the growing population and the absence of a store there by the chain. After a year, the new store is doing only 40 percent of expected business. A subsequent study by the chain shows the store name and image to be relatively unknown in the area and the choice of advertising media to be incorrect. In planning the new branch, these two important factors were not researched.

A Web retailer is doing well with small appliances, portable TVs, and moderately priced cameras. It has a good reputation in these traditional product lines and loyal customers. It wants to add other product lines to capitalize on its name and customer goodwill. Nonetheless, recent expansion into furniture has yielded poor results because the firm did not first conduct consumer research. People will buy standard, branded merchandise via the Web; but they are more reluctant to buy most furniture that way.

A florist cuts the price of two-day-old flowers from $17 a dozen to $5 a dozen because they have a shorter life expectancy when they are bought by customers; but they don't sell. The florist assumes bargain-hunting consumers will want them as gifts or for floral arrangements. What the florist does not know (due to no research) is that people perceive the older flowers to be of poor quality, color, and smell. The reduced price is actually too low and turns off customers!

The conclusion to be drawn from these examples is that nonsystematic or incomplete ways of collecting and analyzing information can cause a firm to enact a bad strategy.

THE RETAIL INFORMATION SYSTEM

Data gathering and analysis should not be regarded as a one-shot resolution of a single issue or problem. They should be viewed as parts of an ongoing, well-integrated process or system. A **retail information system (RIS)** anticipates the information needs of retail managers; collects, organizes, and stores relevant data on a continuous basis; and directs the flow of information to the proper decision makers.

These topics are covered next: building and using a retail information system, data-base management, and gathering information through the UPC and EDI.

Building and Using a Retail Information System

A retail information system requires a lot of background information, which makes the Retailing Resources Web Index (www.crstamu.org/retailin.htm) valuable.

Figure 8.1 presents a general RIS. With such a system, a retailer begins by clearly stating its business philosophy and objectives, both of which are influenced by environmental factors (such as competitors, the economy, and government). The retailer's philosophy and objectives provide broad guidelines, which direct strategic planning. Some aspects of strategic plans are routine and may require little re-evaluation. Others are nonroutine and require careful evaluation each time they arise.

Once a strategy is outlined, the data needed to enact it are collected, analyzed, and interpreted. If data are already available, they are retrieved from storage in company files. Each time new data are acquired, the files are updated. All of this takes place in the firm's information control center. Based on the data in the control center, decisions are then made and put into operation.

Know Your Markets When Moving Away from Home

With the increased retail globalization of markets, it is quite important to understand international etiquette, as well as the history and culture of a foreign country. There are several universal rules for conducting business abroad, such as these:

- Learn a few key phrases in the country's language, such as "Do you speak English?" and "Excuse me." Use the foreign language as much as you can.
- Certain courtesies apply in all cultures. These include dressing conservatively in business settings, using first and last names, and introducing a person of highest rank first, regardless of gender.
- Understand the concept of time. In Spain, one can show up a half hour after the scheduled time and still not be considered late. However, in Germany, a half-hour delay is considered very late.

Here are a few specific examples of how cultural "do's" and "don'ts" vary by country:

- Do not assume that all people with a British accent are from Great Britain (they can be from South Africa, the Caribbean, or Canada).
- "Dinner" in Ireland is a midday meal; the evening meal is referred to as "tea."
- A nodding of the head in Japan means that one is paying attention to you, not necessarily in agreement.

As an executive with a U.S. retailer looking to develop franchises in Poland, what information would you seek in order to learn about Polish culture to better understand the attributes of potential franchisees?

Source: Mary Kay Metcalf, "Etiquette Tips for Today's Global Economy: What to Know Before You Go," *Direct Marketing* (March 1999), pp. 22–24.

Figure 8.1
A Retail Information System

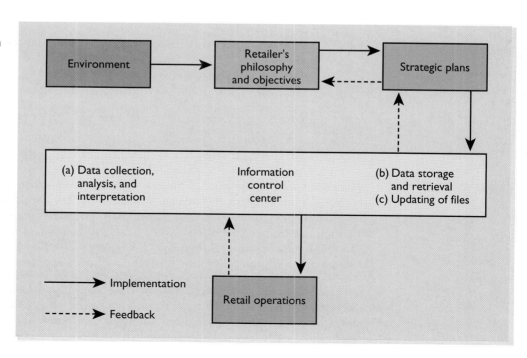

After decisions are enacted, performance results are fed back to the information control center and compared with pre-set criteria. Data are retrieved from files or further data are collected. Routine adjustments are made promptly. Regular reports and exception reports (which explain deviations from expected performance) are given to appropriate managers. Sometimes, a firm may react to performance results in a way that affects its overall philosophy or goals (such as revising its image if the firm is viewed as old-fashioned or sacrificing short-run profits to introduce a computerized checkout system).

All types of data should be stored in the control center for future and ongoing use; and the control center should be integrated with the firm's short- and long-run plans and operations. Data should not be gathered sporadically and haphazardly, but systematically.

A good RIS has several strengths. First, information collection is organized and broad (companywide) in scope. Second, data are regularly gathered and stored. Thus, opportunities can be foreseen and crises avoided. Third, elements of a strategy can be coordinated. Fourth, new strategies can be devised more quickly. Fifth, quantitative results are obtainable, and cost-benefit analysis can be done. However, deploying a retail information system may not be easy. It may require high initial time and labor costs; and complex decisions may be required to set up and follow through on such a system.

In building a retail information system, a number of decisions have to be made:

- *How active a role will the RIS have?* Will it proactively search for and distribute any relevant information pertaining to the firm or will it reactively respond to requests from managers when problems arise? The best systems are more proactive in nature, since the goal is to anticipate events.
- *Should an RIS be managed internally or be outsourced?* Although many retailers continue to perform their own RIS functions, some employ outside specialists to oversee the RIS. Either style can work, as long as the RIS is guided by the retailer's information needs. Several firms have their own RIS and use outside firms for specific tasks (such as conducting surveys or managing network computers).[3]
- *How much should an RIS cost?* Retailers typically spend one-half to one and one-half percent of their revenues on information systems. This lags behind other industries, including most of the manufacturers from which retailers buy goods and services.
- *How technology-driven should an RIS be?* While small firms can gather data from trade association meetings, consumer surveys, and so forth, more firms are placing a greater reliance on technology to drive information gathering and analysis. With the advent of personal computers, inexpensive local area networks, and low-priced software, technology is easier than ever to use in an RIS. Even a neighborhood deli could generate weekly sales data by product category and offer specials on slowing-selling items.
- *How much data are enough?* The purpose of an RIS is to provide enough information, on a regular basis, for a retailer to make the best possible strategy choices—not to overwhelm managers. This means a balancing act between too little information and information overload. To avoid overload, data should be edited to eliminate redundancies.[4]
- *How should data be disseminated throughout the firm?* This requires decisions as to who receives various reports, the frequency of data distribution, and access to data bases. When a firm has multiple divisions or operates in several regions, information access and distribution must be coordinated.
- *How should data be stored for future use?* Relevant data should be stored in a manner that makes retrieval easy and allows for adequate longitudinal (period to period) analysis.

Studies of retailers have found that many firms have set up information systems departments. Larger firms tend to have a chief information officer (CIO) overseeing their RIS. Formal, written annual plans are often produced for information systems departments. Computers are used by most companies conducting information systems analysis; and many firms are using the Web for some RIS functions. Substantial growth in the use of retail information systems is expected. There are many differences in information systems among retailers, on the basis of revenues and retail format.[5]

As computer technology has become more sophisticated and less expensive, more retailers (of all types) have developed comprehensive information systems. For example, 20 years ago, only one percent of U.S. supermarkets had scanning systems; now, virtually all of them have installed such systems. Twenty-five years ago, most computerized systems were used only to reduce cashier errors and improve inventory control. Today, they often form the foundation for a retail information system and are used for surveys, ordering, merchandise transfers between stores, and other diverse activities. These applications are being done by both small and large retailers. According to one study of small- and medium-sized retailers, 80 percent have computerized financial management, 70 percent analyze sales electronically, and 60 percent have computerized inventory management systems.[6]

Visit the "Customer Spotlights" section of its Web site (www. retailpro.com/ vspothome.html) to see the various ways in which actual retailers are applying Retail Pro.

Here are illustrations of how retailers are placing emphasis on computerizing their information systems. Retail Technologies International (www.retailpro.com) markets Retail Pro management information software to retailers. See Figure 8.2. This software is used at 15,000 stores in 50 countries. Although it has been bought by several large retailers, Retail Pro software also has a great appeal among smaller retailers due to flexible pricing—based on the number of users and stores, the type of hardware, and so forth. A small store pays about 2 to 3 percent of one year's sales to buy a complete Retail Pro System, including training and support. Retail Pro has these features, as described at its Web site:

> The Retail Pro Decision Support System has these features: *OLAP* (online analytical processing) processes, analyzes, and views data from different viewpoints on screen instantly without having to generate multiple reports. The *multidimensional data base* can display values by store, vendor, and department for up to 44 dimensions including

Figure 8.2
Retail Pro Management Information Software

Reprinted by permission of Retail Technologies International.

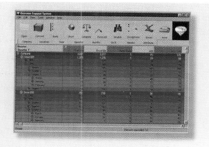

With *Retail Pro* Decision System you can:

▼ Diagnose on-line any department, vendor, style, season, store, or item

▼ Drill down to the exact information you need instantly

▼ Set up models and let DSS automatically watch for exceptions

▼ Instantly rank areas from best to worst using the measurements you choose

▼ Pivot data to see it from different viewpoints, without having to re-run a report

▼ View data in 3D color graphs, with trend lines and moving averages

▼ Drop data, graphs and comparisons into e-mail for relay to managers and staff

▼ Forecast growth trends and track your results against them

▼ Track GMROI*, turn rate, days of supply, stock to sales and sell-through

▼ Export your data into an Excel spreadsheet with a click of the mouse

▼ Compare annual, quarterly, monthly, or weekly numbers year-to-year

▼ Analyze your customer base with laser accuracy at will

store, region, day, month, quarter, year, vendor, department, style, size, color, and season. *Drill down* is able to instantly break out any data dimension into more detail. These views are immediate and can be followed upward or downward in any sequence. *Pivoting* is the ability to switch the hierarchy of how you view data. Assume you are looking at the sales of each department from within a vendor or vendors. With a drag of the mouse, you can see the sales of every vendor from within a department or departments. Ranking can be done instantly by any value. *Forecast* lets the user project performance along any dimension, using past history or other criteria, and automatically track variances from projections. *Watches* are minimum/maximum levels that can be set for any aspect of performance to activate an alert when exceptions occur.

MicroStrategy (www.microstrategy.com) also works with retailers (typically larger ones) to prepare computerized information systems. Its clients include Eddie Bauer, Payless Cashways, Victoria's Secret, Hannaford Bros., PetsMart, ShopKo, and Warner Brothers. One of its leading software products is MicroStrategy Agent, which is described at the firm's Web site:

> MicroStrategy Agent is an integral component of a powerful decision support architecture that goes beyond departmental query and reporting to consumerize the retail information system. Employees, strategic business partners, outside vendors, corporate customers, and individuals all have the potential to access and analyze data at precisely the level of detail they require to make informed decisions. Not only is the tool easy to apply, but it also provides users with the ability to answer any question—regardless of the amount of data needed to satisfy the request (depth), the complexity of the data (breadth), or the required display and visualization to convey the result (reporting range).

Wilsons Leather sells men's and women's outerwear, apparel, and accessories at 550 stores in the United States, Canada, and Great Britain. It recently introduced a new point-of-sale-based RIS. A key advantage of this system is its ability to convey both voice and data communications over one phone line. This supports "trickle polling," whereby sales data are easily extracted from stores. Wilsons' director of business systems says "You can do trickle polling hourly. You can look at sales data and see how stores are doing on a special promotion. You can then turn around and further promote merchandise on a real-time basis." The firm also intends to use its system to better track inventory and ship items that are out of stock in one store to the consumer's home or the store nearest to him or her.[7]

In 1999, Sports Authority spent millions of dollars to upgrade its RIS. Since its founding, the firm has prided itself on having advanced systems to manage information and integrate purchasing, receiving, sales, and inventory planning. Sports Authority has point-of-sale terminals in all stores that can look up prices, provide sales data by item, capture customer ZIP code data, and initiate requests for credit and check authorizations. The firm also has IBM AS/400 computers and hand-held radio frequency terminals as in-store processors to record merchandise sales, print price tags, maintain inventory levels, and for general data inquiry. The in-store processors communicate with central AS/400 computers to exchange data with the retailer's corporate office. This gives local managers the ability to achieve better inventory productivity and merchandise space planning.[8]

Data-Base Management

Data-base management is the procedure used to gather, integrate, apply, and store information related to specific subject areas. It is a key element in a retail information system and may be employed with customer data bases, vendor data bases, product category data bases, and so on. For instance, a retailer may compile and store data on the characteristics and purchase behavior of customers, compute and store sales figures by vendor, and maintain historical records by product category. Each of these would represent a separate data base. Among retailers that maintain data bases, most use them for one or more of these activities: frequent shopper programs, customer analysis, promotion evaluation, trading-area analysis, joint promotions with manufacturers, media planning, and customer communications.

Data-base management should be approached as a series of five steps:

1. Plan the data base and its components and determine information needs.

2. Acquire the necessary information.

3. Retain the information in a usable and accessible format.

4. Update the data base regularly to reflect changing customer demographics, recent purchase behavior, and so forth.

5. Analyze the data base to determine company strengths and weaknesses.

Data-base information can come from internal and external sources. A retailer can develop its data bases internally by keeping detailed records and arranging them properly. To illustrate, a firm could generate data bases with information *by customer*—purchase frequency, goods and services bought, average purchase amount, demographic background, and payment method; *by vendor*—total retailer purchases per time period, total sales to customers per time period, the most popular items, retailer profit margins, average delivery time, and service quality; and *by product category*—total category sales per time period, item sales per time period, retailer profit margins, and the percentage of items discounted.

There are also firms that compile data bases and make them available to retailers for a fee. Donnelley Marketing, a subsidiary of infoUSA, maintains a very comprehensive data base of U.S. households, with detailed information on more than 90 percent of all households: "The accuracy of this massive data base is a result of daily updates and quarterly enrichments. New data added to the system are regularly tested and validated. This data base derives information from a variety of sources. Donnelley Marketing uses over 4,700 telephone directories, state automobile registrations, drivers' license data, voter registrations, birth records, and mail-order buyers to maintain the information. The data base allows selection by many categories such as age, household income, types of auto, and credit card holders—to name a few."[9]

To effectively manage a retail data base, these are important considerations:

- Is senior management knowledgeable in data-base strategies and does it know how company data bases are currently being used?
- Is there a person or department responsible for overseeing the data base?
- Does the firm have data-base acquisition and retention goals?
- Is every data-base initiative analyzed to see if it is successful?
- Is there a mechanism to flag data that indicates potential problems or opportunities?
- Are customer purchases in different product categories or company divisions cross-linked?
- Is there a clear privacy policy regarding the data base, and is this policy communicated to those in a data base? Are there opt-out provisions for those who do not want to be included in a data base?
- Is the data base updated each time there is a customer interaction or some other relevant activity?
- Are customers, personnel, suppliers, and others invited to update their personal data?
- Is the data base periodically checked to eliminate redundant files?[10]

Let us now discuss two specific aspects of data-base management: data warehousing, and data mining and micromarketing. Whereas data warehousing is a mechanism for storing and

Donnelley's parent company, infoUSA (www.infoUSA.com), has a number of resources to help small firms manage data bases.

Figure 8.3
Retail Data-Base Management
in Action

The **data warehouse** is where information is collected, sorted, and stored centrally. Information is disseminated to retailer personnel, as well as to channel partners (such as alerting them to what merchandise is hot and what is not hot) and customers (such as telling them about order status). In **data mining,** retail executives and other employees—and sometimes, channel partners—analyze information by customer type, product category, and so forth in order to determine opportunities for tailored marketing efforts. With **micromarketing,** the retailer applies differentiated marketing: focused retail strategy mixes are planned for specific customer segments—or even for individual customers.

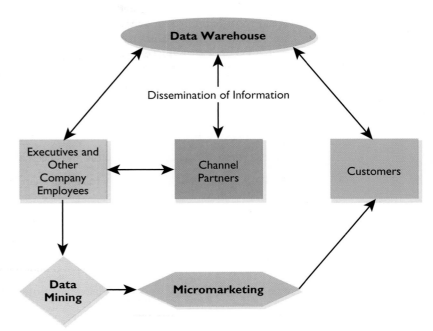

distributing information, data mining and micromarketing are ways in which information can be utilized. Figure 8.3 shows the interplay of data warehousing with data mining and micromarketing.

Data Warehousing One new advance in data-base management is **data warehousing,** whereby copies of all the data bases in a company are maintained in one location and accessible to employees at any locale. The basic premise of data warehousing is "to create a clearinghouse in which to gather and organize critical business data. The data warehouse is a repository of data gathered from various sources, internal and external. Properly designed, implemented, and maintained, a data warehouse is a valuable business intelligence tool."[11]

There are four components to a data warehouse:

- The data warehouse, where data are physically stored.
- Software to copy original data bases and transfer them to the warehouse.
- Interactive software to allow inquiries to be processed.
- A directory for the categories of information maintained in the warehouse.

Data warehousing has three major advantages. First, both information access and inconsistency problems are eliminated by consolidating data in one place. Second, executives and other employees are quickly and easily privy to the same data at the same time no matter where they are located. Third, by storing information centrally, greater data analysis and manipulation are possible. Thus, data can be better broken by customer type, product category, sales location, and so forth.[12]

Computerized data warehouses were once costly to build—and, thus, feasible only for large retailers. In 1996, the average cost to build a data warehouse was $2.2 million. This has changed. A simple data warehouse can now be put together for less than $100,000, making data warehousing affordable to all but very small retailers (and since such retailers tend to operate just one store, centralized data bases and distribution to far-flung executives are not issues, making data warehousing unnecessary for them).[13]

Overseeing Marketing Information Services at Bloomingdale's

Susan Harvey, vice-president of information services at Bloomingdale's, knows the value of a successful data-base marketing program. Her group functions as the internal direct marketing agency for the Bloomingdale's chain and its more than 40 merchandise categories and storewide events. Harvey's division is responsible for more than 400 direct marketing promotions per year.

Harvey also oversees the "Bloomingdale's By Mail" catalog, with a data base of over 3 million names and access to a separate data base of credit-card customers. She evaluates the data base to identify loyal Bloomingdale's customers, create cross-over buyers, reactivate former customers, and prospect for new customers. One of the key challenges has been to plan the correct time interval between customer mailings, while shortening the time between a mailing, a customer response, and analysis of the data.

At Bloomingdale's, Harvey has developed marketing programs aimed at individual customers (as opposed to overall demographic profiles or ZIP codes). This encourages one-to-one marketing programs tailored to specific consumers.

Before joining Bloomingdale's, Susan Harvey had positions on both the advertising agency and client sides of business. In addition, her career encompassed publishing, as well as retailing jobs.

Source: Sharan Barnett and Frank Barnett, "Bloomingdale's Embraces One-to-One Marketing Opportunities: Part 1," *Direct Marketing* (January 1999), pp. 24–27.

Wal-Mart, Sears, American Stores, Hollywood Video, 7-Eleven, and Federated Department Stores are among the growing number of retailers that have adopted data warehousing: "Just a few years ago, if you mentioned data warehousing to a retail audience, most would scratch their heads wondering exactly what you were talking about. Times change. Now the idea of copying all a retailer's data into a massive, master data base is on the radar of almost every retail executive."[14] See Figure 8.4.

At Wal-Mart,

Determining the kinds of products carried by its various stores used to be the job of merchandisers. Today, computers do most of the work. For years, every scrap of information about who buys what has been fed to headquarters in Bentonville, Arkansas, where it is kept in a huge data warehouse. Wal-Mart has over 100 terabytes of data, which if printed on $8\frac{1}{2}$-by-11 sheets of paper and laid end to end would reach the moon and back 15 times. The system was built in-house and works like this:

1. Scanners located at Wal-Mart cash registers across the land read the barcodes on products for price, time of purchase, and the mix of items that were in each shopper's basket.

2. The info is sent to a centralized data warehouse, where computers slice and dice it to glean who's buying what, and when and where they're buying it.

3. This finely sifted purchasing information is sent to manufacturers through an Internet connection, telling them what is selling and where it's selling best. They can then rapidly resupply—or agree to cut prices if a product isn't moving.[15]

Data Mining and Micromarketing **Data mining** involves the in-depth analysis of information so as to gain specific insights about customers, product categories, vendors, and so

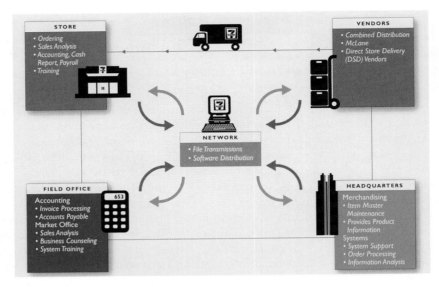

Figure 8.4
7-Eleven's Forward-Looking Approach to Data Warehousing

By electronically connecting all parties in the 7-Eleven supply chain, its retail information system creates a higher level of coordination and much better decision making. Store operators have actual sales information presented in logical formats and are able to order more effectively. Receiving exact orders in an organized fashion allows vendors to provide better service to the stores. Field offices are able to reduce administration costs by receiving information in electronic format. Headquarters merchandising staff are able to judge new product acceptance and communicate upcoming advertising and promotions from manufacturers that will affect sales.

Reprinted by permission.

The Archer Individualized Marketing System (www.nuedgesys-tems.com/prod_serv/ archer) lets retailers easily do data mining and micromarketing.

forth. The goal is to determine whether there are opportunities for tailored marketing efforts that would result in better company performance. One emerging application of data mining is **micromarketing,** whereby the retailer uses differentiated marketing and develops focused retail strategy mixes for specific customer segments, sometimes fine-tuned for the individual shopper.

Data mining relies on software to sift through information in a data warehouse to uncover patterns and relationships among different factors. Vast amounts of data can be quickly searched and consolidated, which would be virtually impossible if done manually. That is why many retailers "are plunging into their data bases to determine who their best customers are and how better to market to them. Most hope to substantiate hunches with hard numbers. But others are venturing into the realm of automated discovery, relying on sophisticated, computer-driven methods that use artificial intelligence to flesh out meaningful, actionable information that can make a difference to the bottom line. 'It's the same algorithm, whether you're trying to predict volcanoes on Venus or a customer's propensity to buy high heels,' says Usama Fayyad, senior researcher in the decision theory and adaptive systems group of Microsoft Research."[16]

Fingerhut, now a division of Federated Department Stores (which acquired Fingerhut mostly because of its data mining prowess), is a leader in data mining:

Fingerhut began studying its data base when the first shopper placed an order in 1948. Today, it sends out 130 different catalogs and has a data warehouse with statistics on more than 65 million shoppers. Hundreds of users from throughout the firm query the data base daily and can crunch more than 3,000 variables on the most active 12 million customers (those buying in the last 4 years). Variables include everything from specific product transactions to demographic data collected from surveys and research vendors. More than 300 predictive models are used to scour data. One predicts the likelihood of someone responding to a given catalog, while another scores the chances of a customer returning merchandise. At least one model is run on each potential recipient of every catalog sent out.[17]

On the basis of its data mining efforts, Fingerhut often engages in micromarketing and creates new catalogs. For example, in one analysis, its researchers found that shoppers who moved tripled the amount they spent with Fingerhut during the three months after they moved. They were especially likely to buy furniture and decorations: "That may seem like a no-brainer, but to Fingerhut, it was a valuable nugget to capitalize on. It developed a new 'mover's catalog' filled with targeted products for this segment. At the same time, it saved money by not mailing other catalogs to these folks right after they relocated."[18]

Gathering Information Through the UPC and EDI

To gather and process data more efficiently for use in their information systems, a growing number of retailers now rely on the Universal Product Code (UPC) and electronic data interchange (EDI).

With the **Universal Product Code (UPC),** products (or tags attached to them) are marked with a series of thick and thin vertical lines, representing each item's identification code. UPC-A labeling—the preferred format—includes numbers, as well as lines. The lines are "read" by scanning equipment at checkout counters. Cashiers do not have to enter transactions manually—although they can, if needed. Because the UPC is not readable by humans, the retailer or vendor must attach a ticket or sticker to every product specifying its size, color, and other information (if the data are not on the package or the product). Given that the UPC does not include price information, this too must be added by a ticket or sticker.

By using UPC-based technology, retailers can record information instantaneously on a product's model number, size, color, and other factors when it is sold, as well as send the information to a computer that monitors unit sales, inventory levels, and other factors. The goals are to produce better merchandising data, improve inventory management and control, speed up transaction time, increase productivity, reduce clerical errors in processing transactions, and coordinate the flow of information.

Since its inception, UPC technology has improved substantially. Today, it is the accepted industry standard for both food retailers and general merchandise retailers (including specialty stores):

At the Marsh Supermarket in Troy, Ohio, several people at the checkout counter on June 26, 1974 were hoping that the never before used UPC code on a package of Wrigley's chewing gum would scan correctly the first time. It did, and the rest is history. Today, the Uniform Code Council estimates that 5 billion scans a day are made of the UPC. The symbol uniquely identifies each product down to its specific stock-keeping unit. For instance, a 16-ounce bottle of shampoo has a different UPC than a 32-ounce bottle of the same brand. It is estimated that food prices to the consumer would have risen almost twice as fast since 1974 without the UPC symbol, says a recently released report from PricewaterhouseCoopers. The value of the information in the UPC is estimated to be 20 times more valuable than originally thought by its creators. "We knew the UPC was going to be vitally important for food distribution," says Alan Haberman, a member of the committee that created the UPC. "However, I don't think we really envisioned how much an impact this technology would have on businesses and consumers."[19]

Figure 8.5
Applying UPC Technology to Gain Better Information

As this photo montage shows, Symbol Technologies has devised a host of scanning products (some of which are wireless) that make UPC data capture and processing quite simple. For example, Symbol products can be used at the point of sale to enter transaction data and transmit them to a central office, at product displays to verify shelf prices, at storage areas to aid in taking physical inventories, at receiving stations to log in the receipt of new merchandise, and at delivery points to track the movement of customer orders.
Reprinted by permission of Symbol Technologies.

Figure 8.5 shows how far UPC technology has come with regard to information gathering and processing.

Virtually every time sales transactions or inventory data are scanned by computer, UPC technology is involved. More than 200,000 manufacturers and retailers worldwide belong to the Uniform Code Council (UCC), an industry association that has taken the lead in setting and promoting inter-industry product identification and communication standards (www.uc-council.org). The UPC is discussed further in Chapter 16 ("Financial Merchandise Management").

GE Global Exchange Services is one of the leaders in EDI technology (www.gegxs.com).

With **electronic data interchange (EDI)**, retailers and suppliers regularly exchange information through their computers with regard to inventory levels, delivery times, unit sales, and so on, of particular items. As a result, both parties enhance their decision-making capabilities, better control inventory levels, and are more responsive to consumer demand trends. UPC scanning is often the basis for generating ongoing product-related data for EDI.

This is how Black & Decker and its interconnected retailers use EDI: "At checkout, a clerk scans in a tool's barcode. Information from the scanning is sent from the store's computer to Black & Decker computers at company headquarters in Maryland, automatically generating a purchase order for new tools to replace those sold. The manufacturer gains invaluable forecasting and merchandising information. Black & Decker's major retailer customers typically provide weekly EDI, point-of-sale reports."[20]

The Internet is beginning to revolutionize manufacturer-retailer uses of EDI:

> The initiatives under way are exciting because they show the potential to reinvent supply chain management in the not too distant future. Exchanging data about inventory levels, sales trends, shipping/receiving times, and item forecasting via the Web rather than by phone and fax could let retailers dramatically reduce supply chain costs and provide better customer service. "Long term, we see the Internet as a portal for sharing information with our partners. Eventually it will be a window our suppliers can look through to gain better insight into our business and for us to get a clearer view of theirs," explains Rachelle Chase, director of electronic commerce at Target Corporation. "Ideally, this will enable us and our suppliers to make better decisions."[21]

EDI is covered further in Chapter 15 ("Implementing Merchandise Plans").

THE MARKETING RESEARCH PROCESS

Marketing research in retailing entails the collection and analysis of information relating to specific issues or problems facing a retailer. At farsighted firms, marketing research is just one element in a thorough retail information system. At other firms, marketing research may be the only type of information gathering and processing that is done.

The **marketing research process** embodies a series of activities: defining the issue or problem to be studied, examining secondary data, generating primary data (if needed), analyzing data, making recommendations, and implementing findings. It is not a single act. The use of this process lets a retailer do research systematically—not haphazardly—and make better decisions. Figure 8.6 outlines the research process. Each activity is done sequentially. Thus, secondary data are not examined until after an issue or problem is defined. The dashed line around the primary data stage means these data are generated only if secondary data do not yield enough information for a decision. The research process is described next.

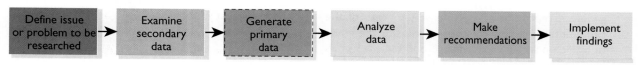

Figure 8.6
The Marketing Research Process in Retailing

Issue (problem) definition involves a clear statement of the topic to be studied. What information does the retailer want to obtain in order to make a decision? Without clearly understanding the topic to be researched, potentially irrelevant and confusing data could be collected. Here are two examples of issue (problem) definitions for a downtown shoe store. Whereas the first one relates to a comparison of three locations and is fairly structured, the second one is much more open-ended:

1. *"Of three potential new store locations, which should we choose?"*

2. *"How can we improve the sales of our men's shoes?"*

After the research issue (problem) has been defined, secondary data sources are examined. **Secondary data** are those that have been gathered for purposes other than addressing the issue or problem currently under study. Secondary data may be internal (such as company records) or external (such as government reports and trade publications). Secondary data are described in more depth in the next section.

Primary data are those collected to address the specific issue or problem under study. This type of data may be generated via surveys, observations, experiments, and simulation. Primary data are discussed more fully later in this chapter.

Sometimes secondary data are relied on; other times, primary data are crucial. Still other times, both are important. Three points are noteworthy. First, the diversity of possible data collection (types and costs) is great. Second, only data relevant to the problem or issue under investigation should be amassed. Third, as indicated earlier, primary data are usually acquired only if the secondary data search yields insufficient information (hence, the dashed box in Figure 8.6).

By gathering data, these kinds of information can be compiled for the two shoe-store issues (problems) that were just stated:

All the Right Data for All the Right Gifts

Diana and Gregg Shapiro are owners of All the Right Gifts (www.alltherightgifts.com), an online shopping directory. All the Right Gifts receives commissions from other retailers based on its referrals.

To effectively manage their shopping directory, the Shapiros carefully track which areas of their Web site are viewed by people, as well as how shoppers reached their site. They use multiple techniques to track visitors. The simplest one is a counter that calculates the number of hits the site receives. The Shapiros also use a log-analysis software program to generate reports that indicate which areas of the site visitors like, how they got to the site, the effect of traffic on server performance, and the site's profitability. The Shapiros have used the information to modify their site. During one recent month, for example, they noticed that the words "automobile" and "airline tickets" were being heavily used by shoppers. As a result, they changed the focus of the "Top 10" gift suggestions and their home page.

Unlike other sites that monitor tracking on an active basis (which require consumers to fill out forms), the Shapiros track All the Right Gifts' visitors more passively. This method relies on Web address tracking mechanisms and cookies (computer programs that track consumers by automatically downloading information).

Should the Shapiros use active, as well as passive, tracking? Explain your answer.

Source: Melissa Campanelli, "Hot on the Trail," *Entrepreneur* (August 1999), pp. 40, 42.

Issue (Problem) Definition	Information Needed to Solve Issue (Problem)
1. Which store location?	1. Data on access to transportation, traffic, consumer profiles, rent, store size, and types of competition are gathered from government reports, trade publications, and observation by the owner for each of the three potential store locations.
2. How to improve sales of shoes?	2. Store sales records for the past five years by product category are gathered. A consumer survey in a nearby mall is conducted.

After data are collected, data analysis is performed to assess that information and relate it to the defined issue or problem. Alternative solutions are also clearly outlined. For example:

Issue (Problem) Definition	Alternative Solutions
1. Which store location?	1. Each site is ranked for all of the criteria (access to transportation, traffic, consumer profiles, rent, store size, and types of competition).
2. How to improve sales of shoes?	2. Alternative strategies to boost shoe sales are analyzed and ranked.

The advantages and disadvantages of each alternative are then enumerated. See Table 8.1.

At this point, recommendations are made as to the strategy the retailer should enact to best address its issue or problem. Of the available options, which is best? Table 8.1 shows recommendations for the shoe-store issues (problems) discussed throughout this section.

Last, but not least, is the implementation of the recommended strategy. If research is to replace intuition in developing and enacting a retail strategy, a decision maker must

Table 8.1 Research-Based Recommendations

Issue (Problem)	Alternatives	Pros and Cons of Alternatives	Recommendation
1. Which store location?	Site A.	Best transportation, traffic, and consumer profiles. Highest rent. Smallest store space. Extensive competition.	Site A: the many advantages far outweigh the disadvantages.
	Site B.	Poorest transportation, traffic, and consumer profiles. Lowest rent. Largest store space. No competition.	
	Site C.	Intermediate on all criteria.	
2. How to improve sales of shoes?	Increased assortment.	Will attract and satisfy many more customers. High costs. High level of inventory. Reduces turnovers for many items.	Lower prices and increase ads: additional customers offset higher costs and lower margins; combination best expands business.
	Drop some lines and specialize.	Will attract and satisfy a specific consumer market. Excludes many segments. Costs and inventory reduced.	
	Slightly reduce prices. Advertise.	Unit sales increase. Markup and profit per item decline. Will increase traffic and new customers. High costs.	

follow recommendations from research studies, even if they seem to contradict his or her own ideas.

Let us now look at secondary data and primary data in greater depth.

Secondary Data

Advantages and Disadvantages Secondary data (information collected for other purposes) have several advantages over primary data:

Through Report Gallery (www. reportgallery.com), a retailer can do competitive intelligence on other firms around the globe. Want the most current annual report? Get it here.

- The assembly of data is inexpensive. Company records, trade journals, and government publications are all rather inexpensive to use. No data collection forms, interviewers, and tabulations are needed.
- Data can be gathered quickly. Company records, library sources, and Web sites can be accessed immediately. Many firms keep past reports and other materials in their retail information systems.
- There may be several sources of secondary data—providing many perspectives and lots of data.
- A secondary source may possess information the retailer would otherwise be unable to get. For example, government publications often have statistics no private firm could acquire.
- When data are assembled by a source such as *Progressive Grocer*, A.C. Nielsen, *Business Week*, or the government, results are quite credible.
- A retailer may have only a rough idea of the topics to investigate. Then, a secondary data search may help it to define issues (problems) more specifically. In addition, background information about a given issue or problem can be gathered from secondary sources before a primary study is undertaken.

Although secondary data have many advantages, there are several potential disadvantages:

- Available data may not suit the purposes of the current study because they have been collected for other reasons. A retailer normally needs local information. Yet, neighborhood statistics may not be found in secondary sources (which typically contain federal, state, and city statistics).
- Secondary data may be incomplete. A service station owner might be interested in how many local adults have cars. He or she would want data broken down by year, model, and mileage driven, so as to stock parts. A motor vehicle bureau could provide data on the models but not the mileage driven.
- Information may be dated. Statistics gathered five or even two years ago may not be valid today. The *U.S. Census of Retail Trade* is conducted every five years. The last retail census contains data gathered in 1997, and many statistics from that census are outdated. Furthermore, there is often a long time delay between the completion of a census and the release of that information to the public. Some of the data from the 1997 retail census do not actually get distributed until 2001.
- The accuracy of secondary data must be carefully evaluated. The retailer needs to decide whether data have been complied in an unbaised, objective way. The purpose of the original research, the data collection techniques used, and the method of analysis should each be examined for bias—if they are available for review. This is crucial if research has been done by a firm with a stake in the findings.
- The secondary data source can be a disadvantage, as well as an advantage. Some sources are known for poor data collection techniques; they should be avoided. If conflicting data are found, the source with the best reputation for accuracy should be used. Conflicting results presented by equally accurate sources may lead a retailer into primary research (the collection of its own data).

- The reliability of secondary data—the ability to replicate a study and get the same outcome—is not always known. In retailing, many research projects are not retested and the user of secondary data has to hope results from one narrow study are applicable to his or her firm.

In sum, a retailer desiring information to resolve an issue has many criteria to consider in contemplating the use of secondary data. In particular, low costs, speed, and access to materials must be weighed against improper fit, datedness, and data accuracy. Whether secondary data resolve an issue or not, their low cost and availability require that primary data not be collected until after studying secondary data. Only if secondary data are unsatisfactory or incomplete should primary data be gathered.

A variety of secondary data sources for retailers are now detailed.

Sources There are various sources and types of secondary data. The major distinctions are between internal and external sources.

Internal secondary data are available within the company, sometimes from the data bank of a retail information system. Thus, before searching for external secondary data or primary data, the retailer should look at information available inside the firm.

At the beginning of the year, most retailers develop budgets for the next 12 months. They are based on sales forecasts and outline planned expenditures for that year. A firm's budget and its performance in attaining budgetary goals are good sources of secondary data.

Retailers use sales and profit-and-loss reports to judge performance. Many have sales data from electronic registers. By studying sales by store, department, and item, and comparing them with prior periods, a firm can get a sense of growth or contraction. Overdependence on sales data may be misleading. Higher sales do not always mean higher profits. Sales data should be examined along with profit-and-loss data. If profit goals are set, achievements can be measured against them. A breakdown of profits and losses can show strengths and weaknesses in operations and management, and lead to improvements.

Customer billing reports offer a lot of data. A retailer could learn about inventory movement, sales by different personnel, peak selling times, and sales volume. For credit customers, it could review sales by geographic area, outstanding debts, repayment time, and types of purchases. Invoices could show the retailer its own purchase history and let it evaluate itself against budgetary or other goals. See Figure 8.7.

Figure 8.7
Internal Secondary Data: A Valuable Source of Information

The sales receipt (invoice) contains a lot of useful data, from the name of the person involved in each sales transaction to the items sold to the selling price. Weekly, monthly, and yearly performance can easily be tracked by carefully storing and retrieving sales receipt data.
Reprinted by permission of Retail Technologies International.

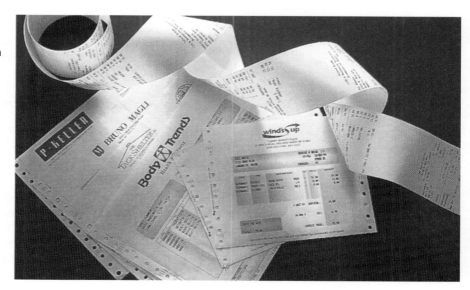

Inventory records indicate the merchandise carried by a firm throughout the year and the turnover of these items. Knowing the lead time to place and receive orders from suppliers, as well as the extra merchandise kept on hand to prevent running out at different times during the year, can aid in planning.

If a firm does primary research, the resultant report should be kept for future use (hopefully in the information control center of a retail information system). When used initially, a report involves primary data. Later reference to it is secondary in nature since the report is no longer used for its primary purpose.

Written reports on company performance are another source of internal secondary data. They may be composed by senior executives, buyers, sales personnel, or stockroom workers. With proper direction, all phases of retail management can be improved through formal report procedures.

External secondary data are available from sources outside the firm. These sources should be consulted if internal information is not sufficient for a decision to be made as to a defined issue. External secondary data sources are comprised of government and non-government categories.

To use external secondary data properly, one should be familiar with appropriate reference guides. They contain listings of written (sometimes computer-based) materials for a specified time. Listings are usually by subject or topic heading. Here are several guides (including computerized data bases), chosen because of their retailing importance. Most are available in any business library or other large library:

- *ABI/INFORM* (data base). Covers hundreds of journals. Articles are classified by subject.
- *Business Index*. Monthly. Completely indexes hundreds of periodicals, including newspapers. Selectively indexes another 900 periodicals.
- *Business Periodicals Index*. Monthly, except for July. Cumulations quarterly, semiannually, and annually. Subject index of hundreds of English-language periodicals.
- *Census Catalog and Guide* (Washington, D.C.: U.S. Bureau of the Census). Cites the programs and services of the Census Bureau. Lists reports, diskettes, microfiche, and maps.
- *Dialog Information Retrieval Service* (data base). Contains hundreds of data bases covering a wide variety of disciplines. Information on public firms, economic data, financial news, and business news.
- *InfoTrac* (data base). Covers hundreds of journals, newspapers, and financial reports in business and other disciplines. Full-text articles and abstracts available (depending on publication).
- *Predicasts F&S Index: Europe*. Monthly. Covers industries and companies. Separate European, International, and U.S. editions.
- *ProQuest* (data base). Covers hundreds of journals, newspapers, and financial reports in business and other disciplines. Full-text articles and abstracts available (depending on publication).
- *Wall Street Journal Index*. Monthly, with quarterly and annual cumulations.

The U.S. Census Bureau has a Web site (www.census.gov/econ/www/retmenu.html) listing its most recent retailing reports, which can be viewed and downloaded from the site.

The government distributes a wide range of printed materials. Here are several publications, chosen for their retailing value. They are available in any business library or other large library:

- *U.S. Census of Retail Trade*. Every five years ending in 2 and 7. Detailed data by retail classification and metropolitan region.
- *U.S. Census of Service Industries*. Every five years ending in 2 and 7. Similar to *Census of Retail Trade* but covers service industries organized by Standard Industrial Classification code.
- *Combined Annual and Revised Monthly U.S. Retail Trade*. Compiled annually. Ten-year statistics on retail sales and retail inventories by kind of business for specified areas and cities.
- *Monthly U.S. Retail Trade Survey*. Retail sales, inventories, and other data by kind of retail category.

- *Statistical Abstract of the United States*. Annually. Detailed summary of U.S. statistics.
- *U.S. Survey of Current Business*. Monthly, with weekly supplements. On all aspects of business.
- *Other*. Registration data (births, deaths, automobile registrations, etc.). Available through federal, state, and local agencies.

Government agencies, such as the Federal Trade Commission, also provide a variety of pamphlets and booklets on topics like franchising, unit pricing, deceptive ads, and credit policies. The Small Business Administration helps smaller retailers, providing literature and managerial advice. Pamphlets and booklets are either distributed free of charge or sold for a nominal fee.

Nongovernment secondary data come from various sources, many of which are listed in reference guides. Four major nongovernment sources are regular periodicals; books, monographs, and other nonregular publications; other channel members; and commercial research houses.

Regular periodicals are available in printed versions at most libraries or by personal subscription. A growing number of publications are also online. Some sites provide free information; others charge a fee. Periodicals may have a broad scope (such as *Business Week*) and discuss diverse business topics; or they may have narrower coverage (such as *Chain Store Age*) and deal mostly with retail topics. It is imperative for readers of periodicals to know the differences in orientation and quality among various publications.

Many organizations publish books, monographs, and other nonregular retailing literature. Some, like Prentice Hall (www.prenhall.com/phbusiness), produce lines of textbooks and practitioner-oriented books. Others have more distinct goals. The American Marketing Association (www.ama.org) distributes information to increase the level of knowledge of readers on various topics. The Better Business Bureau (www.bbb.org) wants to improve the public's image of business and expand industry self-regulation. The International Franchise Association (www.franchise.org) and the National Retail Federation (www.nrf.com) describe industry practices and emerging trends, and act as spokespersons and lobbyists to advocate the best interests of member firms. Besides the associations cited, others can be uncovered by consulting Gale's *Encyclopedia of Associations*.

Retailers can often obtain information from channel members such as advertising agencies, franchise operators, manufacturers, and wholesalers. Whenever these firms do research for their own purposes (such as determining the most effective kind of advertising message) and then present some or all of the findings to their retailers, external secondary data are involved. Channel members will pass on findings to enhance their sales and relations with retailers. They usually do not charge retailers for the information.

The last external source is the commercial research house that conducts ongoing studies and makes results available to many clients for a fee. This source is secondary if the retailer is a subscriber and does not request tailored studies. Among those selling secondary data are Information Resources Inc., A.C. Nielsen, Gallup, and Standard Rate & Data Service. They provide subscriptions at lower costs (and probably with more expertise) than the retailer would incur if data were collected only for its primary use.

Table 8.2 has a listing of selected free online sources of external secondary data—both government and nongovernment. *Please note:* Not all of the information available at these sites may be free.

Primary Data

Advantages and Disadvantages

After a firm has exhausted the available secondary data, its defined issue or problem may still not be resolved. In this instance, primary data (those collected to resolve a specific topic at hand) are necessary. When secondary data research is sufficient, primary data are not collected.

Looking for secondary data on direct marketing (www.colinear.com/resource.htm) or E-commerce (www.webcommercetoday.com/research)? Check out these sites.

Gallup does a variety of syndicated surveys. At its Web site (www.gallup.com), it provides interesting synopses of some of its current work.

Table 8.2 Selected Free Online Sources of External Secondary Data

Advertising Age	www.adage.com
American City Business Journals	www.amcity.com/journals
American Demographics	www.demographics.com
Business Week	www.businessweek.com
Chain Store Age	www.chainstoreage.com
CNN	www.cnn.com
CNN Financial Network	www.cnnfn.com
Convenience Store News	www.csnews.com
Direct	www.directmag.com
Discount Store News	www.discountstorenews.com
DM News	www.dmnews.com
Drug Store News	www.drugstorenews.com
E-Commerce News	www.internetnews.com/ec-news
Entrepreneur	www.enterpreneurmag.com
Fed World	www.fedworld.gov
Forbes	www.forbes.com
Fortune	www.pathfinder.com/fortune
Franchise Handbook	www.franchise1.com
Hoover's Online	www.hoovers.com
Inc.	www.inc.com
Information Please Almanac	www.infoplease.com
International Professional Marketing Journals	marketing.kub.nl/magazine.htm
International Scholarly Marketing Journals	marketing.kub.nl/journal.htm
Library of Congress	www.loc.gov
London Times	www.the-times.co.uk
Marketing News	www.ama.org/pubs/mn
National Home Center News	www.homecenternews.com
NewsPage	www.individual.com
Newsweek International Business Resource Center	www.newsweek-int.com
New York Times	www.nytimes.com
Progressive Grocer	www.progressivegrocer.com
Promo	www.promomagazine.com
Restaurant Business	www.foodservicetoday.com/rb/index.shtml
RT Magazine	www.retailtech.com
Sales & Marketing Management	www.salesandmarketing.com
Stores	www.stores.org
Supermarket Business	www.supermarketbusiness.com
Supermarket News Current Headlines	www.supermarketnews.com/sntodayheadlines.htm
USA Today	www.usatoday.com
U.S. Bureau of the Census	www.census.gov
U.S. Department of Commerce	www.doc.gov
U.S. Small Business Administration	www.sba.gov
Value Retail News	www.valueretailnews.com
Wirthlin Report	www.wirthlin.com/publicns/library.htm

There are several advantages associated with primary data:

- They are collected to fit the retailer's specific purpose.
- Information is current.
- The units of measure and data categories are designed to address the issue or problem being studied.
- The retailer either collects the data itself or hires an outside party to do so. Thus, the source is known and controlled, and the methodology is constructed for the specific study.
- There are no conflicting data from different sources, and research reliability can be determined.
- When secondary data do not resolve an issue or problem, primary data are the only alternative.

There are also several possible disadvantages often associated with primary data:

- They are normally more expensive to obtain than secondary data.
- Information gathering tends to be more time consuming.
- Some types of information cannot be acquired by an individual firm.
- If only primary data are collected, the perspective may be limited.
- Irrelevant information may be collected if the issue is not stated specifically enough.

A retailer desiring information has many criteria to weigh in evaluating the use of primary data. In particular, specificity, currentness, and reliability must be weighed against high costs, time, and limited access to materials. The benefits of primary research must be weighed against the limitations.

A variety of primary data sources for retailers are discussed next.

Want to discover more about the scope of primary data? Go to the Business Research Lab Web site (www.busreslab.com) and click the icons on the left-hand tool bar.

Sources   The first decision is to determine who collects the primary data. A retailer can do this itself (internal) or hire a research firm (external). Internal data collection is usually quicker and cheaper. External data collection is usually more objective and formalized. Second, a sampling methodology is specified. Instead of gathering data from all stores, all products, all customers, and so on, a retailer can obtain accurate data by studying a sample of stores, products, or customers. This saves time and money. With a **probability (random) sample,** every store, product, or customer has an equal or known chance of being chosen for study. In a **nonprobability sample,** stores, products, or customers are chosen by the researcher—based on judgment or convenience. A probability sample is more accurate but is also more costly and difficult to do. Third, the retailer chooses among four basic kinds of data collection: survey, observation, experiment, and simulation. All of these methods are capable of generating data for each element of a retail strategy.

Survey   The **survey** is a research technique whereby information is systematically gathered from respondents by communicating with them. Surveys may be used in a variety of retail settings. For instance, Circuit City surveys thousands of customers each month to determine their satisfaction with the selling process. Spiegel combines an in-house computer-assisted telephone interviewing system with mail questionnaires, small-group personal surveys, and on-site shopper surveys (at its Eddie Bauer stores) to regularly determine customer tastes and needs. Food Lion uses in-store surveys to find out how satisfied its customers are and what their attitudes are on various subjects.

A survey may be conducted in person, over the phone, by mail, or online. In almost all cases, a questionnaire is used. A personal survey is face-to-face, flexible, and able to elicit lengthy responses; and question ambiguity can be explained. It may be costly, and bias is possible (such as interviewers inadvertently suggesting ideas to respondents). A phone survey is fast and relatively inexpensive. Yet, responses are usually short, and nonresponse may be a problem. A mail survey can reach a wide range of respondents, has no interviewer bias, and is relatively inexpensive. Slowness of return, high nonresponse rates, and participation by incorrect respondents are major potential problems. An online survey is very interactive, can be adapted to individual people, and generates fast results. However, the retailer may not have much control over respondent selection (disgruntled customers may use a survey only to gripe rather than to address the overall performance of the retailer), and only certain customers shop online or answer online surveys. The technique chosen depends on the goals and requirements of the research project.

It must also be decided if a survey is to be nondisguised or disguised. In a nondisguised survey, the respondent is told the real purpose of the study. In a disguised survey, the respondent is not told the study's real purpose so that the person does not answer what he or she thinks a firm wants to hear. Disguised surveys can use word associations, sentence completions, cartoon analysis, or projective questions (such as "Do your friends like shopping at this store? Do they find the styles to be in fashion?").

The **semantic differential**—a listing of bipolar adjective scales—is a survey technique that may be disguised or nondisguised. The respondent is asked to rate one or more retailers on several criteria; each criterion is evaluated along a bipolar adjective scale, such as unfriendly–friendly or untidy–neat. By computing the average rating of all respondents for each criterion, an overall store profile can be developed. A semantic differential comparing two furniture retailers appears in Figure 8.8. Store A is a prestige, high-quality store and Store B is a medium-quality, family-run store. The semantic differential reveals the overall images of the stores and graphically portrays them.

Other types of survey-related techniques also can be used, but those described exemplify the usefulness of this primary data tool.

Observation The form of research in which present behavior or the results of past behavior are observed and recorded is known as **observation.** Because people are not questioned as in a survey format, observation may not require the cooperation of respondents, and interviewer or question biases are minimized. In many instances, observation can be used in

Figure 8.8
A Semantic
Differential for Two
Furniture Stores

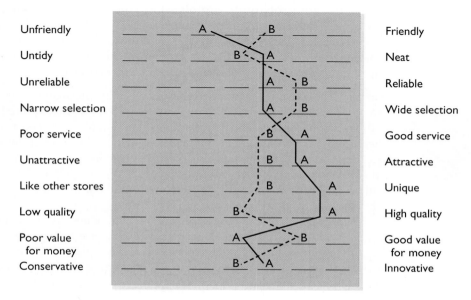

Please check the blanks that best indicate your feelings about Stores A and B.

actual situations, eliminating the influences of artificial environments. The key disadvantage of using observation alone is that attitudes are not elicited.

Retailers can use observation to determine the quality of sales personnel presentations (by having researchers pose as shoppers), to monitor related-item buying by consumers, to determine store activity by time of day and day of week, to make pedestrian and vehicular traffic counts (to measure the potential of new locations), and to determine the proportion of shopping center patrons using public transportation.

With **mystery shoppers,** retailers hire people to pose as customers and observe their operations, from sales presentations to how well displays are maintained to in-home service calls.[22] One marketing research firm, Michelson & Associates, has a nationwide pool of 30,000 mystery shoppers. This is how its mystery shopping research works (rampages.onramp.net/~focus/Mystery_Shopping.html):

> We qualify, train, and manage our shoppers to gather factual information and provide objective observations based on their experience with the front line. Our field reps range from 21 to 70 years of age with the majority being women between age 30 and 45. Our shoppers can be pre-selected based on client criteria such as demographics, type of car, shopping habits, etc. With our program, firms can set customer service guidelines, and monitor and reward excellent performance. Mystery shopping can be used as a marketing and training tool to help ensure a firm's service and operational goals are being met. For best results, management and employees should know they're going to be evaluated by a mystery shopper, but they shouldn't know who the shopper is or when they will be shopped.

Decisions are necessary about whether observation should be disguised or nondisguised, structured or unstructured, direct or indirect, and human or mechanical. In disguised observation, the shopper or company employee is not aware he or she is being watched through a two-way mirror or hidden camera. In nondisguised observation, the participant knows he or she is being observed—such as a department manager observing a cashier's behavior. Structured observation calls for the observer to watch and note specific behavior. Unstructured observation requires the observer to watch and note all of the activities of the person being studied. With direct observation, the observer watches people's present behavior. With indirect observation, the observer examines evidence of past behavior such as food products in consumer pantries. Human observation is carried out by people and is flexible. It may be disguised; but the observer may enter biased interpretations and may miss behavior. Mechanical observation eliminates viewer bias and does not miss behavior. A camera filming in-store shopping is an example of mechanical observation.

Experiment An **experiment** is a type of research in which one or more elements of a retail strategy mix are manipulated under controlled conditions. An element may be an item's price, the layout of a department in a store, a shelf display, or store hours. For instance, if a retailer wants to find out the effects of a price change on a brand's unit sales, only the price of that brand is varied (such as making this week's price $0.99 and next week's $1.19, and then comparing unit sales for each week). The other elements of the retail strategy remain the same. This way, only the effect of the price change is measured.

An experiment may use survey or observation techniques to record data. In a survey, questions are asked about the experiment: Did you buy Brand Z because of its new shelf display? Are you buying more ice cream because it's on sale? In observation, behavior is watched during the experiment: Sales of Brand Z rise by 20 percent when a new display is used. Ice cream sales go up 25 percent during a special sale.

Surveys and observations are experimental if they occur under closely controlled situations. But when surveys ask broad attitude questions or observations of unstructured behav-

Privacy Issues and the Smart Card

A smart card can be as simple as a stored-value credit card and as complex as a student identification card that provides a student with access to campus buildings, serves as payment for meals, and allows library privileges. A single card that can be used for multiple purposes generates a centralized warehouse of data on an individual. For example, sellers could have access to a wide variety of information concerning our names, past purchases, credit card balances, and so on. If all transactions are stored at a single place, the potential for invasion of privacy would be great.

In designing smart cards, retailers need to be concerned about these privacy issues:

- Should they limit their information collection to only those data that are necessary?
- Should they limit their ability to combine information from different data bases?

- Should the disclosure of information to other parties be allowed?

In deciding on smart card regulations, policy makers need to think about these issues:

- Should the government use smart cards to track individuals?
- Should smart card companies be allowed to warehouse data and sell the data to third parties?
- What kinds of disclosure about privacy policies should there be?

As a retailer, how would you assure shoppers that their privacy will not be compromised through smart cards?

Source: "The Smart Card: Is Your Privacy Compromised?" *At Home with Consumers* (December 1998), pp. 1–7.

---

ior occur, experimental procedures are not involved. In a retail setting, an experiment can be hard to undertake since many factors beyond the command of the retailer (such as weather, competition, and the economy) may influence results. On the other hand, a well-controlled experiment can provide a lot of good, specific data.

The major advantage of an experiment lies in its ability to show cause and effect (for instance, a lower price equals higher sales). It is also systematically structured and implemented. The major potential disadvantages are high costs, contrived settings, and uncontrollable factors.

Simulation A type of experiment whereby a computer program is used to manipulate the elements of a retail strategy mix rather than test them in a real setting is **simulation.** Two types of simulations are now being adopted in retail settings: those based on mathematical models and those involving "virtual reality."

For the first type of simulation, a model of the expected controllable and uncontrollable retail environment is constructed. Factors are then manipulated via a computer so their effects on the overall retail strategy and specific elements of it are learned. No consumer cooperation is needed, and many factors and combinations of factors can be analyzed in a controlled, rapid, inexpensive, and risk-free manner. This format is gaining popularity because many retailers' level of mathematical and computer sophistication is improving and good software is more available. Yet, it is still somewhat difficult to use.

With the second type of simulation, a retailer devises or purchases interactive software that lets participants simulate actual behavior in as realistic a format as possible. Although

Figure 8.9
Visionary Shopper:
A Virtual Reality
Simulation

In the Visionary Shopper
application, developed
by Raymond R. Burke
(Indiana University),
consumers use a touch-
screen monitor to pick
up, examine, and pur-
chase products from a
simulated shelf display.
Virtual reality simula-
tions provide marketers
with the realistic com-
petitive context and
behavioral measures of a
test market along with
the low cost, speed,
confidentiality and flexibility of a laboratory
experiment.
Reprinted by permission of
Raymond R. Burke,
Indiana University.

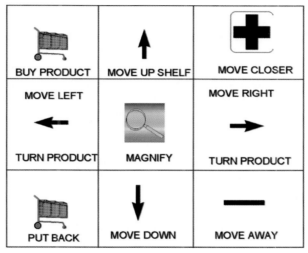

this approach is more futuristic, it creates a "virtual shopping environment." At present, there is limited software for virtual reality simulations and people must be trained to use the software. This is one of the exciting possibilities of virtual reality simulations, from Simulation Research (www.simulationresearch.com):

> Our Visionary Shopper is a unique virtual reality simulation used to test the impact of in-store variables such as price, promotion, and merchandising on consumer pur- chasing behavior. Consumers are seated in front of a large computer monitor and taught to maneuver around the shelf. By using a touchscreen and a small control panel on the monitor screen, they can go left, right, up, down, zoom in or zoom out, just as they would in a normal store. By touching the screen, they can pick up an item from the shelf, turn it around, and look at the product more closely. Touching the magnifying glass icon on the control panel brings up a higher resolution image of the product. Touching the shopping cart icon on the control panel purchases the prod- uct. As of 1999, well over 50 clients in 13 countries had run simulated tests with Visionary Shopper.

See Figure 8.9.

THE DATA COLLECTION ROLE OF RETAILERS IN A DISTRIBUTION CHANNEL

Retailers can have a crucial role in collecting data for members of the value delivery chain due to their position as the last stage in a distribution channel. Of all the firms in a channel, often only retailers have direct contact with and easy access to shoppers.

Retailers can assist other channel members in collecting data by:

- Providing informal feedback on supplier prices, ads, and so on, based on their past experience.
- Allowing data to be gathered on their premises. Many marketing research firms want to conduct interviews at shopping centers because a large and broad base of people is available.
- Gathering specific information requested by suppliers, such as how shoppers react to in-store displays.
- Passing along information on the characteristics of consumers buying particular brands, models, and so on. Because credit transactions account for a major portion of sales, many retailers can link purchases with consumer age, income, occupation, and other factors.
- Participating in single-source data collection by letting their stores have specially equipped computerized checkouts. In **single-source data collection,** a research firm (like Information Resources Inc.) develops a sample of consumer households, determines the demographic and life-style backgrounds of those households via surveys, observes TV viewing behavior via in-home cable hookups to the firm's computers, and monitors shopping behavior by having people make purchases in designated stores. At these stores, consumers present an identification card similar to a credit card; all items bought are then recorded by computerized scanning equipment. This system is more accurate than multi-source data collection (whereby the people surveyed are often different from those whose behavior is observed). It has thus far been mostly limited to purchases in supermarkets and drugstores.

IRI's InfoScan (www.infores.com/public/prodserv/coretrk.htm) is the leading single-source data collection tool in use today.

Through their data warehouses and EDI relationships with suppliers, some retailers are providing extensive data to their channel partners. Over 10,000 suppliers have access to Wal-Mart's data warehouse, which handles more than 120,000 complex information queries each week. Seven thousand suppliers link up with its data warehouse through the Web-based Retail Link program. Sears is also placing greater emphasis on Web communications with suppliers, including 5,500 small vendors who are not computerized enough to get the relevant data in another fashion.[23]

On the negative side, until recently, retailers were unable to obtain information about customer credit card purchases through third-party cards such as MasterCard and Visa. However, in 1999, MasterCard opened up its data warehouse to retailers (and by extension, to the retailers' channel partners). This is how it works:

First, Transactional Data Solutions (TDS) generates a panel of 670,000 randomly selected MasterCard users and tracks their buying habits. To protect consumer privacy, TDS never knows any individual's name or address. "The firewall is always up," says Bill Engel, president and CEO of TDS. By analyzing the panel's aggregated transactions, TDS can cluster consumers by shopping behavior—what they buy, where they shop, how much they spend, and so on. One cluster, for instance, might be 25-to-35-year-old women who shop at upscale department stores. Using a proprietary system, TDS can then mine Simmons research data to define this cluster by looking at media habits, brand preferences, and life-style choices. TDS expects to identify about 40 shopper clusters.[24]

SUMMARY

1. *To show why retailers should systematically collect and analyze information when developing and modifying their strategies.* Whether developing a new retail strategy or modifying an existing one, good information is necessary. Acting on the basis of proper information reduces a retailer's chances of making incorrect decisions. Retailers that rely on nonsystematic or incomplete methods of research, such as intuition, increase their probabilities of failure.

2. *To examine the role of the retail information system, its components, and the recent advances in such systems.* Acquiring useful information should be viewed as an ongoing, well-integrated process. A retail information system anticipates the information needs of retail managers; continuously collects, organizes, and stores relevant data; and directs the flow of information to the proper retail decision makers. Such a system has several components: environment, retailer's philosophy, strategic plans, information control center, and retail operations. The most important component is the information control center. It directs data collection, stores and retrieves data, and updates files.

Data-base management is the procedure used to collect, integrate, apply, and store information related to specific topics (such as customers, vendors, and product categories). Data-base information can come from internal—company-generated—and external—purchased from outside firms—sources. One of the newest advances in data-base management is data warehousing, whereby copies of all the data bases in a firm are maintained in one location and can be accessed by employees at any locale. It is a huge repository separate from the operational data bases set up to support departmental applications. Through data mining and micromarketing, retailers can effectively use their data warehouses to pinpoint the specific needs of customer segments.

In recent years, retailers have greatly increased their use of computerized retail information systems, and the Universal Product Code (UPC) has become the dominant technology for recording and processing product-related data. With electronic data interchange (EDI), the computers of retailers and their suppliers regularly exchange information, sometimes through the Web.

3. *To describe the marketing research process.* Marketing research in retailing involves a process consisting of a series of activities: defining the issue or problem to be researched, examining secondary data, gathering primary data (if needed), analyzing the data, making recommendations, and implementing findings. It is systematic in nature and not a single act. The steps should be sequential.

Secondary data (gathered for other purposes) are inexpensive, can be collected quickly, may have several sources, and may provide otherwise unattainable information. Some sources are quite credible. When the problem is ill defined, a secondary data search can clarify it. There are also potential pitfalls: they may not suit the purposes of the study, units of measurement and categories of data may not be specific enough, information may be old and/or inaccurate, a source may be disreputable and different sources may have conflicting results, and data may not be reliable.

Primary data (gathered for the resolution of the specific topic at hand) are collected if secondary data do not adequately address the issue or problem. They are precise and current, the data are collected and categorized with the units of measures desired, the methodology is known, there are no conflicting results, and the level of reliability can be determined. When secondary data do not exist, primary data are the only alternative. The potential disadvantages of primary data are the costs, time, limited access, narrow perspective, and amassing of irrelevant information.

4. *To discuss the retailer's data collection role.* Retailers often have a vital role in collecting primary data due their position as the final stage in a distribution channel. They can provide informal feedback to suppliers, allow data to be gathered on their premises, assist in monitoring consumer behavior, pass along information on consumer characteristics, and participate in single-source data collection.

Key Terms

retail information system (RIS)
  (p. 252)
data-base management (p. 256)
data warehousing (p. 258)

data mining (p. 259)
micromarketing (p. 260)
Universal Product Code (UPC)
  (p. 261)

electronic data interchange (EDI)
  (p. 263)
marketing research in retailing
  (p. 263)

Key Terms *(continued)*

marketing research process (p. 263)
issue (problem) definition (p. 264)
secondary data (p. 264)
primary data (p. 264)
internal secondary data (p. 267)

external secondary data (p. 268)
probability (random) sample (p. 271)
nonprobability sample (p. 271)
survey (p. 271)
semantic differential (p. 272)

observation (p. 272)
mystery shoppers (p. 273)
experiment (p. 273)
simulation (p. 274)
single-source data collection (p. 276)

Questions for Discussion

1. At the beginning of this chapter, several unsuccessful strategies were described. What types of information gathering and processing would you recommend for each of the following retailers?
   a. Movie theater.
   b. Chain bookstore.
   c. Florist.
   d. Web-based travel agency.

2. Can a retailer ever have too much information? Explain your answer.

3. How could a small retailer devise a retail information system?

4. Explain the relationship among the terms *data warehouse, data mining,* and *micromarketing.*

5. What are the value of the Universal Product Code (UPC) and electronic data interchange (EDI) with regard to the retail information systems of general merchandise retailers?

6. What are the steps in the marketing research process? May any of these steps be skipped? Why or why not?

7. Cite the major advantages and disadvantages of secondary data.

8. As a sporting goods store owner, what kinds of secondary data would you want to obtain from Nike or Reebok?

9. Under which circumstances should a retailer collect primary data?

10. Describe the major advantage of each method of gathering primary data: survey, observation, experiment, and simulation.

11. Develop a 10-item semantic differential for a local restaurant to judge its image. Who should be surveyed? Why?

12. Why would a retailer use mystery shoppers rather than other forms of observation? Are there any instances when you would not recommend their use? Why or why not?

13. Discuss some problems a retailer could face in conducting an in-store display experiment.

14. Comment on "virtual shopping" as a research tool for retailers.

WEB-BASED EXERCISE

A.C. Nielsen (www.acnielsen.com)

Questions

1. Discuss Nielsen's "Retail Measurement" services (part of the "What We Do" section of the Web site).

2. Describe Nielsen's "Consumer Panels" (part of the "What We Do" section of the Web site).

3. Comment on Nielsen's "Multi-Country Services" (part of the "What We Do" section of the Web site).

4. What kinds of retailers are best suited to using the services of A.C. Nielsen? Why?

CHAPTER ENDNOTES

1. Neal Templin, "Undercover with a Hotel Spy," *Wall Street Journal* (May 12, 1999), pp. B1, B6.

2. "Business Intelligence: An Edge for Retailers and Suppliers," *Retail Asia,* as reprinted by Kurt Salmon Associates, *www.kurtsalmon.com/KSA_library/retail_pdf/reprints/Intelligence.PDF* (March 9, 2000).

3. See Susan Reda, "The Outsourcing Solution," *Stores* (*November* 1999), cover story.

4. See Ben Ball, "Drowning in Data," *Progressive Grocer* (September 1999), p. 7.

5. See Matt Nannery, "Star Track," *Chain Store Age* (June 1999), pp. 53–60.

6. "Ernst & Young's 18th Annual Survey of Retail Information Technology," *Chain Store Age* (October 1999), Section 2; and "Ernst & Young's 15th Annual Survey of Retail Information Technology," *Chain Store Age* (September 1996), Section II.

7. Denise Power, "Wilsons Gets Data Faster," *Women's Wear Daily* (June 9, 1999), p. 16.

8. *Sports Authority 1999 Annual Report.*

9. "Donnelley Marketing," *www.nationsjob.com/showcomp.cgi/fids.html* (March 9, 2000).

10. Adapted by the authors from Jeff St. Onge, "Direct Marketing Credos for Today's Banking," *Direct Marketing* (March 1999), p. 56.

11. "Data Warehousing in the Real World," *America's Network* (May 15, 1999), p. 18. See also "Know Your Customer," *Chain Store Age* (January 2000), supplement.

12. Sunny Baker and Kim Baker, "The Best Little Warehouse in Business," *Journal of Business Strategy*, Vol. 20 (May–June 1999), pp. 32–39.

13. Gabrielle Gagnon, "Data Warehousing: An Overview," *PC Magazine* (March 9, 1999), p. 245; and Mark Hammond, "Data Warehousing Braces for Fast Growth," *PC Week* (September 6, 1999), p. 3.

14. "The Consumer in Focus: Making Sense of Data Warehousing," *Chain Store Age* (September 1998), p. 2B; and "Merchandising Systems Spawn Data Warehouses," *Chain Store Age* (September 1999), pp. 80, 82.

15. William J. Holstein, "Data-Crunching Santa," *U.S. News & World Report* (December 21, 1998), pp. 44–45; and William M. Bulkeley, "NCR Pumps Up Its Data Warehousing Drive," *Wall Street Journal* (October 14, 1999), p. B6.

16. Jennifer Lach, "Data Mining Digs In," *American Demographics* (July 1999), p. 39.

17. Ibid., pp. 40, 42.

18. Ibid., p. 42.

19. "Universal Product Code Turns 25," *Industrial Distribution* (October 1999), p. A7.

20. Thomas J. Wall, "The ABCs of EDI," *Sales & Marketing Management* (June 1996), SMT supplement, pp. 30–33.

21. Susan Reda, "Internet-EDI Initiatives Show Potential to Reinvent Supply Chain Management," *Stores* (January 1999), p. 26.

22. For more information, see Adam Finn and Ujwal Kayandé, "Unmasking a Phantom: A Psychometric Assessment of Mystery Shopping," *Journal of Retailing*, Vol. 75 (Summer 1999), pp. 195–217.

23. "Hungry Suppliers Take Byte Out of Wal-Mart," *Chain Store Age* (October 1999), p. 120; and Michael Hartnett, "Outside Firm Helps Sears Bring Small Vendors into EDI Compliance," *Stores* (February 1999), p. 80.

24. Jennifer Lach, "In the (Credit) Cards," *American Demographics* (April 1999), p. 43.

CASE 1

TOURING WITH MOUNTAIN TRAVEL SOBEK

Mountain Travel and Sobek were originally two separate companies—with the former specializing in adventure tours to remote areas and the latter focusing on boating and rafting expeditions. In 1991, the firms merged and became Mountain Travel Sobek (MTS). Today, it is the largest, most comprehensive adventure travel firm in the world. It offers more than 100 different trips to 60 countries on 6 continents.

CASE 1
(CONTINUED)

It is difficult to summarize the demographics of MTS' target market because customers range in age from their late 20s to their middle 80s. Yet, all can be grouped by life-style. They are "spirited" people who like being physically active in touring and who enjoy trekking, rafting, and kayaking. MTS trips include "The Galapagos Islands," "Kenya Wilderness Safari," "Along the Turquoise Coast," "Antarctic Circle & Beyond," "Biking in Provence," "The Everest Escapade," and "Paddling the Heart of Portugal."

Although MTS is best known for its challenging trips aimed at hardy travelers, about one-third of its vacations consist of easier itineraries. MTS measures the extent of physical involvement on a trip using a rating scale from 1 to 5, with 1 being the easiest and 5 denoting the most strenuous activities. A 1 could denote a small boat cruise, a wildlife trip, or a game-viewing safari, while 5 could indicate a high-altitude, long distance trek or a river trip that requires travelers to have previous paddling experience.

One popular tour is the 140-mile trek through tundra, mountain trail, and forest in Arctic National Park, one of Alaska's true wilderness regions. Participants get three days of instruction in dogsled handling, winter survival, and camping techniques from a tour guide who is a veteran of Arctic expeditions. Because dogsleds cannot carry the participants for the entire 16-day trip, travelers are expected to ski alongside the sleds for long stretches of time. The land-only cost of this trip was recently priced at $4,460 per person.

MTS knows that even though most of its participants would rather not travel as part of a group, it can still attract them to group tours through a retail strategy featuring specially selected guides, itineraries, and accommodations. At MTS, the tour guide is seen by travelers as their link to another culture due to the guide's language skills, cultural understanding, environmental understanding, and people skills.

Accommodations on a typical MTS tour are clearly *not* designed for guests who want to be pampered. Lodgings may range from an eco-lodge in the heart of the Ecuadorian Amazon to a deluxe, tented camp site in Africa to a renovated farmhouse in the heart of Tuscany. In larger cities, MTS guests stay at first-class hotels with all the amenities. However, these accommodations are generally away from typical tourist locations, well-traveled routes, and tourist-type lodgings. For example, bathing facilities can range from a bucket bath to a solar-heated shower.

Questions

1. Give an example of how MTS could gather customer information in a nonsystematic manner. Also come up with an example of its engaging in systematic data collection. Which of the two approaches do you think MTS uses? Why?

2. Why should MTS develop a retail information system? What information should be included in it?

3. It is estimated that about 7 million American travelers vacation through the adventure travel business. How can this estimate be validated through secondary data?

4. Devise and explain a 10-item semantic differential for MTS to utilize to learn more about how people perceive its image and services.

Video Questions on MTS

1. Design a research study to determine the special needs of older consumers for adventure travel.

2. Describe the difficulties in researching a customer niche as opposed to a mass market.

NOTE The material in this case is drawn from *www.mtsobek.com;* "Mountain Travel Sobek Puts Clients in the Musher's Seat," *Travel Weekly* (January 20, 1997), p. 55; and Jorge Sidron, "Mountain Travel Sobek Marks 30th Year with One-Time Plans," *Travel Weekly* (March 8, 1999), p. 54.

CASE 2

OBI: DATA WAREHOUSING AT GERMANY'S HOME IMPROVEMENT GIANT

The $3.5 billion, Wermelskirchen, Germany-based OBI chain of more than 300 home improvement stores is allowing its franchisees to remotely access the firm's massive data warehouse. All that the franchisees need are a computer, a Web browser, and an overriding desire to one-up the competition.

Even though most store managers have had access to the data base only since January 1998, OBI chief executive Joachim Zinke says many of them are already milking this innovative marriage of Internet and data-warehousing technologies: "The heavy users are telling me they've been able to lower the value of inventory they are holding by 15 percent with no detrimental effect on sales. They've cut the amount of capital tied up in inventory by identifying lower-turning items and trimming their stocks accordingly. That has freed up space to vary assortments and helped increase the turns of fast-moving items."

All OBI franchisees are required to use the same computer systems to gather point-of-sale data at stores, which makes transfer to the data warehouse easy. "Franchisees can choose their own hardware as long as it meets the requirements of the OBI software they must use," Zinke says. "We give franchisees a pretty free rein. It's up to them to get the most out of the tools we've put in front of them. We don't, for example, produce standard reports and broadcast them to stores. Store managers can go online and access those reports. If the reports don't account for every factor, they can query the warehouse independently. We've taken the position that every single user in the system needs his own individual data and views."

OBI doesn't easily fit into the profile of any U.S. retailer. Its stores look and feel like Home Depot or Lowe's outlets, but the firm is 100 percent franchised. Its highly idiosyncratic mix of merchandise within the stores also contradicts its "chain" identity. The strategy within OBI is to recognize that demand differs considerably from store to store and to encourage franchisees to localize their merchandise.

According to Zinke, "The stores will take a lot of the same merchandise, but the store-specific part of the assortment could be as high as 25 percent. It averages about 10 percent." The unique items that OBI franchisees carry are not available in other parts of the country. They are local products that consumers expect local retailers to offer.

Franchisees have a great deal of flexibility in terms of the information they access and the formats in which they access it. One of the most useful formats allows a store manager to compare how individual SKUs or broad categories are doing in his or her store vs. 5 other OBI stores of the manager's choosing. However, store-to-store comparisons are not available to protect each franchisee's privacy.

Store managers have put the available information to good use. They've remerchandised areas of their stores, adjusted stock levels, enacted store-specific promotions, and experimented with raising and lowering prices. At OBI, those are all decisions made at the store level. "Store managers use the data warehouse to plan promotions and to get a feel for how comparable merchandise from different vendors performs in their stores," Zinke says. "And, by putting together a Web-based solution, we will easily be able to open up warehouse access to our vendors and partners if we choose to in the future. Access is essentially the same for internal and external users."

CASE 2

(CONTINUED)

Questions

1. Describe the pros and cons of OBI's retail information system.

2. How does OBI use its retail information system to do micromarketing? How could it do more?

3. Should a store manager be able to determine how an SKU is doing relative to another particular store (and not just another group of stores)? Explain your answer.

4. State the pros and cons of OBI's opening its retail information system up to suppliers.

NOTE

The material in this case is adapted by the authors from Matt Nannery, "OBI's Uncommon Market" *Chain Store Age* (May 1998), pp. 135–38. Copyright Lebhar-Friedman, Inc., 425 Park Avenue, New York, NY 10022. Reprinted by permission.

PART THREE
COMPREHENSIVE CASE

Streamline, Inc.: Building a Life-Style Solution

INTRODUCTION

Is a retailer's core asset its products or its customers? This is a fundamental strategic issue. Historically, most retailers have been merchandise-driven firms with initiative focused on selling tangible goods. The proliferation of category killers show the maturity of a product-centered orientation. However, a rapid change in customer priorities and the emergence of E-commerce have catalyzed widespread experiments with new business models. While many new designs will fail, this activity has unquestionably increased retail innovation and created fertile opportunities for new entrants who offer a superior value proposition.

One wave to watch will be "solution killers." They understand that the asset with maximum leverage is the consumer relationship, not products or store infrastructure. They focus on value aggregation around a specific target customer. Thus, their focus is on pooling demand, not supply, to acquire and grow a profitable relationship. Emphasis goes from getting new customers to selling more to the same customers.

In this model, the retailer becomes a horizontal brand that bundles highly relevant products and information for a well-defined clientele. This shift in strategy moves a retailer from selling to customer relationship management. In the process, profound changes in traditional business practices will alter the entire way of delivering value, including how a firm selects customers, defines offerings, and configures resources to create customer utility. For retailers willing to defy convention and forge new paths to please customers, the solution killer payoff is significant. The premise of such a strategy is that share of loyal customers, not share of market, maximizes profits. This is manifested in terms of the greater number of items sold per transaction, higher average order size, and increased ordering. Most importantly, sustained cus-tomer satisfaction—the key driver of loyalty and long-term profits—is dramatically enhanced.

STREAMLINE: A HOMEGROWN SUCCESS

In 1993, Streamline founder and CEO, Tim DeMello, originated the concept and mission of Streamline (www.streamline.com)—to consolidate routine household purchases for busy families. He believed the convergence of two major trends—the time famine of dual-income families and the increasing use of technology in the household—would make Streamline's services popular. His vision was to offer a comprehensive life-style solution to let people browse, buy, and receive the precise products, services, and information they need in the most convenient way. The company's proposition consisted of three complementary elements:

- A simpler and better personalized shopping experience.
- A targeted necessity-based offering of products and services.
- Weekly home delivery to a proprietary on-site receptacle accessible at the customer's home.

The consumer paid competitive prices and a $30 monthly subscription fee. DeMello believed such a service would attract a lot of consumer interest and venture financing. To better explore the opportunity, he pulled together $1.7 million from individual investors, in addition to his personal investment of $45,000 as "seed money." His goal was to pilot direct-to-home delivery in the suburban Boston market.

ORIGINATING A LIFE-STYLE SOLUTION BRAND

The original Streamline strategy was to gauge consumer reaction to a company serving as a single source fulfilling multiple needs. Although many advisors argued for conventional research and focus groups, the Streamline team felt the only real test of the radically new customer experience was consumers' actual use of the service. Streamline recruited some customers to test the service concept and the effects of brand, customer segment, pricing, product offering, ordering method, and fulfillment strategy.

After servicing a group of 50 test customers around Westwood, Massachusetts, the Streamline team con-

The material in this case is adapted by the authors from Frank F. Britt, "Building a Life-Style Solution Brand: The Unfolding Story of Streamline, Inc.," *Arthur Andersen Retailing Issues Letter* (July 1998), pp. 1–6. Reprinted by permission.

cluded that it was "an idea waiting to happen." The experiment had worked. Rather than limiting the scope of goods and services, the firm found that customers wanted much more than groceries delivered to their home. The team also began to understand its most valuable asset was not the product it sold but the customer to whom it sold. Insights gained by intensely focusing and understanding a specific target market could accelerate value creation and provide a sustainable competitive advantage.

The customization required by each household made it hard to forecast how the business could be operated at scale or made profitable over time. Moreover, the total capital required for facilities and technology was unclear. The result was a semicoherent direction that remained somewhat unpredictable, maybe even less efficient, but one that would prove more robust and effective. The team sought to raise additional venture capital to study more about how direct delivery of goods might become profitable.

EVOLVING A BUSINESS DESIGN

Streamline, like most early-stage companies, expended significant energy building credibility and stating the merits of its business model and industry opportunity. To support an accelerated rate of development, a framework for real-time strategic management was crafted that focused on four priorities.

Establishing Marketplace Credibility

The company and the emerging consumer-direct industry achieved a milestone when it and 15 leading food and packaged goods providers participated in an industry-wide Andersen Consulting study. The Consumer Direct Cooperative provided Streamline with short-term cash, credibility, and key contacts. The study provided objective analytical validation of the market opportunity and business model, such as:

- Consumer trends that underlie a channel's appeal—having a busy, diverse, technologically enabled population base—will only intensify over the next decade.
- Consumer-direct as a channel is capable of generating substantial sales in the United States, with 15 million to 20 million households becoming regular users by 2007.
- Picking the business model is critical—Streamline's fulfillment center is essential to profitability.

In the meantime, Saul Steinberg, chairman of Reliance Insurance, whose analysts had turned down Streamline for financing a few months earlier, called DeMello after reading about the firm's early results and its involvement in the industry study. Steinberg, a highly successful entrepreneur, agreed to fund $5 million for 40 percent of the company to support the next development phase of the business.

Building a Senior Management Team

Choosing management talent for an early-stage firm affects long-term viability and capital-raising potential. Moreover, beyond the founder, much of the culture and competence of a firm arise from the personalities, desires, and talents of senior management. Accordingly, Streamline set about to build an executive team committed to "investing" their careers in a still unproven business model that could seize a new opportunity. The team had to meld the capabilities and attributes needed to pioneer and profitably grow: expertise and capabilities in early-stage company formation, customer information management, interactive E-commerce, food and packaged goods marketing and operations, and goods/service retailing. Over a one-year period, the company assembled a management team with the credentials and capabilities needed to accelerate business model development.

Acquiring a Portfolio of Strategic Alliances

A third key emphasis was to acquire and foster high-impact partnerships. This would create a barrier to entry and accelerate time-to-scale. Streamline concluded its initial phase of partner acquisition in fall 1997 with the announcement of $10 million in second-round financing from Intel, GE Capital, SAP America, and Paine Webber.

Hardening the Business Model

Streamline's experiment helped move the team toward a business model with three mutually reinforcing elements that together would create superior customer value—a busy suburban family focus, a life-style solution offering, and an innovative set of physical and information processes.

Customer Selection   Streamline organized around a core customer segment and then defined its required business competencies, rather than the more traditional inside-out model. Following the test and supplemental research, the busy suburban family was selected based on a blend of age, income, family composition, and life-style. These consumers had higher levels of education and information technology savvy. Further, a home-based shopping service could better fulfill their unique values, including personalization, relationship, control, choice, service, and stress mitigation. This, together with their purchasing power, made the group ideal.

Life-Style Solutions The company based its goods and service assortment on the overarching principle that Streamline be a "value aggregator" by optimizing the level of choice for a specific audience. This meant subordinating traditional assortment guidelines such as sales volume, gross margins, and product line synergies. Instead, Streamline was guided by the need to deliver a simpler and better shopping experience while growing a high-value relationship. Specifically, the selected offerings needed to be trust-based, purchased often, and either consumable, renewable, or disposable. Items such as groceries, prepared meals, videos, flowers, dry cleaning, specialty pet food, film processing, bottled water, postal pick-up, community programs, and can redemption meet the criteria. The premise of this strategy is that trust, value, and frequency of interaction enhance customer loyalty in nearly any relationship context. The necessity-based nature of the offering virtually ensured substantial recurring revenue and a sustained customer relationship.

Consumers appreciate the company helping sift through the assortment chaos and downsizing their choices to manageable levels. While Streamline carries about one-third of the items of a supermarket, the target consumer views the assortment as robust and well suited to their unique needs. This occurs by ignoring the broad spectrum of the shopping population and appealing to a defined set of households. The tighter selection reduces the cost of complexity in operations and merchandising typically driven by excess numbers of SKUs, the majority of which represent a modest amount of actual sales. In the process, rather than emerge as a narrow retailer offering only groceries, videos, dry cleaning, or even delivery, Streamline was positioned as a life-style solution that bundles physical and information content most relevant to the target audience. In this sense, Streamline makes a promise and delivers on it, saving the consumer a lot of time. As a result, the firm can obtain a bigger share of wallet from the target household.

Ultimately, performance tells the story. On average, a Streamline customer orders 47 out of 52 weeks a year, average order size exceeds $100, and loyalty rates exceed 90 percent annually. In contrast, the average Amazon.com cus-

tomer orders 4 times yearly and spends $30 per order. Attrition at America Online exceeds 15 percent monthly. Peapod gets 8 to 9 orders per customer annually. Streamline's annual $5,000-plus per subscriber ranks among the highest revenue per user of any online merchant.

Two Core Processes The envisioned processes required proprietary physical and information channels connecting Streamline and the busy suburban family. The physical channel would facilitate the distribution of goods and services to customers, as well as the reverse flow of "processed" products, such as videos, dry cleaning, and film. The information channel would let Streamline communicate directly with the household and get feedback from the customer via phone, fax, or online. The virtual channel also would allow Streamline to develop a comprehensive data base and insights into household purchasing patterns and behaviors.

Physical Channel: Making It Work Streamline's physical channel is the single most important factor affecting customer loyalty and profits. Yet, structuring a low-cost, direct fulfillment infrastructure is complex, costly, and not easily duplicated. The current supply chain consists of three elements.

Product fulfillment is the highest direct cost of processing an order. Streamline has implemented a dedicated facility strategy that provides lower cost of real-estate, reduced inventory investment, and enhanced picking productivity via automation scale economics and facility layout. This differs from the conventional grocery distribution center, where the emphasis is on moving pallets and cases in bulk quantities to the store level. Streamline's goal is to pick each 50- to 60-item order perfectly. Doing the math illustrates the challenge. For an average 60-item order, achieving a respectable 99 percent line-item picking accuracy means only 55 percent of orders would be perfect.

Delivery capabilities involve the physical logistics of moving products directly to customer homes. For Streamline, this means placing products from three temperature zones into secure containers and loading them into a multiple-temperature vehicle to maintain quality. In scheduling, home-delivery models such as Peapod are on-demand approaches with higher costs due to not-at-homes and demand uncertainty. Streamline has unattended delivery and guarantees arrival by 6:00 P.M. Enabled by routing software, this allows better load balancing, greater route density, and lower operating costs.

The Streamline service box at the consumer's home (typically in the garage) frees the consumer's time for other activities. Streamline believes the more typical requirement of being at home often cancels out the time saving that makes the service compelling. A patented delivery receptacle enables the driver to deliver orders without interacting with household members. It is a combination refrigerator, freezer, and dry storage cabinet, allowing ordered items to be stored in three temperature environments.

Virtual Channel: Making It Work Streamline's proprietary information channel is the core element of a shopping experience that goes well beyond simply goods and services. It is an interactive relationship that bonds the buyer. At the heart of the customer contact approach is the premise that embedding intelligence, information, and service can increase the value of any product. To achieve this goal, Streamline has built a relationship management system working to create a cogent experience across key customer "touch points." These capabilities enable customer-driven practices in three major areas.

Streamline can be the customer's shopping assistant, making the experience efficient and effective. An interactive marketing capability combined with extensive content, such as digital product images and nutritional information, delivers relevant data at the point of purchase. This yields marketing performance that far exceeds other advertising media such as traditional Web banners, TV, radio, print, and even direct response. In traditional retail outlets, in-store customer assistance is limited. The store is constrained in what it knows, and when and how often it can interact with the consumers. Purchases are largely transactional with no real customer dialog and devoid of effective ways to measure customer satisfaction. This situation is exacerbated by the fact that the traditional marketing model erodes consumer trust by requiring producers to pay retailers up-front for shelf space and co-marketing, which, by definition, means making consumers' needs subordinate to retailers' self-interests.

Order processing takes place either by phone, fax, or computer. Online order acquisition is the least costly and most accurate method because the consumer does the "heavy lifting." Today, more than 65 percent of Streamline's orders are placed online, and that is trending higher due to the superior functionality and faster shopping experience. These orders are automatically synchronized with the product fulfillment systems that aggregate orders by temperature zone, truck route, and customer.

There is a well-defined set of escalation rules, triggered by the severity of issues and customer profiles. A formal recovery management process was developed for counteracting bad experiences such as incorrect orders and mistaken billing. For example, poor quality grapes in a $100 order warrant immediate credit and an apology. But the resolution could be elevated based on the customer value and complaint history to include immediate redelivery and free goods. Understanding the economic, service, and customer-specific tradeoffs has proven essential in transforming mistakes into customer loyalty.

LESSONS LEARNED: A CONSUMER-DIRECT PRACTITIONER'S PERSPECTIVE

The Streamline story provides insights into the lessons of evolving a new retail format rather than assembling all the pieces at once. In the process, it is clearer how this demand-driven strategy and channel will begin reshaping the basic assumptions of store retailing and consumer relationship management.

Online Shopping Reality

Successful online shopping experiences for low-risk items like books will lead consumers through a natural continuum where they logically seek out new categories for online purchases. Given its high frequency and information-dependent nature, online consumable shopping such as groceries is a natural transition for consumers who want simplicity and value. This will push the adoption of online services to achieve critical mass faster than most people currently expect.

No Substitute for Experience

A challenge in the formative stage of a new business and industry such as consumer direct is how to test a customer experience that does not fully exist yet. Therefore, evaluating a consumer-preferred brand and business model cannot be viewed as a single analytical assessment but rather as the encapsulation of an actual, customer-experienced value. It is not only difficult but also impossible to know beforehand how the myriad components will interact to create the final system. In addition, what consumers think of a service hardly matters unless it affects their behavior. Actual experience moves a brand from a cluster of values around a product to fulfillment of consumers' needs. This creates meaning, which then modifies behavior, and it is behavior that generates deeply felt attitudes.

In the near term, it is new competitors, rather than entrenched incumbents, that will likely set off new waves of change based on different assumptions and without the usual physical store constraints. The early winners in the channel will be bold and not simply rely on applying traditional techniques. They may invest in an interactive, personalized shopping experience based on assumptions and capabilities not yet invented. Rather than test in a vacuum or research study, they will seek to understand a consumer's entire experience with the service, including how the firm responds to service issues.

Not a Traditional Store

A consumer-direct experience inherently differs from a store-based one and requires an infrastructure of distribution, support, and service to be in place when and how the consumer wants it. However, online shopping capabilities represent only one element of a viable consumer-direct enterprise that consistently delivers value. While some traditional retail capabilities can be applied to the consumer-direct channel, many points of in-store differentiation such as fast checkout, convenient location, and innovative store merchandising offer no consumer value. In fact, in many cases, the traditional value chain assumptions psychologically impede innovation. Delivering a superior in-home shopping experience requires new capabilities such as in-home merchandising, individualized customer order fulfillment, home delivery, interactive marketing, household-level performance measures, and cross-industry strategic alliances.

At what point do targeted, interactive marketing efforts collide with product-centered category management practices? If category management analysis calls for eliminating an item that a small subset of your best customers favor, how do you balance the need to satisfy the 25 percent of customers that account for 75 percent of profits? Addressing this issue requires a reorientation from viewing categories based on historical transactions and a broad spectrum of the shopping population to analyzing their appeal to a defined set of target households.

Plan for Uncertainty

The enduring competitive advantage in the consumer-direct channel will be the relationship management system, a retail process that brings the right product and information together to make a complex process simple for the consumer. Barriers to entry will be not only the business model but also the ability to adaptively innovate and consistently execute. This mandates investment and integration of vastly different capabilities, such as direct

marketing, more customer-tailored logistics, online shopping, and real-time customer service, which makes managing complexity the key barrier to entry. Service quality, measured in customer satisfaction and loyalty, will emerge as the only true measure of success.

The challenging aspect of planning physical plant, systems, and personnel is the need to build in the assumption of continuing change. Designs must be definitive enough to justify significant investment and commitment but flexible enough to leave the door open for unforeseeable opportunities. What is becoming clearer to most providers is that complexity in fulfillment and electronic commerce cannot be ignored or even greatly reduced; instead, that complexity must be embraced and systematized. Advanced information technology and flexible infrastructure are the key enablers because they permit scaleable personalization that goes far beyond human capabilities and enables excellent service.

Winners will be flexible and innovative. In this journey, the customer, rather than the products, must be at the center of the organizational mission.

Questions

1. Is a retailer's core asset its products or its customers? Explain your answer.
2. Describe the customer market that Streamline is targeting. Do you agree with its choice? Why or why not?
3. What is a "solution killer"? Do you think that Streamline is doing a good job as a solution killer? Explain your answer.
4. Comment on these statements: "While Streamline carries about one-third of the items of a supermarket, the target consumer views the assortment as robust and well suited to their needs. This occurs by ignoring the broad spectrum of the shopping population and appealing to a defined set of households."
5. From a marketing research perspective, what is the value of the Andersen Consulting study reported in the case for Streamline?
6. Do you agree with Streamline that only research conducted in the field under actual conditions was useful to test the "radically new customer experience" it was planning to offer? Why or why not?
7. Discuss the competitive advantage of Streamline's propriety information channel.

CHOOSING A STORE LOCATION

■ Once a retailer conducts a situation analysis, sets goals, and identifies consumer characteristics and needs, it is ready to develop and enact an overall strategy. In Parts Four through Seven, the major elements of such a strategy are examined: choosing a store location, managing a business, merchandise management and pricing, and communicating with the customer. Part Four concentrates on store location.

■ Chapter 9 discusses the crucial nature of store location for retailers and outlines a four-step approach to location planning. Step 1, trading-area analysis, is covered in this chapter. Among the topics studied are the use of geographic information systems, the size and shape of trading areas, how to determine trading areas for existing and new stores, and the major factors to consider in assessing trading areas. Several data sources are described.

■ Chapter 10 deals with the last three steps in location planning: deciding on the most desirable type of location, selecting a general location, and choosing a particular site within that location. Isolated store, unplanned business district, and planned shopping center locales are contrasted. Criteria for evaluating each location are outlined and detailed.

CHAPTER 9

Trading-Area Analysis

CHAPTER OBJECTIVES

1. To demonstrate the importance of store location for a retailer and outline the process for choosing a store location
2. To discuss the concept of a trading area and its related components
3. To show how trading areas may be delineated for existing and new stores
4. To examine three major factors in tradings-area analysis: population characteristics, economic base characteristics, and competition and the level of saturation

Franklin "Chip" Mortimer II (a third-generation retailer) is the president and chief executive officer of Mortimer Lumber (www.mortimerlumber.com), a five-store chain based in Port Huron, Michigan. What has made Mortimer Lumber so successful during its 50-year history are its long-term relationships with its customers and its extensive community involvement.

When an article recently appeared in a local Port Huron newspaper stating that Lowe's was opening across the street from Home Depot, it featured a quote from a Port Huron resident, Barbara Sawher. "I don't know how our community can support these two large stores. But they really don't matter to me and my husband. We believe in participating with businesses that are owned and operated by local people in our community, like Mortimer Lumber."

After seeing the article, Franklin Mortimer sent Mrs. Sawher a letter with a gift certificate, thanking her for the nice comments. Several weeks later, Mrs. Sawher sent back a note expressing appreciation for the gift and acknowledging the friendliness of Mortimer Lumber's staff and their effort to "go the extra mile to help each customer."

According to Chip Mortimer, "We've always had competition, but what are Home Depot and Lowe's going to do for the community? We sit on school boards and Girl Scouts, as well as sports programs in the community. We are constantly telling community organizations, 'yes, we will help.' "[1]

OVERVIEW

Since more than 90 percent of retail sales are made at stores, the selection of a store location is one of the most significant strategic decisions a typical retailer makes. This chapter and Chapter 10 explain why the choice of the proper store location is so crucial; and they describe the steps a retailer should take in choosing a location for a store and deciding whether to build, lease, or purchase facilities.

> *Please Note:* Web site addresses are constantly changing.
> The links in this chapter are current as of the publication of this book.

THE IMPORTANCE OF LOCATION TO A RETAILER

The Site Selection Toolkit (www.bizsites.com/Toolkit/sitetoolkit.html) has a wealth of helpful links for location planning.

The importance of store location must not be underestimated. Location decisions can be complex, costs can be quite high, there is often little flexibility once a location has been chosen, and the attributes of a location have a strong impact on the retailer's overall strategy: "No matter how good its offering, merchandising, or customer service, every retail company still has to contend with three critical elements of success: location, location, and location."[2] See Figure 9.1.

In general, a good location may let a retailer succeed even if its strategy mix is mediocre. A hospital gift shop may do well, although its merchandise assortment is limited, prices are above-average, and it does not advertise. On the other hand, a poor location may be such a liability that even the most able retailer is unable to overcome it. A mom-and-pop grocery store may not do well if it is situated across the street from a food-based superstore; although the small firm features personal service and long hours, it cannot match the superstore's product selection and prices. Yet, at a different site, it might do fine.

The selection of a store location may require extensive decision making due to the number of criteria considered. These include the size and characteristics of the surrounding population, the level of competition, access to transportation, the availability of parking, the attributes of nearby stores, property costs, the length of the agreement, population trends, legal restrictions, and other factors.

Figure 9.1
Atlanta's Perimeter Mall: Demonstrating the Importance of Location

Perimeter Mall is located in northern Atlanta off the 285 Beltway. It has access to office workers and hotel visitors, as well as affluent residents of Atlanta. North Atlanta houses 75 percent of all $50,000+ households in the Atlanta metro area. The central Perimeter area includes 22 million square feet of office space—the largest concentration in the metro area. The 17 hotels with 3,820 rooms in the Perimeter area attract 1.3 million guest visits annually. The Perimeter Mall draws from a large trade area, with a radius of 15+ miles. The more than 900,000 trade area residents account for 50–55 percent of sales. The many corporations and businesses adjacent to Perimeter Mall help the center save 30 percent of sales for Atlanta residents who live outside the trade area. Out-of-town visitors represent another 15–20 percent of sales. They shop Perimeter Mall once per month due to frequent visitation from residents of Augusta (150 miles), Chattanooga (100 miles), and Birmingham (200 miles).
Reprinted by permission of The Rouse Company.

A store location may necessitate a sizable financial investment and a long-term commitment by the retailer. Even a firm seeking to minimize its investment by leasing (rather than owning a building and land) can have a major investment. Besides lease payments that are locked in for the term of an agreement, a retailer must spend money on lighting, fixtures, the storefront, and so on.

Although leases of less than 5 years are common in less desirable retailing locations, leases in good shopping centers or shopping districts are often 5 to 10 years or more. It is not uncommon for a supermarket site to be leased for 15, 20, or 30 years. Department stores and large specialty stores on major downtown thoroughfares have been known occasionally to sign leases longer than 30 years.

Because of its fixed nature, the amount of the investment, and the length of lease agreements, store location is the least flexible element of a retailer's strategy mix. A firm such as a department store cannot easily move to another site or be converted into another type of retail operation. In contrast, advertising, prices, customer services, and the product assortment can be modified more quickly if the environment (consumers, competition, the economy, and so on) changes. Furthermore, if a retailer breaks a lease, it may be responsible to the property owner for any financial damages incurred. In some instances, a retailer may be prohibited from subleasing its location to another party during the term of an agreement.

A retailer owning the building and land on which it is situated may also find it hard to change locations. It would have to find an acceptable buyer, which might take several months or longer; and it may have to assist the buyer in financing the property. It may incur a financial loss, should it sell during an economic downturn.

Any retailer moving from one location to another faces three potential problems. First, some loyal customers and employees may be lost; the greater the distance between the old and the new locations, the greater the loss. Second, a new location may not possess the same characteristics as the original one. Third, the store fixtures and renovations at an old location often cannot be transferred to a new one; their remaining value is lost if they have not been fully depreciated.

Store location has a strong impact on both long-run and short-run planning. In the long run, the choice of a location affects the firm's overall strategy. The retailer needs to be at a store site that will be consistent with its organizational mission, goals, and target market for an extended period. The firm also must regularly study and monitor the status of its location regarding population trends, the distances people travel to the store, and the entry and exit of competitors—and to adapt long-run plans accordingly.

In the short run, store location influences the specific elements of a retail strategy mix (product assortment, prices, promotion, and so on). A retailer in a downtown area populated by office buildings may have little pedestrian traffic on weekends. Therefore, it would probably be improper to sell items such as major appliances at this site (because these items are commonly purchased jointly by husbands and wives). The retailer would have to either close on weekends and not stock certain types of products or remain open on weekends and try to attract customers to the area by extensive promotion or aggressive pricing. If the retailer closes on weekends, it is adapting its strategy mix to the attributes of the location. If it stays open, it must invest additional resources in advertising to attempt to alter consumer buying habits. A retailer trying to overcome its location, by and large, faces greater risks than one adapting to its site.

In choosing a store location, retailers should follow these four steps:

1. Evaluate alternate geographic (trading) areas in terms of the characteristics of residents and existing retailers.

2. Determine whether to locate as an isolated store, in an unplanned business district, or in a planned shopping center within the geographic area.

3. Select the general isolated store, unplanned business district, or planned shopping center location.

4. Analyze alternate sites contained in the specified retail location type.

This chapter concentrates on Step 1. Chapter 10 details Steps 2, 3, and 4. The selection of a store location is a process involving each of these steps.

TRADING-AREA ANALYSIS

A **trading area** is "a geographical area containing the customers of a particular firm or group of firms for specific goods or services."[3] It is also defined as

> A district the size of which is usually determined by the boundaries within which it is economical in terms of volume and cost for a marketing unit or group to sell and/or deliver a good or service.[4]

The first step in the choice of a retail store location is to describe and evaluate alternate trading areas and then decide on the most desirable one. After a trading area is picked, it should be reviewed regularly.

A thorough analysis of trading areas provides the retailer with several benefits:

- Demographic and socioeconomic characteristics of consumers can be detailed, based on government and other published data. For a new store, the study of proposed trading areas reveals market opportunities and the retail strategy necessary for success. For an existing store, it can be determined if the current retail strategy still matches the needs of consumers.

- The focus of promotional activities can be determined. A retailer finding that 95 percent of customers live within three miles of a store would find it inefficient to advertise in a newspaper with a citywide audience. To avoid this problem, the retailer could look at media coverage patterns of proposed or existing locations.

- It can be ascertained whether the location of a proposed branch store will service new customers or take business from existing stores in a chain or franchise. Suppose a supermarket chain currently has a store in Jackson, Mississippi, with a trading area of two miles; and it is considering adding a new store, three miles from the Jackson branch. Figure 9.2 shows the distinct trading areas and expected overlap of the two stores. The shaded portion represents the **trading-area overlap** between the stores, in which the same customers are served by both branches. The chain needs to find out the overall net increase in sales if it adds the proposed location shown in Figure 9.2 (total revised sales of existing store + total sales of new store − total previous sales of existing store).

- Chain executives can anticipate whether competitors want to open stores at nearby locations if the firm does not expand there itself. That is why TJX is willing to have two of its chains, T.J. Maxx and Marshalls, situate within $1\frac{1}{2}$ miles of each other in more than 100 markets throughout the United States, even though they are both off-price apparel chains.

- The proper number of stores operated by a chain retailer in a geographic region can be calculated. How many outlets should a bank, a travel agency, and so on have in a region to provide adequate service for customers (without raising investment costs too much or having too much overlap)? When CVS entered the Atlanta market, it decided to open nine new drugstores in one day. This enabled it to have enough coverage of the city to properly service the residents there, without placing stores too close together. A major competitive advantage for Canadian Tire Corporation is that four-fifths of the Canadian population live within a 15-minute drive of a Canadian Tire store.

- Geographic weaknesses can be highlighted. Suppose a suburban shopping center does a trading-area analysis and discovers that a significant number of people residing south of

Figure 9.2
The Trading Areas of
Current and
Proposed
Supermarket Outlets

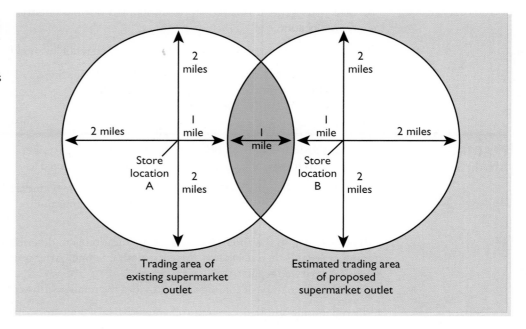

Trading area of
existing supermarket
outlet

Estimated trading area
of proposed
supermarket outlet

town do not shop there; and a more comprehensive study then reveals that people are afraid to drive past a dangerous railroad crossing on the southern outskirts of town. As a result of its research, the shopping center could exert political pressure to make the crossing safer, thus leading to more shoppers from south of town.

- Trading-area analysis can take into account the impact of the World Wide Web; and since the long-run sales relationship between Web-based and store-based retailing is far from certain, store-based retailers must examine their trading areas even more carefully than in the past and plan how much business they anticipate generating from the Web relative to their stores: "To counterbalance the influence of the Web, retailers will have to be more selective when choosing new sites and evaluating existing sites for their physical stores."[5]
- Other factors can be described and weighted. The competition, availability of financial institutions, transporation, availability of labor, location of suppliers, legal restrictions, projected growth, and so on can each be determined for the trading area(s) being examined.

The Use of Geographic Information Systems in Trading-Area Delineation and Analysis

Enter your ZIP code and let TIGER (tiger. census.gov/cgi-bin/ mapbrowse-tbl) map it out.

Increasingly, retailers are using geographic information systems software in their trading-area delineation and analysis. **Geographic information systems (GIS)** combine digitized mapping with key locational data to graphically depict such trading-area characteristics as the demographic attributes of the population, data on customer purchases, and listings of current, proposed, and competitor locations. Thus, GIS software lets retailers quickly research the attractiveness of alternative locations and see the findings on computer-screen maps. Prior to the widespread introduction of GIS software, retailers often placed different color pins on paper maps to show current and proposed locales—as well as competitors' sites—and had to do their own data collection and analysis.[6]

For the most part, GIS software programs are extrapolated from the decennial *Census of Population* and the U.S. Census Bureau's national digital map, which is known as TIGER (topologically integrated geographic encoding and referencing). TIGER incorporates all streets and highways in the United States. GIS software programs can be accessed in two ways: by downloading the maps from Web sites or by purchasing CD-ROM disks.

TIGER maps may be downloaded free from the TIGER Map Service site (tiger.census.gov). These maps can be tailored to reflect census tracts, railroads, highways, waterways, and other physical attributes of any area in the United States. However, TIGER maps do not include retail facilities, other commercial entities, population characteristics, and so on; the site can be cumbersome to use; and since tens of thousands of maps are downloaded daily from the TIGER site, service may be slow. Figure 9.3 shows a sample from the TIGER Map Service.

Sample Claritas reports and maps (www.sitereports.com/ body_onlinereports. html).

Private firms offering GIS mapping software on the Web or through CD-ROM disks include:

- Autodesk (www.autodesk.com/products/mapguide).
- CACI (www.caci.com).
- Caliper Corporation (www.caliper.com).
- Claritas (www.claritas.com).
- Decisionmark (www.decisionmark.com).
- Environmental Systems Research Institute (ESRI) (www.esri.com).
- Geographic Data Technology (www.geographic.com).
- National Decision Systems (www.sitereports.com).
- SRC (www.demographicsnow.com).
- Tetrad Computer Applications (www.tetrad.com).

Do you like colorful trading-area maps? SRC has them. Enter its site (www. demographicsnow.com) and click on "Samples."

Software from private firms has many more enhancements than TIGER. The companies often give free demonstrations, but expect to be paid for current applications. Although GIS

Technology in Retailing

ZIP Coding Through the Marketplace

Boscov's Department Store is a 34-store chain. All of the stores are within 300 miles of its Reading, Pennsylvania, headquarters. Boscov's recently gathered customer information and purchasing patterns for individual stores and incorporated the data into geographic maps. By charting sales by customer ZIP codes, for example, Boscov's can now better visualize its primary and secondary trading areas.

Kim Kolakowski, Boscov's director of credit promotions and marketing, says "In one of our markets, we thought we knew what the market was. But 90 days after the store opened, we determined there were several ZIP codes that we were drawing customers from but where we had no media coverage. We realigned our advertising and had a tremendous sales lift—about 10 percent."

The data analysis and mapping software has also been helpful when the firm seeks out additional locations. According to Kolakowski, "If we are looking at opening a store that is close to an existing store, we can determine whether we would have a huge transfer of the customer base or if there were opportunities to attract new customers." The graphical presentation has even been a useful tool in persuading vendors such as Polo Ralph Lauren and Tommy Hilfiger to sell their products at certain Boscov locations.

How could Boscov's measure trading-area overlap through its data analysis and mapping software?

Sources: "Boscov's Gets Data Graphic," *Women's Wear Daily* (December 16, 1998), p. 32; and www.boscovs.com (March 10, 2000).

Figure 9.3
The TIGER Map
Service

Reprinted by permission.

Click ON THE IMAGE to:
- ○ Zoom in, factor: 2
- ○ Zoom out, factor: 2
- ● Move to new center
- ○ Place Marker (select symbol below)
- ○ Download GIF image

OR
REDRAW MAP
with any option selected below

OFF/ON Layers		OFF/ON Layers	
☐ ☐	City labels	☐ ☐	Interstate labels
☐ ☐	Grid (lat/lon)	☐ ☐	St Hwy labels
☐ ☐	Cens bg points	☐ ☐	State Bounds
☐ ☐	Cens bg bounds	☐ ☐	US Hwy labels
☐ ☐	Congress dist	☐ ☐	Water bodies
☐ ☐	Counties	☐ ☐	Zipcode points
☐ ☐	Indian Resv		
☐ ☐	Highways		
☐ ☐	Parks and Other		
☐ ☐	MSA/CMSA		
☐ ☐	Cities/Towns		
☐ ☐	Railroad		
☐ ☐	Shoreline		
☐ ☐	Streets		
☐ ☐	Census Tracts		

Scale: 1:218074 (Centered at Lat: 38.89000 Lon: -77.02000)

REDRAW MAP

If your browser doesn't support client-side imagemaps, use the controls below to navigate the map.

	NW	N	NE	
Zoom In	W	Pan	E	Zoom Out
	SW	S	SE	

Here is the FAQ and instructions on how to include these maps in your own web documents.
The old mapbrowser has been moved to a new location.

LEGEND

— State   Military Area
— County   National Park
▓ Lake/Pond/Ocean   Other Park
— Expressway   ☐ City
— Highway   — County
— Connector
▓ Stream

Scale 1:218074
*average--true scale depends on monitor resolution
Click on the legend to download it as a GIF file.

Map Census Statistics:
Level: (none)
Theme: (none)
Classify Method:
○ Quintiles or ● Eq Interval

Place a marker on this map:
Latitude(deg):
Longitude(deg):
Symbol: Large Red Dot
Label:
Marker URL:

sorry, but no font control yet

Enter precise coordinates:
Latitude(deg): 38.89000
Longitude(deg): -77.02000
Map Width(deg): 0.360
Map Height(deg): 0.130

Choose a color palette:
Palette #1

REDRAW MAP

• You can also search for a U.S. city or town:
Name: State(optional):
or for a Zip Code: Search

• Or choose from the following preset values:
Washington, D.C. (default), The Mall, United States, Northeast U.S., New York City.

If you have feedback, please check out the Mapsurfer Feedback page.
If you have questions, please check out the service FAQ page.

TIGER Map Service Home Page.

This request serviced by (cyan.census.gov)

software programs differ by vendor (many of which offer trading-area consulting services, besides selling software), software generally can be accessed or bought for as low as under a hundred dollars and as much as several thousand dollars each, is designed to work with PCs, and allows for some manipulation of trading-area data. Illustrations of GIS software appear in Figure 9.4.

GIS software can be applied in various ways. For instance, a chain retailer could use GIS software to learn which of its stores have trading areas containing households with a median annual income of more than $50,000. That firm could derive the sales potential of proposed new store locations and those stores' potential effect on sales at existing branches. It could use GIS software to learn the demographics of customers at its best locations and then derive a model to allow it to scan locations throughout the nation to find the ones with the most desirable trading-area attributes. A retailer could even use GIS software to find its market penetration by ZIP code and to pinpoint its geographic areas of strength and weakness.

Figure 9.4
GIS Software in Action

When delineating and analyzing trading areas, their characteristics need to be studied and compared. Through geographic information systems (GIS) software, such as that represented here, retailers can learn about many trading-area characteristics and then choose the most appropriate area(s) in which to situate. To learn more about how mapping works, visit the Web site developed by Environmental Systems Research Institute, Inc. at *www.esri.com.ims*. There, you can receive a live demonstration of Internet mapping. You can also read about and visit dozens of Web sites around the world that use ESRI's Internet Mapping solutions.

Selected graphic images supplied courtesy of Environmental Systems Research Institute, Inc. (ESRI) and Geographic Data Technology (GDT), Inc., Lebanon, NH. Copyright Environmental Systems Research Institute, Inc. and Geographic Data Technology, Inc. Reprinted by permission.

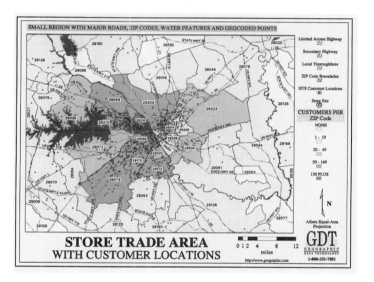

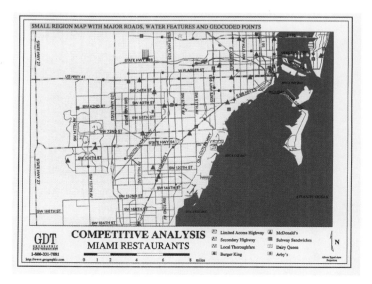

**Figure 9.4
(CONTINUED)**

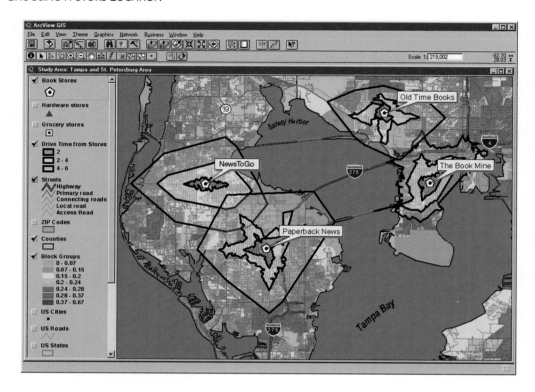

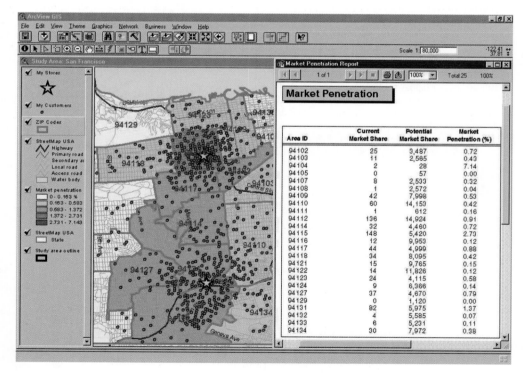

Here are examples of retailers employing GIS software in their trading-area delineation and analysis:

- Tricon uses GIS technology to help pinpoint locations for new KFC, Pizza Hut, and Taco Bell outlets.
- Texaco/Star uses GIS software to determine the time of day people stop for gas, where they are probably going, and what other items they are apt to buy. These data generate consumer profiles that are utilized to explore new locations—with similar people—that might support a Texaco station.[7]
- Crown American Properties owns, operates, and develops regional shopping centers. It currently has 27 centers in eight states. For each center, the firm uses GIS software to map out the competition, highlight household demographics in the area, and indicate street access and visibility. Crown American shows its colorful maps to potential tenants to promote its centers and secure leases.[8]

The Size and Shape of Trading Areas

Each trading area consists of three parts: primary, secondary, and fringe. The **primary trading area** encompasses 50 to 80 percent of a store's customers. It is the area closest to the store and possesses the highest density of customers to population and the highest per capita sales. There is little overlap with other trading areas (both intracompany and intercompany).

The **secondary trading area** contains an additional 15 to 25 percent of a store's customers. It is located outside the primary area, and customers are more widely dispersed. The **fringe trading area** includes all the remaining customers, and they are the most widely dispersed. For example, a store could have a primary trading area of four miles, a secondary trading area of five miles, and a fringe trading area of eight miles. The fringe trading area typically includes some outshoppers, who are willing to travel greater distances to patronize certain stores.

Figures 9.5 and 9.6 show the make-up of trading areas and their segments. In reality, trading areas do not usually follow such concentric or circular patterns. They adjust to the physical environment. The size and shape of a trading area are influenced by such factors as store type, store size, the location of competitors, residential housing patterns, travel time and traffic barriers (such as toll bridges or poor roads), and media availability. These factors are discussed next.

Two types of stores can have different-sized trading areas although they are in the same shopping district or shopping center. One store could offer a better assortment in its product category(ies), promote more extensively, and create a stronger image. This store— known as a **destination store**—would have a trading area much larger than that of a competitor with a less unique appeal. For example, situated in the same shopping center could be an outlet of an apparel chain with a distinctive image and people willing to travel up to 30 miles and a shoe store perceived as average and people willing to travel up to 10 miles. That is why, in comparing itself to other stores, Dunkin' Donuts has used the slogan, "It's worth the trip."

Another type of outlet, called a **parasite store,** does not create its own traffic and has no real trading area of its own. The store depends on people who are drawn to the location for other reasons. A magazine stand in a hotel lobby and a snack bar in a shopping center are both parasites. Customers are not drawn to a location because of them but patronize these stores while they are there.

The extent of a store's or center's trading area is affected by its own size. As a store or center gets larger, its trading area usually increases. This relationship exists because size

Input a location at ArcData Online (www. esri.com/data/online/ quickmap.html) and see why trading areas are rarely concentric! Then, click to move along the dynamic map.

Figure 9.5
The Segments of a
Trading Area

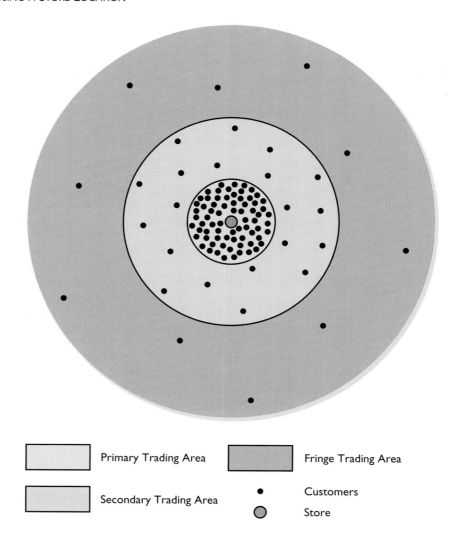

▢	Primary Trading Area	▢	Fringe Trading Area
▢	Secondary Trading Area	•	Customers
		◉	Store

generally reflects the assortment of goods and services. Yet, trading-area size does not rise proportionately with store or center size. As a rule, trading areas for supermarkets are greater than those for convenience stores; because of their size, supermarkets have a better product selection and convenience stores appeal to consumers' needs for fill-in merchandise. In a regional shopping center, department stores typically have the largest trading areas, followed by apparel stores. Gift stores in such a center have comparatively small trading areas. See Figure 9.7.

Competitors' locations determine their effect on the size of a store's trading area. Whenever potential shoppers are situated between two stores, the size of the trading area is often reduced for each; and the size of each store's trading area normally increases as the distance between them grows (target markets then do not overlap as much). On the other hand, when stores are situated very near one another, the size of each trading area does not necessarily shrink due to competition. In this case, the grouping of stores may actually increase the trading area for each store if more consumers are attracted to the general location due to the variety of goods and services. Yet, it is important to recognize that each store's market penetration (its percentage of retail sales in the trading area) may be low with such competition. Also, the entry of a new store may change the shape or create gaps in the trading areas of existing stores.

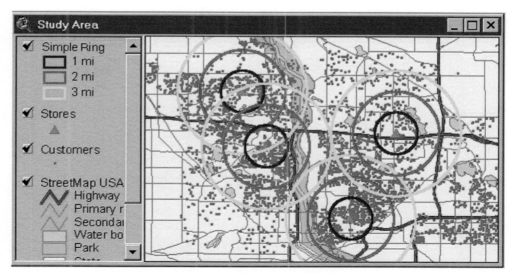

Figure 9.6
Delineating Trading-Area Segments by Customer Willingness to Travel

Remember: To learn more about how mapping works, visit the Web site developed by Environmental Systems Research Institute, Inc. at *www. esri.com/ims*. There, you can receive a live demonstration of Internet mapping. You can also read about and visit dozens of Web sites around the world that use ESRI's Internet Mapping solutions.

Selected graphic image supplied courtesy of Environmental Systems Research Institute, Inc. (ESRI). Copyright Environmental Systems Research Institute, Inc. Reprinted by permission.

Residential housing patterns affect a store's trading area. In many urban communities, people are clustered in multiunit housing near the center of commerce. With such population density, it is worthwhile for a retailer to be quite close to consumers; and trading areas tend to be small because several shopping districts (in close proximity to one another) are likely to exist and prosper, particularly for the most densely populated cities. In many suburbs, people live in single-unit housing—which is more geographically spread out. Thus, to produce satisfactory sales volume, a retailer would need to attract shoppers from a greater distance.

Travel or driving time has an influence on the size of a trading area that may not be clear from a study of just the population's geographic distribution. Physical barriers (toll bridges, tunnels, poor roads, rivers, railroad tracks, one-way streets) usually reduce trading areas and contribute to their odd shapes. Economic barriers (differences in sales taxes between towns) also affect the size and shape of trading areas. If one town has lower taxes, it may entice consumers to travel longer in return for saving money.

Trading-area size is often affected by promotion. In a community where a newspaper or other local advertising media are available, a retailer could afford to use these media and enlarge its trading area. If local media are not available, the retailer would have to weigh the costs and probable waste of advertising in citywide or countywide media against the possibilities of increasing its trading area.

Delineating the Trading Area of an Existing Store

The size, shape, and characteristics of the trading area for an existing store—or shopping district or shopping center—can usually be delineated quite accurately. Store records (secondary data) or a special study (primary data) can be used to measure the trading area. In addition, as

Figure 9.7
Warner Village Outside Rome: Asking Customers to Travel to Shop

Recently, Warner Brothers opened a new mall concept outside of Rome. The Warner Village is anchored by a large Cineplex theater and has over 60 shops. Many of the usual European firms are in its retail lineup: Benetton, Zara, Mango, and Fnac. One feature of this mega-entertainment mall is that people can access the shopping mall only by car. Warner Brothers has selected a site that is approximately 45 minutes outside of Rome by auto route. While the idea of entertainment is important to Italian shoppers, equally important is the idea of community and finding a place to be. So even though the entertainment factor is high for the Warner Brothers Village, the future of this type of format is not certain in Italy.

Reprinted by permission of PricewaterhouseCoopers.

noted earlier in the chapter, many firms offer computer-generated data and maps based on census and other statistics. This information can be tailored to individual retailers' needs.

Store records can reveal the addresses of both credit and cash customers. Addresses of credit customers can be obtained from the retailer's billing department; addresses of cash customers can be acquired by analyzing delivery tickets, cash sales slips, store contests (sweepstakes), and check-cashing operations. In both instances, the analysis of addresses is relatively inexpensive and quick because the data were originally collected for other purposes and are readily available.

Since many big retailers have computerized credit card systems, they can delineate trading areas by studying customer addresses. Primary, secondary, and fringe areas can be described in terms of

- The frequency with which people from various geographic locales shop at a particular store.
- The average dollar purchases at a store by people from given geographic locales.
- The concentration of a store's credit card holders from given geographic locales.

Though it may be easy to get data on credit card customers, conclusions drawn from these data might be invalid if cash customers are excluded from analysis. Credit use may vary among customers from different locales, especially if consumer characteristics in the locales are dissimilar. Thus, an evaluation of only credit customers may overstate or understate the total number of shoppers from a particular locality. This problem is minimized if data are collected for both cash and credit customers.

GDT uses Dynamap/Traffic Counts software (www. geographic.com/ solutions/solutions. cfm?Id=2) to provide vehicular traffic counts. Click on it at GDT's Web site.

A retailer can also collect primary data to determine the size of a trading area. It can record the license plate numbers of cars parked near a store, find the general addresses of the owners of those vehicles by contacting the state motor vehicle office or the local treasurer's office, and then note them on a map. For a few thousand dollars or less, a retailer could have Polk (a marketing research company) record the license plate numbers and determine the general owner addresses and demographics of parked vehicles. In either case, only general addresses (ZIP code and street of residence, but not the exact house number) are given out, to protect people's privacy. When using license plate analysis, nondrivers and passengers must not be omitted. Customers who walk to a store, use public transportation, or are driven by others should be included in research. To collect data on these customers, questions must often be asked (survey).

Use PRIZM (domino. claritas.com/cds.nsf/ regform?openform) to study your area's life-styles and purchasing preferences.

If a retailer desires even more in-depth demographic and life-style data about consumers in particular localities, it can purchase the data from such firms as Claritas. PRIZM is the computerized system devised by Claritas for identifying communities by life-style clusters. Sixty-two different types of neighborhoods have been identified and described using names like "Gray Power," "Starter Families," and "Suburban Sprawl." PRIZM initially was based on ZIP codes; it now is also based on census tracts, block groups and enumeration districts, phone exchanges, and postal routes. Standard online PRIZM reports can be downloaded for as little as $85 per area summary (plus an annual membership fee to Claritas Connect of $195); costs are higher if reports are tailored to the individual retailer.[9]

Dutch Royal Ahold Capitalizes on U.S. Locations

Royal Ahold, a Dutch-based food retailer, has become a powerhouse of U.S. supermarket retailing through its Ahold USA division. Since its entry into the United States, the firm has seen its annual American sales grow to nearly $20 billion.

Here is a timeline of selected Ahold USA activities:

- 1977—acquisition of Bi-Lo, a chain in North and South Carolina and Georgia.
- 1981—acquisition of Giant-Carlisle, a chain with stores in six northeastern states.
- 1991—acquisition of Tops Markets, a chain with stores in upstate New York and in Ohio. Now known as Tops of Finast (with Finast being a chain acquired in 1988).
- 1996—acquisition of Stop & Shop, a New England chain that is now Ahold USA's largest division.

- 1998—acquisition of Giant Food Inc., a chain with stores in Washington, D.C., and Baltimore.
- 1999—announced its intention to acquire Pathmark, a chain with stores in New York and Philadelphia. Due to Ahold's size in the eastern United States, the Federal Trade Commission did not approve and Ahold abandoned this acquisition attempt.

At Royal Ahold, more than a century after its founding, "Entrepreneurial skills, a precise sense of what customers want, and an excellent value-for-money private label policy, are still very much the pillars of our global retail strategy."

What trading-area characteristics should Ahold USA study in deciding what U.S. chains to acquire?

Sources: "Ahold USA," *Hoover's Online* (November 19, 1999); and www.aholdusa.com (March 10, 2000).

No matter how a trading area is delineated, the retailer should realize a time bias may exist. A downtown business district is patronized by different customers during the week (those who work there) than on weekends (those who travel there to shop). Special events may attract people from great distances for only brief time periods; after events are over, trading-area size may drop. Thus, an accurate estimate of a store's trading area can be obtained only through complete and continuous investigation.

After any trading area is delineated, a retailer should map people's locations and densities. This may be done either manually or with a geographic information system. In the manual method, a paper map of the area around a store is used. Different color dots or pins are placed on this map to represent *population* locations and densities, incomes, and other factors. *Customer* locations and densities are then indicated; and primary, secondary, and fringe trading areas are denoted by ZIP code. Customers can be lured by promotions aimed at particular ZIP codes. With a geographic information system, key customer data (such as purchase frequencies and amounts) are combined with other information sources (such as census data) to yield computer-generated digitized maps depicting primary, secondary, and fringe trading areas.

Delineating the Trading Area of a New Store

A new store planning to open in an established trading area can use the methods just noted. This section refers to a trading area with less well-defined shopping and traffic patterns.

Prospective trading areas for a new store must normally be evaluated by judging market opportunities rather than current patronage and traffic (pedestrian and vehicular) patterns. Because the techniques used to delineate the trading area of an established store are often insufficient, additional tools must be utilized.

Trend analysis or surveys can be employed. Trend analysis—estimating the future based on the past—involves examining government and other data concerning predictions about population location, auto registrations, new housing starts, mass transportation, highways, zoning, and so on. Consumer surveys can gather information about the time and distance people would be willing to travel to various possible retail locations, the features attracting people to a new store, the addresses of those most apt to visit a new store, and other topics. Either technique may be a basis for delineating alternate new store trading areas.

There are three types of computerized trading-area analysis models that can be used to assess new store locations: analog, regression, and gravity. An **analog model** is the simplest and most popular trading-area analysis model. Potential sales for a new store are estimated on the basis of revenues of similar stores in existing areas, the competition at a prospective location, the new store's expected market share at that location, and the size and density of the location's primary trading area. A **regression model** uses a series of mathematical equations showing the association between potential store sales and several independent variables at each location under consideration. The impact of such independent variables as population size, average income, the number of households, nearby competitors, transportation barriers, and traffic patterns are studied. A **gravity model** is based on the premise that people are drawn to stores that are closer and more attractive than competitors'. Such factors as the distance between consumers and competitors, the distance between consumers and a given site, and store image are included in this model.

Computerized trading-area analysis offers several benefits to retailers: They operate in an objective and systematic manner. They can offer insights as to how each locational attribute should be weighted. They are useful in screening a large number of locations. They can be used to assess management performance by comparing forecasts with results.

More specific methods for delineating new trading areas are described next.

Reilly's Law The traditional means of trading-area delineation is **Reilly's law of retail gravitation.**[10] Its purpose is to establish a point of indifference between two cities or communities, so the trading area of each can be determined. The **point of indifference** is the geographic breaking point between two cities (communities) at which consumers would be indifferent to shopping at either. According to Reilly's law, more consumers are attracted to the larger city or community because a greater amount of store facilities (assortment) exists there, making the increased travel time worthwhile.

The law may be expressed algebraically as[11]:

$$D_{ab} = \frac{d}{1 + \sqrt{P_b/P_a}}$$

where

D_{ab} = Limit of city (community) A's trading area, measured in miles along the road to city (community) B

d = Distance in miles along a major roadway between cities (communities) A and B

P_a = Population of city (community) A

P_b = Population of city (community) B

Based on this formula, a city with a population of 90,000 (A) would draw people from three times the distance as a city with 10,000 (B). If the cities are 20 miles apart, the point of indifference for the larger city is 15 miles, and for the smaller city, it is 5 miles:

$$D_{ab} = \frac{20}{1 + \sqrt{10,000/90,000}} = 15 \text{ miles}$$

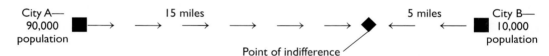

Reilly's law rests on these major assumptions: (1) two competing areas will be equally accessible from the major road; and (2) retailers in the two areas will be equally effective. Other factors (such as the dispersion of the population) are held constant or ignored.

The law of retail gravitation is an important contribution to trading-area analysis because of its ease of calculation and the research that has been conducted on it. Reilly's law is most useful when other data are not available or when the costs of compiling other data are too great. By combining this technique with others, a retailer could generally determine if the most appropriate trading area is being considered.

Despite its usefulness, Reilly's law has at least three key limitations. First, distance is measured by major thoroughfares and does not involve cross streets; yet, some people will travel shorter distances along cross streets. Second, travel time does not necessarily reflect the distance traveled. Today, many people are more concerned about time than distance. Third, actual distance may not correspond with people's perceptions of distance. A store with few services and crowded aisles is apt to be a greater perceived distance from the person than a similarly located store with a more pleasant atmosphere.

Huff's Law In the 1960s, Huff isolated several variables (rather than just one, as Reilly had done) and related them to trading-area size. **Huff's law of shopper attraction** delineates trading areas on the basis of the product assortment (of the items desired by the consumer) carried at various shopping locations, travel times from the shopper's home to alternative locations, and the sensitivity of the kind of shopping to travel time. Assortment is rated by the total square feet of selling space a retailer expects all firms in a shopping area to allot to a product category. Sensitivity to the kind of shopping entails the trip's purpose (restocking versus shopping) and the type of good/service sought (such as furniture versus clothing versus groceries).[12]

Huff's law is expressed as

$$P_{ij} = \frac{\dfrac{S_j}{(T_{ij})^\lambda}}{\displaystyle\sum_{j=1}^{n} \dfrac{S_j}{(T_{ij})^\lambda}}$$

where

P_{ij} = Probability of a consumer's traveling from home i to shopping location j

S_j = Square footage of selling space in shopping location j expected to be devoted to a particular product category

T_{ij} = Travel time from consumer's home i to shopping location j

λ = Parameter used to estimate the effect of travel time on different kinds of shopping trips

n = Number of different shopping locations

λ must be determined through research or by a computer program.

This formula may be applied as follows: Assume a leased department operator is studying three possible locations with 200, 300, and 500 total square feet of store space expected to be allocated to men's cologne (by all retailers in the areas). A group of potential customers lives 7 minutes from the first location, 10 minutes from the second, and 15 minutes from the third. From previous research, the operator estimates the effect of travel time to be 2. Therefore, the probability of consumers' shopping for men's cologne is 43.9 percent at Location 1; 32.2 percent at Location 2; and 23.9 percent at Location 3:

$$P_{i1} = \frac{(200)/(7)^2}{(200)/(7)^2 + (300)/(10)^2 + (500)/(15)^2} = 43.9\%$$

$$P_{i2} = \frac{(300)/(10)^2}{(200)/(7)^2 + (300)/(10)^2 + (500)/(15)^2} = 32.2\%$$

$$P_{i3} = \frac{(500)/(15)^2}{(200)/(7)^2 + (300)/(10)^2 + (500)/(15)^2} = 23.9\%$$

As a result, if 200 males live 7 minutes from Location 1, about 88 of them will shop there.

These points should be considered in using Huff's law:

- To determine Location 1's overall trading area, the same type of computations would be made for people living at a driving time of 5, 10, 15, 20 minutes, and so on. The number of people at each distance who would shop there are then summed. Thus, the stores in Location 1 could estimate their total market, the trading-area size, and the primary, secondary, and fringe areas for a particular product category.
- If new retail facilities (square feet of selling space) in a product category are added to a locale, the percentage of people living at every travel time from that location who would shop there goes up.
- The probability of people shopping at a particular location is highly dependent on the effect of travel time for the product category. In the prior example, if the product is a more important item, such as men's dress watches, consumers would be less sensitive to travel time. A λ value of 1 would result in these probabilities: Location 1, 31.1 percent; Location 2, 32.6 percent; and Location 3, 36.3 percent. Location 3 becomes much more attractive for this product category because of its assortment.

- All the variables are rather hard to calculate; and for mapping purposes, travel time needs to be converted to distance in miles. In addition, travel time depends on the transportation form used.
- Since people buy different items on different shopping trips, the trading area varies from trip to trip.

Other Trading-Area Research Over the years, a number of other researchers have examined trading-area size in a variety of settings. They have introduced additional factors and sophisticated statistical techniques to explain the consumer's choice of shopping location.

In his model, Gautschi added to Huff's analysis by including shopping-center descriptors and transportation conditions.[13] Weisbrod, Parcells, and Kern studied the attractiveness of shopping centers on the basis of expected population changes, store characteristics, and the transportation network.[14] Ghosh developed a consumer behavior model that takes into consideration multipurpose shopping trips.[15] LeBlang demonstrated that consumer life-styles could be used to predict sales at new department store locations.[16] Schneider, Johnson, Sleeper, and Rodgers studied trading-area overlap and franchisees.[17] Albaladejo-Pina and Aranda-Gallego looked at the effects of competition among stores in different sections of a trading area.[18] Bell, Ho, and Tang devised a model with both fixed and variable store choice factors.[19] Ruiz studied the influence of shopping center image on its ability to attract shoppers.[20]

CHARACTERISTICS OF TRADING AREAS

PCensus with MapInfo (www.tetrad.com/ new/franchise.html) is a useful tool for scrutinizing potential franchise locations.

After the size and shape of various alternative trading areas (existing or proposed) have been determined, the retailer studies the characteristics of those areas. Of special interest are the attributes of residents and how well they match with the retailer's definition of its target market. Thus, an auto repair franchisee may compare the opportunities available in several areas by reviewing the number of car registrations; a hearing aid retailer may evaluate the percentage of the population 65 years of age or older; and a bookstore retailer may be concerned with the educational level of residents.

Among the trading-area factors that should be studied by most retailers are the population size and characteristics, availability of labor, closeness to sources of supply, promotion facilities, economic base, competition, availability of locations, and regulations. The **economic base** refers to an area's industrial and commercial structure—the companies and industries that residents depend on to earn a living. The dominant industry (company) in an area is very important since its drastic decline may have adverse effects on a large segment of the area's residents. An area with a diverse economic base, where residents work for a variety of nonrelated industries, is more secure than an area dependent on one major industry. Table 9.1 summarizes a number of the chief factors to consider in evaluating retail trading areas.

Much of the data necessary to describe an area can be obtained from the U.S. Bureau of the Census, the *Survey of Buying Power, Editor & Publisher Market Guide, Rand McNally Commercial Atlas & Market Guide, American Demographics, Standard Rate & Data Service,* regional planning boards, public utilities, chambers of commerce, local government offices, shopping-center owners, and renting agents. In addition, GIS software provides data on potential buying power in an area, the location of competitors, and highway access. Both demographic and life-style information are also included in this software.

Although the yardsticks in Table 9.1 are not equally important in all location decisions, each should be considered (to prevent an oversight). The most important yardsticks should be viewed as "knockout" factors: if a location does not meet minimum standards on key measures, it should be immediately dropped from further consideration.

These are examples of desirable trading-area attributes, according to a diverse mix of retailers:

Table 9.1 Chief Factors to Consider in Evaluating Retail Trading Areas

Population Size and Characteristics

Total size and density	Total disposable income
Age distribution	Per capita disposable income
Average educational level	Occupation distribution
Percentage of residents owning homes	Trends

Availability of Labor

Management
Management trainee
Clerical

Closeness to Sources of Supply

Delivery costs	Number of manufacturers and wholesalers
Timeliness	Availability and reliability of product lines

Promotion Facilities

Availability and frequency of media
Costs
Waste

Economic Base

Dominant industry	Freedom from economic and seasonal fluctuations
Extent of diversification	Availability of credit and financial facilities
Growth projections	

Competitive Situation

Number and size of existing competitors	Short-run and long-run outlook
Evaluation of competitor strengths/weaknesses	Level of saturation

Availability of Store Locations

Number and type of locations	Zoning restrictions
Access to transportation	Costs
Owning versus leasing opportunities	

Regulations

Taxes	Minimum wages
Licensing	Zoning
Operations	

- Twenty percent of Pathmark supermarkets are located in urban communities rather than in the suburbs: "Many of the city communities have incomes very comparable to the suburbs. We just approved a location in Queens, New York, that is home to more than 200,000 people with an average household income over $40,000 with no modern supermarket to shop in. If that's not an opportunity, we don't know what is."[21]
- Krispy Kreme, the fast-growing North Carolina-based donut chain, is looking for "premier locations that have a lot of traffic and density" in markets with 100,000 or more households. It likes "to be around traffic near big-box retailers." It thinks it also draws many customers to the area.[22]
- Finish Line, the sports apparel and shoe chain, looks for sites in mid-sized markets. It evaluates the market areas, shopping mall locations, consumer traffic, competition, and costs associated with opening new stores. It likes to be in enclosed shopping centers.[23]
- Heilig-Meyers, the largest U.S. home furnishings chain, has most of its stores in towns with 5,000 to 50,000 people, at least 25 miles from major markets and within 250 miles from existing or planned distribution centers. Since a distribution center needs 30 to 40

stores to be efficient, the chain tries to expand within each distribution center's zone of market coverage. It has a small percentage of stores in areas such as Chicago, Cleveland, and Atlanta.[24]

- The Syms off-price apparel chain seeks locations near highways or thoroughfares in suburban areas that are populated by a least 1 million persons and that are readily accessible to customers by car. In certain areas, where there are over 2 million people, Syms has opened more than one store.[25]

Several stages of the process involved in gathering data to analyze retail trading areas are shown by the flowchart in Figure 9.8, which incorporates not only the attributes of residents, but also those of the competition. By studying both these factors, a retailer can see how saturated an area is for its business.

We next discuss three factors in trading-area selection: population characteristics, economic base characteristics, and the nature of competition and the level of saturation.

Characteristics of the Population

Considerable knowledge about an area's population characteristics can be gained from secondary sources. They can provide data about the population size, number of households, income distribution, education level, age distribution, and more. Because the *Census of Population* and the *Survey of Buying Power* are such valuable sources, each is briefly described.

Find out about the 2000 U.S. Census (www.census.gov/dmd/www/2khome.htm).

Census of Population   The **Census of Population** supplies a wide range of demographic data for all U.S. cities and surrounding vicinities. These data are organized on a geographic basis, starting with blocks and continuing to census tracts, cities, counties, states, and regions. As a rule, fewer data are available for blocks and census tracts than for larger units because of concerns about individuals' privacy. The major advantage of census data is that they provide demographic information on small geographic units.

Capitalizing on Inner City Opportunities

Fred Westbrook, Jr., a former schoolteacher, decided that an inner-city neighborhood in Nashville, Tennessee, offered a great opportunity to open a pizza restaurant. According to Westbrook, "One day it just hit me. I was going to buy a pizza and I wondered why nobody has opened a pizza franchise here."

Although the Jefferson Street area he chose was home to three major colleges/universities, getting financing was quite difficult. Before ultimately getting approval from Sir Pizza, a regional pizza chain, five national pizza franchisors turned down his proposal. Westbrook then spent months working on preparing a business plan. Yet, despite his father's backing, the banks rejected his loan application. Westbrook was eventually able to open the restaurant with a $28,000 equity loan secured by real-estate he owned. Yet, he still was not able to secure a traditional line of credit from a bank.

According to the Initiative for a Competitive Inner City, there are many advantages to inner-city locations. These include a stable and underutilized work force, and a large underserved local market with substantial purchasing power. A recent study by one consulting firm estimated the annual value of the inner city retail sector at about $100 billion.

In the long-run, Fred Westbrook thinks that "showing appreciation for his customers will give him—and other inner city entrepreneurs—the edge."

Source: Cynthia E. Griffin, "Hidden Treasures," *Entrepreneur* (December 1998), pp. 16–17.

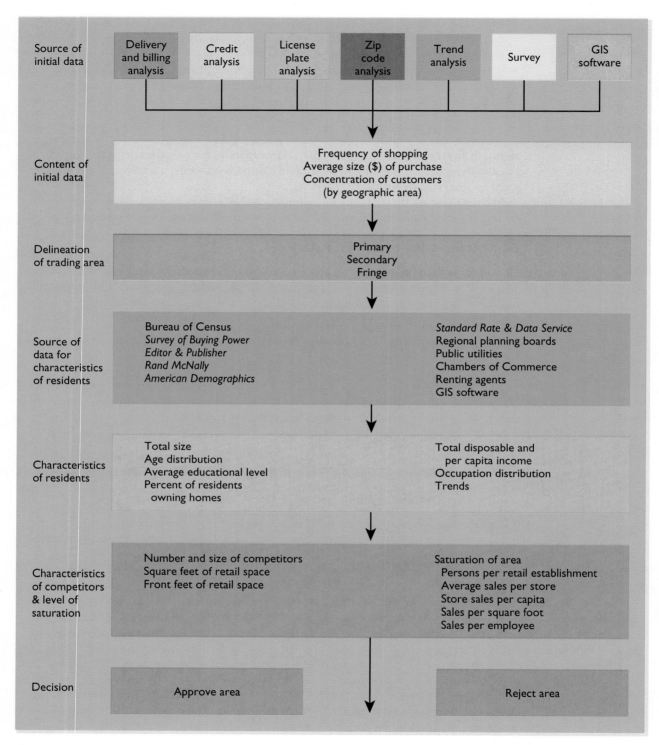

Figure 9.8
Analyzing Retail Trading Areas

Once a retailer has outlined the boundaries of a trading area, it can use census data to gather information for each of the geographic units contained in the area and then study aggregate demographics. A major breakthrough for retailers occurred with the 1970 census, when the U.S. Bureau of the Census created a computer file for the storage and retrieval of population data by geographic area. The 1980 census added useful data categories for retailers interested in segmenting the market—including racial and ethnic data, small-area income data, and commuting patterns. An online computer system was also introduced to make census data more accessible.

The 1990 census expanded the availability of in-depth information through computer formats—such as computer tapes, floppy disks, CD-ROM disks, and online services. But the biggest advance with the 1990 census involved the introduction of TIGER computer tapes, which contain the most detailed physical breakdowns of U.S. areas ever produced. These tapes comprise a computer-readable data base that contains digital descriptions of geographic areas (such as area boundaries and codes, latitude and longitude coordinates, and address ranges). Because TIGER tapes must be used in conjunction with population and other data, GIS software is necessary. As noted earlier in this chapter, many private firms have devised computer-based location analysis programs, based in large part on TIGER. These firms also usually project data to the present year and into the future.

The major drawbacks of the *Census of Population* are that it is undertaken only once every 10 years and that all data are not immediately available when they are collected. For example, information from the 2000 *Census of Population* will be released in phases from 2001 through 2003. Census material can thus be out of date and inaccurate—particularly several years after collection. Therefore, supplementary sources, such as municipal building departments or utilities, state government offices, other U.S. Bureau of the Census reports (including the *Current Population Survey*), and computerized projections by firms like Dun & Bradstreet, must be used to update *Census of Population* data.

The value of actual census tract data (available from the *Census of Population* and updated to 1998 through computerized projections by Dun & Bradstreet) to retailers can be shown by an illustration of Long Beach, New York, a city located 30 miles east of New York City on Long Island's south shore. Long Beach encompasses six census tracts, numbers 4164, 4165, 4166, 4167.01, 4167.02, and 4168. See Figure 9.9 (page 312). Although census tract 4163 is contiguous with Long Beach, it represents Atlantic Beach, another community. Table 9.2 (page 313) contains a variety of population statistics for each of the census tracts in Long Beach. The characteristics of the residents in each tract differ markedly; thus, a retailer might choose to locate in one or more tracts but not in others.

Suppose a growing bookstore chain is evaluating two potential trading areas. Area A corresponds roughly with census tracts 4165 and 4166. Area B is similar to census tracts 4167.01, 4167.02, and 4168. Population data for these two areas have been extracted from Table 9.2 and are presented in Table 9.3 (page 314). Area A is different from Area B, despite their geographic proximity and similar physical size:

- The population in Area B is 24 percent larger.
- Although the population in both areas rose from 1990 to 1998, Area B grew very little.
- Area B has nearly twice as many residents aged 25 and older with college degrees.
- The annual median income in Area A is higher than that in Area B.
- Area B has a greater proportion of workers who are managers or professionals.

The management of the bookstore chain would have a tough time in selecting between the two areas because they both have some of the attributes desired for the target market. Thus, the chain might also have to consider the proximity of the sites available in Area A and Area B relative to the locations of its existing stores, before making a final decision.

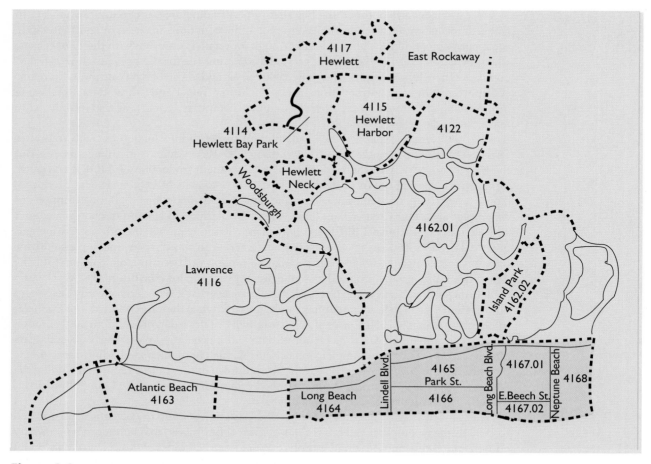

Figure 9.9
The Census Tracts of Long Beach, New York

Survey of Buying Power The ***Survey of Buying Power,*** published yearly by *Sales & Marketing Management* magazine, reports current demographic data on metropolitan areas, cities, and states. It also provides some data not available from the *Census of Population,* such as total annual retail sales by area, annual retail sales for specific product categories, annual effective buying income, and five-year population and retail sales projections. The *Survey's* most critical disadvantage is its use of broad geographic territories, which are often much larger than a store's trading area and cannot be broken down easily.

Let us show the *Survey of Buying Power's* value through an example. Suppose a prospective new car dealer uses it during trading-area analysis for a store location. This dealer wants to investigate three counties near Chicago: Du Page, Kane, and Lake. Table 9.4 lists selected 1998 population and retail sales data (as well as 2003 projections) for each of the counties. The *Survey* updates these data each year.

To fully understand the information in Table 9.4 (page 314), two key terms used in the *Survey of Buying Power* must be defined.[26] **Effective buying income (EBI)** is personal income (wages, salaries, interest, dividends, profits, rental income, and pension income) minus federal, state, and local taxes and nontax payments (such as personal contributions for social security insurance). EBI is commonly known as disposable or after-tax personal income.

Table 9.2 Selected Characteristics of Long Beach, New York, Residents by Census Tract, 1990 and 1998

	TRACT NUMBER					
	4164	4165	4166	4167.01	4167.02	4168
Total Population						
1990	7,082	5,694	5,613	4,162	4,479	6,480
1990 population 25 and older	5,315	3,331	4,306	3,003	3,620	5,074
1998	7,040	5,881	6,365	4,046	4,707	6,457
Number of Households						
1990	2,735	1,812	2,219	1,465	2,295	3,066
1998	2,739	1,887	2,577	1,433	2,437	3,080
Education						
College graduates (% of population 25 and older), 1990	15.2	13.1	17.8	17.1	20.4	19.5
Income						
Median household income, 1990	$45,245	$42,621	$38,642	$47,297	$33,891	$42,471
Median household income, 1998	$55,689	$55,319	$51,516	$54,292	$41,725	$48,400
Selected Occupations						
Managerial and profession specialty occupations (% of employed persons 16 and older), 1990	17.3	12.2	17.3	14.6	17.8	19.6

Sources: Census of Population and Housing (Washington, D.C.: U.S. Bureau of the Census, 1990), Census Tracts Nassau-Suffolk New York Standard Metropolitan Statistical Area; *Market Profile Analysis: Consumer and Business Demographic Reports: Nassau-Suffolk NY DMSA* (Dun & Bradstreet Information Services, 1998 Edition), p. 22; and authors' computations.

Table 9.3 Selected Population Statistics for Long Beach Trading Areas A and B

	Area A (Tracts 4165 and 4166)	Area B (Tracts 4167.01, 4167.02, and 4168)
Total population, 1998	12,246	15,210
Population change, 1990-1998	+8.3%	+0.6%
Number of college graduates, 25 and older, 1990	1,203	2,242
Median household income, 1998	$53,342	$47,902
Managerial and professional specialty occupations (% of employed persons 16 and older), 1990	14.5%	17.8%

Table 9.4 Selected Data from *Survey of Buying Power* Relating to the Automobile Market in Three Illinois Counties, 1998

	COUNTY		
	Du Page	**Kane**	**Lake**
December 31, 1998			
Total population	886,200	396,400	618,400
Number of people 18 and over	651,400	277,900	446,500
Number of households	319,000	132,700	209,800
Total effective buying income (EBI)	$23,013,679,000	$7,582,166,000	$16,727,492,000
Median household EBI	$60,532	$49,324	$57,727
Percentage of households with $35,000–$49,999 EBI	16.2	18.2	16.2
Percentage of households with $50,000+ EBI	62.4	49.1	57.9
Total retail sales	$13,161,089,000	$3,264,509,000	$7,630,681,000
Buying power index (%)	0.4602	0.1473	0.3111
Percentage of U.S. EBI	0.4980	0.1641	0.3620
Percentage U.S. retail sales	0.4882	0.1211	0.2831
Percentage of U.S. population	0.3240	0.1449	0.2261
Automobile retail sales, 1998	$3,769,191,000	$672,528,000	$2,540,124,000
Projections for December 31, 2003			
Total population	931,200	451,600	683,300
Total EBI	$28,942,527,000	$10,118,749,000	$22,511,372,000
Total retail sales	$17,256,552,000	$3,911,202,000	$9,558,841,000
Buying power index (%)	0.4705	0.1544	0.3287

Source: Adapted from *Sales & Marketing Management: 1999 Survey of Buying Power* (September 1999), pp. 84, 169–70. Reprinted by permission of Bill Communications, Inc. ©1999, S&MM Survey of Buying Power; permission conveyed through Copyright Clearance Center, Inc.

The **buying power index (BPI)** is a single weighted measure combining effective buying income, retail sales, and population size into one overall indicator of an area's sales potential, expressed as a percentage of total U.S. sales. Each of the criteria is assigned a weight, based on its relative importance:

Buying power index = 0.5 (the area's percentage of U.S. effective buying income)
  + 0.3 (the area's percentage of U.S. retail sales)
  + 0.2 (the area's percentage of U.S. population)

The buying power index for Du Page is over three times greater than that of Kane and 50 percent greater than that of Lake. As the data in Table 9.4 indicate, Du Page has a larger population and more people 18 and older than either Kane or Lake. These are vital statistics for an auto dealer. In addition, 78.6 percent of Du Page's residents have effective buying incomes of $35,000 or better, compared to 67.3 percent of Kane's residents and 74.1 percent of Lake's. In 1998, automobile sales were $3.8 billion in Du Page, as compared to $673 million in Kane and $2.5 billion in Lake. A Cadillac dealer using *Survey of Buying Power* data might select Du Page and a Chevrolet dealer might select Kane. But, because *Survey* statistics are broad in nature, several subsections of Kane may be superior choices to subsections in Du Page for the Cadillac dealer. The level of competition in each area also must be noted.

Different retailers require different kinds of information about an area's population. The location decision for a bookstore or an auto dealer usually requires more data than those necessary for a fast-food franchise. For the latter, the prime criterion in trading-area analysis is often population density. Thus, fast-food franchisors often seek communities with many people living or working within a three- or four-mile radius of their stores. On the other hand, bookstore owners and auto dealers cannot locate merely on the basis of population density. They must consider a more complex combination of population attributes in evaluating areas and should look at the sources of data described in this chapter.

Economic Base Characteristics It is imperative to study each area's economic base. This base reflects the commercial and industrial infrastructure of the community and the sources of income for its residents. A retailer seeking stability normally prefers an area with a diversified economic base (one with a large number of nonrelated industries and financial institutions) to one with an economic base keyed to a single major industry. The latter area is more affected by a strike, declining demand for an industry, and cyclical fluctuations.

In assessing a trading area's economic base, a retailer should investigate the percentage of the labor force in each industry group, the transportation network, banking facilities, the potential impact of economic fluctuations on the area and particular industries, and the future of individual industries (firms). Data can be obtained from such sources as Easy Analytic Software, *Editor & Publisher Market Guide*, regional planning commissions, industrial development organizations, and chambers of commerce.

Easy Analytic Software (www.easidemographics.com) provides a wide range of inexpensive site selection software and economic reports. It also produces several reports by ZIP code and makes them available for free at its Web site. The free reports must be viewed one ZIP code and one report type at a time. However, the CD-ROM versions are more multifaceted. These are three of the reports that can be downloaded from Easy Analytic's free "The Right Site" section of its Web site: *Employment and Industry Report & Analysis, Quality of Life Report & Analysis*, and *Business Profile Report & Analysis*.

Get free economic data on your community (www. easidemographics. com/reports/easi_ free_reports.phtml).

Ethics in Retailing

The Battle Over Item Price Labeling in New England

In New England, Connecticut has taken the lead in dropping item pricing requirements for supermarkets that have installed electronic shelf labels (ESLs). Unlike in Massachusetts and Rhode Island, where item pricing is still required, labor costs have declined in Connecticut since item pricing requirements were dropped there in 1992.

Elsewhere in the United States, electronic shelf tags are not as popular as in Connecticut, where that state's item pricing exemption enables supermarkets to cost-justify their large investment in new equipment. More than one-half of the ESL systems in the nation have been installed in Connecticut. On average, it takes about $100,000 to equip a typical 40,000-square-foot supermarket with an ESL system. This investment must be offset with lower labor costs to be practical.

An additional benefit of the ESL system used in Connecticut is that it lets supermarkets change the prices on shelf tags and in the point-of-sale price file at the same time. This reduces the scanning errors that occur when the price file is not updated to reflect price changes. Says a spokesperson for the Office of Consumer Affairs in Massachusetts, "We are looking at any way, including technological advances, that promotes accuracy at all times."

As a consumer living on the border of Connecticut and Massachusetts, would you rather shop at a supermarket with or without an ESL system? Explain your answer.

Source: Isabelle Sender, "New England Grocers Fight for ESL Rights," *Chain Store Age* (September 1998), pp. 110, 114.

Editor & Publisher Market Guide provides economic base data for cities on a yearly basis, including principal employment sources, transportation networks, financial institutions and bank deposits, auto registrations, the number of gas and electric meters, newspaper circulation, and major shopping centers. It also has data on population size and total households by city. Like the *Survey of Buying Power, Editor & Publisher Market Guide* has one serious drawback for retailers. Data cover broad geographic areas and are hard to disaggregate. The bookstore chain noted earlier would find *Editor & Publisher* information on shopping centers and retailers to be helpful in analyzing cities. The auto dealer would find *Editor & Publisher* information on the transportation network, the availability of financial institutions, and the number of passenger cars to be very useful. In trading-area analysis, *Editor & Publisher Market Guide* is best used to supplement census and *Sales & Marketing Management* statistics.

The Nature of Competition and the Level of Saturation

An opportunity in an area cannot be accurately assessed until competition is studied. Although a trading area may have residents who match the characteristics of the retailer's desired market and a strong economic base, it may be a poor location for a new store if competition is too extensive. Similarly, an area with a small population and a narrow economic base may be a good location if competition is minimal.

When examining competition in an area, such factors as these should be analyzed: the number of existing stores, the size distribution of existing stores, the rate of new store openings, the strengths and weaknesses of all stores, short-run and long-run trends, and the level of saturation. These factors should be evaluated in relation to an area's population size and growth, not just in absolute terms.

For example, over the past decade, many retailers have expanded into states in the Southeast and Southwest due to their growing populations. Thus, Tiffany, Saks Fifth Avenue, Gumps, Target Stores, Marshall Field's, Lord & Taylor, and Macy's are among the retailers that have entered the New Orleans, Dallas, Orlando, or Phoenix markets. However, there is some concern that these localities may become oversaturated because of the influx of new stores. Furthermore, although the population in the Northeast has been declining relative to the Southeast and the Southwest, one of its major strengths—population density—should not be disregarded by retailers. According to the U.S. Bureau of the Census, population density (the number of persons residing per square mile) in the Northeast is much higher than in the Southeast and Southwest. In New Jersey, there are 1,070 people per square mile; in Massachusetts, 775; in Florida, 262; in Louisiana, 100; in Texas, 72; and in Arizona, 37.

A trading area's saturation can be designated as understored, overstored, or saturated. An **understored trading area** has too few stores selling a specific good or service to satisfy the needs of its population. An **overstored trading area** has so many stores selling a specific good or service that some retailers will be unable to earn an adequate profit. A **saturated trading area** has the proper amount of retail facilities to satisfy the needs of its population for a specific good or service, as well as to enable retailers to prosper.

Despite the large number of areas in the United States that are overstored, there still remain plentiful opportunities in understored communities:

As suburbs become saturated with stores, underserved minority neighborhoods stand out as major opportunities for growth. With high-profile inner city projects such as the Harlem USA development in New York and Baldwin Hills Crenshaw Plaza in Los Angeles raising awareness and attention, retailers, financiers, and developers are showing increasing interest in ethnically oriented shopping centers. Both central city areas, home to middle-class African-Americans and fast-growing Hispanic and Asian communities, are being assessed for their commercial retail potential, as major national retailers learn how to expand in this market. Unlike traditional ethnic shopping districts jammed with small, local merchants catering to a single nationality, the projects now have a broad mix of national retailers in an enclosed mall or power center development.[27]

Measuring Trading-Area Saturation In measuring retail saturation in a trading area, this should be kept in mind: any trading area can support only a given number of stores or square feet of selling space per goods/service category. These are some of the ratios that help to quantify retail store saturation:

- Number of persons per retail establishment.
- Average sales per retail store.
- Average sales per retail store category.
- Average store sales per capita or household.
- Average sales per square foot of selling area.
- Average sales per employee.

Ratios are meaningful only if norms are set. The saturation level in a trading area can then be measured against a standard set by the retailer or it can be compared with that of other trading areas. For example, the owner of an auto accessory chain might find that the current trading area is saturated by computing the ratio of residents to auto accessory stores. On the basis of this calculation, the owner could then decide to expand into a nearby metropolitan area with a lower ratio rather than to add another store in its present trading area.

The data to compute these and other ratios can be obtained from a retailer's records on its own performance, city and state license and tax records, phone directories, personal visits to locales, consumer surveys, economic census data, *Dun & Bradstreet* reference materials, *Editor & Publisher Market Guide*, *County Business Patterns*, trade association publications, and other sources. Sales by product category, population size, and number of households per market area can be found in the *Survey of Buying Power*.

When investigating an area's level of saturation for a specific good or service, ratios must be interpreted carefully. Variations among areas sometimes may not be reliable indicators of differences in saturation. For instance, car sales per capita are different for a suburban area than an urban area because suburban residents have a much greater need for their cars. Thus, each area's level of saturation should be evaluated against different standards—based on optimum per capita sales figures in that area.

In calculating the saturation level in an area based on sales per square foot of selling space, the retailer must take its proposed new store into account. If that proposed store is not part of the calculations, the relative value of each trading area may be distorted. Sales per square foot of selling area decline the most when new outlets are added in small communities. Furthermore, the retailer should consider whether a new store will expand the total consumer market for a specific good or service category in a trading area or just increase the firm's market share in that area without expanding the total market.

These are three examples of how retailers are studying trading-area saturation:

- Meineke Muffler searches for locations with compatible power retailers. It scouts around for areas which already have big-box retailers such as Home Depot or Wal-Mart—but not necessarily direct competitors (such as Midas): "We look to see what creates a regional draw." Meineke uses computer software to gain insights into each area's overall potential (the saturation level), including estimates on auto service demands.[28]
- Wal-Mart carefully studies the number of persons per Wal-Mart store (including Sam's) as an indicator of saturation. It knows that in Alabama, Arkansas, Kansas, Kentucky, Louisiana, Mississippi, Missouri, Oklahoma, Tennessee, and Wyoming, the population to Wal-Mart store ratio is 50,000 or less. In California, Maryland, Massachusetts, New

Jersey, New York, and Washington, the population to store ratio is over 200,000. That is why Wal-Mart is adding many more outlets in the latter states.[29]

- Supermarket chains buy annual data from Trade Dimensions (www.tradedimensions. com) that measures the level of supermarket saturation in cities across the United States. On a per-city basis, Trade Dimensions reports on the number of supermarkets, overall supermarket sales, supermarket sales per capita, weekly sales per square foot, the breakdown of chain supermarkets versus independents, the total square footage of supermarket space, the number of supermarket employees, and more.

SUMMARY

1. *To demonstrate the importance of store location for a retailer and outline the process for choosing a store location.* The choice of location is crucial because of the complex decision making involved, the high costs, the lack of flexibility once a site is chosen, and the impact of a site on a retailer's strategy. A good location may let a retailer succeed even if its strategy mix is relatively mediocre.

The selection of a store location consists of four steps: (1) evaluating alternative trading areas; (2) determining the best type of location; (3) picking a general site; and (4) settling on a specific site. This chapter looks at Step 1. Chapter 10 details Steps 2, 3, and 4.

2. *To discuss the concept of a trading area and its related components.* A trading area is the geographical area from which a retailer draws customers. When two or more shopping locales are near one another, they may have trading-area overlap.

Today, many retailers are utilizing geographic information systems (GIS) software to delineate and analyze trading areas. The software combines digitized mapping with key locational data to graphically depict trading-area characteristics. This lets retailers research alternative locations and display findings on computer screen maps. Several vendors market GIS software (via Web sites and CD-ROM disks), based on enhancements to the TIGER mapping program of the U.S. government.

Each trading area has primary, secondary, and fringe components. The farther people live from a shopping area, the less apt they are to travel there. The size and shape of a trading area depend on store type, store size, competitor locations, housing patterns, travel time and traffic barriers, and media availability. Destination stores have much larger trading areas than parasite stores.

3. *To show how trading areas may be delineated for existing and new stores.* The size, shape, and characteristics of

the trading area for an existing store or group of stores can be identified accurately. A retailer can gather data from store records, sponsoring contests, recording license plate numbers and linking them to addresses, consumer surveys, buying computer-generated data, and so on. Time biases must be considered in amassing data. Results should be mapped and customer densities noted.

Potential trading areas for a new store must often be described in terms of opportunities, rather than current patronage and traffic patterns. Trend analysis and consumer surveys may be used. There are three computerized models that can be used for planning a new store location: analog, regression, and gravity. These models offer several benefits.

Two techniques for delineating new trading areas are Reilly's law of retail gravitation, which relates the population size of different cities to the size of their trading areas, and Huff's law of shopper attraction, which is based on each area's shopping assortment, the distance of people from various retail locales, and the sensitivity of people to travel time.

4. *To examine three major factors in trading-area analysis: population characteristics, economic base characteristics, and competition and the level of saturation.* Once the size and shape of each possible trading area have been set, these factors should be studied. The best secondary sources for population data are the *Census of Population* and the *Survey of Buying Power*, which have complementary strengths and weaknesses for retailers. Census data are detailed and specific, but become dated. Current data are available in the *Survey of Buying Power*, but it reports on broader geographic areas.

A trading area's economic base reflects a community's commercial and industrial infrastructure, as well as residents' income sources. A retailer should look at such economic base factors as the percentage of the labor force in each industry, the transportation network, banking facilities, the potential impact of economic fluctuations on the area, and the future of individual industries. Easy Analytic and *Editor & Publisher Market Guide* are good sources of data on areas' economic bases.

A trading area cannot be properly analyzed without studying the nature of competition and the level of saturation. An area may be understored (too few retail-

ers), overstored (too many retailers), or saturated (the proper number of retailers). Store saturation may be measured in several ways, such as the number of persons per store, the average sales per store, the average store sales per capita or household, average sales per square foot of selling space, and average sales per employee.

Key Terms

trading area (p. 293)
trading-area overlap (p. 293)
geographic information systems (GIS) (p. 294)
primary trading area (p. 299)
secondary trading area (p. 299)
fringe trading area (p. 299)
destination store (p. 299)
parasite store (p. 299)

analog model (p. 304)
regression model (p. 304)
gravity model (p. 304)
Reilly's law of retail gravitation (p. 305)
point of indifference (p. 305)
Huff's law of shopper attraction (p. 305)
economic base (p. 307)

Census of Population (p. 309)
Survey of Buying Power (p. 312)
effective buying income (EBI) (p. 312)
buying power index (BPI) (p. 314)
understored trading area (p. 316)
overstored trading area (p. 316)
saturated trading area (p. 316)

Questions for Discussion

1. If a retailer has a new 20-year store lease, does this mean the next time it studies the characteristics of its trading area should be 15 years from now? Explain your answer.

2. What is trading-area overlap? Are there any advantages to a chain retailer's having some overlap among its various stores? Why or why not?

3. Describe three ways in which a luggage chain could use geographic information systems (GIS) software in its trading-area analysis.

4. How could an off-campus store selling apparel near a college campus determine its primary, secondary, and fringe trading areas? Why should the apparel store obtain this information?

5. Why do few trading areas look like concentric circles?

6. How could a parasite store increase the size of its trading area?

7. Explain Reilly's law. What are its advantages and disadvantages?

8. Use Huff's law to compute the probability of consumers' traveling from their homes to each of three shopping areas: square footage of selling space—Location 1, 4,000; Location 2, 7,000; Location 3,

9,000; travel time—to Location 1, 10 minutes; to Location 2, 15 minutes; to Location 3, 25 minutes; effect of travel time on shopping trip—2. Explain your answer.

9. What are the major advantages and disadvantages of *Census of Population* data in delineating trading areas?

10. Describe the kinds of retail information contained in the *Survey of Buying Power*. What is its most critical disadvantage?

11. Look at the most recent buying power index in the *Survey of Buying Power* for the area in which your college is located. What retailing-related conclusions do you draw?

12. Look at the most recent issue of *Editor & Publisher Market Guide* and study the economic base characteristics for the area in which your college is located. What retailing-related conclusions do you draw?

13. If a retail area is acknowledged to be "saturated," what does this signify for existing retailers? For prospective retailers considering this area?

14. How could a Web-based retailer determine the level of saturation for its product category? What should this retailer do to lessen the impact of the level of saturation it faces?

WEB-BASED EXERCISE

Caliper (www.caliper.com)

Questions

1. Describe Caliper's Maptitude GIS system.

2. What questions should you ask of Caliper's management prior to adopting its system as your retail GIS? Explain your answer.

3. Analyze the relevancy of the data that are used with Maptitude.

4. Should a small gift shop and a department store use Maptitude differently? Explain your answer.

CHAPTER ENDNOTES

1. "Building on Service," *Do-It-Yourself Retailing* (May 1999), pp. 25–27.

2. Sunil Taneja, "Technology Moves In," *Chain Store Age* (May 1999), p. 136.

3. Peter D. Bennett (Editor), *Dictionary of Marketing Terms*, Second Edition (Chicago: American Marketing Association, 1995), p. 287.

4. Ibid., p. 289.

5. "In the Balance: The Net Changes Location Analysis," *Chain Store Age* (May 1999), p. 80.

6. See "Virtual Site Selection for Retailers," *Chain Store Age* (September 1999), pp. 160, 162; "Technology and Site Selection: Mapping Out the Future," *Shopping Centers Today* (September 1999), SCT Technology section; and Erin Strout, "Charting a Course," *Sales & Marketing Management* (August 1999), pp. 46–53.

7. "GIS for Site Analysis," *www.esri.com/industries/business/siteslctn.html* (March 9, 2000).

8. "Crown American Secures Retail Tenants with ArcView Business Analyst," *www.esri.com/news/arcnews/summer99articles/17-crownamerican.html* (Summer 1999).

9. See Pamela DeSmidt, "Claritas for Market Demographic Analysis," *Database* (June 1999), p. 24; and "Claritas Connect Pricing: Economical and Flexible," *www.connect.claritas.com/ratesandfees.htm* (March 9, 2000).

10. William J. Reilly, *Method for the Study of Retail Relationships*, Research Monograph No. 4 (Austin: University of Texas Press, 1929), University of Texas Bulletin No. 2944.

11. Richard L. Nelson, *The Selection of Retail Locations* (New York: F. W. Dodge, 1959), p. 149.

12. David L. Huff, "Defining and Estimating a Trading Area," *Journal of Marketing*, Vol. 28 (July 1964), pp. 34–38; and David L. Huff and Larry Blue, *A Programmed Solution for Estimating Retail Sales Potential* (Lawrence: University of Kansas, 1966). For further information, see Christophe Benavent, Marc Thomas, and Anne Bergue, "Application of Gravity Models for the Analysis of Retail Potential," *Journal of Targeting, Measurement, and Analysis for Marketing*, Vol. 1 (Winter 1992–1993), pp. 305–15; and Eric Cohen, "Miles, Minutes, & Custom Markets," *Marketing Tools* (July–August 1996), pp. 18–21.

13. David A. Gautschi, "Specification of Patronage Models for Retail Center Choice," *Journal of Marketing Research*, Vol. 18 (May 1981), pp. 162–74.

14. Glen E. Weisbrod, Robert J. Parcells, and Clifford Kern, "A Disaggregate Model for Predicting Shopping Area Market Attraction," *Journal of Retailing*, Vol. 60 (Spring 1984), pp. 65–83.

15. Avijit Ghosh, "The Value of a Mall and Other Insights from a Revised Central Place Model," *Journal of Retailing*, Vol. 62 (Spring 1986), pp. 79–97.

16. Paul LeBlang, "A Theoretical Approach for Predicting Sales at a New Department-Store Location Via Life-Styles," *Direct Marketing*, Vol. 7 (Autumn 1993), pp. 70–74.

17. Kenneth C. Schneider, James C. Johnson, Bradley J. Sleeper, and William C. Rodgers, "A Note on Applying Retail Location Models in Franchise Systems: A View from the Trenches," *Journal of Consumer Marketing*, Vol. 15 (No. 3, 1998), pp. 290–96.

18. Isabel P. Albaladejo-Pina and Joaquin Aranda-Gallego, "A Measure of Trade Centre Position," *European Journal of Marketing*, Vol. 32 (No. 5–6, 1998), pp. 464–79.

19. David R. Bell, Teck-Hua Ho, and Christopher S. Tang," Determining Where to Shop: Fixed and Variable Costs of Shopping," *Journal of Marketing Research*, Vol. 35 (August 1998), pp. 352–69.

20. Francisco José Más Ruiz, "Image of Suburban Shopping Malls and Two-Stage Versus Uni-Equational Modelling of the Retail Trade Attraction," *European Journal of Marketing*, Vol. 33 (No. 5–6, 1999), pp. 512–30.

21. Christy Fisher, "City Lights Beckon to Business," *American Demographics* (October 1997), p. 46.

22. Joseph DiStefano, "Doughnuts to Dollars," *Shopping Centers Today* (September 1999), p. 64.

23. *Finish Line 1999 Annual Report.*

24. *Heilig-Meyers Company 1999 Annual Report.*

25. *Syms Corporation 1999 Annual Report.*

26. "Glossary," *Sales & Marketing Management: 1999 Survey of Buying Power* (September 1999), p. 214.

27. Susan Reda, "Ethnically Oriented Centers Draw New Retailer, Developer Interest," *Stores* (January 1997), pp. 122–24.

28. Jennifer Lach, "Reading Your Mind, Reaching Your Wallet," *American Demographics* (November 1998), pp. 39–44.

29. Leslie Kaufman, "Wal-Mart Casts Eye Northward," *New York Times* (February 16, 1999), pp. C1, C10.

CASE 1

ARBY'S: USING GIS MAPPING SOFTWARE

While inexpensive geographic information systems (GIS) mapping software for personal computers has been available since the early 1980s, it has recently gone through a two-stage progression. In the mid-1990s, GIS software packages typically integrated geographic and demographic information on a single CD-ROM disk. Then in the late 1990s, GIS software packages began providing retailers with current data on an area's demographic profiles, lifestyle groups, retail sales, and traffic counts through Web access.

Reports can now be generated on a retail site's trading area characteristics, after the retailer "points and clicks" a computer mouse to identify the borders of a site's trading area. For example, a retailer may wish to determine the total population within given distances (such as 3, 5, and 8 miles) from a specific site. A trading area's current population can also be contrasted with the forecast population.

One active user of GIS software is Arby's, a fast-food franchisor that specializes in fresh, hot roast beef. Conducting trading-area analysis with GIS software presents several advantages for Arby's. First, it can avoid the tedious process of producing handmade maps. Second, the maps can easily be related to Arby's data base, such as the number of residents within a given distance of each site. Third, more potential sites can be identified in terms of desirable trading-area attributes. Fourth, "what if" scenarios—such as the impact of a new location on an existing unit's sales—can more readily be determined.

From its GIS analysis, Arby's knows that 75 percent of its customers usually travel 11 minutes or less from their home or workplace to a store. The firm has also defined each outlet's primary, secondary, and fringe trading areas on the basis of travel time (less than 5 minutes, 5 to 10 minutes, and 10 to 15 minutes). It relies on a detailed data base of road characteristics (outlining each road's normal traffic speed and the distance of a location to an entrance or exit ramp of an interstate highway). The drive times have been placed into its GIS program to prepare driving time maps for every Arby's location.

CASE 1

(CONTINUED)

Arby's regularly uses its findings to segment the market for its food services based on the travel time to each restaurant. Customers living or working less than 5 minutes from an existing Arby's represent a good target market for the firm's quick-service message or for programs to increase customers' frequency of purchase. On the other hand, for people who live or work more than 15 minutes from an existing store, Arby's enacts a marketing program that stresses the fresh preparation and sliced-to-order benefits of its roast beef. In addition, it looks for appropriate locations for new restaurants.

Questions

1. Why should GIS software be used to *supplement* more traditional site selection tools and not to replace them?

2. Develop specific criteria that Arby's can use to evaluate a GIS software vendor.

3. In deciding whether to open additional outlets in a particular trading area, what criteria should Arby's use? How could Arby's use GIS software to aid its decision making in this situation?

4. Would you recommend the use of GIS software for a retailer with one store? Explain your answer.

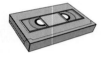

Video Questions on GIS Mapping

1. The video lists five functions for the GIS software that is described. Explain each of them.

2. Give three trading-area applications of GIS software for Arby's that are not cited in the video.

NOTE

The material in this case is drawn from Claritas company reports; and *www.claritas.com* (March 1, 2000).

CASE 2

NEBRASKA'S HILLTOP MALL: COMPETING WITH WAL-MART ACROSS THE STREET

Losing an anchor tenant such as Wal-Mart is usually tough for a 267,000-square-foot shopping center; and Hilltop Mall in Kearney, Nebraska, recently faced this situation. After 10 years in Hilltop Mall, Wal-Mart decided to vacate its 87,000-square-foot store and move directly across the street. Wal-Mart's new supercenter combines general merchandise and supermarket retailing in a single building.

Hilltop Mall's reaction to this action was surprising. According to Bob Slechta, senior vice-president of the firm that manages and leases Hilltop, "If Wal-Mart relocated to another part of town, it might have been different; but if it had to move, this was the best option." Slechta feels the Hilltop Mall benefits from Wal-Mart's presence, even though Wal-Mart draws some shoppers from Hilltop. Says Slechta, "We see lots of customers walking from their parking lot to ours and vice versa. So it's really like we've doubled the size of our shopping center." Since Wal-Mart's departure, average sales per square foot at Hilltop Mall have risen from about $210 to $240 per square foot.

Although Hilltop Mall's trading area encompasses Kearney's local university and medical community, it also draws a large proportion of its store traffic from a geographic area with a 100-mile reach to the north and west. The chief competitive shopping center is the 538,000-square-foot Conestoga Mall, located about 45 miles east of Kearney. The economic base of the surrounding area is heavily agricultural. Kearney has a population of approximately 27,000, and the area within a 45-mile radius adds another 81,000 people. The average household income is about $52,000. Bob Slechta says, "I think Kearney is more of a destination for most of these people. I don't think they're saying, let's jump into the car and go to Wal-Mart. When you come from that far, we all share in that shopping trip as a destination."

After Wal-Mart's relocation, Hilltop Mall made a concerted effort to upgrade its tenant mix, as well as its overall appearance. Slechta believes "that showed a lot of confidence in the market and in our game plan for the shopping center." For example, the expanded Herberger's store now has a greater selection of higher-price apparel, cosmetics, and accessories in its larger store placement. The more upscale appeal of Herberger's and the departure of a full-line discount store have resulted in more apparel stores and other traditional mall retailers being interested in the shopping center. Many Hilltop retailers have expanded or renovated their stores since Wal-Mart's departure.

When Wal-Mart left, 10 years after Hilltop Mall was built, 22 retailer leases were up for renewal. Twenty of these retailers renewed their leases. Currently, Hilltop Mall is 96 percent occupied and anchored by J.C. Penney and Herberger's (which doubled its space by taking on Wal-Mart's former location) and includes 46 other retailers. Furthermore, Herberger's Hilltop Mall store "has had our highest per-square-foot sales of any of our locations."

Questions

1. How can Hilltop Mall determine its primary, secondary, and fringe trading areas?

2. What other factors may explain the economic success of Hilltop Mall after Wal-Mart's departure?

3. Comment on the pros and cons of Kearney's heavily agricultural economic base.

4. As the property manager for Hilltop Mall, develop a plan to increase your market penetration in comparison to Wal-Mart and the Conestoga Mall.

NOTE

The material in this case is drawn from John Dube, "Nebraska Center Finds New Life after Wal-Mart," *Shopping Centers Today* (May 1999), pp. 96, 100.

CHAPTER 10

Site Selection

CHAPTER OBJECTIVES

1. To thoroughly examine the types of locations available to a retailer: isolated store, unplanned business district, and planned shopping center
2. To note the decisions necessary in choosing a general retail location
3. To describe the concept of the one-hundred percent location
4. To discuss several criteria for evaluating general retail locations and the specific sites within them
5. To contrast alternative terms of occupancy

Simon Property Group, the owner and operator of 260 real-estate properties—including regional and community shopping centers, specialty store locations, and mixed-use projects—is one of the leaders in the new strategy of "branding" real-estate properties with the developer's name. Simon's objective is that its "brand will be seen by every shopper who enters our malls."

Each Simon mall entrance now has an 8-foot by 4-foot panel that identifies it as a Simon property and includes the firm's pledge: "We simply promise to maintain a clean, cheerful shopping environment, and to make us your shopping center of choice." The company's properties also indicate their ownership by Simon in other ways. For example, at the firm's regional shopping center in Livingston, New Jersey, red and yellow signs contain the word "Simon" in large letters, with the words "Livingston Mall" in much smaller lettering.

Despite the company's investment and the initial public relations hoopla, many retail consultants wonder about Simon's strategy. As one consultant says, "I would doubt that a customer is going to care whether or not the local mall is owned or managed by a certain company." Referring to his own suburban Atlanta neighborhood, the consultant adds, "We've got two of the most successful malls here, Lenox Square and Phipps Plaza, and 99 percent of Atlantans don't know who owns them and don't care." Each of these shopping centers is owned by Simon. So, you can be sure that many Atlantans now know—or will soon know—the name of the malls' owner.[1]

OVERVIEW

After a retailer investigates alternative trading areas (Step 1), it then determines what type of location is desirable (Step 2), selects the general location (Step 3), and evaluates alternative specific store sites (Step 4). Steps, 2, 3, and 4 are discussed in this chapter.

> *Please Note:* Web site addresses are constantly changing.
> The links in this chapter are current as of the publication of this book.

TYPES OF LOCATIONS

There are three basic location types to distinguish among: the isolated store, the unplanned business district, and the planned shopping center. Each has its own attributes relating to the composition of competing stores, parking facilities, nearness to nonretail institutions (such as office buildings), and other factors. Step 2 in the location process is a determination of which type of location to use.

The Isolated Store

An **isolated store** is a freestanding retail outlet located on either a highway or a street. There are no adjacent retailers with which this type of store shares traffic.[2]

The advantages of this type of retail location are many:

- There is no competition.
- Rental costs are relatively low.
- There is flexibility.
    1. No group rules must be abided by in operation.
    2. Larger space may be attained.
    3. Location is by choice.
- Isolation is good for stores involved in one-stop or convenience shopping.
- Better road and traffic visibility is possible.
- Facilities can be adapted to individual specifications.
- Easy parking can be arranged.
- Cost reductions are possible, leading to lower prices.

There are also various disadvantages to this retail location type:

- Initial customers may be difficult to attract.
- Many people will not travel very far to get to one store on a continuous basis.
- Most people like variety in shopping.
- Advertising costs may be high.
- Operating costs—such as outside lighting, security, maintenance of grounds, and trash collection—cannot be shared.
- The existence of other retailers and community zoning laws may restrict access to desirable locations.
- A store must often be built rather than rented.
- As a rule, unplanned business districts and planned shopping centers are much more popular among consumers; they generate the bulk of retail sales.

The difficulty of attracting and holding a target market is the major reason large retailers (such as Wal-Mart) or convenience-oriented retailers (such as 7-Eleven) are usually those best suited to isolated locations. A small specialty store would probably not be able to develop a customer following at this type of location because people would be unwilling to travel to or shop at a store that does not have a very large assortment of products (width and/or depth) or a strong image for merchandise and/or prices.

Years ago, when discount operations were frowned on by traditional retailers, numerous shopping centers forbade the entry of discounters. This forced numerous discounters to become isolated stores or to build their own centers, and they have been successful. Today, diverse retailers are in isolated locations, as well as at business district and shopping center sites. Examples of retailers using a mixed location strategy are Kmart, Krispy Kreme, McDonanld's, Dairy Queen, Sears, Toys "R" Us, Wal-Mart, and 7-Eleven. Some retailers,

Figure 10.1
Site Selection and Dairy Queen

Dairy Queen situates its stores in various types of locations, from freestanding sites to planned shopping centers. The Dairy Queen/Brazier concept—highlighted here—features the Dairy Queen treat line of soft-serve dairy products and the Brazier fast-food menu. These freestanding stores are designed to include an indoor dining area and a drive-through window. The Dairy Queen/limited Brazier Store is designed for urban markets either in a strip-type shopping center or a freestanding store. These outlets are located in high-traffic sites with good visibility and accessibility. They feature the full line of soft-serve dessert and treat items, frozen cakes, and a limited food menu consisting of hot dogs and barbecue sandwiches. The Treat Center store is designed for larger regional shopping centers and megamalls. This concept combines Dairy Queen soft-serve menu items with Orange Julius fruit beverages and/or Karmelkorn caramel coated popcorn.
Reprinted by permission. All of the store and brand names cited in the caption are registered trademarks of Dairy Queen.

including many gas stations and convenience stores, continue to emphasize isolated locations. See Figure 10.1.

The Unplanned Business District

An **unplanned business district** is a type of retail location where two or more stores situate together (or in close proximity) in such a way that the total arrangement or mix of stores is not due to prior long-range planning. Stores locate based on what is best for them, not the district. Thus, four shoe stores may exist in an area with no pharmacy.

There are four kinds of unplanned business district: the central business district, the secondary business district, the neighborhood business district, and the string. A brief description of each follows.

Central Business District A **central business district (CBD)** is the hub of retailing in a city. It is the largest shopping area in that city and is synonymous with the term *downtown*. The CBD exists in the part of a town or city with the greatest density of office buildings and stores. Both vehicular and pedestrian traffic are very high. The core of a CBD is often no more than a square mile, with cultural and entertainment facilities surrounding it. Shoppers are drawn from the whole urban area and include all ethnic groups and all classes of people.

The CBD has at least one major department store and a broad grouping of specialty and convenience stores. The arrangement of these stores follows no pre-set format; it depends on history (first come, first located), retail trends, and luck.

Here are some strengths that allow CBDs to draw a large number of shoppers and potential shoppers:

- Excellent goods/service assortment.
- Access to public transportation.
- Variety of store types and positioning strategies within one area.
- Wide range of prices.
- Variety of customer services.
- High level of pedestrian traffic.
- Nearness to commercial and social facilities.

In addition, chain headquarters stores are often situated in CBDs.

These are some of the inherent weaknesses of the CBD:

- Inadequate parking.
- Traffic and delivery congestion.
- Travel time for those living in the suburbs.
- Many aging retail facilities.
- Declining condition of some central cities relative to their suburbs.
- Relatively poor image of central cities to some potential consumers.
- High rents and taxes for the most popular sites.
- Movement of some popular downtown stores to suburban shopping centers.
- Discontinuity of offerings (such as four shoe stores and no pharmacy).

Although the CBD remains a major force in retailing, over the past 40 years, its share of overall store sales has fallen substantially, as compared to the planned shopping center. Besides having the weaknesses just cited, much of the CBD's drop-off is due to the continuing suburbanization of the population. In the first half of the 20th century, most urban workers lived near their jobs. But gradually, many people moved to the suburbs—where they are served by planned shopping centers.

Nonetheless, a number of CBDs are doing quite well and others are striving to return to their former stature. Many are using such tactics as modernizing storefronts and equipment, forming cooperative merchants' associations, fixing sidewalks and adding brighter lighting to create "atmosphere," building vertical malls (with several floors of stores), improving transportation networks, closing streets to vehicular traffic (with sometimes disappointing results), bringing in "razzmatazz" retailers such as Nike Town and Warner Bros. Studio Stores, and integrating a commercial and residential environment known as mixed-use facilities.

There are signs of turnarounds and continuing strong retail developments in several cities. According to one consultant, "The most successful downtowns throughout America are those that are moving back to what they were in the beginning. They are returning to much more of a neighborhood feel, as original city centers. 'Pedestrianization' as we define it today is not to close off cars; it is to make it easy to move through." Instead, say other planners: "Most shoppers who arrive downtown in their cars want to park near their shopping area or have easy drop-off access to stores. Pedestrian malls offer neither. Birds and trees are perfectly nice, but no one really goes shopping to see them."[3]

One of the best examples of a strong CBD is New York City, where the business community has worked hard to strengthen the central city to make it more competitive with suburban shopping centers and stimulate office construction. Consider the $200 million renovation of Grand Central Terminal:

When it opened in 1913, Grand Central resembled a village, where a visitor could get a shave, take a Turkish bath, have a hat made, or see a newsreel. By the 1950s, however, airplanes had overtaken long-distance rail travel, and the station fell into disrepair. The diversity of shops dwindled to "five different ways to buy doughnuts and six different ways to buy bagels." Then, the demolition of cross-town Penn Station in the 1960s, ultimately seen as a huge mistake, inspired a long battle to preserve Grand Central. Today, the "city within a city" is sparkling, up to its 100-foot ceiling restored with 2,500 gold-leaf stars. With 120 shops open, one can buy everything from fresh goat meat to Tibetan lamb-trimmed gloves. Some old-time stores have survived, such as Grand Central Optical, which has filled more than 200,000 prescriptions since 1923. The lobby is now a wine shop, with gold-trimmed ceilings and murals of stars and planets. And you can still play tennis on the upper-level courts.[4]

Boston's Faneuil Hall is another thriving CBD renovation. When developer James Rouse took over the 6.5-acre site containing three 150-year-old, block-long former food warehouses, it had been abandoned for almost 10 years. Rouse creatively used landscaping, fountains, banners, open-air courts, informal entertainment (street performers), and colorful graphics to enable Faneuil Hall to capture a festive spirit. Faneuil Hall combines shopping, eating, and watching activities and makes them fun. Today, Faneuil Hall has over 70 shops, 14 full-service restaurants, 40 food stalls, and a popular comedy nightclub. It attracts millions of shoppers and visitors yearly.

Other major CBD projects include Riverchase Galleria (Birmingham, Alabama), Tower City Center (Cleveland), Pioneer Place (Portland), The Gallery at Harborplace (Baltimore), Crown Center (Kansas City), Union Station (Washington, D.C.), Circle Centre (Indianapolis), Peabody Place (Memphis), Horton Plaza (San Diego), New Orleans Centre, Underground Atlanta, and South Street Seaport (New York). See Figure 10.2.

Secondary Business District

A **secondary business district (SBD)** is an unplanned shopping area in a city or town that is usually bounded by the intersection of two major streets. Cities—particularly larger ones—often have multiple SBDs, each having at least a junior department store (which may be a branch of a traditional department store or a full-line discount store), a variety store, and/or some larger specialty stores—in addition to many smaller stores. This type of location has grown in importance as cities have increased in population and "sprawled" over larger geographic areas.[5]

The kinds of goods and services sold in an SBD mirror those in the CBD. However, an SBD has smaller stores, less width and depth of assortment, and a smaller trading area (consumers will not travel as far) and sells a higher proportion of convenience-oriented items.

The SBD's major strengths include good product assortments, access to thoroughfares and public transportation, less crowding and more personal service than a CBD, and placement nearer to residential areas than a CBD. The SBD's major weaknesses include the discontinuity of offerings, the sometimes high rent and taxes (but not as high as in a CBD), traffic and delivery congestion, aging facilities, parking difficulties, and fewer chain outlets than in the CBD. These weaknesses have generally not affected the SBD as much as the CBD—and parking problems, travel time, and congestion are less for the SBD.

Neighborhood Business District

A **neighborhood business district (NBD)** is an unplanned shopping area that appeals to the convenience shopping and service needs of a single residential area. An NBD contains several small stores, such as a dry cleaner, a stationery store, a barber shop and/or a beauty salon, a liquor store, and a restaurant. The leading retailer is typically a supermarket, a large drugstore, or a variety store. This type of business district is situated on the major street(s) of its residential area.

An NBD offers consumers a good location, long store hours, good parking, and a less hectic atmosphere than a CBD or SBD. On the other hand, there is a limited selection of goods

Figure 10.2
Revitalized Central
Business Districts

Large business districts
rely on the customer
traffic drawn by office
buildings, as well as cultural and entertainment
facilities. Two popular,
revitalized business dis-
tricts are depicted here:
The Gallery at
Harborplace in
Baltimore (top photo)
and South Street
Seaport in New York
(bottom photo).
Reprinted by permission of
The Rouse Company.

and services, and prices (on the average) tend to be higher because competition is less than in a CBD or SBD.

String A **string** is an unplanned shopping area comprising a group of retail stores, often with similar or compatible product lines, located along a street or highway. There is little extension of shopping onto perpendicular streets. A string may start with an isolated store,

Placing Small Towns on the Horizon

Rick McCord is the president and the chief executive officer of Horizon Pharmacies, a Princeton, Texas-based chain that acquires and operates profitable independent pharmacies in towns having fewer than 50,000 residents. The chain has 30 stores in 10 states.

According to McCord, "There is less competition in the towns we are targeting, both from a business and acquisition standpoint. The big drug chains aren't that interested in these areas—at least not yet. And the rents or leasing costs in small towns are low, about 1.2 percent of sales. We are not interested in the cookie-cutter approach to drugstore retailing. The stores we buy are tailored to meet the needs of the local community. That's why they succeed. We are not going to change a store to make it fit a master plan." Horizon competes with Wal-Mart in virtually every market.

Rick McCord is certainly an expert in drugstore retailing. After receiving a pharmacy degree in 1976, he joined True Quality Pharmacies. At that time, True Quality operated in some freestanding locations, but mostly as leased departments in Wal-Mart and grocery stores. During his 17-year tenure with True Quality, McCord moved up through the management ladder. McCord and other True Quality executives left that firm in 1994 to start Horizon Pharmacies. Soon thereafter, True Quality was dissolved, with Wal-Mart setting up its own in-store pharmacies. Today, Horizon is flourishing and expanding rapidly.

Source: "Small Towns Mean Big Business for Horizon," *Chain Store Age* (April 1998), p. 44.

success then breeding competitors. Car dealers, antique stores, and clothing stores are examples of retailers often situating in strings.

A string location has many of the advantages of an isolated store site (lower rent, more flexibility, better road visibility and parking, and lower operating costs), along with some disadvantages (limited product variety, increased travel for many consumers, higher advertising costs, zoning restrictions, and the need to build premises). Unlike an isolated store, a string store has competition at its location. This draws more people to the string area and allows for some sharing of common costs among firms. It also means less control over prices and less store loyalty for each outlet there. But an individual store's increased traffic flow, due to being in a string rather than an isolated site, may be greater than the customers lost to competitors. This may explain why four gas stations will locate on opposing corners.

Figure 10.3 shows a map with various forms of unplanned business districts and isolated locations.

The Planned Shopping Center

A **planned shopping center** consists of a group of architecturally unified commercial establishments built on a site that is centrally owned or managed, designed and operated as a unit, based on balanced tenancy, and surrounded by parking facilities. Its location, size, and mix of stores are related to the trading area served. A typical shopping center has one or more anchor stores and a range of smaller stores. Through **balanced tenancy,** the stores in a planned shopping center complement each other as to the quality and variety of their product offerings, and the kind and number of stores are linked to the overall needs of the population. To ensure balanced tenancy, the management of a planned shopping center usually specifies the proportion of total space to be occupied by each kind of retailer, limits the product lines that can be sold by every store there, and stipulates what kinds of firms can acquire

Figure 10.3
Unplanned Business Districts and Isolated Locations

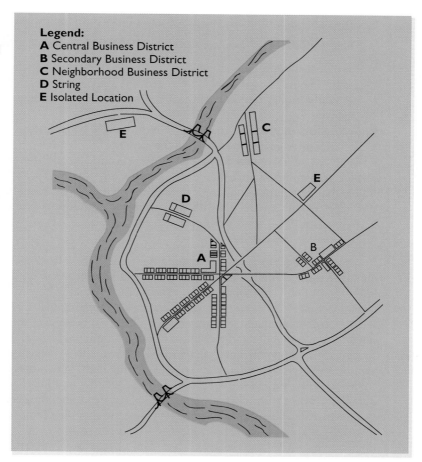

Legend:
A Central Business District
B Secondary Business District
C Neighborhood Business District
D String
E Isolated Location

unexpired leases. At a well-run center, a coordinated and cooperative long-run retailing strategy is followed by all stores.

The planned shopping center has several positive attributes:

- Well-rounded goods and service assortments based on long-range planning.
- Strong suburban population.
- Interest in one-stop, family shopping.
- Cooperative planning and sharing of common costs.
- Creation of distinctive, but unified, shopping center images.
- Maximization of pedestrian traffic for individual stores.
- Access to highways and availability of parking for consumers.
- More appealing than city shopping for some people.
- Generally lower rent and taxes than CBD stores (except for most enclosed regional malls).
- Generally lower theft rates than CBD stores.
- Popularity of malls.
  1. Open (shopping area off-limits to vehicles).
  2. Closed (shopping area off-limits to vehicles and all stores in a temperature-controlled facility).

- Growth of discount malls and other newer types of shopping centers.

There are also some limitations associated with the planned shopping center:

- Landlord-imposed regulations that reduce each retailer's operating flexibility, such as required hours.
- Generally higher rent than an isolated store (with some regional centers being quite expensive).
- Restrictions on the goods/services that can be sold by each store.
- A competitive environment within the center.
- Required payments for items that may be of little or no value to an individual retailer, such as membership in a merchants' association.
- Too many malls in a number of areas (some observers call this "the malling of America").
- Rising consumer boredom with and disinterest in shopping as an activity.
- Aging facilities of some older centers.
- Domination by large anchor stores.

Did you know that shopping centers in some form have existed for over 1,000 years? Learn more about this retailing phenomenon (www.icsc.org/srch/about/impactofshopping centers).

The importance of planned shopping centers is evident from the following. First, according to the International Council of Shopping Centers (www.icsc.org), 40 years ago, there were fewer than 1,000 U.S. shopping centers; now, there are 44,000 (with 5.3 billion square feet of leasable footage), 10 percent of which are closed shopping malls. Shopping center revenues are $1.1 trillion annually and account for almost 40 percent of total U.S. retail-store sales (including automobiles and gasoline). About 10.4 million people work in shopping centers. Second, many shopping center customers are active, with 94 percent of Americans over age 18 visiting some type of center in an average month. Third, individual retail chains have a large shopping center presence. The Limited, Inc., Dillard's, and J.C. Penney are among the vast number of chains with substantial sales and profits from shopping center stores.

Fourth, some big retailers have been involved in shopping center development. Typically, they buy a site of their choosing, years in advance, and contact another major retailer (depending on the center's size). They then bring in a developer, who builds, owns, and leases the center and connects it to the anchor stores. Sears has participated in the construction of dozens of shopping centers, and Publix Supermarkets operates centers with hundreds of small tenants. Fifth, each year, numerous new centers of all kinds and sizes are built and millions of square feet of retail space are added to existing centers.

To sustain their long-term growth, shopping centers are engaging in such practices as these:

Shopping Centers Today, in print and online (www.icsc.org/srch/sct/current/index.html), is the bible of the industry.

- Several older centers have been or are being renovated, expanded, or repositioned. The Florida Mall in Orlando; Market Place Mall in Champaign-Urbana, Illinois; King of Prussia in Pennsylvania; Belle Promenade in New Orleans; County East Mall in Antioch, a San Francisco suburb; Newmarket North Center in Hampton, Virginia; Roosevelt Field in Long Island, New York; Speedway Center in Indianapolis; and University Towne Center in San Diego are among the 10- to 35-year-old centers that have recently been revitalized. As one consultant notes, "You've got to be aware of new competition and be proactive about it, not reactive, and you do that by renovating, repositioning, or remerchandising your center."[6] See Figure 10.4.
- Certain derivative types of centers are being used to foster consumer interest and enthusiasm. Two of these, megamalls and power centers, are discussed a little later in this chapter.
- Shopping centers have been responding to shifting consumer life-styles. They have made parking easier, added ramps for baby strollers and wheel chairs, and included more life-style retailers such as Disney, Warner Bros., Crate & Barrel, Williams-Sonoma, Grand Cuisine, and The Right Start. They have also introduced more information booths and center directories.

Figure 10.4
Roosevelt Field: Renovated, Expanded, *and* Repositioned

Roosevelt Field in Long Island, New York—one of the 10 largest shopping centers in the United States—has been renovated and expanded several times since its opening nearly 45 years ago. In the 1990s alone, $100 million was spent to add a new 170,000-square-foot wing. Today, Roosevelt Field has 2.4 million square feet of store space and it has repositioned itself by adding Bloomingdale's, Nordstrom, Kenneth Cole, Mont Blanc, Tourneau Corner, and Polo Sport (among others) to its mix of 280 stores.
Reprinted by permission of the Simon Property Group.

- The retailer mix is broadening at many centers to attract people interested in one-stop shopping. In particular, more centers than before include such service-oriented businesses as banks, stockbrokers, dentists, doctors, beauty salons, TV repair outlets, and/or car rental offices. Many centers are also heavily involved with "temporary tenants." These are retailers who lease space (often in mall aisles or walkways) and sell from booths or moving carts. The tenants benefit from the lower rent and short-term commitment; the shopping centers benefit by creating more excitement and diversity in shopping. This way, customers often happen on new vendors in unexpected places.
- Some enclosed malls are opening themselves up: "What's driving the renewed focus on shopping al fresco? In part, it is a quest by developers and retailers to lure consumers who find indoor malls stale and homogeneous. Miami resident Carl Zablotny says he doesn't especially like to shop, yet enjoys CocoWalk, a popular open-air center in the city's Coconut Grove district. 'When the wind is blowing and the sun is shining, it's just a more inviting experience than an indoor mall.'"[7] See Figure 10.5.
- More shopping center developers are striving to build their own brand loyalty. Simon, Prime Retail, and Westfield are among the developers that are spending millions of advertising dollars to boost the images of the shopping centers they own by publicizing their own names (rather than just those of the centers). They promote slogans such as "Simply Simon—Simply the best shopping there is." to encourage people to shop their centers, wherever they are.[8] Simon (www.simon.com/company) owns and manages 260 properties in 36 states and Europe, with 190 million square feet of space.
- Shopping centers are turning more to frequent-shopper programs, thereby working to retain customers and track their spending patterns by offering them extra rewards. The prizes range from pre-paid calling cards to Caribbean vacations.[9]

Figure 10.5
CocoWalk: An
Open-Air Shopping
Center

Reprinted by permission of
City Center Retail.

There are three major types of planned shopping centers: regional, community, and neighborhood. Their characteristics are displayed in Table 10.1, and they are described next.

Regional Shopping Center A **regional shopping center** is a large, planned shopping facility appealing to a geographically dispersed market. It has at least one or two full-sized department stores (each with a minimum of 100,000 square feet) and 50 to 150 or more smaller retailers. A regional center has a very broad and deep assortment of shopping-oriented goods, as well as a number of services intended to enhance the consumer's experience at the center. The market for a typical regional center is 100,000+ people, who live or work up to a 30-minute drive from the center. On average, people travel less than 20 minutes.

The regional center is the result of a planned effort to re-create the shopping variety of a central city in suburbia. Some experts even credit the regional shopping center with becoming the social, cultural, and vocational focal point of an entire suburban area. Frequently, a regional center is used as a town plaza, a meeting place, a concert hall, and a place for a brisk indoor walk. Despite people's declining overall interest in shopping (which does pose a significant problem for retailers), on a typical visit to a regional shopping center, many people spend an average of an hour or more there.

Regional malls have existed in the United States for five decades. The first outdoor center opened in 1950 in Seattle, anchored by a branch of Bon Marche, a leading downtown department store. Southdale Center (outside Minneapolis), built in 1956 for the Target Corporation (then known as Dayton Hudson), was the first fully enclosed, climate-controlled mall. Today, there are nearly 21,000 regional centers in the United States. In recent years, this American invention has also been popping up around the world (where small stores still remain the dominant forces)—from Australia to Malaysia to Brazil.

Mall of America's Web site (www. mallofamerica.com) is as impressive as the mall itself.

One newer derivative form of regional center, the megamall, is particularly intriguing. A **megamall** is an enormous planned shopping center with 1 million+ square feet of retail space, multiple anchor stores, up to several hundred specialty stores, food courts, and entertainment facilities. Its goal is to heighten consumer interest in shopping and greatly expand the trading area. There are 395 U.S. megamalls, including the giant Mall of America (www.mallofamerica.com) in Bloomington, Minnesota. It has four anchors (Bloomingdale's, Macy's, Nordstrom, and Sears), over 500 other stores, a 14-screen movie theater, a health club, 57 restaurants and nightclubs, the world's largest indoor amusement park (Camp

Table 10.1 Characteristics of Typical Neighborhood, Community, and Regional Types of U.S. Planned Shopping Centers

Features of a Typical Center	TYPE OF CENTER		
	Regional	Community	Neighborhood
Total site area (acres)	30–100+	10–30	3–10
Total sq. ft. leased to retailers	400,001–2,000,000+	100,001–400,000	30,000–100,000
Principal tenant	One, two, or more full-sized department stores	Branch department store (traditional or discount), variety store, and/or category killer store	Supermarket or drugstore
Number of stores	50–150 or more	15–25	5–15
Goods and services offered	Largest assortment for customers, focusing on goods that encourage careful shopping and services that enhance the shopping experience (such as a food court)	Moderate assortment for customers, focusing on a mix of shopping- and convenience-oriented goods and services	Lowest assortment for customers, emphasizing convenience-oriented goods and services
Minimum number of people living/working in trading area needed to support center	100,000+	20,000–100,000	3,000–50,000
Trading area in driving time	Up to 30 minutes	Up to 20 minutes	Fewer than 15 minutes
Location	Outside central city, on arterial highway or expressway	Close to one or more populated residential area(s)	Along a major thoroughfare in a single residential area
Layout	Mall, often enclosed with anchor stores at major entrances/exits	Strip or L-shaped	Strip
Percentage of all centers	5	33	62
Percentage of all centers' selling space	29	46	25
Percentage of all centers' retail sales	30	41	29

Sources: Percentage data computed by the authors from "NRB Shopping Center Census 1999," *Shopping Centers Today* (April 1999), p. NRB 3.

Snoopy, created by Knott's Berry Farm of California), and 12,750 parking spaces—all on 4.2 million square feet of space. The mall has stores to fit every budget, attracts 37 percent of visitors from outside a 150-mile radius, and draws 600,000 to 900,000 visitors per week (depending on the season). The West Edmonton Mall in Canada is the world's largest megamall. See Figure 10.6.

Community Shopping Center A **community shopping center** is a moderate-sized, planned shopping facility with a branch department store (traditional or discount), a variety store, and/or a category killer store, in addition to several smaller stores (usually similar to those in a neighborhood center). It offers a moderate assortment of both shopping- and convenience-oriented goods and services to consumers from one or more nearby, well-populated, residential areas. About 20,000 to 100,000 people, who live or work within 10 to 20 minutes of the center, are served by this location.

Figure 10.6
West Edmonton Mall: A Canadian Megamall

At 5.3 million square feet, West Edmonton Mall is the largest indoor shopping and entertainment complex in the world, as well as Alberta, Canada's leading tourist attraction. Millions of people come from around the world to visit the mall, which features over 800 stores and services, over 110 restaurants and kiosks, the world's largest indoor amusement park, the world's largest indoor water park, an NHL-size ice arena, four seaworthy submarines in the world's largest indoor manmade lake, dolphin shows, a replica of the Santa Maria ship, a miniature golf course, 26 movie theaters, and a Las Vegas-style casino.
Reprinted by permission of Triple Five Corporation. Photos by the Postcard Factory.

Better long-range planning is used for a community shopping center than for a neighborhood shopping center. Balanced tenancy is usually enforced and cooperative promotion expenditures are more likely. Thus, store composition and the center's image are kept pretty consistent with pre-set goals.

One noteworthy type of community center is the **power center,** a shopping site with (a) up to a half dozen or so category killer stores and a mix of smaller stores or (b) several complementary stores specializing in one product category. A power center usually occupies

200,000 to 400,000 square feet and is situated on a major highway or road intersection. Its goals are to be quite distinctive—thus providing consumers with a strong motivation to go there—and to better compete with regional centers. There are over 2,000 U.S. power centers. For instance, Pennsylvania's Whitehall Square and New York's The Mall at Cross County are category killer power centers run by Kranzco Realty Trust (www.krt.com). The 298,000-square-foot Whitehall Square is anchored by a 50,000-square-foot Sports Authority, a 35,000-square-foot Phar-Mor Drugs, and a 25,000-square-foot Kids "R" Us. The 265,000-square-foot The Mall at Cross County features a 47,000-square-foot Sports Authority, a 46,000-square-foot Circuit City, a 31,000-square-foot T.J. Maxx, and a 25,000-square-foot Kids "R" Us. Each has many smaller stores, as well. The 200,000-square-foot Towne Center Village in Marietta, Georgia, is a specialized home furnishings power center. It features furniture, custom sofa, and Oriental rug stores.

Neighborhood Shopping Center A **neighborhood shopping center** is a planned shopping facility, with the largest store being a supermarket or a drugstore. Other retailers in the center often include a bakery, a laundry, a dry cleaner, a stationary store, a barber shop or beauty parlor, a hardware store, a restaurant, a liquor store, and a gas station. This center focuses on convenience-oriented goods and services for people living or working nearby. It serves 3,000 to 50,000 people who are within a 15-minute drive (usually less than 10 minutes).

A neighborhood shopping center is usually arranged in a strip. When first built, it is carefully planned, and tenants are balanced. Over time, the planned aspects of this center may diminish and newcomers may face fewer restrictions. Thus, a liquor store may be allowed to replace a barber shop. There would then be no barber shop. A center's ability to maintain balance depends on its continuing attractiveness to potential tenants (as expressed by the extent of the store vacancy rate).

In number, but not in selling space or sales, neighborhood centers account for more than 60 percent of all U.S. shopping centers.

THE CHOICE OF A GENERAL LOCATION

The last part of Step 2 in location planning requires a retailer to select one of the three basic locational formats: isolated, unplanned district, or planned center. The decision depends on the firm's strategy and a careful evaluation of the advantages and disadvantages of each alternative.

Once this is done, the retailer chooses a broadly defined site for its store(s), Step 3. Two decisions are needed here. First, the specific kind of isolated store, unplanned business district, or planned shopping center location must be picked. If a retailer wants an isolated store, it must determine whether to locate on a highway or side street. Should the retailer desire an unplanned business area, it must decide whether to locate in a CBD, an SBD, an NBD, or a string. A retailer seeking a planned area must decide whether to locate in a regional, community, or neighborhood shopping center—and whether to situate in a derivative form such as a megamall or power center. Here are the preferences of a variety of retailers:

- The Uni-Mart chain of convenience stores (www.uni-mart.com) favors isolated locations in small towns: "The majority of our stores are located in rural communities where Uni-Mart is the 'store around the corner.' Our strategy is to offer customers a selection of goods and services that meet their everyday needs at convenient locations during extended hours."
- Talbots, Gap, Body Shop, J. Crew, Sam Goody, and Williams-Sonoma are among the mall-based retailers opening more stores in CBDs and SBDs: "They've discovered that many shoppers would rather navigate their own village centers than the sprawling parking lots of regional malls."[10]
- Sterling Jewelers and Helzberg Diamonds are both adding stores in freestanding centers because they can have larger shops there than in regional centers. Sterling's category killer

The Emergence of Power Developers

In recent years, the number of shopping center developers has decreased, mostly due to consolidations. For example, with its acquisition of Corporate Property Investors, Simon now has a controlling interest in 160 regional shopping centers and 50 community shopping centers. Rouse (with 45 regional shopping centers and nearly 20 community shopping centers) and Westfield America (with 40 regional shopping centers) have also grown by acquiring properties from developers such as TrizecHahn. In markets such as San Diego, all but two of the major regional shopping centers are owned by the same firm.

Many retailers are concerned about the impact of developer consolidation on the balance of power between retailers and developers. This particularly bothers the small to medium retailer. Paying higher rents because of less competition among developers is a problem for retailers that want to protect their pricing points. As the real-estate director for a regional sporting goods retailer says, "The more property you control, the more control you have over property. You're gonna be stuck paying what they want."

On the other hand, some retailers see benefits from the consolidation. These include their ability to review multiple properties from a single source, the greater importance of building long-term relationships with developers, easier lease negotiations, and the savings due to economies of scale. Large developers can also provide a higher level of professional management than smaller developers.

In your view, is the growth of the power developer a good or bad trend? Explain your answer.

Sources: Mary Beth Knight, "Is Bigger, Better?" *Chain Store Age* (January 1999), pp. 142–44; and company Web sites.

---

stores, named Jared The Galleria of Jewelry, are five times the size of the firm's mall stores.[11] See Figure 10.7.

> Consolidated Stores has a well-conceived location plan (www.cnstore.com/stores/index.html).

● Consolidated Stores (www.cnstore.com) has a mixed-location strategy. Its Big Lots, Odd Lots, MacFrugal's, and Pic 'N' Save closeout stores are mostly in strip shopping centers. Its K-B toy stores are largely in regional shopping centers. Its K-B Toy Outlets and Toy Liquidators are in factory outlet centers to appeal to serious bargain hunters, who view their trips as major shopping events.

Second, the retailer must determine the general placement of its store(s). For an isolated store, this means selecting a specific highway or side street. For an unplanned district or planned center, this means designating a specific district (e.g., downtown Los Angeles or Pittsburgh) or center (e.g., Seminary South in Fort Worth, Texas, or Chesterfield Mall in Richmond, Virginia).

In Step 3, the retailer narrows down the decisions made in the first two steps and then chooses a general location. Step 4 requires the firm to evaluate specific alternative sites, including their position on a block (or in a center), the side of the street, and the terms of tenancy. The factors to be considered in assessing and choosing a general location and a specific site within that location are described together in the next section because many strategic decisions are similar for these two steps.

LOCATION AND SITE EVALUATION

The assessment of general locations and the specific sites contained within them both require extensive analysis. Site selection is as crucial as the choice of a retail area, especially for stores that rely on customer traffic patterns to generate business.

Figure 10.7
Jared The Galleria
of Jewelry

Reprinted by permission of
Sterling Jewelers, Inc.

In any area, the optimum site for a particular store is called the **one-hundred percent location.** Since different kinds of retailers need different kinds of locations, a location labeled as 100 percent for one firm may be less than optimal for another. An upscale ladies' apparel shop would seek a location with different strengths than those desired by a convenience store. The specialty shop would benefit from heavy pedestrian traffic, closeness to major department stores, and proximity to other specialty stores. The convenience store would rather locate in an area with ample parking and heavy vehicular traffic. It does not need to be close to other stores.

Figure 10.8 contains a checklist for location and site evaluation. In choosing a location, a retailer would rate every alternative location (and specific site) on all the criteria and develop an overall rating for each alternative. Two firms may rate the same site differently, depending on their requirements. This figure should be used in conjunction with the trading-area data noted in Chapter 9, not instead of them.

Pedestrian Traffic

Probably the most crucial measures of a location's and site's value are the number and type of people passing by. Other things being equal, a site with the highest pedestrian traffic is often best.

Because everyone passing a location or site is not necessarily a good prospect for all types of stores, many retailers use selective counting procedures, such as counting only males and females carrying shopping bags. Otherwise, pedestrian traffic totals may include too many nonshoppers. For example, it would be improper for an appliance retailer to count as prospective shoppers all the people who pass a downtown site on the way to work. In fact, much of the pedestrian traffic in a downtown location may be from people who are in the area for nonretailing activities.

A proper pedestrian traffic count should encompass these four elements:

- Separation of the count by age and gender (children under a given age should not be counted).
- Division of the count by time (this allows the study of peaks, low points, and changes in the gender of the people passing by the hour).

Figure 10.8
A Location/Site
Evaluation Checklist

Rate each of the following criteria on a scale of 1 to 10, with 1 being excellent and 10 being poor.		
Pedestrian Traffic	Number of people	_____
	Type of people	_____
Vehicular Traffic	Number of vehicles	_____
	Type of vehicles	_____
	Traffic congestion	_____
Parking Facilities	Number and quality of parking spots	_____
	Distance to store	_____
	Availability of employee parking	_____
Transportation	Availability of mass transit	_____
	Access from major highways	_____
	Ease of deliveries	_____
Store Composition	Number and size of stores	_____
	Affinity	_____
	Retail balance	_____
Specific Site	Visibility	_____
	Placement in the location	_____
	Size and shape of the lot	_____
	Size and shape of the building	_____
	Condition and age of the lot and building	_____
Terms of Occupancy	Ownership or leasing terms	_____
	Operations and maintenance costs	_____
	Taxes	_____
	Zoning restrictions	_____
	Voluntary regulations	_____
Overall Rating	General location	_____
	Specific site	_____

- Pedestrian interviews (these let researchers find out the proportion of potential shoppers).
- Spot analysis of shopping trips (these allow observers to verify the stores actually visited).

Vehicular Traffic

The quantity and characteristics of vehicular traffic must be examined, especially by retailers appealing to customers who drive there. Convenience stores, outlets in regional shopping centers, and car washes are examples of retailers that rely on heavy vehicular traffic. Automotive traffic studies are quite important in suburban areas, where pedestrian traffic is often limited.

As in the analysis of pedestrian traffic, adjustments to the raw count of vehicular traffic must be made. Some retailers count only homeward-bound traffic, some exclude vehicles passing on the other side of a divided highway, and some omit out-of-state license plates. Data on traffic patterns may be available from the state highway department, the county engineer, or the regional planning commission.

Besides traffic counts, the retailer should study the extent and timing of congestion (caused by severe traffic, detours, narrow and poor roads, and so on). Vehicular customers will normally avoid heavily congested areas, and shop where driving time and driving difficulties are minimized.

Parking Facilities

Parking facilities must not be overlooked in assessing a location and specific sites in it. Most the of U.S. retail stores built over the past 50 years include some provision for nearby off-street parking. In many business districts, parking facilities are provided by individual stores, cooperative arrangements among stores, and municipal governments. In planned shopping centers, parking facilities are shared by all stores there. The number and quality of parking spots, their distances from store sites, and the availability of employee parking should all be evaluated.

It is hard to generalize about a retailer's needs for parking facilities because they depend on such factors as the trading area of the store, the type of store, the portion of shoppers using a car, the existence of other parking facilities, the turnover of spaces (which depend on the length of the shopping trip), the flow of shoppers during the day and the week, and parking by nonshoppers. A shopping center normally needs 4 to 5 parking spaces per 1,000 square feet of gross floor area, a supermarket usually requires 10 to 15 spaces per 1,000 square feet, and a furniture store generally needs 3 or 4 spaces per 1,000 square feet.

Sometimes, free parking at shopping locations that are in or close to commercial areas creates problems. Commuters and employees of nearby businesses may park in these facilities, reducing the number of spaces available for shoppers. This dilemma can be lessened by the validation of shoppers' parking stubs and requiring payment from nonshoppers.

Another problem may occur if the total selling space at a location increases due to the addition of new stores or the expansion of current ones. Existing parking facilities may then be inadequate because space formerly allotted to parking might be given to the new stores or extensions and because parking needs rise to accommodate new employees, new shoppers, and longer shopping trips.

Double-deck parking or parking tiers are possible solutions to the problem. Besides saving land, these facilities shorten the distance from a parked car to a store—a crucial factor since customers at a regional shopping center may be unwilling to walk more than a few hundred feet from their cars to the center.

Having too large a parking facility may also cause some difficulties. If the facility is half-full, the location's image may suffer because an illusion of emptiness is created—and people would wonder why. A parking lot may contain 250 cars, but if the capacity of the lot is 500 cars, it might appear that the lot is empty and the stores unpopular.

Transportation

The availability of mass transportation, access from major highways, and ease of deliveries must be examined in assessing a location and specific sites.

In a downtown area, closeness to mass transit is important, particularly for people who do not own cars, who commute to work there, or who would not otherwise shop in an area with traffic congestion and limited parking. The availability of buses, taxis, subways, trains, and other kinds of public transit must be investigated for any area not readily accessible by vehicular traffic. Because most downtown shopping areas are at the hub of a mass transit network, they allow people from all over a city to shop there.

Locations dependent on vehicular traffic should be rated on the basis of their nearness to major thoroughfares. As mentioned in Chapter 9, driving time is a crucial consideration for many people. In addition, drivers heading eastbound on a highway often do not like to make a U-turn to get to a store on the westbound side of that highway.

The transportation network should also be studied for its ability to convey delivery trucks to and from the store. Many thoroughfares are excellent for cars but ban large trucks or cannot bear their weight.

Store Composition

An area's store composition should be studied. How many stores are there? How large are they? The number and size of stores should be consistent with the kind of location selected. A retailer interested in an isolated site would want no stores nearby; a retailer desiring a neighborhood business district would want to locate in an area with 10 or 15 small stores;

Crossing the Border from Mexico to Texas

Polly Adams is a women's specialty store located in Laredo, Texas. The store specializes in a variety of fashions—from contemporary and weekend casual clothing to fancy apparel for special occasions. Over 40 percent of the store's sales are generated by upscale Mexican women who come from Monterrey, an affluent city just south of the Texas border. The other 60 percent of revenues involve sales to customers residing in south Texas. Regardless of where the customers live, they "crave fashion and don't mind paying the price as long as the value is apparent," states Magda Foster, Polly Adams' current owner.

Polly Adams' entire sales staff is bilingual, and all sales associates are urged to keep detailed customer records. Foster conducts morning meetings with her sales staff and explains new store merchandise to each sales associate.

Unlike most other store owners, Foster calls her regular clients and asks them their apparel needs before going to the wholesale markets in Texas and New York. Three times a year, Foster and her sales staff visit the store's key accounts in their homes to show them the season's latest fashions. Foster then sends someone from her staff to the customer's home for a fitting.

Polly Adams currently has one freestanding location. Comment on the pros and cons of its possibly adding a second location in a regional shopping center.

Source: Rusty Williamson, "A Two-Culture Success Story: A Retailer Prospers by Catering to Women on Both Sides of the Tex-Mex Border," *Women's Wear Daily* (May 19, 1999), p. 39S.

and a retailer looking for a regional shopping center would want a location with more than 50 stores, including at least 1 or 2 large department stores (to generate customer traffic).

A firm should weigh its store's compatibility with adjacent or nearby stores when studying locations and sites. If the stores at a given location (be it an unplanned district or a planned center) complement, blend, and cooperate with one another, and each benefits from the others' presence, **affinity** exists. With a strong level of affinity, the sales of each store are greater, due to the high level of customer traffic, than if the stores are apart from each other.

The practice of similar or complementary stores locating near each other is based on two major premises: (1) Customers like to compare the offerings of similar stores with regard to price, style, selection, and service. (2) Customers like one-stop shopping (whereby they purchase a variety of products from different stores on the same shopping trip). Affinities can exist among competing stores, as well as among complementary stores. Because more people travel to shopping areas with large selections than to convenience-oriented areas, the sales of all stores are enhanced.

One measure of compatibility is the degree to which stores exchange customers. The stores in these categories are very compatible with each other and have high customer interchange:

- Supermarket, drugstore, bakery, fruit-and-vegetable store, meat store.
- Department store, apparel store, hosiery store, lingerie shop, shoe store, jewelry store.

A location's retail balance should also be considered. **Retail balance** refers to the mix of stores within a district or shopping center. Proper balance occurs when the number of store facilities for each merchandise or service classification is equal to the location's market potential, a wide range of goods and service classifications is provided to ensure one-stop shopping, there is an adequate assortment within any good or service category, and there is a proper mix of store types (balanced tenancy).

Specific Site

Besides the factors already detailed, the specific site should be reviewed on the basis of visibility, placement in the location, size and shape of the lot, size and shape of the building, and condition and age of the lot and building.

Visibility refers to a site's ability to be seen by pedestrian or vehicular traffic. A site on a side street or at the end of a shopping center does not have the same visibility as one on a major road or at the entrance of a shopping center. High visibility makes passersby aware that a store exists and is open. Furthermore, some people hesitate to go down a side street or to the end of a center.

Placement in the location refers to a site's relative position in the district or center. A corner location may be desirable since it is situated at the intersection of two streets and has "corner influence." A corner site is usually more expensive to own or lease because it offers these advantages: greater pedestrian and vehicular passersby due to converging traffic flows from two streets, increased window display area, and less traffic congestion by the use of two or more entrances. Corner influence is greatest in high-volume retail locations. That is why some Pier 1 stores, Starbucks restaurants, and Walgreen's drugstores occupy corner lots in shopping districts or corner spots in shopping malls. See Figure 10.9.

Some corner assets are reduced in a shopping center. Traffic on streets perpendicular to neighborhood and community centers is usually sparse, and fewer additional customers are attracted to a corner store. Since many stores in larger centers have two entrances (one in the mall and one in the parking area), people walk from the parking lot to the mall without using designated walkways, stores have more window displays without the need for corner sites, and traffic flows to and through the center are eased.

Placement decisions must be keyed to retailer needs. A convenience-oriented firm, such as a stationary store, would be very concerned about the side of the street, the location rela-

Figure 10.9
Corner Influence and Starbucks

At this Japanese Starbucks, pedestrians stroll past the impressive corner storefront—and often stop inside. Reprinted by permission of Starbucks Coffee Company.

tive to other convenience-oriented stores, nearness to parking, access to a bus stop, and the distance from residences. A shopping-oriented retailer, such as a furniture store, would be more interested in the use of a corner site to increase window display space, proximity to wallpaper and other related retailers, the accessibility of its pickup platform to consumers, and the ease of deliveries to the store.

In evaluating the size and shape of the lot, a department store requires significantly more space than a boutique; and it may desire a square site, whereas the boutique may seek a rectangular one. Any site should be viewed in terms of the total space needed: parking, walkways, selling, nonselling, and so on.

When a retailer buys or rents an existing building, its size and shape should be examined. In addition, the condition and age of the lot and the building should be investigated. These characteristics would then be measured against the firm's needs.

Due to the saturation of many desirable locations and the lack of leasing or ownership opportunities in others, some retailers have turned to more nontraditional sites—often to complement their established stores. Here are a few examples:

- TGI Friday's, Staples, and Bally are among the growing number of firms with airport stores.
- McDonald's has outlets in hundreds of Wal-Marts and at dozens of Amoco and Chevron gas stations.
- Some fast-food stores share facilities to give customers more variety, as well as to share costs.

As one observer notes, "The development of retail outlets in nontraditional locations is largely a response to two things: changing consumer demands and fairly saturated local markets. Fast-food chains in particular have developed virtually every profitable piece of real-estate in many markets, yet they still want to increase the number of opportunities for shoppers to see their brand name on the street. Fearing they'll be outnumbered by competitors, these expansion-minded retailers are finding alternatives to freestanding stores. The result is everything from a shopping mall inside Paris' Louvre museum to fast-food restaurants in gas stations. This strategy not only makes chain retailers even more visible, it also appeals to growing consumer demands for ease and convenience. Convenience isn't just about making a store easy to shop in. It's about helping the customer accomplish three or four things that they have to get done over a lunch break or after work. It's about meeting a whole range of needs. And alternative retail sites aren't just for fast-food restaurants. Even upscale retailers are finding new sites."[12]

Terms of Occupancy

Terms of occupancy—including ownership versus leasing, the type of lease, operations and maintenance costs, taxes, zoning restrictions, and voluntary regulations—must be evaluated for each prospective site.

Ownership Versus Leasing A retailer with adequate financial resources can either own or lease premises. Ownership is more common in small stores, in small communities, or at inexpensive locations. It has several advantages over leasing. There is no chance that a property owner will not renew a lease or will double or triple the rent when a lease expires. Monthly mortgage payments are stable. Operations are flexible; the retailer can engage in scrambled merchandising, break down walls, and so on. It is also likely that property value will appreciate over time, giving the retailer a tangible asset if it decides to sell the business. The disadvantages of ownership are the high initial costs, the necessary long-term commitment, and the inflexibility in changing sites. At Home Depot, about 75 percent of its store properties are owned by the retailer.[13]

The Main Street pro-gram (www.mainst. org/about/aboutmain. htm) has revitalized communities across the United States.

If a retailer chooses to own the store premises, it must decide whether to construct a new facility or buy an existing building. In weighing the alternatives, the retailer should consider the purchase price and maintenance costs, zoning restrictions, the age and condition of existing facilities, the adaptability of existing facilities to its needs, and the time to erect a new building. To encourage building rehabilitation in small towns (5,000 to 50,000 people), Congress enacted the Main Street program of the National Trust for Historic Preservation in 1980. Retailers in over 1,400 U.S. communities have benefited from their participation in this program (www.mainst.org) by getting tax credits and low-interest loans.

Despite the advantages of ownership, the great majority of store sites in central business districts and regional shopping centers are leased, mostly due to the high property investments for ownership. Department stores tend to have renewable 30-year leases, supermarkets usually have renewable 20-year leases, and stores such as Finish Line and T.J. Maxx typically have 10-year leases with options to extend for one or more 5-year periods. Some leases give the retailer the right to end an agreement before the expiration date—under given circumstances and for a specified payment by the retailer.

Leasing lets retailers minimize their initial investment, reduce their risk, acquire leases at prime sites that could not accommodate additional stores, gain immediate occupancy and customer traffic, and reduce their long-term commitment (if they desire). Many retailers also feel they can open more stores or spend more on other aspects of their strategies by leasing. Firms that lease also accept these disadvantages: the limits on operating flexibility, the restrictions on subletting and selling the business, possible nonrenewal problems, future rent increases, and not benefiting from the rising value of real estate.

Through a **sale-leaseback,** some large retailers build stores and then sell them to real-estate investors who lease the property back to the retailers on a long-term basis. Retailers using sale-leasebacks build stores to their specifications and have bargaining power in leasing—while lowering capital expenditures.

Tax-exempt industrial revenue bonds have also been used to finance retail facilities. In this arrangement, a state or municipality uses bond proceeds to build stores or warehouses and gives retailers long leases (with payments used to pay bond principal and interest). The practice reduces investment costs for retailers, but requires them to commit to a site for an extended period.

Types of Leases Inasmuch as most retailers lease store facilities, it is vital to be familiar with the basic lease formats used. Property owners no longer rely solely on constant rent leases, partly due to their concern about interest rates and the related rise in many of their operating costs; thus, terms can become quite complicated.

Tiffany (www.tiffany. com), a name synonymous with glamour, is one of the cornerstone retailers on New York's high-rent Fifth Avenue.

The simplest, most direct arrangement is the **straight lease,** whereby a retailer pays a fixed dollar amount per month over the life of the lease. Rent usually ranges from $1 to $75 annually per square foot, depending on factors like the site's desirability and store traffic. At some sites, rents can be much higher (up to hundreds of dollars per square foot). On New York City's Fifth Avenue, from 48th to 58th Streets, the average yearly rent is $600 per square foot! On London's Oxford Street, rent is $400 per square foot!

A **percentage lease** stipulates that rent is related to sales or profits. This differs from a straight lease, which provides for constant payments, regardless of revenues or earnings. Thus, a drugstore may pay 4 percent of sales, a toy store 6 percent, and a camera store 12 percent (with the amounts keyed to the space occupied and sales per square foot). A percentage lease protects a property owner against the effects of inflation, and lets it benefit if a store is successful; it also allows a tenant to view the lease as a variable cost—which means rent is lower when its performance is weak and higher when performance is good. The percentage rate varies by type of shopping district or center and by type of store.

Percentage leases have variations. In one, a minimum or maximum rent is noted. With a specified minimum, low sales are assumed to be partly the retailer's responsibility; the property owner receives minimum payments (as in a straight lease) that at least partially cover the mortgage, taxes, and property maintenance. With a specified maximum, it is assumed that a very successful retailer should not pay more than a maximum rent. Superior merchandising, promotion, and pricing should reward the retailer. A second variation is the sliding scale: the ratio of rent to sales changes as sales rise. A sliding-down scale has a retailer pay a lower percentage as sales go up and is an incentive to the retailer.

A **graduated lease** calls for precise rent increases over a stated period of time. Thus, monthly rent may be $4,000 for the first 5 years, $4,800 for the next 5 years, and $5,600 for the last 5 years of a lease. The rent is known in advance by both the retailer and the property owner, and based on anticipated increases in sales and costs. There is no problem in auditing sales or profits, as there is for percentage leases. A graduated lease is often used with small retailers having weak financial statements and controls.

A **maintenance-increase-recoupment lease** has a provision allowing rent to increase if a property owner's taxes, heating bills, insurance, or other expenses rise beyond a certain point. This provision most often supplements a straight rental lease agreement.

A **net lease** calls for all maintenance costs, such as heating, electricity, insurance, and interior repair, to be paid by the retailer—which is responsible for their satisfactory quality. A net lease frees the property owner from managing the facility and lets the retailer have control over store maintenance. It would be used to supplement a straight lease or a percentage lease.

Other Considerations After assessing ownership and leasing opportunities, a retailer must look at the costs of operations and maintenance. Mortgage or rental payments are only one part of a site's costs. The age and condition of a facility may cause a retailer to have high total monthly costs, even though the mortgage or rent is low. Furthermore, the costs of extensive renovations should be calculated.

What is the sales tax in Utah? California? Go to this site (www. salestaxinstitute. com) to find out the sales tax rates in all 50 states.

Taxes must be evaluated, especially in an ownership situation. Long-run projections, as well as current taxes, must be examined. Differences in sales taxes (those that customers pay) and business taxes (those that retailers pay) among alternative sites must be weighed. Business taxes should be broken down into real-estate and income categories. The highest state sales tax is in Mississippi and Rhode Island (7 percent), while Alaska, Delaware, Montana, New Hampshire, and Oregon have no state sales tax.

Technology in Retailing

Shopping Centers Address Their Cybermall Competition

Shopping centers recognize the increasing popularity of the World Wide Web and its potential impact on their bricks-and-mortar stores. As one shopping center developer says, "People will buy convenience on the Internet. If you are in a convenience business, it will be very difficult for you to compete with the breadth of what it has to offer. I think you have to make the store the whole point of your process. Otherwise, I do see the Internet having an impact."

The pervasiveness of the Web has nudged some developers to rethink the design of their existing shopping centers, as well as the ones they are constructing. TrizecHahn is building Desert Passage, a 500,000-square-foot mall at the Aladdin resort in Las Vegas. This entertainment-filled center will be filled with open-air stalls that resemble a Moroccan market. Another TrizecHahn mall, in Hollywood, will include a Broadway-style theater that will be home to the annual Academy Awards telecast.

Some mall developers have also begun making E-commerce investments. Taubman, for example, recently spent $7 million for a 9.9 percent ownership of fashionmall.com, an online mall. In addition, it has an option to purchase an additional 10 percent of the online firm.

As the manager of a community shopping center, present an overall plan for handling the increased presence of the Web.

Source: Teena Hammond, "Malls of the Future: Shopping Centers Eye Life on the Internet," *Women's Wear Daily* (June 8, 1999), p. 1.

Zoning restrictions should be analyzed. There may be legal limits as to the kind of stores allowed, store size, building height, the type of merchandise carried, and other factors that have to be hurdled (or another site chosen). For example,

> When Kranzco Realty decided to replace an aging 5-plex theater at Barn Plaza in Doylestown, Pennsylvania, with a state-of-the-art 14-plex Regal Cinema, it didn't expect much community resistance. The theater, resembling a barn with a silo and wooden battened-down sides, was falling apart. Surely, no one would object to replacing the old theater with a multiplex having the latest amenities. That was not the case. "They basically said your center is called Barn Plaza, and that barn has been there for 40 years," recalled Kranzco's president. After heated negotiations with township officials and the local community, a new Barn Theater was born. "They made us build the theater like a barn with a new silo on it and we ended up conforming to their wishes." While Barn Plaza may be unique, it illustrates the growing influence that communities are having on shopping center design.[14]

Voluntary restrictions, those not mandated by the government, should also be examined. These are most prevalent in planned shopping centers and may include required membership in merchant groups, uniform store hours, and cooperative security forces. Leases for many stores in regional shopping centers have included clauses protecting anchor tenants (large department stores) from too much competition—especially from discounters. These clauses may involve limits on product lines, bans against discounting, fees for common services, and specifications as to acceptable practices. Anchors have received protective clauses by developers since the latter need their long-term commitments to finance the centers.

Some shopping center practices have been limited by the Federal Trade Commission (FTC). As an illustration, the FTC discourages "exclusives"—whereby only a particular retailer in a shopping center can carry specified merchandise—and "radius clauses"—whereby a tenant agrees not to operate another store within a certain distance of the center.

Because of the overbuilding of retail facilities in many areas, some retailers are now in a better position to bargain over the terms of occupancy. This differs from city to city and from shopping location to shopping location.

Overall Rating

The last task in selecting a general location, and the specific site within it, is to compute overall ratings. First, each location under consideration is given an overall rating based on its performance on all the criteria displayed in Figure 10.8. The overall ratings of alternative locations are then compared, and the best location is chosen. The same procedure is used to evaluate the alternative sites within the location.

It is often difficult to compile and compare composite evaluations because some attributes may be positive while others are negative. For example, the general location may be a good shopping center, but the site in the center may be poor; or an area may have excellent potential, but it will take two years to build a store. Therefore, the attributes in Figure 10.8 need to be weighted according to their importance to the retailer. An overall rating should also include certain knockout factors, those that would preclude consideration of a site. Possible knockout factors are a short-duration lease (fewer than three years), no evening or weekend pedestrian traffic, and poor tenant relations with the landlord.[15]

Lease agreements used to be so simple that they could be written on a napkin—not any more (www.icsc.org/srch/sct/current/sct9905/16.htm).

SUMMARY

1. *To thoroughly examine the types of locations available to a retailer: isolated store, unplanned business district, and planned shopping center.* After a retailer rates alternative trading areas, it decides which type of location is desirable, selects the general location, and chooses a particular site. There are three basic locational types a firm should distinguish among.

An isolated store is freestanding, not adjacent to other stores. This type of location has several advantages, including no competition, low rent, flexibility, road visibility, easy parking, and lower property costs. There are also disadvantages: difficulty in attracting traffic, no variety for shoppers, no shared costs, and zoning restrictions.

An unplanned business district is a shopping area with two or more stores located together or nearby. Store composition is not based on long-range planning. Unplanned business districts can be broken down into four categories: central business district, secondary business district, neighborhood business district, and string.

An unplanned business district generally has these points in its favor: variety of goods, services, and prices; access to public transit; nearness to commercial and social facilities; and pedestrian traffic. Yet, this location's shortcomings have led to the growth of the planned shopping center: inadequate parking, older facilities, high rents and taxes in popular CBDs, discontinuity of offerings, traffic and delivery congestion, high theft rates, and some declining central cities.

A planned shopping center is centrally owned or managed and well balanced. It usually has one or more anchor stores and many smaller stores. During the past several decades, the growth of the planned shopping center has been great, due to extensive goods and service offerings, expanding suburbs, shared strategy planning and costs, attractive locations, parking facilities, lower rent and taxes (except for regional shopping centers), lower theft rates, the popularity of malls (although some people are now bored with them), and the lesser appeal of inner-city shopping. The negative aspects of the planned center include operations inflexibility, restrictions on merchandise carried, and anchor store domination. There are three shopping center forms: regional, community, and neighborhood.

2. *To note the decisions necessary in choosing a general retail location.* First, the specific form of isolated store, unplanned business district, or planned shopping center location is determined, such as whether to locate on a highway or side street; in a CBD, an SBD, an NBD, or a string; or in a regional, community, or neighborhood shopping center. Then, the general location for a store is specified, thereby singling out a particular highway, business district, or shopping center.

3. *To describe the concept of the one-hundred percent location.* Extensive analysis is required when evaluating each general location and the specific sites contained within it. Most importantly, the optimum site for a given store must be determined. This site is called the one-hundred percent location, and it differs by store.

4. *To discuss several criteria for evaluating general retail locations and the specific sites within them.* These factors should be studied: pedestrian traffic, vehicular traffic,

parking facilities, transportation, store composition, the attributes of each specific site, and terms of occupancy. An overall rating is then computed for each location and site, and the best one would be selected.

Affinity occurs when the stores at the same location complement, blend, and cooperate with one another; each benefits from the others' presence.

5. *To contrast alternative terms of occupancy.* Terms of occupancy are critical in choosing a site. A retailer must opt to own or lease. If it leases, terms are specified in a straight lease, percentage lease, graduated lease, maintenance-increase-recoupment lease, and/or net lease. Operating and maintenance costs, taxes, zoning restrictions, and voluntary restrictions also need to be weighed.

Key Terms

isolated store (p. 325)
unplanned business district (p. 326)
central business district (CBD)
  (p. 326)
secondary business district (SBD)
  (p. 328)
neighborhood business district (NBD)
  (p. 328)
string (p. 329)

planned shopping center (p. 330)
balanced tenancy (p. 330)
regional shopping center (p. 334)
megamall (p. 334)
community shopping center (p. 335)
power center (p. 336)
neighborhood shopping center (p. 337)
one-hundred percent location (p. 339)
affinity (p. 343)

retail balance (p. 343)
terms of occupancy (p. 345)
sale-leaseback (p. 345)
straight lease (p. 346)
percentage lease (p. 346)
graduated lease (p. 346)
maintenance-increase-recoupment
  lease (p. 346)
net lease (p. 346)

Questions for Discussion

1. A beauty salon chain has decided to open outlets in a combination of isolated locations, unplanned business districts, and planned shopping centers. Comment on this strategy.

2. Why do computer software stores often locate in shopping centers or business districts, while convenience stores, such as 7-Eleven, often operate at isolated sites?

3. From the retailer's perspective, compare the advantages of locating in unplanned business districts versus planned shopping centers.

4. Differentiate among the central business district, the secondary business district, the neighborhood business district, and the string.

5. Develop a brief plan to revitalize a neighborhood business district near your campus.

6. What is a megamall? What is a power center? Describe the strengths and weaknesses of each.

7. Evaluate a community shopping center near your campus.

8. What are some of the problems that planned shopping centers will probably have to address in the future? How should they respond?

9. Explain why a one-hundred percent location for K-B Toys may not be a one-hundred percent location for a local toy store.

10. What criteria should a small retailer use in selecting a general store location and a specific site within it? A large retailer?

11. What difficulties are there in using a rating scale such as that shown in Figure 10.8? What are the benefits?

Questions for Discussion

12. How do the parking needs for a health club, a consumer electronics store, and a theater differ?

13. Under what circumstances would it be more desirable for a retailer to buy or lease an existing facility rather than to build a new store?

14. What are the pros and cons of a straight lease versus a percentage lease for a prospective retail tenant? For the landlord?

WEB-BASED EXERCISE

West Edmonton Mall (www.westedmontonmall.com)

Questions

1. What should be the role of the West Edmonton Mall Web site? Why?

2. Comment on West Edmonton's overall Web site.

3. Do you like the "Java Mall Map" feature at the Web site? Explain your answer.

4. What are the pros and cons of West Edmonton Mall's overall tenant mix that combines traditional stores with amusement facilities, restaurants, and hotel facilities?

CHAPTER ENDNOTES

1. Barbara Martinez, "Mall Owners Play the Name Game," *Wall Street Journal* (March 10, 1999), p. B10.

2. See Bill Levine, "The Store Stands Alone," *Chain Store Age* (April 1998), pp. 107–108.

3. Jennifer Steinhauer, "When Shoppers Walk Away from Pedestrian Malls," *New York Times* (November 5, 1996), pp. D1, D4. See also Debra Hazel, "Going to Town," *Shopping Centers Today* (June 1999), pp. 7–8.

4. Jill Herbers, "A 'City Within a City': Vanderbilt's Retail Revolution," *Your Company* (July 1, 1999), p. 84.

5. For a fuller discussion of retailing sprawl, see John Springer, "Sprawl Brawl," *Shopping Centers Today* (May 1999), pp. 194–220.

6. Kevin Kenyon, "Off Center?" *Shopping Centers Today* (May 1999), p. 248.

7. Ann Carrns, "Malls Are Going Topless," *New York Times* (March 31, 1999), p. B1.

8. Candace Talmadge, "Centers Strive to Build Brand Identity," *Shopping Centers Today* (May 1999), pp. 109, 116, 127.

9. Sharon R. King, "Shoppers Get Awards; Malls Get Loyalty," *New York Times* (December 23, 1998), pp. C1, C4.

10. Mitchell Pacelle, "More Stores Spurn Malls for the Village Square," *Wall Street Journal* (February 16, 1996), p. B1.

11. Nancy Cohen, "Strip Mining," *Shopping Centers Today* (May 1999), pp. 155, 160, 162.

12. Shelly Reese, "Toilet Paper and a Big Mac," *American Demographics* (July 1996), pp. 14–15.

13. *Home Depot 1999 Annual Report*.

14. Kevin Kenyon, "Local Color," *Shopping Centers Today* (July 1999), p. 25.

15. For more information on site selection practices, see "Retail Real Estate: Awash in Complexity," *Chain Store Age* (May 1999), pp. 106–12.

CASE 1

THE MALL OF AMERICA

The Mall of America is the largest regional shopping center in the United States, with over 500 stores and about 4.2 million square feet of space. The mall is located on a 78-acre site less than two miles from the Twin Cities International Airport and about 10 to 15 minutes from downtown Minneapolis-St. Paul. Approximately 28 million people live within a day's drive of Mall of America. In addition, the mall benefits from a strong tourist market. A recent study conducted by the National Park Service and *Road Smart Magazine* found the Mall of America to be the most visited destination in the United States, attracting tens of millions of people each year.

Unlike smaller regional shopping centers that are predominately retail, the Mall of America is a blend of entertainment, food, and retail facilities. Besides its four anchor department stores (Bloomingdale's, Macy's, Nordstrom, and Sears) and over 500 specialty stores, the mall has a seven-acre Camp Snoopy amusement park (with 50 rides and attractions, including a roller coaster), a four-story LEGO Imagination Center (with 30 full-size LEGO models), a 14-screen movie theater, multiple restaurants, an 18-hole miniature golf course, nightclubs, and even a wedding chapel.

During its planning and early construction stages, many critics were skeptical about whether Mall of America would be a success. Now, however, even the worst skeptics have turned around due to the number of visitors, the length of shopping stays, and retail occupancy statistics. The Mall of America has more visitors per year than Disney World, Graceland, and the Grand Canyon. The average visitor stays for 3 hours (about three times the national average length of stay for a regional mall). No wonder Mall of America is over 95 percent leased.

Tourism from outside a 150-mile radius around Mall of America accounts for 37 percent of the customer traffic to the mall. International visitors account for about 6 percent of the mall's total traffic. This increased tourist base has increased overall retail sales in Minneapolis-St. Paul. Mall of America is now also positioning itself as a convention center, able to handle as many as 7,000 conventioneers at a time. The high level of convention activity is a boon to restaurant and hotel businesses.

Many analysts view Mall of America as a laboratory for stores seeking to involve customers in "hands-on" activities while shopping or offering entertainment combined with eating facilities. For example, Oshkosh's Supersports USA store encourages shoppers to "try before they buy" at its skating rink, basketball court, and Rollerblade track—all situated in the store. The mall also contains a Planet Hollywood and a Rainforest Café, two popular "eatertainment" restaurant facilities.

Questions

1. What are the pros and cons of Mall of America in comparison with a traditional regional shopping center?

2. Would you want to locate a store in Mall of America? Why or why not?

3. Present a seven-point checklist for Mall of America to evaluate potential retailer tenants.

4. What kind of lease terms should Mall of America set? Why?

Video Questions on Mall of America

1. Discuss the advantages and disadvantages to retailer tenants of Mall of America's unique combination of entertainment, food, and retail facilities.

2. Comment on Mall of America's promotional program.

NOTE   The material in this case is drawn from *www.mallofamerica.com* (March 9, 2000).

CASE 2

JUST FRESH: SUCCEEDING WHERE OTHERS HAVE FAILED

Just Fresh is a six-year-old, North Carolina-based bakery-café chain. Its concept is to combine a juice bar with gourmet coffee, bagels, and premium made-to-order sandwiches, salads, pastas, and soups—all with an emphasis on freshness. Although the chain's five partners originally wanted to base Just Fresh on the popular juice bars in the San Francisco area, they realized their chain had to offer more products than just juices and smoothies to be successful in the Southeast. They also saw the need to quickly serve their customers. "What it boiled down to was speed—being able to take a person's order and make their sandwich as fast as they could get it if they went to McDonald's, because that's about the max that people are willing to wait," says Whitney Montgomery, one of Just Fresh's five partners.

In searching for their first location, the partners concentrated on sites with substantial pedestrian traffic. Thus, their choice was in the First Union Atrium, a major pathway between an office building and a hotel in Charlotte, North Carolina's central business district. The Atrium has more than 9,000 people passing through it on a daily basis. According to Montgomery, "The Atrium could be considered one of the best retail spots in all of the Southeast."

Montgomery and his partners were pleasantly surprised when the landlord accepted their proposal. The lease negotiations took close to a year and a significant amount of time was spent on convincing the landlord that Just Fresh deserved a chance. The partners were confident Just Fresh would succeed, but at least three other businesses (including a sandwich restaurant) had recently failed in the same location. Furthermore, the landlord had studied the research done by both Cornell University and Michigan State University—which found that more than one-half of all restaurants fail in their first year of operation. The risk for Just Fresh was even higher because only one of the partners had any restaurant experience!

To protect his interests, the landlord included a clause in the restaurant's lease specifying that he would control the décor. The landlord reasoned that if Just Fresh failed, he could then quickly rent the location to another retailer without the need for costly renovations.

On its first day of business, Just Fresh served only 450 customers. Soon, it was serving more than 1,000 customers per day. Just Fresh's first-year sales were $300,000. Revenues have since grown to $4 million annually. After Just Fresh was established for two years, the partners established their first suburban unit, as well as their second downtown location. Soon after, an additional bakery unit with both self-serve and made-to-order foods was set up in a hospital using the same location that used to house a traditional coffee shop.

Just Fresh's success has come at a price. The partners had to spend considerable resources to fight—and ultimately win—a prolonged zoning battle for a second suburban location at a site formerly occupied by a bank. The partners have also begun to face intense competition for the best retail sites as competitors seek to copy Just Fresh's retail concept.

Questions

1. What are the pros and cons of opening at a retail site where other retailers have recently failed?

2. Could Just Fresh be considered a parasite store in its First Union Atrium location? Explain your answer.

3. What are the differences between an ideal site located in a central business district and one in a suburban location for Just Fresh?

4. What types of retailer present an affinity for Just Fresh?

NOTE   The material in this case is drawn from Elaine W. Teague, "Made From Scratch," *Entrepreneur* (February 1999), pp. 117–19.

PART FOUR
COMPREHENSIVE CASE

A Trading-Area Turnaround: Mom and Pops Are Now Facing "Little Boxes" from Power Retailers

INTRODUCTION

A few weeks ago, Ellen Feuer made a quick stop into a Cleveland-area OfficeMax store with her husband. The couple wasn't looking to do some heavy-duty shopping. Actually, they popped into the store in search of a ballpoint pen. "We weren't in there five minutes," says Ellen's husband, Michael, happily. Under normal circumstances, getting in and out of an OfficeMax superstore with a purchase in a couple of minutes would be impressive. But in this case—the store was the firm's new 7,500-square-foot PDQ store—five minutes could have provided enough time for Ellen to pick out a matching datebook and a few reams of paper.

Michael Feuer had reason to be happy and impressed with the quick shopping trip. He is co-founder, chairman, and CEO of OfficeMax. Still being tested, the PDQ (pretty darn quick) format is to be the horse OfficeMax will ride into high-density urban locations, such as office parks, commercial buildings, and college campuses, both domestically and internationally. The format is also expected to be set up within or near the arteries of major metro markets.

The prototype is stocked with 3,000 SKUs. A regular OfficeMax sells 8,000 SKUs. Feuer says his chain could eventually open 100 PDQs a year. Each unit would be open around-the-clock and also sell merchandise at drive-through windows.

TAKE A GOOD LOOK

Mature markets such as the United States are projected to spur very slow growth over the next decade. A

PricewaterhouseCoopers survey shows the population shopping less, and visiting malls less often but increasing trips to stores in search of a specific item. Translation: For many big-box retailers, a gain in market share will have to come either out of someone else's hide or from new sales avenues created to squeeze additional dollars out of a saturated industry, says Herb Kleinberger, PricewaterhouseCoopers' U.S. retail practice leader.

Say hello to the quick-shop small store (a "little box"), a concept rapidly becoming the focus of much attention within the retail community as a growing number of chains scale down and promote growth through a new miniature format. Retailers have always varied their big box sizes by 10 to 30 percent based on location. In 1998, superstores accounted for only 12.2 percent of new stores, down from a five-year high of 31.4 percent in 1995, according to the Food Marketing Institute. But not until rather recently have chains embraced small-format retailing with such a strong strategic, and financial, commitment.

Small stores cater to customers lacking the time and energy to meander their way through a behemoth of a parking lot en route to a 120,000-square-foot juggernaut—all for a roll of Scotch tape. "Big stores intimidate a lot of people," says PricewaterhouseCoopers economist Carl Steidtmann. "They're overwhelming, fatiguing, and in many cases they offer too many choices, particularly for an aging population. Sometimes wading through a 120,000-square-foot store is maddening."

Western New York supermarket chain Tops Markets, a unit of Ahold USA, apparently agrees. It is abandoning its big boxes. In late 1998, the 110-store Tops said it would focus on smaller, more shopper-friendly stores. The company went ahead and scrapped plans to build some 110,000-square-foot units, as well as any more 77,000-square-foot Tops Friendly Markets. The retailer is betting on a future full of 45,000-square-foot to 65,000-square-foot stores to give its bottom line a fruitful boost.

SMALL SOLDIERS

Sears recently debuted a quartet of small stores. Designed by New York City-based FRCH Design Worldwide, they offer about 60,000 square feet of selling space, focusing primarily on the company's "softer-side" apparel and accessories. Showcased are jewelry and fragrances, as well as Sears' own clothing lines, such as Canyon River Blues, Crossroads, and Apostrophe. The small stores are located in Orangeburg, South Carolina; St. George, Utah; and Lawrence and Garden City, Kansas.

Wal-Mart also has responded. The company recently opened its 40,000-square-foot Neighborhood Market concept, nicknamed "Small-Mart." The first few Markets are now open and being tested near Wal-Mart's Bentonville, Arkansas, headquarters. The food/drug combos are stocked with 20,000 to 23,000 SKUs. General merchandise SKUs are the best-sellers culled from a supercenter's typical 100,000 SKU base. Items include batteries, compact discs, pet products, and a dominant health and beauty care assortment. A stroll through the store last month found panty hose as the sole apparel item. Sales are running at 70 percent food and 30 percent general merchandise items. Wal-Mart says it would eventually like a 60/40 food/GM split.

Neighborhood Markets feature a 2,000-square-foot produce department, a small deli counter, and a fresh meat/produce department. The stores, which have two-lane drive-through pharmacies and photofinishing, are open seven days a week, 7 A.M. to 10 P.M. Units employ 75 associates, have capacity for 220 cars, and house 12 checkout lanes. Pricing mirrors that of Wal-Mart super-centers.

There are two main entrances and a wide but shallow layout with gondola runs ranging from 52 feet to 60 feet. Similar to most supermarkets, aisles are designed front to back (supercenter aisles are side-to-side) to get shoppers in and out as quickly as possible. The design of the store has a "market" feel. Outside, concrete entrances are painted brown to resemble wooden planks. Associates wear green vests, a departure from the well-recognized blue vests of associates in other Wal-Marts. The firm is reportedly looking for each Market to bring in $300 to $400 per square foot, or $15 million in annual revenues.

MOM-AND-POP ALERT

Small stores may satisfy consumers' needs for quick service and convenience, as well as retailers' needs for untapped financial opportunities. But they also serve a strategic purpose. Small stores can be used in areas too small to warrant big units and, look out mom and pop in the remaining trade areas, big box retailers have yet to invade deeply—Main Streets.

Companies such as Hastings Entertainment and Heilig-Meyers' ValueHouse Furniture unit have been thriving in these types of markets for years. Hastings chairman/CEO John Marmaduke says his chain per-

forms best in underserved small and medium-sized markets with populations ranging from 25,000 to 150,000. These markets are usually ignored by existing book, music, and software stores, and generally there is limited competition.

Not for long. "At some point, we will have opened up all the superstores we can open," states CompUSA executive VP-operations Sam Crowley. "When that happens, there will still be markets we're not serving." Dallas-based CompUSA is testing small stores in Texas ranging from 6,000 square feet to 15,000 square feet. The smallest of the group is located in the town of Lufkin (population: 80,000); the largest is in McGallon (population: 350,000). The stores, which Crowley says are profitable, have about half the SKU count of the 5,000 to 6,000 items carried in typical 28,000-square-foot CompUSAs.

Crowley says the company originally expected that the small stores would confine their activity to traditional retail sales. But the units have churned out the same lines of business revenues—corporate sales, training, and tech support—as full-sized CompUSA superstores. "The small markets have turned out to have the same needs as the big ones," he says. "And that taught us something."

Home Depot learned a thing or two when it watched its superstores have little effect on a small hardware chain out West called Fortress Supply. "As we would put stores next to them, they would just keep going," executive VP/chief administrative officer Ron Brill told *Fortune* in November 1998. The result? Home Depot is rolling out a string of 35,000-square-foot hardware stores targeted to small-project fixer-up customers who prefer a smaller, local store. The first of the new hardware c-stores (convenience stores) opened in East Brunswick, New Jersey, in a space formerly occupied by a Rickels home center.

SCALING DOWN

While Home Depot and its fellow big-boxers are looking to wipe independent stores off Main Street, it won't be easy to perform a clean sweep. Seasoned veterans such as Ace Hardware and True Value have carved out a lucrative niche for themselves in the heart of small-town communities. "That's one of the challenges of going into small markets," says Gary Witkin, the president and CEO of Service Merchandise. "You're losing dominance and going into markets where you're competing with good, high-energy retailers."

Across the street from the Neighborhood Market in Springdale, Arkansas, a 61,000-square-foot Harps supermarket has seen little impact to date. With a sign alerting shoppers that Harps has been "your neighborhood market since 1930," the grocer believes Wal-Mart is mostly cannibalizing sales from its surrounding supercenters.

Meanwhile, Service Merchandise is building on its core jewelry category and surrounding it with gift-giving merchandise in a small-store test format of its own. The company is experimenting with Service Select stores in strip centers and malls, in sites close to existing stores, and in sites far away from them. The 12,000-square-foot to 15,000-square-foot Service Select stores feature full-size jewelry departments (2,500 to 3,000 SKUs) accented with track lighting and surrounded by a laminated wood racetrack floor stocked with 1,600 to 1,800 other SKUs, or roughly 20 percent of traditional Service Merchandise stock. Items are delivered three times a week.

Mirroring the recent changes instituted in the chain's larger-format stores, Service Select offers customers a self-service shopping environment where many items are displayed in quantity and can be taken directly to the checkout. The new stores also house kiosks offering direct access to servicemerchandise.com and the chain's complete product offering. Service Merchandise is looking for annual sales of $3 million to $4 million from each Service Select unit and reports some of the test stores have produced higher gross-margin percentages than the company's traditional namesake stores.

Faced with increased low-priced competition from Ikea, Cost-Plus World Market, and even Target Stores, Crate & Barrel is working on Blueprint, a small-format, small-market, 6,000-square-foot store. The first Blueprint is on North Lincoln Avenue in Chicago's North Center area. The store sells "basic" items such as glassware, plates, and flatware culled from the shelves of traditional Crate & Barrel stores. Getting the financing to roll out hundreds of Blueprints shouldn't be a problem, now that Crate & Barrel is owned by affluent German catalog company Otto Versand.

CRUNCH THE NUMBERS

The list of retailers going to small-store formats also includes the likes of Publix and Zellers' Best Value. Staples has its Staples Express stores in central business districts, while Circuit City places its Express units in malls to pick off impulse electronics sales. Chains are betting that small stores can survive on lower volume and smaller selection. With SKU tracking systems more sophisticated than ever, retailers can pack small stores with their best-selling stock. "We can now better mine purchase data and fine-tune what stores carry," says PricewaterhouseCoopers' Steidtmann.

If the sales potential isn't enough to lure retailers to think smaller, consider the cost savings and quicker return on capital investment. Construction costs run, on average, $40 to $50 per square foot, says Juan Romero, president of Architecture Plus International, busy designing Home Depot's hardware convenience stores. Building a 15,000-square-foot store represents a substantial savings compared to building a 60,000-square-foot unit. There's also less inventory to house, reduced utility bills and monthly operations costs, fewer items to buy, and fewer people to employ. "You really do save quite a bit," states Romero. "Even the permits cost less."

But although costs and expenses are a fraction of those found in superstores, so are the sales. The small-store concept certainly has its benefits, but can it produce? Can it bring in the sales volume and profits retailers are looking for? Nobody knows. The power retailer's small stores are still very much in the test mode.

OfficeMax's Feuer doesn't know when there will be hundreds of PDQs scattered around the nation. Famously secretive Wal-Mart says it isn't sure what the future holds for Neighborhood Market, although the company has reportedly already picked out as many as 6,000 potential U.S. sites for the concept. Company spokespeople say that expansion would be limited to areas, both urban and rural, where food distribution centers already exist that service the Wal-Mart super centers.

"You are at the start of something that has the prospect of growing into another great company," said Tom Coughlin, executive VP/COO of the Wal-Mart Stores division, at the Neighborhood Market grand opening in October 1998. Many observers theorize that Neighborhood Markets, with their drive-through pharmacies, would permit Wal-Mart to compete more universally with local grocers in the United States while also being a format that could be brought to Europe, where land considerations might preclude the chain's typical 110,000-square-foot and larger store formats.

CompUSA's Crowley says he's scouting sites for some mini-stores right now, but sees a lot more testing on deck before the company nails down "what the final cookie cutter will look like." CompUSA is still toying with the small stores' assortment and staffing. A Crate & Barrel spokesperson says that if its concept flies, more

Blueprints could sprout up in the near future. Service Merchandise's Witkin says while there appears to be more traffic in mall-based Service Selects, he isn't sure just yet into which markets his small concept will best fit.

The big box no doubt will continue to be the prime growth vehicle for most chains. But if retailers can augment their big boxes with small stores targeted at both dense areas and small-market locales, they may end up with a high-velocity store menu that can serve any city or town, fend off rivals of all sizes, shave costs, slash overhead, and—most importantly—endear itself to a full range of consumers. "This isn't an easy thing to do, but there are small-store opportunities if you're good," says Witkin. "A true retailer has a place in every community in America."

AN OPPOSING APPROACH TO LITTLE BOXES: THE BIGGEST GROCERY STORE IN THE UNITED STATES

Throughout the early 1990s, shoppers in Wisconsin's fourth-largest city were used to seeing smaller, neighborhood grocery stores such as Kohl's Food Stores and Sentry replaced by larger outlets such as Pick'n Save. But they hardly could believe their eyes in August 1997 when Janesville, Wisconsin-based Woodman's Food Market opened in Kenosha, Wisconsin, what is billed as the largest U.S. grocery store.

After all, who had ever walked into a grocery store with a frozen food department nearly a football field in length? Who had strolled the aisles of a food store with 120,000 square feet of selling floor space and about an equal-sized attached warehouse? Who was familiar with the concept of a regional grocery store drawing customers from 30 miles in all directions? Who ever heard of a store where the cashier took the customer's word on a price check and then deducted a few pennies to spare, but did not accept coupons or preferred-customer cards?

Today, the impact of independent grocer Willard Phillip Woodman's unique grocery store, located at the strategic intersection of Interstate 94 and State Highway 50, is still being felt throughout the southeastern Wisconsin marketplace. Although Woodman notes, correctly, that he has driven no competing grocer out of business to date, he also points out that his store has shifted the area's retail grocery price structure downward. "The average grocery basket in our store costs 20 percent less than the competitors," he says.

Why has Woodman, who operates six other slightly smaller stores in other Wisconsin cities, gone beyond big

to gigantic? To achieve economies of scale and compete against larger rivals. By attaching the warehouse to the sales floor, he effectively becomes his own middleman. "The trend is to have large companies," he says. "Having large or small stores is not as important. You have to have some reason for being on the planet, whatever it is. And unless you are part of a large group, it is hard to survive in the high-tech, financial, and legal environment that we are in." Woodman points to the store he has been trying to build in Green Bay for more than two years. "To deal in the political environment, you need legal staff and engineers. The world has become complex."

Gary Fryda, owner of a string of Pick 'n Saves throughout southeastern Wisconsin, says his Kenosha and Racine stores initially lost customers to Woodman's. At 92,000 square feet, Fryda's Pick 'n Save is Kenosha's second-largest grocery store. However, "Our business in Kenosha and Racine has grown back steadily, so it is at about pre-Woodman's levels," Fryda says. "He's got a regional location there at I-94 and Highway 50 with the outlet mall (a 74-store manufacturers' outlet) nearby and his store is drawing people from four counties. Actually, he did the marketplace a favor by pulling shoppers from Chicago and Burlington into the marketplace."

Woodman, a third-generation grocer, says his huge Kenosha store is a few years away from reaching its maximum potential. "That store was built to do $2 million in sales a week," he says. "That means it was built five years in advance. Being 45 minutes [closer to an hour] from downtown Chicago and 45 minutes from downtown Milwaukee, we have the greatest potential of anywhere in the United States. But we have to become more efficient. It's like, 'When I peak, I'm going to be really efficient.' The store is efficient right now. But every time we have another dollar of sales, it becomes more efficient. Because, like in the auto industry or anywhere else, once you cover your fixed costs, everything else is gravy."

Woodman says his store is not designed for the shopper who is in a hurry. "You do not come to Woodman's to buy a few items on convenience. You spend $200 to $500. We don't expect you to be there five times a week. And we don't give anything away. If you give something away here, that means you have to have a price over there that is higher to make up for it. We are not like any other store around. We are a regional-type operator."

Questions

1. Why are power retailers becoming more interested in "little boxes"?
2. How should the locational criteria differ for little-box and big-box stores?
3. Do you agree with Tops Market's decision to abandon big-box supermarkets in favor of little-box ones? Explain your answer.
4. The definition of "little" is clearly in the eye of the beholder. Is a 60,000-square-foot Sears really a little store? What are the ramifications of your answer?
5. What do you think will be the effect of the trend toward little boxes on central business districts? On regional shopping centers? On neighborhood shopping centers? Explain your answers.
6. What do you think will be the impact of this trend on mom-and-pop retailers? How should they respond to this threat?
7. Evaluate Woodman's very-big-box approach to supermarket retailing from both the perspective of Woodman and the stores nearby.

PART FIVE

MANAGING A RETAIL BUSINESS

In Part Five, the elements of managing a retail enterprise are discussed. The steps in setting up a retail organization and the special human resource management environment of retailing are first presented. Operations management is then examined—from both financial and operational perspectives.

Chapter 11 reports how a retailer can use an organizational structure to assign tasks, policies, resources, authority, responsibilities, and rewards to satisfy the needs of the target market, employees, and management. It also shows how human resource management can be deployed to have that structure work properly. Human resource management consists of recruiting, selecting, training, compensating, and supervising personnel.

Chapter 12 focuses on the financial dimensions of operations management in enacting a retail strategy. These topics are discussed: profit planning, asset management (including the strategic profit model, other key business ratios, and financial trends in retailing), budgeting, and resource allocation.

Chapter 13 presents the operational aspects of operations management. These specific concepts are analyzed: operations blueprint; store format, size, and space allocation; personnel utilization; store maintenance, energy management, and renovations; inventory management; store security; insurance; credit management; computerization; and crisis management.

CHAPTER 11

Retail Organization and Human Resource Management

CHAPTER OBJECTIVES

1. To study the procedures involved in setting up a retail organization
2. To examine the various organizational arrangements utilized in retailing
3. To consider the special human resource environment of retailing
4. To describe the principles and practices involved with the human resource management process in retailing

Ace Home Center in Cancun, Mexico, is a hardware retailer that specializes in the do-it-yourself market—and it is known to "go the extra mile with respect to customer service." Many Cancun residents consider Ace to have the best customer service in town.

Ace attributes its excellent reputation to its rigorous continuous training program, which includes daily employee sessions on such topics as customer service, merchandising, teamwork, motivation, and specific product knowledge. The sessions are required for both new and experienced staff members. Employees are required to take examinations based on their training; monthly evaluations are based in part on the test scores. Ace's administrative director says: "We see training as an investment, not as an expense, and that has given us much satisfaction."

Ace believes appearance is a key component in customer perceptions of service. It has a policy requiring employees to wear uniforms (including shoes) that the firm provides. Ace mandates that male employees be clean-shaven; and they cannot wear earrings. No employee—male or female—can wear more than one ring per finger. Ace prohibits employees from smoking or chewing gum within the store.[1]

OVERVIEW

There are three basic steps to managing a retail business properly: setting up an organization structure, hiring and managing personnel, and managing operations—both financially and nonfinancially. In this chapter, the first two steps are covered. Chapters 12 and 13 deal with operations management.

SETTING UP A RETAIL ORGANIZATION

Through a **retail organization,** a firm structures and assigns tasks (functions), policies, resources, authority, responsibilities, and rewards so as to efficiently and effectively satisfy the needs of its target market, employees, and management. Figure 11.1 shows a variety of needs that a retailer should take into account when planning and assessing its organization structure.

> *Please Note:* Web site addresses are constantly changing.
> The links in this chapter are current as of the publication of this book.

Figure 11.1
Selected Factors That Must Be Considered in Planning and Assessing a Retail Organization

TARGET MARKET NEEDS
Are there a sufficient number of personnel (salespeople, deliverypersons, cashiers, etc.)
   available to provide customer service at the appropriate levels?
Are personnel knowledgeable and courteous?
Are store facilities well maintained?
Are the specific needs of branch store customers met?
Are changing needs promptly addressed?

EMPLOYEE NEEDS
Are positions challenging enough?
Is there an orderly promotion program?
Is the employee able to participate in the decision making?
Are the channels of communication clear and open?
Are jobs satisfying?
Is the authority-responsibility relationship clear?
Does the firm promote from within?
Does each employee get treated fairly?
Is good performance rewarded?

MANAGEMENT NEEDS
Is it relatively easy to obtain and retain competent personnel?
Are personnel procedures clearly defined?
Does each worker report to only one supervisor?
Can each manager properly supervise and control the number of workers reporting to
   him (her)?
Do operating departments have adequate staff support (i.e., computerized reports, market
   research, and advertising)?
Are the levels of organization properly developed?
Are the organization's plans well integrated?
Are employees motivated?
Is absenteeism low?
Does the organization provide continuity so that personnel can be replaced in an orderly
   manner?
Is the organization flexible enough to adapt to changes in customer preference and/or
   regional growth patterns?

As a rule, a retailer cannot survive unless its organization structure satisfies the needs of the target market, regardless of how well employee and management needs are met. Thus, an organization structure that reduces costs through centralized buying but results in the firm's being insensitive to geographic differences in customer preferences would probably be improper. Even though many retailers do similar tasks or functions (such as buying, pricing, displaying, and wrapping merchandise), there are many ways of organizing to perform these

Figure 11.2
The Process of
Organizing a Retail
Firm

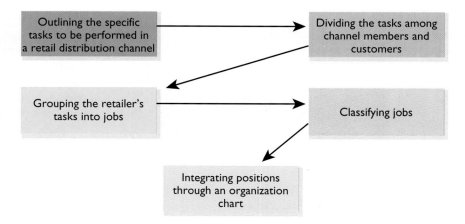

functions and focus on customer, employee, and management needs. The process of setting up a retail organization is outlined in Figure 11.2 and described next.

Specifying Tasks to Be Performed

The general tasks in a retail distribution channel must be enumerated. Among the typical tasks are

- Buying merchandise for the retailer.
- Shipping merchandise to the retailer.
- Receiving merchandise and checking incoming shipments.
- Setting prices.
- Marking merchandise.
- Inventory storage and control.
- Preparing merchandise and window displays.
- Facilities maintenance (e.g., keeping the store clean).
- Customer research and exchanging information.
- Customer contact (e.g., advertising, personal selling).
- Facilitating shopping (e.g., convenient site, short checkout lines).
- Customer follow-up and complaint handling.
- Personnel management.
- Repairs and alteration of merchandise.
- Billing customers.
- Handling receipts and financial records.
- Credit operations.
- Gift wrapping.
- Delivery to customers.
- Returning unsold or damaged merchandise to vendors.
- Sales forecasting and budgeting.
- Coordination.

Fleming is a wholesaler serving more than 3,000 supermarkets. It offers them 11 categories of support services (www.fleming.com/f_rserv.htm).

The proper performance of the preceding activities, keyed to the chosen strategy mix, is necessary for effective retailing to occur.

Dividing Tasks Among Channel Members and Customers

Although the preceding tasks are often performed in a retail channel, they do not have to be done by a retailer. Some can be completed by the manufacturer, wholesaler, specialist, or

Figure 11.3
The Division of
Retail Tasks

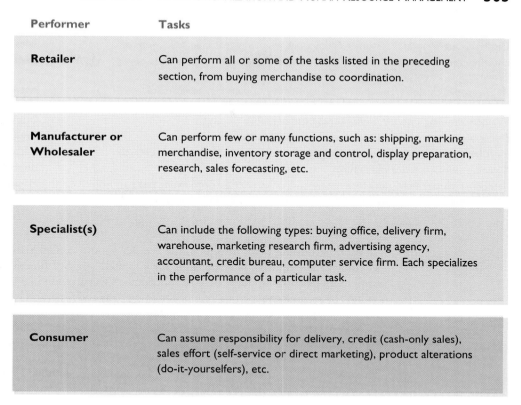

Performer	Tasks
Retailer	Can perform all or some of the tasks listed in the preceding section, from buying merchandise to coordination.
Manufacturer or Wholesaler	Can perform few or many functions, such as: shipping, marking merchandise, inventory storage and control, display preparation, research, sales forecasting, etc.
Specialist(s)	Can include the following types: buying office, delivery firm, warehouse, marketing research firm, advertising agency, accountant, credit bureau, computer service firm. Each specializes in the performance of a particular task.
Consumer	Can assume responsibility for delivery, credit (cash-only sales), sales effort (self-service or direct marketing), product alterations (do-it-yourselfers), etc.

consumer. Figure 11.3 shows the types of activities that could be carried out by each party. Following are some criteria to consider in allocating the functions related to consumer credit.

A task should be carried out only if desired by the target market. Thus, unless a retailer, such as a convenience store, finds a number of customers dislike cash-only sales, it should not accept credit cards. For some firms, liberal credit policies may provide significant advantages over competitors. For others, a cash-only policy may reduce their overhead and lead to lower prices.

A task should be done by the party with proper competence. Credit collection may require a legal staff and computerized records. These are usually most affordable by medium or large retailers. Smaller retailers would more likely rely on bank credit cards. The retailer should consider the loss of control when an activity is delegated to another party. A credit collection agency, pressing hard to receive past-due payments, may antagonize a customer to the point of losing future sales for the retailer.

The retailer's institutional framework can have an impact on task allocation. Franchisees are readily able to get together to have their own credit bureau. Independents cannot do this as easily.

Task allocation should take into account the savings gained by sharing or shifting tasks. The credit function can be better performed by an outside credit bureau if it has expert personnel and ongoing access to financial data, uses tailored computer software, pays lower rent (due to an out-of-the-way site), and so on. Many retailers cannot attain these savings themselves.

Grouping Tasks into Jobs

Home Depot's Web site (www.home depot.com) highlights the range of jobs available in retailing.

After the retailer decides which functions to perform, these tasks are grouped into jobs. The jobs must be clearly defined and structured. Here are some examples of grouping tasks into jobs:

Tasks	Jobs
Displaying merchandise, customer contact, gift wrapping, customer follow-up	Sales personnel
Entering transaction data, handling cash receipts, processing credit purchases, gift wrapping, inventory control	Cashier(s)
Receiving merchandise, checking incoming shipments, marking merchandise, inventory storage and control, returning merchandise to vendors	Inventory personnel
Window dressing, interior display setups, use of mobile displays	Display personnel
Billing customers, credit operations, customer research	Credit personnel
Merchandise repairs and alterations, resolution of complaints, customer research	Customer service personnel
Cleaning store, replacing old fixtures	Janitorial personnel
Personnel management, sales forecasting, budgeting, pricing, coordinating tasks	Management personnel

While grouping tasks into jobs, the retailer should consider the use of specialization, whereby each employee is responsible for a limited range of functions (as opposed to each employee's performing many diverse functions). Specialization has the advantages of clearly defined tasks, greater expertise, reduced training costs and time, and hiring personnel with narrow education and experience. Problems can result due to extreme specialization: poor morale (boredom), people not being aware of their jobs' importance, and the need for an increased number of employees. The use of specialization means assigning specific duties and responsibilities to individuals so a job position encompasses a relatively homogeneous cluster of work tasks. These tasks should have an essential and enduring purpose within the retail organization.

Once work tasks are grouped, job descriptions are constructed. These outline the job titles, objectives, duties, and responsibilities for every position. They are used as a hiring, supervision, and evaluation tool. Figure 11.4 contains a job description for a store manager.

Ethics in Retailing

Raiding the Executive Suite at Federated

When Matthew Serra left his position as chief executive of Stern's, a unit of Federated Department Stores, to become chief executive of Foot Locker, Federated decided to sue Herbert Mines Associates, the executive search firm that recruited Serra. Federated's lawsuit claimed that the head hunter had interfered with Serra's duty to fulfill his responsibilities to Stern's.

The lawsuit is especially troubling to executive search firms because it is one of the first ones addressed at them instead of the displaced executive or the hiring company. Thus, the search firms are concerned that the case will set a precedent.

Some industry observers hope the lawsuit will result in more accountability by search firms.

Although recruiters typically ask job-seeking retail executives if they have a noncompete agreement that would restrict the kinds of work they could do for another retail employer, they are not legally required to ask additional questions. Other observers feel the lawsuit is aimed at scaring search firms from further recruiting of Federated executives. A few say the lawsuit could backfire by creating anxiety in executives contemplating a move to Federated who worry about being sued by their former employers.

What other, less confrontational ways can Federated use to discourage head hunters from seeking its top-performing executives?

Source: "Drawing a Bead on the Headhunters," *Business Week* (January 25, 1999), pp. 108–109.

Figure 11.4
A Job Description for
a Store Manager

JOB TITLE: Store Manager for 34th Street Branch of Pombo's Department Stores

POSITION REPORTS TO: Senior Vice-President

POSITIONS REPORTING TO STORE MANAGER: All personnel working in the
34th Street store

OBJECTIVES: To properly staff and operate the 34th Street store

DUTIES AND RESPONSIBILITIES:

1. Personnel recruitment, selection, training, motivation, and evaluation
2. Merchandise display
3. Inventory storage and control
4. Approving orders for merchandise
5. Transferring merchandise among stores
6. Sales forecasting
7. Budgeting
8. Handling store receipts
9. Preparing bank transactions
10. Locking and unlocking store
11. Reviewing customer complaints
12. Reviewing computer data forms
13. Semiannual review of overall operations
14. Forwarding reports to top management

COMMITTEES AND MEETINGS:

1. Store Managers' Review Committee
2. Attendance at monthly meetings with Senior Vice-President
3. Supervision of weekly meetings with department managers

Classifying Jobs

Jobs are then broadly categorized by a functional, product, geographic, or combination classification system. In a functional classification, jobs are divided by function such as sales promotion, buying, and store operations. Expert knowledge is utilized.

Product classification divides jobs on a goods or service basis. Thus, a department store can hire different personnel for clothing, furniture, gift items, appliances, and so on. Product classification recognizes that differences exist in the personnel requirements for different products. Tighter control and responsibility are also possible.

Geographic classification is useful for chains operating in different locales. Personnel are adapted to local conditions. Job descriptions and qualifications are under the control of individual branch managers.

Some firms, especially larger ones, use a combination of classifications. If a branch unit of an apparel chain hires and supervises its own selling staff, but buying personnel for each product line are centrally hired and controlled by headquarters, the functional, product, and geographic formats are combined.

Table 11.1 Principles for Organizing a Retail Firm

An organization should show interest in its employees. Job rotation, promotion from within, participatory management, recognition, job enrichment, and so forth, improve worker morale.

Employee turnover, lateness, and absenteeism should be monitored, as they may indicate personnel problems.

The line of authority should be traceable from the highest to the lowest positions. In this way, employees know to whom they report and who reports to them (*chain of command*).

A subordinate should only report to one direct supervisor (*unity of command*). This avoids the problem of workers receiving conflicting orders.

There is a limit to the number of employees a manager can directly supervise (*span of control*).

Responsibility should be associated with proper authority. A person responsible for a given objective needs the power to achieve it.

Although a supervisor can delegate authority, he or she is still responsible for subordinates. Handing over authority cannot be an excuse for a manager's failing to achieve a goal.

The number of organizational levels should not grow too rapidly. The greater the number of levels, the longer the time for communication to travel and the greater the coordination problems.

An organization has an informal structure aside from the formal organization chart. Informal relationships exercise power in the organization and may bypass formal relationships and procedures.

Developing an Organization Chart

In planning an overall retail organization, a firm should not look at jobs as individual units but as parts of the whole. The format of a retail organization must be designed in an integrated, coordinated way. Jobs must be defined and distinct; yet, interrelationships among positions must be clear. As a prominent retail executive once remarked, "A successful chief executive does not build a business. He or she builds an organization and the organization builds the business. It is done no other way."[2]

The **hierarchy of authority** outlines the job interactions within a company by describing the reporting relationship among employees (from the lowest level to the store manager or board of directors). Coordination and control are provided by this hierarchy. A firm with a large number of workers reporting to one manager has a *flat organization*. Benefits are good communication, quicker handling of problems, and better employee identification with a job. The major problem tends to be too many people reporting to one manager. A *tall organization* has several management levels. This means close supervision and fewer employees reporting to each manager. The problems include a long channel of communication, an impersonal impression given to workers (regarding access to upper-level personnel), and inflexible rules.

With these factors in mind, a retailer devises an **organization chart,** which graphically displays its hierarchical relationships. Table 11.1 lists the principles to consider in establishing an organization chart. Figure 11.5 shows examples of functional, product, geographic, and combination organization charts.

ORGANIZATIONAL PATTERNS IN RETAILING

Organizational structures differ by institutional type. An independent retailer has a simpler organization than a chain. An independent does not have to manage units far from the main store, the owner-manager usually supervises all employees, and workers have ready access to the owner-manager if there are personal or work problems. In contrast, a chain must specify

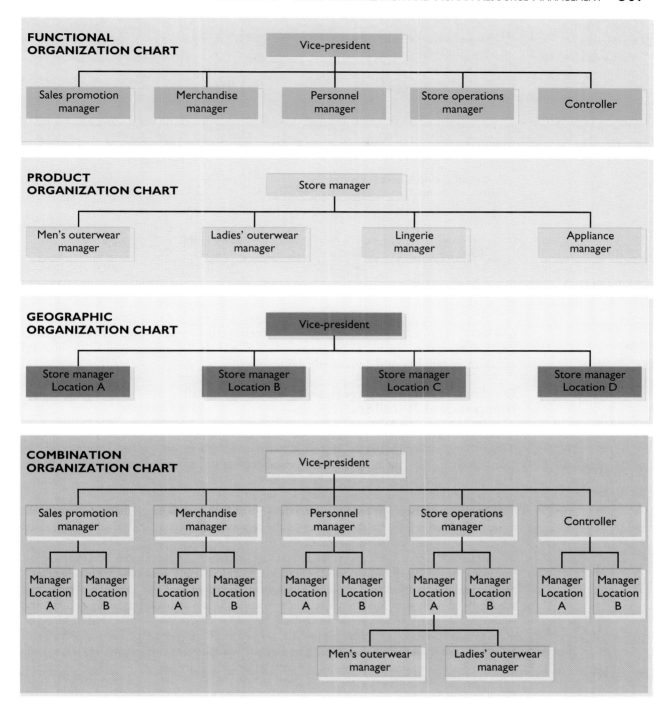

Figure 11.5
Different Forms of Retail Organization

Figure 11.6
Organization
Structures Used by
Small Independents

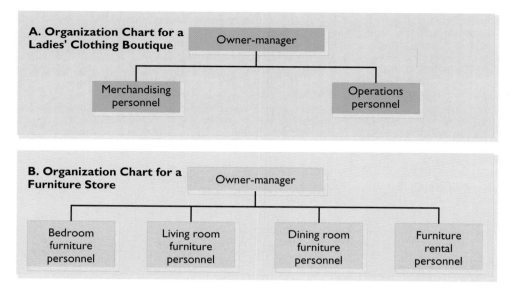

how tasks are delegated, coordinate multiple stores, and use common policies for all employees. A discussion of organizational arrangements used by independent retailers, department stores, chain retailers, and diversified retailers is next.

Organizational Arrangements Used by Small Independent Retailers

Small independent retailers generally use simple arrangements because they contain only two or three levels of personnel (the owner-manager and employees), and the owner-manager personally runs the business and oversees workers. There are few employees and little departmentalization (specialization), and there are no branch units. This does not mean, however, that fewer activities must be performed.

The small independent has little specialization of functions because there are many tasks to be performed relative to the number of workers available to do them. Each worker must allot part of his or her time to several duties.

Figure 11.6 shows the organizations of two small firms. In A, a boutique is organized on a functional basis: merchandising and operations. Merchandising personnel are involved with buying and selling goods and services, assortments, displays, and ads. Operations personnel are involved with store maintenance and operations (such as inventory management and financial reports). In B, a furniture store is organized on a product-oriented basis, with personnel in each category responsible for selected activities. All product categories get proper attention, and some expertise is developed. This expertise is particularly important since different skills are necessary to buy and sell each type of furniture.

Organizational Arrangements Used by Department Stores

Nearly 75 years after its introduction, many medium and large department stores continue to use organizational arrangements that are a modification of the **Mazur plan,** which divides all retail activities into four functional areas—merchandising, publicity, store management, and accounting and control:

1. Merchandising—buying, selling, stock planning and control, planning promotional events.

2. Publicity—window and interior displays, advertising, planning and executing promotional events (in cooperation with merchandise managers), advertising research, public relations.

3. Store management—merchandise care, customer services (such as adjustment bureaus), buying store supplies and equipment, maintenance, operating activities (such as receiving, checking, marking, and delivering merchandise, and overseeing the warehouse), store and merchandise protection (such as insurance and security), training and compensating personnel, workroom operations.

4. Accounting and control—credit and collections, expense budgeting and control, inventory planning and control, recordkeeping.[3]

These four areas are organized in terms of line (direct authority and responsibility) and staff (advisory and support) components. For instance, a controller and a publicity manager provide staff services to the merchandising divisions, but within these areas, personnel are organized on a line basis. This principle can be more clearly understood from an examination of Figure 11.7, which illustrates the Mazur plan.

The merchandising division is responsible for buying and selling. It is headed by a merchandising manager, who is often regarded as the most important area executive in the store. He or she supervises buyers, devises a financial control system for each department, coordinates department merchandise plans and policies (so a store has a consistent image among departments), and interprets economic data and their effect on the store. In some stores, divisional merchandise managers are utilized, so the number of buyers reporting to a single manager does not become unwieldy.

The buyer, in the basic Mazur plan, has complete accountability for controlling expenses and reaching profit goals within his or her department. Duties include preparing preliminary budgets, studying fashion trends, bargaining with vendors over price, planning the number of salespeople needed, and informing sales personnel about the merchandise purchased and fashion trends. The grouping of buying and selling activities into one job (buyer) may present a major problem. Since buyers are not constantly on the selling floor, control of personnel (training, scheduling, and supervision) may suffer.

The growth of branch stores has led to three Mazur plan derivatives: **mother hen with branch store chickens organization,** by which headquarters executives oversee and operate branches; **separate store organization,** by which each branch has its own buying responsibilities; and **equal store organization,** by which buying is centralized and branches become sales units with equal operational status.

In the "mother hen" format, most authority remains with managers at headquarters. Merchandise planning and buying, advertising, financial controls, store hours, and many other tasks are centrally managed. To a great extent, the performance of all outlets is standardized. Branch store managers hire and supervise their employees, but they are responsible for daily operations conforming to company policies. This works well if there are few branches and the buying preferences of branch customers are similar to those at the main store. As branch stores increase in number, buyers, the advertising director, the controller, and others may be overworked and give little attention to branches. Also, since headquarters personnel are located away from branches, differences in customer preferences may be overlooked.

The "separate store" format places merchandise managers in branch stores, which have autonomy for merchandising and operations. Customer needs are quickly noted, but duplication by managers at headquarters and branch stores is possible. Coordination can also be a problem (such as having a consistent image). Transferring goods between branches is more complex and costly. This format is best if stores are large, branches are geographically separated, or local customer tastes vary widely.

In the "equal store" format, department stores want to gain the benefits of both centralization and decentralization. It is the most popular method among department store chains.

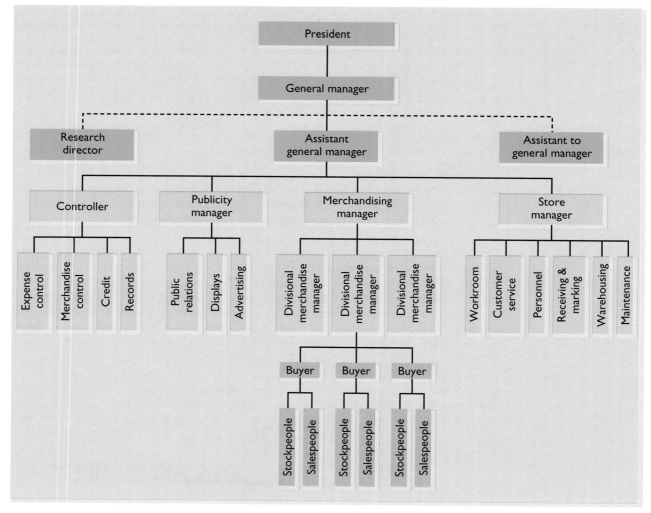

Figure 11.7
The Basic Mazur Organization Plan for Department Stores

Source: Adapted from Paul Mazur, *Principles of Organization Applied to Modern Retailing* (New York: Harper & Brothers, 1927), frontispiece. Reprinted by permission.

Buying—forecasting, planning, purchasing, pricing, distribution to branches, and promotion—is centrally managed. Selling—presenting merchandise, selling, customer services, and store operations—is managed locally. All outlets, including headquarters, are treated equally. Buyers are freed from supervising as many personnel. Data gathering is critical since buyers have less customer contact. Responsibility is more dispersed.

Organizational Arrangements Used by Chain Retailers

Chain retailers of various types often use a version of the equal-store organizational format, as depicted in Figure 11.8. Although chain store organizations may differ, they generally have these attributes:

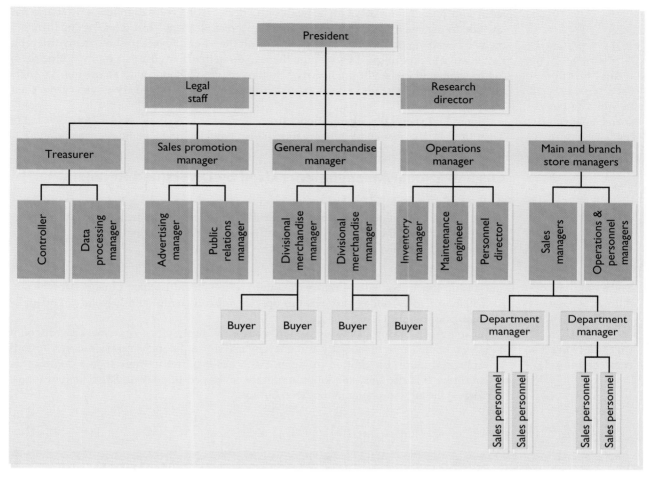

Figure 11.8
The Equal-Store Organizational Format Used by Many Chain Stores

- There are a large number of functional divisions, such as sales promotion, merchandise management, distribution, store operations, real-estate, personnel, and information systems.
- Overall authority and responsibility are centralized. Store managers have selling responsibility.
- Many operations are standardized (fixtures, store layout, building design, merchandise lines, credit policy, and store service).
- An elaborate control system keeps management informed.
- Some decentralization lets branches adapt to localities and increases store manager responsibilities. For example, though large chains standardize most of the items their outlets carry, store managers can often fine-tune the rest of the mix to appeal to local markets—rural or urban, African-American or Hispanic-American, high income or low. This is employee empowerment at the store manager level.

To emphasize the last point above, consider the case of Ken Potter, recently honored as a Young Retailer of the Year by the National Retail Hardware Association. The now 36-year-old Potter is manager of the ACO Hardware store in Dearborn, Michigan—the leading out-

To discover how Toys "R" Us operates, go to the "Investor Relations" section of its Web site (www. shareholder.com/toy/ index-new.cfm).

let in a 63-unit chain. Although he has a series of operating rules to follow, Potter also has latitude to use his initiative to adapt the chain's overall plan: "In exercising his management-by-walking philosophy, Potter works with the 41 employees to show them different, better ways to do things. 'I try to urge them to do better than just getting by. I urge them not to wallow in the sea of mediocrity.' Employees credit Potter with an on-the-go, energetic store atmosphere and also appreciate the time he is willing to spend answering their questions."[4]

Figure 11.9 shows the organizational structure for the U.S. Toys "R" Us store division of Toys "R" Us, Inc. It is an equal-store format organized by function and geographic area.

Organizational Arrangements Used by Diversified Retailers

A **diversified retailer,** also known as a retail conglomerate, is a multiline firm operating under central ownership. Like a chain, a diversified retailer has more than one store; however, unlike a typical chain, stores cover different types of retail operations. Here are two examples of diversified retailers:

The who, what, where, and why of Burlington Coat's diversified divisions are described at its Web site (www.coat. com/corpinfo/qf).

- Burlington Coat Factory (www.coat.com) operates five other retail businesses, besides its flagship Burlington Coat Factory discount apparel chain: Luxury Linens, Baby Depot, Totally 4 Kids, Cohoes Fashions (an upscale apparel chain), and Decelle (an off-price chain). See Figure 11.10.
- Japan's Aeon Group (www.jusco.co.jp) comprises superstores, supermarkets, discount stores, home centers, specialty and convenience stores, financial services stores, restaurants, and more. In addition to Japan, Aeon has facilities in more than a dozen other countries. It is also a leading shopping center developer. Jusco, with $21 billion in annual sales, is the largest retailer in the Aeon Group.

A Penney Spent Is a Dollar Earned in Latin America

As part of its global retailing strategy, J.C. Penney bought a 27 percent equity interest in Lojas Renner SA, a 21-unit Brazilian department store chain with annual sales of $190 million. Lojas Renner has been expanding at the rate of 3 to 5 stores per year. This adds to its 22 border stores in Texas, Arizona, and California, as well as its stores in Puerto Rico, Mexico, and Chile.

This was an interesting development because of Penney's previous lack of success in Latin America. Although Penney has had upscale stores in Puerto Rico for more than 30 years, it had backed away from Latin American operations due to the softening in the economies there. Now, Penney feels there are new Latin American opportunities for it to acquire strong existing chains: "We believe Brazil is a key to

our strategy for South American development because of its extremely large population base, expected to hit 200 million by 2010."

Penney does not plan to change the name of the Lojas Renner chain. However, it does plan to stock these Brazilian stores with Penney private-label merchandise. Penney also intends to use Lojas Renner's credit operations as a central base for its credit business in neighboring Chile, where Penney operates one department store and one home store.

What are the pros and cons of Penney's centralized decision making for its Latin American and border stores?

Source: Rusty Williamson, "Penney's Buys Equity Stake in Brazil's Lojas Renner Chain," *Women's Wear Daily* (December 9, 1998), p. 29.

Figure 11.9
The Organizational
Structure of Toys
"R" Us (United States
Only), Selected
Positions

Source: Compiled by the
authors from the *Toys
"R" Us, Inc. 1999
Annual Report.*

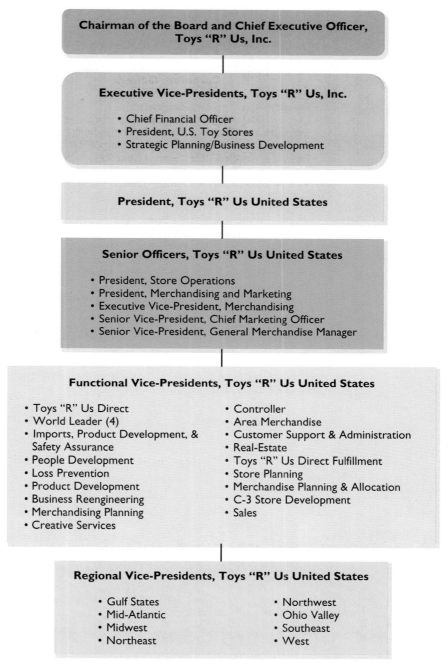

Due to the multiple strategy mixes, diversified retailers face unique considerations in implementing an organization structure. First, interdivision control is needed. Operating procedures and clear goals must be communicated among divisions. Second, interdivision competition must be coordinated (e.g., Should a firm's department stores and discount stores carry the same brands?). Third, resources must be divided among different divisions. Fourth, potential image and advertising conflicts must be avoided. Fifth, management skills

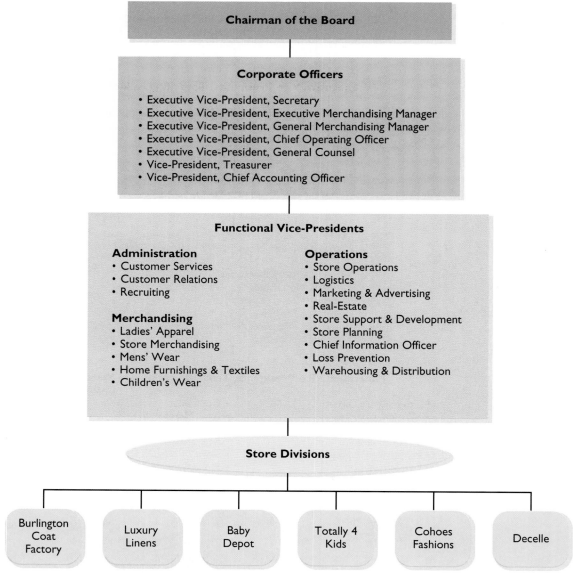

Figure 11.10

The Organizational Structure of Burlington Coat Factory

Source: Compiled by the authors from the *Burlington Coat Factory 1999 Annual Report.*

must be adapted to rather different operations. Accordingly, a diversified retailer usually has a very complex organization structure.

HUMAN RESOURCE MANAGEMENT IN RETAILING

Human resource management involves recruiting, selecting, training, compensating, and supervising personnel in a manner consistent with the retailer's organization structure and strategy mix. It is required of all retailers, with policies dependent on their line of business, the number of employees, the location of outlets, and other factors.

Because good personnel are needed to develop and carry out retail strategies, and labor costs can amount to 50 percent or more of some retailers' operating expenses, the value of effective human resource management is clear. This is further illustrated through the following:

The Bureau of Labor Statistics compiles current employment data on such jobs as retail sales worker supervisors and managers (www.bls.gov/oco/ocos025.htm).

- U.S. retailing employs more than 22 million people, and this figure is rising. There is a constant need to attract new employees—as well as to retain existing ones. For example, over 2 million fast-food workers are aged 16 to 20, and they must be regularly replaced since they stay in their jobs for only short periods. In general, retailers need to reduce the turnover rate for their employees. When workers quickly—and in great numbers—exit a firm, the results can be disastrous. See Table 11.2.
- The Pizzeria Uno chain is committed to employee development and advancement: "The increasingly tight labor market in recent years has given impetus to our programs to train hourly workers and to promote from within. These multilevel programs provide advancement opportunity, build employee loyalty, and provide the human resources Uno needs to fuel its growth. In addition, we have implemented 'Quality of Life' programs that reward employees for performance and longevity."[5]
- The highest entry-level position at Home Depot is usually assistant store manager; store managers are typically not hired from outside the firm. Although Home Depot is a large and growing chain, senior executives have been personally involved in training virtually every manager. They want to be sure the basic operating philosophy is clearly communicated to and carried out by all employees.
- At Nordstrom, there is decentralized buying, and salespeople have considerable input. They can place special orders, decide when products are delivered, get extra merchandise if needed, and resolve customer problems.

The Special Human Resource Environment of Retailing

Retailers face a special human resource environment—characterized by a large number of inexperienced workers, long hours, highly visible employees, many part-time workers, and variability in customer demand. These factors often make the hiring, staffing, and supervision of employees a complex process.

The greatest personnel difficulty for many retailers is the inexperience of a lot of their workers. Because there is a need for a large labor force in retailing, persons with little or no prior experience are often hired. For some new workers, a position in retailing represents

Table 11.2 The True Cost of Employee Turnover

Recruiting and hiring new employees.

Training costs—including management time.

Full pay and benefits during training, before full productivity is reached.

Lost sales and alienated customers during off-site training.

Costs of mistakes made by new, inexperienced employees.

Loss of customers loyal to departing employees.

Loss of knowledge and experience of departing employees.

Lost or damaged relationships with suppliers.

Employee morale and customer perception of that morale.

Source: Terri Kabachnick, "Turning Against the Tide," *Arthur Andersen Retailing Issues Letter* (Center for Retailing Studies, Texas A&M University, September 1995), p. 3. Reprinted by permission.

their first "real" job. People are attracted to retailing because they find jobs near to home; and retail positions (such as checkout clerks, wrappers, stock clerks, and some types of sales personnel) may require limited education, training, and skill. Also, the low wages paid for some positions call for the hiring of inexperienced people. Thus, high employee turnover and cases of poor performance, lateness, and absenteeism may be the result.

The long working hours encountered in retailing, sometimes including Saturdays and Sundays, turn off certain prospective employees; and there is a strong trend toward longer store hours since family shoppers and working women shoppers want stores with evening and weekend hours. Accordingly, some retailers must have at least two shifts of full-time employees.

In retailing, employees are highly visible to the customer. Therefore, when a retailer selects and trains personnel, special care must be taken with regard to their manners and appearance. Unfortunately, some small retailers may not recognize the importance of employee appearance (such as being neatly groomed and appropriately attired).

Due to the long hours of retail stores, firms often must hire part-time workers. In many supermarkets, over half the workers are part-time; and problems can arise accordingly. Some part-time employees may be more lackadaisical, late, absent, or likely to quit their jobs than full-time employees (who are more career-oriented). This means they must be closely monitored.

Last, variations in customer demand by day, time period, or season may cause planning problems. For example, most consumers make major supermarket trips on Thursday, Friday, or Saturday. So, how many employees should a supermarket have on Sunday (or Monday) through Wednesday, and how many on Thursday through Saturday? Demand differences during the day (morning, afternoon, evening) and by season (fall, Christmas) also affect planning. Sometimes, when stores are especially busy, "every staffer, including the bookkeeper and administrative employees, may need to work on the selling floor."[6]

As a rule, retailers should consider points such as these:

- Recruitment and selection procedures must generate a sufficient number of applicants efficiently.
- Some training programs must be intensive and short because workers are inexperienced and temporary.
- Compensation must be perceived as "fair" by employees.
- Advancement opportunities must be available to employees who look at retailing as a career.
- Employee appearance and work habits must be explained and reviewed.
- Morale problems may result from high employee turnover and the large number of part-time workers.
- Full- and part-time workers may have conflicts, especially if part-timers replace some full-timers.

In retailing, there is a broad range of career opportunities available to women and minorities—and there is less of a "glass ceiling" than in many other industries. Nonetheless, there is still room for improvement.

Women in Retailing Women now have more career options in retailing than ever before, as exemplified by Melissa Myers:

There was no doubt in Melissa Myers' mind that she would pursue a retailing career. "I knew I wanted to go into retail since high school, and I find retail exciting because it's different every day." But she never expected to join an electronics chain. "I thought I would go into soft goods." However, after graduating in 1997 from Purdue, she joined Electronics Boutique. "When I was in college, I knew something about electronics, but not a lot. Now I am able to have an intelligent conversation about so many different categories of products—I can't believe how much I've learned. Now, I'm

Electronics Boutique is proving that there is a prominent place for women in consumer electronics retailing (www.ebworld.com/ebx/abouteb/hiring/jobs.asp).

really into it." As store manager, Myers is responsible for ensuring that her store is in stock and that merchandise is displayed properly. She also manages the sales associates at her store. "I love my job because it's ever-changing. It's quick-paced and exciting. I'm out there in the field making decisions." Myers is also continuing to learn. "Electronics Boutique sends associates to other parts of the country to meet with vendors and attend courses on topics such as loss prevention. I like traveling and learning more about the industry." Since joining Electronics Boutique, Myers has unearthed some skills she never knew she had and is putting them to use on the job. "I didn't realize that I could be so good at multitasking. It's great to be able to manage so many things at once."[7]

Mary Kay Ash was a true pioneer, beginning her now billion-dollar business in 1963. Learn about her story (www.marykay.com/marykay/About/marykay/bio.html).

Debbi Fields (Mrs. Fields' Cookies) and Mary Kay Ash (Mary Kay Cosmetics) founded retailing empires. At Avon, the chief executive officer is an Asian-American woman, and 43 percent of its corporate officers are women. J.C. Penney's new president of the men's division is a woman—and she reports to the president of merchandising, who is also a woman. The president of Target Corporation's department store division is a woman; and during her tenure, she has boosted performance significantly:

Before Linda Ahlers took over the division, the stores—Dayton's, Hudson's, and Marshall Field's—were limping along with operating margins of 5 percent, three points behind the industry leaders. Ahlers dumped the Macy's and Lord & Taylor strategy of stuffing maiboxes with promotion fliers nearly every week. She cut sale days from 120 to 60, focusing on merchandising and becoming the second-best service provider behind Nordstrom. By deploying style watchers across the globe to spot trends, she made sure stores had the items gracing the pages of fashion glossies and a knowledgeable, all-smiles, we'll-take-anything-back sales force. This strategy was a hit, enabling Ahlers to pull off the equivalent of a retailing hat trick: boosting operating margins to 8 percent while focusing on service and slashing promotions.[8]

According to recent studies, retailers have made a lot of progress in career advancement for women. Five retailers are among the top 13 U.S. public companies in terms of the percentage of women who are corporate officers: Avon, Nordstrom, Target Corporation, Venator (parent company of Foot Locker), and BJ's Wholesale Club. For restaurateurs such as Carlson, Starbucks, Advantica, and IHOP, at least 30 percent of corporate officers are women. The female:male mix for managerial jobs in the lodging and food service sectors is now approaching 50 percent each. More than two-thirds of supervisors at eating and drinking establishments are women. *Working Mother* considers Target Corporation, Gymboree, Marriott, Nordstrom, Sears, and Stride Rite to be among the best companies for which working mothers can work.[9]

Despite the progress being made, women still account for less than 15 percent of corporate officers at retail firms. But this is expected to change, "There is a wave at the vice-president level that is about to go over the top." As the vice-president of franchise sales and administration for Mrs. Winner's Chicken & Biscuits recently remarked, "Now, I come across women who are role models all the time."[10]

These are some of the issues that retailers must address with regard to female workers:

- Meaningful training programs.
- Advancement opportunities.
- Flex time—the ability of employees to adapt their hours.
- Job sharing among two or more employees who each work less than full-time.
- Child care.

Minorities in Retailing As with women, retailers have done many good things in the area of minority employment, with more still to be accomplished. Consider these examples.

DiversityInc.com presents a lot of useful information about minorities in the workplace (www.diversityinc.com).

Supermarket chain H-E-B (www.hebgrocery.com), also known as H.E. Butt, is quite involved with ensuring diversity in its workforce:

We have always considered ourselves as a leader in our industry in terms of creativity and innovation. That is difficult to achieve without capitalizing on the diversity of our work force, workplace, and marketplace. Our work force differs by race, gender, religion, sexual orientation, physical abilities, marital status, parental status, and in many other ways. We must have an organizational culture designed to develop the unique talents of each individual. For example, offering training only during the day denies access to those who work different shifts. Fixed working hours may be difficult for families with varying needs. There are times when our similarities require another approach. For example, employees doing the same work with comparable skill and time on the job should be equally paid. We must understand and become sensitive to issues of culture, language, values, beliefs, holidays, and traditions if we are to stay committed to our customers and our employees. Diversity management shouldn't be something we do; rather, it should be a part of everything we do.

The Lark is a small chain of upscale apparel shops located in low-income, minority neighborhoods in Gary, Indiana, and Chicago. "Because many black shoppers say they feel slighted or even mistrusted by sales help in mainstream stores, they are particularly receptive to retailers that treat them well." At The Lark, "good service begins with good treatment of employees, 90 percent of whom are black. Managers are paid $30,000 to $70,000 a year and salespeople $15,000 to $40,000. The Lark also offers employees health insurance, pays half the tuition for any outside education they seek, and has a $500 no-questions-asked loan policy should employees get in a jam."[11] Turnover is quite low.

Toyota is striving to increase its number of minority-owned U.S. car dealerships. According to one Hispanic-American dealer, who is also a member of Toyota's minority advisory board: "Toyota's got many hands out to try to locate capable, viable minority dealer candidates. The company will go outside the automobile industry to get somebody who is energetic and who shows promise and wants to become a dealer. Then that person will get an awful lot of schooling and training."[12]

After some tough times in the mid-1990s, Denny's has become a model franchise chain for minority employees (www.dennys.com/who/philosophy_main.html).

A recent survey found that more minority workers in retailing rate the opportunities for career advancement as favorable than unfavorable—and they have a more positive view of career opportunities than nonminority workers: Asian-Americans, 45.4 percent favorable, 24.6 percent unfavorable; Hispanic-Americans, 37.8 percent favorable, 27.3 percent unfavorable; African-Americans, 36.3 percent favorable, 34.4 percent unfavorable; Caucasian-Americans, 35.5 percent favorable, 34.7 percent unfavorable. In addition, a *Fortune* study of the best large U.S. firms for minority employees found 4 of the top 10 to be retailers: Toyota, Advantica (parent of Denny's, El Pollo Loco, and other restaurants), Darden restaurants, and Wal-Mart. Minority workers represent one-third or more of the employees at these firms.[13]

These are some of the issues that retailers must address with regard to minority workers:

- Clear policy statements from top management as to the value of diversity among employees.
- Active recruitment programs to stimulate minority applications.
- Meaningful training programs.
- Advancement opportunities.
- Zero tolerance for insensitive workplace behavior.

The Human Resource Management Process in Retailing

The **human resource management process** consists of these interrelated personnel activities: recruitment, selection, training, compensation, and supervision. The goals of this process are to obtain, develop, and retain employees.

When applying this process, diversity, labor laws, and employee privacy should all be kept in mind. Diversity involves two fundamental premises: (1) that employees be hired and promoted in a fair and open way, without regard to their gender, ethnic background, and other related factors; and (2) that in an increasingly diverse society, the workplace should be representative of such diversity.

There are several aspects of labor laws for retailers to satisfy:

- Not hiring underage workers.
- Not paying workers "off the books."
- Not requiring workers to engage in illegal acts (such as bait-and-switch selling).
- Not discriminating in hiring or promoting workers.
- Not violating worker safety regulations.
- Not dealing with suppliers that disobey labor laws.

Retailers must also be careful not to violate employees' right to privacy with regard to their personal information. Only necessary data should be gathered and stored, and it should not be freely disseminated.

Next, each activity in the human resource management process is discussed for retail sales and middle-management positions.

Recruiting Retail Personnel

Recruitment is the activity whereby a retailer generates a list of job applicants. Sources of potential employees include educational institutions, other channel members, competitors, advertisements, employment agencies, unsolicited applicants, and current and former employees who are looking for new positions or who recommend friends. Table 11.3 indicates the characteristics of these sources.

CarMax relies heavily on its Web site (www. carmax.com/careers/ index.html/) for recruiting personnel.

Besides these sources, the Web is beginning to play more of a role in recruitment. Many retailers have a career or job opportunities section at their Web site; and some of these sections are as elaborate as the retailers' overall sites. Check out Target Stores' Web site (www.target.com/jobs), for example.

For entry-level sales jobs, retailers are apt to rely on educational institutions, ads, walk-ins (or write-ins), Web sites, and employee recommendations. For middle-management positions, retailers are likely to use employment agencies, competitors, ads, and current employee referrals.

Often during recruitment, the retailer's major goal is to generate a large list of potential employees, which will be sharply reduced during selection. However, retailers that accept applicants for further consideration only if they meet minimum background standards (such as education and experience) can save a lot of time and money during selection.

Selecting Retail Personnel

The firm next selects new employees from those recruited. The goal at this stage is to match the traits of potential employees with the requirements of the jobs to be filled. The procedure should encompass job analysis and description, the application blank, interviewing, testing (optional), references, and a physical exam (optional). The steps should be integrated.

Job analysis consists of gathering information about each job's functions and requirements: duties, responsibilities, aptitude, interest, education, experience, and physical tasks. It is used to select personnel, set performance standards, and assign salaries. Department managers at general merchandise stores often oversee other sales associates, serve as the main sales associates for their departments, have some administrative and analytical duties, report directly to the store manager, are eligible for bonuses, and are paid from $25,000 to $40,000+ annually. Most have been with their firms for two or more years.

Job analysis should lead to written job descriptions. A **traditional job description** contains a position's title, supervisory relationships (superior and subordinate), committee

Table 11.3 Recruitment Sources and Their Characteristics

Sources	Characteristics
Outside the Company	
Educational institutions	a. High schools, business schools, community colleges, universities, graduate schools b. Good for training positions; ensure minimum educational requirements are met; especially useful when long-term contacts with instructors are developed
Other channel members, competitors	a. Employees of wholesalers, manufacturers, ad agencies, competitors; leads from each of these b. Reduce extent of training; can evaluate performance with prior firm(s); must instruct in company policy; some negative morale if current employees feel bypassed for promotions
Advertisements	a. Newspapers, trade publications, professional journals, Web sites b. Large quantity of applicants; average applicant quality may not be high; cost/applicant is low; additional responsibility placed on screening; can reduce unacceptable applications by noting job qualifications in ads
Employment agencies	a. Private organizations, professional organizations, government, executive search firms b. Must be carefully selected; must be determined who pays fee; good for applicant screening; specialists in personnel
Unsolicited applicants	a. Walk-ins, write-ins b. Wide variance in quality; must be carefully screened; file should be kept for future positions
Within the Company	
Current and former employees	a. Promotion or transfer of existing full-time employees, part-time employees; rehiring of laid-off employees b. Knowledge of company policies and personnel; good for morale; honest appraisal from in-house supervisor
Employee recommendations	a. Friends, acquaintances, relatives b. Value of recommendations depend on honesty and judgment of current employees

assignments, and the specific ongoing roles and tasks. Figure 11.4 showed a traditional job description for a store manager. Yet, using a traditional description alone has been criticized. This may limit a job's scope, as well as its authority, responsibility, and decision-making power; be static and not let a person grow; limit activities to those listed; and not describe how positions are coordinated. To complement a traditional description, many personnel experts suggest a **goal-oriented job description** that enumerates basic functions, the relationship of each job to overall goals, the interdependence of positions, and information flows. Figure 11.11 illustrates a goal-oriented job description.

An **application blank** is usually the first tool used to screen applicants; providing data on education, experience, health, reasons for leaving prior jobs, outside activities, hobbies, and references. It is rather short, requires little interpretation, and can be used as the basis for probing in an interview. A refinement is the **weighted application blank,** in which factors having a high relationship with success are given more weight than others. Retailers that use such a form have analyzed the performance of current and past employees and determined the criteria (education, experience, and so on) best correlated with job success (as measured by longer tenure, higher sales, less absenteeism, and so on). After weighted scores are awarded to all job applicants (based on data they provide), a minimum total score becomes a cutoff point for hiring. An effective application blank aids retailers in lessening turnover and selecting high achievers.

Figure 11.11
A Goal-Oriented Job Description for a Management Trainee

Attributes Required	Ability	Desire	In the Retailing Environment
ANALYTICAL SKILLS: ability to solve problems; strong numerical ability for analysis of facts and data for planning, managing, and controlling.			Retail executives are problem solvers. Knowledge and understanding of past performance and present circumstances form the basis for action and planning.
CREATIVITY: ability to generate and recognize imaginative ideas and solutions; ability to recognize the need for and be responsive to change.			Retail executives are idea people. Successful buying results from sensitive, aware decisions, while merchandising requires imaginative, innovative techniques.
DECISIVENESS: ability to make quick decisions and render judgments, take action, and commit oneself to completion.			Retail executives are action people. Whether it's new fashion trends or customer desires, decisions must be made quickly and confidently in this ever-changing environment.
FLEXIBILITY: ability to adjust to the ever-changing needs of the situation; ability to adapt to different people, places, and things; willingness to do whatever is necessary to get the task done.			Retail executives are flexible. Surprises in retailing never cease. Plans must be altered quickly to accommodate changes in trends, styles, and attitudes, while numerous ongoing activities cannot be ignored.
INITIATIVE: ability to originate action rather than wait to be told what to do and ability to act based on conviction.			Retail executives are doers. Sales volumes, trends, and buying opportunities mean continual action. Opportunities for action must be seized.
LEADERSHIP: ability to inspire others to trust and respect your judgment; ability to delegate and to guide and persuade others.			Retail executives are managers. Running a business means depending on others to get the work done. One person cannot do it all.
ORGANIZATION: ability to establish priorities and courses of action for self and/or others; skill in planning and following up to achieve results.			Retail executives are jugglers. A variety of issues, functions, and projects are constantly in motion. To reach your goals, priorities must be set and work must be delegated to others.
RISK-TAKING: willingness to take calculated risks based on thorough analysis and sound judgment and to accept responsibility for the results.			Retail executives are courageous. Success in retailing often comes from taking calculated risks and having the confidence to try something new before someone else does.
STRESS TOLERANCE: ability to perform consistently under pressure, to thrive on constant change and challenge.			Retail executives are resilient. As the above description should suggest, retailing is fast-paced and demanding.

An application blank should be used in conjunction with a job description. Those meeting the minimum job requirements are processed further (interview). Those who do not are immediately rejected. In this way, the application blank provides a quick and inexpensive method of screening.

Making Retailing a Serious Career Option

Are young retail employees happy at their jobs? Robert Tillman, the chief executive of Lowe's, says "more than 70 percent of high school students, in preparation for college, begin their working careers in retailing, but only 3 percent of them wanted to be there." When employees are not really interested in their jobs, they often do not deliver effective customer service. The situation is exacerbated by the tight U.S. job market of recent years.

To overcome this problem, firms must enact better plans to motivate current and prospective employees to consider retailing careers. Attracting the right employees means that retailers not only need to offer competitive salaries, but they must also provide a compensation package (including health benefits and profit sharing) demonstrating the firms' commitment to suitable career opportunities. Retailers must communicate their career growth plans to employees by showing them specific opportunities. Training programs that provide employees with product, sales, and managerial knowledge are important. Finally, a retailer should offer career ladder positions with increasing responsibility and fulfillment.

Source: Mark D. Parrott, "Retailing Career," *Do-It-Yourself Retailing* (January 1999), p. 8.

The interview seeks information that can be amassed only by personal questioning and observation. It lets the prospective employer determine the candidate's verbal ability, note his or her appearance, ask questions keyed to the application, and probe career objectives. Several decisions about interviewing must be made: the level of formality, the number and length of interviews, the interview location, the person(s) to do the interviewing, the use of a relaxed or intense atmosphere, and the degree to which interviews are structured. These decisions often depend on the interviewer's ability and the job's requirements.

Many, particularly smaller, retailers hire an applicant if he or she performs well during the interview. Other, usually larger, retailers use an additional selection device: testing. In this case, a candidate who does well during an interview is asked to complete psychological tests (that measure personality, intelligence, interest, and leadership skills) and/or achievement tests (that measure learned knowledge).[14]

Tests must be administered and interpreted by qualified people. Standardized exams should not be used unless proven as effective predictors of job performance. Because achievement tests deal with specific skills or information, such as industry knowledge, the ability to make a sales presentation, and insights on retailing practices, they are easier to interpret than psychological tests; and direct relationships between knowledge and ability can be shown. In giving tests to job applicants, retailers must not violate any federal, state, or local law. For example, the federal Employee Polygraph Protection Act of 1988 bars firms from using lie detector tests in most retail hiring situations (drugstores are exempt from this law).

To save time and operate more efficiently, some retailers—both large and small—are turning to computerized application blanks and testing. Home Depot and Target Stores have in-store kiosks in all of their outlets that allow people to apply for jobs, complete application blanks, and answer several questions. Says a Target spokesperson, "It really speeds up the hiring process and captures more people. Someone could apply and get an offer the same day. Before, it took 10 days or so." At Hot Topic, an apparel and accessories chain targeting teens, there is a computerized questionnaire that asks whether applicants could "work in an environment where we play loud alternative music."[15]

In conjunction with interviewing and testing, retailers often get references from applicants that can be checked either before or after the interview stage. References are contacted to see how enthusiastically they recommend an applicant, check the applicant's honesty, ask a prior employer why the applicant left the job, and review the types of people who will vouch for an applicant. Mail and phone checks are inexpensive, fast, and easy.

When a candidate successfully completes the interview, testing, and reference check steps, some firms require a physical exam before giving a job. This is especially due to the physical activity, long hours, and tensions involved in many retailing positions. A clean bill of health would mean the candidate is offered a job. Again, federal, state, and local laws must be followed.

Each step in the selection process complements the others; together, they give the retailer a total information package to aid in choosing personnel. As a rule, retailers should use job descriptions, application blanks, interviews, and reference checks. The use of follow-up interviews, psychological and achievement tests, and physical exams depends on the retailer and the position. Inexpensive tools (such as application blanks) are used in the early screening stages, whereas more costly, in-depth tools (such as interviews) are used after reducing the applicant pool. Federal and state laws require that questions be linked to job performance. Equal opportunity, nondiscriminatory practices must be followed.

Training Retail Personnel When a new employee first joins a firm, he or she should receive **pre-training,** which is an indoctrination on the firm's history and policies, as well as a job orientation on hours, compensation, the chain of command, and job duties. In addition, the new employee is introduced to co-workers: "An effective orientation program should inspire recruits to work for the company and provide information that they still do not know about their jobs and the retailer. What kind of first impression do orientation programs make? Do they confirm the new hire's choice that XYZ company is a good place to work? Or are the programs so foreign to most new employees' mindsets that they can dampen, if not negate, enthusiasm for the job?"[16]

Training programs are used to teach new (and existing) personnel how best to perform their jobs or how to improve themselves. Training can range from one- or two-day sessions on writing up sales orders, operating a cash register, personal selling techniques, or compliance with affirmative action programs to two-year programs for executive trainees on all aspects of the retailer and its operations. For example,

- At Wal-Mart (www.wal-mart.com), assistant store manager trainees receive 17 weeks of instruction in three main areas: merchandising, people development, and operations. Part of training is computerized and part is with a management sponsor. Once the program is completed, each trainee becomes an assistant store manager and has responsibility for his or her own section of a store, known as a "store-within-a-store"—with fiscal, merchandising, and human resource responsibility for it.
- Sears University "opened" in January 1995. It offers regular retail education courses plus self-study options. Annually, 20,000 managers enroll in hands-on programs ranging from one day to one week. Some programs provide managers with core skills in buying, merchandising, and human resource management. Others help participants function as strategic leaders. Courses are taught by seasoned line managers, training and development experts, and university faculty consultants.[17]

Effective retailers realize training is an ongoing activity. New equipment, changes in laws, and new product lines (as well as motivating current personnel, employee promotions, and employee turnover) necessitate not only training but retraining as well. Thus, Federated Department Stores has a program called "clienteling," whereby sales associates are tutored on how to develop better long-term relationships with specific repeat customers. Core vendors of Federated are regularly involved in teaching sales associates about the features and benefits of new merchandise when it is introduced.

Table 11.4 Selected Training Decisions

When does training occur? (At the time of hiring and/or after being at the workplace?)

How long should training be?

What training programs are for new employees? For existing employees?

Who should conduct each training program? (Supervisor, co-worker, training department, or outside specialist?)

Where should training take place? (At the workplace or in a training room?)

What material (content) should be learned? How should it be taught?

Should audiovisuals be used? If yes, how?

Should elements of the training program be computerized? If yes, how?

How can the effectiveness of training be measured?

Several training decisions need to be made, as shown in Table 11.4. They can be divided into three categories: identifying needs, devising appropriate training methods, and evaluation.

Short-term training needs for both new and existing employees can be identified by measuring the gap between the skills those workers already have and the skills desired by the firm (for each job). Training should prepare workers for possible job rotation, promotions, and emerging changes in the company. A longer plan for personnel development lets a firm identify future needs and train workers. Short- and long-run training needs can be unearthed by communicating with top management, formal evaluations, informal observations, group discussions, employee requests, and employee performance.

After needs are identified, the best way(s) to address them must be uncovered from among lectures, demonstrations, films, programmed instruction, conferences, sensitivity training, case studies, role playing, behavior modeling, and competency-based instruction. These techniques may be personalized; some may be computerized (as more firms are doing). The methods' attributes are noted in Table 11.5. Retailers often use two or more techniques of training to reduce boredom and cover the material better.

To promote its Cashier Training Software, Strategic Systems offers an online demonstration (www.ssaweb.com/web/tryus.html).

Computer-based training has two formats: personal computer and Web. For example, Strategic Systems Associates markets Cashier Training Software for less than $2,000. Its multimedia CD-ROM for supermarkets has modules on the checkout counter, register systems, scanning, tendering, adjustments, age-related sales (such as beer), and cashier responsibilities. At the same time, the National Retail Federation is making its Performance TRAC training programs available—for a fee—on the Web for potential retail employees.[18]

For retail training to succeed, an environment conducive to learning is necessary. These are essential principles for enacting a positive training environment:

- All people can learn if taught properly.
- A person learns better when motivated; intelligence alone is not sufficient.
- Learning should be goal-oriented.
- A trainee learns more when he or she participates and is not a passive listener.
- The teacher must provide guidance.
- Learning should be approached as a series of steps rather than a one-time occurrence.
- Learning should be spread out over a reasonable period of time rather than be compressed.
- The learner should be encouraged to do homework or otherwise practice.
- Different methods of learning should be combined.
- Performance standards should be set and good performance recognized.
- The learner should feel a sense of achievement.
- The teacher should adapt to the learner and to the situation.

Table 11.5 The Characteristics of Retail Training Methods

Method	Characteristics
Lecture	Factual, uninterrupted presentation of material; can use professional educator or expert in the field; no active participation by trainees
Demonstration	Good for showing how to use equipment or do a sales presentation; applies relevance of training; active participation by trainees
Video	Animated; good for demonstration; can be used many times; no active participation by trainees
Programmed instruction	Presents information in a structured manner; requires response from trainees; provides performance feedback; adjustable to trainees' pace; high initial investment
Conference	Useful for supervisory training; conference leader must encourage participation; reinforces training
Sensitivity training	Extensive interaction; good for supervisors as a tool for understanding employees
Case study	Actual or hypothetical problem presented, including circumstances, pertinent information, and questions; learning by doing; exposure to a wide variety of problems
Role playing	Trainees placed into real-life situations and act out roles
Behavior modeling	Trainees taught to imitate models shown on videotape or in role-playing sessions
Competency-based instruction	Trainees given a list of tasks or exercises that are presented in a self-paced format

A training program must be systematically evaluated for effectiveness. Comparisons can be made between the performance of those who have received training and those who have not. They may also be made among employees receiving different types of training for the same job. When a retailer measures the success of a training program, evaluations should always be made in relation to stated training goals. In addition, training effects should be measured over several time intervals (such as immediately, 30 days later, and 6 months later), and proper records maintained.

Compensating Retail Personnel Total compensation should be fair to both the retailer and its employees to be effective. **Compensation** includes direct monetary payments (such as salaries, commissions, and bonuses) and indirect payments (such as paid vacations, health and life insurance benefits, and retirement plans). To better motivate employees, some firms also have profit-sharing plans. Smaller retailers often pay salaries, commissions, and/or bonuses, and have less emphasis on fringe benefits. Bigger firms generally pay salaries, commissions, and/or bonuses and have more emphasis on fringe benefits.

This site (www.dol. gov/dol/esa/public/ minwage/america. htm) shows the minimum wage in every state.

For some time, there have been unsuccessful efforts to raise the federal minimum wage, which has remained at $5.15 per hour since 1997. These efforts (opposed by many retailers) continue. Besides the federal minimum wage law, 43 states have their own minimum wage laws—with about 10 being higher than the federal minimum and 6 being lower. The minimum wage has the most impact on retailers hiring entry-level, part-time workers (which encompass millions of people). However, full-time, career-track retailing jobs are *always* paid an attractive market rate; and to attract part-time workers during good economic times, retailers must often pay salaries above the minimum.

At some large firms, compensation for certain positions is set through collective bargaining. According to the U.S. Bureau of Labor Statistics, about 1.25 million retail employees are represented by labor unions; and union membership varies greatly. As an example, unionized grocery stores account for more than 60 percent of total U.S. supermarket sales. Yet, independent supermarkets are not apt to be unionized. Union contracts also frequently affect nonunion personnel, who ask for similar compensation.

Technology in Retailing

Employee Training Made as Easy as CBT

Many retailers that once considered computer-based training (CBT) as nonessential, now view it as an effective technique to boost profits by reducing costs and employee turnover. According to Maggie Lunt, manager of education at the Food Marketing Institute, "Once people use it, they view it as a training method that's here to stay, a viable way to train people at a lower cost. And because they're embracing the technology, they're anxious to see more CBT products."

CBT programs are often used to familiarize entry-level retail employees on the basics of a particular job. For example, one CBT provider—Payback Training Systems—has devised a number of CBT programs tailored to supermarkets. These include specific skill-related programs for cashiers, grocery clerks, dairy personnel, and produce clerks.

Through CBT, Supervalu has been able to cut the *trainer* time for cashier positions from 24 to 6 hours and the *trainee* time from 24 to 12 hours. In addition, Supervalu reports an 18 percent faster scan time, a 44 percent reduction in over-rings and under-rings, and an 11 percent reduction in employee turnover because of CBT.

Describe other criteria that retailers can use to determine the success of CBT.

Source: Barry Janoff, "User-Friendly," *Progressive Grocer* (March 1999), pp. 65–70.

In a *straight-salary plan,* a worker is paid a fixed amount per hour, week, month, or year. Earnings are not directly tied to productivity. Advantages of this plan are retailer control, employee security, and known expenses. Disadvantages are retailer inflexibility, limited worker incentive to lift productivity, and fixed costs. Lower-level retail workers (such as clerks and cashiers) are usually paid salaries.

With a *straight-commission plan,* earnings are directly tied to productivity (such as sales volume). A fixed amount is not paid. Advantages of this plan are retailer flexibility, the link to worker productivity, no fixed costs, and employee incentive. Disadvantages are the retailer's potential lack of control over the tasks employees perform, the risk of low earnings to employees, the variability of retail costs, and the lack of limits placed on worker earnings. Sales personnel for autos, real-estate, insurance, furniture, jewelry, and other expensive items are often paid on straight commission—as are direct-selling personnel.

To combine the attributes of both salary and commission plans, some retailers pay their employees a *salary plus commission.* Shoe salespeople, major appliance salespeople, and some management personnel are among the employees paid in this manner. Sometimes, bonuses are awarded as supplements to salary and/or commission. These are normally given for outstanding performance. At Finish Line stores, national, regional, district, and store managers receive fixed salaries and earn bonuses based on the sales, payroll, and theft rate goals of their stores. In certain cases, top retail management is paid via a "compensation cafeteria," whereby those executives can choose their own combination of salary, bonus, deferred bonus, fringe benefits, life insurance, stock options, and retirement benefits.

Target Stores has a generous benefits package for employees (target.com/jobs/benefits.asp).

One of the thorniest issues facing retailers today involves the benefits portion of employee compensation, especially as related to pensions and health care. It is very challenging in this era with intense price competition, the growing use of part-time workers, and escalating medical costs for retailers to balance their employees' life-style needs with company financial needs.

Supervising Retail Personnel **Supervision** is the manner of providing a job environment that encourages employee accomplishment. The goals are to oversee personnel, achieve good performance, maintain employee morale and motivation, control expenses, minimize redundancies, communicate policies, and resolve problems. Supervision is provided by personal contact, meetings, and written reports between managers and subordinates.

One key element of supervision is to continually motivate employees to achieve company objectives and thereby harness their energy to the retailer's needs. **Job motivation** is the drive within people to attain work-related goals. It may be positive or negative. Sears believes that 10 attitude questions can help to predict employee behavior, based on their motivation:

1. Do you like the kind of work you do?
2. Does your work give you a sense of accomplishment?
3. Are you proud to say you work at Sears?
4. How does the amount of work you are expected to do influence your overall attitude about your job?
5. How do your physical working conditions influence your overall attitude about your job?
6. How does the way you are treated by those who supervise you influence your overall attitude about your job?
7. Do you feel good about the future of the company?
8. Do you think Sears is making the changes necessary to compete effectively?
9. Do you understand Sears' business strategy?
10. Do you see a connection between the work you do and the company's strategic objectives?[19]

Employee motivation should be approached from two perspectives: (1) What job-related factors cause employees to be satisfied or dissatisfied with their positions? (2) What supervision style is best for both the retailer and its employees? See Figure 11.12.

Each employee looks at job satisfaction in terms of minimum expectations ("dissatisfiers") and desired goals ("satisfiers"). True satisfaction—and a motivated employee—require fulfillment of both factors. *Minimum expectations* relate mostly to the work environment itself, including the right to a safe workplace, equitable treatment for those having the same jobs, some flexibility in policies (e.g., a person is not docked pay if he or she arrives 10 minutes after the required time), an even-tempered boss, some freedom in attire, a fair compensation package, basic fringe benefits (such as vacation time and some form of medical coverage), clear communications, job security, and so forth. By themselves, these elements can generally influence motivation in only one way—negatively. If minimum expectations are not met, the person will be unhappy. If minimum expectations are met, they are taken for granted and do little to motivate the person to go "above and beyond."

Desired goals relate more to the job than to the work environment. These elements include whether an employee likes the job itself, is recognized for good performance, feels a sense of achievement, is empowered to make decisions in his or her area of work, is trusted, has a defined career path, receives extra compensation when performance is exceptional, and is given the chance to learn and grow at the company. These elements can have a tremendous positive impact on job satisfaction and worker motivation—and stimulate a person to go "above and beyond." Nonetheless, should the person's minimum expectations not be met, he or she might still be dissatisfied enough to leave the company, even if the job itself is quite rewarding. As one expert points out:

> Human resources professionals apparently still underestimate the value of recognition programs in employee motivation and, therefore, in enhanced productivity. It appears that praise and a thank you continue to be the most neglected social gestures in the workplace. Recognition is distinctly different from reward in that the former reinforces the desired behavior or performance while the latter is given after results have been achieved. Recognition programs need not entail substantial resources. The key is

Figure 11.12
A.C. Moore: Fostering a Motivated Labor Force

A.C. Moore operates 40 arts and crafts super-stores that offer a vast assortment of tradi-tional and contempo-rary arts, crafts, and flo-ral merchandise for a wide range of cus-tomers. It believes strongly in employee development and empowerment.
Reprinted by permission of Masters Group Design. Photography: Theo Anderson. Art Direction: Lisa M. Weinberger.

to make them creative, consistent, and timely. Each firm—depending on its history, culture, and personality—can develop a program tailored to its specific needs.[20]

There are three basic styles of supervising retail employees:

- Management assumes employees must be closely supervised and controlled, and that only economic inducements really motivate. Management further believes that the aver-age worker lacks ambition, dislikes responsibility, and prefers to be led. This is the tradi-tional view of motivation and has been applied to lower-level retail positions.
- Management assumes employees can be self-managers and assigned authority, motiva-tion is social and psychological, and supervision can be decentralized and participatory. Management also thinks that motivation, the potential for development, the capacity for assuming responsibility, and a readiness to achieve company goals are all present in peo-ple. The critical supervisory task is to create a work environment in which people can achieve their own goals by attaining company objectives. This is a more modern view of motivation and applies to all levels of retail personnel.
- Management applies a self-management approach and also advocates more employee involvement in defining jobs and sharing decision making. There is mutual loyalty between the firm and its workers, and both parties enthusiastically cooperate for the long-term benefit of each. This is a modern view and applies to all levels of personnel.

It is imperative that supervision motivates employees in a manner that yields job satisfac-tion, low turnover, low absenteeism, and high productivity:

Retailers spend millions of dollars training workers. But today, those workers are apt to pick up and leave at the most unpredictable time. It's called the law of turnover, and it's especially applicable in a strong economy. Annual rates are staggering—commonly in the range of 100 percent to 200 percent among hourly associates. We often ask retailers how they retain good workers. The common response is "Pay more," but plenty offer premium wages and still can't attract top talent. On the other hand, retailers that create an appealing job atmosphere—also known as an environment of choice—cannot only entice recruits to sign on, but can encourage experienced employees to stay.[21]

The key to turnover is that retailers not only recruit and train workers more effectively, but also manage them better. The force behind a quiet rebellion in retailing is the younger generation of workers, those the popular press calls Generation X to distinguish them from the baby boomers who are their bosses. Boomers keep saying things about working long and hard to get ahead, paying your dues before getting responsibility and higher pay. Younger colleagues retort: "Get a life. I don't mind working, even working hard, but where is my family, where is my happiness?" They want more flexibility in their schedules and time for themselves, their interests, and priorities.[22]

SUMMARY

1. *To study the procedures involved in setting up a retail organization.* A retail organization structures and assigns tasks, policies, resources, authority, responsibilities, and rewards to efficiently and effectively satisfy the needs of a firm's target market, employees, and management. There are five steps in setting up an organization: outlining specific tasks to be performed in a distribution channel, dividing tasks among channel members and customers, grouping tasks into jobs, classifying jobs, and integrating positions through an organization chart.

Specific tasks include buying, shipping, receiving and checking, pricing, and marking merchandise; inventory control; display preparation; facilities maintenance; research; customer contact and follow-up; personnel management; merchandise repairs; finances and credit; gift wrapping; delivery; returns; forecasting; and coordination. These tasks may be divided among retailers, manufacturers, wholesalers, specialists, and customers.

Tasks are next grouped into jobs, such as sales personnel, cashiers, inventory personnel, display personnel, credit personnel, customer service personnel, janitorial personnel, and management. Then jobs are categorized by functional, product, geographic, or combination classification. Finally, an organization chart graphically displays the hierarchy of authority and the relationship among jobs, and coordinates personnel.

2. *To examine the various organizational arrangements utilized in retailing.* Retail organization structures differ by institutional type. Small independents generally use simple organizations, with little specialization. Many department stores use a version of the Mazur plan, whereby they place functions into four categories: merchandising, publicity, store management, and accounting and control. The equal store format, a version of the Mazur plan, is used by numerous chain stores. Diversified firms have very complex organizations.

3. *To consider the special human resource environment of retailing.* Retailers have a unique human resource environment due to the large number of inexperienced workers, long hours, highly visible employees, many part-time workers, and variations in customer demand. There is a broad range of career opportunities available to women and minorities, although improvement is still needed.

4. *To describe the principles and practices involved with the human resource management process in retailing.* This process comprises several interrelated activities: recruitment, selection, training, compensation, and supervision. In applying the process, diversity, labor laws, and employee privacy should be kept in mind.

Recruitment is the activity of generating job applicants. Sources include educational institutions, channel members, competitors, ads, employment agencies, unsolicited applicants, current and former employees, and Web sites.

The selection of retail personnel requires thorough job analysis, creating job descriptions, using application

SUMMARY (CONTINUED)

blanks, interviews, testing (optional), reference checking, and physical exams. After personnel are selected, they go through pre-training (orientation) and job training. Effective training revolves around identifying needs, devising proper methods, and evaluating the results. Training is usually necessary for continuing, as well as, new personnel.

Employees are compensated by direct monetary payments and/or indirect payments. The alternative direct compensation plans are straight salary, straight commission, and salary plus commission and/or bonus. Indirect payments involve such items as paid vacations, health benefits, and retirement plans. The latter are now much more controversial.

Supervision and motivation are needed to gain good employee performance. A main task of supervision is employee motivation. The causes of job satisfaction/dissatisfaction and the supervisory style must be reviewed.

Key Terms

retail organization (p. 360)
hierarchy of authority (p. 366)
organization chart (p. 366)
Mazur plan (p. 368)
mother hen with branch store chickens
   organization (p. 369)
separate store organization (p. 369)
equal store organization (p. 369)

diversified retailer (p. 372)
human resource management (p. 374)
human resource management process
   (p. 378)
recruitment (p. 379)
job analysis (p. 379)
traditional job description (p. 379)
goal-oriented job description (p. 380)

application blank (p. 380)
weighted application blank (p. 380)
pre-training (p. 383)
training programs (p. 383)
compensation (p. 385)
supervision (p. 386)
job motivation (p. 387)

Questions for Discussion

1. Cite at least five objectives a small independent camera retailer should set when setting up its organization structure.

2. Why are employee needs important in developing a retail organization?

3. Are the steps in setting up an organization the same for small and large retailers? Explain your answer.

4. Present a seven-item checklist to use in assigning tasks to members in a retail channel of distribution.

5. What are the pros and cons of analyzing a retailer on the basis of its organization chart?

6. Describe the greatest similarities and differences in the structures of small independents, department stores, chain retailers, and diversified retailers.

7. How can retailers attract and retain more women and minority workers?

8. How would small and large retailers act differently for each of the following?
   a. Diversity.
   b. Recruitment.
   c. Selection.
   d. Training.
   e. Compensation.
   f. Supervision.

9. Why are the job description and the application blank so important in employee selection?

10. What problems can occur while interviewing and testing prospective employees?

11. Present a plan for the ongoing training of both existing lower-level and middle management employees without making it seem punitive.

12. Describe the major goals of a compensation plan (both direct and indirect components) in a retail setting.

13. Are the minimum job expectations of entry-level workers and middle-level managers similar or dissimilar? What about the desired goals? Explain your answers.

14. How would you supervise and motivate a 19-year-old supermarket cashier?

WEB-BASED EXERCISE

Careers in Retailing (www.careersinretailing.com)

Questions

1. How could a retail employer most effectively use this site?

2. How could a job searcher seeking a retail career best use this site?

3. Examine the career opportunities at two different retailers. Comment on the pros and cons of each.

4. Discuss the diversity of retail careers represented on this Web site.

CHAPTER ENDNOTES

1. "A Satisfying Experience: Cancun Retailer Relies on Attention to Detail, Broad Assortment to Help Differentiate Business from Competition," *Do-It Yourself Retailing* (June 1999), pp. 66–67.

2. *Levitz 1995 Annual Report.* See also Jennifer Laabs, "The HR Side of Sears' Comeback," *Workforce* (March 1999), pp. 24–28; and Arthur Blank, "They Sweat the Small Stuff," *Canadian Business* (May 28, 1999), pp. 51–54.

3. Paul M. Mazur, *Principles of Organization Applied to Modern Retailing* (New York: Harper & Brothers, 1927).

4. Doug Donaldson, "Ken Porter: Young Retailers of the Year," *Do-It-Yourself Retailing* (August 1999), p. 252.

5. *Uno Restaurant Corporation 1998 Annual Report*

6. Angela Y. Hardin, "Stores Scramble for Seasonal Help," *Crain's Cleveland Business* (November 8, 1999), p. 3.

7. "Retailing Career Electrifying at Electronics Boutique," *Careers in Retailing* (January 1999), pp. 19, 22.

8. Michelle Conlin and Wendy Zellner, "The Glass Ceiling: The CEO Still Wears Wingtips," *Business Week Online* (November 22, 1999).

9. "Women in Power: A Score Card," *Business Week Online* (November 22, 1999); Victor Wishna, "Dollars and Census," *Restaurant Business* (July 1, 1999), p. 18; Jacqueline Dulen, "Strength in Numbers," *Restaurants & Institutions* (March 15, 1999), p. 39; "100 Best Companies," *www.working-mother.com* (November 23, 1999); and "Shattering the Glass Ceiling," *Chain Store Age* (January 2000), pp. 57–59.

10. Dulen, "Strength in Numbers," p. 39.

11. Robert Berner, "Urban Rarity: Stores Offering Spiffy Service," *Wall Street Journal* (July 25, 1996), pp. B1, B10.

12. "The 50 Best Companies for Asians, Blacks, and Hispanics," *Fortune* (July 19, 1999), p. 52.

13. David P. Schulz, "Employee Attitude Surveys Focus on the Human Side of the Retail Equation," *Stores* (April 1999), pp. 96–97; and Edward Robinson and Jonathan Hickman, "The Diversity Elite," *Fortune* (July 19, 1999), p. 62.

14. See Christopher Caggiano, "Psycho Path," *Inc.* (July 1998), pp. 77–85.

15. Jim McCartney, "Retailers Using Computers to Screen Applicants," *Shopping Centers Today* (October 1999), p. 50; David P. Schulz, "Small Retailers Turn to Pre-Employment Screening Services," *Stores* (May 1998), pp. 72, 74; and Matt Richtel, "Online Revolution's Latest Twist: Computers Screening Job Applicants," *New York Times* (February 6, 2000), pp. A1, A21.

16. Marilyn Moats Kennedy, "Setting the Right Tone, Right Away," *Across the Board* (April 1999), pp. 51–52.

17. Valerie Seckler, "Sears' Campus Courtship Blossoms," *Women's Wear Daily* (August 4, 1998), p. 15.

18. "CTS—Supermarket Edition," *www.ssaweb.com/products/products01a.html* (March 9, 2000); and Jeanette Hye, "NRF Moves to Web-Based Training," *Women's Wear Daily* (November 3, 1999), p. 20.

19. Anthony J. Rucci, Steven P. Kirn, and Richard T. Quinn, "The Employee-Customer-Profit Chain at Sears," *Harvard Business Review*, Vol. 76 (January–February 1998), pp. 82–97.

20. Brenda Paik Sunoo, "Praise and Thanks—You Can't Give Enough!" *Workforce* (April 1999), p. 56.

21. John Jones and Stacey Kaplan, "Buck the Turnover Plague—Become a Retailer of Choice," *Discount Store News* (March 22, 1999), p. 17.

22. David P. Schulz, "Generational Tensions Add to 'Quiet Rebellion' in Retail Work Force," *Stores* (March 1999), pp. 61–62.

CASE 1

BECOMING AN EMPLOYER OF CHOICE, NOT CHANCE

Every year, retailers spend millions of dollars training their workers, only to have them leave for other job opportunities. The annual turnover is staggering, with 100 percent being typical—and even 200 percent being common—among part-time retail employees. One reason for the high turnover is that working in retailing can mean long hours, as well as weekend and holiday shifts, that encroach on one's personal life.

How can a retailer attract good workers willing to make the commitment and encourage them to stay once they are on board? How can a firm stimulate part-time workers to consider full-time careers in retailing? A common response is: "Pay more! If we could raise our starting hourly rate by 25 cents, our problems would be solved." However, throwing money at the problem may be more of a temporary fix than a long-term solution. A better response is to create an appealing atmosphere, "an environment of choice," that entices recruits to sign on and provides sufficient reasons for experienced employees to stay. In a competitive job market, retailers must work harder to differentiate themselves from the competition and to become an "employer of choice" by developing a "persona" that epitomizes each retailer's values.

Developing a persona and leveraging it to attract and retain good employees should translate into a win–win situation for both the retailers and employees. For example, Target Stores coined the phrase "Fast, Fun, and Friendly" to explain its customer service philosophy to the workforce (and potential employees). Target carries that persona over to its relationship with employees. While the company refers to customers as "guests," it considers employees to be "team members," communicating the notion of community. Management strives to treat team members with dignity and respect, and it empowers them to take action they feel appropriate to help the guests (employee empowerment). The goal is to make team members know that their contributions matter.

Many people become interested in working for a retailer after shopping at its stores. As potential employees, customers get to view the prospective employer and the work environment before they are hired. If people don't feel comfortable shopping in the environment, if their experience with the sales staff or human resources staff is unpleasant, or even if the application form itself doesn't reflect the quality or image they expect, then they are unlikely to complete the application process. On the other hand, if the environment suits their personality, they may very well apply.

The power of the work environment must not be underestimated. Retail employees who are worth keeping want to learn on the job and grow personally and professionally. Because they are constantly in the public eye, these workers want to be proud of the surroundings in which they work. Environment is not just physical; it's also emotional. Arlene Stem, president and CEO of Gantos, a women's specialty apparel chain, explains her company's retention strategy for salespeople this way: "You must create the right environment, one that creates 'ownership' in the company and a passion for the business."

Traditionally, many of the part-time employees in retailing have been younger people, from their late teens to their early thirties. Many of those in today's retail workforce would be classified as Generation X-ers, members of the generation following the well-documented baby boom generation. Generation X-ers are said to provide daily challenges to their baby boomer supervisors with their independence, confidence, and creativity. Therefore, they must be managed differently if they are to succeed and thrive as productive employees in the desired retail environment.

Questions

1. How can a fast-food retailer seek to minimize turnover of entry-level employees?

2. Describe how a small local independent retailer can develop a "persona."

3. How can a discount apparel retailer maximize its work environment for employees and still keep costs low?

4. Comment on the difficulties of managing Generation X employees and how these potential problems can be overcome.

NOTE

The material in this case is adapted by the authors from Stacey L. Jones and John M. Kaplan, "Workers Are Seeking Employers of Choice," *Chain Store Age* (October 1998), pp. 72, 74. Copyright Lebhar-Friedman, Inc., 425 Park Avenue, New York, NY 10022.

CASE 2

SUPERVALU: APPRAISING EMPLOYEE PERFORMANCE

Supervalu is the nation's largest food distribution company. Supervalu supplies about 3,500 different supermarkets. In addition, the firm operates approximately 470 company-owned supermarkets and 800 limited-assortment food stores.

Supervalu uses a management by objectives (MBO) process to assess its buyers and other key personnel. This process is based on four concepts: (1) establishment of clear priorities through the quantification of goals (wherever possible), (2) a results orientation, (3) an appreciation of the critical skills needed to succeed in these jobs, and (4) open discussions between employees and their managers.

This case (based on composite characters devised by Supervalu to illustrate its procedures) focuses on Supervalu's use of the MBO process in appraising Bill Edwards, a Supervalu buyer. A year ago, as part of an MBO performance appraisal process, Bill Edwards and Teresa Harrison, his supervisor, mutually agreed to hold Edwards accountable for fulfilling specific and quantifiable goals for the coming year relating to gross profits, inventory turnover, vendor complaints, and vendor relations in his department.

Two incidents are noteworthy in portraying Edwards' performance during the year. In one incident, Edwards initiated a meeting with a major Supervalu supplier to complain about late deliveries and back orders. Although Edwards ultimately resolved the problem, some ill will was created when he initially suggested that Supervalu temporarily switch vendors until the supplier could resolve the problem. In another situation, Edwards initially refused to immediately inspect damaged freight at a loading dock. Instead, he tried to get the loading dock supervisor to accept the freight "as is," arguing that ultimately it would be accepted in its damaged condition by his customers. Only after he was reminded that this was against company policy did Edwards work out another solution to the problem.

CASE 2

(CONTINUED)

About 11 months after Edwards and Harrison discussed Edwards' goals for the year, Harrison began to prepare for Edwards' performance evaluation meeting. She gathered information from a variety of sources, including financial data from Edwards' department, letters from vendors, specific behavior that Harrison had observed, and information from Edwards' co-workers.

One letter she received indicated that Edwards had done an outstanding job in getting products needed quickly and that his ideas were original and fresh. Another letter, however, was critical. It noted that he had minimized Supervalu's needs and sidestepped Supervalu's management policies.

Harrison decided to call Sara Karnsby, one of Edwards' co-workers, to ask about his performance. Karnsby's evaluation of Edwards was rather mixed. These are some of the comments she made: "Bill's been a lot better lately, in that he has great ideas and is more organized. But he is still hard for us to deal with sometimes. While Bill is light on detail work, he gets things done. His customers really like him."

At the annual performance evaluation, Edwards was very upset when he was only judged to be "average" on overall performance. He said he had "made his numbers," worked hard, established relations with vendors, and demonstrated his creativity. Although Harrison agreed that he had made his numbers, she was critical of his human relations skills. She was especially concerned about his relations with co-workers and vendors—and his domineering personality.

As part of the MBO process for the next year, Edwards and Harrison have agreed that his key area for development will be building human relations skills. They plan to meet in two months to discuss what he has learned from a training seminar on negotiating skills and how he will apply the material to his job.

Questions

1. Describe the pros and cons of an MBO system of employee assessment.

2. Describe the relationship between an MBO evaluation system and a goal-oriented job description.

3. How can this appraisal system be tied into developing and evaluating management training programs?

4. Was Edwards fairly evaluated? Explain your answer.

Video Questions on Supervalu

1. Evaluate Supervalu's performance appraisal system.

2. What other suggestions could Harrison have given Edwards?

NOTE

The material in this case is drawn from *www.supervalu.com* (March 9, 2000); and data supplied by Supervalu.

Operations Management: Financial Dimensions

CHAPTER OBJECTIVES

1. To define operations management
2. To discuss profit planning
3. To describe asset management, including the strategic profit model, other key business ratios, and financial trends in retailing
4. To look at retail budgeting
5. To examine resource allocation

Nordstrom, the upscale department store chain, has been systematically working to reduce its overall costs—not a simple task: "The biggest challenge is to keep the culture in the organization while making the necessary changes for the new millennium." Although Nordstrom's sales per square foot have been nearly double those of competitor May Department Stores, its operating profits as a percent of sales have been among the industry's lowest (with May's being two-and-a-half times higher).

Nordstrom is looking to increase its productivity by slashing inventories 9 percent, reducing the size of its merchandise buying staff from 900 to 735 employees, and consolidating its 16 different buying regions into 4. Nordstrom also wants to get better pricing terms from its suppliers and to negotiate lower rental terms from the owners of its mall-based stores.

Part of the process of improving productivity requires the Nordstrom family, which owns 35 percent of the company, to more openly embrace change. A positive sign is Nordstrom's recently hiring a former Starbucks executive to head its private-label apparel group. Nordstrom's private brands are more costly to the chain than its purchasing some traditional manufacturer brands, but the high quality and distinctive image justify the cost.[1]

OVERVIEW

Once a retailer devises an organization structure and forms a human resource management plan, it concentrates on **operations management**—the efficient and effective implementation of the policies and tasks necessary to satisfy the firm's customers, employees, and management (and stockholders, if it is a publicly owned company).

The way retailers operate their businesses has a huge impact on sales and profitability. For example, high inventory levels, long store hours, expensive fixtures, extensive customer services, and extensive advertising may encourage consumers to shop and lead to higher sales volume. But at what cost? If a store pays night-shift salaries of 25 percent more than day-shift salaries, is being open 24 hours per day worthwhile (do the increased sales justify the costs and add to overall profit)?

Please Note: Web site addresses are constantly changing. The links in this chapter are current as of the publication of this book.

This chapter covers the financial aspects of operations management, with emphasis on profit planning, asset management, budgeting, and resource allocation. The operational dimensions of operations management are explored in detail in Chapter 13.

PROFIT PLANNING

A **profit-and-loss (income) statement** represents a summary of a retailer's revenues and expenses over a particular period of time, usually a month, quarter, or year. It lets the firm review its overall and specific revenues and costs for similar periods (such as January 1, 2000, to December 31, 2000, versus January 1, 1999, to December 31, 1999), as well as analyze profitability. By having frequent profit-and-loss statements, a firm can monitor progress toward goals, update performance estimates, and revise strategies and tactics.

In comparing profit-and-loss performance over time, it is crucial that the same time periods be used (such as the third quarter of 2000 with the third quarter of 1999) due to seasonality considerations. The retailer should also note that some yearly periods may have an unequal number of weeks (such as 53 weeks in one fiscal year versus 52 weeks in another). In addition, retailers that have increased the number of stores or the square footage of existing stores between accounting periods should take into account the larger facilities in their analysis. Thus, yearly sales growth should reflect both the total revenue growth and the rise in same store sales.

A profit-and-loss statement consists of these major components:

- **Net sales**—The revenues received by a retailer during a given period after deducting customer returns, markdowns, and employee discounts.
- **Cost of goods sold**—The amount a retailer has paid to acquire the merchandise sold during a given period. It is based on purchase prices and freight charges, less all discounts (such as quantity, cash, and promotion).
- **Gross profit (margin)**—The difference between net sales and the cost of goods sold. It consists of operating expenses plus net profit.
- **Operating expenses**—The cost of running a retail business.
- **Net profit before taxes**—The profit earned after all costs have been deducted.

Table 12.1 shows the most recent annual profit-and-loss statement for Donna's Gift Shop, an independent retailer. The firm uses a fiscal year (September 1 to August 31) rather

Learn more about the profit-and-loss statement. Click "Points to Ponder" (phl.smginc.com/smginc/marketing/fiqnet/demo/fiqnet/learning/moduleb/b_2.htm).

Table 12.1 Donna's Gift Shop, Fiscal 2000 Profit-and-Loss Statement

Net sales	$220,000
Cost of goods sold	$120,000
Gross profit	$100,000
Operating expenses	
Salaries	$ 50,000
Advertising	3,300
Supplies	1,100
Shipping	1,000
Insurance	3,000
Maintenance	3,400
Other	1,700
Total	$ 63,500
Other costs	$ 17,500
Total costs	$ 81,000
Net profit before taxes	$ 19,000

Moving ShopKo Away from a Focus on Short-Term Earnings

Bill Podany, ShopKo's chief executive, feels that the head of a regional discount retail chain often encounters significantly different challenges than the head of a larger national chain. In today's economy, forming relationships with journalists who write about the retail industry and with stock analysts who influence shareholders is especially important for medium-sized firms:

> We are pigeonholed into being a regional discounter, even though we don't like to be typified as that anymore. We're bludgeoned into that sector, which has more failures than it has winners. My level of exposure to that world—telling our story, hawking our story—takes up a big part of my time. Investor relations is very, very important for us. Ten years ago, we shied away from it. Today it's different.

Podany further believes that Wall Street analysts pressure publicly owned retailers to rely too much on their quarterly earnings. Thus, many CEOs are forced to make decisions that increase short-term sales and profits to the detriment of long-term interests. He strongly rejects this philosophy and plans for the long-term: "Changing times require a new set of leadership skills than in the past. I've probably reinvented myself 3 or 4 times in 30 years. I was trained in a classic command-and-control environment, that the guy with the biggest title and salary knew more than everybody else. That he or she was omnipotent, imperialistic, and shouted parables out of his or her office, and people jumped. It was probably appropriate for those times, but it certainly isn't appropriate today."

Source: "The New Breed of the Old School," *Discount Store News* (May 24, 1999), pp. 57–59.

than a calendar year in preparing its accounting reports. These observations can be drawn from the table:

- Donna's annual net sales for fiscal 2000 were $220,000—computed by deducting returns, markdowns on the items sold, and employee discounts from total sales.
- Donna's cost of goods sold was computed by taking the total purchases for merchandise sold, adding freight, and subtracting quantity, cash, and promotion discounts. Cost of goods sold was $120,000.
- Donna's gross profit was $100,000, calculated by subtracting the cost of goods sold from net sales. This sum was used for operating and other expenses, with the remainder accounting for net profit and the payment of local, state, and federal taxes.
- Donna's operating expenses included salaries, advertising, supplies, shipping, insurance, maintenance, and other operating costs—for a total of $63,500.
- Donna's unassigned costs were $17,500.
- Donna's net profit before taxes was $19,000, computed by deducting total costs of $81,000 from gross profit. This amount covered federal, state, and local taxes, as well as profits.

Overall, fiscal 2000 was a pretty good year for Donna; her personal salary was $35,000 and the store's before-tax profit was $19,000. A further analysis of Donna's Gift Shop's profit-and-loss statement will be conducted in the budgeting section of this chapter.

ASSET MANAGEMENT

Each retailer has assets to manage and liabilities to control. This section presents the basic components of a retailer's balance sheet, and describes the strategic profit model and other key business ratios.

Try out the Business Owner's Toolkit's downloadable Excel-based balance sheet template (www. toolkit.cch.com/ tools/balshe_m.asp).

A **balance sheet** itemizes a retailer's assets, liabilities, and net worth at a specific time—based on the principle that assets = liabilities + net worth. Table 12.2 has a balance sheet for Donna's Gift Shop.

Assets are any items a retailer owns with a monetary value. Current assets are cash on hand (or in the bank) and items readily converted to cash in the short run, such as inventory on hand (or in transit to the retailer) and accounts receivable (amounts owed to the firm by customers). Fixed assets are property, buildings (a store, warehouse, and so on), store fixtures, and equipment such as cash registers and trucks; these are used in operations for a long period. The major fixed asset for many retailers is real-estate.

Unlike current assets, which are recorded on a balance sheet on the basis of cost, fixed assets are recorded on the basis of cost less accumulated depreciation. This may create some difficulties in asset management, as records may not accurately reflect the true value of a firm's assets. For instance, many retailing analysts use the term **hidden assets** to describe depreciated assets, such as store buildings and warehouses, that are reflected on a retailer's balance sheet at low values relative to their actual worth. In some instances, investors are enticed to acquire retailers because of the high value of these hidden assets.

Liabilities are financial obligations a retailer incurs in operating a business. Current liabilities are payroll expenses payable, taxes payable, accounts payable (amounts owed to suppliers), and short-term loans; these must be paid in the coming year. Fixed liabilities comprise mortgages and long-term loans; these are generally repaid over several years.

A retailer's **net worth** is computed as assets minus liabilities. It is also called owner's equity and represents the value of a business after deducting all financial obligations.

In operations management, the retailer's goal is to use its assets in the manner providing the best results possible. There are three basic ways to measure those results: net profit margin, asset turnover, and financial leverage. Each component is discussed next.

Net profit margin is a performance measure based on a retailer's net profit and net sales:

$$\text{Net profit margin} = \frac{\text{Net profit}}{\text{Net sales}}$$

Table 12.2 A Retail Balance Sheet for Donna's Gift Shop (as of August 31, 2000)

Assets		Liabilities	
Current		**Current**	
Cash on hand	$ 13,300	Payroll expenses payable	$ 4,000
Inventory	24,100	Taxes payable	9,000
Accounts receivable	1,100	Accounts payable	21,400
Total	$ 38,500	Short-term loan	700
		Total	$ 35,100
Fixed (present value)			
Property	$125,000	**Fixed**	
Building	42,000	Mortgage	$ 65,000
Store fixtures	9,700	Long-term loan	4,500
Equipment	1,700	Total	$ 69,500
Total	$178,400		
		Total liabilities	$ 104,600
Total assets	$216,900	**Net Worth**	$ 112,300
		Liabilities + net worth	$ 216,900

In the case of Donna's Gift Shop, fiscal year 2000 net profit margin was just over 8.6 percent—a very good percentage for a gift shop. To enhance net profit margin, a retailer could seek to either raise gross profit as a percentage of sales or reduce operating expenses as a percentage of sales.[2] It could try to lift gross profit by purchasing opportunistically, selling exclusive product lines, avoiding price competition by excellent customer service, minimizing markdowns, and selling a mix of goods with high margins. It could reduce operating costs by stressing self-service, lowering labor costs (through better scheduling and automation), refinancing a mortgage to take advantage of lower interest, cutting energy costs, and so on. The firm must be careful not to lessen customer service to the extent that sales and profit would decline.

Asset turnover is a performance measure based on a retailer's net sales and total assets:

$$\text{Asset turnover} = \frac{\text{Net sales}}{\text{Total assets}}$$

Donna's Gift Shop had a very low asset turnover, 1.0143, meaning the store averaged $1.01 in sales per dollar of total assets. To improve its asset turnover ratio, a firm would have to generate increased sales from the same level of assets or keep the same sales with a reduced asset base. A firm might increase sales by having longer hours, accepting orders at its Web site, training employees to cross-sell additional products to consumers, or stocking better-known brands. None of these tactics requires the asset base to be expanded. Or a firm might maintain sales on a lower asset base by moving to a smaller store (less wasted space), simplifying fixtures (or having suppliers install and own fixtures), keeping a smaller inventory on hand, and negotiating with property owners for them to pay part of the costs of a renovation.

By looking at the relationship between net profit margin and asset turnover, **return on assets (ROA)** can be computed:

$$\text{Return on assets} = \text{Net profit margin} \times \text{Asset turnover}$$

$$\text{Return on assets} = \frac{\text{Net profit}}{\text{Net sales}} \times \frac{\text{Net sales}}{\text{Total assets}}$$

$$= \frac{\text{Net profit}}{\text{Total assets}}$$

Thus, Donna's Gift Shop had an ROA of 8.8 percent, computed as:

$$= .0864 \times 1.0143 = 0.0876 = 8.8\%$$

This return on assets is below average for gift stores because the firm's good net profit margin does not adequately offset its low asset turnover.

Financial leverage is a performance measure based on the relationship between a retailer's total assets and net worth:

$$\text{Financial leverage} = \frac{\text{Total assets}}{\text{Net worth}}$$

Donna's Gift Shop had a financial leverage ratio of 1.9314. This means assets were just under twice Donna's net worth, and total liabilities and net worth were almost equal. Thus, Donna's financial leverage was slightly above-average for gift stores (which are conservative as a group). The store is in no danger.

A retailer with a high financial leverage ratio has substantial debt, while a ratio of 1 means it has no debt—assets equal net worth. If the ratio is too high, there may be too much focus on cost-cutting and short-run sales so as to make large interest payments, net profit margins may suffer due to interest charges, and a firm may even be forced into

Figure 12.1
The Strategic Profit Model

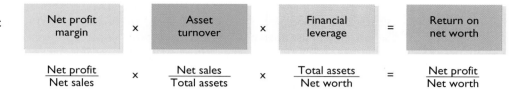

| Net profit margin | × | Asset turnover | × | Financial leverage | = | Return on net worth |

$$\frac{\text{Net profit}}{\text{Net sales}} \times \frac{\text{Net sales}}{\text{Total assets}} \times \frac{\text{Total assets}}{\text{Net worth}} = \frac{\text{Net profit}}{\text{Net worth}}$$

bankruptcy if debts cannot be paid in an orderly manner. On the other hand, when financial leverage is low, a retailer may be too conservative, thereby limiting its ability to renovate and expand existing stores—as well as to enter new markets. In general, leverage is too low if owner's equity is relatively high. In that case, equity could be partly replaced by increasing the amount of short- and long-term loans and/or accounts payable. Some equity funds could be taken out of a business by the owner (stockholders, if a public firm).

The Strategic Profit Model

The numerical relationship among net profit margin, asset turnover, and financial leverage is expressed by the **strategic profit model,** which reflects a performance measure known as **return on net worth.** See Figure 12.1. The strategic profit model can be used in planning or controlling assets. Thus, a retailer could learn that the major cause of its poor return on net worth is less-than-satisfactory asset turnover or too low financial leverage.

According to the strategic profit model, a firm can raise return on net worth by raising the net profit margin, asset turnover, or financial leverage. Because these measures are multiplied to determine a return on net worth, doubling any of them—for example—would result in doubling the return on net worth.

This is how the strategic profit model can be applied to Donna's Gift Shop:

$$\text{Return on net worth} = \frac{\text{Net profit}}{\text{Net sales}} \times \frac{\text{Net sales}}{\text{Total assets}} \times \frac{\text{Total assets}}{\text{Net worth}}$$

$$= \frac{\$19,000}{\$220,000} \times \frac{\$220,000}{\$216,900} \times \frac{\$216,900}{\$112,300}$$

$$= .0864 \times 1.0143 \times 1.9314$$

$$= .1692 = 16.9\%$$

Donna's return on net worth was somewhat below average for all gift stores, due to low asset turnover.

Table 12.3 applies the strategic profit model to various retailers. In evaluating these data, it is best to make comparisons among firms within given retail institutional categories. For example, the net profit margins of apparel retailers such as The Limited, Inc. and Gap, Inc. have historically been much higher than those of food retailers. Because financial performance differs from year to year, caution is advised in studying these data. Furthermore, the individual components of the strategic profit model must be reviewed, not just the return on net worth, as these two Table 12.3 illustrations reveal:

• A comparison of Sears and Federated Department Stores shows Sears' 1998 return on net worth to be far superior to that of Federated Department Stores. Yet, an analysis of the individual components of the strategic profit model reveals that Sears' better return on net worth was largely due to high financial leverage. Federated's net profit margin was much greater than Sears'.

Table 12.3 Application of Strategic Profit Model to Selected Retailers, 1998 Data

Retailer	Net Profit Margin	×	Asset Turnover	×	Financial Leverage	=	Return on Net Worth
Apparel Retailers							
The Limited, Inc.	21.99		2.05		2.04		91.96
Gap, Inc.	9.11		2.28		2.52		52.34
TJX	5.34		2.89		2.25		34.72
Consumer Electronics Retailers							
Best Buy	1.13		4.06		3.69		16.93
Circuit City	1.18		2.74		1.87		6.05
Drugstore Retailers							
Walgreen	3.34		3.12		1.72		17.92
CVS	2.60		2.27		2.16		12.75
Rite Aid	2.78		1.49		2.62		10.85
Food Retailers							
Safeway	3.29		2.15		3.70		26.17
Albertson's	3.54		2.57		2.22		20.20
Publix	3.14		3.34		1.55		16.26
Winn-Dixie	1.46		4.44		2.24		14.52
American Stores	1.17		2.25		3.29		8.66
General Merchandise Retailers							
May Department Stores	6.33		1.27		2.75		22.11
Wal-Mart	3.18		2.83		2.33		20.97
Target Corporation (formerly Dayton Hudson)	3.02		1.98		2.94		17.58
Sears	2.53		1.10		6.21		17.28
Nordstrom	4.11		1.61		2.37		15.68
Costco	1.88		3.89		2.12		15.50
Federated Department Stores	4.19		1.17		2.37		11.62
Kmart	1.69		2.37		2.37		9.49
J.C. Penney	1.94		1.30		3.29		8.30
Dillard's	1.68		0.98		2.88		4.74
Home Improvement Retailers							
Home Depot	5.33		2.25		1.54		18.47
Lowe's	3.94		1.93		2.02		15.36
Office Supplies Retailers							
Office Depot	2.59		2.19		2.03		11.51
Staples	2.60		2.24		1.92		11.18

Source: Computed by the authors from data in "The Fortune 500 Largest U.S. Corporations," *Fortune* (April 26, 1999), pp. F1–F23.

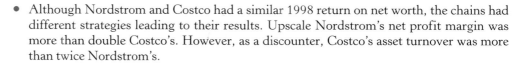

- Although Nordstrom and Costco had a similar 1998 return on net worth, the chains had different strategies leading to their results. Upscale Nordstrom's net profit margin was more than double Costco's. However, as a discounter, Costco's asset turnover was more than twice Nordstrom's.

Other Key Business Ratios

Other ratios may also be used to measure retailer success or failure in reaching performance goals. Such ratios have a strong impact on short- and long-run performance. Accordingly, here are the definitions of several key business ratios—besides those covered in the preceding discussion:

- *Quick ratio*—cash plus accounts receivable divided by total current liabilities, those due within one year. A ratio greater than 1 to 1 means the firm is liquid and easily able to cover short-term liabilities.
- *Current ratio*—total current assets (cash, accounts and notes receivable, merchandise inventories, and marketable securities) divided by total current liabilities. A ratio of 2 to 1 or more is good.
- *Collection period*—accounts receivable divided by net sales and then multiplied by 365. It shows the amounts owed by customers. If most sales are on credit, a collection period one-third or more over normal terms (such as 40.0 for a store with 30-day credit terms) means slow-turning receivables.
- *Accounts payable to net sales*—accounts payable divided by annual net sales. This compares how a retailer pays suppliers relative to volume transacted. A figure above the industry average indicates that a firm relies on suppliers to finance operations.
- *Overall gross profit*—net sales minus the cost of goods sold and then divided by net sales. This companywide average takes markdowns, discounts, and shortages into account. It is used by retailers to cover both operating costs and net profit.[3]

The Census Bureau, online, provides more than a decade of gross profit (gross margin) percentage data by line of business (www.census.gov/svsd/retlann/view/gmper.txt).

Table 12.4 presents several median key business ratios—including net profit margin, asset turnover, and return on net worth—for a number of retailer categories. From this table, a hardware store manager or owner would learn that the industry average is a marginal quick ratio of 0.8; liquid assets are slightly less than current liabilities. The current ratio of 3.2 is quite good, mostly because of the value of inventory on hand. The collection period of 18.3 days is moderate, considering that many small sales are paid for in cash. Accounts payable of 5.1 percent of sales is good. The overall gross profit of 33.2 percent is used to cover both operating costs and profit. The net profit margin of 2.3 percent is a rather low figure for nonfood retailing. The asset turnover ratio is conservative, 2.1, another indicator of the value of inventory. The return on net worth percentage of 8.6 is quite low. In sum, on average, hardware stores require high inventory and other investments and yield low to medium returns.

Financial Trends in Retailing

Entrepreneur (www.entrepreneurmag.com) has a lot of valuable advice for small businesses. Click on "Your Business".

Several current financial trends relating to retailers' asset management merit discussion: new funding sources, initial public offerings, mergers and consolidations, spinoffs, bankruptcies, and liquidations.

Many retailers are benefiting from new sources of funding for their businesses. As one expert says, "There is a ton of money—so much liquidity throughout the marketplace—that there is now private equity money available for companies at every stage of development." This is far different from the usual situation faced by most startups and growing retailers, which have been required to deal with insufficient funding or have been too dependent on the founder. This is a trend that keeps swelling, mostly due to two parties: (a) pension funds, insurers, and other big investors interested in startups and growth companies; and (b) investment professionals who regularly set up new funds. Vulnerable retailers do have to be careful to avoid "vulture funds" that lend money for exorbitant rates or overly high equity stakes.[4]

One funding source that has exploded over the past decade is the **initial public offering (IPO),** whereby a company raises money by selling stock to the public. In particular, during the late 1990s, IPOs started to become quite popular for Web retailers due to the long-run potential of those firms, although the excessive use of IPOs has dampened some investors'

Table 12.4 Median Key Business Ratios for Selected Retailer Categories, 1998

Line of Business	Quick Ratio (times)	Current Ratio (times)	Collection Period (days)	Accounts Payable to Net Sales (%)	Overall Gross Profit (%)[a]	Net Profit Margin (%)	Asset Turnover (times)	Return on Net Worth (%)
Auto & home supply stores	0.9	2.3	23.4	6.3	35.9	2.1	2.8	11.1
Car dealers (new and used)	0.2	1.3	4.8	0.7	12.3	1.0	4.3	16.5
Catalog firms	0.8	2.2	12.4	6.0	41.0	2.8	3.4	21.6
Department stores	0.8	3.1	11.2	5.8	33.1	1.5	2.1	6.8
Direct-selling companies	1.1	2.1	33.8	4.1	48.0	6.2	2.6	24.1
Drug & proprietary stores	1.0	2.9	14.6	4.2	25.4	2.2	4.3	17.2
Eating places	0.7	1.1	4.8	3.1	52.5	3.4	2.9	18.0
Family clothing stores	1.2	5.4	10.2	4.3	35.3	4.0	1.9	10.2
Florists	1.2	2.3	21.2	4.4	51.2	3.5	2.7	15.6
Furniture stores	0.9	2.8	25.0	4.8	37.8	3.1	2.3	10.7
Gasoline service stations	0.8	1.5	6.2	2.8	17.6	1.2	4.6	11.9
Gift, novelty, & souvenir shops	0.8	3.2	6.0	4.3	43.4	5.5	2.3	19.4
Grocery stores	0.5	1.7	3.3	3.4	22.5	1.5	4.9	12.6
Hardware stores	0.8	3.2	18.3	5.1	33.2	2.3	2.1	8.6
Hobby, toy, & game shops	0.7	3.4	2.9	4.9	40.4	3.6	2.7	14.8
Jewelry stores	0.6	3.0	15.7	9.4	43.5	4.2	1.6	11.8
Lumber & other materials dealers	0.9	2.5	25.6	4.4	29.0	2.1	2.6	10.5
Men's & boys' clothing stores	0.8	3.7	11.7	4.8	39.3	4.4	2.2	13.7
Radio, TV, & electronics stores	0.8	2.1	14.2	5.6	35.5	2.8	3.0	14.1
Sewing & needlework stores	0.6	4.0	6.6	5.6	41.0	2.6	2.2	9.0
Shoe stores	0.5	3.7	5.1	5.8	36.7	3.6	2.4	12.9
Sporting-goods & bicycle stores	0.5	2.6	7.3	6.8	33.7	3.1	2.5	13.3
Variety stores	0.8	3.8	5.5	4.2	34.2	2.7	2.6	11.2
Women's clothing stores	0.9	3.8	10.6	4.0	37.1	4.0	2.7	13.4

[a] Gross profit is reported as means rather than medians and represents net figures, which take into account all deductions (such as markdowns, discounts, and shortages).

Source: *Industry Norms and Key Business Ratios: Desk-Top Edition 1998–99* (New York: Dun & Bradstreet, 1999), pp. 147–163. Reprinted by permission.

Financing the Malls of Europe

Joseph Kaempfer (a developer of several office buildings in Washington, D.C.) and Alan Glen (a developer of U.S. discount shopping malls) teamed up to develop discount malls in Europe. The partners realized that although discount malls were not yet popular in Europe, many firms with successful factory outlets in the United States were eager to pursue European markets.

Kaempfer sought additional capital from British Airports Authority (BAA), a European retail airport developer. Soon thereafter, Kaempfer bought out Glen's interest, as well as the equity interests of other investors.

Within 16 months, Kaempfer built five European discount malls, each having as many as 120 tenants—including Polo Ralph Lauren, Armani, Nike, and Gap. These malls are now generating yearly sales of $500 million and an annual rental income of $60 million for Kaempfer. New malls are being planned in France, Italy, Britain, Spain, the Netherlands, and Germany.

Once each mall is established, Kaempfer plans to sell a majority interest to an international financial institution. This will raise additional financing for him to build more malls.

Describe the pros and cons of a financial institution's owning a European discount mall.

Source: Howard Banks, "The Malling of Europe," *Forbes* (February 22, 1999), p. 66.

---

enthusiasm. Among the Web retailing IPOs that immediately soared were eBay (the auction site) and Webvan (the online grocer). In fact, Webvan achieved a total market valuation of $7.9 billion on November 5, 1999, its first day of trading—despite expected 1999 losses of $65 million. On the other hand, 1-800-flowers.com and BarnesandNoble.com had disappointing results from their IPOs.[5]

To do well with an IPO, the following is suggested:

Initial public offerings can make you rich; they make you famous for a little while. They offer the unmistakable signal that you and your company have arrived. But don't confuse matters. Just because you meet with success doesn't mean an IPO is in the offing. Aside from size, scope, and industry issues, the timing for an IPO has to be right. At the broad-brush level, the issue of timing would seem to be a simple one. *Is the market receptive to IPOs or isn't it?* However, there are other key points to ponder: *Is your industry in favor?* If not, you'll have a hard time getting an appointment with an investment banker to discuss an IPO, let alone pull one off. *Are you about to turn the corner to profitability?* Companies sometimes go public when they're posting losses. You hear about them, not because it's so common, but because it's so uncommon. It's better to go public and report improving earnings than it to go public and report narrowing losses. *Does your firm have a layer of professional management in place?* Going public is an incredible drain on human resources. So if you're the visionary who is also responsible for executing the strategy, monitoring it, and tinkering with it—while selling this to investors, keeping them updated, and feeling good about it—then your IPO is a 911 call waiting to happen. *Is there a logical set of buyers?* This is difficult to explain but nonetheless an important point. Does the nature of your firm make the deal proper for institutional or retail investors, and is it appropriately sized for the buyers?[6]

Mergers and consolidations represent a way for strong retailers to add to their asset base without building new facilities or waiting for new business units to turn a profit. They also present a way for weak retailers to receive financial transfusions. For example, in recent years, CompUSA acquired Computer City, Camelot Music purchased The Wall, Toys "R" Us bought Baby Superstore, Ames Department Stores acquired Hills, and Gart Sports obtained Sportmart. All deals were driven by the weakness of the acquired firms. In some cases (such as with Computer City), the acquired party was converted to the name and format of the acquiring party (CompUSA). In others, the acquired firm (The Wall) continued operating under its own name and format. Typically, mergers and consolidations lead to some stores being shut, particularly those with trading-area overlap, and cutbacks among management personnel.

Over the past 20 years, the **leveraged buyout (LBO),** in which a retail ownership change is mostly financed by loans from banks, investors, and others, has had a major effect on retail budgeting and cash flow. At times, because debts incurred with LBOs can be high, some well-known retailers have had to focus more on paying interest on their debts than on investing in their businesses, run sales to generate enough cash to cover operating costs and buy new merchandise, and sell store units to pay off debt. Among the retailers whose operations in the 1990s were affected by LBOs were Macy's, Ralphs, Stop & Shop, and Montgomery Ward. In their weakened state, some of them were acquired by others (such as Macy's acquisition by Federated Department Stores). Safeway, also involved in an LBO, seems to have done well by cutting costs, reducing prices, and improving customer service. While its financial leverage remains high, its 1998 ratio of 3.70 was lower than its 1995 ratio of 6.53 and its 1992 ratio of 21.50.[7]

Sometimes, successful retailers use spinoffs to generate more money or to sell a division that is no longer meeting expectations. The Limited, Inc., spun off the very healthy Limited Too (among other divisions) and raised funds that were reinvested in its core businesses. Tandy Corporation, the parent of Radio Shack, sold Computer City to CompUSA because its losses there kept mounting.

When they want to continue in business, weak retailers file Chapter 11. If they want to liquidate, they file Chapter 7 (www.abiworld.org/media/chapters.html).

To safeguard themselves against mounting debts, as well as to continue in business, faltering retailers may seek bankruptcy protection under Chapter 11 of the Federal Bankruptcy Code. With this protection, retailers can renegotiate their bills, get out of leases, and work with creditors in planning for the future. Declaring bankruptcy has major ramifications: "While some believe that filing for bankruptcy results in the loss of key executives, disruptions in supply, and the demoralization of those who stay, others say it fends off creditors and lets firms pay off debt and survive what may be a temporary upheaval. Executives who are not in favor of filing for Chapter 11 also cite the heavy cost of legal and financial advisory fees that bankruptcy protection entails."[8] Montgomery Ward is an example of a retailer that recently emerged from bankruptcy, after devising a strategy to close 39 stores, cut 4,000 jobs, renovate existing stores, and secure an agreement to repay creditors at 29 cents on the dollar. It was in bankruptcy for one year.[9]

Not all bankruptcies end up with rejuvenated retailers. Many end up in liquidations, where the firms ultimately go out of business. A short time ago, this happened with Caldor (the full-line discount store chain), County Seat (the apparel chain), and Hechinger (the home improvement chain). When a retailer goes out of business, it is painful for all parties: the owner/stockholders, employees, creditors, and customers. Hechinger's departure from the marketplace cost Kmart $230 million—the amount of the lease guarantees it made at the time Hechinger acquired Kmart's failing Builders Square chain.[10]

Viable retailers may liquidate poorly performing units in order to devote more attention to their strong businesses. Venator (formerly Woolworth Corporation) did this when it closed down its Woolworth variety stores to concentrate on the successful chains shown in Figure 12.2.

Figure 12.2
The New Venator: A Focus on Strong Business Units

Reprinted by permission of Venator Group Retail, Inc.

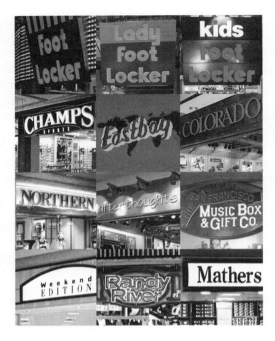

BUDGETING

Why does a new business need a formal budget? Find out here (www.entrepreneur. com:80/Magazines/ MA_SegArticle/ 0,1539,227579-1,00. html).

Budgeting outlines a retailer's planned expenditures for a given time based on expected performance. Thus, a firm's costs can be linked to satisfying target market, employee, and management goals. What should planned personnel costs be if a firm wants a certain level of customer service, such as no shopper waiting in a checkout line for more than 10 minutes? What compensation should be planned to motivate salespeople? What total planned expenses will generate intended revenues and reach profit goals?

There are several reasons for a retailer to meticulously prepare a budget:

- Expenditures are clearly related to expected performance, and costs can be adjusted as goals are revised. This enhances productivity.
- Resources are allocated to the appropriate departments, product categories, and so on.
- Spending for various departments, product categories, and so on is coordinated.
- Because management plans in a structured and integrated manner, the goal of efficiency can be given more prominence.
- Cost standards are set, such as advertising equals 5 percent of sales.
- A firm prepares for the future rather than reacts to it.
- Expenditures are monitored during a budget cycle. If a firm allots $50,000 to buy new merchandise over a budget cycle, and it has spent $33,000 on such items halfway through that cycle, it has planned expenditures of $17,000 remaining.
- A firm can analyze the differences between its expected and actual costs and performance.
- A firm's expected and actual costs and performance can be compared with industry averages.

In budgeting, a retailer should consider the effort and time involved in the process, recognize that forecasts may not be fully accurate (due to unexpected demand, competitors' tactics, and so on), and be willing to modify plans as needed. It should not let itself become

The Double-Sided Sword of Chapter 11 Filings

There are two views of the effect of Chapter 11 filings on retailers. The positive view is that when a retailer files for bankruptcy, creditors are prevented from taking any action to secure repayment of outstanding debts (they are put on "hold"), the retailer can cancel leases at poorly performing locations, and the retailer may be able to pay off debt at a discount (such as 30 cents on the dollar). To some extent, the firm is given a fresh start to revive itself.

On the other hand, a retailer that files for bankruptcy may face the loss of its most marketable executives, find an unmotivated workforce, have a tough time getting creditors to ship new merchandise, and face millions of dollars in legal fees. In addition, because of the publicity a Chapter 11 filing generates, the retailer's image among stockholders, customers, and the general public usually suffers.

Neil Moses, chief financial officer of Bradlees (a firm that has successfully emerged from bankruptcy) says, "There are some very good reasons to use the Chapter 11 process, but principally, the reason why a company files for Chapter 11 is that it can't reach agreement with its vendors and, particularly, with its bank group about how to do an out-of-court restructuring. There is a lot of animosity, there is a lack of trust, and all this culminates in a Chapter 11 filing."

Should a retailer hoping to get additional goods from its suppliers prior to a peak selling season, delay a Chapter 11 filing? Comment on the pros and cons of this strategy.

Source: Michael Hartnett, "Value of Chapter 11 Protections for Retailers Sparks Sharp Debate," *Stores* (April 1999), pp. 92–93.

overly conservative (or inflexible) or simply add a percentage to each current expense category to arrive at the next year's budget, such as increasing expenditures by 3 percent across the board based on an anticipated sales growth of 3 percent.

The budgeting process is shown in Figure 12.3 and described next.

Preliminary Budgeting Decisions

There are six preliminary budgeting decisions.

First, the personnel responsible for budgeting decisions are specified. Top-down budgeting places financial decisions with upper management; these decisions are then communicated down the line to succeeding levels of managers. Bottom-up budgeting requires lower-level executives to develop budget requests for their departments; these requests are then assembled, and an overall companywide budget is designed. With top-down budgeting, senior management centrally oversees budgets. With bottom-up budgeting, varied perspectives are included, managers are held accountable for their own decisions, and employee morale is enhanced. Many firms combine aspects of the two approaches.

Second, the time frame is defined. Most firms have budgets with yearly, quarterly, and monthly components. Annual spending is then planned, while expected versus actual costs and performance are regularly reviewed. As a result, the retailer controls overall costs and responds to seasonal or other fluctuations. Sometimes, the time frame can be longer than a year or shorter than a month. For example, when a firm decides to open new stores over a five-year period, it specifies capital spending (property, construction, and so forth) for the entire five years. And when a supermarket chain such as Safeway orders milk, baked goods, and other perishable goods, it has daily or weekly budgets for each item.

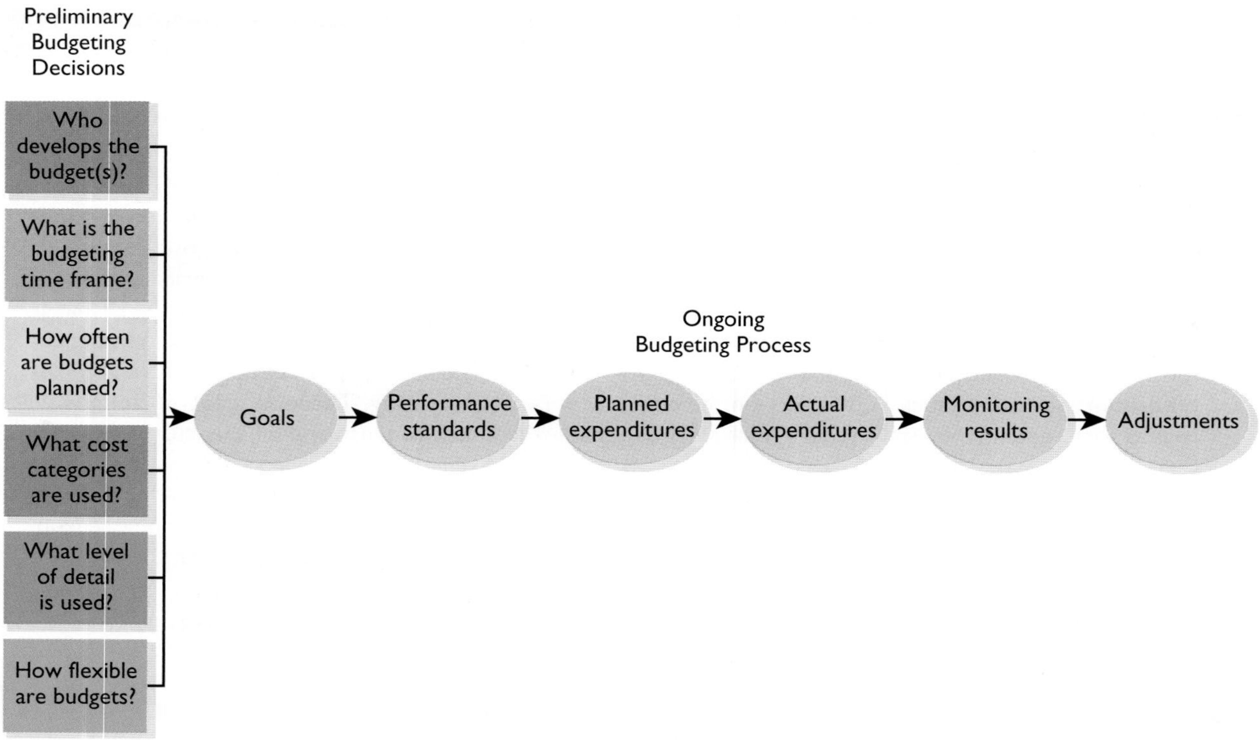

Preliminary
Budgeting
Decisions

Figure 12.3
The Retail Budgeting Process

Third, the frequency with which budgets are planned is determined. Though many retailers review budgets on an ongoing basis, most companies plan them yearly. In some firms, several months may be set aside each year for the budgeting process to be undertaken; this lets all participants have ample time to gather data and enables retailers to take their budgets through several drafts before giving final approval.

Fourth, cost categories are established:

- *Capital expenditures* are major long-term investments in land, buildings, fixtures, and equipment. *Operating expenditures* are the short-term selling and administrative expenses of running a business.
- *Fixed costs* such as store security expenses and real-estate taxes remain constant for the budget period regardless of the retailer's performance. *Variable costs* such as sales commissions are based on the firm's performance over the budget period. If performance is good, these expenses often rise.
- *Direct costs* are incurred by specific departments, product categories, and so on, such as the earnings of department-based salespeople. *Indirect costs* such as centralized cashiers are shared by multiple departments, product categories, and so on.
- *Natural account expenses* are reported by the names of the costs, such as salaries, and not assigned by purpose. *Functional account expenses* are classified on the basis of the purpose or activity for which expenditures are made, such as cashier salaries.

Tables 12.5 and 12.6 show the expense categories set by the National Retail Federation. Individual firms may use different categories from those in the tables.

Table 12.5 Natural Account Expense Categories

01	Payroll
03	Media costs
04	Taxes
06	Supplies
07	Services purchased
08	Other
09	Travel
10	Communications
11	Pensions
12	Insurance
13	Depreciation
14	Professional services
16	Bad debts
17	Equipment rentals
20	Real property rentals
90	Expense transfers (net)
92	Credits and outside revenues

Source: Alexandra Moran (Editor), *FOR 1996 Edition* (New York: Wiley, 1996).

Fifth, the level of detail is set. Should planned spending be assigned by department (produce), product category (fresh fruit), product subcategory (apples), or product item (McIntosh apples)? If a retailer has a very detailed budget, it must be sure every expense subcategory is adequately covered.

Sixth, budget flexibility is prescribed. On the one hand, a budget should be strict enough to serve its purpose in guiding planned expenditures and linking costs to goals. On the other hand, a budget that is too inflexible would not let a retailer adapt to changing market conditions, capitalize on unexpected opportunities, or minimize the costs associated with a strategy poorly received by customers. Many firms express their budget flexibility in quantitative terms. Thus, a buyer could increase his or her quarterly budget by a certain maximum percentage if customer demand is higher than anticipated.

Table 12.6 Functional Account Expense Categories (Expense Centers)

010	Property and equipment
100	Company management
200	Accounting and management information
300	Credit and accounts receivable
400	Sales promotion
500	Service and operations
600	Personnel
700	Merchandise receiving, storage, and distribution
800	Selling and supporting services
900	Merchandising

Source: Alexandra Moran (Editor), *FOR 1996 Edition* (New York: Wiley, 1996).

Ongoing Budgeting Process

After preliminary budgeting decisions are made, the retailer engages in the ongoing budgeting process shown in Figure 12.3:

- Goals are set based on customer, employee, and management needs (as discussed in Chapter 11).
- Performance standards to achieve the goals are specified. These include customer service levels, the compensation needed to motivate employees and minimize turnover, and the sales and profits needed to satisfy management. Frequently, the budget is related to a sales forecast, which projects expected revenues for the next period. Forecasts are usually broken down by department or product category.
- Expenditures are planned in terms of performance goals. In **zero-based budgeting,** a firm starts each new budget from scratch and outlines the expenditures needed to reach that period's goals. All costs are justified each time a budget is done. With **incremental budgeting,** a firm uses current and past budgets as guides and adds to or subtracts from them to arrive at the coming period's expenditures. Most retailers use incremental budgeting because it is easier, less time-consuming, and not as risky.
- Actual expenditures are made. The retailer pays rent and employee salaries, buys merchandise, places advertisements, and so on.
- Results are monitored: (1) Actual expenditures are compared with planned spending for each expense category previously specified by the retailer, and reasons for any deviations are reviewed. (2) The firm learns whether goals and performance standards have been met and tries to explain deviations.
- The budget is adjusted. Major or minor revisions in the original budget are made, depending on how closely a firm has come to reaching goals. The funds allotted to

Table 12.7 Donna's Gift Shop, Fiscal 2000 Budgeted Versus Actual Profit-and-Loss Statement (in Dollars and Percent)

	BUDGETED		ACTUAL		VARIANCE[a]	
	Dollars	**Percent**	**Dollars**	**Percent**	**Dollars**	**Percent**
Net Sales	$200,000	100.00	$220,000	100.00	+$20,000	—
Cost of goods sold	$110,000	55.00	$120,000	54.55	−$10,000	+0.45
Gross profit	$ 90,000	45.00	$100,000	45.45	+$10,000	+0.45
Operating expenses:						
Salaries	$ 50,000	25.00	$ 50,000	22.73	—	+2.27
Advertising	3,500	1.75	3,300	1.50	+$ 200	+0.25
Supplies	1,200	0.60	1,100	0.50	+$ 100	+0.10
Shipping	900	0.45	1,000	0.45	−$ 100	—
Insurance	3,000	1.50	3,000	1.36	—	+0.14
Maintenance	3,400	1.70	3,400	1.55	—	+0.15
Other	2,000	1.00	1,700	0.77	+$ 300	+0.23
Total	$ 64,000	32.00	$ 63,500	28.86	+$ 500	+3.14
Other costs	$ 17,500	8.75	$ 17,500	7.95	—	+0.80
Total costs	$ 81,500	40.75	$ 81,000	36.81	+$ 500	+3.94
Net profit before taxes	$ 8,500	4.25	$ 19,000	8.64	+$10,500	+4.39

[a] Variance is a positive number if actual sales or profits are higher than expected or actual expenses are lower than expected. Variance is a negative number if actual sales or profits are lower than expected or actual expenses are higher than expected.

some expense categories may be reduced, while greater funds may be provided to other categories.

Table 12.7 compares budgeted (planned) and actual revenues, expenses, and profits for Donna's Gift Shop during fiscal 2000. The actual data come from Table 12.1. The variance figures in Table 12.7 compare expected and actual results for each profit-and-loss item. Variances are positive numbers if actual performance is better than expected and negative numbers if performance is worse than planned.

As Table 12.7 indicates, in *dollar terms,* net profit before taxes was $10,500 higher than anticipated. Sales were $20,000 higher than expected; thus, the cost of goods sold was $10,000 more than anticipated. Because of solid cost controls, actual operating expenses were $500 lower than expected. Table 12.7 also shows Donna's performance in *percentage terms.* This lets a firm set goals and performance standards—and evaluate budgeted versus actual performance—on a percent-of-sales basis. As can be seen, actual net profit before taxes was 8.64 percent of sales; this compares very favorably to the planned level of 4.25 percent. Most of the increased net profit before taxes was due to actual operating costs being 36.81 percent of sales versus planned operating costs of 40.75 percent of sales.

Learn more about cash flow management (www. entrepreneur.com:80/ Magazines/MA_ SegArticle/ 0,1539,265227,00. html).

In planning and applying a budget, a firm must think about **cash flow,** which relates the amount and timing of revenues received to the amount and timing of expenditures made during a specific time. In cash flow management, the intention is usually to make sure revenues are received prior to expenditures being made.[11] Otherwise, short-term loans may have to be taken or profits tied up in the business to pay inventory and other expenses. For seasonal businesses, this may be unavoidable. According to the Small Business Administration, underestimating costs and overestimating revenues, both of which affect cash flow, are the leading causes of new business failures. Table 12.8 has two examples of cash flow.

RESOURCE ALLOCATION

In allotting financial resources, both the magnitude of various costs and productivity should be examined. Each has significance for asset management and budgeting.

The Magnitude of Various Costs

As we noted earlier, retail expenditures can be divided into capital and operating categories. **Capital expenditures** are the long-term investments in fixed assets. **Operating expenditures** are the short-term selling and administrative costs of running a business. Before making decisions, it is imperative to have a sense of the magnitude of various capital and operating costs. The following examples illustrate the point.

In 1999, these were the average capital expenditures for erecting a single store for a range of retailers. The amounts include the basic building shell; heating, ventilation, and air-conditioning; lighting; flooring; fixtures; ceilings; interior and exterior signage; and roofing:

- Supermarket—$3.3 million.
- Department store—$7.2 million.
- Full-line discount store—$2.8 million.
- Apparel specialty store—$765,000.
- Drugstore—$685,000.
- Home center—$1.9 million.[12]

Thus, a typical home center chain must be prepared to invest $1.9 million to build each new outlet (which averaged 47,341 square feet industrywide in 1999) it opens. This does not

Table 12.8 The Effects of Cash Flow

A.

A retailer has rather consistent sales throughout the year. Therefore, the cash flow in any given month is positive. This means no short-term loans are needed, and the owner can withdraw funds from the firm if she so desires:

Linda's Luncheonette, Cash Flow for January

Cash inflow:		
Net sales		$11,000
Cash outflow:		
Cost of goods sold	$2,500	
Operating expenses	3,500	
Other costs	2,000	
Total		$ 8,000
Positive cash flow		$ 3,000

B.

A retailer has highly seasonal sales that peak in December. Yet, to have a good assortment of merchandise on hand during December, it must order merchandise in September and October and pay for it in November. As a result, it has a negative cash flow in November that must be financed by a short-term loan. All debts are paid off in January, after the peak selling season is completed:

Dave's Party Favors, Cash Flow for November

Cash inflow:		
Net sales		$14,000
Cash outflow:		
Cost of goods sold	$12,500	
Operating expenses	3,000	
Other costs	2,100	
Total		$17,600
Net cash flow		−$ 3,600
Short-term loan (to be paid off in January)		$ 3,600

include land and merchandise costs, and the total could be higher if a larger-than-average store is built.

Besides new building construction costs, remodeling can also be expensive. Remodeling is prompted by competitive pressures, mergers and acquisitions, consumer trends, the requirement of complying with the Americans with Disabilities Act, environmental concerns, and other factors.

To easily study the financial operating performance of publicly owned retailers, go to Annual Report Service (www.annualreportservice.com) and select the companies to analyze.

To reduce their investments, some retailers insist that real-estate developers help pay for building, renovating, and fixturing costs. These demands by retail tenants reflect some areas' oversaturation, the amount of retail space available due to the liquidation of some retailers (as well as mergers), and the interest of developers in gaining retailers that generate consumer traffic (such as category killers).

Operating expenses are usually expressed as a percentage of sales and range from 20 to 25 percent in supermarkets to well over 40 percent in some specialty stores. To succeed, a firm's operating costs must be in line with competitors'. May Department Stores has an edge over many rivals due to lower SGA (selling, general, and administrative expenses as a percentage

Automating Payments Won't Sink Retailers' Float

Karen Moore, the merchandise electronic data interchange coordinator for 7-Eleven (the convenience store chain), says: "Automating payments is probably the easiest process for retailers to implement, yet is one of the last things we do." She believes too many retailers fear they will weaken their cash flow if they pay bills electronically since snail-mail payments require time for mailing and processing. This fear is mostly unfounded.

7-Eleven has improved its float (cash flow) by using electronics fund transfer (EFT), because the firm can now determine when funds are actually transferred to suppliers and creditors. Since EFT eliminates the uncertainty of mail delivery, 7-Eleven no longer has to issue payments early. By ensuring that suppliers are paid on time, 7-Eleven can even negotiate better payment terms from suppliers. Finally, EFT results in savings by eliminating the need to manually calculate amounts due and to manually post accounts payable and cash ledgers.

Some retail executives look mainly at the savings in employee costs when implementing an EFT system. However, many experts think the savings that result from better vendor terms and improved controls are more important than employee cost savings.

How could a small grocery store calculate its savings from the use of EFT?

Source: "Piloting Your Cash Boat," *Chain Store Age* (June 1999), p. 133.

---

of sales): May, 19 percent; Saks, 21 percent; Dillard's, 27 percent; Nordstrom, 28 percent; and Federated, 30 percent.[13]

Resource allocation must also take into account a retailer's **opportunity costs,** which are the possible benefits the firm forgoes if it invests in one opportunity rather than another. If a supermarket chain decides to renovate 10 existing stores at a total cost of $3.3 million, it could not open a new outlet requiring a $3.3-million investment (excluding land and merchandise costs). Since financial resources are finite, firms often face either/or decisions. If the supermarket chain expects to earn greater profits by renovating than by building a new store, the latter becomes a lost opportunity—at least for now.

Productivity

Due to erratic sales, mixed economic growth, rising labor costs, intense competition, and other factors, many retailers place great priority on improving **productivity,** the efficiency with which a retail strategy is carried out. Productivity can be described in terms of costs as a percentage of sales, the time it takes a cashier to complete a transaction, the percentage of customers a salesperson sees in an average day who purchase, profit margins, sales per square foot, inventory turnover, sales growth, and so on. For each of these measures, productivity goals would require a firm to apply its strategy as efficiently as possible. The key question is: How can sales and profit goals be reached while keeping control over costs?

Because different retail strategy mixes have distinct resource needs as to store location, fixtures, the level of personnel, and other elements, productivity measures must be related to norms for each type of strategy mix (like department stores versus full-line discount stores). Sales growth should also be measured on the basis of comparable seasons, using the same stores as in previous periods. Otherwise, the data will be affected by seasonality and/or the increased square footage of stores.

Circuit City operates four prototypes with square footage and merchandise assortments tailored to population and volume expectations for specific trade areas: The 'D' format

By using four different store prototypes, Circuit City (www. circuitcity.com) is able to operate 600 stores in 45 states. Use the "Store Locator" to see whether there's one near you.

serves the most-populated trade areas. Selling space averages 23,000 square feet. The 'C' format accounts for the largest percentage of the store base. Selling space averages 15,000 square feet. The 'B' format is often situated in smaller markets or those on the fringe of larger metropolitan markets. Selling space averages 12,500 square feet. 'B' stores have a broad merchandise assortment to maximize return on investment in lower-volume areas. The 'A' format is located in the least populated areas. Selling space averages 9,500 square feet. 'A' stores have a layout, staffing, and assortment that yields high productivity in the smallest markets.[14]

Productivity can be enhanced in two ways: (1) A firm can improve employee performance, sales per foot of space, and other factors by upgrading training programs, increasing advertising, and so on. (2) It can reduce costs by automating, having suppliers do certain tasks, taking advantage of discounts, seeking cheaper suppliers, being flexible in operations, and so forth. An example would be a retailer using a small core of full-time workers during nonpeak times and supplementing them with many part-time workers in peak periods.

Retailers need to consider that productivity must not be measured just from a cost-cutting perspective. Excessive cost-cutting can undermine customer loyalty. One of the complex dilemmas for bricks-and-mortar retailers that are also online is how to handle customer returns. To control costs, some of them have decided not to allow online purchases to be returned at their stores. This policy has gotten a lot of customers upset. Barnes & Noble, with 520 bricks-and-mortar stores, does not accept returns of purchases made at its Web site (www.barnesandnoble.com). Furthermore, its policy is not well communicated to potential customers. To find out about the Web site's return policy, a shopper has to enter the "Help" section and then scroll all the way down to the bottom of the screen.

These are two strategies that retailers have used to raise productivity:

- Department stores such as Sears are paying more attention to space productivity. Sears has cleared hundreds of thousands of square feet of space in its stores—by moving some furniture departments into freestanding stores, converting space that was previously used by its affiliated home improvement contractors to retail use, and better managing and displaying its merchandise categories.

Tuesday Morning has a *very* unique philosophy about store dates (www.tuesdaymorning.com/hours.html).

- Tuesday Morning, a chain selling quality closeout merchandise, opens its stores for four seasonal sales events, totaling about 225 selling days a year. The stores are closed for all of January and July—and parts of several other months (for restocking). Operating costs are low because the stores save on labor expenses (part-time workers are used extensively), utilities, and insurance. The firm further reduces its costs by locating in low-rent sites. Tuesday Morning realizes it operates destination stores that are sought out by loyal customers.[15]

What lessons can be learned? "If you're not completely sure what your organizational goals ought to be or the costs associated with achieving those goals, and you have not devised accurate measurements to assess your progress either internally and/or with your trading partners, it's difficult to achieve the desired productivity."[16]

SUMMARY

1. *To define operations management.* Operations management involves efficiently and effectively implementing the tasks and policies to satisfy the retailer's customers, employees, and management. This chapter covered the financial aspects of operations management. Operational dimensions are studied in Chapter 13.

2. *To discuss profit planning.* The profit-and-loss (income) statement summarizes a retailer's revenues and expenses over a specific time, typically on a monthly, quarterly, and/or yearly basis. It consists of these major components: net sales, cost of goods sold, gross profit (margin), operating expenses, and net profit before taxes.

3. *To describe asset management, including the strategic profit model, other key business ratios, and financial trends in retailing.* Each retailer has assets and liabilities to manage. A balance sheet shows a retailer's assets, liabilities, and net worth at a given time. Assets are items with a monetary value owned by a retailer; some assets appreciate and may have a hidden value. Liabilities are financial obligations incurred in running a business. The retailer's net worth, also known as owner's equity, is computed as assets minus liabilities.

Asset management may be measured by reviewing a firm's net profit margin, asset turnover, and financial leverage. Net profit margin equals net profit divided by net sales. Asset turnover equals net sales divided by total assets. By multiplying the net profit margin by asset turnover, a retailer can find its return on assets—which is based on net sales, net profit, and total assets. Financial leverage equals total assets divided by net worth. The strategic profit model incorporates asset turnover, profit margin, and financial leverage to yield the return on net worth. As an overall measure, with three specific components, it allows a retailer to better plan or control its asset management.

These are among the other key ratios with which retailers should be familiar: quick ratio, current ratio, collection period, accounts payable to net sales, and overall gross profit (in percent).

Current financial trends in asset management involve funding sources, initial public offerings, mergers and consolidations, spinoffs, bankruptcies, and liquidations. Many retailers are benefiting from new sources of funding for their businesses. With an initial public offering (IPO), a company raises money by selling stock to the public. Mergers and consolidations are a way for strong retailers to add to their asset base and for weak ones to receive financial transfusions. The leveraged buyout (LBO), in which an ownership change is mostly financed by loans, has had a major effect on retail budgeting and cash flow. Retailers may use spinoffs to generate more

money or to sell a division that is no longer meeting expectations. To continue in business, faltering retailers may file for bankruptcy protection under Chapter 11 of the Federal Bankruptcy Code. Some bankruptcies allow retailers to revive themselves, while others lead to liquidations as the firms go out of business.

4. *To look at retail budgeting.* Budgeting outlines a retailer's planned expenditures for a given time based on its expected performance; costs are linked to satisfying goals.

There are six preliminary decisions: (1) Responsibility is defined by top-down and/or bottom-up methods. (2) The time frame is specified. (3) The frequency of budgeting is set. (4) Cost categories are established. (5) The level of detail is ascertained. (6) The amount of flexibility is determined.

The ongoing budgeting process then proceeds: goals, performance standards, planned spending, actual expenditures, monitoring results, and adjustments. With zero-based budgeting, each budget starts from scratch; with incremental budgeting, current and past budgets are guides. The budgeted versus actual profit-and-loss (income) statement and the percentage profit-and-loss (income) statement are vital tools. In all budgeting decisions, the impact of cash flow, which relates the amount and timing of revenues received with the amount and timing of expenditures made, must be considered.

5. *To examine resource allocation.* In resource allocation, both the magnitude of costs and productivity need to be examined. Costs can be divided into capital and operating categories; the amount of both must be regularly reviewed. Opportunity costs mean forgoing possible benefits that may occur if a retailer invests in one opportunity rather than another. Productivity is the efficiency with which a retail strategy is carried out; the goal is to maximize sales and profits while keeping costs in check.

Key Terms

operations management (p. 395)
profit-and-loss (income) statement
  (p. 396)
net sales (p. 396)
cost of goods sold (p. 396)
gross profit (margin) (p. 396)
operating expenses (p. 396)
net profit before taxes (p. 396)
balance sheet (p. 398)
assets (p. 398)

hidden assets (p. 398)
liabilities (p. 398)
net worth (p. 398)
net profit margin (p. 398)
asset turnover (p. 399)
return on assets (ROA) (p. 399)
financial leverage (p. 399)
strategic profit model (p. 400)
return on net worth (p. 400)
initial public offering (IPO) (p. 402)

leveraged buyout (LBO) (p. 405)
budgeting (p. 406)
zero-based budgeting (p. 410)
incremental budgeting (p. 410)
cash flow (p. 411)
capital expenditures (p. 411)
operating expenditures (p. 411)
opportunity costs (p. 413)
productivity (p. 413)

Questions for Discussion

1. Describe the relationship of assets, liabilities, and net worth for a retailer. How is a balance sheet useful in examining these items?

2. A retailer has net sales of $750,000, net profit of $125,000, total assets of $600,000, and a net worth of $200,000.
   a. Calculate net profit margin, asset turnover, and return on assets.
   b. Compute financial leverage and return on net worth.
   c. Evaluate the financial performance of this retailer.

3. How can a furniture store increase its asset turnover?

4. Is too high a financial leverage necessarily bad? Why or why not?

5. Distinguish among these terms: quick ratio, current ratio, and collection period.

6. Differentiate between an IPO and an LBO.

7. Under what circumstances would you recommend top-down budgeting rather than bottom-up budgeting?

8. What is zero-based budgeting? Why do most retailers utilize incremental budgeting, despite its limitations?

9. What is the value of a percentage profit-and-loss statement?

10. How could a seasonal retailer improve its cash flow during periods when it must buy goods for future selling periods?

11. Distinguish between capital spending and operating expenditures. Why is this distinction important to retailers?

12. What factors should retailers consider when assessing opportunity costs?

13. How can these retailers improve their productivity?
   a. Carpet store.
   b. Laundromat.
   c. Bakery.
   d. Upscale apparel store.

14. What are the pros and cons of Barnes and Noble's return policy for products bought at its Web site (www.barnesandnoble.com)?

WEB-BASED EXERCISE

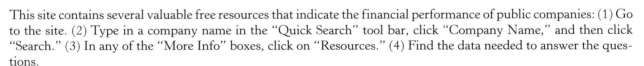

EDGAR Online (www.edgar-online.com)

This site contains several valuable free resources that indicate the financial performance of public companies: (1) Go to the site. (2) Type in a company name in the "Quick Search" tool bar, click "Company Name," and then click "Search." (3) In any of the "More Info" boxes, click on "Resources." (4) Find the data needed to answer the questions.

Questions

1. Do a "Quick Search" for Wal-Mart. Comment on the information obtained from the "Market Guide's Company Snapshot Report".

2. Do a "Quick Search" for Safeway, Inc. (SWY). Comment on the information obtained from "Zacks".

3. Do a "Quick Search" for Wet Seal. Comment on the information obtained from the "Wall Street Research Net".

4. Do a "Quick Search" for Hertz. Comment on the information obtained from the "Yahoo! Finance Message Board".

CHAPTER ENDNOTES

1. Calmetta Y. Coleman, "Nordstrom Tries to Cut Costs While Maintaining Service," *Wall Street Journal* (April 8, 1999), p. B4.

2. See Douglas J. Tigert, Lawrence Ring, and Colson Hillier, "The Profit Wedge: How Five Measure Up," *Chain Store Age* (May 1998), pp. 60–68.

3. *Industry Norms and Key Business Ratios: Desk-Top Edition 1998-99* (New York: Dun & Bradstreet, 1999).

4. Jill Andresky Fraser, "How to Finance Anything," *Inc.* (February 1998), pp. 34–42; and "Vulture Funds: A Friend of Retailers," *HFN* (October 19, 1998), p. 1.

5. Mindy Charski, "Catching the IPO Wave," *U.S. News & World Report* (October 18, 1999), p. 97; Matt Richtel, "Webvan Stock Price Closes 65% Above Initial Offering," *New York Times on the Web* (November 6, 1999); and Leslie Kaufman, "Many Internet Entrepreneurs Are Not Getting Really, Really Rich," *New York Times on the Web* (July 20, 1999).

6. David R. Evanson and Art Beroff, "Synchronize Your Watches," *Entrepreneur* (November 1999), pp. 74–77.

7. "The 50 Largest Retailing Companies," *Fortune* (May 31, 1993), p. 220; "The Fortune 500 Largest U.S. Corporations," *Fortune* (April 29, 1996), pp. F3–F4; and "The Fortune 500 Largest U.S. Corporations," *Fortune* (April 26, 1999), pp. F3–F4.

8. Michael Hartnett, "Value of Chapter 11 Protections for Retailers Sparks Sharp Debate," *Stores* (April 1999), p. 92. See also Kevin Kenyon, "Retail Bankruptcy Brings Challenge, Opportunities," *Shopping Centers Today* (October 1999), pp. 55, 58; and John A. Pearce II and Samuel A. DiLullo, "When a Strategic Plan Includes Bankruptcy," *Business Horizons*, Vol. 41 (September–October 1998), pp. 67–73.

9. "As Ward Exits Ch. 11, Creditors Eye Cash Pot," *Discount Store News* (July 26, 1999), p. 2; and "Wards to Emerge from Bankruptcy Protection by Midyear," *HFN* (February 8, 1999), p. 4.

10. Calmetta Y. Coleman and James R. Hagerty, "Kmart to Take $230 Million Charge to Cover Guarantees on Store Leases," *Wall Street Journal* (June 14, 1999), p. A4.

11. See Julie H. Hertenstein and Sharon M. McKinnon, "Solving the Puzzle of the Cash Flow Statement," *Business Horizons*, Vol. 40 (January–February 1997), pp. 69–76.

12. Computed from "Building and Equipment," *Chain Store Age* (July 1999), pp. 102–104.

13. Company 1999 annual reports.

14. *Circuit City 1999 Annual Report*, p. 9.

15. Debbie Howell, "Part-Time Tuesday Morning Produces Year-Round Sales," *Discount Store News* (September 20, 1999), p. 8.

16. Ryan Mathews, "The Final Frontier," *Progressive Grocer* (September 1996), p. 69.

CASE 1

TODAY'S MAN: A FINANCIAL OPERATIONS TURNAROUND

Today's Man, a men's wear superstore chain located mostly in the Northeast, filed for Chapter 11 bankruptcy protection in January 1996. Two years later, the retailer emerged from bankruptcy with a better strategy and focus. The revitalization of Today's Man surprised many analysts and creditors. Some thought that it would be impossible for the firm to sustain itself during a period when advertising was cut by 50 percent. Others doubted that Today's Man would last longer than three months. This case describes the factors leading to Today's Man's bankruptcy, as well as its superior restructuring strategy.

In late 1994, Today's Man had multiple symptoms of impending financial difficulties. These included reduced profit margins, low inventory turnover, and declining same-store sales. According to industry analysts, its retail market area was oversaturated. There were also some high-profile retail bankruptcies in its trading area at this time.

At that point, Today's Man abandoned its traditional everyday low pricing strategy and began using aggressive price-oriented promotions such as "buy one, get one free," to attract customers. David Feld, the founder and chief executive officer of Today's Man, now

CASE 1

(CONTINUED)

acknowledges that: "We lost our value proposition and we lost our focus. We were spending too much money on promotional advertising and too much on markdowns and we weren't making a sales plan. And for some reason I still do not understand, we continued to spend the money anyway." Today's Man was soon forced into bankruptcy.

As part of the restructuring, Feld decided to close new stores in the Chicago market. As one retailing analyst describes it: "The decision to close Chicago was gut-wrenching for Feld, but it sent a clear signal to vendors and creditors that he was willing to take some difficult steps for the greater good of the firm." Feld also decided to make Today's Man the dominant brand—and later on, the only brand—in its stores. This shift in emphasis clearly demonstrated the chain's value proposition to its customer base.

Today's Man never communicated its poor financial condition to customers. Instead of conducting "Going Out of Business" promotions in Chicago, the merchandise there was shipped to the chain's Northeast stores. This approach also provided Today's Man's other stores with valuable inventory at a key time. In addition, Today's Man reduced its advertising expenditures by 50 percent and refocused its advertising on value-based institutional messages.

The retailer was well aware of the value of honest and open communications with its vendors and employees. According to Frank Johnson, Today's Man's executive vice-president/chief financial officer, "We sat down with each of them and we went through the business plans, the P&Ls [profit-and-loss statements], and the cash flow, and we showed them the balance sheet. We told them what our problems were and what we could and couldn't do. As a result, they became partners with us and I believe that today we have the best vendor relationships we've had as a company in as long as I can remember." Today's Man also communicated openly with its store managers and salespeople to rekindle their spirits and minimize employee turnover.

Johnson believes the keys to making a restructuring process work are control and execution. He states wistfully, "First and foremost, it takes execution. Second, it takes execution, and then it takes executing the numbers you told everyone you were going to execute."

Questions

1. Evaluate Today's Man's decision to rapidly close its Chicago stores.

2. What key business ratios should Today's Man have evaluated in late 1994 to anticipate its financial difficulties?

3. Discuss the importance of cash flow planning to Today's Man in late 1994—and today.

4. What is the value of the strategic profit model to Today's Man as it pursues its current strategy?

NOTE

The material in this case is adapted by the authors from *www.todaysman.com* (March 7, 2000); and Susan Reda, "Tough Restructuring Regimen Guides Today's Man Revival Effort," *Stores* (March 1999), pp. 68–69. Copyright 1999, NRF Enterprises Inc. Reprinted by permission.

CASE 2

ELECTRONIC SHELF LABELING

Electronic shelf labeling (ESL) systems transmit information from a retailer's product price file to wireless electronic shelf labels that are located on a product's shelf-facing. Retailers can select among different display sizes, as well as choose among labels that can be mounted on peg hooks, existing store fixtures, refrigerator units, and freezers.

There are several advantages to the use of ESL systems in place of traditional pricing labels:

- An electronic system reduces the high labor costs associated with initial price labels and with revised labels that reflect price changes.
- Because ESL continuously monitors and compares each shelf label against a computer-generated price file, both retailers and shoppers are assured of pricing accuracy.
- An ESL system gives retailers the ability to more quickly respond to competitive pressures, changes in costs, and changes in demand.
- Electronic shelf-facing labels can help retailers with their in-store planograms.
- ESLs enable retailers to display special promotional messages (including those that flash both the regular and sale prices) on shelf-facings.
- Some retailers use ESLs to comply with state pricing legislation. For example, Pennsylvania has pricing accuracy laws for retailers, and Connecticut requires that supermarkets meet item-pricing laws that list both total price and price per unit of measure. Some states mandate that if there is a pricing discrepancy between the posted and scanned price and the scanned price is higher, the retailer must give the item to the customer for free.

An early adopter of ESLs was Dill's Food City, a five-store Georgia supermarket chain. Other retailers, including Wal-Mart and BJ's, have also tested ESLs. According to published reports, the cost of an electronic price tag is about $5; this would mean a $75,000 investment for a retailer with 15,000 labels. Dill's shelf labels display both price per ounce and price per unit. Although pricing accuracy was never a problem for Dill's (an audit on its manual-entry labeling system found only seven discrepancies between scanned and posted prices), Dill's is still concerned about this issue. Its vice-president of operations says that 70 percent of pricing errors are undercharges that favor the customer.

The capital investment required to equip a supermarket with an ESL system ranges from $80,000 to $110,000. There are alternative ways to finance this investment aside from leasing arrangements. One supplier has introduced a "toll" fee structure that is based on a per-tag monthly fee plus a per-use monthly rate. The toll fee varies due to the number of price changes a store makes per week. The first 1,000 changes are priced at one level, the second 1,000 changes are priced at a lower level, and price changes exceeding 4,000 per week carry no additional toll fee. Due to fewer ESL changes, the toll fees for retailers utilizing everyday low prices would be lower than for those with a high-low pricing strategy.

Questions

1. What is the impact of an ESL system on productivity?

2. Outline the potential cost savings associated with ESL systems over manual ones.

3. Comment on the pros and cons of ownership, leasing, and toll fees for an ESL system from a financial perspective.

4. Apply the concept of opportunity costs to a supermarket chain's decision about whether to acquire an ESL system.

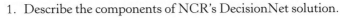

CASE 2
(CONTINUED)

Video Questions on ESL

1. Describe the components of NCR's DecisionNet solution.

2. What types of promotional messages are appropriate for an ESL system?

NOTE

The material in this case is drawn from *www.ncr.com* (March 3, 2000); Patrick Sciacca, "Fleming Offers Retailers ESL Option," *Supermarket News* (May 3, 1999), p. 80; and Denise Zimmerman, "Dill's Food Expands Test of New ESL Prototype," *Supermarket News* (February 17, 1997), p. 17.

Operations Management: Operational Dimensions

CHAPTER OBJECTIVES

1. To describe the operational scope of operations management
2. To examine several specific aspects of operating a retail business: operations blueprint; store format, size, and space allocation; personnel utilization; store maintenance, energy management, and renovations; inventory management; store security; insurance; credit management; computerization; outsourcing; and crisis management

Kmart recently completed its strategy to convert stores to the Big K format. In addition to the usual Kmart full-line department store, the Big K format includes a large grocery and consumables department called the Pantry. The new format has already been credited with increasing Kmart's sales per square foot and the frequency of shopper visits.

Kmart thinks its new uniform format can increase productivity by the improved use of in-store planograms. The format also better enables Kmart to reduce labor costs, improve customer service, lower pilferage, and improve merchandise handling. Each Big K store has a replenishment team manager who is responsible for the stockroom processing area and pilferage control; and the sales floor in each Big K is divided into soft-line and hard-line team managers.

Team managers are evaluated monthly on customer service through a mystery shopper program. They are paid a large percentage of their bonus based on this evaluation. In addition, Kmart wants to improve customer service by devising specific standards for hiring employees and keying employee coverage of selected departments to the number of items promoted in its weekly freestanding newspaper insert.[1]

OVERVIEW

PerformanceWorks software lets retailers study their operating strengths and weaknesses (www.landmark.com/solutions/productsDIS.htm).

As defined in Chapter 12, operations management is the efficient and effective implementation of the policies and tasks that satisfy a retailer's customers, employees, and management (and stockholders, if it is publicly owned). While Chapter 12 examined the financial dimensions of operations management, this chapter covers the operational aspects.

For firms to ensure their long-run success, operational areas need to be managed as well as possible. Thus, a decision to change a store format or to introduce new anti-theft equipment must be carefully reviewed since these acts could greatly affect retail performance. In running their businesses, retail executives must make a wide range of operational decisions, such as these:

Please Note: Web site addresses are constantly changing. The links in this chapter are current as of the publication of this book.

- What operating guidelines are used?
- What is the optimal format and size of a store? What is the relationship among shelf space, shelf location, and sales for each item in the store?
- How can personnel best be matched to customer traffic flows? Would increased staffing improve or reduce productivity? What impact does self-service have on the sales of each product category?
- What effect does the use of various building materials have on store maintenance? How can energy costs be better controlled? How often should facilities be renovated?
- How can inventory best be managed?
- How can the personal safety of shoppers and employees be ensured?
- What levels of insurance are required?
- How can credit transactions be managed most effectively?
- How can computer systems improve operating efficiency?
- Should any aspects of operations be outsourced?
- What kinds of crisis management plans should be in place?

OPERATING A RETAIL BUSINESS

To address the preceding operational questions, we now look at the operations blueprint; store format, size, and space allocation; personnel utilization; store maintenance, energy management, and renovations; inventory management; store security; insurance; credit management; computerization; outsourcing; and crisis management.

Operations Blueprint

To encourage more compatibility among different retail hardware and software systems, the National Retail Federation has established its ARTS program (www. nrf-arts.org).

A good tool in running a retail business is the **operations blueprint,** which systematically lists all the operating functions to be performed, their characteristics, and their timing. As a blueprint is developed, the retailer specifies, in detail, every operating function from the store's opening to its closing—and those responsible for carrying them out. For example, who opens the store? When? What are the steps at the opening (turning off the alarm, turning on the power, setting up the computer system, displaying items that have been locked away overnight, and so forth)? The performance of these tasks must not be left to chance.

If a retailer is large or diversified, it may use multiple operations blueprints. The firm then has separate blueprints for such areas as store maintenance, inventory management, credit management, and store displays. Furthermore, whenever a retailer modifies its store format or operating procedures (for example, relying more on self-service), it must also adjust the operations blueprint(s).

Figure 13.1 has an operations blueprint for a quick-oil-change firm's workers to follow. It identifies employee and customer tasks (in order), as well as expected performance times for each activity. Among the advantages of this blueprint—and others—are that it can standardize activities (within a location and between locations), isolate points at which operations are weak or prone to failure (Do employees actually check transmission, brake, and power-steering fluids in one minute?), outline a plan that can be evaluated for completeness (Should the customer be offered options for grades of oil?), evaluate personnel needs (Should one person change the oil and another wash the windshield?), and help recommend productivity improvements (Should the customer or an employee drive a car into and out of the service bay?).

Store Format, Size, and Space Allocation

With regard to store format, a retailer should consider whether productivity can be raised by such tactics as locating in a planned shopping center rather than in an unplanned business

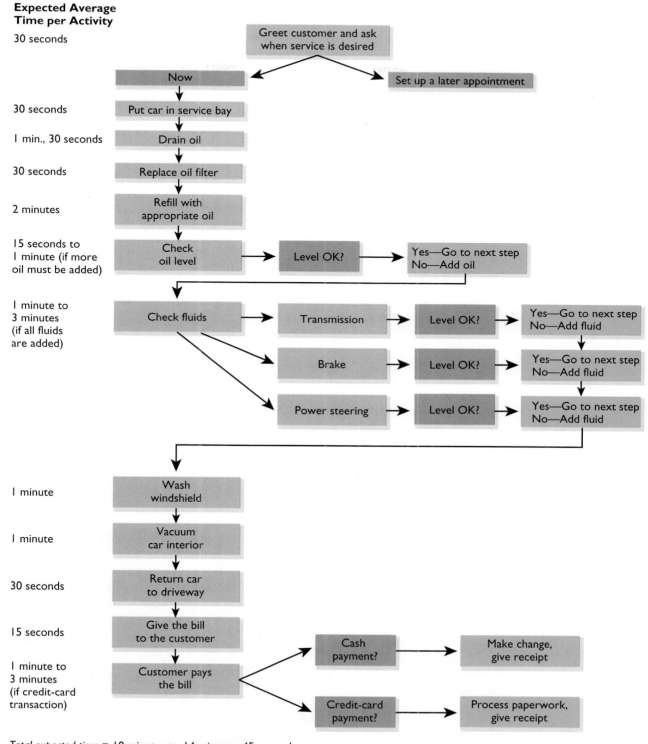

Expected Average Time per Activity

30 seconds

30 seconds

1 min., 30 seconds

30 seconds

2 minutes

15 seconds to 1 minute (if more oil must be added)

1 minute to 3 minutes (if all fluids are added)

1 minute

1 minute

30 seconds

15 seconds

1 minute to 3 minutes (if credit-card transaction)

Total expected time = 10 minutes to 14 minutes, 45 seconds.

Figure 13.1
An Operations Blueprint for a Quick-Oil-Change Firm's Employees

district, using prefabricated materials rather than customized ones in construction, and applying certain kinds of store design and display layouts (covered in Chapter 18). As always, decisions must be related to the retail strategy mix.

A crucial store format decision for chain retailers is whether to use **prototype stores,** whereby multiple outlets conform to relatively uniform construction, layout, and operations standards. Prototype stores offer several benefits. They make construction and centralized management control easier, reduce construction costs, standardize operating methods, facilitate the interchange of employees among outlets, allow fixtures and other materials to be bought in quantity, and display a consistent chain image. Yet, a strict reliance on prototypes may lead to inflexibility, failure to adapt to or capitalize on local customer needs, and too little creativity. Nike, Pep Boys (an auto accessory and repair center chain), Radio Shack, Toys "R" Us, fast-food outlets, and various supermarket chains are among those with prototype stores.[2]

Together with prototype stores, some chains use **rationalized retailing** programs that combine a high degree of centralized management control with strict operating procedures for every phase of business. Most aspects of these chains' operations are performed in a virtually identical manner in its outlets. Rigid control and standardization make this technique easy to enact and manage. In addition, a firm can add a significant number of units in a rather short time. Radio Shack and Toys "R" Us both use rationalized retailing. They operate many stores that are similar in size, the number of items carried, store layout, merchandising, and sales approaches to others in that chain. See Figure 13.2.

In their quest to be distinctive, and due to rents in many major metropolitan markets, various firms use one or both of two contrasting store-size approaches. Home Depot, Barnes & Noble, Sports Authority, and others use category killer stores to try to dominate smaller stores by having extensive assortments. Food-based warehouse stores and large discount-oriented stores often situate in secondary sites, where rents are low. They are confident they can draw customers from large trading areas. Cub Foods (a food-based warehouse chain), Wal-Mart, and others are engaged in this approach.

At the same time, a number of retailers (including those cited in the prior paragraph) believe large stores are not efficient in serving saturated (or small) markets or have been opening smaller stores or downsizing existing ones because of high rents:

The Retail Group (www.theretailgroup. com/work) has collaborated with a number of retailers to develop prototype stores.

Figure 13.2
Radio Shack: A Prime Practitioner of Prototype Stores

Reprinted by permission of Tandy Corporation.

In the hunt for higher sales, it's not how far and wide you cast the net, but where it lands. Such is the theory behind Saks Fifth Avenue's Main Street stores. In an environment of bloated expansion plans throughout the industry, the upscale fashion retailer is slowly branching out beyond the mall and locating smaller stores in the heart of affluent suburbia. "It is simply a matter of fishing where the fish are," says vice-chairman Brian E. Kendrick. The Main Street format is less a new concept than a slice of the existing one. The stores average about 46,000 square feet compared to full-line Saks' stores which start at about 120,000 square feet and top out at 250,000 square feet. Main Street merchandise is not new or different from full-line stores, it is simply "edited," as Kendrick likes to say. There also is an emphasis on high frequency purchases such as cosmetics, shoes, and intimate apparel. The concept's innovation lies in strategic site selection. Rather than breaking into new markets in search of fresh customers, Saks builds where its core customers already live and shop: suburbs and towns with affluent women and men between 35 and 45 years old that spend, well, a lot.[3]

Retailers often place considerable emphasis on allocating store space. They want to use facilities as productively as possible and determine the amount of space and its placement for each product category.[4] Sometimes, retailers decide to drop merchandise lines altogether because they occupy too much store space in relation to their sales and profit. That is why J.C. Penney eliminated home electronics, large sporting goods, and photographic equipment from its department stores.

With a **top-down space management approach,** a retailer starts with its total available store space (by outlet and for the overall firm, if a chain), divides the space into categories, and then works on in-store product layouts. This is in contrast to a **bottom-up space management approach,** in which planning starts at the individual product level and then proceeds to the category, total store, and overall company levels.

TelePizza Reigns in Spain

TelePizza is one of Europe's hottest growth stocks with a total market capitalization of approximately $2 billion. The firm's founder, Leopoldo Fernandez Pujas, has built TelePizza by borrowing concepts from McDonald's (cleanliness), Domino's (on-time delivery), and Pizza Hut (sit-down locations).

Pujas has always had an obsession with details. Before opening his first outlet, he had children taste and rate different pizzas, each with a different recipe. He then refined the recipe until all of the taste testers preferred the same one. Now, Pujas routinely monitors sales on a street-by-street basis to determine the success of TelePizza's flyer promotions, evaluate complaints against managers by the firm's part-time staff, and learn which stores and personnel sell the most garlic bread. Any store manager whose sales drop is quickly fired. As a result of the attention to details such as these, TelePizza accounts for 60 percent of Spain's pizza market.

TelePizza plans to open U.S. mall-style food courts that combine several fast-food menus at one location. These locations will have separate kitchens and cash registers, but the eating areas, phone operators, computer systems, and delivery service will be centralized.

What are some of the operational decisions that TelePizza must make in developing its mall-style food courts?

Source: Richard C. Morris, "Sizzler," *Forbes* (March 22, 1999), pp. 96, 98.

These are just some tactics being used to improve the productivity of store space: Many retailers employ vertical displays, which occupy less room than horizontal ones; they may hang displays on store walls or from ceilings. Formerly free space now goes to small point-of-sale displays and vending machines; and, sometimes, product displays are being located in front of stores. Open doorways, mirrored walls, and vaulted ceilings give small, cramped stores the appearance of being larger. Some retailers allot up to 75 percent or more of their total floor space to selling; the rest is used for storage, rest rooms, and so on. Scrambled merchandising (with high-profit, high-turnover items) occupies more space in stores, in mail-order catalogs, and at Web sites than before. By staying open longer, retailers also use space better.

Personnel Utilization

Kronos' Workforce Smart Scheduler (www.kronos.com/products/sscase.htm) allows retailers to better manage employee scheduling.

From an operations perspective, efficiently utilizing retail personnel is vital: (1) Labor costs are high. In department stores, wages and benefits account for 46 percent of operating costs; in specialty stores, they account for 43 percent of operating costs.[5] (2) High employee turnover leads to increased recruitment, training, and supervision costs. (3) Poor personnel may have bad selling skills, mistreat customers, misring sales transactions, and make other errors. (4) Productivity gains in technology have been more rapid than those in labor; yet, many retailers are labor intensive. (5) Labor deployment is often subject to unanticipated demand. While retailers know they must increase the sales staff in peak periods and reduce it in slow ones, they may still be over- or understaffed if weather changes, competitors run specials, or suppliers increase promotion support. (6) There is less flexibility for firms with unionized employees. Working conditions, compensation, tasks, overtime pay, performance measures, termination procedures, seniority rights, promotion criteria, and other factors are generally specified in written labor contracts.

These are among the tactics being used by retailers to maximize their personnel productivity:

- Hiring process—By carefully screening potential employees before they are offered jobs, turnover can be reduced and better performance secured.
- Workload forecasts—For each season, week, day, and time period, the needed number and type of employees can be pre-determined. A drugstore may have one pharmacist, one cashier, and one stockperson in the store from 2 P.M. to 5 P.M. on Wednesdays and add a pharmacist and a cashier from 5 P.M. to 7:30 P.M. (to accommodate people shopping after work). In doing workload forecasts, personnel costs must be balanced against the possibilities of lost sales if customer waiting time is excessive. The key is to be both efficient (cost-oriented) and effective (service-oriented). Today, a number of retailers use computer software as an aid in scheduling personnel.
- Job standardization and cross-training—Through **job standardization,** the tasks of personnel with similar positions in different departments, such as cashiers and stockpeople in clothing and candy departments, are kept rather uniform. With **cross-training,** personnel learn tasks associated with more than one job, such as cashier, stockperson, gift wrapper, and customer complaints handler. A firm can increase personnel flexibility and reduce the total number of employees needed at any given time by job standardization and cross-training. If one department is slow, a cashier could be assigned to another that is busy; and a salesperson could also process transactions, help set up displays, and handle customer complaints. Cross-training can even reduce employee boredom. See Figure 13.3.
- Employee performance standards—Each worker must have clear performance goals and be accountable for them. Cashiers can be judged on transaction speed and misrings, buyers on department revenues and markdowns, and senior executives on the firm's reaching sales and profit targets. Personnel tend to be more productive when working toward specific goals.

Figure 13.3
Enhancing Job
Standardization

The NCR 7450 uses
DynaKey technology, a
combined display and
keyboard that guides
cashiers through trans-
actions. By learning this
technology, cashiers can
be interchangeable in
different departments
or store branches.
Reprinted by permission of
NCR Corporation.

- Compensation—Financial remuneration, promotions, and recognition can reward good performance to help motivate employees. A cashier will be motivated to reduce misrings if he or she knows there is a bonus for keeping mistakes under a certain percentage of all transactions processed.
- Self-service—Personnel costs as a percentage of sales can be reduced significantly if self-service facilities are used, thereby lessening the need for personnel. However, two points should be taken into account: (1) Self-service requires better in-store displays, popular brands, ample assortments on the selling floor, and goods/services with clear features. (2) By reducing or eliminating sales personnel, some shoppers may feel they get inadequate service; and there is no cross-selling (whereby customers are encouraged to buy complementary goods they may not have been thinking about).
- Length of employment—Long-term employment can be encouraged. Generally, full-time workers who have been with a firm for an extended time are more productive than those who are part-time or who have worked there for a short time. The former are often more knowledgeable, are more anxious to see the firm succeed, need less supervision, are popular with customers, can be promoted, and are more apt to accept and adapt to retailing's special environment. The high productivity associated with full-time, long-term workers normally far outweighs their relatively high compensation.

Store Maintenance, Energy Management, and Renovations

Domco is a leading
maker of retail floor-
ing. Visit its Azrock
Commercial Flooring
Products division site
(www.domco.com/
azrock), select a type
of retail building,
then choose a floor-
ing application, and
see the variety of
flooring available.

Store maintenance encompasses all the activities in managing physical facilities. These are just some facilities that must be managed well: exterior—parking lot, points of entry and exit, outside signs and display windows, and common areas adjacent to a store (e.g., sidewalks); interior—windows, walls, flooring, climate control and energy use, lighting, displays and signs, fixtures, and ceilings. Table 13.1 shows several maintenance decisions.

The quality of store maintenance affects consumer perceptions of the firm, the life span of facilities, and operating costs. Consumers do not like to patronize stores that are unsanitary, decaying, or otherwise poorly maintained. This means regularly cleaning light fixtures, replacing burned-out lamps, and periodically cleaning or repainting room surfaces to optimize light reflection. Some chains even go so far as to replace all lamps at the same time to ensure constant color and light levels throughout the stores.

Table 13.1 Selected Store Maintenance Decisions

What responsibility should the retailer have for maintaining outside facilities? For instance, does a lease agreement make the retailer or the property owner accountable for snow removal in the parking lot?

Should store maintenance activities be done by the retailer's personnel or by outside specialists? Will that decision differ by type of facility (e.g., air-conditioning versus flooring) and by type of service (e.g., maintenance versus repairs)?

What repairs should be classified as emergencies? How promptly should nonemergency repairs be made?

How frequently is store maintenance required for each type of facility (e.g., daily vacuuming of floors versus weekly or monthly washing of exterior windows)? How often should special maintenance activities be done (e.g., waxing floors and restriping spaces in a parking lot)?

How should store maintenance vary by season and by time of day (e.g., when a store is open versus when it is closed)?

How long should existing facilities be utilized before acquiring new ones? What schedule should be followed?

What performance standards should be set for each element of store maintenance? Do these standards adequately balance costs against a desired level of maintenance?

Ongoing and thorough maintenance can let a retailer use current facilities for an extended period before having to invest in new ones. At home centers, for instance, the heating, ventilation, and air-conditioning equipment lasts an average of 16 years; display fixtures an average of 11 years; and interior signs an average of 7 years. But maintenance can be rather costly. In a typical year, a 35,000-square-foot home center spends about $10,000 on floor maintenance alone.[6]

Due to the rise in costs over the past two decades (although prices have stabilized in recent years), energy management is now a major consideration in store operations for retailers. For firms with special needs, such as food stores and florists, it is especially critical. As the energy systems and utilities manager for BJ's membership club says: "For most folks, utilities are the third largest controllable cost, usually behind leasing and payroll. It's a sizable number that you could shave some cost off."[7]

To manage their energy resources more effectively, many retailers now:

- Use better insulation in constructing and renovating stores to gain long-run savings on energy bills.
- Carefully adjust interior temperature levels during nonselling hours. In summer, air-conditioning is reduced at off-hours; in winter, heating is lowered at off-hours.
- Use computerized systems, that can be programmed by store department and to fractions of a degree, to closely monitor temperature levels.
- Have centralized computer-controlled systems, so operators monitor and adjust temperature, lighting, heat, and air-conditioning in multiple stores from one office. The systems even let the operators learn whether managers have left on lights in closed stores and turn those lights off from their consoles.
- Substitute high-efficiency bulbs and fluorescent ballasts for traditional lighting.
- Install "targeted desiccant" air-conditioning systems to control humidity levels in specific store areas, such as refrigerated and freezer locations, thus minimizing moisture condensation.

Here is an example of how seriously retailers are taking energy management:

TGI. Friday's wants to decrease energy consumption even as it enhances lighting quality. The restaurant chain did just that at its units in Florida, where high-efficiency

Operating in an Environmentally Friendly Manner

Some industry experts believe retailing has been one of the more gluttonous industries in its use of natural resources in headquarters, retail stores, and distribution centers. To remedy this, retailers can reduce their negative impact on the environment by focusing on three specific areas: the physical environment, air quality, and energy, water, and waste usage. Let's look at each of these areas:

- Retailers can protect the physical environment by using recycled goods or goods with recycled components for their fixtures, interior furnishings, and even floor coverings. In a 10,000-square-foot store, for example, installing new carpeting with recycled content can save 80,000 pounds of natural resources.
- The use of wall paints with low volatile organic compounds (VOCs) and carpeting with a glue-free "peel and stick" system (that eliminates the VOCs in wet adhesives) can improve air quality.
- Retailers can monitor usage of electricity, water, and paper to reduce waste. High-efficiency heating, ventilating, and air-conditioning systems; clock timers; and fluorescent fixtures can reduce energy consumption.

What else do you think retailers can do to improve their environmental efforts?

Source: "Are You Environmentally Challenged?" *Chain Store Age* (December 1998), p. 240.

lighting and window film are saving each of the 28 locations about $7,000 to $9,000 in annual operating costs. The system has also improved the quality of illumination. "Before we installed the new lighting, our incandescent floodlights accented the decor memorabilia and tables, but the rest of the space was fairly dark. Now, it is more evenly lit. You can see everything that is supposed to be highlighted and have good vision throughout the restaurant," says Tim Reckner, Friday's Southeast project facilities manager. Customized 5-watt and 9-watt compact fluorescent lamps have replaced incandescent lamps in high hats, track lighting, and Tiffany-style lamps in the rest rooms and dining and bar areas. The lower wattage and heat load have reduced energy consumption by 90 percent in public areas.[8]

Figure 13.4 describes Eddie Bauer's efforts at energy management.

Besides undertaking everyday store maintenance and energy management, retailers must set decision rules regarding renovations. These are just some of the issues to be addressed: How often are renovations necessary? What areas require renovations more frequently than others? How extensive will renovations be at any one time? Will the retailer be open for business as usual during renovations? How much money must be set aside in anticipation of future renovations? Will renovations result in higher revenues, lower operating costs, or both?

The complexities—and opportunities—of store renovations may be illustrated by the recent activities of Royal Ahold:

The tricky part of any renovation is keeping customers happy and satisfied while work is in progress: Is it better to close a store for the duration of a project and risk losing customers to competitors? Or is it better to keep a unit open and work piecemeal, forcing customers to navigate partially-opened floor space with items shifted to nonfamiliar areas? The debate is particularly vexing for supermarkets. Grocers fear disrupting their customers' patterns, for they know that the numerous shopping alternatives available to them could translate into a permanent change of shopping pattern.

Figure 13.4
Eddie Bauer's
Corporate
Headquarters

At its Redmond,
Washington, headquar-
ters, Eddie Bauer has an
integrated, extremely
efficient, energy system
with a design that
encourages natural light.
Reprinted by permission.
Photo credit to Ann
Hopping/Callison
Architecture, Inc.

Royal Ahold has begun to export its successful Next Week Open supermarket renovation plan to the United States. It commences the moment a store is closed on Saturday
night, assuring that it is ready to open again one week later with almost no resemblance
to the old store inside and out. "It is like a military operation," says Hans Gobes,
senior VP of Royal Ahold. "First, you get all the things out. Immediately after closing
the store on Saturday night, people are ready to take products off the shelves and tear
down the store." By Sunday night, everything has been cleaned up and made ready for
the first new elements to be brought into the store. "It takes very detailed planning and
lots of preparation. Carpenters, electricians, painters, the associates, all are very much
part of the whole. Everybody has a very specific spot and time schedule in the program. Everything is all so well prepared that you can do the renovation in one-tenth
the time you needed before."[9]

Inventory Management

From an operations vantage point, a retailer uses inventory management to maintain a
proper merchandise assortment while ensuring that its operations are efficient and effective.
While the role of inventory management in merchandising is discussed in Chapter 15, these
are some operational factors to consider:

- How can the handling of merchandise received from different suppliers be coordinated?
- How much inventory should be on the selling floor versus in a warehouse or storage area?
- How often should inventory be moved from nonselling to selling areas of a store?
- What inventory functions can be done during nonstore hours rather than while a store
  is open?
- What are the tradeoffs between faster delivery times from suppliers and higher shipping
  costs?
- What support is expected from suppliers in storing merchandise or setting up displays?

- What level of in-store merchandise breakage is acceptable?
- Which items require customer delivery? How should this be accomplished with regard to timing and responsibility?

Store Security

Store security relates to two basic issues: personal security and merchandise security. Personal security is examined here. Merchandise security is covered in Chapter 15.

Many consumers and employees feel less safe at retail establishments than they did a decade age, with these results: Fewer people are willing to shop at night. Many stores with Sunday hours ring up most of that day's sales by early afternoon due to people feeling more comfortable with daytime shopping. Almost one-half of shoppers believe malls are not as safe as they were. Some people age 60 and older no longer go out at all during the night. Consumers often stop going to malls they feel are unsafe or visit them only at specific hours. As one mall manager says: "Every study ever done about how people choose where to shop have 'security' and 'safety' at the top of the list."[10] And "despite the falling national crime rates, many stores that used to do a lot of business after dark are not doing so any more. People are shopping fewer stores and for fewer hours. Parking areas are a major source of angst for people, who are far more scared of walking through a large parking lot than anything else about shopping."[11]

These are some of the practices retailers are utilizing to address the issue of personal safety:

- Uniformed security guards provide a visible presence that is reassuring to customers and employees, and a warning to potential thieves and muggers. Some malls even have horse-mounted guards to further protect people. This is a big change from the past: "There was a time when every effort was made to minimize thoughts by the general public that security was even an issue for U.S. shopping centers. If a mall advertised that it had top-notch security, the assumption was that shoppers would start to wonder why they needed to promote that concept at all—and begin to feel that maybe they were at risk. That theory no longer holds true. Says one mall security director, 'We want to make the public aware that their safety is a priority.' "[12]
- Undercover personnel are used to thwart criminal attempts that wait for uniformed guards to pass by.
- Brighter lighting is used in parking lots, which are also patrolled more frequently by guards on foot and in vehicles. The guards more often work in teams to better head off potential problems.
- TV cameras and other devices scan the in-store and outside areas visited by shoppers and employees. 7-Eleven has an in-store cable TV and alarm monitoring system, complete with audio capabilities.
- Some shopping areas have imposed curfews for teenagers. At the Mall of America in Minneapolis, on Friday and Saturday nights after 6:00 P.M., anyone under 16 years of age must be accompanied by a person who is at least 21 years old. This is a controversial, but thus far, successful tactic.
- Access to store facilities (such as storage rooms) has been tightened.
- Bank deposits are made more frequently—often by armed security guards.

Insurance

The purchase of insurance that covers the retailer in case of losses due to fire, customer lawsuits regarding on-premises accidents, and other causes must be carefully planned. Among the types of insurance retailers buy are workers' compensation, public liability, product liability, property, and directors' and officers' liability. In addition, many retailers offer some health insurance option to their full-time employees; sometimes, the retailers pay the entire premiums, other times employees pay part or all of the premiums.

Insurance decisions are vital for several reasons: (1) Over the past decade, premiums have risen dramatically—in some cases, doubling. (2) Several insurers have reduced the scope of their coverage; they now require higher deductibles before paying claims or will not provide coverage on all aspects of operations (such as the professional liability of pharmacists). (3) There are fewer insurance carriers servicing retailers today than a decade ago; this limits the choice of carrier. (4) Insurance against environmental risks (such as leaking tanks) is now more important due to government rules. Overall, at department stores and specialty stores, insurance costs (excluding health) are 1 percent of revenues.

To protect themselves financially, a number of retailers have enacted costly programs aimed at lessening their vulnerability to employee and customer insurance claims due to dangerous or unsafe conditions, as well as to hold down insurance premiums. These programs include using no-slip carpeting, flooring, and rubber entrance mats; frequently mopping and inspecting wet floors; doing regular elevator and escalator maintenance checks; conducting fire drills; having fire-resistant facilities; setting up separate storage structures for dangerous items; discussing safety issues in employee training; and keeping records that proper maintenance has been done, in case there is legal action.

Credit Management

Visa presents a lot of advice (www.visa.com/fb/merch/practice) for retailers to reduce their administrative costs and the costs associated with the fraudulent use of credit and debit cards.

Credit management involves the policies and practices retailers follow in receiving payments from their customers. These are some of the major operational decisions to be made:

- What form of payment is acceptable? A retailer may accept cash only, cash and personal checks, cash and credit card(s), cash and debit cards, or all of these.
- Who administers the credit plan? The firm can have its own credit system and/or accept major credit cards (such as Visa, MasterCard, American Express, and Discover).
- What are customer eligibility requirements to make a check or credit purchase? For a check purchase, identification such as a photo ID might be sufficient. For a credit purchase, a new customer would have to meet requirements as to age, employment, annual income, and so on; and an existing customer would be evaluated in terms of his or her outstanding balance and credit limit. A minimum purchase amount may also be specified for a credit transaction.
- What are the tradeoffs between the cost of permitting credit transactions and the increased profits generated by credit sales?
- What credit terms will be used? A retailer with its own plan must determine when interest charges will begin, what the rate of interest will be, and minimum monthly payments.
- How are late payments or nonpayments to be handled? Some retailers with their own credit plans rely on outside collection agencies to follow up on past-due accounts.

In credit management, a retailer generally must weigh the ability of credit to generate added revenues against the cost of processing payments. The latter can include screening, transaction, and collection costs, as well as bad debts. If a retailer completes all credit functions itself, it will incur these costs; if outside parties (such as Visa) are used, the retailer covers the costs via its fees to the credit organization.

The *Nilson Report* presents information on retail payment methods. At its site (www.nilsonreport.com/recent_issues.html), you can access highlights from recent issues.

According to studies on retailing payment methods, in the United States, there are now 1.3 billion credit and debit cards in use, 89 percent of adults use credit cards, 61 percent of adults use ATMs, 37 percent of adults use debit cards, and 33 percent of adults use pre-paid cards. During the Christmas holiday season alone (the day after Thanksgiving to the day before Christmas), there are 2.2 billion retail credit and debit card transactions, yielding $127 billion in purchases. In general, the average sales transaction involving a check is 75 percent higher than one with cash; and the average sales transaction involving a credit card is more than double the amount with cash. Overall, 50 percent of retail transactions and 40 percent of revenues are in cash, 22 percent of transactions and 25 percent of revenues are by check, and 28 percent of transactions and 35 percent of revenues are by credit and debit card. At supermarkets, 59 percent of transactions and 30 percent of revenues are in cash, 22 percent of transactions and 46 percent of revenues are by check, and 9 percent of transactions and 17 percent of revenues are by credit and debit card—with other formats (such as food stamps) comprising the balance. Among retailers accepting credit cards, a third have their own card, 98 percent accept MasterCard and/or Visa, 80 percent accept Discover, and just over one-half accept American Express. Most retailers that accept credit cards, handle two or more cards.[13]

Credit card fees paid by retailers generally range from 1.5 to 5.0 percent of sales for Visa, MasterCard, Discover, and American Express—depending mostly on the retailer's credit volume and the card provider. There may also be transaction fees of 5 to 35 cents per charge and monthly statement fees of $5 to $35. In contrast, the total costs of retailers' own credit operations as a percent of credit sales are usually lower, at 2.0 percent. Costco has a Merchant Credit Processing program for small businesses so they may carry Visa or MasterCard at competitive costs. For store-based retailers, Costco has a 1.57 percent of sale fee, a per item charge of 21 cents, and no monthly statement fee.[14]

Many supermarkets, gas stations, and drugstores—among others—have begun placing greater emphasis on some form of **debit card system,** whereby the purchase price of a good or service is immediately deducted from a consumer's bank account and entered into a retailer's account via an appropriate computer terminal. The retailer's risk of nonpayment is eliminated and its costs are reduced with debit rather than credit transactions. For traditional credit cards, end-of-month billing is employed (with no interest charges if payments are made promptly); with debit cards, monetary account transfers are made at the time of the purchase—delayed billing carries interest charges from the day an item is bought. There has been, and will continue to be, some resistance to debit transactions by consumers who like the delayed-payment benefit of conventional credit cards. Some people may also dislike debit cards because of privacy or security issues (such as: Can a retailer look at a customer's bank balance? Can a retail clerk gain access to a customer's checking account by learning the person's access code?).[15]

As the payment landscape evolves, several new operational challenges must be dealt with properly:

Click on "About Deluxe" (www.deluxe.com) to learn about one of the premier payment systems support companies for retailers.

- Retailers can choose from a broadening array of options for processing shopper payments: "From ATMs and debit cards to credit cards, and on to emerging technologies such as smart cards and mag-stripe electronic gift cards, the payment field is growing ever more complex. Most retailers want to provide customers with as many payment options as are reasonable and that are likely to be used. The result is a mix of online and off-line activity at the point of sale for the vast majority of chain retailers. The key driver in every instance is minimizing the time customers spend in line."[16] Yet, from an operations standpoint, training cashiers is more complicated due to all the payment formats.
- There are now hardware and software to process paper checks electronically. This results in cost savings for the retailer and faster payments from the bank.
- Visa and MasterCard are being sued by some retailers for requiring the latter to accept both credit and debit cards, if the retailers want to continue carrying Visa and MasterCard credit cards.
- Nonstore retailers have less legal protection against credit card fraud than store-based retailers that secure written authorization.
- Credit card transactions on the Web must instantly take into account different sales tax rates and currencies (for global sales).

- In Europe, retailers are grappling with the intricacies of converting to the common euro currency. Credit card transactions have more readily been converted to the euro, while cash transactions are still often in the currency of the country where the store is located.

Computerization

CAM Commerce Solutions (www. camcommerce.com) offers *free* operations software to small retailers in the hope that as these retailers grow, they will pay for advanced software.

Many retailers are improving their operations productivity through computerization; and with the declining prices of computer systems and related software, even more firms will do so in the near future. At the same time, retailers need to make sure that this prophecy does not come true: "Technology's like a merry-go-round. The faster it goes, the more you invest. The more you invest, the more dependent you get on it and the more you upgrade in the future."[17] Let us present a variety of examples of the operational benefits of computerization.

Videoconferencing is being used by retailers such as Home Depot, Wal-Mart, and J.C. Penney. It lets them link store employees with central company headquarters, as well as communicate with vendors. Videoconferencing can be deployed through satellite technology and by computer (using special hardware and software). In both cases, audio/video communications are used to train workers, spread news, stimulate employee morale, and so on.

SpectraLink (www. spectralink.com) has wireless "Solutions" for "Retail" businesses.

In-store telecommunications are aiding operations by offering low-cost, secure in-store transmissions. See Figure 13.5. SpectraLink Corporation is one of the firms marketing lightweight pocket phones that enable personnel to talk to one another anywhere in a store. There are no air time charges or monthly fees because the SpectraLink system is linked to the retailer's existing phone network. SpectraLink clients include Barnes & Noble, Borders, Ikea, Kmart, Neiman Marcus, and Toys "R" Us.

Through PC-based software such as Retail Pro (www.retailpro.com), many firms are using computerized inventory control: With a keystroke, "complex inventory can be sorted by vendor, department, class, subclass, style, season, color, size, etc. Retail Pro displays inventory on a lineal display or in a matrix such as a size/color grid. There is no extra data

Technology in Retailing

Making Retail Checkouts Gooey (GUI)

Two leading vendors of point-of-sale (POS) equipment are scheduled to introduce high graphic interactive touchscreen devices for use by consumers. One of these POS devices will enable customers to sign their names with an inkless electronic pen, and view either generic or specific messages. An example of a specific message would be an offer for an instant discount for selected photographic accessories to a customer who has just purchased a camera. Other possible applications include advertising, personal messages, loyalty programs, electronic couponing, and instant credit offers. The POS system can even accept an application for a retailer's credit card.

There is some concern that the introduction of a graphics interface could frustrate rather than encourage consumers. According to one industry observer, retailers have for some time now made interactive kiosks, touch-screen information terminals, and other devices available to consumers. "In almost all cases, the technology was ignored by customers over the age of 50 and used infrequently by 25-to-50-year-olds.

Describe the necessary balance between ease of use and sophisticated features for these new terminals.

Source: Patricia A. Murphy, "Interactive Touchscreens Seen Reshaping Retail Checkout," *Stores* (July 1998), p. 56.

Figure 13.5
Effective In-Store
Communications

Foot Locker employees
are equipped with
battery-powered head-
sets that enable them to
communicate easily
within individual stores.
Reprinted by permission of
Venator Group, Inc.

entry needed to update inventory movement; the actions of ordering, receiving, ticketing, and selling on the system are all that are needed to keep the data base current." Raymark's Xpert Series Integrated Retail Suite is highlighted in Figure 13.6.

But nowhere are the operational effects of retail computerization more important than in the area of the checkout process. Let us specifically look at the computerized checkout, the electronic point-of-sale system, and scanning formats.

Figure 13.6
Computerized
Inventory Control
with Xpert Series

Reprinted by permission
of Raymark.

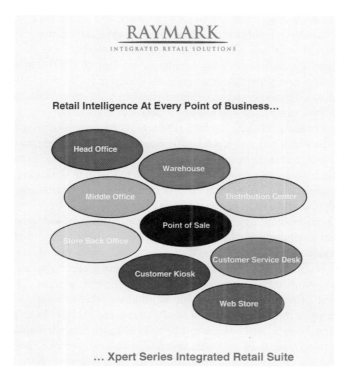

RAYMARK
INTEGRATED RETAIL SOLUTIONS

Retail Intelligence At Every Point of Business...

Head Office

Warehouse

Middle Office

Distribution Center

Point of Sale

Store Back Office

Customer Service Desk

Customer Kiosk

Web Store

... Xpert Series Integrated Retail Suite

Figure 13.7
The Computerized
Checkout at Kmart

Kmart has installed
state-of-the-art comput-
erized checkouts at all
of its 2,200 Kmart, Big
Kmart, and Super Kmart
stores.
Reprinted by permission.

The **computerized checkout** is used by many types of retailers (large and small), so
they can efficiently process transactions and monitor inventory status. Firms rely on UPC-
based systems, whereby cashiers manually ring up sales or pass items over or past optical
scanners. Computerized registers instantly record and display sales, customers get detailed
receipts, and all inventory data are stored in a computer memory bank. See Figure 13.7.

This type of checkout lowers costs by reducing transaction time, employee training, misrings, and the need for item price markings. In addition, retailers can increase productivity
because of better inventory control, reduced spoilage, and improved ordering. They also get
data on an item-by-item basis—which aids in determining store layout and merchandise
plans, setting the amount of shelf-space per item, and automatically replenishing inventory.

There have been a number of recent technological developments related to computerized
checkouts. These include wireless scanners that let workers scan heavy items without having
to pick them up, radio frequency identification tags (RFID) that emit a unique radio frequency code when placed near a receiver (which is faster than UPC codes and better for
harsh climates), and speech recognition (that can tally up an order for one hamburger and a
diet Coke, for example, on the basis of a clerk's verbal order).

Two potential problems do face retailers using computerized checkouts. First, UPC-
based systems will not reach peak efficiency until all suppliers attach UPC labels to merchandise; otherwise, retailers incur labeling costs. Second, because UPC symbols are
unreadable by humans, some states have enacted laws making price labeling on individual
packages mandatory; others are considering legislation. This lessens the labor savings of
retailers that would like to post only shelf prices.

Many retailers have upgraded to an **electronic point-of-sale system,** which performs all
the tasks of a computerized checkout and also verifies check and charge transactions, provides instantaneous sales reports, monitors and changes prices, sends intra- and interstore
messages, evaluates personnel and profitability, and stores data. Most times, a point-of-sale
system is used in conjunction with a retail information system. The terminals in the electronic point-of-sale system can either stand alone (the "intelligent" type) or be integrated
with an in-store minicomputer or a headquarters mainframe. In any case, keyboards, printers, scanners, wands, and screens can be used as needed by the retailer.

In computerizing their payment systems, retailers have more scanning options than ever
before: "As scanning systems, in their many shapes and sizes, have become integral to most

Symbol Technologies
(www.symbol.com) is
one of the leaders in
retail scanning equip-
ment, with an exten-
sive product line.

point-of-sale operations, retailers now look to the newest technology for help in achieving increased productivity, reduced training cycles, and accurate data collection throughout the entire distribution pipeline. In effect, the dramatic gains in increased efficiency made possible by scanners have served to raise the bar on retailers' expectations. They want systems that are smaller, faster, easier to use, more durable, more affordable, and as useful in distribution centers and backroom storage areas as they are at the point of sale." These are among the advances in scanning: handheld scanners; wearable, hands-free scanners; miniaturized data transceivers; and in-home scanners (for online ordering—shoppers scan the barcodes of the items they want to replenish rather than typing out a list).[18]

As noted in Chapter 2, the emerging scanning option in which many retailers are quite interested is **self-scanning,** whereby the consumer himself or herself scans the items being purchased at a checkout counter, pays electronically by credit or debit card, and bags the items. This is why a number of retailers (including Wal-Mart) are testing self-scanning:

> The technology, which first emerged more than a decade ago, has streaked from the pilot-program stage to full-blown installation in Safeway UK and appears to be on the same track at major retailers such as Kroger, H.E. Butt, A&P, and Shaw's in the United States. The initial numbers are impressive. Labor savings of between 20 and 40 hours a week per station appear to be the norm. Payback is between a year and 13 months on average. In addition, there are very good security methods that prevent customers from accidentally or purposely bypassing an item. There is a mechanism in the system that looks at the size and weight so that one item can't be passed off as another. Furthermore, a self-checkout system can work with fewer employees, which means lower payroll—and an alternative for retailers having trouble finding workers.[19]

Retailers are quite pleased that one especially vexing operational issue is behind them: the "Y2K problem." During the period leading up to January 1, 2000, the retailing industry spent hundreds of millions of dollars to fix computer software bugs that existed because two-digit date codes were often used in early software programs. Supervalu alone spent over $26 million to correct its software. Why the concern? Left uncorrected, any 1999 or prior information stored in a retailer's computer system might have been automatically deleted when the clock struck midnight on December 31, 1999.

Outsourcing

GE Capital's Card Services (www.ge.com/capital/retailer/index.html) handles the credit operations for a number of retailers.

In recent years, more retailers have turned to outsourcing for some of the operating tasks they previously performed themselves. With **outsourcing,** a retailer pays an outside party to undertake one or more of its operating functions. The goals are to reduce the costs and employee time devoted to particular tasks. For example, Kmart has entered into agreements with logistics firms to consolidate small shipments and to process returned merchandise; it has also outsourced electronic data interchange tasks. Home Depot is outsourcing most of its trucking operations. J.C. Penney, which for decades fully managed its credit operations, has just entered into a long-term outsourcing arrangement with GE Capital.

The Eckerd drugstore chain well illustrates the benefits of outsourcing:

> Cost savings. Reduced liability. Improved store appearance. These are just a few of the benefits Eckerd has realized since it switched from in-house lighting maintenance to an outsourced program. "We have found better lighting at reduced costs through outsourcing," says Ray Morgan, corporate manager. In the past, Eckerd took a regional approach. It had 6 maintenance offices with technicians responsible for changing lamps and ballasts and doing repairs. Lamps were changed if they burned out. Store managers changed lamps when technicians were not available. Along with opening the chain up to potential liability, it made for inconsistency. The switch began 5 years ago

when Eckerd decided to outsource all maintenance services, including lighting. Almost overnight, it began to see cost savings from staff reductions and lower overhead expenses related to inventory, service trucks, warehouse space, and administration.[20]

Crisis Management

Despite their best intentions, retailers may sometimes be faced with crisis situations that need to be managed as smoothly as possible. Crises may be brought on by such events as an in-store fire or broken water pipe, bad weather breaking the store's front window, access to a store being partially blocked due to picketing by striking workers, a car accident in the parking lot, a burglary, a sudden illness by the owner or a key employee, a storm that knocks out a retailer's power, unexpectedly high or low consumer demand for a good or service, a sudden increase in a supplier's prices, a natural disaster like a flood or an earthquake, or other factors.

Although crises cannot always be anticipated, and some adverse effects may occur regardless of retailer efforts, these principles should be adhered to in devising operations management plans:

1. There should be contingency plans for as many different types of crisis situations as possible. That is why retailers buy insurance, install backup generators in anticipation of power failures, and prepare management succession plans in the event of sudden illnesses of key officers. Thus, a firm can have a checklist of steps to follow if there is an incident such as an in-store fire or a parking-lot accident.

2. Essential information should be communicated to all affected parties, such as the fire or police department, employees, customers, and the media, as soon as a crisis occurs.

3. Cooperation—not conflict—among the involved parties is essential.

4. Responses should be as swift as feasible; indecisiveness may worsen the situation.

Climbing the CVS Operations Career Ladder

Shannon Bonacci originally thought of a career in a more corporate environment, but was attracted to retailing by the thought of working with both customers and fellow employees. She also could not see herself being behind a desk all day. On graduation from Western New England College in 1998, she accepted a position at CVS, one of the largest drugstore chains in the United States.

Six months after joining CVS, Bonacci was an assistant store manager in a 24-hour CVS store that is one of the largest in its district: "The environment is supportive and the management team fits and works together like one unit. I like the fact that I work for a company that's so large. It allows a lot of different options for growth."

Bonacci's career plans are to remain in the operations end of retailing (rather than the merchandising side) and become a store manager, then a district manager, and eventually move into upper management at CVS. The value the firm places on its "promotion from within" philosophy can be verified by looking at the background of Tom Ryan, the current chairman of the board. He was originally hired by CVS as a pharmacist upon his college graduation.

Source: "Prescribing Change at CVS," *Careers in Retailing* (January 1999), p. 23.

5. The chain of command for decisions should be clear and the decision maker given adequate authority.

Crisis management is also a task for small retailers, not just for large ones. As one crisis management expert notes, "It's very important for small businesses or startups to be prepared for a crisis because the margin of error is so tiny. They're dealing with a fragile environment, where even a minor crisis could put them out of business."[21]

SUMMARY

1. *To describe the operational scope of operations management.* As defined in Chapter 12, operations management efficiently and effectively seeks to enact the policies needed to satisfy customers, employees, and management. In contrast to Chapter 12, which dealt with financial aspects, Chapter 13 covered operational facets.

2. *To examine several specific aspects of operating a retail business.* An operations blueprint systematically lists all operating functions, their characteristics, and their timing. The responsibility for performing the functions is also specified in an operations blueprint.

Store format and size considerations include the use of prototype stores and store size. Firms using prototype stores often do so under the aegis of rationalized retailing. Some retailers emphasize category killer stores; others open smaller stores. In space allocation, retailers deploy a top-down or a bottom-up approach. They are always searching for ways to optimize the productivity of store space.

Personnel utilization activities to improve productivity range from better screening job applicants to workload forecasts to job standardization and cross-training. Job standardization means the tasks of people with similar positions in different departments are kept rather uniform. Cross-training means people learn tasks associated with more than one job. A firm can advance its personnel flexibility and minimize the total number of workers needed at any given time by these techniques.

Store maintenance includes all the activities in managing physical facilities. The quality of store maintenance influences people's perceptions of the retailer, the life span of facilities, and operating expenses. Energy management is an operational concern for many retailers. At firms with special energy needs, it is crucial. To better control energy resources, retailers are doing everything from using better-quality insulation materials when building and renovating stores to substituting

high-efficiency bulbs and fluorescent ballasts for traditional lighting. Besides everyday facilities management, retailers need to set decision rules as to the frequency and manner of store renovations.

Operationally, inventory management requires that retailers strive to acquire and maintain the proper merchandise while ensuring efficient and effective operations. There are many factors to consider, from coordinating different supplier shipments to planning customer deliveries (if needed).

Store security measures are needed to protect both personal and merchandise safety. Because of safety concerns, fewer people now shop at night and some avoid shopping in areas they view as unsafe. To improve personal safety, retailers are employing security guards, better lighting parking lots, tightening access to store facilities, and deploying other tactics.

Insurance covers retailers against losses from fire, lawsuits, and other causes. Among the types of insurance that retailers buy are workers' compensation, public liability, product liability, property, and directors' and officers' liability. Many firms also have some type of employee health insurance.

Credit management pertains to the policies and practices retailers follow in receiving customer payments. Nearly 90 percent of U.S. adults use credit cards. Check and credit payments generally mean larger transactions than cash payments. One-half of retail transactions are in cash, 22 percent by check, and 28 percent by credit or debit card. Retailers pay various fees to be able to offer noncash payment options to customers; and there are a wide range of payment systems available for retailers.

A growing number of retailers are computerizing elements of operations. Videoconferencing and wireless in-store telephone communications are gaining in popularity. Computerized checkouts and electronic point-of-sale systems are quite useful. Electronic point-of-sale systems perform all the tasks of computerized checkouts—as well as verify check and charge transactions, provide

S U M M A R Y *(CONTINUED)*

instant sales reports, monitor and change prices, send intra- and interstore messages, evaluate personnel and profitability, and store data. Self-scanning is undergoing serious testing.

With outsourcing, the retailer pays another party to handle one or more operating functions. The goals are to reduce costs and better utilize employees' time.

Crisis management must handle unexpected situations as smoothly as possible. There should be contingency plans, information should be communicated to all affected, all parties should cooperate, responses should be as swift as feasible, and the chain of command for decisions should be clear.

Key Terms

operations blueprint (p. 422)
prototype stores (p. 424)
rationalized retailing (p. 424)
top-down space management
    approach (p. 425)

bottom-up space management
    approach (p. 425)
job standardization (p. 426)
cross-training (p. 426)
store maintenance (p. 427)

debit card system (p. 433)
computerized checkout (p. 436)
electronic point-of-sale system (p. 436)
self-scanning (p. 437)
outsourcing (p. 437)

Questions for Discussion

1. Present a brief operations blueprint for an online luggage retailer.

2. What are the pros and cons of prototype stores? For which kind of firms is this type of store most desirable?

3. Differentiate between the top-down and bottom-up space management approaches.

4. Why would a retailer be interested in job standardization and cross-training for its employees?

5. Comment on this statement: "The quality of store maintenance efforts affects consumer perceptions of the retailer, the life span of facilities, and operating expenses."

6. Talk to two local retailers and ask them what they have done to maximize their energy efficiency. Present your findings.

7. As a restaurant owner, you are planning a complete renovation of the dining room. What decisions must you make?

8. Present a five-step plan for a retailer to reassure customers that it is safe to shop there.

9. A mom-and-pop store does not accept checks because of the risks involved. However, it does accept Visa and MasterCard. Evaluate this strategy.

10. As the owner of a local supermarket, how would you persuade customers to use debit cards (because you are interested in expanding business, but do not want to accept credit cards)?

11. What potential problems may result if a retailer relies on its computer system to implement too many actions (such as employee scheduling or inventory reordering) automatically?

12. What operations criteria would you use to evaluate the success of self-scanning at Wal-Mart?

13. Are there any operating functions that should *never* be outsourced? Explain your answer.

14. Outline the contingency plan a retailer could have in the event that each of these occurs:
    a. A shopper's fainting in the store.
    b. Vandalism of the storefront.
    c. A firm's Web site being down for five hours.
    d. The bankruptcy of a key supplier.

WEB-BASED EXERCISE

Retail Pro (www.retailpro.com)

Questions

1. Evaluate the features of Retail Pro.

2. How can Retail Pro be used to improve customer loyalty?

3. How can Retail Pro improve a retailer's overall productivity?

4. Evaluate the special functions of Retail Pro.

CHAPTER ENDNOTES

1. Mike Troy, "Below Kmart's Surface, Hidden Benefits Arise," *Discount Store News* (March 22, 1999), pp. 62, 64.

2. See "Prototypes: From Concept to Rollout," *Chain Store Age* (May 1999), p. 199.

3. Joanne Gordon, "Saks Appeal," *Chain Store Age* (May 1998), p. 85.

4. Karen M. Kroll. "New Stockroom Model Offers Guide to Better Use of Store Space," *Stores* (August 1999), pp. 82, 84.

5. Alexandra Moran (Editor), *FOR 1996 Edition* (New York: Wiley, 1996), pp. 6, 9.

6. "Building and Equipment Costs Rise as Store Size Shrinks," *Chain Store Age* (July 1999), pp. 102–104.

7. Patrick Sciacca, "Energy to Save: Effort, Deregulation, and Technology Are Cutting Energy Costs for Savvy Retailers," *Supermarket News* (August 2, 1999), p. 21.

8. "T.G.I.F.'s Recipe for Savings," *Chain Store Age* (September 1999), p. 108.

9. "Royal Facelift," *Chain Store Age* (December 1998), p. 176.

10. Iver Peterson, "Walking the Beat from Macy's to Sears," *New York Times* (December 23, 1998), p. B1.

11. Robert Langreth, "Shoppers' Concerns Over Safety Persist Despite Declining National Crime Statistics," *Wall Street Journal* (May 13, 1996), p. B4B.

12. Kevin Kenyon, "Close Watch," *Shopping Centers Today* (June 1999), pp. 19, 22.

13. Tom Coyle, "Surveys and Trends," *America's Community Banker* (July 1999), p. 39; "1999 Christmas Plastic Charges Top $126 Billion," *www.cardweb.com* (November 23, 1999); Ernst & Young, "Survey of Payment Methods," *Chain Store Age* (January 1996), Section Two; and Susan Reda, "Mission Critical: Supermarket Payments," *Stores* (February 1999), pp. 22–26.

14. "Credit Card Processing," *www.costco.com* (March 9, 2000).

15. See Patricia A. Murphy, "New Breeds of Debit Cards Offer Expanded Opportunities for Retailers," *Stores* (May 1999), pp. 76, 78; Jan M. Rosen, "The Siren Swipe of the Debit Card," *New York Times* (October 31, 1999), Section 3, p. 15; and "E-Payments 2000: Moving Money and More," *Chain Store Age* (June 1999), supplement.

16. Sunil Taneja, "The Payment Evolution," *Chain Store Age* (September 1999), p. 178.

17. Len Lewis, "High-Tech or Too Tech?" *Progressive Grocer* (June 1998), p. 35.

18. "Special Section: Scanners," *Stores* (August 1999), p. P2.

19. Terry Hennessy, "Taking Control," *Progressive Grocer* (December 1998), p. 83; and Jim McCartney, "Self-Scanning Tests at Wal-Mart, Supermarkets Register Approval," *Shopping Centers Today* (November 1999), p. 65.

20. "Advantages of Outsourcing," *Chain Store Age* (July 1999), pp. 106, 108.

21. Brian Ruberry, "Danger Zone," *Entrepreneur* (November 1998), p. 153.

CASE 1

CAN SHEETZ CONTINUE PLAYING SWEET MUSIC?

Convenient for whom? That was the question everyone from store managers to corporate executives was asking at Sheetz Inc., the 192-store, Altoona, Pennsylvania-based convenience store retailer. According to Charlie Campbell, a one-time store manager, "Store managers were taking three to four hours to close out their sales day. We would spend an hour looking for a $5 error." That is just one very vivid example of the inefficient practices that kept Sheetz's profits down. It has worked hard to turn this situation around.

In 1995, Sheetz planned dual reengineering projects. The store-level project began that year; a corporate initiative began in 1997. Campbell, now director of organizational efficiency at Sheetz, said the projects were through and yielded impressive results. He said the company saved $5.1 million in payroll costs between 1996 and 1998 by redefining tasks and streamlining business practices.

Sheetz has also partnered with KPMG Peat Marwick to identify inefficient practices—organizing 12 cross-functional project teams. The store operations team uncovered gross inefficiencies that were more the fault of procedures than the store managers themselves. For example, Sheetz store managers had to input data for no fewer than 40 computer screens to close out their day. "We were forcing the store managers to look at information that had no value to them," Campbell says. "Now, we've reduced those 40 screens to 18 and hope to reduce that number to one. And we are saving 158,704 manager pay hours annually." While these "saved" hours did not reduce payroll expenses, store managers can now spend that time on the sales floor rather than hunched over a computer.

Prior to the reengineering, much of the information that filtered down to store managers was of questionable value. "There were too many redundant reports," Campbell remarks. "240 reports were available on the store managers' computers. We've gotten that number down to 23."

Sheetz even embarked on a series of detailed time studies to get a feel for how store-level tasks were being done and how they could be improved. As Charlie Campbell says, "The task-specific time studies enabled Sheetz to standardize all store operations. We actually produced laminated index cards outlining exactly how each task should be performed. The time study helped us align labor costs with needs. The end result of our efforts was an average reduction of 55 man-hours per week per store—and we accomplished that while increasing customer service at a time when our sales were growing."

In addition, Sheetz wanted to align store tasks with corporate procedures. Paying for direct store delivery (DSD) shipments is a prime example of processes that were woefully out of sync prior to the reorganization. Before, Sheetz would pay vendor invoices without corroborating information from store computers that the goods were actually received. "If the vendor sent its hard copy to our offices, the vendor was paid," Campbell states. "We were not using the computers at the stores to manage our inventory." Now, all Sheetz stores scan DSD shipments into their systems when the goods are received, and payment is based on electronic information sent from the stores to the corporate office.

Sheetz's operational adjustments, for the most part, are complete. Nonetheless, Campbell believes the company must be ever vigilant to ensure that the processes it adds in the future are efficient: "We will constantly evaluate new processes and procedures." That will ensure that Sheetz never again has to mount such an extensive reengineering project.

Questions

1. What factors could account for any retailer's needing to reengineer its operations?

2. What are the pros and cons of extensive reengineering in a retail environment?

3. Evaluate the Sheetz reengineering approach.

4. What are the pros and cons of standardizing operations across all Sheetz stores?

NOTE   The material in this case is adapted by the authors from "Rap Sheetz," *Chain Store Age* (June 1999), pp. 78–82. Copyright Lebhar-Friedman, Inc., 425 Park Avenue, New York, NY 10022. Reprinted by permission.

CASE 2

SELF-SCANNING COMES OF AGE

Although self-scanning is in widespread use in Europe, it is still in relative infancy in the United States. Self-scanning is undergoing rigorous testing at a number of U.S.-based retailers, especially supermarket chains. As Barb Ramsour, the director of information systems for 23-unit Balls Food Stores, notes, "Three years ago, the technology was still too expensive, but now here we are, actually using the technology." During the two months after self-scanning was installed at one of the chain's stores, it was responsible for 2,300 customer grocery orders per day (about 7 percent of customer transactions). Balls has been testing self-scanning at two special self-serve lanes that are used in place of one traditional checkout lane.

With self-checkouts, shoppers can scan, bag, and pay for merchandise without human assistance. These checkouts incorporate a scanner and scale into an integrated point-of-sale system. To protect the retailer from fraud, systems include a security camera that displays an on-screen image of a customer making a purchase. Unlike traditional point-of-sale systems that require shopper training, a self-checkout touchscreen guides the shopper through all the steps needed to complete a transaction, including payment. After all items are scanned, the customer receives a printed receipt. The shopper can then choose among several payment options including credit and debit cards, and cash (change is returned automatically).

A supermarket can also obtain optional equipment that accepts checks and food stamps as payment. Depending on the size of a store and its sales volume, a retailer can choose to have either a floating attendant (who oversees several checkout lanes) or an attendant station (with a permanently stationed attendant). The attendant must verify a customer's age when alcohol or tobacco is purchased. Some vendors offer optional weight data bases that can compare the actual weight of a cart's contents to its weight based on the scanned purchases. Store security personnel are then alerted to any discrepancies.

If self-scanning becomes widespread in the United States, it could have major implications for labor costs, as well as customer service. The self-scanning benefits for the retailer and the consumer include lower labor costs, improved customer service (since all checkout lanes are open all of the time—even during low-traffic periods), and the ability to shift cashiers to other functions. In addition, self-scanning provides privacy for the shopper.

A recent survey of frequent shoppers at five supermarkets (representing three chains and two independents) found that 61 percent of those questioned thought self-scanning improves customer service. However, only 10 percent of the shoppers interviewed used the self-scanning lanes exclusively. Customers who did not use the system often believed that

CASE 2

(CONTINUED)

the presence of self-checkout lanes led to shorter lines at the traditional checkout counters. They were happy to know that an option existed if the regular lanes became especially crowded.

The president of Lees Supermarkets sees self-scanning as a big plus from the customer's perspective. "It's kind of like taking a shortcut around a traffic jam. It might take you as long to get there as if you waited with everyone else, but it seems better because you are moving."

Questions

1. Describe the impact of self-scanning on the utilization of personnel.

2. What is the impact of self-scanning on cross-training?

3. Develop a store security policy for a retailer utilizing self-scanning.

4. What criteria should be used to determine whether self-scanning be adopted across all units of a chain?

Video Questions on Self-Scanning

1. Describe the security features of the NCR self-scanning system.

2. Why is human factors engineering especially critical in the design of a self-scanning system?

NOTE

The material in this case is drawn from *www.ncr.com* (March 9, 2000); Deena Amato-McCoy, "Balls Getting Good Results with Self-Scanning Technology," *Supermarket News* (March 23, 1998), p. 19; and Kim Ann Zimmerman, "Frequent Shoppers Like Self-Scanning Option," *Supermarket News* (May 17, 1999), p. 28.

PART FIVE
COMPREHENSIVE CASE
The Strategic Role of Human Resources

INTRODUCTION

Workers are softly rebelling, creating shifts and changes with companies that remind me of the beach erosions caused by storms. No matter how well developers plan and execute, nature eventually determines the landscape. Human nature, like any natural system, is powerful and complex. When unleashed, it can strike with deadly force or it can slowly and systematically pound away until the landscape changes.

Today's workers are slowly altering their workplace environment by their behavior. Their deeply held beliefs in self-reliance, independence, life balance, and individualism support their actions. Many attribute these beliefs and behaviors to the generation of 23- to 32-year-olds—Generation X-ers. However, I disagree. Changing the workplace is not just one generation's agenda. These behaviors and beliefs are cross-generational responses to life's changing demands. By studying and understanding these evolving trends, human resource professionals can redefine their roles and become key leaders in helping their firms prepare for and manage their people power. However, to accomplish this goal, human resources (HR) must transform.

DISTURBING PATTERN

When I consider all the retail organizations that I have studied, surveyed, and worked with, a disturbing pattern emerges—weak human resource departments. Most retailers do not view the HR department as a strategic business partner or as an indispensable part of the firm. My executive assessments usually show merchandising, finance, or marketing in the top spot when I rate each department's value and contribution to the

The material in this case is adapted by the authors from Terri Ka-bach-nick, principal and founder of the consulting firm, Terri Kabach-nick & Company, "The Strategic Role of Human Resources," *Arthur Andersen Retailing Issues Letter* (January 1999), pp. 1–6. Reprinted by permission.

retailer's success as perceived by the firm. HR inevitably ranks last, coupled with loss prevention.

I believe these ratings do not reflect HR competence but the perceived relevance. Senior management generally cites numerous examples of personal benefits and company values when asked specifically about HR's contribution. Meanwhile, management rarely involves HR in strategic planning and hardly ever asks HR to contribute to marketing or growth decisions. HR is involved when it's time to implement. Management views HR as an expense—a drain on profits. It needs to become a profit center.

In the following sections, I will discuss why and how HR must change and the quality-of-life issues affecting business today, show the significance of HR expertise, and demonstrate how HR as an integral part of the company gets direct results at the bottom line. HR transformation begins with every HR practitioner. It starts with a clear, deep understanding of people and their quality-of-life choices.

QUALITY OF WORK LIFE

Work to live or live to work? Employees' opposing views complicate management. Many older managers perceive younger workers as having a poor or nonexistent work ethic. Younger workers say "get a life" and refuse to be caught in what they perceive as an imbalanced existence. Younger managers face difficulties with older workers who are unwilling to accept change.

My research reveals that these workers are quietly influencing each other. Older workers often regret the dues they paid to the firm at the expense of family and happiness. They now want a fuller life. Younger workers want to control the work affecting their lives. They want flexibility. Both are faced with family pressures and responsibilities, such as child care or parent care or both. Today's workers reflect a hybrid of values, beliefs, and behaviors—not as a result of age but of the quality-of-life issue.

Our study of 1,400 retail executives, managers, and associates of all ages found that:

- 84 percent—the most important finding—like what they do but not where they do it. Specifically, they cite policies that inhibit creativity, rules, and procedures that make no sense, and executives who exist on a planet called *entitlement*.
- 42 percent would leave their job and follow a good boss rather than build a new relationship.

- 76 percent would leave their present job for less money to work for a company that offers personal development and flexibility.
- 58 percent believe that an outsider has a better chance of getting the job or promotion that they want.
- 72 percent of managers have no clue about their future with the company.
- 81 percent feel that the way to the top is strictly political.
- Many firms forecast that part-timers will account for up to 80 percent of their workers in the future.
- Part-timers' overall job performance scores are about 30 percent higher as compared to full-timers'.

In the recent past, many workers, on all levels, simply left their employers if their needs were not met. This trend is now reversing. As we learned, although conditions can be disappointing and frustrating, many workers are opting to stay, chip away, and transform the firm. They find this task challenging, stimulating, and "cool." They feel they can nudge a firm to change for the better, by creating loosely organized, cross-departmental teams that, in their own venues, contest existing policies and politics.

One such team, in addition to polling fellow workers on issues ranging from schedules to meetings, has collected money and hired a labor attorney as an adviser. As a result, management has made changes. Afterwards, the CEO told me, "I didn't know what hit me. But when I put my ego aside, I realized they made sense. They were prepared, had facts, and were very polite. We need more of this type of caring."

Erosion in the labor pool is also forcing retailers to rethink policies and demands that no longer work. Consider these real-life examples of practices that employees question and many refuse to accept: A policy requiring every store manager to work three weekends a month because that is the retailer's busiest time. A silent standard that working a normal 8-hour day means you are not serious about your career and should not expect to get promoted. A career path forcing an employee to learn jobs in which he or she has no interest or natural aptitude. The practice of treating part-time workers as a necessary but insignificant commodity. Annual reviews based on job descriptions irrelevant to work performed.

According to our surveys, many of today's younger workers exhibit persistence, and older workers are adopting this newfound attitude. They believe their desired changes are good for everyone—company and employees. If they don't win change immediately, they regroup, rethink their strategy, and try again. They believe in being pragmatic, not cynical. They want to be treated as customers, not commodities. Many senior managers complain about the arrogance. Today's workers view assertive-

ness as their right. They prefer to persist rather than quit because they know it doesn't get better elsewhere.

By understanding today's workers, HR professionals can help firms find ways to balance employees' increasing work and family challenges so they are satisfying and profitable to employee and employer.

HR'S STRATEGIC ROLES

Workers and line managers, not necessarily senior management, are forcing HR to transform. They are questioning traditional orientation and training programs, requesting more learning tools, and demanding faster response and communication. They are forcing HR to be what it should be—a resource.

Future HR management will shift most of the routine, time-consuming bureaucracy to technology. They will stress the human element. The new HR will focus on personnel development and retention. HR professionals will be coaches, counselors, mentors, and succession planners. They will be the knowledge source for complicated labor laws and government policies. They will promote and fight for values, ethics, beliefs, and spirituality within their corporate community—and effectively build relationships with the outside community, schools, nonprofit organizations, and families.

To succeed, HR must be a business-driven function with a thorough understanding of the firm's big picture. It must be a strategic consulting partner providing innovative solutions and influencing decisions and policies. Consider the diagnostic questions at the end of the following role descriptions.

Trusted Insiders

HR practitioners prove their credibility by careful attention to response time, quality and effectiveness of casual communication, rule enforcement, openness to diverse opinions, and personal conduct—thereby contributing to perceptions of HR's professionalism and trustworthiness. HR professionals earn trust by:

- Being well informed.
- Taking a position on issues.
- Communicating directly.
- Demonstrating high integrity.
- Challenging the status quo.

Key Issues: Is HR viewed as a partner or an enforcer? Do employees seek out HR as a confidante? Does HR participate fully within the inner circle of management?

Quality-of-Life Experts

HR becomes the in-house expert on workers' time requirements, family and social obligations, team responsibilities, and developmental needs. It learns how workers perceive the firm and its management. With this competence, HR provides alternative insights on business issues, educates management on the consequences of new policies and directives, and influences decision making.

Key Issues: How will our employees react to a given decision? Are we sending clear, consistent messages to everyone? What is the ratio of cost to productivity gains in our decisions? Are we demonstrating heart and soul?

Job Matchmakers

HR installs systems to measure applicant beliefs and values for comparison with the firm's beliefs and values. HR assessments match applicants' behavior, attitudes, and job suitability to position templates. This replaces "gut instinct" hiring decisions, which significantly improves employee retention rates. For example, I consulted with a Midwestern retailer to help reduce turnover and boost retention through a more effective hiring process. We developed position templates and taught hiring and interview techniques. Within one year, the test stores retained 76 percent of new hires while nontest stores retained only 34 percent. The test stores also reduced interview time from an average of 45 minutes to 20 minutes.

Key Issues: How are employees selected? Who currently creates job descriptions? Does our current process match person to position? Have we recently trained our interviewers in effective techniques?

Company Communicators

Too often, HR is viewed as a management puppet dispensing information on command. To change this perception, HR consistently works with senior management to communicate policies, decisions, and plans with honesty, sensitivity, and timing.

Key Issues: Are our messages tailored to our audience? Do we include background information and fully explain our reasoning? Are our workers the first to know or do they receive information from the news media or the rumor mill?

Information Source

HR becomes the information source rather than the recipient. It stays immersed in facts from all key areas of business—including marketing strategies, expansion plans, customer data, P/E (price/earnings) ratios, sales focus, and results. It creates and maintains a safe environment where workers can come for information that they choose not to get elsewhere. "Resource" is its last name.

Key Issues: Is HR the first place workers come for answers or clarification? Does HR consistently answer questions correctly? Does HR think in terms of commercial success?

Prepared Mediators

HR builds its own radar system to help predict tumultuous activity that can change a firm's landscape. Some of the predictable storms include, but are not limited to, sexual harassment grievances; gender, age, or race inequities; biased performance reviews; probation and termination policies; and compensation discrimination. The radar's effectiveness is a result of a foundation of trust and sensitivity.

Key Issues: Is HR attuned to daily office interactions? Does HR teach and maintain—with strong corporate backing—a "no exceptions to the rules" policy across position lines? Is HR well versed in current behavior rules, laws, and guidelines? Is it well connected to experts on these issues?

Business Sleuths

HR goes beyond competition awareness. It studies similar industries and is curious about banking, hospitality, entertainment, communication, technology, and automotive. All of these have customers and employ people. All struggle daily with worker and customer issues. My point is that HR practitioners are well served when learning lessons from varied sources. In the words of one CEO from a major retailer: "Increasingly, I look to my HR executive for advice. I expect that advice to be backed by facts and examples. Her ongoing involvement in professional organizations outside of retailing provides her with a unique perspective and information that is of great value to me and to the company."

Key Issues: Does HR network with HR professionals from other industries? Participate in conferences and meetings not limited to HR? Promote an ongoing company policy for learning and development?

Business Strategists

HR challenges policies—written and unwritten—if they no longer make sense. For example, a senior VP of HR in a department store chain wanted to eliminate a long-standing policy against job sharing. The firm's senior executive committee opposed the change. The VP stood his ground and argued that the policy caused productive and good management people to leave. Proving that these employees left even though compensation from the new employer was lower, he gained the committee's attention. He then successfully argued that two people sharing responsibilities of one position would improve productivity, increase output, strengthen decision making, and serve as a role model for teamwork. He explained that employees with added responsibilities of child or parent care often could not afford to hire help. Job sharing provided a solution. He also stated that putting in "face time" demoralizes employees and makes no sense to today's workers who insist on a balance between working and other life pursuits. Results became evident quickly. Turnover in junior and senior management was reduced substantially, profit margins in the shared job areas have improved, and higher morale has become evident.

Key Issues: Can we find a better way to do this job? How can we innovate and reach company goals? What can we do to positively affect worker and company bottom lines? What is the worker's bottom line?

Education Customizers

A new approach begins with the premise that workers need to learn only what they need to learn. HR rethinks training and education programs that assume all workers require the same training. It provides employee education by first assessing what the individual knows and does well. Then, HR provides tools allowing individuals to pace and control their learning. Following training, HR assesses and measures improvement. HR shows it is more than a training department. It develops and retains productive workers.

Key Issues: Are we implementing strategic business educational plans? Have we produced measurable results? Are we cost effective?

Management Partners

HR builds partnerships with line managers and executive management. It shows each manager's impact on each employee. It provides opportunities for managers to learn leadership skills, then assesses their employee retention rates. Thus, HR improves departmental recruitment, employee satisfaction, and profits. Our recent research points out that the biggest deterrent to successful recruitment of college graduates is their perception of the retail industry gained from part-time retail job experience. At fault are poor store managers who mismanage young part-timers and cause disenchantment with retailing.

Key Issues: Are managers held accountable for people development? Who are they coaching? Who are they mentoring? Do they ask for HR help in analyzing employees' needs?

Technology Experts

HR studies, analyzes, and lobbies for investment in HR technology. Many retail HR departments are behind in software, systems, and technological tools because budget allocations generally favor profit producers over HR administrative functions. Few retailers truly believe an investment in improved HR systems will significantly improve productivity and profit. Yet, in companies making this investment, the benefits include reduced operating costs, greater efficiency in service, improved communication at all levels, shifting priorities to development of people instead of paper, and elimination of costly duplication of work. In one retail organization with 48 department stores, a computer-based hiring system reduced hiring costs by 52 percent and improved employee retention by 38 percent within two years.

Key Issues: Which tasks and roles would most benefit from a shift to technological systems? What are the state-of-the-art tools? How will customers benefit from this investment?

IN CONCLUSION—A MESSAGE FOR CEOs

My final message is directed to chief executives. HR professionals cannot accomplish this transformation alone. They need your direction and commitment. Your HR executive is your link into your entire organization. Have you created a safe environment that allows this individual to tell you the truth? Does he or she trust and believe in you? Maybe this example will relay my message best.

Consider this example: A retailer—147 stores—was being acquired and restructured. The CEO was meeting with 400 managers to announce the news and address the questions of workforce stability. He knew that retaining many talented people was part of the acquisition deal and critical to a successful transition. He also knew the best always leave first. Professionals drafted his speech, which he edited.

A draft of the speech found its way to the HR director. After reading the planned speech, she knew it would not be well received by the audience and would probably result in negativity, fear, and a quick loss of good people. She felt the CEO was not addressing every attendee's primary concern: *what about me?* She had two worries—the employees' feelings and the CEO's resulting image. She also knew that criticizing the speech was not an option because the CEO was focused on the reaction of the board, the shareholders, and the media. Taking a big risk, she stayed up all night writing a speech she felt would be forthright, caring, visionary, and direct. The next morning she requested an emergency meeting with the CEO. He gave her 15 minutes. Handing him the rewritten speech, she said simply, "Please just read this and then I'll explain." Questions, not explanations, followed. The most memorable was, "Why did you do this?" Her answer was simple: "I was afraid of the consequences for you and for the company."

For profits, you need people who perform. Table 1 shows a scorecard for assessing human resources.

Table 1 A Human Resources Scorecard

Does HR have an identity? What is it known for?

Does HR predict outcomes, inform management, and communicate a strong point of view?

Do both management and front-line employees trust HR? What's the proof?

Is HR a constant, reliable information source? How do we know this?

Is HR verbalizing and living our company values? Do all employees clearly understand them?

Does HR read and understand the company balance sheet?

Does HR know the company's profit-to-earnings ratio?

Does HR know and understand the focus and vision of other key divisions—merchandising, marketing, finance, RIS, and others?

What are our CEO's chief concerns? Why?

What are the three top business goals of HR this year? How are these linked to company goals?

What is HR's focus in training and development?

Are current educational programs producing results? If so, have these results been documented and communicated to senior management and all employees?

Is HR teaching managers how to grow talent and lead people? Are managers held accountable for employee retention and development?

How does HR's education and development strategy influence individual behavior?

What are the costs of employee replacement at all levels? Is everyone aware of these costs and their impact on profitability?

Is HR a truly diverse and unbiased organization?

Does HR teach tolerance and respect for differences in others? How? What evidence is there that these efforts are working?

Does HR have a clear and well-understood succession strategy?

Does HR provide individual leadership and executive coaching?

Are the core competencies of all jobs well defined and measurable?

Do reward/recognition programs match worker needs? How do they compare to competitors?

Is HR a professional communicator who tailors all messages to each audience?

What recent investments have been made in technology and systems? How proficient is HR in using them and monitoring results?

How does HR learn, develop, and nurture an individual's growth as a professional?

Is HR delivering or just doing?

Questions

1. According to the case, what should be the strategic role of HR? Do you agree? Explain your answers.
2. Comment on this statement from a retailing perspective: "Today's workers are slowly altering their workplace environment by their behavior."
3. How would you resolve the perceptual conflicts between younger and older retailing employees?
4. What are the implications of the case in terms of the definition of operations management at the beginning of Chapter 12?
5. How would you measure the productivity of a retailer's cashiers? Its sales personnel? Its customer service personnel?
6. In light of the discussion in the case, is job standardization a good idea? Is cross-training? Why or why not?
7. What technology should be used by a state-of-the-art HR department? Explain your answer.

MERCHANDISE MANAGEMENT AND PRICING

■ In Part Six, the merchandise management and pricing aspects of the retail strategy mix are presented. Merchandise management consists of the buying, handling, and financial aspects of merchandising. Pricing decisions are crucial due to their impact on the financial aspects of merchandise management and their interaction with other retailing elements.

■ Chapter 14 covers the development of merchandise plans. It begins with a discussion of merchandising philosophy. It then looks at buying organizations and their processes, as well as the considerations in formulating merchandise plans. The chapter concludes by describing category management and merchandising software.

■ Chapter 15 focuses on implementing merchandise plans. Each stage in the buying and handling process is detailed: gathering information, selecting and interacting with merchandise sources, evaluation, negotiation, concluding purchases, receiving and stocking merchandise, reordering, and re-evaluation. The chapter also examines logistics and inventory management, and their effects on merchandising.

■ Chapter 16 concentrates on financial merchandise management. The cost and retail methods of accounting are introduced. The merchandise forecasting and budgeting process is presented. Unit control systems are discussed. Dollar and unit financial inventory controls are integrated.

■ Chapter 17 deals with pricing. The outside factors affecting decisions are reviewed: consumers, government, suppliers, and competitors. A framework for developing a price strategy is shown: objectives, broad policy, basic strategy, implementation, and adjustments.

CHAPTER 14

Developing Merchandise Plans

CHAPTER OBJECTIVES

1. To demonstrate the importance of a sound merchandising philosophy
2. To study various buying organization formats and the processes they use
3. To outline the considerations in devising merchandise plans: forecasts, innovativeness, assortment, brands, timing, and allocation
4. To discuss category management and merchandising software

Susan Foslien, owner of Susan Stores (based in San Francisco and Burlingame, California), says, "It's time for a new crop of retail stores. We need to look for young people who aren't afraid to make a statement and take some risks."

Two such stores are Kirna Zabete and Jeffrey New York. They are not afraid to show vivid colors, focus on unknown designers, treat fashion in a totally nontraditional manner, or to mix merchandise that normally would not be found in the same store. Kirna Zabete has been compared to Colette, a Paris boutique that sells a wide range of items (from Nike sneakers to couture fashions), while Jeffrey New York more closely resembles the women's shop at Barney's.

Kirna Zabete is a 5,000-square-foot store that sells apparel by both lesser-known and more established designers, French flowers, bulk candy, and dog accessories. Its owners, Beth Sheperd and Sarah Hailes, are both under 30 years old.

Jeffrey New York is an 18,000-square-foot store that sells men's and women's apparel from such designers as Sander, Jean Paul Gaultier, and Gucci, as well as shoes, accessories, and home products. Jeffrey's founder, Jeffrey Kalinsky, is also under 30 years old. At an earlier point in his retail career, Kalinsky was a shoe buyer at Barney's.[1]

OVERVIEW

Information Resources, Inc. offers a full range of merchandising advice to its retail clients (www.infores.com/public/ret3.htm).

Developing and implementing a merchandise plan is a key phase in a retail strategy. To succeed, a firm must have the proper assortments of goods and services when they are in demand and sell them in a manner consistent with its overall strategy. **Merchandising** consists of the activities involved in acquiring particular goods and/or services and making them available at the places, times, and prices and in the quantity that enable a retailer to reach its goals.

For virtually all retailers, merchandising decisions dramatically affect performance: "Why do investments in merchandising skills and talent often produce better returns than investments in technology or other skill specialties? In retailing organizations, merchandis-

---

Please Note: Web site addresses are constantly changing.
The links in this chapter are current as of the publication of this book.

ers are in a critical role because they are responsible for bringing to market the products that will excite and please target consumers. Rarely is there a situation, as with retail merchandising, where so few individuals drive so many decisions and outcomes. A small fraction of the employee population controls as much as 70 to 80 percent of a firm's destiny. Retailers may be called on to place multimillion dollar bets—at times, even hundred million or billion dollar wagers."[2]

In this chapter, the *planning* aspects of merchandising are discussed. The *implementation* aspects of merchandising are laid out in Chapter 15. The *financial* aspects of merchandising are described in Chapter 16. Retail *pricing* is covered in Chapter 17.

MERCHANDISING PHILOSOPHY

A **merchandising philosophy** sets the guiding principles for all the merchandise decisions that a retailer makes. This philosophy must reflect the desires of the target market, the retailer's institutional type, its marketplace positioning, its defined value chain (both expected and augmented elements), supplier capabilities, costs, competitors, product trends, and a host of other factors. The retailer's merchandising philosophy drives every product decision, from what product lines to carry to the shelf space allotted to different products to inventory turnover to pricing—and much more.

The intricacies of a merchandising philosophy are borne out by these observations about just one aspect of merchandising—the assortment: "Retailers have to decide on the breadth of assortment across the store (narrow or wide) and the depth of the assortment within each category (deep or shallow). In addition, retailers have to select the quality of the items stocked within the assortment—high or low, national brands or store brands. Related to this, retailers need to decide on their pricing policies, across categories and within. Finally, retailers have to decide if assortments should generally be stable over time or whether there should be surprise, specials, or customization in their assortments."[3] See Figure 14.1.

At Cost Plus, "you never know what you'll find" (www.costplus.com).

Cost Plus, a 100-store chain, flourishes with its highly unusual, but effective, merchandising philosophy:

Baskets hang from the ceiling, rhythmic world music pulses, and ethnic exotica (such as a $120 tribal headdress from Indonesia) crowd the concrete floors. You can also find furniture, kitchenware, and nibbles from around the world—care for some Poky (chocolate-covered Japanese biscuit sticks)?—as well as a huge wine and beer section. While Crate & Barrel and Pottery Barn are doing pretty well in the housewares business, Cost Plus CEO Murray Dashe excels by sticking to his formula. Three-quarters of goods are home furnishings and collectibles. But it's the unlikely assortment of consumables—from private label salsa to Beringer wines—that generate repeat visits from customers, who spend an average of 50 minutes prowling the aisles. Some goods overlap with Pottery Barn, but many cost less. To differentiate itself, Cost Plus designs a lot of what it sells and revamps 60 percent of its products every year. "Traditional merchandise is the kiss of death for us," says Dashe.[4]

In forming its merchandising philosophy, a retailer must determine the scope of responsibility for its merchandise personnel. Are these personnel to be involved with the full array of *merchandising functions*, both buying and selling goods and services (including selection, pricing, display, and customer transactions)? Or are these personnel to focus on the *buying function*, with other people responsible for displays, personal selling, and so on? Many firms consider merchandising to be the foundation for their success, and buyers (or merchandise managers) engage in both buying and selling tasks. However, some retailers consider their buyers to be highly skilled specialists who should not be active in the selling function, which is done by other skilled specialists. For instance, store managers at full-line discount stores

Figure 14.1
Foot Locker: A Global Merchandising Philosophy

About a quarter of a century ago, Foot Locker pioneered the art of specialty athletic retailing by offering customers something that was then unheard of—the ability to select from hundreds of different athletic shoes under one roof. Foot Locker grew to become the largest athletic footwear and apparel retailer in the world—with more than 2,600 stores worldwide. The company continues to offer customers a huge selection of footwear for most sports including running, basketball, tennis, aerobics, fitness, track, baseball, football, soccer, and more, for both competition and casual wear. The stores carry an array of branded athletic footwear, apparel, and accessories from all major brands including Nike, Reebok, Adidas, Fila, Converse, New Balance, Asics, Champion, Starter, and others, as well as branded and private-label products made exclusively for Foot Locker. Each store reflects an inventory customized to fit its market, whether it's in Los Angeles, Rome, or Tokyo.
Reprinted by permission of Venator Group Retail, Inc.

often have great influence as to the way items are displayed, but have rather little influence as to whether to stock or promote particular brands.

The advantages of a merchandising-oriented philosophy are that there is a smooth chain of command; the buyer's expertise is used in selling, responsibility and authority are clear (a buyer does not blame sales personnel for poor sales efforts and vice versa), the buyer ensures that items are properly displayed, costs are reduced (fewer specialists), and the buyer is close to consumers through his or her selling involvement. The advantages of separating buying and selling are that similar skills are not needed for each task, the morale of store personnel goes up as they get more authority, selling is not viewed as a secondary task, salespeople are closer to customers than buyers, there can be specialists, and merchandisers may not be good supervisors due to the time away from the store and the differences in managing buying and selling personnel. An individual firm must evaluate which format is better for carrying out its own strategy.

To capitalize on merchandising opportunities, more retailers are now turning to micromerchandising and cross-merchandising. With **micromerchandising,** a retail firm adjusts its shelf-space allocations to respond to customer and other differences among local markets. Dominick's Finer Foods, a supermarket chain, allots shelf space to children's and adult's cereals on the basis of the demand patterns at its different stores; sales and inventory turnover have gone up accordingly. Wal-Mart adapts the space it allots to various product lines at its various stores to reflect the demographics, weather, and popularity of different customer recreational activities. Micromerchandising is easier to do these days because of the information generated through data warehouses.

In **cross-merchandising,** a retailer carries complementary goods and services so that shoppers are encouraged to buy more. That is why apparel stores also stock accessories. Cross-merchandising, like scrambled merchandising, can be ineffective if it is taken too far. Nonetheless, it has tremendous potential:

> "What beverages are sold in supermarkets is limited only by how far someone's imagination goes. As long as the economy is good and people will pay $1 or $2 a bottle, the possibilities are endless," says Ken Ferrera, president of James Ferrera & Sons. These comments echo widespread sentiments within the industry that the dynamics of the entire beverage category are changing, and that in the future, the category will be quite different than it is today in terms of new products, space allocations, and how and where products are marketed and merchandised in supermarkets. "Beverages are no longer just one store aisle. It's the water aisle, the soda aisle, what used to be the juice section, and the ethnic aisle. There's a lot of cross-merchandising and many candidates for multiple stocking, with spot coolers in stores and drinks all over the store," says Ferrera. In the future, beverages will play a larger role in meal solutions, enhancing the supermarkets' image as one-stop meal centers.[5]

BUYING ORGANIZATION FORMATS AND PROCESSES

A retail merchandising plan cannot be properly devised and implemented unless the buying organization and its processes are well defined—specifying who is responsible for merchandise decisions, the tasks of these people, the authority to make decisions, and the relationship of merchandising to overall retail operations. Figure 14.2 highlights the range of organization attributes from which retailers may choose.

Figure 14.2
The Attributes and Functions of Buying Organizations

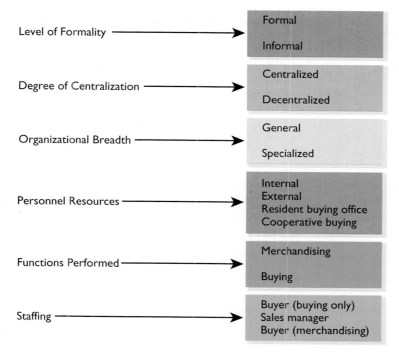

Level of Formality	→	Formal Informal
Degree of Centralization	→	Centralized Decentralized
Organizational Breadth	→	General Specialized
Personnel Resources	→	Internal External Resident buying office Cooperative buying
Functions Performed	→	Merchandising Buying
Staffing	→	Buyer (buying only) Sales manager Buyer (merchandising)

Level of Formality

With a **formal buying organization,** merchandising (buying) is a distinct retail task and a separate department is set up. The functions involved in acquiring merchandise and making it available for sale are then under the control of this department. A formal organization is most often used by larger firms and involves distinct personnel. In an **informal buying organization,** merchandising (buying) is not a distinct task. The same personnel handle both merchandising (buying) and other retail tasks; responsibility and authority are not always clear-cut. Informal organizations generally occur in smaller retailers.

The major advantages of a formal organization are the clarity of responsibilities and authority and the use of full-time, specialized merchandisers. The major disadvantage is the cost of having a separate department. Key advantages of an informal format are the low costs and flexibility. Key disadvantages are less-defined responsibilities and authority, and the de-emphasis on merchandise planning.

Both structures exist in great numbers. It is not crucial for a firm to use a formal department. It is crucial that the firm recognizes the role of merchandising (buying) and ensures that responsibility, activities, authority, and the interrelationship with operations are aptly defined and enacted.

Degree of Centralization

Multiunit retailers must choose whether to have a centralized buying organization or a decentralized one. In a **centralized buying organization,** all purchase decisions emanate from one office. For instance, a chain may have eight stores, with all merchandise decisions made at the headquarters store. In a **decentralized buying organization,** purchase decisions are made locally or regionally. Thus, a 12-store chain may allow each outlet to select its own merchandise or divide the branches into geographic territories (such as four branches per region) with regional decisions made by the headquarters store in each territory.

Careers in Retailing

Climbing Bloomingdale's Merchandising Career Ladder

Lori Swersky was always interested in fashion. So, when Bloomingdale's recruited her as an undergraduate at the University of Michigan, she accepted the offer and started working in 1997. Swersky is now senior assistant buyer in men's designer clothing. Her responsibilities include selecting the merchandise for all of the two dozen Bloomingdale's stores and ensuring that the proper merchandise gets to each location. "I am responsible for everything that happens to the merchandise until the customer buys it. I have to be in touch with the business day to day so I know what's moving." As part of her responsibilities, Swersky travels to various Bloomingdale's locations to see how the stores look and to meet employees.

Swersky feels that her current position gives her the opportunity to be creative and proactive. "You can use your creativity to grow and change the business. My job is exciting because it changes every day, and I'm able to experience it and learn so much." The job has also helped Swersky develop her organizational skills. "It's hard to develop that skill, at first, and during training I wasn't sure I'd be able to adapt so quickly to whatever is the priority of the moment. It's much easier for me to handle that now."

Source: "Sizing Up Bloomingdale's for Fashionable Jobs," *Careers in Retailing* (January 1999), p. 17.

Among the advantages of centralized buying are the integration of effort, strict controls, consistent image, proximity to top management, staff support, and discounts through volume purchases. Among the possible disadvantages are the inflexibility, time delays, poor morale at local stores, and excessive uniformity. Decentralized buying has these advantages: adaptability to local conditions, quick order processing, and improved morale because branches have autonomy. Potential disadvantages are disjointed planning, an inconsistent image, limited controls, little staff support, and a loss of volume discounts.

Many chains combine the benefits of both formats by deploying a centralized buying organization while also giving store managers the power to revise orders or place their own orders:

> Every retailer struggles with how to incorporate input from store personnel into merchandising decisions. Some firms use a local decision model, while others often have a centrally directed model. To improve local merchandising, consider a hybrid model, one that consolidates information in a central data warehouse, yet allows both headquarters decision makers and regional operations people to manipulate data to meet their own needs. Headquarters buying staff typically have the most vendor leverage, and thus can most effectively source most merchandise to meet consumer needs. But when individual stores have some purchasing flexibility, make sure that local purchases and inventories are visible in the data warehouse so results are known and actors are accountable. Local merchandising is primarily a function of better communications between local stores and corporate headquarters.[6]

Organizational Breadth

A choice must be made between a general buying organization and a specialized one. In a general organization, one or several people buy all of a firm's merchandise. Thus, the owner of a small hardware store may buy all the merchandise for his or her store. With a specialized organization, each buyer is responsible for a product category. For instance, a department store usually would have separate buyers for girls', juniors', and women's clothes.

The general approach is better if the retailer is small or there are few different goods/services involved. The specialized approach is better if the retailer is large or many goods/services are handled. Through specialization, knowledge is improved and responsibility well defined; however, costs are higher and extra personnel are normally required.

Personnel Resources

A retailer can choose an inside buying organization and/or an outside one. The **inside buying organization** is staffed by a retailer's own personnel, and merchandise decisions are made by permanent employees of the firm. See Figure 14.3. With an **outside buying organization,** a company or personnel external to the retailer are hired, usually on a fee basis. Although most retailers use either an inside or an outside buying organization, some employ a combination of the two.

An inside buying organization is most often utilized by large retailers and very small retailers. Large retailers do this to have greater control over merchandising decisions, as well as to be more distinctive. They have the financial clout to employ their own specialists. At very small retailers, such as bakeries and stationery stores, the owner or manager does all merchandising functions to save money and keep close to the market. Here are two examples of large retailers with inside buying organizations:

- Zellers (hbc.com/zellers/corporate) is a Canadian firm with more than 350 full-line discount department stores nationwide. All merchandising tasks are done internally. Its buyers are given the latitude to exercise their marketing and merchandising skills to

Figure 14.3

Michaels Stores' Inside Buying Organization

Michaels Stores is a growing chain of arts, crafts, and decorative products shops. Each of its outlets carries about 36,000 items that are selected by the firm's full-time buyers. Michaels has a corporate merchandising group to choose products from and negotiate purchase terms with about 1,000 vendors. Merchandising personnel often travel to meet with vendors. Shown here is a buying trip to the Orient.
Reprinted by permission.

"identify the mix of product assortments to maintain leadership in their categories and meet the needs of the customers." There are 14 buying departments, including shoes, electronics, housewares, ladies' wear, fashion accessories, men's wear, home décor, and children's wear.

Ross Stores has merchandising career opportunities in New York and Los Angeles. Scroll down to "Buying Office" and click on a job category (www.rossstores.com/jo_jb.jsp).

- At Ross Stores (www.rossstores.com), the off-price apparel chain with stores in 17 states, "Our commitment to the buying function is key to the company's competitive position. As a team, we provide name brand merchandise at a good price through strong negotiations and vendor relationships. As market specialists for a multistate retailer, we employ an entrepreneurial buying strategy reflecting regional preferences and trends. Career opportunities often exist in these positions: merchandise managers, buyers, assistant buyers, and merchandise control analysts/planning analysts."

An outside organization is most frequently used by small or medium-sized retailers or those far from their sources of supply. In these cases, it is more efficient for the retailers to hire outside buyers than to use company personnel. An outside organization has clout in dealing with suppliers (because of purchase volume), usually services noncompeting retailers, offers marketing research expertise, and sometimes sponsors private-label goods. Outside buying organizations may be paid by retailers that subscribe to their services or by vendors that give commissions. Sometimes, an individual retailer decides to set up its own internal organization if it feels its outside group is dealing with direct competitors or the firm finds it can buy items more efficiently on its own. The two leading outside buying organizations are the Doneger Group and Frederick Atkins:

Learn more "About Doneger" (www.doneger.com/index_guest.asp), the world's largest outside buying organization.

- The Doneger Group (www.doneger.com) is "the largest, most dynamic independent resident buying office and fashion merchandising consulting firm in the industry. We advise over 700 retailers on merchandising concepts and specific trends and offer sourcing capabilities and a breadth of opportunities. Our retailers have over 7,000 locations throughout the world and generate combined annual sales of over $2.5 billion dollars. Through our daily involvement in all market categories of women's, men's, and children's apparel, accessories, and home furnishings, our merchandising and market research specialists are able to offer clients a broad range of services to help them make the right decisions and meet the ever-changing challenges of the fashion and retail business. It is our goal to help retailers generate greater sales, increase profits, and gain market share."

- Frederick Atkins, on the other hand, is owned by its more than 100 retail members. Until recently, the company provided buying, distribution, and marketing programs, and designed and produced several private-label clothing lines. But today, Atkins is "shifting totally into product development and no longer advises stores about which vendors might provide them with the most appropriate merchandise." It provides products with landed costs exceeding $150 million annually.[7]

Associated Merchandising Corporation (AMC) is a hybrid buying organization. For more than 70 years, it was a nonprofit organization co-owned by numerous retailers. It was then acquired in 1998 by Target Corporation, primarily to service the firm's Target Stores, Mervyn's, Marshall Field's, Dayton's, and Hudson's chains. Yet, it still provides global merchandising functions for several other retailers, as well. AMC employs 1,200 people who are involved with international trend identification, product design and development, global sourcing of products, quality assurance, and production, delivery, and order tracking. Products sourced include apparel, accessories, and home goods.

A **resident buying office,** which can be an inside or outside organization, is used when a retailer wants to keep in close touch with key market trends and cannot do so through just its headquarters buying staff. Such offices are usually situated in important merchandise centers (sources of supply) and provide valuable data and contacts. There are a few major resident buying offices in the United States, serving several thousand retailers. Each organization just cited (Zellers, Ross, Doneger, Frederick Atkins, and AMC) has multiple resident buying offices to get a better sense of local markets and merchandise sources.

Why should a retailer hire a resident buying office? (www. minskybuying.com/ reasons.html)

Besides the major players, there are many smaller outside resident buying offices that can assist retailers, as exemplified by Denise Minsky Buying Group (www.minskybuying.com):

We provide a broad spectrum of services predicated on experience, performance, professionalism, and personal service. I have had 20 years of corporate buying experience with national retail chains including Marshall's and T.J. Maxx. Ten years ago, I opened my own office in the heart of the garment center catering to operations from single stores to multistore chains. We offer working relationships with over 2,000 sources in the budget and moderate markets. We constantly seek value buys for our regular and off-price accounts in every classification and category. Our goal is to help you save existing costs, relieve some of the burden that you endure, and increase your profit.

The Chain Drug Marketing Association (www.chaindrug.com) provides many services for its members.

Independent retailers and small chains are involved with cooperative buying to a greater degree than before to compete with large chains. In **cooperative buying,** a group of retailers gets together to make quantity purchases from suppliers.[8] Volume discounts are then achieved. It is most popular among food, hardware, and drugstore retailers. For example, the Chain Drug Marketing Association acts as a cooperative for 110 small chains. Sometimes, retailers initiate cooperatives; other times, a wholesaler or manufacturer may form a cooperative as a way to cut costs. The National Retail Federation's Group Buying Service (www.nrf.com/services/group) enables small and medium-sized retailers to "pool their purchasing power" for packaging, delivery, and similar goods and services that aid in everyday merchandising operations. It is not yet involved with actual merchandise buying.

Functions Performed

When forming its merchandising philosophy, a retailer outlines the roles of merchandise and in-store personnel. At this juncture, the responsibilities and functions of both areas are assigned. To reiterate, if a retailer takes a "merchandising" view, its merchandise personnel oversee all buying and selling functions, including assortments, advertising, pricing, point-of-sale displays, the deployment of personnel, and personal selling approaches. If a retailer takes a "buying" view, its merchandise personnel oversee the buying of products, advertising, and pricing, while in-store personnel oversee assortments, displays, personnel deployment, and sales presentations. Functions must also reflect the level of formality, the degree of centralization, and personnel resources, as enumerated in setting up the buying organization.

Staffing

The last organizational decision centers on staffing. What positions must be filled, and what qualifications should be required? Firms with a merchandising vantage point are most concerned with hiring good buyers. Firms that take a buying perspective are interested in hiring both buyers and sales managers.

Many large firms hire college graduates whom they place in training programs and promote internally to positions as buyers and sales managers. A buyer must be attuned to the marketplace, must be assertive in bargaining with suppliers, must use buying plans (detailed shopping lists that completely outline purchases) extensively, and may have to travel to major marketplaces. A sales manager must be a good organizer, supervisor, and motivator. A merchandising buyer must possess the attributes of each. Today, more retailers than ever feel the critical qualification for good merchandisers is their ability to relate to customers and methodically anticipate future needs. In addition, to some extent, buyers are involved with each of the remaining activities described in this chapter and many of those detailed in Chapter 15.

Federated Department Stores (www.retailology.com/career/career_paths.asp) has exciting career paths in both merchandising and operations.

Federated Department Stores, which operates several leading department store chains, including Bloomingale's and Macy's, has career tracks that recognize the value of both merchandising and in-store personnel. Here are selected positions in two distinct career tracks (www.retailology.com/career):

Merchandising

- Assistant Buyer—Aids buyer in selecting and procuring merchandise, which supports overall sales volume, gross margin, and turnover objectives. Provides operational support to buyers. Assumes buying responsibility of key classification, once buyer determines proficiency level.
- Associate Buyer—Responsible for merchandise development, marketing, and financial management of a particular area of business. This is a developmental step for a buyer position.
- Buyer—Expected to maximize sales and profitability of a given area of business through the development and implementation of a strategy, analysis, and appropriate reaction to sales trends. Overall support of the company sales, gross margin, and turnover objectives.
- Divisional Merchandise Manager—Responsible for overseeing the execution of merchandise selection and procurement for a particular segment of business. Sets the merchandise direction to ensure a focused continuity on the selling floor within the family of business. Develops strategy to ensure customer satisfaction and maximize performance and profits, maximize promotional strategy, competitively dominant assortments, and store-by-store profit maximization.

Store Management

- Assistant Sales Manager—Responsible for supervising all daily store activities in a specific merchandise area. Includes selling and service management, selecting and developing associates, merchandising, and business management.
- Sales Manager—In charge of all daily store activities in a specific merchandise area. Includes merchandise presentation, employee development, customer service, operations, and inventory control.
- Assistant Store Manager—Directs all activities related to merchandise flow, store maintenance, expense management, shortage prevention, and store sales support functions

for a significant portion of the total store's volume. Assumes Store Manager responsibilities in his or her absence.

- Store Manager—Senior-level executive responsible for all aspects of running a profitable store. Sets the tone and leads the store's culture/environment to ensure success in customer service, profits, operations, people development, merchandise presentation, and merchandise assortment.

DEVISING MERCHANDISE PLANS

Clothestime (www.clothestime.com) is always looking to stay current with its youthful customers.

There are several factors to consider in devising merchandise plans: forecasts, innovativeness, assortment, brands, timing, and allocation. See Figure 14.4.

Forecasts

Forecasts are projections of expected retail sales for given periods. Because retailers' purchases are based on their sales expectations, forecasts are the foundation of merchandise plans. They include these components: overall company projections, product category projections, item-by-item projections, and store-by-store projections (if a chain). Consider the case of Clothestime, a 300-store apparel chain:

> The planning process starts when the top merchandise planners sit down with financial planners. The group brainstorms—trying to figure out months in advance how the retailer can profit from fashion trends that could fade away before the upcoming season gets under way. "We start by meeting with the finance staff to come up with a corporate goal," says Sandie Sorenson, director of planning and allocation. "Then we sit down with the buyer and his or her merchandise planner to talk about where they see their mix going." The buyer and the merchandise planner formulate an SKU-level plan, which is then reviewed and reworked to make sure it's in sync with the financial goals the company has outlined for the upcoming season. "This takes about six weeks from beginning to end. We could do that faster, but we want all the people involved to really think through their plan."[9]

Figure 14.4
Considerations in Devising Merchandise Plans

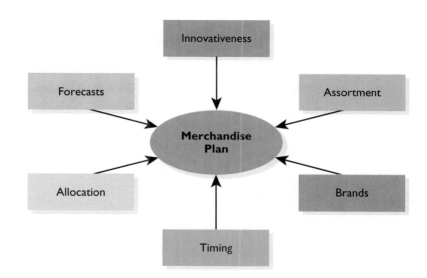

In this section, forecasting is examined from a general planning perspective. In Chapter 16, the financial dimensions of forecasting are reviewed.

When preparing forecasts, it is essential to distinguish among different types of merchandise. **Staple merchandise** consists of the regular products carried by a retailer. For a supermarket, staples are products such as milk, bread, canned soup, and facial tissues. For a department store, staples are products such as luggage, cameras, glassware, and housewares. Because these items have relatively stable sales (sometimes seasonal) and their nature may not change much over time, a retailer can clearly outline the quantities for these items. A **basic stock list** specifies the inventory level, color, brand, style category, size, package, and so on for every staple item carried by the retailer.

Assortment merchandise consists of apparel, furniture, autos, and other products for which the retailer must carry a variety of products in order to give customers a proper selection. This merchandise is harder to forecast than staples due to demand variations, style changes, and the number of sizes and colors to be carried. Decisions are two-pronged: (1) Product lines, styles, designs, and colors must be projected. (2) A **model stock plan** is used to project specific items, such as the number of green, red, and blue pullover sweaters of a certain design by size. With a model stock plan, many items of popular sizes and colors are ordered; and small amounts of less popular sizes and colors are ordered to fill out the assortment. A specialty store may stock one size 18 dress and six size 10 dresses for each style carried.

Fashion merchandise consists of products that may have cyclical sales due to changing tastes and life-styles. Sales of products such as bow ties or miniskirts are often high for a number of years, become unpopular for a while, and then become popular again. For these items, forecasting can be hard. **Seasonal merchandise** consists of products that sell well over nonconsecutive time periods. Items such as ski equipment and air-conditioner servicing have excellent sales during one season per year. Since the strongest sales of seasonal items usually occur at the same time each year, forecasting is straightforward.

Retailing Around the World

In South Africa, It's Cool to Be Imported

Unlike in the United States or Europe, where retailers often do not like to promote that a garment is made from imported fabric, this is a major selling point in South Africa. For example, the boutique Sprita clearly labels its store brands as being made from "100 percent imported fabric." Another boutique also labels its store brands as being made from all-imported fabric, even though the garments are sewn in South Africa to reduce labor costs.

Most apparel in South Africa is casual. Among the major jeans brands sold there, Levi's is the priciest (about $50), while Lee sells for about $28. Store brands sell at around $17 and are sold in very large volume. Woolworth's, a division of the British retailer Marks & Spencer (and no connection to the former U.S. variety store chain), sells only private labels and has a 10 percent market share of the jeans market.

According to the managing director of Levi Strauss South Africa, "The market there has been tough because of the fluctuating rand [the unit of currency]. There are a lot of opportunities in South Africa for American brands, but consumers are discerning. Perceptions of South Africa usually have no relation to reality. There is a sophisticated first world and a disenfranchised fourth or fifth world."

Develop a merchandise plan for jeans for a South African retailer that targets the mass market.

Source: Joyce Barrett, "South Africa Plays Catch-Up—Johannesburg Slowly Builds Its Retail with an International Flavor," *Women's Wear Daily* (January 19, 1999), p. 10.

With **fad merchandise,** a high level of sales is generated for a short time. Often, toys and games are short-lived fads, such as the *Toy Story 2* products that flew off store shelves in 1999 and 2000. The retailer must be careful not to be overly optimistic or pessimistic about fads. The difficulty in forecasting fads is determining whether such products will actually be hits and for how long. Sometimes, fads turn into extended fads, whereby residual sales continue for a longer period at a fraction of earlier sales. Cabbage Patch Kids dolls and Trivial Pursuit board games are in the extended fad category.

In forecasting for best-sellers (which may be staples, fad items, etc.), many retailers use a **never-out list** to determine the amount of merchandise to purchase for resale. The goal is to purchase enough of these products so they are always in stock. Products are added to and deleted from a never-out list as their popularity and importance to the retailer change. Before a new Danielle Steele novel is released, stores order large quantities to be sure they can meet anticipated demand. After it disappears from newspaper best-seller lists, smaller quantities are kept. For virtually all types of retailers, it is a good strategy to use a combination of a basic stock list, a model stock plan, and a never-out list. These lists may overlap.

Innovativeness

A retailer's determination of the innovativeness of its merchandise plan involves a number of factors: target market(s), goods/service growth potential, fashion trends and theories (if applicable), the retailer's image, competition, customer segments, responsiveness to consumers, investment costs, profitability, risk, constrained decision making, and declining goods/services. See Table 14.1.

Table 14.1 Factors to Bear in Mind When Planning Merchandise Inovativeness

Factor	Relevance for Planning
Target market(s)	Evaluate whether the target market is conservative or progressive.
Goods/service growth potential	Consider each new offering on the basis of rapidity of initial sales, maximum sales potential per time period, and length of sales life.
Fashion trends and theories	Understand the "trickle-down" and "trickle-across" theories, if selling fashion merchandise.
Retailer image	The kinds of goods/services a retailer carries are influenced by its image. The level of innovativeness should be consistent with this image.
Competition	Lead or follow competition in the selection of new goods/services.
Customer segments	Customers can be segmented by dividing merchandise into established-product displays and new-product displays.
Responsiveness to consumers	New offerings should be carried when requested by the target market.
Amount of investment	These types of investment are possible for each new good/service: product costs, new fixtures, and additional personnel (or further training for existing personnel).
Profitability	Each new offering should be assessed for potential profits (for the particular item, as well as the overall profits of the retailer).
Risk	The major risks involve the possible tarnishing of the retailer's image, investment costs, and opportunity costs.
Constrained decision making	Franchise and chain operators may be restricted in the new goods/services they can purchase.
Dropping declining goods/ services	Older goods/services should be deleted if sales and/or profits are too low.

An innovative firm, one that carries new goods and services and plans for upcoming trends, faces a great opportunity—distinctiveness (by being first in the market)—and a great risk—possibly misreading customers and being stuck with large inventories. By assessing each factor in Table 14.1 and preparing a detailed plan for merchandising new goods and services, a firm should capitalize on its opportunities and reduce its risks.[10] As illustrated in Figure 14.5, Wendy's takes innovativeness quite seriously.

One of today's most innovative retailers was founded in 1848. Hammacher Schlemmer (www.hammacher-schlemmer.com) offers an eclectic mix of housewares, personal care products, home and office products, apparel, sports and leisure goods, and gift items. It has stores in New York, Los Angeles, and Chicago, as well as catalogs and a Web site: "To our customers, Hammacher Schlemmer means shopping from one of the most unique and innovative collections of products available anywhere in the world. It is our mission to enhance our customers' lives by bringing them unique products that either solve problems or further their life-style, and eliminate their need to comparison shop by providing them with, not only the best products in the marketplace, but the information showing why these products are truly the best." The firm carries such items as a $4,000 standup snowmobile, an $800 Nordic drying closet, a $21,000 authentic German organ grinder, and a $250 Black Forest cuckoo clock.

Retailers should assess the growth potential for each new good or service they carry. Three issues are of particular interest: How fast will a new good or service generate sales? What are the most sales (dollars and units) to be achieved in a season or a year? Over what period will a good or service continue to sell?

A useful tool for assessing growth potential is the **product life cycle,** which shows the expected behavior of a good or service over its life. The traditional cycle has four stages: introduction, growth, maturity, and decline—as depicted and described in Figure 14.6.

During introduction, the retailer should anticipate a more limited target market, with higher-income, more innovative consumers. The good or service will probably be supplied in one basic version, not a choice of alternatives. The manufacturer (supplier) may limit distribution to "finer" stores. Yet, new convenience items such as food and housewares products are normally mass distributed. Items initially distributed selectively tend to have a high-end price strategy. Mass distributed products typically involve low-end pricing to fos-

Check out Hammacher Schlemmer's list of current "Top Picks" (www.hammacher schlemmer.com/ toppicks).

Figure 14.5
R&D at Wendy's

Wendy's Research & Development Department is dedicated to continually improving products by refining cooking and serving procedures and ingredients. R&D regularly comes up with new products for testing and possible addition to the menu.
Reprinted by permission.

Figure 14.6
The Traditional
Product Life Cycle

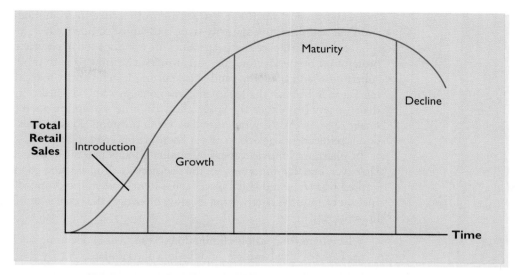

Strategy Variable	Life Cycle Stage			
	Introduction	Growth	Maturity	Decline
Target market	High-income innovators	Middle-income adopters	Mass market	Low-income and laggards
Good or service	One basic offering	Some variety	Greater variety	Less variety
Distribution intensity	Limited or extensive	More retailers	More retailers	Fewer retailers
Price	Penetration or skimming	Wide range	Lower prices	Lower prices
Promotion	Informative	Persuasive	Competitive	Limited
Supplier structure	Monopoly-oligopoly	Oligopoly-competition	Competition	Oligopoly

ter faster consumer acceptance. In either case, early promotion must be explanatory, geared to informing consumers. At this stage, there is only one or very few possible suppliers.

As innovative consumers buy a new good or service and recommend it to their friends, sales increase rapidly and the cycle enters the growth stage. The target market expands to include middle-income consumers who are somewhat more innovative than the average. Width and depth of assortment expand. The number of retailers carrying the product increases. Price discounting is not widely used, but a variety of retailers offer a large range of prices, customer services, and quality. Promotion is more persuasive and aimed at acquainting shoppers with availability and services. The number of suppliers increases.

In maturity, sales reach the maximum level and the largest portion of the target market is reached. Lower-, middle-, and upper-income shoppers select from very broad product offerings. All types of retailers (discount to upscale) carry the good or service in some form. Prestige retailers continue stressing brand names and customer services, but others enter into active price competition. Price is more often cited in promotional activities. For retailers and their suppliers, the maturity stage is the most competitive.

According to the traditional product life cycle, a good or service then enters decline, often brought on by two factors: the target market shrinks (due to product obsolescence, newer substitutes, and boredom) and price cutting lessens profit margins. In decline, the target market may become the lowest-income consumer and laggards. Some retailers cut back on their variety (to reduce the space allotted); others drop the good or service for profit and image reasons. At the retailers still carrying the items, lower prices are offered, and promotion is reduced and geared to price. There are fewer suppliers.

In planning innovativeness, a retailer's focus is too often on new-product additions. However, equally important are the decisions to drop existing goods or services. Because of limited resources and shelf space, some items have to be dropped when others are added. Instead of intuitively removing existing offerings, the retailer should use structured guidelines:

- Select items for possible elimination on the basis of declining sales, prices, and profits; the appearance of substitutes; and the loss of usefulness.
- Gather and analyze detailed financial and other data about these items.
- Consider nondeletion strategies such as cutting costs, revising promotion efforts, adjusting prices, and cooperating with other retailers.
- After a deletion decision is made, do not overlook timing, parts and servicing, inventory, and holdover demand.

Sometimes, a seemingly obsolete good or service can be revived. An innovative retailer will recognize potential in this area and merchandise accordingly. For example, direct marketers often use TV commercials to sell cassettes and compact discs featuring the music of artists who were previously successful. They also heavily promote "greatest hits" recordings featuring combinations of artists.

Apparel retailers must be familiar with fashion trends, which may be divided into vertical and horizontal categories; fashions may go through one or a combination of the two. A vertical trend occurs when a fashion is first accepted by an upscale market segment and undergoes changes in its basic form before it is sold to the general public. The fashion passes through three stages: distinctive—original designs, designer dress shops, custom-made, worn by upscale consumers; emulation—modification of original designs, finer stores, alterations, worn by the middle class; and economic emulation—simple copies of originals, discount and bargain stores, mass produced, mass marketed.

In recent years, horizontal fashion trends have grown in importance. A horizontal trend occurs when a new fashion is accepted by a broad spectrum of people on its introduction, while retaining its basic form. Within any social class, there are innovative customers who act as opinion leaders. New fashions must be accepted by these leaders, who then convince other members of the same social class (who are more conservative) to buy the items. Fashion is sold across the class and not from one class down to another.

By understanding both theories and learning which is more appropriate for its positioning niche in the marketplace, a retailer can better predict fashion successes and the types of customers who will buy from it. Figure 14.7 contains a checklist for predicting fashion adoption.

Assortment

An **assortment** is the selection of merchandise a retailer carries. It includes both the breadth of product categories and the variety within each category.[11]

A firm must first choose its quality of merchandise. Should it carry top-line, expensive items and sell to upper-income customers? Or should it carry middle-of-the-line, moderately priced items and cater to middle-income customers? Or should it carry bottom-line,

Figure 14.7
A Checklist for
Predicting Fashion
Adoption

		Yes	No
1.	Does the fashion satisfy a consumer need?	__	__
2.	Is the fashion compatible with emerging consumer life-styles?	__	__
3.	Is the fashion oriented toward the mass market? Toward a market segment?	__ __	__ __
4.	Is the fashion radically new?	__	__
5.	Are the reputations of the designer(s) and the retailers carrying the fashion good?	__	__
6.	Are several designers marketing some version of the fashion?	__	__
7.	Is the price range for the fashion appropriate for the target market?	__	__
8.	Will extensive advertising be used?	__	__
9.	Will the fashion change over time?	__	__
10.	Will consumers view the fashion as a long-term trend?	__	__

inexpensive items and attract lower-income customers? Or should it try to draw more than one market segment by offering a variety in quality, such as middle- and top-line items for middle- and upper-income shoppers? The firm must also decide whether to carry promotional products (low-priced closeout items or special buys used to generate store traffic).

Several factors must be reviewed in choosing merchandise quality: desired target market(s), competition, image, store location, stock turnover, profit margins, manufacturer versus private brands, customer services, personnel, perceived product benefits, and constrained decisions. See Table 14.2.

For example, Dollar General (the variety store chain) has an overall merchandising strategy that is very consistent with its approach to merchandise quality:

> Dollar General is a discount retailer of general merchandise at everyday low prices. Through nearly 4,000 conveniently located stores, it offers a focused assortment of consumable basic merchandise including health and beauty aids, packaged food products, cleaning supplies, housewares, stationery, seasonal goods, basic apparel, and domestics. Stores serve primarily low-, middle-, and fixed-income families. The average customer transaction is approximately $8. The company encourages customers to shop Dollar General for their everyday household needs, leading to frequent customer visits.[12]

Dollar General is so successful that its annual sales exceed $3.5 billion.

After a retailer decides on the product quality to carry consistent with its merchandising philosophy, it determines the width and depth of assortment. **Width of assortment** refers to the number of distinct goods/service categories (product lines) with which a retailer is involved. **Depth of assortment** refers to the variety in any one goods/service category (product line) with which a retailer is involved. As noted in Chapter 5, an assortment can range from wide and deep (a department store) to narrow and shallow (a box store). Selected advantages and disadvantages of each assortment strategy are shown in Table 14.3.

Table 14.2 Factors to Take into Account When Planning Merchandise Quality

Factor	Relevance for Planning
Target market(s)	Merchandise quality must be matched to the wishes of the desired target market(s).
Competition	A retailer can sell similar quality (follow the competition) or different quality (to appeal to a different target market).
Retailer's image	Merchandise quality must be directly related to the perception that customers have of the retailer.
Store location	The location affects the retailer's image and the number of competitors, which, in turn, relate to quality.
Stock turnover	High quality and high prices usually yield a lower turnover than low quality and low prices.
Profitability	High-quality merchandise generally brings greater profit per unit than low-quality merchandise; however, turnover may cause total profits to be greater for low-quality merchandise.
Manufacturer versus private brands	For many consumers, manufacturer (national) brands connote higher quality than private (dealer) brands.
Customer services offered	High-quality merchandise requires personal selling, alterations, delivery, and so on. Low-quality merchandise may not.
Personnel	Skilled, knowledgeable personnel are necessary for high-quality merchandise. Limited personnel (self-service) are needed for low-quality merchandise.
Perceived goods/ service benefits	Low-quality merchandise attracts customers who desire functional product benefits (e.g., warmth, comfort). High-quality merchandise attracts customers who desire extended product benefits (e.g., status, services, style).
Constrained decision making	a. Franchisees or chain store managers have limited or no control over product quality. They either buy directly from the franchisor or must abide by company quality standards.
	b. Independent retailers who buy from a few large wholesalers will be limited to the range of quality offered by those wholesalers.

Assortment strategies vary widely. For example, KFC's thousands of worldwide outlets emphasize chicken and related quick-service products. They do not sell hamburgers, pizza, or other popular fast-food items; these do not fit with KFC's merchandising approach. As a single-focus Web retailer, eToys concentrates strictly on family-oriented toys. On the other hand, Wal-Mart's huge supercenters feature thousands of general merchandise and food items, and Amazon.com is a Web-based department store that offers 18 million items for sale. This is the dilemma that retailers face in determining how big an assortment to carry:

"Why settle for conventional furniture stores selling conventional furniture?" (www.choiceseating. com)

A common strategy has been to compete by offering a wide variety of items within a category, designed to appeal to every consumer taste. Large assortment strategies can backfire, however, if the complexity causes information overload such that a customer feels overwhelmed and dissatisfied, or chooses not to make a choice at all. For example, Choice Seating, a sofa shop, makes this offer: "Choose from 5,000 fabrics, 300 superior leathers, 500 different frames." The problem is that each customer ultimately only wants one sofa. Accordingly, the huge number of potential options (2.5 million different fabric sofas; 150,000 leather sofas) may be confusing and overwhelming rather than beneficial. Research shows that dissatisfaction with the shopping process is attributed largely to the retailer, which can ultimately impact store traffic and the percentage of customers who purchase. The key to customer satisfaction with the entire shopping interaction is to ensure that the customer is equipped to handle the variety.

Table 14.3 Retail Assortment Strategies

Advantages	Disadvantages
Wide and Deep (many goods/service categories and a large assortment in each category)	
Broad market	High inventory investment
Full selection of items	General image
High level of customer traffic	Many items with low turnover
Customer loyalty	Some obsolete merchandise
One-stop shopping	
No disappointed customers	
Wide and Shallow (many goods/service categories and a limited assortment in each category)	
Broad market	Low variety within product lines
High level of customer traffic	Some disappointed customers
Emphasis on convenience customers	Weak image
Less costly than wide and deep	Many items with low turnover
One-stop shopping	Reduced customer loyalty
Narrow and Deep (few goods/service categories and a large assortment in each category)	
Specialist image	Too much emphasis on one category
Good customer choice in category(ies)	No one-stop shopping
Specialized personnel	More susceptible to trends/cycles
Customer loyalty	Greater effort needed to enlarge the size of the trading area
No disappointed customers	Little (no) scrambled merchandising
Less costly than wide and deep	
Narrow and Shallow (few goods/service categories and a limited assortment in each category)	
Aimed at convenience customers	Little width and depth
Least costly	No one-stop shopping
High turnover of items	Some disappointed customers
	Weak image
	Limited customer loyalty
	Small trading area
	Little (no) scrambled merchandising

To do so, we propose that retailers which offer a large variety in each category ask non-expert consumers to explicitly indicate attribute preferences as a way to help them sort through the variety and figure out which option best fits their needs. Accordingly, category killers such as Circuit City may see fit to provide more information and sales support than general merchandise retailers who carry smaller assortments in any category.[13]

Retailers should take several factors into account in planning their width and depth of assortment. The impact on sales and profit should be evaluated. If variety is increased, will overall sales go up? Will overall profits? Carrying 10 varieties of cat food will not necessarily yield greater sales or profits than stocking 4 varieties. Thus, the retailer must look at the investment costs that occur with a large variety.

Space requirements must be examined. How much space is required for each good or service category? How much space is available? Because selling space is limited, it should be allocated to those goods and services generating the greatest customer traffic and sales. The inventory turnover rate should also be considered in assigning shelf space. See Figure 14.8.

Figure 14.8
Assortment Planning
at Walgreens

In many product cate-
gories, Walgreens drug-
stores carry a deep
assortment. The chain
annually sells 100 million
Hallmark greeting cards.
Reprinted by permission of
Walgreen Company.

In planning, a distinction should be made among scrambled merchandising, complementary goods and services, and substitute goods and services. With scrambled merchandising,
a retailer adds unrelated items to generate more customer traffic and lift profit margins (such
as a florist carrying umbrellas). Handling complementary goods/services lets the retailer sell
basic items and related offerings (such as a stereo and CDs, a lawn service and tree spraying)
through cross-merchandising. While scrambled merchandising and cross-merchandising
are both intended to increase the retailer's overall sales, carrying too many substitute
goods/services (such as competing brands of toothpaste) may simply shift sales from one
brand to another and have little impact on a retailer's overall sales. For some firms, the proliferation of substitute products has created a difficult problem: how to offer consumers an
adequate choice without tying up too much investment and floor space in one product category.

These factors are also important if a retailer moves toward a wider, deeper merchandising
strategy:

- Risks, merchandise investments, damages, and obsolescence may increase dramatically.
- Personnel may be spread too thinly, sometimes over dissimilar goods and services.
- Both the positive and negative ramifications of scrambled merchandising may occur.
- Inventory control may be more difficult; and overall merchandise turnover probably will
  slow down.

A retailer may sometimes have no choice about stocking a full assortment within a product line. A powerful supplier may insist that the retailer carry its entire line or else it will not
distribute through that retailer at all. But large retailers—and smaller ones that belong to
cooperative buying groups—are now standing up to suppliers; and many retailers stock their
own brands next to manufacturers'. As retail chains and buying groups have gotten bigger,
this has occurred more frequently.

Brands

As part of its assortment planning, a retailer must choose the proper mix of manufacturer,
private, and generic brands to carry—a challenge that is becoming more complex with the
proliferation of brands in each grouping. **Manufacturer (national) brands** are produced

and controlled by manufacturers. They are usually well known, supported by manufacturer ads, somewhat pre-sold to consumers, require limited retailer investment in marketing, and often represent maximum product quality to consumers. Such brands dominate sales in many product categories. Among the most popular manufacturer brands are Barbie, Liz Claiborne, Coke, Gillette, Kodak, Levi's, Microsoft, Nike, Pampers, and Sony. The retailers most likely to feature manufacturer brands are small firms, Web firms, discounters, and others wanting the credibility that carrying well-known brands confers on them or having strategies geared to low pricing (whereby consumers compare the prices of different retailers on name-brand items).

Although they face extensive competition from private bands, manufacturer brands remain the dominant type of brand, accounting for 85 percent of all retail sales worldwide. As Tropicana's CEO says, "What would a supermarket without national brands look like? I can describe it in one lonely word—empty. It's hard to imagine a store without national brands. No Pepsi-Cola, Cheerios, Fritos, or Tide. No Colgate, Oreos, Tylenol, or Hellmann's. No Hershey bars, Campbell's soup, Heinz ketchup, Quaker oatmeal, or (forgive my own loyalty) Tropicana orange juice. The list goes on. Where are this imaginary store's shoppers? Try down the street at a supermarket where the aisles are lined with national brands."[14]

Private (dealer) brands, also known as **store brands,** contain names designated by wholesalers or retailers, are more profitable to retailers, are better controlled by retailers, are not sold by competing retailers, are less expensive for consumers, and lead to customer loyalty to retailers (rather than to manufacturers). Yet, with most private-label products, retailers must line up suppliers, arrange for physical distribution and warehousing, sponsor ads, create in-store displays, and absorb losses from unsold items. Retailers' growing interest in their own brands' sales is evident from the following:

Is That Tommy Hilfiger in Wal-Mart?

According to Judge John E. Sprizzo, Wal-Mart never told the buyers or the store managers about his November 1996 injunction forbidding the retailer from knowingly selling counterfeit Tommy Hilfiger clothes or infringing on any Hilfiger trademarks. As a result, in 1998, Judge Sprizzo found Wal-Mart in civil contempt of court.

During 1998, Hilfiger executives became aware that fake Tommy Hilfiger apparel was being sold again by Wal-Mart. As recorded in their pre-trial depositions, buyers at Wal-Mart's headquarters stated that they had purchased diverted Tommy Hilfiger apparel from brokers. Wal-Mart's buyers acknowledged that they did not ask the source of the merchandise.

Although Hilfiger does not sell its apparel to Wal-Mart because of the chain's image, Hilfiger cannot legally bar Wal-Mart from selling its genuine goods if they are obtained from distributors. Thus, to obtain Tommy Hilfiger apparel, some of Wal-Mart's sources were diverters who had bought the apparel from multiple sources (such as bankrupt retailers, retailers that overpurchased the brand and wanted to sell off the excess, and retailers seeking to dispose of leftover and discontinued merchandise). These middlemen typically purchase apparel from unauthorized channels; thus, some of their goods can be counterfeit.

Should Wal-Mart continue to sell Tommy Hilfiger apparel when it has so much difficulty assuring the designer that the apparel is genuine? Explain your answer.

Source: Emily Nelson, "Why Tommy Hilfiger Just Can't Seem to Stay Out of Local Wal-Mart," *Wall Street Journal* (January 28, 1999), pp. A1, A8.

- Private brands are typically priced 20 to 30 percent lower than manufacturer brands. This benefits consumers, as well as retailers (costs are lower and revenues are shared by fewer parties). Retailer profits are higher from private brands than manufacturer brands, despite the lower prices.
- According to a survey of U.S. adults, 9 out of 10 shoppers are aware of private brands, 8 out of 10 buy them regularly, and 6 out of 10 say price has a major impact on the purchase of private brands.[15]
- In the United States and Canada, private brands account for 20 percent of sales. In Northern Europe, the figure is 24 percent (with private brands in Switzerland at 54 percent of sales). Private brands account for only 1.4 percent of sales in Eastern Europe and under 1 percent in Brazil and Argentina.[16]
- For retailers such as Old Navy, The Limited, and McDonald's, private brands represent most or all of company revenues. This is also true for Europe's Decathlon, which is featured in Figure 14.9.
- At virtually all large retailers, both private brands and manufacturer brands are strong. In fact, Sears' Kenmore appliances—the market-leading brand—outsell GE, Whirlpool, Maytag, and KitchenAid. J.C. Penney, which already generates $8 billion in annual private-brand sales, has set a goal of private brands' accounting for 50 percent of company revenues (up from the current 27 percent). Penney has about 35 private brands, such as Stafford and Hunt Club. Even Amazon.com is now selling private brands along with its millions of manufacturer-branded items.[17] How many retailers and brands in Table 14.4 can you match? Take our private-brand test.
- In the past, private brands were exclusively discount versions of mid-tier products. Yet, today, a new form of branding has emerged—the premium private brand: "A premium private brand may have once been an oxymoron, but that's no longer the case. Following

The best-selling appliance brand is not GE or Whirlpool (www.sears.com/ kenmore).

Figure 14.9
Decathlon's Approach to Private Brands

Decathlon, owned by Auchan, is a magnet for European sports shoppers. With operations in six countries, it features footwear, apparel, accessories, and sporting goods equipment. The chain is known for its extensive private-label products which look like name brands but are 30 to 40 percent less expensive. The chain is innovative because it capitalizes on hot trends. In addition, its large-format selling space allows distinctiveness in the product assortment and private labels.
Reprinted by permission of PricewaterhouseCoopers LLP.

Table 14.4 The Berman/Evans Private Brand Test

Think you know a lot about private brands? Then, take our test. Match the retailers and the brand names. The answers are at the bottom of the table. No peeking. First, take the test.

Please note: Some retailers have more than one brand on the list.

Retailer	Brand
1. Costco	a. Arizona jeans
2. Kmart	b. Charter Club apparel
3. Macy's	c. Craftsman tools
4. Nordstrom	d. Evergreen sports wear
5. J.C. Penney	e. Jaclyn Smith women's apparel
6. Sears	f. Kathy Lee women's apparel
7. Target Stores	g. Kirkland tires
8. Wal-Mart	h. Martha Stewart home furnishings
	i. Michael Graves home products
	j. Sam's American Choice detergent
	k. St. John's Bay sports wear

Answers: 1—g; 2—e, h; 3—b; 4—d; 5—a, k; 6—c; 7—i; 8—f, j

the lead of their European counterparts, North American retailers have been introducing store brands whose quality matches or even exceeds that of brand-name goods, while still selling for a slightly lower price. Safeway, Wal-Mart, and others have realized that many consumers have the willingness and cash to pay extra for higher quality, and they want to capture a share of that spending."[18]

Despite the exciting possibilities, care must be taken by retailers in deciding how much emphasis to place on their own private brands. There are many consumers who are loyal to manufacturer brands and would shop elsewhere if those brands are not stocked or their variety is pruned. See Figure 14.10.

Figure 14.10
Kmart: Applying a Mixed-Brand Strategy

Kmart realizes that it must carry strong manufacturer brands, as well as its own popular private brands, in order to provide a superior shopping experience for its customers.
Reprinted by permission.

Generic brands feature products' generic names as brands (such as canned peas or instant coffee); they are no-frills goods stocked by some retailers. They are a form of private brand. These items usually receive secondary shelf locations, have little or no promotion support, are sometimes of less quality than other brands, are stocked in limited assortments, and have plain packages. Generics are controlled by retailers and are priced well below other brands. In U.S. supermarkets carrying them, generics have stabilized at less than 1 percent of sales. However, in the prescription drug industry, where the product quality of manufacturer brands and generics is similar, generics account for one-third of unit sales.

The competition between manufacturers and retailers for shelf space and profits has led to a phenomenon known as the **battle of the brands,** whereby manufacturer, private, and generic brands fight each other for more space and control. Nowhere is this battle clearer than at Wal-Mart: "Brand marketers should be afraid, says consultant Christopher Hoyt, as Wal-Mart transforms itself from their biggest customer to their biggest competitor. The retailer will become even more of a threat as it nears 60 percent U.S. household penetration, making network TV advertising cost-effective. 'In five years, the consumer isn't going to be able to tell the difference between a Wal-Mart brand and a national brand.' "[19]

Timing

A retailer must ascertain when each type of merchandise is to be stocked. For new goods and services, it must be decided when they are first displayed and sold. For established goods and services, the firm must plan the merchandise flow during the year.

To properly plan the timing of merchandise, the retailer should take into account its forecasts and various other factors: peak seasons, order and delivery time, routine versus special orders, stock turnover, discounts, and the efficiency of inventory procedures.

As noted earlier in the chapter, some goods and services have peak seasons during the year. For these items (like winter coats), a retailer should plan large inventories for peak times and less for off-seasons. Because some people like to shop during the off-season, the retailer should not eliminate the items.

Purchases should be planned on the basis of order and delivery time. How long does it take the retailer to process an order request? After the order is sent to the supplier, how long does it take to receive merchandise? By adding these two time periods together, the retailer can get a good idea of the lead time to restock shelves. If it takes a retailer 7 days to process an order and the supplier another 14 days to deliver goods, the retailer should begin a new order at least 21 days before the old inventory runs out.

Planning differs for routine versus special orders. Routine orders involve restocking staples and other regularly sold items. Deliveries are received weekly, monthly, and so on. Planning and problems are thus minimized. Special orders involve merchandise not sold regularly. These orders need more planning and close cooperation between retailer and supplier. Specific delivery dates are usually arranged. Custom furniture is a product requiring special orders.

Stock turnover (how quickly merchandise sells) greatly influences how often items must be ordered. Convenience items such as milk and bread (which are also highly perishable) have a high turnover rate and must be restocked quite often. Shopping items such as refrigerators and color TVs have a lower turnover rate and are restocked less often.

In deciding when and how often to buy merchandise, a retailer should consider quantity discounts. Large purchases may mean lower per-unit costs. Using efficient inventory procedures, such as electronic data interchange and quick response planning procedures, also decreases costs and order times while increasing merchandise productivity.

Allocation

The last part of merchandise planning is the allocation of items. A single-unit retailer usually must choose how much merchandise to place on the sales floor, how much to place in a stockroom, and whether to use a warehouse. A chain must also allot items among stores. Allocation is covered further in Chapter 15.

Some retailers focus almost entirely on warehouses as central—or regional—distribution centers. Products are shipped from suppliers to these warehouses, and then allotted and shipped to individual outlets. Other retailers, including many supermarket chains, do not rely as much on central or regional warehouses. Instead, they have at least some goods shipped directly from suppliers to individual stores.

It is vital for chains, whether engaged in centralized or decentralized merchandising, to have a clear store-by-store allocation plan. Even if merchandise lines are standardized across the chain, store-by-store assortments must reflect the variations in the size and diversity of the customer base, in store size and location (such as an isolated site versus placement in a regional mall), in the climate, and in other factors.

CATEGORY MANAGEMENT

As noted briefly in Chapter 2, an emerging merchandising technique that some firms—including several supermarkets, drugstores, hardware stores, and general merchandise retailers—are using to improve their productivity is **category management.** This is a method of managing a retail business that focuses on product category results rather than the performance of individual brands or models. It arranges groupings of products into strategic business units, so as to better meet consumer needs and achieve sales and profit goals. Category management orients retail managers toward the merchandising decisions necessary to maximize the total return on the assets assigned to them:

> A category framework will convert a series of facts into a business development story where sources of untapped consumer demand are revealed. Consider a retailer whose category sales consistently lag during Christmas. Further analysis shows that during the holiday season a particular product segment in the category—which has significant "stocking stuffer" appeal—enjoys a strong sales surge despite the absence of merchandising support from any retailer in the market. Yet the retailer we are focusing on doesn't even carry this segment, which partly explains the poor sales. However, there is an opportunity for the retailer to do more than just catch up with competitors if it can be the first one to support the segment during the next holiday. "Win–win" can be overused, but this is a time where it rings true. If a category management program can identify and validate this opportunity, the retailer can benefit from being made aware of it and then being given a detailed action plan to exploit it.[20]

According to one expert, successful category management is predicated on these ten points:

1. Categories should be arranged as they would be if consumers could stock the shelf themselves.

2. Category configuration should be a function of time, space, and product utilization.

3. Category management should seek to drive multiple item purchases, not the selection of a single SKU from a like-item category set.

4. Category management is a fluid, dynamic, proprietary set of decisions, not a standard, universal, institutionalized practice.

5. The ultimate aim of category management is to create unique consumer value not just to bolster manufacturer-retailer sales.

6. A retailer's category management plan ought to be based on overall trading-area scenarios.

7. Category management is an exclusionary process—as much a way of deciding what not to sell as what to sell to everyone.

8. The fundamental data base for category management should be drawn from a pre-customer interface analysis of trading-area needs.

9. The supplier's goal is to make the most of purchases and margins within a given geographic area. The retailer's goal is to raise total store or store cluster profitability and productivity.

10. Category management is a strategy of differentiation.[21]

A fundamental notion in category management is that a firm must empower specific personnel to be responsible for the financial performance of every product category. As with micromerchandising, category management means adapting a retailer's merchandising strategy in each store or region to best satisfy customers. In deciding the proper space allocation per product category, these are several of the crucial measures of performance to retailers. Comparisons can be made by studying company data from period to period and by looking at categorical statistics published in trade magazines:

- Sales per linear foot of shelf space—annual sales divided by the total linear footage devoted to the product category.
- Gross profit per linear foot of shelf space—annual gross profit divided by the total linear footage devoted to the product category.
- Return on inventory investment—annual gross profit divided by average inventory at cost.
- Inventory turnover—the number of times during a given period, usually one year, that the average inventory on hand is sold.
- Days' supply—the number of days of supply of an item on the shelf; it is a similar measure to inventory turnover.
- Direct product profitability (DPP)—an item's gross profit less its direct retailing costs (such as warehouse and store support, occupancy, inventory, and direct labor costs, but not general overhead).

Although a lot of firms are using the concept in selected product categories, relatively few retailers have fully integrated category management programs—due to the detailed planning, setup costs, and channel relationships necessary to enact these programs. According to surveys of manufacturers and retailers, some collaborative aspects of category management are working well, while others are not[22]:

What Manufacturers Feel About Retailers
Successful applications of category management
- Retailers act as equal partners and not as sponsors that delegate to category "captains."
- Retailers get input from manufacturers to ensure that they put the best possible plan together.
- Retailers have an open mind and are willing to change. Those that test new ideas and are enthusiastic about learning more about customers get the most out of category management.
- Since a full category business plan requires three to six months, retailers that give manufacturers proper lead time—as well as timely goals and suggestions—receive the highest-quality work.
Unsuccessful applications of category management
- Retailers fail to communicate a consistent strategy to manufacturers. Different goals among the retailers' senior managers, category managers, and operations managers impede the process.

- Retailers have a "template fixation." Yet, a template is nothing more than a structured way to gather measurement data. By itself, a template cannot explain why shoppers choose a given product or category from a retailer. Retailers must move beyond templates.
- Retailers expect manufacturers to do more than their share or to pay more than their share for gathering and analyzing data.

What Retailers Feel About Manufacturers

Successful applications of category management

- Manufacturers gather data on consumer purchasing behavior and make recommendations to the retailers. Those that do are invited to "take a seat" at the table.
- Manufacturers with clearly defined and supported plans are viewed favorably by retail partners.
- Manufacturers help the retailers to understand how to get more out of shopper traffic and build shopper loyalty, incremental volume, and return on merchandising assets.

Unsuccessful applications of category management

- Manufacturers make recommendations that consistently favor their brands and therefore lose credibility with retailers. The complexity of category management and the resources required for it to work make it critical that unbiased recommendations are made.
- Manufacturers just drop a completed template off with their retailers. This shows that they are not committed to the retail category manager and that they are not very involved in the process.
- Manufacturers do not maintain confidentiality regarding shared data or recommendations. Thus, they are not acting as valued partners.

Figure 14.11 indicates how a firm could use category management to better merchandise liquid detergent. One axis relates to direct product profitability (DPP). For the supermarket in this example, $0.69 per item is the average DPP for all liquid detergents. Those with higher amounts would be placed in the top half of the grid; those with lower amounts would be placed in the lower half. The other axis classifies the detergents in terms of unit sales (an indicator of inventory turnover), with 12.3 items per week being the dividing line between slow- and fast-moving detergents. On the basis of this two-by-two grid, all detergents could be placed into one of four categories: high potential ("sleepers")—products with high profitability but low unit sales; winners—products with high profitability and high weekly sales; underachievers ("dogs")—products with low profitability and low weekly sales; and traffic builders—products with low profitability and high weekly sales. Specific strategies are recommended in the figure.

MERCHANDISING SOFTWARE

One of the most significant advances in merchandise planning is the widespread availability of computer software, typically PC- or Web-based. With merchandising software, retailers have an excellent support mechanism that enables them to systematically prepare forecasts, try out various assortment scenarios, coordinate the data needed to engage in category management, and so forth. In an environment where many retailers carry thousands of items, merchandising software is a vital part of everyday business life.

Some merchandising software is provided by suppliers and trade associations at no charge, as part of the value delivery chain and relationship retailing. Other software is sold by marketing firms, often for a cost of $2,500 or less (although some software sells for $25,000 or more). In this section, we demonstrate the far-reaching nature of merchandising software as it relates to selected aspects of merchandise plans.

Figure 14.11
Applying Category
Management to
Heavy-Duty Liquid
Detergent

Source: Walter H.
Heller, "Profitability:
Where It's Really At,"
Progressive Grocer
(December 1992),
p. 27. Copyright
Progressive Grocer.
Reprinted by
permission.

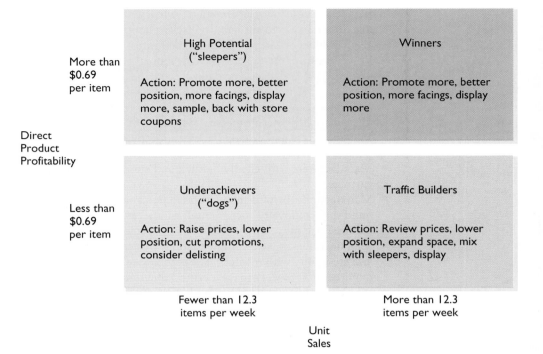

Note: The criteria are based on the average profit and movement of the items in the product
category of heavy-duty liquid detergent. The averages change for each product category.

General Merchandise Planning Software

Many retailers prefer functionally driven software, while others deploy integrated software
packages. The Limited, Inc., is an example of the latter. It uses a software package from
Island Pacific Systems that encompasses merchandise planning and forecasting, purchase
order management, allocation, inventory management, and price management. Several of
the company's divisions, including The Limited, Lerner New York, and Lane Bryant, utilize
the software. As the firm's chief information officer says, "The seamless flow of information
through the company and our various businesses is essential."[23]

Forecasting Software

A number of retailers employ their data warehouses to make merchandise forecasts. JDA
Software is one of the firms that produces software that enables them to do so: "Before the
advent of data warehousing, buyers, merchandise managers, and corporate financial analysts working on hunches had to ask information technology (IT) staffers to query departmental data bases to ferret out telling information regarding sales trends. The situation was
difficult. Queries were often run at night so as not to disrupt the work of the department
served by the operational data base. The buyer who requested the query often felt hand-
cuffed. He or she usually had to drop the information into an Excel spreadsheet to understand how it compared to other factors. Retailers reacted to the problem by setting up data
warehouses 'populated' with copies of information from disparate operational data bases.
Users generally access the information via desktop query tools, thereby negating the need for
IT departments to produce paper reports. Sometimes, the data warehouse is programmed to

Technology in Retailing

Connecting with Retail Buyers

Apparel manufacturers are stepping up their use of the Internet as a means of providing product information and photographs for retail buyers. As one partner in a marketing consulting firm says, "This type of system really offers a department store buyer the same advantage as the consumer—the ability to do quick and easy shopping without the hassle."

VF Corporation, for example, has a business-to-business E-commerce site for retail buyers of its Healthtex children's line. Buyers can view images of the firm's Health-Tex products, get information about these products, and even place orders over the Internet. VF intends to open additional sites for its Wrangler, Lee, Vanity Fair, Rustler, and other brands for both retail buyers and final consumers.

VF is using work-flow management software to aid in overseeing the retail buyer's approval process for the images used on its sites. It hopes this software can reduce the approval time by 40 percent. Approvals are necessary due to the large number of photographs and images that accompany each site.

How will the Health-Tex Web site change the relationship between VF's sales force and retail buyers? What do you recommend?

Source: Kim Ann Zimmerman, "VF Taps Internet to Reach Retail Buyers," *Women's Wear Daily* (March 3, 1999), p. 14.

---

notify merchandise managers of unexplained activity or a lack of activity. This is referred to as 'exception reporting.' "[24]

Software firms such as Forseon offer sophisticated software specifically for forecasting purposes. Forseon's Forseer Software System "is built on 'Retail Intelligent' forecasting methodology, which analyzes the historical performance of inventory and generates forecasts based on sales patterns, profits, inventory levels, markdowns, markups, geography, store location, price points, fashion/business trends, weather, consumer interest, and other factors. Forseer's ability to perform adjustments for data anomalies and excessive markdowns and compare its findings to Forseon's data base of merchandising models adds to the accuracy of results and lets retailers see what is most apt to occur in sales and inventory."[25]

Forseon's RMSA division has forecasting solutions for retailers in several different sectors (www.forseon. com/retail_industries. htm).

Innovativeness Software

Because a lot of software provides detailed data more quickly than ever before, such software enables retailers to monitor and quickly react to trends. Processes that once took months to complete now can be done in weeks or days. Instead of missing a selling season, retailers can be prepared for the latest craze.

Target Corporation, for example, uses Web-based color control software from Datacolor International: "It requests a color wanted for a product by sending a digital sample via the Internet to the dye house. Colorite technology ensures that the color sent is the exact same color received. The wanted color is scanned/photographed by a spectrophotometer (a device designed to measure color). The color then appears as a digital swatch on the computer monitor. Once the color standard is set, it is sent to the dye house, where digital samples are made until a match is found. The dye house sends a digital sample of the color to the retailer, and if the color isn't exactly right, more dyeing is done. Only after the right color is found is an actual swatch sent to the retailer. This compresses the time it takes to send swatches back and forth. The time it usually takes to communicate and match a retailer's requested color and for the supplier to find a match is often 8 to 12 weeks. Now, the process takes about 3 weeks, sometimes less."[26]

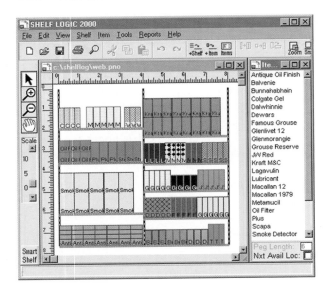

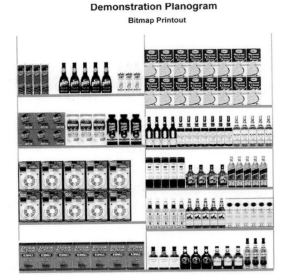

Demonstration Planogram
Bitmap Printout

Figure 14.12
Shelf Logic 2000: Software for Category Management Planning

Reprinted by permission of Logical Planning Systems.

Assortment Software

A number of retailers employ merchandising software to better plan assortments. One application is from JDA Software (www.jda.com): "Arthur Assortment Planning optimizes the art of merchandise selection to meet your target customers' needs and your strategic financial goals. It provides a 'best practice' process within which your buyers and planners can work together to build effective assortments that satisfy both qualitative and quantitative goals. Getting the right product presentation for customers is no longer a complex task. Arthur Assortment Planning helps your buyers and planners create balanced and targeted assortments that take into account store personalities, space, seasonality, and the right mix of products for your customer, including price point, brand, theme, and color. With flexible reviewing functionality and the ability to consolidate assortments, you can view your merchandise through your customer's eyes, from every angle, for any store or store group, for any level of your business."

Allocation Software

Chains of all sizes and types want to improve the ways in which they allocate merchandise to their stores. There are several software programs to let them do so. Consider Clothestime, the apparel chain using STS Systems software. According to Clothestime's director of planning and allocation: "Allocation software takes a unit plan and divvies up merchandise according to the needs of the stores. It sort of prorates the plan. Although the mix can vary considerably from store to store, individual merchandise planners can override it as necessary. Obviously, we would only sell T-shirts that say California in California. That's a pretty basic example of how a merchandise planner might choose to customize a plan."[27]

Category Management Software

At A.C. Nielsen's Category Manager site (acnielsen.com/ products/tools/ categorymanager), click on the "Image Gallery" to learn about the software's features.

There is a wide range of software programs to help manufacturers and retailers deal with the complexities of category management. A few retailers have even developed their own software. Programs typically base space allocation on sales, inventory turnover, and profits at individual stores. Because data are store specific, space allocations can reflect actual purchases.

These are some examples of category management software:

- A.C. Nielsen (www.acnielsen.com) software programs include Category Manager, Spaceman (in multiple versions), and Shelf Builder.
- Information Resources, Inc. (www.infores.com) offers several versions of its Apollo software, as well as Account Traffic Builder.
- Logical Planning Systems (www.shelflogic.com) markets Shelf Logic 2000 category management software for only $750. See Figure 14.12.

SUMMARY

1. *To demonstrate the importance of a sound merchandising philosophy.* Developing and implementing a merchandise plan is a key element in a successful retail strategy. Merchandising consists of the activities involved in a retailer's buying goods and services and making them available for sale. A merchandising philosophy sets the guiding principles for all merchandise decisions and must reflect the desires of the target market, the retailer's institutional type, its marketplace positioning, its defined value chain, supplier capabilities, costs, competitors, product trends, and other factors.

2. *To study various buying organization formats and the processes they use.* The buying organization and its processes must be well defined in terms of the level of formality, degree of centralization, organizational breadth, personnel resources, functions performed, and staffing.

With a formal buying organization, merchandising (buying) is a distinct retail task and a separate department is set up. In an informal buying organization, merchandising (buying) is not a distinct task. The same personnel handle both merchandising (buying) and other retail tasks. Multiunit retailers must choose whether to have a centralized buying organization or a decentralized one. In a centralized buying organization, all purchase decisions emanate from one office. In a decentralized buying organization, purchase decisions are made locally or regionally. For a general organization, one or several people buy all of a firm's merchandise. With a specialized organization, each buyer is responsible for a product category.

An inside buying organization is staffed by a retailer's personnel and decisions are made by permanent employees of the firm. An outside buying organization involves a company or personnel external to the retailer. Although most retailers use either an inside or an outside buying organization, some employ a combination of the two. A resident buying office, which can be an inside or outside organization, is used when a retailer wants to keep in close touch with key market trends and cannot do so through just its headquarters buying staff. Independent retailers and small chains are involved with cooperative buying to a greater degree than before to compete with large chains.

The responsibilities and functions of merchandise and in-store personnel are assigned. If a retailer has a "merchandising" view, merchandise personnel oversee all buying and selling functions. If a retailer has a "buying" view, merchandise personnel oversee the buying of products, advertising, and pricing, while in-store personnel oversee assortments, displays, personnel deployment, and sales presentations. Then, staffing is undertaken. Firms with a merchandising view are most concerned with hiring good buyers. Firms with a buying view are interested in hiring both buyers and sales managers.

3. *To outline the considerations in devising merchandise plans: forecasts, innovativeness, assortment, brands, timing, and allocation.* Forecasts are projections of expected retail sales and form the foundation of merchandise plans. Forecasts include overall projections, category projections, item-by-item projections, and store projec-

SUMMARY *(CONTINUED)*

tions. Staple merchandise consists of the regular products carried by a retailer. A basic stock list specifies the inventory level, color, brand, and so on for every staple item carried by the retailer. Assortment merchandise consists of products for which there must be a variety so as to give customers a proper selection. A model stock plan is used to project specific assortment merchandise. Fashion merchandise has cyclical sales due to changing tastes and lifestyles. Seasonal merchandise sells well over nonconsecutive periods. With fad merchandise, a high level of sales is generated for a short time. In forecasting for best-sellers, many retailers use a never-out list.

A retailer's determination of its merchandise innovativeness is related to the target market(s), product growth potential, fashion trends, the retailer's image, competition, customer segments, responsiveness to consumers, investment costs, profitability, risk, constrained decision making, and declining goods/services. Three issues are of particular interest: How fast will a new good or service generate sales? What are the most sales to be achieved in a season or a year? Over what period will a good or service continue to sell? A useful tool for assessing growth potential when devising a merchandising plan is the product life cycle.

An assortment is the selection of merchandise a retailer carries. A firm must first choose its quality of merchandise. It then determines the width and depth of assortment. Width of assortment refers to the number of distinct goods/service categories carried. Depth of assortment refers to the variety in any one category. As part of assortment planning, a retailer chooses the proper mix of brands. Manufacturer (national) brands are produced and controlled by manufacturers. Private (dealer) brands, also known as store brands, contain names designated by wholesalers or retailers. Generic brands feature generic names as brands and are a form of private brand. The competition between manufacturers and retailers is called the battle of the brands.

A retailer must ascertain when merchandise is stocked. For new goods and services, it must be decided when they are first to be displayed and sold. For established goods and services, the firm must plan the merchandise flow during the year. In deciding when and how often to buy merchandise, a retailer should consider quantity discounts. A single-unit retailer usually must choose how much merchandise to allocate to the sales floor and how much to the stockroom, and whether to use a warehouse. A chain must also allocate items among stores.

4. *To discuss category management and merchandising software.* Category management is an emerging technique for managing a retail business that focuses on product category results rather than the performance of individual brands or models. It arranges product groups into strategic business units to better address consumer needs and meet financial goals. Category management orients retail personnel toward the merchandising decisions needed to maximize the total return on the assets. There is now plentiful PC- and Web-based merchandising software available for retailers, in just about every aspect of merchandise planning.

Key Terms

merchandising (p. 452)
merchandising philosophy (p. 453)
micromerchandising (p. 454)
cross-merchandising (p. 455)
formal buying organization (p. 456)
informal buying organization (p. 456)
centralized buying organization (p. 456)
decentralized buying organization (p. 456)
inside buying organization (p. 457)

outside buying organization (p. 457)
resident buying office (p. 459)
cooperative buying (p. 459)
forecasts (p. 461)
staple merchandise (p. 462)
basic stock list (p. 462)
assortment merchandise (p. 462)
model stock plan (p. 462)
fashion merchandise (p. 462)
seasonal merchandise (p. 462)
fad merchandise (p. 463)

never-out list (p. 463)
product life cycle (p. 464)
assortment (p. 466)
width of assortment (p. 467)
depth of assortment (p. 467)
manufacturer (national) brands (p. 470)
private (dealer, store) brands (p. 471)
generic brands (p. 474)
battle of the brands (p. 474)
category management (p. 475)

Questions for Discussion

1. Describe and evaluate the merchandising philosophy of your college bookstore.

2. What is the distinction between *merchandising functions* and the *buying function?*

3. Is cross-merchandising a good approach? Why or why not?

4. What are the advantages and disadvantages of a decentralized buying organization?

5. What do you think are the pros and cons of a retailer's having its own resident buying offices?

6. How could a sporting goods store use a basic stock list, a model stock plan, and a never-out list?

7. How innovative should each of these be in planning merchandise? Explain your answers.
   a. Deli.
   b. Men's shoe store.
   c. Small luggage store.
   d. Web-based music retailer.

8. Under what circumstances could a retailer carry a wide range of merchandise quality without hurting its image? When should the quality of merchandise carried be quite narrow?

9. How should a furniture retailer use the product life cycle concept?

10. What are the tradeoffs in a retailer's deciding how much to emphasize private brands rather than manufacturer brands?

11. What kinds of problems may occur if a retailer mistimes its purchases?

12. Present a checklist of five factors for a chain retailer to review in determining how to allocate merchandise among its stores.

13. What is the basic premise of category management? Why do you think that supermarkets have been at the forefront of the movement to use category management?

14. What do you think are the risks of placing too much reliance on merchandising software?

WEB-BASED EXERCISE

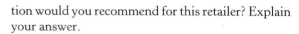

Merchandise Mart (www.merchandisemart.com)

Questions

1. What are the benefits of the Merchandise Mart to a buyer of casual furnishings?

2. Describe the Merchandise Mart's "Attractions" section.

3. Suppose an independent retailer views the Merchandise Mart as an important source of market information. However, its store is located 1,500 miles from Chicago. What type of buying organization would you recommend for this retailer? Explain your answer.

4. A major chain retailer with stores throughout the United States views the Merchandise Mart as a key source of market information. What type of buying organization would you recommend for this retailer? Explain your answer.

CHAPTER ENDNOTES

1. Sharon Edelson, "New Entrepreneurs Shake Up Retail Scene by Ignoring Old Rules," *Women's Wear Daily* (April 26, 1999), p. 1.

2. Mary A. Tolan, "Developing High-Powered Merchants," *Stores* (June 1998), p. S3; and "Thought Leadership," *www.ac.com/services/retail/reta_thought.html* (March 9, 2000).

3. Barbara E. Kahn, "Introduction to the Special Issue: Assortment Planning," *Journal of Retailing*, Vol. 75 (Fall 1999), p. 289.

4. Kelly Barron, "The Prince of Peddlers," *Forbes* (October 18, 1999), p. 144.

CHAPTER ENDNOTES

5. "Breaking the Rules," *Progressive Grocer* (August 1998), p. 58.

6. Marie Beninati, Paul Evans, and Joseph McKinney, "A Blueprint for Local Assortment Management," *Chain Store Age* (February 1997), p. 30.

7. Ginger Koloszyc, "Ordering System Slashes Costs for Retail Buying Co-Op," *Stores* (May 1999), pp. 28, 30; and Valerie Seckler, "Bernard to Head Atkins," *Women's Wear Daily* (May 7, 1999), p. 4.

8. See Laura Klepacki, "CDMA: Member Buying Power," *Women's Wear Daily* (April 16, 1999), p. 6; and Umberto Gallo, "Cooperative Buying," *Chain Store Age* (August 1999), p. 80.

9. "Trend-Spotting," *Chain Store Age* (July 1999), p. 80.

10. See also Erik Jan Hultink, Jürg M. Thölke, and Henry S. J. Robben, "Retailers' Adoption Decision of New Consumer Durables," *Journal of Product Innovation Management,* Vol. 16 (September 1999), pp. 483–90.

11. For a good, wide-ranging discussion on this topic, see "Special Issue: Assortment Planning," *Journal of Retailing,* Vol. 75 (Fall 1999).

12. *Dollar General Corporation 1999 Annual Report.*

13. Cynthia Huffman and Barbara E. Kahn, "Variety for Sale: Mass Customization or Mass Confusion?" *Journal of Retailing,* Vol. 74 (Fall 1998), pp. 491–92; and *www.choiceseating.com* (March 9, 2000).

14. Gary Rodkin, "A Balancing Act," *Progressive Grocer* (June 1999), p. 29.

15. Murray Raphel, "Branded!" *Direct Marketing* (July 1999), p. 29.

16. "Private Label Continues to Gain Share, A.C. Nielsen Study Shows," *www.acnielsen.com* (August 19, 1999).

17. "The Top Major Appliance Brands," *HFN* (September 20, 1999), p. 76; Rusty Williamson, "Penney's Labels, Online Getting Push This Year," *Women's Wear Daily* (March 12, 1999), p. 17; Allison Zisko, "Private Label Prospers at Retail," *HFN* (August 30, 1999), p. 38; and "Amazon's Own Label Soon to Debut Online," *Discount Store News* (October 4, 1999), p. 2.

18. David Dunne and Chakravarthi Narasimhan, "The New Appeal of Private Labels," *Harvard Business Review,* Vol. 77 (May–June 1999), p. 42.

19. Jack Neff, "Wal-Mart Stores Go Private (Label)," *Advertising Age* (November 29, 1999), pp. 1, 34, 36, 38.

20. Edward Bettigole, "21st Century Category Management," Progressive Grocer (November 1999), p. 7.

21. "Toward a Revised Theory of Category Management," *Progressive Grocer* (August 1995), p. 36.

22. Information Resources, Inc., "Manufacturer and Retailer Report Cards," *NeoBrief* (Issue 1, 1999), pp. 3–6.

23. Kim Ann Zimmerman, "Limited Links Systems," *Women's Wear Daily* (April 28, 1999), p. 11.

24. "Merchandising Systems Spawn," *Chain Store Age* (September 1999), p. 80.

25. Julie Ritzer Ross, "Advanced Forecasting Systems Seek Better Merchandising Decisions," *Stores* (April 1998), pp. 52–53.

26. Shawn Nelson, "Internet-Based System Speeds Color Selection Process," *Stores* (August 1999), pp. 74, 76.

27. "Trend-Spotting," p. 82.

CASE 1

NORDSTROM REMAKES ITS BUYING ORGANIZATION

Nordstrom, the Seattle-based chain, has decided to centralize its designer buying team. This strategy may bring more fashionable, high-ticket labels such as Chloe, Michael Kors, and Yves Saint Laurent to Nordstrom's suburban locations. Previously, these locations generally featured big-volume brands and their assortment of designer lines was limited.

The revamped buying team is a reflection of the new attitude fostered by Pete Nordstrom and the other fourth-generation Nordstrom family members who have led the chain since mid-1995. "We've been stepping out for the last year and a half and will be stepping out a lot more. We're very open-minded," says Sue Patneaude, Nordstrom's vice-president of designer apparel. "If you stay safe, you get into trouble. The firm has not changed its philosophy about decentralization, but designer is acknowledged to be a different business." The rest of Nordstrom's buying organization remains decentralized, with four teams, one for each Nordstrom region: California, Northwest, Central, and East Coast.

According to Patneaude, "The designer business is very specialized, and we need to reflect the way the market likes to work." She also acknowledges that the reorganization makes it easier for designers, who will see one buyer instead of four. The designer team consists of six buyers, with an average of 10 years' experience at Nordstrom. Each one covers a specific segment of the designer market: European designer sportswear, European ready-to-wear collections, American ready-to-wear collections, American designer sportswear, advanced American collections, and progressive designers.

There are also six retail coordinators, covering different regions of the country. They operate like planners and help the buyers identify the needs of individual stores. The buyers and coordinators both report to a retail director, who is a gatekeeper between the two groups. In addition, the team includes a sales promotion director for designer apparel, as well as a financial planning and technology manager.

Patneaude has singled out the progressive designer category as adding "a new dimension" to Nordstrom, and representing a price level between bridge and designer collections. "We really feel it will be important to a number of our suburban stores. We've grown and grown and grown. Now it is time to refine and customize the mix." Progressive designer departments, each about 2,500 square feet, were planned for 12 stores as of July 1999. Patneaude believes the designer dress category has "tremendous potential for us" and says there are plans to develop stronger businesses with other designers.

The designer business represents a tiny fraction of the total apparel volume for Nordstrom, which has been planning its inventories more carefully. It is attempting to sell more goods while buying less. Executives call the strategy an emphasis on "quality sales." This approach appears to be working. For example, during one recent selling period, Nordstrom's comparable store inventories were reportedly down 5 percent, while earnings rose by 7 percent. Expense and inventory controls accounted for the enhanced profitability. The lower inventory level facilitated a better flow of fresh merchandise and raised expectations for more-sustained full-price merchandise sales.

The company also installed a new computerized merchandise planning system in fall 1998. The system updates markdowns and merchandise receipts every 15 minutes, facilitating improved assortments at the store level and better open-to-buy planning.

Questions

1. What are the pros and cons of Nordstrom's centralizing its designer buying organization?

2. Describe the need for coordination between the retail planners and the buyers.

3. Should Nordstrom consider centralizing its overall buying responsibilities? Explain your answer.

4. Explain how Nordstrom's new merchandising software is helpful in its quest for "quality sales."

NOTE The material in this case is drawn from David Moin, "Nordstrom Revamps Buying Team in Effort to Build Designer Mix," *Women's Wear Daily* (February 10, 1999), p. 1.

CASE 2

CATEGORY MANAGEMENT FOR CONDIMENTS

The main purpose of category management is to determine the optimal assortment of products that will maximize sales and eliminate unnecessary product duplication. The condiments category consists of ketchup, barbecue sauce, mustard, steak sauce, Worcestershire sauce, cocktail sauce, and chili sauce. It accounts for over $1.7 billion in annual U.S. sales. Within the category, ketchup accounts for 32 percent of sales, barbecue sauce for 26 percent, mustard for 19 percent, steak sauce for 14 percent, Worcestershire sauce for 4 percent, cocktail sauce for 3 percent, and chili sauce for 1 percent.

Let's look at some of the general characteristics of condiments buyers:

- They spend $1,500 more per year in grocery expenditures than the average U.S. household.
- Households with children are the largest condiments buyers.
- Condiments buyers seek flavor and variety. Many customers stock different varieties within the same condiments groupings (such as multiple styles of mustard) in their homes at any point in time.
- Customers make 80 percent of their condiments purchases at regular prices.

Consumer behavior differs for each condiment product category. Ketchup buyers first decide on whether to purchase a premium versus a value brand and then choose the product's size. On the other hand, mustard buyers focus first on the choice of flavor (yellow, Dijon, brown, spicy, or specialty), then on the package type (glass or plastic), and finally on package size. Each segment of the mustard market also appeals to a different target audience. Although yellow mustards appeal more to households with children, Dijon and specialty mustards appeal more to one- and two-person households.

The condiments category can be better managed by determining whether an SKU is a core item, a unique item, or an unnecessary duplication. Core items have mass market appeal, while unique items increase variety and selection for the mass market and further extend a product's shopper base to include additional profitable market segments. In contrast, unnecessary duplications can be safely eliminated.

Category management can be illustrated by a supermarket stocking five kinds of hickory-flavored barbecue sauce in two price tiers. By eliminating the slowest-selling item in each tier (an unnecessary duplication), the store can raise its return on inventory investment and inventory turnover, reduce its days' supply of inventory, and decrease total inventory costs. Another principle of category management is that the top-selling 50 percent of items in a category may comprise up to 95 percent of a category's sales.

There are three vital considerations with regard to assortment decision making: (1) Stocking goods in a product subcategory should reflect the behavior of that subcategory's shoppers. Since package type is a more important buying factor to a mustard buyer than to a ketchup buyer, the latter must be offered multiple packages in each size. (2) Retailers should leverage manufacturer research to improve category performance. Manufacturers have lots of data that they are willing to share. (3) Retailers should study product placement alternatives. One recent study showed that ketchup and mustard should be placed at opposite ends of an aisle (with steak sauce, Worcestershire sauce, and chili located between them).

Questions

1. List and describe three other measures of category performance that could be used, besides those cited in this case.

2. Explain the relationship among return on inventory investment, inventory turnover, days of inventory supply, and inventory costs.

3. What lessons in this case can be applied to another category such as detergent?

4. How can a store manager differentiate among core, unique, and unnecessary duplication items?

Video Questions on Category Management

1. Comment on recent trends in the consumption of mustard, steak sauce, and barbecue sauce.

2. Explain the principles of product placement for condiments.

NOTE   The material in this case is drawn from data supplied by H.J. Heinz.

CHAPTER 15

Implementing Merchandise Plans

CHAPTER OBJECTIVES

1. To describe the steps in the implementation of merchandise plans: gathering information, selecting and interacting with merchandise sources, evaluation, negotiation, concluding purchases, receiving and stocking merchandise, reordering, and re-evaluation

2. To examine the prominent roles of logistics and inventory management in the implementation of merchandise plans

Noodle Kidoodle (www.noodlekidoodle.com) is a specialty toy retailer with a very distinctive merchandising strategy. During fiscal year 1999, Noodle Kidoodle's sales exceeded $100 million. By the end of 1999, the fast-growing chain operated 50 stores in 12 states, including New York, Texas, and Florida.

The firm's merchandising approach is to offer a wide selection of nonviolent educational toys, to make each store a "fun" place to visit for children and parents alike, and to provide excellent customer service. All Noodle Kidoodle stores have a "please touch" philosophy that encourages children to "test drive" toys and games. Every store also has special events featuring programs by local celebrities, crafts, a large-screen TV, and a reading area.

Besides carrying popular lines of toys such as Barbie, Noodle Kidoodle also sells science laboratory kits that most toy retailers would not stock. As a matter of policy, Noodle Kidoodle refuses to sell violent movie- or TV-based toys. For example, it does not carry Power Rangers toys. In addition, the chain has not built its business around toys that are either "hot" or "promotionally driven," states its chief executive officer.

Noodle Kidoodle's largest store is located in Plano, Texas. The 13,000-square-foot location has bright interior signs marking its well-defined categories of products. Within each category, products are subdivided by toy type or by manufacturer.[1]

OVERVIEW

Enter the Seven-Eleven Japan Web site (www.sej.co.jp) and check out its "News Release" section to see what this innovative retailer is doing.

This chapter builds on Chapter 14 and covers the implementation of merchandise plans, as well as the roles of logistics and inventory management in enacting such plans. Sometimes, it is relatively simple to enact the prescribed merchandise plans. But in many cases, it requires hard work, perseverance, and creativity. Web retailing in Japan is a good example of the latter situation:

In a country where neither credit cards nor Internet use are all that popular, how would online shopping work? In Japan, the answer is coming from, of all places, convenience

Please Note: Web site addresses are constantly changing. The links in this chapter are current as of the publication of this book.

stores (*combinis*). Japanese consumers have been slow getting on the Internet, a result of the high cost of phone service and hardly any fixed-price Web access. However, many more Japanese are expected to soon be ordering books, videos, and all sorts of things over the Internet. So, the combinis are vying to be the place they go to pay in cash for the items they order online. Seven-Eleven Japan, the largest combini chain, got the ball rolling in June 1999 by announcing an agreement with Softbank and other partners to sell books and videos on the Internet. Starting in November 1999, the venture, called e-Shopping! Books, let shoppers on the Web site of partner Yahoo Japan choose one of the 8,000 Seven-Eleven locations in Japan where they'd like to have merchandise delivered. Another partner, book wholesaler Tohan, would deliver individual online orders to Seven-Eleven along with the wholesale orders of magazines and paperbacks it delivers to the combinis. The combini model of E-retailing sits well with Japanese shoppers, many of whom never use credit cards at all.[2]

IMPLEMENTING MERCHANDISE PLANS

The implementation of merchandise plans comprises these sequential steps: (1) gathering information, (2) selecting and interacting with merchandise sources, (3) evaluation, (4) negotiation, (5) concluding purchases, (6) receiving and stocking merchandise, (7) reordering, and (8) re-evaluation. See Figure 15.1.

Gathering Information

After overall merchandising plans are set, more specific information about ongoing target market needs and prospective suppliers is required. A retailer should gather appropriate data before buying or rebuying any merchandise. Information-gathering techniques, as related to retailing, were detailed in Chapter 8.

In gathering data for merchandising decisions, a retailer has several possible information sources. The most valuable is the consumer. By regularly researching the target market's demographics, life-styles, and potential shopping plans, a retailer can study consumer demand directly. Loyalty programs are especially useful in tracking consumer purchases and interests.

Other sources of information can be used when direct consumer data are unavailable or insufficient. Suppliers (manufacturers and wholesalers) usually do their own sales forecasts and marketing research (such as test marketing). They also know how much outside promotional support a retailer will get, and this affects sales. In closing a deal with the retailer, a

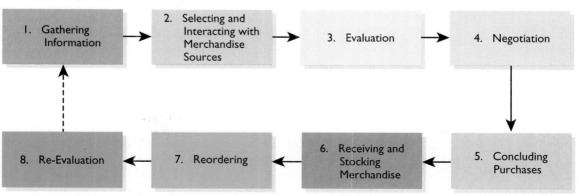

Figure 15.1
The Process for Implementing Merchandise Plans

supplier may present charts and graphs, showing forecasts and promotional support. Yet, the retailer should remember one significant point: It is the retailer that has direct access to the target market and its needs.

Retail sales and display personnel interact with consumers and can pass their observations along to management. A **want book (want slip)** system is a formal way to record consumer requests for unstocked or out-of-stock merchandise. The want book is used in smaller firms; want slips are utilized by larger retailers. These tools are very helpful to a retailer's buyers. Due to their involvement with consumers, personnel should be encouraged to offer feedback and not be shut off from making comments. Outside of customers, salespeople may provide the most useful information for merchandising decisions.

Buying personnel can learn a lot about consumer demand by visiting suppliers, talking with sales personnel, and observing customer behavior. Usually, buyers are responsible for complete sales forecasts and merchandise plans in their product categories; top management combines the forecasts and plans of individual buyers to obtain overall company projections.

Competitors are another information source. A conservative retailer may not stock an item until competitors do. Comparison shoppers, who look at the offerings and prices of competitors, may be employed. The most sophisticated type of comparison shopping involves the use of shopping bots such as mySimon.com on the Web, whereby competitors' offerings and prices are tracked electronically.[3] Buy.com, for one, constantly checks its prices against those of competitors to make sure that it is not undersold. In addition, trade publications report on trends in each area of retailing and provide another way of gathering data from competitors. See Figure 15.2 for an example of a competition shopping report.

Other sources may offer useful pieces of consumer-related information: government sources indicate unemployment, inflation, and product safety data; independent news sources conduct their own consumer polls and do investigative reporting; and commercial data can be purchased.

To gain information about prospective suppliers and their merchandise, retailers can

See why High Point (www.ihfc.com/welcome.html) is a world-class market.

- Talk to the suppliers, get specification sheets, read trade publications, and seek out references.
- Attend trade shows featuring multiple suppliers that take place in major cities. For example, there are hundreds of trade shows annually in New York. In Leipzig, Germany, the annual Fashion Fair attracts nearly 200 exhibitors and about 700 buyers. The National Hardware Show in Chicago has 3,000 exhibits and 70,000 attendees each year. The High Point Market in North Carolina has semi-annual shows that attract 2,400 manufacturers and 71,000 attendees—from all 50 states and from 106 countries.

CaliforniaMart (www.californiamart.com/retailer) offers a lot of online information for retailers.

- Visit permanent merchandise marts that are open year-round. Among the leading merchandise marts are AmericasMart in Atlanta (www.americasmart.com), CaliforniaMart in Los Angeles (www.californiamart.com), Dallas Market Center (www.dallasmarket-center.com), and Merchandise Mart in Chicago (www.merchandisemart.com). Each of these facilities has daily hours for its permanent vendor showrooms, as well as large areas for periodic trade shows.

1-800-Database (www.1-800-database.com/html/imagegallery.html) has an interesting collection of product images that retailers can access.

- Search the Web. One interesting new application is the SKUfinder (www.skufinder.com) from 1-800-Database: "A business-to-business Internet search engine is being rolled out to provide a cost-effective way for retailers to access manufacturer product information and images. SKUfinder enables users to search for data and images by a variety of identifiers, including UPC, brand, and description. Analysts say that quick and cost-effective access to data and images is a key competitive tool for retailers. Positioned to address this market is 1-800-Database, with a data base of 250,000 product images and information from such industries as hardware, grocery, housewares, health and beauty care, auto accessories, beverages, pet products, and school products. The firm spent a year and a half developing its search engine. 'It's like Yahoo for products,' says chairman Steve

Figure 15.2
A Competition
Shopping Report

COMPETITION SHOPPING REPORT

Store #_____   Date_____

Dept. #_____   Qualified Competition Shopped:

1._____

2._____

Our Style No.	Mfr. Model or Style	Description	Our Price	1st Compet. Price	2nd Compet. Price	Store's Recom. Price	Buyer's Recom. Price

Item Seen at Our Competitor's Store Which We Should Carry:					
Manufacturer	Mfr. Model or Style	Description	Reg. or List Price	Sale Price	Buyer's Comments

_____   _____
Signature of Shopper   *Store Manager*

Kirschner, referring to the popular Web guide."[4] SKUfinder requires a password to enter the data base.

Whatever the amount of information acquired, the retailer should feel comfortable that it is sufficient for making decisions as accurately as possible. For routine merchandising decisions (staple products), limited information may be adequate. On the other hand, new car sales can fluctuate widely and require extensive data for sales forecasts.

Selecting and Interacting with Merchandise Sources

The next step is to select sources of merchandise and to interact with them. Three major options exist:

Take a "Live Demo" of the outside suppliers that Buying-Office.com services for retailers (www.buying-office.com/files/demo.htm).

- *Company-owned*—A large retailer owns a manufacturing and/or wholesaling facility. A company-owned supplier handles all or part of the merchandise the retailer requests.
- *Outside, regularly used supplier*—This supplier is not owned by the retailer but used regularly by it. The retailer knows the quality of the goods and services and the reliability of the supplier through firsthand experience.
- *Outside, new supplier*—This supplier is not owned by the retailer; and the retailer has not bought from it before. The retailer may be unfamiliar with the supplier's merchandise quality and reliability.

A retailer can rely on one kind of supplier or utilize a combination of them (the biggest retailers often deal with all three formats). The basic types of outside suppliers (regularly used and new) are described in Figure 15.3. In choosing vendors, such criteria as those listed in Table 15.1 should be considered.

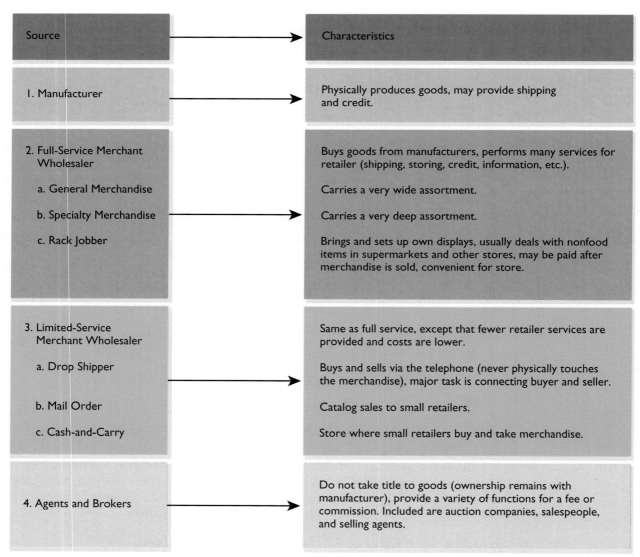

Figure 15.3
Outside Sources of Supply

Table 15.1 Points to Review in Choosing Vendors

Reliability—Will a supplier consistently fulfill all written promises?

Price–quality—Who provides the best merchandise at the lowest price?

Order-processing time—How fast will deliveries be made?

Exclusive rights—Will a supplier give exclusive selling rights or customize products?

Functions provided—Will a supplier undertake shipping, storing, and other functions, if needed?

Information—Will a supplier pass along important data?

Ethics—Will a supplier fulfill all verbal promises and not engage in unfair business or labor practices?

Guarantee—Does a supplier stand behind its offerings?

Credit—Can credit purchases be made from a supplier? On what terms?

Long-term relations—Will a supplier be available over an extended period?

Reorders—Can a supplier promptly fill reorders?

Markup—Will markup (price margins) be adequate?

Innovativeness—Is a supplier's line innovative or conservative?

Local advertising—Does a supplier advertise in local media?

Investment—How large are total investment costs with a supplier?

Risk—How much risk is involved in dealing with a supplier?

Consolidated Stores, which buys merchandise to stock its 2,500 stores (several retail closeout chains and K-B Toys), is a good example of how complicated it can be to choose suppliers:

> An integral part of our business is buying quality, branded merchandise directly from manufacturers and other vendors at prices substantially below those paid by conventional retailers. We have built strong relationships with many manufacturers and capitalize on our purchasing power in the closeout and toy marketplace. We have the ability to buy all of a manufacturer's closeouts in specific product categories and to control distribution according to vendor instructions. Also, the success of our toy business depends in part on the ability to buy on competitive terms. We supplement branded closeout purchases with a limited amount of private label goods. Our merchandise is bought from more than 3,000 foreign and domestic suppliers, resulting in multiple sources for each product category. The top 10 vendors account for 18.5 percent of purchases, with no one vendor accounting for more than 4 percent. We buy 20 percent of products directly from overseas suppliers, and a material amount of domestically purchased goods is also made abroad. Thus, a significant portion of our merchandise supply is subject to certain risks, including increased import duties and more restrictive quotas.[5]

Sometimes, retailers and their suppliers interact well together. Other times, there are conflicts. As we have discussed throughout this book, the benefits of relationship building between retailers and their suppliers can be invaluable—well worth the effort necessary to make the relationships work:

Miami International Fashion Week

The first Miami International Fashion Week (a trade show) highlighted 110 exhibitors, including 25 designers from South America, Mexico, and the Caribbean, a diverse group of U.S. fashion manufacturers, and several local Florida designers. As Carolina Herrera, a well-known designer, says: "This is the only show highlighting Latin American talent. We need to present Latin American design as truly international, rather than folkloric."

The show's promoters said that between 2,500 and 3,000 retail buyers attended the event. However, this included all *registered* buyers—not necessarily the buyers who actually attended the show. Some exhibitors felt the show had a scarcity of buyers due to its poor timing. The show was held between a large New York trade show and Mother's Day weekend. Despite this concern, the four daily fashion displays of Latin American designers drew crowds of several hundred people each, including other designers and the Latin American media.

The garments shown at the show were largely eveningwear designed for an affluent clientele. The designers stated that this segment is more immune to economic fluctuations than less-affluent consumer segments.

What are the pros and cons of using shows as a major source of market information for retail merchandisers?

Source: Georgia Lee, "Latino Talent on Display," *Women's Wear Daily* (May 28, 1999), p. 14.

The 1990s witnessed some good things happening among retailers, wholesalers, and suppliers. At the start of the decade, only a few companies were handling their relationships constructively, with most giving collaboration lip service. But today, many have moved from talk into the real world. Basically, what they have done is replaced vituperation with collaborative action. At the same time, all is not rosy. Many collaborative efforts have involved the biggest companies on both sides of the street, a situation that has been exacerbated by consolidations, particularly on the chain retailer side. As a result, the brave new world is not apparent for some smaller firms who, to an extent, remain in the Middle Ages.[6]

Despite the progress toward better relationships, there remain issues that are sore points between retailers and suppliers, as these two examples indicate. On the one hand, many retailers have beefed up their use of private brands because they are upset with companies such as Polo Ralph Lauren and Gucci for opening their own stores in the same shopping centers. Two-thirds of Gucci sales are now generated from its company-owned and franchised shops. On the other hand, many manufacturers are distressed by what they believe is retailers' excessive use of **chargebacks,** whereby the retailers, at their discretion, make deductions in their bills for infractions ranging from late shipments to damaged and expired merchandise. Rite Aid, the drugstore chain, has deducted as much as 10 percent when paying some bills.[7]

Evaluating Merchandise

Whatever source is chosen, the retailer needs a procedure for evaluating the merchandise under purchase consideration. Should each individual unit be examined, or can an item be bought by description?

Three forms of evaluation are possible: inspection, sampling, and description. The technique depends on the item's cost, its attributes, and the regularity of purchase. Inspection occurs when every single unit is examined before purchase and after delivery. Jewelry and art are two examples of expensive, relatively unique purchases for which the retailer carefully inspects all items.

A retailer uses sampling when it regularly buys a large quantity of breakable, perishable, or expensive items. Inspecting each piece of merchandise is inefficient. So, items are sampled for quality and condition. Thus, a retailer ready to buy several hundred light fixtures, bunches of bananas, or inexpensive watches does not inspect each fixture, banana, or watch. Instead, a number of units are sampled. The entire selection is bought if the sample is satisfactory. An unsatisfactory sample might cause a whole shipment to be rejected (or a discount negotiated). Sampling may also occur on receipt of merchandise.

A retailer engages in description buying when it buys standardized, nonbreakable, and nonperishable merchandise. The items are not inspected or sampled; they are ordered in quantity from a verbal, written, or pictorial description. For example, a stationery store can order paper clips, pads, and typing paper from a catalog or Web site. After it receives an order, a count of only those items is conducted.

Negotiating the Purchase

Once a merchandise source is chosen and pre-purchase evaluation is conducted, a retailer negotiates the purchase and its terms. A new or special order usually results in a negotiated contract. In this case, a retailer and a supplier carefully discuss all aspects of the purchase. However, a regular order or reorder often involves a uniform contract. Terms are then standard or have already been agreed on, and the order is handled routinely.

For off-price retailers and other deep discounters, negotiated contracts are normally required with every purchase. That is because these firms employ **opportunistic buying,** by which especially low prices are negotiated for merchandise whose sales have not lived up to expectations, end-of-season goods, items consumers have returned to the manufacturer or another retailer, and closeouts.

A number of purchase terms have to be specified, whether a negotiated or a uniform contract is involved. These include the delivery date, quantity purchased, price and payment arrangements, discounts, form of delivery, and point of transfer of title. There may also be special clauses.

The delivery date and the quantity purchased must be clearly stated. A retailer should be able to cancel an order if either provision is not carried out properly. The retailer's purchase price, payment arrangements, and permissible discounts are also important. What is the retailer's cost per item (including handling charges)? What forms of payment are permitted (such as cash versus credit)? What discounts are given? Often, retailers' purchase prices are discounted for early payments (for example, "2/10/net 30" means a 2 percent discount is given if the full bill is paid in 10 days; the full bill is due in 30 days), trade activities (such as setting up displays), and quantity purchases. Stipulations are needed for the form of delivery (water, air, truck, rail, and so on) and the party responsible for shipping charges (for instance, FOB factory—free on board—means a supplier places merchandise with the shipper, but the retailer pays the freight). Last, the point of transfer of title—when ownership changes from supplier to buyer—should be noted in a contract.

Special clauses may be inserted by either party. Sometimes, these clauses are beneficial to both parties (such as an agreement regarding how much advertising support each party will provide). Other times, the clauses are insisted on by the party that is more powerful. As noted in Chapter 1, a major bone of contention between vendors and large retailers is the latter's increasing use of **slotting allowances,** which are payments that retailers require of vendors for providing shelf space in stores:

> Imagine a real-estate market so tight that its inhabitants pay landowners thousands of dollars just to reserve a spot no more than a foot square. But the fee would not guaran-

To learn more about the slotting allowance controversy, read this online *Candy Business* article (www.retailmerchandising.net/cbus/archives/0599/599slot.asp).

tee the tiny space would be theirs even a month down the road. This expensive real-estate market won't be found in Manhattan or Tokyo. It's on the shelves of your local supermarket. Slotting allowances, ranging from $1,000 to $20,000, are charged by supermarkets and other big retailers to manufacturers wanting to stock new products on their shelves. Small businesses say slotting fees conspire to keep their products off the shelves. Retailers reply that the introduction of a new product is a risky business and requires investment to succeed.[8]

Concluding Purchases

A discussion on "EDI (General)" is available at *ec/edi Insider* (www.wpc-edi.com/insider), an industry newsletter.

For many medium-sized and large firms, purchases are concluded automatically. Computers are used to complete and process orders (based on electronic data interchange [EDI] and quick response [QR] inventory planning), and each purchase is fed into the computer's data bank. Smaller retailers often conclude purchases manually. Orders are written up and processed manually, and purchases are added to the store's book inventory in the same manner. However, with the rapid advances in computerized ordering software, even small retailers can sometimes place orders electronically—especially if they are tied to large wholesalers that supply them with EDI and QR capabilities.

Multiunit retailers must determine whether to use central, regional, or local approval to conclude purchases: Should central or regional management have the final okay in a purchase, or should the local manager have the final say? Advantages and disadvantages accrue to each approval technique.

As mentioned in the previous section, transfer of title should be specified with the supplier. Several alternatives are possible:

- The retailer takes title immediately on purchase.
- The retailer assumes ownership after merchandise is loaded onto the mode of transportation.
- The retailer takes title when a shipment is received.
- The retailer does not take title until the end of a billing cycle, when the supplier is paid.
- The retailer accepts merchandise on consignment and does not own the items. The supplier is paid after merchandise is sold.

It is essential that the retailer understand the differences among these options, because its responsibilities and rights differ in each case.

A consignment or memorandum deal can be made if a vendor is in a weak position and wants to persuade retailers to carry its items. In a **consignment purchase,** a retailer has no risk because title is not taken; the supplier owns the goods until sold. A new electronic version of the consignment purchase, known as scan-based trading, is being actively tested at various supermarkets. It saves time and money for all parties due to paperless steps in the purchase process.[9] In a **memorandum purchase,** risk is still low, but a retailer takes title on delivery and is responsible for damages. In both options, retailers do not pay for items until they are sold and can return items.

Receiving and Stocking Merchandise

At this point, a firm physically receives and handles items, which involves such varied tasks as receiving and storing goods, checking and paying invoices, price and inventory marking, setting up displays, figuring on-floor amounts and assortments, completing transactions, arranging delivery or pickup, processing returns and damaged goods, monitoring pilferage, and controlling merchandise. Distribution management is key, whether it entails retail distribution centers or direct store delivery. See Figure 15.4.

Figure 15.4

Receiving and Stocking Merchandise at Category Killer Stores

Italian-based Salmoiraghi and Vigano operates a chain of category killer eyewear stores. These stores carry prescription and nonprescription glasses, including an extensive line of designer glasses. Because the company carries the products of numerous manufacturers from around the globe, it must coordinate shipments, set up the many displays in each store, and monitor inventory levels by item—challenging tasks.

Reprinted by permission of PricewaterhouseCoopers LLP.

Items are usually shipped from suppliers to warehouses, for storage and disbursement, or directly to retailers' store(s). For example, the Walgreen drugstore chain has fully automated warehouses to stock thousands of products and speed their delivery to the stores. On the other hand, rather than rely exclusively on deliveries from suppliers, The Limited, Inc., orders some apparel by satellite and computer; uses common and contract carriers to pick it up from manufacturers in the United States and Asia (using chartered jets); ships items to its own warehouses in Columbus, Ohio; and then delivers them to stores. At J.C. Penney, there are separate distribution centers for its store and catalog operations.

When orders are received, they must be checked for completeness and product condition. Invoices must also be checked for accuracy and payments made as specified. This step cannot be taken for granted:

> To improve efficiency, cut costs, and enhance service, manufacturers are seeking to define the "perfect order" and create processes to let them consistently deliver it to retailers and wholesalers. So far, the definition that major firms have agreed upon considers order completeness, timeliness and condition, and invoice accuracy. Many manufacturers have measured order completeness and on-time delivery for years, but the perfect order bundles a number of factors that haven't been considered in relation to each other. While they may have looked to improve on-time delivery, for example, they may not have considered if that has affected the condition in which merchandise arrives. Conversely, in the effort to ship complete, undamaged orders, they may be missing customer deadlines.[10]

Next, prices and inventory information are marked on merchandise. Supermarkets estimate that price marking on individual items costs them an amount equal to their annual profits, and they look forward to the time when shelf prices will be legally sufficient in all markets. Price and inventory marking can be done in various ways. Small firms may hand-post prices and manually keep inventory records. Some retailers use their own computer-generated price tags and rely on pre-printed UPC data on packages to keep inventory records. Others buy tags, with computer- and human-readable price and inventory data, from outside suppliers. Still others expect vendors to provide source tagging.

Monarch Marking (www.monarch.com/products/retbarproducts.htm) markets an extensive line of printing devices.

The more information labels or tags possess, the better the inventory control system. For example, with portable printers from Monarch Marking Systems (www.paxar.com/solutions_monarch.htm), a retailer can use hand-held devices to print UPC-based labels; and the devices can be connected to store computers. Seagull Scientific's Bar Tender for Windows software (www.seagullscientific.com) enables retailers to easily print product tags containing a wide range of data. See Figures 15.5 and 15.6.

Store displays and on-floor quantities and assortments depend on the type of retailer and merchandise involved. Supermarkets usually have bin and rack displays and place most inventory on the selling floor. Traditional department stores have all kinds of interior displays and place a lot of inventory in the back room, off the sales floor. Displays and on-floor merchandising are discussed in Chapter 18.

Merchandise handling is not complete until the customer buys and receives it from a retailer. This means order taking, credit or cash transactions, packaging, and delivery or pickup. Automation has improved retailer performance in each of these areas.

A procedure for processing returns and damaged goods is also needed. The retailer must determine the party responsible for customer returns (supplier or retailer) and the situations

Figure 15.5
The Monarch 1130 Series Labeler

The 1130 Series labelers represent a complete family of identification and pricing solutions. The labelers are simple and easy to use. They have ergonomic handle grips, lift-up covers for quick maintenance, label-viewing windows, and other features.
Reprinted by permission of Monarch Marking Systems.

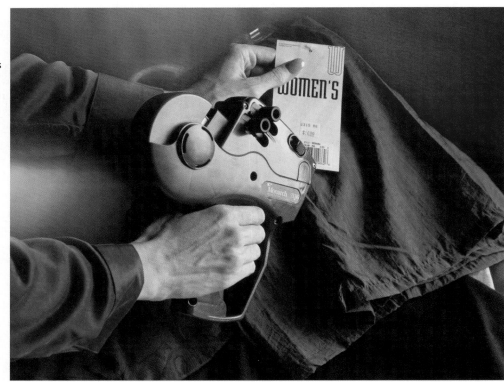

Figure 15.6

Bar Tender for Windows

Seagull Scientific Systems' Bar Tender for Windows printing software can be used to generate a wide variety of label designs.

Reprinted by permission of Seagull Scientific Systems, author of "Bar Tender" label printing software.

in which damaged goods would be accepted for refund or exchange (such as the length of time a warranty is honored).

As discussed later in the chapter, monitoring and reducing inventory losses due to theft is an aspect of merchandising that has grown in significance. More retailers than before are taking aggressive actions to deal with this problem due to the high costs of merchandise theft.

Merchandise control involves evaluating revenues, profits, turnover, inventory shortages, seasonality, and costs for each goods/service category and item carried by a retailer. Control is generally achieved by preparing inventory data, and then periodically conducting a physical inventory count to check the accuracy of the figures. The latter usually must be adjusted to reflect damaged goods, pilferage, customer returns, and other factors. An in-depth discussion of this topic appears in Chapter 16.

Merchandise receiving and handling is covered further later in this chapter.

Pursuing a Merchandising Career to the (Car) Max

Joe Wilson is a purchasing manager for CarMax, the car and truck retailer. Wilson feels that his current career is the perfect application of his University of Richmond finance degree. He is also impressed with CarMax's rapid growth. When Wilson started at CarMax in 1995, the retailer had only 3 units. By 1999, it had 25 units, as well as continued plans for expansion. The chain's growth has helped propel Wilson's career from his starting position as a buyer in training to buyer, and now to lead buyer. Wilson's present responsibilities include balancing the supply and demand for the chain's inventory of both cars and trucks. This requires that Wilson travel to car auctions to purchase used vehicles.

Before joining CarMax, Joe Wilson assumed that he would have a corporate job wearing a suit. But he left the door open for other opportunities. "And that's the advice I'd give students in college now." According to Wilson, "Before people take a position, they have to decide if they want a career or job. You have to do something you really love and where you can have fun. Open your mind to new ideas."

Source: "Taking Careers to the Max," *Careers in Retailing* (January 1999), pp. 20, 22.

Reordering Merchandise

A procedure for reordering merchandise is necessary for items the retailer purchases more than once. Four factors are critical in devising such a plan: order and delivery time, inventory turnover, financial outlays, and inventory versus ordering costs.

Order and delivery time must be studied. How long does it take for a retailer to process an order and a supplier to fulfill and deliver it? It is possible for delivery time to be so lengthy that a retailer must reorder while having a full inventory. On the other hand, overnight delivery may be available for some items.

The turnover rate for each type of merchandise must be calculated. How long does it take for a retailer to sell out its inventory? A fast-selling product gives a retailer two choices: order a surplus of items and spread out reorder periods, or keep a low inventory and order frequently (short order periods). A slow-selling item may let a retailer reduce its initial inventory level and spread out the reorder period.

The financial outlays under various purchase options must be reviewed. A large order, with a quantity discount, may require a large cash outlay. A small order, while more expensive per item, results in lower total costs at any one time (since less inventory is held).

Finally, inventory holding versus ordering costs must be weighed. Advantages of having a large inventory are customer satisfaction, quantity discounts in purchases, low per-item shipping charges, and easier control and handling. Potential disadvantages are high investment costs; the greater possibility of obsolescence, deterioration, and damages; and storage, insurance, and opportunity costs. Advantages of placing many orders and keeping a small inventory are low investment costs, low opportunity costs, low storage costs, and low damages and obsolescence. Potential disadvantages are disappointing customers by being out of stock, higher per-unit costs, the impact of order delays, the need for partial shipments, extra service charges, and more complex control and handling. Retailers normally try to trade off the two costs by keeping enough stock to satisfy customers while not having a high surplus inventory. Quick response inventory planning lowers both inventory and ordering costs through closer retailer-supplier relationships.

Re-Evaluating on a Regular Basis

Once a merchandising plan is enacted, it should be re-evaluated regularly, with management reviewing the buying organization and that organization assessing the implementation. The overall procedure, as well as the handling of individual goods and services, should be monitored. Any conclusions reached while re-evaluating a merchandise plan become part of the information-gathering stage for future efforts.

LOGISTICS

Logistics is the total process of planning, implementing, and coordinating the physical movement of merchandise from manufacturer (wholesaler) to retailer to customer in the most timely, effective, and cost-efficient manner possible. Logistics regards order processing and fulfillment, transportation, warehousing, customer service, and inventory management as interdependent functions in the value delivery chain. It oversees inventory management decisions as items travel through a retail supply chain. If a logistics system works well, firms reduce stockouts, hold down inventories, and improve customer service—all at the same time. See Figure 15.7.

Logistics can be quite challenging—with plenty of points at which potential breakdowns may occur:

> Amazon.com's new warehouses are a wonder of automation. On the third level, for example, is a box of Raggedy Ann dolls with a red light in front of it. When the light goes on, it means that someone, somewhere in the world, has gone to Amazon's Web site and ordered the doll. Quickly, a worker comes by, picks out a doll, puts it into a cart, and deposits it on a conveyor belt that rushes through the vast warehouse. The doll moves from belt to belt until it drops into a long chute-like bin, one of 2,000 used to assemble orders. As the conveyer moves, other items for the same customer also fall into the bin. When the order is complete, another light flashes below the bin, and a

Figure 15.7
The Sophisticated Logistics System of Reitmans

As Canada's largest women's specialty retailer, Reitmans Limited operates stores in five divisions: Reitmans, Smart Set, Dalmys, Penningtons Superstores, and RW & Co. The firm's distribution center consists of 210,000 square feet in Montreal. It ships over 26,000,000 garments and accessories to 600 stores across Canada. This requires sophisticated technology, proven conveyor systems, and dedicated employees. Automated receiving, processing, and shipping systems—with three flat-goods sorters, two hanging-goods sorters, and powered trolleys—have produced excellent results, including increased distribution accuracy, a 30 percent reduction in labor requirements, a 50 percent increase in peak processing throughput, and a two-day reduction in processing time.
Reprinted by permission.

worker puts all the items into a box, which travels down another series of belts through machines that pack it, tape it, weigh it, and affix a mailing label. Yet more conveyers carry it to a truck at one of the loading docks. The warehouses are still working out some kinks. About two weeks ago, the shrink wrapper, which encloses books in plastic to protect them in shipping, wasn't getting the wrap to shrink. And a device that affixes shipping labels onto boxes was malfunctioning. But, in general, the place was humming.[11]

In this section, these aspects of logistics are discussed: performance goals, the supply chain, order processing and fulfillment, transportation and warehousing, and customer transactions and customer service. Inventory management is covered in the following section.

Performance Goals

Among retailers' major logistics goals are to

- Relate the costs incurred to specific logistics activities, thereby fulfilling all activities as economically as possible, given the firms' other performance objectives.
- Place and receive orders as easily, accurately, and satisfactorily as possible.
- Minimize the time between ordering and receiving merchandise.
- Coordinate shipments from various suppliers.
- Have enough merchandise on hand to satisfy customer demand, without having so much inventory that heavy markdowns will be necessary.
- Place merchandise on the sales floor efficiently.
- Process customer orders efficiently and in a manner satisfactory to customers.
- Work collaboratively with other members of the supply chain, including regular communications.
- Handle returns effectively and minimize damaged products.
- Monitor accomplishments.
- Have backup plans in case of breakdowns in the system.

South Park Merchandise Goes South

After receiving complaints from customers that the *South Park* merchandise it was carrying was in poor taste, J.C. Penney decided to stop ordering *South Park* items. Before deciding to discontinue the line, Penney had carried the *South Park* brand for 15 months. Although all the *South Park* merchandise had been ordered through Penney's men's wear division, individual stores were selling the items in various departments based on the store managers' discretion.

Among the items affected were T-shirts (priced at $17 and $18), boxer shorts (priced at $10), and stuffed animals (priced between $18 and $50). All of the merchandise featured characters and images from Comedy Central's *South Park* television series, which some viewers found to often be rude and violent. The *South Park* movie from Paramount was also "R" rated. Penney continued to sell all of the affected merchandise until the inventory ran out.

Rather than selling the *South Park* merchandise until the inventory was depleted, what other options were available to J.C. Penney? Comment on the ethical ramifications of each option.

Source: "Penney's Halts South Park Orders," *Women's Wear Daily* (April 29, 1999), p. 4.

Consider these examples.

Sears employs a formal procedure for setting logistics goals. Vice-presidents for transportation, distribution, maintenance, information systems, customer relations, vendor relations, and the buying organization meet periodically to set quantifiable logistics goals, such as reducing the cost of moving single cartons through a distribution center or between two points by a given date. The vice-presidents suggest goals for one another and vote on each of the ideas proposed. Objectives that "pass" are recorded on the executives' evaluation reports and analyzed monthly to see if they are being met.[12]

At Uptons, the full-line discount store chain, the chief executive's favorite term is "throughput." It embodies his passion for speed and accessibility and a growing interest in logistics. The CEO is always searching for ways to reduce the time to move merchandise "through the distribution center, into the store, onto the floor, and out the door." "It's about concentration and enormous focus. And, it's about collaborating with major alliances on how to cut lead times, how to get sharper prices, and how to get the goods on the floor three hours quicker. It's terribly important, and it's how we intend to win."[13]

The Bon-Ton department store chain (www.bonton.com) has prepared a detailed *Logistics Guide* for its vendors. As it says at the company Web site:

In any partnership and any supplier/retailer working relationship, it is very important to define expectations. Product quality, shipping windows, production, and product availability are just some of the expectations that are defined. In retail, the role of logistics is taking on a greater importance in producing higher levels of productivity, improving product flow to the selling floor, and reducing inventories and overall cost reduction for both the retailer and supplier. To this end, these logistical requirements have been developed for vendors. All of the standards are consistent with standard practices prevalent in the retail industry. While critical to our mutual success, these provisions allow us to optimize freight expense, and receive and process merchandise in a timely and cost-effective manner, thus assuring a continuous flow of merchandise to stores. All instructions, terms, and expectations must be fully complied with and become applicable to all shipments to Bon-Ton. Failure to comply in full with these instructions may create an additional and unnecessary freight cost, unacceptable delays in transit time, and/or unnecessary labor cost, which will be passed on to the shipper in the form of a chargeback.

Bon-Ton (www.bonton.com/logistics/logistics.htm) is very serious about maximizing its logistics performance.

Supply Chain Management

The **supply chain** is the logistics aspect of a value delivery chain. It comprises all of the parties that participate in the retail logistics process: manufacturers, wholesalers, third-party specialists (shippers, order-fulfillment houses, and so forth), and the retailer. The following are key supply chain trends.

Many retailers and suppliers are striving for closer logistical relationships. One emerging technique for larger retailers is known as **collaborative planning, forecasting, and replenishment (CPFR),** whereby there is a holistic approach to supply chain management among a network of trading partners. According to the Collaborative Planning, Forecasting, and Replenishment Committee, a nonprofit trade organization with more than 60 member firms (including Best Buy, H.E. Butt, Kmart, Staples, and Wal-Mart),

The CPFR Committee (www.cpfr.org) is actively working to expand the use of integrated supply chain planning.

CPFR has the potential to deliver increased sales, organizational streamlining and alignment, administrative and operational efficiency, improved cash flow, and improved return-on-assets performance. How does CPFR work? It begins with an agreement between trading partners to develop a market-specific plan based on sound category management principles. A key to success is that both partners agree to own the process and the plan. This plan fundamentally describes what is going to be sold, how it will be merchandised and promoted, in what marketplace, and during what time frame. This plan becomes operational through each company's existing systems but is accessible by either party.[14]

Third-party logistics (outsourcing) is becoming more popular. For example, in dealing with its vendors, Sears has very precise standards regarding invoices, purchase orders, advance shipping orders, and barcode labeling. The retailer also prefers conducting routine transactions electronically. Because these stipulations can be difficult for small suppliers, Sears uses St. Paul Software as an outside logistics specialist. St. Paul contacts the small firms, determines their abilities, and assists them in meeting Sears' requirements—including, in some cases, converting vendor faxes into electronic purchase orders (which can then be tracked). Third-party logistics is not limited to just big retailers. Companies such as GATX Logistics and Ryder Dedicated Logistics work with small and medium retailers to ship and warehouse merchandise.[15]

The Web is a growing force in supplier-retailer communications. A number of manufacturers and retailers have set up dedicated sites exclusively to interact with their channel partners. For confidential information exchanges, passwords and secure encryption technology are utilized. Target Corporation, for one, has a very advanced Web site called Partners Online that it has set up in stages. By the time the site is fully rolled out in 2001, Target Corporation will have spent four years in developing and testing it. At the Web site, vendors can access weekly sales data and inventory reports, accounts payable figures, invoices, and report cards on their performance. There are also manuals and newsletters.[16]

Order Processing and Fulfillment

To optimize order processing and fulfillment, a number of retailers now engage in **quick response (QR) inventory planning,** by which a retailer reduces the amount of inventory it keeps on hand by ordering more frequently and in lower quantity. A QR system requires a retailer to have good relationships with suppliers, coordinate shipments, monitor inventory levels closely to avoid running out of stock, and regularly communicate with suppliers via electronic data interchange and other means.

For the retailer, a QR system reduces inventory costs, minimizes the space required for product storage, and lets the firm better match its orders with market conditions—by replenishing stock more quickly. For the manufacturer, a QR system can also improve inventory turnover and better match supply and demand by giving the vendor the data to track actual sales. These data were less available to the manufacturer in the past. In addition, a QR system that operates effectively makes it more difficult for a retailer to switch suppliers.

Overall, the most active users of QR are department stores, full-line discount stores, specialty apparel stores, home centers, supermarkets, and drugstores. Among the individual firms using QR with at least some products are Cub Foods, Dillard's, Federated Department Stores, Giant Food, Home Depot, Kmart, The Limited, Inc., J.C. Penney, Sears, Shaw's Supermarkets, Target Corporation, and Wal-Mart.

A QR system is most effective if used in conjunction with floor-ready merchandise, lower minimum order sizes, newly formatted store fixtures, and electronic data interchange. **Floor-ready merchandise** refers to items that are received at the store in condition to be put directly on display without any preparation by retail workers. Thus, with this approach, apparel manufacturers are responsible for preticketing garments (with information specified by the retailer) and placing them on hangers. Similarly, Safeway supermarkets require that vendors put Safeway tags on fruit such as apples and grapefruit, freeing produce clerks for other tasks.

Quick response also means suppliers need to rethink the minimum order sizes they will accept. For instance, while a minimum order size of 12 for a given size or color was once required by sheet and towel makers, minimum order size is now as low as 2 units. Likewise, minimum order sizes for men's shirts have been reduced from 6 to as few as 2 units.

The new minimum order sizes have led some retailers to refixture in-store departments. Prior to quick response, fixtures were often configured on the basis of a retailer's stocking full inventories. Today, retailers need to make an impact with smaller inventories.

Electronic data interchange, EDI (described in Chapter 8), lets retailers use QR inventory planning efficiently—via a paperless, computer-to-computer relationship between retailers and their vendors. Research studies suggest that retail prices could be reduced by an average of 10 percent or so with the industrywide usage of QR and EDI. These two illustrations show the value of QR and EDI:

Big 5 Sporting Goods has cut the time between ordering and receiving goods from 3 weeks to 3 days with the help of its EDI system. The retailer sells sports shoes, apparel, and other related items, in 9 western states. "Sporting goods has lagged behind in EDI," the firm's Andrea Weeks says. "But Nike gave us a big push when it told us it wanted us to start using EDI." Rather than risk losing Nike as a supplier, Weeks sold the notion of EDI to her bosses. "I didn't promise more accuracy, complete shipments, or a shorter order time, though we've seen those things, because I didn't want to oversell. I just said it would save buying associates a lot of time. Formerly, we wrote orders and entered data in our system. Then, we'd fax orders to vendors and data would be entered again."[17]

A buyer is ready to purchase goods from abroad. Instead of picking up the phone or sending a fax, she issues a request for a price quote through a Web site. Not long afterward, she receives a reply and executes an order with a mouse click. As this scenario shows, industry players are recognizing that cyberspace EDI for orders, inventory levels, sales trends, shipping/receiving times, item forecasts, and the like can yield cost reduction, better customer service, and streamlined delivery. Extranets (private networks using Internet technology) have gained considerable ground, as well. While many major vendors and retailers have had EDI in place for some time, the Internet empowers smaller firms that could not finance the programming inherent in supporting EDI. "The beauty of the Internet is that it takes a company's size out of the equation," says Karen Norman, a manager at Tastee Apple, which produces apple cider, apple chips, and caramel apples for Sam's Clubs and other membership clubs.[18]

Take a look at the "Newsletter" at this site (www.ecr-central. com) to gain further insights on ECR.

In the supermarket sector of retailing, a number of firms are striving to apply their own form of order processing and fulfillment, known as **efficient consumer response (ECR).** Through ECR, supermarkets are incorporating aspects of quick response inventory planning, electronic data interchange, and logistics planning. Here is how: "ECR builds on QR techniques but addresses a much wider scope of issues. Not only is the order cycle addressed, but so are a wide variety of business processes involving new product introductions, item assortments, and promotions. The key enabling methods are similar, however. ECR uses technology to improve every step of the cycle (or business process), which results in making every step faster and more accurate. ECR also uses collaborative relationships in which any combination of retailer, wholesaler, broker, and manufacturer works together to seek out inefficiencies and reduce costs by looking at the net benefits for all players in the relationship. The idea is that true efficiency comes only when overall costs are reduced for all the parties in the relationship."[19] Although U.S. supermarkets believe ECR may let them cut tens of billions of dollars in distribution costs, implementing it has not been easy. Many supermarkets are still unwilling to trade their ability to negotiate special short-term purchase terms with vendors in return for routine order fulfillment without special deals.

There are two other aspects of order processing and fulfillment that retailers are also addressing. One, with *advanced ship notices,* retailers involved with QR and EDI receive a "heads up," whereby complete bills of lading are sent electronically as soon as a shipment leaves the vendor. This gives the retailers more time to efficiently receive and allocate merchandise.[20] Two, because more retailers are buying from multiple suppliers, from multilocation sources, and from overseas, they must coordinate the placement and fulfillment of their orders. Home Depot, among others, has even added an import logistics group to form a coordinated method for forecasting, ordering, sourcing, and logistics. Supervalu is grappling with its practice of buying such products as fruit from many different countries—from Australia to Uruguay.[21]

Sometimes, there are glitches in order processing and fulfillment that cause major headaches. That recently occurred with Hershey Foods:

Just a few days before Halloween, the biggest candy binge of the year, the Great North Foods warehouse in Alpena, Michigan, displayed empty shelves where there should have been Hershey's bars. Reese's Peanut Butter Cups were missing, too. The trouble? An order for 20,000 pounds of candy the regional distributor had placed with Hershey in September hadn't arrived. Great North had to stiff 100 of the 700 stores it supplies on candy orders it couldn't fill. Only on October 28 did a Hershey shipment show up at Great North—the first in five weeks—and the distributor still didn't know if Hershey had sent enough to meet its needs. For the nation's largest candy maker, new technology that came on line in July had gummed up its ordering and distribution systems, leaving many stores nationwide reporting spot shortages of Kisses, Kit Kats, Twizzlers, and other stalwarts."[22]

Transportation and Warehousing

Several transportation decisions are necessary:

- How often will merchandise be shipped to the retailer?
- How will small order quantities be handled?
- What type of shipper will be used (the manufacturer, the retailer itself, or a third-party specialist)?
- What transportation form will be used? Are multiple forms required (such as manufacturer trucks to retailer warehouses and retailer trucks to individual stores)?
- What special considerations must be taken into account for perishables and expensive merchandise?
- How often will special shipping arrangements be necessary (such as rush orders)?
- How are shipping terms negotiated with suppliers?
- What delivery options will be available for the retailer's customers? This is a critical decision for nonstore retailers, especially those selling through the Web.

Transportation effectiveness is influenced by the caliber of the logistics infrastructure (including the availability of refrigerated trucks, airports, waterway docking facilities, and superhighways), traffic congestion, parking, and other factors. Retailers operating outside the United States must come to grips with the logistical problems in many foreign countries. For example, "Food shipments can take 5 days to get across Brazil because there's no superhighway or rail system. In China, 90 percent of the roads are dirt. You can't just put up a sign and say you're in business."[23]

With regard to warehousing, some retailers focus almost entirely on warehouses as central—or regional—distribution centers. Products are shipped from suppliers to these warehouses, and then allotted and shipped to individual outlets. Burlington Coat Factory's 420,000-square-foot New Jersey central warehouse processes 54 percent of the firm's dollar volume of merchandise to its stores nationwide. Toys "R" Us has a system of separate regional distribution centers for its U.S. Toys "R" Us stores, its international Toys "R" Us stores, and its Kids "R" Us chain. Most centers are owned; some are leased.[24] Figure 15.8 shows how Claire's central warehousing system works.

Other retailers, including many supermarket chains, do not rely as much on central or regional warehouses. Instead, they have at least some goods shipped directly from suppliers to individual stores. This is known as **direct store distribution (DSD),** and it works best with retailers that also utilize EDI. Direct store delivery is a way to move high turnover, high bulk, perishable products from the manufacturer directly to the store. Industrywide, DSD supermarket items (such as beverages, bread, and snack foods) have an average shelf life of 70 days, while warehoused items have an average shelf life of more than a year. About 25 percent of the typical supermarket's sales are from items with DSD.[25]

The advantages of central warehousing include efficiency in transportation and storage, mechanized processing of goods, improved security, efficient marking of merchandise, the ease of returns, and smooth and coordinated merchandise flow. Central warehousing's key disadvantages are the excessive centralized control, the extra handling of perishables, the high operating costs for small retailers, and potential order-processing delays. In addition, centralized warehousing may reduce the capability of quick response systems by adding another stage in distribution. These are the pros and cons of direct store delivery:

> DSD offers great promise, both as a way to ensure that fresh products are always on the shelf and as a significant step toward realizing the potential of micromerchandising. Depending on the brands represented, a DSD vendor may be in a store as often as 2 or

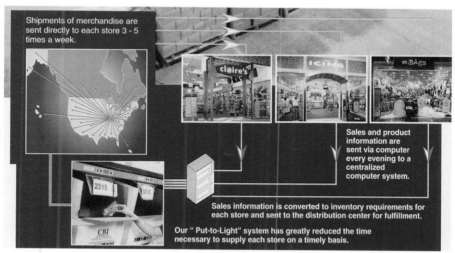

Figure 15.8
Claire's Aggressive Use of Central Warehousing

Claire's Stores has a central warehouse in Hoffman Estates, Illinois. The mammoth warehouse has been designed to accommodate a second level and can support up to 6,000 stores. At present, the firm operates more than 2,200 shops, mostly in shopping malls. They sell inexpensive jewelry and accessories for girls. Its stores include Claire's Boutiques, Claire's Accessories, Dara Michelle, The Icing, Bijoux One, and Bow Bangle (in Europe). Apparel and other items are sold at Mr. Rags. It acquired the rival Afterthoughts chain from Venator in 1999.
Reprinted by permission.

Technology in Retailing

Merchandise Software Brooks New Bounds

Brooks Brothers recently revised the way it implements its merchandise plans. The retailer has installed an integrated software suite of retail applications that include purchase orders, supplier contracts, inventory replenishment, electronic data interchange, and promotions management. These programs have been designed to be integrated with the retailer's financial accounting programs, as well as its warehouse management systems.

Michelle Garvey, Brooks Brothers' vice-president of information systems, says: "Everyone at Brooks Brothers, from the CEO to the IS department to the buyers and merchandisers, was ready for a change. Our core merchandising system ran on an obsolete hardware platform, the software vendor was out of business, and the system was heavily customized." In selecting its new system, Brooks Brothers resisted customization due to past difficulties with customer support and upgrading.

The new system incorporates some enhancements to the vendor's "plain vanilla" system. These enhancements enable Brooks Brothers to markdown a specific color that has not been selling well while allowing a classic color to be sold at full price.

What are the pros and cons of a customized merchandising planning system for a retailer such as Brooks Brothers?

Source: Matt Nannery, "Brooks Bros.' Big Bang," *Chain Store Age* (April 1999), pp. 43–46.

---

3 times a week. This should guarantee that DSD products are among the freshest in the store. The knowledge of DSD vendors ought to be a valuable source of information to store managers. It should also open the door to selling individual stores slightly differently in response to their unique target populations. However, DSD is a system that, currently at least, adds layers of complexity to backroom receiving and vendor/distributor relations and can be the main cause of the mountains of invoices and receiving documents.[26]

Customer Transactions and Customer Service

Besides inbound logistics, retailers must plan for outbound logistics: completing customer transactions by turning over merchandise to the customer. This can be as simple as having a shopper take an item from the display area to the checkout counter or driving his or her car to a loading area where the product is dispensed. It can also be as complex as concluding one Web transaction that entails shipments from multiple vendors directly to the customer. A shopper's purchase of a computer, a fax machine, and a telephone answering machine from Buy.com, for instance, may result in three separate shipments. That is why such firms as UPS, Federal Express, DHL, and Airborne are doing more retail deliveries than ever before. They can readily handle the diversity of shipping requests, which retailers often cannot.[27]

The UPS Logistics Group (www.wwlog.com) is expanding its operations targeted at retailers.

Even the simplest customer deliveries can have a breakdown. Think of the local pharmacy that has its high school delivery person fail to show up for work one day—or the pizzeria that gets no customer orders between 2:00 P.M. and 5:00 P.M. and 25 delivery orders between 5:00 P.M. and 7:00 P.M.

There are considerable differences between retail stores and nonstore retailers. Most retail stores expect the customer to take the purchase with him or her, or to pick it up when it is ready (such as a new car). All direct marketers, including Web retailers, are responsible for ensuring that products are delivered to the shopper's door or another convenient nearby location.

Customer service expectations are very much affected by the retailer's logistical effectiveness. This can be quite a challenge: "Analysts say online grocery shopping is a tough market to crack because customers expect high quality and are unwilling to pay extra for the convenience. Grocery stores already operate on razor-thin profit margins without the added expense of delivery, and the perishable nature of many foods does not make operating from a central location feasible. By some estimates, an online grocer must do 10 times the volume of a typical store to be successful."[28]

INVENTORY MANAGEMENT

As part of its logistics efforts, a retailer employs **inventory management** to acquire and maintain a proper merchandise assortment while ordering, shipping, handling, storing, displaying, and selling costs are kept in check. First, a retailer places an order with a supplier based on a sales forecast or actual customer behavior. Both the number of items and their variety (such as assorted colors and materials) are requested in ordering. Order size and frequency depend on quantity discounts and inventory costs. Second, a supplier fills the retailer's order and sends merchandise to a warehouse or directly to the store(s). Third, the retailer receives merchandise, makes items available for sale (by removing them from shipping cartons, marking prices on them, and placing them on the selling floor), and completes customer transactions. Some transactions are not complete until items are delivered to the customer. The cycle starts anew when a retailer places another order. Let us examine these elements of inventory management: retailer tasks, inventory levels, merchandise security, reverse logistics, and inventory analysis.

Retailer Tasks

Due to the comprehensive nature of inventory management, and as part of their efforts to be more cost-effective, various retailers now expect suppliers to perform more tasks or they outsource at least part of their inventory management activities: "A decade ago, producers shipped products to retailers in a *warehouse-ready* mode. Retailers then reprocessed merchandise to package and price it for sale in the store where consumers make purchases. Today, in the era of *floor-ready*, producers ship products that have already been packaged and prepared for immediate movement to the sales floor, thus bypassing some traditional channels and creating new alliances between retailers and producers. As we move to the new millennium, there will be a shift to *consumer-ready* manufacturing where the links between producer and consumer are even more direct than in traditional selling channels."[29] Here are some examples:

- Wal-Mart and other retailers are counting on key suppliers to actively participate in their inventory management programs. Procter & Gamble even has its own employees stationed at the headquarters of Wal-Mart to manage the inventory replenishment of Procter & Gamble products. Industrywide, this practice is known as **vendor-managed inventory (VMI).** It is rapidly growing in popularity.

- Wal-Mart is also at the forefront of another trend, store-based retailers outsourcing customer order fulfillment for their online businesses. Wal-Mart hired Fingerhut Business Services (a subsidiary of Federated Department Stores) because, even though it "is considered technologically advanced in many areas, online is not one of them." Wal-Mart is using Fingerhut until it can build up its own online order fulfillment facilities, a task taking longer than it anticipated.[30]

- According to the National Association for Retail Merchandising Services (www.narms.com), third-party specialists provide more than $1 billion in retail merchandising

The National Association for Retail Merchandising Services offers a national online "JobBank" (www.narms.com/jobbank.html) by category and job location.

services each year, ranging from stocking shelves and reordering items to designing in-store displays. One of these specialists is Field Marketing (www. fieldmktg.com), which provides shelf maintenance, stocking and restocking, category management, visual merchandising, and other services for such clients as Dunkin' Donuts, Lowe's, KFC, and Home Depot.

One controversial inventory management activity involves who is responsible for source tagging, the manufacturer or the retailer. *Source tagging* occurs when anti-theft tags are placed on products when they are produced, rather than at the retail store. Although both sides agree on the benefits of manufacturers doing source tagging, in terms of the reduced costs and the floor-readiness of merchandise, there are disagreements about who should pay for the tags.[31]

Inventory Levels

Having the proper levels of inventory is a difficult balancing act: (1) The retailer wants to be appealing and never lose a sale because of being out of stock. Yet, it does not want to be "stuck" with excess merchandise that must be marked down drastically to be sold. (2) The balancing act is even harder for retailers that carry fad merchandise, that handle new items for which there is no track record, and that operate in new business formats (such as Web retailing) where demand estimates are often quite inaccurate. This is why the retailer must plan inventory levels in relation to the type of product involved: staples, assortment merchandise, fashion merchandise, fad merchandise, and best-sellers. (3) Customer demand is *never* completely predictable—even for staples. Weather, special sales, and other factors all have an impact on even the most stable items. (4) Shelf space allocations should be linked to current sales performance, which means that space allocations need to be reviewed and adjusted on a regular basis.

As previously noted, one of the main advantages of QR and EDI is that retailers can maintain "leaner" inventories since they receive new merchandise more often. However, when merchandise is especially popular or the supply chain breaks down, out of stocks are likely to occur (consider the Hershey example earlier in the chapter). A study by the Food Marketing Institute found that even supermarkets, which carry more staples than most other retailers, lose about 3 percent of sales due to out-of-stock merchandise.[32]

These two opposing perspectives show just how baffling inventory management can be:

The supply chain is bloated. But, with a little will power, retailers and the manufacturers that supply them can trim down and shape up. "Inventory positions are just too high," says the managing director of Global Supply Chain Management at KPMG Consulting. "Pretty typically, most retailers, as well as consumer packaged goods companies, can reduce inventory another 20 to 25 percent. There's a lot of inventory sitting around out there that is just not being productively deployed."[33]

[The question is, which 20 to 25 percent should be reduced? As Toys "R" Us sadly learned.] In fall 1998, shoppers at Toys "R" Us, armed with holiday wish lists, often left the chain's cavernous stores frustrated and empty-handed. Not just the hot sellers like Furby stuffed animals were in short supply; the stores even ran out of stocking-stuffers like Crayola Crayons. And the company felt the pain acutely in its bottom line. What of 1999? As the retailer headed into the crucial Christmas season, with Wal-Mart Stores and eToys continuing to snatch a big share of its business, Toys "R" Us strove mightily to do things differently. It hoped to avoid a repeat of 1998 by placing bigger bets on top-selling toys like Furby and Pokemon, as well as classics like Potato Head.[34]

Merchandise Security

Each year, $30 billion in U.S. retail sales are lost due to **inventory shrinkage** caused by employee theft, customer shoplifting, and fraud and administrative errors by vendors. Employees account for $18 billion, customers $10 billion, and vendors $2 billion of the total. The average employee theft is much larger than the average shopper theft. Shrinkage ranges from under 1 percent of sales at supermarkets to more than 2 percent of sales at sporting goods stores. At supermarkets, cigarettes and health and beauty care items represent 60 percent of the items shoplifted.[35] Thus, some form of merchandise security program is needed by all retailers.

To reduce theft, there are three key points to include in inventory planning. First, loss prevention should be weighed as stores are designed and built. Thus, the placement of store entrances, dressing rooms, and delivery areas should be planned from a security standpoint. Second, a combination of security measures should be enacted, such as employee background checks, in-store guards, electronic security equipment, and merchandise tags. Third, retailers need to communicate the importance of loss prevention to employees, customers, and vendors, as well as the actions they will to take to reduce losses (such as firing workers and prosecuting shoplifters).

Here are some activities that reduce losses due to merchandise theft:

Sensormatic (www. sensormatic.com) is a leader in electronic security.

- Product tags, security guards, video cameras, point-of-sale computers, employee surveillance, and burglar alarms are each being used by more firms. Storefront protection is also popular.
- Many general merchandise retailers and some supermarkets use **electronic article surveillance,** by which specially designed tags or labels are attached to products. The tags can be sensed by electronic devices that are placed at store exits. If the tags are not removed by store personnel or desensitized by electronic scanning equipment, an alarm goes off. Retailers now also have greater access to nonelectronic tags. These are tightly attached to products and must be removed by special detachers; otherwise, the products are unusable. Dye tags will permanently stain products, if not removed properly. See Figure 15.9.

Figure 15.9
Sensormatic: The Leader in Store Security Systems

These aesthetically pleasing, acrylic pedestals (part of Sensormatic's Euro Pro Max system) provide an unobstructed vision of exits, as well as the ultimate electronic article surveillance system. An alarm goes off if a person tries to leave a store without a product's security tag being properly removed.
Reprinted by permission of Sensormatic Electronics Corporation.

- Several retailers are doing detailed background checks for every employee. Some are using loss prevention software that detects suspicious employee behavior.
- Various retailers have employee training programs on the impact of losses and offer incentives for reducing them. Others distribute written policies on ethical behavior that are signed by all personnel, including owners and senior management. For example, Target Stores has enrolled managers at problem stores in a Stock Shortage Institute. Neiman Marcus has shown workers a film with interviews of convicted shoplifters in prison to highlight the problem's seriousness.
- More retailers are apt to fire employees and prosecute shoplifters involved with theft. Courts are imposing stiffer penalties; and in some areas, store detectives are empowered by police to make arrests. In over 40 states, there are civil restitution laws, whereby shoplifters must pay for stolen goods or face arrests and criminal trials. In most states, fines are higher if goods are not returned or they are damaged. Shoplifters must also contribute to court costs. By imposing its own fines, Jack Eckerd (the drugstore chain) saves time and immediately gets its merchandise back, rather than handing goods to police for evidence.
- Some mystery shoppers are hired to watch for shoplifting, not just to observe shopping behavior for research purposes.

Figure 15.10 presents a detailed list of tactics retailers can use to combat employee and shopper theft, by far the leading causes of losses.

When devising and enacting a merchandise security plan, a retailer must assess the plan's impact on its image, employee morale, shopper comfort, and vendor relations. For instance, by setting strict rules for fitting rooms (by limiting the number of garments brought in at one time) or placing chains on expensive furs and suede coats, a firm may cause some people to try on and buy less clothing—or visit another store. See Figure 15.11.

Reverse Logistics

The term **reverse logistics** encompasses all merchandise flows that go from the retailer back through the supply channel. It typically involves items returned because of damages, defects, or less-than-anticipated retail sales. Sometimes, retailers may use closeout firms to buy back unpopular merchandise (at a fraction of the original cost) that the supplier will not take back and then resell it at a deep discount. To avoid channel conflicts, the conditions for reverse logistics should be specified in advance.

Research by the Reverse Logistics Executive Council indicates that U.S. firms spend about $35 billion per year for the handling, transportation, and processing costs associated with return products. The University of Nevada's Center for Logistics Management says that customer returns are about 6 percent for retailing overall, with up to a 30 to 35 percent return rate for some catalog and Web retailers.[36]

These are among the decisions that must be made in this area:

Showcase (www. the-showcase.com) buys merchandise from failing retailers and sells it at its stores in North Carolina and Virginia.

- Under what conditions (such as the permissible time, the condition of the product, and so forth) are returns accepted by the retailer and by the manufacturer?
- What refund or reimbursement policy is followed? Is there a restocking fee for returning an opened package?
- What party is responsible for shipping the product back to the manufacturer?
- What documentation is necessary to prove the date of purchase, the price paid, and so on?
- How are repairs handled? (for example, an immediate exchange, a third-party repair, or a refurbished product sent by the manufacturer)
- To what extent are employees empowered to process returns?

Figure 15.10
Ways Retailers Can
Deter Employee and
Shopper Theft

A. Employee Theft

- Using pencil-and-paper honesty tests, voice stress analysis, and psychological tests as employee screening devices.
- Developing a system of locking up trash to prevent merchandise from being thrown out and then retrieved.
- Verifying through use of undercover personnel whether all sales are rung up.
- Utilizing cameras and mirrors to monitor activities.
- Implementing central control of all exterior doors to monitor opening and closing.
- Properly identifying deliverypeople.
- Verifying receipts and goods taken out.
- Sealing all trucks after they are loaded with goods.
- Inspecting worker packages, tool boxes, lunch boxes.
- Dividing responsibilities (e.g., having one employee record sales, another making deposits).
- Giving rewards for spotting thefts.
- Having training programs.
- Vigorously investigating all known losses.
- Firing offenders immediately.

B. Shopper Theft While Store Is Open

- Using in-store detectives or uniformed guards.
- Prosecuting all individuals charged with theft.
- Using electronic article surveillance wafers, electromagnets, or stick-ons for high-value and theft-prone goods.
- Developing comprehensive employee training programs.
- Providing employee bonuses based upon overall reduction in shortages or based on value of recovered merchandise.
- Inspecting all packages brought into store.
- Utilizing self-closing/self-locking showcases for high-value items such as jewelry.
- Chaining down expensive samples, such as high-fidelity equipment, to fixtures.
- Placing goods with high value/small size in locked showcases.
- Attaching expensive clothing together.
- Alternating the direction of hangers on clothing near doors.
- Limiting the dollar value and quantity of merchandise displayed near exits.
- Limiting the number of entrances and exits to the store.
- Utilizing cameras and mirrors to increase visibility, especially in low-traffic areas.

C. Employee/Shopper Theft While Store Is Closed

- Conducting thorough check of the building at night to make sure no one is left in store.
- Locking all exits, even fire exits, at night.
- Utilizing ultrasonic/infrared detectors, burglar alarm traps, or guards with dogs when store is closed.
- Placing valuables in safe.
- Using shatterproof glass and/or iron gates on display windows to prevent break-ins.
- Making sure exterior lighting is adequate when store is closed.
- Periodically testing burglar alarms.

Figure 15.11
Store Security Gates
Can Be Attractive

Dynaflair Corporation
manufactures a variety
of retail security gates.
These gates can be cus-
tomized to fit the per-
sonality of each store.
They do not detract in
any way from the
retailer's image.
Reprinted by permission.

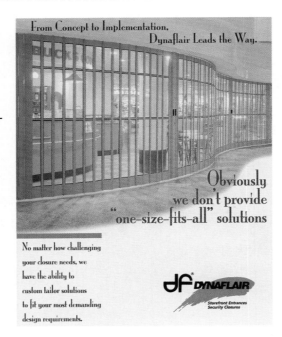

Inventory Analysis

Inventory status and performance must be analyzed regularly to gauge the success of inventory management. Recent advances in computer software have made this activity much more accurate and timely. According to retailer surveys by Arthur Andersen Consulting, these are the elements of inventory performance that firms deem most important: gross margin dollars, inventory turnover, gross profit percentage, gross margin return on inventory, the weeks of supply available, and the average in-stock position.

Inventory analysis is discussed further in the next chapter, "Financial Merchandise Management."

SUMMARY

1. *To describe the steps in the implementation of merchandise plans.* (1) Information is gathered about target market needs and prospective suppliers. Data about shopper needs can come from customers, sources of supply, personnel, competitors, and others. A want book (want slip) is particularly useful. To acquire information about suppliers, the retailer can talk to prospects, attend trade shows, visit permanent merchandise marts, and search the Web.

(2) The retailer chooses firm-owned; outside, regularly used; and/or outside, new supply sources. Relationships may sometimes be strained with suppliers because their goals are different from those of retailers.

(3) The merchandise under consideration is evaluated through inspection, sampling, and/or description. The choice of method depends on the product and situation.

(4) Purchase terms are set. They may have to be negotiated in their entirety (as with opportunistic buying) or uniform contracts may be used. Terms must be clear, including the delivery date, quantity purchased, price and payment arrangements, discounts, form of delivery, and point of transfer. There may also be special provisions.

(5) The purchase can be concluded automatically or manually. In some instances, management approval is

needed. The transfer of title can take place as soon as the order is shipped or it may not occur until after the merchandise is actually sold.

(6) Merchandise handling decisions include receiving and storing, price and inventory marking, displays, on-floor assortments, customer transactions, delivery or pickup, returns and damaged goods, monitoring pilferage, and control.

(7) Reorder procedures depend on order and delivery time, inventory turnover, financial outlays, and inventory versus ordering costs.

(8) Both the overall merchandising procedure and specific goods and services need to be regularly reviewed.

2. *To examine the prominent roles of logistics and inventory management in the implementation of merchandise plans.* Logistics is the overall process of planning, implementing, and coordinating the physical movement of merchandise from supplier to retailer to customer. Among the major logistics goals are to relate costs to specific activities, place and receive orders easily and accurately, minimize ordering/receiving time, coordinate shipments, have proper merchandise levels, place merchandise on the sales floor, process customer orders, work collaboratively within the supply chain, handle returns effectively and minimize damaged products, monitor accomplishments, and have backup plans.

The supply chain comprises all the parties in the logistics process. With collaborative planning, forecasting, and replenishment, there is a holistic approach. Third-party logistics is becoming popular. A number of manufacturers and retailers have Web sites to interact with their channel partners.

Some retailers engage in quick response inventory planning. Floor-ready merchandise is received at the store ready to be displayed. Electronic data interchange lets retailers use quick response planning through computerized supply chain relationships. A number of supermarkets use efficient consumer response. Several transportation decisions are needed, as are warehousing choices. Certain retailers have goods shipped by direct store distribution. Retailers must also plan for outbound logistics: completing customer transactions by turning over merchandise to the customer.

As part of logistics, a retailer uses inventory management. Due to its complexity, and to reduce costs, retailers may expect suppliers to perform more tasks or they may outsource at least some inventory activities. Vendor-managed inventory (VMI) is rapidly growing in popularity.

Having the proper inventory is a hard balancing act: The retailer wants to not lose sales due to being out of stock. Yet, it does not want to be stuck with excess merchandise. Each year, $30 billion in U.S. retail sales are lost due to employee theft, customer shoplifting, and vendor fraud and errors. Many retailers use electronic article surveillance, with special tags or labels attached to products.

Reverse logistics encompasses all merchandise flows—from the retailer back through the supply channel. It involves items returned because of damages, defects, or less-than-anticipated retail sales.

Inventory status and performance must be analyzed regularly.

Key Terms

want book (want slip) (p. 490)
chargebacks (p. 494)
opportunistic buying (p. 495)
slotting allowances (p. 495)
consignment purchase (p. 496)
memorandum purchase (p. 496)
logistics (p. 501)
supply chain (p. 503)

collaborative planning, forecasting,
 and replenishment (CPFR) (p. 503)
quick response (QR) inventory
 planning (p. 504)
floor-ready merchandise (p. 504)
efficient consumer response (p. 505)
direct store distribution (DSD)
 (p. 507)

inventory management (p. 509)
vendor-managed inventory (VMI)
 (p. 509)
inventory shrinkage (p. 511)
electronic article surveillance (p. 511)
reverse logistics (p. 512)

Questions for Discussion

1. Why is the implementation of merchandise plans sometimes quite difficult?

2. What information should a specialty store gather before adding a new computer brand to its product mix?

Questions for Discussion *(continued)*

3. What are the pros and cons of a retailer's relying too much on a want book?

4. Cite the advantages and disadvantages associated with these merchandise sources for Burger King. How would your answers differ for a small fast-food chain?
   a. Company-owned.
   b. Outside, regularly used.
   c. Outside, new.

5. Devise a checklist a retailer could use to negotiate opportunistic buying terms with suppliers.

6. Under what circumstances should a retailer try to charge slotting allowances? How may this strategy backfire?

7. Which is more difficult, implementing a merchandise plan for a small bookstore or a book superstore? Explain your answer.

8. Distinguish between these two terms: *logistics* and *inventory management*. Give an example of each.

9. What are the benefits of quick response inventory planning? What do you think are the risks?

10. Why are some retailers convinced that distribution centers must be used as the shipping points for merchandise from manufacturers while other retailers favor direct store distribution?

11. How could a local pharmacy be prepared for the variations in customer demand for home delivery during the day?

12. What is vendor-managed inventory? How do both manufacturers and retailers benefit from its use?

13. How would you avoid out-of-stock situations while not being stuck with excessive merchandise?

14. Present a seven-item checklist for a retailer to use with its reverse logistics.

WEB-BASED EXERCISE

Menlo Logistics (www.menlolog.com)

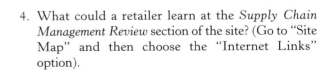

Questions

1. Describe Menlo Logistics' functions as an independent logistics provider.

2. Discuss the pros and cons of outsourcing logistics to a firm such as Menlo Logistics.

3. What could a retailer learn at the *Logistics Management* section of the site? (Go to "Site Map" and then choose the "Internet Links" option.)

4. What could a retailer learn at the *Supply Chain Management Review* section of the site? (Go to "Site Map" and then choose the "Internet Links" option).

CHAPTER ENDNOTES

1. Debbie Howell, "Noodle Kidoodle Finds Success on Road Less Traveled," *Discount Store News* (February 8, 1999), p. 46.

2. Peter Landers, "In Japan, the Hub of E-Commerce Is a 7-Eleven," *Wall Street Journal* (November 1, 1999), pp. B1, B4.

3. See Saul Hansell, "In Shopping Bots We Trust?" *New York Times* (November 18, 1999), p. D1; and Chris Taylor, "Bot Till You Drop," *Time* (October 11, 1999), p. 52.

4. David Gunn, "New Internet Search Engine Eases Access to Vast Store of Product Data," *Stores* (August 1999), pp. 86–87.

5. *Consolidated Stores 1999 Annual Report.*

6. Steve Weinstein, "The State of Trade Relations," *Progressive Grocer* (June 1999), p. 19.

7. See Christopher Palmeri, "Retailer's Revenge," *Forbes* (May 3, 1999), pp. 62, 66; and Mark Maremont and Robert Berner, "Leaning on Suppliers, Rite Aid Deducts Cash at Bill-Paying Time," *Wall Street Journal* (March 31, 1999), pp. A1, A6.

8. Eric Petersen, "Square Peg in a Round Slot," *ColoradoBiz* (August 1999), p. 48.

9. Duana Lohn, "Scan-Based Trading: A Vision Whose Time Has Come?" *www.kpmg.com/cm/article-archives/actual-articles/Scan.html* (August 1999).

10. Shelly Reese, "Grocery Suppliers Seek the Perfect Order," *Stores* (March 1998), pp. 53–54.

11. Saul Hansell, "Amazon's Risky Christmas," *New York Times* (November 28, 1999), Section 3, pp. 1, 15.

12. Julie Ritzer Ross, "Pagonis Stresses Logistics Role in Controlling Costs," *Stores* (April 1998), pp. 76–77.

13. Susan Reda, "Focus on Logistics Helps Uptons Score Dramatic Gains," *Stores* (August 1998), pp. 68–72.

14. "Executive Summary," *www.cpfr.org* (December 9, 1999).

15. Michael Hartnett, "Outside Firm Helps Sears Bring Small Vendors into EDI Compliance," *Stores* (February 1999), pp. 80–81; and Julie Ritzer Ross, "Logistics Providers Take Expanded Role in Supply Chain Management," *Stores* (March 1998), pp. 57–58.

16. "Keeping in Touch," *Chain Store Age* (May 1999), p. 258.

17. Jean Thilmany, "Big 5: EDI Delivers the Goods," *Women's Wear Daily* (June 30, 1999), p. 9.

18. "Internet Revolutionizes EDI," *Discount Store News*, (May 24, 1999), p. 3.

19. "FMI Media Backgrounder: Efficient Consumer Response," *www.fmi.org/media/bg/ecr1.html* (March 9, 2000).

20. Sunil Taneja, "Speedy Delivery," *Chain Store Age* (July 1999), pp. 90, 92.

21. Michael Hartnett, "Home Depot Strengthens Global Sourcing System," *Stores* (March 1998), pp. 55–56; and Len Lewis, "Produce Possibilities," *Progressive Grocer* (January 1999), pp. 51–58.

22. Emily Nelson and Evan Ramstad, "Hershey's Biggest Dud Has Turned Out to Be New Computer System," *Wall Street Journal* (October 29, 1999), pp. A1, A6.

23. Len Lewis, "Growing Global," *Progressive Grocer* (September 1999), p. 22.

24. *Burlington Coat Factory 1999 Annual Report;* and *Toys "R" Us 1999 Annual Report.*

25. "The ABCs of DSD," *Progressive Grocer* (November 1998), p. 7; and David Wellman, "The Direct Approach to the Bottom Line," *Supermarket Business* (August 1999), p. 15.

26. Ryan Mathews, "DSD: Toward a Unified Distribution System," *Progressive Grocer* (November 1995), p. 4.

27. Dan Scheraga, "Taking Stock," *Chain Store Age* (October 1999), pp. 172–74.

28. Lawrence M. Fisher, "Online Grocer Is Setting Up Delivery System for $1 Billion," *New York Times* (September 10, 1999), p. C1.

29. Kurt Salmon Associates, "Vision for the New Millennium," *KSA Brochure* (n.d.).

30. David Moin and Thomas Cunningham, "Fingerhut to Service Wal-Mart," *Women's Wear Daily* (June 22, 1999), p. 2.

31. Faye Bookman, "Retailers, Suppliers Sort Out Issue of Who Pays for Source Tagging," *Stores* (October 1998), pp. 84, 86.

32. "Turning Out-of-Stocks into a Huge Opportunity," *Progressive Grocer ECR '99* (December 1998), p. 10.

33. "Dieting for Dollars," *Chain Store Age* (October 1998), p. 4C.

34. Dana Canady, "Toys "R" Us Decks Its Shelves," *New York Times on the Web* (October 1999).

35. Harris Fleming, Jr., "Stop, Thief!" *Drug Topics* (October 4, 1999), p. 94; Dick Silverman, "Retail Theft Price Tag: $26 Billion," *Women's Wear Daily* (June 9, 1999), p. 17; and Ginger Koloszyc, "Supermarkets Find Growing Payoff in EAS Anti-Shoplifting Systems," *Stores* (February 1999), pp. 28, 30.

36. Harvey Meyer, "Many Happy Returns," *Journal of Business Strategy*, Vol. 20 (July–August 1999), pp. 27–31; and Connie Robbins Gentry, "Reducing the Cost of Returns," *Chain Store Age* (October 1999), pp. 124, 126.

CASE 1

SEARS AND BENETTON: A NEW MERCHANDISING PARTNERSHIP

Sears is paying greater attention to the young fashion customer with the rollout of its exclusive Benetton USA collection. Robert Mettler, Sears' president of merchandising, explains the company's reasoning: "We need to attract a younger customer. It is important to do this with a brand like Benetton that has created excitement among fashion customers around the world. The real issue is to create fashion at a value-oriented position in the market." Benetton executives believe the brand could generate as much as $100 million in annual retail sales. To reach this goal, Sears must successfully compete with such specialty apparel retailers as The Buckle, Pacific Sunwear, and Abercrombie & Fitch. The new brand should also benefit Benetton's merchandising approach because during the past decade Benetton's number of freestanding U.S. stores has dropped from 800 to 140 units.

These are the details of the 1999 Benetton USA introduction:

- Ad campaign launched on August 1 with nontraditional media such as billboards and bus shelters, as well as broadcast spots and print ads.
- The collection showcased in concept shops within Sears that have sleek display fixtures.
- Highlighting the Benetton USA junior apparel line in windows flanking the mall entrances of between 75 and 100 Sears stores.
- A loyalty card program initiated and aimed at 12-to-19-year-old junior customers to coincide with the Benetton USA rollout.

The fixtures displaying Benetton USA apparel consist of streamlined modular shelving and hanging units, made of a neutral wood veneer and Plexiglas. The cases are housed within the Benetton USA concept shops, as part of a larger shift in Sears' merchandising strategy that calls for installing more apparel concept shops. Previously, Sears had merchandised apparel mostly by classification. The Benetton USA concept shops occupy 1,000 square feet in the junior departments, 600 square feet in young men's, and 200 to 300 square feet in boys' and girls'. Industry sources report that Sears spent about $8.5 million on the fixturing, lighting, and other elements of the concept shops.

The new line, which has similar designs to the United Colors of Benetton, is priced at one-half of typical Benetton apparel. It is also especially designed to attract a younger target market and be more casual. Prices for the junior apparel range from $18 for ribbed T-shirts to $64 for blazers. In between, there are sweaters priced from the mid-$20s to $48, bottoms at $20 to $38, blazers starting in the high $50s, and outerwear from $30 to the high $50 range.

A major challenge in developing Benetton USA, according to Euro-America (the company that holds the master license for Benetton USA's apparel line), is "producing the quality Benetton is seeking at the price points Sears is targeting." Sears wants items priced 10 to 15 percent below comparable items at Gap while Benetton wants to keep the products at Gap's level of quality. "If all goes well, as we expect," Euro-America projects, "restocking will be the next big challenge." The line is being sourced in China, the Philippines, South Korea, Indonesia, Guatemala, and Brazil.

Questions

1. What are the pros and cons of the Benetton USA strategy for Sears?

2. What are the pros and cons of the Benetton USA strategy for Benetton?

3. Comment on the statement that the biggest challenge in developing Benetton USA "is producing the quality Benetton is seeking at the price points Sears is targeting."

4. Describe some of the logistical difficulties in sourcing this line from China, the Philippines, South Korea, Indonesia, Guatemala, and Brazil.

NOTE

The material in this case is drawn from Anne D'Innocenzio, "Another Life in a Lower Tier," *Women's Wear Daily* (March 31, 1999), p. 1; and Valerie Seckler, "Sears' 'Megabrand' Move: Benetton USA," *Women's Wear Daily* (June 9, 1999), p. 6.

CASE 2

PILFERAGE CONTROL THE SENSORMATIC WAY

Sensormatic Electronics is a maker of electronic article surveillance (EAS) products, with annual sales exceeding $1 billion. Its wide product mix includes Sensor Ink and Inktag products that mark thieves with ink and damage stolen goods, sophisticated cameras that monitor stores and warehouses, and unobtrusive labels that can be hidden under a product label. The firm's most popular EAS device is the Ultra-Max.

The Ultra-Max system uses raised plastic tags that resemble chicklet gum in both size and shape. Unlike many other EAS products, Ultra-Max tags can be reactivated if a customer returns a product to the store. Because the tags are clearly visible to shoppers, they are an active deterrent to theft. The Ultra-Max system employs acousto-magnetic technology. When an Ultra-Max tag that has not been deactivated enters a magnetic field located near a store exit, the material inside the tag vibrates. This then sets off an alarm. The success of the Ultra-Max system is due to its low rate of false alarms, its ability to properly cover wide-area store exits (up to 9 feet between two pedestals), and the ease of deactivating the alarm by retail personnel.

One of the emerging developments in theft control is source tagging, whereby manufacturers place anti-theft devices on products before their shipment to retailers. More than 1,800 consumer goods manufacturers currently insert Sensormatic's anti-theft labels into their products. Recently, Wal-Mart informed its suppliers that it wants to receive products with anti-theft tags already installed. Wal-Mart plans to phase in the use Ultra-Max in all of its stores within a 5-year period. The Sports Authority and Home Depot have also endorsed source tagging.

There are several benefits to the use of source tagging for retailers:

- Because EAS tags are attached by manufacturers as part of their usual production process, retailers no longer have to attach EAS devices by hand.
- They can reduce order lead time since items no longer have to go to a separate area for tagging.
- Without source tagging, many firms lock small valuable products in glass cases that must be opened by sales clerks. With source tagging, one home center chain, for example, reports significantly higher sales due to the use of open merchandising on a variety of plumbing and electrical items.
- This process offers better protection against professional shoplifters who can override detection from Ultra-Max by placing stolen merchandise in foil-lined bags.

There is no uniform industry standard for source tagging at present. As a result, source tags from Sensormatic's major competitor, Checkpoint Systems, are not compatible with Sensormatic equipment. The lack of a standard requires manufacturers to purchase multiple

CASE 2
(CONTINUED)

tags or risk alienating retailers since the tag chosen may not match the retailer's security system. Eastman Kodak, Johnson & Johnson, and Procter & Gamble recently announced the formation of the Consumer Product Manufacturers' Consortium. This group seeks to create an industrywide standard for security tags.

Questions

1. What are the advantages and the disadvantages of source tagging versus tagging by retailers?

2. What are the obstacles to the increased use of source tagging?

3. How can a specialty store determine the value of source tagging for music CDs?

4. What are the pros and cons of the development of a uniform industry standard for source tags?

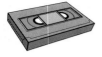

Video Questions on Ultra-Max

1. Describe the guidelines for installing Sensormatic labels.

2. Develop a procedure for a sales clerk to approach a customer who has set off a store alarm.

NOTE

The material in this case is drawn from L. A. Lorek, "Sensormatic Prepares to Launch 60 New Products," *Knight-Ridder/Tribune Business News* (June 8, 1999), p. 1; and *www.sensormatic.com* (March 11, 2000).

Financial Merchandise Management

CHAPTER OBJECTIVES

1. To describe the major aspects of financial merchandise planning and management
2. To explain the cost and retail methods of accounting
3. To study the merchandise forecasting and budgeting process
4. To examine alternative methods of inventory unit control
5. To integrate dollar and unit merchandising control concepts

Until recently, most Web retailers accepted merchandise returns only if they were received in saleable condition and shipped back within 30 to 60 days of the consumers' initial receipt of the items. Now, some Web retailers have liberalized their policies. For example, Amazon.com will accept the return of any of its recommended books at any time, regardless of condition, for a full refund.

The change in refund policies is largely due to the poor ratings Web retailers have gotten regarding customer service. They need to find a financially sound way to deal with this issue:

Online stores are subject to all the flaws of any direct marketer—shipments that may have the wrong or damaged goods, or arrive late, or are lost forever. What is exasperating for many customers is the way some firms are dealing with the problems. "You walk away feeling this is so ducky that I didn't leave my house and got all my shopping done at 10 P.M.," said one shopper, who bought her twin daughters two hot Nintendo Game Boy units, as well as cameras and printers, from Amazon.com. "Then the box arrives, and there is only one stupid Game Boy, without all the pieces, and you say this is no good." When she logged back on to Amazon, the site would say only that her other Game Boy had been delayed, along with the cameras and printers. "I just freaked. They didn't contact me to say it's possible you won't ever get these. And they never said they were sorry." She eventually canceled the order and found some items in a local Best Buy store and others at eToys.com.[1]

OVERVIEW

Peachtree offers integrated accounting software for small businesses. Try out the free "Trial Version" (www.peachtree.com/trial).

Through **financial merchandise management,** a retailer specifies exactly which products (goods and services) are purchased, when products are purchased, and how many products are purchased; both dollar and unit controls are employed. **Dollar control** involves planning and monitoring a retailer's financial investment in merchandise over a stated period.

> *Please Note:* Web site addresses are constantly changing.
> The links in this chapter are current as of the publication of this book.

Unit control relates to the quantities of merchandise a retailer handles during a stated period. Dollar controls usually precede unit controls, as a retailer must plan its dollar investment before making assortment decisions.

Well-structured financial merchandise plans offer such benefits as these:

- The value and amount of inventory in each department and/or store unit during a given period can be delineated. Stock is thus balanced, and fewer markdowns may be necessary.
- The amount of merchandise (in terms of investment) a buyer can purchase during a given period can be stipulated. This gives a buyer direction.
- A buyer can study the inventory investment in relation to planned and actual revenues. This improves the return on investment.
- The retailer's space requirements can be partly determined by estimating beginning-of-month and end-of-month inventory levels.
- A buyer's performance can be rated. Various measures may be used as performance standards.
- A buyer can determine stock shortages, giving an estimate of bookkeeping errors and pilferage.
- Slow-moving items can be classified—thus leading to increased sales efforts or markdowns.
- A proper balance between inventory levels and out-of-stock conditions can be maintained.

This chapter divides financial merchandise management into four areas: methods of accounting, merchandise forecasting and budgeting, unit control systems, and financial inventory control. The hypothetical Handy Hardware Store is used to illustrate the concepts.

INVENTORY VALUATION: THE COST AND RETAIL METHODS OF ACCOUNTING

The Internal Revenue Service—yes, the IRS—has an excellent online primer about inventory accounting (www.irs.ustreas.gov/forms_pubs/pubs/p53806.htm).

Retail inventory accounting systems can be complex because they entail a great deal of data (due to the number of items sold). A typical retailer's dollar control system must provide such data as the sales and purchases made by that firm during a budget period, the value of beginning and ending inventory, the extent of markups and markdowns, and merchandise shortages.

Table 16.1 shows a profit-and-loss statement for Handy Hardware Store for the period from January 1, 2000, through June 30, 2000. The sales amount represents total receipts over this time. Beginning inventory was computed by counting the merchandise in stock on January 1, 2000—recorded at cost. Purchases (at cost) and transportation charges (costs incurred in shipping items from suppliers to the retailer) were derived by adding the invoice slips for all merchandise bought by Handy in the period.

Together, beginning inventory, purchases, and transportation charges equal the cost of **merchandise available for sale.** Because Handy does a physical inventory twice yearly, ending inventory was figured by counting the merchandise in stock on June 30, 2000—recorded at cost (Handy codes items so costs can be derived for each item in stock). The **cost of goods sold** equals the cost of merchandise available for sale minus the cost value of ending inventory. Sales less cost of goods sold yields **gross profit,** while **net profit** is gross profit minus retail operating expenses.

Retailers usually have different data needs than manufacturers. Assortments are larger. Costs cannot be printed on cartons unless coded (due to customer inspection). Stock shortages are higher. Sales are conducted more often. Retailers require monthly, not quarterly, profit data.

Two inventory accounting systems are available to a retailer: the cost and retail methods of accounting. The cost accounting system values merchandise at cost plus inbound transportation charges. The retail accounting system values merchandise at current retail prices.

Table 16.1 Handy Hardware Store Profit-and-Loss Statement, January 1, 2000–June 30, 2000

Sales		$417,460
Less cost of goods sold:		
Beginning inventory (at cost)	$ 44,620	
Purchases (at cost)	289,400	
Transportation charges	2,600	
Merchandise available for sale	$336,620	
Ending inventory (at cost)	90,500	
Cost of goods sold		246,120
Gross profit		$171,340
Less operating expenses:		
Salaries	$ 70,000	
Advertising	25,000	
Rental	16,000	
Other	26,000	
Total operating expenses		137,000
Net profit before taxes		$ 34,340

Let us now study the cost and retail inventory methods in terms of the frequency with which data are obtained, the difficulties of a physical inventory and recordkeeping, the ease of settling insurance claims (if there is inventory damage), the extent to which shortages can be computed, and system complexities.

The Cost Method

With the **cost method of accounting,** the cost to the retailer of each item is recorded on an accounting sheet and/or is coded on a price tag or merchandise container. As a physical inventory is done, item costs must be learned, the quantity of every item in stock counted, and total inventory value at cost calculated.

One way to code merchandise cost is to use a 10-letter equivalency system, such as M = 0, N = 1, O = 2, P = 3, Q = 4, R = 5, S = 6, T = 7, U = 8, and V = 9. An item coded with the letters STOP would have a cost value of $67.23. The technique is useful as an accounting tool and for retailers that allow price bargaining by customers (profit per item is easy to compute).

A retailer can use the cost method while it does physical or book inventories. A physical inventory involves an actual merchandise count; a book inventory relies on recordkeeping entries.

A Physical Inventory System Using the Cost Method In a **physical inventory system,** ending inventory is measured by actually counting the merchandise still in stock at the close of a selling period; ending inventory is recorded at cost. The retailer cannot compute gross profit until after ending inventory is valued. Thus, a firm using the cost method and relying on a physical inventory system can derive gross profit only as often as it does a full inventory count. Since most firms do so just once or twice yearly, a physical inventory system alone imposes limits on planning.

By using only a physical inventory system, a firm might also be unable to compute inventory shortages (due to pilferage, unrecorded breakage, and so on) because ending inventory value is set by simply adding the costs of all items in stock. What the ending inventory level *should be* is not computed.

A Book Inventory System Using the Cost Method A **book inventory system** (also known as a **perpetual inventory system**) avoids the problem of infrequent financial analysis by keeping a running total of the value of all inventory on hand at cost at a given time. Therefore, end-of-month inventory values can be computed without a physical inventory, and frequent financial statements can be prepared. In addition, a book inventory lets a retailer uncover stock shortages by comparing projected inventory values with actual inventory values through a physical inventory.

A retailer maintains a perpetual system by regularly recording purchases and adding them to existing inventory value; sales transactions are then subtracted to arrive at the new current inventory value (all at cost). Table 16.2 shows Handy Hardware's book (perpetual) inventory system for July 1, 2000, through December 31, 2000. *Note:* The ending inventory in Table 16.1 is the beginning inventory in Table 16.2.

Table 16.2 assumes merchandise costs are rather constant and monthly sales at cost are easily computed. Yet, suppose merchandise costs rise. How would inventory then be valued? Two ways to value inventory are the FIFO (first-in-first-out) and LIFO (last-in-first-out) methods.

The **FIFO method** logically assumes old merchandise is sold first, while newer items remain in inventory. The **LIFO method** assumes new merchandise is sold first, while older stock remains in inventory. FIFO matches inventory value with the current cost structure—the goods in inventory are the ones bought most recently, while LIFO matches current sales with the current cost structure—the goods sold first are the ones bought most recently. During periods of rising inventory values, LIFO offers retailers a tax advantage because lower profits are shown.

In Figure 16.1, the FIFO and LIFO methods of inventory valuation are illustrated for Handy Hardware's snow blowers for the period January 1, 2000, through December 31, 2000; the store carries only one model of snow blower. Handy has found that it sold 220 snow blowers in 2000 at an average price of $320. Handy knows it started 2000 with a beginning inventory of 30 snow blowers, which it had bought for $150 each. During January 2000, it bought 100 snow blowers at $175 each; from October to December 2000, Handy bought

View Skandata's online perpetual inventory screens or download the "Evaluation Demo" (www.skandata.com/invdemo.html).

Lifo Systems has a comprehensive "Learn More About LIFO" section at its Web site (www.lifosystems.com/learn.htm).

Table 16.2 Handy Hardware Store Perpetual Inventory System, July 1, 2000–December 30, 2000[a]

Date	Beginning-of-Month Inventory (at Cost)	+	Net Monthly Purchases (at Cost)	−	Monthly Sales (at Cost)	=	End-of-Month Inventory (at Cost)
7/1/00	$90,500		$ 40,000		$ 62,400		$68,100
8/1/00	68,100		28,000		38,400		57,700
9/1/00	57,700		27,600		28,800		56,500
10/1/00	56,500		44,000		28,800		71,700
11/1/00	71,700		50,400		40,800		81,300
12/1/00	81,300		15,900		61,200		36,000
	Total		$205,900		$260,400		(as of 12/31/00)

[a] Transportation charges are not included in computing inventory value in this table.

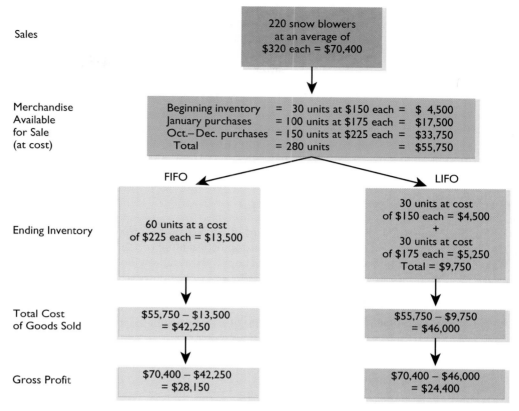

Figure 16.1

Applying FIFO and LIFO Inventory Methods to Handy Hardware, January 1, 2000–December 31, 2000

another 150 snow blowers for $225 apiece. Because Handy sold 220 snow blowers in 2000, as of the close of business on December 31, it had 60 units left in inventory.

Using the FIFO method, Handy would assume its beginning inventory and initial purchases were sold first. The 60 snow blowers remaining in inventory would have a cost value of $225 each, resulting in a total cost of goods sold of $42,250 and a gross profit of $28,150. Using the LIFO method, Handy would assume the most recently purchased items were sold first and the remaining inventory would consist of beginning goods and early purchases. Of the snow blowers remaining in inventory, 30 would have a cost value of $150 each and 30 a cost value of $175 apiece, resulting in a total cost of goods sold of $46,000 and a gross profit of $24,400. The FIFO method presents a more accurate picture of the cost of goods sold and the true cost value of ending inventory. The LIFO method indicates a lower profit, leading to the payment of lower taxes, but an understated ending inventory value at cost.

The retail method of inventory, which combines FIFO and LIFO concepts, is explained shortly. A fuller discussion of FIFO and LIFO may be found in a basic accounting textbook.

Disadvantages of Cost-Based Inventory Systems Cost-based physical and book systems have significant disadvantages. First, both require a retailer to assign costs to each item in stock (and to each item sold). During periods when merchandise costs change, cost-based valuation systems are most useful for firms with low inventory turnover, limited assortments, and high average prices. Retailers with these attributes are car dealers, furriers, furniture stores, and major appliance dealers.

Second, neither cost-based method adjusts inventory values to reflect style changes, end-of-season markdowns, or sudden surges of demand (which may raise prices). Thus, ending inventory value, based on merchandise cost, may not reflect its actual worth. This discrepancy could be troublesome if the ending inventory value is used in computing insurance coverage or in filing insurance claims for losses.

Despite these factors, retailers making the products they sell—such as bakeries, restaurants, and furniture showrooms—often keep records on a cost basis. A department store with these operations (or others involved in manufacturing) can use the cost method for them and the retail method for other areas.

The Retail Method

With the **retail method of accounting,** closing inventory value is determined by calculating the average relationship between the cost and retail values of merchandise available for sale during a period. Though the retail method overcomes the disadvantages of the cost method, it requires detailed recordkeeping. It is more complex because ending inventory is first valued in retail dollars and then converted to cost in order to compute gross margin (gross profit).

There are three basic steps to determine an ending inventory value by the retail method:

1. Calculating the cost complement.

2. Calculating deductions from retail value.

3. Converting retail inventory value to cost.

Calculating the Cost Complement The value of beginning inventory, net purchases, additional markups, and transportation charges are all included in the retail method. Beginning inventory and net purchase amounts (purchases less returns) are recorded at both cost and retail levels. Additional markups represent the extra revenues received by a retailer when it increases selling prices over the period covered, due to inflation or unexpectedly high demand. Transportation charges are the retailer's costs for shipping the goods it buys from suppliers to the retailer. Table 16.3 shows the total merchandise available for sale at cost and at retail for Handy Hardware over the period from July 1, 2000, through December 31, 2000, based on Table 16.2 costs.

By using Table 16.3 data, the average relationship of cost to retail value for all merchandise available for sale by Handy Hardware in the six months can be computed. This is called the **cost complement:**

Table 16.3 Handy Hardware Store, Calculating Merchandise Available for Sale at Cost and at Retail, July 1, 2000–December 31, 2000

	At Cost	At Retail
Beginning inventory	$ 90,500	$139,200
Net purchases	205,900	340,526
Additional markups	—	16,400
Transportation charges	3,492	—
Total merchandise available for sale	$299,892	$496,126

Buy It in Spain, Sell It in Germany

Wolfgang Marshall is general manager of Auto Friesen, a large German car dealership that practices "auto arbitrage." This is how auto arbitrage works. Instead of ordering Volkswagen models from German factories, an auto arbitrager, such as Wolfgang Marshall, purchases these automobiles from other car dealers that are located in Spain, Italy, or Denmark. These cars are then imported back to Germany.

Because incomes in a country such as Spain are about 75 percent of the European average, most car manufacturers offer lower prices on models sold there. Auto arbitragers also take advantage of the lower prices offered by auto makers on cars sold in Denmark to offset Denmark's high luxury taxes. Auto arbitragers ship their vehicles directly to Germany, so they are exempt from these taxes.

Wolfgang Marshall and other auto arbitragers are able to undercut a typical dealer's prices due to their low costs. By using this practice, Auto Friesen can sell a Ford Mondeo for about 30 percent less than a standard Frankfort dealer's price.

What impact do you think Auto Friesen's use of auto arbitrage has on its financial merchandise management strategy?

Source: Edmund L. Andrews, "Buying a Car? Location, Location, Location," *New York Times* (December 27, 1998), Section 3, p. 7.

$$\text{Cost complement} = \frac{\text{Total cost valuation}}{\text{Total retail valuation}}$$

$$= \frac{\$299,892}{\$496,126} = 0.6045$$

Because the cost complement is 0.6045 (60.45 percent), on average, 60.45 cents of every retail sales dollar was made up of Handy Hardware's merchandise cost.

Calculating Deductions from Retail Value Ending retail value of inventory must reflect all deductions from the total merchandise available for sale at retail. Besides sales revenues, deductions include markdowns (such as special sales and reduced prices on discontinued, end-of-season, and shopworn goods), employee discounts, and stock shortages (due to pilferage, unrecorded breakage, and so on). Although sales, markdowns, and employee discounts can be recorded throughout an accounting period, a physical inventory is needed for a retailer to learn about stock shortages.

From Table 16.3, it is known that Handy Hardware had a retail value of merchandise available for sale of $496,126 during the period from July 1, 2000 through December 31, 2000. As shown in Table 16.4, this was reduced by sales of $422,540 and recorded markdowns and employee discounts of $14,034. The ending book value of inventory at retail as of December 31, 2000, was $59,552.

After a physical inventory is taken, stock shortages are simple to compute with the retail method. A firm compares the retail book value of ending inventory with the actual physical ending inventory value at retail. If the book inventory exceeds the physical inventory, a stock shortage exists. Table 16.5 shows the results of a physical inventory by Handy Hardware. Shortages were $3,082 (at retail), and book value was adjusted accordingly. Although Handy knows the shortages were from shopper and employee pilferage, bookkeeping errors (not recording markdowns, employee discounts, and breakage), and overshipments not billed to customers, it cannot learn the proportion of shortages from each factor.

Table 16.4 Handy Hardware Store, Computing Ending Retail Book Value, as of December 31, 2000

Merchandise available for sale (at retail)		$496,126
Less deductions:		
Sales	$422,540	
Markdowns	11,634	
Employee discounts	2,400	
Total deductions		436,574
Ending retail book value of inventory		$ 59,552

Occasionally, a physical inventory may reveal a stock overage, which is an excess of physical ending inventory value over book value. An overage may be due to errors in a physical inventory or in keeping a book inventory. If overages occur, the ending retail book value of inventory must be adjusted upward.

Inasmuch as a retailer has to conduct a physical inventory to compute stock shortages (overages), and a physical inventory is usually taken only once or twice a year, shortages (overages) are often estimated for monthly merchandise budgets.

Converting Retail Inventory Value to Cost The retailer must next convert the adjusted ending retail book value of inventory to cost so as to compute dollar gross profit (gross margin). The ending inventory at cost equals the adjusted ending retail book value multiplied by the cost complement. For Handy Hardware, this was:

$$\text{Ending inventory (at cost)} = \text{Adjusted ending retail book value} \times \text{Cost complement}$$
$$= \$56,470 \times .6045 = 34,136$$

The preceding equation does not yield the exact ending inventory value at cost for Handy but approximates it based on the average relationship between cost and the retail selling price for all merchandise available for sale.

The adjusted ending inventory at cost can be used to find gross profit. See Table 16.6. For Handy Hardware, the July 1, 2000, through December 31, 2000, cost of goods sold was $265,756, resulting in gross profit of $156,784. By deducting operating expenses of $139,000, Handy sees that the net profit before taxes for this six-month period was $17,784.

Advantages of the Retail Method Several strengths of the retail method are evident in comparing the cost and retail accounting methods:

Table 16.5 Handy Hardware Store, Computing Stock Shortages and Adjusting Retail Book Value, as of December 31, 2000

Ending retail book value of inventory	$59,552
Physical inventory (at retail)	56,470
Stock shortages (at retail)	3,082
Adjusted ending retail book value of inventory	$56,470

Table 16.6 Handy Hardware Store Profit-and-Loss Statement, July 1, 2000–December 31, 2000

Sales		$422,540
Less cost of goods sold:		
Total merchandise available for sale (at cost)	$299,892	
Adjusted ending inventory (at cost)[a]	34,136	
Cost of goods sold		265,756
Gross profit		$156,784
Less operating expenses:		
Salaries	$ 70,000	
Advertising	25,000	
Rental	16,000	
Other	28,000	
Total operating expenses		139,000
Net profit before taxes		$ 17,784

[a] Adjusted ending inventory (at cost) = Adjusted retail book value × Cost complement = $56,470 × .6045 = $34,136

- The retail method is easier to use when taking a physical inventory. The chances of making errors in valuing merchandise are reduced since the physical inventory is recorded at retail value and costs do not have to be decoded.
- Because undertaking a physical inventory is simpler, it can be completed more often. This lets a firm be more aware of slow-moving items and stock shortages and take appropriate corrective actions.
- The physical inventory method at cost requires a physical inventory to prepare a profit-and-loss statement. In contrast, the retail method lets a firm set up a profit-and-loss statement based on book inventory figures, which can be adjusted to include estimated stock shortages between physical inventories. A book inventory system is better than a physical system at cost because frequent statements are needed if a firm is to study profit trends by department.
- A complete record of ending book values is important in determining the proper insurance coverage and in settling insurance claims. The retail book method gives a firm an estimate of inventory value throughout the year. Since physical inventories are usually taken when merchandise levels are low, the book value at retail allows firms to plan insurance coverage for peak periods and shows the values of goods on hand (in case of a claim adjustment). The retail method is accepted in insurance claims.

Limitations of the Retail Method The greatest weakness of the retail method is the bookkeeping burden of recording a lot of cost and price data. Ending book inventory figures can be correctly computed only if these items are accurately noted: the value of beginning inventory (at cost and at retail), purchases (at cost and at retail), shipping charges, markups, markdowns, employee discounts, transfers from other departments or stores, returns, and sales. Though personnel are freed from the burden of taking many physical inventories, ending book value at retail may be inaccurate unless all required data are precisely recorded. With computerization, this potential problem is lessened.

A second limitation of the retail method is that the cost complement is an average figure based on the total cost of merchandise available for sale and its total retail value. It is possible for the resultant ending cost value to only approximate the true cost of items on hand. This is especially so if fast-selling items have different markups from slow-selling items and/or if there are wide variations among the markups of goods within a single department.

Familiarity with the retail and cost methods of inventory is essential for understanding the financial merchandise management material described in the balance of this chapter.

MERCHANDISE FORECASTING AND BUDGETING: DOLLAR CONTROL

As noted in the chapter overview, dollar control means planning and monitoring a firm's inventory investment over time. Figure 16.2 shows the dollar control process for merchandise forecasting and budgeting, comprising six stages: designating control units, sales forecasting, inventory-level planning, reduction planning, planning purchases, and planning profit margins.

It is necessary to follow the sequential nature of this process since a change in one stage affects all the stages after it. For instance, if a sales forecast is too low, a firm may run out of items because it does not plan to have enough merchandise during a selling season and its planned purchases will also be too low.

Designating Control Units

Merchandise forecasting and budgeting requires the selection of **control units,** the merchandise categories for which data are gathered. Such classifications must be narrow enough to isolate opportunities and problems with specific merchandise lines. A retailer wishing to control goods within departments must record data on dollar allotments separately for each category.

As an example, knowing that total markdowns in a department are 20 percent above last year's level is less valuable than knowing the specific merchandise lines in which large markdowns are being taken. A retailer can broaden its control system by summarizing categories that comprise a department. However, a broad category cannot be broken down into components. It is better to err on the side of too much information than too little.

It is helpful to select control units consistent with other internal company data and with trade association data, if possible. Internal comparisons are meaningful only when classifica-

Figure 16.2
The Merchandise Forecasting and Budgeting Process: Dollar Control

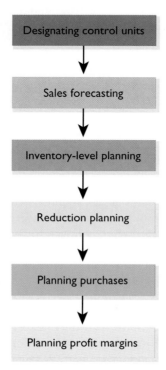

Re'SKU'ing Inventory Costs

Tyringham Holdings operates five jewelry and gift shops that sell watches, stemware, and flatware. It decided, not long ago, to reduce the 15,000 stock-keeping units (SKUs) that were used to track inventory and sales. Tyringham's stores formerly had a separate SKU for each unit of merchandise because the firm viewed each piece of jewelry as unique. Now, under the new system, the firm is categorizing all one-carat diamonds within the same SKU and then subdividing this classification by cut, color, and clarity within the single SKU. The reduction in SKUs is made possible by Tyringham's point-of-sale and merchandising system.

Brad Kallus, the vice-president of finance for three Tyringham stores, feels the new system will allow important inventory data to be upgraded faster and then distributed to the firm's executives and associates on a more timely basis. The new system also includes frequent information on what is selling at each store, as well as how long specific inventory has remained unsold.

What are the pros and cons of Tyringham's reducing its number of SKUs?

Source: Jean Thilmany, "Cutting the Diamond SKUs," *Women's Wear Daily* (April 21, 1999), p. 12.

tion categories are stable. A classification system that shifts over time does not permit comparisons between periods. Valid external comparisons can be made only if control units are similar for a retailer and its trade associations. Control units may be set up on the basis of departments, classifications within departments, price line classifications, and standard merchandise classifications. A discussion of each follows.

At the very least, retailers should keep financial records for specified departmental categories. Even the small Handy Hardware needs to acquire data on a departmental basis (tools and equipment, supplies, housewares, and so on) for buying, inventory control, and markdown decisions. The broadest practical division is the department, which lets a retailer assess each general merchandise grouping or buyer.

To obtain more financial data than available in departmental categories, **classification merchandising** can be used, whereby each specified department is subdivided into further categories for related types of merchandise. In planning merchandise for its tools and equipment department, Handy Hardware can keep financial records not only on the overall performance of that department but also on the individual performance of such categories as lawn mowers/snow blowers, power tools, hand tools, and ladders.

A special form of classification merchandising uses *price line classifications*, whereby retail sales, inventories, and purchases are analyzed by retail price category. This is valuable if a firm offers the same type of product at vastly different prices to different target markets (such as Handy Hardware having $20 power tools for do-it-yourselfers and $135 models for contractors). Retailers with deep assortments most often use price line control. As a case in point, a men's clothing store may want to differentiate between sports jackets selling in the $99–$129 range and those in the $219–$249 range. Such diverse categories of sports jackets are usually sold to different customers or to the same customers for different purposes.

To best contrast its data with industry averages, a firm's merchandise categories should conform to those cited in trade publications. The National Retail Federation devised a *standard merchandise classification* to list the most common merchandise-reporting categories for a wide range of retailers and products. It annually produces *Merchandising and Operating Results of Retail Stores,* using its classifications. More specific classifications are also popular for some retailers. Published each year is *Progressive Grocer's* "Supermarket Sales Manual," based on standard classifications for that industry.

Once appropriate dollar control units are set, all transactions—including sales, purchases, transfers, markdowns, and employee discounts—must be recorded under the proper classification number. Thus, if house paint is Department 25 and brushes are 25-1, all transactions must carry these designations.

Sales Forecasting

Nonstop Solutions has helped Longs Drugs upgrade its forecasting processes (www. nonstop.com).

A retailer estimates its expected future revenues for a given time period by *sales forecasting.* Forecasts may be companywide, departmental, and for individual merchandise classifications. Perhaps the most important step in any financial merchandise planning process is accurate sales forecasting. Because of its effect on subsequent steps, an incorrect estimate of future sales throws off the entire process. That is why many retailers, including Longs Drug Stores, are investing in state-of-the-art forecasting systems. Longs has dramatically improved its cash flow by deploying the system from Nonstop Solutions.[2]

Firmwide and departmentwide sales of larger retailers are often forecast by the use of statistical techniques such as trend analysis, time series analysis, and multiple regression analysis. A discussion of these techniques is beyond the scope of this book. It should be noted that few small retailers use those methods; they rely more on "guesstimates," projections based on experience.

Sales forecasting for merchandise classifications within departments (or price lines) generally relies on more qualitative techniques, even for larger firms. One way of forecasting sales for these narrower categories is first to project sales on a companywide basis and by department, and then to break down these figures judgmentally into merchandise classifications.

Sales forecasts must carefully anticipate and take into account external factors, internal company factors, and seasonal trends. Among the external factors that could affect a retailer's future sales are consumer demographic and life-style trends, competitors' actions, the state of the economy, the weather, and new supplier offerings. For example, many retailers now place greater emphasis on weather forecasts. Strategic Weather Services offers a patented methodology to analyze and forecast the relationship among consumer demand, store traffic, and the weather.[3]

Among the internal company factors that could have an impact on a retailer's future sales are additions and deletions of merchandise lines, revised promotion and credit policies, changes in business hours, opening new outlets, and remodeling existing stores. With a number of retailers, seasonal variations must be considered in developing monthly or quarterly sales forecasts. For instance, Handy Hardware's yearly snow blower sales should not be estimated from December sales alone.

A retailer can develop a sales forecast by examining past trends and projecting future growth (based on external and internal factors). Table 16.7 shows such a forecast for Handy Hardware. It should be regarded as an estimate, subject to revisions. That is why a financial merchandise plan needs some flexibility. The firm should be aware that various factors may be rather hard to incorporate when devising a forecast, such as merchandise shortages, consumer reactions to new products, strikes by suppliers' personnel, the rate of inflation, and new government legislation.

After a yearly forecast is derived, it should be broken into quarterly or monthly planning periods. In retailing, monthly sales forecasts are usually required. Jewelry stores know December typically accounts for one-fifth of annual sales, while drugstores know December usually provides one-tenth or so of annual sales (slightly above the monthly average).

Table 16.7 Handy Hardware Store, a Simple Sales Forecast Using Product Control Units

Product Control Units	Actual Sales 2000	Projected Growth/ Decline (%)	Sales Forecast 2001
Lawn mowers/snow blowers	$200,000	+10.0	$220,000
Paint and supplies	128,000	+3.0	131,840
Hardware supplies	108,000	+8.0	116,640
Plumbing supplies	88,000	−4.0	84,480
Power tools	88,000	+6.0	93,280
Garden supplies/chemicals	68,000	+4.0	70,720
Housewares	48,000	−6.0	45,120
Electrical supplies	40,000	+4.0	41,600
Ladders	36,000	+6.0	38,160
Hand tools	36,000	+9.0	39,240
Total year	$840,000	+ 4.9[a]	$881,080

[a] There is a small rounding error.

Stationery stores are aware that Christmas cards account for 38 percent of annual card sales, and Valentine's Day cards account for 13 percent.[4]

To acquire more specific estimates, a retailer could use a **monthly sales index,** which divides each month's actual sales by average monthly sales and multiplies the results by 100. Table 16.8 shows Handy Hardware's 2000 actual monthly sales and monthly sales indexes. The data indicate the store is seasonal, with peaks in late spring and early summer (for lawn mowers, garden supplies, house paint and supplies, and so on), as well as December (for lighting fixtures, snow blowers, and gifts).

According to Table 16.8, average monthly 2000 sales were $70,000 ($840,000/12). Thus, the monthly sales index for January is 67 [($46,800/$70,000) × 100]; other monthly

Table 16.8 Handy Hardware Store, 2000 Sales by Month

Month	Monthly Actual Sales	Sales Index[a]
January	$ 46,800	67
February	40,864	58
March	48,000	69
April	65,600	94
May	112,196	160
June	103,800	148
July	104,560	149
August	62,800	90
September	46,904	67
October	46,800	67
November	66,884	96
December	94,792	135
Total yearly sales	$840,000	
Average monthly sales	$ 70,000	
Average monthly index		100

[a] Monthly sales index = (Monthly sales/Average monthly sales) × 100

Table 16.9 Handy Hardware Store, 2001 Sales Forecast by Month

Month	Actual Sales 2000	Monthly Sales Index	Monthly Sales Forecast for 2001[a]		
January	$ 46,800	67	$73,423 × .67	=	$ 49,193
February	40,864	58	73,423 × .58	=	42,585
March	48,000	69	73,423 × .69	=	50,662
April	65,600	94	73,423 × .94	=	69,018
May	112,196	160	73,423 × 1.60	=	117,477
June	103,800	148	73,423 × 1.48	=	108,666
July	104,560	149	73,423 × 1.49	=	109,400
August	62,800	90	73,423 × .90	=	66,081
September	46,904	67	73,423 × .67	=	49,193
October	46,800	67	73,423 × .67	=	49,193
November	66,884	96	73,423 × .96	=	70,486
December	94,792	135	73,423 × 1.35	=	99,121
Total sales	$840,000		Total sales forecast		$881,080[b]
Average monthly sales	$ 70,000		Average monthly forecast		$ 73,423

[a] Monthly sales forecast = Average monthly forecast × (Monthly index/100). In this equation, the monthly index is computed as a fraction of 1.00 rather than 100.
[b] There is a small rounding error.

indexes are computed similarly. Each monthly index shows the percentage deviation of that month's sales from the average month's. A May index of 160 means May sales are 60 percent higher than the average month. An October index of 67 means sales in October are 33 percent below the average.

Once monthly sales indexes are determined, a retailer can forecast monthly sales, based on the yearly sales forecast. Table 16.9 shows how Handy Hardware's 2001 monthly sales can be forecast if average monthly sales are expected to be roughly $73,423. May sales are projected at $117,477 ($73,423 × 1.60) and October sales at $49,193 ($73,423 × 0.67).

Inventory-Level Planning

Dynacom's Accounting 2000 for Windows comes in a free downloadable "Shareware Version" (www.dynacom.ca/ English/winbasicen. html).

Following its derivation of a sales forecast, a retailer plans the inventory levels for the period. Inventory must be sufficient to meet sales expectations, allowing a margin for error. Among the techniques to plan inventory levels are the basic stock, percentage variation, weeks' supply, and stock-to-sales methods.

With the **basic stock method,** a retailer carries more items than it expects to sell over a specified period. This gives the firm a cushion if sales are more than anticipated, shipments are delayed, or customers want to select from a variety of items. It is best when inventory turnover is low or sales are erratic over the year. Beginning-of-month planned inventory equals planned sales plus a basic stock amount:

$$\text{Basic stock (at retail)} = \text{Average monthly stock at retail} - \text{Average monthly sales}$$

$$\text{Beginning-of-month planned inventory level (at retail)} = \text{Planned monthly sales} + \text{Basic stock}$$

If Handy Hardware, with an average monthly 2001 sales forecast of $73,423, wants to have extra stock on hand equal to 10 percent of its average monthly forecast ($7,342) and expects January 2001 sales to be $49,193:

$$\text{Basic stock (at retail)} = (\$73,423 \times 1.10) - \$73,423 = \$7,342$$

$$\text{Beginning-of-January planned inventory level (at retail)} = \$49,193 + \$7,342 = \$56,535$$

In the **percentage variation method,** beginning-of-month planned inventory during any month differs from planned average monthly stock by only one-half of that month's variation from estimated average monthly sales. This method is recommended when stock turnover is more than six times a year or relatively stable, since it results in planned inventories closer to the monthly average than other techniques:

$$\text{Beginning-of-month planned inventory level (at retail)} = \text{Planned average monthly stock at retail} \times \tfrac{1}{2} \left[1 + (\text{Estimated monthly sales} / \text{Estimated average monthly sales})\right]$$

If Handy Hardware plans average monthly stock of $80,765 and November 2001 sales are expected to be 4 percent less than average monthly sales of $73,423, the store's planned inventory level at the beginning of November 2001 would be:

$$\text{Beginning-of-November planned inventory level (at retail)} = \$80,765 \times \tfrac{1}{2} \left[1 + (\$70,487/\$73,423)\right] = \$79,150$$

For Handy Hardware, the percentage variation method is not a good one to use because of its variable sales. With that method, Handy would plan a beginning-of-December 2001, inventory of $94,899 (based on planned average monthly stock of $80,765), less than it expects to sell ($99,121).

The **weeks' supply method** forecasts average sales on a weekly basis, so beginning inventory equals several weeks' expected sales. It assumes inventory is in direct proportion to sales. Thus, too much merchandise may be stocked in peak selling periods and too little during slow selling periods:

$$\text{Beginning-of-month planned inventory level (at retail)} = \text{Average estimated weekly sales} \times \text{Number of weeks to be stocked}$$

If Handy Hardware forecasts average weekly sales of $10,956.92 during the period from January 1, 2001, through March 31, 2001, and it wants to stock 13 weeks of merchandise (based on expected turnover in the first part of 2001), beginning inventory would be $142,440:

$$\text{Beginning-of-January planned inventory level (at retail)} = \$10,956.92 \times 13 = \$142,440$$

With the **stock-to-sales method,** a retailer wants to maintain a specified ratio of goods on hand to sales. A ratio of 1.3 means that if Handy Hardware plans sales of $69,018 in April 2001, it should have $89,723 worth of merchandise (at retail) available during the month. Like the weeks' supply method, the stock-to-sales ratio tends to adjust inventory more drastically than changes in sales require.

Yearly industrywide stock-to-sales ratios are provided by sources such as *Merchandising and Operating Results of Retail Stores* (New York: National Retail Federation), *Industry Norms and Key Business Ratios* (New York: Dun & Bradstreet), and *Annual Statement Studies* (Philadelphia: Robert Morris Associates). A retailer can thus compare its ratios with other firms'.

Reduction Planning

Besides forecasting sales, a firm should estimate the extent of its expected **retail reductions,** which represent the difference between beginning inventory plus purchases during the period and sales plus ending inventory. Planned reductions incorporate anticipated markdowns (price discounts to stimulate merchandise sales), employee and other discounts (price cuts given to employees, senior citizens, clergy, and others), and stock shortages (caused by pilferage, breakage, and bookkeeping errors). It is essential for a retailer to estimate and plan reductions, not just wait for them to occur:

$$\text{Planned reductions} = \begin{array}{l}(\text{Beginning inventory} + \text{Planned purchases}) \\ - (\text{Planned sales} + \text{Ending inventory})\end{array}$$

Reduction planning revolves around two key factors: estimating expected total reductions by budget period and assigning the estimates monthly. The following should be studied in planning total reductions:

- Past experience.
- Markdown data for similar retailers.
- Changes in company policies.
- Merchandise carryover from one budget period to another.
- Price trends.
- Stock-shortage trends.

Past experience is a good starting point. This information can then be compared with that of similar firms—by reviewing available data on markdowns, discounts, and stock shortages in trade publications. For instance, a retailer with more (higher) markdowns than competitors could investigate and correct the situation by adjusting its buying practices and price levels or training sales personnel better.

In reviewing prior reductions, a retailer must consider its own procedures. Policy changes in a budget period often affect the quantity and timing of markdowns. If a firm expands its assortment of seasonal and fashion merchandise, this would probably lead to a rise in necessary markdowns.

Merchandise carryover, price trends, and stock shortage trends also affect planning. If such items as gloves and antifreeze are stocked in off seasons, markdowns are often not used to clear out inventory. Yet, the carryover of fad items merely postpones reductions. Price trends of product categories have a strong impact on retail reductions. For example, many full computer systems now sell for less than $1,000, down considerably from earlier amounts. This means higher-priced computers have to be marked down to be saleable.

A firm can use recent stock shortage trends (determined by comparing book and physical inventory values over previous budget periods) to project future reductions due to employee, customer, and vendor theft; breakage; and bookkeeping mistakes. Up to one-quarter of all stock shortages in retailing are due to clerical and handling errors. If a firm has total stock shortages of less than 2 percent of annual sales, it is usually deemed to be doing well. Figure 16.3 shows a checklist to reduce shortages from clerical and handling errors. Suggestions for reducing shortages from theft were covered in Chapter 15.

Figure 16.3
A Checklist to
Reduce Inventory
Shortages Due
to Clerical and
Handling Errors

Answer yes or no to each of the following questions. A no answer to any question means corrective measures must be taken.

Buying

1. Is the exact quantity of merchandise purchased always specified in the contract?
2. Are purchase quantities recorded by size, color, model, etc.?
3. Are special purchase terms clearly noted?
4. Are returns to the vendor recorded properly?

Marking

5. Are retail prices clearly marked on merchandise?
6. Are the prices marked on merchandise checked for correctness?
7. Are markdowns and additional markups recorded by item number and quantity?
8. Does a cashier check with a manager if a price is not marked on an item?
9. Are the prices shown on display shelves checked for consistency with those marked on the items themselves?
10. Are old price tags removed when an item's price is changed?

Handling

11. After receipt, are purchase quantities checked against contract specifications?
12. Is merchandise handled in a systematic manner?
13. Are goods separated by merchandise classification?
14. Are all handling operations monitored properly (e.g., receiving, storing, distribution)?
15. Is enough merchandise kept on the selling floor (to reduce excessive handling)?
16. Are items sold in bulk (such as produce, sugar, candy) measured accurately?
17. Are damaged, soiled, returned, or other special goods handled separately?

Selling

18. Do sales personnel know correct prices or have easy access to them?
19. Are markdowns, additional markups, etc., communicated to sales personnel?
20. Are misrings by cashiers made on a very small percentage of sales?
21. Are special terms noted on sales receipts?
22. Do sales personnel confirm that all items are rung up by cashiers?
23. Are employee discounts noted?
24. Is the addition on sales receipts done mechanically or double checked if computed by hand?
25. Are sales receipts numbered and later checked for missing invoices?

Inventory Planning

26. Is a physical inventory conducted at least annually?
27. Is a book inventory maintained throughout the year?
28. Are the differences between physical inventory counts and book inventory always accounted for?
29. Are sales and inventory records reviewed regularly?

Accounting

30. Are permanent records on all transactions kept?
31. Are both retail and cost data maintained?
32. Are all types of records monitored for accuracy?
33. Are inventory shortages compared with industry averages to determine acceptability of performance?

After determining total reductions, they must be planned by month because reductions as a percentage of sales are not the same each month. Stock shortages may be much higher during busy periods, when stores are more crowded and transactions happen more quickly.

Planning Purchases

The formula for calculating planned purchases for a period is:

$$\begin{aligned}\text{Planned purchases} \\ \text{(at retail)}\end{aligned} = \begin{aligned}&\text{Planned sales for the month} + \text{Planned reductions for the month} \\ &+ \text{Planned end-of-month stock} - \text{Beginning-of-month stock}\end{aligned}$$

If Handy Hardware projects June 2001 sales to be $108,666 and total planned reductions to be 5 percent of sales, plans end-of-month inventory at retail to be $72,000, and has a beginning-of-month inventory at retail of $80,000, planned purchases for June are

$$\begin{aligned}\text{Planned purchases} \\ \text{(at retail)}\end{aligned} = \$108,666 + \$5,433 + \$72,000 - \$80,000 = \$106,099$$

Because Handy Hardware expects 2001 merchandise costs to be about 60 percent of retail selling price, it is planning to purchase $63,659 of goods at cost in June 2001:

$$\begin{aligned}\text{Planned purchases} \\ \text{(at cost)}\end{aligned} = \begin{aligned}&\text{Planned purchases at retail} \\ &\times \text{Merchandise costs as a percentage of selling price}\end{aligned}$$

$$= \$106,099 \times 0.60 = \$63,659$$

Take an online tour of *The OTB Book* (www. otb-retail.com/tour1. htm).

Open-to-buy is the difference between planned purchases and the purchase commitments already made by a buyer for a given time period, often a month. It represents the amount the buyer has left to spend for that month and is reduced each time a purchase is made. At the beginning of a month, a firm's planned purchases and open-to-buy are equal if no purchases commitments have been made prior to the start of that month. Open-to-buy is recorded at cost.

At Handy Hardware, the buyer has made commitments for June 2001 valued in the amount of $55,000 at retail. Accordingly, Handy's open-to-buy at retail for June is $51,099:

$$\begin{aligned}\text{Open-to-buy} \\ \text{(at retail)}\end{aligned} = \begin{aligned}&\text{Planned purchases for the month} \\ &- \text{Purchase commitments for the month}\end{aligned}$$

$$= \$106,099 - \$55,000 = \$51,099$$

To calculate the June 2001 open-to-buy at cost, $51,099 is multiplied by Handy Hardware's merchandise costs as a percentage of selling price:

$$\begin{aligned}\text{Open-to-buy} \\ \text{(at cost)}\end{aligned} = \begin{aligned}&\text{Open-to-buy at retail} \\ &\times \text{Merchandise costs as a percentage of selling price}\end{aligned}$$

$$= \$51,099 \times 0.60 = \$30,659$$

The open-to-buy concept has two significant strengths. First, it assures the retailer that a specified relationship between stock on hand and planned sales is maintained, which avoids overbuying and underbuying. Second, it lets a firm adjust merchandise purchases to reflect changes in sales, markdowns, and so on. If Handy Hardware revises its June 2001 sales forecast to $120,000 (from $108,666), it automatically increases planned purchases and open-to-buy by $11,334 at retail and $6,800 at cost.

From a strategic perspective, it is usually advisable for a retailer to keep at least a small open-to-buy figure for as long as possible. This enables the firm to take advantage of special deals, purchase new models when introduced, and fill in items that sell out. An open-to-buy

Forecasting a Career at Macy's

Sylmarie Sasso is a planner for junior denim at Macy's. As a 1996 accounting graduate from the University of the State of New York at Albany, she feels that her facility with numbers has helped her at work: "Every day when I get in, I check my numbers to see how we are doing. You really have to be a sponge and soak up so much information. I had no idea how much information I could handle and process. Planning is really number-oriented. I use accounting skills every day."

Sasso's responsibilities in her current position include getting the right assortment of goods to the right stores at the right time. For example, "Boston needs cold weather clothing first, and Florida may need very little of it. In addition, there are adjustments to the assortment based on differences in the characteristics of the population. Urban stores need slightly different size mixes than suburban stores.

Sylmarie Sasso is also involved in supplier negotiations: "With vendors, everything is negotiation. Small points can become a major deal, so it's important to learn how to negotiate with people."

Source: "Employment at Macy's East Adds Up to Success," *Careers in Retailing* (January 1999), pp. 16, 18.

limit sometimes must be exceeded due to underestimates of demand (low sales forecasts). As with the budgeting process, a retailer should not be so rigid that merchandising personnel are unable to have the discretion (employee empowerment) to purchase below-average priced items when the open-to-buy is not really open.

Planning Profit Margins

In developing a merchandise budget, a retailer is quite interested in profitability (expressed by dollar and percentage profit margins) and thus must consider planned net sales, retail operating expenses, profit, and retail reductions in pricing merchandise:

$$\text{Required initial markup percentage} = \frac{\text{Planned retail expenses} + \text{Planned profit} + \text{Planned reductions}}{\text{Planned net sales} + \text{Planned reductions}}$$

The required markup is a companywide average. Individual items may be priced according to demand and other factors, as long as the average is met. A fuller markup discussion is in Chapter 17. The concept of initial markup is introduced at this point for continuity in the description of merchandise budgeting.

Handy has an overall 2001 sales forecast of $881,080 and expects annual operating expenses to be $290,000. Reductions are projected to be $44,000. The total net dollar profit margin goal is $60,000, amounting to 6.8 percent of sales. Therefore, its required initial markup is 42.6 percent:

$$\text{Required initial markup percentage} = \frac{\$290,000 + \$60,000 + \$44,000}{\$881,080 + \$44,000} = 42.6\%$$

$$\begin{array}{l}\text{Required initial} \\ \text{markup percentage} \\ \text{(all factors expressed} \\ \text{as a percentage of} \\ \text{net sales)}\end{array} = \frac{32.9\% + 6.8\% + 5.0\%}{100.0\% + 5.0\%} = 42.6\%$$

Figure 16.4
The Merchandise
Forecasting and
Budgeting Process:
Dollar Control

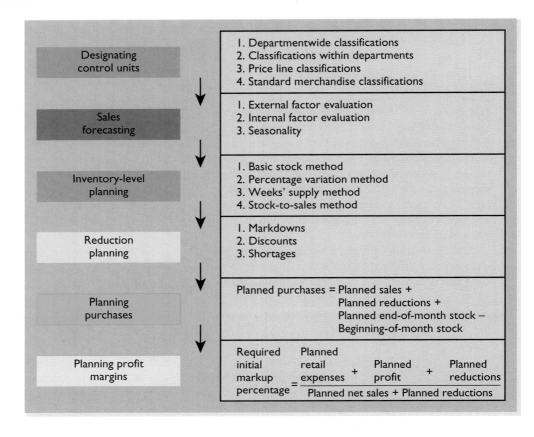

Figure 16.4 summarizes the merchandise forecasting and budgeting process. It expands on Figure 16.2 by including the bases for each decision stage.

UNIT CONTROL SYSTEMS

RWS Information Systems offers unit control software capabilities in its POS-IM program (www.rwsinfo.com/invcon2.html).

Unit control systems deal with quantities of merchandise in units rather than in dollars. Information typically contained in unit control systems includes

- The identification of items selling well and those selling poorly.
- A focus on opportunities and problem areas in terms of price, color, style, size, and so on.
- The computation of the quantity of goods on hand (if a perpetual inventory system is used). This minimizes overstocking and understocking.
- An indication of inventory age, highlighting candidates for markdowns or special promotions.
- A determination of the optimal time to reorder merchandise.
- A synopsis of experiences with alternative sources (vendors) when problems arise.
- The level of inventory and sales for each item in every store branch. This improves the transfer of goods between branches and alerts salespeople as to which branches have desired products. Also, less stock can be held in individual stores, reducing costs.

Physical Inventory Systems

A physical inventory unit control system is similar to a physical inventory dollar control system. But a dollar control system is concerned with the financial value of inventory, while a unit control system looks at the number of units by item classification. With unit control, the retailer assigns the task of monitoring inventory levels, either by visual inspection or actual count. See Figure 16.5.

In a typical visual inspection system, merchandise is placed on pegboard (or similar) displays, with each item numbered on the back of its package or on a stock card. Minimum inventory quantities are clearly noted, and sales personnel reorder when the number of items on hand reaches the minimum level. Accuracy occurs only if merchandise is placed in numerical order on displays (and sold accordingly). The system is used in the houseware and hardware displays of various discount, variety, and hardware stores.

Although a visual inspection system is easy to maintain and inexpensive, it has shortcomings: (1) It does not provide data on the rate of sales of individual items. (2) Minimum stock quantities may be arbitrarily defined and not drawn from in-depth analysis.

The other physical inventory system, actual counting, means regularly compiling the number of units on hand. A stock-counting system records—in units—inventory on hand, purchases, sales volume, and shortages during specified periods. Thus, Handy Hardware could use the system for its insulation tape:

	Number of Rolls of Tape for the Period 12/1/00–12/31/00
Beginning inventory, December 1, 2000	100
Total purchases for period	70
Total units available for sale	170
Closing inventory, December 31, 2000	60
Sales and shortages for period	110

A stock-counting system requires more clerical work than a visual system, but lets a firm obtain sales data for given periods and stock-to-sales relationships as of the time of each count. A physical system is not as sophisticated as a perpetual one. It is more useful with low-value items having predictable sales.

Perpetual Inventory Systems

A *perpetual inventory unit control system* keeps a running total of the number of units handled by a retailer through ongoing recordkeeping entries that adjust for sales, returns, transfers to other departments or stores, receipt of shipments, and other transactions. All additions to and subtractions from beginning inventory are recorded. Perpetual (book) inventory systems can be done manually, use merchandise tags processed by computers, or rely on point-of-sale devices such as optical scanners. Technological advances have greatly aided retailers in applying computer-based perpetual inventory systems.

A manual system requires employees to gather data by examining sales checks, merchandise receipts, transfer requests, and other documents. Data are then coded and tabulated.

A merchandise tagging system relies on pre-printed tags attached to each item. Tags include data by department, classification, vendor, style, date of receipt, color, and material. When an item is sold, a copy of the tag is removed and sent to a tabulating facility, where information is analyzed by computer. Since pre-printed tags are processed in batches, they can be used by small and medium retailers (that subscribe to independent service bureaus) and by branches of chains (with data processed at a central location).

Point-of-sale systems, from firms such as IBM, Digital Equipment, and NCR, feed data from merchandise tags or product labels directly to in-store computer terminals for immediate data processing. Computer-based systems are quicker, more accurate, and of higher quality than manual ones. Due to the access to computers, computerized checkouts, and service bureaus, costs are reasonable for smaller retailers.

Figure 16.5
Physical Inventory Systems Made Simpler

Taking a physical inventory using a Retail Pro portable terminal takes only a fraction of the time required for a traditional manual count. It also yields a more accurate result. After each scan with the laser gun, the physical count is recorded in the portable terminal. Once a section of inventory is complete, an employee connects the portable terminal to a computer and Retail Pro compares the recorded inventory with the physical counts. Any discrepancies are immediately isolated and reported. When the firm is ready, it can automatically adjust the recorded inventory to reflect the physical counts and record this adjustment. The portable terminal can also perform quantity and price verifications by pre-loading inventory quantity and price information. When merchandise is scanned, the unit displays the correct retail price and the expected quantity on hand. This makes it easy to detect pricing errors and missing merchandise.

Reprinted by permission of Retail Technologies International.

Newer point-of-sale (POS) systems can be easily networked, have battery backup capabilities (in case of power outages), and use standard components (meaning a better choice of printers, keyboards, and monitors). Many POS systems use optical scanners to transfer data from products to computers by wands or other devices that interact with sensitized strips on the items. Figure 16.6 shows how barcoding works. As noted earlier in the text, the UPC is the dominant format for coding data onto merchandise.

A retailer does not have to use a perpetual system for all of its inventory. Many firms combine perpetual and physical systems, whereby key items (accounting for a large proportion of sales) are controlled by a perpetual system and other items are controlled by a physical inventory system. In this way, attention is properly placed on the retailer's most important products.

Unit Control Systems in Practice

Inventory Management Services (www.practicalorganization.com/retail.html) provides third-party physical inventory services for retailers.

Arthur Andersen annually surveys a broad cross-section of retailers about their inventory management practices. According to its 1999 survey of leading department stores, discount stores, specialty stores, supermarkets, convenience stores, and home centers:

- 96 percent of the firms engage in "wall-to-wall" physical inventories, with 32 percent doing so yearly, 27 percent semiannually, 20 percent monthly, and 17 percent quarterly.

Figure 16.6
How Does a UPC-
Based Scanner System
Work?

Courtesy Giant Food Inc.

When the checker passes an item with the UPC symbol over a scanning device, the symbol is read by a low-energy laser.
The UPC symbol is found on many supermarket products and looks like this.

Each product has its own unique identification number. For example, the first five digits, 11146, represent the manufacturer, Giant in this case. The second five digits represent the specific items; 01345 identifies 24 ounce iced tea mix.
Note that the price is not in the symbol. The symbol identifies the product, not the price.

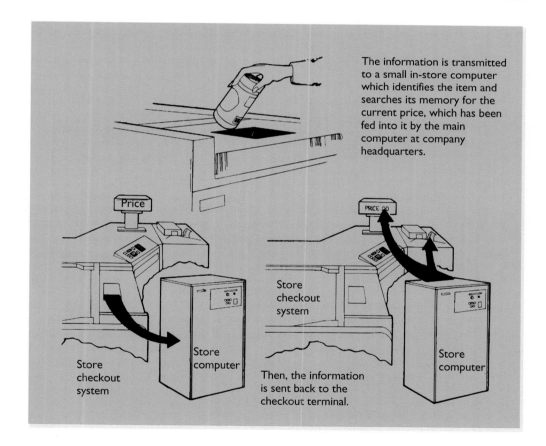

The information is transmitted to a small in-store computer which identifies the item and searches its memory for the current price, which has been fed into it by the main computer at company headquarters.

Then, the information is sent back to the checkout terminal.

- During physical inventories, 64 percent of the firms record retail prices, 54 percent record SKU codes, 34 percent record item costs, and 8 percent note the age of the inventory.
- 50 percent of physical inventories are done by company employees; and 50 percent are outsourced.
- 74 percent of the firms use a perpetual inventory system.[5]

FINANCIAL INVENTORY CONTROL: INTEGRATING DOLLAR AND UNIT CONCEPTS

Technology Strategy Incorporated (www. grossprofit.com) markets sophisticated inventory analysis software. Check out its "News" and "Clients" sections for applications.

Up to this point, dollar and unit control concepts have been discussed separately. Yet, in practice, they are directly linked. The decision on how many units to buy at a given time affects and is affected by dollar investments, inventory turnover, quantity discounts, warehousing and insurance costs, and so on.

Three aspects of financial inventory control are described next: stock turnover and gross margin return on investment, when to reorder, and how much to reorder.

Stock Turnover and Gross Margin Return on Investment

Stock turnover represents the number of times during a specific period, usually one year, that the average inventory on hand is sold. It can be measured by store, product line, department, and vendor. High stock turnover has several virtues. Inventory investments are productive on a per-dollar basis. Merchandise on shelves is fresh. Losses due to changes in styles and fashion are less. Costs associated with maintaining inventory (such as interest, insurance, breakage, and warehousing) are reduced.

Stock turnover can be computed in units or dollars (at retail or cost):

$$\text{Annual rate of stock turnover (in units)} = \frac{\text{Number of units sold during year}}{\text{Average inventory on hand (in units)}}$$

$$\text{Annual rate of stock turnover (in retail dollars)} = \frac{\text{Net yearly sales}}{\text{Average inventory on hand (at retail)}}$$

$$\text{Annual rate of stock turnover (at cost)} = \frac{\text{Cost of goods sold during the year}}{\text{Average inventory on hand (at cost)}}$$

The choice of a turnover formula depends on the retailer's accounting system.

In computing stock turnover, the average inventory level for the entire period covered in the analysis needs to be reflected. Turnover rates are invalid if the true average is not used, as occurs if a firm mistakenly views the inventory level of a peak or slow month as the yearly average.

Table 16.10 shows annual stock turnover rates for various retailer types. Eating places, gasoline service stations, and grocery stores have very high rates. They rely on sales volume for their success. Jewelry stores, drugstores, shoe stores, and family clothing stores have very low rates. They require larger profit margins on each item sold and maintain a sizable assortment for customers.

A retailer can raise stock turnover by a number of different strategies, such as reducing its assortment, eliminating or having minimal inventory for slow-selling items, buying in an efficient and timely way, applying quick response inventory planning, and using reliable suppliers.

Despite a high turnover's advantages, there are instances in which it can have adverse effects. Buying items in small amounts could increase merchandise costs because quantity discounts may be lost and transportation charges may rise. Since a high turnover rate might be due to low assortment, some customer sales may be lost. High turnover could lead to low profits if prices must be lowered to move inventory quickly. A retailer's return on investment depends on both turnover and profit per unit.

Learn more about GMROI (www.martec-international.com/ Improving%20GMROI %20E1P.htm) from Martec International.

Gross margin return on investment (GMROI) shows the relationship between the gross margin in dollars (also known as total dollar operating profits) and the average inventory investment (at cost) by combining profitability and sales-to-stock measures:

Table 16.10 Annual Median Stock Turnover Rates for Selected Types of Retailers

Type of Retailer	Annual Median Stock Turnover Rate (Times)
Auto and home supply stores	7.5
Department stores	4.4
Drugstores	3.6
Eating places	74.0
Family clothing stores	3.6
Furniture stores	4.8
Gasoline service stations	40.2
Grocery stores	18.7
Hardware stores	4.4
Household appliance stores	6.0
Jewelry stores	2.5
Lumber and other building materials dealers	7.4
Men's and boys' clothing stores	4.1
New and used-car dealers	6.4
Shoe stores	3.6
Women's clothing stores	5.1

Source: Industry Norms & Key Business Ratios: Desk-Top Edition (New York: Dun & Bradstreet, 1998–99), pp. 147–63.

$$\begin{aligned}
\text{Gross margin} \\
\text{return on investment} \\
\text{(GMROI)}
\end{aligned} = \frac{\text{Gross margin in dollars}}{\text{Net sales}} \times \frac{\text{Net sales}}{\text{Average inventory at cost}}$$

$$= \frac{\text{Gross margin in dollars}}{\text{Average inventory at cost}}$$

In this formula, the gross margin in dollars is defined as net sales minus the cost of goods sold. The gross margin percentage (a profitability measure) is derived by dividing dollar gross margin by net sales. A sales-to-stock ratio is provided by dividing net sales by average inventory at cost. It may be converted to stock turnover by multiplying the sales-to-stock ratio by [(100 − Gross margin percentage)/100].

GMROI is a useful concept for several reasons:

- It shows how diverse retailers can prosper with different gross margins and sales-to-stock ratios. A supermarket may have a gross margin percentage of 20 and a sales-to-stock ratio of 25, resulting in a GMROI of 500 percent (20% × 25). A women's clothing store may have a gross margin percentage of 50 and a sales-to-stock ratio of 10, yielding a GMROI of 500 percent (50% × 10). The GMROIs of the firms are the same due to the trade-off between profitability per item and turnover.
- It is a good indicator of a manager's performance since it focuses on factors controlled by that person. Interdepartmental comparisons can also be made.
- It is simple to plan and understand, and data collection is easy.
- A retailer can determine if GMROI performance is consistent with other company goals, such as its image and cash flow.

The gross margin percentage and the sales-to-stock ratio must be studied individually. If only overall GMROI is reviewed, performance may be assessed improperly. Some experts

With Some Payment Plans, Consumers Need to Say Grace

With a retail deferred payment plan, a consumer can purchase a big-ticket item such as a major appliance or furniture and delay payment until a later date. Some retailers give consumers grace periods ranging from one month up to two years from the date of purchase. As long as the full bill is paid before the end of the grace period, there is no interest. In that case, the consumer is getting a free loan. However, that is not necessarily the intent of this payment plan.

Typically, the appliance or furniture retailer contracts with an outside finance company that buys its customer-deferred payment accounts for a discount. If the accounts begin payment in two years, for example, the finance company may discount the payment to the retailer by 10 percent. This means the retailer receives 90 percent of the product's purchase price in return for the finance company's obtaining the right to collect the full amount due plus the interest on the loan from the consumer.

Retailers typically work the discount into their pricing strategy. Thus, a $2,000 dining room set may be marked up by an additional 10 percent to reflect the grace period. In addition, shoppers often mistakenly believe that interest on the bill does not start until the end of the grace period. In fact, consumers who do not pay the full amount on time are charged interest from the date of purchase. A person with a two-year payment deferral who pays the bill one month after the grace period will have to pay for 25 months of interest.

How aggressively should a retailer disclose the interest charges that build up for deferred payment plans? Explain your answer.

Source: Lucinda Harper, "Retailers Play 'Can You Top This?' with Payment Plans," *Wall Street Journal* (December 24, 1998), pp. A2, A4.

suggest that the formula noted here be expanded to include accounts receivable, accounts payable, and inventory carrying costs.

When to Reorder

One way to control inventory investment is to systematically set stock levels at which new orders must be placed. Such a stock level is called a **reorder point.** Determining a reorder point depends on the order lead time, usage rate, and safety stock. **Order lead time** is the period from the date an order is placed by a retailer to the date merchandise is ready for sale (received, price-marked, and put on the selling floor). **Usage rate** refers to average sales per day, in units, of merchandise. **Safety stock** is the extra inventory kept on hand to protect against out-of-stock conditions due to unexpected demand and delays in delivery. It is planned according to the firm's policy toward running out of items (service level).

This is the formula if a retailer does not plan to carry safety stock, believing customer demand is stable and its orders are promptly filled by suppliers:

Reorder point = Usage rate × Lead time

If Handy Hardware sells 10 paintbrushes a day and needs 8 days to order, receive, and display them, it has a reorder point of 80 brushes. It would reorder brushes once inventory on hand reaches 80. By the time brushes from that order are placed on shelves (8 days later), stock on hand will be zero, and the new stock will replenish the inventory.

This strategy is correct only when Handy has a perfectly steady customer demand of 10 paintbrushes daily and it takes exactly 8 days for all stages in the ordering process to be completed. Yet, this does not normally occur. If customers buy 15 brushes per day during a given month, Handy would run out of stock in $5\frac{1}{3}$ days and be without brushes for $5\frac{2}{3}$ days. Similarly, if an order takes 10 days to process, Handy would have no brushes for 2 full days, despite correctly estimating demand. Figure 16.7 shows how stockouts may occur if safety stock is not planned.

For a retailer interested in maintaining safety stock, the reorder formula becomes:

Reorder point = (Usage rate × Lead time) + Safety stock

As a rule, retailers should include safety stock in merchandise planning because demand is rarely constant from day to day or week to week and deliveries from suppliers can be delayed.

Suppose Handy Hardware decides on safety stock of 30 percent for paintbrushes; its reorder point is:

Reorder point = (10 × 8) + (.30 × 80) = 80 + 24 = 104

Handy still expects to sell an average of 10 brushes per day and receive orders in an average of 8 days. A safety stock of 24 extra brushes is kept on hand to protect against unexpected demand or a late shipment.

By combining a perpetual inventory system and reorder point calculations, merchandise ordering can be programmed into a computer and reordering done automatically when stock-on-hand reaches the reorder point. This is an **automatic reordering system.**

Figure 16.7
How Stockouts
May Occur

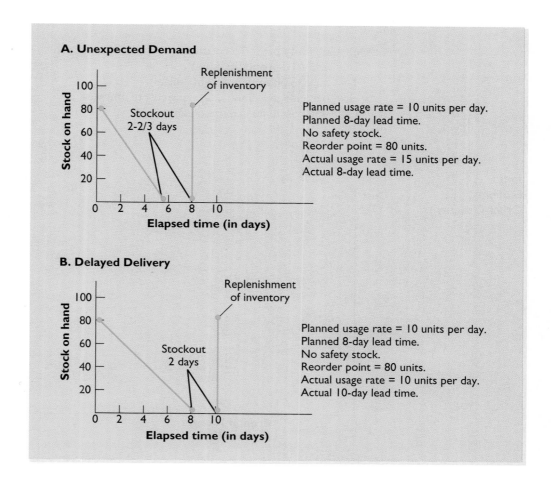

However, intervention by a buyer or a store manager must be possible, especially if monthly sales fluctuate greatly.

How Much to Reorder

The decision about how much to order affects how often a retailer buys merchandise. A firm placing large orders generally reduces ordering costs but increases inventory-holding costs. A firm placing small orders often minimizes inventory-holding costs while ordering costs may rise (unless electronic data interchange and a quick response inventory system are used).

Economic order quantity (EOQ) is the quantity per order (in units) that minimizes the total costs of processing orders and holding inventory. Order-processing costs include computer time, order forms, labor, and handling new goods. Holding costs include warehousing, inventory investment, insurance, taxes, depreciation, deterioration, and pilferage. EOQ calculations can be done by large and small firms.

As Figure 16.8 shows, order-processing costs drop as the quantity per order (in units) goes up because fewer orders are needed to buy the same total annual quantity, and inventory-holding costs rise as the quantity per order goes up because more units must be held in inventory and they are kept for longer periods. The two costs are summed into a total cost curve.

Mathematically, the economic order quantity is

$$EOQ = \sqrt{\frac{2DS}{IC}}$$

where

EOQ = quantity per order (in units)
D = annual demand (in units)
S = costs to place an order (in dollars)
I = percentage of annual carrying cost to unit cost
C = unit cost of an item (in dollars)

Figure 16.8
Economic
Order Quantity

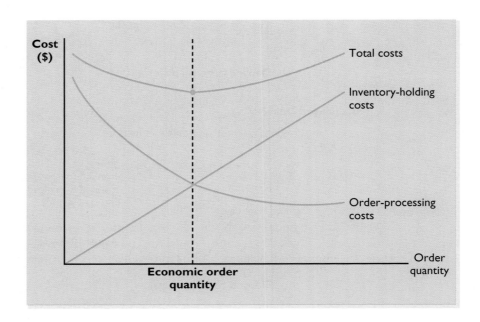

Handy estimates it can sell 150 power tool sets per year. They cost $90 each. Breakage, insurance, tied-up capital, and pilferage equal 10 percent of the costs of the sets ($9 each). Order costs are $25 per order. The economic order quantity is

$$\text{EOQ} = \sqrt{\frac{2(150)(\$25)}{(0.10)(\$90)}} = \sqrt{\frac{\$7,500}{\$9}} = 29$$

The EOQ formula must often be modified to take into account changes in demand, quantity discounts, and variable ordering and holding costs.

SUMMARY

1. *To describe the major aspects of financial merchandise planning and management.* Financial merchandise management stipulates which products are bought by the retailer, when they are bought, and what quantity is bought. Dollar control plans and monitors the inventory investment for a given period, while unit control relates to the amount of merchandise handled during that period. Financial merchandise management encompasses methods of accounting, merchandise forecasting and budgeting, unit control systems, and integrated dollar and unit controls.

2. *To explain the cost and retail methods of accounting.* The two accounting techniques for retailers are the cost and retail methods of inventory valuation. Physical and book (perpetual) procedures are possible with each. Physical inventory valuation requires actually counting merchandise at prescribed intervals. Book inventory valuation relies on accurate bookkeeping and a smooth flow of data.

The cost method obligates a retailer to have careful records for each item bought or code its cost on the package. This must be done to find the exact value of ending inventory at cost. Many firms use the LIFO accounting method to approximate that value, which lets them reduce taxes by having a low ending inventory value. In the retail method, closing inventory value is tied to the average relationship between the cost and retail value of merchandise available for sale. This more accurately reflects market conditions, but is more complex.

3. *To study the merchandise forecasting and budgeting process.* Merchandise forecasting and budgeting is a form of dollar control with six stages: designating control units, sales forecasting, inventory-level planning, reduction planning, planning purchases, and planning profit margins. Adjustments at any point in the process require all later stages to be modified accordingly.

Control units are merchandise categories for which data are gathered. They must be narrow enough to isolate problems and opportunities with specific product lines. Sales forecasting may be the key stage in the merchandising and budgeting process because its accuracy affects many other stages. Through inventory-level planning, a firm sets merchandise quantities for specified periods; techniques include the basic stock, percentage variation, weeks' supply, and stock-to-sales methods. Reduction planning estimates expected markdowns, discounts, and stock shortages. Planned purchases are linked to planned sales, reductions, ending inventory, and beginning inventory. Profit margins are related to a retailer's planned net sales, operating expenses, profit, and reductions.

4. *To examine alternative methods of inventory unit control.* A unit control system involves physical units of merchandise. It includes designating best-sellers and poor-sellers, the quantity of goods on hand, inventory age, reorder time, and so on. A physical inventory unit control system may use visual inspection or a stock-counting procedure. A perpetual inventory unit control system keeps a running total of the number of units a firm handles by ongoing recordkeeping entries that adjust for sales, returns, transfers, new items received, and so on. A perpetual system can be applied manually, by merchandise tags processed by computers, or by point-of-sale devices. Virtually all larger retailers conduct regular "wall-to-wall" physical inventories; three-quarters use a perpetual inventory system.

5. *To integrate dollar and unit merchandising control concepts.* The aspects of financial inventory control that integrate dollar and unit control concepts are stock turnover and gross margin return on investment, when to reorder, and how much to reorder. Stock turnover is the number of times during a specified period that the

SUMMARY *(CONTINUED)*

average inventory on hand is sold. Gross margin return on investment shows the relationship between the gross margin in dollars (total dollar operating profits) and average inventory investment (at cost). A reorder point calculation—when to reorder—includes the retailer's usage rate, order lead time, and safety stock. The economic order quantity—how much to reorder—aids a retailer in choosing how big an order to place, based on both ordering and inventory costs.

Throughout Chapter 16, mathematical merchandising equations were introduced and illustrated.

Key Terms

financial merchandise management (p. 521)
dollar control (p. 521)
unit control (p. 522)
merchandise available for sale (p. 522)
cost of goods sold (p. 522)
gross profit (p. 522)
net profit (p. 522)
cost method of accounting (p. 523)
physical inventory system (p. 523)
book inventory system (perpetual inventory system) (p. 524)

FIFO method (p. 524)
LIFO method (p. 524)
retail method of accounting (p. 526)
cost complement (p. 526)
control units (p. 530)
classification merchandising (p. 531)
monthly sales index (p. 533)
basic stock method (p. 534)
percentage variation method (p. 535)
weeks' supply method (p. 535)
stock-to-sales method (p. 535)
retail reductions (p. 536)
open-to-buy (p. 538)

stock turnover (p. 544)
gross margin return on investment (GMROI) (p. 544)
reorder point (p. 546)
order lead time (p. 546)
usage rate (p. 546)
safety stock (p. 546)
automatic reordering system (p. 547)
economic order quantity (EOQ) (p. 548)

Questions for Discussion

1. What are the benefits of good financial merchandise plans?

2. Which retailers can best use a perpetual inventory system based on the cost method? Explain your answer.

3. The FIFO method seems more logical than the LIFO method, because it assumes the first merchandise purchased is the first merchandise sold. So, why do more retailers use LIFO?

4. What are the advantages and disadvantages of the retail method of accounting in comparison with cost-based retail accounting?

5. Why should a small camera store designate control units, even though this may be time-consuming?

6. Why use sophisticated weather forecasting services if daily weather predictions tend to be inaccurate?

7. Contrast the weeks' supply method and the stock-to-sales supply method of merchandise planning.

8. Present two situations in which it would be advisable for a retailer to take a markdown, instead of carry over merchandise from one budget period to another.

9. What are the pros and cons of a high stock turnover?

10. A retailer has yearly sales of $550,000. Inventory on January 1 is $250,000 (at cost). During the year, $450,000 of merchandise (at cost) is purchased. The ending inventory is $275,000 (at cost). Operating costs are $90,000. Calculate the cost of goods sold and net profit, and set up a profit-and-loss statement. There are no retail reductions in this problem.

11. A retailer has a beginning monthly inventory valued at $50,000 at retail and $35,000 at cost. Net purchases during the month are $120,000 at retail and $70,000 at cost. Transportation charges are $5,000. Sales are $130,000. Markdowns and discounts equal $20,000. A physical inventory at the end of the month shows merchandise valued at $10,000 (at retail) on hand. Compute the following:
   a. Total merchandise available for sale—at cost and at retail.
   b. Cost complement.

c. Ending retail book value of inventory.
d. Stock shortages.
e. Adjusted ending retail book value.
f. Gross profit.

12. The sales of a full-line discount store are listed here. Calculate the monthly sales indexes. What do they mean?

January	$180,000	July	$180,000
February	190,000	August	220,000
March	190,000	September	240,000
April	220,000	October	200,000
May	220,000	November	260,000
June	200,000	December	340,000

13. If the planned average monthly stock for the discount store in Question 11 is $260,000 (at retail),

how much inventory should be planned for August if the retailer uses the percentage variation method? Comment on this retailer's choice of the percentage variation method.

14. The discount store in Questions 12 and 13 knows its cost complement for all merchandise purchased last year was 0.64; it projects this figure to remain constant. For the current year, it expects to begin and end December with inventory valued at $160,000 at retail and estimates December reductions to be $12,000. The firm already has purchase commitments for December worth $120,000 (at retail). What is the open-to-buy at cost for December?

WEB-BASED EXERCISE

Dun & Bradstreet Small Business Services (www.dnb.com)

For the following questions, first click on the "Products & Services" option and then go to the second "Products & Services" scrollbar. Return to this scrollbar prior to answering each question.

Questions

1. Select the Dun & Bradstreet "Learn About D&B Reference Products" option. Describe a reference product that is helpful to a retailer.

2. Select the "Evaluate & Qualify Suppliers" option. Describe a Dun & Bradstreet supply chain solution that is applicable to a retailer.

3. Select the "Focus on Your Industry" option. Describe a Dun & Bradstreet solution applicable to a retailer.

4. Select the "View All Products & Services" option. Describe two Dun & Bradstreet solutions applicable to retailers that you did not discuss in Questions 1 to 3.

CHAPTER ENDNOTES

1. "Back to Basics," *Chain Store Age* (March 1999), p. 188; and Saul Hansell, "Electronic Sales Are Up, as Are Customer Gripes," *New York Times on the Web* (December 17, 1999).

2. Amy Doan, "Vitamin Efficiency," *Forbes* (November 1, 1999), pp. 176–86.

3. Dick Silverman, "Weather Forecasts Can Make a Bottom Line Sunnier," *Women's Wear Daily* (June 9, 1999), p. 17.

4. Greeting Card Association, "Seasons Greetings," *American Demographics* (November 1999), p. 72.

5. "Inventory Management: Critical Processes for Retailers," *Chain Store Age* (December 1999), Section Three, pp. 3B–5B.

CASE 1

SCHNUCK MARKETS MOVES TO CPFR

Collaborative planning, forcasting, and replenishment (CPFR) is based upon a five-stage process involving retailers and their major suppliers:

- *Developing a front-end agreement*—Trading partners allocate responsibilities among each other in terms of goals, information needs, and the measurement of success.
- *Creating a business plan*—A joint business plan is set up for each major category.
- *Preparing a sales forecast*—A sales forecast is devised based on specific promotional events.
- *Collaborating on order forecasting*—Order forecasts are jointly compiled.
- *Establishing order-generation plans*—Shipment execution is planned and forecasts are updated.

Although CPFR is still in its infancy, some retailing experts feel it has the potential to eliminate costly supply chain variations and distortions. According to these observers, CPFR goes beyond the more popular continuous replenishment system (CRS) in reducing excess inventory and stockouts. Among the early proponents of CPFR are leading manufacturers such as Procter & Gamble, Nabisco, Pillsbury, Warner-Lambert, and Sara Lee. Ernst & Young and the Uniform Code Council also support CPFR.

Schnuck Markets, a St. Louis-based supermarket chain, operates 94 stores and its own distribution centers. In 1984, Schnuck developed a CRS in cooperation with Procter & Gamble. With this system, Schnuck took data from its distribution centers and provided it to Procter & Gamble, which then managed Schnuck's inventory using that data. The system enabled Schnuck to lower inventory while it doubled sales. Yet, the system often caused stockouts. Bob Drury, Schnuck's vice-president of management information systems, thinks CRS did a great job of demand forecasting, but a horrible job on promotions. This is a major problem for a chain with 5,000 promotions a month.

Schnuck's current CPFR model uses point-of-sale (POS) data relating to sales, markdowns, and inventories. As Drury reports, "The power of CPFR is that it uses POS both for everyday replenishment decisions and historical POS data to provide a much better predictor of future demand, which allows the entire supply chain to operate differently." The older system was based on reductions in warehouse inventories.

A major advantage of CPFR in comparison to its CRS predecessor is its better potential to accurately forecast changes in demand from new promotions. Nonetheless, Ralph Drayer, vice-president for product supply and ECR worldwide at Procter & Gamble, says an early test of CPFR for the paper products carried by one retail chain resulted in a 77.4 percent accuracy level for a sales forecast. This meant that the retailer would still be out of stock nearly 23 percent of the time.

The long-term goal is to have CPFR enable retailers to reduce inventory by an additional 50 percent as compared to CRS levels. As Schunck's Drury says, "Our division and store managers tell us our backrooms are empty—and we're not even doing the promotions side of it yet. So there's a lot of opportunity."

The inventory reductions in a typical CPFR system are accomplished through a variety of initiatives including post-promotion planning to improve future events, work process improvement that reduces the time between when an order is placed and it is received, and better data exchange between retailers and suppliers.

Questions

1. Why would a vendor such as Procter & Gamble work with Schnuck to develop and improve a CPFR system?

2. Describe the relationship among low inventory levels, high inventory turnover, and stockouts.

3. How can Schnuck improve its performance in terms of stockouts?

4. What is the difference between an inventory system based on POS data versus one based on warehouse withdrawals?

NOTE   The material in this case is drawn from Len Lewis, "CPFR: One Giant Business Plan," *Progressive Grocer* (April 1999), pp. 69–72.

CASE 2

PLANNED PURCHASES AND OPEN-TO-BUY

Some retailing analysts believe that too many retailers simply guess at the proper amount of buying dollars instead of computing open-to-buy levels. According to these analysts, "shooting from the hip" generally results in a significant amount of overbuying. Thus, when a retail buyer asks, "Do I really need an open-to-buy system," the simple answer should be "Yes, you do."

An open-to-buy system enables a retail buyer to plan his or her buying dollars in a manner that provides for adequate inventory turnover while minimizing the possibility of stockouts and excessive markdowns—because inventories are based on sales projections and merchandise is fresh. Open-to-buy planning also helps ensure that correct quantities are purchased by each department for each delivery date. Delivery date planning is especially important for seasonal merchandise such as apparel or gift items.

A proper open-to-buy system avoids both overstocking and understocking. Overstocking increases inventory carrying costs, lowers inventory turnover, and results in excessive markdowns. Understocking results in lost sales (due to stockouts or not having merchandise in the proper size, color, and styles) and leads to dissatisfied customers.

The two key factors that most affect open-to-buy are projections of sales and inventory turnover. If sales are greater than planned, a retailer needs to increase its orders so that the new inventory levels are sufficient to support the added sales activity. One way to plan sales in rising periods is to revise a department's sales projections by a conservative percentage based on past trends. In contrast, if sales are less than planned, future ordering should be curtailed or even cancelled, if possible, to avoid the possibility of excessive markdowns, shortages of cash, and out-of-date merchandise. Many experts recommend this strategy even though it may generate ill will with suppliers.

A procedure to control inventory turnover is for a buyer to compare both actual and projected sales and inventory levels monthly on a department-by-department basis. If sales are increasing, inventory turnover should also increase unless a buyer has begun the month with an unrealistically high inventory level. However, if inventory turnover rates do not meet projected levels, buyers should not lower turnover projections. This will cause a negative spiral. Instead, buyers should seek to sell off excess inventory or to reduce or cancel existing orders before committing to new expenditures.

A buyer needs to determine whether the difference between actual and projected sales is due to trends or to unusual situations such as bad weather, competitor price cuts, the economic prosperity in the region, and the effectiveness of the retailer's overall strategy. This helps the buyer learn whether a prior year's performance is a good indication of this year's,

CASE 2
(CONTINUED)

whether sales increases will continue into future months, and whether the buyer has the right merchandise.

Questions

1. What types of retailers do you think are most prone to guess rather than compute open-to-buy? Explain your answer.

2. Why does guessing open-to-buy more commonly result in overbuying rather than in underbuying?

3. Under what circumstances should a buyer seek to cancel an existing order to maintain a desired inventory turnover level?

4. Compare the costs of overbuying with the costs of underbuying. State your assumptions.

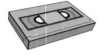

Video Questions on Open-to-Buy

1. Should a buyer commit his or her entire open-to-buy early in the selling season? Explain your answer.

2. Under what circumstances should open-to-buy planning be based on monthly time periods? Quarterly time periods?

NOTE

The material in this case is drawn from Mort Haaz, "There's Time to Change," *Gifts & Decorative Accessories* (June 1999), pp. 33–35.

CHAPTER 17

Pricing in Retailing

CHAPTER OBJECTIVES

1. To describe the role of pricing in a retail strategy and to show that pricing decisions must be made in an integrated and adaptive manner
2. To examine the impact of consumers; government; manufacturers, wholesalers, and other suppliers; and current and potential competitors on pricing decisions
3. To present a framwork for developing a retail price strategy: objectives, broad policy, basic strategy, implementation, and adjustments

Even on the "Wild Wild Web," price is not everything. If you do not believe it, ask Shopping.com. During the 1998 Christmas holiday season, Shopping.com's customers complained about busy signals, billing errors, and missing shipments. There were even 270 consumer complaints to the Better Business Bureau. Shopping.com simply could not handle its volume.

In 1999, Compaq Computer Corporation acquired Shopping.com for $220 million and immediately set out to restore the levels of customer service and shopper confidence. To do so, Compaq initiated a "125 percent satisfaction guaranteed" program, whereby dissatisfied shoppers would receive the purchase price plus another 25 percent as payment for their time, effort, and aggravation. A $250 gift certificate was also offered to any customer with a complaint on file with the Better Business Bureau.

According to retailing experts, more Web retailers need to understand that online customers require the same level of customer support as traditional retail shoppers—even if they purchase at very low prices. One study of Web shoppers found there is a high correlation between the likelihood of rebuying from the same retail Web site and these factors: the level and quality of customer service, on-time delivery, product presentation, product information, product shipping and handling, and posted privacy policies. As a result, some online retailers have begun to hire additional customer service representatives, respond more quickly to E-mail messages, and enable customers to better track shipped orders.[1]

OVERVIEW

Find out how to tell if the price is right (www.smartbiz.com/sbs/arts/jab26.htm).

A retailer must price goods and services in a way that achieves profitability for the firm and satisfies customers, while adapting to various constraints. Pricing is a crucial strategic variable due to its direct relationship with a firm's goals and its interaction with other retailing elements. A pricing strategy must be consistent with the retailer's overall image (positioning), sales, profit, and return on investment goals.

> *Please Note:* Web site addresses are constantly changing.
> The links in this chapter are current as of the publication of this book.

Motel 6

There are three basic pricing options for a retailer. Each has advantages and disadvantages: (1) A discount orientation uses low prices as the major competitive advantage. A low-status image, fewer shopping frills, and low per-unit profit margins mean a target market of price-based customers, low operating costs, and high inventory turnover. Off-price retailers and discount department stores are in this category. (2) With an at-the-market orientation, the firm has average prices. It offers solid service and a nice atmosphere to middle-class shoppers. Margins are moderate to good, and average to above-average quality products are stocked. A firm may find it hard to expand the price range of products sold; and it may be squeezed by retailers positioned as discounters or prestige stores. Traditional department stores and many drugstores are in this category. (3) Through an upscale orientation, a prestigious image represents the firm's major competitive advantage. A smaller target market, higher operating costs, and lower inventory turnover mean customer loyalty, distinctive services and product offerings, and high per-unit profit margins. Upscale department stores and specialty stores are in this category.

As we have mentioned several times (especially in Chapter 2), one of the keys to successful retailing is providing a good VALUE in the consumer's mind—for the particular price orientation chosen. Every customer, whether spending $4.00 for an inexpensive ream of paper or $40 for a ream of embossed, personalized stationery, wants to feel he or she is getting a good value for the money. The consumer is not necessarily looking for the best price. He or she is often more interested in the best value:

- "Research on the importance of price in buying decisions yields almost as many different consumer motivations as market segments. Yet, one attitude eclipses all others. Price may be vital, but people are unwilling to sacrifice on quality, convenience, and a pleasant shopping experience. They want it all." Two-thirds of Americans say, "The key thing about a brand or store is that it gives good value for the money."[2] That is why Motel 6, illustrated in Figure 17.1, does well.

- "No question about it. Before we make any purchase—a house, a car, a dress, a tie—even a meal in a restaurant—we just about always think about the value of what we are getting for the price we are paying. So why shouldn't this question of price versus value be raised by prospects who are looking at a hotel to rent a sleeping room, buy a meal at the restaurant, book a wedding reception, or have a conference? It stands to reason, in our business

Figure 17.1
Motel 6 Means Value

"No-frills" is the Motel 6 virtue. For over 36 years, the firm has sent a message to the public, selling a nice room at a low price. Motel 6 has become a household name, synonymous with value. It enjoys the highest recognition factor of any budget chain. As the company's Web site notes, "If you're like millions of other travelers, you've 'seen the light' and know you can get a clean, comfortable room without the high price. No matter why or where you travel, Motel 6 has over 800 convenient locations where you can always get the best price of any national chain."
Reprinted by permission.

of selling rooms, food, beverages, space, recreation, and all the other outlets at a facility, that we need to understand how to fit value to the needs of prospects. Frankly, we do not do such a great job. There must be value to everything we sell. It may be a real value or even a perceived value, but it only works when it can fit a customer's needs."[3]

- With the Web's popularity, many consumers have a greater price awareness and are more apt to do comparison shopping. All they have to do is visit a site such as CNET or mySimon. Within seconds, they can learn the prices at dozens of online retailers. This means a "fair value" to the shopper will be lower price with traditional comparison shopping, whereby consumers visit a few stores. For years, Syms (the off-price apparel chain) has used the slogan, "An educated consumer is our best customer." Now, all retailers have to recognize how educated their customers may be. See Figure 17.2.

- The Web is not always the definitive source for good value: "Want the cheapest prices on computers? Conventional wisdom says shop the Web. But it's hard to bargain with a Web site, and highly hyped sites like Buy.com don't always undercut competitors by as much as it might seem. Pick up the phone after the mouse, and firms with long track records and human sales staffs may give you deals they're unwilling to advertise. They may even sell you an item the Web retailers can't keep in stock."[4]

- Retailers must be careful in their pricing activities, since in some instances, the consumers' sense of entitlement raises their expectations quite high. What is a fair value then? In 1999, "Buy.com ran afoul of customer expectations when it listed a $588 Hitachi PC monitor on its site for $164. Buy.com began taking orders, but after realizing the error, the firm agreed to sell only what it had in stock at the time to the first customers who ordered at the lower price. It refused to honor the other orders. It is now in the midst of a class-action lawsuit based, in part, on its handling of the matter."[5]

Figure 17.2
Comparison Shopping
Online with mySimon
Reprinted by permission.

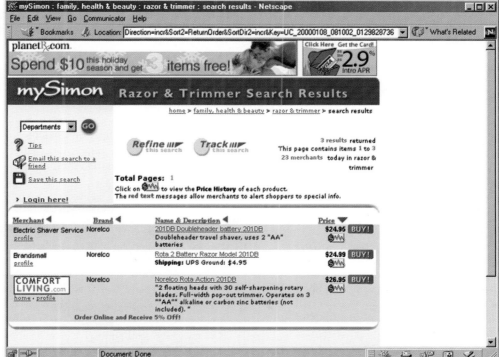

The interaction of price with other retailing mix elements can be shown by BE's Toy City, a hypothetical discount specialty store. Its two partners have set a broad strategy consisting of:

- A target market of price-conscious families.
- Selling inexpensive toys (in the $9 to $12 range).
- A limited range of merchandise quality (BE's "better" merchandise consists of end-of-season closeouts and manufacturer overruns).
- Self-service.
- An outlet mall location.
- A deep assortment.
- Quantity purchases at discount from suppliers.
- An image of efficiency and variety.

Chapter 17 divides retail pricing into two major sections: the external factors affecting a price strategy and the steps in developing a price strategy.

EXTERNAL FACTORS AFFECTING A RETAIL PRICE STRATEGY

Before describing how a retail price strategy is developed, let us explore the external factors influencing price decision making. Consumers, government, manufacturers and wholesalers, and competitors each have an impact on a retail pricing strategy, as shown in Figure 17.3. Sometimes, these factors may have only a minor effect. In other cases, they may severely restrict the options in setting prices.

The Consumer and Retail Pricing

Retailers should understand the price elasticity of demand that they face because there is often a relationship between price and consumer purchases and perceptions.[6]

One look at Godiva's Web site (www. godiva.com) and you'll know why demand for its products is inelastic.

The **price elasticity of demand** relates to the sensitivity of customers to price changes in terms of the quantities they will buy. If relatively small percentage changes in price result in substantial percentage changes in the number of units bought, price elasticity is high. This occurs when the urgency to purchase is low or acceptable substitutes exist. If large percentage changes in price have small percentage changes in the number of units bought, demand is considered inelastic. This occurs when purchase urgency is high or there are no acceptable substitutes (as takes place with brand or retailer loyalty). Unitary elasticity occurs in cases where percentage changes in price are directly offset by percentage changes in quantity.

Price elasticity is computed by dividing the percentage change in the quantity demanded by the percentage change in the price charged. Because the quantities bought generally decline as prices go up, elasticity tends to be a negative number:

Figure 17.3
Factors Affecting Retail Price Strategy

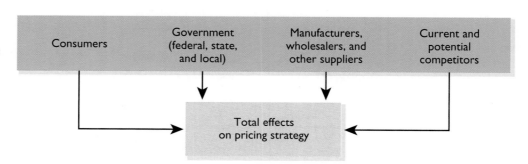

Paying for "Fast" Food at Japanese Restaurants

One fascinating new strategy used by some Japanese restaurants to counteract the industry's high prices is "all-you-can-eat-by-the-minute" pricing. With this approach, patrons can eat all the items they want from a buffet at a fixed cost per minute. The "eat-by-the-minute" strategy requires customers to punch timecards, just like factory workers, when they enter and leave the restaurant. Thus, the fastest eater gets the lowest restaurant bill.

The "eat-by-the-minute" restaurants are changing the behavior of their customers. Some people take large helpings to avoid going back to the buffet. Others come by themselves, so they can eat faster.

And customers are quick to complain about slow service that could affect their meal cost.

According to a popular restaurant guide, as of 1999, there were about 200 "all-you-can-eat" restaurants in the Tokyo area alone. Even some fancy restaurants that once catered to expense account customers now offer this plan: "With the restaurant economy this bad, you need to give consumers a good deal."

What are the pros and cons of this unique pricing strategy? Would you recommend bringing the concept to the United States? Explain your answer.

Source: Yumiko Ono, "We're Eating Out Tonight, So Please Bring a Stopwatch," *Wall Street Journal* (December 23, 1998), pp. A1, A4.

$$\text{Elasticity} = \frac{\dfrac{\text{Quantity 1} - \text{Quantity 2}}{\text{Quantity 1} + \text{Quantity 2}}}{\dfrac{\text{Price 1} - \text{Price 2}}{\text{Price 1} + \text{Price 2}}}$$

Table 17.1 shows the calculation of price elasticity for a 1,000-seat movie theater (with elasticities converted to positive numbers). The quantity demanded (tickets sold) declines at every price level from $5.00 to $9.00. Fewer customers patronize the theater at $9.00 than at $5.00. Demand is inelastic from $5.00 to $6.00; total ticket receipts increase since the percentage change in price is greater than the percentage change in tickets sold. Demand is uni-

Table 17.1 A Movie Theater's Elasticity of Demand

Price	Tickets Sold (Saturday Night)	Total Ticket Receipts	Elasticity of Demand[a]
$5.00	1,000	$5,000	E = 0.60
6.00	896	5,376	E = 1.00
7.00	768	5,376	E = 1.84
8.00	600	4,800	E = 3.40
9.00	400	3,600	

Computation example = [(1,000 − 896)/(1,000 + 896)]/[($5.00 − $6.00)/($5.00 + $6.00)] = 0.60

[a]Expressed as a positive number.

tary from $6.00 to $7.00; total ticket receipts are constant since the percentage change in tickets sold exactly offsets the percentage change in price. Demand is elastic from $7.00 to $9.00; total ticket receipts decline since the percentage change in tickets sold is greater than the percentage change in price.

For this example, total ticket receipts are highest at $6.00 or at $7.00. But what about total theater revenues? If patrons spend an average of $3.50 each at the concession stand, the best price is $6.00 (total overall revenues of $8,512). The theater is most interested in total revenues generated since operating costs are the same whether there are 896 or 768 patrons. But as a rule, retailers should evaluate the costs, as well as the revenues, from serving additional customers.

In retailing, computing price elasticity is difficult for two reasons. First, as in the case of the movie theater, demand for individual events or items may be hard to predict. One week, the theater may attract 1,000 patrons to a movie, and the next week, it may attract 400 patrons to a different movie. Second, retailers such as supermarkets and department stores sell thousands of items and could not possibly compute elasticities for every one. As a result, they usually rely on average markup pricing, competition, tradition, and industrywide data to indicate price elasticity.

Price sensitivity varies by market segment, based on shopping orientation. Here are several segments:

- *Economic consumers*—They perceive competing retailers as similar to one another and shop around for the lowest possible prices. This segment has grown dramatically in recent years.
- *Status-oriented consumers*—They perceive competing retailers as quite different from one another. They are more interested in prestige brands and customer services than in price.
- *Assortment-oriented consumers*—They seek retailers with strong assortments in the product categories being considered. They look for fair prices.
- *Personalizing consumers*—They shop where they are known. There is a strong personal bond with retail personnel and the firm itself. These shoppers will pay slightly above-average prices.
- *Convenience-oriented consumers*—They shop only because they must. They want nearby locations and long hours, and may shop by catalog or the Web. These people will pay higher prices.

After identifying potential segments, retailers determine which of them form their target market.

The Government and Retail Pricing

In studying the impact of the government on pricing, it must be remembered that three levels exist: federal, state, and local. Because many laws are federal, they apply to interstate commerce. A retailer operating exclusively within the boundaries of one state may not be restricted by some federal legislation.

Government activity entails seven main areas: horizontal price fixing, vertical price fixing, price discrimination, minimum price levels, unit pricing, item price removal, and price advertising.

Horizontal Price Fixing **Horizontal price fixing** involves agreements among manufacturers, among wholesalers, or among retailers to set certain prices. Such agreements are illegal under the Sherman Antitrust Act and the Federal Trade Commission Act, regardless of how "reasonable" prices may be. It is also illegal for retailers to reach agreements with one another regarding the use of coupons, rebates, or other price-oriented tactics.

Although few large-scale legal actions have been taken in recent years, the penalties for horizontal price fixing can be severe. For example,

- To settle a class-action lawsuit, 20 pharmaceutical manufacturers agreed to pay hundreds of millions of dollars to thousands of independent and chain pharmacies throughout the United States that had accused the manufacturers of price fixing.[7]
- The Attorney General of Minnesota settled an antitrust suit with the state's leading dairies that had accused the dairies of fixing milk prices for more than a decade. The dairies agreed to donate 250,000 gallons of milk annually for five years (a total value of $2.8 million) to the Minnesota Food Bank.[8]
- The U.S. Department of Justice accused the National Automobile Dealers Association (which represented 84 percent of all car dealers) of violating antitrust laws by encouraging members to limit price competition in selling to consumers. The Association settled out of court, signing a consent decree—effective for 10 years—prohibiting it from urging members to enact pricing or advertising programs to restrict competition. It also agreed not to punish dealers for their pricing policies.[9]

Vertical Price Fixing **Vertical price fixing** occurs when manufacturers or wholesalers seek to control the retail prices of their goods and services. Until 1976, manufacturers and wholesalers in the United States had the right to set minimum retail prices for their products in order to protect their brands' reputations—and to not have their reputations diluted through indiscriminate price cutting by retailers. This practice also protected small and full-service retailers against discounters. However, this system was criticized by consumer groups and many manufacturers, wholesalers, and retailers as being anticompetitive, keeping prices artificially high, and allowing inefficient retailers to stay in business. As a result, the Consumer Goods Pricing Act ended the interstate use of fair trade practices and resale price maintenance. Retailers cannot be required to adhere to *minimum retail prices* set by manufacturers and wholesalers.

In 1997, the U.S. Supreme Court, in a unanimous decision, approved one specific type of vertical pricing—setting *maximum retail prices:*

> The Supreme Court opened the door for manufacturers to cap the prices retailers charge for their products. The ruling reverses a decision that barred such limits and left retailers and franchisees free to raise prices above suppliers' suggested prices. Now manufacturers will be able to set a maximum price as long as they can show they aren't stifling competition. "The ruling returns to the manufacturer or franchisor a greater degree of control over how its product is portrayed, is priced, and is presented to the American people," said James M. Spears, a Washington antitrust lawyer who is former general counsel of the Federal Trade Commission.[10]

Other than by setting maximum prices, manufacturers and wholesalers today can legally control retail prices only by one of these methods: They can screen retailers. They can set realistic list prices. They can pre-print prices on products (which retailers do not have to use). They can set regular prices that are accepted by consumers (such as 50 cents for a newspaper). They can use consignment selling, whereby the supplier owns items until they are sold and assumes costs normally associated with the retailer. They can own retail facilities. They can refuse to sell to retailers that advertised discount prices in violation of written policies. The supplier has a right to announce a general policy as to dealer pricing and can refuse to sell to those that do not comply with it, but it cannot use coercion or conspire with other dealers to prohibit a retailer from advertising low prices.

Price Discrimination The **Robinson-Patman Act** bars manufacturers and wholesalers from discriminating in price or purchase terms in selling to individual retailers if these retailers are purchasing products of "like quality" and the effect of such discrimination is to injure competition. The intent of the Robinson-Patman Act is to stop large retailers from using their power to gain discounts not justified by the cost savings achieved by suppliers due to big orders. There are exceptions that allow justifiable price discrimination if:

- Products are physically different.
- The retailers paying different prices are not competitors.
- Competition is not injured.
- Price differences are due to differences in supplier costs.
- Market conditions change—whereby costs rise or fall, or competing suppliers shift their prices.

Discounts themselves are not illegal, as long as suppliers follow the preceding rules, make discounts available to competing retailers on an equitable basis, and offer discounts sufficiently graduated so small (as well as large) retailers can qualify. Discounts for cumulative purchases (total orders during the year) and for multistore purchases by chains may be hard to justify.

While the Robinson-Patman Act restricts sellers more than buyers, retailers are covered under Section 2(F) of the Act: "It shall be unlawful for any person engaged in commerce, in the course of such commerce, knowingly to induce or receive a discrimination in price which is prohibited in this section." From a strategic perspective, a retail buyer must try to get the lowest prices charged to any competitor in its class, yet be careful not to bargain so hard that discounts cannot be justified by acceptable exceptions.

Minimum-Price Laws   About half the states have **minimum-price laws** that prevent retailers from selling certain items for less than their cost plus a fixed percentage to cover overhead. Merchandise costs are defined in various ways. They are often purchase or replacement costs, whichever are less. Besides general laws, some state rules set minimum prices for specific products. For instance, in New Jersey and Connecticut, the retail price of liquor cannot be less than the wholesale cost (including taxes and delivery charges).

With **loss leaders,** retailers price selected items below cost to lure more customer traffic for those retailers. Firms such as supermarkets often use loss leaders to increase overall sales

---

Shoe Store Owners Take on Nine West

Peter Polities, as owner of a shoe store in New Jersey, decided to reduce the price of a pair of Nine West shoes from $60 to $49.99. However, after getting complaints from other retailers carrying Nine West shoes, Vincent Camuto, the president of Nine West, demanded that he end the sale. When Polities refused, he was told by Camuto that, "We can't ship you those shoes."

According to information compiled by Polities and the owners of two other stores selling Nine West shoes, Nine West and some department stores had agreed on minimum prices for selected styles. These styles were then placed on an "off-limits" list. The off-limits list also included specific dates that these shoes could be placed on sale, as well as their minimum selling prices for these special sales. Adherence to the off-limits prices was policed by Nine West employees. Retailers offering off-limits merchandise below the minimum price levels were warned by Nine West that future shipments would be either delayed or cancelled.

Although it is illegal for Nine West and some of its retailers to agree on minimum prices, it is legal for Nine West to demand that its price lists be followed—and for it to stop doing business with those that violate its policy.

As Peter Polities' retailing consultant, advise him as to how he should deal with Nine West.

Source: Melody Peterson, "Treading a Contentious Line," *New York Times* (January 13, 1999), pp. C1, C2.

and profits under the assumption that people will buy more than one item once drawn to a store. For example, at auto supply stores, "oil has been considered a loss leader. Because it is sold in large quantities, oil is used as a tool to help drive store traffic. And since most U.S. consumers don't expect to pay much more than a buck a quart, any attempt to boost the price will meet as much resistance as an Ohio State fan cheering for the Buckeyes in Michigan Stadium. That's just the way it is."[11] Although loss leaders are restricted by some minimum-price laws, because this approach is usually consumer-oriented, the laws are rarely applied (as long as there is no predatory pricing).

Minimum-price laws aim to protect small retailers from **predatory pricing,** in which large retailers seek to reduce competition by selling goods and services at very low prices, thus causing small retailers to go out of business. In one widely watched case, three independent pharmacies in Conway, Arkansas, filed a predatory pricing suit claiming Wal-Mart had sold selected products below cost in an attempt to reduce competition. During 1993, Wal-Mart was found guilty in an Arkansas court, ordered to pay $289,407 in damages to the pharmacies, and ordered to stop selling health and beauty aids and over-the-counter drugs at prices below cost in its Conway store. This was the first time Wal-Mart was unable to settle a predatory pricing case out of court. Wal-Mart agreed it had priced selected products below cost to meet or beat rivals' prices, but not to harm small competitors. After Wal-Mart appealed the verdict to the Arkansas Supreme Court, it was overturned. In 1995, that court ruled Wal-Mart had not engaged in predatory pricing because the three pharmacies were still profitable and "competition appears to be thriving."[12]

Unit Pricing The proliferation of package sizes has led to **unit pricing** laws in many states. The aim of such legislation is to let consumers compare the prices of products available in many sizes. Food stores are most affected by unit price rules. In many cases, these stores must express both the total price of an item and its price per unit of measure. Thus, a 6.5-ounce can of tuna fish priced at 99 cents also has a shelf label showing this as $2.44 per pound. With unit pricing, a person learns that a 12-ounce can of soda selling for 35 cents (2.9 cents per ounce) is costlier than a 67.6-ounce—2-liter—bottle selling for $1.49 (2.2 cents per ounce).

The intent of unit pricing laws is to give more information to consumers. Although early research studies questioned the effectiveness of unit pricing, later findings have indicated it is advantageous for both retailers and consumers.

Not all retailers must comply with unit pricing laws. There are exemptions for firms with low-volume sales. In addition, grocery items are more heavily regulated than nongrocery items. Retailer costs include computing per unit prices, printing product and shelf labels, and keeping computer records. The costs are influenced by the way prices are attached to goods (by the supplier or the retailer), the number of items subject to unit pricing, the frequency of price changes, sales volume, and the number of stores in a chain. Supermarkets report that unit pricing is not expensive, but smaller food stores report that costs are high.

Unit pricing can be a good strategy for retailers to follow, even when not required by law. For instance, Giant Food's unit pricing system more than pays for itself in terms of decreased price-marking errors, better inventory control, and improved space management.

Item Price Removal The boom in computerized checkout systems has led many firms, especially supermarkets, to advocate **item price removal**—whereby prices are marked only on shelves or signs and not on individual items. Scanning equipment reads pre-marked codes on product labels and enters price data at the checkout counter. This practice is banned in several states and local communities.

Supermarkets say item price removal would significantly reduce labor costs and let them offer lower prices. Opponents feel this would lead to more errors against consumers and make it harder for shoppers to verify prices as they are rung up. Giant Food uses item price removal in its supermarkets—with little consumer resistance and considerable cost savings.

Giant maintains accurate, highly visible shelf prices and gives items free to consumers if the prices processed by its electronic cash registers (equipped with scanners) are higher than those posted on shelves.

Price Advertising There are FTC guidelines pertaining to advertising price reductions, advertising prices in relation to competitors' prices, and bait-and-switch advertising.

These guidelines generally state that a retailer cannot claim or imply a price has been reduced from some former level (such as a manufacturer's list or suggested list price) unless the former price was an actual, bona fide one at which the retailer offered a good or service to the public on a regular basis during a reasonably substantial, recent period of time.

When a retailer claims its prices are lower than those of other firms, FTC guidelines say it must make certain that its price comparisons pertain to competitors selling large quantities in the same trading area. A particularly controversial, but basically legal, practice is price matching. For the most part, firms make three assumptions when using a policy that "guarantees to match the lowest price of any competing retailer" on the same item: (1) This approach gives shoppers the impression that the firms always offer low prices or else they would not make such a commitment. (2) Most shoppers will not return to a store after a purchase if they see a lower price advertised elsewhere. (3) They can exclude most deep discounters, such as membership clubs and direct marketers, from the guarantee by saying they are not really competitors. As *Consumer Reports* says, "One customer shopping strategy is to ask the store to match a competitor's advertised price, which many chains pledge to do. But be sure to have the ad in hand, and don't necessarily expect an exact match. Some stores refuse to match warehouse club prices, for example, while others sell exclusive models in part to thwart price matching."[13]

Bait advertising, or **bait-and-switch advertising,** is an illegal practice in which a retailer lures a customer by advertising goods and services at exceptionally low prices; then, once the customer contacts the retailer (by entering a store or calling a toll-free number or going to a Web site), he or she is told the good/service of interest is out of stock or of inferior quality. A salesperson (or Web script) tries to convince the person to buy a better, more expensive substitute that is available. In bait advertising, the retailer has no intention of selling the advertised item. In deciding whether a promotion constitutes bait advertising, the FTC can consider how many sales were made at the advertised price, whether a sales commission was paid on sale items, and the total amount of sales relative to advertising costs.

Manufacturers, Wholesalers, and Other Suppliers—and Retail Pricing

There may be conflicts between manufacturers (and other suppliers) and retailers in setting final prices since each would like some input and control. Manufacturers usually want to have a certain image and to let all retailers, even ones that are rather inefficient, earn profits. In contrast, most retailers want to set prices based on their own image, goals, and so forth.

A supplier can control prices by using an exclusive distribution system, not selling to price-cutting retailers, or being its own retailer. A retailer can gain control by being vital to its suppliers as a customer, threatening to stop carrying suppliers' lines, stocking private brands, or selling gray market goods.

Many manufacturers set their selling prices to retailers by estimating retail prices and then subtracting required retailer and wholesaler profit margins. In the men's apparel industry, the common retail markup is 50 percent of the final price. Thus, a man's shirt retailing at $30 can be sold to the retailer for no more than $15. If a wholesaler is involved, the manufacturer's price to the wholesaler must be far less than $15.

Retailers sometimes carry manufacturers' brands and place high prices on them so rival brands (such as private labels) can be sold more easily. This is called "selling against the brand" and is disliked by manufacturers since sales of their brands are apt to decline. Some retailers also sell **gray market goods,** brand-name products bought in foreign markets or goods transshipped from other retailers. Manufacturers dislike gray market goods because they are often sold at low prices by unauthorized dealers. Firms such as Givenchy now limit gray market goods on the basis of copyright and trademark infringement.

When suppliers are unknown or products are new, retailers may seek price guarantees to ensure that inventory values and profits are maintained. Price guarantees protect retailers against possible price declines. Suppose a new supplier sells a retailer radios having a suggested retail price of $30 and guarantees the price to a retailer. If that retailer cannot sell the radios at this price, the manufacturer pays the difference. Should the retailer have to sell the radios at $25, the manufacturer gives a rebate of $5 per unit. Another type of price guarantee is one in which a supplier guarantees to a retailer that no competitor will be able to buy an item for a lower price. If anyone does, the retailer gets a rebate. The relative power of the retailer and its suppliers determines whether such guarantees are provided.

A retailer also has suppliers other than manufacturers and wholesalers. They include employees, fixtures manufacturers, landlords, and outside parties (such as advertising agencies). Each of them has an effect on price because of their costs to the retailer.

Competition and Retail Pricing

See how differently Auto-by-Tel (www. autobytel.com) and CarsDirect.com (www. carsdirect.com) approach the selling of cars.

The degree of control an individual firm has over prices often depends on the competitive environment. In *market pricing,* there is a lot of competition; and because people have a large choice as to the retailer to patronize, they often seek the lowest prices. Thus, firms price similarly to each other and have less control over price. Supermarkets, fast-food firms, and gas stations use market pricing because they are in competitive industries and sell similar goods and services. Demand for specific retailers may be weak enough so that a number of customers would switch to a competitor if prices are raised much.

In *administered pricing,* firms seek to attract consumers on the basis of distinctive retailing mixes. If there is strong differentiation from competitors, a retailer can control the prices it charges. This occurs when people consider image, assortment, personal service, and other factors to be more important than price and will pay above-average prices for the goods and services of distinctive retailers. Traditional department stores, fashion apparel stores, and upscale restaurants are among those that seek to have unique offerings and have some control over their prices.

Most price-oriented strategies can be quickly copied. Thus, the reaction of competitors is predictable when the leading firm is successful. This means a retailer should view price strategy from a long-run, as well as a short-run, perspective. If the competitive environment becomes too intense, a price war may erupt—whereby various firms continually lower prices below regular amounts and sometimes below their cost to attract consumers away from competitors. Price wars are sometimes difficult to end and can lead to low profits, losses, or even bankruptcy for some competitors. This is especially so for Web retailers.[14]

DEVELOPING A RETAIL PRICE STRATEGY

As Figure 17.4 shows, a retail price strategy has five steps: objectives, policy, strategy, implementation, and adjustments. Like any other strategic activity, pricing begins with clear goals and ends with an adaptive or corrective mechanism. Pricing policies must be integrated with the total retail mix, which occurs in the second step of price planning. The process can be complex due to the often erratic nature of demand, the number of items carried, and the fact that all aspects of the process are affected by the external factors already noted.

Figure 17.4
A Framework for Developing a Retail Price Strategy

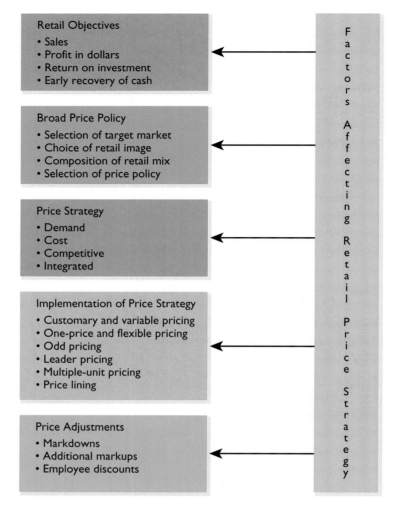

Retail Objectives
• Sales
• Profit in dollars
• Return on investment
• Early recovery of cash

Broad Price Policy
• Selection of target market
• Choice of retail image
• Composition of retail mix
• Selection of price policy

Price Strategy
• Demand
• Cost
• Competitive
• Integrated

Implementation of Price Strategy
• Customary and variable pricing
• One-price and flexible pricing
• Odd pricing
• Leader pricing
• Multiple-unit pricing
• Price lining

Price Adjustments
• Markdowns
• Additional markups
• Employee discounts

Factors Affecting Retail Price Strategy

Nielsen's Priceman (acnielsen.com/products/tools/priceman) is a powerful software tool for strategic pricing.

Retail Objectives and Pricing

A retailer's pricing strategy must reflect its overall goals; and these goals can be stated in terms of sales and profits. Besides its broad objectives, a retailer needs to set more specific pricing goals to avoid such potential problems as confusing people by having too many prices, spending excessive time bargaining with customers, employing frequent sales to stimulate customer traffic, having inadequate profit margins, and placing too much emphasis on price in the strategy mix.

Overall Objectives and Pricing Sales goals are often stated in terms of revenues and/or unit volume. An example of a sales goal and a resultant pricing strategy is a car dealer's desire to achieve large revenues by setting low prices and selling a high unit volume. This aggressive price strategy is known as **market penetration.** It is proper if customers are highly sensitive to price, low prices discourage actual and potential competition, and retail costs do not rise as much as sales volume increases.

Profit in dollars objectives are sought when a retailer concentrates on total profit or profit per unit. With a **market skimming** strategy, a firm charges premium prices and attracts customers less concerned with price than service, assortment, and status. Though this

CDnow (www.cdnow.
com) sells its "Top
100" for 30 percent
off list price. The
Cheesecake Factory
(www.thecheescake
factory.com) has
great cakes—
although they can be
a little pricey.

approach typically does not maximize sales, it does achieve high profit per unit. It is appropriate if the market segment a retailer defines as its target market is insensitive to price, new competitors are unlikely to enter the market, and additional sales will greatly increase retail costs. See Figure 17.5.

Return on investment and early recovery of cash are two other profit-based goals. Return on investment is sought if a firm stipulates that profit must be a certain percentage of its investment, such as 20 percent of inventory investment. Early recovery of cash is used by retailers that may be short on funds, wish to expand, or be uncertain about the future. A market skimming strategy is often applied by retailers with return on investment or early recovery of cash as a goal.

BE's Toy City, the discount toy store introduced at the beginning of the chapter, may be used to illustrate how a retailer can set sales, profit, and return-on-investment goals. BE's Toy City sells inexpensive toys and overruns to avoid competition with mainstream toy stores and full-line discount stores, has a single selling price for all toys (to be set for the next year from within the range of $9 to $12), minimizes operating costs, maximizes self-service, and carries a large selection to generate traffic.

Table 17.2 has data on BE's Toy City pertaining to demand, costs, profit, and return on inventory investment at prices from $9 to $12. The retailer must select the most appropriate

Figure 17.5
A Marketing Skimming Approach in an Upscale Shopping Environment

The $1.4 billion Venetian Resort-Hotel-Casino opened in Las Vegas during 1999. It is a fully integrated resort that focuses on world-class dining, upscale shopping, luxurious rooms, and upscale spa services. The Venetian appeals to global travelers, business professionals, conventioneers, and families—people who enjoy going far beyond the simple "must see" attractions to experience a "must see, stay, dine, shop, and enjoy" resort destination. By bringing the best Las Vegas has to offer to one location, under one roof, the Venetian is looking to set a new standard for entertainment and hospitality. The Grand Canal Shoppes is the Venetian's 500,000-square-foot themed, indoor retail mall. The area features cobbled walkways, a reproduction of Venice's Grand Canal, and a replica of St. Mark's Square. Shoppers are transported to another time and place in a festival-like atmosphere, including serenading gondoliers, artisans, glassblowers, and masque makers. Approximately 65 exclusive retailers, many new to the United States, and brand name restaurants now make their home in the Grand Canal Shoppes. Reprinted by permission.

Table 17.2 BE's Toy City: Demand, Costs, Profit, and Return on Inventory Investment[a]

Selling Price (in $)	Quantity Demanded (in units)	Total Sales Revenue (in $)	Average Cost of Merchandise (in $)	Total Cost of Merchandise (in $)	Total Nonmerchandise Costs (in $)	Total Costs (in $)
9.00	114,000	1,026,000	7.60	866,400	104,000	970,400
10.00	104,000	1,040,000	7.85	816,400	94,000	910,400
11.00	80,000	880,000	8.25	660,000	88,000	748,000
12.00	60,000	720,000	8.75	525,000	80,000	605,000

Selling Price (in $)	Average Total Costs (in $)	Total Profit (in $)	Profit/Unit (in $)	Markup at Retail (in %)	Profit/Sales (in %)	Average Inventory on Hand (in units)
9.00	8.51	55,600	0.49	16	5.4	12,000
10.00	8.75	129,600	1.25	22	12.5	13,000
11.00	9.35	132,000	1.65	25	15.0	14,000
12.00	10.08	115,000	1.92	27	16.0	16,000

Selling Price (in $)	Inventory Turnover (in units)	Average Investment in Inventory at Cost (in $)	Inventory Turnover (in $)	Return on Inventory Investment (in %)
9.00	9.5	91,200	9.5	61
10.00	8.0	102,050	8.0	127
11.00	5.7	115,500	5.7	114
12.00	3.8	140,000	3.8	82

Note: Average cost of merchandise reflects quantity discounts. Total nonmerchandise costs include all retail operating expenses.

[a]Numbers have been rounded.

price within that range. Table 17.3 shows how BE's Toy City arrived at the figures in Table 17.2.

From Table 17.2, several conclusions concerning the best price for BE's Toy City can be drawn:

- A sales goal would lead to a price of $10. Total sales are highest ($1,040,000).
- A dollar profit goal would lead to a price of $11. Total profit is highest ($132,000).
- A return on inventory investment goal would also lead to a price of $10. Return on inventory investment is 127 percent.
- Although a large quantity can be sold at $9, that price would lead to the least profit ($55,600).
- A price of $12 would yield the highest profit per unit and as a percentage of sales, but total dollar profit is not maximized at this price.
- High inventory turnover would not necessarily lead to high profits.

As a result, BE's Toy City's partners have decided a price of $11 would let them earn the highest dollar profits, while generating good profit per unit and profit as a percentage of sales.

Specific Pricing Objectives Table 17.4 has a list of specific pricing goals other than sales and profits. While a number of objectives are enumerated here, each firm must determine their relative importance given its particular situation—and plan accordingly. Furthermore,

Table 17.3 Derivation of BE's Toy City Data

Column in Table 17.2	Source of Information or Method of Computation
Selling Price	Trade data, comparison shopping, experience
Quantity demanded (in units) at each price level	Consumer surveys, trade data, experience
Total sales revenue	Selling price $\times$ Quantity demanded
Average cost of merchandise	Contacts with suppliers, quantity discount structure, estimates of order sizes
Total cost of merchandise	Average cost of merchandise $\times$ Quantity demanded
Total nonmerchandise costs	Experience, trade data, estimation of individual retail operating expenses
Total costs	Total cost of merchandise $+$ Total nonmerchandise costs
Average total costs	Total costs/Quantity demanded
Total profit	Total sales revenue $-$ Total costs
Profit per unit	Total profit/Quantity demanded
Markup (at retail)	(Selling price $-$ Average cost of merchandise)/Selling price
Profit as a percentage of sales	Total profit/Total sales revenue
Average inventory on hand	Trade data, merchandise turnover data (in units), experience
Inventory turnover (in units)	Quantity demanded/Average inventory on hand (in units)
Average investment in inventory (at cost)	Average cost of merchandise $\times$ Average inventory on hand (in units)
Inventory turnover (in $)	Total cost of merchandise/Average investment in inventory (at cost)
Return on inventory investment	Total profit/Average investment in inventory (at cost)

Table 17.4 Specific Pricing Objectives from Which Retailers May Choose

To maintain a proper image.

To not encourage customers to become overly price-conscious.

To be perceived as fair by all parties (including suppliers, employees, and customers).

To be consistent in setting prices.

To increase customer traffic during slow periods.

To clear out seasonal merchandise.

To match competitors' prices without starting a price war.

To promote a "we-will-not-be-undersold" philosophy.

To be regarded as the price leader in the market area by consumers.

To provide ample customer service.

To minimize the chance of government actions relating to price advertising and antitrust matters.

To discourage potential competitors from entering the marketplace.

To create and maintain customer interest.

To encourage repeat business.

some goals may be incompatible with one another, such as "to not encourage customers to become overly price-conscious" and a " 'we-will-not-be-undersold' philosophy."

Broad Price Policy

Click on Phoenix Retail Systems' "Automated Price Information Systems" (www.apisys.com/ priceintro.html) to see a good visual of the pricing process.

Through a broad price policy, a retailer generates a coordinated series of actions, a consistent image (especially vital for chains and franchises), and a plan including short- and long-run perspectives (thereby balancing immediate and future goals). In this stage, a firm must be sure its price policy is interrelated with the target market, the retail image, and the other elements of the retail mix.

A broad price policy translates price decisions into an integrated framework. For example, a firm must decide whether prices should be established for individual items, interrelated for a group of goods and services, or based on an extensive use of special sales. These are some of the price policies from which a retailer could choose:

- No competitors will have lower prices; no competitors will have higher prices; or prices will be consistent with competitors'.
- All items will be priced independently, depending on the demand for each; or the prices for all items will be interrelated to maintain an image and ensure proper markups.
- Price leadership will be exerted; competitors will be price leaders and set prices first; or prices will be set independently of competitors.
- Prices will be constant over a year or season; or prices will change if merchandise costs change.

Price Strategy

A price strategy can be demand, cost, and/or competitive in orientation. In **demand-oriented pricing,** a retailer sets prices based on consumer desires. It determines the range of prices acceptable to the target market. The top of this range is called the demand ceiling, the most people will pay for a good or service.

With **cost-oriented pricing,** a retailer sets a price floor, the minimum price acceptable to the firm so it can reach a specified profit goal. A retailer usually computes merchandise and retail operating costs and adds a profit margin to these figures.

For **competition-oriented pricing,** a retailer sets its prices in accordance with competitors'. Price levels of key competitors and how they influence the firm's sales are studied.

As a rule, retailers should use a combination of these approaches in enacting a price strategy. The approaches should not be viewed as operating independently of one another.

Demand-Oriented Pricing Demand-oriented pricing seeks to estimate the quantities customers would buy at various prices and focuses on the prices associated with stated sales goals. Whereas cost-oriented pricing relies on costs, a demand-oriented approach looks more at customer interest. In using demand-oriented pricing, it is critical to understand the psychological implications. Two aspects of psychological pricing are the price-quality association and prestige pricing.

According to the **price-quality association** concept, many consumers feel high prices connote high quality and low prices connote low quality. This association is especially important if competing firms or products are hard to judge on bases other than price, consumers have little experience or confidence in judging quality (as with a new retailer or product), shoppers perceive large differences in quality among retailers or products, and brand names are an insignificant factor in product choice. Though various studies have documented a price-quality relationship, research also indicates that if other quality cues, such as retailer or product features and the stocking of well-known brands, are introduced, these factors may be more significant than price in a person's judgment of overall retailer or product quality.

Prestige pricing, in which it is assumed consumers will not buy goods and services at prices deemed too low, is based on the price–quality association. Its premise is that consumers may feel too low a price means poor quality and status. In addition, some people want prestige pricing in selecting retailers and do not patronize those with prices viewed as too low. Saks Fifth Avenue and Neiman Marcus do not generally carry the least expensive versions of items because their customers may feel they are inferior.

Prestige pricing does not apply to all shoppers. Thus, the target market must be considered before a retailer reaches a decision here. Some people may be economizers and always shop for bargains; and neither the price-quality association nor prestige pricing may be applicable for them.

Cost-Oriented Pricing One form of cost-oriented pricing, markup pricing, is the most widely practiced retail pricing technique. In **markup pricing,** a retailer sets prices by adding per-unit merchandise costs, retail operating expenses, and desired profit. The difference between merchandise costs and selling price is the **markup.** If a retailer buys a desk for $200 and sells it for $300, the extra $100 is used to cover its operating costs and profit. The markup is $33\frac{1}{3}$ percent at retail or 50 percent on cost. The markup percentage depends on a product's traditional markup, the supplier's suggested list price, inventory turnover, competition, rent and other overhead costs, the extent to which a product must be altered or serviced, and the selling effort.

Markups can be computed on the basis of retail selling price or cost, but are typically calculated using the retail price: (1) Retail expenses, markdowns, and profit are always stated as a percentage of sales. Thus, if markups are expressed as a percentage of sales, they are more meaningful. (2) Manufacturers quote their selling prices and trade discounts to retailers as percentage reductions from retail list prices. (3) Retail price data are more readily available than cost data. (4) Profitability seems smaller if expressed on the basis of price. This can be useful in dealing with the government, employees, and consumers.

This is how a **markup percentage** is calculated. The difference is in the denominator. For both formulas, merchandise cost is the per unit invoice and freight cost to a retailer, less per unit trade or quantity discounts:

$$\frac{\text{Markup percentage}}{\text{(at retail)}} = \frac{\text{Retail selling price} - \text{Merchandise cost}}{\text{Retail selling price}}$$

$$\frac{\text{Markup percentage}}{\text{(at cost)}} = \frac{\text{Retail selling price} - \text{Merchandise cost}}{\text{Merchandise cost}}$$

Table 17.5 shows a range of markup percentages at retail and at cost. As markups go up, the disparity between the percentages grows. Suppose a retailer buys a watch for $20 and considers whether to sell it for $25, $40, or $80. The $25 price yields a markup of 20 percent at retail and 25 percent at cost, the $40 price yields a markup of 50 percent at retail and 100 percent at cost, and the $80 price yields a markup of 75 percent at retail and 300 percent at cost.

The markup concept has various applications in pricing and purchase planning. These examples indicate its usefulness:

- A discount clothing store can buy a shipment of men's jeans at $12 each and wants a 30 percent markup at retail.[15] What retail price should the store charge to achieve this markup?

$$\frac{\text{Markup percentage}}{\text{(at retail)}} = \frac{\text{Retail selling price} - \text{Merchandise cost}}{\text{Retail selling price}}$$

Table 17.5 Markup Equivalents

Percentage at Retail	Percentage at Cost
5.0	5.3
10.0	11.1
15.0	17.6
20.0	25.0
25.0	33.3
30.0	42.9
35.0	53.8
40.0	66.7
45.0	81.8
50.0	100.0
60.0	150.0
75.0	300.0
80.0	400.0
90.0	900.0

$$0.30 = \frac{\text{Retail selling price} - \$12.00}{\text{Retail selling price}}$$

$$\text{Retail selling price} = \$17.14$$

- A stationery store desires a minimum 40 percent markup at retail.[16] If it feels envelopes should retail at 79 cents per box, what is the maximum price the firm can pay for the envelopes?

$$\frac{\text{Markup percentage}}{\text{(at retail)}} = \frac{\text{Retail selling price} - \text{Merchandise cost}}{\text{Retail selling price}}$$

$$0.40 = \frac{\$0.79 - \text{Merchandise price}}{\$0.79}$$

$$\text{Merchandise cost} = \$0.474$$

- A sporting goods store has been offered a closeout purchase on a line of bicycles. The per unit cost of each bike is $105, and they should retail for $160 each. What markup at retail would the store obtain?

$$\frac{\text{Markup percentage}}{\text{(at retail)}} = \frac{\text{Retail selling price} - \text{Merchandise cost}}{\text{Retail selling price}}$$

$$= \frac{\$160.00 - \$105.00}{\$160.00} = 34.4$$

The retailer's markup percentage may also be determined by examining planned retail operating expenses, profit, and net sales. Suppose a florist estimates retail operating expenses (rent, salaries, electricity, cleaning, bookkeeping, and so on) to be $55,000 per year. The desired profit is $50,000 per year, including the owner's salary. Net sales are forecast to be $250,000. The planned markup would be:

$$\frac{\text{Markup percentage}}{\text{(at retail)}} = \frac{\text{Planned retail operating expenses} + \text{Planned profit}}{\text{Planned net sales}}$$

$$= \frac{\$55,000 + \$50,000}{\$250,000} = 42$$

If potted plants cost the florist an average of $8.00 each, the retailer's selling price per plant would be:

$$\text{Retail selling price} = \frac{\text{Merchandise cost}}{1 - \text{Markup}}$$

$$= \frac{\$8.00}{1 - 0.42} = \$13.79$$

The florist will need to sell about 18,129 plants at $13.79 apiece to achieve its sales and profit goals. To reach these goals, all plants must be sold at the $13.79 price.

It is highly unusual for a retailer to sell all items in stock at their original prices. Therefore, the initial markup, maintained markup, and gross margin should be computed. **Initial markup** is based on the original retail value assigned to merchandise less the costs of the merchandise. **Maintained markup** is based on the actual prices received for merchandise sold during a time period less merchandise cost. Maintained markups are related to actual prices received; so they can be hard to estimate in advance. The difference between initial and maintained markups is that the latter reflect adjustments from original retail values caused by markdowns, added markups, shortages, and discounts.

The initial markup percentage depends on planned retail operating expenses, profit, reductions, and net sales:

$$\begin{array}{l}\text{Initial markup} \\ \text{percentage} \\ \text{(at retail)}\end{array} = \frac{\begin{array}{c}\text{Planned retail operating expenses } + \text{ Planned profit} \\ + \text{ Planned retail reductions}\end{array}}{\text{Planned net sales } + \text{ Planned retail reductions}}$$

If planned retail reductions are 0, the initial markup percentage equals planned retail operating expenses plus profit, both divided by planned net sales. This results in the basic markup percentage formula.

To resume the florist example, suppose the firm projects that its retail reductions will be 20 percent of estimated sales, or $50,000. To reach its goals, the initial markup and the original selling price would be:

$$\begin{array}{l}\text{Initial markup} \\ \text{percentage} \\ \text{(at retail)}\end{array} = \frac{\$55,000 + \$50,000 + \$50,000}{\$250,000 + \$50,000} = 51.7$$

$$\text{Retail selling price} = \frac{\text{Merchandise cost}}{1 - \text{Markup}} = \frac{\$8.00}{1 - 0.517} = \$16.56$$

This means the original retail value of 18,129 plants would be about $300,000. Retail reductions of $50,000 would lead to net sales of $250,000. Thus, the retailer must begin selling plants at $16.56 apiece if it wants to have an average selling price of $13.79 per plant and a maintained markup of 42 percent.

The maintained markup percentage can be viewed as:

$$\begin{array}{l}\text{Maintained markup} \\ \text{percentage} \\ \text{(at retail)}\end{array} = \frac{\text{Actual retail operating expenses } + \text{ Actual profit}}{\text{Actual net sales}}$$

or

$$\begin{array}{l}\text{Maintained markup} \\ \text{percentage} \\ \text{(at retail)}\end{array} = \frac{\text{Average selling price } - \text{ Merchandise cost}}{\text{Actual selling price}}$$

Gross margin is the difference between net sales and the total cost of goods sold. The total cost of goods sold figure, as opposed to the gross cost figure, adjusts for cash discounts and additional expenses:

Gross margin (in $) = Net sales − Total cost of goods

For the florist, gross margin (the dollar equivalent of maintained markup) would be about $250,000 − $145,000 = $105,000. The total cost of goods is merchandise cost times the number of units bought.

Although a retailer must set an overall company markup goal, markups for categories of merchandise or even individual products may differ. In fact, product markups can vary dramatically. For instance, at many full-line discount stores, maintained markup as a percentage of sales ranges from under 20 percent for consumer electronics to more than 40 percent for jewelry and watches.

With a **variable markup policy,** a retailer purposely adjusts markups by merchandise category to achieve four major purposes. A variable markup policy:

1. Recognizes that costs associated with separate goods/service categories may fluctuate widely. Some items require extensive alterations (such as clothing) or installation (such as carpeting). Even within a product line like women's clothing, expensive fashions require higher end-of-year markdowns than inexpensive items. The more expensive line would receive a higher initial markup.

2. Allows for differences in product investments. In a major appliance department, where the retailer orders regularly from a wholesaler, lower markups would be needed than in a fine jewelry department, where the retailer would have to maintain a complete stock of merchandise.

3. Accounts for differences in sales efforts and merchandising skills. Selling a food processor may take a substantial sales effort, whereas selling a toaster may involve much less effort and skill.

4. May enable a retailer to generate more customer traffic by advertising certain products at especially attractive prices. This entails leader pricing, which is discussed later in the chapter.

One method for planning variable markups is **direct product profitability (DPP),** whereby a retailer finds the profitability of each category or unit of merchandise by computing adjusted per-unit gross margin and assigning direct product costs for such expense categories as warehousing, transportation, handling, and selling. The proper markup for each category or item can then be set. DPP is used by some supermarkets, discounters, and other retailers. The major problem is the complexity of assigning costs.

Figure 17.6 shows how DPP works. In this example, two items have a selling price of $20. With Item A, the retailer has a merchandise cost of $12. The per-unit gross margin is $8. Since it gets a $1 per-unit allowance to set up a special display, the adjusted gross margin is $9. Total direct retail costs are estimated at $5. Direct product profit is $4, or 20 percent of sales. With Item B, the merchandise costs $10. The per-unit gross margin is $10, and there are no special discounts or allowances. Since Item B needs more selling effort, total direct retail costs are $6. The direct profit is $4, or 20 percent of sales. To attain the same direct profit per-unit, Item A has a markup of 40 percent (per-unit gross margin/selling price) and Item B has a markup of 50 percent.

For many reasons, cost-oriented (markup) pricing is popular among retailers. It is fairly simple, especially because a retailer can apply a standard markup for a category of products more easily than it can estimate demand at various prices. The firm can also adjust prices according to demand or segment a market. Markup pricing has a sense of equity in that the

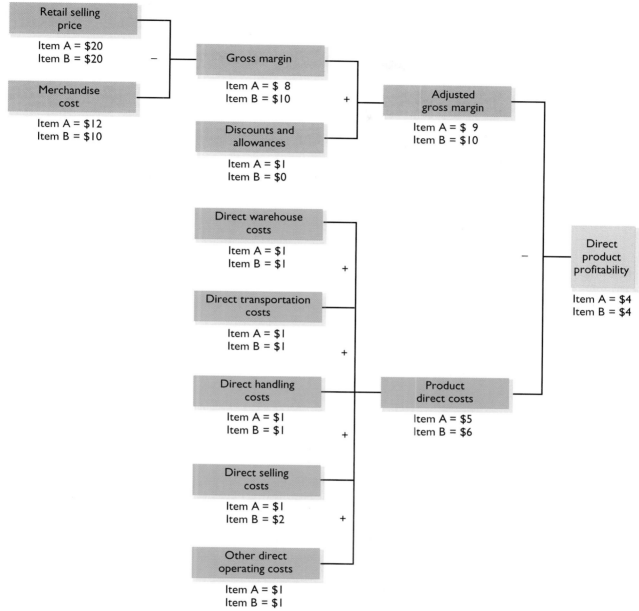

Figure 17.6
How to Determine Direct Product Profitability

retailer earns a fair profit. In addition, when retailers have similar markups, price competition is reduced. Last, markup pricing is efficient if it takes into account the competition, seasonal factors, and difficulties in selling specific merchandise categories.

Competition-Oriented Pricing In competition-oriented pricing, a retailer uses competitors' prices as a guide, rather than demand or cost considerations. A competition-oriented firm might not alter its prices to react to changes in demand or costs unless competitors alter

Table 17.6 Competition-Oriented Pricing Alternatives

Retail Mix Variable	ALTERNATIVE PRICE STRATEGIES		
	Pricing Below the Market	**Pricing at the Market**	**Pricing Above the Market**
Location	Poor, inconvenient site; low rent	Close to competitors, no locational advantage	Absence of strong competitor convenient to consumers
Customer service	Self-service, little product knowledge on part of salespeople, no displays	Moderate assistance by sales personnel	High levels of personal selling, delivery, exchanges, etc.
Product assortment	More emphasis on best-sellers	Medium or large assortment	Small or large assortment
Atmosphere	Inexpensive fixtures, little or no carpeting or paneling, racks for merchandise	Moderate atmosphere	Attractive, pleasant decor with many displays
Role of fashion in assortment	Fashion follower, conservative	Concentration on accepted best-sellers	Fashion leader
Special services	Not available	Not available or extra charge to customers	Included in price
Merchandise lines carried	Some name brands, private labels, closeouts, small manufacturers	Selection of name brands, private labels	Exclusive name brands and private labels

Bi-Lo, the southeastern supermarket chain, offers everyday low prices and "Weekly Specials" (www.bi-lo.com). Click on the icon to see this week's.

theirs. Similarly, such a retailer might change its prices when competitors do, even if demand or cost factors remain the same.

A competition-oriented retailer can price below the market, at the market, or above the market. Table 17.6 outlines the factors influencing a firm's choice. It is clear from this table that competition-oriented pricing must be coordinated with the overall strategy mix. A firm with a strong site, superior service, good assortments, a favorable image, and exclusive brands could set prices above competitors. However, above-market pricing is not suitable for a retailer that has an inconvenient site, relies on self-service and best-sellers, is a fashion follower, and offers no real product distinctiveness.

A competition-oriented pricing approach could be used for several reasons. It is rather simple since there are no calculations of demand curves or concern with price elasticity. The ongoing market price is assumed to be fair for both the consumer and the retailer. Pricing at the market level does not disrupt competition and therefore does not usually lead to retaliation.

Integration of Approaches to Price Strategy The preceding three approaches should be integrated, so demand, cost, and competition are all taken into account. To do this, a firm should answer questions such as these before enacting a price strategy:

- If prices are reduced, will revenues increase greatly? (Demand orientation)
- Should different prices be charged for a product based on negotiations with customers, seasonality, and so on? (Demand orientation)
- Will a given price level allow a traditional markup to be attained? (Cost orientation)
- What price level is necessary for a product requiring special costs in purchasing, selling, or delivery? (Cost orientation)

Dollar General's General of EDLP

According to Cal Turner, his grandfather and father, who opened the predecessor to Dollar General stores over 50 years ago, were just "unsophisticated country folks." Today, Dollar General operates thousands of stores in two dozen states, and its annual revenues are in the billions of dollars. While Turner may be more sophisticated than his predecessors, he is certainly following in their price-oriented footsteps.

As a teenager, Turner helped his father in the chain's first stores. He was drawn full-time to the family business in 1965 after graduation from Vanderbilt University and a three-year stint in the Navy. Turner succeeded his father as president of Dollar General in 1977 and as chairman of the board

in 1988. Since his son decided not to join Dollar General, management executives have been both recruited and developed internally to replace Cal Turner when he decides to retire.

Dollar General understands the needs of its customers. About one-half have household incomes of less than $20,000; and according to Cal Turner, they "understand true everyday low price." As a result, pricing at Dollar General is simple: "We'll clothe you from the waist up for five bucks and from the waist down for 10 bucks." Core merchandise price points go from 4 for $1 up to $20 per item. Noncore items go as high as $35.

Source: Debbie Howell, "The Right Reverend of EDLP," *Discount Store News* (May 24, 1999), pp. 46, 76.

- What price levels are competitors setting? (Competitive orientation)
- Can above-market prices be set due to a superior image? (Competitive orientation)

By no means is this list complete, but it demonstrates how a retailer can integrate demand, cost, and competitive price orientations.

Implementation of Price Strategy

Implementing a price strategy involves a variety of separate but interrelated specific decisions, in addition to those broad concepts already discussed. A checklist of selected decisions is shown in Table 17.7. In this section, the specifics of a pricing strategy are detailed.

Table 17.7 A Checklist of Selected Specific Pricing Decisions

1. How important is price stability? How long should prices be maintained?
2. Is everyday low pricing desirable?
3. Should prices change if costs and/or customer demand vary?
4. Should the same prices be charged of all customers buying under the same conditions?
5. Should customer bargaining be permitted?
6. Should odd pricing be used?
7. Should leader pricing be utilized to draw customer traffic? If yes, should leader prices be above, at, or below costs?
8. Should consumers be offered discounts for purchasing in quantity?
9. Should price lining be used to provide a price range and price points within that range?
10. Should pricing practices vary by department or product line?

Customary and Variable Pricing **Customary pricing** is used when a retailer sets prices for goods and services and seeks to maintain them for an extended period. Prices are not altered during this time. Examples of goods and services with customary prices are newspapers, candy, pay phones, arcade games, vending machine items, and foods on restaurant menus. In each of these cases, a retailer seeks to establish customary prices and have consumers take them for granted.

A version of customary pricing is **everyday low pricing (EDLP),** in which a retailer strives to sell its goods and services at consistently low prices throughout the selling season. Under EDLP, the retailer sets low prices initially; and there are few or no advertised specials, except on discontinued items or end-of-season closeouts. The retailer reduces its advertising and product relabeling costs, while the manufacturer reduces the added production and shipping costs caused by erratic sales levels. EDLP also increases the credibility of the retailer's prices to the consumer. On the other hand, with EDLP, manufacturers tend to eliminate the special trade allowances designed to encourage retailers to offer price promotions during the year. Wal-Mart and Ikea are among the retailers successfully utilizing EDLP. See Figure 17.7.

In many instances, a retailer cannot or should not use customary pricing. A firm *cannot* maintain constant prices if its costs are rising. A firm *should not* hold prices constant if customer demand varies. Under **variable pricing,** a retailer alters its prices to coincide with fluctuations in costs or consumer demand. Variable pricing may also provide excitement due to special sales opportunities for customers.

Cost fluctuations can be seasonal or trend-related. Seasonal fluctuations affect retailers selling items whose production peaks at certain times during the year. Thus, supermarket and florist prices vary over the year due to the seasonal nature of many agricultural and floral products. When items are scarce, their costs to the retailer go up. Trend-related fluctuations refer to the steady upward (or downward) spiral of costs to the retailer. If costs contin-

Figure 17.7
Everyday Low Pricing: It's
Always On Sale
Reprinted by permission.

ually rise (as with luxury cars) or fall (as with personal computers), the retailer must change prices permanently (unlike with seasonal fluctuations, which cause temporary changes).

Demand fluctuations can be place- or time-based. Place-based fluctuations exist for retailers selling seat locations (such as concert sites) or room locations (such as hotels). Different prices can be charged for different locations; for example, tickets close to the stage command higher prices. If variable pricing is not followed, location is based on a policy of first come, first served. Time-based fluctuations occur if consumer demand differs by hour, day, or season. Demand for a movie theater is greater on Saturday than on Wednesday; demand for an airline is greater during December than during February. Thus, prices should be lower during periods of low demand.

Yield management pricing is a computerized demand-based variable pricing technique, whereby a retailer (typically a service firm) determines the combination of prices that would yield the greatest total revenues for a given period. It is widely used in the airline and hotel industries. For instance, a crucial airline decision is how many first-class, full-coach, intermediate-discount, and deep-discount tickets to sell on each flight. Through yield management pricing, an airline would offer fewer discount tickets for flights during peak periods than for ones in nonpeak times. The airline has two goals: to try to fill as many seats as possible on every flight and to sell as many full-fare tickets as it can ("You don't want to sell a seat for $119 when a person will pay $500"). Yield management pricing is efficient and consumer-oriented, but it may be too complex for small retailers, and it requires sophisticated software.[17]

It is possible to combine customary and variable pricing. For instance, a theater can charge $4 every Wednesday night and $8 every Saturday. A bookstore can lower prices by 20 percent for books that have been out for three months.

One-Price Policy and Flexible Pricing   Under a **one-price policy,** a retailer charges the same price to all customers buying an item under similar conditions. This policy may be used together with customary pricing or variable pricing. For example, with variable pricing, all customers interested in a particular section of theater seats would pay the same price. The system is easy to manage, does not require skilled salespeople, makes shopping quicker, permits self-service, puts consumers under less pressure, and is tied to the firm's price goals. Throughout the United States, one-price policies are the rule for most retailers, and bargaining is often not permitted.

In contrast, **flexible pricing** lets consumers bargain over selling prices, and those who are good at bargaining obtain lower prices than those who are not. Many jewelry stores, auto dealers, housepainters, online auctions, and consumer electronics stores use flexible pricing. Retailers using this approach do not clearly post bottom-line prices; shoppers need prior knowledge to bargain successfully. Flexible pricing encourages shoppers to spend more time, gives an impression the firm is discount-oriented, and generates high margins from shoppers who do not like haggling. It requires high initial prices and good salespeople.

A special form of flexible pricing is **contingency pricing,** an arrangement by which a service retailer does not get paid until after the service is performed and payment is contingent on the service's being satisfactory. In some cases, such as real-estate and lawn care, consumers prefer contingency payments so they can be assured the service is properly performed. This represents some risk to the retailer since considerable time and effort may be spent without payment. A real-estate broker may show a house 25 times, may not sell it, and therefore is not paid.

Odd Pricing   Retail prices are set at levels below even dollar values, such as $0.49, $4.98, and $199, in **odd pricing.** The assumption is that people will feel these prices represent discounts or that the amounts are beneath consumer price ceilings. Realtors hope consumers with a price ceiling of less than $200,000 will be attracted to houses selling for $199,500. From this perspective, odd pricing is a form of psychological pricing. See Figure 17.8.

Looking to bargain? Go to eBay (www.ebay.com) or Haggle Online (www.haggle.com).

Figure 17.8
Odd Pricing: A Popular
Retailing Tactic
Reprinted by permission of Golf Day.

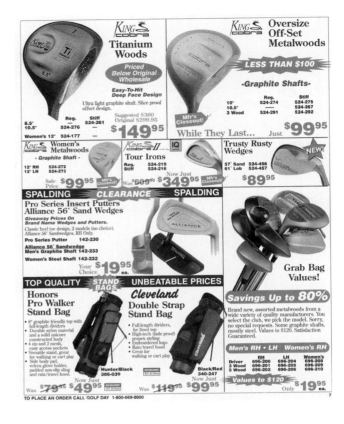

Originally, odd prices were used to force sales clerks to give change on each purchase, thus preventing them from pocketing receipts without ringing up sales. Odd prices are now accepted as part of the U.S. system of retailing and are used more for psychological reasons.

Odd prices that are 1 cent or 2 cents below the next highest even price (e.g., $0.29, $0.99, $2.98) are common up to $10.00. Beyond that point and up to $50.00, 5-cent reductions from the highest even price (e.g., $19.95, $49.95) are more usual. For more expensive items, prices are in dollars (e.g., $399, $4,995).

Despite the widespread use of odd pricing in retailing, there has been limited research on its psychological effects.[18]

Leader Pricing In **leader pricing,** a retailer advertises and sells selected items in its goods/service assortment at less than the usual profit margins. The goal is to increase customer traffic for the retailer so as to sell regularly priced goods and services in addition to the specially priced items. Leader pricing is different from bait-and-switch, in which sale items are not sold.

Leader pricing often involves frequently purchased, nationally branded, high turnover goods and services because it is easy for customers to detect low prices, thereby generating high customer patronage. Supermarkets, home centers, discount department stores, toy stores, drugstores, and fast-food restaurants are just some of the retailers that utilize leader pricing to draw shoppers. There are two kinds of leader pricing: loss leaders and sales at lower than regular prices (but higher than cost). As noted earlier in this chapter, loss leaders are regulated on a statewide basis under minimum-price laws.

Multiple-Unit Pricing With **multiple-unit pricing,** a retailer offers discounts to customers who buy in quantity or who buy a product bundle. For example, by selling items at two for $0.75 or six for $2.19, a retailer would attempt to sell more products than at $0.39 each.

There are three reasons to use multiple-unit pricing: (1) A firm could seek to have customers increase their total purchases of an item. Yet, if people buy multiple units to stockpile them, instead of consuming more, the firm's overall sales would not increase. (2) Multiple-unit pricing can help sell slow-moving and end-of-season merchandise. (3) Price bundling may increase the sales of related items.

In **bundled pricing,** a firm combines several elements in one basic price. A 35-mm camera bundle could include a camera, batteries, a telephoto lenses, a case, and a tripod for $289. A $60 air-conditioner tune-up could include in-home servicing, vacuuming the unit, replacing the air filter, unclogging tubing, lubricating the unit, and checking air circulation. This approach increases overall sales and offers people a discount over unbundled prices. However, it is unresponsive to different customers. As an alternative, many firms use **unbundled pricing,** whereby they charge separate prices for each item sold. A TV rental firm could charge separately for the TV rental, home delivery of the set, and a monthly service contract. This lets the retailer closely link prices with costs and gives people more choice. Unbundled pricing may be harder to manage and may result in people buying fewer related items. See Figure 17.9.

Marriott International (www.marriott.com) really knows how to use price lining.

Price Lining Rather than stock merchandise at all different price levels, retailers often employ **price lining** and sell merchandise at a limited range of price points, with each point representing a distinct level of quality. With price lining, retailers first determine their price

Figure 17.9
Price Bundling from wine.com
Reprinted by permission.

floors and ceilings in each product category. They then set a limited number of price points within the range. Department stores generally carry good, better, and best versions of merchandise consistent with their overall price policy—and set individual prices accordingly. Marriott International operates luxury Ritz-Carlton hotels, moderate Courtyard by Marriott hotels, and budget Fairfield Inn hotels.

Price lining benefits both consumers and retailers. It lessens shopping confusion for consumers. If the price range for a box of handkerchiefs is $6 to $15 and the price points are $6, $9, and $15, consumers would know that distinct product qualities exist. However, should a retailer have prices of $6, $7, $8, $9, $10, $11, $12, $13, $14, and $15, the consumer may be confused about product qualities and differences.

For retailers, price lining aids in merchandise planning. Retail buyers can seek out those suppliers carrying products at appropriate prices; and the buyers can keep in mind final selling prices in negotiating with suppliers. They can automatically disregard products not fitting within price lines and thereby reduce inventory investment. Also, stock turnover goes up when the number of models carried is limited.

Four difficulties do exist with price lining. First, depending on the price points selected, price lining may leave gaps between prices that are perceived as too large by consumers. A parent shopping for a graduation gift might find a $30 briefcase to be too inexpensive and a $150 briefcase to be too expensive. Second, inflation can make it tough to maintain price points and price ranges. When costs rise, retailers can either eliminate lower-priced items or reduce markups. Third, markdowns or special sales may disrupt the balance in a price line, unless all items in that line are reduced proportionally. Fourth, price lines must be coordinated for complementary product categories, such as blazers, skirts, and shoes.

Price Adjustments

Price adjustments allow retailers to use price as an adaptive mechanism. Markdowns and additional markups may be needed due to such factors as competition, seasonality, demand patterns, merchandise costs, and pilferage. Figure 17.10 shows a price change authorization form.

A **markdown** from the original retail price of an item can meet the lower price of another retailer, adapt to inventory overstocking, clear out shopworn merchandise, reduce assortments of odds and ends, and increase customer traffic. An **additional markup** is an increase in a retail price above the original markup when demand is unexpectedly high or costs are rising. In today's competitive marketplace, markdowns are applied by retailers much more frequently than additional markups.

A third price adjustment, the employee discount, is noted here since it may affect the computation of markdowns and additional markups. Also, although an employee discount is not an adaptive mechanism, it influences morale. Some firms give employee discounts on all items and also let workers buy sale items before they are made available to the general public.

Computing Markdowns and Additional Markups Markdowns and additional markups can be expressed in dollars (total dollar markdown or markup) or percentages.

The **markdown percentage** is the total dollar markdown as a percentage of net sales (in dollars):

$$\text{Markdown percentage} = \frac{\text{Total dollar markdown}}{\text{Net sales (in \$)}}$$

A difficulty with this formula is that net sales must reflect additional markups and employee discounts (along with dollar markdowns). Also, the formula does not enable a retailer to learn the percentage of items that are marked down as compared to those sold at the original price.

Essentus (www. essentus.com/ solutions/ merchandising/price. html) helps small and medium apparel retailers plan for price adjustments.

Figure 17.10
A Price Change Authorization Form

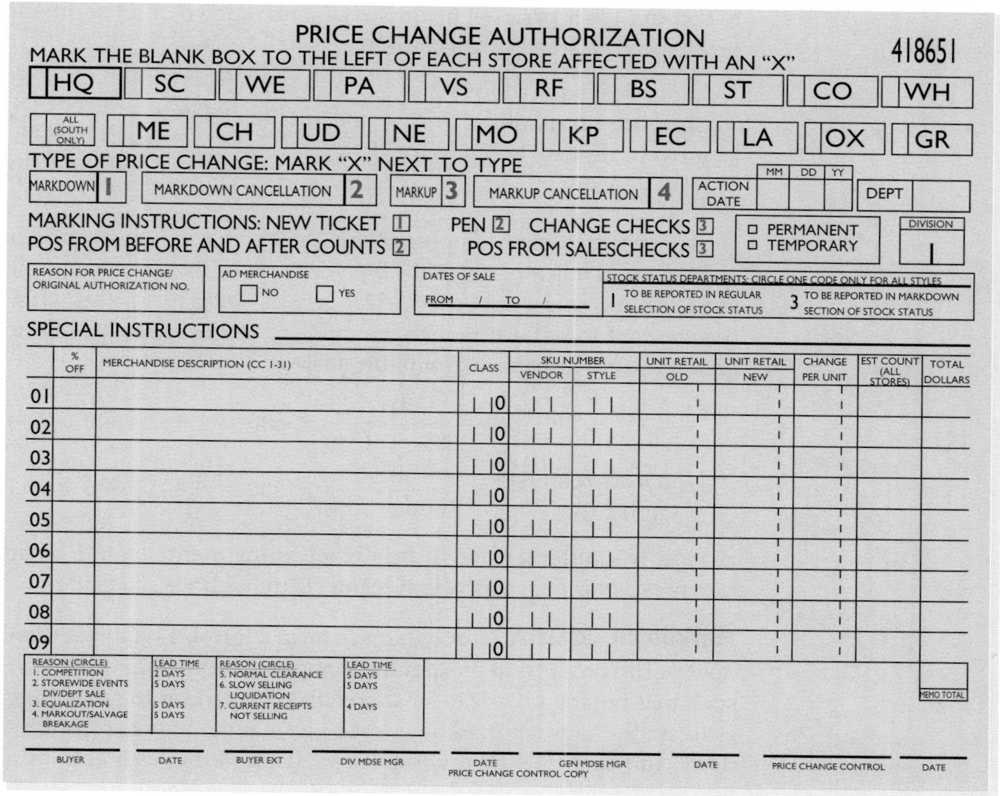
PRICE CHANGE AUTHORIZATION 418651

MARK THE BLANK BOX TO THE LEFT OF EACH STORE AFFECTED WITH AN "X"

HQ SC WE PA VS RF BS ST CO WH

ALL (SOUTH ONLY) ME CH UD NE MO KP EC LA OX GR

TYPE OF PRICE CHANGE: MARK "X" NEXT TO TYPE

MARKDOWN 1 MARKDOWN CANCELLATION 2 MARKUP 3 MARKUP CANCELLATION 4 ACTION DATE MM DD YY DEPT

MARKING INSTRUCTIONS: NEW TICKET 1 PEN 2 CHANGE CHECKS 3 □ PERMANENT □ TEMPORARY DIVISION 1

POS FROM BEFORE AND AFTER COUNTS 2 POS FROM SALESCHECKS 3

REASON FOR PRICE CHANGE/ ORIGINAL AUTHORIZATION NO. | AD MERCHANDISE □ NO □ YES | DATES OF SALE FROM / TO / | STOCK STATUS DEPARTMENTS: CIRCLE ONE CODE ONLY FOR ALL STYLES 1 TO BE REPORTED IN REGULAR SELECTION OF STOCK STATUS 3 TO BE REPORTED IN MARKDOWN SECTION OF STOCK STATUS

SPECIAL INSTRUCTIONS

	% OFF	MERCHANDISE DESCRIPTION (CC 1-31)	CLASS	SKU NUMBER VENDOR	SKU NUMBER STYLE	UNIT RETAIL OLD	UNIT RETAIL NEW	CHANGE PER UNIT	EST COUNT (ALL STORES)	TOTAL DOLLARS
01			10							
02			10							
03			10							
04			10							
05			10							
06			10							
07			10							
08			10							
09			10							

REASON (CIRCLE)	LEAD TIME	REASON (CIRCLE)	LEAD TIME
1. COMPETITION	2 DAYS	5. NORMAL CLEARANCE	5 DAYS
2. STOREWIDE EVENTS DIV/DEPT SALE	5 DAYS	6. SLOW SELLING LIQUIDATION	5 DAYS
3. EQUALIZATION	5 DAYS	7. CURRENT RECEIPTS NOT SELLING	4 DAYS
4. MARKOUT/SALVAGE BREAKAGE	5 DAYS		

MEMO TOTAL

BUYER DATE BUYER EXT DIV MDSE MGR DATE GEN MDSE MGR DATE PRICE CHANGE CONTROL DATE

PRICE CHANGE CONTROL COPY

A complementary measure is the **off-retail markdown percentage,** which looks at the markdown for each item or category of items as a percentage of original retail price:

$$\text{Off-retail markdown percentage} = \frac{\text{Original price} - \text{New price}}{\text{Original price}}$$

With this formula, the markdown percentage for every item can be computed, as well as the percentage of items marked down.

Suppose a gas barbecue grill sells for \$200 at the beginning of the summer and is reduced to \$140 at the end of the summer. The off-retail markdown is 30 percent [(\$200 − \$140)/\$200]. If 100 grills are sold at the original price and 20 are sold at the sale price, the percentage of items marked down is 17 percent, and the total dollar markdown is \$1,200.

The **additional markup percentage** looks at total dollar additional markups as a percentage of net sales, while the **addition to retail percentage** measures a price rise as a percentage of the original price:

$$\text{Additional markup percentage} = \frac{\text{Total dollar additional markups}}{\text{Net sales (in \$)}}$$

$$\text{Addition to retail percentage} = \frac{\text{New price} - \text{Original price}}{\text{Original price}}$$

Retailers need to be aware that price adjustments affect their markups per unit and that many more customers would have to buy at reduced prices to have a total gross profit equal to that at higher prices. The impact of a markdown or an additional markup on total gross profit can be learned by this formula:

$$\begin{array}{c}\text{Unit sales required to} \\ \text{earn the same total} \\ \text{gross profit with a} \\ \text{price adjustment}\end{array} = \frac{\text{Original markup (\%)}}{\begin{array}{c}\text{Original markup (\%)} \\ +/- \text{ Price change (\%)}\end{array}} \times \begin{array}{c}\text{Expected unit} \\ \text{sales at} \\ \text{original price}\end{array}$$

At a specialty store, suppose a Sony Walkman with a cost of $50 has an original retail price of $100, which is a markup of 50 percent. The firm expects to sell 500 units over the next year, leading to a total gross profit of $25,000 ($50 × 500). How many units would the retailer have to sell if it reduces the price to $85 or raises it to $110 and still earn a $25,000 gross profit? This is how to find the answer:

$$\begin{array}{c}\text{Unit sales required} \\ \text{(at \$85)}\end{array} = \frac{50\%}{50\% - 15\%} \times 500 = 1.43 \times 500 = 714$$

$$\begin{array}{c}\text{Unit sales required} \\ \text{(at \$110)}\end{array} = \frac{50\%}{50\% + 10\%} \times 500 = 0.83 \times 500 = 417$$

A retailer's judgment regarding price adjustments would be affected by its operating expenses at various sales volumes and customer price elasticities.

Markdown Control Through markdown control, a retailer evaluates the number of markdowns, the proportion of sales involving markdowns, and the causes. The control must be such that buying plans can be altered in later periods to reflect markdowns. A good way to evaluate the cause of markdowns is to have retail buyers record the reasons for each markdown and examine them periodically. Possible buyer notations are "end of season," "to match the price of a competitor," "worn merchandise," and "obsolete style."

Technology in Retailing

Costco.com Goes to Phase II

Costco, the deep discounter, has overhauled its Web site (www.costco.com) as part of its self-proclaimed "second phase transition." One of Costco's main goals in redesigning its site—according to Courtland Newberry, Costco's senior vice-president of E-commerce, business delivery, and quality assurance—is to ensure that shoppers can more easily order merchandise.

In general, the updated Web site offers higher-ticket items, including high-end jewelry and computer equipment, that are not carried in Costco's membership clubs. Susan Castillo, Costco's general merchandise manager, says that less than 5 percent of the products carried on Costco's Web site are also carried in its warehouses: "We can move in and out of items quickly, which is so critical with the way technology changes every ten minutes. The site will not be everything for everyone. It will be item-driven with great values that go beyond the warehouse walls."

The average purchase on Costco's Web site is between $350 and $400, versus an average purchase of between $90 to $100 at its traditional stores. Although online shoppers often order only one item, most warehouse purchasers buy multiple items.

Comment on the differences in pricing strategy for Costco's Web site and its membership clubs.

Source: Shani Weiss, "Costco Online's Phase II Set for Spring Launch," *Discount Store News* (March 22, 1999), pp. 7, 93.

Table 17.8 Ten Ways to Control Markdowns

1. Adhere to a buying plan regarding the quantities ordered and the timing of merchandise receipt. Do not buy too much merchandise to secure a greater quantity discount or promotional allowance. Learn to say "no" to vendors' salespeople.

2. Be an important customer. Limit the number of vendors with which you deal. Bargain for the right to exchange slow-selling merchandise during the season, if necessary.

3. Evaluate the reasons for slow-selling merchandise. Can additional displays or sales incentives quicken the sales pace?

4. Carefully study the impact of special purchases on the sale of traditional merchandise.

5. Be careful in size selection. It may be wise to risk being out of stock, for example, in very small and very large sizes versus having to take drastic markdowns.

6. Maintain a perpetual inventory to avoid large markdowns.

7. Limit spoilage by properly caring for and displaying perishable or breakable goods, and by using proper packaging and containers.

8. Monitor layaway payments. Beware of an item being saved for a long time and then not being wanted by a customer. Request partial pre-payments to hold a layaway item.

9. Make sure salespeople are properly motivated and trained.

10. Staple merchandise can generally be carried over to next year. Inventory costs must be weighed against the size of the necessary markdowns, potential increases in price next year, shelf space occupied, shipping costs, etc.

Source: Adapted by the authors from William Burston, *A Checklist of 38 Ways of Controlling Markdowns* (New York: National Retail Federation, n.d.).

Markdown control lets a firm monitor its policies, such as the way items are stored and late acceptance of fashion shipments. Careful planning may also enable a retailer to avoid some markdowns by running more ads, training workers better, shipping goods more efficiently among branch units, and returning items to vendors. Table 17.8 cites 10 ways to control markdowns.

The need for markdown control should not be interpreted as meaning that all markdowns can or should be minimized or eliminated. In fact, too low a markdown percentage may indicate that a retailer's buyers have not assumed enough risk in purchasing goods.

Timing Markdowns Although there is some disagreement among retailers about the best markdown timing sequence, much can be said about the benefits of enacting an early markdown policy: (1) This policy offers merchandise at reduced prices when demand is still fairly active. (2) It requires lower markdowns to sell products than markdowns late in the season. (3) Early markdowns free selling space for new merchandise. (4) The retailer's cash flow position can be improved.

The main advantage of a late markdown policy is that a retailer gives itself every opportunity to sell merchandise at original prices. Yet, the advantages associated with an early markdown policy cannot be achieved under a late markdown policy.

Retailers can also use a staggered markdown policy, whereby prices are discounted throughout an item's selling period. One pre-planned staggered markdown policy for reducing prices over a selling period involves an **automatic markdown plan.** In such a plan, the amount and timing of markdowns are controlled by the length of time merchandise remains in stock. Syms applies markdowns in this manner:

Our pricing policy is to affix a ticket to each item displaying Syms' selling price, as well as the price we regard as the traditional full retail price of that item at department or specialty stores. All garments are sold with the brand name affixed by the manufacturer. Syms has long utilized a 10-day automatic markdown pricing policy to promote movement of merchandise. The date of placement on the selling floor of each item is stamped on the back of the price ticket. The front of each ticket contains what we believe to be the nationally advertised price, the initial Syms price, and three reduced prices. Each reduced price becomes effective after the passage of 10 selling days. The Company also offers "dividend" prices consisting of additional price reductions on various types of merchandise.[19]

Syms' plan ensures fresh stock and early markdowns.

A storewide clearance, conducted once or twice a year, is another way to time markdowns. Often a storewide clearance takes place after peak selling periods like Christmas and Mother's Day. The goal is to clean out merchandise before taking a physical inventory and beginning the next season. The advantages of a storewide clearance over an automatic markdown policy are that a longer period is provided for selling merchandise at original prices and that frequent markdowns can destroy a consumer's confidence in a retailer's regular prices: "Why buy now, when it will be on sale next week?" An automatic policy may also encourage a steady stream of bargain hunters who are not potential customers for the firm's regular merchandise, while clearance sales limit bargain hunting to once or twice a year.

Retailers should be concerned about frequent markdowns. In the past, many retailers would introduce merchandise at high prices and then mark down prices on many items by as much as 60 percent to increase store traffic and improve inventory turnover. This caused customers to wait for price reductions and treat initial prices skeptically. Today, a great number of retailers utilize lower initial markups, run fewer sales, and apply fewer markdowns than before. Nonetheless, one of the biggest problems facing some retailers is that they have gotten consumers too used to buying when items are discounted.

SUMMARY

1. *To describe the role of pricing in a retail strategy and to show that pricing decisions must be made in an integrated and adaptive manner.* Pricing is crucial to a retailer because of its interrelationship with overall objectives and the other components of the retail strategy. A price plan must be integrated and responsive— and provide a good value to customers.

2. *To examine the impact of consumers; government; manufacturers, wholesalers, and other suppliers; and current and potential competitors on pricing decisions.* Before designing a price plan, a retailer must study the factors affecting its decisions. Sometimes, the factors have a minor effect on pricing discretion; other times, they severely limit pricing options.

With regard to consumers, retailers should be familiar with the price elasticity of demand and the different market segments that are possible. Government restrictions deal with horizontal and vertical price fixing, price discrimination, minimum prices, unit pricing, item price removal, and price advertising. There may be conflicts about which party controls retail prices; and manufacturers, wholesalers, and other suppliers may be required to provide price guarantees (if they are in a position of weakness). The competitive environment may foster market pricing, which could lead to price wars, or administered pricing.

3. *To present a framework for developing a retail price strategy.* This framework consists of five stages: objectives, broad price policy, price strategy, implementation of price strategy, and price adjustments.

Retail pricing goals can be chosen from among sales, dollar profits, return on investment, and early recovery of cash. After they are chosen, a broad policy is set and a coordinated series of actions is outlined, consistent with the retailer's image and oriented to the short and long run.

A good price strategy integrates demand, cost, and competitive concepts. Each of these orientations must be understood separately and jointly. Psychological pricing, markup pricing, alternative ways of computing markups, gross margin, direct product profitability, and pricing below, at, or above the market are among the key aspects of strategy planning.

When enacting a price strategy, several specific tools can be used to supplement the broad base of the strategy. Retailers should know when to use customary and variable pricing, one-price policies and flexible pricing, odd pricing, leader pricing, multiple-unit pricing, and price lining.

Price adjustments may be required for a firm to adapt to various internal and external conditions. Adjustments include markdowns, additional markups, and employee discounts. It is important that adjustments are controlled by a budget, the causes of markdowns are noted, future company buying reflects earlier errors or adaptations, adjustments are properly timed, and excessive discounting is avoided.

Key Terms

price elasticity of demand (p. 558)
horizontal price fixing (p. 560)
vertical price fixing (p. 561)
Robinson-Patman Act (p. 561)
minimum-price laws (p. 562)
loss leaders (p. 562)
predatory pricing (p. 563)
unit pricing (p. 563)
item price removal (p. 563)
bait advertising (bait-and-switch
    advertising) (p. 564)
gray market goods (p. 565)
market penetration (p. 566)
market skimming (p. 566)
demand-oriented pricing (p. 570)
cost-oriented pricing (p. 570)
competition-oriented pricing (p. 570)

price–quality association (p. 570)
prestige pricing (p. 571)
markup pricing (p. 571)
markup (p. 571)
markup percentage (p. 571)
initial markup (p. 573)
maintained markup (p. 573)
gross margin (p. 574)
variable markup policy (p. 574)
direct product profitability (DPP)
    (p. 574)
customary pricing (p. 578)
everyday low pricing (EDLP) (p. 578)
variable pricing (p. 578)
yield management pricing (p. 579)
one-price policy (p. 579)

flexible pricing (p. 579)
contingency pricing (p. 579)
odd pricing (p. 579)
leader pricing (p. 580)
multiple-unit pricing (p. 580)
bundled pricing (p. 581)
unbundled pricing (p. 581)
price lining (p. 581)
markdown (p. 582)
additional markup (p. 582)
markdown percentage (p. 582)
off-retail markdown percentage
    (p. 583)
additional markup percentage (p. 583)
addition to retail percentage (p. 583)
automatic markdown plan (p. 584)

Questions for Discussion

1. Why should retailers understand the concept of price elasticity even if they cannot compute it?

2. Comment on each of the following from the perspective of a small retailer:
   a. Horizontal price fixing.
   b. Vertical price fixing.
   c. Price discrimination.
   d. Minimum-price laws.
   e. Unit pricing.

3. Why do some retailers sell gray market goods?

4. Give an example of a price strategy that integrates demand, cost, and competitive criteria.

5. Explain why markups are usually computed as a percentage of selling price rather than of cost.

6. A floor tile retailer wants to receive a 40 percent markup (at retail) for all merchandise. If one style of tile retails for $8 per tile, what is the maximum that the retailer would be willing to pay for a tile?

7. A car dealer purchases multiple-disc CD players for $175 each and desires a 35 percent markup (at retail). What retail price should be charged?

8. A photo store charges $11.00 to process a roll of slides; its cost is $7.35. What is the markup percentage (at cost and at retail)?

9. A firm has planned operating expenses of $220,000, a profit goal of $160,000, and planned reductions of $50,000 and expects sales of $900,000. Compute the initial markup percentage.

10. At the end of the year, the retailer in Question 9 determines that actual operating expenses are $200,000, actual profit is $160,000, and actual sales are $880,000. What is the maintained markup percentage? Explain the difference in your answers to Questions 9 and 10.

11. What are the pros and cons of everyday low pricing to a retailer? To a manufacturer?

12. Under what circumstances do you think bundled pricing is a good idea? A poor idea? Why?

13. What is the difference between markdown percentage and off-retail percentage?

14. A retailer buys items for $30. At an original retail price of $50, it expects to sell 1,000 units.
    a. If the price is marked down to $40, how many units must the retailer sell to earn the same total gross profit it would attain with a $50 price?
    b. If the price is marked up to $60, how many units must the retailer sell to earn the same total gross profit it would attain with a $50 price?

WEB-BASED EXERCISE

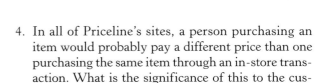

Priceline (www.priceline.com)

Questions

1. Describe Priceline's grocery site. Compare it with Peapod's (www.peapod.com).

2. Evaluate Priceline's new car site. Compare it with Auto-By-Tel's (www.autobytel.com).

3. Discuss Priceline's airline ticket site. How does its pricing strategy for airline tickets differ from that for grocery items?

4. In all of Priceline's sites, a person purchasing an item would probably pay a different price than one purchasing the same item through an in-store transaction. What is the significance of this to the customer? To the retailer?

CHAPTER ENDNOTES

1. Timothy Hanrahan, "Price Isn't Everything," *Wall Street Journal* (July 12, 1999), p. R20.

2. Michael Hartnett, "Expectation Is the Key to Pricing," *Discount Store News* (September 7, 1998), p. 16.

3. Howard Feiertag, "Price–Value Relationship Remains Cornerstone Consideration," *Hotel & Motel Management* (November 16, 1998), p. 24.

4. Stephen Manner, "Off-Web Dickering," *Forbes* (April 1999), p. 134.

5. Bob Tedeschi, "Pricing Errors on the Web Can Be Costly," *New York Times on the Web* (December 13, 1999).

6. See Byung-Do Kim, Kannan Srinivasan, and Ronald T. Wilcox, "Identifying Price Sensitive Consumers: The Relative Merits of Demographic vs. Purchase Pattern Information," *Journal of Retailing,* Vol. 75 (Summer 1999), pp. 173–93.

7. Michael F. Conlan, "Antitrust Settlement Expected to Be Slow in Distributing Money," *Drug Topics* (September 20, 1999), p. 20.

8. Lee Egerstrom, "Minnesota Dairies Settle Milk Price-Fixing Case with State," *Knight-Ridder/Tribune Business News* (November 3, 1999), p. OKRB9930717A.

9. Stephen Labaton, "Car Dealers' Group Settles U.S. Antitrust Suit," *New York Times* (September 21, 1995), p. D7.

10. Edward Felsenthal, "Manufacturers Allowed to Cap Retail Prices," *Wall Street Journal* (November 5, 1997), pp. A3, A8.

11. Michael Willins, "Motor Oil Update," *Aftermarket Business* (June 1, 1998), p. 48.

12. Louise Lee, "Arkansas Court Rules Wal-Mart Didn't Use Illegal Pricing Practices," *Wall Street Journal* (January 10, 1995), p. B10; and Norman W. Hawker, "Wal-Mart and the Divergence of State and Federal Predatory Pricing Law," *Journal of Public Policy & Marketing,* Vol. 15 (Spring 1996), pp. 141–47.

13. "Getting the Gear," *Consumer Reports* (October 1998), p. 16.

14. See George Anders, "Eager to Boost Traffic, More Internet Firms Give Away Services," *Wall Street Journal* (July 28, 1999), pp. A1, A8.

15. Selling price may also be computed by transposing the markup formula into

$$\text{Retail selling price} = \frac{\text{Merchandise}}{1 - \text{Markup}} = \$17.14$$

16. Merchandise cost may also be computed by transposing the markup formula into

$$\text{Merchandise cost} = (\text{Retail selling price})(1 - \text{Markup}) = \$0.474$$

17. See Ramarao Desiraju and Steven M. Shugan, "Strategic Service Pricing and Yield Management," *Journal of Marketing,* Vol. 63 (January 1999), pp. 44–56.

18. See Karen Gedenk and Henrik Sattler, "The Impact of Price Thresholds on Profit Contribution—Should Retailers Set 9-Ending Prices?" *Journal of Retailing,* Vol. 75 (Spring 1999), pp. 33–57.

19. *Syms 1999 Annual Report.*

CASE 1

PRICING AT BOJANGLES'

Bojangles' is a fast-food chain headquartered in North Carolina. It specializes in a Cajun-style menu with homemade biscuits, spicy fried chicken, Cajun gravy, and seasoned french fries. Most of its foods are made in each restaurant from basic ingredients. Unlike some other fast-food chains, Bojangles' serves all three meals effectively: Breakfast typically features biscuits. Lunch stresses chicken sandwiches. Dinner features a complete chicken dinner.

With nearly 300 stores worldwide (60 percent company-owned and 40 percent franchised), Bojangles' is one of the largest chicken-based restaurant chains, with annual systemwide sales of $250 million. Its overall sales have been increasing steadily.

The chain has passed through a succession of owners since its 1977 start. In 1981, the restaurant's founders sold the chain to Horn & Hardart for $12 million. In 1990, Horn & Hardart sold its interest to a venture management firm, Interwest and Sienna, for $24 million. Finally, in 1998, the chain was acquired by local investors for $85 million. The leading investor, Glenn Gulledge, has taken over as president and chief executive officer. Gulledge was employed by Bojangles' in 1980, but then left to work at Wendy's International and with local Wendy's franchiseees. He did that for nearly 20 years. Gulledge's partner, James H. "Hezzy" Miller, is senior vice-president of administration and finance.

Part of the new strategy for Bojangles' is to improve sales performance at each store through special pricing offers. Hezzy Miller explains: "We think there's a lot of capacity [for growth] within the existing stores." Bojangles' priced-based promotions are now designed to increase unit sales throughout the year.

One type of promotion focuses on "buy one, get one free." In a recent promotion of this kind, "Ham it up for free," Bojangles' gave away more than 100,000 ham biscuits during a one-day promotion at 200 of its then 251 U.S. units (since franchisees do not have to participate in each promotion). This promotion was accompanied by a five-day radio advertising blitz.

A second type of promotion features a different item at a reduced sale price every month. Although this increases sales, some critics feel that it also conditions customers to visit the chain only when their favorite food is on sale.

CASE 1
(CONTINUED)

A third type of promotion focuses on combo meals. Bojangles' typical combo meal includes a main course (such as a chicken sandwich), a side dish, and a beverage for 10 to 15 percent below the cost of the three items if purchased individually. Combo pricing is effective in increasing profits if customers who would normally purchase two items buy the combo pack (since gross profits on beverages and side orders are typically higher than on main courses). However, a difficulty associated with combo pricing is that customers who would normally order all three items now receive a discount.

Questions

1. What are the problems associated with Bojangles' having too many price promotions?

2. Since franchisee participation in promotions is voluntary, how can Bojangles' stimulate the maximum participation?

3. Comment on the economics of combo pricing.

4. Should Bojangles' offer special family packs, where multiple combo meals are sold at an additional discount? Explain your answer.

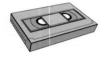

Video Questions on Bojangles'

1. How can Bojangles' estimate its demand curve (the relationship between price and quantity sold)?

2. If value is a function of quality, service, and price, should Bojangles' sell its products at prices above, below, or the same as competitors? Explain your answer.

NOTE

The material in this case is drawn from "Bojangles' Thanks Customers with Biscuits," *Nation's Restaurant News* (September 14, 1998), p. 26; Mark Hamstra, "Investors Buy Bojangles' for $85 Million," *Nation's Restaurant News* (April 13, 1998), pp. 1, 77; and Alan Liddle, "Chicken Chains Beat Their Wings as Sales Soar in 1999," *Nation's Restaurant News* (July 26, 1999), p. 122.

CASE 2

TARGET CORPORATION COMPUTERIZES TO AVOID "MARKDOWN MADNESS"

While many retailers grudgingly accept markdowns as an unfortunate cost of doing business, Minneapolis-based Target Corporation is aggressively doing something about them. The firm has worked with California's Santa Clara University to produce a forecasting model to minimize both the cost of taking markdowns and the time it takes to clear out underperforming merchandise from its shelves.

Target Corporation's new approach is very different from how it used to handle markdowns. The forecasting model now looks at two years of promotional and markdown performance and at weekly store sales by item to see how deep a markdown is needed to clear out slow-selling items by a specific date. All of the company's major divisions—Dayton's, Hudson's, Target Stores, Marshall Field's, and Mervyn's California—use the system. According to the firm's Paul Lamoureux, "We wanted to find a way to maximize profits during the clearance cycle. In the past, clearance prices were determined by each buyer's budget. If a buyer had, say, a $100,000 markdown budget, he or she might have marked down a product 25 percent. If there was more money in the budget, he or she would go higher, say 40 percent."

Lamoureux says that "the system does not make markdowns go away. It tells us what we need to do to liquidate clearance items in the time frame we set. I liken the system to an escalator. The merchant decides when to start clearing out an item—when to put it on the escalator. The system takes it down to the next pricing level. It sets the prices, decides when they should fall based on how that item is moving in different stores, and does all the paperwork." As the various divisions at Target Corporation have gone to the system, "we saw a drastic increase in the depth of first markdowns. We weren't hit with second and third markdowns because the first markdown often accomplished the job of moving the merchandise off the shelves. It was quite a revelation once the system took over."

Dale Achabal, a professor at Santa Clara University, says that is exactly the way markdowns should work: "There is no combination of two markdowns that is more profitable than one markdown. If you have to take a second markdown, it's because the first markdown didn't do what you thought it was going to do. If a markdown budget is causing a retailer to delay taking a markdown, it's costing that company more money over the course of the clearance. The longer you wait in the season, the less value that item has to the customer."

"This system looks at weekly movement information and self-corrects," Lamoureux adds. For many of our buyers, this is the first exposure they've had to intelligent computer systems. Once it's clear to them that a product is a dog, they can turn it over to the system. They never have to look at it again."

Despite the effectiveness of the computerized markdown management system, Target Corporation occasionally chooses to specify markdowns manually. "There are limitations to systems like this," Lamoureux remarks. "A high-end chain like Marshall Field's might only have 6 dresses in a particular style in a store. When you are talking about a fashion item like that, the system is not going to have a lot of historical information to base a decision on. In cases like that, we'd manage the markdown manually."

Questions

1. Why do you think that more retailers have not emulated Target Corporation's computerized markdown system?

2. What are the pros and cons of taking a large markdown on an item early in the selling season?

3. Evaluate Target Corporation's strategy of basing markdowns on two years of weekly sales experience at each store.

4. Present five guidelines that specify when Target Corporation should not rely solely on its computerized markdown management system.

NOTE   The material in this case is adapted by the authors from "Managing Markdown Madness," *Chain Store Age* (March 1999), p. 118. Copyright Lebhar-Friedman, Inc., 425 Park Avenue, New York, NY 10022. Reprinted by permission.

PART SIX
COMPREHENSIVE CASE
Category Management in Action

INTRODUCTION

In the space of a year, category management has become a cornerstone of perishables strategy for leading supermarket companies of all sizes. Major gaps in data that kept category management at bay for years in the meat, produce, bakery, and deli departments are being rapidly bridged or resolved. Firms are modifying dry grocery category management methods or developing whole new systems to deal with the perishables marketplace.

National perishables industry associations say they have moved beyond explaining category management principles to members and are now helping them implement plans. Why are companies swarming to category management? Profit and survival, according to industry experts.

Consider the economics. Perishables account for about one-half of total supermarket sales. Inventory shrinkage can drain as much as 15 percent. Mistakes at the checkout stand with random-weight items can cost 1 percent of category sales. And that doesn't take into account the increased sales generated by providing more of the perishables that customers want. Industry consultants say category management can increase sales from 5 to 15 percent.

"We will probably never have data as good as dry grocery," says Anne Lightburn of the Food Marketing Institute (FMI). "But perishables are the point of difference for stores, and the bang for the buck for the data gathered is much greater than for dry grocery. Small gains in data on perishables—especially produce—can give stores quantum leaps in sales." That kind of return on investment is drawing firms to category management faster than the raging bull market attracted investors to Wall Street.

THE RAPID GROWTH OF CATEGORY MANAGEMENT IN SUPERMARKETS

FMI estimates that two-thirds of supermarket companies have implemented category management plans for produce. FMI's *Industry Speaks* study found that 57.9 percent of companies with average annual sales of less than $10 million had or were in the process of implementing category management plans. At the top end of the scale, 75 percent of the companies with annual sales of more than $1 billion already had category management plans. Tables 1 to 4 show some of the highlights from the FMI study.

Table 1 Level of Supermarkets' Category Management Implementation by Annual Sales

Category Management Practice	Total	ANNUAL SALES				
		Under $10 Million	$10–$50 Million	$51–$250 Million	$251 Million– $1 Billion	More Than $1 Billion
Total number of companies that have begun to implement category management	26	4	6	9	5	2
% of companies that have divided produce offerings into formal categories	73.1	50.0	83.3	77.8	80.0	50.0
% of companies that have developed formal category business plans with defined goals	19.2	—	16.7	22.2	20.0	50.0

Source: Food Marketing Institute, *Food Marketing Industry Speaks,* 1998.

The material in this case is adapted by the authors from Terry Hennessy, "Getting to the Core," *Progressive Grocer* (May 1999), pp. 105–116. Reprinted by permission of Bill Communications, Inc.; permission conveyed through Copyright Clearance Center, Inc.

Table 2 Level of Supermarkets' Category Management Implementation by Number of Stores

Category Management Practice	Total	NUMBER OF STORES			
		1	2–10	11–49	50+
Total number of companies that have begun to implement category management	26	4	11	4	7
% of companies that have divided produce offerings into formal categories	73.1	75.0	72.7	75.0	71.4
% of companies that have developed formal category business plans with defined goals	19.2	—	9.1	25.0	42.9

Source: Food Marketing Institute, *Food Marketing Industry Speaks,* 1998.

Table 3 Supermarkets' Category Management in Produce Operations by Annual Sales

Category Management Practice	Total	ANNUAL SALES				
		Under $10 Million	$10–$50 Million	$51–$250 Million	$251 Million–$1 Billion	More Than $1 Billion
Total companies	66	19	18	17	8	4
% of companies that had begun to use category management as of the time of the FMI study	39.4	21.1	33.3	52.9	62.5	50.0
% of companies that had not begun to use category management as of the time of the FMI study but planned to do so during the following year	27.3	36.8	16.7	35.3	12.5	25.0
% of companies that had no plans to use category management as of the time of the FMI study	33.3	42.1	50.0	11.8	25.0	25.0

Source: Food Marketing Institute, *Food Marketing Industry Speaks,* 1998.

Table 4 Supermarkets' Category Management in Produce Operations by Number of Stores

Category Management Practice	Total	NUMBER OF STORES			
		1	2–10	11–49	50+
Total companies	66	19	25	9	13
% of companies that had begun to use category management as of the time of the FMI study	39.4	21.1	44.0	44.5	53.8
% of companies that had not begun to use category management as of the time of the FMI study but planned to do so during the following year	27.3	21.1	32.0	22.2	30.8
% of companies that had no plans to use category management as of the time of the FMI study	33.3	57.8	24.0	33.3	15.4

Source: Food Marketing Institute, *Food Marketing Industry Speaks,* 1998.

As the owner of several hundred supermarkets and the primary supplier for 3,500 other stores, Supervalu, the Minneapolis-based wholesaler and retailer, has completed the training of category managers and key retailers in hundreds of stores in its northern and central regions. "The first step was rolling out the training program," says Judy Farniok, Supervalu's manager of category management development. "We worked intensively with a limited group on some pilot projects, with the idea that as they complete the tests, we would expand to more retailers."

THE CHALLENGES OF CATEGORY MANAGEMENT

One of the category management hurdles Roundy's faces in Wisconsin is getting the stores it supplies to adopt compatible data collection systems. "A lot of the independents have different front-end systems," says Frank Gillespie, Roundy's corporate director of produce. "We are trying to get them all compatible, but it will take a couple of years."

Meanwhile, Roundy's is using PLU (price look-up) codes to help reduce shrinkage by almost 1 percent of sales, and it is concentrating on developing individual perishable category information and strategies. "We saved 1 percent of our gross from better shrink control," says Gillespie. "People at the front checkout stands don't know one apple from another, so the PLU codes help them record the right price and item."

Apples are also on the leading edge of another Roundy's experiment. "We have 15 stores working with the Washington Apple Commission on a pilot program that reviews apple category sales, feeds the information to the commission, and compares their sales to others in the region and nationally," Gillespie says. "We are beginning to get some pretty good feedback and are able to measure things such as square footage display of the category versus profit. It's going exceptionally well in the apple category." The next step for Roundy's is to begin studying the value-added categories in produce, such as the pre-packaged salads in the 24-foot upright displays, notes Gillespie.

The Roundy's and Supervalu experiences illustrate the innovations companies are developing to capitalize on category management strategies. "Category management is not meant to be applied in a vacuum," says Meredith Eriksen, FMI's manager of education. "Category management for produce is never going to be as clean and neat and tidy as the center store, with all its

brands. But applied to perishables, it can make a huge difference in the bottom line."

One of the most dramatic developments in recent years is the development of accurate market-level data for meat. "This is the first time we have market-level data for fresh meat to use in category management analysis and to make decisions," says Kevin Yost, executive director of channel marketing for the National Cattlemen's Beef Association (NCBA), Chicago.

Last year, the NCBA went into partnership with Information Resources Inc. (IRI) to help three retailers in each of seven metro areas adopt Uniform Retail Meat Identity Standards (URMIS). The retail stores have adopted the standards, and IRI has been collecting the standardized data and converting it into the first market-level fresh meat reports. Yost remarks: "People who have been in the business for 30 years are amazed by the data."

Major obstacles remain. Generic 4-digit PLU codes on random-weight items may help cashiers, but they don't provide the kind of detailed information needed for sophisticated category management plans, says John Clutts, director of ECR (Efficient Consumer Response) for Giant Food, based in Washington, D.C., and co-chair of the ECR operating committee. There is precious little information available to compare perishable categories locally, regionally, and nationally—though data bases are slowly growing. "We still have a huge uphill struggle," says Clutts. "One of the big obstacles is the availability of data," states FMI's Eriksen. "We are still trying to standardize codes, we are struggling to determine the best way to use information gathered through loyalty cards, and there is not a vast pool of syndicated data."

WORKING AROUND THE OBSTACLES

Faced with these hurdles, companies are forced to leapfrog over some data gaps and customize their approaches to get the full value from perishables category management. "We are seeing more of a perishables approach, rather than a grocery model," says Bruce Axtman, a category management consultant with Willard Bishop Consulting. "There is a much greater degree of focus on shrink and supply chain for perishables."

Customized approaches can pay off in a big way, according to Axtman, with companies seeing gains of up to 15 percent in perishable sales. But category management for perishables isn't some simple one-step-works-for-all program, Axtman notes: "There are different levels of involvement in category management. Level one is understanding definitions and strategies, and beginning to collect data. Level two is to begin looking at the data to find out what is working and to develop strategies. This is where companies can begin to see some big returns—as much as a 5 to 15 percent increase in sales."

"Then there is the third level, in which companies begin to understand the supply chain and deal with shrink. At this level, they move from strategic to operational planning; they look at store clusters and individual stores, and they use comparison data to help find out why one store—or set of stores—is performing worse than others," says Axtman. "The newcomers are in level one; we are starting to see a fair number of people in level two and the leaders are in level three."

Fortunately, a bevy of perishables industry organizations have come to the aid of grocery companies that want to develop effective category management plans. In just the past year, the International Dairy, Deli, Bakery Association (IDDBA) spent $400,000 to set up a turn-key category management computer program for retailers. "One of the things we found out early about category management plans was that people usually asked 'How do we get there?'" says Carol Christison, IDDBA executive director. "Our mission was to make the program affordable and get it out there to help get retailers up to speed quickly."

The IDDBA's *Category Planning Workbook for the Supermarket Deli & Bakery* uses a common Excel database software program and costs $95 for members and $545 for nonmembers. The *Workbook* is broken into three sections: Data Sources, Category Planning, and a Sample Category Plan. "We haven't asked retailers about the results of using the workbook, yet, but it will help them identify the items that fill those black holes of emotional needs that drive shoppers to buy," says Christison.

Three other large associations—the Produce Marketing Association, Food Marketing Institute, and National Cattlemen's Beef Association—combined forces to sponsor the Third Annual Category Management for Perishables Conference in Chicago on August 19–20, 1999. "We've changed our format to be more responsive," says FMI's Lightburn. "It's no longer an introductory course, Category Management 101; we've taken it to a higher level." FMI said between 175 and 200 people attended the seminar, about the same number as in 1998. The seminar, with both presentations and workshops, explored strategy development, performance measurement, data challenges, promotion planning and evaluation, and shrinkage management.

"One of the problems has been that companies believe category management plans give them a competitive advantage, so they are reluctant to come to industry conferences and share information," says Terry Humfeld, Produce Marketing Association vice-president.

The Washington Apple Commission is working with several companies, such as Roundy's, to track sales patterns and identify category trends. In addition, the Apple Commission released a *Washington Apple Best Practices Recommendations* manual in autumn 1998, based on data gathered over the previous 5 years. "We looked at the things we learned while developing our data base and identified those practices that are yielding the best results," says Jean Ashby, category management director for the Apple Commission, based in Wenatchee, Washington. "This manual is for retailers who don't have the ability to develop their own category management plan for apples. They still have to understand the strategic part of the plan to implement the tactical recommendations."

The New York Apple Commission is developing data on taste preferences for different varieties of apples. "We are finding that the customers don't care where the apples come from, or whether they are bright red, or pink or yellow," says Jim Allen, retail promotions director of the New York Apple Association, based in Fischers, New York. "They care about the taste and the condition of the apple—especially whether it was bruised or discolored."

One of the emerging sources of information in the data-scarce random weight categories is global research company A.C. Nielsen. Since 1997, Nielsen has been gathering information from 52,000 households. "We gave our panelists barcoded booklets so that when they buy a product without a UPC code, such as an apple, they simply scan the barcode for that particular apple in the booklet," says Meredith Spector, Nielsen's vice-president of marketing for Homescan Core Services. Spector says the households were going to begin gathering information on home-meal replacement in spring 1999, detailing if the food came from restaurants, pizza parlors, grocery stores, or convenience markets. The information gathered by Nielsen is being sold to 15 to 20 manufacturers and retailers to help develop category management, product placement, and store placement.

WHAT'S AHEAD

In a world of thin margins, increasingly sophisticated competition, and marketing strategies backed by reams of reports, category management may seem like a natural step in the supermarket industry's evolution. But at least one voice is rising in warning. "Most of the focus of category management is on creating profit, not creating demand," says Glen Terbeek, a Hilton Head, South Carolina, consultant formerly with Andersen Consulting in Chicago. He has specialized in the food industry for 33 years.

"When you get into perishables, you have the opportunity to demonstrate merchandising skills that are an art form," says Terbeek. Perishables merchandising includes such things as assortment, display, attitude of workers, and creating an environment in the store. "Making a store look like a country market may be 180 degrees different than what it would look like if you use regular category management, which concentrates on the supply chain. Are we trying to apply scientific methods to an art form?"

One of the most visual art forms in produce sections is displays of colorful, individual apples, stacked high and shiny. Ashby, of the Washington Apple Commission, admits that using category management principles could spell the demise of apple—or other perishables—displays if they are not profitable enough. "If it is a beautiful display, but not yielding dollars, the store will have to use another display." But she doesn't think that's likely: "They won't let that happen. They know the importance of creating a big splash." The payoff of category management is worth it: "We are finally getting over the data hurdles. We are getting to the core of category management and we are going to reap the benefits."

Questions

1. How can category management be incorporated into a retailer's overall merchandising philosophy?

2. What are the pros and cons of using category management?

3. Comment on the data in Tables 1 to 4.

4. What special impediments do smaller retailers face in deploying category management? How would you overcome these obstacles?

5. Does the use of category management make inventory accounting more or less difficult or have no effect? Explain your answer.

6. How is category management related to these concepts: variable pricing, price lining, and automatic markdown plan?

7. Present and describe a flowchart showing the steps a retailer should follow in implementing category management.

PART SEVEN

COMMUNICATING WITH THE CUSTOMER

In Part Seven, the elements involved in a retailer's communicating with its customers are discussed. First, the role of a retail image and how it is developed and maintained are covered. Various aspects of a promotional strategy are then detailed.

Chapter 18 discusses the importance of communications for a retailer. The significance of image in the communications effort and the components of a retailer's image are reviewed. Creating an image depends heavily on a firm's atmosphere—which is comprised of all of its physical characteristics, such as the store exterior, the general interior, layouts, and displays. This applies to both store and nonstore retailers. Ways of encouraging customers to spend more time shopping and the value of community relations are also described.

Chapter 19 focuses on promotional strategy, specifically how a retailer can inform, persuade, and remind its target market about its strategic mix. The first part of the chapter deals with the four basic types of retail promotion: advertising, public relations, personal selling, and sales promotion. The second part describes the steps in a promotional strategy: objectives, budget, mix of forms, implementation of mix, and review and revision of the plan.

CHAPTER 18

Establishing and Maintaining a Retail Image

CHAPTER OBJECTIVES

1. To show the importance of communicating with customers and examine the concept of retail image
2. To describe how a retail store image is related to the atmosphere it creates via its exterior, general interior, layout, and displays, and to look at the special case of nonstore atmospherics
3. To discuss ways of encouraging customers to spend more time shopping
4. To consider the impact of community relations on a retailer's image

The husband-and-wife team of Linda and Steve Anderson purchased King's Drugs, a 40-year-old pharmacy on midtown Atlanta's Peachtree Street, in 1989. Although approximately 2,000 independent pharmacies go out of business each year, King's is flourishing.

Since acquiring King's Drugs, the Andersons have cross-marketed cosmetics and gifts, added more hard-to-find products, and increased the displays of impulse items. In an area of the store that is called "Favorite Things," products such as bath salts are sold alongside candles and needlepoint computer covers. These items are nicely arranged on dry sinks, dressers, and hand-painted tables—which can also be bought. As Pat Abernathy, the artist responsible for the store's visual merchandising, says: "Most people go to a drugstore on a mission. We made the front of the store so aesthetically pleasing that it compels the 'mission' shopper to stop and look around." As a result, cosmetics products, which had been neglected until the Andersons purchased the store, now account for 20 percent of total sales.

Customer service at King's is quite special for a drugstore. The Andersons know the names of their loyal customers and greet them personally. The cosmetics salespeople notify regular customers of special offers. Shoppers who are looking to find particular products are taken directly to the items, instead of being told where to find the merchandise.[1]

OVERVIEW

There are many trade associations (www. visualstore.com/ events/associations. html) in the retail image arena. Visit a few.

A retailer needs a superior communications strategy to properly position itself in customers' minds, as well as to nurture their shopping behavior. The firm must present information about itself to the target market, and this information must be interpreted by the target market in the manner intended. Once customers are attracted, it is then imperative for the retailer to create a proper shopping mood for them. A variety of physical and symbolic cues can be used to do this. As we mentioned in Chapter 1, it is imperative to maximize the customer's total retail experience:

Please Note: Web site addresses are constantly changing. The links in this chapter are current as of the publication of this book.

From Nike's pervasive swoosh and the towering Golden Arches of McDonald's to the sultry retail environs of Victoria's Secret, firms are shedding the hobgoblin of mediocrity, reinventing themselves, and creating a total retail experience in which to immerse consumers. The stars of retailing have built unique shopping experiences through a combination of entertainment, smart merchandising, store brands, decor, and old-fashioned customer service.[2]

When you're building a brand [retail image], what exactly is it that you are building? Let's start with what it is not. It is not a person, not even the founder of the company. Founders die. It is not the firm. Companies are bought and sold. It is not the store. They burn down. It is not the merchandise within the store's walls. Goods become outdated. If it's not these things, what is it? I believe a brand [retail image] is a promise conveyed to customers by everything they observe: the retailer's name and logo, advertising, the way they are treated by salespeople, signs, the storefront, billing statements, displays, the shopping environment, catalogs, news articles, the Web, and other shoppers. This promise encompasses all the thoughts, feelings, associations, and expectations a person experiences when exposed to it. An image is either strengthened or weakened by every point of customer contact.[3]

This chapter describes how to establish and maintain a retail image. Retail atmosphere, storefronts, store layouts, and displays are examined, as they relate to communicating with customers. We also explore the challenge of how to encourage customers to spend more time shopping and the role of community relations. Chapter 19 focuses on the common promotional tools available to retailers in reaching customers: advertising, public relations, personal selling, and sales promotion.

Please note that although our discussion in this chapter looks more at store-based retailers, the overall principles also apply to nonstore retailers. For a mail-order firm, the cover of each catalog is its storefront, and the interior layouts and displays are the pages devoted to product categories and the individual items and brands within them. For a Web retailer, the home page is its storefront, and the interior store layouts and displays are represented by the individual links within the site.

THE SIGNIFICANCE OF RETAIL IMAGE

Display & Design Ideas (www.ddimagazine.com) is a leading trade magazine, with "News" stories at its Web site.

As defined in Chapter 3, *image* refers to how a retailer is perceived by customers and others; and *positioning* refers to a firm's devising its strategy in a way that projects an image with regard to its retail category and its competitors, and that elicits consumer responses to this image. To succeed, a firm must communicate a distinctive, clear, and consistent image. Once its image is established in consumers' minds, a retailer is placed in a niche relative to competitors. It is rather difficult to break out of that niche if it is firmly implanted in people's minds. It is also challenging to convey a consistent image globally, given the different backgrounds and expectations of consumers around the world.[4]

Components of a Retail Image

Numerous factors contribute to a retailer's image, and it is the totality of these factors that forms an overall image:

1. Characteristics of the target market.

2. Retail positioning and reputation of the firm.

3. Customer service.

4. Store location and geographic coverage.

5. Merchandise assortment, fashionability, and quality.

6. Price levels.

7. Attributes of physical facilities (atmosphere).

8. Shopping experiences.

9. Community service.

10. Mass advertising and public relations.

11. Type and extent of personal selling.

12. Sales promotion.

Items 1 to 6 and their relation to retail image were examined in earlier chapters of this book. Items 7 to 12 are the focal points for our discussion of communications issues in Chapters 18 and 19. Figure 18.1 shows all the elements of a retail image (incorporating Items 1 through 12).

The Dynamics of Creating and Maintaining a Retail Image

Creating and maintaining a retail image is a complex, multistep, ongoing process that applies market segmentation and distinguishes a firm from competitors. It encompasses far more than store "atmosphere," which is discussed shortly. Furthermore, with so many consumers having little time for shopping and others having less interest in it, retailers must work hard to *entertain* shoppers:

> The way a store looks goes beyond its fixturing, lighting, carpeting, and decor treatments. It is the result of a vision from the men and women charged with translating the message behind the merchandise or the brand into a format that will draw the customer. That's not easy in today's overstored, competitive marketplace. Architects,

Figure 18.1
The Elements of a
Retail Image

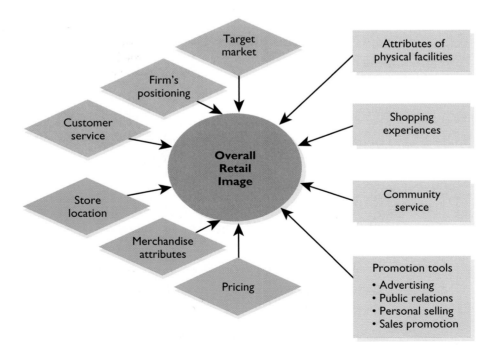

store planners, and designers are under great pressure to create winning environments that not only sell merchandise but also attract and entertain people. Such designs take the retail experience beyond buying and selling transactions—evoking a mood, an image, or an attitude to keep busy shoppers coming back for more.[5]

As the president of The Retail Group, a design firm, says: "A shopper should be able to determine the following about a store *in three seconds:* its name, its line of trade, its claim to fame, its price position, and its personality. All that must be conveyed quickly because people are generally unwilling to buy things from retailers. Those who need what you are selling will find you. Thus, everyone else must be enticed—in very short order—to enter your store. The glut of pitches out there only ups the ante. Without a distinct image, you don't have a chance of being seen or heard through all the clutter that is retailing."[6]

Let's look at three examples. The Gap's Old Navy is one of retailing's rising stars: " 'In the theatre of life, you, too, will have your moment.' That's written on the floor of Old Navy's new Manhattan flagship. In a way the chain probably never intended, it couldn't be more appropriate—because this is Old Navy's moment." It may be hard to believe, but this seemingly well-entrenched chain was only founded in 1994! So, how did Old Navy come so far, so fast? "From its zany ads to its right-on, bargain fashions, the chain is making all the right moves. For instance, its Manhattan store is dwarfed in size when compared to the huge Macy's across the street. But it stands on its own when it comes to fun and shopping appeal. From mannequins that move to rocket ship-styled listening stations, the store is a delight. And a textbook example of total branding. The format—an industrial-looking design tempered with retro graphics and lots of fun, nostalgic props—has the same tongue-in-cheek appeal as Old Navy ads. Its egalitarian hip image cuts across all demographics. So do its fashions. Signs have just the right amount of fashion attitude. 'Dare to flare' proclaims a sign for girls' jeans. Few retailers do mannequins better than that. Mannequins bob up and down and run in place in the Manhattan store. There are also revolving displays." By 2004, Old Navy's annual sales may even exceed those of Gap, babyGap, and GapKids combined.[7]

Would you name a store Chapter 11? An Atlanta-based bookstore chain has: "Some would consider it a temptation of fate to name a business after a bankruptcy term, but Barbara Babbit Kaufman, founder of Chapter 11 Books, has never been superstitious: 'I wanted a name that would draw people's attention and make them curious. I also wanted something that would get across the idea that we sell at bargain prices. Chapter 11 fit the bill.' Her disregard for omens has been rewarded. The 13-store chain has found a way to thrive in a land ruled by giants." There are several reasons for the firm's success. "We fulfill a niche that large bookstores would find impossible to fill by virtue of their superstore format," Babbit Kaufman says. "When the customer comes into the store, she can turn her head from side to side and see the entire store. Plus, there's clear signage over everything, so every section is easy to find." There is also a help desk near the entrance. Chapter 11 communicates its discount image through the slogan, "Prices so low, you'd think we were going bankrupt." Its strategy is also based more on in-store events than on ads. "We spend less on advertising in one year than our Atlanta neighbor Wolf Camera spends every week," Babbit Kaufman boasts. "But our brand recognition in the area we serve is nearly 100 percent, anyway." When the firm held a launch party for J.K. Rowling's novel *Harry Potter and the Prisoner of Azkaban,* it not only attracted coverage by the local media, but *Time* magazine and CNN, as well.[8]

In contrast with Chapter 11 Books' conscious effort to exploit the term "Chapter 11," Montgomery Ward & Co. is working to overcome the stigma of having recently emerged from bankruptcy protection: "The public remaking of Wards began August 20, 1999, as remodeled stores celebrated grand openings. Using the slogan 'Same Space, New Face,' Wards is encouraging consumers to come see the changes for themselves." The renovated Wards store in San Diego's Mission Valley Center shopping center illustrates how the firm is

Take a look at the new Wards (www. wards.com). Click on "Wards Today" and then "Our New Stores."

Powering J.C. Penney's Selling Floor

Cathy Mills, J.C. Penney's vice-president and director of updated store environment, says: "Right now, our store environment doesn't intrinsically communicate with consumers most effectively. We want our environments to convey fashionability and convenience of shopping."

In her position, Mills is responsible for recasting Penney's "stale selling floors" into an updated and compelling shopping experience. Part of this strategy involves designing in-store fashion shops that feature power brands such as Liz Claiborne's Crazy Horse and Evan-Picone. Under Penney's "street-of-shops" layout, these display areas feature high-technology lighting, modern displays, and more rational product groupings. Mills has brought together a team of employees with visual layout, merchandising, financial, and planning backgrounds to work on this project.

Mills began her career with J.C. Penney in 1972 as a personnel associate. She rose through the ranks in the store operations and communications areas. In her previous position, Mills was vice-president of merchandising of women's accessories and beauty. She moved into her present position in 1997, and now reports directly to Penney's senior vice-president and director of stores.

Source: Rusty Williamson, "Penney's Sets Prototypes for Power Brands," *Women's Wear Daily* (May 4, 1999), p. 15.

---

converting its older units. That two-story store opened in 1960 and was the first Wards unit in San Diego. Today, "A wide race track has improved customer mobility, lower shelving has improved sightlines, and better lighting has made the store brighter. Peachwood fixtures and displays have been used to create a unified look that presents the feel of a department store within a discount store environment." Fashion is now the main emphasis, with brand names throughout, including Lee jeans and private brands. The firm's repositioning is being marketed as an intelligent choice for busy shoppers: "You can't shop smarter than Wards." In locales with remodeled stores, Wards has sent a promotional video to all households in the trading area. It has also mailed a 64-page fashion-only brochure to consumers, and its Web site offers virtual tours of the new stores. Finally, "Wards' image change also involves dropping the Montgomery from the name to limit confusion between old stores and new."[9]

Of particular concern to chain retailers, franchisors, and global retailers is maintaining a consistent image among all branches. Yet, despite the best planning, a number of factors may vary widely among branch stores and affect an image. They include management and employee performance, consumer profiles, competitors, the convenience in reaching stores, parking, safety, the ease of finding merchandise, and the qualities of the surrounding area. Sometimes, retailers with good images receive negative publicity. This must be countered in order for them to maintain their desired standing with the public.

ATMOSPHERE

A retailer's image depends heavily on the atmosphere it establishes. For a store-based retailer, **atmosphere** (also known as **atmospherics**) refers to the store's physical characteristics that are used to develop an image and draw customers. For a nonstore-based firm, the physical characteristics of such retailing tools as catalogs, vending machines, and Web sites affect its image. A retailer's sights, sounds, smells, and other physical attributes contribute to the image projected to consumers. "Atmosphere" is the psychological feeling a customer gets when visiting a retailer (the personality of a store, catalog, vending machine, or Web site), whereas a "retail image" is a much broader and all-encompassing term relative to the communication tools a retailer uses to position itself.

Many people form impressions of a retailer before entering its facilities (due to the store location, storefront, and other factors) or just after entering (due to merchandise displays, the width of aisles, and other things). These people often judge a retailer prior to closely examining merchandise and prices. Atmosphere may thus influence people's shopping enjoyment, their time spent browsing and examining a firm's offerings, their willingness to converse with personnel and to use facilities such as dressing rooms, their tendency to spend more money than originally planned, and their likelihood of future patronage.

When a retailer takes a proactive, integrated approach to atmospherics so as to create a certain "look," properly display products, stimulate shopping behavior, and enhance the physical environment, it engages in **visual merchandising.** According to Cahill, an interior design firm, "Visual merchandising is more than the enhancement of retail space for the purpose of increasing sales. With the creative use of lighting, props, and customized displays, the retail selling space can be transformed into space which informs, stimulates the senses, entertains, and ultimately reinforces the shopper's relationship with the product. Visual merchandising today is as much about communicating the brand experience as it is about selling the product."[10] It includes everything from store display windows to the width of aisles to the materials used for fixtures to merchandise presentation. See Figure 18.2.

The National Association of Visual Merchandisers (www.visualmerch.com) profiles the real-world experiences of its members through the "Quarterly Info" section of its site.

Figure 18.2
Visual Merchandising Means Business

Claire's Accessories stores use visual merchandising to target young people ages 9 to 20, with the core customer being about 14 years of age. The chain has 1,600 locations throughout North America, the Caribbean, Japan, Europe, and Great Britain. The typical North American store is about 960 square feet in size, is mall-based, and has more than 10,000 SKUs. The units operating in Great Britain and Japan average 570 square feet in size. All of the stores sell compelling fashion accessories in a colorful environment. Claire's Accessories recently introduced a new prototype store, creating a "cool," "hip," and fun place for teens to shop. On a regular basis, the prototype is being rolled out to more units.
Reprinted by permission of Claire's Stores.

Figure 18.3
The Elements of
Atmosphere

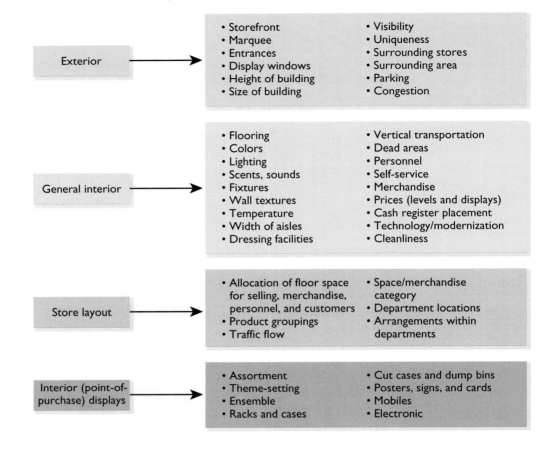

A Store-Based Retailing Perspective

Check out the colorful
"Architectural
Examples" and
"Merchandising
Design" of Visual Arts
(members.aol.com/
visualarts/main.htm). Store atmosphere (atmospherics) can be divided into these key elements: exterior, general interior, store layout, and displays. Figure 18.3 contains a detailed breakdown of them.

Exterior A store's exterior characteristics have a powerful impact on its image and should be planned accordingly.

A **storefront** is the total physical exterior of the store itself. It includes the marquee, entrances, windows, lighting, and construction materials. With its storefront, a retailer can present a conservative, trendy, lavish, discount, or other image to the consumer. A firm should not underestimate the significance of the storefront as a component of image, especially for new customers. When passing through an unfamiliar business district or shopping center, consumers often judge a store by its exterior. Besides the storefront itself, atmosphere can be enhanced by trees, fountains, and benches in front of the store. These intensify consumer feelings about shopping and about the store by establishing a relaxed environment.

There are various alternatives to consider in planning a basic storefront. Here are a few of them:

- Modular structure—a one-piece rectangle or square that may attach several stores.
- Prefabricated (prefab) structure—a store frame built in a factory and assembled at the store site.
- Prototype store—used by franchisors and chains. Because a consistent atmosphere is sought, uniform storefronts are built.

Figure 18.4
Using Marquees to
Generate Powerful
Retail Images

Reprinted by permission of
Track 'n Trail, Inc.

- Recessed storefront—lures people by being recessed from the level of other stores. In this case, the store is one of many at its locale. Customers must walk in a number of feet to examine the storefront.
- Unique building design—a round structure, for example.

A **marquee** is a sign used to display the store's name. It can be painted or a neon light, printed or script, and alone or mixed with a slogan (trademark) and other information. To be effective, the marquee should stand out and attract attention, as Track 'n Trail does with its various chains. See Figure 18.4. Image is influenced because a marquee can be gaudy and flashy or subdued and subtle. The world's most widely known marquee is McDonald's golden arch, which some communities consider overpowering.

Store entrances require three major decisions. First, the number of entrances is determined. Many small stores have only one entrance. Department stores may have four to eight or more entrances. A store hoping to draw vehicular and pedestrian traffic may need at least two entrances (one to lure pedestrians, another near the parking lot). Because front and back entrances serve different purposes, they should be designed separately. A factor that may limit the number of entrances is potential pilferage.

Second, the type of entrance(s) is chosen. The doorway can be revolving; electric, self-opening; regular, push-pull; or climate-controlled. The latter is an open entrance with a curtain of warm or cold air, set at the same temperature as inside the store. This entry makes a store inviting, reduces pedestrian traffic congestion, and lets customers see inside the store. Entrance flooring can be cement, tile, or carpeting. Lighting can be traditional or fluorescent, white or colors, and/or flashing or constant. Look at how impressive Sephora's entrances are, as depicted in Figure 18.5.

Third, the walkways are considered. A wide, lavish walkway creates a different atmosphere and mood than a narrow, constrained one. In the construction of the storefront, ample room must be provided for the walkway. Large window displays may be attractive, but customers would not be pleased if there is insufficient space for a comfortable entry into the store.

Figure 18.5
How a Store
Entrance Can
Generate Shopper
Interest

Sephora store entrances
are visually appealing
and inviting.
Reprinted by permission of
PricewaterhouseCoopers
LLP.

Display windows have two main purposes: to identify the store and its offerings, and to induce people to enter. See Figure 18.6. By showing a representative merchandise offering, a store can create an overall mood. By showing fashion or seasonal goods, it can show it is contemporary. By showing sale items, a store can lure price-conscious consumers. By showing eye-catching displays that have little to do with its merchandise offering, a store can attract

Figure 18.6
Eye-Catching Window
Displays from Celio
Sport

The French-based Celio
Sport chain uses its
exterior store displays
to portray its image and
identify its offerings.
Reprinted by permission of
PricewaterhouseCoopers
LLP.

pedestrians' attention. By showing public service messages (e.g., a window display for the Jerry Lewis Telethon), the store can indicate its concern for the community.

Considerable planning is needed to develop good display windows, which leads many retailers to hire outside specialists. Decisions include the number, size, shape, color, and themes of display windows—and the frequency of changes per year. Retailers in shopping malls may not use display windows for the side of the building facing the parking lot; there are solid building exteriors. They feel vehicular patrons are not lured by expensive outside windows; but they do invest in displays for storefronts inside the malls.

Exterior building height can be disguised or nondisguised. Disguised building height occurs if part of a store or shopping center is beneath ground level. The building is then not intimidating to people who dislike a large structure. Nondisguised building height occurs if the entire store or center can be seen by pedestrians (all floors at ground level or higher). Since overall building size cannot really be disguised, customers should be researched to see how people feel about different-sized facilities. An intimate image cannot be fostered with a block-long building. Nor can a department store image be linked to a small site.

Few firms can succeed without good visibility. This means pedestrian and/or vehicular traffic clearly see storefronts or marquees. A store located behind a bus stop has poor visibility for vehicular traffic and pedestrians across the street. Many firms near highways use billboards since drivers pass by quickly.

In every case, the goal is to have the store or center appear unique and catch the shopper's eye. A distinctive store design, an elaborate marquee, recessed open-air entrances, decorative windows, and unusual building height and size are one set of storefront features that could attract consumers by their uniqueness. In the process, a retail image is reinforced. Nonetheless, uniqueness may not be without its shortcomings. An example is the multilevel "shopping-center-in-the-round." Because this center (which often occupies a square city block) is round, parking is provided on each floor level to make the walking distances very short. However, a rectangular center would provide greater floor space on a lot of the same size, convenient on-floor parking may minimize shopping on other floors, added entrances increase chances for pilferage, many people dislike circular driving, and architectural costs are higher.

As a retailer plans its exterior, surrounding stores and the surrounding area should both be studied. Surrounding stores present image cues due to their price range, level of service, and so on. The surrounding area includes the demographics and life-styles of those who live nearby. An overall area image rubs off on the individual firm because people tend to have a general perception of a shopping center or a business district. An unfavorable atmosphere would exist if vandalism and crime are high, people living near the store are not in the target market, and the area is rundown.

Parking facilities can add to or detract from store atmosphere. Plentiful, free, nearby parking creates a more positive image than scarce, costly, distant parking. Some potential shoppers may never enter a store if they drive around looking for parking and, not finding it, go elsewhere or return home. Other customers may run in and out of a store to finish shopping before parking meters expire.

Allied with the potential parking problem is that of congestion. Store atmosphere is diminished if the parking lot, sidewalks, and/or entrances are jammed. Consumers who feel crushed in the crowd generally spend less time shopping and are in poorer moods than those who feel comfortable.

Trauth Associates (www.trauth.com/interior/portfolio.htm) has designed interiors for a variety of retailers. Several are profiled here.

General Interior Once customers are inside a store, there are numerous elements that affect their perceptions. At Sephora, the French cosmetics chain that is rapidly expanding in the United States, the stores "are chicly decorated, easy-to-navigate bazaars for the sale of scores of brands of makeup and fragrance. Music is low, lighting is flattering, and merchandise, much of which is helpfully arranged by category rather than brand, is out for the touching and taking. Sales clerks leave you alone unless you need them; and if you'd prefer to avoid the staff,

Figure 18.7
Kay Jewelers:
Maximizing the Store
Interior

At the more than 550
Kay Jewelers shops
around the United
States, the store interior
plays a prominent role
in creating a total retail
experience. From the
carpeted floors to the
high-gloss fixtures, Kay
sets the proper tone for
its shoppers.
Reprinted by permission of
Sterling Jewelers, Inc.

touch-activated video monitors can guide you through product selection. Sephora's ambition is to create an experience that is exciting—visually, sensually, spiritually, intellectually."[11]

The general interior elements of store atmosphere were cited in Figure 18.3. They are illustrated in Figure 18.7 and described next.

Flooring can be cement, wood, linoleum, carpet, and so on. A plush, thick carpet creates one kind of atmosphere, and a concrete floor creates another. Because people use cues to form store perceptions, flooring materials and designs are important. Thus, 95 percent of department stores have carpeted floors, 90 percent of discount stores have vinyl floors, and 85 percent of home centers have concrete floors.[12]

Colors and lighting affect a store's image. Bright, vibrant colors contribute to a different atmosphere than light pastels or plain white walls. Lighting can be direct or indirect, white or colors, constant or flashing. For instance, a teen-oriented apparel boutique could use bright colors and vibrant, flashing lights to foster one atmosphere, and a maternity dress shop could use pastel colors and indirect lighting to form a different atmosphere. At the children's section of Nike Town, Honolulu, "the ceiling is fashioned as a solar system of sports balls, with the sun in the middle. The planets are represented by different balls with glowing stars on a low-voltage wire system with diffuse- and clear-bulb lamps strung around the planets. The filament glows through the clear lamps, creating a sparkle effect."[13]

Scents and sounds influence the customer's mood and contribute to the atmosphere. A restaurant can use food scents to increase people's appetites. A cosmetics store can use an array of perfume scents to attract shoppers. A pet store can let its animals' natural scents and sounds woo customers. A beauty salon can play soft music or rock, depending on its target market. Slow-tempo music in supermarkets encourages people to move more slowly.

Store fixtures can be planned on the basis of their utility, as well as their aesthetics. Pipes, plumbing, vents, beams, doors, storage rooms, and display racks and tables should be considered part of interior decorating. A store with an upscale image dresses up and disguises its fixtures. A store with a discount image might leave fixtures exposed because this is inexpensive and portrays the desired image.

Wall textures can enhance or diminish atmospherics. Prestigious stores often use fancy, raised wallpaper. Department stores are more apt to use flat wallpaper, while discount stores may have barren walls. Chic stores might have elaborate chandeliers, while discount stores have simple lighting fixtures.

The customer's mood is affected by the store's temperature and the way of achieving it. A person would be uncomfortable if there was insufficient heat in winter and coolness in summer. This can shorten a shopping trip. In another vein, the store image is influenced by the use of central air-conditioning, unit air-conditioning, fans, or open windows.

The width of the aisles has an impact on retail image. Wide, uncrowded aisles create a better atmosphere than narrow, crowded ones. People shop longer and spend more if they are not pushed and shoved while walking or looking at merchandise. In Boston, although the basement in Filene's department store has many bargains, overcrowding keeps some customers away.

Dressing facilities can be elaborate, plain, or nonexistent. A prestigious store has carpeted, private dressing rooms. An average-quality store has linoleum-floored, semiprivate rooms. A discount store has small stalls or no facilities at all. For some apparel shoppers, dressing facilities (and their maintenance) are a big factor in store selection. To them, atmosphere and the type of dressing facility are intertwined.

Multilevel stores must have some form of vertical transportation: elevator, escalator, and/or stairs. Larger stores may have a combination of all three. Traditionally, finer stores relied on operator-run elevators and discount stores on stairs. Today, escalators are quite popular and gaining stature. They provide shoppers with a quiet ride and a panoramic view of the store. Finer stores decorate around their escalators with fountains, shrubs, and trees. The placement and design of vertical transportation determine its contribution to atmosphere. Stairs remain important for some discount and smaller stores.

Light fixtures, wood or metal beams, doors, rest rooms, dressing rooms, and vertical transportation can cause **dead areas** for the retailer. These are awkward spaces where normal displays cannot be set up. Sometimes, it is not possible for such areas to be deployed profitably or attractively. However, retailers have learned to use dead areas better. Mirrors are attached to exit doors. Vending machines are located near rest rooms. Ads appear in dressing rooms. One creative use of a dead area involves the escalator. It lets shoppers view each floor, and sales of impulse items go up when placed at the escalator entrance or exit. Many firms plan escalators so customers must get off at each floor and pass by appealing displays.

The number, manner, and appearance of personnel reflect a store's atmosphere. Polite, well-groomed, knowledgeable personnel generate a positive atmosphere. Ill-mannered, poorly groomed, unknowing personnel engender a negative one. A store using self-service minimizes its personnel and creates a discount, impersonal image. A store cannot develop a prestigious image if it is set up for self-service.

The goods and services a retailer sells influence its image. Top-line items yield one kind of image, and bottom-line items yield another. The mood of the customer is affected accordingly.

Store prices contribute to image in two ways. (1) Price levels yield a perception of retail image in consumer minds. (2) The way prices are displayed is a vital part of atmosphere. Prestigious stores have few or no price displays and rely on discrete price tags. Discount stores accentuate price displays and show prices in large print. Cash register placement is also associated with the pricing strategy used. Prestigious stores place cash registers in inconspicuous areas such as behind posts or in employee rooms. Discounters locate cash registers centrally, with big signs pointing to them.

The technology used by the store and the modernization of its building and fixtures also affect image. A store with state-of-the-art technology impresses people with its operations efficiency and speed. One with slower, older technology may have impatient shoppers. A store with a modern building (new storefront and marquee) and new fixtures (lights, floors, and walls) fosters a more favorable atmosphere than one with older facilities. Renovations are easier, faster, and less costly than building or opening new stores. The main reasons for remodeling are improving store appearance, updating facilities, expansion, and the need to reallocate space. It results in strong sales and profit increases after completion.

Last, but certainly not least, there must be a plan for keeping the store clean. No matter how impressive a store's exterior and interior may be, an unkempt store will be perceived poorly by customers. As the chief executive of Casey's General Stores once remarked, "Even a great marketing plan won't keep a store spotless. We sell clean. People open the door and form an image right away."[14]

Store Layout   At this point, the specifics of store layout are planned and set up.

Allocation of Floor Space   Each store has a total square footage of floor space available and must allot it among selling, merchandise, personnel, and customers. Without that allocation, the firm would have no conception of the space available for displays, signs, rest rooms, and so on:

- *Selling space* is the area for displays of merchandise, interactions between salespeople and customers, demonstrations, and so on. Self-service retailers often apportion a large amount of space to selling.
- *Merchandise space* is the area where nondisplayed items are stocked. A traditional shoe store is an example of a retailer whose merchandise space takes up a large percentage of total space.
- *Personnel space* is often required for employees to change clothes and to take lunch and coffee breaks, and for rest rooms. Firms may try to minimize this space by insisting on off-the-job clothes changing and other tactics. Because floor space is so valuable, personnel space is usually controlled strictly. Yet, when planning personnel space, a retailer should consider employee morale and appearance.
- *Customer space* contributes toward the shopping mood. It can include a lounge, benches and/or chairs, dressing rooms, rest rooms, a restaurant, vertical transportation, a nursery, parking, and wide aisles. Discount retailers are more apt to skimp on these areas; those with upscale images provide their customers with ample amounts of space for many or all of these factors.

Bringing the Tiffany Aura to Paris

For the first time in nearly 50 years, Tiffany's again has a store in Paris. Tiffany's new store is just steps away from its previous Paris store, which opened in the mid-1800s and closed in the mid-1950s. The present location is in a building constructed in 1825 in an area considered as a prime location for an upscale fine jewelry store.

Tiffany's Paris store differs from its traditional format in several ways. While most of Tiffany's retail locations feature a slate-gray exterior and a huge steel door, the Paris store utilizes a restored building façade. The store interior, on the other hand, incorporates Tiffany's traditional cherry wood and steel design elements. Most Tiffany stores occupy only one floor (with notable exceptions being its stores in New York and Chicago), but the Paris location has three floors. Lastly, Tiffany stores generally carry a full range of jewelry, china, crystal, gifts, and stationery. In contrast, the Paris store is completely devoted to jewelry and hand-painted porcelain.

What factors do you think account for the different atmospherics at Tiffany Paris store?

Source: Wendy Hessen, "Tiffany's to Return to Paris in the Fall," *Women's Wear Daily* (February 8, 1999), p. 19.

Visual Effects markets planogram services (www.merchandise-solutions.com). Click on "Planogram System" and then on one of the listed products for a sample.

More firms now use planograms to assign space. **A planogram** is a visual (graphical) representation of the space for selling, merchandise, personnel, and customers—as well as for product categories. It also lays out their in-store placement. A planogram may be hand-drawn or computer-generated, as with Pro/space software from Intactix (www.intactix.com).

Classification of Store Offerings A store's offerings are next classified into product groupings. Four types of groupings and combinations of them can be employed:

- **Functional product groupings** categorize and display merchandise by common end use. A men's clothing store might carry these functional groups: shirts, ties, cuff links, and tie pins; shoes, shoe trees, and shoe polish; T-shirts, undershorts, and socks; suits; and sports jackets and slacks.
- **Purchase motivation product groupings** appeal to the consumer's urge to buy products and the amount of time he or she is willing to spend in shopping. A committed customer with time to shop will visit a store's upper floors; a disinterested person with less time to shop will look at displays on the first floor. A firm can capitalize on this by grouping items by purchase motivation. Look at the street level of a department store. The merchandise there includes impulse products and other rather quick purchases. The third floor has items encouraging and requiring more thoughtful shopping.
- **Market segment product groupings** place together various items appealing to a given target market. A clothing store divides products into juniors', misses', and ladies' apparel. A music store separates CDs into rock, jazz, classical, R&B, country and western, gospel, and other music sections. An art gallery places paintings into different price groups.
- **Storability product groupings** may be used for products needing special handling. A supermarket has freezer, refrigerator, and room-temperature sections. A florist keeps some products in a refrigerator and others at room temperature; so do a bakery and a fruit store.

Many retailers use a combination of product groupings and plan store layouts accordingly. In addition to the considerations just mentioned, provisions must be made for minimizing shoplifting and pilferage. This means positioning vulnerable product groupings away from corners and doors.

Determination of a Traffic-Flow Pattern The traffic-flow pattern of the store is then determined. There are two basic options: straight and curving. In a **straight (gridiron) traffic flow,** displays and aisles are placed in a rectangular or gridiron pattern, as shown in Figure 18.8. With a **curving (free-flowing) traffic flow,** displays and aisles are placed in a free-flowing pattern, as shown in Figure 18.9.

A straight traffic pattern is most often used by food retailers, discount stores, hardware stores, and other convenience-oriented retailers (such as stationery stores). It has several advantages:

- An efficient atmosphere is created.
- More floor space is devoted to product displays.
- People can shop quickly; regular customers especially desire clearly marked, distinct aisles and develop a routine way of walking through the store.
- Inventory control and security are simplified.
- Self-service is easy, thereby reducing labor costs.

The disadvantages of a gridiron pattern are the impersonal atmosphere, the more limited browsing by customers, and the rushed shopping behavior.

A curving traffic pattern is most often used by boutiques, department stores, apparel stores, and other shopping-oriented stores. For example, apparel retailer Wet Seal uses store interiors that are "intentionally chaotic to echo the atmosphere of a teenage girl's bedroom."[15] There are several benefits of this approach:

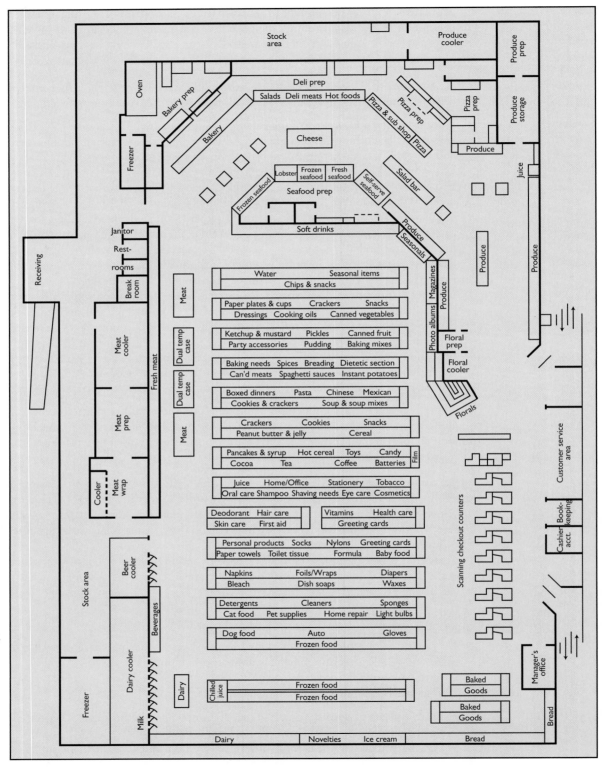

Figure 18.8
How a Supermarket Uses a Straight (Gridiron) Traffic Pattern

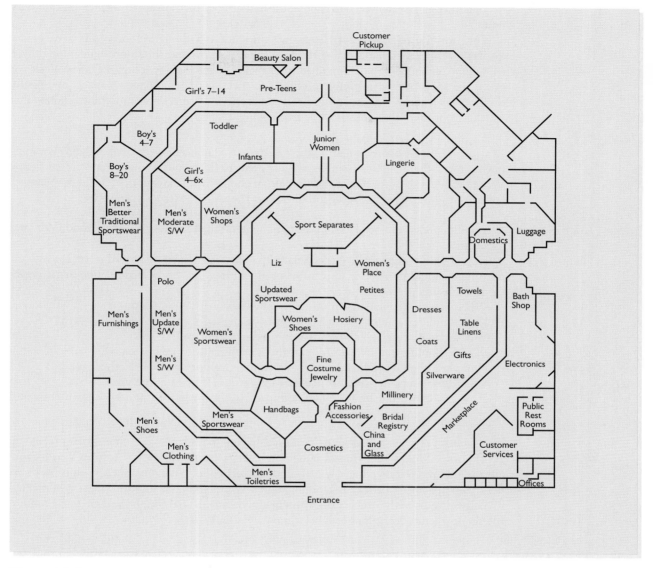

Figure 18.9
How a Department Store Uses a Curving (Free-Flowing) Traffic Pattern

- A friendly atmosphere is presented.
- Shoppers do not feel rushed and will browse around.
- People are encouraged to walk through the store in any direction or pattern they desire.
- Impulse or unplanned purchases are enhanced.

The disadvantages of a free-flowing pattern are the possible customer confusion, the wasted floor space, the difficulties in inventory control and security, the higher labor intensity, and the potential loitering. Also, free-flow displays often cost more than standardized gridiron displays.

Determination of Space Needs The space for each product category is now ascertained. Selling, as well as nonselling, space must be considered in any calculations. There are two major approaches from which to choose: the model stock method and the space-productivity ratio.

The **model stock approach** determines the amount of floor space necessary to carry and display a proper merchandise assortment. Apparel stores and shoe stores are among those using this method. The **sales-productivity ratio** assigns floor space on the basis of sales or profit per foot. Highly profitable product categories get large chunks of space; marginally profitable categories get less space. Food stores and bookstores are among the retailers that use this technique in planning floor space.

Mapping Out In-Store Locations Next, department locations are mapped out. For multilevel stores, that includes assigning departments to floors and laying out individual floors. What products should be on each floor? What should be the layout of each floor? A single-level store addresses only the second question. These are the issues to consider:

- What items should be placed in the basement, on the first floor, on the second floor, and so on?
- How should groupings be placed relative to doors, vertical transportation, and so on?
- Where should impulse or unplanned product categories be located relative to categories that consumers plan to buy?
- Where should convenience products be situated?
- How should associated product categories be aligned?
- Where should seasonal and off-season products be placed?
- Where should space-consuming categories such as furniture be located?
- How close should product displays and stored inventory be to each other?
- What shopping patterns do consumers follow once they enter the store?
- How can consumer lines be avoided near the cash register, and how can the overall appearance of store crowding be averted?

Saks Fifth Avenue knows men "don't like having to walk past perfume spritzers or go up 10 flights." Meijer food-based superstores have been testing a "store-within-a-store approach that cross-merchandises all products related to a category (such as all baby products from diapers to formula to clothing) and keeps them in one location. Instead of picking up baby formula in the grocery department and having to go through the store to get to toys, the shopper finds everything in one location."[16]

Arrangement of Individual Products The last step in store layout planning is arranging individual products within departments. Various criteria may be used. For instance, the most profitable items and brands could get favorable spots where consumer traffic is heavy; and products may be arranged by package size, price, color, brand, level of personal service required, and/or customer interest.

End-aisle display positions, eye-level positions, and checkout-counter positions are the most apt to increase sales for individual items. Continuity of locations is also important; shifts in store layout may decrease sales by confusing shoppers. The least desirable display position is often knee or ankle level, because consumers do not like to bend down.

Individual retailers need to do research to learn the sales impact of different product positions; and it must be kept in mind that manufacturer and retailer goals often differ. A manufacturer wants its brand's sales to be maximized and pushes for eye-level, full-shelf, end-aisle locations. On the other hand, a retailer wants to maximize total store sales and profit, regardless of brand.

Self-service retailers have special considerations. Besides using a gridiron layout to minimize customer confusion, aisles, displays, and merchandise must be clearly marked. A large selling space, with on-floor assortments, is necessary. Cash registers must be plentiful and accessible. It is hard to sell complex or expensive items through self-service.

Consider some of the tactics employed by supermarkets:

- Sixty percent begin with produce, most of the rest with flowers. "The idea is to tantalize the customer, to draw you in with eye-catching displays and a promise of bounty and freshness."
- "Cereal theory" means placing boxes on lower shelves, which are at eye level for children.
- People buy more soup if the varieties are not shelved in alphabetical order.
- Store brands do better when located to the left of manufacturer brands. "After seeing the name brand, the eye—habituated by a lifetime of reading—will automatically move left (as it would on a new page) to compare prices."
- Since "the best viewing angle is 15 degrees below the horizontal, the choicest display level has been measured at 51 to 53 inches off the floor."[17]

Interior (Point-of-Purchase) Displays Once store layout is fully detailed, a retailer devises its interior displays. Each **point-of-purchase (POP) display** provides shoppers with information, adds to store atmosphere, and serves a substantial promotional role:

> The significance of POP displays lies in the fact that many shopping decisions are made at the point of sale. According to Gallup, 62 percent of grocery shoppers and 56 percent of mass merchandise shoppers notice point-of-purchase displays in stores. What constitutes POP material? It runs the spectrum of visual intercepts, including in-store posters and banners, product display (including the ubiquitous end-aisle supermarket display), table tent cards in restaurants, shelf talkers that indicate a special item or a special price, and coupon dispensers (either take-one pads or the little blinking red light devices that automatically dispense coupons from a shelf).[18]

> All over the store, there are eye-catching promotional traps to snare impulse purchases. "We're the last 5 seconds of marketing before a purchase," says Rob Olejniczak, director of promotional services at Miller Brewing. But store aisles, ceilings, and cases have become so cluttered that some retailers have drawn up strict rules about what kind of signs they'll accept. Marketers negotiate with retailers months in advance about placing their in-store advertising. Big retail chains keep a schedule of which product displays go where, and when. Because many displays are accompanied by discounts, retailers try to prevent simultaneous promotions for rival products. Manufacturers often pay stores to display their ads, especially if they occupy prime retailing real-estate, like end-aisle displays.[19]

Several types of displays are described here. Most retailers use a combination of some or all of these displays. This is illustrated in Figure 18.10.

At this site (dir.
yahoo.com/Business_
and_Economy), retailers can choose from many display firms. Click on "Business to Business," "Retail Management," and then "Point of Purchase Displays."

The **assortment display** exhibits a wide range of merchandise. With an open assortment, the customer is encouraged to feel, look at, and/or try on a number of products. Greeting cards, books, magazines, and apparel are the kinds of products for which firms use open assortments. In recent years, food stores have expanded the use of open displays for fruit, vegetables, and candy; and department stores have opened up cosmetics and perfume displays. With a closed assortment, the customer is encouraged to look at a variety of merchandise but not touch it or try it on. Computer software and CDs are pre-packaged items a shopper is not allowed to open before buying. Jewelry is usually displayed in closed glass cases that must be unlocked by store employees.

The **theme-setting display** depicts a product offering in a thematic manner and portrays a specific atmosphere or mood. Firms often change their displays to reflect seasons or special

Figure 18.10
Displays at PS Plus Stores

Catherines Stores Corporation is a leading specialty retailer of large-size women's apparel, operating 432 stores in 40 states and the District of Columbia. The company operates four separate divisions, with distinct merchandising concepts and marketing strategies. The PS Plus Sizes division—shown here—operates 111 stores in major metropolitan areas such as Chicago, Washington, D.C., Houston, Dallas, Detroit, Seattle, and Los Angeles. It competes principally on the basis of merchandise selection and price. In Plus Sizes stores, there are open assortments, neatly arranged on rack displays. Some accessories are placed in closed displays. In keeping with the chain's image, there is no use of cut cases or bin displays.
Reprinted by permission.

events; some even have employees dress to fit the occasion. All or part of a store may be adapted to a theme, such as Washington's Birthday, Columbus Day, Valentine's Day, the Fourth of July, or another concept. Each special theme is enacted to attract attention and make shopping more enjoyable (and not a chore).

With the **ensemble display,** which has become very popular, a complete product bundle (ensemble) is presented rather than showing merchandise in separate categories (such as a shoe department, sock department, pants department, shirt department, sports jacket department). Thus, a mannequin is dressed in a matching combination of shoes, socks, pants, shirt, and sports jacket, and these items are readily available in one department or adjacent departments. Customers are pleased with the ease of a purchase and like being able to envision an entire product bundle.

The **rack display** has a primarily functional use: to neatly hang or present products. It is often used by apparel retailers, houseware retailers, and others. The major problems are possible cluttering and customers' returning items to the wrong place, thus disrupting the proper product sequence. Current technology allows retailers to use sliding, disconnecting, contracting/expanding, lightweight, attractive rack displays. A **case display** exhibits heavier, bulkier items than racks hold. Records, books, prepackaged goods, and sweaters typically appear in case displays.

A **cut case** is an inexpensive display, in which merchandise is left in the original carton. Supermarkets and discount stores frequently set up cut-case displays. These cases do not create a warm atmosphere. Neither does a **dump bin,** which is a case that houses piles of sale clothing, marked-down books, or other products. Instead of neat, precise displays, dump bins have open assortments of roughly handled items. Advantages of cut cases and dump bins are reduced display costs and a low-price image.

See the E-POP options from DCI Marketing (www.dcimarketing. com/e_pop.htm).

Posters, signs, and cards can be used to dress up all types of displays, including cut cases and dump bins. These tools provide information about in-store product locations and stimulate customers to shop. A mobile, a type of hanging display with parts that move, especially in response to air currents, serves the same purpose—but is more appealing to the eye and stands out. Electronic POP displays are also widely utilized today. They can be interactive, grab the shopper's attention, be tailored to individual stores, provide product demonstrations, answer customer questions, and incorporate the latest in multimedia capabilities. These displays are much easier to reprogram than traditional displays are to remodel.

A Nonstore-Based Retailing Perspective

Many of the principles of atmospherics apply to both store and nonstore retailers. However, there are also some key distinctions. Let us look at these factors from the perspective of one type of direct marketer, the Web retailer: the storefront, general interior, store layout, displays, and checkout counter.

Storefront The storefront for a Web retailer is the home page. Thus, it is important that the company name be highlighted and the positioning of the firm made clear.

A Web retailer's home page must:

Interact with the eMarketEdge demo E-store (demo. previewsystems.com) to experience the many components of online retailing.

- Prominently show the company name and indicate the positioning of the firm.
- Be inviting. As with a physical storefront, a virtual storefront must encourage customers to enter the "store."
- Make it easy to enter the store.
- Show the product lines carried.
- Use graphics as display windows and icons as entry points.
- Have a distinctive look and feel.
- Include the retailer's address and phone number.
- Be accessible through various search engines.

General Interior As with store-based retailers, the general interior of a Web retailer sets a shopping tone and mood. Colors run the gamut from plain white backgrounds to stylish black backgrounds. Some retailers use audio to generate shopper interest. "Fixtures" relate to how simple or elaborate the Web site looks. "Width of aisles" means how cluttered the site appears and the size of the text and images.

For a Web retailer, the general interior also involves elements such as the following:

- Instructions about how to use the site.
- Information about the company.
- Product icons.
- News items.
- The shopping cart (how orders are placed).
- A product search engine.
- Locations of physical stores (for dual channel retailers).
- A shopper login for firms that use loyalty programs and track their customers.

Store Layout The store layout for a Web retailer has two components: the layout of each individual Web page and the links to move from one page to another. Web retailers spend a lot of time planning the traffic flow for their stores. Online shoppers want to be as efficient as possible in shopping, and they get impatient or frustrated if the "store" is not laid out properly.

Some online firms use a systematic gridiron approach, while others have more free-flowing Web pages and links. Many companies have a store directory on the home page that indicates their product categories. The shopper clicks on an icon to enter the section of the site housing the category (department) of interest. A number of retailers encourage customers to shop for any product from any section of the Web site by providing an interactive search engine. The person types in the product name or category and is automatically sent to the relevant Web page.

Like their physical store colleagues, online retailers allocate more display space to popular product categories and brands, and give them a more distinctive position on their Web pages. On Web pages that require scrolling down, best-sellers usually appear at the top of the page and slower-sellers at the bottom.

Displays Web retailers can display full product assortments or let consumers choose from more selective assortments. The decision in this area greatly affects the open or cluttered appearance of a site, as well as the level of choice and possible confusion a shopper encounters. Online firms frequently use special themes, such as Valentine's Day or Mother's/Father's Day. It is easy for them to show ensembles—and for shoppers to interactively mix and match to create their own ensembles. Likewise, through its graphics and photos, a site can give the appearance of cut cases and dump bins for items on sale.

Checkout Counter The checkout counter is much more complicated for Web retailers than for most physical store retailers. There are three reasons why: (1) Online shoppers tend to worry more about the security and privacy of their purchase transactions than those who buy in a store. (2) Online shoppers often have to work harder to complete transactions. At a minimum, they must carefully enter the model number and quantity, and their shipping address, E-mail address, shipping preference, and credit card number. They may also be asked for their phone number, job title, and so on, because some retailers are anxious to build their data bases. (3) Online shoppers may feel surprised by the shipping and handling costs, which, typically, are not revealed until they go to the checkout.

Companies such as Amazon.com have patented their order checkout procedures. They consider the ease of completing purchases to be a significant competitive advantage. Amazon.com's "1-Click" program enables shoppers to securely store their shipping address, preferred shipping method, and credit card information. Each purchase then requires just one click to set up an order form.

Learn how Amazon.com (www.amazon.com) enables shoppers to use "1-Click Settings" for easy ordering.

Special Considerations Let us examine two issues: how to set up a proper Web site, and the advantages and disadvantages of Web atmospherics versus those of traditional stores.

Unlike with conventional bricks-and-mortar stores, online retailers usually have little experience with Web design or the fundamentals of store design and layout. To a greater extent than bricks-and-mortar stores, online firms hire Web specialists to design their sites. As their businesses grow, they may then take Web design functions in-house. Here is just a sampling of the resources available to small retailers in designing Web stores: Bigstep.com (www.bigstep.com), eCongo.com (www.econgo.com), Global Mall (www.globalmall.com), Storefront Developments (www.store-front.com), Yahoo! Store (store.yahoo.com), and CobWeb (e-storefront.com). In this grouping, design costs range from free for Bigstep.com and eCongo.com to $25,000 and up for CobWeb.

In comparison with traditional store retailers, online retailers have several advantages. A Web site:

- Can be tailored to the individual customer.
- Can be much more current.
- Can be modified regularly, from day to day (or even hour to hour) to reflect changes in consumer demand, new offerings from suppliers, and competitors' actions.

- Has almost unlimited space to present product assortments, displays, and information.
- Can promote cross-merchandising and impulse purchases with little effort on the part of the shopper.
- Enables a shopper to enter and exit an online store in a matter of minutes.

Compared to traditional store retailers, online retailers also have potential disadvantages. A Web site:

- Can be slow. This situation worsens as more graphics, photos, and audio and video clips are added.
- Can be difficult to navigate. This problem is growing as online firms add more product lines. How many clicks must a shopper make from the time he or she enters a site until a purchase is completed?
- Cannot display the three-dimensional aspects of products as well as physical stores.
- Requires constant attention and updating to reflect out-of-stock conditions, new merchandise, and price changes.
- Is more likely to be exited without a purchase because it is easier to visit another site than another bricks-and-mortar store.

ENCOURAGING CUSTOMERS TO SPEND MORE TIME SHOPPING

Underhill's Envirosell Inc. (www.envirosell.com) is a leader in shopping behavior research.

Paco Underhill, the guru of retail anthropology, has a simple explanation for why it is crucial for retailers to encourage consumers to spend more time in the store or at the Web site: "The amount of time a shopper spends in a store (assuming he or she is shopping, not waiting in a line) is perhaps the single most important factor in determining how much he or she will buy. In an electronics store that we studied, nonbuyers spent an average of 5 minutes and 6 seconds in the store, compared with the 9 minutes and 29 seconds buyers spent there. In a toy store, buyers spent on average more than 17 minutes, compared with 10 minutes for nonbuyers. In some stores, buyers are there three or four times longer than nonbuyers. The majority of the advice we give to retailers involves ways of getting shoppers to shop longer."[20] See Figure 18.11.

Figure 18.11
Making the Shopping Experience More Pleasant

At the Parque Corredor mall in Spain, the emphasis is on creating a family-oriented shopping complex. By offering facilities such as this carousel, the mall helps parents keep their children entertained in between stops at various stores—thereby extending the length of the overall shopping visit. Reprinted by permission of PricewaterhouseCoopers LLP.

Technology in Retailing

The Digital Age of Jewelry Retailing

Michelson Jewelers is a 10-unit chain that is headquartered in Paducahm, Kentucky. It sells midpriced jewelry, watches, and crystal keepsakes. In an effort to increase sales with its current inventory, Michelson now photographs each piece of merchandise with a digital camera, as it is received in its warehouse.

This digitization enables sales associates to retrieve all photographs on their point-of-sale screens. The photographs can show customers the merchandise that is out-of-stock at a particular store, but available at other units. Deann Moore, Michelson's controller, says: "We're the kind of store where obviously we can't have everything in stock at all times, so with these photos, we can show our other stores' inventory to customers."

Digital photography also has other vital applications for Michelson. It assists store-level executives during physical inventories in their search for missing merchandise. Retail buyers can view the items intended for reorder or for store transfer from one location to another. The move to digital photography is only Michelson's latest technological advance. It recently installed new point-of-sale inventory, accounting, and accounts receivable systems.

What impact will the digital photography system have on Michelson's company image? Explain your answer.

Source: Jean Thilmany, "Michelson: A Jewelry 'Screen' Pass," *Women's Wear Daily* (February 24, 1999), p. 24.

Among the tactics being used to persuade people to spend more time shopping are experiential merchandising, solutions selling, an enhanced shopping experience, retailer co-branding, and wish list programs.

The intent of **experiential merchandising** is to convert shopping from a passive activity into a more interactive one, by better engaging the customer. Some retailers are doing this especially well:

> Research shows consumers have cut shopping time—Kurt Salmon Associates reveals they average only 45 minutes a week shopping for themselves, or just over an hour including shopping for others. But retailers who offer entertaining activities, such as Nike Town, where customers shop 45 minutes to one hour; REI, where they stay one to two hours; or Oshman's Sporting Goods, where customers shop at least 30 minutes, find longer stays mean bigger sales. "We call this 'experiential merchandising,' the art of providing merchandise in a creative environment that encourages the customer to interact with the store items and personnel," says Alvin Lubetkin, Oshman's chief executive.[21]

> "What makes Barnes & Noble and Borders entertaining is that they invite people to spend a long time and enjoy not only their products, the books, but also the social interaction of other people in the store," says Courtney Lord of Lord Associates. "It's hip fashion stores that are now having a lot of runway feel, and Limited Too with a lot of interaction for young kids. Good retailers in excitingly designed retail environments are going to be the successful retail venues of the future." [22]

> Levi's new San Francisco flagship store is full of gadgets and gizmos designed to entertain, amuse, and help Levi's learn about its customers. Fingerprint identification and personal data are solicited at in-store kiosks. Detailed body measurements are logged in the 3-D body scanner chamber. Listening stations track music tastes. From waist

size to CD preference, it can devise in-depth customer profiles that are likely to play a crucial role in its marketing. Customers are engulfed in a high-energy, frenetic environment complete with multicolor spotlights, flashing images, and pulsating music. Images, materials, and even the music change by floor to reflect the products and activities there. [23]

Solutions selling takes a customer-centered approach and presents "solutions" rather than "products." It goes a step beyond cross-merchandising. For example, at holiday times, some retailers group gift items by price ("under $25, under $50, under $100, $100 and above") rather than by product category. This provides a solution for the shopper who has a budget to spend but a fuzzy idea of what to buy. Many supermarkets sell fully prepared, complete meals that just have to be heated and served. This solves the problem of "What's for dinner?" without requiring the consumer to shop for individual meal components. At Ulta beauty stores (formerly Ulta3), "Before, the store was about selection and price. Now, the store is about selection, but its also about fulfillment, where a woman is in control. Help is here if she needs it. It'll be a place women can come and meet a buddy. Before, it was a store. Now, it's a place to be."[24]

An enhanced shopping experience means the retailer does everything possible to make the shopping trip pleasant—and to minimize annoyances or frustrations. Given the retail choices that consumers have these days, a pleasing experience is a must: "Consider the process that you, as a consumer, go through when shopping. A well-designed merchandising system might attract you, but what happens next? Don't you need to be engaged? Don't you need to know all of your options? Don't you need information, presented in the right way? And don't you need all of this in a matter of seconds?"[25]

The Retail Group (www.theretailgroup.com/work) has helped many retailers offer an enhanced shopping experience. Stop by some of its clients to see how.

Various firms provide an enhanced shopping experience by setting up wider aisles so people do not feel as cramped, adding benches and chairs so those accompanying the main shopper can relax while he or she looks around, using kiosks to stimulate impulse purchases and answer questions, having activities for young children (such as Ikea's playroom), and opening more checkout counters so customers do not get agitated waiting to make a purchase. And what 70-year-old shopping accessory is turning out to be one of the greatest enhancements of all? It is the humble shopping cart, as highlighted in Figure 18.12:

Figure 18.12
The Shopping Cart's Role in an Enhanced Shopping Experience

One look at this Kmart photo shows why the "humble" shopping cart can be such a powerful in-store marketing tool.
Reprinted by permission.

A month from now, as Santa Claus crawls back up the last chimney and heads home, the retail world will begin its annual postmortem: How did discounters once again manage to trounce traditional department stores? Was it sophisticated pricing, the latest in-store design, or cutting-edge inventory management? Actually, after 20 years of growing discounter dominance, a simpler explanation rolls into view: the shopping cart. As old-fashioned as they seem, carts are perfectly suited for the way people shop today. They're pressed for time and buy more in fewer trips. Mothers struggling to corral children love them. The growing ranks of senior citizens lean on carts for support and appreciate not having to carry their purchases. Carts empower an impulse. Carts also make many of the newer retailing strategies work. From category killers such as Home Depot to mass merchandisers such as Target Stores and Kmart, stores are getting bigger, carrying a wider array of goods, and pushing prices lower. They need customers to stay longer, cruise through the whole store, and load up. So, why would any sane retailer deny its customers a cart? Some, it seems, are just too classy to have stainless steel contraptions junking up their stores. "I'm not sure I could see someone buying a $2,000 suit and hanging it over a cart," says Carolyn Biggs, director of stores for Saks Fifth Avenue.[26]

More firms are participating in co-branding, whereby two or more known retailers situate under the same roof to share costs and stimulate consumers to spend more time in the store: "McDonald's inside a Wal-Mart. Starbucks inside a Barnes & Noble. Pier 1 Imports inside a Sears Mexico. Polo Shops inside a Bloomingdale's. For several years, retailers have blended branded concepts under one roof. Recent moves bring GNC inside Rite Aid stores and Blockbuster Video inside Kroger stores in Atlanta. Now, the industry appears to be exploring a new form of convergence, the coming together of service establishments and traditional retail formats. First-time callers dialing up Willowbee & Kent in Boston often get more than they thought. Those looking to find out which brands of luggage may be on sale don't expect to hear a computerized voice say 'press 7 for the travel agency.' And callers looking to price a trip to the Cayman Islands are sometimes surprised to hear 'press 6 for the retail department.' "[27]

Another tactic in use by a growing number of retailers is the wish list program. It is a technique borrowed from Web retailers that enables customers to prepare shopping lists for gift items they'd like to *receive* from a particular store or shopping center:

A me-generation update of the bridal registry, the wish list allows a consumer to record his or her gift choices by simply checking size, color, and model number. Dan Swaab, a 29-year-old architect, recently put a black pullover from clothing outlet Butch Blum and a customized picture frame from a store called Fireworks, among other items, on his list. But instead of signing up on a computer site, he did so at the University Village shopping mall outside Seattle, which has been providing forms since November 1999 for visitors to fill in as they visit their favorite boutiques. The completed lists can be dropped off at locations throughout the complex and are entered into a data base (at no cost to shoppers) available both on the mall's Web site and at kiosks. Swaab, who says he is familiar with the Internet but "not a full bore browser," sees no advantage to doing a wish list solely on the Internet. "Returns can be such a hassle. This way, I've tried everything on."[28]

COMMUNITY RELATIONS

The manner in which retailers interact with the communities around them has an impact on their image—and performance. Firms can enhance their images by engaging in such community-oriented actions as these:

- Making sure that stores are barrier-free for disabled shoppers.
- Showing a concern for the environment by recycling trash and cleaning streets.

Age Verification for Alcohol and Tobacco Sales

7-Eleven is now turning to high-technology solutions to better meet age verification laws for the sale of alcohol and tobacco products. It started by installing age verification equipment in its 1,200 California stores. The equipment, which costs about $200 per store, reads the magnetic stripe on the back of a driver's license and instructs the sales clerk as to whether or not to accept a purchase of age-restricted merchandise.

As a corporate spokesperson for 7-Eleven, Inc., says, "At 7-Eleven, we have a mandatory ID program. But we handle between 1,000 and 1,500 customers in a store in a typical day. Sometimes, problems come up. A store clerk may not be able to calculate a customer's age quickly enough with other customers waiting or may make a math error."

There are several benefits to the use of the age verification equipment. In California, for example, a store will lose its liquor license if it is caught selling alcohol to underage customers three times. The equipment also puts the blame for a rejection on the equipment, not on the sales clerk.

What do you think is the impact on 7-Eleven's overall image of its using age verification equipment?

Source: Shelly Reese, "Age Verification Units Counter Alcohol, Tobacco Sales to Minors," *Stores* (June 1998), pp. 66, 68.

- Supporting charities and noting that support at the company Web site.
- Participating in antidrug programs.
- Employing area residents.
- Running special sales for senior citizens and other groups.
- Sponsoring Little League and other youth activities.
- Cooperating with neighborhood planning groups.
- Donating money and/or equipment to schools.
- Carefully checking IDs for purchases with age minimums.

7-Eleven is a top corporate sponsor of the Muscular Dystrophy Association, participates in Mothers Against Drunk Driving (MADD) public awareness programs, and supports organizations that promote literacy and multicultural understanding. Wal-Mart, Kmart, and Consolidated Stores are among the numerous retailers participating in some type of antidrug program. Borders, Barnes & Noble, Target Stores, and others participate in the national "Read-In" literacy program. Safeway and Giant Food are just two of the many supermarket chains that give money and/or equipment to schools in their neighborhoods.

As with any aspect of retail strategy planning, community relations efforts can be undertaken by companies and organizations of any size and format. Here's an illustration:

When one hears the words "teenager" and "mall" uttered in the same breath, chances are "loitering" or "cruising" fall somewhere in between them. However, if you live in Grandville, Michigan, a suburb of Grand Rapids, the words bridging teens and a new mall have expanded to include "merchandising," "marketing," and "design." Open since late 1999, River Town Crossings Mall counts among its tenants a 1,118-square-foot store called School Spirit!!! that is operated by students from three area school districts. The store sells merchandise, from pencils to sweatshirts to stadium blankets, emblazoned with the participating schools' logos. It is open during regular mall hours, with employment available to students from the three high schools involved in the program. There is an adult store manager. So far, the effort has been successful in turning around what could have been a tense relationship between education and retail in

Grandville. When the developer announced its plan for a mall directly across the street from the high school under construction, many parents had reservations. "To diffuse concern, we launched a campaign to sell ourselves to the community," says Ron DenAdel, the developer's vice-president, "that it wasn't just a mall, but a neighbor." His discussions with a school administrator, who also chaired the town planning commission, brought about meetings between the developer and Grandville High School. Eventually, the two parties hammered out the store idea as the most effective way to cooperate, inviting nearby Hudsonville and Jenison school districts to participate. Then came the lease deal itself. Negotiated in much the same way as a normal retail tenant deal would be, rent for the store was set at a "very reduced rate."[29]

SUMMARY

1. *To show the importance of communicating with customers and examine the concept of retail image.* Customer communications are crucial for a retailer (store- or nonstore-based) to position itself in customers' minds. Various physical and symbolic cues can be used when communicating.

Creating and maintaining the proper image, the way a firm is perceived by its customers and others, is an essential aspect of the retail strategy mix. The components of a firm's image are its target market characteristics, retail positioning and reputation, store location, merchandise assortment, price levels, physical facilities, shopping experiences, community service, mass advertising and public relations, personal selling, and sales promotion. Accordingly, a retail image requires a multistep, ongoing process. For chains, it is essential that there be a consistent image among branches.

2. *To describe how a retail store image is related to the atmosphere it creates via its exterior, general interior, layout, and displays, and to look at the special case of nonstore atmospherics.* A retail image depends on the atmosphere (atmospherics) projected. For a store-based retailer, atmosphere is defined as the physical attributes of the store utilized to develop an image; it is composed of the exterior, general interior, store layout, and displays. For a nonstore-based firm, the physical attributes of such strategic mix factors as catalogs, vending machines, and Web sites affect its image.

The store exterior is comprised of the storefront, marquee, entrances, display windows, building height and size, visibility, uniqueness, surrounding stores and area, parking, and congestion. It sets a mood or tone before a prospective customer even enters a store.

The general interior of a store encompasses its flooring, colors, lighting, scents and sounds, fixtures, wall textures, temperature, width of aisles, dressing facilities,

vertical transportation, dead areas, personnel, self-service, merchandise, price displays, cash register placement, technology/modernization, and cleanliness. The interior of an upscale retailer is far different from that of a discounter—portraying the image desired, as well as the costs of doing business.

In laying out a store's interior, six steps are followed. (1) Floor space is allocated among selling, merchandise, personnel, and customers; and the space provided for each is based on a firm's overall strategy. More firms now use planograms to allot store space. (2) Product groupings are set, based on function, purchase motivation, market segment, and/or storability. (3) Traffic flows are planned, using a straight or curving pattern. (4) Space per product category is computed by a model stock approach or sales-productivity ratio. (5) Departments are located. (6) Individual products are arranged within departments.

Interior (point-of-purchase) displays provide information for consumers, add to store atmosphere, and have a promotional role. Interior display possibilities include assortment displays, theme displays, ensemble displays, rack and case displays, cut case and dump bin displays, posters, mobiles, and electronic displays.

For Web retailers, many principles of atmospherics are similar to those for bricks-and-mortar retailers. There are also key differences. The home page is the Web retailer's storefront. The general interior consists of site instructions, company information, product icons, the shopping cart, the product search engine, and other factors. The store layout comprises the layout of individual Web pages, as well as the links that connect these pages. Displays can feature full or more selective assortments. Many sales are lost if the checkout counter does not function well. There are specialists that help in Web site design. Compared to traditional stores, Web stores have various pros and cons.

3. *To discuss ways of encouraging customers to spend more time shopping.* The more time that consumers spend shopping, the more they are likely to purchase. To persuade customers to devote more time with the retailer, these tactics are often employed: experiential merchandising, solutions selling, enhancing the shopping experience, retailer co-branding, and wish list programs.

4. *To consider the impact of community relations on a retailer's image.* Customers are likely to react favorably to retailers showing community interest and involvement in such activities as establishing stores that are barrier-free for disabled persons, supporting charities, and running special sales for senior citizens.

Key Terms

atmosphere (atmospherics) (p. 602)
visual merchandising (p. 603)
storefront (p. 604)
marquee (p. 605)
dead areas (p. 609)
planogram (p. 611)
functional product groupings (p. 611)
purchase motivation product group
   ings (p. 611)
market segment product groupings
   (p. 611)

storability product groupings (p. 611)
straight (gridiron) traffic flow (p. 611)
curving (free-flowing) traffic flow
   (p. 611)
model stock approach (p. 614)
sales-productivity ratio (p. 614)
point-of-purchase (POP) display
   (p. 615)
assortment display (p. 615)
theme-setting display (p. 615)
ensemble display (p. 616)

rack display (p. 616)
case display (p. 616)
cut case (p. 616)
dump bin (p. 616)
experiential merchandising (p. 620)
solutions selling (p. 621)

Questions for Discussion

1. Why is it sometimes difficult for a retailer to convey its image to consumers? Give an example of an on-campus retailer with a fuzzy image.

2. How could a new car dealer project an upscale retail image? How could a used car dealer project such an image?

3. Define the concept of *atmosphere*. How does this differ from that of *visual merchandising*?

4. Which aspects of a store's exterior are controllable by a retailer? Which are uncontrollable?

5. How would the following differ for an upscale restaurant and a fast-food chain?
   a. Flooring.
   b. Lighting.
   c. Fixtures.
   d. Personnel.
   e. Level of self-service.

6. What are meant by selling, merchandise, personnel, and customer space?

7. Present a planogram for a nearby music store.

8. Develop a purchase motivation product grouping for a consumer electronics Web retailer.

9. Which stores should *not* use a curving (free-flowing) layout? Explain your answer.

10. Visit the Web site of eToys (www.etoys.com) and then comment on its storefront, general interior, store layout, displays, and checkout counter.

11. What do you think are the advantages and disadvantages of experiential merchandising?

12. How could a neighborhood hardware store engage in solutions selling?

13. Do you agree with upscale retailers' decision not to provide in-store shopping carts? What realistic alternatives would you suggest? Explain your answers.

14. Why should a retailer contribute to a charity or pay to sponsor a Little League team?

WEB-BASED EXERCISE

Lettuce Entertain You (www.leye.com/restaurants/index.html)

Questions

1. Evaluate this site from the perspective of creating a retail atmosphere.

2. What are the advantages and disadvantages of communicating the components of a restaurant's image through a Web site?

3. How would you enhance this Web site to portray the restaurants' image in even more innovative ways?

4. Comment on the virtual tour component of the Web site.

CHAPTER ENDNOTES

1. Georgia Lee, "King's Drugs Thrives with Promotions, Service," *Women's Wear Daily* (April 23, 1999), p. 14S.

2. Len Lewis, "Designing a Difference," *Progressive Grocer* (June 1998), p. 17.

3. Rodney W. Underhill, "Who's Minding the Brand?" *Arthur Andersen Retailing Issues Letter* (July 1999), p. 1–2.

4. See A. Coskun Samli, J. Patrick Kelly, and H. Keith Hunt, "Improving the Retail Performance by Contrasting Management- and Customer-Perceived Store Images: A Diagnostic Tool for Corrective Action," *Journal of Business Research*, Vol. 43 (September 1998), pp. 27–38; Lisa Bertagnoli, "A Delicate Balance," *Women's Wear Daily* (August 12, 1999), p. 14S; and Peter J. McGoldrick, "Spatial and Temporal Shifts in the Development of International Retail Images," *Journal of Business Research*, Vol. 42 (June 1998), pp. 189–96.

5. "The Image Makers," *Chain Store Age* (April 1996), p. 44.

6. Edward O. Welles, "The Diva of Retail," *Inc.* (October 1999), p. 48.

7. Marianne Wilson, "Old Navy Earns Right to Bask in Spotlight," *Chain Store Age* (October 1999), p. 152; and Carol Emert, "Old Navy's Model Plan," *San Francisco Chronicle* (October 20, 1999), p. C1.

8. "Turn the Page," *Chain Store Age* (November 1999), pp. 80, 84.

9. Robert Scally, "Post-Chapter 11 Wards Hard at Work on Image," *Discount Store News* (September 6, 1999), p. 4.

10. Tom Lyons, "Visual Merchandising Today," *www.cahilldisplay.com/resources.htm* (March 10, 2000).

11. Ginia Bellafonte, "Stores Are Wooing Customers by Making the Shopping Less Forbidding, More Friendly—and Fun," *Time* (December 7, 1998), p. 64; and "More Trouble Ahead for Department Stores: Sephora's New Style of Retailing Eats Away at Their Most Profitable Business," *Forbes* (April 9, 1999), p. 82.

12. "Types of Flooring Used," *Chain Store Age* (July 1999), p. 130.

13. "Nike Town Turns on Spotlight," *Chain Store Age* (March 1999), p. 132.

14. "Retail Entrepreneur of the Year: Donald F. Lamberti," *Chain Store Age* (December 1997), p. 54.

15. Miles Socha, "Display: Engaging All the Senses," *Women's Wear Daily* (May 24, 1999), p. 13.

16. Jean E. Palmieri, "Saks Out to Be Men's Best Friend in Chicago," *Daily News Record* (December 3, 1999), p. 24; and Lisa Vicenti, "Cross-Merchandising Adds to Meijer Appeal," *HFN* (July 5, 1999), p. 1.

17. Jack Hitt, "The Theory of Supermarkets," *New York Times Magazine* (March 10, 1996), pp. 56–61, 94, 98.

18. Alf Nucifora, "Enticing Shoppers to Stop, Look, Buy with POP," *LI Business News* (January 15, 1999), p. 6C.

19. Yumiko Ono, "'Wobblers' and 'Sidekicks' Clutter Stores, Irk Retailers," *Wall Street Journal* (September 8, 1998), p. B1.

20. Paco Underhill, *Why We Buy* (New York: Simon & Schuster, 1999). See also Kirk L. Wakefield and Julie Baker, "Excitement at the Mall: Determinants and Effects on Shopping Response," *Journal of Retailing,* Vol. 74 (Fall 1998), pp. 515–39.

21. Dick Silverman, "Making Shopping Fun Again," *Footwear News* (November 9, 1998), p. 31.

22. Sunil Taneja, "Reinventing the Experience," *Chain Store Age* (November 1998), p. 156.

23. Marianne Wilson, "Levi's Fashions a New Attitude," *Chain Store Age* (October 1999), p. 135.

24. Pete Born, "Ulta3's Retail Makeover," *Women's Wear Daily* (June 11, 1999), p. 10.

25. "Category Merchandising: The Finishing Touch to Category Management," *Aftermarket Business* (October 1999), p. 63.

26. Joseph B. Cahill, "The Secret Weapon of Big Discounters: Lowly Shopping Cart," *Wall Street Journal* (November 24, 1999), pp. A1, A10.

27. Dan Hanover, "That's the Ticket," *Chain Store Age* (April 1999), p. 31.

28. Leslie Kaufman, "Decking the Malls with Real Shoppers," *New York Times on the Web* (November 24, 1999).

29. "School Ties," *Chain Store Age* (April 1999), p. 84.

CASE 1

ATMOSPHERICS ARE ON TARGET AT TARGET STORES

Customers who never visit Wal-Mart or Kmart are often proud of the fact that they shop at Target Stores, and its in-store merchandising is a big part of what separates that chain from the rest of the discount pack. While Target may sell many of the same routine commodities as its competitors, it is how the overall assortment is presented that makes the difference. "It's the image that counts," says Ken Stone, a professor at Iowa State University. Target Stores' positioning as an upscale discount store stems from parent Target Corporation's origin's as a department store retailer. Displays, lighting, and customer ease of access are almost always better in Target Stores than in competitors such as Kmart or Circuit City, Stone notes.

"Target doesn't block the aisle with dump bins the way Wal-Mart or Kmart does, and that gives the stores a much cleaner image," he states. The chain keeps a close eye on the look of its stores, and Target is the only one of the big three discount chains to employ its own in-house staff of merchandisers rather than rely on third-party merchandisers, vendors, and store associates.

Target's advanced data-mining techniques help fine-tune the mix in each individual store while maintaining a consistent look across the chain, according to Sid Doolittle, a retail analyst. "Target has the ability to analyze sales performance on a store-by-store basis, and because of that each store is merchandised very carefully from a style and color standpoint according to the demand patterns."

Customers may not realize that Target's lighting is better and that the gondolas and dump bins are absent, but they have the feeling that the shopping environment is better. "The upshot of it is there are a lot of professional people, women in particular, who will buy a lot of work clothes and things there," Stone remarks. "Some of these same people wouldn't think of buying these items at Wal-Mart or Kmart."

Target Stores' approach is part of a growing trend in apparel, along with strip malls and power center retailers such as Marshall's, Kohl's, and T.J. Maxx, states Doug Tigert, a professor at Babson College. However, he believes that Target's distinctiveness only goes so far: "When we did a major fashion study, it did show that Target was upscale from Wal-Mart, Kmart, and Venture and had a better quality image, but it didn't show that it was in the range of J.C. Penney. It's a very difficult exercise to get positioning between the discount stores and Sears and Penney." Target's private labels—such as Merona and Furio—are perceived

CASE 1

(CONTINUED)

as having a higher quality and value, in part because of the environment where the products are sold. Dolittle notes: "Target offers value in styles, but not necessarily using brands as the main thrust. Instead, it has house brands. Target has carefully managed the development of the private lines to offer better value than the name brands."

In the past, one factor that set Target Stores apart from its competitors was its ability to market merchandise across numerous categories in order to enable consumers to create a coordinated look. "Target ties things together and they do appear more stylish," Stone says. Target also often uses licensing as a tool to create exclusive products that reinforce its position as an upscale discounter. Today, other discounters are following Target's lead and adopting similar programs.

Questions

1. What factors contribute to Target Stores' upscale image? Use the components of retail image in this chapter in answering this question.

2. What are the pros and cons of Target Stores having its own in-house staff merchandisers?

3. How else could Target Stores use atmospherics to foster its image as a distinctive discounter?

4. What could Target Stores do to increase the amount of time that shoppers spend in the store?

NOTE

The material in this case is adapted by the authors from Robert Scally, "Upscale Mix Lifts Image Above the Fray," *Discount Store News* (April 19, 1999), p. 58. Reprinted by permission.

CASE 2

PATAGONIA: AN ENVIRONMENT-ALLY-FOCUSED SPECIALTY RETAILER

Patagonia (www.patagonia.com) is a marketer of high-quality outdoor apparel with a well-established reputation for environmental consciousness. Besides a large mail-order operation, Patagonia has 24 stores (10 in the United States, 5 in Japan, 3 in Europe, 4 in South America, and 2 in Australia).

Patagonia was founded by Yvon Chouinard in 1957 in Ventura, California, as an outlet for the sale of his handmade mountain climbing equipment. In 1972, Chouinard began to manufacture, distribute, and sell apparel items aimed at consumers who had a passion for mountaineering, skiing, snowboarding, and other outdoor sports. From the outset, Chouinard insisted that his clothing be as technically sound as his climbing gear. The firm prides itself on field testing its products under extreme conditions.

Chouinard thinks Patagonia exists to serve as a model for corporate responsibility. His long-standing philosophy has been to run the firm along "self-sustaining" principles. In 1984, Patagonia began tithing—distributing 10 percent of pre-tax profits (now about one percent of sales) to preserving and restoring the natural environment through a program it calls an "earth tax."

In the mid-1980s, Patagonia's sales were growing at 30 percent per year. To capitalize on this, it decided to reposition itself away from appealing only to outdoor enthusiasts. It developed a line of casual wear targeted at the mass market. Not only was the new line unsuccessful, but it also diluted the firm's favorable image among its core outdoor-oriented clientele. As a result, Patagonia was forced to reorganize in 1991 and to lay-off one-fifth of its workers.

As part of its recovery strategy, Patagonia refocused on its "technical" clothing products and expanded its environmental consciousness by redesigning products to minimize the detrimental environmental effects associated with their manufacture or use.

Beginning in spring 1996, Patagonia made a commitment to use only organically grown cotton in its cotton garments. The company switched to organic cotton because it believed the pesticides, herbicides, and other chemicals used in growing traditional cotton are detrimental to the soil, air, and ground water. Patagonia also developed an internal environmental program, whereby two-thirds of its waste is reused (by reusing boxes, recycling paper, and having composts at its main offices).

In 1998, a Patagonia catalog received the *Catalog Age* annual best catalog award. In commenting on the Patagonia catalog, one of the award competition's judges stated: "It's what a great catalog should be: an excellent marriage of product, market, and creative." In one of the award-winning catalog's spreads, Patagonia featured its Activist fleece collection (tops, tights, and bibs), described the fabric and its various functions, and then showed a photograph of a daredevil parachuter wearing the apparel. The environmental influence is also evident throughout all of its catalogs today. For example, organic cotton goods and post-consumer recycled fabrics are clearly labeled.

Questions

1. Evaluate Patagonia's Web site (www.patagonia.com) in terms of its retail image.

2. What are the differences in developing a retail image for a catalog versus a bricks-and-mortar retailer?

3. How do Patagonia's environmental efforts benefit the firm? Are there any potential negatives associated with such an image?

4. Contrast the atmospherics of Patagonia's Web site with L.L. Bean's (www.llbean.com).

Video Questions on Patagonia

1. What are the pros and cons of Patagonia's hiring personnel with a serious passion for outdoor sports?

2. Discuss the pros and cons of Patagonia's no-growth marketing strategy from the perspective of its retail image.

NOTE　This case was prepared and written by Professor Gail H. Kirby, Santa Clara University. The material is drawn from Laura M. Beaudry, "13th Annual Catalog Awards: Gold Award, Apparel Over $100—Patagonia," *Catalog Age* (September 1998), p. 70; and Larry Armstrong, "Patagonia Sticks to Its Knitting," *Business Week* (December 7, 1998), p. 68. Reprinted by permission.

CHAPTER 19

Promotional Strategy

CHAPTER OBJECTIVES

1. To explore the scope of retail promotion
2. To study the elements of retail promotion: advertising, public relations, personal selling, and sales promotion
3. To discuss the strategic aspects of retail promotion: objectives, budgeting, the mix of forms, implementing the mix, and reviewing and revising the plan

To say the least, the media response to the first ad for Wendy's that featured R. David (Dave) Thomas, the firm's founder, as its corporate spokesperson was especially critical of Thomas. Some press reports criticized his Middle-American delivery, his open-faced expression, and his stocky build. One critic went so far as to call him "a steer in a short-sleeved shirt." Even executives at Bates USA, Wendy's advertising agency, conceded that Dave Thomas' "speech, pacing, and rhythm were way off."

But Dave Thomas has certainly demonstrated that media criticism is not always on target! He has appeared in more than 640 TV commercials, making this the longest-running advertising campaign to feature a company founder as its spokesperson. Unlike the media critics, retailing experts attribute the success of the Wendy's campaign to Thomas' high believability. Wendy's senior vice-president for marketing says the ads work because "They're not about Dave; they're about Wendy's quality."

Bates has learned the best way to use Dave Thomas. The ads often poke fun at his simplistic philosophy and his love for the food he created. For example, one commercial showed Thomas responding to B. B. King, the famous blues singer, after getting a letter from him describing his fondness for Wendy's food. Thomas replies: "Keep smiling, you'll beat the blues yet."

Now, the media critics suggest that Wendy's use of Dave Thomas is "getting a little stale" and that the campaign misses the children's market. Nonetheless, Wendy's plans to continue marketing the wit and wisdom of Dave Thomas.[1]

OVERVIEW

U.S. newcomer Sephora has an integrated promotion plan, from its colorful Web site (www.sephora.com) to its stores.

Retail promotion is broadly defined as any communication by a retailer that informs, persuades, and/or reminds the target market about any aspect of that firm. This chapter deals with preparing and enacting a promotional strategy. In the first part of the chapter, elements of promotion (advertising, public relations, personal selling, and sales promotion) are detailed. The second part centers on the strategic aspects of promotion: objectives, budget, mix of forms, implementation of mix, and review and revision of the plan.

> *Please Note:* Web site addresses are constantly changing. The links in this chapter are current as of the publication of this book.

Consider the effort that Wal-Mart, *Promo* magazine's "Marketer of the Decade," puts into its promotion strategy. The firm does not rely on low prices alone. Here are excerpts from an interview with Mike Cockrell, Wal-Mart's vice-president of marketing:

How has Wal-Mart's promotion philosophy changed during the decade? Perhaps we're a little more sophisticated, but not so much that our customers aren't able to feel relaxed and enjoy themselves in our stores. This is all very hometown-driven. At the same time, we've come a ways from the free donkey rides and free sliced watermelon event we featured in the early 1960s.

What has Wal-Mart learned about consumers and about marketing in the last 10 years? We believe customers want to feel a connection with associates in their store, their community. Take our Good Works Program. We need to let our customers know our stores have charitable programs that benefit their hometowns. We also are able to achieve that connection with retailtainment—our Oreo Stacking Contest, Grandparents Day, and our Wal-Mart Live broadcasts of exclusive concert performances from Garth Brooks, Britney Spears, Faith Hill, and others.

Why has Wal-Mart been so successful getting companies to partner on promotions and tailor campaigns? That's the result of our marketing managers cultivating strong, more tandem-driven relationships with buyers and suppliers. They explain up-front what the parameters are at Wal-Mart, what we expect out of the promotion, what we are able to do at our stores with respect to operations.

What role do marketing managers play in promotion? Ideas often originate with marketing managers, who also coordinate the marketing plan to be executed in stores. Our success is the result of this collaborative effort that typically begins with our marketing managers, but sometimes with suppliers or buyers. Promotions are coordinated by marketing managers, but managed at store level. We give stores a core program and challenge them to enhance it.

What promotion has been Wal-Mart's best? Not every promotion has sold a lot, but that's all right. Most times, it's about retailtainment—letting customers know Wal-Mart is a place for socializing.[2]

ELEMENTS OF THE RETAIL PROMOTIONAL MIX

This site (www. smartbiz.com/sbs/ arts/kline2.htm) is a good place to start learning about Web promotion options.

Advertising, public relations, personal selling, and sales promotion are the four elements of promotion. Each is discussed here in terms of goals, advantages and disadvantages, and basic forms. Although these elements are described individually, a good promotional plan integrates them—based on the retailer's overall strategy. A movie theater concentrates more on ads and sales promotion (point-of-purchase displays to prompt food and beverage sales), while an upscale specialty store stresses personal selling. See Figure 19.1.

Retailers devote significant sums to promotion. For example, a typical department store spends nearly 4 percent of sales on ads and 8 to 10 percent on personal selling and support services. In addition, most department store chains invest heavily in sales promotions (such as special events) and use internal or external public relations offices to generate favorable publicity and reply to media information requests.

Advertising

Advertising is paid, nonpersonal communication transmitted through out-of-store mass media by an identified sponsor. Four aspects of the definition merit further clarification:

Figure 19.1
Communicating Through the Retail Promotion Mix

Peapod uses its logo and slogan in all of its promotion efforts. The company advertises on a regular basis, seeks out publicity from the media, uses its delivery personnel as customer service representatives, and runs special promotions.
Reprinted by permission.

(1) Paid form—This distinguishes advertising from publicity (an element of public relations), for which no payment is made by the retailer for the time or space used to convey a message. (2) Nonpersonal presentation—In advertising, a standard message is delivered to the entire audience, and it cannot be adapted to individual customers (except when the World Wide Web is involved). (3) Out-of-store mass media—These include newspapers, radio, TV, the Web, and other mass communication channels, rather than personal contacts. In-store communications (such as displays and audio announcements) are considered sales promotion. (4) Identified sponsor—Advertising clearly divulges the sponsor's name, unlike publicity. See Figure 19.2.

Sears has the highest annual dollar advertising expenditures among U.S. retailers—$1.6 billion. About 4 percent of its U.S. sales is spent on ads. In contrast, many firms have higher advertising-to-sales ratios, despite lower dollar spending. These include Montgomery Ward (6.1 percent) and Federated Department Stores (5.0 percent). On the other hand, Wal-Mart spends just 0.3 percent of sales on ads, relying more on word of mouth, in-store events, and everyday low prices.[3] Table 19.1 shows 1998 advertising-to-sales ratios for a number of retailing categories.

Differences Between Retailer and Manufacturer Advertising Strategies Although the definition cited applies to all advertising, it is important to examine some of the key distinctions between retailer and manufacturer advertising strategies. First, retailers usually have more geographically concentrated target markets than manufacturers. This means they can adapt better to local needs, habits, and preferences than manufacturers. However, many retailers are unable to utilize national media as readily as manufacturers. For example, only the largest retail chains and franchises can advertise on national TV programs. An exception is direct marketing (including the World Wide Web) because trading areas for even small firms can be geographically dispersed.

Figure 19.2
Using Advertising to Create Awareness of
Store Locations—and More!

Shoe Carnival stores offer popular name-brand
footwear, shopping convenience, a large selection of
current fashions, great customer service, plus a fun
and entertaining store environment. Shoe Carnival is
a publicly held, retail footwear company with over
100 stores, and aggressive growth planned for the
future. It has stores in 20 states. Through ads such as
the one shown here, the company promotes its Web
site, *www.shoecarnival.com,* where people can obtain
company information, find out store locations, discover employment opportunities, and read about
weekly promotions.
Reprinted by permission.

Second, retail ads stress immediacy. Individual items are placed for sale and advertised over specific, short time periods. Timely purchases are sought. In contrast, manufacturers are more often concerned with developing favorable product or company attitudes and not with short-run sales increases.

Third, many retailers stress prices in ads, whereas manufacturers usually emphasize several product attributes. In addition, retailers often display a number of different products in

Table 19.1 Selected U.S. Advertising-to-Sales Ratios by Type of Retailer

Type of Retailer	Advertising Dollars as Percentage of Sales Dollars[a]	Advertising Dollars as Percentage of Margin[b]
Apparel and accessories stores	6.3	14.2
Auto and home supply stores	1.1	2.7
Department stores	3.7	13.0
Drug and proprietary stores	0.9	3.2
Eating places	4.2	16.4
Family clothing stores	3.7	10.0
Furniture stores	6.9	17.4
Grocery stores	1.1	3.8
Hobby, toy, and game shops	3.0	11.3
Hotels and motels	2.7	11.4
Lumber and building materials	0.7	2.3
Mail-order firms	8.4	27.8
Movie theaters	2.8	15.8
Music stores	1.4	3.7
Radio, TV, and consumer electronics stores	3.9	15.5
Shoe stores	3.0	7.8
Variety stores	1.1	5.0

[a]Advertising dollars as percentage of sales = Advertising expenditures/Net company sales
[b]Advertising dollars as percentage of margin = Advertising expenditures/(Net company sales − Cost of goods sold)

Source: Schonfeld & Associates, "1999 Advertising-to-Sales Ratios for the 200 Largest Ad Spending Industries," *Advertising Age* (June 28, 1999), p. 58. Reprinted by permission.

Technology in Retailing

Feeding Hungry College Students in Cyberspace

Food.com (www.food.com) is a new online restaurant-ordering service that deals with students at over 50 college campuses, including Boston University, New York University, Florida State University, and the University of Texas at Austin. As a spokesperson for Food.com states, "Our service is a natural fit for college kids. They do a lot of ordering out and they're also early adopters of technology."

Food.com's promotional program utilizes CollegeStudent.com and *College Directory Publishing*. Its promotional arrangement was negotiated through Future Pages, an advertising network of newspaper Web sites and college newspapers. Food.com has devised print advertisements that run in college newspapers as part of the Future Pages program. CollegeStudent.com handles Food.com's on-campus promotion events, including the creation of flyers, posters, and events. CollegeStudent.com sends promotional E-mails to students who subscribe to its network. Food.com also has an on-line co-branded restaurant and dining guide that appears in the college newspapers and at CollegeStudent.com.

Besides its college campus program, Food.com focuses on office meals in areas where there is a high concentration of employees and where a large number of Internet connections exist. Food.com has relationships with over 11,000 restaurants.

Evaluate Food.com's promotional program targeting college students. What would you add to it?

Source: Patricia Riedman, "Cybermalls Go After Colleges, Office Workers," *Advertising Age* (February 8, 1999), p. 60.

---

one ad, whereas manufacturers tend to minimize the number of products mentioned in a single ad.

Fourth, media rates tend to be lower for retailers than for manufacturers. Because of this factor and the desire of many manufacturers and wholesalers for wide distribution, the costs of retail advertising are sometimes shared by manufacturers or wholesalers and retailers. Two or more retailers may also share costs. This is known as **cooperative advertising.**

Objectives Retail advertising may be tied to specific goals, including:

- Short-term sales increases.
- Greater customer traffic.
- Developing and/or reinforcing a retail image.
- Informing customers about goods and services and/or company attributes.
- Easing the job for sales personnel.
- Developing demand for private brands.

A retailer would select one or more goals and base advertising efforts on it (them).

Advantages and Disadvantages The major advantages of advertising are that:

- A large audience is attracted. Also, for print media, circulation is supplemented by the passing of a copy from one reader to another.
- The costs per viewer, reader, or listener are low.
- A large number of alternative media are available. Therefore, a retailer can match a medium to the target market.
- The retailer has control over message content, graphics, timing, and size (or length), so a standardized message in a chosen format can be delivered to the entire audience.
- In print media, a message can be studied and restudied by the target market.

Find out how to devise ads that sell (www.smartbiz.com/sbs/arts/bly65.htm).

- Editorial content (a TV show, a news story, and so on) often surrounds an ad. This may increase its credibility or the probability it will be read.
- Self-service or reduced-service operations are possible since a customer can become aware of a retailer and its offerings before shopping.

The major disadvantages of advertising are that:

- Because the message is standardized, it is inflexible (except for the Web, whose interactive nature can be tailored to people's needs). The retailer cannot focus on the needs of individual customers.
- Some ads require large investments. This may reduce the access of small firms to certain media (such as TV).
- Media may reach large geographic areas, and for retailers, waste may occur. Thus, a small supermarket chain may find that only 40 percent of a paper's readers reside in its trading area.
- Some media require a long lead time for placing ads. This reduces the retailer's ability to advertise fad items or to react to some current events themes.
- Some media have a high throwaway rate. For instance, circulars and mail ads may be discarded without being read.
- Ads often are brief. A 30-second TV commercial or small newspaper ad does not have many details.

These are broad generalities about advertising. The pros and cons of specific media are described next.

Media Retailers can choose from among papers, phone directories, direct mail, radio, TV, the World Wide Web, transit, outdoor, magazines, and flyers/circulars. A summary of the attributes of these media appears in Table 19.2.

Papers can be classified as dailies, weeklies, and shoppers. Among retailers, the paper is the most preferred medium, having the advantages of market coverage, short lead time, reasonable costs, flexibility, longevity, graphics, and editorial association (ads near columns or articles). Disadvantages include the possible waste (circulation to a wider geographic area than that containing the target market), the competition among retailers, the black-and-white format, and the appeal to fewer senses than TV. To maintain their dominant position, many papers have redesigned graphics, and some run a limited number of color ads. Free-distribution shopper papers ("penny savers")—with little news content and delivery to all households in a geographic area—are growing in use, sometimes at the expense of other papers.

Phone directories (the White and Yellow Pages) are key advertising media. In the White Pages, retailers get free alphabetical listings along with all other phone subscribers, commercial and noncommercial. The major advantage of the White over the Yellow Pages is that people who are familiar with a retailer's name are not exposed to competitors' names. The major disadvantage, in contrast with the Yellow Pages, is the alphabetical rather than type-of-business listing. A customer unfamiliar with repair services in his or her area will usually look in the Yellow Pages under "Repair" and choose a firm.

With the Yellow Pages, firms pay for alphabetical listings (and larger display ads, if desired) in their business category. Most retailers advertise in the Yellow Pages. The advantages include their widespread usage by people who are ready to shop and their long life (one year or more). The disadvantages are that retailer awareness is not stimulated and there is a lengthy lead time for new ads. Retailers have multiple Yellow Pages firms vying for their business—at competitive rates.

Direct mail is the medium whereby retailers send catalogs or ads to customers by the mail or private delivery firms. Advantages are the targeted audience, tailored format, controlled

Table 19.2 Advertising Media Comparison Chart

Medium	Market Coverage	Particular Suitability	Major Advantages	Major Disadvantages
Daily papers	Single community or entire metro area; local editions may be available.	All larger retailers.	Wide circulation, short lead time.	Nonselective audience, heavy ad competition.
Weekly papers	Single community usually; may be a metro area.	Retailers with a strictly local market.	Targeted readers, local identification.	Limited audience, little ad creativity.
Shopper papers	Most households in one community; chain shoppers can cover a metro area.	Neighborhood retailers and service businesses.	Targeted readers, low costs.	Small audience, a giveaway and not always read.
Phone directories	Geographic area or occupational field served by the directory.	All types of goods and service-oriented retailers.	Attract consumers who are ready to shop or purchase, permanent message.	Limited to active shoppers, long lead time needed.
Direct mail	Controlled by the retailer.	New and expanding firms, those using coupons or special offers, mail order.	Targeted readers, personalized and aimed at good prospects, can be tied to data base.	High throwaway rate, low image to many consumers.
Radio	Definable market area surrounding the station.	Retailers focusing on identifiable segments.	Relatively low costs, good market coverage.	No visual effect, must be used regularly to be of value.
TV	Definable market area surrounding the station.	Retailers of goods and services with wide appeal.	Dramatic impact, wide market coverage.	High cost of time and production, audience waste.
World Wide Web	Global.	All types of goods and service-oriented retailers.	Wide market coverage, interactive, low costs, multimedia capabilities.	Privacy issues, need for continuous updating, hard to measure results.
Transit	Urban or metro community served by transit system.	Retailers near transit routes, especially those appealing to commuters.	Targeted audience, repetition and length of exposure.	Clutter of ads, distracted or uninterested audience.
Outdoor	Entire metro area or single neighborhood.	Amusement and tourist-oriented retailers, well-known firms.	Dominant size, frequency of exposure.	Clutter of ads, distracted or disinterested audience.
Local magazines	Entire metro area or region, zoned editions sometimes available.	Restaurants, entertainment-oriented firms, specialty shops, mail-order firms.	Special-interest audience, creative options.	Long lead time, less sense of immediacy.
Flyers/circulars	Single neighborhood.	Restaurants, dry cleaners, service stations, and other neighborhood firms.	Very targeted audience, low costs.	High throwaway rate, poor image.

costs, quick feedback, and potential tie-ins (such as including ads with billing statements). Computerized data bases have raised the efficiency of direct mail ads. Among the disadvantages are the high throwaway rate ("junk mail"), poor image to some people, low response rate, and outdated mailing lists (addressees may have moved).

Radio is used by a variety of retailers. Advantages are the relatively low costs, its value as a medium for car drivers and riders, its ability to use segmentation, its rather short lead time, and its wide reach. Disadvantages include no visual impact, the need for repetition, the need for brevity, and waste. The use of radio by retailers has gone up in recent years.

TV ads, although increasing due to the rise of national and regional retailers, are far behind papers in retail promotion expenditures. Among the advantages are the dramatic effects of messages, the large market coverage, creativity, and program affiliation (for sponsors). Disadvantages include high minimum costs, audience waste, the need for brevity and repetition, and the limited availability of popular times for nonsponsors. Because cable TV is more focused than conventional stations, it appeals to local retailers.

From an advertising perspective, retailers are utilizing the World Wide Web to provide information to customers about store locations, to describe the products carried, to let people order catalogs, and so forth. More firms are also selling products through the Web. Retailers have two opportunities to reach customers by the Web: advertising on search engines, browsers (such as Netscape and Microsoft Explorer), and other firms' Web sites; and communicating with customers at their own sites. As discussed in Chapter 6, retailer participation in the Web is growing quickly.

Transit advertising is used in areas with mass transit systems. Ads are displayed on buses and in trains and taxis. Advantages are the captive audience, mass market, high level of repetitiveness, and geographically defined market. Disadvantages are the ad clutter, a distracted or uninterested audience, a lack of availability in small areas, restricted travel paths, and graffiti. In addition to traditional transit ads, retailers often advertise on their delivery trucks, sometimes in a very unusual manner:

> With dozens of Web startups overloading TV, radio, and newsprint with the most frantic advertising boom in history, Web retailers fret that consumers just aren't paying attention. And with nothing but a Web address to tout, they all know they may be very forgettable. The solution: a bit of virtual bricks-and-mortar. A faux fleet of delivery trucks is doing the trick for BigStar Entertainment, which sells videotapes and DVDs online, and sends them off via UPS. To set itself apart from the clutter of competitors, BigStar paid a trucking company to plaster the BigStar name on 23 local delivery trucks in New York—and to make it look as if it owned the fleet. The trucks don't carry BigStar movies; it's probably pizza boxes or office equipment inside. But BigStar figures they give it a certain stature. It trains the truck drivers to answer questions about BigStar's business—even though they don't work for the firm—and to hand out coupons. BigStar is so pleased with the results that it expanded its fake fleet to 203 trucks in Dallas, San Francisco, and Los Angeles. "What I wanted to do was create a sense of permanence," explains Donna Williams, senior vice-president of marketing and business development—"to give people the impression that BigStar is actually out there in the real world."[4]

Outdoor (billboard) advertising is sometimes used by retailers. Posters and signs may be displayed in public places, on buildings, and alongside highways. Advantages are the large size of the ads, the frequency of exposure, the relatively low costs, and the assistance in directing new customers. Disadvantages include the clutter of ads, a distracted or uninterested audience, the limited information, and some legislation banning outdoor ads. See Figure 19.3.

Magazine usage is growing for retailers due to three factors: the rise in national and regional firms, the creation of regional and local editions, and the use by nonstore firms.

Figure 19.3
Billboard Advertising for Pedestrians and Motorists

Around the globe, billboard advertising is a rather inexpensive and attention-getting medium. Shown here is a Burger King billboard in Lugano, Switzerland. Photo by Barry Berman.

Advantages of magazines are their tailoring to specific markets, creative options, editorial associations, longevity of messages, and use of color. Disadvantages include the long lead time, less sense of consumer urgency, and waste.

Flyers/circulars are also a major medium. Single-page (flyers) or multiple-page (circulars) ads can be distributed in parking lots or right to consumer homes. Advantages include a very targeted audience, low costs, flexibility, and speed. Among the disadvantages are the level of throwaways, the poor image to some consumers, and clutter. Flyers are good for smaller firms, while circulars are used by larger ones.

Types Advertisements can be classified by content and payment method. See Figure 19.4.

Figure 19.4
Types of Advertising

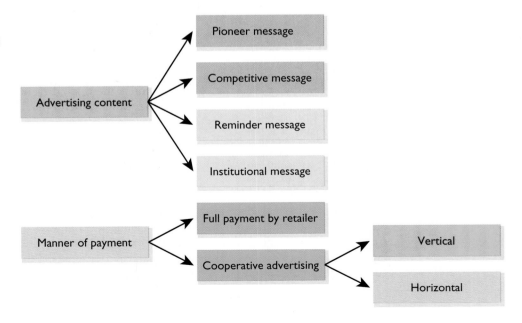

Ads may be pioneering, competitive, reminder, or institutional. *Pioneer ads* have awareness as a goal and offer information (usually on new firms or locations). *Competitive ads* have persuasion as a goal. *Reminder ads* are geared to loyal customers and stress the attributes that have made the retailers successful. *Institutional ads* strive to keep retailer names before the public without emphasizing the sale of goods or services. Public service messages are institutional in nature.

In placing ads, retailers may pay their own way or seek cooperative ventures. For firms paying their own way, the major advantages are control and flexibility. The major disadvantages are the costs and efforts required. Cooperative ventures are those in which two or more parties share the costs and the decision making. It is estimated that $12 billion is spent annually on U.S. cooperative advertising, most in vertical agreements. Newspapers are preferred over other media for cooperative ads related to retailing.

In a **vertical cooperative advertising agreement,** a manufacturer and a retailer or a wholesaler and a retailer share an ad.[5] Each party's duties and responsibilities are usually specified contractually. Retailers are typically not reimbursed until after ads are run and invoices are provided to the manufacturer or the wholesaler. Vertical cooperative advertising is subject to the Robinson-Patman Act; manufacturers and other suppliers must offer similar arrangements to all retailers on a proportional basis. The advantages of a vertical agreement to a retailer are reduced ad costs, the assistance in preparing ads, greater coverage of the market, and less time in planning. Disadvantages to a retailer include less control, flexibility, and distinctiveness. Some retailers are concerned about the requirements they must meet to be eligible for support and the emphasis on the supplier's name in ads. Manufacturers and other suppliers are responding by being more flexible and understanding of retailers concerns. For instance, in the American Express cooperative program, restaurants can choose from among dozens of border designs and copy blocks (tailored to a wide variety of cuisines). Restaurants can also insert their own logos and add other copy.

Carol Wright (www.carolwright.com) is a leader in horizontal cooperative promotions.

With a **horizontal cooperative advertising agreement,** two or more retailers share an ad. A horizontal agreement is most often used by small noncompeting retailers (such as independent hardware stores), retailers situated in the same shopping center, and franchisees of a given franchising firm. Advantages and disadvantages are similar to those in a vertical agreement. Two further benefits are the bargaining power of retailers in dealing with the media and the synergies of multiple retailers working together.

When planning a cooperative advertising strategy, retailers should consider such questions as these:

- What ads qualify, in terms of merchandise and special requirements?
- What percentage of advertising is paid by each party?
- When can ads be run?
- What media can be used?
- Are there special provisions regarding message content?
- What documentation is required for reimbursement?
- How does each party benefit?
- Do cooperative advertisements obscure the image of individual retailers?

Public Relations

Public relations entails any communication that fosters a favorable image for the retailer among its publics (consumers, investors, government, channel members, employees, and the general public). It may be nonpersonal or personal, paid or nonpaid, and sponsor controlled or not controlled. **Publicity** is any nonpersonal form of public relations whereby

Promoting the Burger King

Paul Clayton wrote his college thesis on why Burger King was an underperformer. He then joined the chain as assistant manager of advertising and promotion. Over the next ten years, he rose to the position of senior vice-president of worldwide marketing and in 1997, at age 39, Clayton became president of Burger King North America. Soon thereafter, *Brandweek* named him one of the top marketers of the year.

Although Burger King is very successful, with $11 billion in sales and nearly 8,000 outlets in the United States alone, Paul Clayton is in a challenging position. Look at the events he faced in late 1999:

Just 7 weeks after Burger King launched a new ad campaign, the firm was already in search of ways to change it. "We need to get our ads right," said Paul Clayton. "I think we have some work to do." He wanted Burger King and its advertising agency to create more "relevant and likable" commercials, and to do work that breaks through "the enormous clutter that exists." Long dependent on network TV, Burger King also plans to bolster local advertising, particularly on the West Coast. That's where competition is most brutal, with regional chains like Jack in the Box and Carl's Jr. "We need to understand the consumer perception of our brand that is unique to the West Coast to determine what we need to do to properly position Burger King." Clayton attributed soft sales to lack of big product news and the failure of ads to emotionally connect with consumers.

Source: Louise Kramer, "Burger King President Loses Taste for Ads," *Advertising Age* (September 27, 1999), p. 1.

At Wendy's (www. wendys.com), public relations means community relations. From the lower left scroll bar, select "In Touch with the Community" and click "Go."

messages are transmitted through mass media, the time or space provided by the media is not paid for, and there is no identified commercial sponsor.

The basic distinction between advertising and publicity is the nonpaid nature of the latter. Due to this difference, publicity messages are not as readily controllable by a retailer. A story on a store opening may not appear at all, appear after the fact, or not appear in the form desired. Yet, to consumers, publicity is often more credible and valuable than ads. Thus, advertising and publicity (public relations) should be complements, not substitutes, for each other. Many times, publicity should precede advertising.

Public relations can benefit both large and small retailers. While the former often spend a lot of money to publicize events such as the Macy's Thanksgiving Day Parade and the mailing of the annual Neiman Marcus Christmas catalog, small firms can creatively generate attention for themselves on a limited budget. For example, Joe Greenwald, president of a company specializing in restaurant marketing, public relations, and advertising, recommends that restaurants do the following public relations activities. These recommendations can easily be adapted to any small retailer:

1. *Eliminate junk mail to editors.* Limit your press releases to only news they can use, thereby increasing your chances of getting coverage.

2. *Never violate the 10-second rule.* That's how much time an editor will spend to determine whether your item will be used. The headline and first sentence of your release better be interesting.

3. *Get the chef out of the kitchen.* Do cooking demonstrations in the restaurant and the community—at stores and shopping malls. It's a good way to gain new patrons, as well as PR exposure.

4. *Promote your signature dish like crazy.* What, you don't have a signature dish? Get one! Choose your most popular entree, publicize it on your menu and through PR. Become famous for it.

5. *TV or not TV?* Local TV programmers and cable shows often look for restaurants to feature. Contact your local stations and let them know that your restaurant is both unique and interesting.

6. *Adopt a charity.* Two or three times a year, support a charity with a percentage of one night's or one week's profits. The charity will usually publicize this.

7. *Don't just open a restaurant, make it an event.* Some time ago, we did an opening for a restaurant client and produced "the world's longest ribbon-cutting" by stretching a 150-yard ribbon past the restaurant and across a marina. We had the mayor cut the ribbon from aboard a Coast Guard cutter.

8. *Stop procrastinating.* It's time you created a Web site. It need not be as expensive as you might think. It can be as low as $1,000. Use it to display your menu, feature special promotions or events (such as wine tastings), and show a favorite recipe from your chef.

9. *Look for news potential in your patrons.* Recently, a 102-year-old man visited one of our clients for dinner. The general manager called me at home. I grabbed my camera, hurried out, interviewed the man, and took his picture. The story and photograph appeared in the paper the following week.

10. *Host meetings and parties.* Offer special menus and prices for lunches, dinners, or happy hours to business, civic, and community groups. Then, send press releases with photos.

11. *Create a cookbook of your chef's favorite recipes.* Make it available for sale at the restaurant and have the chef autograph it. Publicize the availability of the book.

12. *Celebrity patrons are news.* When VIPs such as athletes, entertainers, TV and radio personalities, and government officials visit, send press releases to the local paper, and display photos on the wall.[6]

Objectives Public relations seeks to accomplish one or more of these goals:

- Increase awareness of the retailer and its strategy mix.
- Maintain or improve a company's image.
- Show the retailer as a contributor to the public's quality of life.
- Demonstrate innovativeness.
- Present a favorable message in a highly believable manner.
- Minimize total promotion costs.

Advantages and Disadvantages The major advantages of public relations are that:

- An image can be presented or enhanced.
- A more credible source presents the message (such as a good restaurant).
- There are no costs for the message's time or space.
- A mass audience is addressed.
- Carryover effects are possible (if a store is perceived as community-oriented, its value positioning is more apt to be perceived favorably).
- People pay more attention to news stories than to clearly identified ads.

The major disadvantages of public relations are that:

- Some retailers do not believe in spending any funds on image-related communication.

- With publicity, there is little retailer control over the message and its timing, placement, and coverage by a given medium.
- It may be more suitable for short-run, rather than, long-run planning.
- Although there are no media costs for publicity, there are costs for a public relations staff, planning activities, and the activities themselves (such as store openings).

Types Public relations can be classed as planned or unexpected, and image enhancing or image detracting.

With planned public relations, a retailer outlines its activities in advance, strives to have the media report on them, and anticipates that certain events will result in media coverage. Community services, such as donations and special sales; parades on holidays (such as the Macy's Thanksgiving Day Parade); the sales of "hot" new goods and services; and the opening of a new store, are activities a retailer hopes will gain media coverage. The release of quarterly sales figures and publication of the annual report are events a retailer can anticipate will be covered by the media.

Unexpected publicity takes place when the media report on a firm's performance without its having advance notice of the coverage. TV and newspaper reporters may anonymously visit restaurants and other retailers to rate their performance and quality. A fire, an employee strike, or other newsworthy event may be mentioned in a story. Investigative reports on company practices may appear.

There is positive publicity when the media report on the firm in a complimentary manner, with regard to the excellence of its retailing practices, its efforts on behalf of its community, and so on. However, the media may also provide negative publicity. For instance, with a store opening, the media could describe the location in less than glowing terms, rap the store's environmental impact, and otherwise be critical. The firm has no control over the message, and the media may not cover this or any other company event. That is why public relations must be viewed as a component of the promotion mix, not as the whole mix.

Personal Selling

Personal selling involves oral communication with one or more prospective customers for the purpose of making sales. The level of personal selling utilized by a retailer depends on the image it wants to convey, the types of products sold, its level of self-service, and its interest in long-term customer relationships—as well as expectations of customers.[7]

At J.C. Penney, this means better programs for sales associates. Why? First, higher levels of selling are needed to reinforce its image as a more fashion-oriented department store. Unlike discounters that rely on self-service merchandising, Penney wants to stress the advice given by its sales staff. Second, Penney wants to stimulate cross-selling, whereby sales associates recommend related-item purchases to customers. Effective cross-selling increases the average sales transaction. Third, Penney wants sales associates to better "save the sale," by suggesting to customers who are returning merchandise to try different colors, styles, or quality. Four, through top-notch personal selling, Penney believes it can foster further customer loyalty. Table 19.3 highlights Penney's tips for its sales associates.

Objectives Among the goals of personal selling are to:

- Persuade customers to make purchases (because they often enter a store after acquiring some information through advertising).
- Stimulate sales of impulse items or products related to customers' basic purchases.
- Complete transactions with customers.
- Feed back information to company decision makers.
- Provide adequate levels of customer service.
- Improve and maintain customer satisfaction.

Table 19.3 J.C. Penney's Tips for Sales Associates

1. Greet the customer to make him or her feel welcome. This sets the tone for the customer's visit to your department.
2. Listen to customers to determine their needs.
3. Know your merchandise. For example, describe the quality features of Penney's private brands.
4. Know merchandise in related departments, as well. This can increase sales, as well as lessen a customer's shopping time.
5. Learn to juggle several shoppers at once.
6. Pack the customer's merchandise carefully. Ask if the customer would want the merchandise on a hanger to prevent creasing.
7. Constantly work at keeping the department looking its best.
8. Refer to the customer by his or her name; this can be gotten from the person's credit card.
9. Stress Penney's "hassle-free" return policy.

Source: J.C. Penney.

- Create awareness of items also marketed through the Web, mail, and telemarketing.

Advantages and Disadvantages The major advantages of selling are related to the nature of personal contact:

- A salesperson can adapt a message to the needs of the individual customer.
- A salesperson can be flexible in offering ways to address customer needs.
- The attention span of the customer is higher than with advertising.
- There is often little or no waste; most people who walk into a store are potential customers.
- Customers respond more often to personal selling than to ads.
- Immediate feedback is provided.

The major disadvantages of personal selling are that:

- Only a limited number of customers can be reached at a given time.
- The costs of interacting with each customer can be high.
- Customers are not initially lured into a store through personal selling.
- Self-service may be discouraged.
- Some customers may not view salespeople as helpful and knowledgeable but as too aggressive.

Types Most retail sales positions can be categorized as either order taking or order getting. An **order-taking salesperson** engages in routine clerical and sales functions, such as setting up displays, placing inventory on shelves, answering simple questions, filling orders, and ringing up sales. This type of selling most often occurs in stores that have a strong mix of self-service with some personnel on the floor.

An **order-getting salesperson** is actively involved with informing and persuading customers, and in closing sales. This is the true "sales" employee. Order getters usually sell higher-priced or complex items, such as real-estate, autos, apparel, appliances, and consumer electronics. On average, they are much more skilled and better paid than order takers. See Figure 19.5.

A manufacturer may sometimes help fund personal selling by providing **PMs** (defined as promotional money, push money, or prize money) for retail salespeople selling that manufacturer's brand. PMs are in addition to the compensation received from the retailer. Many retailers are concerned about this practice because it encourages their sales personnel to be

Figure 19.5
Personal Selling:
When Self-Service
Isn't Appropriate

Despite the greater
emphasis on self-service
retailing, many products
(such as Goodyear tires)
lend themselves to a
more personal
approach, where sales-
people can present
information and answer
questions.
Reprinted by permission
of Goodyear.

loyal to the manufacturer, and salespeople may be less responsive to actual customer desires
(if customers desire brands not yielding PMs).

Salespeople may work in a store, visit consumer homes or places of work, or engage in
telemarketing.

Functions   Store sales personnel may be responsible for all or many of these tasks: greeting
customers, learning customer wants, showing merchandise, giving a sales presentation,
demonstrations, answering objections, and closing the sale. See Figure 19.6. Nonstore sales
personnel may also have to generate customer leads (by knocking on doors in residential
areas or calling people who are listed in a local phone directory).

On entering a store or a department in it (or being contacted at home), a customer is
greeted by a salesperson. Typical in-store greetings are: "Hello, may I help you?" "Good
morning [afternoon]. If you need any help, please call on me." "Hi, is there anything in particular you are looking for?" With any greeting, the salesperson seeks to put the customer at
ease and to build rapport.

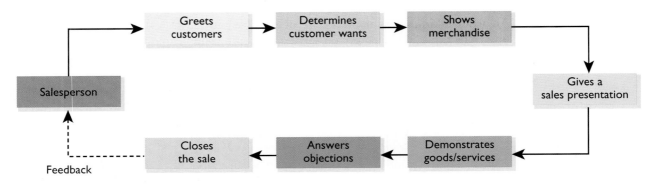

Figure 19.6
Typical Personal Selling Functions

The salesperson next finds out what the person wants. From the perspective of the retailing concept, a salesperson cannot succeed without first ascertaining customer wants: Is the person just looking, or is there a specific good or service in mind? For what purpose is the item to be used? Is there a price range in mind? What other information can the shopper provide to help the salesperson?

At this point, the salesperson may show merchandise. Based on customer wants, he or she selects the product most apt to satisfy that customer. The salesperson may try to trade up (discuss a more expensive version) or offer a substitute (if the retailer does not carry or is out of the requested item).

The salesperson now makes a sales presentation to motivate the customer to purchase. These are the two most common sales techniques: The **canned sales presentation** is a memorized, repetitive speech given to all customers interested in a particular item. It works best when sales force turnover is high and customers require little assistance. The **need-satisfaction approach** is based on the principle that each customer has a different set of wants; thus, a sales presentation should be geared to the demands of the individual customer. This approach is being utilized more in retailing.

In a presentation, a demonstration can show the utility of an item and allow customer participation. Demonstrations are often used with stereos, autos, health clubs, dishwashers, video games, and watches.

A customer may have questions during the selling process, and the salesperson must address them properly. After all questions are answered, the salesperson closes the sale. This means getting the shopper to conclude the purchase. Typical closing lines are: "Will you take it with you or have it delivered?" "Cash or charge?" "Would you like this gift wrapped?" "Have you decided on the color, red or blue?"

For the personal selling process to be completed effectively, salespeople must be enthusiastic, knowledgeable about their firm and its offerings, interested in customers, and able to communicate effectively. Table 19.4 contains a selected list of ways retail sales can be lost through poor personal selling and how to avoid these problems.

Table 19.4 Selected Reasons Why Retail Sales Are Lost—and How to Avoid Them

Poor qualification of the customer: Information should be obtained from the customer so the salesperson can gear a presentation to the prospective buyer.

Salesperson does not demonstrate the good or service: A good sales presentation should be built around the item shown in use; benefits can then be easily visualized.

Failure to put feeling into the presentation: The salesperson should be sincere and consumer-oriented in his or her presentation.

Poor knowledge: The salesperson should know the major advantages and disadvantages of his or her goods and services, as well as competitors', and be able to answer questions.

Arguing with a customer: The salesperson should avoid arguments in handling customer objections, even if the customer is completely wrong.

No suggestion selling: The salesperson should attempt to sell related items (such as service contracts, product supplies, and installation) along with the basic product.

Giving up too early: If an attempt to close a sale is unsuccessful, it should be tried again.

Inflexibility: The salesperson should be creative in analyzing alternative solutions to a customer's needs, as well as in adapting his or her message to the requirements of the individual customer.

Poor follow-up: The salesperson should be sure an order is correctly written, merchandise arrives at the agreed-on time, and the customer is satisfied.

Sales Promotion

Dash off and glance at this sales promotion site for online shoppers (www.dash.com).

Sales promotion encompasses the paid communication activities other than advertising, public relations, and personal selling that stimulate consumer purchases and dealer effectiveness. Included are displays, contests, sweepstakes, coupons, frequent shopper programs, prizes, samples, demonstrations, referral gifts, and other limited-time selling efforts outside of the ordinary promotion routine. Considerable information on sales promotion is available from *Promo* magazine (www.promomagazine.com).

The value and complexity of sales promotion are clear from this *Promo* commentary:

Three of every four shoppers are open to new experiences as they browse the aisles of supermarkets and search for bargains at drugstores and mass merchandisers. This means an opportunity to make a measurable impact when they're free of distractions and most receptive to new ideas. The last best chance to make a difference is in the store. But behavior changes as people enter different types of stores. Of those who browse supermarket aisles, only 19 percent browse at a chain drug or discount store. Three of five supermarket browsers turn into destination shoppers when they enter a chain drugstore, and two-fifths are destination shoppers in mass merchandise stores. The upshot: Firms must work harder to get shoppers' attention in a drug or discount store by using more intrusive techniques such as displays or special signs. While shopping varies by store, there are exceptions based on the product. For shampoos and pain relievers bought at drugstores and mass merchandisers, more browsing takes place than at supermarkets. Shampoos and pain relievers need more intrusive promotion at supermarkets. In drug and discount stores, it's the food items that need to use them.[8]

Objectives Sales promotion goals include:

- Increasing short-term sales volume.
- Maintaining customer loyalty.
- Emphasizing novelty.
- Complementing other promotion tools.

Advantages and Disadvantages The major advantages of sales promotion are that:

- It often has eye-catching appeal.
- Themes and tools can be distinctive.
- The consumer may receive something of value, such as coupons or free merchandise.
- It helps draw customer traffic and maintain loyalty to the retailer.
- Impulse purchases are increased.
- Customers can have fun, particularly with contests and demonstrations.

The major disadvantages of sales promotion are that:

- It may be difficult to terminate certain promotions without adverse customer reactions.
- The retailer's image may be hurt if corny promotions are used.
- Sometimes, frivolous selling points are stressed rather than the retailer's product assortment, prices, customer services, and other factors.
- Many sales promotions have only short-term effects.
- It should be used mostly as a supplement to other promotional forms.

Types Figure 19.7 describes the major types of sales promotions. Each is described here.

Point-of-purchase promotion consists of in-store displays designed to increase sales. The effect of the displays on retail image was discussed in Chapter 18. From a promotional perspective, the displays may remind customers, stimulate impulse behavior, facilitate self-service, and reduce retail promotion costs if manufacturers provide displays. The long-term

Marketing U.S. Shopping Centers to Foreign Tourists

A recent study sponsored by a traditional shopping center developer and the U.S. Department of Commerce found that more than 21 million people visit the United States annually from outside North America, and nearly 90 percent of this group go shopping during their U.S. visit. Retail analysts believe currency fluctuations and economic downturns have little effect on shopping by these tourists because many plan their trips well in advance. Shopping centers attracting a diversified group of tourists are also protected since declines in tourism from one country can be offset by increases from other countries.

Some shopping centers are particularly successful in attracting foreign tourists. For example, many international visitors to New York take a one-hour bus trip to Woodbury Common Premium Outlets in Central Valley, New York. To lure foreign tourists, the mall's vice-president of marketing advertises the center in foreign magazines and offers translators in such languages as Japanese. Other centers even cross-promote their retail locations with museums and historical sites. Some give additional airline frequent flyer miles and work with tour operators to route tourists to their malls.

As the marketing director for a leading department store in downtown San Francisco, present a promotional plan to attract foreign tourists.

Source: Maura K. Ammenheuser, "Foreign Affairs," *Management & Marketing* (May 1999), pp. 109, 112, 114.

impact of point-of-purchase promotions must be studied. For instance, in some product categories, total sales may not rise if special displays are used; instead, customers could stockpile items and buy less when the special displays are removed.

These data show the extent of point-of-purchase displays:

Visit the site of the leading point-of-purchase trade association (www.popai.org).

- The Point-of-Purchase Advertising Institute (POPAI) estimates that manufacturers and retailers together annually spend $14 billion on in-store displays in the United States.
- Virtually all retailers deploy some type of POP display.
- Among the retail categories with above-average use of in-store displays are restaurants, apparel stores, music/video stores, toy stores, and sporting goods stores.
- Retailers spend one-sixth of their sales promotion budgets on displays.
- Display ads appear on shopping carts in the majority of U.S. supermarkets. Also, thousands of supermarkets have in-store electronic signs above their aisles promoting well-known brands.
- Retailers use about two-thirds of all displays provided by manufacturers.[9]

Contests and sweepstakes are similar in nature; they seek to attract and retain customers who participate in events that have large prizes. A contest requires a customer to demonstrate some skill in return for a reward. A sweepstakes requires only participation, with the lucky winner chosen at random. Disadvantages of contests and sweepstakes are their costs, customer reliance on these tools as the reason for continued patronage, the effort required of consumers, and entries by nonshoppers. Together, manufacturers and retailers spend over $200 million each year on contests and sweepstakes.

Coupons present discounts from the regular selling prices of manufacturer and retailer brands. Each year, 275 billion coupons are distributed in the United States, with grocery products accounting for 75 percent of that amount. U.S. consumers actually redeem 5 billion coupons, resulting in their saving $3.5 billion; retailers receive $500 million to $600 million for handling redeemed coupons. Coupons are offered to consumers by freestanding inserts

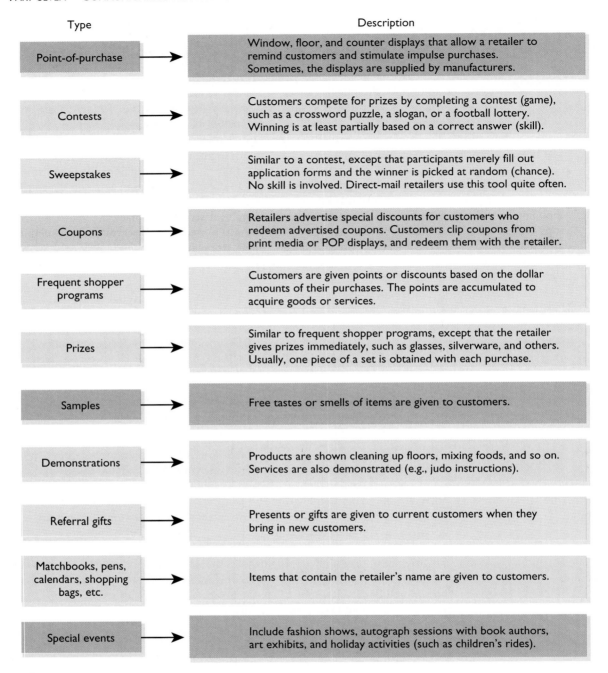

Type	Description
Point-of-purchase	Window, floor, and counter displays that allow a retailer to remind customers and stimulate impulse purchases. Sometimes, the displays are supplied by manufacturers.
Contests	Customers compete for prizes by completing a contest (game), such as a crossword puzzle, a slogan, or a football lottery. Winning is at least partially based on a correct answer (skill).
Sweepstakes	Similar to a contest, except that participants merely fill out application forms and the winner is picked at random (chance). No skill is involved. Direct-mail retailers use this tool quite often.
Coupons	Retailers advertise special discounts for customers who redeem advertised coupons. Customers clip coupons from print media or POP displays, and redeem them with the retailer.
Frequent shopper programs	Customers are given points or discounts based on the dollar amounts of their purchases. The points are accumulated to acquire goods or services.
Prizes	Similar to frequent shopper programs, except that the retailer gives prizes immediately, such as glasses, silverware, and others. Usually, one piece of a set is obtained with each purchase.
Samples	Free tastes or smells of items are given to customers.
Demonstrations	Products are shown cleaning up floors, mixing foods, and so on. Services are also demonstrated (e.g., judo instructions).
Referral gifts	Presents or gifts are given to current customers when they bring in new customers.
Matchbooks, pens, calendars, shopping bags, etc.	Items that contain the retailer's name are given to customers.
Special events	Include fashion shows, autograph sessions with book authors, art exhibits, and holiday activities (such as children's rides).

Figure 19.7
Types of Sales Promotion

in Sunday papers and placements in daily papers, direct mail, Web sites, regular magazines, and Sunday newspaper magazines. They are also placed in or on packages and dispensed from electronic in-store machines.[10] See Figure 19.8.

Figure 19.8
The Latest Phase of Couponing

Catalina Marketing Corporation, a leading coupon distributor, has introduced a new program called SuperMarkets Online®, *www.supermarkets.com*. This is how it works: The consumer visits any Web site that features the ValuPage® program, clicks on the ValuPage banner, and enters a zip code. Participating retailers are chosen. The consumer then selects the offers of interest, prints the ValuPage—which is a shopping list with a barcode, and takes the list to the selected retailer. The barcode is scanned at the checkout along with the products purchased. The combination of the barcode from the ValuPage and the barcodes from the promoted products triggers the Catalina Marketing printer, located at the checklane, to issue WebBucks®. These are cash rewards that are good on any purchase on the next visit to the issuing grocery chain.
Reprinted by permission.

These are the key advantages of coupons. One, in many cases, manufacturers pay to advertise and redeem coupons. Two, coupons are helpful to an ongoing ad campaign and increase store (Web) traffic. According to surveys, 99 percent of consumers redeem coupons at least once during the year. Three, the use of coupons increases the consumer's perception that a retailer offers good value. Four, ad effectiveness can be measured by counting redeemed coupons.

Disadvantages of coupons include their possible negative effect on the retailer's image, consumers shopping only if coupons are available, low redemption rates, the clutter of coupons, retailer and consumer fraud, and handling costs. Less than 2 percent of coupons are redeemed by consumers due to the large number of them that are received by each American household.

As described in Chapter 2, frequent shopper programs foster customer relationships by awarding discounts or prizes to people for continued patronage. In most programs, customers accumulate points (or their equivalent)—which are redeemed for cash, discounts, or prizes. Some programs, such as the one from Blockbuster (www.blockbuster.com), are very successful:

Blockbuster Rewards is a frequency program designed to give you three great ways to earn free rentals: (1) Get 1 free rental after 5 paid rentals of any movies and/or games during each calendar month—up to 2 free rentals per month! (2) You get a free Blockbuster Favorites rental every month for a year—12 in all—just for joining! (3) Get 1 free Blockbuster Favorites rental with each paid movie or game rental every

Monday through Wednesday all year long, including holidays! *Automatic Tracking— No Punch Cards!* We'll keep track of your rentals and tell you when you've earned a free one. Use your free rental immediately or anytime by the end of the next calendar month. Check your receipt to see how close you are to your next free rental and when existing free rentals will expire. Simply pay the $9.95 annual fee at the checkout counter. There are no forms to fill out. You'll get 2 Blockbuster Rewards Membership Cards, plus 2 key ring cards. Give the extra cards to household members authorized to rent on your account—their paid rentals help you earn free rentals even faster!

Loyalty programs are used by online retailers (www.passpoints. com), as well as bricks-and-mortar retailers (www.hbc. com/zellers). At the Zellers site, click on "Club Z Rewards."

Advantages of frequent shopper programs are the loyalty bred (customers can amass points only by shopping at a specific firm or firms), the "free" nature of awards to many consumers, and the competitive edge for a retailer similar to others. However, some consumers feel frequent shopper programs are not really free and would rather shop at lower-priced stores without these programs, it may take customers a while to gather enough points to get meaningful gifts, and profit margins may be smaller if retailers with these programs try to price competitively with firms that do not have the programs.

Prizes are similar to frequent shopper programs, but they are given with each purchase. Giveaways are most effective when sets of glasses, silverware, dishes, place mats, and so on are distributed one at a time to shoppers. These encourage loyalty. Problems are the cost of prizes, the difficulty of termination, and the possible impact on image.

As a complement to personal selling, free samples (such as a taste of a cake or a smell of a perfume) and demonstrations (such as cooking lessons) may be used. About $700 million is spent annually on sampling and demonstrations in U.S. stores—mostly at supermarkets, membership clubs, specialty stores, and department stores.[11] They are effective because customers become involved and impulse purchases increase. Loitering and costs may be problems.

Referral gifts are used to encourage existing customers to bring in new ones. Direct marketers, such as book and music clubs, often use this tool. It is a technique that has no important shortcomings and recognizes the value of friends in influencing purchasing decisions.

Items such as matchbooks, pens, calendars, and shopping bags may be given to customers. They differ from prizes since they promote retailers' names and are not part of a set. These items should be used as supplements. The advantage is longevity. There is no real disadvantage. See Figure 19.9.

Retailers may use special events to generate consumer enthusiasm. Events can range from store grand openings to fashion shows to art exhibits. When Toys "R" Us opens stores, it has giveaways and activities for children, and there is always a guest appearance by the firm's Geoffrey the giraffe (a human in a costume). Generally, in planning a special event, the potential increase in consumer awareness and store traffic needs to be weighed against that event's costs.

PLANNING A RETAIL PROMOTIONAL STRATEGY

To communicate successfully with customers, the retailer's overall promotional strategy must be formed carefully. A systematic approach to promotional planning is shown in Figure 19.10 and explained next.

Determining Promotional Objectives

Broad goals include increasing sales, stimulating impulse and reminder buying, raising customer traffic, getting leads for sales personnel, presenting and reinforcing the retailer image, informing customers about the attributes of goods and services, popularizing new store and Web sites, capitalizing on manufacturer support, offering customer service and enhancing

Figure 19.9
The Promotional
Value of
Shopping Bags

Reprinted by permission
of Venator Group Retail,
Inc. Photo by Dick Lauria
Photography Inc.

customer relations, maintaining customer loyalty, and having consumers pass along positive information to their friends and others. In developing a promotional strategy, a retailer must determine which of these are most important.

It is crucial to state goals clearly to give direction to the choice of promotional types, media, and messages. Thus, increasing company sales is not a specific enough goal.

Figure 19.10
Planning a Retail
Promotional Strategy

However, increasing sales by 20 percent is directional, quantitative, and measurable. With such an objective, a firm could devise a thorough promotional plan and evaluate its success.

McDonald's, which has won numerous awards over the years for its creative advertising, sets multiple goals for its efforts. The firm wants ads and promotions to drive sales, introduce new products, push special offers, and create an emotional bond with customers:

> Without changing its overall ad strategy, the latest batch of McDonald's commercials has attempted to evoke a feel-good connection with consumers. The move is part of an ongoing effort by McDonald's to exude more emotion, much the way past ads did. For instance, the chain introduced "First Book," a TV spot featuring a blind girl reading a book all by herself for the first time. Her reward: a trip to McDonald's for a Happy Meal. The spot shows her making the selection from a Braille menu as mom looks on with pride. "We've always had a tremendous, rich tradition, and even a heritage, of producing ads that do more than just sell our products," says Lany Zwain, senior vice-president of marketing. "Over the last couple of years, we were very good on the humor side but we really hadn't done a lot to reach out and touch people with heart-warming or wholesome or romantic or heart-tugging emotions. We want to connect our brand to our customers and create special moments at McDonald's that are also special moments in people's lives."[12]

See what leads to good WOM (www. geocities.com/ wallstreet/6246/ tactics1.html).

Perhaps the most vital long-term goal for any retailer is to gain positive **word of mouth (WOM)**, which occurs when one consumer talks to others.[13] If a satisfied customer refers his or her friends to that retailer, this can build into a chain of customers. No retailer can succeed if it receives extensive negative WOM (for example, "The hotel advertised that everything was included in the price. Yet it cost me $35 to play golf"). Negative WOM will cause a firm to lose substantial business. HCS, an E-commerce consulting firm, is right on target with this remark (www.hcsweb.net/wordofmouth.htm): "Please a visitor and they will tell a few friends. Anger a visitor and they will tell everyone!"

A service retailer, even more than its goods-oriented counterparts, must have positive word of mouth to attract new customers and retain existing ones. Most service firms credit WOM referrals with generating the majority of new customers/clients/patients. As author/consultant Michael Cafferky says (www.geocities.com/WallStreet/6246/main.html): "We are bombarded with thousands of advertising messages (some of them wasteful) every day. So many advertising messages rush at us daily, we cut through all that hype (which often we don't trust) to get to the essence of the messages we need. Word of mouth (which usually we trust) allows us to sort it all out."

Establishing an Overall Promotional Budget

Five procedures for setting the size of a retail promotional budget are discussed here.

With the **all-you-can-afford method,** a retailer first allots funds for each element of the retail strategy mix except promotion. The funds that are left go to the promotional budget. This is the weakest of the five techniques. Its shortcomings are that little emphasis is placed on promotion as a strategic mix variable; expenditures are not linked to goals; and if little or no funds are left over, the promotion budget is too small or nonexistent. The method is used predominantly by small, conservative retailers.

The **incremental method** relies on prior budgets for the allocation of funds. A percentage is either added to or subtracted from one year's budget to determine the next year's. If this year's promotion budget is $100,000, next year's budget would be calculated by adding or subtracting a percentage to or from that amount. A 10 percent rise means that next year's budget would be $110,000. This technique is useful for a small retailer. A reference point is used. The budget is adjusted based on the firm's feelings about past successes and future trends. It is easy to use. Yet, the budget is rarely tied to specific goals. Intuition or "gut feelings" are used. It is hard to assess effectiveness.

For the **competitive parity method,** a retailer's budget is raised or lowered based on competitors' actions. If the leading firm in an area raises its budget by 8 percent, competitors in the area could follow suit. This method is useful for small and large firms. Advantages are that it uses a comparison point and is market-oriented and conservative. Disadvantages are that it is an imitative, not a leading, philosophy; it may be tough to get competitive data; and it is assumed that competitors are similar (in terms of the number of years in business, size, target market, location, merchandise, prices, and so on). That last point is particularly critical because competitors may actually need quite different promotional budgets.

In the **percentage-of-sales method,** a retailer ties its budget to sales revenue. First, the firm develops a promotion-to-sales ratio. During each succeeding year, the ratio of promotion dollars to sales dollars then remains constant, while the dollar amount varies. A firm could set promotion costs at 10 percent of sales. If this year's sales are expected to be $600,000, there is a $60,000 promotion budget. If next year's sales are projected at $720,000, a $72,000 budget is planned. Benefits of this process are using sales as a base, the adaptability, and correlating promotion to sales. Shortcomings are that there is no relation to goals (for an established firm, a sales increase may not require an increase in promotion); promotion is not used to lead sales, but follow them; and promotion drops during poor sales periods, when increases might be helpful. This technique provides excess financing in times of high sales and too few funds in periods of low sales.

Under the **objective-and-task method,** a retailer clearly defines its promotion goals and prepares a budget to satisfy them. A retailer may decide its goal is to have 70 percent of the people in its trading area know its name by the end of a one-month promotion campaign, up from 50 percent currently. To do so, it calculates what tasks and costs are required to achieve that goal:

Objective	Task	Cost
1. Gain awareness of working women.	Use eight ¼-page ads in four successive Sunday editions of two area papers.	$12,000
2. Gain awareness of motorists.	Use twenty 30-second radio ads during prime time on local radio stations.	8,000
3. Gain awareness of pedestrians.	Give away 5,000 shopping bags.	5,000
	Total budget	$25,000

The objective-and-task method is the best budgeting technique. Advantages are that goals are clearly stated, spending is related to goal-oriented tasks, it is adaptable, and success or failure can be assessed. The major shortcoming is the complexity in setting goals and specific tasks, especially for small retailers.

When deciding how to plan their promotion budgets, retailers should weigh the strengths and weaknesses of each method in relation to their own requirements and constraints. To assist firms in their budgeting efforts, there is now computer software available.

Selecting the Promotional Mix

After a budget is set, a retailer must determine the promotional mix: its combination of advertising, public relations, personal selling, and sales promotion. A firm with a rather limited budget may rely on store displays, flyers, targeted direct mail, and publicity to generate customer traffic, while a firm with a big promotion budget may rely more on newspaper and TV ads.

Table 19.5 The Promotion Mixes of Selected Small Retailers

Type of Retailer	Favorite Media	Emphasis on Personal Selling	Special Considerations	Promotional Opportunities
Apparel store	Weekly papers; direct mail; radio; Yellow Pages; exterior signs.	High.	Cooperative ads available from manufacturers.	Fashion shows for community groups and charities.
Auto supply store	Local papers; Yellow Pages; POP displays; exterior signs.	Moderate.	Cooperative ads available from manufacturers.	Direct mail.
Bookstore	Local papers; shoppers; Yellow Pages; radio; exterior signs.	Moderate.	Cooperative ads available from publishers.	Author-signing events.
Coin-operated laundry	Yellow Pages; flyers in area; local direct mail; exterior signs.	None.	None.	Coupons in newspaper ads.
Gift store	Weekly papers; Yellow Pages; radio; direct mail; exterior signs.	Moderate.	None.	Special events; Web ads.
Hair grooming/ beauty salon	Yellow Pages; mentions in feature articles; exterior signs.	Moderate.	Word-of-mouth communication key.	Participation in fashion shows; free beauty clinics.
Health food store	Local papers; shoppers; direct mail; POP displays; exterior signs.	Moderate.	None.	Display windows.
Restaurant	Newspapers; radio; Yellow Pages; outdoor; entertainment guides and theater programs; exterior signs.	Moderate.	Word-of-mouth communication key.	Write-ups in critics' columns; special events.

Freestanding inserts (www.fsicouncil.org) offer retailers many advertising and sales promotion possibilities.

The mix is often affected by the type of retailer involved. Table 19.5 shows how small firms vary in terms of their promotion mixes—such as coin-operated laundries emphasizing Yellow Pages and flyers; and health food stores relying on local papers, as well as point-of-purchase displays. In supermarkets, sampling, frequent shopper promotions, theme sales, and bonus coupons are among the techniques used most; these promotions do vary between independent and chain outlets. At upscale retail stores, there is more attention to personal selling and less to advertising and sales promotion as compared with discounters.

Retailers often use an assortment of promotional forms to reinforce each other. A melding of media ads and POP displays may be more effective in getting across a message than either one form alone.

In reacting to a retailer's communication efforts, consumers often go through a sequence of steps called the **hierarchy of effects,** which takes them from awareness to knowledge to liking to preference to conviction to purchase. Different promotional mixes are needed in each step. Ads and public relations are most effective in developing awareness, while personal selling and sales promotion are most effective in changing attitudes and stimulating desires. This is especially true for expensive, complex goods and services. See Figure 19.11.

Implementing the Promotional Mix

The implementation of a promotional mix involves choosing which specific media to use (such as, Newspaper A and Newspaper B), the timing of promotion, the content of messages, the makeup of the sales force, specific sales promotion tools, and the responsibility for coordination.

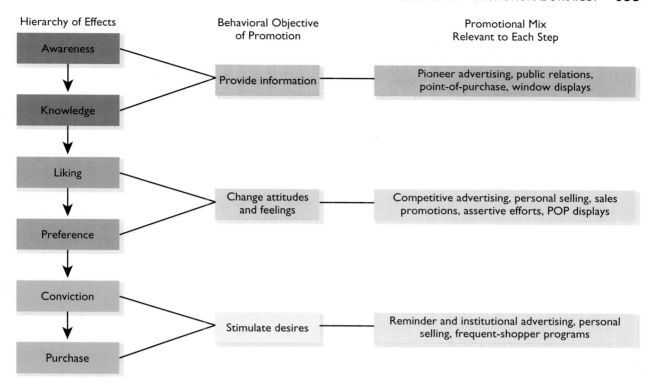

Figure 19.11
Promotion and the Hierarchy of Effects

Consider this example:

When New Jersey-based Summit Bankcorp decided to open branches in supermarkets, in-store bank employees were turned into active partners in the promotion. Shoppers never quite knew when a Summit employee would pop up in the meat department or dairy section to dispense brochures on equity loans, checking accounts, or certificates of deposit. With 30,000 monthly shoppers, grocery aisles provided a captive audience for Summit's marketing efforts, and many employees became truly skilled at working the floor. Summit staffers used juice and soup cans as props for their sales pitches. They donned supermarket aprons and gave out flowers or vegetable seeds to show the "home-gown" quality of home loans or other Summit services. In-store efforts were supported with a jungle safari instant-win game tied to the Walt Disney Animal Kingdom theme park. The game gave Summit sales and account reps an opportunity to interact with consumers in a fun and compelling way. Summit couldn't be more pleased so far. A branch manager in Kenilworth, New Jersey, says the campaign "has definitely raised sales and delivered a retail theme that is very important to us."[14]

Is 3D shopping on the Web ahead of its time or on target (www. 3dshopping.com)?

Media Decisions The choice of specific media is based on such factors as overall costs, efficiency (the cost to reach the target market), lead time, and editorial content. Overall costs are important since extensively using one expensive medium may preclude a balanced promotional mix. In addition, a firm may not be able to repeat a message in a costly medium, and ads are rarely effective when shown only once.

Ethics in Retailing

Substantiating Ad Claims Means Not Overstating Promises

In 1999, the Home Shopping Network (HSN) agreed to pay the government a fine of $1.1 million as a settlement for charges relating to its making unsubstantiated claims when selling acne preparations, diet pills, and other health-and-beauty-related products. Although HSN did not admit guilt, it stated that it would agree to a previous government order to back its assertions with "competent and reliable scientific evidence."

Among the claims the Federal Trade Commission scrutinized was a statement that a male skin-care product would "clear anyone's acne and razor bumps." Another unsubstantiated claim was that a vitamin spray could cure a hangover. Other products under investigation were a line of sprays that were said to help people stop smoking and recover from hangovers. HSN stated that these statements were made by an overly enthusiastic celebrity host. The media director for the manufacturer of one of the affected products stated that "they [HSN] were saying things we had no backup for."

HSN markets its products through multiple media, including TV programs and mail-order brochures. The spray vitamins and stop smoking products were marketed on the program's "Spotlight on Ruta Lee."

Present several ethical guidelines for HSN's celebrity hosts.

Source: "Home Shopping Network Settles Suit," *New York Times on the Web* (April 16, 1999).

A medium's efficiency relates to the cost of reaching a given number of target customers. Media rates are typically expressed in terms of cost per 1,000 readers, watchers, or listeners:

$$\text{Cost per thousand} = \frac{\text{Cost per message} \times 1,000}{\text{Circulation}}$$

A newspaper with a circulation of 400,000 and a per-page advertising rate of $10,000 has a per-page cost per thousand of $25.

In this computation, total circulation was used to measure efficiency. Yet, because a retailer usually appeals to a limited target market, only the relevant portion of circulation should be considered. Thus, if 70 percent of a newspaper's readers are target customers for a particular firm (and the other 30 percent live outside its trading area), the real cost per thousand is

$$\text{Cost per thousand (target market)} = \frac{\text{Cost per page} \times 1,000}{\text{Circulation} \times \dfrac{\text{Target market}}{\text{Circulation}}}$$

$$= \frac{\$10,000 \times 1,000}{400,000 \times 0.70} = \$35.71$$

Different media need different lead times. A newspaper ad can be placed shortly before publication, whereas a magazine ad sometimes must be placed months in advance. In addition, the retailer must decide what kind of editorial content it wants near its ads (such as a sports story or a personal care column).

Media decisions are not as simple as they seem. For instance, despite spending billions of dollars on TV and radio commercials, banner ads at search engines, and other media, many

Web retailers are finding that the most valuable medium for them may be common E-mail. It is fast, inexpensive, and targeted.

To generate *awareness* of unknown Web retailers, costly advertising may be necessary in today's intensively competitive and cluttered landscape of E-commerce:

> Send.com is buying its 15 minutes of fame. The year-old Internet gift site has raised only $10 million in venture capital funding so far, but it is spending $20 million for TV ads on such top-rated shows as *Ally McBeal, Frasier,* and *Monday Night Football* in the next eight weeks. Although he has borrowed against investors' pledges of more capital to pay for his ad spending spree, Send.com chief executive Michael Lannon sees little choice. "Not every company is going to survive this Christmas. We are treating the next eight weeks like an election campaign. Both we and our investors believe that customers are going to vote on who the leading gift site is, and only one candidate wins."[15]

Once customers have visited a Web site, E-mail can help *sustain relationships:*

> Web retailers have learned that E-mail may be the best way to cut through the clutter of the medium and deliver a personalized pitch to the consumer—not to mention retailer profits. "Opt-in E-mail [which, unlike unsolicited ads, consumers agree to receive] is a critical part of our marketing strategy going forward," says the president of Macys.com. It sends 12 to 15 E-mails annually to each person on a customer list that numbers hundreds of thousands of people. Shoppers sign up for E-mail updates and offers when they visit Macys.com, they can unsubscribe at any time, and they can stipulate that Macy's not share any personal data with other firms. Customers who respond to opt-in messages by visiting Macys.com purchase, on average, 5 to 7 times more often than other visitors to the site.[16]

Timing of the Promotional Mix Promotion decisions must take reach and frequency into account. **Reach** is the number of distinct people exposed to a retailer's promotion efforts in a specific period. **Frequency** is the average number of times each person who is reached is exposed to a retailer's promotion efforts in a specific period.

A retailer can advertise extensively or intensively. Extensive media coverage often means ads reach many people but with relatively low frequency. Intensive media coverage generally means ads are placed in selected media and repeated frequently. Repetition is important, particularly for a retailer seeking to develop an image or sell new goods or services.

In enacting its mix, a retailer must consider peak seasons and whether to mass or distribute efforts. When peak seasons occur, all elements of the promotional mix are usually utilized; in slow periods, promotional efforts are typically reduced. A **massed promotion effort** is used by retailers, such as toy retailers, that promote mostly in one or two seasons. A **distributed promotion effort** is used by retailers, such as fast-food restaurants, that promote throughout the year.

Though they are not affected by seasonality as much as other retailers, massed advertising is practiced by supermarkets, many of which use Wednesday for weekly newspaper ads. This takes advantage of the fact that a high proportion of consumers do their major shopping trip on Thursday, Friday, or Saturday.

Sales force size can vary by time (morning versus evening), day (weekdays versus weekends), and month (December versus January). Sales promotions also vary in their timing. Store openings and holidays are especially good times for sales promotions (and public relations).

The CarMax message is clear and information-packed (carmax.com/reasons/index.html).

Content of Messages Whether written or spoken, personally or impersonally delivered, message content is important. Advertising themes, wording, headlines, the use of color, size, layout, and placement must be selected. Publicity releases need to be written. In personal selling, the greeting, the sales presentation, the demonstration, and the closing need to be applied. With sales promotion, the firm's message must be composed and placed on the promotional device.

To a large extent, the characteristics of the promotional form influence the message. A shopping bag often contains no more than a retailer's name, a billboard (seen while driving at 55 miles per hour) is good for visual effect but can hold only limited information, and a salesperson may be able to maintain a customer's attention for a while, thus expanding the content of the message that is conveyed. Some shopping centers use a glossy magazine format to communicate a community-oriented image, introduce new stores to consumers, and promote the goods and services carried at stores in the center.

In advertising and public relations, distinctiveness can aid a retailer due to message proliferation. Cluttered ads displaying many products suggest a discounter's orientation, while fine pencil drawings and selective product displays suggest a specialty store focus.

Some retailers are involved with comparative advertising, whereby messages contrast their offerings with competitors'. These ads can help position a retailer relative to competitors, increase awareness of the firm, maximize the efficiency of a limited budget, and provide credibility. Yet, they provide visibility for competitors, may confuse people, and may lead to legal action by competitors. Fast-food and off-price retailers are among those using comparative ads.

Makeup of Sales Force Qualifications for sales personnel must be detailed, and these personnel must be recruited, selected, trained, compensated, supervised, and monitored. Personnel should also be classified as order takers or order getters and assigned to the appropriate departments. An in-depth discussion regarding human resource management was provided in Chapter 11.

Sales Promotion Tools Specific sales promotion tools must be chosen from among those cited in Figure 19.7. The combination of tools depends on short-term goals and the other aspects of the promotion mix. If possible, cooperative ventures with manufacturers or other suppliers should be sought. Tools inconsistent with the firm's image should never be used; and retailers should recognize the types of promotions that customers really want: "Reality check for nervous store owners: Even the novelty of electronic commerce can't dim the appeal of the shopping mall at the kickoff of the holiday season. "We like to be out with all the crazies," says Herb Filipponi of San Luis Obispo, California, shopping with his wife, Diane, braving the crowd in San Francisco's Union Square. "You can't get the warm and fuzzies from a computer box. You can't feel fabrics and sit on Santa's lap with your little girl," says Jan Wohlwend-Cycon, general manager of Valley View Center, a Dallas mall with more than 170 stores.[17]

Responsibility for Coordination Regardless of the retailer's size or organizational form, someone at the firm must have responsibility for the promotion function. Larger retailers often assign this job to a vice-president of promotion, who oversees display personnel, works with the firm's ad agency, supervises the firm's own advertising department (if there is one), and supplies branch outlets with the necessary in-store materials. In a large retail setting, personal selling is usually under the jurisdiction of the store manager.

For a promotional strategy to succeed, its components have to be coordinated with other retail mix elements. Sales personnel must be informed of special sales and know product features; featured items must be received, marked, and displayed; and accounting entries must be made.

Often, a shopping center or a shopping district runs theme promotions, such as "Back to School." In those instances, someone must coordinate the activities of all retailers participating in the event.

Reviewing and Revising the Promotional Plan

An analysis of the success of a promotion plan depends on its objectives, and that analysis is simplified if goals are stated in advance (as suggested in this chapter). Revisions would be made for promotional tools not achieving their pre-set goals.

Here are some ways to test the effectiveness of a promotional effort:

Examples of Retail Promotion Goals	Approaches for Evaluating Promotion Effectiveness
Inform current customers about new credit plans; acquaint potential customers with new offerings.	Study company and product awareness before and after promotion; evaluate extent of audience.
Develop and reinforce a particular image; maintain customer loyalty.	Study image through surveys before and after public relations and other promotion efforts.
Increase customer traffic; get leads for sales-people; increase revenues above last year's; reduce customer returns from prior year's.	Evaluate sales performance and the number of inquiries; study customer intentions to buy before and after promotion; study customer trading areas and average purchases; review coupon redemption.

Advertising Age's Net Results (adage.com/dataplace/netresults) presents current data that measure advertising on the Web.

Although it may sometimes be tough to assess promotion efforts (for instance, increased revenues might be due to a variety of factors, not just promotion), it is crucial for retailers to systematically study and adjust their promotional mixes when appropriate. Here is what three retailers are doing to assess their promotion effectiveness:

- Wal-Mart provides its suppliers with store-by-store data and sets up-front goals for cooperative programs. Actual sales are then compared against the goals.
- Lowe's, the home center chain, applies a computerized technique called "multiple-variable testing" to review thousands of different ideas affecting the design of circulars and media mix options.
- Pizza Hut uses data-base retailing to make promotions more effective. It recently trimmed promotional offers from 650 to 16: "We've cut our spending by 40 percent, increased coupon redemption by 50 percent, and our coupons are consistently more profitable than they used to be."[18]

It is also beneficial to study consumer surveys regarding the impact of retail promotion programs. For instance, in 1999, an International Communications Research television advertising survey of women found that 36 percent of respondents say music is the best attention-getter in ads, while 30 percent say a sale is the best message to attract them to a store.[19]

SUMMARY

1. *To explore the scope of retail promotion.* Retail promotion involves any communication by a retailer that informs, persuades, and/or reminds the target market about any aspect of the retailer through ads, public relations, personal selling, and sales promotion.

2. *To study the elements of retail promotion.* Advertising involves any paid, nonpersonal communication. It has the advantages of a large audience, low costs per person, many alternative media, and other factors. Disadvantages include message inflexibility, high absolute costs, and the wasted portion of the audience. Key advertising media are papers, phone directories, direct mail, radio, TV, the World Wide Web, transit, outdoor, magazines, and flyers/circulars. Especially useful are cooperative ads, in which a retailer shares the costs and message with manufacturers, wholesalers, or other retailers.

SUMMARY (CONTINUED)

Public relations includes all communications fostering a favorable image for a retailer with its publics. It may be nonpersonal or personal, paid or nonpaid, and sponsor controlled or not controlled. Publicity is the nonpersonal, nonpaid form of public relations. Advantages of public relations include the awareness created, the enhanced image presented, the credibility of the source to the consumer, and no costs for messages. Disadvantages include a lack of control over messages, the short-term nature, and nonmedia costs. Publicity can be expected or unexpected, and positive or negative.

Personal selling involves oral communication with one or more potential customers and is critical for persuasion and in closing sales. Advantages are adaptability, flexibility, and immediate feedback. Disadvantages are the small audience, high per-customer costs, and an inability to help lure customers into the store. Order-taking (routine) and/or order-getting (creative) salespeople can be employed. Sales functions include greeting the customer, determining wants, showing merchandise, making a sales presentation, demonstrating goods and/or services, answering objections, and closing the sale.

Sales promotion comprises the paid communication activities other than advertising, public relations, and personal selling. Advantages are that it may be eye-catching, unique, and valuable to the customer. Disadvantages are that it may be hard to end, have a negative effect on image,

and rely on frivolous selling points. Types of sales promotion include POP displays, contests and sweepstakes, coupons, frequent shopper programs, prizes, samples, demonstrations, referral gifts, matchbooks, pens, calendars, shopping bags, and special events.

3. *To discuss the strategic aspects of retail promotion.* There are five steps in planning a promotion strategy.
  (1) Goals are stated in specific and measurable terms. Positive word of mouth (WOM) is an important long-term goal.
  (2) An overall promotion budget is set on the basis of one of these techniques: all you can afford, incremental, competitive parity, percentage of sales, and objective and task.
  (3) The promotional mix is outlined, based on the firm's budget, the type of retailing involved, the coverage of the media, and the hierarchy of effects.
  (4) The promotional mix is enacted. Included are decisions involving specific media, promotional timing, message content, sales force composition, particular sales-promotion tools, and the responsibility for coordination.
  (5) The retailer systematically reviews and adjusts the promotional plan, consistent with its preset goals.

Key Terms

retail promotion (p. 630)
advertising (p. 631)
cooperative advertising (p. 634)
vertical cooperative advertising
  agreement (p. 639)
horizontal cooperative advertising
  agreement (p. 639)
public relations (p. 639)
publicity (p. 639)

personal selling (p. 642)
order-taking salesperson (p. 643)
order-getting salesperson (p. 643)
PMs (p. 643)
canned sales presentation (p. 645)
need-satisfaction approach (p. 645)
sales promotion (p. 646)
word of mouth (WOM) (p. 652)
all-you-can-afford method (p. 652)

incremental method (p. 652)
competitive parity method (p. 653)
percentage-of-sales method (p. 653)
objective-and-task method (p. 653)
hierarchy of effects (p. 654)
reach (p. 657)
frequency (p. 657)
massed promotion effort (p. 657)
distributed promotion effort (p. 657)

Questions for Discussion

1. Are there any retailers that should *not* use advertising? Explain your answer.

2. How would an advertising plan for a Web retailer differ from that for a bricks-and-mortar chain?

3. How do manufacturer and retailer cooperative advertising goals overlap? How do they differ?

4. How may a movie theater try to generate positive publicity?

5. Give three examples each of order-taking salespeople and order-getting salespeople. Under which circumstances should each type be used?

6. How can advertising, public relations, personal selling, and sales promotion complement each other for a retailer?

7. Are there any retailers that should *not* use sales promotion? Explain your answer.

8. What are the pros and cons of sweepstakes and contests?

9. Develop sales promotions for each of the following:
   a. A revitalized neighborhood business district.
   b. An existing dry cleaner now open on Sunday for the first time.
   c. A new pharmacy.

   d. A new outlet mall in a moderate-sized suburb.

10. Which method of promotional budgeting should a small retailer use? A large retailer? Why?

11. Explain the hierarchy of effects from a retail perspective. Apply your answer to a new gift store.

12. Describe the difference between massed promotion and distributed promotion in retailing. How may a retailer combine both methods?

13. Develop a checklist for a full-line discount store to coordinate its promotional plan.

14. For each of these promotional goals, explain how to evaluate promotional effectiveness:
    a. Maintain customer traffic.
    b. Develop an innovative image.
    c. Increase customer loyalty by 8 percent.

WEB-BASED EXERCISE

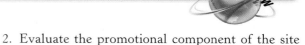

My Points (www.mypoints.com)

Go to the My Points site and sign up for membership (there is no cost or obligation). Then, answer the questions.

Questions

1. Evaluate the promotional component of the site from a retailer's perspective.

2. Evaluate the promotional component of the site from a final consumer's perspective.

3. Select the "Shop and Earn" option. Evaluate a computer retailer's site.

4. Select the "Shop and Earn" option. Evaluate a travel and vacation retailer's site.

CHAPTER ENDNOTES

1. Patricia Winters Lauro, "Wendy's Founder Wasn't a Hit, Except with Customers," *New York Times* (March 16, 1999), p. C10.

2. "10 Years in Five Questions," *Promo* (December 1999), p. 65.

3. "100 Leading National Advertisers," *Advertising Age* (September 27, 1999), various pages.

4. Suein L. Hwang, "A New Spin for Web Firms: Not.com." *Wall Street Journal* (November 11, 1999), p. B1.

5. See Barry Janoff, "Dynamic Duos," *Progressive Grocer* (October 1999), p. 115; and Judith Rosen, "Co-op on the Edge of a New Millennium," *Publishers Weekly* (July 12, 1999), p. 21.

6. Joe Greenwald, "12 Public Relations Tactics That Will Guarantee Your Restaurant's Success," *Nation's Restaurant News* (April 26, 1999), p. 38.

7. See Kristy E. Reynolds and Sharon E. Beatty, "Customer Benefits and Company Consequences of Customer-Salesperson Relationships in Retailing," *Journal of Retailing*, Vol. 75 (Spring 1999), pp. 11–32.

8. "Special Report: Impact in the Aisles," *Promo* (January 1996), pp. 25, 28.

9. *Promo's Sourcebook 2000;* and authors' estimates.

10. Ibid.

11. Ibid.

12. Louise Kramer, "McD's Ad Goal: 'Touch People,'" *Advertising Age* (November 15, 1999), p. 22.

13. See Mary C. Gilly, John L. Graham, Mary Finley Wolfinbarger, and Laura J. Yale, "A Dyadic Study of Interpersonal Information Search," *Journal of the Academy of Marketing Science,* Vol. 26 (Spring 1998), pp. 83–100.

14. Richard Sale, "Bankers Go to Market," *Promo* (August 1999), pp. 85–86.

15. Leslie Kaufman, "Online Retailers Emptying Their Wallets on Advertising," *New York Times on the Web* (November 2, 1999).

16. Bob Tedeschi, "E-Commerce Report," *New York Times* (August 9, 1999), p. C5.

17. "Shoppers Still Love to Sit on Santa's Lap," *Wall Street Journal* (November 29, 1999), p. B1.

18. Richard Sale, "Check This Out," *Promo* (October 1999), pp. 39–44; James R. Hagerty, "Home Improvement Chain Puts Science to Work on Its Marketing," *Wall Street Journal* (March 11, 1999), p. B18; and Carol Krol, "Pizza Hut's Data Base Makes Its Couponing More Efficent," *Advertising Age* (November 30, 1998), p. 27.

19. Ira P. Schneiderman, "What Grabs the Customer?" *Women's Wear Daily* (May 28, 1999), p.13.

CASE 1

THE PROMOTIONAL EFFORTS OF SAN DIEGO'S LA CASA MARIA RESTAURANT

Established in 1987 by Maria and Hernando Lopez, La Casa Maria is one of the most popular Mexican restaurants in San Diego, California. The owners seek to serve fresh food with a "home flavor." Thus, the restaurant features the type of food that would be served in a Mexican home on a special occasion. Unlike other restaurants with extensive menus, La Casa Maria features a limited menu (that generally includes a choice from among two appetizers, salads, soups, and main dishes). All of the food at La Casa Maria is prepared to order.

La Casa Maria also has a special ambience. All guests are personally greeted by either Maria or Hernando. The restaurant has two dining areas: a main dining area and an outdoor terrace. Both have spectacular ocean and mountain views.

The promotional activities of La Casa Maria include a combination of Yellow Pages advertising, word-of-mouth communication, local newspaper advertising, sponsorship of local baseball and soccer teams, and providing food free-of-charge to local elementary schools for fund-raising activities. La Casa Maria's largest single advertising expenditure is with the Yellow Pages. The owners believe Yellow Pages advertising is particularly important because it enables them to attract consumers who do not have a particular restaurant in mind.

These are the basic objectives of La Casa Maria's Yellow Pages advertising:

- To clearly communicate important facts about the restaurant.
- To convey the restaurant's friendly image.
- To stand out among the other restaurant ads and break through the clutter.

La Casa Maria's Yellow Pages ad contains a map of its location, its address and phone number, a listing of the hours open, its credit card acceptance policy, its reservations policy, a listing of its awards, and pricing information for both adult and children's meals.

Through research studies on behalf of the Yellow Pages Publishers Association, this is known about restaurant advertising:

- The most visited heading in the Yellow Pages is "Restaurants." Most consumers read at least five ads.
- 41 percent of all people turn to the "Restaurants" heading without the name of a restaurant in mind. The rest have a specific restaurant in mind and want to contact the restaurant and learn more about it.

- Individuals who refer to the "Restaurants" heading tend to be both male and female, aged 18 to 34 (particularly 18 to 24), have a household income of over $40,000, and have attended college.
- 74 percent of all references to the "Restaurants" heading result in an actual purchase; 37 percent of the references that result in a purchase are from new customers.
- On the basis of a 10-point rating scale (with a score of 10 being the highest possible score), consumers assign these ratings with regard to the usefulness of elements that could be included in a Yellow Pages restaurant ad: days and hours open—8.8, the type of food served—8.1, the need for reservations—8.0, menu items/specialties—7.7, location—7.4, the type of restaurant (bar/family/formal)—7.4, the price range—7.2, and credit card acceptance—7.0. Elements with relatively low ratings are listing either the E-mail address (3.4) or the fax number (2.7).

Questions

1. Evaluate La Casa Maria's promotional objectives for the Yellow Pages.

2. Evaluate La Casa Maria's overall media usage.

3. How would you change the elements in La Casa Maria's Yellow Pages ad based on the research data cited in this case.

4. What criteria should be used to evaluate La Casa Maria's Yellow Pages expenditures?

NOTE   The material in this case is drawn from *Student Brief: La Casa Maria Authentic Mexican Restaurant* (Troy, Mich.: Yellow Pages Publishers Association, n.d.).

CASE 2

RETAIL NEWSPAPER ADVERTISING   Newspapers are the most important U.S. advertising medium, accounting for 25 percent of media spending. Eighty-five percent of all newspaper ads are placed in local markets, 15 percent in national markets. Newspaper advertising is particularly important for retailers due to its large readership, the local nature of circulation, and the attractive options that are available. Let's look at these factors.

Although 62 percent of adults read a daily newspaper, this number increases to 70 percent on Sundays. Men and women prefer different sections of a newspaper. The highest degree of readership among men is general news, followed by sports, editorial, and business sections. Among women, general news is also the most read, followed by food, arts and entertainment, and home living.

Newspapers can be classified by frequency of publication, size, and circulation. There are 1,600 daily newspapers and approximately 7,500 weekly newspapers. The most widely read daily newspaper is the *Wall Street Journal,* followed by *USA Today.* Weekly newspapers are especially important for small-town retailers and for firms seeking niche markets. One type of weekly newspaper is the advertising-laden shopper. Shoppers have low advertising rates, but they may not be read since households do not pay for this medium. There are two sizes of newspapers: the larger broad sheet and the less popular tabloid.

In preparing newspaper media plans, retailers can choose among classified ads, display ads, and supplements. Classified ads are often used for employment, real-estate, and used car sales. Local display advertising generates the most advertising revenue for daily papers.

CASE 2
(CONTINUED)

National display ads can be used by larger firms to supplement the advertising of local branches or franchises and to provide better store recognition. National display ads are typically 75 percent more costly than local ads with the same circulation. Supplements such as *Parade* and *USA Weekend* are distributed to newspapers by independent publishers. Another form of supplement is a freestanding insert. Freestanding inserts typically contain offers from one store or a collection of pre-printed coupons.

Newspaper advertising has several advantages over other media. These include geographic selectivity, extensive market coverage, flexibility, a short lead time, and the impact on stimulating consumers to act. Geographic selectivity is achieved through zoned editions whereby retailers target specific geographic regions. Thus, retailers can eliminate waste circulation. Newspapers offer high market penetration. Some newspapers even offer free versions to nonsubscribers as a way of increasing market coverage. Flexibility is enhanced by enabling retailers to select among various ad sizes, color alternatives, freestanding inserts, and supplement options. Many newspapers allow retailers to fax in their ads as close as one day prior to publication. Lastly, newspapers can induce consumers to buy through coupon-based offers. About 80 percent of all redeemed coupons are distributed through newspapers.

Retailers can choose among four different types of newspaper advertising: institutional, regular price, special promotion, and deep markdown price. Institutional advertising is image-related and is generally the most creative of all ad forms. Regular price advertising seeks to explain the benefits consumers derive from buying goods and services at a specific retailer. Special promotions seek to develop high sales volume and store traffic through discounts, special purchases, and markdowns of regular merchandise. Deep markdown price advertising seeks to clear end-of-season inventories.

Questions

1. How should a tire retailer use the information on newspaper readership patterns by men and women in creating its advertising strategy?

2. What do you think are the pros and cons of using a freestanding insert to a retailer such as Kmart?

3. What types of image-related advertising appeals can a major department store use?

4. When should a retailer employ radio ads rather than newspaper ads? Explain your answer.

Video Questions on Newspaper Advertising

1. Discuss the pros and cons of the use of photographs, drawings/artwork, and reverse type for a small independent retailer.

2. Describe the basic principles of newspaper layout (illustration, headline, copy, and logo).

PART SEVEN COMPREHENSIVE CASE

The Power of Being Different

INTRODUCTION

Most retailers know they need to innovate. Many just don't have the stomach to carry it through. It's not about change for change's sake. Retailers have to be passionate about it. Innovation needs a well-planned strategic direction, a unique store design that makes the strategy work, and proper operational concept execution. We all know what the success stories are. The common element among them is the commitment they have made to change and to innovation. Successful retailers change the rules of the game, exploiting all opportunities for innovation.

Retailing is undergoing a time of unprecedented change. Firms are facing hard, perplexing choices, and the number of casualties grows daily. Some are no longer around—they did not innovate, or change, or develop a winning strategy and are no longer in business. Others have significantly diminished in size.

It's nearly impossible to pick up a paper or magazine without headlines blaring that retailing is in a tumultuous state of change. Quick to predict the potential of Web retailing, sometimes referred to as the "gold rush in cyberspace," editors of business publications "stir the pot" by printing speculative forecasts that are usually outdated as soon as they are made.

Recent years have seen a new era of "retail polarity," causing us to re-examine the changing needs of consumers and their shopping habits. Clearly, retailers are moving to the extremes, leaving in the center a "no man's land." This middle ground is a spot where retailers do not want to be, and we liken it to a "sea of sameness," a vast wasteland where there is virtually no difference in product, pricing, assortment, or availability. Retailers that fail to innovate may find themselves being pulled under the waves of change.

The material in this case is adapted by the authors from D. Lee Carpenter, founder and chairman, Design Forum, "Return on Innovation—The Power of Being Different," *Arthur Andersen Retailing Issues Letter,* (May 1998), pp. 1–6. Reprinted by permission.

LEFT BRAIN, RIGHT BRAIN

We divide consumers into two groups: left brain and right brain. Left-brain shoppers are looking for the low-impact, low-service, low-cost shopping experience and usually go to places like Costco, Sam's Club, Kmart, and the Internet. They want the retailer that offers a functional, analytical, need-fulfilling, value-oriented experience. Shoppers who are "right brainers" buy for creative and emotional reasons. They want "high touch" or the "wow" experience. With price not a primary concern, these shoppers usually frequent stores like Disney, Gander Mountain, Golf Galaxy, and FAO Schwarz, to name a few.

Everyone has a left brain and a right brain, and, therefore, when shopping, crosses from pole to pole. Those who cross seek two different retail experiences to meet an immediate need. For instance, a shopper may visit Sam's Club to buy commodity products and other discounted merchandise, and then spends the money saved there at Saks Fifth Avenue for a makeover or a fashion show. It is because of this buying behavior that retailers today find it difficult to understand their customers.

So how does strategic store design fit into this current climate? Stores are "the stage" for the consumers' retail experience. That stage must be set to tell a story. When developing a productive store environment, retailers must carve their own niche and create a suitable, stimulating experience for the customer. Strategic design must target the polar extremes of shopping behavior. Design is the "visual personality" of the store. Left-brain shoppers want an environment meeting specific, functional needs. For right-brain shoppers, an enticing, imaginative, spirited store design creates a powerful image, which, in turn, creates a definite advantage over competitors. Retailers can reach each segment using fresh design ideas to build long-term relationships, staking their claim, and getting out of the middle ground.

In my 20 years in retailing, I've observed first-hand the destructiveness of six long-standing myths. My purpose here is to show how these myths block the innovative vitality essential to long-term success.

MYTH ONE: BRANDING IS FOR SOAP, NOT STORES

For years, people at Procter & Gamble have known the power and importance of branding. We all know their brands: Tide, Zest, Cheer, Safeguard—the list goes on.

They've understood that you're only as good as your brand, and they've devoted much attention to managing that brand at all levels of their business. It has worked well for them.

However, in business author Tom Peters' latest book, *The Circle of Innovation,* he states that in an increasingly crowded market, product and service distinction alone are not enough: "If you build it, they will not necessarily come." As a result, branding is more—not less—important than ever. Branding means nothing more than creating a distinct personality and telling the world about it.

Branding today has expanded beyond just soaps and other consumer products. It is moving in new directions and being extended to new areas, including stores and people. Martha Stewart has become a "brand." Sears, although carrying brand names such as Kenmore, Craftsman, and Diehard, is also a brand. Other retailers are beginning to understand that branding is crucial to success, and those who don't are likely to be forgotten in the "sea of sameness."

An example of effective branding through design is Land Rover, a company whose Range Rover Discovery and Land Rover products were sold from the back of Jaguar or other luxury vehicle dealership facilities. Its U.S. presence was nearly nonexistent. Several years ago, however, this company of only 60 U.S. dealers made an important realization: In a country with a growing sport-utility vehicle market, the lack of a strong brand position and brand equity would eventually leave it in the dust. Land Rover needed to create its own brand equity and stand for its core values.

The response was an entirely new image. Today, with approximately 160 dealers (120 of which are new, stand-alone Land Rover Centres), the image boasts authenticity, entertainment, and customer service. Each showroom features a dramatic product display using rocks and boulders to set vehicles at steep angles to imply motion, capturing the feeling of the true off-road driving experience. Externally, rustic outdoor architecture is complemented by a test track that allows customers to actually drive the vehicle on unusual and challenging "terrain" to fully appreciate the integrity of the product—and to have fun!

The showroom uses "artifacting," or the creative display of authentic outdoor equipment, including canoes, travel trunks, telescopes, and antique maps to convey a sense of long distance and adventure. Unique flooring features a giant compass displaying each dealership's actual latitudinal and longitudinal coordinates. Jackets, luggage, adventure books, and packages have become added ways for Land Rover to sell not just a vehicle but the whole outdoor discovery experience. Employees have been trained to create the ultimate four-wheel drive showroom in every market. They are featured in newspaper ads and on TV to extend the brand from the product to the retail point-of-sale, and into the customer's awareness level.

Land Rover has come a long way in a short time, extending the brand franchise effectively. The firm has met its goal: to create themed retail showrooms that show the Land Rover brand as a unique point of difference from competing brands. And it seems to be working.

MYTH TWO: GOOD POSITIONING ENDURES FOREVER

Good positioning means a company's name, reputation, and niche are well recognized. Positioning also means that this well-known, distinct personality is followed up with a reliable, high-quality product. Positioning is the effort aimed to help customers know the real differences between a retailer and its competitors, so they will perceive the product and the experience as possessing the attributes they want.

However, a good positioning strategy does not last forever. As markets change, so must the retailers, and so must their positioning. Monitoring trends enables retailers to strive for innovation, modify their well-established positioning, and have a successful future. Good positioning that is continually modified to move with consumers' changing tastes and perspectives can guarantee a firm a long, lucrative future.

For 40 years, Dunkin' Donuts has offered a very popular product—the donut. Yet, as people's attitudes toward healthy eating changed, so did the demand for the product. Customers began looking for healthier alternatives and expected the almost 4,000 franchised Dunkin' Donuts outlets to provide them. A "more relevant position" was the answer, with the company crafting its stance around its enhanced menu, specifically the new coffee offerings. It quickly went from "America's Number One Donut Shop" to the new tagline of "Dunkin' Donuts: Something Fresh Is Always Brewing Here."

A contemporary, energetic design now invigorates the overall Dunkin' Donuts experience. Modifying the menu was the first step; it now features not only coffee and donuts but also hot and cold specialty coffee drinks, bagels, and muffins. The next step was to incorporate upbeat, new design elements into the store environment, including brighter menu boards, backlit signage, and more visible displays to refocus on merchandising the expanded menu. Moving on from the well-known pink and orange colors, the firm created "ripe raisin," a rich, warm tone that now serves as the basis of a fresh new color palette and communicates the enhanced coffee presence—while modernizing the atmosphere. This signature color is used externally on roofs and signs and internally on countertops and walls. In addition, these design elements are combined with the value strategy of charging a fair price for the product.

The overall design strategy aids in positioning Dunkin' Donuts to an entirely new customer base and the results are promising: increased customer loyalty and better customer frequency, as well as substantially higher sales volumes.

MYTH THREE: THE CUSTOMERS WILL TELL US WHAT THEY WANT

Yes, customers will express what they want, but will that feedback really provide the retailer with what is truly needed—strategic direction and creative concept development? Although customers can give you good ideas, they should not be responsible for driving long-range planning. Many times, when customer input is sought, that feedback usually relates to merchandise selection and pricing, not the "big picture." Today's unforgiving retail world demands "breakthrough thinking" to remain competitive. Design based on innovative thinking and creativity, not solely on customer feedback, brings to retailers new concepts for retail strategy and, ultimately, success.

Could customers have told toy maker FAO Schwarz that it needed to launch "FAO Schweetz," one of retailing's most exciting new candy concepts? Probably not. Design makes inanimate candies come alive by showing enormous, playful characters who seem happiest living in a candy store. Every imaginable flavor of jellybeans, 30 gummy bear flavors, and 21 colors of M&Ms fill gigantic letters spelling "FAO Schweetz" in the display window. A Godiva chocolate vault invites exploration. There's a Sour Patch Fruit Stand with 24 sour patch candies; and a dancing Jelly Belly chorus line provides entertainment. Customers can't pass by the oversized gumball machine or the tall lollipops that pop up from the floor, beckoning children (and some adults) to stay longer. This breakthrough from the typical toy store, complemented by the design, has taken FAO Schwarz into a new arena, one with much potential.

MYTH FOUR: DESIGN IS THE ICING ON THE CAKE

This is the most common myth—that design is "glitter" and really has nothing to do with concept. The "cake," many business owners claim, is the product they sell and, thus, design does not bring in new customers or encourage current ones' continued support. Many firms think they can get by with a fresh coat of paint, new signs, and rearranged displays, call it strategic design, and enhance results dramatically. Nothing is further from the truth. Design has an integral role in the strategic plan. It is the thread that helps hold a store concept together, supporting other elements and helping blend them to achieve the goal.

Called the pre-eminent music and entertainment store, the Virgin Records Megastore in New York City's Times Square has hit the mark for strategic, innovative design. Often touted as a New York landmark, the exterior features a huge, fire-red neon Virgin logo, an enormous analog clock stating "It's Time to Fly," and gigantic, illuminated color displays of newly released album covers. Walking inside the tri-level, 75,000-square-foot store is like entering music heaven, with blaring pop music, theatrical lighting, and arty graphics. All elements combined scream, "It's show time!"

Design showcases the extensive product offerings and was planned with an indigenous architectural theme, using stone, concrete, and other textures—even graffiti—to give it a New York City appeal. The ceiling was created to resemble an urban sky at night with telephone lines and trolley car wires. A tall, open store center serves as the nucleus of activity. A 50-foot, glass and steel disk jockey tower belting out "Virgin Radio" in sizzling red letters reaches from floor to ceiling and serves as the focal point. The sides of the cylindrical center post merchandise available on each level. With 600 listening stations and 100 video/laser viewing stations, a person could spend hours poring over the 150,000 music titles on CD and cassette in 40 music categories, as well as the largest selection of laser disk and video titles in the world.

The main floor, on the street level, is home to pop, rock, dance, soul, rap, and singles collections. A towering Sony Trinitron screen broadcasts music videos, with hundreds of smaller monitors following suit throughout the store. One level down features classical and specialty music sections such as jazz, blues, folk, vocals, and spoken word, all encased in environments that evoke the tone and mood of each genre. A performance space in the classical section provides an area for special events and features a replica of Michelangelo's famous ceiling painting. The third level houses video/laser, new media, books, and children's sections, all complemented by lunch at the "sidewalk" tables of the Virgin Cafe and the option to catch a movie in the four-screen Sony theater complex.

MYTH FIVE: IT HAS TO BE A COOKIE-CUTTER

The question many retailers still ask is, why not cookie-cutter? It seems to have worked for McDonald's and Kmart. And the fact is, it has worked for these powerful retailers—ten years ago. During the past several years, the economics behind the golden arches have been a bit shaky and though sales and income have more than tripled since 1987, growth has slowed. This struggle comes from various problems, including food quality and failed initiatives like the Arch Deluxe. The point is that customers have no other reason to go to a cookie-cutter store if the product quality and price do not satisfy their needs. Even cookie-cutter stores must innovate. A tone must be cultivated to reflect the personality of the store and the target customer. Design must be held to the same standards that the retailer demands of products.

Although it has 850 stores, Kinko's avoids cookie-cutter design by focusing on customer needs and location. Its growth has been exceptional since modest beginnings in 1970 when the first store was so small that it barely housed the copier. The reason for the monumental success has been because the firm found a niche and built stores around customer needs: Early stores were often near colleges and they were open 24 hours—as college students usually needed copying services in the middle of the night. Next, Kinko's continued to grow with its customers and began looking at the trend of more and more people opening small businesses and working from their homes. It immediately went after this market, coining the phrase, "The New Way to Office."

With store size varying from 500 to 3,000 square feet, Kinko's has a variety of design formats to provide the right service and the right products to meet different customer needs. Although many stores are still near universities, growth has taken place in urban and metropolitan areas, as well as by offering business and technical support services. Kinko's helps not just with "copies" but with "documents." Two new services are Kinkonet, for fast transmission of electronic documents, and Kinko's Express, a self-service section with an assortment of

paper and color/black-and-white printing. Consistent adaptation to changing customer needs makes Kinko's the perfect example of a noncookie-cutter concept.

MYTH SIX: OUR PEOPLE ARE THE BEST

As retail design strategists, the first statement we often hear from new clients is "whatever design you develop for us, our people will be able to carry it out." Unless you have a spectacular customer service training program—and I mean "out of this world," like Disney —the typical retailing staff more than likely will not be able to get the job done. Retailers must take a critical look at their sales force, without bias. Can each staff member really implement a new plan? What obstacles will arise? Will noncompliance become an issue? Many issues can crop up, even with the most cooperative, enthusiastic sales team.

Coupled with a unique design approach, the Saturn Corporation has taken a page out of the Disney book, giving birth to a new breed of—not auto dealerships but—automobile *retailers*. Using this term, along with the term *sales consultants*, sets Saturn apart. Realizing that people are truly at the heart of the success of its product, the company created a strategy to benefit the customer, the Saturn service team, suppliers, retailers, and neighbors. The Saturn philosophy of customer service begins with distinctive, welcoming canopies that create the impression of an accessible, comfortable environment. This first impression supports the ultimate goal of "no pressure" service, and consumers are not pushed when buying a Saturn vehicle. Saturn is unique, especially in the auto industry, because its goal is to be more responsible in treating customers. To ensure a no-hassling environment, vehicles have fixed prices, the sales force is noncommissioned, and sales offices are situated away from the merchandise displays.

Competent, thorough professionals proudly provide exemplary service with courtesy, cooperation, and friendliness. The overall climate is relaxed, and customers are warmly enveloped in this "feeling" by atmosphere subtleties, down to a casual conversational style and "no neckties" policy. When cars are bought, a ceremony ensues. New owners arrive to pick up their cars and find them washed and sitting in the middle of the showroom. The Saturn team congratulates and thanks them with thunderous applause.

A special pride has been instilled in the Saturn team through various methods. Production workers are asked for their input to improve the product, for example, and executives often sit in cubicles with the same amenities as student interns. An environment of equality can be found at Saturn, and it all carries over to the precise implementation of the highest customer service standards. A refreshing outlook on how to do business has helped Saturn position itself as the auto retailer that builds and sells the best cars, and it backs up that positioning with solid customer service. This strategy, especially in the highly competitive auto industry, has enabled Saturn to offer an unmatched purchase and service experience and, as a result, to enjoy greater customer loyalty than any other vehicle.

TRUTH: SUCCESS IS ONE INNOVATIVE STEP AWAY

In light of the evolving retail landscape, innovation remains the critical factor to survival. Retailers cannot continue to cling to these common industry myths. Initial steps to innovation may be small or large scale, gradual or accelerated. Becoming creative in retail happens with extensive monitoring of the marketplace and customer behavior and continues with thoughtful, careful planning.

But you have to be able to take some risks, too. As noted in the examples, change also stems from breakthrough thinking and must deliver bottom-line results. It must reinvigorate and revitalize the retail experience, jumpstart store traffic volume, and ignite sales. And it absolutely must carry the retailer into the new millennium with creativity and confidence.

Retailers should open the door to innovation and walk away from the "sea of sameness." Find a niche for the new millennium and create a retail experience that will adapt with the polarity shift that will undoubtedly continue to evolve. Retailers cannot sit back or drift with the tide, for if they do, drowning in the sea of sameness is inevitable. Innovate or evaporate.

Questions

1. From the perspective of atmospherics, state four lessons a retailer could learn from reading this case.
2. In planning a store layout, which traffic flow (straight or curving) would be better in appealing to "left-brain" shoppers? To "right-brain" shoppers? Why?
3. "If you build it, they will not necessarily come." What are the ramifications of this statement for store-based retailers? For Web retailers?
4. Why does a "cookie-cutter" approach work for McDonald's, while Kinko's avoids this type of store design? What can retailers with prototype stores learn from Kinko's?
5. How has Dunkin' Donuts' promotional focus changed over the years? Today, Dunkin' Donuts and Baskin-Robbins are co-branded in many outlets. Present a slogan and a theme for a TV ad that capitalize on this partnership.
6. According to the case, this statement is a myth: "Whatever design you develop for us, our people will be able to carry it out." Why? Apply your answer to the personal selling aspect of the promotion mix.
7. What criteria should innovative retailers use to measure the success of their promotion efforts? Explain your answer.

PUTTING IT ALL TOGETHER

◻ In Part Eight, we "put it all together."

◻ Chapter 20 ties together the elements of a retail strategy that have been described all through this book. The chapter examines planning and opportunity analysis, productivity, performance measures, and scenario analysis. The value of data comparisons (benchmarking and gap analysis) is indicated. Strategic control via the retail audit is covered.

CHAPTER 20

Integrating and Controlling the Retail Strategy

CHAPTER OBJECTIVES

1. To demonstrate the importance of integrating a retail strategy
2. To examine four key factors in the development and enactment of an integrated retail strategy: planning procedures and opportunity analysis, defining productivity, performance measures, and scenario analysis
3. To show how industry and company data can be used in strategy planning and analysis (benchmarking and gap analysis)
4. To explain the principles of a retail audit, its utility in controlling a retail strategy, the difference between horizontal and vertical audits, and the possible difficulties with auditing
5. To provide examples of audit forms

When David Glass, Wal-Mart's chief executive officer, was asked in 1990 to comment on the state of retailing, he remarked, "Half of all U.S. retail companies now in existence will be out of business by the year 2000." Years later, he corrected his earlier statement by stating that "I was too conservative." This sentiment was echoed by Wal-Mart's chief financial officer, when he said that Wal-Mart's 1999 sales accounted for 5 percent of total U.S. retail sales, and "We're now focused on capturing the remaining 95 percent."

Given Wal-Mart's ambitious—but somewhat tongue-in-cheek—plans for its domination of U.S. retailing, it is interesting that Sam Walton (the company's founder) laid out a blueprint for other retailers so they could survive in the era of Wal-Mart. In his autobiography, *Made in America*, Walton recommended that retailers follow these 10 rules to stay competitive. Wal-Mart already practices them:

1. *Commitment*—Be enthusiastic about your business.

2. *Share*—Involve your staff in decision making.

3. *Listen*—Listen to your staff and your customers.

4. *Communicate*—Have an "open door" relationship with your employees.

5. *Appreciate*—Congratulate employees when they do something right.

6. *Celebrate*—Make sure that employees have fun. For example, your retail operation should celebrate each employee's birthday.

7. *Motivate*—Set high goals for your staff and give high performers appropriate rewards.

8. *Exceed*—Promise a lot, but actually deliver more than promised.

9. *Control*—Control your costs.

10. *Swim upstream*—Evaluate what the competition is doing and do something different.[1]

> *Please Note:* Web site addresses are constantly changing.
> The links in this chapter are current as of the publication of this book.

OVERVIEW

Throughout *Retail Management: A Strategic Approach,* we have examined a number of individual factors pertaining to the development of retail strategies. This chapter focuses on integrating and controlling the retail strategy. It ties together the material detailed previously, shows why retailers need to plan and enact coordinated strategies, and describes how to assess success or failure.

By having an integrated strategy and regularly monitoring it, firms of any size or format can take a proper view of the retailing concept and create a superior total retail experience. Consider the independent hardware store, a format that is threatened by the inroads made by Home Depot and other power retailers:

> Independent hardware retailers should not just focus on the day-to-day operations of their stores. More importantly, they should plan their strategic direction and devote more time on researching and thinking of ways of staying competitive. Attending industry events such as the International Hardware Week and the National Hardware Show and making store calls will help them fulfill these functions since these are ways of seeing new products and category developments: What does the new Home Depot Villager's Hardware mean to you? Does the new Stambaugh Hardware upscale convenience hardware format have applications in your business? Will Maggie's Building Solutions Showroom format at 84 Lumber change how you do things? Are there new niche product lines being offered this season that your wholesaler isn't selling that might be right for you? One wonderful aspect of owning your own business is the ability to be an independent. To think and act independently is an important strategic advantage in today's competitive landscape. Large firms are encumbered by their very size. Decisions take a long time to make and an even longer time to implement. In the case of public firms, Wall Street is always looking over their shoulder. Independents, on the other hand, are free to move quickly and to enact new strategies without wading through levels of bureaucracy. Unfortunately, too many owners are so consumed by their daily operations that they never seem to find time to perform the most important function of a chief executive officer—plotting the strategic direction. If owners know where they are and where they are headed, they are more likely to reach the destination.[2]

As today's retailers look to the future, they must deal with many strategic choices and decision dilemmas due to the globalization of world markets, evolving consumer life-styles, competition among formats, and rapid technology changes. There are both opportunities and threats from these developments: "The lines between traditional retailing segments are blurring. Interesting new partnerships unite the strengths of seemingly diverse firms. Standard Oil and McDonald's combine to form a convenient and fun place for families to service their car while getting a low-cost meal. Starbucks and Barnes & Noble partner to nourish the book-browsing experience. Life experience formats like Container Store and Eatzi's draw customers because they solve problems for them—they save people time, they reduce the effort to shop, and they lessen the risk of failure. They take away the hassle and replace it with fun."[3]

INTEGRATING THE RETAIL STRATEGY

It is essential for a retailer to view strategic planning as an integrated and ongoing process—not as a fragmented and one-time-only concept. A major goal of *Retail Management* has been to describe the relationships among the many elements of a retail strategy and show the need to act in an integrated way. Figure 20.1 highlights the integrated strategy of bebe, the

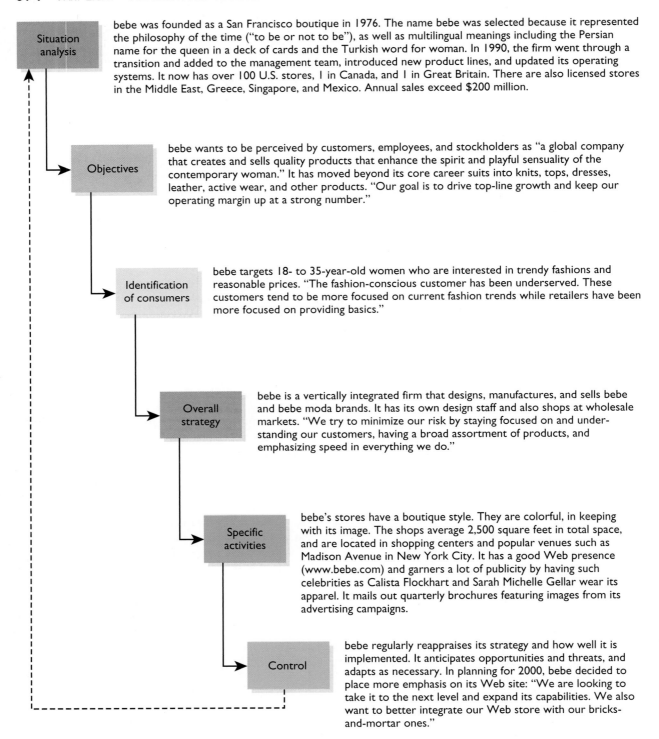

Situation analysis

bebe was founded as a San Francisco boutique in 1976. The name bebe was selected because it represented the philosophy of the time ("to be or not to be"), as well as multilingual meanings including the Persian name for the queen in a deck of cards and the Turkish word for woman. In 1990, the firm went through a transition and added to the management team, introduced new product lines, and updated its operating systems. It now has over 100 U.S. stores, 1 in Canada, and 1 in Great Britain. There are also licensed stores in the Middle East, Greece, Singapore, and Mexico. Annual sales exceed $200 million.

Objectives

bebe wants to be perceived by customers, employees, and stockholders as "a global company that creates and sells quality products that enhance the spirit and playful sensuality of the contemporary woman." It has moved beyond its core career suits into knits, tops, dresses, leather, active wear, and other products. "Our goal is to drive top-line growth and keep our operating margin up at a strong number."

Identification of consumers

bebe targets 18- to 35-year-old women who are interested in trendy fashions and reasonable prices. "The fashion-conscious customer has been underserved. These customers tend to be more focused on current fashion trends while retailers have been more focused on providing basics."

Overall strategy

bebe is a vertically integrated firm that designs, manufactures, and sells bebe and bebe moda brands. It has its own design staff and also shops at wholesale markets. "We try to minimize our risk by staying focused on and under-standing our customers, having a broad assortment of products, and emphasizing speed in everything we do."

Specific activities

bebe's stores have a boutique style. They are colorful, in keeping with its image. The shops average 2,500 square feet in total space, and are located in shopping centers and popular venues such as Madison Avenue in New York City. It has a good Web presence (www.bebe.com) and garners a lot of publicity by having such celebrities as Calista Flockhart and Sarah Michelle Gellar wear its apparel. It mails out quarterly brochures featuring images from its advertising campaigns.

Control

bebe regularly reappraises its strategy and how well it is implemented. It anticipates opportunities and threats, and adapts as necessary. In planning for 2000, bebe decided to place more emphasis on its Web site: "We are looking to take it to the next level and expand its capabilities. We also want to better integrate our Web store with our bricks-and-mortar ones."

Figure 20.1
The Integrated Strategy of bebe

Sources: Figure developed by the authors based on data from Marianne Wilson, "bebe: Simply the Best," *Chain Store Age* (November 1999), pp. 55–58; and *www.bebe.com* (March 9, 2000).

This site (www.
bizmove.com/
marketing/m2c.htm)
raises a lot of good
questions for retailers
to think about in
integrating their
strategies.

California-based apparel chain. In 1999, *Chain Store Age* cited bebe as the leading "high performance retailer" among all publicly-held U.S. firms.[4]

Four fundamental factors especially need to be taken into account in devising and enacting an integrated retail strategy: planning procedures and opportunity analysis, defining productivity, performance measures, and scenario analysis. These factors are discussed next.

Planning Procedures and Opportunity Analysis

Planning procedures can be optimized through various coordinated activities. By doing so, planning is more systematic and reflects input from multiple parties:

- Senior executives first outline the firm's overall direction and goals. This provides written guidelines for middle- and lower-level managers, who get input from all types of internal and external sources. These managers are thus encouraged to generate ideas at an early stage.
- Top-down plans (by upper managers) and bottom-up or horizontal plans (by middle- and lower-level managers) are then combined.
- Specific plans are enacted, including checkpoints and dates.

Opportunities need to be carefully examined with regard to their impact on overall strategy, and not in an isolated manner. See Figure 20.2. For example, Just for Feet stumbled badly by overexpanding and adding smaller stores not as conducive to its category killer merchandising philosophy. As a result, Just for Feet hired a new management team, closed a number of small, unprofitable stores, and filed for Chapter 11 bankruptcy protection. The company has returned to its earlier heritage in the hope of restoring the business.

Figure 20.2
Opportunity Analysis
with the SBA

While evaluating opportunities, retailers should utilize some form of **sales opportunity grid,** which rates the promise of new and established goods, services, procedures, and/or store outlets across a variety of criteria. In this way, opportunities may be evaluated on the basis of the integrated strategies the firms would follow if the opportunities are pursued. Computerization makes it possible to apply such a grid.

Table 20.1 shows a sales opportunity grid for a supermarket that wants to decide which of two salad dressing brands to carry. The store manager has outlined the integrated strategy to be used for each brand; A is established, whereas B is new. Due to its newness, the manager believes initial Brand B sales would be lower, but first year sales would be similar. The brands would be priced the same and occupy identical space. Brand B requires higher display costs but offers a larger markup. Brand B would return a greater gross profit ($781 to $613) and net profit ($271 to $193) than Brand A by the end of the first year. Based on the overall grid, the manager picks Brand B. Yet, if the store is more concerned about immediate profit, Brand A might be chosen because it is expected to take Brand B a while to gain acceptance.

Table 20.1	**Supermarket's Sales Opportunity Grid for Two Brands of Salad Dressing**	
Criteria	**Brand A (established)**	**Brand B (new)**
Retail price	$1.29/8-ounce bottle	$1.29/8-ounce bottle
Floor space needed	8 square feet	8 square feet
Display costs	$10.00/month	$20.00/month for 6 mos.
		$10.00/month thereafter
Operating costs	$0.12/unit	$0.12/unit
Markup	19%	22%
Sales estimate		
During first month		
Units	250	50
Dollars	$323	$65
During first six months		
Units	1,400	500
Dollars	$1,806	$645
During first year		
Units	2,500	2,750
Dollars	$3,225	$3,548
Gross profit estimate		
During first month	$61	$14
During first six months	$343	$142
During first year	$613	$781
Net profit estimate		
During first month	$21	−$12
During first six months	$115	−$38
During first year	$193	$271

Example 1:
Gross profit estimate = Sales estimate − [(1.00 − Markup percentage) × (Sales estimate)]
Brand A gross profit estimate during first six months = $1,806 − [(1.00 − 0.19) × ($1,806)] = $343

Example 2:
Net profit estimate = Gross profit estimate − (Display costs + Operating costs)
Brand A net profit estimate during first six months = $343 − ($60 + $168) = $115

Defining Productivity in a Manner Consistent with the Strategy Chosen

As noted in Chapters 12 and 13, productivity refers to the efficiency with which a retail strategy is carried out; and it is in any retailer's interest to reach sales and profit goals while keeping control over costs. Productive strategies are well integrated with regard to target market, location(s), and operations, merchandising, pricing, and communications efforts.

Intellilink's Easy 1 system (www.ilsa. com) can improve a retailer's productivity. See how.

A retailer must be careful in enacting its strategy. On the one hand, it looks to avoid unnecessary expenses. A firm does not want to have eight salespeople working at one time if four can satisfactorily handle all customers. Likewise, it does not want to pay high rent for a site in a regional shopping center if customers would be willing to travel a few miles farther to a less costly site. On the other hand, a retailer does not wish to lose customers due to insufficient sales personnel to handle the rush of shoppers during peak hours. It also does not seek to be in a low rent site if this leads to a significant drop in customer traffic.

This tradeoff often means neither the least expensive strategy nor the most expensive one may be the most productive strategy, since the former approach might not adequately service customers and the latter might be wasteful. A productive strategy for an upscale firm is far different from that for a discounter. An upscale retailer would not succeed with self-service operations, and it would be unnecessary (and inefficient) for a discounter to have a large sales staff. The most productive approach applies a specific integrated retail strategy (such as a full-service jewelry store) as efficiently as possible. See Figure 20.3.

Food Lion is one of the pre-eminent U.S. retailers. It has a well-integrated, productive strategy. Here are some reasons why (www.foodlion.com/companyinfo.htm):

Figure 20.3
Micro Warehouse: A Well-Conceived Approach to Improving Productivity

Reprinted by permission.

The Strategic Pull of Burdines

Prior to graduation, Brent Hoover thought his career would be in commercial lending. As a marketing major who graduated from Florida State University in 1996, Hoover interviewed with only one retailer—Burdines. However, after meeting with the Burdines recruiting team, he quickly became convinced that he wanted to pursue a retailing career path.

Hoover, now an assistant buyer at Burdines, estimates that 90 percent of his current responsibilities involve financial forecasting: "My job consists of projecting how profitable something will be, presenting ideas to management for extra funding, and projecting markdowns."

He enjoys the fast pace of retailing: "One second it's numbers-oriented, the next second it is an advertising function. I am always looking for new ways to drive the bottom line." Although he has always been good at concurrently performing multiple tasks, the assistant buyer's position challenges his ability to manage multiple responsibilities. What is he learning? "You never have time to focus on just one thing at a time." As a result, Hoover is trying to delegate tasks to others, whenever possible.

Brent Hoover plans to become a buyer and then move into Burdines' upper management levels.

Source: "Retail Offered Creative Options," *Careers in Retailing* (January 1999), pp. 15, 18.

Our success has always been based on the principle of offering customers quality products at extra low prices in clean, convenient stores. Food Lion is now one of the largest U.S. supermarket chains, with 1,120 stores in 11 states. The stores sell more than 24,000 different products and offer branded merchandise, as well as a growing number of high-quality private label products. Price leadership and quality assurance have made the stores welcome in our Southeast and Mid-Atlantic operating regions. We have maintained low price leadership and quality assurance through technological advances and operating efficiencies such as standard store formats, efficient warehouse design, and computer links with vendors. Food Lion is a leader in implementing quality assurance by monitoring critical points in the movement of food from the farm to the dinner table. We look with confidence to a future of continued innovation, growth, price leadership, and service to customers and communities.

Performance Measures

By determining relevant **performance measures**—the criteria used to assess effectiveness—and setting standards (goals) for each of them, a retailer can better develop and integrate its strategy. Among the measures frequently used by retailers are total sales, average sales per store, sales by goods/service category, sales per square foot, gross margins, gross margin return on investment, operating income, inventory turnover, markdown percentages, employee turnover, financial ratios, and profitability.

To properly gauge the effectiveness of a strategy, a firm should use **benchmarking,** whereby the retailer sets its own standards and measures performance based on the achievements of its sector of retailing, specific competitors, high-performance firms, and/or the prior actions of the firm itself. The goal is to learn from experience (www.eprs.com/benchmarking.htm): "Benchmarking helps managers evaluate overall profitability, efficiency, and productivity. It also helps them to better control costs by benchmarking them against the best practices being achieved by other retailers. This information can be very powerful as it allows managers to know business better, so as to identify what is working and what isn't.

Table 20.2 Benchmarking Through Annual Operating Statements of Typical Small Retailers (Expressed in Terms of Revenues = 100%)

Type of Retailer	Total Revenues	Cost of Goods Sold	Gross Profit	Total Operating Expenses	Net Income
Apparel stores	100	66.7	33.3	29.2	4.1
Auto parking	100	32.9	67.1	59.1	8.0
Auto repair shops	100	53.9	46.1	33.7	12.4
Barber shops	100	4.1	95.9	41.3	54.6
Bars/drinking places	100	54.3	45.7	41.2	4.5
Beauty salons	100	20.0	80.0	54.0	26.0
Bicycle stores	100	69.8	30.2	24.5	5.7
Coin laundries	100	11.3	88.7	85.1	3.6
Dentists	100	8.5	91.5	49.6	41.9
Drugstores	100	69.0	31.0	22.5	8.5
Eating places	100	53.0	47.0	41.4	5.6
Gas stations	100	84.0	16.0	12.2	3.8
Gift stores	100	63.2	36.8	34.0	2.8
Grocery stores	100	83.1	16.9	14.4	2.5
Hardware stores	100	74.8	25.2	20.9	4.3
Motels	100	12.8	87.2	84.4	2.8
Photography studios	100	29.0	71.0	54.8	16.2
Real-estate brokers	100	9.1	90.9	52.2	38.7
Repair services	100	40.1	59.9	41.5	18.4
Used car dealers	100	83.5	16.5	14.3	2.2

Source: U.S. Internal Revenue Service, as reported at *www.sbaonline.sba.gov/SCORE/ca/typop.html* (March 11, 2000).

It can also serve as an alert to trends that might remain hidden. It is important for various industry groups to have reliable, accurate, timely, and impartial performance figures available."

One of the most useful information sources for retailers is the *Annual Benchmark Report for Retail Trade,* which is available through a free download from the U.S. Census Bureau Web site (www.census.gov/mp/www/pub/bus/msbus19c.html). The *Benchmark Report* shows a 10-year monthly comparison of sales, inventories, and inventory ratios by retail category. It also reveals 10 years of annual purchases, gross margins, and per-capita sales by category.

In addition to the *Benchmark Report,* retailers of varying sizes and in different goods or service lines can obtain comparative data from such sources as the Internal Revenue Service, Small Business Administration, *Progressive Grocer, Stores, Chain Store Age, Discount Store News,* Dun & Bradstreet, the National Retail Federation, Robert Morris Associates, and annual reports. This information lets retailers compare their performance with others.

Table 20.2 contains benchmarking data for small retailers in 20 business categories. The cost of goods sold as a percentage of revenues is highest for gas stations and grocery stores, gross profit is greatest for barber shops and dentists, operating expenses are the most for coin laundries and motels, and net income is highest for barber shops and dentists.

Table 20.3 reveals the customer satisfaction with leading department/discount stores, supermarkets, hotels and motels, and restaurants/fast-food firms. It is based on an ongoing benchmarking survey that yields the American Customer Satisfaction Index (ACSI):

Look at several typical operating statements for small firms by retail format (www.sbaonline.sba.gov/SCORE/ca/typop.html).

- Overall expectation of quality.
- Expectation regarding customization.
- Expectation regarding reliability (how often things go wrong).
- Overall evaluation of experience.

Table 20.3 Benchmarking Through the American Customer Satisfaction Index

Retailer	1997 Index Score	1998 Index Score	1999 Index Score
Department/Discount Stores	74	72	73
Nordstrom	82	80	79
J.C. Penney	78	75	75
Wal-Mart	74	76	75
Target Corporation (discount stores)	77	73	74
Target Corporation (department stores)	74	72	74
Sears	74	71	74
May	75	72	72
Dillard's	74	73	71
Kmart	72	68	71
Army & Air Force Exchange Service	69	69	68
Federated	73	66	67
Supermarkets	74	73	73
Publix	80	79	79
Supervalu	75	74	77
Wal-Mart	75	72	75
Winn-Dixie	75	74	74
Food Lion	73	73	73
Kroger	74	74	73
Safeway	73	70	71
Albertson's	77	72	70
Hotels and Motels	68	72	70
Promus (Doubletree, Embassy Suites, etc.)	77	78	79
Marriott	76	76	77
Hilton	75	72	74
Hyatt	77	75	73
Starwood Hotels (ITT-Sheraton, Westin)	NM	67	69
Holiday Inn	NM	69	68
Ramada Inns	64	67	67
Restaurants/Fast-Food Firms	66	68	69
Wendy's	71	69	73
Little Caesars	69	73	71
Pizza Hut	63	71	71
Domino's Pizza	68	68	70
Burger King	67	68	64
KFC	69	67	64
Taco Bell	66	67	64
McDonald's	60	60	61

Sources: University of Michigan Business School and American Society for Quality Control. Reprinted by permission.

- Evaluation of customization experience.
- Evaluation of reliability experience.
- Rating of quality given the price.
- Rating of price given the quality.
- Overall satisfaction.
- Expectancy disconfirmation (performance falling short or exceeding expectations).
- Performance versus the customer's ideal.
- The customer's level of complaining.

- Repurchase likelihood.
- Price tolerance (increase) given a repurchase.
- Price tolerance (decrease) to induce repurchase.[5]

ACSI addresses two questions: "Are customer satisfaction and evaluations of quality improving or declining in the United States? Are they improving or declining for particular sectors of industry, for specific industries, and for specific companies?" It is based on a scale of 0 to 100, with 100 the highest possible score. A national sample of nearly 50,000 people takes part in phone interviews, with at least 100 interviews of current customers for each of the 200 firms studied (acsi.asq.org). Table 20.3 shows that the highest 1999 scores achieved by any of the listed retailers were the 79 for Nordstrom, Publix, and Promus; the lowest were the 61 to 64 for McDonald's, Burger King, KFC, and Taco Bell.

During the past decade, there has been more interest in measuring and benchmarking service retailing. The most well-known measurement tool is **SERVQUAL,** which lets retailers assess the quality of their service offerings by asking customers to react to a series of statements in five areas of performance:

- *Reliability*—Providing services as promised. Dependability in handling service problems. Performing services right the first time. Providing services at the promised time. Maintaining error-free records.
- *Responsiveness*—Keeping customers informed about when services will be done. Prompt service. Willingness to help customers. Readiness to act on customer requests.
- *Assurance*—Employees who instill customer confidence. Making customers feel safe in their transactions. Employees who are consistently courteous. Employees who have the knowledge to answer customer questions.
- *Empathy*—Giving customers individual attention. Employees who deal with customers in a caring way. Having the customer's best interest at heart. Employees who understand the needs of their customers. Convenient business hours.
- *Tangibles*—Modern equipment. Visually appealing facilities. Employees who have a neat, professional appearance. Visually appealing materials associated with the service.[6]

Learn about best practices, both retail and nonretail, from APQC (www.apqc.org/best).

In reviewing the performance of others, a firm should look at the *best practices* in retailing—whether involving companies in its own business sector or other sectors: "It's a simple proposition. Find someone who does a great job, observe and monitor them, benchmark their results, and apply the most appropriate techniques they use. From the firm that scrutinizes a best practice in one territory or store and tries to clone it to the rest of its organization, to the merchant that scrupulously studies the best of its competitors, the value of analyzing, adopting, or adapting best practices is a technique that cannot be overestimated."[7]

Chain Store Age publishes an annual best practices list of "high performance retailers." These are publicly-owned U.S. firms performing well above average on a **retail performance index,** encompassing 5-year trends in revenue growth and profit growth, and a 6-year average return on assets. Due to its importance for publicly held firms, return on assets is weighted twice as much as revenue growth or profit growth in the retail performance index. An overall performance index of 100 is average. Table 20.4 shows leading high performance retailers for 1998. A review of the table reveals there are various ways to be a high performance retailer. For example, bebe stores (the overall leader) had very consistent results. It was first in profit growth, second in revenue growth, and fifth in return on assets. On the other hand, Intimate Brands (the fourth-best retailer) was first in return on assets, but 16th in profit growth and 19th in revenue growth. By learning about high performance firms in different retail categories, a prospective or existing company can study the strategies of those retailers and try to emulate their best practices.

Table 20.4 Benchmarking High Performance Retailers

Company	Compound Annual Revenue Growth, 1993–1998	Compound 5-Year Revenue Growth Index	Annual Profit Growth, 1993–1998	5-Year Profit Growth Index	Average Annual Return on Assets, 1993–1998	5-Year Return on Assets Index	Retail Performance Index[a]
bebe stores	43.92	424	84.06	563	18.79	508	501
Dollar Tree	40.51	391	48.79	327	20.93	566	463
CDW Computer Centers	44.95	434	39.22	263	20.44	553	451
Intimate Brands	18.96	183	24.75	166	23.35	632	403
99 cent Only Stores	21.33	206	23.36	157	21.03	569	375
Bed Bath & Beyond	35.51	343	34.78	233	16.62	450	369
800-JR Cigar	30.89	298	52.47	352	14.20	384	354
American Eagle Outfitters	28.44	274	54.97	368	13.23	358	340
Pacific Sunwear of Calif.	42.36	409	54.03	362	10.27	278	332
K&G Men's Center	30.29	292	40.03	268	14.14	383	331
Gap, Inc.	22.40	216	26.12	175	16.63	450	323
Claire's Stores	18.63	180	21.38	143	17.06	462	312
Gateway 2000	33.95	328	18.04	121	14.50	392	308
The Buckle	21.12	204	36.42	244	14.14	383	303
Dollar General	23.24	224	30.25	203	14.27	386	300
Funco	32.56	314	61.64	413	8.57	232	298
Wild Oats Markets	53.20	513	64.13	430	3.69	100	286
Urban Outfitters	19.86	192	15.09	101	15.65	423	285
O'Reilly Automotive	35.06	338	30.03	201	9.85	266	268
Shoe Pavilion	23.21	224	70.43	472	6.50	176	262
Total Retailing Medians	*10.37*	*100*	*14.92*	*100*	*3.70*	*100*	*100*

[a] Retail performance index = [Revenue growth index + Profit growth index + 2(Return on assets index)]/4

Source: "bebe: Simply the Best," *Chain Store Age* (November 1999), p. 57. Copyright Lebhar-Friedman, Inc., 425 Park Avenue, New York, NY 10022. Reprinted by permission.

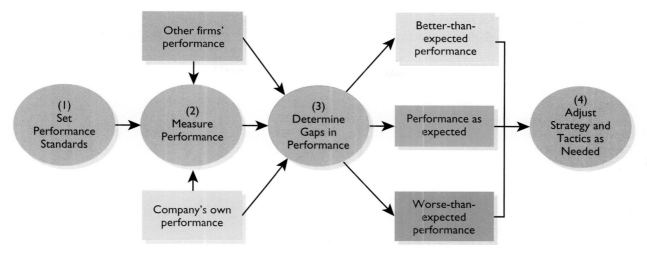

Figure 20.4
Utilizing Gap Analysis

What makes a good retail Web site? Companies can close the gap by checking here (www.waller.co.uk/eval.htm).

Finally, by benchmarking its own internal performance and conducting gap analysis, a retailer can measure its results and plan for the future. Through **gap analysis,** a company can compare its actual performance against its potential performance, and then determine the areas in which it must improve. As Figure 20.4 indicates, gap analysis has four main steps: (1) set performance standards, (2) measure performance (the company's and other firms), (3) determine gaps in performance (whether the company has done better, the same, or worse than desired), and (4) adjust strategy and tactics as needed.

Let us apply gap analysis to Home Depot. Table 20.5 indicates Home Depot's financial results for the period from 1996 through 1998. The data in the table may be used to benchmark Home Depot in terms of its own performance. For instance, between 1996 and 1998, Home Depot increased its gross margin percentage, while maintaining its general and administrative expenses and its pre-opening expenses as a percentage of sales. Net earnings rose accordingly. However, the current ratio and inventory turnover fell. These results were due to "gaps" that Home Depot must correct to sustain its financial momentum. Overall, Home Depot's 1996 to 1998 performance was outstanding.

To ensure that gaps are minimized in the relationship retailing process, retailers should undertake the following approach:

> Specific steps are needed to successfully travel the relationship retailing journey. When fully enacted, technology can be a linchpin for building life-long profitable relationships with individual customers.

1. *Customer Insight:* Analyze customer segments and the information known about customers, including segmentation by revenue, cost, and profitability.

2. *Customer Profiling:* Collect customer information on an ongoing and consistent basis. Customer transaction data are merged with life-style information to build a complete picture of individual customers. This also identifies people who are not currently customers but who fit the profile of the retailer's most profitable segment.

3. *Customer Life-Cycle Model:* Define how customers interact with the retailer at various stages in their life span. Demographic data are used to construct life cycles for each market segment. The cost to service each life cycle within each segment is carefully studied,

Table 20.5 Home Depot: Internal Benchmarking and Gap Analysis

	1996	1997	1998
Statement of Earnings Data			
Net sales (in hundred thousands)	$19,535	$24,156	$30,219
Earnings before taxes (in hundred thousands)	$1,535	$2,002	$2,654
Net earnings (in hundred thousands)	$938	$1,224	$1,614
Gross margin (% of sales)	27.8	28.1	28.5
General and administrative expenses (% of sales)	1.7	1.7	1.7
Preopening expenses (% of sales)	0.3	0.3	0.3
Net earnings (% of sales)	4.8	5.1	5.3
Balance Sheet Data and Financial Ratios			
Total assets (in hundred thousands)	$9,372	$11,229	$13,465
Working capital (in hundred thousands)	$1,867	$2,004	$2,076
Merchandise inventories (in hundred thousands)	$2,708	$3,602	$4,293
Current ratio (times)	2.01	1.82	1.73
Inventory turnover (times)	5.6	5.4	5.4
Return on invested capital (%)	16.3	17.0	19.3
Customer and Store Data			
Number of stores	512	624	761
Square footage at year-end (in hundred thousands)	54	66	81
Number of customer transactions (in hundred thousands)	464	550	665
Average sale per transaction	$42.09	$43.63	$45.05
Comparable-store sales increase (%)	7	7	7
Weighted-average sales per square foot	$398	$406	$410

Source: Home Depot 1998 Annual Report.

yielding a customer profit and loss for each segment. This determines the life-cycle value for each segment.

4. *Extended Business Model:* Use the results of steps 3 and 4 to draw a conclusion about which customers belong in the retailer's business model, the best ways to interact with them, and the best approach to building lasting relationships. Individual customers are surveyed to learn what customization will best meet their needs, and what type of interactions best suit their life-styles. Specific interaction plans build on the integrity of the offer and the intimacy of the relationship.

5. *Relationship Program Planning and Design:* Identify all the electronic and physical channels that form the link between a retailer and customers, and the messages that need to flow back and forth. Touch points are defined (in person, pick-up, delivery, kiosk, phone, fax, TV, personal computer) and software applications are specified to support interactions. Process re-engineering, organizational changes, and employee training are defined. Processes are selected that focus on pleasing customers, attracting new customers, higher retention rates, increased spending per visit/transaction, and increased profitability per customer.

6. *Implementation:* Integrate marketing, customer service, and sales into a common view. Rapid prototyping of the relationship marketing program can then be tested and incremental rollouts can ensure a steady crescendo to the program.[8]

Scenario Analysis

In **scenario analysis,** a retailer projects the future by studying factors that affect long-run performance and then forms contingency ("what if") plans based on alternate scenarios (such as low, moderate, and high levels of competition in the trading area).[9] Scenario analysis is not easy. Consider these forecasts:

Pricewaterhouse-Coopers (www.pwcris.com/FreeContent/SpecialReports_files/specialreports.asp) makes various forward-looking retail research reports available online. Click on "Special Reports" for free downloads.

Economics of Plenty—In the new era, space and information are virtually unlimited. We have reached a point where supply exceeds demand. *Consumer Up For Grabs*—Fickle, less loyal, and more selfish than ever, the consumer is out there. They are more than willing to try new things and to embrace change that benefits them. *One Size Doesn't Fit All*—That approach will no longer work in terms of retail space, promotion, and pricing. Advances in technology and information will deepen firms' understanding of consumers and deliver value in new ways to small segments, possibly down to the level of a market of one. *Communication Dialog*—One-way communication will be displaced by a two-way interactive dialog. *No One-Trick Ponies*—There will be multiple points of customer contact, the convergence of clicks and mortar. Firms must be available where and when the consumer wants to shop (24/7/365). *Virtually Boundless*—Retailers will be less hierarchical and more collaborative, structured around outsourcing. Firms will begin to unbundle operations and reconnect virtually. *Supply and Demand Chains*—The focus will move from the integration of the supply chain to the integration of supply and demand chains. The consumer will be the vital link in the new value chain. *High Value Solutions*—More people will want complete bundles of products and services. They will seek out relationships with retailers that make their lives easier and benefit them as consumers. *Customers, Not Transactions*—We will track shoppers with great precision, focusing on sales per customer, profit per customer, and customer acquisition costs.[10]

Wal-Mart Works to Conquer the Globe

Wal-Mart entered South Korea by acquiring four Makro stores and six other undeveloped sites. H. S. Chang, the Korean businessman who owned the Makro stores and the undeveloped land, is retaining a minority interest in Wal-Mart's venture. The Makro stores had total annual sales of approximately $160 million at the time of their purchase.

Eventually, Wal-Mart will change the name of the Makro stores and adapt its own retail format to them. As a Wal-Mart spokesperson says, "This is one more step in our Asia expansion program. We are committed to Asia for the long term, and when that's the case, Korea jumps up quickly. It's the third largest economy in Asia, and the ninth largest in the world."

Wal-Mart plans to open 50 to 60 stores per year in foreign markets and to continue its search for acquisitions. It also plans to dramatically increase its number of store units in China by adding super-centers and Sam's Club outlets. The company spokesperson states, "There are three phases to our growth in international markets: learning, ramping up, and rapid expansion." Thus, Wal-Mart acknowledges that it is still in the early phase in China.

From a strategic planning perspective, what are the pros and cons of Wal-Mart's expansion into Korea and China?

Source: Valerie Seckler, "Wal-Mart Adds South Korea to Its International Markets," *Women's Wear Daily* (July 13, 1998), p. 175.

Despite all of the problems in the world, our overall view is one of optimism. These are among the likely aspects of the global economy of the early 21st century:

- Retailing will be more global, more consolidated, more efficient, and more focused.
- Consumers the world over will be more sophisticated, more price-conscious, more discerning about shopping experiences, and more demanding of efficient shopping experiences.
- There are still competitive surprises that remain for retailers. Some of these surprises will come from the home-grown retailers of the emerging markets.
- There will be fewer currencies. Not only has the euro reduced the number of independent currencies, but currency union in other parts of the world is likely—especially in Latin America.
- Remaining independent currencies will float rather than be fixed, causing fewer currency crises.
- Asia will recover. Russia will not—at least not anytime soon. Japan will muddle along.
- Inflation will remain dead and commodity prices will remain weak.
- Growth will be strong in areas with strong human capital, transparent financial markets, strong banking laws and weak regulation of other industries, and independent central banks. Good potential retail markets are Poland, Argentina, Chile, Philippines, China, Korea, and Thailand.[11]

Ten years ago, prognosticators sounded overzealous to suggest that a network of computers would recast society. While the most futuristic and utopian predictions may never play out, the Net is bringing irrevocable change to one part of life: buying stuff. So far, the Web has been the province of more affluent, better-educated people who are likeliest to have PCs. Yet, trends seem likely to make E-retailing a mass market. Firms will continue tinkering with the so-called free PC and free Internet access business models—whereby people get simple PCs or no-frills Web access at low or no cost in exchange for being captive to advertisers or specific retailers. Despite the weak track record of such approaches, marketers will persevere until they establish a technological link to the masses. With a more diverse socioeconomic mix, users can expect a wider range of Internet services and products.[12]

KPMG (www.us.kpmg. com/cm/home.html) also offers free downloads of selected retail research reports.

Retailers must face one significant reality—the consumer is in charge. Consumers enjoy more choice and have access to a greater amount of information upon which to base decisions. People have a clear view of value. What is value? Is it price? Yes. Is it quality? Yes. Is it information? Yes. But it's also selection, convenience, service, and entertainment. Providing value is a challenge for retailers.[13]

How are firms reacting to these forecasts? Consider the vision of Hertz, as expressed in Figure 20.5. Let's also look at Kohl's (www.kohls.com), one of the leading U.S. department store chains. In 1999, Kohl's generated sales of $4.6 billion. As of early 2000, it operated 260 stores, primarily in the Midwest and Mid-Atlantic regions. Kohl's has a well-conceived plan that it will continue in the future:

- *Organizational Mission and Positioning*: "Our mission is to be a value-oriented, family-focused department store chain. Our goal is to offer our customers the best value in any given market. Our pricing strategy emphasizes value by offering attractive prices and name brand merchandise—in a department store atmosphere."
- *Overall Strategy:* Kohl's aims at middle-income customers. It carries apparel and shoes for women, children, and men; accessories; housewares; and soft goods such as towels. It has fewer departments than other department stores. It uses central cash registers to facil-

Figure 20.5
The Hertz Vision for
the Long Haul

Hertz has built a global brand on five basic beliefs:

1 Treat the customer honestly and ethically;

2 Treat employees with the dignity and respect with which we expect them to treat the customer;

3 Provide the highest level of customer service and quality of vehicles;

4 Differentiate ourselves through innovation;

5 Use profits and market share to measure how efficiently we achieve these goals.

Ethics in Retailing

Is Diverting a Diversionary Tactic?

For years, diverters (distributors that purchase and resell products outside the normal distribution channel) have been portrayed as working on the fringes of retailing, and as making shady deals on low-quality goods. They have also been accused of taking advantage of unsuspecting retailers.

Let's look at some of these notions from the perspective of a grocery wholesaler that practices diverting:

- *Diverters operate on the fringe of legal and ethical business practices*—Diverting simply involves the transferring of products from one market to another based on differences in prices and allowances. It's a form of market arbitrage.
- *Retailers are suffering financially due to diverters' high profits*—Diverting enables retailers to increase their profits due to lower costs and higher sales opportunities.
- *Food items purchased from diverters are commonly outdated*—Diverters depend on repeat business and could not survive in the long term if the merchandise was unsafe or outdated.
- *Diverting is a fad*—Price-oriented promotions and special allowances generate opportunities for diverting. These programs may increase in the future due to better sales tracking by both wholesalers and diverters.

Under what circumstances would you, as a grocery store buyer, purchase goods through a diverter? Explain your answer.

Source: K. C. Potts, "Who's Afraid of the Big, Bad Diverter?" *Progressive Grocer* (March 1998), p. 19.

itate transactions and reduce staff costs. Kohl's carries many name brands and sells them at lower prices than other department stores.

- *Growth*: Kohl's believes that it has saturated its core trading areas in Illinois, Ohio, Indiana, and Wisconsin (its home base). Therefore, it has been placing emphasis on expanding into other markets. By the end of 2000, it plans to be operating about 300 stores (up from 108 at the beginning of 1995) in 27 states, including heavy expansion in Texas, New York, New Jersey, Colorado, Georgia, and Connecticut. For the fiscal year ending January 28, 1995, revenues were $1.6 billion. For the fiscal year ending January 31, 2001, revenues will be well in excess of $5 billion.
- *Technology*: "We are tying together the technology of our merchandising, planning, and allocation, logistics, and distribution functions. Examples of this include our comprehensive planning and allocation system to facilitate planning for inventory, forecasting with vendors, allocation of seasonal merchaidse, and continued replenishment of our stock of basic items."
- *Management Team*: "Because Kohl's associates are the key to our future, developing a strong management team has been critical. Our associate program is a comprehensive, detailed initiative that involves evaluation of every manager twice each year. Our goal is twofold: to plan for our future growth and to assure our associates find their jobs both challenging and rewarding."[14]

CONTROL: USING THE RETAIL AUDIT

After a retail strategy is devised and put into action, it must be continuously assessed and necessary adjustments made. A vital evaluation tool is the **retail audit,** which systematically examines and evaluates a firm's total retailing effort or a specific aspect of it. The purpose of an audit is to study what a retailer is presently doing, appraise how well the firm is performing, and make recommendations for future actions.

An overall audit investigates a retailer's objectives, strategy, implementation, and organization. Goals are reviewed and evaluated for their clarity, consistency, and appropriateness. The strategy and the methods for deriving it are analyzed. How well the strategy has been enacted and actually received by customers is reviewed. The organizational structure is analyzed with regard to lines of command, types of organization charts, and other factors.

Good auditing includes these elements: Audits are conducted regularly. In-depth analysis is involved. Data are amassed and analyzed systematically. An open-minded, unbiased perspective is maintained during the audit process. There is a willingness to uncover weaknesses to be corrected, as well as strengths to be exploited. After an audit is completed, the appropriate decision makers are responsive to the recommendations made in the audit report.

Undertaking an Audit

There are six steps in retail auditing. See Figure 20.6 for an overview of the process:

1. Determining who does the audit.
2. Determining when and how often the audit is conducted.
3. Determining areas to be audited.
4. Developing audit form(s).
5. Conducting the audit.
6. Reporting to management.

Figure 20.6
The Retail Audit
Process

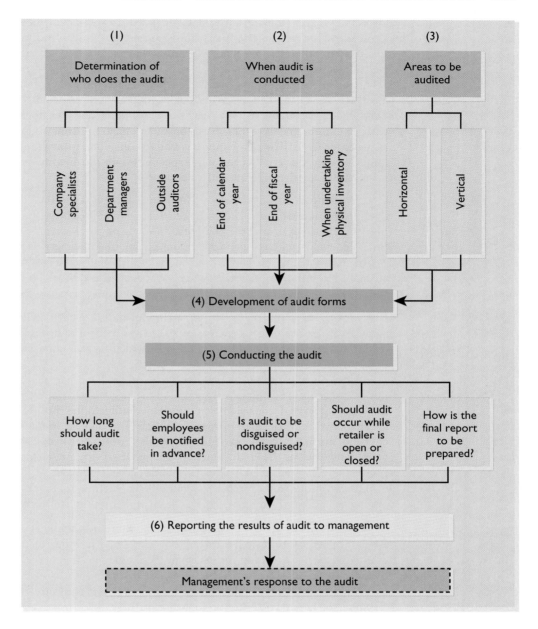

Determining Who Does the Audit In conducting a retail audit, one or a combination of three parties can be involved: a company audit specialist, a company department manager, and an outside auditor.

A company audit specialist is an internal employee whose prime responsibility is the retail audit. The advantages of this person include the auditing expertise, the thoroughness, the level of knowledge about the firm, and the ongoing nature (no time lags). Disadvantages include the costs (very costly for small retailers that do not need full-time auditors) and the limited independence of these auditors.

A company department manager is an internal employee whose prime job is operations management, but he or she may also be asked to participate in the retail audit. The advantages of this source are that added personnel expenses are not needed and that the manager is knowledgeable about the firm and has a full understanding of daily operations. Disadvantages include the manager's time away from his or her primary role, the potential lack of objectivity, time pressure, and the complexity of doing companywide audits.

An outside auditor is a person who is not a retailer's employee but rather a consultant (for a fee). Advantages include the auditor's broad experience, objectivity, and thoroughness. Disadvantages include the high costs per day or hour (however, for small retailers, it may be cheaper to hire expensive, per-diem consultants than full-time auditors; the opposite is usually true for larger firms), the time lag while a consultant gains familiarity with the firm, the failure of some retailers to use outside specialists on a continuous basis, and the reluctance of some employees to cooperate with outsiders.

Determining When and How Often the Audit Is Conducted Logical times for conducting an audit are at the end of the calendar year, at the end of the retailer's annual reporting year (fiscal year), or at the point of a complete physical inventory. Each of these is appropriate for evaluating a retailer's operations during the previous period.

An audit must be enacted at least annually, although some retailers desire more frequent analysis. It is important that the same period(s), such as January–December, be studied each year if meaningful comparisons, projections, and adjustments are to be made.

Determining Areas to Be Audited A retail audit typically includes more than financial analysis; it reviews various aspects of a firm's strategy and operations. It can also be used during successful and unsuccessful periods to identify strengths and weaknesses. There are two basic types of audits—horizontal and vertical.

This site has a detailed online vertical pricing audit (www.bizmove.com/marketing/m2y3.htm) for retailers.

A **horizontal retail audit** analyzes a firm's overall performance, from the organizational mission to goals to customer satisfaction to the basic retail strategy mix and its implementation in an integrated, consistent way. Since this audit studies the interrelation of many strategic elements and their relative importance, it is also called a "retail strategy audit." A **vertical retail audit** analyzes—in depth—a firm's performance in one area of the strategy mix or operations, such as the credit function, customer service, merchandise assortment, or interior displays. A vertical audit is focused and specialized in nature.

The two audits should be used in conjunction with one another because a horizontal audit often reveals areas that merit further investigation by a vertical audit.

Developing Audit Forms To be orderly and thorough, a retailer should use detailed audit forms. An audit form lists the area(s) to be examined and the exact information required in evaluating each area. Audit forms usually resemble questionnaires, and they are completed by the auditor.

Without audit forms, analysis is more haphazard and subjective, and not as standardized. Key questions may be omitted or poorly worded. Auditor biases may show through. Most significantly, questions may differ from one audit period to another, which limits comparisons over time. Examples of retail audit forms are presented shortly.

Conducting the Audit Once the auditor is selected, the timing of the audit is determined, the areas of analysis chosen, and audit forms constructed, the audit itself is undertaken.

Management should specify in advance how long the audit will take and conform to a timetable. Prior notification of employees depends on management's perception of two factors: the need to compile some data in advance to increase audit efficiency and save time versus the desire to get a true picture and not a distorted one (which may occur if there is too much prior notice).

A disguised audit is one in which employees are not aware it is taking place. It is useful if the auditor investigates an area like personal selling and wishes to act as a customer to elicit employee responses. A nondisguised audit is one in which a firm's employees know an audit

Computer-Aided Auditing Is Passing the Test

In the past, many retailers employed outside auditing firms. But now, a growing number of software programs enable retailers to undertake these responsibilities on their own. One example relates to Carson Pirie Scott's payment of sales taxes to the state of Missouri for customer purchases at its stores located there. Until recently, the department store chain was required to send the total sales tax on goods sold, regardless of when a Carson Pirie Scott's credit card customer paid his or her bill. Thus, the chain could receive payment on a customer's credit card balance several months after the goods were sold. This difference in timing could result in unnecessarily large tax bills. By using its new software, Carson Pirie Scott can recalculate its payment of sales tax to more accurately reflect the timing of actual final customer payment patterns.

Carson Pirie Scott is also employing the software to recoup hundreds of thousands of dollars in accounts payable. For instance, the firm has used the auditing software to evaluate a medical insurance provider's adherence to contract terms and to verify employee benefits under Social Security.

What other applications for audit recovery (gap analysis) exist for a department store retailer?

Source: Julie Ritzer Ross, "Analysis Tools to Improve Real Audit Process," *Stores* (August 1998), pp. 96–97.

is being conducted. This is desirable if employees are asked specific operational questions and help in gathering data for the auditor.

The decision as to whether to perform an audit when the firm is open or closed depends on the data sought. Some audits should be done while a retailer is open, such as assessing parking adequacy, in-store customer traffic patterns, the use of vertical transportation, and customer relations. Other audits should be done while a retailer is closed, such as analyses of the condition of fixtures, inventory levels and turnover, financial statements, and employee records.

The format for the audit report must be determined. It can be formal or informal, brief or long, oral or written, and a statement of findings or a statement of findings plus recommendations. The report has a better chance of acceptance if presented in the format desired by management.

Reporting Audit Findings and Recommendations to Management The last auditing step is presenting findings and recommendations to management. It is management's role, not the auditor's, to see what adjustments (if any) to make. The proper company executives must read the report thoroughly, consider each point made, and enact the needed strategy changes.

Management should treat each audit seriously and react accordingly. It is a mistake if only lip service is paid to findings. A firm's long-term success is predicated on evaluating the present and adapting to the future. No matter how well an audit is done, it is a worthless exercise if not acted on by management.

Responding to an Audit

After management studies the audit findings, appropriate actions should be taken. Areas of strength should be continued and areas of weakness revised. All actions must be consistent with the retail strategy and recorded and stored in the retail information system.

For example, TJX Companies, Inc., the parent company of several off-price apparel chains, places great reliance on its retail audits. Here is what it stated in one recent annual report:

TJX (www.tjx.com) is very open about its performance. Enter the "Corporate Web Site" and see how much information is available about the firm's plans and results.

TJX is the largest off-price retailer of apparel and home fashions in the United States and worldwide. The firm operates 604 T.J. Maxx stores, 475 Marshalls stores, and 87 Winners Apparel stores. The latter is a Canadian off-price family apparel chain. TJX also operates HomeGoods, a U.S. off-price home fashion chain with 35 stores, and T.K. Maxx, an off-price family apparel chain with 39 stores in Great Britain, Ireland, and the Netherlands. In addition, during fiscal 1999, the company opened 6 A.J. Wright stores, a new United States off-price family apparel chain targeted to moderate income customers. The firm strives to offer value through brand names, fashion, quality, and compelling prices. During fiscal 1999, 32.4 percent of sales were in the Northeast, 17.5 percent in the Midwest, 27.9 percent in the South, 1.1 percent in Central states, 13.4 percent in the West, 4.9 percent in Canada, and 2.8 percent in Europe (primarily Great Britain). Due to the acquisition of Marshalls in 1995, TJX has continued to realize improved operating efficiencies for the combined T.J. Maxx/Marshalls entity by integrating many administrative and operational functions, as well as through increased purchasing leverage—all of which have allowed the company to provide improved value to customers. The company has kept the separate identities of T.J. Maxx and Marshalls stores, including certain elements of merchandising, product assortment, marketing, and store appearance. Since the Marshalls acquisition, TJX has initiated a store closing program to reduce excess retail space. The company also continually reviews store performance and periodically identifies underperforming locations for closing. During fiscal 1999, 4 T.J. Maxx stores and 2 Marshalls stores were closed. In total, over the past five years, T.J. Maxx has opened 153 stores and closed 61, while Marshalls, since the date of the acquisition, has opened 46 stores and closed 76. In common with apparel retailers generally, the company's business is subject to seasonal influences, with higher sales and income generally realized in the second half of the year.[15]

Possible Difficulties in Conducting a Retail Audit

Several potential obstacles may occur in doing a retail audit. A retailer should be aware of them:

- An audit may be costly to undertake.
- It may be quite time-consuming.
- Performance measures may be inaccurate.
- Employees may feel threatened and not cooperate as much as desired.
- Incorrect data may be collected.
- Management may not be responsive to the findings.

At present, many retailers—particularly smaller ones—do not understand or perform systematic retail audits. But as these retailers begin the 21st century, this must change if they are to assess themselves properly and plan correctly for the future.

ILLUSTRATIONS OF RETAIL AUDIT FORMS

In this section, a management audit form and a retailing effectiveness checklist are presented. They demonstrate how small and large retailers can inexpensively, yet efficiently, conduct retail audits.

An internal or external auditor (or department manager) can complete one of the forms in a thorough, periodic way and then discuss the findings with management. The examples noted are both horizontal audits. A vertical audit is an in-depth analysis of any one area in the forms.

A Management Audit Form for Small Retailers

This site (www.salesdoctors.com/surgery/4check.htm) contains a "Power Retailing Checklist."

The *Management Audit for Small Retailers* was prepared by the Small Business Administration. This booklet, although written for small firms, provides a series of questions and discussions applicable to all retailers. It comprehensively details the components of a retail audit. Figure 20.7 shows selected questions from each area covered in the *Management Audit for Small Retailers*. It should be viewed as an overall horizontal audit, not as fragmented pieces. "Yes" is the desired answer to each question. For questions answered negatively, the firm must learn the causes for the responses and adjust the strategy.

These questions cover areas that are the basis for retailing. You can use this form to evaluate your current status and, perhaps, to rethink certain decisions. Answer YES or NO to each question.

A Look at Yourself and Your Ability to Grow

____ Do you keep abreast of changes in your field by subscribing to leading trade and general business publications?

____ Do you plan for a profit (your net income) above a reasonable salary for yourself as manager?

____ Are you an active member of a trade association?

Customer Relations

____ Do you purposely cater to selected groups of customers rather than to all groups?

____ Do you have a clear picture of the retail image you seek to implant in the minds of your customers?

____ Do you evaluate your own performance by asking customers about their likes and dislikes and by shopping competitors to compare their assortments, prices, and promotion methods with your own?

Personnel Management and Supervision

____ Do employees in your firm know to whom they each report?

____ Do you delegate authority to those immediately responsible to you, freeing yourself from unnecessary operating details?

____ Do you seek employees' opinions of stock assortments, choice of new merchandise, layout, displays, and special promotions?

____ Do you apply the concept of "management by objectives," that is, do you set work goals for yourself and for each employee for the month or season ahead and at the end of each period check the actual performance against these goals?

Merchandise Inventory Control

____ Do you keep sales, inventory, and purchase records by types of merchandise within your departments?

____ Do you control your purchases in dollars by means of an open-to-buy system?

____ For staple and reorder items, do you prepare a checklist (never-out list) that you check against the actual assortment on hand?

____ Do you make certain best-sellers are reordered promptly and that slow-sellers are processed swiftly for clearance?

____ Are you taking adequate safeguards to reduce shoplifting and pilferage in your store?

Budgetary Control and Productivity

____ In controlling your operations, do you frequently compare actual results with the budget projections you have made; and do you then adjust your merchandising, promotion, and expense plans as indicated by deviation from these projections?

(continued)

Figure 20.7

A Management Audit Form for Small Retailers

Source: Adapted by the authors from John W. Wingate and Elmer O. Schaller, *Management Audit for Small Retailers* (Washington, D.C.: Small Business Administration, Small Business Management Series No. 31).

_____ Do you study industry data and compare the results of your operation with them?

_____ Do you think in terms of ratios and percentages, rather than exclusively in dollars-and-cents?

_____ Do you use a variety of measures of performance, such as net profit as a percent of your net worth, stock turnover, gross profit margin per dollar of cost investment in merchandise, and sales per square foot of space?

Buying

_____ Do you regularly search the market for merchandise, prices, and sources rather than relying too much on established sources?

_____ When reordering new items that have shown volume potential, do you make it a point to order a sufficient number?

_____ Do you keep up assortments through important selling seasons, despite the possibility of markdowns on the remainders?

_____ For goods having a short selling season, do you predetermine when first orders are to be placed, when retail stocks are to be complete, the extent of the peak selling period, the start of clearance, and final cleanup?

_____ Do you take advantage of all available discounts and do you include them on your written orders?

Pricing

_____ Do you figure markup as a percentage of retail selling price rather than as a percentage of costs?

_____ Do you set price lines or price zones?

_____ Do the prices you set provide adequate markups within the limits of competition?

_____ In pricing new items and evaluating cost quotations, are you guided by what you think the customer will consider good value?

_____ Before marking down goods for clearance, do you consider alternate ways of selling them—special displays, repackaging, or including them in a deal?

Display and Layout

_____ Are window displays planned to attract attention, develop interest, create desire, and prompt a customer to enter your store for a closer inspection?

_____ Do you give as much attention to your interior display as to your windows?

_____ Are items that customers may not be specifically looking for but are likely to buy on sight (impulse) displayed near store entrances and at other points that have heavy traffic?

_____ Are your cash registers well located?

_____ Are nonselling and office activities kept out of valuable selling space?

_____ Do you receive, check, and mark incoming goods at central points rather than on the selling floor?

Advertising and Sales Promotion

_____ Do you advertise consistently in at least one appropriate medium: newspapers, direct mail, flyers, local television, or radio?

_____ Does each of your ads specifically "sell" your firm in addition to the merchandise advertised?

_____ Do you regularly and systematically familiarize your salespeople with your plans for advertised merchandise and promotions?

_____ Do you consult your suppliers about dealer aids helpful to the promotion of their merchandise in your store?

_____ Do you use cooperative ads with other merchants in your community?

_____ Do you conduct a continuing effort to obtain free publicity in the local press or broadcast media?

Figure 20.7 (continued)

Cash and Finance

____ Does someone other than the cashier or bookkeeper open mail and prepare a record of receipts to be checked against deposits?

____ Do you deposit all of each day's cash receipts in the bank without delay?

____ Do you calculate your cash flow regularly and take steps to provide enough cash for each period's needs?

____ Do you have a line of credit at your bank, not only to meet seasonal requirements but also to permit borrowing at any time for emergency needs?

Credit

____ Do you have a credit policy?

____ Are your bad-debt losses comparable with those of other similar retailers?

____ Periodically, do you review your accounts to determine their status?

Insurance

____ Is your company's insurance handled by a conscientious and knowledgeable agent?

____ Have you updated your insurance needs to ensure adequate protection for buildings, equipment, merchandise, and other assets, as well as for public liability?

Accounting Records

____ Do you have your books balanced and accounts summarized each month?

____ Do you use a modern point-of-sale register for sales transactions and modern equipment to record accounts receivable?

____ Do you keep data on sales, purchases, inventory, and direct expenses for different types of merchandise?

Taxes and Legal Options

____ Do you retain a tax accountant to review your accounting records and prepare your more complicated tax returns?

____ Do you retain a good lawyer to confer with on day-to-day problems that have legal implications?

Planning for Growth

____ Over the past few years, have you done much long-range planning for growth?

____ When you find that change is called for, do you act decisively and creatively?

____ Do you make most of your changes after thoughtful analysis rather than as reactions to crises?

____ Are you grooming someone to succeed you as manager in the not-too-distant future?

Figure 20.7 *(continued)*

A Retailing Effectiveness Checklist

Figure 20.8 contains another type of audit form, a retailing effectiveness checklist, which can be used to assess overall strategy performance and preparedness for the future. It can also be used by small and large firms alike. The checklist is more strategic in nature than the *Management Audit for Small Retailers,* which is more tactical. Unlike the yes–no answers in Figure 20.7, the effectiveness checklist lets a retailer rate its performance from 1 to 5 in each area, thus providing more in-depth information. However, a total score would not be computed because all items are not equally important. A simple summation would not present a meaningful score.

Rate your company's effectiveness in each of the following areas on a scale of 1 to 5, with 1 being strongly agree (excellent effort) and 5 being strongly disagree (poor effort). An answer of 3 or higher signifies that improvements are necessary.

1. A long-term organizational mission is clearly articulated. ____
2. The current status of the firm is taken into consideration when setting future plans. ____
3. The firm's role in the business system is understood. ____
4. Sustainable competitive advantages are actively pursued. ____
5. Company weaknesses have been identified and minimized. ____
6. The management style is compatible with the firm's way of doing business. ____
7. There is a logical short-run and long-run approach to the firm's chosen line of business. ____
8. There are specific, realistic, and measurable short- and long-term goals. ____
9. These goals guide strategy development and resource allocation. ____
10. The characteristics and needs of the target market are known. ____
11. The strategy is tailored to the chosen target market. ____
12. There are systematic plans prepared for each element of the strategy mix: ____
   a. Location. ____
   b. Managing the business. ____
   c. Merchandise management and pricing. ____
   d. Communicating with the customer. ____
13. Uncontrollable factors are monitored: ____
   a. Consumers. ____
   b. Competition. ____
   c. Technology. ____
   d. Economic conditions. ____
   e. Seasonality. ____
   f. Legal restrictions. ____
14. The overall strategy is integrated. ____
15. Short-, moderate-, and long-term plans are compatible. ____
16. The firm knows how each merchandise line, for-sale service, and business format stands in the marketplace. ____
17. Tactics are carried out in a manner consistent with the strategic plan. ____
18. The strategic plan and its elements are adequately communicated. ____
19. Unbiased feedback is regularly sought for each aspect of the strategic plan. ____
20. Information about new opportunities and threats is sought out. ____
21. After enacting a strategic plan, company strengths and weaknesses, as well as successes and failures, are studied on an ongoing basis. ____
22. Results are studied in a manner that reduces the firm's chances of overreacting to a situation. ____
23. Strategic modifications are made when needed. ____
24. Strategic plans are modified before crises occur. ____
25. The firm avoids strategy flip-flops (that confuse customers, employees, suppliers, and others). ____
26. The company has a Web site or plans to have one shortly. ____
   a. The site properly communicates the firm's image. ____
   b. The site is easy to use. ____
   c. The site provides fast, reliable customer service. ____
   d. The site is regularly updated. ____

Figure 20.8
A Retailing Effectiveness Checklist

SUMMARY

1. *To demonstrate the importance of integrating a retail strategy.* This chapter shows why it is necessary for retailers to plan and apply coordinated strategies, and describes how to assess success or failure. The stages of a retail strategy must be viewed as an ongoing, integrated system of interrelated steps—not as a fragmented, one-time-only concept.

2. *To examine four key factors in the development and enactment of an integrated retail strategy: planning procedures and opportunity analysis, defining productivity, performance measures, and scenario analysis.* Planning procedures can be optimized by adhering to a series of specified actions, from situation analysis to control. Opportunities need to be studied in terms of their impact on overall strategy, and not in an isolated way. The sales opportunity grid is a good tool for comparing various strategic options.

To maximize productivity when enacting their strategies, retailers need to define exactly what productivity represents to them. Though firms should be as efficient as possible, this does not necessarily mean having the lowest possible operating costs (which may lead to customer dissatisfaction), but rather keying spending to the performance standards required by a retailer's chosen strategy mix and niche in the market (such as upscale versus discount).

By picking the proper performance measures and setting standards for them, a retailer can better integrate its strategy. Measures include total sales, average sales per store, sales by goods/service category, sales per square foot, gross margins, gross margin return on investment, operating income, inventory turnover, markdown percentages, employee turnover, financial ratios, and profitability. The *Chain Store Age* performance index combines sales growth, profit growth, and return on assets

With scenario analysis, a retailer projects the future by examining the major factors that will have an impact on its long-term performance and then prepares contingency plans keyed to alternative scenarios. It is not easy to do.

3. *To show how industry and company data can be used in strategy planning and analysis (benchmarking and gap analysis).* A firm should utilize benchmarking, whereby it sets its own standards and measures performance based on the achievements of its sector of retailing, specific competitors, high performance companies (best practices), and/or its own prior actions. Plentiful data are available to do this. Through gap analysis, a retailer can compare its actual performance against its potential performance, and then see areas in which it must improve.

4. *To explain the principles of a retail audit, its utility in controlling a retail strategy, the difference between horizontal and vertical audits, and the possible difficulties with auditing.* A retail strategy needs to be regularly monitored, evaluated, and fine-tuned or revised. The retail audit is one way to accomplish this control function. It is a systematic, thorough, and unbiased review and appraisal. Through an audit, a firm's goals, strategy, implementation, and organization can each be investigated.

The retail audit process consists of these six sequential steps: (1) determining who does the audit, (2) determining when and how often it is conducted, (3) setting the areas to be audited, (4) developing audit forms, (5) conducting the audit, and (6) reporting results and recommendations to management. After the right executives read the audit report, necessary revisions in strategy should be made.

In a horizontal audit, a retailer's overall strategy and performance are assessed. In a vertical audit, one element of a strategy is reviewed in detail. Among the potential difficulties of auditing may be the costs, the time commitment, the inaccuracy of performance standards, the poor cooperation from some employees, the collection of incorrect data, and unresponsive management. A number of firms do not conduct audits; as a result, they may have difficulties evaluating their positions and planning for the future.

5. *To provide examples of audit forms.* Two audit forms are presented in the chapter: a management audit for retailers and a retailing effectiveness checklist.

Key Terms

sales opportunity grid (p. 676)
performance measures (p. 678)
benchmarking (p. 678)

SERVQUAL (p. 681)
retail performance index (p. 681)
gap analysis (p. 683)
scenario analysis (p. 685)

retail audit (p. 688)
horizontal retail audit (p. 690)
vertical retail audit (p. 690)

Questions for Discussion

1. Why is it imperative for a firm to view its strategy as an integrated and ongoing process?

2. Present an integrated strategy for bebe to increase sales by 12 percent annually for each of the next three years. Refer to Figure 20.1 in your answer.

3. Develop a sales opportunity grid for a neighborhood stationery store planning to add an ATM to its services mix.

4. Comment on this statement: "Often neither the least expensive strategy nor the most expensive strategy may be the most productive strategy." Does this mean upscale stores should downgrade their strategies? Explain your answer.

5. Cite five performance measures commonly used by retailers, and explain what can be learned by studying each.

6. What is benchmarking? Present a five-step procedure to do retail benchmarking.

7. What do you think are the pros and cons of the retail performance index described in this chapter and highlighted in Table 20.4?

8. How are the terms *gap analysis* and *scenario analysis* interrelated?

9. Distinguish between horizontal and vertical retail audits. Develop a vertical audit form for an online jewelry retailer.

10. What are the attributes of good retail auditing?

11. Distinguish among these auditors. Under what circumstances would each be preferred?
    a. Outside auditor.
    b. Company audit specialist.
    c. Company department manager.

12. Under what circumstances should a nondisguised audit be used?

13. How should management respond to the findings of an audit? What can happen if the findings are ignored?

14. Why do many retailers not conduct any form of retail audit? Are these reasons valid? Explain your answer.

WEB-BASED EXERCISE

Starbucks (www.starbucks.com)

Questions

1. Evaluate Starbucks' overall retail strategy and describe its organizational mission based on its Web site.

2. Is Starbucks' target market clear? Explain your answer.

3. What performance measures can Starbucks use to evaluate its Web site?

4. Prepare a retail audit to evaluate Starbucks' Web site.

CHAPTER ENDNOTES

1. Murray Raphel, "Up Against the Wal-Mart," *Direct Marketing* (April 1999), pp. 52–53.

2. John P. Hammond, "Think Strategically," *Do-It-Yourself Retailing* (August 1999), p. 10.

3. Austen Mulinder, "Hear Today . . . Or Gone Tomorrow? Winners Listen to Customers," *Arthur Andersen Retailing Issues Letter* (September 1999), p. 2.

4. Marianne Wilson, "bebe: Simply the Best," *Chain Store Age* (November 1999), pp. 55–58.

5. Claes Fornell, Michael D. Johnson, Eugene W. Anderson, Jaesung Cha, and Barbra Everitt Bryant, "The American Customer Satisfaction Index: Nature, Purpose, and Findings," *Journal of Marketing*, Vol. 60 (October 1996), pp. 7-18.

6. A. Parasuraman, Valarie A. Zeithaml, and Leonard L. Berry, "Alternative Scales for Measuring Service Quality: A Comparative Assessment Based on Psychometric and Diagnostic Criteria," *Journal of Retailing*, Vol. 70 (Fall 1994), pp. 201–30. See also Terry Grapentine, "The History and Future of Service Quality Assessment," *Marketing Research* (Winter 1998/Spring 1999), pp. 5–20; Robert F. Hurley and Hooman Estelami, "Alternative Indexes for Monitoring Customer Perceptions of Service Quality: A Comparative Evaluation in a Retail Context," *Journal of the Academy of Marketing Science*, Vol. 26 (Summer 1998), pp. 209–21; and Richard S. Lytle, Peter W. Hom, and Michael P. Mokwa, "SERV*OR: A Managerial Measure of Organizational Service-Orientation," *Journal of Retailing*, Vol. 74 (Fall 1998), pp. 455–89.

7. "Best Practices in Retailing," *Chain Store Age* (November 1995), pp. 49–108. See also "Global Supply Chain Benchmarking and Best Practices Study: Phase II," *Stores* (September 1999), pp. K1–K22.

8. Mulinder, "Hear Today . . . Or Gone Tomorrow? Winners Listen to Customers," p. 5.

9. See Robert Gertner, "Scenario—Telling a Good Story," *Financial Times* (November 15, 1999), p. 14.

10. Tom Rubel, "Retailing at the End of an Era," *Retailing 2010: A Consumer-Centric Outlook* (Columbus, Ohio: PricewaterhouseCoopers, 1999), p. 6.

11. Ira Kalish, "Global Outlook: The Economy and the Retail Industry," *Winning Strategies for the New World of Global Retailing* (Columbus, Ohio: PricewaterhouseCoopers, 1999), pp. 15–16.

12. Bob Tedeschi, "Electronic Retailing to a Truly Mass Market Is Expected," *New York Times on the Web* (December 20, 1999). See also Philip Evans and Thomas S. Wurster, "Getting Real About Virtual Commerce," *Harvard Business Review*, Vol. 77 (November–December 1999), pp. 85–94.

13. Theresa Williams and Mark J. Larson, "Preface," *Retail Technology in the Next Century* (Indiana University-KPMG Study, 1999), p. 1.

14. "Kohl's Corporation," *www.hoovers.com* (March 9, 2000); *www.kohls.com* (March 9, 2000); and "Kohl's Corporation January Sales Report," *Business Wire* (February 3, 2000).

15. *TJX Companies, Inc. 1999 Annual Report.*

CASE 1

LANDS' END'S RETAIL STRATEGY: PREPARING FOR THE FUTURE

Lands' End's plans call for long-term annual growth of 10 to 15 percent. To achieve this goal, the company wants to increase sales from current customers, attract customers who have not purchased goods within the past three years, and expand its international sales.

Here is some key financial information that can be used in assessing Lands' End's retail strategy:

	1999	1998	1997
Percent sales increase over previous fiscal year	+8.5	+13.0	+8.5
Gross profit as a percent of sales	45.0	46.6	45.5
Selling, general administration, and advertising expense as a percent of sales	39.7	38.8	37.9
Income from operations as a percent of sales	4.4	7.8	7.5
Net income after tax as a percent of sales	2.3	5.1	4.6

In planning its overall retail strategy, Lands' End sees itself as a direct merchant. According to its 1999 annual report, "We deal with the manufacturers who make our products according to our specifications and to our quality requirements. This type of partnership eliminates the costly middleman markups that are part and parcel of buying branded

CASE 1
(CONTINUED)

merchandise." As a direct merchant, consumers can order goods from Land's End via phone, mail, fax, or the Internet. Consumers benefit from Lands' End transactions due to the savings in driving time, no parking or traffic hassles, and no waiting in lines. As the annual report states, "We devote our energies to making it as easy to shop from Lands' End, regardless of the channel our customer wants to use."

The Internet is seen by Lands' End as an increasingly important part of its overall retail strategy. The company plans to generate a significant portion of its business from E-commerce by the year 2004. The retailer also believes that its Web efforts have low risk and great profit potential. Currently, over 40 percent of Lands' End's operating costs consist of creating, printing, and mailing its paper catalogs.

Both E-commerce selling costs and order processing costs are significantly less than those associated with print catalogs. E-commerce also reduces Lands' End's uncertainty associated with rising paper and postage costs for its print catalogs. In addition, the firm can communicate its Web address through the over 250 million catalogs it distributes each year and in the millions of packages sent to its customers.

Lands' End has consistently been one of the top apparel retailers on the Web. In a typical October (a nonholiday period), the Land's End site has had more than 1.1 million visitors. This number exceeded the traffic on sites run by Gap, Eddie Bauer, and Macy's. Unlike many other retailers, Lands' End is in a unique position to develop its Web business due to the logistics system already in place to handle its direct marketing activities. Lands' End is capable of shipping up to 150,000 orders on a very busy day.

According to one retail analyst, "Lands' End has a well-developed E-commerce site that is better than many of the well-known sites out there." The site, for example, lets female shoppers "try on" outfits through a three-dimensional model that contains the shopper's measurements. The Web site also recommends styles based on a person's body proportions.

Despite its many far-sighted efforts, early in the fourth quarter of 1999, Lands' End reported that its overall sales had dropped by 18 percent from the same five-week period in 1998. The sales decline was attributed to Lands' End's decision to control costs by reducing both the number of catalogs that it sent to its customers, as well as the number of pages per catalog.

Questions

1. Do you feel that Lands' End's growth-related objectives are attainable? Explain your answer.

2. Interpret the data in the case.

3. Evaluate Lands' End's strategy of increased reliance on Web-related sales.

4. How could Lands' End have avoided its 1999 fourth-quarter sales dip while still cutting costs?

Video Questions on Lands' End

1. Describe how Lands' End implements its customer service strategy.

2. Develop a retail audit form to evaluate Lands' End's new advertising strategy.

NOTE   The material in this case is drawn from *www. landsend.com* (March 6, 2000); *Lands' End 1999 Annual Report;* and Associated Press, "Surfing Lands' End," *Newsday* (December 15, 1999), p. A73.

CASE 2

DOES SPARKS DEPARTMENT STORE HAVE A FUTURE?

Among the casualties in retailing have been many independent family-owned department stores. Kurt Barnard, a retail consultant, says such stores are an "endangered species" due to the increased competition from malls and chains. According to the U.S. Department of Commerce, the number of small retailers has declined by about 50 percent in recent years.

Countering the trend is one independent department store that is doing well: Sparks Department Store, located in a two-story building in Malden, Massachusetts, a working class city 10 miles from Boston. The store is owned by Albert Sparks, whose father started the business over 80 years ago, and has been at the same site for 50 years. There are several factors that account for its success: its closeness to customers, the low-price emphasis, the high employee loyalty, and the management succession plan.

Albert Sparks is close to his customers, who desire basic fashions at low prices. Thus, his store does not carry trendy merchandise. He is also responsive to special customer requests: "If someone is looking for a particular ladies' slacks and we are out of her size, within 5 minutes, we'll be on the phone with the manufacturer reordering that item." Sparks is also quick to assess a trend and capitalize on it. Several years ago, he created a printed T-shirt with a local logo. He ordered 12 dozen to judge market acceptance, and reordered them as the shirts were sold. In all, 12,000 shirts were sold within one year.

Because the store attracts customers by outpricing the national chains for the same or comparable goods, Albert Sparks is well aware of the need to keep a close watch on costs: "Our customers aren't looking for a fancy store. They're looking for good deals." The store's atmosphere can be described as no-frills and consists of metal racks, wooden tables, and a decades-old linoleum floor. Costs are so low that the store is profitable at much lower markup levels than at a traditional department store.

Albert Sparks believes strongly in employee retention. The retailer's 25 employees have an average annual turnover rate of 5 percent versus a turnover rate as high as 90 percent with other retailers. As a result, employees know shoppers by name, they better understand shopper needs, and a mutual trust develops among the worker, the shopper, and the store's management. One tactic used to keep employees is to assure them that they will keep their jobs in the event that an illness or other circumstance prevents them from working, regardless of the length of the absence.

Like Albert Sparks, who learned the business working in his father's store, his children have been employed in the store in varying capacities. Now, he is grooming one of his daughters to take over the business when he retires.

Despite the firm's success, Sparks has to resolve some difficulties. Although downtown Malden was once a thriving city with a large textile manufacturing base, it is now a fairly quiet town. Malden's population is also aging. The percent of the population reaching retirement age each year has almost doubled since 1980.

CASE 2

(CONTINUED)

Questions

1. Evaluate Sparks Department Store's overall retail strategy.

2. What types of performance evaluation measures should Sparks use? Explain your answer.

3. Discuss how Sparks can apply the retailing effectiveness checklist highlighted in Figure 20.8.

4. Describe a retail audit regarding Sparks' cost control strategy.

NOTE

The material in this case is drawn from Debra Sparks, "A Mom-and-Pop Store Defies the Odds," *Business Week* (April 12, 1999), pp. 16E2, 16E6.

PART EIGHT
COMPREHENSIVE CASE

Is Toys "R" Us Poised for a Turnaround?

INTRODUCTION

As of the end of 1999, Toys "R" Us operated 1,536 stores, including 1,084 in the United States (707 Toys "R" Us toy stores, 205 Kids "R" Us children's clothing stores, 127 Babies "R" Us infant-toddler stores, and 45 Imaginarium educational toy stores). Internationally, the company operated 452 toys stores (some of which were franchised and joint ventures).

From a financial perspective, fiscal 1999 (February 1, 1998, through January 30, 1999) continued a long period of disappointing performance at the company. For example, during one seven-quarter period, each quarter was marked by a decline in earnings. Furthermore, over the past decade, the firm's market share has declined from 25 percent to less than 17 percent. In 1998, Wal-Mart overtook Toys "R" Us as the largest toy retailer in the United States. Prior to 1998, Toys "R" Us was the largest U.S. toy retailer for more than 15 years. The Toy Manufacturers of America estimates that Wal-Mart's market share for toys is 17.4 percent versus Toys "R" Us' 16.8 percent.

The material in this case is drawn from Patti Bond, "Toys "R" Us Unveils Redesign at Alphretta, Ga., Test Store," *Knight-Ridder/Tribune Business News* (June 8, 1999); Dana Canedy, "Seeking Mr. Potato Head in All the Wrong Aisles," *New York Times* (September 5, 1999), p. BU4; Cecile B. Corral, "Toys "R" Us Aims for No. 1 Toy Spot," *Discount Store News* (June 21, 1999), p. 1; Saul Hansell, "Toys "R" Us Falls Behind on Shipping," *New York Times* (December 23, 1999), p. C5; Patty de Llosa, "Toys Were Us: The Bad News Keeps on Coming at the Nation's Biggest—Oops, Second Biggest—Toy Retailer," *Fortune* (September 27, 1999), pp. 145 ff.; Betty Liu, "Toys "R" Us to Revamp 525 Stores," *Financial Times* (June 9, 1999), p. 33; Lauren Coleman-Lochner, "Toys "R" Us Plays with New Store Layouts, Sleeker Marketing Appeals," *Knight-Ridder/Tribune Business News* (June 9, 1999); Bernadette Smith, "Paramus, N.J.-Based Toys "R" Us Looks to Improve Its Customer Service," *Knight-Ridder/Tribune Business News* (June 13, 1999); *Toys "R" Us 1999 Annual Report; Toys "R" Us Quarterly Report for the Period Ended October 30, 1999;* and Dana Canedy, "Toys "R" Us Hires R.O.M. Chief, Hoping to Coax Back Customers," *New York Times* (January 11, 2000), pp. C1, C7.

Although total sales were $11.2 billion in fiscal 1999, they grew by only 1.2 percent over the level in the previous year. Furthermore, same-store sales declined by 4 percent in its U.S. toy stores and 2 percent in its international toy stores. Comparable sales at its Kids "R" Us stores were also down by 2 percent. Comparable store sales were only strong in two of its businesses: its 65 combo Toys "R" Us/Kids "R" Us stores and its Babies "R" Us stores (where comparable store sales were up almost 20 percent). See Table 1.

The weak performance was a major reason for the unexpected resignation of Toys "R" Us' chief executive officer, Robert Nakasone, in late August 1999. Nakasone had worked at Toys "R" Us for 14 years when he assumed the CEO position in summer 1998. According to Michael Goldstein, former chief executive officer and current chairman of the board of directors, Nakasone resigned because of differences with the board "regarding the direction of the company." Goldstein was named acting CEO until a permanent replacement was found. Nakasone was the fourth senior manager to leave Toys "R" Us in 1999.

THE CHALLENGES FACING THE DOMESTIC OPERATIONS OF TOYS "R" US

Although Toys "R" Us pioneered the concept of the category killer store (in 1957) and brought supermarket-style self-service merchandising to the selling of toys, some critics now believe that the chain is like a "faded rose" that was successful in an era prior to the Web and susceptible to tough competition from firms such as Wal-Mart. A recent report by Paine Webber, a securities firm, expressed concern over Toys "R" Us' long-term outlook in the face of increased competition from Web retailers, as well as toy vendors that ship directly. The report also foresaw potential disruptions due to the renovation activity at many of its domestic toy stores.

The company has been criticized as having entered the E-commerce business late in comparison to Amazon.com (which introduced a toy store in June 1999) and eToys, an online retailer that went public in May 1999. Toys "R" Us' Web site also has had a number of major difficulties. For example, its Web site crashed in the middle of the December 1998 holiday rush, and was up and down intermittently for the following four weeks. Then, its newly hired E-commerce chief quit after just eight weeks on the job. Toys "R" Us' Web difficulties continued through late December 1999, when it announced that it would be unable to fulfill all of its Web

Table 1 Net Sales, Net Income, and Number of Stores for Toys "R" Us, Fiscal Years Ending January 29, 1994, through January 30, 1999

	Year Ending 1-30-99	Year Ending 1-31-98	Year Ending 2-1-97	Year Ending 2-3-96	Year Ending 1-28-95	Year Ending 1-29-94
Operations						
Net sales ($ millions)	11,170	11,038	9,932	9,427	8,746	7,946
Net income ($ millions)	−132	490	427	148	532	483
Number of Stores at Year End						
Toys "R" Us—U.S.	704	700	682	653	618	581
Toys "R" Us—International	452	441	396	337	293	234
Kids "R" Us—U.S.	212	215	212	213	204	217
Babies "R" Us—U.S.	113	98	82	—	—	—
Total Stores	1,481	1,454	1,372	1,203	1,115	1,032

Source: Toys "R" Us 1999 Annual Report.

orders. According to John Barbour, current chief executive of Toysrus.com, the problem was largely in the fulfillment area, since most of the goods were in stock. Toys "R" Us sent free gift certificates for $100 worth of merchandise to the affected consumers to restore lost goodwill.

Increasingly, Toys "R" Us' domestic toy operations have been subject to competition from discounters such as Wal-Mart. One retailing analyst sums it up by saying: "Wal-Mart sells Pokemon, Furby, Barbie, and Hot Wheels—most of the toys that Toys "R" Us has—at cheaper prices." In addition, Wal-Mart stores offer one-stop shopping convenience for time-sensitive parents.

Toys "R" Us just recently settled a large antitrust suit that was filed against the firm in 44 states, Washington, D.C., and Puerto Rico. The suit alleged that Toys "R" Us and some toy manufacturers had colluded to withhold several best-selling toys from other retailers. Toys "R" Us settled the suit by donating $27 million in toys to the U.S. Marine Corps' Toys for Tots Foundation and paying out $13.5 million in damages.

The company still has another major antitrust case pending. The Federal Trade Commission has alleged that Toys "R" Us violated fair trade practices by threatening to stop carrying some popular toys if their manufacturers also sold these toys to membership clubs such as Costco. When a federal judge ruled in the Federal Trade Commission's favor, Toys "R" Us said it would appeal the verdict.

THE LONG-TERM DOMESTIC STRATEGY OF TOYS "R" US

There are stores in every state but Wyoming, ranging from 1 each in Alaska, Hawaii, Montana, North Dakota, Rhode Island, and Vermont to 87 stores in California.

Items are arranged in stores according to blueprints and most store units use similar displays and layouts. Toys "R" Us' standard prototype store in the United States is 46,000 square feet of space, with 20,000- and 30,000-square-foot stores being the norm in smaller markets. Of the 707 stores currently operated by Toys "R" Us in the United States, 277 are in the traditional format, 200 are in the company's new C-3 format (which stands for customer-focused, cost-effective, and concept of the future), and 230 are front-end retrofits with an improved checkout and traffic flow. The new formats facilitate both operations and shopping for customers.

Most Toys "R" Us stores are located either within strip shopping centers or are freestanding units. A significant number of its properties are owned. Of its 707 domestic toy stores, for example, 62 percent are owned. The company also owns 13 of its 15 distribution centers. This strategy enables the company to have increased flexibility in land use, lowers taxes through depreciation allowances, and provides security from high rent increases at lease renewals.

Unlike many competitors, Toys "R" Us owns and maintains a fleet of trucks. The firm believes this arrangement provides it with the maximum flexibility to meet seasonal peak loads.

The retailer's sophisticated computer system records sales on an item-by-item basis and compares actual against projected sales. This system monitors current sales and inventory levels by individual store and region. Shelf space for items with better-than-expected sales performance is expanded, while items with poorer-than-anticipated results are marked down and receive less shelf space in the future.

Through supply chain management initiatives, the company has been able to drastically reduce its overall inventory. As an example, its Toys "R" Us stores had 31 percent less inventory at the end of fiscal year 1999 than at the same time one year earlier. This approach increases the chain's merchandise flexibility by expanding its open-to-buy position.

Toys "R" Us is investing to achieve better customer service. This includes increased levels of sales floor staffing, increased product knowledge training for the sales staff, and new in-store informational graphics. The firm hired Disney's Magic Institute to provide seminars to Toys "R" Us executives, store managers, and sales associates on how to treat guests.

THE SHORT-RUN DOMESTIC TURNAROUND STRATEGY OF TOYS "R" US

During 1998, Toys "R" Us announced an overall retail strategy to reposition its toy business. The plan consisted of reformatting the U.S. toy stores into the new C-3 format, closing 9 unprofitable U.S. toy stores, and closing/disposing of about 50 toy stores (mostly in Europe). In addition, the firm decided to convert 28 existing stores to a combination Toys "R" Us/Kids "R" Us format, thus enabling the company to close 31 Kids "R" Us stores located nearby.

The firm decided to convert 525 of its existing 46,000-square-foot stores to its new C-3 format. It renovated 200 existing U.S. toy stores to this format in 1999 and 325 additional stores were scheduled for 2000—at a cost of $650,000 to $700,000 per store. In addition, all new U.S. toy stores will be in the C-3 format. This layout features wider aisles and more end-cap displays. The C-3 stores also have a sales floor that is 20 percent larger than its current stores and a back room that is one-third smaller.

The C-3 prototype stores have a revised layout for adjacent departments that should result in a more effective customer traffic flow. In the new layout, each department targets a different age group. Thus, "Juvenile World" seeks to attract mothers with its deeper assortment of toddler clothing. According to Toys "R" Us' past president, "Our research shows that apparel drives 30 percent of mothers' shopping trips. It's also a way to generate more year-round sales for a retailer that depends on seasonal traffic." The stores even include an interactive format where, for example, parents can click on a monitor to learn about an infant car seat or teenagers can get additional information concerning the purchase of a bicycle.

Toys "R" Us also introduced a merchandise "world" concept in its C-3 stores during 1999. Under the merchandise world concept, each store has decentralized product sourcing, consumer advertising and promotion plans, and support teams for each key department "world." Department worlds have been established for each of the following areas:

- R Zone—Video, electronics, computer software, and related products for children nine and older.
- Action and Adventure—action figures, die-cast cars, and related products.
- Girls—dolls, collectibles, accessories, and life-style products.
- Outdoor Fun—bikes, sports, and play sets.
- Pre-School—toys and accessories.
- Seasonal—Christmas, Halloween, and summer accessories.
- Baby Apparel—apparel for newborns through toddlers.
- Learning Center—Educational and developmental products for babies through kindergarten children.
- Family Fun—games and puzzles.
- Deal/Seasonal—$1 to $5 specials and in-season products located near the front entrance.

THE STRATEGY FOR KIDS "R" US

Toys "R" Us entered the children's clothing market by opening two Kids "R" Us discount stores in 1983. These stores have a similar overall strategy to that of Toys "R" Us stores. This includes the use of both national and private label brands, wide assortments, a liberal return policy, self-selection, shopping carts, the use of freestanding or strip center locations, and the close monitoring of sales and inventory levels.

Unlike Toys "R" Us stores (with its warehouse format), Kids "R" Us stores are carpeted and have play areas, music videos, funhouse mirrors, and soft rock music. The stores are several times larger than most clothing discounters, with each Kids "R" Us store occupying between 15,000 and 25,000 square feet. Although Kids "R" Us stores carry a large selection of in-season, name-brand clothing and accessories for children up to age 12, they do not carry irregular or off-season merchandise, as do many off-price retailers.

As part of its plan to improve profits, Kids "R" Us closed 3 weak stores in 1998 and an additional 28 units in 1999. These stores are being replaced by converting nearby existing Toys "R" us stores into combination stores with both Toys "R" Us and Kids "R" Us stores. There are Kids "R" stores in 30 states.

THE STRATEGY FOR BABIES "R" US

In 1997, the firm acquired Baby Superstore in an exchange of common stock valued at approximately $376 million. This division targets newborn to preschool children with a prototype store between 38,000 and 42,000 square feet. Each store is designed so low-profile merchandise is displayed in the center to enable consumers to have a wide view of the entire merchandise selection when in the middle of the store.

Each outlet features as many as 40 room settings of juvenile furniture such as cribs and dressers, and children's accessories such as bumper seats, strollers, and car seats. Each store devotes over 5,000 square feet to national brand and private label clothing, as well as feeding supplies, health and beauty aids, and infant care products. In addition, a computerized baby registry service for gifts is offered in each store.

Babies "R" Us' growth was accelerated by the purchase of Baby Superstore, which operated 76 stores in 23 states as of its acquisition in 1997. Since then, Toys "R" Us has converted virtually all the Baby Superstores into the Babies "R" Us format. The firm now operates 127 Babies "R" Us stores. The company is the market share leader in the juvenile specialty category. There are stores in 33 states.

THE STRATEGY FOR IMAGINARIUM

In July 1999, Toys "R" Us acquired New Jersey-based Imaginarium Toy Centers, a leading educational specialty toy retailer with 41 stores in 13 states (at the time of the acquisition). Toys "R" Us did this to:

accelerate our strategy to establish a leadership position in the learning and educational toy category in our new store prototype. The integration of Imaginarium within our C-3 stores will strengthen our initiative to provide a dedicated, customer friendly "discovery and learning center" by providing a strong brand name featuring products that enhance child development in an interactive environment. The acquisition of Imaginarium will support this initiative and solidify our "store within a store" strategy. This investment also enables Toys "R" Us to further tap into the multi-billion dollar learning and specialty toy market, which is experiencing between 10 and 15 percent annual growth. The purchase of Imaginarium provides Toys "R" Us with opportunities for exciting new growth vehicles and concepts. In addition to integrating the Imaginarium concept into our existing toy stores, we will also nurture its promising stand-alone "neighborhood store" prototype under the Imaginarium name.

THE STRATEGY FOR TRU DIRECT

TRU Direct sells merchandise directly to the public via the firm's Web site at www.toysrus.com. The site, due to disappointing results, has been revamped multiple times. Thousands of products from hundreds of vendors are offered at the site. Toys "R" Us spent $30 million to get toysrus.com ready for the 1999 holiday season. Thus far, it has lagged far behind eToys in online sales.

The company recently entered the mail-order business with the introduction of two catalogs, both of which were also posted on the firm's Web site. Thus, consumers can enter an order for this merchandise either through the phone or at the Web. In the future, the company plans to add several other catalogs featuring juvenile and collectible products.

The Imaginarium acquisition was also made because of its synergies with www.toysrus.com: "Along with the advantages inherent to the Toys "R" Us traditional bricks-and-mortar stores, the purchase in development of the specialty toy categories through the Internet channel. Linking www.imaginarium.com with www.toysrus.com gives us an instant entree into this important segment of toy E-commerce. This initiative will strengthen our Internet positioning and give us one of the broadest toy offerings available anywhere online."

THE FOREIGN STRATEGY OF TOYS "R" US STORES

In 1999, Toys "R" Us operated or franchised toy stores in 25 countries outside the United States. See Table 2. Most of these stores are similar to the prototype designs used domestically. As in the United States, Toys "R" Us owns and maintains its own fleet of trailers in most of the countries where it operates. The international division also uses a computerized inventory system that is similar to the American one. Toys "R" Us recently began to offer a catalog program globally comparable to that in the United States.

Toys "R" Us planned to open a number of international toy stores in 1999, including 10 franchise sites. It also set out to close underperforming international toy stores as part of its overall strategic restructuring.

CONCLUSION

During the first three-quarters of fiscal 2000 (February 1, 1999, through October 31, 1999), Toys "R" Us had a strong performance. Its U.S. comparable toy store sales were up 13 percent for the third quarter and 6 percent for the first nine months. The increase for the quarter was the highest in over 10 years. Sales of video games, Pokemon trading cards, games and toys, Furby, Barbie, and Star Wars all contributed to the gains. Customer response to the new C-3 format was very positive. Internationally, comparable store sales were up 5 percent for the third quarter and 4 percent for the first nine months.

Nonetheless, some analysts wonder why Toys "R" Us has been so late at recognizing its problems. Others believe Toys "R" Us can't get beyond its glory days.

RoAnn Costin, a Toys "R" Us board member, says "It's hard when you've got a founder—a genius who built the company—to try to tell him that things have to change. It's hard to bring it up with Charles Lazarus [the firm's chairman emeritus]." Even though Lazarus is officially retired, the board is made up largely of his old friends and former employees. He also sometimes intervenes in business matters. In one recent incident, Lazarus tried to block the retailer from selling a new line of educational toys (which make up the fastest-growing segment of the toy market). When the toys were finally stocked, Lazarus was "shocked at their success" according to one report. Some observers suggest that Nakasone was seen as overstepping his authority when he tried to replace some members of the Lazarus-dominated board and even tried to hire a search firm to look for new directors.

Getting a successor to Nakasone was complicated by the firm's ongoing weaknesses and the potential strained relations with the board. As one retail consultant noted, "Who's going to take that job? With that board, that kind of security, who would want it?" The answer turned out to be John Eyler, the chairman and chief executive of F.A.O. Schwarz. He was hired as the Toys "R" Us president and chief executive in January 2000.

It's hard not to be rooting for a company with these goals:

- *"Our Vision:* Put joy in kids' heads and a smile on parents' faces."
- *"Our Mission:* We believe our business is built one customer at a time, and we are committed to making each and every customer happy. The goal is to be the Worldwide Authority on Kids, Families, and Fun."
- *"Our Culture:* Yes, we spend a lot of time around toys. And sure, Toys "R" Us is a fun and friendly place to work. After all, when you like what you do, you have a good time doing it. Our 60,000 associates come from all walks of life. Drawing on their own backgrounds and experiences, each individual adds to our rich cultural diversity and better positions us to move in new directions and explore new markets. This atmosphere encourages new ideas and enables us to learn from our differences."

Table 2 Toys "R" Us International Locations (as of January 30, 1999)

Australia	24	Netherlands	9[a]
Austria	8	Portugal	6
Belgium	3	Saudi Arabia	3[a]
Canada	64	Singapore	4
Denmark	10[a]	South Africa	8[a]
France	44	Spain	29
Germany	59	Sweden	5
Hong Kong	5[a]	Switzerland	5
Indonesia	3[a]	Taiwan	6[a]
Israel	5[a]	Turkey	5
Japan	76[b]	United Arab Emirates	4[a]
Luxembourg	1	United Kingdom	61
Malaysia	5[a]	Total	452

[a] Franchise or joint venture
[b] 80% owned

Source: Toys "R" Us 1999 Annual Report.

- *"Giving Back to Kids:* Toys "R" Us cares about the overall well-being of the people and communities that make our business possible. To show our support, we have contributed for many years to several national nonprofit organizations that benefit children, including pediatric cancer research. We also furnish playrooms in many hospitals to brighten young patients' stays there. The company shares with its associates a vision for a better world by matching their contributions to these types of charities and organizations geared toward the needs of children, including health and education."

Questions

1. How could a well-established retailer like Toys "R" Us find itself in such a precarious position? What lessons could other firms learn from the example of Toys "R" Us?

2. Analyze the data in Tables 1 and 2.

3. Do all the pieces of Toys "R" Us' current company-wide strategy fit together? Explain your answer.

4. Evaluate the new strategy for Toys "R" Us' U.S. toy business. Comment also on its recent acquisition of Imaginarium.

5. What synergies are possible for all of Toys "R" Us' various divisions?

6. What are the advantages and disadvantages of Toys "R" Us' ownership of many of its store locations and distribution centers?

7. What are the pros and cons of Toys "R" Us' current international strategy?

APPENDIX A

CAREERS IN RETAILING

OVERVIEW

A person looking for a career in retailing has two broad possibilities: owning a business or working for a retailer. One alternative does not preclude the other. Many people open their own retail businesses after getting experience as employees. A person can also choose franchising, which has elements of both entrepreneurship and managerial assistance. Franchising was discussed in Chapter 4.

Regardless of the specific retail career path chosen, recent college graduates often gain personnel and profit-and-loss responsibilities faster in retailing than in any other major industry. For instance, after an initial training program, an entry-level manager supervises personnel, works on in-store displays, interacts with customers, and reviews sales and other data on a regular basis. An assistant buyer helps in planning merchandise assortments, interacting with suppliers, and outlining the promotion effort. Typically, new merchandise selections must be made at least once every four to six months. Our Web site (www.prenhall.com/bermanevans) has loads of career-related materials.

THE BRIGHT FUTURE OF A CAREER IN RETAILING

From the needs of time-pressed consumers to the growth of electronic shopping, the nation's retail industry faces formidable challenges as it prepares to do business in the new millennium. With those challenges come unparalleled opportunities for success and growth. American retailing has never been as vibrant as it is today. Accounting for a substantial percentage of the country's gross domestic product, retailing is an important driver of our economy.[1]

Not too long ago, doomsayers were predicting the death of traditional bricks-and-mortar stores. Faced with so many look-alike choices, shoppers were becoming bored and disinterested. It was the end of shopping as we knew it—or so said the pessimists of the time.

But retailers fought back, using state-of-the-art technology to transform the shopping experience, improving the way goods are ordered and delivered, as well as overall store operations. This technology has put retailers more in tune with consumers' wants and needs, quickening the flow of goods from suppliers to shoppers and allowing a more targeted and immediate response. The increased emphasis on technology is just part of retailers' new-found focus on providing value to consumers. Other ways include quality customer service, brand equity, unique and compelling merchandise selection, and exciting store designs. Many stores are luring shoppers by providing one-of-a-kind experiences that are often as entertaining as more traditional forms of amusement.

The retail industry has truly transformed itself over the past decade. Consolidations and mergers in all segments have weeded out poor performers and created powerful players that bring an important degree of professionalism to all phases of operations. These retailers know the battle for market share cannot be won without engaged and motivated employees—people who view retail as a career as opposed to a transitory job. Thus, there has been an added emphasis on employee recruitment and human resources, which in turn has resulted in increased opportunities for job satisfaction and advancement.

OWNING A BUSINESS

Owning a retail business is popular, and many opportunities exist. Four-fifths of retail outlets are sole proprietorships; and many of today's retail giants began as independents. Wal-Mart, J.C. Penney, Kmart, Filene's, Toys "R" Us, McDonald's, Sears, and Mrs. Fields illustrate this. Consider the saga of Mrs. Fields Original Cookies (www.mrsfields.com/the_story):

> Debbi Fields, a young mother with no business experience, opened her first cookie store in Palo Alto, California, in 1977. They told her she was crazy. No business could survive just selling cookies. Humble beginnings launched Mrs. Fields into a worldwide celebrity and made her company a premier chain of cookie and baked goods stores. Headstrong determination. A dynamic personality. A sincere concern for people. They all played a role in Debbi Fields' success. But quality, more than anything, accounts for Mrs. Fields' worldwide acceptance. The mission has always been to create the highest quality product possible—every time. To extend her vision, Mrs. Fields began franchising in 1990. It's now that rarest of franchise opportunities. A dynamic opportunity backed by name recognition and approval from worldwide consumers. Today, Mrs. Fields has over 650 domestic locations and over 65 international locations in 11 different countries.

> People too often overlook the possibility of owning a retail business. Many times, initial investments can be quite modest (several thousand dollars). Direct marketing (both mail order and Web retailing), direct selling, and service retailing often require relatively low initial investments—as do various franchises. Financing may also be available from banks, manufacturers, store-fixture firms, and equipment companies. Chapter 3 contained a discussion of starting and operating a retail business.

OPPORTUNITIES AS A RETAIL EMPLOYEE

Retailing is a major employer. In the United States, over 22 million people work for traditional retailers. This does not include millions of others employed by firms such as banks, insurance companies, and airlines. By any measure, more people work in retailing than in any other industry.

Retail career opportunities are plentiful because of the number of new retail businesses opening each year and the labor-intensive nature of retailing. Nationally, thousands of new outlets open every year in the United States. Furthermore, certain segments of retailing are growing at particularly rapid rates. Thus, general merchandise retailers such as Wal-Mart and Kmart plan to open many new stores in foreign markets during the next decade.

The increases in employment due to new store openings and the sales growth of retail formats (such as power retailing) also mean there are significant opportunities for personal advancement for talented retail personnel. For instance, each time a chain opens a new outlet, there is a need for a store manager and other management-level people.

Selected retailing positions, career paths, and compensation ranges are described next.

Types of Positions in Retailing

Retailing employment is not confined to buying and merchandising. Career opportunities with retailers also encompass advertising, public relations, credit analysis, marketing

Table 1 Selected Positions in Retailing

Job Title	Description
Accountant (internal)	Records and summarizes transactions. Verifies reports. Provides financial information, budgets, forecasts, and comparison reports.
Advertising manager	Develops and implements an advertising program. Determines media, copy, and message frequency. Recommends ad budget and choice of ad agency.
Assistant buyer	Works under the direction of a buyer, usually in a specific product category. Assists in sales analysis, order handling, buying, and setting up displays.
Assistant department manager	Works under the supervision of a department manager. Assists in managing personnel, controlling inventory, and other store operations.
Assistant store manager	Helps implement merchandising strategy and policies; interviews, hires, and trains sales personnel; takes inventory; and orders supplies.
Auditor (internal)	Analyzes data, interprets reports, verifies accuracy of data, and monitors adherence to the retailer's regular policies and practices.
Buyer	Devises and controls sales and profit projections for a product category (generally for all stores in a chain); plans proper merchandise assortment, styling, sizes, and quantities; negotiates with and evaluates vendors; and supervises in-store displays.
Catalog manager	Selects merchandise for inclusion in catalogs, works with vendors, orders catalogs, and monitors order fulfillment (particularly, timely shipments).
Commercial artist	Creates illustrations, layouts, and types of print to be used in the retailer's ads and catalogs, as well as on private-label packages.
Credit manager	Supervises the credit process, including credit eligibility, credit terms, late payment fees, and consumer credit complaints.
Data-processing manager	Oversees daily operations of the computer facility. Generates appropriate accounting, credit, financial, inventory, and sales reports. Recommends hardware and software.
Department manager	Responsible for a department's merchandise displays, analyzing merchandise flow, and the training and direction of the sales staff. Assists buyers in selecting merchandise for branch stores.
District store manager	Responsible for management personnel, sales generation, merchandise presentation, expense control, and customer services in all stores in district.
Divisional merchandise manager	Plans, manages, and integrates buying for an entire merchandise division (comprising many departments).
Fashion coordinator	Directs buyers in evaluating fashion trends. Oversees fashion shows.
Fashion director	Responsible for developing and maintaining a retailer's overall fashion perspective.
Franchisee	Purchases a business from a franchisor. Benefits by common format, joint ads, and trouble shooting of franchisor. Decisions constrained by franchisor.
Franchisor	Develops a business format and image, then licenses the right to utilize this format and name to independent businesspeople. Oversees franchises, maintains operating standards, and receives royalty fees.
Group manager	Manages a number of department managers in different merchandise classifications. Trains, supervises, and evaluates these department managers.
Management trainee	First position for most college graduates entering retailing. Involves company orientation, classroom and on-the-job training, and close contact with buyers and group managers. Leads to department manager or assistant buyer.
Marketing research director	Acquires and analyzes relevant and timely data to assist executives in making important decisions. Very involved in methodology and data collection.
Merchandise administrator	Coordinates and evaluates and work of buyers in several related merchandise classifications (in a division).

Table 1 (CONTINUED)

Job Title	Description
Merchandise analyst	Plans and evaluates merchandise allocation to stores to ensure items are shipped at the right time, in proper amounts, and in the right assortment. Sets assortment strategy based on trends. Monitors reorder systems.
Merchandise manager	Coordinates selling efforts among different departments (merchandise categories). Acts as liaison between store managers and buyers. Similar to group manager, but, there are expanded merchandise responsibilities.
Operations manager	Responsible for receiving, checking, marking, and delivering merchandise; customer service; workroom operations; personnel; and maintaining the retailer's physical plant.
Personnel manager	Devises a personnel policy. Analyzes long-term personnel needs. Recruits, selects, and trains employees. Works on compensation scales and supervision rules.
Public relations director	Keeps the public aware of the retailer's positive accomplishments. Measures public attitudes. Seeks to maintain a favorable image of the company.
Real-estate director	Evaluates retail sites. Negotiates leases or purchases. Works with builder on construction projects.
Salesperson	Enables customers to make proper choices. Handles minor complaints. Stocks some items and sets up some displays. Notes understocked items. May also serve as a cashier.
Sales promotion manager	Plans and enacts special sales, themes, and sales promotion tools (such as contests).
Security supervisor	Responsible for minimizing pilferage among employees and customers. Recommends security systems and procedures. Manages a retailer's security personnel.
Senior vice-president for merchandising	Responsible for developing and evaluating all of the merchandise categories for performance. Has direct accountability for growth and profit.
Store manager	Oversees all store personnel and operations in a given outlet. Coordinates activities with other units in a chain. Responsible for customer service; implements merchandising and human resource policies.
Warehouser	Stores and moves goods within a warehouse. Keeps inventory records and rotates stock.
Web specialist	Involved with firm's Web site, from design of pages to oversight of customer interactions.

research, warehouse management, data processing, personnel management, accounting, and real-estate. See Table 1 for a list and description of various retailing positions. From the table, one can see the range of career options available. However, some highly specialized positions may be available only in large retail firms.

To a certain extent, the type of position a person seeks should be matched with the type of retailer likely to have such a position. For example, chain stores and franchises may have real-estate divisions. Department stores and chain stores may have large personnel departments. Mail-order firms may have large advertising production departments. If one is interested in travel, a buying position or a job with a retailer having geographically dispersed operations should be sought.

Figures 1 to 3 show the entry-level retailing experiences of three recent college graduates.

Career Paths and Compensation in Retailing

For college graduates, executive training programs of larger retailers offer good learning experiences and potential for advancement. These firms often offer careers in merchandising and nonmerchandising areas.

Here is how a new college graduate could progress in a career path at a typical department store or specialty store chain: He or she usually begins with a training program (lasting from

Figure 1
Ames

Reprinted by permission of
Discount Store News.

Discount Store News

Careers in Retailing

Ames

Aiming High at Ames

Fast pace. Rapid advancement possibilities. Good income potential. All three ideas appealed to David Fisher when he interviewed with the Ames recruiter who visited the University of Albany.

I was a communications major, but our department centered around human communications as the root of society. I wasn't sure what I wanted to do when I graduated, but I had held some part-time jobs in retailing and found it to be really exciting. The Ames recruiter had such energy and excitement about the company that I thought it would be a great place to work," Fisher says.

Fisher joined Ames as a management trainee in May 1998. "They offered an outstanding training program that recognizes and meets the needs of recent college graduates," says Fisher. While Fisher accepted a retail management position in the store management training program, Ames also has buying, finance and information systems programs at its corporate offices in Rocky Hill, Conn.

After accepting the position of management trainee, Fisher qualified for Ames relocation assistance program. "That made a big difference for me," he says. "They worked with me to make it easier for me to take the job. The training program also prepares people who may not have much employment experience to enter the workplace."

Fisher enjoys the problem-solving aspect of his job as an assistant manager. I like having the opportunity to respond to situations and stand by those decisions," he says. Fisher also finds managing staff and merchandising the sales floor to be both exciting and challenging.

"When I was interviewing, the company was portrayed as a place where each employee could make a difference, and that is true," says Fisher.

"People notice your achievements. Our CEO Joe Ettore, believes in an open line of communication and that trickles down. Where else can an associate e-mail the CEO and get a response?"

Fisher may not need to look beyond Ames for career advancement. "As long as Ames keeps providing me with opportunities, I plan to keep moving to the next level."

three months to a year or more) on how to run a merchandise department. That program often involves on-the-job and classroom experiences. On-the-job training usually includes working with records, reordering stock, planning displays, and supervising salespeople. Classroom activities normally include learning how to evaluate vendors, analyze computer reports, forecast fashion trends, and administer store policy.

At the completion of initial training, the employee becomes an entry-level operations manager (often called a sales manager, assistant department manager, or department manager—depending on the firm) or an assistant buyer. An entry-level manager or assistant buyer works under the direction of a seasoned department (group) manager or buyer and analyzes sales, assists in purchasing goods, handles reorders, and helps with displays. The entry-level manager supervises personnel and learns store operations; the assistant buyer is more involved in purchases than operations. Depending on a retailer's philosophy, either person may follow the same type of career path, or the entry-level operations manager may progress up the store management ladder and the assistant buyer up the buying ladder.

During this time, responsibilities and duties depend on the department (group) manager's or buyer's willingness to delegate and teach. They also depend on the autonomy given to that manager (buyer) to plan and enact a strategy. In a situation in which a manager or buyer has authority to make decisions, the entry-level manager or assistant buyer will usually

Figure 2
Babies "R" Us

Reprinted by permission of *Discount Store News.*

Discount Store News

Careers in Retailing

BABIES Я US

Developing careers at Babies "R" Us

Alicia Hitt has parlayed her collegiate psychology major into a successful career at Babies "R" Us. As regional human resources assistant manager, this 1996 graduate of Texas A&M finds she is able to "facilitate a lot of change and development."

Says Hitt, "It's great to be a support system for the stores. It's so important that employees know there is someone behind them willing to help them with their career development."

The ability to solve problems, motivate people and contribute to the company's overall success were all factors in Hitt's decision to postpone graduate school indefinitely to continue on her career track at the chain.

"This is a diverse environment," she says. "I didn't always want to be behind a desk. Now I'm out learning the business and helping people solve problems."

In fact, Hitt is rarely behind her desk these days. Her job requires a hectic travel schedule. She currently travels 80 percent the time. In addition to recruiting, she is involved in facilitating a number of training programs. "It's a lot of travel because we are growing so quickly," she explains. "Traveling is exciting because you get to visit different parts of the country and meet and work with a variety of employees, from management to hourly associates."

Organizational, communication and interpersonal skills are all important in Hitt's position. "It's great to be working with the public," she says. "My past experience was as an assistant manager of a store. Now I work with the public in a different way."

Although retailing wasn't her first career direction, it is one that has put her on a promising path.

---

be given more responsibility. If a firm has centralized management, a manager (buyer) is more limited in his or her responsibilities, as is the entry-level manager or assistant buyer. Further, an assistant buyer will gain more experience if he or she is in a firm near a wholesale market center and can make trips to the market to buy merchandise.

The next step in a department store or specialty store chain's career path is a promotion to department (group) manager or buyer. This position can be viewed as entrepreneurial, the running of a business. The manager or buyer selects merchandise, develops a promotional campaign, decides which items to reorder, and oversees personnel and recordkeeping. For some retailers, *manager* and *buyer* are synonymous terms. For others, the distinction is as just explained for entry-level positions. Generally, a person is considered for promotion to manager or buyer after two years.

Large department store and specialty store chains have additional levels of personnel to plan, supervise, and control merchandise departments. On the store management side, there can be group managers, store managers, branch vice-presidents, and others. On the buying side, there can be divisional managers, merchandising vice-presidents, and others.

At many firms, advancement is indicated by specific career paths. This lets employees monitor their performance, know the next career step, and progress in a systematic, clear manner. Selected career paths at Saks Incorporated (the parent of Saks Fifth Avenue, Proffitt's, McRae's, Younkers, Parisian, Herberger's, Carson Pirie Scott, Bergner's, Boston Store, and others), PetsMart (a chain of pet supply stores), and Pep Boys (an auto supply and service chain) are shown in Figures 4 through 6.

Table 2 (page A11) lists compensation ranges for personnel in a number of retailing positions.

Figure 3
Franklin Mint

Reprinted by permission of
Discount Store News.

Discount Store News

Careers in Retailing

Banking on the Franklin Mint

"Get your foot in the door early," is the advice Jon Munn would give college seniors looking to pursue a career in retailing. Munn, assistant manager at one of The Franklin Mint's retail stores, started part-time as a stockperson while in college.

After graduating in 1997 with a degree in English from the University of Maryland, Munn interviewed for a few editing positions, then decided that an inviting career path was right in front of him. "I had worked at the Mint during college and was always attracted to the merchandise," says Munn. "The wide-range of items gives you an opportunity to attract a unique clientele."

Munn is learning about collecting as he's learning about retail. "I've learned about what people collect to pass down to their children and what are good investments. It's a very interesting field and it's fun to develop relationships with the collectors," he says.

Starting on the ground floor has imbued Munn with a strong understanding of the store's needs. "It's good to have experience in all areas of running the store. It's important, for example, to know the challenges the stockpeople face so you can help them solve their problems in getting the merchandise to the sales floor," Munn explains.

In his position, Munn is responsible for ensuring that merchandise gets to the store and is displayed properly. He must master the delicate balance between consumer demand and stock on-hand.

Another large part of his job is maintaining client contact by keeping track of what customers are collecting. "We create a collector list so that we can contact collectors when something new comes in," he says. "Written communication to collectors is a big part of what we do."

Maintaining a client base is an important function of associates, particularly during slower-selling seasons. It's also an area many of the associates find rewarding because it is one more step that Munn thinks makes The Franklin Mint retail experience even more personal.

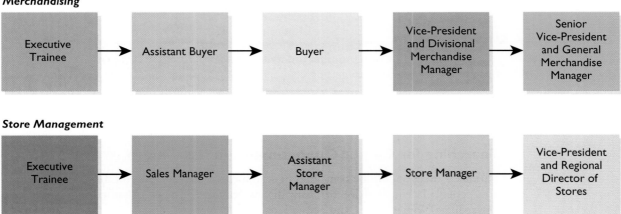

Merchandising

| Executive Trainee | → | Assistant Buyer | → | Buyer | → | Vice-President and Divisional Merchandise Manager | → | Senior Vice-President and General Merchandise Manager |

Store Management

| Executive Trainee | → | Sales Manager | → | Assistant Store Manager | → | Store Manager | → | Vice-President and Regional Director of Stores |

Figure 4
Two Typical Career Paths at Saks Incorporated

Source: Adapted by the authors from *www.saksincorporated.com/hr/careers.html* (March 9, 2000).

Figure 5
PetsMart's Fast-Track
Career Ladder

Source: Adapted by the
authors from *www.
petsmart.com* (March 9,
2000).

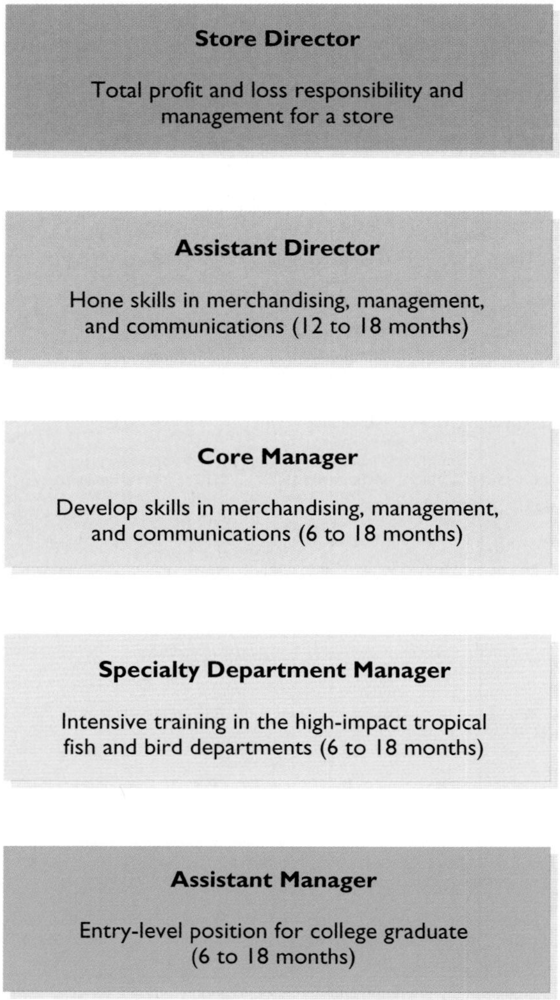

Store Director

Total profit and loss responsibility and
management for a store

Assistant Director

Hone skills in merchandising, management,
and communications (12 to 18 months)

Core Manager

Develop skills in merchandising, management,
and communications (6 to 18 months)

Specialty Department Manager

Intensive training in the high-impact tropical
fish and bird departments (6 to 18 months)

Assistant Manager

Entry-level position for college graduate
(6 to 18 months)

**GETTING YOUR
FIRST POSITION
AS A RETAIL
PROFESSIONAL**

The search for career opportunities, interview preparation, and the evaluation of the options open to you are key steps in getting your first professional position in retailing. It is essential that you devote sufficient time to these steps so your job hunt progresses as quickly and as smoothly as possible.

Searching for Career Opportunities in Retailing

Various sources should be consulted in searching for career opportunities. These include your school placement office, company directories and Web sites, classified ads in your local newspapers, Web job sites, and networking (with professors, friends, neighbors, and family members).

Here are some hints to consider in searching for career opportunities in retailing:

• Do not "place all your eggs in one basket." Do not rely too much on friends and relatives to get you a job. They may be able to get you an interview, but not a guaranteed job offer.

- Treat your career search in a serious and systematic manner. Plan in advance and do not wait until the recruiting season at your school has started to generate a list of potential retail employers.
- Use directories with lists of retailers and current job openings. Online directories include *Careers in Retailing* (www.careersinretailing.com), *Retail Jobnet* (www. retailjobnet.com), *Retail Job Mart* (www.retailjobmart.com), *RetailSeek.com* (www.retailseek.com/index. html), and *Peterson's Careers & Jobs* (www. petersons.com/career/search.html). Also consult our Web site (www.prenhall. com/bermanevans).
- Rely on the "law of large numbers." In sending out resumés, you may have to contact at least 10 to 20 retailers to get just two to four interviews.
- Make sure your resumé and accompanying cover letter highlight your most distinctive qualities. These may include school honors, officer status in a key organization, appropriate work experience, special computer expertise, and the proportion of college tuition you paid for yourself. Figure 7 shows a sample resumé geared to an entry-level position in retailing.
- Show your resumé to at least one professor for his or her reaction. Be receptive to the constructive comments made. Remember, your professor's goal is to help you get the best possible first job.

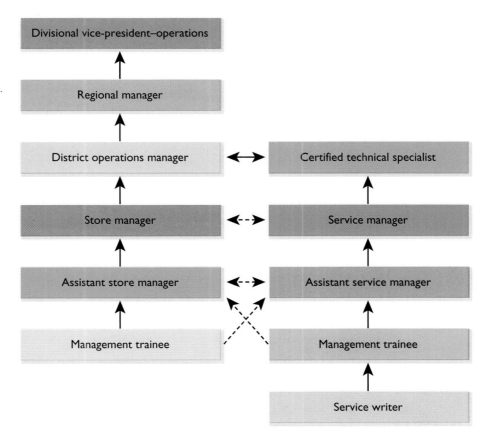

Figure 6
Pep Boys' Executive Career Ladder

Source: Pep Boys. Reprinted by permission.

Preparing for the Interview

The initial and subsequent interviews for a retail position, which may last for 20 to 30 minutes or longer, play a large part in determining if you are offered a job. For that reason, it is necessary that you prepare properly for all interviews. Keep the following hints in mind:

- Adequately research each firm. Be aware of its goods/service category, current size, overall retail strategy, competitive developments, and so on.
- Anticipate questions and plan general responses in advance: "Tell me about yourself." "Why are you interested in a retailing career?" "Why do you want a job with us?" "What are your major strengths?" "What are your major weaknesses?" "What do you want to be doing five years from now?" "Are you willing to relocate?" "Which college courses did you like most?" "Which courses did you like least?" "What would your previous employers say about you?" In pre-interview preparation, role-play your answers to these questions with someone. Listen to his or her comments.
- Get ready for every interview as if it is the most important one you will have. Otherwise, you may not be properly prepared if the position turns out to be more desirable than you originally thought. Also, remember that you represent both your college and yourself at all interviews.
- Be prepared to raise your own questions when asked to do so in the interview. These questions should relate to career paths, training programs, and opportunities for advancement.
- Dress appropriately and be well groomed.
- Verify the date and place of the interview. Be prompt.
- Have a pen and pad available to record information after the interview has been completed.
- Write a note to the interviewer within a week to thank him or her for spending time with you and to express a continuing interest in the company.

Evaluating Retail Career Opportunities

Job seekers often place too much emphasis on initial salary or the firm's image (as to fashion orientation or target market) in assessing career opportunities. Many other factors should be considered, as well.

These questions should be linked to the attributes of each specific job offer you may receive:

- What activities do you like?
- What are your personal strengths and weaknesses?
- What are your current and long-term goals?
- Do you want to work for an independent, a chain, or a franchise operation?
- Does the opportunity offer an acceptable and clear career path?
- Does the opportunity include a formal training program?
- Will the opportunity enable you to be rewarded for good performance?
- Will you have to relocate?
- Will each promotion in the company result in greater authority and responsibility?
- Is the compensation level fair relative to other offers?

Table 2 Typical Compensation Ranges for Personnel in Selected Retailing Positions

Position	Compensation Range ($)	
Department manager—soft-line retailer	16,000–	30,000+
Store management trainee	18,000–	30,000+
Assistant buyer	20,000–	35,000+
Department manager—department store	20,000–	35,000+
Department manager—mass merchandiser	20,000–	35,000+
Store manager—specialty store, home center, drugstore	20,000–	55,000+
Market research junior analyst	22,000–	32,000+
Department manager—hard-line retailer	22,000–	35,000+
Store manager—soft-line retailer	25,000–	50,000+
Buyer—specialty store, home center, drugstore, department store	25,000–	60,000+
Warehouse director	27,000–	90,000+
Market research analyst	30,000–	45,000+
Buyer—discount store	32,000–	55,000+
Market research senior analyst	32,000–	55,000+
Market research assistant director	35,000–	65,000+
Security director	40,000–	70,000+
Buyer—national chain	40,000–	75,000+
Store manager—department store	40,000–	75,000+
Market research director	45,000–	75,000+
Senior human resources executive	50,000–	140,000+
Divisional merchandise manager	55,000–	90,000+
Senior advertising executive	55,000–	110,000+
Operations director	60,000–	90,000+
General merchandise manager—drugstore, home center	60,000–	90,000+
Senior real-estate executive	60,000–	120,000+
General merchandise manager—specialty store, department store	65,000–	125,000+
General merchandise manager—discount store, national chain	65,000–	125,000+
Senior financial executive	75,000–	200,000+
Senior merchandising executive	75,000–	250,000+
President	150,000–	800,000+
Chairman of the board	150,000–	10,000,000+

Source: Estimated by the authors from various publications.

- Can a superior employee move up the career path significantly faster than an average one?
- If ownership of a retail firm is a long-term goal, which opportunity provides the best preparation?

JENNIFER MARCUS
17 HART DRIVE
WEST HARTFORD, CONNECTICUT 06117
(860) 555-7416

Employment Objective:	Assistant Buyer Position, Formal Training Program Desired

Education:	Bachelor of Business Administration, December 2000
	Hofstra University, Hempstead, New York 11549
	    Major: Marketing Minor: Psychology
	    Class Rank: Top 10%

Scholarships and Awards:	Hofstra University Distinguished Scholar Academic Award
	    Dean's List for 6 semesters
	    Cum laude graduate

Extracurricular Activities:	Vice-President, Retail Management Society. Spring 1999-Fall 2000
	    Responsible for recruitment of members, arranging for guest speakers, and
	    budget preparation and control.
	Member, American Marketing Association

Computer Skills:	Proficient in Word; working knowledge of Lotus and SPSS
Work Experience:	

January 1999–present	Assistant to Store Manager, Fashion World
	200 Main Street, Hempstead, New York
	    Responsible for setting up displays, providing product information to the sales
	    staff, interacting with certain vendors, and handling returns.

January 1997–
December 1998
	Cashier, Thrifty Drug Stores
	Green Fields Shopping Center, Valley Fields, New York
	    Responsible for customer transactions, processing credit card sales, and
	    restocking shelves.
	
	Paid half of tuition expenses by working 20 hours per week while attending college

Personal:	Willing to relocate. Hobbies include photography and personal computers.
References:	Will be furnished upon request.

Figure 7
A Sample Resumé

ENDNOTE

1. The material in this section is adapted by the authors from "Retail Growth Brings New Opportunities," *Careers in Retailing* (January 1999), p. 9. Copyright Lebhar-Friedman, Inc., 425 Park Avenue, New York, NY 10022. Reprinted by permission of *Discount Store News.*

APPENDIX B

ABOUT THE WEB SITE THAT ACCOMPANIES *RETAIL MANAGEMENT*

(www.prenhall.com/bermanevans)

OVERVIEW

Accompanying *Retail Management: A Strategic Approach* is a comprehensive, interactive Web site that includes everything from career data to a comprehensive listing of company sites on the World Wide Web. Once you have connected to the Internet, it is designed to run on your Web browser (such as Netscape or Internet Explorer).

The Web site is user-friendly, real-world in nature, and keyed to the concepts covered in *Retail Management*. In this appendix, we describe how to use the Web site and present an overview of each of its components.

DIRECTIONS FOR USE

To utilize the Web site, you need to be connected to the Internet and have access to a Web browser such as Netscape or Internet Explorer. You will also need a printer if you want to reproduce material for your own reference or for class submissions.

Follow these steps:

- After booting up your computer, connect to the Internet and access your Web browser.
- From within your browser, enter the Web site by going to the "Location" or "Address" tool bar at the top of the browser screen and then typing the address of the *Retail Management* site (www.prenhall.com/bermanevans).
- When you visit the site for the first time, read the description at the home page. It explains the components of the site and how to access them. You should print this discussion for later reference.
- Print any file by clicking on the "Print" icon at the top of the browser screen. (You can also click on the "File" icon and "Print" on the menu bar.) You can print one screen or all the screens in a file.
- From the menu screen, you can click your mouse on the icon of any of the components of the Web site. You then enter that specific section.
- All descriptions, instructions, and so forth appear at the home page or in the various sections and can be quickly and simply accessed and printed.

WEB SITE COMPONENTS

The site has these components:

- A chapter-by-chapter listing (including the appendixes).
- For each chapter, there is (are)
  - A chapter overview (summary).
  - Chapter objectives.
  - A listing of key terms.
  - Interactive study guide questions.
  - Access to the glossary (which may be used by typing in the first letter of a word and then scrolling down).
  - Hot links to relevant Web sites (several hundred in all).
  - Access to the computer exercises.
- Links to real-world software downloads and demos.
- Career material and a directory of 500 retailers, complete with links to their home pages.
- Sixteen computer exercises linked to the text.
- The full glossary.
- Author biographies and photos.
- Resources for professors.

Interactive Study Guide

The interactive study guide contains 20 multiple choice, 20 true–false, and 15 fill-in questions per chapter (with answers and text references). By looking up the text page references, you can study for exams and go over topics that are giving you difficulty. And you can look at the glossary section of this Web site to further brush up on key terms. You may even E-mail your results to yourself or your professor.

Chapter Overviews/Chapter Objectives

These two sections enable you to view the overviews and objectives of each of the 20 chapters in *Retail Management*.

Key Terms and Glossary

There is a listing of key terms by chapter. In addition, you may access the full glossary from *Retail Management*. Glossary items can be selected alphabetically by scrolling to the relevant words.

Text-Related Web Site Links

This section has links to well over 1,000 retailing-related Web sites, divided into several categories. By clicking on the link to any of the Web sites, you are immediately transported there.

Careers in Retailing

This section contains advice on resumé writing, how to take an interview, and internships. In addition, there is a lot of information from the U.S. Bureau of Labor Statistics' *Occupational Outlook Handbook*, as well as links to popular career sites.

Real-World Career Examples

This section contains links directly to the career sections of 120 retailers' Web sites. These links have been chosen for their information value.

Retail Resources on the Web

Still more information on the world of retailing is contained in this section. There are four main categories: a retailer directory, Federal Trade Commission business tips, Small Business Administration business tips, and links to 30 free software downloads and demonstrations.

Computer Exercises

Sixteen text-based exercises noted by a computer symbol throughout this book can be downloaded from our Web site. Look at the site (www.prenhall.com/bermanevans) for more information on installing and running the exercises. The program is complete with instructions and questions. The exercises are divided by part:

Part One
- Store Positioning (Chapter 3)

Part Two
- Franchising (Chapter 4)
- Wheel of Retailing (Chapter 5)
- Scrambled Merchandising (Chapter 5)
- Direct Marketing (Chapter 6)

Part Three
- Attitude Survey (Chapter 8)

Part Four
- Reilly's Law (Chapter 9)
- Buying Power Index (Chapter 9)
- Measuring Trading-Area Saturation (Chapter 9)

Part Five
- Strategic Planning Model (Chapter 12)
- Key Business Ratios (Chapter 12)
- Budgeting and Cash Flow (Chapter 12)

Part Six
- Retail Method of Accounting (Chapter 16)
- Open to Buy (Chapter 16)

Part Seven
- Seasonal Promotional Planning (Chapter 19)

Part Eight
- Sales Opportunity Grid (Chapter 20)

GLOSSARY

Additional Markup Increase in a retail price above the original markup when demand is unexpectedly high or costs are rising.

Additional Markup Percentage Looks at total dollar additional markups as a percentage of net sales:

$$\text{Additional markup percentage} = \frac{\text{Total dollar additional markups}}{\text{Net sales (in \$)}}$$

Addition to Retail Percentage Measures a price rise as a percentage of the original price:

$$\text{Addition to retail percentage} = \frac{\text{New price} - \text{Original price}}{\text{Original price}}$$

Advertising Paid, nonpersonal communication transmitted through out-of-store mass media by an identified sponsor.

Affinity Exists when the stores at a given location complement, blend, and cooperate with one another, and each benefits from the others' presence.

All-You-Can-Afford Method Promotional budgeting procedure in which a retailer first allots funds for each element of the strategy mix except promotion. The funds that are left go to the promotional budget.

Analog Model Computerized site selection tool in which potential sales for a new store are estimated based on sales of similar stores in existing areas, competition at a prospective location, the new store's expected market share at that location, and the size and density of a location's primary trading area.

Application Blank Usually the first tool used to screen applicants. It provides data on education, experience, health, reasons for leaving prior jobs, outside activities, hobbies, and references.

Assets Any items a retailer owns with a monetary value.

Asset Turnover Performance measure based on a retailer's net sales and total assets. It is equal to net sales divided by total assets.

Assortment Selection of merchandise carried by a retailer. It includes both the breadth of product categories and the variety within each category.

Assortment Display An open or closed display in which a retailer exhibits a wide range of merchandise.

Assortment Merchandise Apparel, furniture, autos, and other products for which the retailer must carry a variety of products in order to give customers a proper selection.

Atmosphere Store's physical characteristics that are used to develop an image and draw customers. It is also known as atmospherics.

Atmospherics *See* Atmosphere.

Attitudes (Opinions) Positive, neutral, or negative feelings a person has about the economy, politics, goods, services, institutions, and so on.

Augmented Customer Service Encompasses the actions that enhance the shopping experience and give retailers a competitive advantage.

Automatic Markdown Plan Controls the amount and timing of markdowns on the basis of the length of time merchandise remains in stock.

Automatic Reordering System Computerized approach that combines a perpetual inventory and reorder point calculations.

Bait Advertising Illegal practice in which a retailer lures a customer by advertising goods and services at exceptionally low prices, and then tries to convince the person to buy a better, more expensive substitute that is available. The retailer has no intention of selling the advertised item.

Bait-and-Switch Advertising *See* Bait Advertising.

Balanced Tenancy Occurs when stores in a planned shopping center complement each other as to the quality and variety of their product offerings.

Balance Sheet Itemizes a retailer's assets, liabilities, and net worth at a specific time—based on the principle that assets equal liabilities plus net worth.

Basic Stock List Specifies the inventory level, color, brand, style category, size, package, and so on for every staple item carried by a retailer.

Basic Stock Method   Inventory level planning tool wherein a retailer carries more items than it expects to sell over a specified period:

$$\text{Basic stock} = \frac{\text{Average monthly stock at retail} -}{\text{Average monthly sales}}$$

Battle of the Brands   The competition between manufacturers and retailers for shelf space and profits, whereby manufacturer, private, and generic brands fight each other for more space and control.

Benchmarking   Occurs when the retailer sets its own standards and measures performance based on the achievements in its sector, specific competitors, high performance firms, and/or its own prior actions.

Bifurcated Retailing   Denotes the decline of middle-of-the-market retailing due to the popularity of both mass merchandising and niche retailing.

Book Inventory System   Keeps a running total of the value of all inventory at cost as of a given time. This is done by recording purchases and adding them to existing inventory value; sales are subtracted to arrive at the new current inventory value (all at cost). It is also known as a perpetual inventory system.

Bottom-Up Space Management Approach   Exists when planning starts at the individual product level and then proceeds to the category, total store, and overall company levels.

Box (Limited-Line) Store   Food-based discounter that focuses on a small selection of items, moderate hours of operation (compared to supermarkets), few services, and limited manufacturer brands.

BPI   *See* Buying Power Index.

Budgeting   Outlines a retailer's planned expenditures for a given time based on expected performance.

Bundled Pricing   Involves a retailer combining several elements in one basic price.

Business Format Franchising   Arrangement in which the franchisee receives assistance in site location, quality control, accounting, startup practices, management training, and responding to problems—besides the right to sell goods and services.

Buying Power Index (BPI)   Single weighted measure combining effective buying income, retail sales, and population size into one overall indicator of an area's sales potential. It is expressed as:

BPI = 0.5 (the area's percentage of U.S. effective
        buying income)
      + 0.3 (the area's percentage of U.S. retail sales)
      + 0.2 (the area's percentage of U.S. population)

Canned Sales Presentation   Memorized, repetitive speech given to all customers interested in a particular item.

Capital Expenditures   Retail expenditures that are long-term investments in fixed assets.

Case Display   Interior display that exhibits heavier, bulkier items than racks hold.

Cash Flow   Relates the amount and timing of revenues received to the amount and timing of expenditures made during a specific time.

Category Killer   Very large specialty store featuring an enormous selection in its product category and relatively low prices. It draws consumers from wide geographic areas.

Category Management   Merchandising technique that some firms—including supermarkets, drugstores, hardware stores, and general merchandise retailers—are using to improve their productivity. It focuses on product category results rather than the performance of individual brands or models.

CBD   *See* Central Business District.

Census of Population   Supplies a wide range of demographic data for all U.S. cities and surrounding vicinities. These data are organized on a geographic basis.

Central Business District (CBD)   Hub of retailing in a city, and its largest shopping area. It is synonymous with "downtown." The CBD has the greatest density of office buildings and stores.

Centralized Buying Organization   Occurs when a retailer makes all purchase decisions from one office.

Chain   Retailer that operates multiple outlets (store units) under common ownership. It usually engages in some level of centralized (or coordinated) purchasing and decision making.

Channel Control   Occurs when one member of a distribution channel can dominate the decisions made in that channel by the power it possesses.

Channel of Distribution   Comprises all of the businesses and people involved in the physical movement and transfer of ownership of goods and services from producer to consumer.

Chargebacks   Practice of retailers, at their discretion, making deductions in the manufacturers' bills for infractions ranging from late shipments to damaged and expired merchandise.

Class Consciousness   Extent to which a person desires and pursues social status.

Classification Merchandising   Allows firms to obtain more financial data by subdividing each specified department into further categories for related types of merchandise.

Cognitive Dissonance Doubt that occurs after a purchase is made, which can be alleviated by customer after-care, money-back guarantees, and realistic sales presentations and advertising campaigns.

Collaborative Planning, Forecasting, and Replenishment (CPFR) Emerging technique for larger firms whereby there is a holistic approach to supply chain management among a network of trading partners.

Combination Store Unites supermarket and general merchandise sales in one facility, with general merchandise typically accounting for 25 to 40 percent of total sales.

Community Shopping Center Moderate-sized, planned shopping facility with a branch department store, a variety store, and/or a category killer store, in addition to several smaller stores. About 20,000 to 100,000 people, who live or work within 10 to 20 minutes of the center, are served by this location.

Compensation Includes direct monetary payments to employees (such as salaries, commissions, and bonuses) and indirect payments (such as paid vacations, health and life insurance benefits, and retirement plans).

Competition-Oriented Pricing Approach in which a firm sets prices in accordance with competitors'.

Competitive Advantages Distinct competencies of a retailer relative to competitors.

Competitive Parity Method Promotional budgeting procedure by which a retailer's budget is raised or lowered based on competitors' actions.

Computerized Checkout Used by large and small retailers to efficiently process transactions and monitor inventory. Cashiers ring up sales or pass items by scanners. Computerized registers instantly record and display sales, customers get detailed receipts, and inventory data are stored in a memory bank.

Concentrated Marketing Selling goods and services to one specific group.

Consignment Purchase Items not paid for by a retailer until they are sold. The retailer can return unsold merchandise. Title is not taken by the retailer; the supplier owns the goods until sold.

Constrained Decision Making Excludes franchisees from or limits their involvement in the strategic planning process.

Consumer Behavior Involves the process by which people determine whether, what, when, where, how, from whom, and how often to purchase goods and services.

Consumer Cooperative Retail firm owned by its customer members. A group of consumers invests in the company, elects officers, manages operations, and shares the profits or savings that accrue.

Consumer Decision Process Stages a consumer goes through in buying a good or service: stimulus, problem awareness, information search, evaluation of alternatives, purchase, and post-purchase behavior. Demographics and life-style factors affect this decision process.

Consumerism Relates to the activities of government, business, and other organizations that are designed to protect individuals from practices infringing on their rights as consumers.

Consumer Loyalty (Frequent Shopper) Programs Rewards for a retailer's best customers, those with whom it wants long-lasting relationships.

Contingency Pricing Arrangement by which a service retailer does not get paid until after the service is satisfactorily performed. This is a special form of flexible pricing.

Control Phase in the evaluation of a firm's strategy and tactics in which a semiannual or annual review of the retailer takes place.

Controllable Variables Aspects of business that the retailer can directly affect (such as hours of operation and sales personnel).

Control Units Merchandise categories for which data are gathered.

Convenience Store Well-located food-oriented retailer that is open long hours and carries a moderate number of items. It is small, with average to above-average prices and average atmosphere and services.

Conventional Supermarket Departmentalized food store with a wide range of food and related products; sales of general merchandise are rather limited.

Cooperative Advertising Occurs when manufacturers or wholesalers and their retailers, or two or more retailers, share the costs of retail advertising.

Cooperative Buying Procedure used when a group of retailers make quantity purchases from suppliers.

Core Customers Consumers with whom retailers seek to nurture long relationships. They should be singled out in a firm's data base.

Corporation Retail firm that is formally incorporated under state law. It is a legal entity apart from individual officers (or stockholders).

Cost Complement Average relationship of cost to retail value for all merchandise available for sale during a given time period.

Cost Method of Accounting Requires the retailer's cost of each item to be recorded on an accounting sheet and/or coded on a price tag or merchandise container. When a physical inventory is done, item costs must be learned, the quantity of every item in stock counted, and total inventory value at cost calculated.

Cost of Goods Sold   Amount a retailer has paid to acquire the merchandise sold during a given time period. It equals the cost of merchandise available for sale minus the cost value of ending inventory.

Cost-Oriented Pricing   Approach in which a retailer sets a price floor, the minimum price acceptable to the firm so it can reach a specified profit goal. A retailer usually computes merchandise and retail operating costs and adds a profit margin to these figures.

CPFR   *See* Collaborative Planning, Forecasting, and Replenishment.

Cross-Merchandising   Exists when a retailer carries complementary goods and services so that shoppers are encouraged to buy more.

Cross-Shopping   Occurs when consumers shop for a product category through more than one retail format or visit multiple retailers on one shopping trip.

Cross-Training   Enables personnel to learn tasks associated with more than one job.

Culture   Distinctive heritage shared by a group of people. It passes on beliefs, norms, and customs.

Curving (Free-Flowing) Traffic Flow   Presents displays and aisles in a free-flowing pattern.

Customary Pricing   Used when a retailer sets prices for goods and services and seeks to maintain them for an extended period.

Customer Loyalty   Exists when a person regularly patronizes a particular retailer (store or nonstore) that he or she knows, likes, and trusts.

Customer Satisfaction   Occurs when the value and customer service provided through a retailing experience meet or exceed consumer expectations.

Customer Service   Identifiable, but sometimes intangible, activities undertaken by a retailer in conjunction with the basic goods and services it sells.

Cut Case   Inexpensive display, in which merchandise is left in the original carton.

Data-Base Management   Procedure used to gather, integrate, apply, and store information related to specific subject areas. It is a key element in a retail information system.

Data-Base Retailing   Way of collecting, storing, and using relevant information on customers.

Data Mining   Involves the in-depth analysis of information so as to gain specific insights about customers, product categories, vendors, and so forth.

Data Warehousing   Advance in data-base management whereby copies of all the data bases in a company are maintained in one location and accessible to employees at any locale.

Dead Areas   Awkward spaces where normal displays cannot be set up.

Dealer Brands   *See* Private Brands.

Debit Card System   Computerized process whereby the purchase price of a good or service is immediately deducted from a consumer's bank account and entered into a retailer's account.

Decentralized Buying Organization   Lets purchase decisions be made locally or regionally.

Demand-Oriented Pricing   Approach by which a retailer sets prices based on consumer desires. It determines the range of prices acceptable to the target market.

Demographics   Objective, quantifiable, easily identifiable, and measurable population data.

Department Store   Large store with an extensive assortment (width and depth) of goods and services that has separate departments for purposes of buying, promotion, customer service, and control.

Depth of Assortment   The variety in any one goods/service category (product line) with which a retailer is involved.

Destination Retailer   Firm that consumers view as distinctive enough to become loyal to it. Consumers go out of their way to shop there.

Destination Store   Retail outlet with a trading area much larger than that of a competitor with a less unique appeal. It offers a better merchandise assortment in its product category(ies), promotes more extensively, and creates a stronger image.

Differentiated Marketing   Aims at two or more distinct consumer groups, with different retailing approaches for each group.

Direct Marketing   Form of retailing in which a customer is first exposed to a good or service through a nonpersonal medium and then orders by mail, phone, or fax—and increasingly by computer.

Direct Product Profitability (DPP)   Method for planning variable markups whereby a retailer finds the profitability of each category or unit of merchandise by computing adjusted per-unit gross margin and assigning direct product costs for such expenses as warehousing, transportation, handling, and selling.

Direct Selling   Includes both personal contact with consumers in their homes (and other nonstore locations such as offices) and phone solicitations initiated by a retailer.

Direct Store Distribution (DSD)   Exists when retailers have at least some goods shipped directly from suppliers to individual stores. It works best with retailers that also utilize EDI.

Discretionary Income   Money left after paying taxes and buying necessities.

Distributed Promotion Effort Used by retailers that promote throughout the year.

Diversification Way in which retailers become active in business outside their normal operations—and add stores in different goods/service categories.

Diversified Retailer Multiline firm with central ownership. It is also known as a retail conglomerate.

Dollar Control Planning and monitoring the financial merchandise investment over a stated period.

Downsizing Unprofitable stores closed or divisions sold off by retailers unhappy with performance.

DPP *See* Direct Product Profitability.

DSD *See* Direct Store Distribution.

Dual Vertical Marketing System Involves firms engaged in more than one type of distribution arrangement. This enables those firms to appeal to different consumers, increase revenues, share some of their costs, and maintain a good degree of control over their strategy.

Dump Bin Case display that houses piles of sale clothing, marked-down books, or other products.

Ease of Entry Occurs due to low capital requirements and no, or relatively simple, licensing provisions.

EBI *See* Effective Buying Income.

Economic Base Area's industrial and commercial structure—the companies and industries that residents depend on to earn a living.

Economic Order Quantity (EOQ) Quantity per order (in units) that minimizes the total costs of processing orders and holding inventory:

$$EOQ = \sqrt{\frac{2DS}{IC}}$$

where

EOQ = Economic order quantity (in units)
  D = Annual demand (in units)
  S = Costs to place an order (in dollars)
  I = Percentage of annual carrying cost to unit cost
  C = Unit cost of an item (in dollars)

ECR *See* Efficient Consumer Response.

EDI *See* Electronic Data Interchange.

EDLP *See* Everyday Low Pricing.

Effective Buying Income (EBI) Personal income (wages, salaries, interest, dividends, profits, rental income, and pension income) minus federal, state, and local taxes and nontax payments (such as personal contributions for social security). It is commonly known as disposable or after-tax personal income.

Efficient Consumer Response (ECR) Form of order processing and fulfillment by which supermarkets are incorporating aspects of QR inventory planning, EDI, and logistics planning.

Electronic Article Surveillance Involves attaching specially designed tags or labels to products.

Electronic Banking Includes both automatic teller machines (ATMs) and the instant processing of retail purchases.

Electronic Data Interchange (EDI) Lets retailers and suppliers regularly exchange information through their computers with regard to inventory levels, delivery times, unit sales, and so on, of particular items.

Electronic Point-of-Sale System Performs all the tasks of a computerized checkout and also verifies check and charge transactions, provides instantaneous sales reports, monitors and changes prices, sends intra- and interstore messages, evaluates personnel and profitability, and stores data.

Employee Empowerment Way of improving customer service in which workers have discretion to do what they feel is needed—within reason—to satisfy the customer, even if this means bending some rules.

Ensemble Display Interior display whereby a complete product bundle (ensemble) is presented rather than showing merchandise in separate categories.

EOQ *See* Economic Order Quantity.

Equal Store Organization Centralizes the buying function. Branch stores become sales units with equal operational status.

Ethics Involves activities that are trustworthy, fair, honest, and respectful for each retailer constituency.

Evaluation of Alternatives Stage in the decision process where a consumer selects one good or service to buy from a list of alternatives.

Everyday Low Pricing (EDLP) Version of customary pricing whereby a retailer strives to sell its goods and services at consistently low prices throughout the selling season.

Exclusive Distribution Takes place when suppliers enter agreements with one or a few retailers to designate the latter as the only firms in specified geographic areas to carry certain brands or product lines.

Expected Customer Service Level of service that customers want to receive from any retailer, such as basic employee courtesy.

Experiential Merchandising Tactic whose intent is to convert shopping from a passive activity into a more interactive one, by better engaging the customer.

Experiment Type of research in which one or more elements of a retail strategy mix are manipulated under controlled conditions.

Extended Decision Making Occurs when a consumer makes full use of the decision process, usually for expensive, complex items with which the person has had little or no experience.

External Secondary Data Available from sources outside a firm.

Factory Outlet Manufacturer-owned store selling its closeouts, discontinued merchandise, irregulars, canceled orders, and, sometimes, in-season, first-quality merchandise.

Fad Merchandise Items that generate a high level of sales for a short time.

Family Life Cycle How a traditional family moves from bachelorhood to children to solitary retirement.

Fashion Merchandise Products that may have cyclical sales due to changing tastes and life-styles.

Feedback Signals or cues as to the success or failure of part of a retail strategy.

FIFO Method Logically assumes old merchandise is sold first, while newer items remain in inventory. It matches inventory value with the current cost structure.

Financial Leverage Performance measure based on the relationship between a retailer's total assets and net worth. It is equal to total assets divided by net worth.

Financial Merchandise Management Occurs when a retailer specifies exactly which products (goods and services) are purchased, when products are purchased, and how many products are purchased.

Flea Market Location where many vendors offer a range of products at discount prices in plain surroundings. Many flea markets are located in nontraditional sites not normally associated with retailing. They may be indoor or outdoor.

Flexible Pricing Strategy that lets consumers bargain over selling prices; those consumers who are good at bargaining obtain lower prices than those who are not.

Floor-Ready Merchandise Items that are received at the store in condition to be put directly on display without any preparation by retail workers.

Food-Based Superstore Retailer that is larger and more diversified than a conventional supermarket but usually smaller and less diversified than a combination store. It caters to consumers' complete grocery needs and offers them the ability to buy fill-in general merchandise.

Forecasts Projections of expected retail sales for given time periods.

Formal Buying Organization Views merchandising (buying) as a distinct retail task; a separate department is set up.

Franchising Contractual arrangement between a franchisor (a manufacturer, a wholesaler, or a service sponsor) and a retail franchisee, which allows the franchisee to conduct a given form of business under an established name and according to a given pattern of business.

Free-Flowing Traffic Flow *See* Curving Traffic Flow.

Frequency Average number of times each person who is reached by a message is exposed to a retailer's promotion efforts in a specific period.

Frequent Shopper Programs *See* Consumer Loyalty Programs.

Fringe Trading Area Includes customers not found in primary and secondary trading areas. These are the most widely dispersed customers.

Full-Line Discount Store Type of department store with (1) a broad product assortment; (2) the range of products expected at department stores; (3) centralized checkout service; (4) self-service; (5) private-brand nondurables and well-known manufacturer-brand durables; (6) less-fashion-sensitive merchandise; (7) relatively inexpensive building, equipment, and fixtures; and (8) less emphasis on credit.

Functional Product Groupings Categorize and display a store's merchandise by common end use.

Gap Analysis Enables a company to compare its actual performance against its potential performance, and then determine the areas in which it must improve.

Generic Brands No-frills goods stocked by some retailers. These items usually receive secondary shelf locations, have little or no promotion support, are sometimes of less quality than other brands, are stocked in limited assortments, and have plain packages. They are a form of private brand.

Geographic Information Systems (GIS) Combine digitized mapping with key locational data to graphically depict such trading-area characteristics as the demographic attributes of the population, data on customer purchases, and listings of current, proposed, and competitor locations.

GIS *See* Geographic Information Systems.

GMROI *See* Gross Margin Return on Investment.

Goal-Oriented Job Description Enumerates a position's basic functions, the relationship of each job to overall goals, the interdependence of positions, and information flows.

Goods Retailing Focuses on the sale of tangible (physical) products.

Goods/Service Category Retail firm's line of business.

Graduated Lease Calls for precise rent increases over a stated period of time.

Gravity Model Computerized site selection tool based on the premise that people are drawn to stores that are closer and more attractive than competitors'.

Gray Market Goods Brand-name products bought in foreign markets or goods transshipped from other retailers. They are often sold at low prices by unauthorized dealers.

Gridiron Traffic Flow *See* Straight Traffic Flow.

Gross Margin Difference between net sales and the total cost of goods sold. It is also called *gross profit*.

Gross Margin Return on Investment (GMROI) Shows relationship between total dollar operating profits and the average inventory investment (at cost) by combining profitability and sales-to-stock measures:

$$\text{GMROI} = \frac{\text{Gross margin in dollars}}{\text{Net sales}} \times \frac{\text{Net Sales}}{\text{Average inventory at cost}}$$

$$= \frac{\text{Gross margin in dollars}}{\text{Average inventory at cost}}$$

Gross Profit Difference between net sales and the total cost of goods sold. It is also known as *gross margin*.

Hidden Assets Depreciated assets, such as store buildings and warehouses, that are reflected on a retailer's balance sheet at low values relative to their actual worth.

Hierarchy of Authority Outlines the job interactions within a company by describing the reporting relationships among employees. Coordination and control are provided.

Hierarchy of Effects Sequence of steps a consumer goes through in reacting to retail communications, which leads him or her from awareness to knowledge to liking to preference to conviction to purchase.

Horizontal Cooperative Advertising Agreement Enables two or more retailers (most often small, situated together, or franchisees of the same company) to share an ad.

Horizontal Price Fixing Agreement among manufacturers, among wholesalers, or among retailers to set certain prices. This is illegal, regardless of how "reasonable" prices may be.

Horizontal Retail Audit Analyzes a retail firm's overall performance, from mission to goals to customer satisfaction to basic retail strategy mix and its implementation in an integrated, consistent way.

Household Life Cycle Incorporates the life stages of both family and nonfamily households.

Huff's Law of Shopper Attraction Delineates trading areas on the basis of the product assortment carried at various shopping locations, travel times from the shopper's home to alternative locations, and the sensitivity of the kind of shopping to travel time.

Human Resource Management Recruiting, selecting, training, compensating, and supervising personnel in a manner consistent with the retailer's organization structure and strategy mix.

Human Resource Management Process Consists of these interrelated activities: recruitment, selection, training, compensation, and supervision. The goals are to obtain, develop, and retain employees.

Hypermarket Combination store pioneered in Europe that blends an economy supermarket with a discount department store. It is even larger than a supercenter.

Image Represents how a given retailer is perceived by consumers and others.

Impulse Purchases Occur when consumers buy products and/or brands they had not planned to before entering a store, reading a catalog, seeing a TV shopping show, turning to the Web, and so forth.

Income Statement *See* Profit-and-Loss Statement.

Incremental Budgeting Process whereby a firm uses current and past budgets as guides and adds to or subtracts from them to arrive at the coming period's expenditures.

Incremental Method Promotional budgeting procedure by which a percentage is either added to or subtracted from one year's budget to determine the next year's.

Independent Retailer that owns only one retail unit.

Infomercial Program-length TV commercial (most often, 30 minutes in length) for a specific good or service that airs on cable television or on broadcast television, often at a fringe time. It is particularly worthwhile for products that benefit from visual demonstrations.

Informal Buying Organization Does not consider merchandising (buying) as a distinct retail function; the same personnel handle both merchandising (buying) and other retail tasks.

Information Search Consists of two parts: determining alternatives to solve the problem at hand (and where they can be bought) and learning the characteristics of alternatives. It may be internal or external.

Initial Markup (at Retail) Based on the original retail value assigned to merchandise less the merchandise costs, expressed as a percentage of the original retail price:

$$\text{Initial markup percentage (at retail)} = \frac{\begin{array}{c}\text{Planned retail operating} \\ \text{expenses} + \text{Planned profit} + \\ \text{Planned retail reductions}\end{array}}{\begin{array}{c}\text{Planned net sales} + \text{Planned} \\ \text{retail reductions}\end{array}}$$

Initial Public Offering (IPO) Method whereby a firm raises money by selling stock to the public.

Inside Buying Organization Staffed by a retailer's own personnel; merchandise decisions are made by permanent employees of the firm.

Intensive Distribution Takes place when suppliers sell through as many retailers as possible. This often maximizes suppliers' sales and lets retailers offer many brands and product versions.

Internal Secondary Data Available within a company, sometimes from the data bank of a retail information system.

Internet Global electronic superhighway of computer networks that use a common protocol and that are linked by telecommunications lines and satellite.

Inventory Management Process whereby a firm seeks to acquire and maintain a proper merchandise assortment while ordering, shipping, handling, storing, displaying, and selling costs are kept in check.

Inventory Shrinkage Encompasses employee theft, customer shoplifting, and fraud and administrative errors by vendors.

IPO *See* Initial Public Offering.

Isolated Store Freestanding retail outlet located on either a highway or a street. There are no adjacent retailers with which this type of store shares traffic.

Issue (Problem) Definition Step in the marketing research process that involves a clear statement of the topic to be studied.

Item Price Removal Practice whereby prices are marked only on shelves or signs and not on individual items. It is banned in several states and local communities.

Job Analysis Consists of gathering information about each job's functions and requirements: duties, responsibilities, aptitude, interest, education, experience, and physical tasks.

Job Motivation Drive within people to attain work-related goals.

Job Standardization Keeps tasks of employees with similar positions in different departments rather uniform.

LBO *See* Leveraged Buyout.

Leader Pricing Occurs when a retailer advertises and sells selected items in its goods/service assortment at less than the usual profit margins. The goal is to increase customer traffic so as to sell regularly priced goods and services in addition to the specially priced items.

Leased Department Site in a retail store—usually a department, discount, or specialty store—that is rented to an outside party.

Leveraged Buyout (LBO) Ownership change mostly financed by loans from banks, investors, and others.

Liabilities Financial obligations a retailer incurs in operating a business.

Life-Styles Ways that individual consumers and families (households) live and spend time and money.

LIFO Method Assumes new merchandise is sold first, while older stock remains in inventory. It matches current sales with the current cost structure.

Limited Decision Making Occurs when a consumer uses every step in the purchase process but does not spend a great deal of time on each of them.

Limited-Line Store *See* Box Store.

Logistics Total process of planning, enacting, and coordinating the physical movement of merchandise from supplier to retailer to customer in the most timely, effective, and cost-efficient manner possible.

Loss Leaders Items priced below cost to lure more customer traffic. Loss leaders are restricted by some state minimum price laws.

Maintained Markup (at Retail) Based on the actual prices received for merchandise sold during a time period less merchandise cost, expressed as a percentage:

$$\text{Maintained markup percentage (at retail)} = \frac{\text{Actual retail operating expenses} + \text{Actual profit}}{\text{Actual net sales}}$$

or

$$\frac{\text{Average selling price} - \text{Merchandise cost}}{\text{Average selling price}}$$

Maintenance-Increase-Recoupment Lease Has a provision allowing rent to increase if a property owner's taxes, heating bills, insurance, or other expenses rise beyond a certain point.

Manufacturer (National) Brands Produced and controlled by manufacturers. They are usually well known, supported by manufacturer ads, somewhat pre-sold to consumers, require limited retailer investment in marketing, and often represent maximum product quality to consumers.

Markdown Reduction from the original retail price of an item to meet the lower price of another retailer, adapt to inventory overstocking, clear out shopworn merchandise, reduce assortments of odds and ends, and increase customer traffic.

Markdown Percentage Total dollar markdown as a percentage of net sales (in dollars):

$$\text{Markdown percentage} = \frac{\text{Total dollar markdown}}{\text{Net sales (in \$)}}$$

Marketing Concept   Customer-centered, companywide approach to strategy development and implementation that is value-driven and has clear goals.

Marketing Research in Retailing   Collection and analysis of information relating to specific issues or problems facing a retailer.

Marketing Research Process   Embodies a series of activities: defining the issue or problem, examining secondary data, generating primary data (if needed), analyzing data, making recommendations, and implementing findings.

Market Penetration   Pricing strategy in which a retailer seeks to achieve large revenues by setting low prices and selling a high unit volume.

Market Segment Product Groupings   Place together various items that appeal to a given target market.

Market Skimming   Pricing strategy wherein a firm charges premium prices and attracts customers less concerned with price than service, assortment, and status.

Markup   Difference between merchandise costs and retail selling price.

Markup Percentage (at Cost)   Difference between retail price and merchandise cost expressed as a percentage of merchandise cost:

$$\text{Markup percentage (at cost)} = \frac{\text{Retail selling price} - \text{Merchandise cost}}{\text{Merchandise cost}}$$

Markup Percentage (at Retail)   Difference between retail price and merchandise cost expressed as a percentage of retail price:

$$\text{Markup percentage (at retail)} = \frac{\text{Retail selling price} - \text{Merchandise cost}}{\text{Retail selling price}}$$

Markup Pricing   Form of cost-oriented pricing in which a retailer sets prices by adding per-unit merchandise costs, retail operating expenses, and desired profit.

Marquee   Sign used to display a store's name and/or logo.

Mass Customization   Ability to efficiently and economically offer goods and services more tailored to individual consumers.

Massed Promotion Effort   Used by retailers that promote mostly in one or two seasons.

Mass Marketing   Selling goods and services to a broad spectrum of consumers.

Mass Merchandising   Positioning approach whereby retailers offer a discount or value-oriented image, a wide and/or deep merchandise assortment, and large store facilities.

Mazur Plan   Divides all retail activities into four functional areas: merchandising, publicity, store management, and accounting and control.

Megamall   Enormous planned shopping center with 1-million+ square feet of retail space, multiple anchor stores, up to several hundred specialty stores, food courts, and entertainment facilities.

Membership (Warehouse) Club   Appeals to price-conscious consumers, who must be members to shop.

Memorandum Purchase   Occurs when items are not paid for by the retailer until they are sold. The retailer can return unsold merchandise. However, it takes title on delivery and is responsible for damages.

Merchandise Available for Sale   Equals beginning inventory, purchases, and transportation charges.

Merchandising   Activities involved in acquiring particular goods and/or services and making them available at the places, times, and prices and in the quantity to enable a retailer to reach its goals.

Merchandising Philosophy   Sets the guiding principles for all the merchandise decisions a retailer makes.

Mergers   The combinations of separately owned retail firms.

Micromarketing   Emerging application of data mining whereby the retailer uses differentiated marketing and focused strategy mixes for specific segments, sometimes fine-tuned for the individual shopper.

Micromerchandising   Strategy whereby a retailer adjusts its shelf-space allocations to respond to customer and other differences among local markets.

Minimum Price Laws   State regulations preventing retailers from selling certain items for less than their cost plus a fixed percentage to cover overhead. These laws restrict loss leaders and predatory pricing.

Model Stock Approach   Method of determining the amount of floor space necessary to carry and display a proper merchandise assortment.

Model Stock Plan   Planned composition of fashion goods, which reflects the mix of merchandise available based on expected sales. It indicates product lines, colors, and size distributions.

Monthly Sales Index   Measure of sales seasonality that is calculated by dividing each month's actual sales by average monthly sales and then multiplying the results by 100.

Mother Hen with Branch Store Chickens Organization   Exists when headquarters executives oversee and operate the branches. This works well if there are few branches and the buying preferences of branch customers are similar to those of the main store.

Motives   Reasons for consumer behavior.

Multiple-Unit Pricing   Discounts offered to customers who buy in quantity or who buy a product bundle.

Mystery Shoppers   People hired by retailers to pose as customers and observe their operations, from sales presentations to how well displays are maintained to in-home service calls.

National Brands   *See* Manufacturer Brands.

NBD   *See* Neighborhood Business District.

Need-Satisfaction Approach   Sales technique based on the principle that each customer has a different set of wants; thus, a sales presentation should be geared to the demands of the individual customer.

Neighborhood Business District (NBD)   Unplanned shopping area that appeals to the convenience shopping and service needs of a single residential area. The leading retailer is typically a supermarket, a large drugstore, or a variety store and it is situated on the major street(s) of its residential area.

Neighborhood Shopping Center   Planned shopping facility with the largest store being a supermarket or a drugstore. It serves 3,000 to 50,000 people within a 15-minute drive (usually less than 10 minutes).

Net Lease   Calls for all maintenance costs, such as heating, electricity, insurance, and interior repair, to be paid by the retailer—which is responsible for their satisfactory quality.

Net Profit   Equals gross profit minus retail operating expenses.

Net Profit Before Taxes   Profit earned after all costs have been deducted.

Net Profit Margin   Performance measure based on a retailer's net profit and net sales. It is equal to net profit divided by net sales.

Net Sales   Revenues received by a retailer during a given time period after deducting customer returns, markdowns, and employee discounts.

Net Worth   Retailer's assets minus its liabilities.

Never-Out List   Used when a retailer plans stock levels for best-sellers. The goal is to purchase enough of these products so they are always in stock.

Niche Retailing   Enables retailers to identify customer segments and deploy unique strategies to address the desires of those segments.

Nongoods Services   Area of service retailing in which intangible personal services (not goods) are offered to consumers—who experience the services rather than possess them.

Nonprobability Sample   Approach in which stores, products, or customers are chosen by the researcher—based on judgment or convenience.

Nonstore Retailing   Utilizes strategy mixes that are not store-based to reach consumers and complete transactions. It occurs via direct marketing, direct selling, and vending machines.

Objective-and-Task Method   Promotional budgeting procedure by which a retailer clearly defines its promotional goals and prepares a budget to satisfy them.

Objectives   Long-term and short-term performance targets that a retailer hopes to attain. Goals can involve sales, profit, satisfaction of publics, and image.

Observation   Form of research in which present behavior or the results of past behavior are observed and recorded. It can be human or mechanical.

Odd Pricing   Retail prices set at levels below even dollar values, such as $0.49, $4.98, and $199.

Off-Price Chain   Features brand-name apparel and accessories, footwear, linens, fabrics, cosmetics, and/or housewares and sells them at everyday low prices in an efficient, limited-service environment.

Off-Retail Markdown Percentage   Markdown for each item or category of items computed as a percentage of original retail price:

$$\text{Off-retail markdown percentage} = \frac{\text{Original price} - \text{New price}}{\text{Original price}}$$

One-Hundred Percent Location   Optimum site for a particular store. A location labeled as 100 percent for one firm may be less than optimal for another.

One-Price Policy   Strategy wherein a retailer charges the same price to all customers buying an item under similar conditions.

Open Credit Account   Requires a consumer to pay his or her bill in full when it is due.

Open-to-Buy   Difference between planned purchases and the purchase commitments already made by a buyer for a given time period, often a month. It represents the amount the buyer has left to spend for that month and is reduced each time a purchase is made.

Operating Expenditures (Expenses)   Short-term selling and administrative costs of running a business.

Operations Blueprint   Systematically lists all the operating functions to be performed, their characteristics, and their timing.

Operations Management   Process used to efficiently and effectively enact the policies and tasks to satisfy a firm's customers, employees, and management (and stockholders, if a publicly owned company).

Opinions *See* Attitudes.

Opportunistic Buying Negotiates low prices for merchandise whose sales have not met expectations, end-of-season goods, items returned to the manufacturer or another retailer, and closeouts.

Opportunities Marketplace openings that exist because other retailers have not yet capitalized on them.

Opportunity Costs Possible benefits a retailer forgoes if it invests in one opportunity rather than another.

Option Credit Account Form of revolving account that allows partial payments. No interest is assessed if a person pays a bill in full when it is due.

Order-Getting Salesperson Actively involved with informing and persuading customers, and in closing sales. This is a true "sales" employee.

Order Lead Time Period from when an order is placed by a retailer to the date merchandise is ready for sale (received, price marked, and put on the selling floor).

Order-Taking Salesperson Engages in routine clerical and sales functions, such as setting up displays, placing inventory on shelves, answering simple questions, filling orders, and ringing up sales.

Organizational Mission Retailer's commitment to a type of business and a distinctive marketplace role. It is reflected in the attitude to consumers, employees, suppliers, competitors, government, and others.

Organization Chart Graphically displays the hierarchical relationships within a firm.

Outshopping When a person goes out of his or her hometown to shop.

Outside Buying Organization Company or person external to the retailer hired to fulfill the buying function, usually on a fee basis.

Outsourcing Situation whereby a retailer pays an outside party to undertake one or more operating tasks.

Overstored Trading Area Geographic area with so many stores selling a specific good or service that some retailers will be unable to earn an adequate profit.

Owned-Goods Services Area of service retailing in which goods owned by consumers are repaired, improved, or maintained.

Parasite Store Outlet that does not create its own traffic and has no real trading area of its own.

Partnership Unincorporated retailer owned by two or more persons, each with a financial interest.

Perceived Risk Level of risk a consumer believes exists regarding the purchase of a specific good or service from a given retailer, whether or not the belief is actually correct.

Percentage Lease Stipulates that rent is related to a retailer's sales or profits.

Percentage-of-Sales Method Promotional budgeting method in which a retailer ties its budget to revenue.

Percentage Variation Method Inventory level planning method where beginning-of-month planned inventory during any month differs from planned average monthly stock by only one-half of that month's variation from estimated average monthly sales. Under this method:

$$\text{Beginning-of-month planned inventory level (at retail} = \text{Planned average monthly stock at retail} \times \tfrac{1}{2}[1 + (\text{Estimated monthly sales}/\text{Estimated average monthly sales})]$$

Performance Measures Criteria used to assess effectiveness, including total sales, sales per store, sales by product category, sales per square foot, gross margins, gross margin return on investment, operating income, inventory turnover, markdown percentages, employee turnover, financial ratios, and profitability.

Perpetual Inventory System *See* Book Inventory System.

Personality Sum total of an individual's traits, which make that individual unique.

Personal Selling Oral communication with one or more prospective customers to make sales.

Physical Inventory System Actual counting of merchandise. A firm using the cost method of inventory valuation and relying on a physical inventory can derive gross profit only when it does a full inventory.

Planned Shopping Center Group of architecturally unified commercial facilities on a site that is centrally owned or managed, designed and operated as a unit, based on balanced tenancy, and surrounded by parking.

Planogram Visual (graphical) representation of the space for selling, merchandise, personnel, and customers—as well as for product categories.

PMs Promotional money, push money, or prize money that a manufacturer provides for retail salespeople who sell that manufacturer's brand.

Point of Indifference Geographic breaking point between two cities (communities), so that the trading area of each can be determined. At this point, consumers would be indifferent to shopping at either area.

Point-of-Purchase (POP) Display Interior display that provides shoppers with information, adds to store atmosphere, and serves a substantial promotional role.

POP Display See Point-of-Purchase Display.

Positioning Enables a retailer to devise its strategy in a way that projects an image relative to its retail category and its competitors, and elicits consumer responses to that image.

Post-Purchase Behavior   Further purchases or reevaluation based on a purchase.

Power Center   Shopping site with (a) up to a half dozen or so category killer stores and a mix of smaller stores or (b) several complementary stores specializing in one product category.

Power Retailer   *See* Category Killer.

Predatory Pricing   Involves large retailers that seek to reduce competition by selling goods and services at very low prices, thus causing small retailers to go out of business.

Prestige Pricing   Assumes consumers will not buy goods and services at prices deemed too low. It is based on the price-quality association.

Pre-Training   Indoctrination on the history and policies of the retailer and a job orientation on hours, compensation, the chain of command, and job duties.

Price Elasticity of Demand   Sensitivity of customers to price changes in terms of the quantities bought:

$$\text{Elasticity} = \frac{\dfrac{\text{Quantity 1} - \text{Quantity 2}}{\text{Quantity 1} + \text{Quantity 2}}}{\dfrac{\text{Price 1} - \text{Price 2}}{\text{Price 1} + \text{Price 2}}}$$

Price Lining   Practice whereby retailers sell merchandise at a limited range of price points, with each point representing a distinct level of quality.

Price-Quality Association   Concept stating that many consumers feel high prices connote high quality and low prices connote low quality.

Primary Data   Those collected to address the specific issue or problem under study. This type of data may be gathered internally or externally via surveys, observations, experiments, and simulation.

Primary Trading Area   Encompasses 50 to 80 percent of a store's customers. It is the area closest to the store and possesses the highest density of customers to population and the highest per-capita sales.

Private (Dealer, Store) Brands   Contain names designated by wholesalers or retailers, are more profitable to retailers, are better controlled by retailers, are not sold by competing retailers, are less expensive for consumers, and lead to customer loyalty to retailers (rather than to manufacturers).

Probability (Random) Sample   Approach whereby every store, product, or customer has an equal or known chance of being chosen for study.

Problem Awareness   Stage in the decision process at which the consumer not only has been aroused by social, commercial, and/or physical stimuli, but also recognizes that the good or service under consideration may solve a problem of shortage or unfulfilled desire.

Problem Definition   *See* Issue Definition.

Productivity   Efficiency with which a retail strategy is carried out.

Product Life Cycle   Shows the expected behavior of a good or service over its life. The traditional cycle has four stages: introduction, growth, maturity, and decline.

Product/Trademark Franchising   Arrangement in which franchisees acquire the identities of franchisors by agreeing to sell the latter's products and/or operate under the latter's names.

Profit-and-Loss (Income) Statement   Summary of a retailer's revenues and expenses over a particular period of time, usually a month, quarter, or year.

Prototype Stores   Used with an operations strategy that requires multiple outlets in a chain to conform to relatively uniform construction, layout, and operations standards.

Publicity   Any nonpersonal form of public relations whereby messages are transmitted by mass media, the time or space provided by the media is not paid for, and there is no identified commercial sponsor.

Public Relations   Any communication that fosters a favorable image for the retailer among its publics (consumers, investors, government, channel members, employees, and the general public).

Purchase Act   Exchange of money or a promise to pay for the ownership or use of a good or service. Purchase variables include the place of purchase, terms, and availability of merchandise.

Purchase Motivation Product Groupings   Appeal to the consumer's urge to buy products and the amount of time he or she is willing to spend in shopping.

QR Inventory Planning   *See* Quick Response Inventory Planning.

Quick Response (QR) Inventory Planning   Enables a retailer to reduce the amount of inventory it keeps on hand by ordering more frequently and in lower quantity.

Rack Display   Interior display that neatly hangs or presents products.

Random Sample   *See* Probability Sample.

Rationalized Retailing   Combines a high degree of centralized management control with strict operating procedures for every phase of business.

Reach   Number of distinct people exposed to a retailer's promotional efforts during a specified period.

Recruitment   Activity whereby a retailer generates a list of job applicants.

Reference Groups Influence people's thoughts and behavior. They may be classified as aspirational, membership, and dissociative.

Regional Shopping Center Large, planned shopping facility appealing to a geographically dispersed market. It has at least one or two full-sized department stores and 50 to 150 or more smaller retailers. The market for this center is 100,000+ people, who live or work up to a 30-minute drive time from the center.

Regression Model Computerized site selection tool that uses equations showing the association between potential store sales and several independent variables at each location under consideration.

Reilly's Law of Retail Gravitation Traditional means of trading-area delineation that establishes a point of indifference between two cities or communities, so the trading area of each can be determined.

Relationship Retailing Exists when retailers seek to establish and maintain long-term bonds with customers, rather than act as if each sales transaction is a completely new encounter with them.

Rented-Goods Services Area of service retailing in which consumers lease and use goods for specified periods of time.

Reorder Point Stock level at which new orders must be placed:

Reorder point = (Usage rate × Lead time) + Safety stock

Resident Buying Office Inside or outside buying organization used when a retailer wants to keep in close touch with market trends and cannot do so with just its headquarters buying staff. Such offices are usually situated in important merchandise centers (sources of supply) and provide valuable data and contacts.

Retail Audit Systematically examines the total retailing effort or a specific aspect of it to study what a retailer is presently doing, appraise how well it is performing, and make recommendations.

Retail Balance The mix of stores within a district or shopping center.

Retail Information System (RIS) Anticipates the information needs of managers; collects, organizes, and stores relevant data on a continuous basis; and directs the flow of information to proper decision makers.

Retailing Business activities involved in selling goods and services to consumers for their personal, family, or household use.

Retailing Concept Based on a customer orientation, coordinated effort, value-driven, and goal orientation.

Retail Institution Basic format or structure of a business. Institutions can be classified by ownership, store-based

retail strategy mix, and nonstore-based, electronic, and nontraditional retailing.

Retail Life Cycle Theory asserting that institutions—like the goods and services they sell—pass through identifiable life-cycle stages: innovation, accelerated development, maturity, and decline.

Retail Method of Accounting Determines closing inventory value by calculating the average relationship between the cost and retail values of merchandise available for sale during a period.

Retail Organization How a firm structures and assigns tasks, policies, resources, authority, responsibilities, and rewards so as to efficiently and effectively satisfy the needs of its target market, employees, and management.

Retail Performance Index Encompasses five-year trends in revenue growth and profit growth, and a six-year average return on assets.

Retail Promotion Any communication by a retailer that informs, persuades, and/or reminds the target market about any aspect of that firm.

Retail Reductions Difference between beginning inventory plus purchases during the period and sales plus ending inventory. They encompass anticipated markdowns, employee and other discounts, and stock shortages.

Retail Strategy Overall plan guiding a retail firm. It influences the firm's business activities and its response to market forces, such as competition and the economy.

Return on Assets (ROA) Performance ratio based on net sales, net profit, and total assets:

$$\frac{\text{Return}}{\text{on assets}} = \frac{\text{Net profit}}{\text{Net sales}} \times \frac{\text{Net sales}}{\text{Total assets}} = \frac{\text{Net profit}}{\text{Total assets}}$$

Return on Net Worth Performance measure based on net profit, net sales, total assets, and net worth:

$$\frac{\text{Return on}}{\text{net worth}} = \frac{\text{Net profit}}{\text{Net sales}} \times \frac{\text{Net sales}}{\text{Total assets}} \times \frac{\text{Total assets}}{\text{Net worth}}$$

Reverse Logistics Encompasses all merchandise flows from the retailer back through the supply channel.

Revolving Credit Account Allows a customer to charge items and be billed monthly on the basis of the outstanding cumulative balance.

RIS *See* Retail Information System.

ROA *See* Return on Assets.

Robinson-Patman Act Bars manufacturers and wholesalers from discriminating in price or purchase terms in selling to individual retailers if these retailers are purchasing products of "like quality" and the effect of such discrimination is to injure competition.

Routine Decision Making Takes place when a consumer buys out of habit and skips steps in the purchase process.

Safety Stock   Extra inventory to protect against out-of-stock conditions due to unexpected demand and delays in delivery.

Sale-Leaseback   Practice of retailers building stores and then selling them to real-estate investors who lease the property back to the retailers on a long-term basis.

Sales Opportunity Grid   Rates the promise of new and established goods, services, procedures, and/or store outlets across a variety of criteria.

Sales-Productivity Ratio   Method for assigning floor space on the basis of sales or profit per foot.

Sales Promotion   Encompasses the paid communication activities other than advertising, public relations, and personal selling that stimulate consumer purchases and dealer effectiveness.

Saturated Trading Area   Geographic area with the proper amount of retail facilities to satisfy the needs of its population for a specific good or service, as well as to enable retailers to prosper.

SBD   *See* Secondary Business District.

Scenario Analysis   Lets a retailer project the future by studying factors that affect long-term performance and then forming contingency plans based on alternate scenarios.

Scrambled Merchandising   Occurs when a retailer adds goods and services that may be unrelated to each other and to the firm's original business.

Seasonable Merchandise   Products that sell well over non-consecutive time periods.

Secondary Business District (SBD)   Unplanned shopping area in a city or town that is usually bounded by the intersection of two major streets. It has at least a junior department store, a variety store, and/or some larger specialty stores—in addition to many smaller stores.

Secondary Data   Those gathered for purposes other than addressing the issue or problem currently under study.

Secondary Trading Area   Geographic area that contains an additional 15 to 25 percent of a store's customers. It is located outside the primary area, and customers are more widely dispersed.

Selective Distribution   Takes place when suppliers sell through a moderate number of retailers. This lets suppliers have higher sales than in exclusive distribution and lets retailers carry some competing brands.

Self-Scanning   Enables the consumer himself or herself to scan the items being purchased at a checkout counter, pay electronically by credit or debit card, and bag the items.

Semantic Differential   Disguised or nondisguised survey technique, whereby a respondent is asked to rate one or more retailers on several criteria; each criterion is evaluated along a bipolar adjective scale.

Separate Store Organization   Treats each branch as a separate store with its own buying responsibilities. Customer needs are quickly noted, but duplication by headquarters and branch stores is possible.

Service Retailing   Involves transactions in which consumers do not purchase or acquire ownership of tangible products. It encompasses rented goods, owned goods, and nongoods.

SERVQUAL   Lets retailers assess the quality of service offerings by asking customers to react to a series of statements in five areas of performance: reliability, responsiveness, assurance, empathy, and tangibles.

Simulation   Type of experiment whereby a computer program is used to manipulate the elements of a retail strategy mix rather than test them in a real setting.

Single-Source Data Collection   Occurs when a research firm develops a sample of consumer households, determines the demographic and life-style backgrounds of those households through surveys, observes TV-viewing behavior by in-home cable hookups to the firm's computers, and monitors shopping behavior by having people make purchases in designated stores.

Situation Analysis   Candid evaluation of the opportunities and threats facing a prospective or existing retailer.

Slotting Allowances   Payments that retailers require of vendors for providing shelf space in stores.

Smart Card   New version of electronic payment that contains an electronic strip that stores and modifies information as transactions take place.

Social Class   Informal ranking of people based on income, occupation, education, and other factors.

Social Responsibility   Occurs when a retailer acts in society's best interests—as well as its own. The challenge is to balance corporate citizenship with fair profits.

Sole Proprietorship   Unincorporated retail firm owned by one person.

Solutions Selling   Takes a customer-centered approach and presents "solutions" rather than "products." It goes a step beyond cross-merchandising.

Sorting Process   Involves the retailer's collecting an assortment of goods and services from various sources, buying them in large quantity, and offering to sell them in small quantities to consumers.

Specialog   Enables a retailer to cater to the specific needs of customer segments, emphasize a limited number of items, and reduce catalog production and postage costs.

Specialty Store   Retailer that concentrates on selling one goods or service line.

Staple Merchandise   Consists of the regular products carried by a retailer.

Stimulus   Cue (social or commercial) or a drive (physical) meant to motivate or arouse a person to act.

Stock-to-Sales Method   Inventory level planning technique wherein a retailer wants to maintain a specified ratio of goods on hand to sales.

Stock Turnover   Number of times during a specific period, usually one year, that the average inventory on hand is sold. It can be computed in units or dollars (at retail or cost):

$$\text{Annual rate of stock turnover (in units)} = \frac{\text{Number of units sold during year}}{\text{Average inventory on hand (in units)}}$$

$$\text{Annual rate of stock turnover (in retail dollars)} = \frac{\text{Net yearly sales}}{\text{Average inventory on hand (at retail)}}$$

$$\text{Annual rate of stock turnover (at cost)} = \frac{\text{Cost of goods sold during the year}}{\text{Average inventory on hand (at cost)}}$$

Storability Product Groupings   Used for products that need special handling.

Store Brands   See Private Brands.

Storefront   Total physical exterior of a store, including the marquee, entrances, windows, lighting, and construction materials.

Store Maintenance   Encompasses all the activities in managing a retailer's physical facilities.

Straight Lease   Requires the retailer to pay a fixed dollar amount per month over the life of a lease. It is the simplest, most direct leasing arrangement.

Straight (Gridiron) Traffic Flow   Presents displays and aisles in a rectangular or gridiron pattern.

Strategic Profit Model   Expresses the numerical relationship among net profit margin, asset turnover, and financial leverage. It can be used in planning or controlling a retailer's assets.

Strategy Mix   Firm's particular combination of store location, operating procedures, goods/services offered, pricing tactics, store atmosphere and customer services, and promotional methods.

String   Unplanned shopping area comprising a group of retail stores, often with similar or compatible product lines, located along a street or highway.

Supercenter   Combination store blending an economy supermarket with a discount department store.

Supermarket   Self-service food store with grocery, meat, and produce departments and minimum annual sales of $2 million. The category includes conventional supermarkets, food-based superstores, combination stores, box (limited-line) stores, and warehouse stores.

Supervision   Manner of providing a job environment that encourages employee accomplishment.

Supply Chain   Logistics aspect of a value delivery chain. It comprises all of the parties that participate in the retail logistics process: manufacturers, wholesalers, third-party specialists, and the retailer.

Survey   Research technique which systematically gathers information from respondents by communicating with them.

Survey of Buying Power   Reports current demographic data on metropolitan areas, cities, and states. It also provides such information as total annual retail sales by area, annual retail sales for specific product categories, annual effective buying income, and five-year population and retail sales projections.

Tactics   Actions that encompass a retailer's daily and short-term operations.

Target Market   Customer group that a retailer seeks to attract and satisfy.

Terms of Occupancy   Consist of ownership versus leasing, the type of lease, operations and maintenance costs, taxes, zoning restrictions, and voluntary regulations.

Theme-Setting Display   Interior display that depicts a product offering in a thematic manner and portrays a specific atmosphere or mood.

Threats   Environmental and marketplace factors that can adversely affect retailers if they do not react to them (and sometimes, even if they do).

Top-Down Space Management Approach   Exists when a retailer starts with its total available store space, divides the space into categories, and then works on in-store product layouts.

Total Retail Experience   All the elements in a retail offering that encourage or inhibit consumers during their contact with a retailer.

Trading Area   Geographic area containing the customers of a particular firm or group of firms for specific goods or services.

Trading-Area Overlap   Occurs when the trading areas of stores in different locations encroach on one another. In the overlap area, the same customers are served by both stores.

Traditional Department Store   Type of department store in which merchandise quality ranges from average to quite good, pricing is moderate to above-average, and customer service ranges from medium levels of sales help, credit, delivery, and so forth to high levels of each.

Traditional Job Description   Contains each position's title, supervisory relationships (superior and subordinate), committee assignments, and the specific ongoing roles and tasks.

Training Programs   Used to teach new (and existing) personnel how best to perform their jobs or how to improve themselves.

Unbundled Pricing   Involves a retailer's charging separate prices for each item sold.

Uncontrollable Variables   Aspects of business to which the retailer must adapt (such as competition, the economy, and laws).

Understored Trading Area   Geographic area that has too few stores selling a specific good or service to satisfy the needs of its population.

Unit Control   Looks at the quantities of merchandise a retailer handles during a stated period.

Unit Pricing   Practice required by many states, whereby retailers (mostly food stores) must express both the total price of an item and its price per unit of measure.

Universal Product Code (UPC)   Classification for coding data onto products via a series of thick and thin vertical lines. It lets retailers record information instantaneously on a product's model number, size, color, and other factors when it is sold, as well as send the information to a computer that monitors unit sales, inventory levels, and other factors. The UPC is not readable by humans.

Unplanned Business District   Type of retail location where two or more stores situate together (or nearby) in such a way that the total arrangement or mix of stores is not due to prior long-range planning.

UPC   See Universal Product Code.

Usage Rate   Average sales per day, in units, of merchandise.

Value   Represented by the activities and processes—a value chain—that provide a given level of value for the consumer from the manufacturer, wholesaler, and retailer perspectives. From the customer's perspective, it is the perception the shopper has of a value chain.

Value Chain   Total bundle of benefits offered to consumers through a channel of distribution.

Value Delivery System   All the parties that develop, produce, deliver, and sell and service particular goods and services.

Variable Markup Policy   Strategy whereby a firm purposely adjusts markups by merchandise category.

Variable Pricing   Strategy wherein a retailer alters prices to coincide with fluctuations in costs or consumer demand.

Variety Store   Outlet that handles a wide assortment of inexpensive and popularly priced goods and services, such as stationery, gift items, women's accessories, health and beauty aids, light hardware, toys, housewares, confectionery items, and shoe repair.

Vending Machine   Format involving the coin- or card-operated dispensing of goods and services. It eliminates the use of sales personnel and allows around-the-clock sales.

Vendor-Managed Inventory (VMI)   Practice of retailers counting on key suppliers to actively participate in their inventory management programs. Suppliers have their own employees stationed at retailers' headquarters to manage the inventory replenishment of the suppliers' products.

Vertical Cooperative Advertising Agreement   Enables a manufacturer and a retailer or a wholesaler and a retailer to share an ad.

Vertical Marketing System   All the levels of independently owned businesses along a channel of distribution. Goods and services are normally distributed through one of three types of systems: independent, partially integrated, and fully integrated.

Vertical Price Fixing   Occurs when manufacturers or wholesalers seek to control the retail prices of their goods and services.

Vertical Retail Audit   Analyzes—in depth—performance in one area of the strategy mix or operations.

Video Kiosk   Freestanding, interactive, electronic computer terminal that displays products and related information on a video screen; it often uses a touchscreen for consumers to make selections.

Visual Merchandising   Proactive, integrated approach to atmospherics taken by a retailer to create a certain "look," properly display products, stimulate shopping, and enhance the physical environment.

VMI   See Vendor-Managed Inventory.

Want Book   Notebook in which retail store employees record requests for unstocked or out-of-stock merchandise.

Want Slip   Slip on which retail store employees enter requests for unstocked or out-of-stock merchandise.

Warehouse Club   See Membership Club.

Warehouse Store   Food-based discounter offering a moderate number of food items in a no-frills setting.

Web   *See* World Wide Web.

Weeks' Supply Method   An inventory level planning method wherein beginning inventory equals several weeks' expected sales. It assumes inventory is in direct proportion to sales. Under this method:

Beginning-of-month planned inventory level (at retail) = Average estimated weekly sales × Number of weeks to be stocked

Weighted Application Blank   Form whereby criteria best correlating with job success get more weight than others. A minimum total score becomes a cutoff point for hiring.

Wheel of Retailing   Theory stating that retail innovators often first appear as low-price operators with low costs and low profit margins. Over time, they upgrade the products carried and improve facilities and customer services. They then become vulnerable to new discounters with lower cost structures.

Wholesaling   Intermediate stage in the distribution process during which goods and services are not sold to final consumers but to business customers—such as manufacturers and retailers—for their use in running the business or for resale to others.

Width of Assortment   Number of distinct goods/service categories (product lines) a retailer carries.

WOM   *See* Word of Mouth.

Word of Mouth (WOM)   Occurs when one consumer talks to others.

World Wide Web (Web)   Way of accessing the Internet, whereby people work with easy-to-use Web addresses and pages. Users see words, colorful charts, pictures, and video, and hear audio.

Yield Management Pricing   Computerized demand-based variable pricing technique whereby a retailer (typically a service firm) determines the combination of prices that yield the greatest total revenues for a given period.

Zero-Based Budgeting   Practice followed when a firm starts each new budget from scratch and outlines the expenditures needed to reach that period's goals. All costs are justified each time a budget is done.

PHOTO CREDITS

Chapter 1
Fig. 1-1 (page 4) Reprinted by permission of the Taubman Company. **Fig. 1-2 (page 5)** Reprinted by permission. **Fig. 1-8 (page 15)** Reprinted by permission. **Fig. 1-9 (page 16)** Photo by Barry Berman. **Fig. 1-11 (page 19)** Reprinted by permission of Pricewaterhouse-Coopers LLP.

Chapter 2
Fig. 2-1 (page 29) Reprinted by permission. **Fig. 2-2 (page 30)** Reprinted by permission of Moto Photo, Inc. **Fig. 2-3 (page 33)** Reprinted by permission. **Fig. 2-4 (page 36)** Reprinted by permission. **Fig. 2-5 (page 36)** Reprinted by permission of NCR Corporation, NCR is a copyright of NRC Corporation. **Fig. 2-6 (page 42)** Reprinted by permission. **Fig. 2-8 (page 46)** Reprinted by permission of the American Marketing Association. **Fig. 2-9 (page 47)** Reprinted by permission. **Fig. 2-10 (page 49)** Reprinted by permission of Carolina First Corporation. **Fig. 2-11 (page 50)** Reprinted by permission. **Fig. 2-12 (page 53)** Reprinted by permission of Eddie Bauer, Inc. **Fig. 2-13 (page 57)** Reprinted by permission of Target Stores.

Chapter 3
Fig. 3-2 (page 72) Reprinted by permission. **Fig. 3-6 (page 83)** Reprinted by permission of Simon Property Group. **Fig. 3-7 (page 84)** Reprinted by permission from *Chain Store Age.* Copyright Lebhar-Friedman, Inc., 425 Park Avenue, New York, NY 10022. **Fig. 3-8 (page 85)** Reprinted by permission. **Fig. 3-10 (page 88)** Reprinted by permission of MeriStar Hospitality Corporation.

Chapter 4
Fig. 4-3 (page 120) Reprinted by permission of Pricewaterhouse-Coopers LLP. **Fig. 4-4 (page 121)** Reprinted by permission of Regis Corporation. **Fig. 4-5 (page 123)** Reprinted by permission of AmeriHost Properties, Inc.

Chapter 5
Fig. 5-4 (page 152) Reprinted by permission of Eckerd Corporation. **Fig. 5-5 (page 156)** Reprinted by permission of Wendy's International. **Fig. 5-6 (page 156)** Reprinted by permission. **Fig. 5-7 (page 161)** Reprinted by permission of PricewaterhouseCoopers LLP. **Fig. 5-8 (page 166)** Reprinted by permission.

Chapter 6
Fig. 6-1 (page 176) Reprinted by permission. **Fig. 6-2 (page 177)** Reprinted by permission. **Fig. 6-3 (page 178)** Reprinted by permission. **Fig. 6-5 (page 191)** Reprinted by permission of Mary Kay Cosmetics. **Fig. 6-9 (page 200)** Reprinted by permission. **Fig. 6-10 (page 201)** Reprinted by permission. **Fig. 6-11 (page 204)** Reprinted by permission of PricewaterhouseCoopers LLP.

Chapter 7
Fig. 7-3 (page 226) Reprinted by permission. **Fig. 7-4 (page 227)** Reprinted by permission. **Fig. 7-7 (page 241)** Reprinted by permission.

Chapter 8
Fig. 8-2 (page 255) Reprinted by permission of Retail Technologies International. **Fig. 8-4 (page 260)** Reprinted by permission. **Fig. 8-5 (page 262)** Reprinted by permission of Symbol Technologies. **Fig. 8-7 (page 267)** Reprinted by permission of Retail Technologies International. **Fig. 8-9 (page 275)** Reprinted by permission of Raymond R. Burke, Indiana University.

Chapter 9
Fig. 9-1 (page 292) Reprinted by permission of Rouse Company. **Fig. 9-3 (page 296)** Reprinted by permission. **Fig. 9-4 (page 297)** Selected graphic images supplied courtesy of Environmental Systems Research Institute, Inc. (ESRI) and Geographic Data Technology (GDT). Copyright Environmental Systems Research Institute, Inc. and Geographic Data Technology. Reprinted by permission. **Fig. 9-6 (page 301)** Reprinted by permission. **Fig. 9-7 (page 302)** Reprinted by permission of PricewaterhouseCoopers.

Chapter 10
Fig. 10-1 (page 326) Reprinted by permission. All of the store and brand names cited in the caption are registered trademarks of Dairy Queen. **Fig. 10-2 (page 329)** Reprinted by permission of the Rouse Company. **Fig. 10-4 (page 333)** Reprinted by permission of the Simon Property Group. **Fig. 10-5 (page 334)** Reprinted by permission of City Center Retail. **Fig. 10-6 (page 336)** Reprinted by permission of Triple Five Corporation. Photos by the Postcard Factory. **Fig. 10-7 (page 339)** Reprinted by permission of Sterling Jewelers. **Fig. 10-9 (page 344)** Reprinted by permission of Starbucks Coffee Company.

Chapter 11
Fig. 11-7 (page 370) Reprinted by permission. **Fig. 11-12 (page 387)** Reprinted by permission of Master Group Design. Photography: Theo Anderson. Art Direction: Lisa M. Weinberger.

Chapter 12
Fig. 12-2 (page 406) Reprinted by permission of Venator Group.

Chapter 13
Fig. 13-2 (page 424) Reprinted by permission of Tandy Corporation. **Fig. 13-3 (page 427)** Reprinted by permission of NCR Corporation. **Fig. 13-4 (page 430)** Reprinted by permission. **Fig. 13-5 (page 435)** Reprinted by permission of Venator Group. **Fig. 13-6 (page 435)** Reprinted by permission of Raymark. **Fig. 13-7 (page 436)** Reprinted by permission.

Chapter 14
Fig. 14-1 (page 454) Reprinted by permission of Venator Group. **Fig. 14-3 (page 458)** Reprinted by permission. **Fig. 14-5 (page 464)** Reprinted by permission. **Fig. 14-8 (page 470)** Reprinted by permission of Walgreen Company. **Fig. 14-9 (page 474)** Reprinted by permission of PricewaterhouseCoopers LLP. **Fig. 14-10 (page 473)** Reprinted by permission. **Fig. 14-11 (page 478)** Reprinted by permission. **Fig. 14-12 (page 480)** Reprinted by permission of Logical Planning Systems.

Chapter 15
Fig. 15-4 (page 497) Reprinted by permission of PricewaterhouseCoopers LLP. **Fig. 15-5 (page 498)** Reprinted by permission of Monarch Marking Systems. **Fig. 15-6 (page 499)** Reprinted by permission of Seagull Scientific Systems, author of "Bar Tender" label printing software. **Fig. 15-7 (page 501)** Reprinted by permission. **Fig. 15-8 (page 507)** Reprinted by permission. **Fig. 15-9 (page 511)** Reprinted by permission of Sensormatic Electronics Corporation. **Fig. 15-11 (page 514)** Reprinted by permission.

Chapter 16
Fig. 16-5 (page 542) Reprinted by permission Retail Technologies International. **Fig. 16-6 (page 543)** Courtesy Giant Food. Inc.

Chapter 17
Fig. 17-1 (page 556) Reprinted by permission. **Fig. 17-2 (page 557)** Reprinted by permission. **Fig. 17-5 (page 567)** Reprinted by permission. **Fig. 17-7 (page 578)** Reprinted by permission. **Fig. 17-8 (page 580)** Reprinted by permission of Golf Day. **Fig. 17-9 (page 581)** Reprinted by permission.

Chapter 18
Fig. 18-2 (page 603) Reprinted by permission of Claire's Stores. **Fig. 18-4 (page 605)** Reprinted by permission of Track 'n Trail, Inc. **Fig. 18-5 (page 606)** Reprinted by permission of PricewaterhouseCoopers LLP. **Fig. 18-6 (page 606)** Reprinted by permission of PricewaterhouseCoopers LLP. **Fig. 18-7 (page 608)** Reprinted by permission of Sterling Jewelers. **Fig. 18-10 (page 616)** Reprinted by permission. **Fig. 18-11 (page 619)** Reprinted by permission of PricewaterhouseCoopers LLP. **Fig. 18-12 (page 621)** Reprinted by permission.

Chapter 19
Fig. 19-1 (page 632) Reprinted by permission. **Fig. 19-2 (page 633)** Reprinted by permission. **Fig. 19-3 (page 638)** Photo by Barry Berman. **Fig. 19-5 (page 644)** Reprinted by permission of Goodyear. **Fig. 19-8 (page 649)** Reprinted by permission. **Fig. 19-9 (page 651)** Reprinted by permission of Venator Group.

Chapter 20
Fig. 20-3 (page 677) Reprinted by permission. **Fig. 20-5 (page 687)** Reprinted by permission.

Appendix
Fig. 1 (page A5) Reprinted by permission of *Discount Store News*. **Fig. 2 (page A6)** Reprinted by permission of *Discount Store News*. **Fig. 3 (page A7)** Reprinted by permission of *Discount Store News*.

NAME INDEX

SUBJECT INDEX

Note: An asterisk before term indicates Glossary entry.

An asterisk before a term indicates Glossary entry.

An asterisk before a term indicates Glossary entry.

An asterisk before a term indicates Glossary entry.

An asterisk before a term indicates Glossary entry.

An asterisk before a term indicates Glossary entry.

An asterisk before a term indicates Glossary entry.

An asterisk before a term indicates Glossary entry.

An asterisk before a term indicates Glossary entry.

An asterisk before a term indicates Glossary entry.

An asterisk before a term indicates Glossary entry.

An asterisk before a term indicates Glossary entry.

An asterisk before a term indicates Glossary entry.

An asterisk before a term indicates Glossary entry.

An asterisk before a term indicates Glossary entry.

An asterisk before a term indicates Glossary entry.

An asterisk before a term indicates Glossary entry.

An asterisk before a term indicates Glossary entry.

ASSOCIATIONS

American Association of Franchisee Dealers	www.aafd.org
Better Business Bureau	www.bbb.org
Direct Marketing Association	www.the-dma.org
Direct Selling Association	www.dsa.org
Federation of European Direct Selling Assoc.	www.fedsa.be
Food Marketing Institute	www.fmi.org
Institute for Business and Professional Ethics	www.depaul.edu/ethics
International Council of Shopping Centers	www.icsc.org
International Franchise Association	www.franchise.org
International Small Business Consortium	www.isbc.com
National Association for Female Executives	www.nafe.com
National Association of Chain Drug Stores	www.nacds.org
National Association of Convenience Stores	www.cstorecentral.com
National Automatic Merchandising Association	www.vending.org
National Automobile Dealers Association	www.nada.org
National Foundation for Women Business Owners	www.nfwbo.org
National Mail Order Association	www.nmoa.org
National Retail Federation	www.nrf.com
National Small Business United	www.nsbu.org
Point-of-Purchase Advertising Institute POPAI	www.popai.com

GEOGRAPHIC INFORMATION SYSTEMS

CACI Marketing Systems	www.demographics.caci.com
Claritas	www.claritas.com
Easy Analytics	www.easidemographics.com
ESRI	www.esri.com
Geographic Data Technology	www.geographic.com
SRC	www.demographicsnow.com
Tetrad Computer Applications	www.tetrad.com

SMALL BUSINESS RESOURCES

Bizresource	www.bizresource.com
Business Owner's Toolkit	www.toolkit.cch.com
Business Research Lab	www.busreslab.com
Business Resource Center	www.morebusiness.com
Power Retailing Checklist	www.salesdoctors.com/surgery/4check.htm
Small Business Search	www.smallbizsearch.com
SmallbizNet	www.lowe.org/smbiznet
Smart Business Supersite	www.smartbiz.com
UPS Logistics Group	www.wwlog.com
Visa Small Business Site	www.visa.com/cgi-bin/vee/fb/smbiz/main.html

RETAIL SOFTWARE

Buying-Office.com live demo	www.buying-office.com
Descartes Systems Group	www.descartes.com
Dynacom Technologies	www.dynacom.ca
Intactix	www.intactix.com
Intellilink	www.ilsa.com

Continued on next page